Erin
DeMasi

SOCIAL PROBLEMS

TENTH EDITION

William Kornblum
City University of New York, Graduate School and University Center

Joseph Julian
San Francisco State University

In collaboration with
Carolyn D. Smith

Prentice
Hall

Upper Saddle River, New Jersey 07458

Library of Congress Cataloging-in-Publication Data
Kornblum, William.
    Social problems/William Kornblum, Joseph Julian.—10th ed.
      p.   cm.
    Includes bibliographical references and index.
    ISBN 0-13-026313-3
     1. Social problems—United States. 2. United States—Social conditions—1980- I. Julian,
Joseph. II. Title.

HN59.2.K66   2001
361.1—dc21   00-055792

VP, Editorial Director: *Laura Pearson*
Publisher: *Nancy Roberts*
Managing Editor: *Sharon Chambliss*
Director of Marketing: *Beth Gillett Mejia*
Project Manager: *Serena Hoffman*
AVP, Director of Production
  and Manufacturing: *Barbara Kittle*
Prepress and Manufacturing Manager: *Nick Sklitsis*
Prepress and Manufacturing
  Buyer: *Mary Ann Gloriande*

Copy Editor: *Barbara Connor*
Creative Design Director: *Leslie Osher*
Interior and Cover Design: *Ximena Tamvakopoulos*
Line Art Director: *Guy Ruggiero*
Illustrations: *ElectraGraphics, Inc.*
Photo Researcher: *Beaura K. Ringrose*
Director, Image Resource Center: *Melinda Reo*
Image Specialist: *Beth Boyd*
Manager, Rights and Permissions: *Kay Dellosa*
Cover Art: © *Brad Holland*

This book was set in 10/12 New Baskerville
by Pine Tree Composition, Inc.,
and was printed and bound by Courier Companies, Inc.
The cover was printed by The Lehigh Press, Inc.

©2001, 1998, 1995, 1992, 1989, 1986,
1983, 1980, 1977, 1974 by Prentice-Hall, Inc.
A Division of Pearson Education
Upper Saddle River, New Jersey 07458

Printed in the United States of America

10 9 8 7 6 5 4 3 2

ISBN 0-13-026313-3

Prentice-Hall International (UK) Limited, *London*
Prentice-Hall of Australia Pty. Limited, *Sydney*
Prentice-Hall Canada Inc., *Toronto*
Prentice-Hall Hispanoamericana, S.A., *Mexico*
Prentice-Hall of India Private Limited, *New Delhi*
Prentice-Hall of Japan, Inc., *Tokyo*
Pearson Education Asia Pte. Ltd., *Singapore*
Editora Prentice-Hall do Brasil, Ltda., *Rio de Janeiro*

BRIEF CONTENTS

1 SOCIOLOGICAL PERSPECTIVES ON SOCIAL PROBLEMS   2

2 PROBLEMS OF PHYSICAL HEALTH   26

3 MENTAL ILLNESS   60

4 SEX-RELATED SOCIAL PROBLEMS   88

5 ALCOHOL AND OTHER DRUGS   120

6 CRIME AND CRIMINALS   150

7 VIOLENCE   188

8 POVERTY AMID AFFLUENCE   220

9 RACISM, PREJUDICE, AND DISCRIMINATION   254

10 SEX ROLES AND INEQUALITY   286

11 AN AGING SOCIETY   312

12 THE CHANGING FAMILY   340

13 PROBLEMS OF EDUCATION   368

14 PROBLEMS OF WORK AND THE ECONOMY   396

15 URBAN PROBLEMS   422

16 POPULATION AND IMMIGRATION   452

17 TECHNOLOGY AND THE ENVIRONMENT   476

18 WAR AND TERRORISM   506

GLOSSARY   529

BIBLIOGRAPHY   534

CONTENTS

BOX FEATURES   xii
PREFACE   xiv

1   SOCIOLOGICAL PERSPECTIVES ON SOCIAL PROBLEMS   2

What Is a Social Problem? 3

Perspectives on Social Problems, 5

The Functionalist Perspective, 7   The Conflict Perspective, 10
The Interactionist Perspective, 12

The Natural History of Social Problems, 14

The Media and Social Problems, 16

Research on Social Problems, 17

Demographic Studies, 19   Survey Research, 19   Field Observation, 19
Social Experiments, 20

Social Policy, 22

Beyond Left and Right, 24

Summary, 24   Key Terms, 25   Internet Exercise, 25

2   PROBLEMS OF PHYSICAL HEALTH   26

Health Care as a Global Social Problem, 27

The Scope of Health-care Problems in America, 29

Unequal Access to Health Care, 30   The High Cost of Health Care, 32
Inadequate Protection, 37   Women and Health Care, 40
The Disabled and Handicapped, 42   Ethical Issues, 43

AIDS—A Modern Plague, 45

Explanations of Health-care Problems, 49

Class and Class Conflict, 49   Institutions and Health Care, 50
Health and Social Interaction, 51

Social Policy, 52

Managed Care, 53   Insurance Reform, 53   The Disabled and Handicapped, 55
Social Policy and AIDS, 56

Beyond Left and Right, 57

Summary, 58   Key Terms, 58   Internet Exercise, 59

3   MENTAL ILLNESS   60

Mental Illness as a Social Problem, 61

Suicide and Mental Illness, 63

The Social Construction of Mental Illness, 66

Defining Mental Illness, 66   Classification of Mental Disorders, 68
Diagnosis or Label? 70

Inequality, Conflict, and Mental Illness, 71

Social Class and Mental Disorder, 72   Mental Disorder and Urban Life, 73
Other Factors, 74

Institutional Problems of Treatment and Care, 75

Methods of Treatment, 75   Changes in Mental-health Professions, 76
Treatment Institutions, 77   Deinstitutionalization and Homelessness, 81

Social Policy, 84

Beyond Left and Right, 86

Summary, 86   Key Terms, 87   Internet Exercise, 87

4   SEX-RELATED SOCIAL PROBLEMS   88

Sex as a Social Problem, 91

Tolerated Sex Variance, 92   Asocial Sex Variance, 92
Structured Sex Variance, 94

Homosexuality, 94

Social-Scientific Perspectives on Homosexuality, 96   Who Becomes a Homosexual? 97
Lesbianism, 99   The Homosexual Subculture, 99

Prostitution, 102

Social-Scientific Perspectives on Prostitution, 102   Norms of Prostitution, 103
Why Do People Become Prostitutes? 104   The Prostitute Subculture, 106
The Impact of AIDS, 108

Pornography, 109

Social-Scientific Perspectives on Pornography, 110   Pornography and Censorship, 111
Research on Pornography, 111   Pornography and Public Opinion, 112

Social Policy, 113

Homosexuality, 113   Prostitution, 115   Pornography, 116

Beyond Left and Right, 118

Summary, 118   Key Terms, 119   Internet Exercise, 119

5   ALCOHOL AND OTHER DRUGS   120

The Nature of the Problem, 122

Drug Abuse, 122   Abuse, Addiction, and Dependence, 123

Alcohol Use and Abuse, 126

Problem Drinkers and Alcoholics, 127   Who Drinks? 127
Drinking among Young People, 129   Alcohol-related Social Problems, 130
Treatment of Alcoholism, 132

Illegal Drug Use and Abuse, 135

Commonly Abused Drugs, 135   Patterns of Drug Abuse, 137   Drug Use and Crime, 141
Drug Use and AIDS, 142   Treatment of Drug Abuse, 143

Social Policy, 145

Beyond Left and Right, 148

Summary, 148   Key Terms, 149   Internet Exercise, 149

6 CRIME AND CRIMINALS 150

The Nature of Crime, 154

Police Discretion, 157   Problems of Accuracy, 159

Types of Crimes and Criminals, 160

Violent Personal Crimes, 160   Occasional Property Crimes, 161
Occupational (White-collar) Crimes, 161   Corporate Crimes, 162   Public-order Crimes, 163
Conventional Crimes, 163   Organized Crime, 164   Professional Crimes, 165
Juvenile Delinquency, 166   Hate Crimes, 167

Conditions and Causes of Crime, 167

Biological Explanations of Crime, 167   Gender and Crime, 168   Age and Crime, 169
Sociological Explanations of Crime, 170

Controlling Crime, 176

Retribution-Deterrence, 176   Rehabilitation, 179   Prevention, 181

Social Policy, 182

Conventional Crimes, 183   Occupational and Corporate Crimes, 184
Organized Crime, 184   Public-order and Juvenile-justice Reforms, 185

Beyond Left and Right, 186

Summary, 186   Key Terms, 187   Internet Exercise, 187

7 VIOLENCE 188

The Concept of Violence, 191

Explanations of Violence, 192

The Biological Viewpoint, 192   Frustration–Aggression and Control Theories, 193
Violence as a Subculture, 194   Violence as Rational Choice, 195
The Influence of the Mass Media, 195

Criminal Violence, 196

Criminal Homicide, 197   Hate Crimes, 199   Assault and Robbery, 202   Rape, 202

Family Violence, 204

Child Abuse, 204   Spouse Abuse, 206   Elder Abuse, 207

Gangs, Guns, and Violent Death, 207

Social Policy, 211

Gun Control, 211   Media Violence, 214   Dealing with Family Violence, 215
Race, Poverty, and Violence: The Unfinished Agenda, 216

Beyond Left and Right, 218

Summary, 218   Key Terms, 219   Internet Exercise, 219

8

POVERTY AMID AFFLUENCE 220

The Haves and the Have-nots, 223

The Rich, 223   The Poor, 225

Poverty and Social Class, 227

The Nature of Poverty, 229

The Poverty Line, 229   Who Are the Poor? 232

Concomitants of Poverty, 240

Health Care, 240   Education, 241   Housing and Homelessness, 241
Justice, 243

Explanations of Persistent Poverty, 243

Structural Explanations, 243   Cultural Explanations, 245

Social Policy, 246

Reform of "Welfare as We Know It," 246   Dependency, Work, and Responsibility, 249
Moving to Opportunity? 250

Beyond Left and Right, 251

Summary, 251   Key Terms, 252   Internet Exercise, 252

9

RACISM, PREJUDICE, AND DISCRIMINATION 254

The Meaning of *Minority*, 257

Defining Racism, Prejudice, and Discrimination, 259

Origins of Prejudice and Discrimination, 261

Prejudice and Bigotry in the Individual, 261   Prejudice and Bigotry in Social
Structures, 262   Cultural Factors: Norms and Stereotypes, 263

Institutional Discrimination, 266

Education, 267   Housing, 269   Employment and Income, 271
Justice, 274

Some Consequences of Prejudice and Discrimination, 276

Social Policy, 278

Job Training, 278   Affirmative Action, 278   Education for Equality, 280
Some Trends and Prospects, 282

Beyond Left and Right, 284

Summary, 284   Key Terms, 285   Internet Exercise, 285

10

SEX ROLES AND INEQUALITY 286

Traditional Sex Roles, 288

The Nature of Sexism, 290

Power and Male Hegemony, 291   Stereotyping, 292   Sexism and Employment, 292
Sexual Harassment, 294   Homemaking, 295   The Women's Movement, 297

Sources of Sexism, 299

Socialization, 299   Education, 300   The Family, 301   Language and the Media, 301
Organized Religion, 302   Government, 302   The Legal System, 303

Social Policy, 304

Changes in Child-rearing Practices, 304   Changes in the Educational System, 305
Changes in the Legal System, 306   Reproductive Control, 307
Social Policy and the Women's Movement, 308   Changes in Men's Roles, 308

Beyond Left and Right, 309

Summary, 310   Key Terms, 311   Internet Exercise, 311

11   AN AGING SOCIETY   312

Aging as a Social Problem, 314

Perspectives on Aging, 315

The Elderly in America Today, 315

Age Stratification, 318   Who Are the Elderly? 319   Ageism, 321

Dimensions of the Aging Process, 323

Physiological Aspects of Aging, 323   Psychological Dimensions of Aging, 324
Social and Cultural Dimensions of Aging, 325

Concomitants of Aging, 326

Victimization of the Elderly, 326   Elder Abuse, 327   Health Care and the Aged, 327
Economic Discrimination, 328   Family Problems, 330

Retirement, 330

Death, 331

Social Policy, 333

Housing, 333   Health Care, 334   Retirement and Social Security, 335

Beyond Left and Right, 337

Summary, 337   Key Terms, 338   Internet Exercise, 338

12   THE CHANGING FAMILY   340

The Nature of Families, 342

Adequate Family Functioning, 344   Effects of Women's Employment, 345
The Black Family, 348

Divorce, 350

Stepfamilies, 352   Explanation of Trends in Divorce Rates, 352
The Impact of Divorce, 353   Cohabiting Couples, 354

Postponement of Marriage, 354

Changing Norms of Parenthood, 355

Births to Unmarried Women, 355   Teenage Pregnancy, 356
Gay and Lesbian Families, 358

Homeless Families, 358

Reproductive Issues, 359

Advances in Reproductive Technology, 359   The Morning-after Pill, 360

Social Policy, 361

Divorce Law, 361   Efforts to Reduce Teenage Pregnancies, 363
Child Care and Family Support, 364

Beyond Left and Right, 365

Summary, 366   Key Terms, 367   Internet Exercise, 367

PROBLEMS OF EDUCATION   368

Sociological Perspectives on Education, 372

Functionalist Approaches, 372   Conflict Approaches, 372   Interactionist Approaches, 373

Education and Inequality: The Issue of Equal Access, 374

Black Students, 375   Hispanic Students, 375   Preschool Programs, 377   Desegregation, 379
Educational Attainment Today, 379

School Reform: Problems of Institutional Change, 381

Schools as Bureaucracies, 381   Classroom and School Size, 383   School Choice, 384
The "Technological Fix," 384   Teachers' Professionalsim and Unions, 387
School Violence, 387

Social Policy, 389

Educational Conservatism and "Back to Basics," 390   Humanism and Open Education, 391
Access to Higher Education, 392   Trends and Prospects, 392

Beyond Left and Right, 393

Summary, 393   Key Terms, 394   Internet Exercise, 394

PROBLEMS OF WORK AND THE ECONOMY   396

The American Free-Enterprise System, 397

Global Markets and Corporate Power, 398

Multinational Corporations, 399   Global Factory, Global Sweatshops, 400

Effects on American Workers, 401

From Manufacturing to Services, 402   Women in the Global Labor Market, 405
Technology and Specialization, 406

Problem Aspects of Work, 408

Job Insecurity, 409   Job Stress, 409   Alienation, 410   Unemployment, 411
Occupational Safety and Health, 413

Consumers and Credit, 415

Problems of Debt Entanglement, 416   Possessions and Self-expression, 417

Social Policy, 418

Beyond Left and Right, 420

Summary, 420   Key Terms, 421   Internet Exercise, 421

15 URBAN PROBLEMS 422

An Urbanizing World, 424

The American City, 426

Urban Growth and Social Problems, 426   Antiurban Bias, 426
The Composition of Urban Populations, 427

Theories of Urbanism, 429

Wirth's Theory, 429   Compositionalism, 430   Subcultural Theory, 430

Metropolitan Growth, 431

The Transportation Boom, 434   The Impact of Suburban Growth, 435

Problems of Cities, 437

Deconcentration, 438   Relocation of Manufacturing, 439   Financial Problems, 440
Government, 442

Shelter Poverty, Homelessness, and Neighborhood Distress, 443

Shelter Poverty, 443   Homelessness, 444   Distressed Neighborhoods, 445

Social Policy, 446

Housing, 447   Homelessness, 448

Beyond Left and Right, 449

Summary, 449   Key Terms, 451   Internet Exercise, 451

16 POPULATION AND IMMIGRATION 452

The World's Population, 453

Measures of Population Growth, 453   The Demographic Transition, 455
Rising Expectations, 458   Food and Hunger, 459

The U.S. Population, 460

Population Control, 462

Family Planning, 463   ZPG, 463   Population Control in LDCs, 464

Immigration and Its Consequences, 465

Immigration to the United States: A Brief History, 466
Recent Trends in Immigration to the United States, 468   Urban Concentration of Immigrants, 469
Undocumented Immigrants, 470

Social Policy, 472

Beyond Left and Right, 474

Summary, 474   Key Terms, 475   Internet Exercise, 475

17 TECHNOLOGY AND THE ENVIRONMENT 476

Defining Technology, 478

Technology and Global Inequality, 478

Technological Dualism, 479

The Digital Divide, 479

Controlling Technology, 481

Autonomous Technology, 481   Automation, 482   Whistle-blowers, 483
Bureaucracy and Morality, 484

Technology and Institutions, 485

Technology and the Natural Environment, 487

Environmental Stress, 489

Origins of the Problem, 489   Air Pollution, 490   Water Pollution, 492
Solid-waste Disposal, 493   Other Hazards, 495

The United States and the World Environment, 496

Social Policy, 500

Appropriate Technology, 500   Technology Assessment, 501   Policy on Global Warming, 501
Environmental Action, 501

Beyond Left and Right, 503

Summary, 504   Key Terms, 504   Internet Exercise, 505

18 WAR AND TERRORISM   506

The Nature of the Problem, 508

Direct Effects of War, 508   Indirect Effects of War, 509   Effects of Nuclear War, 510

Military Technology and the Conduct of War, 511

Controlling Warfare, 512

Theories About War and Its Origins, 514

Ethological and Sociobiological Theories, 514   Clausewitz: War as State Policy, 515
Marx and Lenin on War, 516   Institutional and International Perspectives, 516

Terrorism: Undeclared War, 520

Social Policy, 523

Arms Control: A Promise Unfulfilled, 523   Alternatives to the Arms Race, 525
Dealing with Terrorism, 525

Beyond Left and Right, 526

Summary, 527   Key Terms, 528   Internet Exercise, 528

GLOSSARY   529

BIBLIOGRAPHY   534

PHOTO CREDITS   547

INDEX   548

BOX FEATURES

SOCIAL PROBLEMS ONLINE

Researching Social Problems	21
AIDS on the Internet	48
Information about Mental Health and Homelessness	80
Gays on the Internet	100
Youth and Alcohol on the Internet	133
Crime and Criminal Justice on the Internet	160
Information about Guns and Violence on the Internet	208
Poverty and Welfare on the Internet	230
Race and Ethnicity	275
Information about Women on the Internet	298
Information about Aging on the Internet	317
Families and the Internet	351
Education and the Internet	380
Economics on the Internet	408
Urban Problems and the Internet	437
Population and the Internet	457
Environmental Information on the Internet	488
Information about War and Terrorism	521

Unintended Consequences

Life-saving Technologies	44
Drug Control in a Borderless World	147
Is There a Case for Discretion?	158
Effects of Welfare Reform	248
Greater Equality Increases Domestic Burdens	309
Welfare Reform and Job Creation	419
Making Family Unification More Difficult	473
Terrorism and the Internet	526

CURRENT CONTROVERSIES

Caring for the Homeless Mentally Ill   83
Homosexuality and Child Custody   114
The Myth of Black Violence   217
Immigration   283
Do We Have a Right to Die?   336
Family Support and Day Care   364
Reinstitutionalization versus Community Care   448
Market Approaches to Pollution   502

CRITICAL RESEARCH

Profits and Health-Care   54
Women and Depression—A Critical View   65
Sex Tourism Exploits Vulnerable Populations   108
The Critical View of Marijuana   144
Racial Profiling   172
Crisis of Youth Violence or Adult Panic?   200
Single Mothers Making Ends Meet   234
Stigmatizing Minority Women as Welfare Queens   265
Catherine MacKinnon: Anti-Harassment Warrior   296
Dying with Dignity   322
Life Without Father   362
Closing the Digital Divide in the Classroom   385
The Maquilladora Effect   403
Destructive Urban Design   441
Starvation in the Midst of Plenty   461
The Global Food Fight   497
Globalization and the Hope of World Peace   519

This tenth edition of *Social Problems* appears during an almost unprecedented stretch of economic good times for the United States and most
urban industrial nations. Despite the relative prosperity, however, prospects for addressing the nation's and the world's social problems are far from rosy.
The continuing failure of health-care reform has resulted in increasing numbers of
people who lack health insurance. The Welfare Reform Act of 1996 continues to have
consequences that are positive in terms of numbers of people working but negative
for the children of poor families. Indeed, children have been hit hardest by recent
changes in social policy, particularly cuts in child support for low-income families.
Elsewhere in the world, there is a widening gap between the haves and the have-
nots—a gap that can be seen between entire nations as well as between the rich and
the poor within nations—and this poses a major threat to world security. The threat
of a renewed arms race, especially between India and Pakistan, and continuing ethnic
strife in the nations of the former Soviet empire and throughout much of Africa are
testing the capabilities of the United Nations and the world's most powerful nations,
especially the United States.

For every major social problem confronting Americans and citizens of other nations, there are groups of people dedicated to seeking a solution. Some of them are
experts on particular social problems, like the members of the medical profession
who each day confront the tragedy of AIDS, or the law enforcement professionals
who cope with crime and violence. Others are nonprofessionals, often citizens who
have decided to devote themselves to doing something about a particular situation or
problem. Among these activists are people who have experienced the condition they
seek to improve—women who have suffered sexual abuse, people who know what it is
to be homeless, drug and alcohol abusers who want to help themselves and others,
and neighbors confronted with the dumping of toxic wastes. Such groups may include elected officials and other political leaders who are expected to formulate
sound social policies to address social problems. This book is written in an effort to
make their work more effective and in the hope that some readers will be moved to
take up their causes. We dedicate it to the citizens of the world who devote some of
their precious time on earth to helping others.

Organization of the Book

The first few chapters of this book focus on relatively individual behaviors, such as
drug use and crime. The social institutions and other factors that affect these behaviors are noted and described. The middle chapters focus on inequality and discrimination, discussing such topics as poverty, prejudice, sexism, and ageism. Every attempt
has been made to indicate the effects of large-scale discrimination on individuals, as
well as to deal with the concept of institutionalized inequalities. Later chapters discuss
problems that are common to many societies, such as those related to family life and
work. The final chapters—on the problems of cities, environmental pollution, and
war and terrorism—focus on matters of global significance. It seems best to discuss
each subject in a separate chapter in order to deal with it comprehensively and in
depth. Throughout the book, however, an attempt has been made to indicate how the
different problems overlap and are interrelated.

Pedagogical Devices

Social Problems has been designed to be as helpful as possible to both students and teachers. Each problem is discussed in a well-organized and readable manner. As much as possible, unnecessary terminology has been avoided. The treatment of each problem is analytical as well as descriptive, and includes the most up-to-date findings available.

Each chapter begins with an outline and a set of significant facts and ends with a summary that lists the important concepts presented. Important terms within the chapter are boldfaced and listed at the end of the chapter, and their definitions are included in the Glossary at the end of the book. In addition, boxed discussions in each chapter deal with Current Controversies or Unintended Consequences of efforts to alleviate social problems. New to this edition, a Critical Research feature in each chapter adds a dimension of critical thinking based on sociological research that should enliven debates about social problems and citizens' responsibilities in dealing with them.

In keeping with the book's effort to achieve as much sociological objectivity as possible, there is a feature at the end of each chapter called Beyond Left and Right. Its purpose is to help students think critically about the partisan debates over the problems discussed in the chapter they have just read. Each chapter also includes a pedagogical aid titled Social Problems Online, which will help students use the World Wide Web to inquire more deeply into particular social problems. Internet Exercises are provided at the end of each chapter.

Changes in the Tenth Edition

The reception given to previous editions of *Social Problems* by both colleagues and students has been encouraging, and many of their suggestions and criticisms have been incorporated in subsequent revisions. This edition represents a continuing effort to create a comprehensive, up-to-date text. To this end, the text has been thoroughly revised. Our aim has been to retain the book's emphasis on the sociological analysis of social problems, as well as the policies designed to alleviate or eliminate them. Although policies change continually, we have attempted to update the discussions of policy to reflect the most recent thinking about solutions to social problems.

In the preparation of this edition, certain areas of the text have received special attention. Chapter 2 (Problems of Physical Health) has been extensively revised in light of the rapid rise of managed care, the growing number of uninsured or inadequately insured Americans, and the sharp debate about insurance company influence on medical care. The chapter also has a thoroughly updated section on AIDS as a global plague, as well as more material on patients' rights. Chapter 3 (Mental Illness) has a new section on suicide and more discussion of sensational crimes by the mentally ill. Chapter 4 (Sex-Related Social Problems) has an extended discussion of homophobia and its consequences and a Critical Research feature on sex tourism that is likely to generate much student interest.

Chapter 5 (Alcohol and Other Drugs) reflects renewed debate over the justifications for extremely harsh punishment of drug users, especially marijuana users, and new material on the genetic factors in alcoholism. Chapter 6 (Crime and Criminals) has new material on interventions against violent gangs, research on racial profiling, and a new section on hate crimes. Chapter 7 (Violence) includes new material on school killings. Chapter 8 (Poverty Amid Affluence) has an expanded discussion of the impact of welfare reform, more material about the working poor, and a Critical Research feature on the problems of single mothers, to name only some of the extensive changes made in this key chapter. Chapter 9 (Racism, Prejudice, and Discrimination) has been extensively updated with new material about affirmative action and far more emphasis on racism in contemporary life in the United States and elsewhere. Chapter 10 (Sex Roles and Inequality) has an expanded discussion of child-care issues under workfare and a new section on power and male hegemony.

Later chapters reflect important changes in social problems, both global and domestic: an expanded discussion of the implications of aging populations worldwide in Chapter 11 (An Aging Society); a new Critical Research feature on fatherless families and more about worldwide divorce patterns in Chapter 12 (The Changing Family); and a Critical Research feature on the digital divide and its impact on education and inequality in Chapter 13 (Problems of Education). Chapter 14 (Problems of Work and the Economy) has been completely revamped, with new sections on corporate power and wealth in a globalizing economy, plus far more material about the effects of globalization on women in the labor force, job stress, and job insecurity, as well as more on the impacts of new technologies. Chapter 15 (Urban Problems) has more material about ethnic enclaves in major cities, with some emphasis on the Miami Cubans. Chapter 16 (Population and Immigration) has a new section on worldwide hunger and a Critical Research feature on starvation in the midst of plenty. There are extensive reports on new environmental problems in Chapter 17 (Technology and the Environment). Chapter 18 (War and Terrorism) has updated material on globalization and worldwide patterns of terrorism and the growing threat of rogue states.

Throughout the text, statistical material, figures, and tables have been updated wherever necessary, and recent research has been cited throughout. The Social Policy sections incorporate recent programs and proposals.

Supplements

Instructors and students who use this textbook have access to a number of materials designed to complement the classroom lectures and activities and to enhance the students' learning experience:

For the Instructor

Instructor's Resource Manual. This essential instructor's tool includes chapter outlines, teaching objectives, discussion questions, classroom activities, and film/video suggestions.

Test Item File. This carefully prepared manual consists of over 1,300 multiple-choice and essay questions. All multiple-choice questions are page referenced to the text. **Prentice Hall Custom Test** is a test generator designed to allow the creation of personalized exams. It is available in Windows and Macintosh formats.

Prentice Hall Color Transparencies: Social Problems, Series III. Full color illustrations, charts, and other visual materials have been selected to offer an effective means of amplifying lecture topics.

ABCNEWS **ABC News/Prentice Hall Video Library for Social Problems.** Selected video segments from award-winning ABC News programs such as *Nightline, ABC World News Tonight/American Agenda,* and *20/20* accompany topics featured in the text. Please contact your local Prentice Hall sales representative for more details.

For the Student

Student Study Guide. This carefully written guide helps students better understand the material presented in the text. Each chapter consists of chapter summaries, learning objectives, detailed chapter outlines, key terms, and self-test questions page referenced to the text.

The New York Times Supplement. *The New York Times* and Prentice Hall are sponsoring *Themes of the Times*, a program designed to enhance student access to current information of relevance in the classroom. Through this program, the core subject matter provided in the text is supplemented by a collection of time-sensitive articles from one of the world's most distinguished newspapers, *The New York Times*. These articles demonstrate the vital, ongoing connection between what is learned in the classroom and what is happening in the world around us.

To enjoy the wealth of information of *The New York Times* daily, a reduced subscription rate is available. For information call toll-free: 1-800-631-1222.

Prentice Hall and *The New York Times* are proud to cosponsor *Themes of the Times*. We hope it will make the reading of both textbooks and newspapers a more dynamic, involving process.

Media Supplements

Sociology on the Internet: Evaluating Online Resources. This guide focuses on developing the critical thinking skills necessary to evaluate and use online sources effectively. The guide provides a brief introduction to navigating the Internet, along with complete references related specifically to the Sociology discipline and how to use the companion websites available for many Prentice Hall textbooks. This brief supplementary book is free to students when shrinkwrapped as a package with *Social Problems, Tenth Edition.*

Companion Website™. In tandem with the text, students can now take full advantage of the World Wide Web to enrich their studies through the *Social Problems* website: **http://www.prenhall.com/kornblum**. This study resource will correlate the text with related material available on the Internet. Features of the website include chapter objectives, study questions, as well as links to interesting material and information from other sites on the web that reinforce and enhance the content of each chapter.

Distance Learning Solutions. Prentice Hall is committed to making our outstanding text content available to the growing number of courses being delivered over the Internet. By developing relationships with the leading venders—Blackboard ™, Web CT™, and ecollege.com ™—we provide premium, book-specific content in the delivery method of your choice. Please contact your local Prentice Hall representative to find out more about our products in this area, or visit our online demo site at **http://www.prenhall.com/demo**.

Acknowledgments

Revising and updating a social problems textbook is a formidable task. Social problems is a far-ranging field with myriad findings and concepts that accumulate rapidly and are often changing. This edition has benefited from the reviews of many sociologists, all of whom have contributed useful comments and suggestions. We are happy to number among them the following: Barbara K. Chesney, University of Toledo; James E. Floyd, Macon College; Marie Pease Lewis, Macon College; Edward Ponczek, William Rainey Harper College; Steven C. Seyer, Lehigh Carbon Community College; and John Tenuto, DePaul University.

To the following, whose suggestions have enriched all nine previous editions, a special thank-you: Mark Abrahamson, University of Connecticut; Lynn Anderson, Navarro College; Howard Bahr, Brigham Young University; Jeanne Ballantine, Wright State University; Nancy Bartkowski, Northern Michigan University; William Bielby, University of California-Santa Barbara; Susan L. Blackwell, Delgado Community College; Edwin Boling, Wittenberg University; Bradley Jay Buchner, Cheyney University of Pennsylvania; Walter F. Carroll, Bridgewater State College; Carol E. Chandler,

McHenry County College, Verghese J. Chirayath, John Carroll University; William T. Clute, University of Nebraska–Omaha; William Cockerham, University of Illinois, Urbana–Champaign; William L. Collins, Asheville-Buncombe Technical Community College; Paul L. Crook, San Diego Mesa College; William M. Cross, Illinois College; Phillip W. Davis, Georgia State University; Lois Easterday, Onondaga Community College; John Farley, Southern Illinois University; Michael P. Farrell, State University of New York–Buffalo; William Feigelman, Nassau Community College; Morris A. Forslund, University of Wyoming; Sidney Forsythe, Wheaton College; John Galliher, University of Missouri; Harry Gold, Oakland University; Erich Goode, State University of New York–Stony Brook; Norman Goodman, State University of New York–Stony Brook; Marshall Graney, Wayne State University; James Greenley, University of Wisconsin; Julia Hall, Drexel University; John Hedderson, University of Texas–El Paso; John Hendricks, University of Kentucky; Mary R. Holley, Montclair State College; Nils Hovik, Lehigh County Community College; Gary Jensen, University of Arizona; Richard I. Jolliff, El Camino College; Russell I. Johnson, Washington University; Daniel J. Klenow, North Dakota State University; Louis Kriesberg, Syracuse University; Patricia Lengermann, George Washington University; and Betty Levine, Indiana University.

Also, Peter Maida, University of Maryland; Wilfred Marston, University of Michigan–Flint; Edward J. McCabe, Eastern Michigan University; Richard L. Meile, Indiana University, Northwest; Steven Messner, State University of New York, Albany; Robert G. Miller, Baker University; Linda Mooney, East Caroline University; George C. Myers, Duke University; Charles Nam, Florida State University; Steven Nock, University of Virginia; Donald Noel, University of Wisconsin; Donald Olmsted, Michigan State University; Barry Perlman, Community College of Philadelphia; Robert Perucci, Purdue University; Karen Predow, formerly of Rutgers University; Robert Rothman, University of Delaware; Nora Roy, Tennessee University; Laura Sanchez, Tulane University; Earl R. Schaeffer, Columbus State Community College; David Schulz, University of Delaware; Mary Sellers, Northampton County Area Community College; John W. Shepard, Jr., Baylor University; Edward G. Stockwell, Bowling Green State University; Russell Stone, State University of New York–Buffalo; Ann Sundgren, Tacoma Community College; Kenrick S. Thompson, Arkansas State University, Mountain Home; Kevin Thompson, North Dakota State University; Miriam G. Vosburgh, Villanova University; William Waegel, Villanova University; Ruth Wallace, George Washington University; and Irving Zola, Brandeis University.

Finally, thanks are due to the many skilled publishing specialists who contributed their talents to this edition. Much of the research on which the revision is based was provided by Joseph Compton. Administrative aspects of the project were skillfully handled by Publisher Nancy Roberts and Managing Editor Sharon Chambliss. Ximena Tamvakopoulos created a pleasing interior design. Serena Hoffman, the project manager, did an enormous amount of work to get the book out on time. Kathy Ringrose took charge of rounding up the photographs that complement the text, and Mary Ann Gloriande was responsible for the manufacturing process. The book owes much to the efforts, creativity, and perseverance of each of them.

SOCIAL PROBLEMS

1

Sociological Perspectives on Social Problems

SOCIAL PROBLEMS

- When most people in a society agree that a condition threatens the quality of their lives and their most cherished values and that something should be done to remedy it, the society has defined that condition as a social problem.

- Social problems often seem to develop in a series of phases or stages based largely on public perception of conditions that come to be defined as problems.

- Social conditions that are thought of as problems can improve over time—as well as worsen.

OUTLINE

What Is a Social Problem?

Perspectives on Social Problems
The Functionalist Perspective
The Conflict Perspective
The Interactionist Perspective

The Natural History of Social Problems

The Media and Social Problems

Research on Social Problems
Demographic Studies
Survey Research
Field Observation
Social Experiments

Social Policy

Victor Ayala is a sociologist who knows through long and bitter experience how difficult it is to find lasting solutions to our most pressing social problems. In addition to teaching sociology and counseling at a community college, Ayala worked for many years as a volunteer on the AIDS ward of a large public hospital. There he encountered patients in advanced stages of the disease and was responsible for helping them establish contact with family members, find housing, deal with the notification of former lovers, and cope with many other difficult tasks. Ayala's book, *Falling Through the Cracks* (1996), documents his experiences in reaching and comforting indigent AIDS patients. Very often the people he helped in the hospital were able to spend some months in hospices or in the care of their own families. But even more often they died alone in a darkened hospital room with no one but Ayala to hold their hand.

Many of Ayala's patients were also drug addicts, often with long-standing heroin or crack habits. Most commonly they were homeless or had spent long periods as street vagrants. In some cases they had criminal records. Often they had illegitimate children. Many of the most poverty-stricken AIDS patients had been abused as children and had engaged in abusive behavior toward others as adults. It was clear to Ayala that AIDS was only one of the many problems they faced.

What Is a Social Problem?

We will see throughout this book that social problems are often closely interrelated. Crime, poverty, lack of medical care, violence, drug abuse, and many other behaviors or situations that we commonly think of as social problems rarely exist in isolation. And for any one of the problems just named or others we could cite, there are vigorous debates about causes and responsibilities. Are we responsible, some ask, for the sins of others? Are not many people with AIDS to blame for their illness since it is often spread through casual, unprotected sex? Others might point out that the consequences of AIDS and other illnesses are problems that should concern everyone. These and similar arguments deal not only with the causes of social problems but also with what should be done about them.

Sociologist Victor Ayala combines research and social action by writing about the needs of poor people with AIDS while counseling them and working as their advocate for more equitable health care.

Most people will agree that AIDS is a problem that society must somehow address, and this is true for all the other issues mentioned earlier. Most members of society agree that they are conditions that ought to be remedied through intentional action.

Of course, agreement that remedies are necessary does not imply that people agree on what the remedies should be. Most people would like to see a reduction in rates of poverty and homelessness, but far fewer agree that welfare or Aid to Families with Dependent Children (AFDC) was a reasonable way of dealing with these social problems in the absence of work requirements. However, work requirements, in turn, introduce the difficulty of ensuring that there actually is work available that can be done by poor people with little education. The same controversies arise in connection with almost all social problems. Many Americans are appalled at the level of gun violence in their nation, but many others are equally appalled at the prospect of more government restrictions on their freedom to buy and use guns as they wish. In short, recognition that a social problem exists is far different from arriving at a consensus about a solution.

When most people in a society agree that a condition exists that threatens the quality of their lives and their most cherished values, and they also agree that something should be done to remedy that condition, sociologists say that the society has defined that condition as a **social problem.** In other words, the society's members have reached a broad consensus that a condition that affects some members of the population is a problem for the entire society, not just for those who are directly affected.

The importance of this definition will become clear if we consider one or two examples. In China before the Communist revolution of the mid–twentieth century, opium use and addiction were widespread. In Shanghai alone there were an estimated 400,000 opium addicts in the late 1940s. Everyone knew that the condition existed, and many responsible public figures deplored it; but few outside the revolutionary parties believed that society should intervene in any way. After all, many of the country's richest and most powerful members had made their fortunes in the opium trade. The Chinese Communists believed that society should take responsibility for eradicating opium addiction, however, and when they took power they did so, often through drastic and violent means. What had previously been seen as a social condition had been redefined as a social problem that had to be solved.

To take an example from our own society, before 1920 women in the United States did not have the right to vote. Many women objected to this condition and opposed it whenever possible, but most men and many women valued the traditional pattern of male dominance and female subservience. To them, there was nothing unusual about women's status as second-class citizens. It took many years of painstaking organization, persuasion, and demonstration by the leaders of the woman suffrage movement to convince significant numbers of Americans that women's lack of voting rights was a social problem that the society should remedy through revision of its laws. We will see later in the book, especially in Chapter 10, that the conditions that affect women's lives continue to be viewed by some members of society as natural and inevitable and by others as problems that require action by society as a whole (Lorber, 1994).

It is worth noting that the idea that a society should intervene to remedy conditions that affect the lives of its citizens is a fairly recent innovation. Until the eighteenth century, for example, most people worked at exhausting tasks under poor conditions for long hours; they suffered from severe deprivation all their lives, and they often died young, sometimes of terrible diseases. But no one thought of these things as problems to be solved. They were accepted as natural, inevitable conditions of life. It was not until the so-called "enlightenment" of the late eighteenth century that philosophers began to argue that poverty is not inevitable but a result of an unjust social system. As such, it could be alleviated by changing the system itself through such means as redistribution of wealth and elimination of inherited social status.

The founders of the American nation applied these principles in creating a form of government that was designed to "establish justice, insure domestic tranquility . . . promote the general welfare . . . and secure the blessings of liberty." The U.S. Constitution guaranteed the rights of individual citizens and established the legal basis for remedying conditions that are harmful to society's members. Moreover, through the system of representative government that it also created, the Constitution established a means by which citizens could define a condition like poverty as one that society should attempt to remedy. Later in this chapter and at many points throughout the book, we will see how this process is carried out and the effects it has had and continues to have on American society.

We will also see many instances of the interconnections among social problems. This interconnectedness is evident in the example of AIDS at the beginning of the chapter. Very often, when government leaders seek solutions to social problems, they must consider multifaceted approaches that address entire sets of problems rather than a single problem by itself, a situation that makes the formulation of effective social policy quite difficult.

Perspectives on Social Problems

Everybody has opinions about the causes of social problems and what should be done about them. Some people will argue, for example, that the problems of a homeless single mother are her own fault. She may be morally loose or mentally unsound, not very bright, or not motivated to work hard and lift herself and her family out of poverty. These are all familiar explanations of individual misfortune. At worst, they blame the individual for his or her situation. At best, they explain individual troubles in terms of traits that the person cannot control. In fact, for this one unfortunate woman any of these simple explanations might be true. But even if they are true for particular individuals, none of them tells us why the same pattern is repeated for entire groups of people.

Why are increasing numbers of women becoming single mothers, and why are increasing numbers of single mothers becoming homeless as well? Why is it that women who are born into poor and minority families are more likely to become single mothers, and possibly heads of homeless families, than women who are born into middle-class families of any racial or ethnic group? And does the experience of being homeless inflict hardships on women and children that make it more difficult for them to perform productive roles in society and attain the good life?

These are sociological questions. They ask why a condition like homelessness exists. They ask how the condition is distributed in society and whether some people are more at risk than others. They are questions about the social rather than the individual aspects of a problem. And they are not important merely from an academic or social-scientific viewpoint. Answers to these questions are a prerequisite for effective action to eliminate social problems. Note, however, that research on these issues is not limited to sociology. Other social-scientific approaches to the study of social problems are described in the accompanying box.

Contemporary sociology is founded on three basic perspectives, or sets of ideas, that offer theories about why societies hang together and how and why they change. These perspectives are not the only sociological approaches to social problems, but they can be extremely powerful tools for understanding them. Each of these perspectives—functionalism, conflict theory, and interactionism—gives rise to a number of distinctive approaches to the study of social problems. (See Table 1–1.) We explore several of those approaches in the following sections, devoting special attention to how they seek to explain one of society's most pressing problems: criminal deviance.

Other Approaches to the Study of Social Problems

In addition to sociology, other disciplines in the social sciences are concerned with the analysis of human behavior, and sociologists often draw on the results of their research. The work of historians, for example, is vital to an understanding of the origins of many social problems. The research of anthropologists on nonindustrial and tribal societies offers contrasting views of how humans have learned to cope with various kinds of social problems. Perhaps the greatest overlap is between sociology and political science, both of which are concerned with the processes by which policies deal with social problems that arise in different societies. Following are brief descriptions of several social-scientific disciplines whose research findings have a bearing on the study of social problems.

History

History is the study of the past. However, historical data can be used by sociologists to understand present social problems. In studying homelessness, for example, historians would focus on changes in how people obtained shelter in a society and what groups or individuals tended to be without shelter in different historical periods.

Cultural Anthropology

Cultural anthropologists study the social organization and development of smaller, nonindustrial societies, both past and present. Since cultural anthropology is closely related to sociology, many of the same techniques can be used in both fields, and the findings of cultural anthropologists regarding primitive and traditional cultures shed light on related phenomena in more complex, modern societies. An anthropological study of homelessness would be likely to look very closely at one or a few groups of homeless people. The anthropologist might be interested in how the homeless and others in their communities understand their situation and what might be done about it.

Psychology and Social Psychology

Psychology deals with human mental and emotional processes, focusing primarily on individual experience. Rooted in biology, it is more experimental than the other social sciences. An understanding of the psychological pressures that underlie individual responses can illuminate social attitudes and behavior. Thus, a psychologist would tend to study the influences of homelessness on the individual's state of mind or, conversely, how the individual's personality and ways of looking at life might have contributed to his or her situation.

Social psychology—the study of how psychological processes, behavior, and personalities of individuals influence or are influenced by social processes and social settings—is of particular value for the study of social problems. A social psychologist would be likely to study how life on the streets damages the individual in various ways.

Economics

Economists study the levels of income in a society and the distribution of income among the society's members. To understand how the resources of society—its people and their talents; its land and other natural resources—can be allocated for the maximum benefit of that society, economists also study the relationship between the supply of resources and the demand for them. Confronted with the problem of homelessness, an economist would tend to study how the supply of and demand for housing of different types influence the number of homeless people in a given housing market. *(continued)*

> **Other Approaches to the Study of Social Problems (*continued*)**
>
> **Political Science**
>
> Political scientists study the workings of government at every level of society. As Harold Lasswell (1941), a leading Amerian political scientist, put it, "Politics is the study of who gets what, when, and how." A political scientist, therefore, would be likely to see homelessness as a problem that results from the relative powerlessness of the homeless to influence the larger society to respond to their needs. The political scientist would tend to focus on ways in which the homeless could mobilize other political interest groups to urge legislators to deal with the problem.

The Functionalist Perspective

From the day we are born until the day we die, all of us hold a position—a **status**—in a variety of groups and organizations. In a hospital, for example, the patient, the nurse, the doctor, and the orderly are all members of a social group that is concerned with health care. Each of these individuals has a status that requires the performance of a certain set of behaviors, known as a **role.** Taken together, the statuses and roles of the members of this medical team and other teams in hospitals throughout the country make up the social institution known as the health-care system. An **institution** is a more or less stable structure of statuses and roles devoted to meeting the basic needs of people in a society. The health-care system is an institution; hospitals, insurance companies, and private medical practices are examples of organizations within this institution.

TABLE 1–1   Major Perspectives on Social Problems

Perspective	View of Society and Social Problems	Origins of Social Problems	Proposed Solutions
Functionalist	Views society as a vast organism whose parts are interrelated; social problems are disruptions of this system. Also holds that problems of social institutions produce patterns of deviance and that institutions must address such patterns through strategic social change.	Social expectations fail, creating normlessness, culture conflict, and breakdown. Social problems also result from the impersonal operations of existing institutions, both now and in the past.	Engage in research and active intervention to improve social institutions.
Conflict	Views society as marked by conflicts due to inequalities in class, race, ethnicity, gender, age, and other divisions that produce conflicting values. Defines social problems as conditions that do not conform to society's values.	Groups with different values and differing amounts of power meet and compete.	Build stronger social movements among groups with grievances. The conflicting groups may then engage in negotiations and reach mutual accommodations.
Interactionist	Holds that definitions of deviance or social problems are subjective; separates deviant and nondeviant people not by what they do but by how society reacts to what they do.	Society becomes aware that certain behaviors exist and labels them as social problems.	Resocialize deviants by increasing their contacts with accepted patterns of behavior; make the social system less rigid. Change the definition of what is considered deviant.

The functionalist perspective looks at the way major social institutions like the family, the military, the health-care system, and the police and courts actually operate. According to this perspective, the role behavior associated with any given status has evolved as a means of allowing a particular social institution to fulfill its function in society. Thus, the nurse's role requires specific knowledge and behaviors that involve treatment of the patient's immediate needs and administration of care according to the doctor's orders. The patient, in turn, is expected to cooperate in the administration of the treatment. When all members of the group perform their roles correctly, the group is said to be functioning well.

In a well-functioning group, there is general agreement about how roles are to be performed by each member. These expectations are reinforced by the society's basic values, from which are derived rules about how people should and should not behave toward each other in different situations. The Ten Commandments, the Golden Rule, the Bill of Rights, and the teachings of all of the world's religions are examples of sets of rules that specify how people should behave in different social roles.

But if society is made up of groups in which people know their roles and adhere to the underlying values, why do we have social problems like crime and warfare, and why does it seem so difficult to make social organizations function effectively? From the functionalist perspective, the main reason for the existence of social problems is that societies are always changing and having to adapt to new conditions; failure to adapt successfully leads to social problems.

The French social theorist Émile Durkheim observed that changes in a society can drastically alter the goals and functions of human groups and organizations. As a society undergoes a major change—say, from agricultural to industrial production—the statuses people assume and the roles they play also change, with far-reaching consequences. Thus, for example, the tendency for men and women from rural backgrounds to have many children, which was functional in agrarian societies because it produced much-needed farmhands, can become a liability in an urban-industrial society, where housing space is limited and the types of jobs available are constantly changing. From the standpoint of society's smooth functioning, it can be said that the roles of the father and mother in the rural setting, which stresses long periods of childbearing and many children, become dysfunctional in an urban setting.

Wars, colonial conquest, disease and famine, population increases, changing technologies of production or communication or health care—all these major social forces can change societies and thereby change the roles their members are expected to perform. As social groups strive to adapt to the new conditions, their members may feel that they are adrift—unsure of how to act or troubled by conflict over how to perform as parents or wage earners or citizens. They may question the values they learned as children and wonder what to teach their own children. This condition of social disequilibrium can lead to an increase in social problems like crime and mental illness as individuals seek their own, often antisocial, solutions to the dilemmas they face.

Criminal Deviance: A Functionalist View.   From the functionalist perspective, all societies produce their own unique forms of crime and their own ways of responding to them. All sociologists recognize that there are causes within the individual that help explain why one person becomes a criminal while another, who may have experienced the same conditions, does not. But for the sociologist, especially one who applies the functionalist perspective, the question of why particular crimes are committed and punished in some societies and not in others is an important research topic. Why is it that until quite recently a black man who was suspected of making advances to a white woman was often punished more severely than one who was suspected of stealing? Why was the theft of a horse punishable by immediate death on the western frontier? Why was witchcraft considered such a heinous crime in the

Puritan settlements of colonial New England? And why is it that these crimes occurred at all when those who committed them were punished so severely?

The functionalist answer is that societies fear most the crimes that seem to threaten their most cherished values, and individuals who dare to challenge those values will receive the most severe punishment. Thus, the freedom to allow one's horses to graze on common land was an essential aspect of western frontier society that was threatened by the theft of horses. The possibility that a white woman could entice a black man and that their affair could be interpreted as anything other than rape threatened the foundations of the American racial caste system, which held that blacks were inferior to whites. In both cases immediate, sometimes brutal punishment was used to reinforce the central values of the society.

Social Problems as Social Pathology.   The functionalist perspective on problems like criminal deviance has changed considerably since the nineteenth century. In the late 1800s and early 1900s, functionalist theorists regarded such behavior as a form of "social disease" or **social pathology.** This view was rooted in the organic analogy that was popular at the time. Human society was seen as analogous to a vast organism, all of whose complex, interrelated parts function together to maintain the health and stability of the whole. Social problems arise when either individuals or social institutions fail to keep pace with changing conditions and thereby disrupt the healthy operation of the social organization; such individuals or institutions are considered to be "sick" (hence the term *social pathology*). In this view, for example, European immigrants who failed to adjust to American urban life were considered to be a source of "illness," at least insofar as they affected the health of their adopted society. Underlying this concept was a set of moral expectations; social problems violated the expectations of social order and progress.

Although many people who comment on social problems today are tempted to use the organic analogy and the disease concept, most sociologists reject this notion. The social-pathology approach is not very useful in generating empirical research; its concepts of sickness and morality are too subjective to be meaningful to many sociologists. Moreover, it attempts to apply a biological analogy to social conditions even when there is no empirical justification for doing so. More important, it is associated with the idea that the poor and other "deviant" groups are less fit to survive from an evolutionary perspective and hence should not be encouraged to reproduce. The social-pathology approach therefore has been largely discredited. Modern functionalists do not focus on the behaviors and problems of individuals; instead, they see social problems as arising out of the failure of institutions like the family, the schools, and the economy to adapt to changing social conditions.

Social-disorganization Theory.   Rates of immigration, urbanization, and industrialization increased rapidly after World War I. Many newcomers to the cities failed to adapt to urban life. European immigrants, rural whites, and southern blacks were often crowded together in degrading slums and had trouble learning the language, manners, and norms of the dominant urban culture. Many of those who managed to adjust to the city were discriminated against because of their religion or race, and others lost their jobs because technological advances made their skills obsolete. Because of these conditions, many groups formed their own subcultures or devised other means of coping. Alcoholism, drug addiction, mental illness, crime, and delinquency rates rose drastically. Some sociologists believed that the social-pathology viewpoint could not adequately explain the widespread existence of these social problems. They developed a new concept that eventually became known as social-disorganization theory.

This theory views society as being organized by a set of expectations or rules. **Social disorganization** results when these expectations fail, and it is manifested in three major ways: (1) *normlessness,* which arises when people have no rules that tell them how to behave; (2) *culture conflict,* which occurs when people feel trapped by contradictory rules; and (3) *breakdown,* which takes place when obedience to a set of rules is not rewarded or is punished. Rapid social change, for example, might make traditional standards of behavior obsolete without providing new standards, thereby giving rise to normlessness. The children of immigrants might feel trapped between the expectations of their parents and those of their new society—an example of culture conflict. And the expectations of blacks might be frustrated when they do well in school but encounter job discrimination; their frustration, in turn, might lead to breakdown.

The stress experienced by victims of social disorganization may result in a form of personal disorganization such as drug addiction or crime. The social system as a whole also feels the force of disorganization. It may respond by changing its rules, keeping contradictory rules in force, or breaking down. Disorganization can be halted or reversed if its causes are isolated and corrected.

Modern Functionalism: Building Institutions.   In this book we will see many instances in which social-disorganization theory has been used to explain social problems. However, this approach is not widely used today. A more modern version of the functionalist perspective attempts to show how people reorganize their lives to cope with new conditions. Often this results in new kinds of organizations and, sometimes, whole new institutions. This research focus is known as the *institutional* or **institution-building** approach (Goodin, 1995; Janowitz, 1978). Research on how to improve the organization of public schools to meet new educational demands is an example.

The Conflict Perspective

By no means do all sociologists accept the functionalist view of society and social problems. There is an alternative set of theories, often known as the **conflict perspective,** that rejects the idea that social problems can be corrected by reforming institutions that are not functioning well. The conflict perspective is based on the belief that social problems arise out of major contradictions in the way societies are organized, contradictions that lead to large-scale conflict between those who have access to the good life and those who do not. This perspective owes much to the writings of Karl Marx (1818–1883), the German social theorist who developed many of the central ideas of modern socialism.

In *The Communist Manifesto* (1848), *Capital* (1867), and other works, Marx attempted to prove that social problems like unemployment, poverty, crime, corruption, and warfare are not usually the fault of individuals or of poorly functioning organizations. Instead, he argued, their origins may be found in the way societies arrange access to wealth and power. According to Marx, the social problems of modern societies arise from capitalism. An inevitable outcome of capitalism is class conflict, especially conflict between those who own the means of production (factories, land, and the like) and those who sell their labor for wages. In such a system workers are exploited by their bosses, for whom the desire to make a profit outweighs any humanitarian impulse to take care of their employees.

In the capitalist system as Marx described it, the capitalist is driven by the profit motive to find ways to reduce labor costs—for example, through the purchase of new machinery that can do the work of several people or by building factories in places where people will work for less money. These actions continually threaten the livelihood of workers. Often they lose their jobs, and sometimes they resort to crime or even begin revolutions to overturn the system in which they are the have-nots and the owners of capital are the haves. In sum, for Marx and modern Marxian sociologists, social problems may be attributed to the ways in which wealth and power become concentrated in the hands of a few people and to the many forms of conflict engendered by these inequalities.

The view from the new SuperMax prison facility in rural Wisconsin. With inmate populations at record levels, new prison construction is a booming industry.

Marxian conflict theory can be a powerful tool in the analysis of contemporary social problems. To illustrate this point, let us look at how this theory explains criminal deviance in societies like the United States.

Deviance: A Marxian Conflict View.   Marxian students of crime and deviance believe that situations such as those described at the beginning of the chapter do not occur merely because such organizations as the police and the courts function in certain ways or do not function as they were intended to. Instead, Marxian theorists believe that such situations are a result of differences in the power of different groups or classes in society. For example, top organized-crime figures have the money and power to influence law enforcement officials or to hire the best attorneys when they are arrested. Street drug dealers, in contrast, are relatively powerless to resist arrest. Moreover, they serve as convenient targets for an official show of force against drug trafficking. From the Marxian perspective, the rich and powerful are able to determine what kinds of behaviors are defined as social problems because they control major institutions like the government, the schools, and the courts. They are also able to shift the blame for the conditions that produce those problems to groups that are less able to defend themselves, namely, the poor and the working class (D. R. Gordon, 1994; Quinney, 1986; Turk, 1978).

Scholars who adopt a Marxian perspective tend to be critical of proposals to reform existing institutions. Since they attribute most social problems to underlying patterns of class conflict, they do not believe that existing institutions like prisons and courts can address the basic causes of those problems. Usually, therefore, their research looks at the ways in which the material conditions of society, such as inequalities of wealth and power, seem to account for the distribution of social problems in a population. Or they conduct research on social movements among the poor and the working class in an attempt to understand how those movements might mobilize large numbers of people into a force that could bring about major changes in the way society is organized (Piven & Cloward, 1977, 1982).

Value Conflict Theory.   The Marxian theory of class conflict cannot explain all the kinds of conflict that occur around us every day. In families, for example, we see conflicts that may range from seemingly trivial arguments over television programs to intense disputes over issues like drinking or drug use; in neighborhoods we may see conflict between landlords and tenants, between parents and school administrators, or between groups of parents who differ on matters of educational policy such as sex education or the rights of female athletes. Such conflict often focuses not on deep-seated class antagonisms but on differences in values. For most feminist groups, for example, abortion is a social problem if women cannot freely terminate a pregnancy within some reasonable time. In contrast, many religious groups define legal abortion as a social problem. The debate over legalization versus criminalization of abortion reflects the conflicting values of important groups in society.

Value conflict theorists define social problems as "conditions that are incompatible with group values" (Rubington & Weinberg, 1987, 1995). Such problems are normal, they add, since in a complex society there are many groups whose interests and values are bound to differ. According to value conflict theory, social problems occur when groups with different values meet and compete. To return to the example of criminal deviance, value conflict theorists would say that deviance from society's rules results from the fact that some groups do not agree with those rules and therefore feel free to break them if they can. For example, whenever a society prohibits substances like alcohol or drugs, some groups will break the rules to obtain the banned substance. This stimulates the development of criminal organizations that employ gangsters and street peddlers to supply the needs of those who deviate. The underlying cause of the problem is conflicting values concerning the use of particular substances.

From the value conflict viewpoint, many social problems need to be understood in terms of which groups hold which values and have the power to enforce them against the wishes of other groups. Once this has been determined, this approach leads to suggestions for adjustments, settlements, negotiations, and compromises that will alleviate the problem. These, in turn, may result in new policies, such as civilian review boards, arbitration of disputes, open hearings on issues, and changes in existing laws to reflect a diversity of opinions (Larana, Johnston, & Gusfield, 1994).

The Interactionist Perspective

Why do certain people resort to criminal deviance while the vast majority seek legitimate means to survive? A functionalist would point out that individuals who do not adhere to society's core values or have been uprooted by social change are most likely to become criminals. When they are caught, their punishment reinforces the desire of the majority to conform. But this explanation does not help us understand why a particular individual or group deviates.

Conflict theorists explain deviance as the result of conflict over access to wealth and power (in the Marxian version) or over values (in the non-Marxian version). But how is that conflict channeled into deviant behavior? Why do some groups that experience value conflict act against the larger society while others do not? Why, for example, do some homosexuals come out publicly while others hide their sexual preference? Presumably both groups know that their sexual values conflict with those of the larger society, but what explains the difference in behavior? The conflict perspective cannot provide an adequate answer to this question.

The interactionist perspective offers an explanation that gets closer to the individual level of behavior. Research based on this perspective looks at the processes whereby different people become part of a situation that the larger society defines as a social problem. The interactionist approach focuses on the ways in which people actually take on the values of the group of which they are members. It also explores how different groups define their situation and in so doing "construct" a version of life that promotes certain values and behaviors and discourages others.

A key insight of the interactionist perspective originated in the research of W. I. Thomas and his colleagues in the early decades of this century. In their classic study of the problems of immigrants in the rapidly growing and changing city of Chicago, these pioneering sociologists found that some groups of Polish immigrant men believed that it would be easier to rob banks than to survive in the mills and factories, where other immigrants worked long hours under dangerous conditions. The sociologists discovered that the uneducated young immigrants often did not realize how little chance they had of carrying out a successful bank robbery. They defined their situation in a particular way and acted accordingly. "Situations people define as real," Thomas stated, "are real in their consequences" (Thomas & Znaniecki, 1922). Thus, from the interactionist perspective an individual or group's definition of the situation is central to understanding the actions of that individual or group.

Another early line of interactionist research is associated with Charles Horton Cooley and George Herbert Mead. Cooley, Mead, and others realized that although we learn our basic values and ways of behaving early in life, especially in our families, we also participate throughout our lives in groups made up of people like ourselves; these are known as *peer groups*. From these groups we draw much of our identity, our sense of who we are, and within these groups we learn many of our behaviors and values. Through our interactions in peer groups—be they teams, adolescent friendship groups, or work groups—we may be taught to act in ways that are different from those our parents taught us. Thus, when interactionists study social problems like crime, they focus on the ways in which people are recruited by criminal groups and learn to conform to the rules of those groups.

Labeling: An Interactionist View of Deviance.   Labeling theory is an application of the interactionist perspective that offers an explanation for certain kinds of social deviance. Labeling theorists feel that the label "deviant" reveals more about the society applying it than about the act or person being labeled. In certain societies, for example, homosexuality is far more accepted than it is in the United States. Labeling theorists suggest that there are groups and organizations in American society that benefit from labeling homosexuals deviant—religious and military institutions, for example. Similarly, deviant acts are not always judged in the same way; prison sentences for black offenders, for instance, tend to be longer than sentences for white offenders who commit the same crimes. In the view of labeling theorists, this difference has to do with the way power is distributed in our society. In short, labeling theory separates deviant and nondeviant people not by what they do but by how society reacts to what they do.

According to labeling theorists, social problems are conditions under which certain behaviors or situations become defined as social problems. The cause of a social problem is simply society's awareness that a certain behavior or situation exists. A behavior or situation becomes a social problem when someone can profit in some way by applying the label "problematic" or "deviant" to it. Such labeling causes society to suffer in two ways. First, one group unfairly achieves power over another—"deviants" are repressed through discrimination, prejudice, or force. Second, those who are labeled deviant may accept this definition of themselves, and the label may become a self-fulfilling prophecy. The number and variety of deviant acts may be increased to reinforce the new role of deviant. A person who is labeled a drug addict, for example, may adopt elements of what is popularly viewed as a drug addict's lifestyle: resisting employment or treatment, engaging in crime, and so on. Sociologists term this behavior **secondary deviance.**

According to labeling theory, the way to solve social problems is to change the definition of what is considered deviant (Rubington & Weinberg, 1995). It is thought that acceptance of a greater variety of acts and situations as normal would automatically

The practice of parading a crime suspect in public (sometimes called the "perp walk") often has the effect of implying guilt before a trial is held.

eliminate concern about them. Decriminalization of the possession of small amounts of marijuana for personal use is an example of this approach. Note, however, that many people would consider marijuana use a social problem even if it were decriminalized. At the same time, discouraging the tendency to impose labels for gain would reduce the prevalence of labeling and cause certain problems to become less significant. Communism, for example, was a matter of great concern to Americans in the 1950s; many people won popularity or power by applying the label "Communist" to others. When it became clear that the label was being misapplied and that the fear it generated was unjustified, the label lost its significance and the "social problem" of internal Communist influence largely disappeared.

Labeling theory is only one of numerous applications of the interactionist perspective to social problems. Another common approach focuses on the processes of socialization that occur in groups and explores the possibility of resocialization through group interaction—as occurs, for example, in groups like Alcoholics Anonymous. At many points in this book we will encounter situations in which intentional resocialization has been used in efforts to address social problems.

The Social Construction of Social Problems. The interactionist perspective also contributes to what is known as the "social construction" approach to social problems. This approach argues that some claims about social problems become dominant and others remain weak or unheeded. Our perceptions of what claims about social problems should be heeded develops through the activities of actors and institutions in society that shape our consciousness of the social world. The press, television, radio, universities and colleges, government agencies, and civic voluntary associations are examples of institutions that often have a stake in defining what social problems are. Journalists, television commentators, editorial writers, professors who take public stands on issues, scientists who appear before the cameras, and many other lobbyists and "opinion makers" are in fact involved in selecting some claims and rejecting others. In so doing, they "construct" the way we think about the issues.

Consider an example: The issue known as global warming is extremely complex and requires knowledge that is too technical for most people to understand fully. But as members of the media and concerned, vocal scientists develop a consensus that the atmosphere is warming because of pollution, the public begins to get that message and to share the opinion that climatic change is occurring. Droughts and wildfires, which may have seemed severe but not out of the ordinary, come to be viewed as part of a social problem known as global warming, independent of whether the earth's atmosphere can actually be proven to be heating up because of the effects of carbon dioxide and other greenhouse gases.

Critics of the social construction view often argue that there are real trends and changes behind the emergence of social problems like global warming, pollution, or gun violence. Still, the influence of the media and universities does account for some tangible social construction of what we perceive as problematic in our society or in the world (B. Allen, 1999; Richardson & May, 1999).

The Natural History of Social Problems

To readers of daily newspapers and faithful watchers of television news, social problems may often resemble fads. We hear a great deal about a particular problem for a while, and then it fades from public attention, perhaps to reappear some time later if there are new developments in its incidence or control. With AIDS, crack cocaine, driving while intoxicated (DWI), serial killers, financial scandals, racial violence, terrorism, and so many other problems demanding attention, it is little wonder that the focus on any given subject by the press and the public tends to last only a few days or weeks.

To a large extent, the short attention span of the media can be explained by the need to attract large numbers of viewers or readers; the media can be expected to be rather fickle and to constantly pursue stories that will capture the attention of the public. However, sociologists distinguish between the nature of media coverage of a social problem and the way a problem is perceived by the public and political leaders. They have devoted considerable study to the question of how social problems develop from underlying conditions into publicly defined problems that engender social policies and sustained social movements. This subject is often referred to as the "natural history" of social problems.

Early in the twentieth century sociologists recognized that social problems often seemed to develop in a series of phases or stages. They called the study of this process the natural history approach because their effort was analogous to the work of biologists who study the development of a great many individual organisms to chart the stages of development of a species (Edwards, 1927; Park, 1955; C. R. Shaw, 1929; Wirth, 1927). But whereas sociologists recognize that social problems often follow certain regular stages of development, they also know that there are many deviations from the usual sequence.

In a useful formulation of the natural history approach, Malcolm Spector and John Kitsuse (1987) outlined the following major stages that most social problems seem to go through:

Stage 1—Problem definition. Groups in society attempt to gain recognition by a wider population (and the press and government) that some social condition is "offensive, harmful, or otherwise undesirable." These groups publicize their claims and attempt to turn the matter into a political issue.

Stage 2—Legitimacy. When the groups pressing their claims are considered credible and their assertions are accepted by official organizations, agencies, or institutions, there may be investigations, proposals for reform, and even the creation of new agencies to respond to claims and demands.

Stage 3—Reemergence of demands. Usually the original groups are not satisfied with the steps taken by official agencies; they demand stronger measures, more funding for enforcement, speedier handling of claims, and so on. They renew their appeals to the wider public and the press.

Stage 4—Rejection and institution building. The complainant groups usually decide that official responses to their demands are inadequate. They seek to develop their own organizations or counterinstitutions to press their claims and enact reforms.

Let us briefly apply this natural history model to the development of the idea that the easy availability of guns, especially handguns, automatic rifles and pistols, and assault weapons, contributes to higher murder rates and to sensational crimes like school shootings. In the 1980s, during the height of the crack cocaine epidemic, many teenagers and young adults were being killed in street shootings and drive-by killings. John Hinkley's shooting of President Reagan and his press secretary, James Brady, increased awareness of the problem of gun violence. At the same time, the rise of armed militia groups and an increase in the frequency of serial killings, some of which involved firearms, helped define the problem of violence as due to the easy availability of guns. Despite persistent lobbying by the National Rifle Association and other pro-gun groups, the problem definition gained credibility and legitimacy as citizen groups pressed their lawmakers for gun control legislation. The Brady Bill, which requires identity checks for gun purchasers, and the controversial ban on certain types of assault weapons resulted from this new sense of legitimacy for gun control advocates and their ideas. But the continued shootings in public schools–notably the one in Littleton, Colorado, in 1999—led to demands for more stringent gun control legislation, an issue that played an important role in the presidential campaigns of 2000.

The Media and Social Problems

In the second half of the twentieth century there was a communications revolution. The advent of television after World War II made far more news more immediately available to people in advanced industrial nations than had ever been possible before. In subsequent decades we have seen the advent of cable television, TV magazine shows like "60 Minutes," the Internet, and specialized magazines catering to a wide variety of interests. This communications revolution has had a lasting impact on our perception of social problems.

One effect is the speed of communication. Information about new diseases like AIDS can be disseminated throughout the population far faster than would have been possible in the past. The rapid availability of information can help people avoid certain kinds of problems, but it can also spread fear and lead to copycat behavior. The rapid spread of crack cocaine during the 1980s and early 1990s may have been due to some extent to the power of movies and the media to produce a fad in narcotics use; some sociologists believe that this also occurred in the 1960s with the spread of marijuana use among young Americans. But just as the media can accelerate the rise of social problems, so also they can educate the public about how to help solve such problems as crime, delinquency, and drug abuse. Throughout this text, where appropriate, we will point out the involvement of the media in social problems and in policies designed to solve or alleviate them.

Sociologist Barry Glassner (2000) argues that the media's passion for sensational stories about crime and violence and the public's ever-growing appetite for sensational coverage of violence actually mask important changes in social problems and divert public attention from problems that can be addressed through social policy. The recent killings in schools, for example, occurred as the actual rate of murder was decreasing rapidly, but the public was shocked by a few sensational crimes into overreacting to school crime and demanding measures that infringe on personal freedom and contribute to a decline in public optimism. We will revisit this argument elsewhere in the book, but it is important to note here that it only touches on the very complex relationship between public opinion and media coverage of social problems.

Table 1–2 traces the rise, fall, and often reemergence of a number of social problems as they were ranked by the American public in the second half of the twentieth century. Note that in 1999 the Gallup poll showed that only 17 percent rated crime as the "most important social problem facing the country today." But in 1950, at the height of the cold war after World War II, 40 percent rated war as the most serious problem, and in 1965, at the height of the civil rights movement, fully 52 percent of the public rated civil rights as the number one social problem. So do the media shape public opinion, or do the major events and social movements covered by the media determine how people rate the seriousness of social problems? The evidence in this series of data suggests that although the media play an important role in bringing information about events to the public, actual events such as rampant inflation, rising unemployment rates, the possible outbreak of war, and high rates of crime that affect people in their communities (as opposed to more sensational but isolated crimes covered on TV) shape the public's perception of how severe different social problems are.

TABLE 1–2 Topics Named When Respondents Were Asked: "What Do You Think Is the Most Important Problem Facing the Country Today?"

1950	1954*	1959*	1965	1970	1975
War: 40%	Threat of war: 18%	Keeping the peace: 38%	Civil rights: 52%	Campus unrest: 27%	High cost of living: 60%
The economy: 15%	Communism in U.S.: 17%	High cost of living: 17%	Foreign affairs: 39%	Vietnam War: 22%	Unemployment: 20%
Unemployment: 10%	Unemployment: 16%	Integration: 10%	Immorality, crime, juvenile delin-quency: 4%	Other international problems: 14%	Dissatisfaction with government: 7%
Communism: 8%	High cost of living: 13%	Unemployment: 9%	High cost of living: 3%	Racial strife: 13%	Energy crisis: 7%

1980	1985	1990	1995	1999
Foreign policy: 44%	Threat of war, inter-national tensions: 23%	Budget deficit: 21%	Crime, violence: 27%	Ethics, morality, family decline: 18%
High cost of living, inflation: 39%	Unemployment: 21%	Drug abuse: 18%	Unemployment: 15%	Crime, violence: 17%
Energy problems: 12%	High cost of living: 11%	Poverty, homeless-ness: 7%	Budget deficit: 14%	Education: 11%
Unemployment: 4%	Budget deficit: 10%	The economy: 7%	Health care: 12%	Guns, gun control: 10%

Some Events That May Have Been an Influence: 1950 Korean War. Senator Joseph R. McCarthy issues his first accusations of Communists in government. **1954** Secretary of State John Foster Dulles vows "massive retaliation" against Soviet aggression. **1955** The Supreme Court orders school desegregation to proceed "with all deliberate speed." **1957** Senator Strom Thurmond of South Carolina sets all-time filibuster record (24 hours, 27 minutes) with speech against civil rights. **1960** U-2 spy plane, with the American pilot Francis Gary Powers, is shot down over the Soviet Union. **1963** The Rev. Dr. Martin Luther King Jr. leads civil rights marches in the South and delivers his "I Have a Dream" speech at the March on Washington. **1965** U.S. troops are authorized to undertake offensive operations in South Vietnam. **1970** Four students are killed by National Guard units at Kent State University in Ohio. **1973** Senator Sam Ervin of North Carolina heads Senate investigation of the Watergate scandal on national television. **1973** Gas prices skyrocket after Arab nations embargo oil exports to U.S. **1973–75** The nation is stuck in recession. **1977** President Carter calls for "moral equivalent of war" in energy conservation. **1979** Iranian militants seize U.S. Embassy in Teheran, taking American hostages. U.S. inflation reaches its highest level in 33 years. **1983** Muslim terrorists kill 240 U.S. Marines in a suicide bombing in Lebanon. **1987** President Reagan submits first trillion-dollar budget to Congress as deficits mount. **1994** The Bureau of Justice Statistics announces that the number of inmates topped one million, giving the U.S. the highest incarceration rate in the world. **1999** Two students open fire in a Colorado high school, killing 15, including themselves.

*Data for 1955 and 1960 not available.

Source: *New York Times,* August 1, 1999. Copyright © 1999 by The New York Times Co. Reprinted by permission.

Research on Social Problems

Katherine Newman (1999) is a professor of anthropology and sociology at Harvard University's Kennedy School. She works closely with William Julius Wilson, the nation's leading expert on inner-city poverty. Newman has spent the last few years studying the kinds of jobs young people from ghetto neighborhoods get when they do find jobs. The majority of those jobs are in the fast-food industry. Contrary to what many critics assert, young people often learn valuable skills at these jobs. Moreover, such jobs are not easy to obtain because of the lack of alternatives in the local labor market. As a result, young people often find that they are better off staying on the job and learning the habits of the workplace, including punctuality and cleanliness. With that experience, they stand a better chance of landing other, perhaps more interesting work later on. Newman's research uses the methods of **ethnography,** the close observation of interactions among people in a social group or organization.

Lyn Lofland and her students at the University of California at Irvine are conducting research on the way women and men cope with the pressures and problems of urban living. They are particularly interested in the way gender influences people's experiences on city streets. Through careful observation of the street life of cities like

The effects of natural disasters in densely populated urban areas are an increasingly important aspect of the study of social problems such as homelessness.

San Francisco, the researchers hope to help urban planners find ways to enable members of both sexes to feel safe in public places.

Yale University sociologist Kai Erikson (1995) recently investigated the effects of a local bank's failure on migrant farm workers and sharecroppers in rural Florida. Erikson was asked to conduct this research by the law firm representing the people who lost their savings as a result of the bank's failure. The firm's attorneys learned about him through his famous study of the effects of the dam rupture at Buffalo Creek, West Virginia, in 1972. Erikson's book about the resulting flood, *Everything in Its Path,* won a National Book Award for social research and helped make lawmakers more sensitive to the human costs of major natural and economic disasters.

These three examples illustrate some of the ways in which sociological research is brought to bear on social problems. We could add many more. When the media seek an expert to comment on changes in crime rates from one year to the next, they often call on criminologists such as Hans Zeisel, whose work we will encounter in Chapter 6. When members of Congress debate the merits of different proposals for reforming the welfare system, they often turn to the work of sociologists such as Mary Jo Bane, an expert on trends in welfare dependency, or they may consult Sheldon Danziger and his colleagues at the University of Washington's Institute for Research on Poverty. In these and countless other areas, sociologists are asked to conduct empirical research and to supply information that can be referred to in debates on these issues.

In this age of rapid social change, information about social problems is in ever-increasing demand. Even if you do not go on to a career that requires expertise in social research, as an informed citizen you will benefit from the ability to evaluate its findings. In this section, therefore, we will briefly introduce the most frequently used research methods: demographic studies, survey research, field observations, and social experiments.

Demographic Studies

Demography is the subfield of sociology that studies how social conditions are distributed in human populations and how those populations are changing. When we ask how many people are affected by a particular condition or problem—for example, when we want to know how many people are affected by crime or unemployment—we are asking a demographic question. The answers to such questions consist of numerical data about the people affected compared to those who are not affected. Demographers frequently supply data about the *incidence* of a social phenomenon; that is, how many people are affected and to what extent. Incidence can be given in absolute numbers; for example, in 1997 there were 3,335 people under sentence of death in the United States, of whom 1,876 were white and 1,459 were nonwhite (*Statistical Abstract*, 1999). The incidence of a phenomenon can also be expressed as a *rate*. According to the National Center on Child Abuse and Neglect, for example, in 1999 the rate of reported cases of child abuse was 430 per 10,000 children in the U.S. population; in 1976 it was 101 per 10,000. Rates are often more useful than absolute numbers because they are not affected by changes in population size. Thus, in the example just given, the increase in reported cases of child abuse is not due to the growth of the population during the period covered but must have some other cause.

Survey Research

We often take for granted the availability of statistics about social conditions and problems. Every month we see reports on the latest unemployment figures or crime rates or trends in the cost of housing, and we are given statistics on what people think about these and other issues. Political campaigns rely heavily on measures of public opinion, both on the issues and on the popularity of the candidates. All this information, including the basic information about the U.S. population derived from the national census, is obtained through a sociological method known as **survey research.**

Survey research was developed early in the twentieth century as a way of gathering information from a number of people, known as a **sample,** who represent the behavior and attitudes of the larger population from which they are selected. Today survey research is a major industry in much of the world. The techniques of sampling and interviewing are used routinely by market research firms, political polling organizations, media corporations of all types, university research centers, and many other organizations, including the Census Bureau and other government agencies. Whenever we encounter statistics about what people in a society believe about a problem or how different groups within a population behave, there is a good chance that those statistics are based on the results of a survey.

In a survey, people speak to interviewers—in person, on the telephone, or by mail—and provide them with information, which is aggregated and converted into numerical data. When looking at survey data, therefore, be sure to ask who was interviewed and for what reasons. You should also ask whether the survey reports the results of a set of questions asked about conditions prevailing at one time or whether matched samples of respondents were interviewed on more than one occasion. A questionnaire that is given to a sample of respondents on a single occasion yields what sociologists call **cross-sectional data** on behavior and opinion at a particular time. Comparisons of matched samples over time yield **longitudinal data,** which tell us what changes have occurred in a particular social condition over a specific period.

Field Observation

When sociologists seek to understand the processes that occur among the people who are directly involved in a social problem, they may attempt to observe social behavior as it is actually taking place. This often requires the sociologist to participate directly in the social life of the individuals or groups in question, a technique known as **participant observation** or **field research.** (The term *field* refers to the social settings in which the observed behavior occurs.) Neighborhoods; communities; organizations like police headquarters, hospital emergency rooms, prisons, or schools—all are examples of field settings. The technique of participant observation requires skill in gaining and keeping the trust of the people whose behavior is being observed; practice in careful observation and recording of the behaviors in question; and skill at conducting interviews that may range over many issues, some of which may be highly personal or controversial.

Research based on participant observation usually seeks to discover how the processes of human interaction contribute to particular social conditions or problems. Thus, field research frequently, though not always, applies the interactionist perspective. This approach is illustrated in the following example.

In a classic study of how people become drug users, sociologist Howard Becker interacted with groups of musicians and other people who were likely to use marijuana. A jazz musician himself, Becker was readily accepted in the groups whose behavior he wished to observe. As he watched first-time users take their first puffs on a joint, he noted that they often claimed not to feel any effect, even when Becker himself observed changes in their behavior. But when more experienced users explained to the novice what the "proper" feelings were, the new smokers began to feel the sensation of being high. Becker concluded that to some extent the experience of using marijuana is a social construction; the drug may have certain physiological effects on everyone, but social interaction must occur for the new smoker to define what the appropriate feelings are and then to experience them. Becker's (1963a) famous article, "Becoming a Marijuana User," was among the first empirical descriptions of the degree to which the experience and extent of drug use are determined by users' definitions of the situation. It is an excellent example of how sociologists can discover important aspects of behavior through observation in the field.

In the chapters to come, whenever we refer to a field research study or to participant observation research, remember that the researcher has actually observed the behavior in question. Also, since the research describes the behavior of real people, note how careful the researcher has been to disguise the identities of the individuals who were observed and interviewed.

Social Experiments

There are times when it is possible for a sociologist or other social scientist to apply experimental methods to the study of a social problem. In an experiment, the investigator attempts to systematically vary the conditions that are of interest in order to determine their effects. In a controlled experiment, the investigator applies a "treatment" to one group—that is, exposes its members to a certain condition, to which they must somehow respond—but does not apply the treatment to a second group that is identical to the first in every other way. The subjects who receive the treatment are known as the **experimental group;** those who do not are the **control group.** When the investigator compares the experiences of the experimental and control groups, it can be assumed that any differences between them are due to the effects of the treatment.

We will have occasion in later chapters to describe controlled experiments that have applied this model to human subjects to study social problems. Here we will briefly present two examples of social experiments. One of them was able to use both experimental and control groups; the other could establish only an experimental group.

To study the influence of jobs on ex-offenders, the Vera Institute of Justice undertook the Wildcat experiment, in which individuals serving jail terms were allowed to take part in various forms of "supported work." Instead of being placed individually in unfamiliar jobs, Wildcat workers were assigned to jobs in groups of three to seven and received guidance and evaluation while they were working. Other prisoners were assigned to individual jobs under traditional work-release arrangements; they constituted a control group. The results of the experiment were mixed: Although the Wildcat workers earned more, had more stable jobs, and were less likely to become dependent on welfare than members of the control group, they were also more likely to be arrested and returned to prison (L. N. Friedman, 1978).

In sharp contrast to the Wildcat experiment is the famous "prison" study conducted by Philip Zimbardo and his colleagues. The researchers created a simulated prison in the basement of a building at Stanford University. Twenty-four students who had volunteered to take part in the experiment were divided into two groups: "prisoners" and "guards." The prisoners were confined to the simulated prison, and the guards were instructed in their duties and responsibilities. In this experiment it was not possible to form a control group; in fact, the experiment itself was canceled after six days. In that brief time both the guards and the prisoners had become unable to distinguish between the experiment and reality, with the result that "human values

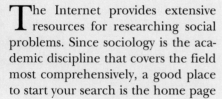

SOCIAL PROBLEMS ONLINE

Researching Social Problems

The Internet provides extensive resources for researching social problems. Since sociology is the academic discipline that covers the field most comprehensively, a good place to start your search is the home page of Princeton University's Sociology Department, **http://www.princeton.edu/~sociolog/**. The page includes links with other sociology departments on each continent, domestic and international research institutes, data archives, and web pages for academic journals.

If you are interested in the theoretical antecedents to the study of social problems, a web page with a sense of humor is that of the Dead Sociologists' Society at **http://www.diogenes.baylor.edu/WWWproviders/ Larry_Ridener/DSS/DEADSOC.HTML**. It provides links to pages devoted to some of the founders of sociology, such as Émile Durkheim and Karl Marx, as well as organizations like the Society for the Study of Social Problems (**http://funnelweb.utcc.utk.edu/~sssp/**).

The Urban Institute, one of the nation's premier think tanks for social problems, has a website (**http://www.urban.org**) that contains many of its publications on civil rights, crime, education, poverty, and government policy in a downloadable format. Current and back issues of its periodicals are also available. The site is updated regularly and has a search feature that functions much like a high-powered index.

Studying social problems requires knowledge of public opinion. The Gallup Organization, sponsor of the world-famous Gallup poll, has a home page at **http://www.gallup.org/** with reports on its weekly surveys of political developments in the United States. Besides election polls and surveys of public opinion in the United States and abroad, links are available to some of the marketing research done by the firm's foreign affiliates. Roper Search Worldwide, whose motto is "Turning Data into Intelligence Worldwide," is located at **http:// www.roper.com/** and features data on international public opinion and marketing.

Should you be interested in analyzing public opinion research data on your own, Queens College of the City University of New York has a downloadable personal computer (PC) version of the General Social Survey (GSS) data at **http://www.soc.qc.edu/QC_ Software/GSS.html.** The GSS is an annual survey of approximately 30,000 families in the United States that collects data on political and social attitudes. The survey has been conducted annually since the early 1970s by the National Opinion Research Center (**http:// www.norc.uchicago.edu/**). The Queens College site also has a free and easy-to-learn downloadable statistical software package.

were suspended, self-concepts were challenged, and the ugliest, most base, pathological side of human nature surfaced" (Zimbardo, 1972, p. 243).

As informative as experimental studies like these may be, they raise major questions about the ethical limits of social research. Sociologists and other social scientists realize that they must not infringe on the basic rights of human subjects. Under the rules of professional associations like the American Sociological Association and the guidelines of government agencies like the National Institute of Mental Health, people who conduct research with human subjects must guarantee the following rights:

1. *Privacy*—the right of the individual to define, with only extraordinary exceptions in the interest of society, when and on what terms his or her acts should be revealed to the general public.

2. *Confidentiality*—the assurance that information supplied by a subject or respondent will not be passed on to anyone else in a form that could be traced to that respondent.

3. *Informed consent*—the right of subjects and respondents to be informed beforehand about what they are being asked and how the information they supply will be used.

SOCIAL POLICY

Much of the research conducted by sociologists is designed to provide information to be used in formulating social policies, as well as in evaluating existing policies and suggesting improvements and new directions. **Social policies** are formal procedures designed to remedy a social problem. Generally they are designed by officials of government at the local, state, or federal level, but they can also be initiated by private citizens in voluntary associations, by corporations, and by nonprofit foundations.

There is generally a good deal of debate about any proposed social policy. Much of the debate consists of discussion and analysis of how well a proposed policy appears to address the problem. Such analysis tends to be considered technical in the sense that, although there is general agreement on the need to address the problem, the debate hinges on the adequacy of the proposed means to achieve the agreed-upon ends. Increasingly, however, we are witnessing policy debates that are ideological rather than technical, and in the United States such debates frequently pit conservatives against liberals or socialists.

Conservatives usually seek to limit the involvement of government in the solution of social problems. They believe that private firms, governed by the need to compete in markets and make profits, are the best type of organization for coping with the problems of prisons, schools, and the like. Liberals and socialists reject the dominance of the market (and, hence, the profit motive) in social-welfare institutions. However, the policies they propose may expand government bureaucracies without always delivering adequate services to the populations that need them.

Throughout this century the government's role in attempting to solve social problems has increased steadily, despite the ideological stands of various administrations. America's role as a world military power, for example, has required the continual expenditure of public funds on military goods and services. These costs have increased dramatically with every war and every major change in military technology. Similarly, the fight against drug commerce has added greatly to the cost of maintaining the society's judicial and penal institutions.

Every function of government has a similar history of escalating costs because of increases in the scale of the society or the scope of the problem. During the 1980s, for example, the Reagan administration sought to decrease the cost of government involvement in regulating economic institutions such as airlines, banks, and financial markets. Among other measures taken were those designed to decrease the regulation of the banking industry. Banks and savings and loan associations were allowed to operate in markets that had previously been barred to them because of the risks involved. At the same time, personnel cuts were made in the federal bank regulatory agencies. The risk to depositors was held to a minimum by the continued existence of government guarantees in the form of deposit insurance. The combination of deregulation and deposit insurance, along with regional recessions in the oil-producing states, caused many savings and loan associations to become insolvent, exposing the often corrupt practices of their directors. Amid escalating costs to the government and American taxpayers—estimated in the hundreds of billions of dollars—Congress once again passed legislation designed to increase regulation of the banking industry and to prevent future financial disasters of such magnitude.

Policy decisions of similar scope are responsible for unemployment insurance, Social Security, community mental-health systems, and numerous other benefits that Americans have come to view as "entitlements" of citizenship. But these benefits are costly. They require the transfer (via taxation) of funds from the well-off to the less well-off. As the overall cost of government has increased, so has the tax burden on individual citizens. This increase in the cost of government comes from policies that serve specific segments of the population, as well as from those designed to be of benefit to the entire population. For example, organized labor has consistently promoted policies that regulate industry in the interests of workers, whereas industrialists claim that any regulations that increase their costs of doing business will hurt their ability to compete in domestic or world markets.

These women are working together in the Mentor Project of the Coalition for the Advancement of Economic Self-Sufficiency, a program that matches volunteers, one-on-one, in helping move people off welfare rolls.

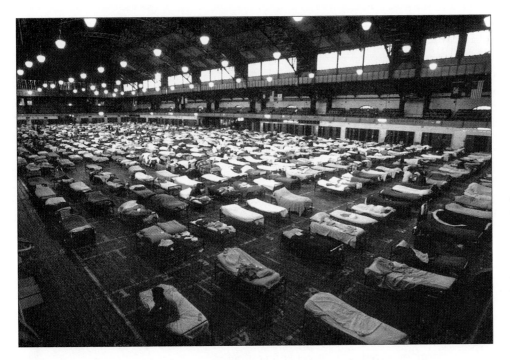

As homelessness has come to be recognized as a major social problem, efforts have been made to provide shelter for homeless people, including a growing number of children. Vast "congregate shelters" like the one shown here are unable to cope effectively with the complex mental and physical problems of many homeless people.

This conflict is typical of many current controversies over the best ways to handle social issues, with conservatives stressing private or market solutions and liberals calling for public or government actions. Some of the conflicting approaches to the solution of various social problems that have been proposed by conservatives, liberals, and others will be discussed in the Social Policy sections that conclude each chapter of this book, as well as in boxed features that focus on particular controversies.

Beyond Left & Right

Social problems evoke strong moral reactions from people. Whether the issue is homelessness, drug abuse, bankruptcy, or any of the other controversial problems dealt with in this book, discussions of the problem raise many difficult moral and ideological questions. Voices on the conservative side of the ideological spectrum of American politics—that is, on the right—tend to take a moral stance on many social problems and often insist on individual responsibility for solving them. Voices on the liberal side—that is, on the left—are more likely to argue that social problems arise from social conditions as well as individual weaknesses, and are more likely to advocate public efforts to address those problems. People in the middle may simply be cautious or undecided about where they stand.

Where do you stand? Are you more likely to argue from a conservative or a liberal position about social problems? Do you feel torn when issues are debated from conservative and liberal positions? How can a course in the sociology of social problems help sort out the arguments and go beyond the shouting?

Sociologists have personal views about the major social issues of their time, but they try to keep those views in the background in order to assess the facts. When sociologists examine the social policies directed at solving social problems, they recognize that laws and policies reflect the ideological and moral divisions of the people who make them. A sociological stance on social problems tries to go beyond the ideological divisions in society by examining the consequences of different policies. By adopting a sociological view of issues, you will not have to abandon your own moral positions, but you will have to question how far you can push these beliefs onto others and still make progress toward solving difficult social problems.

SUMMARY

- When most people in a society agree that a condition exists that threatens the quality of their lives and their most cherished values, and they also agree that something should be done to remedy it, sociologists say that society has defined that condition as a social problem.

- Sociologists who study social problems ask questions about the social rather than the individual aspects of a problem. The primary sociological approaches to the study of social problems are the functionalist, conflict, and interactionist perspectives.

- The functionalist perspective looks at the way major social institutions actually operate. From this perspective, the main reason for the existence of social problems is that societies are always changing; failure to adapt successfully to change leads to social problems.

- In the early 1900s, functionalist theorists saw social problems like criminal deviance as a form of social pathology. Later they tended to emphasize the effects of immigration, urbanization, and industrialization; this emphasis formed the basis of social-disorganization theory. Modern functionalists often conduct institutional research designed to show how people and societies reorganize their lives and institutions to cope with new conditions.

- The conflict perspective is based on the belief that social problems arise out of major contradictions in the way societies are organized, which lead to large-scale conflict. This perspective owes a great deal to the writings of the German social theorist Karl Marx.

- Marxian conflict theory attributes most social problems to underlying patterns of class conflict. A broader view is taken by value conflict theorists, who believe that social problems occur when groups with different values meet and compete.

■ Research based on the interactionist perspective looks at the processes whereby different people become part of a situation that the larger society defines as a social problem. It focuses on the ways in which people actually take on the values of the group of which they are members.

■ According to labeling theory, social problems are conditions under which certain behaviors or situations become defined as problems. In this view, the cause of a social problem is simply society's awareness that a certain behavior or situation exists. The labels applied to certain behaviors act as self-fulfilling prophecies because people who are so labeled accept society's definition of themselves and behave accordingly.

■ The most frequently used research methods in the study of social problems are demographic studies, survey research, field observation, and social experiments.

People who conduct research with human subjects must guarantee the rights of privacy, confidentiality, and informed consent.

■ Social policies are formal procedures designed to remedy a social problem. They are formulated by officials of governments at all levels, as well as by voluntary associations, corporations, and nonprofit foundations. Much of the research conducted by sociologists is designed to provide information to be used in formulating and evaluating social policies.

■ The natural history approach to the analysis of social problems focuses on public perception of conditions that come to be defined as problems. In this view, there are four stages in the development of a social problem: problem definition, legitimacy, reemergence of demands, and rejection and institution building.

KEY TERMS

social problem, p. 4
status, p. 7
role, p. 7
institution, p. 7
social pathology, p. 9
social disorganization, p. 9
institution building, p. 10

conflict perspective, p. 10
secondary deviance, p. 13
ethnography, p. 17
demography, p. 19
survey research, p. 19
sample, p. 19
cross-sectional data, p. 19

longitudinal data, p. 19
participant observation, p. 20
field research, p. 20
experimental group, p. 20
control group, p. 20
social policies, p. 22

INTERNET EXERCISE

The web destinations for Chapter 1 are related to different aspects of sociological perspectives on social problems. To begin your explorations, go to the Prentice Hall Companion Website: **http://prenhall.com/kornblum**. Then choose **Chapter 1** (Sociological Perspectives on Social Problems). Next, select **destinations** from the menu on the left side of the screen. There are a variety of sites to investigate. We suggest that you begin with **SocioRealm**. After you have accessed this site, click on *Social Theory*. Chapter 1 discusses three core perspectives on social problems: functionalist, conflict, and interactionist. From the *Social Theory* screen, click on *Durkheim* for a review of functionalism; click on *Marx* for further discussion of the conflict perspective; scroll down to *Charles H. Cooley* for a

different look at the interactionist perspective. If you have time, you may wish to explore other social theorists who are highlighted within this website. After you have explored the SocioRealm site, answer the following questions:

■ What are the core assumptions of each major theoretical perspective (functionalist, conflict, and interactionist)?

■ All of the early social theorists, such as Émile Durkheim, Karl Marx, and Max Weber, had certain concerns in common. What are some of these common concerns, and how do they relate to the perceived social problems during the time periods involved?

2 Problems of Physical Health

HEALTH AND HEALTH CARE

- A person born in Sierra Leone in 1997 can expect to live less than 40 years. In the United States, a person born in 1997 can expect to live about 77 years.

- More than 44 million Americans have no health insurance, and millions more have inadequate coverage.

- The infant mortality rate for blacks is 15.1 per 1,000 live births; for whites, it is 6.3.

- Expenditures on health care in the United States increased by about 200 percent between 1980 and 1996.

- Throughout the world, about 30 million people are infected with the HIV virus, 90 percent of them in the developing nations of Asia and sub-Saharan Africa.

OUTLINE

Health Care as a Global Social Problem

The Scope of Health-care Problems in America
Unequal Access to Health Services
The High Cost of Health Care
Inadequate Protection
Women and Health Care
The Disabled and Handicapped
Ethical Issues

AIDS—A Modern Plague

Explanations of Health-care Problems
Class and Class Conflict
Institutions and Health Care
Health and Social Interaction

Social Policy
Managed Care
Insurance Reform
The Disabled and Handicapped
Social Policy and AIDS

A mericans are spending more on health care each year. Increasingly, however, they feel that they are getting less care and more worry in return for their dollars. Little wonder that health-care issues are becoming more and more important in voters' ratings of political candidates. The problems associated with reforming the health-care system are vastly complicated by specific health problems that affect many Americans. The spread of AIDS, babies born with fetal alcohol syndrome or drug addiction, new strains of virulent diseases like tuberculosis, the moral dilemmas of prolonging or terminating life—these and other developments that we discuss in this chapter are all serious problems in themselves. But from a sociological standpoint the most significant problems are those that stem from the inadequacies of the existing health-care system or from the growing social inequalities that produce increasingly unequal access to health care.

Health Care as a Global Social Problem

Health care presents a variety of social problems to all of the world's societies. In more affluent regions like western Europe, North America, and Australia, the problems associated with physical health often involve reducing inequalities in access to high-quality health care. In impoverished regions of the world, where high-quality medical care is often lacking, the social problems associated with physical health are even more profound. These problems include the spread of infectious diseases, high rates of infant and maternal death, low life expectancies, scarcities of medical personnel and equipment, and inadequate sewage and water systems.

It is true that in the past half century there have been increases in life expectancy in most regions of the world. These improvements often reflect better water and sewage systems, as well as child vaccination programs. But recent reviews of the global health situation warn that continued improvements in public health systems and in the delivery of medical services will be necessary, especially in poor regions, if these gains are to continue (United Nations, 1999).

The United Nations rates nations on the basis of a series of indicators of health, education, equality of political participation, and many other factors. The nations are then grouped into high, medium, and low levels of human development for purposes of comparison. The figures in Table 2–1 indicate how much or little improvement various nations have made in two key health indicators, life expectancy and infant mortality.

Life expectancy is highly correlated with the quality of health care in a society. As a population's health improves as a result of better medical care and improved living conditions, the average age to which its members live (i.e., the life expectancy of the population) rises dramatically. For example, Table 2–1 indicates that a person born in Sierra Leone in 1997 can expect to live less than 40 years; in contrast, a person born in the United States in 1997 can expect to live about 77 years.

Differences in life expectancy between developed and less developed nations are due largely to the increasing chance that people in the former will survive the childhood diseases and parasites that cause such high death rates in the latter. Table 2–1 shows the wide gap between the industrial and low-income countries in infant mortality rates, the most important comparative indicator of health. In Sierra Leone the infant mortality rate is 182, more than twice the rate in India, 26 times the rate in the United States, and 46 times the rate in Argentina.

Infant mortality rates are highly correlated with the number of health-care professionals in a society, which serves as a measure of the quality of the health care available to its members. However, other factors besides the availability of health-care professionals may affect the health of a population. In the poorest regions of the world, malnutrition, a decline in breast-feeding, and inadequate sanitation and health facilities are associated with high infant and child mortality. In the case of breast-feeding, companies that sell infant milk formulas have been implicated in the negative change. However, poor maternal health and lack of prenatal care contribute even more to persistent high rates of infant mortality. International health organizations have been

TABLE 2–1   Health Indicators for Selected Nations

	Life Expectancy at Birth		Infant Mortality Rate (per 1,000 live births)	
	1970	1997	1970	1997
High human development	70.6	77.0	25	7
United States	70.7	76.7	20	7
Sweden	74.4	78.5	11	4
Argentina	66.3	72.9	59	21
Costa Rica	66.7	76.0	58	12
Medium human development	57.3	66.6	101	51
Hungary	69.3	70.9	36	10
Mexico	61.1	72.2	79	29
China	62.0	69.8	85	38
India	49.1	62.6	130	71
Low human development	42.8	50.6	147	106
Nepal	42.1	57.3	156	75
Nigeria	42.7	50.1	120	112
Sierra Leone	34.4	37.2	206	182

Source: United Nations, 1999.

urging more affluent nations to assist poorer ones in expanding maternal health care and promoting basic literacy and health-education programs for women.

At the International Conference on Population and Development in 1995, delegates agreed that countries with the highest levels of mortality "should aim to achieve by 2005 a maternal mortality rate below 125 per 100,000 live births and by 2015 a rate below 75 per 100,000" (United Nations, 1999). But these improvements will require far more health-care resources than are currently available in the poor nations of Africa, Latin America, and Asia. Moreover, the emergence of new and extremely deadly epidemics, especially AIDS and other sexually transmitted diseases, diverts scarce medical resources away from basic health care and preventive public health programs.

In the United States, our comparatively poor health is due largely to the way we live; sedentary occupations, fattening, nonnutritious foods, and lack of proper exercise contribute to the high incidence of heart disease and other ailments. Environmental pollution and cigarette smoking contribute to the high incidence of respiratory disease and cancer. There can be little doubt, however, that many of our health problems are aggravated by the kind of medical care that is—or is not—available.

Medical sociology is the subfield of sociology that specializes in research on the health-care system and its impact on the public, especially access to health care (Cockerham, 1998; Matcha, 1999) and the evolution of health-care institutions (Starr, 1995). In describing problems of physical health, sociologists are particularly interested in learning how a person's social class (as measured by income, education, and occupation) influences his or her access to medical care and its outcome. Sociologists also work with economists and health-care planners in assessing the costs of different types of health-care delivery systems (Bergthold, 1990).

Medical sociologists often point out that health-care institutions themselves are the source of many of the problems we associate with health in the United States. They emphasize that the health-care system has evolved in such a way that doctors maintain private practices while society supports the hospitals and insurance systems that allow them to function (Fox, 1997). In other words, American health care never developed as a purely competitive industry or a regulated public service. Instead, as we will see shortly, it became a complex institution comprising many private and public organizations.

As great strides were made in the ability to treat illnesses—especially through the use of antibiotics—and to prevent them through improved public health practices, doctors began to develop narrow specialties and to refer patients to hospitals with special facilities. This created a situation in which doctors and hospital personnel became highly interdependent and developed a need to "assert their long-run collective interests over their short-run individual interests" (Starr, 1982, p. 230). All efforts to change our health-care system, to make it less costly or more efficient or more humane, must deal with the power of insurance companies, doctors, and other health-care providers, which derives not from their wealth or their ownership of health-care facilities but from their mode of relating to one another and to the public (Marmor, 1994). This is a subject that will become clear once we have discussed some of the specific problems of health care in American society.

The Scope of Health-Care Problems in America

The range of situations in which health care can be viewed as a social problem is extremely wide. At the micro, or individual, level, where people we know and love are affected, we think of such problems as whether to terminate life-support systems or whether the correct medical treatment is being applied or whether an elderly parent should be placed in a nursing home. But people's experiences at the micro level are influenced by larger forces that act throughout society and touch the lives of millions. These are the macro problems of health care. At the micro level we may worry about elderly loved ones, but at the macro level the issue is how effectively health care is distributed among all people (including the elderly and the poor) and what can be done to improve the delivery of needed medical services.

In this section we explore several aspects of health care in the United States that contribute to social problems at both the micro and macro levels. Unequal access to health services, the high cost of health care, inadequate insurance coverage, the special problems of women and the disabled and handicapped, and ethical issues arising from medical technology are among the problems that must be addressed if more Americans are to receive more and better health care. And as we will see in the next section, these issues become even more critical in the context of the AIDS epidemic.

Unequal Access to Health Care

Health care is distributed very unevenly in the United States. More than 44 million citizens have no health insurance, and millions more have inadequate coverage (Pear, 1999b). The poor, the near-poor, members of racial and ethnic minority groups, and residents of depressed rural areas are most likely to fall into the uninsured category. Economic class and race are also correlated with the risk of becoming seriously ill. For example, industrial workers are more likely to contract certain forms of cancer and respiratory diseases than other population groups, and lack of prenatal care is a serious problem in minority communities (Wellner, 1999). Thus, to a large extent health care as a social problem can be viewed in terms of inequality of access to health-care services.

Inequalities of Class and Race. The use and availability of medical care are directly related to socioeconomic class and race. The racial aspect is most directly illustrated by a comparison of life expectancy for whites and nonwhites: on average, the life expectancy for white males is about six years longer than that for black males; the

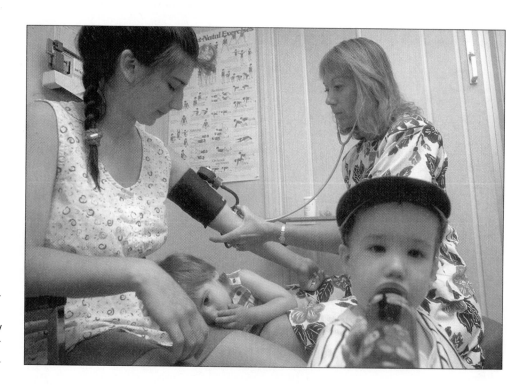

Changes in the U.S. health-care system and cuts in funding for health services are increasing the difficulty of obtaining decent health care for lower-income families like this one.

life expectancy for white females is about four years longer than that for black females. In addition, the infant mortality rate for blacks is more than twice that for whites: 13.7 per 1,000 live births, compared to 6.0 (*Statistical Abstract,* 1999). Nonwhites suffer proportionately more from almost every illness than do whites; and because they are less likely to have been immunized, nonwhites suffer higher rates of death from infectious diseases. Such differences cannot be ascribed to income differences alone since even in cases in which income is the same, death rates remain higher for nonwhites.

To be black and poor places one at the greatest risk of not receiving adequate health care or emergency treatment. In a study of patients at U.S. hospitals, medical researchers found that only 47 percent of very sick black and poor patients were put in intensive-care units, whereas 70 percent of white and poor Medicare patients were so placed. And even in federal Veterans Administration hospitals, where care is supposedly more uniformly distributed, blacks were less likely than whites to receive more costly medical procedures like catheterization of the heart for blocked arteries (Blakeslee, 1994). Reflecting on these and other disparities, former Secretary of Health and Human Services Louis W. Sullivan observed that "everybody believes that because we are all human beings, we are all the same. But the research shows that when we are sick we are very different" (Noble, 1999, p. F12).

From a socioeconomic point of view, there is a strong relationship between membership in a lower class and a higher rate of illness. People in the lower classes tend to feel sicker and have higher rates of untreated illnesses than people in the middle and upper classes. They also tend to be disabled more frequently and for longer periods. Moreover, mortality rates for almost all diseases are higher among the lower classes. In a classic study of social class and mortality, British researchers tracked almost 18,000 male civil service employees over a ten-year period. They found that mortality rates varied directly with the individual's job classification, a measure of social class (Marmot, Shipley, & Rose, 1984).

These findings are presented in Figure 2–1. They show that in the population studied, the risk of dying was more than twice as high for manual workers in the civil service as for professionals and administrative personnel, especially in middle age (40–64 years old). A more recent survey of class and illness found that people who had been unemployed for a month or more were 3.8 times more susceptible to a virus than people who were not experiencing the stress of joblessness (Goode, 1999; Marmot, 1998).

Low income affects the health of the poor from birth. The high rate of infant mortality among the poor is due to a number of factors associated with poverty.

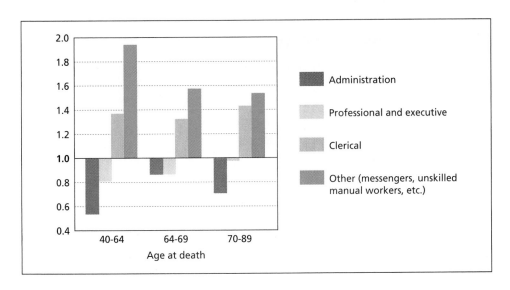

Figure 2–1 Relative Risk of Dying (1 = average of all groups)

Source: Goode, 1999. Copyright © 1999 by The New York Times Co. Reprinted by permission.

Inadequate nutrition appears to account for the high death rates among the new-born children of low-income mothers. The babies most at risk are those with a low birthweight. Among the causes of low birthweight are the low nutritional value of the mother's diet, smoking or other drug use by the mother during pregnancy, and lack of prenatal care. After the neonatal period (the first three months), the higher rate of infant death among the poor is linked with a greater incidence of infectious diseases. Such diseases, in turn, are associated with poor sanitation and lack of access to high-quality medical care, as well as, in some cases, drug use.

Before the creation of Medicaid, poor people who could not afford private physicians relied on a "meager combination of charity care, public hospitals and clinics, and limited public welfare-based assistance for the financing and provision of health care" (Rowland, 1994, p. 191). After the passage of Medicaid in 1965, the poor increased their consumption of medical services dramatically. Medicaid accounted for about 12 percent of the nation's health-care spending and served slightly over 30 million people. Just over half of the expenses were contributed by the federal government and the remainder by individual states (Rowland, 1994). However, with the passage of welfare reform in 1996, Medicaid funding has been reduced, with the result that many poor people are receiving less medical care now than in recent decades (Birenbaum, 1995). (The Social Policy section of this chapter presents more analysis of this situation.)

The High Cost of Health Care

Unequal access to health care is related to its cost, which is very high. In fact, because of the rapid rates of increase in the cost of medical care in recent years, the American health-care system is often said to be in crisis. Expenditures on health care in the United States amounted to $3,800 per capita in 1997, an increase of about 200 percent over the 1980 level of $1,002 per capita (*Statistical Abstract,* 1999). It is true that all the highly developed nations have had high levels of health-care spending, as can be seen in Figure 2–2. Nevertheless, the United States has seen the highest increases in these expenditures, despite a slowing in the rate of inflation in medical costs in the past five years.

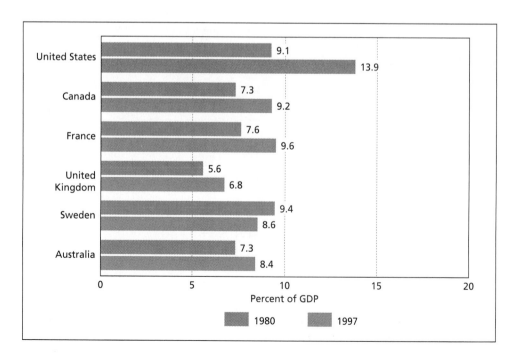

Figure 2–2 Spending on Health Care, Selected Countries

Source: Data from *Statistical Abstract,* 1999.

Runaway health-care costs began to be a serious social problem in the United States during the 1970s and 1980s. Before then, medical costs as a share of gross domestic product (GDP) were not out of line with those in other highly developed Western nations. Why have health-care costs risen so sharply in the United States, and why have they proven so difficult to control? One answer may be found in the third-party, fee-for-services system that resulted from the expansion of medical insurance in the 1960s. As the cost of health care was increasingly separated from the patient's household budget through coverage by third parties (public and private insurers), more people were receiving more medical services but at a greater cost to the third parties, which paid doctors and hospitals fees for services. Thus, as Paul Starr (1982) explains, "Since under fee-for-services, doctors and hospitals make more money the more services they provide, they have an incentive to maximize the volume of services. Third-party, fee-for-service payment was the central mechanism of medical inflation" (p. 385). The clearest example of this problem is the cost of hospital care.

Hospitals.   Spending for personal health care accounts for almost 89 percent of total national health-care expenditures, and hospital charges account for about 38 cents of every dollar spent on personal health care (*Statistical Abstract*, 1999). As the population continues to age, the costs of nursing-home care and related services will continue to escalate. These trends combine to make health-care reform and control of health-care expenditures an urgent national priority (White House Domestic Policy Council, 1993).

Until the mid-1980s, hospital costs rose at a dramatic pace, primarily because hospitals had little incentive to keep costs down. Both patients and physicians were often discouraged from using hospitals on an outpatient basis, and hospitals offered few self-care facilities for patients who could look after themselves. This situation was aggravated by health insurance programs like Blue Cross, which enabled hospitals to raise their fees almost at will. Expensive medical technologies are another important factor in the increase in hospital costs, as is the aging of the population, which increases the demand for hospital services.

In recent years the rate of increase in hospital costs has slowed somewhat, largely as a result of improvements in the efficiency of hospital administration. Among the techniques that have been used to reduce the level of hospital costs are preadmission testing in outpatient departments and physicians' offices and a reduction in the average length of hospital stays. In addition, many procedures that formerly were performed on an inpatient basis have been moved to outpatient and office settings. Other factors in the reduction of the overall level of hospital care are the increased use of second opinions and an increase in care by nonhospital providers such as nursing homes and home health agencies (Atkins, 1999; Craig, 1993).

Unfortunately, these various measures to control costs have not been fully successful. And as more patients are treated outside of hospitals or stay in hospitals for shorter periods, the costs of home care of the ill are rising rapidly. Another problem is that severe measures to reduce hospital costs have a disproportionate impact on the poor and the elderly, who are more likely to suffer from chronic illnesses that may require hospitalization. These and similar situations illustrate the tendency of cost-control efforts in one area to result in higher costs elsewhere, and they provide an argument for comprehensive reform of the nation's health-care system.

Physicians.   Another factor in the high cost of health care is the fees charged by physicians. Of each dollar spent by individuals on health care in 1996, about 22 cents went for physicians' services; moreover, this cost has increased more rapidly than the costs of other goods and services. In 1985, the mean net income of practicing physicians was $112,200; in 1996, it was $199,000. This 11-year increase represents a gain of about 56 percent (Kilborn, 1998a). In 1994 physicians' incomes began to decrease for the first time in decades as a result of pressures from insurance companies, a dramatic increase in managed-care systems, and the steadily increasing supply of doctors. At present, doctors' earnings are increasing slowly, as can be seen in Figure 2–3.

During much of the twentieth century a shortage of physicians, together with an increasing demand for medical services, helped doctors command high fees. The supply of doctors has grown significantly since 1950, but this growth has not necessarily led to improved access to medical care or to lower costs. A look at the distribution of physicians will indicate why. People living in cities and suburbs can afford high-cost, specialized medical care. These places also tend to be more attractive to physicians than rural locales. As a result, physicians who engage in private practice tend to be clustered in metropolitan areas, producing shortages elsewhere. Even in densely settled urban areas, poor sections may have too few practicing physicians. However, it should be noted that rural areas have small populations that cannot support major institutions like teaching hospitals, where many physicians practice and conduct research.

Another cause of the increase in the cost of physicians' services is specialization. At the turn of the century, the majority of the nation's doctors were general practitioners; by 1996, only 8.3 percent were. One reason for the high degree of specialization is the rapid increase in medical knowledge, which means that physicians can become competent only in limited areas. Another reason is that high-quality medical care often requires the availability of specialists. The fact remains, however, that specialists command more income than doctors who engage in primary care. A specialist's income may be up to one and one-half times that of a general practitioner. Specialization also increases costs in another way. Patients must consult several physicians for a variety of ailments instead of one physician for all of them. Visiting several different physicians multiplies the cost of treatment many times.

A major factor in the high cost of physicians' services is the cost of malpractice insurance. Malpractice litigation has become more frequent, for several reasons. Ineffective insurance programs play a significant role. If more people were adequately covered, they would be less likely to go to court to recover their health-care costs. The increasing sophistication of medical technology also plays a part in the rise of

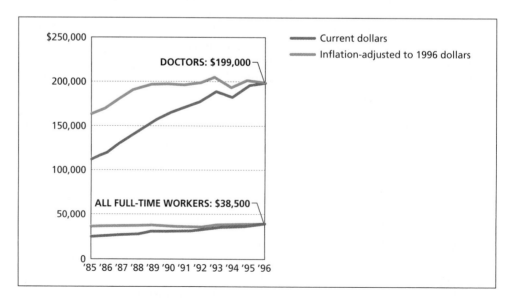

Figure 2–3 Average Incomes of Doctors Compared with the Average Incomes of Year-Round, Full-Time Workers Age 15 and Up.

Source: Kilborn, 1998a. Copyright © 1998 by The New York Times Co. Reprinted by permission.

malpractice litigation. Although recent advances enable doctors to perform treatments that once would have seemed miraculous, the treatments can be more hazardous for the patients if they are performed incorrectly or without sufficient skill and care. Public expectations about the powers of modern medicine also increase the likelihood of malpractice suits. When the new technology fails, people tend to feel angry and frustrated and to blame the most available representatives of medical science—their physicians. Although many experts believe that the cost of malpractice suits accounts for less than 2 percent of total health-care costs, this proportion is huge in dollar terms (Birenbaum, 1995).

Other Factors.   Steadily improving medical technologies are another reason for high medical costs. Medical sociologists and economists argue that the costs of these technologies account for a disproportionate share of total medical costs in the United States. Because the rate of hospital use, measured in hospital days per person, has remained fairly constant since the 1960s, it is clear that patients are receiving more expensive tests and medical procedures than ever before (Fox, 1992). The list of advanced medical technologies that did not exist a few decades ago is impressive. It includes invasive cardiology (e.g., open heart surgery and angioplasty), renal dialysis, noninvasive imaging (e.g., sonograms, CAT scans, and MRI imaging), organ transplantation, intraocular lens implants, motorized wheelchairs, and biotechnologies that are yielding new but costly drugs like AZT. Although some of these technologies may reduce the costs of medical care, most studies indicate that they have caused total health-care spending to rise (Freudenheim, 1999).

The cost of prescription drugs is a major factor in the high cost of health care. Throughout the industrialized world, advances in pharmaceutical research and technologies are bringing new and more effective drugs to market each year. These remedies often result in major savings for employers and individuals when measured in terms of lower rates of absence from work. But their costs threaten to accelerate the rate of increase in overall medical expenses. Total spending for prescription drugs increased at a rate of 14.1 percent in 1997, due especially to the demand for new drugs to combat depression, allergies, arthritis, hypertension, and elevated cholesterol. The drug component of health-care expenditures is growing at a rate of about 8 percent anually—significantly faster than the 3 percent growth rate expected for hospital care and physicians' services (Worsham, 1999).

Another set of explanations for the high cost of health care in the United States can be traced to specific cultural traits. The tendency of Americans to believe in taking action, to view illness as an invasion or threat to the individual, and to have an almost childlike faith in the magical powers of science helps explain the aggressive nature of American medicine compared to medical practices in other industrialized nations (Payer, 1988). In her study of medical practices in different Western cultures, Lynn Payer attributes this characteristic of American medicine to the frontier experience, which favored aggressive individuals who could take charge in dangerous situations. She notes that Dr. Benjamin Rush, a signer of the Declaration of Independence "and a doctor whose influence on American medicine lasted for decades, believed that one of the hindrances to the development of medicine had been 'an undue reliance upon the powers of nature in curing disease'" (p. 127). From the heroic frontier physician who battled ferocious diseases like yellow fever to contemporary surgeons who advocate radical mastectomy to combat breast cancer, Payer and other students of medical practice believe that the desire to "do something" is an outstanding feature of American medicine and one that inevitably increases the cost of health care.

Demographic factors also contribute to rising health-care costs. The baby boom cohort, the generation of Americans born in the 15-year period after World War II, includes a disproportionately large number of dependent and working poor people.

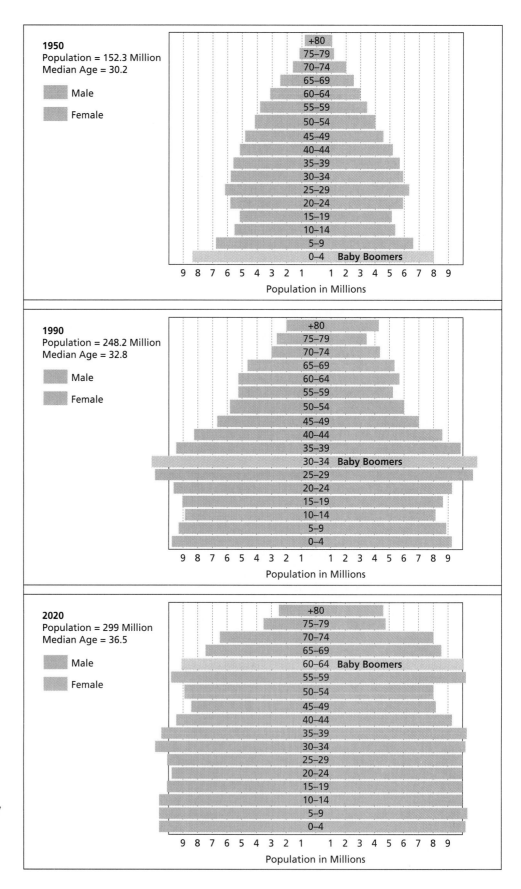

Figure 2–4 Impact of the Baby Boom on the U.S. Population, 1950–2020

Source: Data from the Census Bureau and the United Nations.

As shown in Figure 2–4, as this extremely large segment of the population passes through the life span it exerts a strong influence on national social issues. Members of this cohort are living longer than previous generations and are likely to require costly medical services as they encounter the chronic illnesses of old age. Now entering middle age, they are becoming more concerned about health care and income security. The resulting pressure on the nation's health-care system, according to some analysts, threatens to bankrupt the Social Security and Medicare systems unless changes are made in the taxation system that funds these entitlement programs.

Unequal access to medical services is another important cause of the rising cost of health care. As the number of poor people without medical insurance increases, so does the cost of treating illnesses that could have been avoided with better preventive care (e.g., tuberculosis, asthma, AIDS, and hypertension). Also, poor people are more likely to suffer from the effects of inadequate diet, lack of exercise, and exposure to harmful and addictive drugs (especially tobacco and alcohol) than more affluent Americans. On the world scene, the United States stands out among the advanced nations as the one that does the least to ensure adequate health coverage for the neediest segments of its population. The causes and consequences of this situation are discussed in later sections of the chapter.

Inadequate Protection

We often hear it said that an ounce of prevention is worth a pound of cure. It is certainly true that the heavy burden on the American health-care system would be alleviated if greater emphasis were placed on the prevention of illness. (This will become especially clear in the discussion of AIDS later in the chapter.) Figure 2–5 presents some comparisons between the cost of early preventive medicine (or related social services for young children) and the much higher costs society incurs when it does not invest in prevention. In an ideal society all citizens would have comprehensive health insurance that would encourage preventive measures, as well as the treatment of disease and injury. But if prevention is not possible, at least there should be some form of protection. Given the fact that both as individuals and as a society we seem to

Early or Late Intervention: Pay Now or Pay Later	
$600	Prenatal care for a pregnant woman for 9 months
$2,500	Medical care for a premature baby for 1 day
$842	A small child's nutritious diet for 1 year
$4,000	Special education for a child with a mild learning disability for 1 year
$8	A measles shot
$5,000	Hospitalization for a child with measles
$5,000	Drug treatment for an addicted mother for 9 months
$30,000	Medical care for a drug-exposed baby for 20 days
$135	School-based sex education per pupil for 1 year
$50,000	Public assistance for a teenage parent's child for 20 years
$2,000	Six weeks of support services so parents and children can stay together
$10,000	Foster care for a child for 18 months

Figure 2–5 Potential Cost Savings from Early Preventive Medicine or Social Services

Source: Children's Defense Fund.

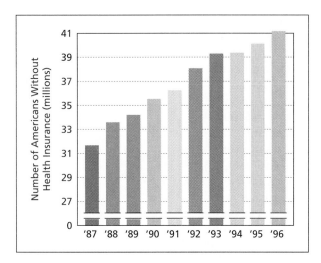

Figure 2–6   Americans Without Health Insurance.

Source: Kilborn, 1998b. Copyright © 1998 by The New York Times Co. Reprinted by permission.

be unable to prevent a wide variety of illnesses and chronically disabling conditions, there is clearly a need for some means of protecting citizens from the potentially devastating economic impact of major health-care expenditures.

For much of the nation's history, individuals paid for their own health care, or if they had insurance they paid for the insurance themselves. As a result, the poor and the near-poor often received medical care only in the most extreme emergencies. Along with the New Deal legislation of the 1930s—which included the establishment of Social Security, the extension of pension benefits for employed Americans, and other social-welfare legislation—the United States began to establish a system of health insurance whose costs were shared by employers, individuals, and government.

There are now four categories of health insurance: commercial insurance companies that sell both individual and group policies; public insurance (Blue Cross and Blue Shield); independent prepaid groups, or health maintenance organizations (HMOs); and public insurance. Public insurance includes two programs designed to help the medically needy—Medicare and Medicaid—which were enacted by Congress in 1965. Medicare is paid for by Social Security taxes. It is designed to cover some of the medical expenses of people aged 65 and over. Those over 65 who are ineligible for Medicare may voluntarily enroll in the program by paying premiums. Medicaid, an assistance program financed from tax revenues, is designed to pay for the medical costs of people who cannot afford even basic health care.

The Uninsured.   Despite the existence of public insurance programs, the number of Americans who are not covered by health insurance is rising rapidly. As Figure 2–6 shows, between 1987 and 1996 the number of uninsured Americans rose by almost 10 million, bringing the total of uninsured individuals to about 41 million.

Contrary to what many people believe, the largest proportion of uninsured people are members of families in which one or more members work full time. In 1999 the poorest Americans were more likely to have insurance coverage than in 1989, largely because of Medicaid eligibility. Those whose income was twice the official poverty level (the "working poor") were likely to be uninsured because employers began to reduce the number of employees for whom they provided health insurance (Pear, 1998). The very poor who are out of the labor force qualify for Medicaid, and the elderly are eligible for Medicare. Young people who are subject to frequent periods of unemployment and minority workers who are employed at jobs with no health benefits are especially likely to be uninsured (see Figure 2–7). Figure 2–8 shows that children, the most vulnerable segment of the population, have been losing out the most as the proportion of uninsured people in the U.S. population has risen. Note also that some of the wealthiest and fastest-growing states, especially California, Arizona, and Texas, have the highest proportions of individuals with no health insurance.

Another group that lacks sufficient health insurance is the elderly population. Many older people believe, incorrectly, that Medicare and other insurance programs will cover the cost of long-term care in nursing homes. As a result, elderly people whose families are unable to care for them may find their savings exhausted after less than a year in a nursing home (Pear, 1998).

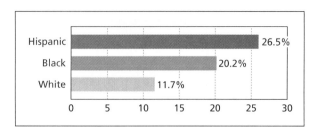

Figure 2–7   Persons Lacking Medical Insurance in the United States, by Race

*Hispanic people can be of any race.

Source: Data from the Census Bureau.

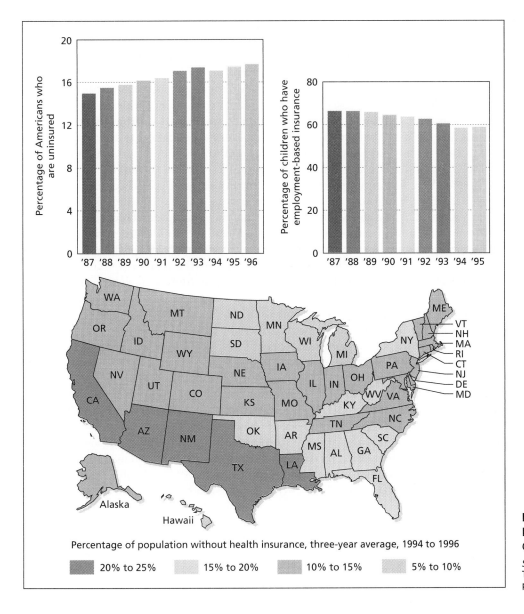

Figure 2–8 Percent and Location of Americans Without Coverage

Source: Pear, 1998. Copyright © 1998 by The New York Times Co. Reprinted by permission.

Medicaid and Medicare have been helpful to many Americans, but a number of ills plague these programs. First, there is inequity in the distribution of services. The poorest people continue to receive the fewest services. There are also inequities in geographic distribution. In addition, a number of factors have caused the Medicare program to fall short of its goal of providing full access to health care for the elderly. Among them is the requirement of deductible payments and coinsurance (additional insurance policies that must be purchased to ensure complete medical coverage). People who are financially secure can meet this requirement, and the poor can turn to Medicaid for this portion of their expenses. But the near-poor aged must still forfeit the care they need because they cannot pay for it and are not eligible for Medicaid.

A second problem with Medicare and Medicaid is their cost to the public and their impact on health-care costs in general. Both programs have been criticized for waste and abuse by administrators and physicians, who have no incentive to keep costs down and few auditing controls to keep them ethical. Hospitals, for example, have used Medicare funds to construct new buildings, purchase superfluous equipment, and hire nonmedical personnel such as public-relations directors. Some physicians operate "Medicaid mills"—clinics that serve the poor—often carrying out unnecessary tests and treatments. Many physicians refuse to treat patients under Medicaid because of the paperwork and regulations involved, and since many doctors' offices are inaccessible to the poor, the Medicaid mills are often their only source of health care.

The tendency for the costs of treating people with serious illnesses to be transferred from one insurance system to another is called **cost shifting.** Because many doctors and hospitals believe that they have a moral obligation to treat sick people even if they do not have insurance, hospitals end up with over $10 billion a year in treatment costs that are not reimbursed by public or private insurance. These costs are passed along to insured patients in the form of higher fees, driving up the premiums charged by insurance companies. This has the effect of shifting the burden to private firms that provide health coverage for their employees (Birenbaum, 1995). This situation, in turn, causes employers to reduce their health insurance costs, often by reducing the number of employees covered under their benefit plans. Since the uninsured tend to use hospital emergency rooms as their main source of primary medical care, the rising number of uninsured people only worsens the problem of cost shifting. So does the tendency for insurance companies to try to avoid insuring patients with AIDS and other major illnesses.

The practice whereby insurance companies attempt to limit hospital stays and otherwise seek to influence the course of a patient's medical care—for example, by reviewing doctors' treatment plans—has created widespread controversy in recent years. Many health-care professionals, as well as patients' groups, are pressing for reform of the managed-care system, in which insurance companies have increased control over medical decisions (Rovner, 1999). We will return to this controversy and the proposed patients' bill of rights in the Social Policy section.

Insurance companies also attempt to increase premiums for categories of people that they believe will create a financial burden in the future, such as those who have been infected with human immunodeficiency virus (HIV) or families with disabled children. This is accomplished through a practice known as "policy churning," in which the insurance company raises its rates each year and then invites some policyholders to reapply for an attractive low rate, but denies that rate to people who are ill or fall into other high-risk categories (Kolata, 1992).

In sum, although insurance plans, both public and private, were originally intended to solve many of the problems and inequities of the American health-care system, in many ways they have compounded existing difficulties.

Women and Health Care

Since the late 1960s some of the strongest criticisms of the health-care system have come from the women's movement. Feminists argue that in American society women are forced to play subordinate roles in every social institution, including health care. As part of an effort to enhance the power of women, they have campaigned for the legal right to terminate unwanted pregnancies through abortion, as well as for more control over their own medical care, especially in the areas of obstetrics and gynecology. This activism has had some influence on the delivery of health care to women, but the permanence of these gains is far from assured.

One of the first issues around which the women's movement was able to mobilize mass support was abortion. Although the majority of the American public opposed the procedure during the 1960s, increased publicity about birth defects (notably those caused by the use of thalidomide, a tranquilizer, during pregnancy) helped change many people's attitudes. In the late 1960s, as state legislatures began to liberalize restrictions on abortion, a number of women's groups demonstrated and lobbied aggressively not merely for a loosening of restrictions but also for outright repeal of all limitations on access to abortion. In 1973, in *Roe* v. *Wade*, the United States Supreme Court affirmed the right of all women to obtain abortions early in pregnancy. Since then, however, opponents of abortion have succeeded in gaining the passage of legislation that restricts federal funding of abortion.

In 1990 a number of decisions on abortion seemed to pave the way toward a reversal of the *Roe* decision. In particular, the decision in *Webster* v. *Reproductive Health Services* allows states to ban the use of public funds for counseling or encouraging women to have an abortion and to prohibit abortions in publicly owned hospitals and by doctors paid with public funds. According to Chief Justice William Rehnquist, the *Webster* decision would not return the states to the "dark ages" in which abortion was outlawed; it merely "allows more governmental regulation of abortion than was permissible before."

Abortion is an issue that continues to create rancorous conflict in American society and politics. Recognizing that the Democrats have an advantage because of their support of pro-choice policies, in the political campaigns of 2000 the Republicans attempted to move closer to the majority's tolerance of abortion rights—at the risk of alienating the conservative, pro-life wing of their party (Germond & Witcover, 1999). At the same time, anti-abortion forces have begun to concentrate their efforts on visible protests outside abortion clinics and at other locations where they believe they can have an impact and gain popular support. Few medical issues so divide the American people, as well as those in other societies. (The abortion issue is discussed further in Chapter 10.)

The controversy over abortion awakened many women to larger problems in the health-care system, and the women's movement has continued its efforts to make medical personnel more sensitive to the physical and psychological needs of women. Feminists point out that in many ways health-care organizations have placed their own interests ahead of the needs and preferences of their clients. In the case of childbirth, in most states infants must be delivered by a licensed doctor. Because the birthing process usually occurs in a hospital with the participation of a number of specialists, mothers lack the supportive presence of one person from the beginning of labor until the birth of the infant. Moreover, until recently the hospital was dominated by high-status male physicians who retained exclusive command of relevant medical knowledge, making it difficult for women to challenge established procedures (Gabay & Wolfe, 1997). Thus, efforts to win acceptance of midwives, who perform deliveries in the home and are present throughout the childbirth process, have been only moderately successful. The work of nurse midwives, for example, is usually limited to hospitals and performed under medical supervision, whereas that of lay midwives, who practice outside of medical control, is not fully legal in all states (Katz Rothman, 1994).

Other critics of the health-care system as it relates to women have called for less intervention in the birth process itself. Anesthesia, induced labor, and surgical practices such as Caesarian sections and the use of forceps have come under attack. Some of these forms of intervention not only can cause harm to both mother and infant but also inflate the cost of delivery. As a result of these criticisms, classes in prepared childbirth taught by nurse practitioners have become widespread. Such classes prepare a woman (and often her partner as well) for the experience of childbirth by describing the process in detail and teaching a variety of techniques for reducing or eliminating pain during labor and delivery. These techniques not only make it possible to avoid excessive use of anesthetics but also greatly reduce the woman's fear and anxiety about giving birth. Some hospitals have also granted women a greater say in decisions that affect their deliveries, such as whether a mate or friend may be present in the delivery room.

Women's groups have also criticized the nature of gynecological care in the United States. It is argued that the simple fact of being female has been "medicalized"; that is,

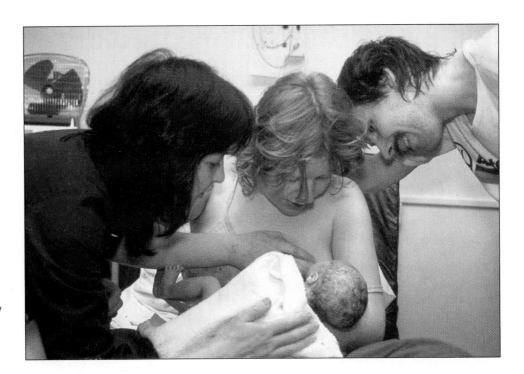

A growing minority of women are choosing to have their babies with the help of a midwife because they feel that the midwife can be more responsive to their needs during labor and delivery.

certain conditions, such as pregnancy and menstruation, have been defined in terms of health and illness (Katz Rothman, 1994). This has permitted "experts," especially gynecologists and psychiatrists (see Chapter 3), to achieve professional dominance over women, with results that not only are economically beneficial to physicians but also contribute to women's relative lack of power in society (Riessman, 1983).

Although many politically active women concern themselves with issues of reproductive care and abortion, medical researchers and health administrators point out that women and their needs are vastly underrepresented in medical research. Eighty percent of health-care workers are women, yet women remain largely absent from the leadership ranks of medicine. The National Institutes of Health (NIH), the most important source of funds for medical research, spend less than 20 percent of their research budget on women's health issues, even though breast cancer alone claims the lives of about 40,000 women a year. Moreover, until recently most of the studies of heart disease and smoking used only male subjects, and the possible unique needs of women were unresearched (Ness & Kuller, 1999). In 1990, in response to the latter criticism, the NIH created an Office of Research on Women's Health. The office provides funds for studies designed to fill gaps in scientific knowledge that result from the exclusion of women from past experiments. In addition, proposals for studies that use only male subjects must be justified on scientific grounds.

The Disabled and Handicapped

Another important population from the standpoint of health-care needs is people who are disabled or handicapped, usually as a result of automobile and industrial accidents. Automobile accidents are a major cause of paralysis and other permanent disabilities, in addition to other serious injuries that often require hospitalization and costly surgery. Until recently the disabled and handicapped were literally forgotten people. They were excluded from work, school, and society both by active discrimination and by barriers imposed by a world designed for the able-bodied. Steps, curbs, and narrow doorways and aisles—impassable obstacles to wheelchairs, for example—are only a few of the aspects of everyday life that still impede the physically disabled.

Although the situation has improved since the 1960s as a result of the political organization of the disabled themselves, many problems remain.

The disabled suffer from extremely high unemployment rates. Of the 16 million people with a work disability, fewer than one-third are employed (Stafford, 1999). In addition, many handicapped people are underemployed—assigned to low-level, low-paying jobs—because employers are afraid to offer them challenges. In many instances Social Security regulations contribute to the problem by limiting the amount of money a handicapped person can earn and still receive benefits. For all these reasons, the majority of the handicapped are poor.

Numerous studies have shown that when disabled people are hired, they usually dispel all the negative myths that surround them. An overwhelming majority prove to be dedicated, capable workers; they have only a slightly higher-than-average absentee rate, and their turnover rate is well below average. The disabled are neither slower nor less productive than other workers and have excellent safety records.

Almost 30 million Americans have deformities or orthopedic impairments; another 30 million have visual or hearing impairments (*Statistical Abstract*, 1999). In addition, advances in medical science have made it possible for many people to survive serious accidents, usually with handicaps. Technology is also making it possible for many disabled people, who would have been bedridden or housebound in the past, to be mobile and to acquire new skills. Improved health care and prevention of disease have meant that more people than ever before are living to an advanced age and are incurring the disabilities that often occur in old age.

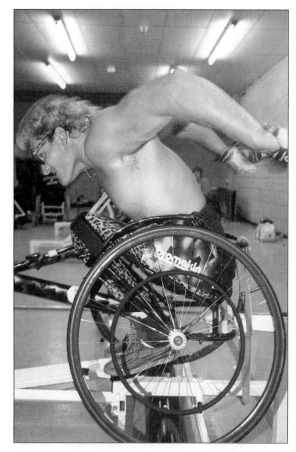

Today disabled people refuse to be denied active and productive roles in society.

The disabled and handicapped have emerged as a recognized minority group. Like women and blacks, they are demanding an end to the discrimination that keeps them out of jobs and out of the mainstream of life. They oppose efforts to place them in special programs or schools, except during the necessary phases of rehabilitation or therapy. Special programs, they claim, are the ghettos of the handicapped. As we will see in the Social Policy section of the chapter, in recent decades some far-reaching legislation has been enacted in an attempt to address the problems of the disabled and handicapped.

Ethical Issues

As medical technology has improved and life-prolonging procedures have become more available and dependable, a number of complex ethical issues have arisen. Some of the new medical technologies, such as heart and kidney transplants, are extremely costly and cannot be provided to all patients who might benefit from them. Thus, the question arises of how to choose the patients who will undergo these procedures (Callahan, 1994).

The availability of life-prolonging equipment and procedures has also given rise to questions about the meaning of life and death. State legislatures across the country have been debating the question of whether death occurs when the heart stops beating or when the brain stops functioning. Courts have been required to decide whether patients should have the right to die by ordering life-prolonging treatments to be terminated.

In recent years a related issue, assisted suicide, has come to the fore. Michigan doctor Jack Kevorkian became the personification of the right-to-die issue when he helped a 54-year-old woman with Alzheimer's disease kill herself, using an intravenous device that allowed the patient to receive a lethal drug by pressing a button. The doctor was arrested and charged with first-degree murder; later the charges were dropped, but the doctor was ordered to refrain from using the suicide device in the future. Kevorkian continued to defy the authorities in Michigan and eventually was sentenced to a term in prison. Although many doctors and health authorities condemn the practice, Kevorkian's sensational methods have brought the "right to die" issue to national attention.

Some court decisions have upheld this right. For example, in 1990 a Las Vegas judge granted the request of a 31-year-old quadriplegic that he be allowed to end his life by being disconnected from a respirator. In another case, a Missouri court allowed the family of a comatose woman to stop having chemical nutrition and water pumped into her stomach; the decision was based on evidence that the young woman, if she had been mentally able, would have wished to terminate life-support measures.

As the populations of the urban industrial nations continue to age, and given the appearance of ever more sophisticated methods for prolonging life, the number of ethical, legal, and technical questions about life's end grows as well. Imagine that your elderly parent has had a stroke. Doctors express little hope that consciousness can be restored or that life-support systems could be removed without causing death. This is not a rare situation. Unless your family and the terminally ill parent have

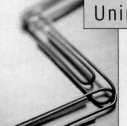

Unintended Consequences

Life-saving Technologies

All medical policies and technologies have both intended and unintended consequences. The new life-saving technologies also create situations in which people who wish to die can do so by refusing treatment. Policies and laws designed to protect people's rights can also become a means of protecting their right to die.

Medical researcher Daniel Callahan has long been one of the nation's strongest advocates of patients' rights and the use of advanced directives. He notes, however, that after ten years of efforts to educate patients and their families about their rights to care in the face of death, over 40 percent of terminally ill patients do not have advanced directives. Even when such directives exist, doctors and other hospital personnel are often unwilling to implement them if it means not trying heroic measures to sustain life. "The culture of medicine," Callahan (1995) writes, "in league with that of American hospitals and the health care system, all push in the direction of aggressive treatment, of frequent deafness to patient wishes, and toward a curious unwillingness to take prognosis information as seriously as it should be" (p. 533; see also 1997).

For Callahan and other medical ethicists, the problems of advanced life-saving technologies are hardly limited to the dying patients. He is one of a growing number of health-care experts who believe that new policies will have to be established to determine who has access to many life-saving medical procedures. In his view, priority should be given to preventive medicine and to the needs of groups that are particularly at risk—for example, prenatal care for the poor—rather than to high-cost efforts to save the lives of individuals whose chances of surviving and leading a comfortable life are minimal. Every person should have the right to humane care, not cure, he believes; expensive medical resources should not be devoted to marginal cases such as 18-ounce babies or quadriplegic teenage victims of automobile accidents.

Callahan and other researchers and policymakers have yet to agree on an equitable system for rationing expensive medical treatments. However, this failure does not deny the importance of the issue so much as it points to the immense political and ethical difficulties involved.

prepared advanced directives for dealing with the situation, much agony and prolonged suffering can ensue for everyone concerned. Advanced directives have two parts: a living will, which tells doctors and hospitals how the patient wants to be cared for should he or she become terminally ill, and a health-care proxy, which designates an advocate, usually a close family member, who can make sure that those wishes are honored (Aitken, 1999). Daniel Callahan, one of the nation's leading experts on medical ethics, comments further on these points in the Unintended Consequences feature on page 44.

AIDS—A Modern Plague

The social problems related to health care became especially acute in the mid-1980s with the spread of a previously unknown disease: *acquired immune deficiency syndrome (AIDS)*. This disease is caused by the *human immunodeficiency virus (HIV)*, which attacks the body's immune system. An unusual feature of HIV is the long period of latency—up to ten years—between the time of infection and the appearance of the disease. During this period there may be no visible symptoms. Once it has been rendered ineffective by the virus, however, the immune system is unable to combat other diseases that routinely infect humans, such as pneumonia, cancer, and tuberculosis, and death is almost inevitable.

It is not certain what proportion of people infected with HIV will actually develop AIDS-related illnesses, but the number who do so remains high. In 1996 AIDS researchers discovered that treatment with a combination of anti-AIDS drugs, all costly, is effective in preventing the onset of AIDS symptoms and, in some cases, in eliminating the presence of HIV altogether. But these treatments are available mainly in more affluent nations and to more affluent patients; they are not widely available in Africa and other regions where the spread of HIV continues at epidemic rates and is associated with heterosexual transmission through unprotected sex.

AIDS is a global epidemic. In the United States, deaths from AIDS dropped 47 percent between 1996 and 1997. The drop was due primarily to expensive drug treatments, which are available mainly in more affluent nations. Elsewhere in the world, especially in impoverished African and Asian countries, the rate of infection is soaring. The World Health Organization (WHO) estimates that more than 30 million people are infected with HIV; almost 90 percent of them are in the developing nations of Asia and sub-Saharan Africa. In Zimbabwe, for example, 25 percent of the adult population is thought to be HIV positive, largely through heterosexual transmission. Infection rates are rising rapidly in the economically and politically chaotic nations of the former Soviet Union. India, with an estimated 4 million cases, has the world's highest number of cases, although given India's huge population, the rate of infection is relatively low (Glausiusz, 1999).

Prospects for coping with the AIDS epidemic in poor nations are particularly gloomy because of the high cost of advanced treatments. In the United States, the cost of the multidrug therapy that has proven to be effective in suppressing the deadly AIDS symptoms can average $750 a month. This is a fortune for people in poor nations like South Africa, where about 8 percent of the population is HIV positive and the annual per capita income is $6,000. (See Figure 2–9.) But some encouraging changes are occurring. It appears that a short, four-week course of even one anti-AIDS drug, AZT, during late pregnancy and delivery can halve the rate of HIV

As medical researchers strive to find a cure for AIDS, educators and policymakers use posters like this to make people more aware of the need to engage in "safer" forms of sexual behavior.

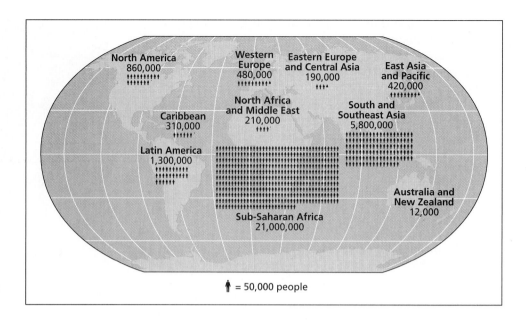

Figure 2–9 HIV Cases Worldwide

Source: Glausiusz, 1999. Ian Warpole © 1999. Reprinted with permission of *Discovery Magazine.*

transmission from mothers to their babies. And there is also evidence from some third-world nations that rates of condom use are rising as AIDS education finally begins to take effect. In the urban parts of Senegal and in Uganda, studies show that there has been an enormous increase in safe sex practices. Unfortunately, these vital changes are slow to occur, and there has not been nearly enough investment in programs to change the behaviors that lead to infection.

In the United States, almost 400,000 people have died of AIDS since 1981 (Bozette, 1998). In 1997, however, the number of AIDS deaths in the United States fell below 17,000. (The record high of about 43,000 was reached in 1995.) These changes are due primarily to the spread of new treatments and to lower rates of infection as a result of intensive education and safe sex campaigns begun years ago. But AIDS experts now fear that complacency and a return to unsafe sexual practices could once again increase the HIV infection rate (Altman, 1999). It is clear that in the United States, as elsewhere, the epidemic is not over.

The HIV virus is transmitted through the exchange of body fluids, that is, directly from an infected person's blood, semen, or vaginal secretions into another person's bloodstream. Transmission can occur through sexual activity that leads to torn membranes; through blood transfusions, sharing of hypodermic needles, and other means; or from an infected mother to her unborn or newborn infant. The disease is not transmitted by mere contact with skin—by a handshake or a hug, for example—or through the air as a result of a sneeze or cough. It is not transmitted by sharing meals, bathrooms, and beds with infected individuals or by casual contact in the home, school, or workplace. The primary means of transmission are sexual intercourse, especially anal intercourse, and sharing of needles by drug users.

AIDS is sometimes referred to as a "gay disease" because in the United States it first appeared in male homosexuals between the ages of 20 and 49, and the majority of AIDS deaths have occurred among this population. But AIDS is by no means limited to homosexuals. The data in Table 2–2 show that users of intravenous drugs are also infected by the virus in large numbers.

AIDS has spread among heterosexual individuals in a variety of ways. One way is prostitution: The Centers for Disease Control have found that over half of all prostitutes in the United States are serum positive; that is, they have been infected by HIV even if they are not yet showing outward symptoms of AIDS. However, the primary bridge between homosexual and heterosexual transmitters is intravenous drug users,

TABLE 2–2   AIDS Cases by Exposure Category, United States[a]

Exposure Category	Percent
Men who have sex with men	51
Injecting drug use	25
Men who have sex with men and inject drugs	7
Hemophilia/coagulation disorder	1
Heterosexual contact	8
Sex with injecting drug user (45)	
Sex with bisexual male (5)	
Sex with HIV-infected person (47)	
Other (3)	
Receipt of blood transfusion, blood components, or tissue	1
Other/risk not reported or identified	7

[a]Adults and adolescents.

Source: Data from Centers for Disease Control.

who transmit the disease to their sexual partners and to others with whom they share needles. Intravenous drug users and their mates, as well as their babies, account for 25 percent of AIDS cases in the United States.

Most people want to know whether AIDS is going to become widespread among heterosexuals, as it seems to have done in some segments of the population in Africa and Brazil. "The answer," says Thomas C. Quinn, an AIDS researcher at the National Institute of Allergy and Infectious Diseases, "is not a yes or a no. Heterosexuals will get infected, but they will not be your everyday person. It will be the people already at risk for syphilis, gonorrhea, chlamydia, and with life styles that include risky sexual partners. Among those, it will be an epidemic" (quoted in Hilts, 1990, p. C1). The epidemic will also affect the children of some AIDS victims. An estimated 100,000 orphans have already been produced by the disease.

Quinn and his colleagues studied almost 5,000 patients in two inner-city clinics that treat sexually transmitted diseases (Hilts, 1990). They found that heterosexuals with syphilis who did not use drugs intravenously (IV) were seven to nine times more likely to have AIDS than other patients at the clinics, suggesting that heterosexual intercourse played a role in transmitting both syphilis and AIDS to those patients. Similar conditions have been found among IV drug and crack users and their partners. Promiscuity occurs in combination with untreated disease. The realization that non-IV drugs like crack are implicated in the AIDS epidemic (because women and men in crack houses engage in sex with many partners, thereby greatly increasing their risk of infection) emerged in part from the pioneering research of sociologist Claire Sterk (1988, 2000), who spent hundreds of hours interviewing street women about their drug and sexual behavior.

For AIDS victims and their families, the impact of the disease is devastating. Not only must they deal with fear and grief, but they must also cope with shame. Because AIDS is associated with homosexuality and drug abuse, relatives and close friends of the patients feel stigmatized. They may become angry at the patient and blame themselves for failing to rescue him or her from a dangerous lifestyle (Ayala, 1996). "Having AIDS is a little bit like being treated as if you're a leper," says a therapist who works with AIDS patients and family members (quoted in Walker, 1987).

SOCIAL PROBLEMS ONLINE

AIDS on the Internet

An enormous range of material about AIDS is available to students and professors on the Internet. For example, there are home pages for organizations of AIDS activists in the United States and throughout the world. But for basic information about the disease, its spread, its control, and the latest research developments, a good place to start is the home page of a major public agency like the Centers for Disease Control (CDC) in Atlanta.

The CDC has a home page at **http://www.cdc.gov** with numerous links to specific AIDS/HIV web sites. Each web page has links to the other CDC sites (e.g., the CDC's mission, addresses of regional centers, information for travelers, and news bulletins about infectious diseases), as well as links to non-CDC web pages or e-mail addresses. Each CDC web page has a search tool that allows the user to find related resources such as additional web pages, online articles and reports, press releases, and graphics.

After connecting to the CDC home page, one of the first places the user might want to browse is the National Center for HIV, STD, and TB Prevention (NCHSTP) page. Click on the center's highlighted name or enter its address—**http://www.cdc.gov/nchstp/od/ nchstp.html.** The NCHSTP page contains links to fact sheets and brochures about AIDS/HIV and other sexually transmitted diseases. There are links to U.S. and worldwide statistics on AIDS/HIV and resources for religious communities, women, and the sports world. There are also connections to non-CDC web pages, some maintained by organizations like the American Social Health Association and the Johns Hopkins School of Medicine STD Research Group, and to others devoted to specific diseases like herpes.

Another interesting site with a more international focus is the World Health Organizaiton's Global Programme on AIDS. It can be reached at **http://gpawww .who.ch/.** Its resources range from relatively simple topics like the ABCs of HIV/AIDS and how to use a condom to sophisticated reports on HIV-1 generic variability.

The Gay Men's Health Crisis has a web page at **http://www.gmhc.org** that stresses education and activism. In addition to providing basic information about AIDS/HIV, it contains useful discussions about HIV testing and living with AIDS/HIV.

Although certain drugs, such as AZT, may slow the onset of AIDS symptoms, to date there is no cure for AIDS. The only defense against it is prevention. At present, therefore, behavioral changes are the only means of stopping the spread of the virus. Indeed, AIDS is different from most other diseases in that individuals can, at least in theory, choose to avoid infection. The battle against the AIDS epidemic, thus, is a social as well as a biological one. While scientists conduct research in an effort to find a cure, educators, social scientists, and policymakers are attempting to influence the behavior of large numbers of people. But efforts to control behavior—especially sexual behavior—raise a variety of moral and ethical issues: Should people be required to undergo testing for the presence of the HIV virus? Should they be required to reveal the names of individuals with whom they have had sexual contacts? Should drug addicts be given clean needles? Should condoms be distributed in public schools? Just how controversial this subject is will become clear in discussions of AIDS-related issues at several points in this book.

Thus, AIDS is having a major impact not only on individuals and their loved ones but also on the health-care system itself. The HIV virus can be detected almost immediately, and in most cases months or years go by before severe symptoms appear. Therefore, there is ample time for medical intervention. But treatment for AIDS is complex and prolonged. Because it destroys the body's ability to fight disease, the presence of AIDS is signaled by the onset of many different illnesses, ranging from pneumonia to various forms of cancer. In the terminal stages, the patient often suffers from acute illnesses like meningitis. Thus, treatment for the illnesses associated with AIDS is complex and usually requires long periods of hospitalization and intensive care. The health-care system, already overburdened, is severely strained by the need to provide expensive care for hundreds of thousands of AIDS patients. Health insurance costs are also increasing as more AIDS cases develop.

Clearly, AIDS is a great deal more than a serious illness. It can, in fact, be viewed as three epidemics rolled into one: the spread of the HIV virus; the epidemic of the disease AIDS; and the social, political, psychological, and ethical reactions to the disease and those who suffer from it (Bozette, 1998). AIDS has had a profound effect on American society—on its ways of living and dying and on its debates over health care, sex education, drug abuse, and social justice. It has had an especially dramatic effect on sexual behavior. There has been a resurgence of traditional sexual mores and values not only among the groups most at risk but throughout the population (Laumann et al., 1994). These changes will be discussed more fully in Chapter 4, which deals with sex-related social problems.

Explanations of Health Care Problems

Why do we have such difficulty improving the quality of health-care services and providing more equal access to them? The explanations offered by medical sociologists depend to a large extent on the perspective from which they view the problem. Conflict theorists, for example, tend to view the problem as a feature of capitalism: The poor get less medical care because they get less of everything in American society. Those who approach this question from a functionalist perspective have sought the answers in medicine's development into a complex and costly social institution. And from an interactionist perspective, many of the problems of health care in the United States and other highly developed nations can be traced to cultural factors, including the way people are taught to interact with one another. In this section we will briefly discuss each of these approaches to the explanation of health-care problems.

Class and Class Conflict

Sociologists often point out that social class, measured by the income and wealth a household has at its disposal, goes a long way toward explaining the types of illnesses experienced by members of that household and the kinds of health care they receive. We have already suggested that lack of access to good medical care causes higher rates of illness and death among the poor. Until the early twentieth century, the ill health of the poor was caused largely by infectious diseases. Today medical science is able to control and cure such diseases much more effectively, with the result that by themselves they no longer account for tremendous differences in health between the poor and the nonpoor:

> Access to good medical care, preventive medical action, health knowledge, and limitation of delay in seeking treatment have become increasingly important in combating mortality, as chronic diseases have become the chief health enemy in the developed world. In these areas, lower class people may well be at a disadvantage. (Antonovsky, 1974, p. 178; see also Cockerham, 1998)

In fact, as control of chronic diseases like cancer becomes more important, the differences between the health of the poor and that of the nonpoor are likely to increase; that is, the poor will still have higher rates of illness and death than the nonpoor because of their relative lack of access to high-quality medical care.

In an analysis of the relationship between social class and ill health, Lee Rainwater (1974) suggested that lack of access to medical care is not the only factor that affects the health of the poor: Just being poor promotes poor health. The poor, for example,

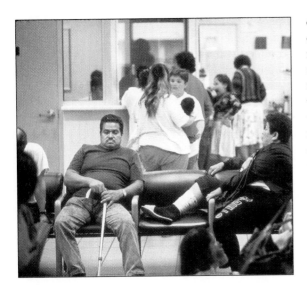

Crowding in hospital emergency rooms reflects the tendency of people who lack medical insurance to seek primary care at an emergency room in lieu of visiting a private physician.

cannot afford to eat properly, so they are likely to be weak. They often live in the most polluted areas and hence are susceptible to respiratory diseases. Because they cannot afford proper housing, they are exposed to disease-carrying refuse and rodents. Perhaps most important, their lives are filled with stress due to constant worry about getting enough money to pay for necessities. Such long-term stress can cause both physical and mental illness. It also makes it difficult to react to minor signs of ill health (Birenbaum, 1995). A cough is likely to be dismissed if one does not have enough to eat; only a much worse cough will prompt a visit to a clinic, and by then it may be too late. The poor also seem to feel middle-aged earlier than the nonpoor. As a result, they are likely to accept illness and disability as somehow natural, even in their 30s.

Social scientists who see class conflict as a basic cause of social-class differences in health and unequal access to medical care are skeptical of the increasing privatization of the American health-care system. They point out that as public hospitals are replaced by hospitals run for profit, there is a tendency to avoid treatment of less profitable patients.

Studies have shown that as more hospitals are managed by for-profit or not-for-profit corporations, as opposed to the public sector, they are indeed less likely to provide services like drug counseling, suicide prevention, and AIDS treatment (Himmelstein et al., 1999). Both public and private hospitals share the duty to accept all patients who require emergency care, but private hospitals can decide to eliminate their emergency facilities altogether, and the requirement for emergency care does not extend to nonemergencies.

Social scientists who view health-care problems from a conflict perspective often explain the outcomes of conflicts over medical policy in terms of conflict between classes. For example, in a study of the social, political, and psychological impact of AIDS in America, Dennis Altman (1987) showed that as long as AIDS was perceived as a disease of homosexuals and intravenous drug users, members of the middle and upper classes did not put pressure on the government to invest heavily in its treatment and cure. Altman and others have pointed out that because AIDS strikes disproportionately at less advantaged citizens and members of minority groups, it is often thought of as "their" disease.

Institutions and Health Care

Functionalist explanations of health-care problems focus on features of health-care institutions themselves. Sociologists with this institutional orientation point out that every society is faced with the problem of distributing health-care services among its members. The United States uses a marketplace approach, which views health care as a commodity that is subject to the demands and spending power of consumers. Canada, by contrast, views health care as an entitlement of citizenship and extends full coverage to all its legal residents.

Since health-care costs are lower in Canada and many medical professionals feel that the quality of care in that nation is at least equal to the quality of care in the United States, there are many advocates for a comparable "universal and single payer" insurance system in the United States (Wolfe, cited in Spero, 1993). Opponents of the Canadian system point out, however, that it deprives the well-off of the higher-quality health care they can afford. The broad sociological issue here is how to improve health-care institutions in order to provide the best possible care for the greatest number of people. Most medical sociologists do not agree that health care should be treated as a commodity available in higher amounts and quality to those most able to afford it. But this does not mean that they believe that the Canadian model could be imported to the United States without a great deal of compromise.

There are a number of functionalist arguments for why a service that has come to be viewed as a basic human right should not be treated as a commodity:

■ *Information*—A consumer is not in a position to shop for medical treatment in the same way that one shops for other products or services, since the need for such treatment cannot be evaluated by the consumer.

■ *Product uncertainty*—The consumer does not have sufficient knowledge to judge the effectiveness of sophisticated treatments.

■ *Norms of treatment*—Medical care is performed under the control of a physician. A patient does not direct his or her own treatment.

■ *Lack of price competition*—Prices for doctors' services are not advertised and are not subject to true competition.

■ *Restricted entry*—There are numerous barriers to entry to medical school. Many qualified applicants are turned down because of a limited number of places.

■ *Professional dominance*—Many health-care services that are restricted to physicians could be performed by trained technicians. This restriction has created a monopoly.

■ *Misallocated supply*—An abundance of specialists encourages the use of expensive and sophisticated treatments when simpler ones would be just as effective. (Himmelstein et al., 1999)

Health and Social Interaction

The relatively poor health of Americans is due in part to features of our lifestyle, including sedentary occupations, nonnutritious diets, lack of proper exercise, environmental pollution, and cigarette smoking (Gochman, 1997). But if activities like smoking are detrimental to health, why do people engage in them? Interactionist explanations of social problems related to health care often draw on studies of patterns of sociability (i.e., interaction among people in groups) and the ways in which people are socialized in different societies and communities. Features of a society's lifestyle, such as smoking, drinking, and diet, are deeply ingrained in the way people interact with one another. Very often we eat, drink, or smoke as much to be sociable as to sustain ourselves. Advertising reinforces these patterns by associating consumption with sociability, as you can see by completing the following phrases: "It's ——— Time"; "Welcome to ——— Country."

Excessive eating, leading to obesity, and high rates of alcohol consumption are among the health problems related to patterns of sociability in an affluent society. But the most pervasive and serious problems are created by smoking. Despite the efforts of health professionals both in and out of government, 45 million Americans continue to smoke cigarettes. Each year thousands of adolescents ignore warnings about the health risks associated with smoking; one study found that the percentage of eighth-graders who had smoked in the previous 30 days rose by 30 percent in just 3 years (Verhovek, 1995). In addition, women often expose unborn infants to the negative effects of smoking, especially low birthweight. More than 1,100 deaths a day and a greater number of serious illnesses are directly attributable to cigarette smoking, and recent research has shown that passive smoking (breathing air that contains cigarette smoke) is a serious environmental hazard.

Interactionist perspectives on issues like smoking and health typically focus on the way communications (e.g., advertising images and messages) seek to connect the use of tobacco with particular lifestyles. They may also take a more explicitly critical look at the way tobacco companies directly or indirectly influence those communications. For example, a study by Kenneth E. Warner at the University of Michigan found that "the higher the percentage of cigarette advertising revenues, the lower the likelihood that a magazine will publish an article on the dangers of smoking" (quoted in Carmody, 1992, p. D22).

It is helpful to think of the major sociological perspectives as conceptual tools to be used in analyzing a complex social problem like the prevention and treatment of physical illnesses. No single perspective explains all the important issues, but together they go a long way toward a full explanation. The functionalist view is most helpful in pointing out how social institutions like hospitals should function, why they do not function effectively, and how they could be improved. The conflict perspective allows for more insight into the influence of inequalities of wealth, education, and power on access to and quality of medical care. The interactionist perspective points to the way differences in people's perception of social conditions such as the AIDS epidemic influence their behavior toward others.

SOCIAL POLICY

Medical sociologists have been deeply involved in evaluating proposed and existing health-care policies. And as the merits of various approaches to health-care delivery have been debated, medical sociologists have increasingly engaged in research designed to supply empirical data on prevention and care systems of all kinds. This has usually involved providing data on what classes of people benefit from a given policy and in what ways, and on how those benefits or losses compare to the situation that existed before the new policy was implemented.

The findings of medical sociology concerning widespread reforms such as those proposed during the 1990s also suggest the inevitability of compromise and improvisation (Starr, 1995). After a thorough review of the evolution of health-care systems in many of the world's advanced democratic nations—including Great Britain, Sweden, Canada, West Germany, France, and the United States—medical sociologist Odin W. Anderson (1989) concluded that none of these nations has a central "blueprint" for how its health-care system should develop or how costs could be controlled. Although all of the nations studied have developed highly complex systems with a wide array of trained specialists, Anderson observes, they now "are wondering how to manage multiple chronic illnesses in an aging population" (p. 160).

In Canada and some of the social democracies of western Europe, the problems arising from aging populations, lack of coverage for the poor, the challenge of controlling health-care costs, and a host of other issues are addressed through what is known as a single-payer system. In 1946 Canada introduced national legislation to extend health care to all, regardless of age, occupation, preexisting conditions, or income. Today all citizens and legal residents of Canada are covered by the Canadian Medicare system; doctors who provide direct, fee-for-service medical care to private patients cannot participate in the national system. Each of Canada's provinces has its own system of health-care providers, but to receive federal funding the system must provide comprehensive services for anyone in the province. In this way everyone is entitled to the same quality of services. Relatively few Canadians complain about the system or about lack of access to doctors. In the United States, in contrast, 7 percent of survey respondents say that they have not visited a doctor because of inability to pay (Birenbaum, 1995).

There are some drawbacks to the Canadian system. It is less well equipped with advanced medical technologies. Moreover, hospitals and doctors are allocated a fixed amount for their services, which helps keep costs in check. But greater physician autonomy also results in longer hospital stays and a higher rate of hospital admissions than in the United States. On the other hand, because there are no insurance forms or billing procedures, there are far fewer clerks and other nonmedical service workers employed in the system (Birenbaum, 1995). Administrative costs are thus far lower than they are in the United States (less than 1 percent of all medical expenses compared to over 6 percent in the United States). In recent years, however, the rising costs of medical care have placed strains on the Canadian system and have contributed to already high federal and provincial tax rates, something that frightens American lawmakers who might otherwise be attracted to the more equitable Canadian system (Craig, 1993).

Managed Care

In place of a comprehensive and universal health-care system, the United States has been moving toward a system termed *managed care*, the dominant feature of which is the **health maintenance organization (HMO),** which provides both insurance and medical services. HMOs contract with payers (employers, employees, or both) to provide an agreed-upon set of services at a fixed, prepaid annual fee. They incur the risk that the costs of providing medical services may exceed their revenues, so they attempt to control costs by requiring primary-care providers (general practitioners, nurse practitioners, and others) to act as gatekeepers who decide whether to refer patients to other health services. In the 1990s enrollment in HMOs has doubled, reaching over 51 million, mainly because employers are increasingly turning to HMOs to cut their medical insurance costs. In addition, changes in the system for funding Medicaid and Medicare (which insure basic health care for about 73 million Americans) have given the states more autonomy.

Although Medicare costs continued to increase steadily during this period, by 1999 there was some evidence that government attempts to regulate the Medicare program, combined with low rates of inflation, had at last succeeded in reducing the annual rate of increase in Medicare spending from 10 percent to a mere 1 percent between 1998 and 1999. At this writing, however, no similar progress has been made by private insurers (Pear, 1999a).

The trend toward managed care has greatly altered the practice of medicine. A steadily decreasing proportion of doctors are in private practice, in which they depend on the traditional fee-for-service system. Instead, more doctors are joining HMOs, medical groups, or other forms of managed care. The American Medical Association (AMA) and many of its physician members have historically opposed any form of "socialized" or national health-care system like that in Canada. But as their autonomy is diminished through managed-care systems, many doctors are frustrated by their loss of control. Many fear a loss of income as well. The need to compete for patients has led to more advertising for medical services, which further commercializes a profession that once prided itself on being different from other businesses (Williams et al., 1995). (See the Critical Research feature on page 54.)

Insurance Reform

As noted earlier, the increase in membership in HMOs is due largely to the efforts of employers to decrease their health insurance costs, along with the tendency of states to shift Medicaid patients into HMOs. But the lack of comprehensive health-care reform has had dramatic consequences as well. The proportion of uninsured people in the U.S. population is growing, and this problem is related to other social problems, particularly changes in the economy that are increasing the number of low-wage workers who lack health benefits.

CRITICAL RESEARCH

Profits and Health-Care

Do health maintenance organizations that are run for profit offer the same level and quality of care as those that are run as nonprofit businesses? This is a controversial question. It raises the possibility that those who invest in medical insurance companies and HMOs might be more interested in profits than in delivery of the best possible medical care. But it is clearly an empirical question. It can be addressed by research that compares the two types of health-care providers. And it is exactly the type of question that motivates Dr. Sidney Wolfe, the founder (with Ralph Nader) of the Public Citizen Health Research Group. Dr. Wolfe is one of the nation's most respected critics of existing health-care policies. He supports a single-payer health system based on the Canadian model. He is also an extremely active medical researcher who collaborates on studies that ask critical questions such as whether the profit motive in medical care is associated with lower levels and quality of medical service.

To test the hypothesis that nonprofit HMOs provide higher-quality care than for-profit HMOs, Wolfe and his colleagues compared 248 investor-owned and 81 nonprofit HMOs on 14 quality-of-care indicators. They found that after a heart attack, 59 percent of for-profit HMO members and 71 percent of nonprofit HMO members received the appropriate treatment, beta-blocker drugs. However, for-profit HMO members were less likely to receive regular immunizations, mammograms, Pap tests, and annual eye examinations for diabetics. In short, the investigators found that nonprofit HMOs provide better-quality health care than for-profit HMOs.

These findings were published in the *Journal of the American Medical Association*, the nation's most prestigious medical journal. Although they are hardly the final word in the controversy, they demonstrate through solid empirical research what Wolfe has been claiming all along: By forcing Americans to accept lower-quality care and by depriving many others of any health insurance and regular care, current policies increase the overall cost of health care because people are far sicker and come to hospitals for more serious illnesses than they might have otherwise (Himmelstein et al., 1999).

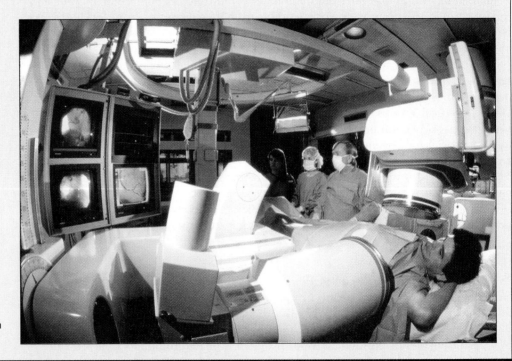

This digital biplane angioscope is an example of the multimillion-dollar equipment investments that make it difficult for not-for-profit HMOs to compete with for-profit HMOs.

Despite intense debate, few actual policies have been developed to provide a safety net for those who cannot afford high-quality medical care. The only significant recent legislation is the Kassebaum-Kennedy bill, enacted in 1996, which prohibits health insurance plans from limiting or denying coverage or charging higher premiums for an existing medical condition diagnosed or treated in the previous six months. This is a vital policy for people with AIDS, cancer, and other debilitating diseases who previously were at risk of being denied insurance if they changed jobs and a new insurance company discovered their costly medical condition. But the bill contains a serious loophole in that coverage can be denied for up to a year during the transition from one job to another (Clymer, 1996).

At present the major controversy over medical insurance reform concerns patients' rights to adequate medical care through their insurer, and especially through their HMO. Many doctors and patients have found that managed care has resulted in situations in which hospital stays are limited or other forms of treatment are curtailed, not on doctors' orders but because of decisions by insurance companies (Rovner, 1999). In 1997 Texas adopted a patients' rights law. This policy allows clients to challenge HMO decisions by appealing to an independent, board-certified physician; patients can also sue their HMOs. Studies indicate that Texans are generally satisfied with the policy. At the federal level, however, in 1999 the Republican-dominated Senate killed a Democratic-sponsored measure that would have created a similar policy for all Americans. Instead, it passed what most observers consider a watered-down version that only allows patients to appeal insurance companies' decisions through a system of internal review. The Democrats continue to oppose this weaker patients' rights bill (Pedersen, 1999).

The Disabled and Handicapped

The first significant measure that affected the disabled and handicapped was the Rehabilitation Act of 1973, which prohibited government agencies and contractors from discriminating against the handicapped and mandated affirmative-action plans for hiring and promotion. The act was strengthened in 1977, when the Department of Health and Human Services (HHS) issued regulations that required all recipients of HHS funds to provide equal access to employment or services—or lose their subsidies. The new regulations extended the term *handicapped* to include people who are disfigured, retarded, mentally ill, emotionally disabled, or drug or alcohol addicted, as well as those with histories of cancer and heart disease.

In practical terms, the HHS rulings meant that new buildings constructed with HHS grants must be equipped with such features as ramps and elevators. Old buildings had to be remodeled. Employers had to provide assistance for handicapped employees or potential employees, such as braille literature, telephone amplifiers, and special parking or furniture.

A related act, the Education for All Handicapped Children Act of 1975, required that handicapped children be provided with a "free appropriate public education" in the least restrictive environment appropriate to their needs—often an ordinary classroom in a public school. This policy is sometimes called *mainstreaming*. Critics of this act point out that it costs twice as much to educate a handicapped child in the public school system as it does to educate a nonhandicapped child; supporters emphasize the substantial reduction in Medicaid and disability costs that it can achieve.

The most far-reaching legislation affecting people with physical and mental disabilities is the Americans with Disabilities Act (ADA), which was passed in 1990. This act bars discrimination against the disabled in employment, transportation, public accommodations, and telecommunications. It requires employers that receive federal funds to provide equal opportunity for employment and for participation in programs and services to otherwise qualified people with disabilities. Employers must make reasonable accommodations to the disabilities of those individuals—that is, they must make facilities physically accessible; restructure job duties and modify work schedules; purchase or modify equipment; and provide readers, interpreters, or other support services. In addition, public accommodations and transportation facilities must be accessible to people in wheelchairs, and telephone companies must provide relay services that allow hearing- or voice-impaired people to place and receive calls.

At the end of the 1990s there were signs that judges were in a mood to curtail somewhat the rights of disabled people under the ADA. The Supreme Court ruled in 1998 that people with medically treatable disabilities (as opposed to permanent ones) are not eligible to sue their employers under the act. And as we will see in the next chapter, many states are seeking to curtail the rights of people with mental disabilities (Falk, 1999).

Social Policy and AIDS

The discovery of new treatments for people with HIV, based on intensive drug therapies and costly medications, raises many difficult policy issues. As more low-wage workers, immigrants, and indigent people are moved off Medicare or have their Medicare support reduced as a result of welfare reform, it becomes less likely that they will receive the new treatments. Even more affluent HIV and AIDS patients may not receive the new treatments if their insurance plans are inadequate or delayed.

Elsewhere in the world, changes in the pattern of HIV transmission mean that more babies will be born with AIDS in coming years, and more costly treatment will be required for AIDS patients in nations that can hardly afford to treat existing cases. Most world health authorities acknowledge that in the absence of a vaccination against AIDS, the only realistic policy to prevent the further spread of the disease is education, especially through programs directed at young women and adolescents.

Since the incidence of AIDS is increasing most rapidly among very poor people, particularly members of minority groups, many AIDS activists fear that the disease will become a neglected issue (Ayala, 1996). But the spread of AIDS among the poor in the more affluent nations means that the policies needed to prevent or slow its spread throughout the world are similar in both rich and poor nations. Again the key is more effective education about the risks of unprotected sex, needle sharing among drug users, and promiscuous sex. Increasingly these messages will need to be directed at women everywhere. Thus, the World Health Organization (WHO) recommends the following measures:

- *Prevent HIV infection in women* by protecting the human rights of women and girls, increasing education opportunities for girls and young women, increasing women's access to economic activities, and other measures.

- *Reduce the impact of HIV/AIDS on women* by including women living with HIV/AIDS in the development of HIV/AIDS policy and prevention and care programs; encouraging voluntary, confidential testing; and supporting programs that work with families of women living with the disease.

- *Care for women with HIV/AIDS* by providing appropriate health and welfare services, ensuring that women have access to contraceptive measures, increasing access to child care and other support services, and similar policies. (WHO, 1994)

Effective educational programs are often hampered by ideological and religious differences within a population. In the United States, for example, to avoid arousing the anger of conservative groups, the government has been careful not to issue AIDS brochures and materials that seem to promote sexual activity. The AIDS Commission has pointed out that this restriction actually serves to prolong the epidemic. Many groups at risk of contracting AIDS need very straightforward verbal and pictorial descriptions of the kinds of behavior they must avoid. They need plain language and blunt warnings. But pictures of people shooting drugs and engaging in sexual contact are not likely to gain the approval of local panels. The commission strongly urges policies that would reduce the power of local panels and permit the creation of more effective communications to target populations.

Numerous other policy issues are related to the AIDS epidemic. One area of controversy is how to prevent AIDS among intravenous drug users and their sex partners. Proposals include increasing the availability of treatment for drug users, providing for safer injection, and initiating more prevention programs (Des Jarlais, 1987). Programs in which addicts exchange old needles for new, sterile needles have been extremely controversial. They have been initiated in some American cities on a demonstration basis but have not yet received adequate support to increase their scope, as they have in Holland and some other European nations.

Another area of concern is how to speed up the production, testing, and distribution of medicines that can prolong the lives of AIDS patients. The Department of Health and Human Services (HHS) has done relatively little to expedite this process, nor has action been taken to make existing AIDS medications available to patients who cannot afford them. However, in 1990 the federal Food and Drug Administration (FDA) approved a vastly accelerated process for testing and emergency administration of two somewhat promising AIDS drugs, and a number of pharmaceutical companies that produce the medicines agreed to make them available at lower prices to indigent patients. Both developments signal an increased resolve to move more quickly in response to the continuing spread of AIDS, especially among the very poor.

Beyond Left & Right

The Clinton health-care plan of 1994 was the most comprehensive proposal for reforming the U.S. medical insurance system since the advent of Medicare and Medicaid. But it was strongly criticized by conservative opponents, both in and outside of Congress, who believed that it would vastly expand the health-care bureaucracy and decrease access to private doctors. On the left, the plan was criticized by those who favored a single-payer system of universal health insurance such as those in Canada and western Europe. The plan was defeated in Congress, and now the federal and state governments are attempting to make piecemeal reforms such as increasing enrollment in managed-care plans and reducing the costs of Medicare coverage. Meanwhile, the number of Americans without any medical insurance continues to grow.

What lessons can be learned from the failure of comprehensive medical reform? Are conservatives more likely to feel that we must improve a system in which the economically advantaged have the best medical care? Are liberals likely to give up the dream of a single-payer system of national health care? What are your opinions about these issues?

In the foreseeable future, health-care policy will continue to move in small but important steps, avoiding major ideological confrontations. Legislators on both sides of the dispute know that the Medicare fund must be augmented and additional revenues found, which will entail higher payments by those who can afford them. And measures that allow unemployed workers to retain their medical benefits for a specified length of time while they find new jobs will ease anxiety for hundreds of thousands of people. Another likely change will be increasing competition among managed-care providers in many states and regions. None of these changes is likely to aggravate ideological tensions. The nation is moving slowly toward improving its health-care system, and perhaps in this case ideological differences have prevented hasty policies with many unintended consequences.

SUMMARY

- Health care is considered a social problem when members of a society have unequal access to health-care institutions and the quality of the care provided is low relative to its cost.

- Health care is distributed very unequally in the United States. The use and availability of medical care are directly related to socioeconomic class and race. People in the lower classes tend to have higher rates of untreated illnesses and disabilities and higher mortality rates for most diseases than people in the middle and upper classes.

- Unequal access to health care is related to the cost of obtaining it. Health-care costs have increased by 200 percent since 1980. Hospital charges are a major factor in the high cost of health care in the United States, as are the fees charged by physicians and the rising cost of prescription drugs. Among the factors contributing to high fees are specialization and unnecessary surgery.

- Many Americans lack adequate health insurance. Public insurance programs (Medicaid and Medicare) have helped the poor and the elderly obtain greater access to health care, but there remain large numbers of people who are not covered by health insurance, either public or private.

- The controversy over legalized abortion has revealed many problems in the treatment of women by the medical establishment and has led to efforts to make medical personnel more sensitive to women's physical and psychological needs. These include efforts to win acceptance of midwives, to decrease medical intervention in the birth process, and to increase research on women's health issues.

- The disabled and handicapped encounter special problems related to their condition. They suffer high unemployment rates, and the majority are poor.

- Improved medical technology and life-prolonging procedures give rise to ethical issues such as how to determine when death occurs and whether individuals have a right to die.

- The social problems related to health care have become especially acute as a result of the AIDS epidemic. The disease is especially prevalent among homosexuals and intravenous drug users, but it is also spreading among the heterosexual population. There is no cure for it, and at present behavioral changes are the only defense against the spread of the virus.

- Conflict theorists believe that social class goes a long way toward explaining the types of illnesses experienced by members of a household and the kinds of health care they receive.

- Functionalist explanations of health-care problems focus on features of health-care institutions themselves, such as the marketplace approach to health care in the United States.

- The interactionist perspective on health-care problems points to the role of lifestyle features such as poor diet; lack of exercise; and smoking, including passive smoking, or breathing air that contains cigarette smoke.

- Since the defeat of the comprehensive health-care plan proposed by the Clinton administration, the nation has turned increasingly toward a managed-care system. Its dominant feature is the health maintenance organization, or prepaid group practice, which provides complete medical services to subscribers in a specific region who pay a monthly fee. There have also been some reforms in the laws that affect health insurance.

- Policy measures that affect the disabled and handicapped include the Education for All Handicapped Children Act of 1975, which requires that handicapped children be provided with free public education in the least restrictive environment appropriate to their needs, and the Americans with Disabilities Act of 1990, which bars discrimination against the disabled in employment, public accommodations, and other areas.

- Policy issues related to the AIDS epidemic include how to give costly treatment to those who cannot afford it and how to educate the general public, especially women, about ways to avoid infection.

KEY TERMS

cost shifting, p. 40
health maintenance organization
  (HMO), p. 53

INTERNET EXERCISE

The web destinations for Chapter 2 are related to different problems of physical health. To begin your explorations, go to the Prentice Hall Companion Website: **http://prenhall.com/kornblum.** Then choose **Chapter 2** (Problems of Physical Health). Next, select **destinations** from the menu on the left side of the screen. There are a number of interesting sites to investigate. We suggest that you begin with **CNN-Health-HMOs.** In Chapter 2, the *Critical Research* feature deals with profits and health care; specifically, do health maintenance organizations that are run for profit offer the same level and quality of care as those that are run as nonprofit businesses? The CNN site offers a broad look at the debate surrounding HMOs in particular and managed care in general. Check out the "Stories" section for discussions involving the controversy surrounding health maintenance organizations. There is also a "Glossary" section that you may click on in order to bring up topics of interest. After you have explored the CNN/HMO Debate site, answer the following questions:

- Respond to the question posed in the *Critical Research* feature: Do HMOs run for profit offer the same quality and level of care as those that are run as nonprofit businesses?

- What are the advantages and disadvantages of managed-care programs for health-care consumers?

3 Mental Illness

MENTAL ILLNESS

- One out of every four Americans suffers some form of mental disorder in a given year.

- Severe disorders like schizophrenia and manic-depressive illness affect 3.5 percent of the adult population.

- Overall rates of mental illness are about the same for men and women, but women are more likely to suffer from depression, anxieties, and phobias.

- Only about 30 percent of individuals afflicted by diagnosable mental disorders seek mental-health or substance abuse services.

OUTLINE

**Mental Illness
as a Social Problem**
Suicide and Mental Illness

**The Social Construction
of Mental Illness**
Defining Mental Illness
Classification of Mental
  Disorders
Diagnosis or Label?

**Inequality, Conflict,
and Mental Illness**
Social Class and Mental
  Disorder
Mental Disorder and Urban
  Life
Other Factors

**Institutional Problems
of Treatment and Care**
Methods of Treatment
Changes in Mental-health
  Professions
Treatment Institutions
Deinstitutionalization
  and Homelessness

Social Policy

Approximately one out of every four Americans suffers some form of mental disorder in a given year. These disorders range from mild depression and anxiety to severely debilitating psychoses like schizophrenia and manic depression (Regier et al., 1993). An estimated 3.5 million Americans suffer from severe mental illnesses, especially schizophrenia and manic-depressive illness. At least 40 percent of these individuals are not being treated for their illness, and many of them are found among the homeless on the streets of the nation's cities (Torrey & Zdanowicz, 1999).

Around the world, mental illness is a growing but largely unheralded social problem. Approximately 80 percent of the world's 350 million mentally disabled people live in developing nations. While basic physical health has improved worldwide, mental health has remained stagnant or deteriorated. Ironically, increases in the incidence of clinical depression, schizophrenia, dementia, and other forms of chronic illness have been a side effect of improved physical health in many parts of the world. More people are living to the ages at which the risk of severe mental illness increases (*United Nations Chronicle,* 1999).

The mental problems of the aging U.S. population are also a growing concern for researchers and policymakers, as well as for millions of elderly people and their families. Depression is extremely common in the elderly, usually worsened by isolation and chronic pain. Alzheimer's disease, a degenerative brain disorder that destroys memory, has been increasing in prevalence. Recent progress in research and development of treatments for depression and possible treatments for Alzheimer's is encouraging, but the problems brought on by mental illnesses among the elderly are likely to increase as the elderly population grows, a subject to which we return in Chapter 11.

Mental Illness as a Social Problem

The terms **mental disorder** and **mental illness** are often used interchangeably, and that is how they are used here. However, in formal social-scientific writing, *mental illness* is usually reserved for mental disorders that require hospitalization or for which close medical supervision would normally be recommended. Most people who seek help from mental-health institutions are unlikely ever to be hospitalized (Horowitz & Scheid, 1999).

Until the mid-twentieth century a large proportion of people who were classified as mentally ill and admitted to mental hospitals were actually suffering from physical ailments like epilepsy and brain tumors (Grob, 1985). Today researchers are learning about the biological origins of many mental illnesses, including schizophrenia, autism, and alcoholism (Berrios, 1995). As we discover the biological bases of some mental illnesses, we also gain information about the social conditions—such as physical abuse, neglect, and severe stress—that may bring on the mental breakdowns that cause people to cease functioning "normally."

The specific relationships between biological factors and certain types of mental illness are considered in detail in psychology and genetics courses. For our purposes here, it is enough to be aware that mental illness, whatever its causes, is a source of serious social problems not only in terms of the number of people affected but also the extent to which social institutions are strained by efforts to care for them.

The mental disorders that cause severe social problems are the most extreme forms of mental illness. Of these, the most sensational are those that threaten the social order—sociopaths who become serial killers (e.g., Jeffrey Dahmer) or "mad bombers" like the infamous Unabomber. The number of individuals with such disorders may be small, but they constitute an especially serious social problem because they are so violent and irrational.

Less threatening to public safety and perceptions of security, but far more widespread as a social problem, are severely ill individuals (often diagnosed as psychotic) who cannot care for themselves without specialized attention. They include people who are classified as mentally ill and chemically addicted, who are also especially likely to be indigent and homeless (Ries, 1994).

For the mentally ill themselves, their problem is a terrible affliction. They experience such symptoms as unimaginable fear, uncontrollable hallucinations, panic, crushing sadness, wild elation, and roller-coaster mood swings. For society as a whole, their illness presents a range of social problems: stress in family life, heavy demands on health-care institutions, moral and ethical problems (e.g., whether to permit the plea of insanity in criminal cases), the cost of treatment to society, and so on. All of these can be aggravated by the social stigma attached to mental illness. It can be said that the mentally ill suffer twice: They suffer from the illness itself, and they also suffer rejection, as if their illness were their own fault. This is not nearly as true for physical illness, and this factor alone marks off mental illness for special consideration in the study of social problems.

In the United States, panic attacks and phobias are the most common form of mental problem. Phobias include severe fears such as fear of going outside, fear of heights, or fear of being in an enclosed space. Phobias and panic attacks affect an estimated 20 million Americans in any given year. Another 18 million suffer from depression, including manic depression, major depression, and minor depression. Alcoholism, classified as a mental illness, has been diagnosed in approximately 14 million people. To complicate matters, about 6 million Americans have a substance abuse disorder along with one or more severe or relatively severe mental disorders like schizophrenia. These individuals are often referred to as mentally ill chemical abusers (MICA) and are a particularly problematic population in major urban centers (Horowitz & Scheid, 1999; Regier, 1991).

A distressing aspect of the general problem of mental illness is the social impact of **deinstitutionalization,** or discharging patients from mental hospitals directly into the community. Some of these patients are not able to function as normal members of society, and the consequences can be painful both for them and for those who come into contact with them. Others may suffer from less severe problems caused by rejection and stigma. As we will see later in the chapter, it has been difficult to develop (or consistently fund) effective means of treating such individuals outside of mental hospitals.

Policymakers at every level of society look to sociologists and other social scientists for basic research on the causes of mental illness and on the effects of major policy initiatives like deinstitutionalization or community treatment, as well as recommendations on how to deal with trends in mental illness. Thus, in addition to sponsoring research on medical approaches to treatment and rehabilitation, the National Institute of Mental Health (NIMH) funds studies of the social epidemiology of mental illness—by which we mean not simply its distribution in the population but also its impact on families and communities and welfare institutions, as well as the associated problems of homelessness and social dependency.

In studying social problems related to mental illness, the basic sociological perspectives can help

Mentally ill patients like this woman experience a degree of anguish that is difficult to comprehend for those who are not mentally ill.

clarify the relevant issues and explain some aspects of the origins of mental disorders. The interactionist perspective focuses on the social construction of mental illness, that is, on how our definitions of "normal" and "deviant" behavior in social situations lead to definitions of mental disorders. To a large extent, the definition of mental illness is the province of psychologists and psychiatrists. Their diagnoses result in labels like "schizophrenic" or "depressed." Research by sociologists who have studied the interactions among people who are thought of as mentally ill suggests that such a label may cause one to define oneself as ill and to behave in ways that confirm the self-definition (White, 1998).

Conflict theorists tend to focus on how mental illness may be associated with deprivation and inequality, including unequal access to appropriate care. The emergence of a two-class system of mental-health care in the United States is a central concern of this sociological perspective. Typically, more affluent patients with less severe mental illnesses receive higher-quality private care, whereas severely ill patients, often reduced to poverty by their illnesses, are shunted into budget-starved public institutions (National Advisory Mental Health Council, 1993).

From a functionalist perspective, mental illnesses constitute a social problem because they challenge our ability to provide effective treatment. This is especially true in societies that are marked by rapid social change, in which people do not have long-standing attachments to others in their immediate social surroundings or are often separated from their families, or in which systems of treatment have been changing rapidly and it is not clear how people with mental disorders should be helped (Sperry, 1995). One area in which these problems are especially evident is suicide prevention.

Suicide and Mental Illness

In October 1999, on the stressful anniversary of the shootings and suicides at Columbine High School, the mother of a student who had been paralyzed in the shootings walked into a pawn shop that sold handguns. As she was examining a pistol, she took bullets from her purse, inserted them into the gun, and shot herself. This grisly and public suicide is an example of a much larger social problem. Many social scientists believe that suicide has reached epidemic proportions in the United States and other nations. The sensational suicide of Carla June Hochhalter is a reminder of the complexity of suicide and its links to mental illness. Just that week, her daughter had shown some important progress in her recovery. But for severely depressed individuals like this mother of a shooting victim, small signs of hope can produce unexpected and irrational reactions. Suicide is the most extreme of such behaviors.

Every 17 minutes someone commits suicide in the United States. Suicide ranks third among causes of death for young people, and it is the second highest cause of death among college students. Contrary to popular belief, the rate of suicide, especially among teenagers and young adults, is not decreasing; in fact, since 1950 it has been increasing steadily. Men and women report suicidal thoughts with equal frequency, but young men are over three times more likely to kill themselves than are women. The likelihood of a male teenager or young adult committing suicide has increased by over 200 percent since midcentury (King, 1999). In the United States this year, suicide will claim more young men than AIDS, heart disease, and all other major illnesses. Around the world, the World Health Organization estimates that suicide is responsible for almost 2 percent of all deaths. This puts suicide well ahead of war and homicide (Solomon, 1999).

Mental illness seems to account for a great deal of suicide, but by no means does it explain all cases. Many people might believe that anyone who commits suicide or murder is insane, but the causes of suicide are far more complex. Kay Redfield Jamison, an expert on the subject, notes that half of all people with bipolar disease (manic depression) will make a suicide attempt, as will about one in five people with major depression. People who have suffered neurological damage before birth, often because of alcohol or cocaine use by the mother, may experience severe mood disorders that can lead to suicide. And there is mounting evidence that genetic factors are responsible for some mental illnesses, as well as for impulsiveness, aggression, and violence, which increase the risk of suicide. Unfortunately, our knowledge of the possible biological antecedents of suicide is still developing while the toll of suicide mounts. Although drugs like lithium and antidepressants are somewhat effective in decreasing rates of suicide among risk-prone individuals with histories of mental disorder, there are as yet no therapies to correct genetic damage at the neurological level (Jamison, 1999).

Research by Jamison and others calls attention to the social aspects of suicide's causes and treatment. Depression, for example, can be brought on by chronic anxieties over money and loss of work, as can marital discord. It often engenders further depression or abusive behavior and substance abuse, which can accelerate a downward spiral toward suicide. Among the elderly, loss of mental capabilities (dementia) is associated with depression and suicidal tendencies. But not all suicide is irrational and related to mental illness. People commit suicide to avoid severe embarrassment, to escape debt, to express strong political protest, and to avoid severe suffering due to physical illness. These reasons suggest that suicide can be the result of rational choices, even though the act itself requires an extremely strong emotional state if it is to succeed. In the young, however, suicide is almost always the result of depression or other forms of mental illness.

The shootings and suicides at Columbine and the hidden epidemic of suicides by teenagers and young adults inevitably raise questions about intervention and prevention. It is extremely difficult, however, to predict who will commit suicide among the far larger population of individuals who cope with suicidal thoughts. It is also true that suicide can produce localized suicide epidemics among peers. Strategies for peer counseling and suicide awareness, therefore, are extremely important. Jamison (1999) and other researchers tend to be highly critical of federal health-care policies that have decreased insurance coverage for the treatment of mental illness and deny adequate coverage and therapies to the mentally ill, a subject to which we return in the Social Policy section of the chapter. (See the Critical Research feature on page 65.)

CRITICAL RESEARCH

Women and Depression—A Critical View

Kay Redfield Jamison (1999) knows at first hand why mental illness is not only an individual problem but also a social problem of enormous importance. She has experienced the ravages of mental illness in her own life and has conducted research on the inadequacies of existing systems of mental-health insurance and treatment, especially for women. Here is a brief account, in her words, of what it is like to suffer from manic depression (bipolar disorder):

Depression, somehow, is much more in line with society's notions of what women are all about: passive, sensitive, hopeless, helpless, stricken, dependent, confused, rather tiresome, and with limited aspirations. Manic states, on the other hand, seem to be more the province of men: restless, fiery, aggressive, volatile, energetic, risk-taking, grandiose and visionary, and impatient with the status quo. Anger or irritability in men, under such circumstances, is more tolerated and understandable; leaders or takers of voyages are permitted a wider latitude for being temperamental. Journalists and other writers, quite understandably, have tended to focus on women and depression, rather than women and mania. This is not surprising: depression is twice as common in women as in men. But manic-depressive illness occurs equally often in women and men, and, being a relatively common condition, mania ends up affecting a large number of women. They, in turn, often are misdiagnosed; receive poor, if any, psychiatric treatment; and are at high risk for suicide, alcoholism, drug abuse, and violence. But they, like men who have manic-depressive illness, also often contribute a great deal of energy, fire, enthusiasm, and imagination to the people and world around them. . . .

When I was depressed, nothing came to me, and nothing came out of me. When manic, or mildly so, I would write a paper in a day; ideas would flow. I would design new studies, catch up on my patient charts and correspondence, and chip away at the mindless mounds of bureaucratic paperwork that defined the job of a clinic director. Like everything else in my life, the grim was usually set off by the grand; the grand, in turn, would yet again be canceled out by the grim. It was a loopy but intense life: marvelous, ghastly, dreadful, indescribably difficult,

gloriously and unexpectedly easy, complicated, great fun, and a no-exit nightmare. (p. 14)

Jamison's no-exit nightmare became so severe that, like many who suffer from manic depression, she tried to commit suicide. Eventually she began to be treated with lithium, a drug that is effective in treating the illness but for which it is difficult to determine the correct doses; moreover, it can have severe side effects. In Jamison's case, the drug diminished the severity of her symptoms but made it almost impossible for her to read for a number of years, depriving her of her career during that time. Eventually she and her doctors arrived at a balanced treatment, but not before she had experienced years of needless frustration with the nation's faulty system of mental-health treatment and inadequate insurance for those suffering mental illness. Her critical analysis of the mental-health system leads her to believe that an affluent society like ours should be doing far more to address the multiple individual and social problems of mental illness. Rather than simply throwing severely mentally ill people on the streets, she believes that hospitalization under highly improved conditions should be a desirable option. Community care, better insurance systems, and vastly improved access to the most up-to-date drug therapies are also high on her agenda.

The Social Construction of Mental Illness
Defining Mental Illness

When social scientists say that mental illness is socially constructed, they are highlighting aspects of those illnesses that help define how both mentally ill and "normal" people behave. The usefulness of this approach will become clear if we consider some alternative views of mental illness. In this section we look briefly at three different explanations of mental illness: (1) the medical model, which asserts that mental illness is a disease with physiological causes; (2) the deviance approach, which asserts that mental illness results from the way people who are considered mentally ill are treated; and (3) the controversial argument that mental illness is not a disease but a method governments use to define certain people as being in need of isolation and "treatment."

The Medical Model.   The most familiar school of thought holds that a mental disorder should be viewed as a disease with biological causes. That is, a mental disorder is primarily a disturbance of the normal personality that is analogous to the physiological disturbance caused by physical disease. It can be remedied primarily by treating the patient. Once this has been done, the patient will be able to function adequately.

Research in the biological sciences, especially genetics, has uncovered strong evidence to support biological explanations of mental illnesses like schizophrenia, manic depression, childhood autism, senility, and even alcoholism (to which we will return in Chapter 5). In addition to disorders that are classified as mental illnesses, many of which have been found to have somatic causes, there are a host of mental disabilities that usually appear at birth, such as Down syndrome, cerebral palsy, and brain damage caused by birth trauma; such disorders present unusual and difficult challenges to those afflicted by them.

Research on the medical model of mental disorders arose in reaction to the older notion that mentally disturbed people are mad or "possessed" and should be locked up, beaten, or killed. It made possible serious investigation of the causes and cures of mental disorders and was responsible for the development of virtually all the systems of mental-health care and therapeutic treatment in existence today—systems that are still largely in the hands of medically oriented personnel. It has helped reduce the stigma and shame of mental disorder since, after all, "illness can happen to anyone."

Nevertheless, the concept of mental disorder as a disease has certain disadvantages. Because it concentrates on individuals and their immediate environment (often their childhood environment), it tends to disregard the wider social environment as a possible source of the problem. In addition, especially for hospitalized patients, the medical model can lead to impractical criteria of recovery—people may have gained considerable insight into their inner tensions but are still unable to function adequately when they return to the outer tensions of home, job, or society. It is also true that many mental illnesses, which may or may not be caused by an individual's physiology, may be brought on, alleviated, or worsened by conditions in that person's social environment.

Mental Illness as Deviance.   Neither social nor biological scientists know precisely what kinds of interactions among the multitude of physical and social conditions that affect human beings may cause mental illness in some cases or lead to remission or recovery in others. We do know, however, that the way a mentally ill person is treated once the illness has been diagnosed can have a lasting impact on that person's behavior and on his or her chances of leading a happy and productive life.

The concept of mental disorder as a disease holds that something about a person is abnormal and that the fundamental problem lies in his or her emotional makeup, which was twisted, repressed, or otherwise wrongly developed as a result of genetic or

Federal law requires that communities provide training and education for individuals suffering from mental disorders with genetic or physiological causes, such as Down syndrome.

chemical factors or events early in life. Although this theory seems to explain some mental disorders, many observers believe that other factors need to be taken into account, especially the constant pressure exerted by modern society. Out of this has developed the view that mental disorder represents a departure from certain expectations of society—that it is a form of social deviance.

In this connection the idea of **residual deviance** is useful. According to Thomas Scheff (1963), who formulated the concept, most social conventions are recognized as such, and violation of those conventions carries fairly clear labels: People who steal wallets are thieves, people who act haughtily toward the poor are snobs, and so on. But there is a large residual area of social convention that is so completely taken for granted that it is assumed to be part of human nature. To use Scheff's example, it seems natural for people holding a conversation to face each other rather than to look away. Violation of this norm seems contrary to human nature.

Scheff (1963) suggests that residual deviance occurs in most people at one time or another and usually passes without treatment. What causes it to become a mental disorder in some cases is that *society decides to label it as such*. When this happens, the role of "mentally ill person" is offered to the deviant individual. Since such people are often confused and frightened by their own behavior during a time of stress—as well as by other people's reactions to their behavior—they are likely to be particularly impressionable and may accept the role that is offered to them. Once this happens, it becomes difficult for them to change their behavior and return to their "normal" role.

If this is so, mental disorder may actually be caused by some of the attempts to cure it. By treating a patient in a separate institution, the mental-health profession certifies that the individual is indeed a patient and that he or she is mentally ill (Berrios, 1995). The point of the concept of mental disorder as deviance, thus, is that the disorder may be a function not only of certain individuals' inability to comply with societal expectations but also of the label attached to those who deviate (Scull, 1988).

Problems in Living. A third approach to understanding mental disorder has been offered by Thomas Szasz, a psychiatrist who has generated considerable controversy by contending that mental illness is a myth. Although this is not a widely accepted view, it does call attention to the relationship between diagnosis and repression. Szasz does not claim that the social and psychological disturbances referred to as mental illness do not exist; rather, he argues that it is dangerously misleading to call them illnesses. Instead, he believes, they should be regarded as manifestations of unresolved problems in living.

The significance of Szasz's basic argument is that it concerns justice and individual freedom. As he sees it, a diagnosis of mental disorder involves a value judgment based on the behavioral norms held by psychiatrists. Referring to certain behaviors as illnesses allows doctors to use medicine to correct what are essentially social, ethical, or legal deviations. Not only is this logically absurd, Szasz contends, but it is also dangerous.

Szasz (1994, 1998) believes that individual liberty can be unwittingly sacrificed through too great a concern for the "cure" of "mental illness." This issue has come to the fore in connection with the forcible removal of homeless individuals from city streets. The presence of these people, who are often shabby and dirty and may behave in bizarre ways, offends "normal" citizens. As we will see later in the chapter, the interpretation of this lifestyle as a sign of mental illness has been used to justify the involuntary placement of the homeless in shelters or hospitals, where they are out of sight. We will also see that sensational crimes by mentally ill people, such as incidents of sudden violence in which schizophrenic individuals push unsuspecting pedestrians off train platforms, along with public concern about links between mental illness and violent crimes in schools, have produced renewed efforts to enforce mandatory institutionalization (Phillips, 1998).

When sociologists speak of the social construction of mental illness, they incorporate all these approaches into their explanations. They recognize that there is often a biological basis for mental illness. In fact, medical and genetic discoveries are making possible more effective treatments. But social-scientific research also finds that mental illness is often aggravated by the fact that mentally ill people are treated as social deviants. They also recognize and study instances in which the label of mental illness is a convenient way of ridding society of people who are troublesome. (The nations of the former Soviet Union were notorious for this technique, but it has been used in societies all over the world at one time or another.) Most important, sociologists recognize that the classification of mental illnesses and decisions about how they should be treated are determined by how we think about the causes, consequences, and possibilities of treating mental disorders. Even the diagnosis of mental illness requires the emergence of a common set of perceptions among mental-health professionals, a point that will become clear if we look in more detail at the problems of diagnosis.

Classification of Mental Disorders

Clinicians and researchers need a common language to discuss mental disorders. It is impossible to plan a consistent program of treatment for a patient without an accurate diagnosis, and it is impossible to evaluate the effectiveness of various forms of treatment without clearly defined diagnostic terms.

In 1973, in an effort to deal with these problems, the American Psychiatric Association (APA) embarked on a controversial and ambitious revision of its manual of mental disorders. The new manual, released in 1980 and referred to as the *Diagnostic and Statistical Manual of Mental Disorders,* third edition, or simply as *DSM-III,* represented the work of hundreds of scientists and professionals in the field of mental-health care. A revised edition, *DSM-IV,* was published in 1994. Widely regarded as a major advance in the scientific description and classification of mental disorders, *DSM-III* had a significant impact on treatment. Among other things, it made an important contribution to the separation of mental disorders from behaviors (such as homosexuality) that deviate from societal norms but are not necessarily a result of mental illness.

Although, as we will see shortly, labeling theorists continue to believe that the diagnostic categories of psychiatrists reflect the biases of the people who make them up, *DSM-III* and *DSM-IV* resolved some of the more controversial issues in the classification of mental disorders. In general, however, the manual continues to represent the illness model. To a large extent it seeks to attribute mental dysfunctions to physiological, biochemical, genetic, or profound internal psychological causes. The major categories of the illness model, as presented in *DSM-IV*, are shown in Figure 3–1.

DISORDERS EVIDENT IN INFANCY, CHILDHOOD, OR ADOLESCENCE
These disorders that begin prior to adulthood include mental retardation, attention-deficit hyperactivity, anorexia nervosa, bulimia nervosa, stuttering, sleepwalking, and bedwetting.

ORGANIC MENTAL DISORDERS
Psychological or behavioral abnormalities associated with temporary or permanent dysfunction of the brain resulting from aging, disease, or drugs; include delirium and dementia.

PHSYCHOACTIVE SUBSTANCE USE DISORDER
Disorders resulting from excessive and persistent use of mind-altering substances like alcohol, barbiturates, cocaine, or amphetamines.

SCHIZOPHRENIA
Characterized by symptoms such as delusions or hallucinations and deterioration from a previous level of functioning, with symptoms existing for more than six months. Examples include catatonic schizophrenia and paranoid schizophrenia.

DELUSIONAL DISORDERS
The key feature is the presence of a delusion (e.g., belief that one is being persecuted). It is often difficult to clearly differentiate delusional disorders from paranoid schizophrenia.

MOOD DISORDERS
These disorders, also known as affective disorders, involve extremes in emotion; they include major depression and bipolar (manic-depressive) disorder.

ANXIETY DISORDERS
The key symptom, anxiety, is manifest in phobias, generalized anxiety disorder, panic attacks, or obsessive-compulsive disorder.

SOMATOFORM DISORDERS
The presentation of physical symptoms such as paralysis without medical explanation. Examples include somatization disorder, hypochondriasis, and conversion disorder.

DISSASSOCIATIVE DISORDERS
Involves a splitting or disassociation of normal consciousness; includes psychogenic amnesia, psychogenic fugue, and mutliple personality.

PSYCHOSEXUAL DISORDERS
Disorders characterized by sexual arousal by unusual objects or situations (fetishism) or by sexual dysfunctions such as inhibition of sexual desire.

PERSONALITY DISORDERS
Chronic, inflexible, and maladaptive personality patterns that are generally resistant to treatment, such as the antisocial personality disorder.

DISORDERS OF IMPULSE CONTROL
These include kleptomania, pyromania, and pathological gambling.

Figure 3–1 Categories of Psychological Disorders Listed in the *Diagnostic and Statistical Manual of Mental Disorders,* 4th ed.

Source: Adapted from American Psychiatric Association, 1994.

A number of familiar terms are not used in *DSM-IV*. Chief among them is *neurosis,* the older term for a wide range of disorders in which the individual suffers from severe anxiety but continues to attempt to function in the everyday world, usually through a variety of subterfuges or defense mechanisms, such as denial of problems or projection of one's own problems onto another person (e.g., perceiving others as hostile or angry rather than acknowledging these traits in oneself). The new classification system replaces this term with more specific ones like *affective disorder, anxiety disorder, somatoform disorder,* and *psychosexual disorder.* In everyday usage, however, the term *neurosis* continues to appear with some frequency.

Diagnosis or Label?

Just as some physical illnesses may be culturally defined, so may certain mental disorders. The medical model assumes that patients present symptoms that can be classified into diagnosable categories of mental illness. But there is a growing belief that at least some psychiatric diagnoses are pigeonholes into which certain behaviors are placed arbitrarily. The diagnosis of schizophrenia has, according to labeling theorists, been especially subject to misuse. Although there is little agreement about its origins, causes, and symptoms, it is the most commonly used diagnosis for severe mental illness. To labeling theorists, this suggests that diagnoses of mental illnesses tend to reflect cultural values, not scientific analysis. People are not "schizophrenic" in the sense that they manifest definite symptoms; instead, their behavior violates society's norms and expectations. For example, a person who sees visions might be considered perfectly normal, even admirable, in many cultures, although in the United States he or she would probably be regarded as disturbed.

The problem with labeling people as mentally ill is threefold: it makes us perceive certain behaviors as "sick," something to be eliminated rather than understood; it gives public agencies the right to incarcerate people against their will simply for not conforming; and it causes those people to define themselves as rule breakers and undesirables and allows them to fulfill that image. Many studies have demonstrated the influence of societal factors on the diagnosis of mental illness, as well as the vagueness of such diagnoses. Rosenhan (1973), in a classic study that will be described more fully later in the chapter, found that psychologists and psychiatrists on the staffs of several mental hospitals were unable to determine accurately which of the people they interviewed were mentally healthy and which were mentally ill. Greenley (1972) found that the attitudes of the families of patients in a mental hospital were a critical factor in how the patients' illnesses were defined. If the family insisted that the patient be released, the psychiatrist in charge would generally agree. Upon being discharged, the patient would be defined, both in the doctor's conversations and in official records, as being well enough to leave. When there was no pressure for a patient to be released, the patient generally was defined as being too sick to leave the hospital.

Despite the undeniable influence of labeling on the diagnosis and treatment of mental illness, recent large-scale research has shown that interviewers with basic training in the diagnosis of mental illness can spot people with serious mental disorders like schizophrenia and severe depression quite accurately. Such research is vital to our knowledge of the extent of mental illness in a population (Goleman, 1993; Horowitz & Scheid, 1999).

In a fascinating episode in the history of psychiatry, a group of people who had long been considered mentally ill successfully challenged that label and convinced the APA to remove it from the *DSM*. For a number of years homosexuals had demonstrated at psychiatric conventions, demanding that homosexuality no longer be considered a mental disorder. In 1973, after several years of heated controversy, the Board of Trustees of the APA voted to strike homosexuality from its official list of mental diseases. But this decision infuriated large numbers of conservative psychiatrists, who viewed homosexuality not as a label applied to a deviant group by a dominant group but as an illness that requires treatment and, if possible, cure. They insisted that the question be considered in a referendum by the entire membership of the APA. After intensive maneuvering that resembled efforts to garner support at political conventions, the medical model was voted down and the label "mental disorder" was no longer officially applied to homosexuality by psychiatrists (Bayer, 1987).

Incidents like this one remind us that the members of a society, especially mental-health professionals and political leaders, are continually negotiating the definitions and, thus, the possible treatments of mental disorders. We will see in the next section that a large number of factors—including whether people are rich or poor, live in a central city or a suburb or a rural area, are black or white or Hispanic, male or female—can affect how, or even if, their illnesses are diagnosed and treated.

Inequality, Conflict, and Mental Illness

Sociologists and experts on mental-health care estimate that in a typical year about 28 percent of adults are affected by a diagnosable mental disorder, including alcohol and other substance abuse disorders (Goldman, Frank, & McGuire, 1994). But only about 40 percent of these individuals seek mental-health or substance abuse services. Additional millions of people without diagnosable mental disorders seek care, increasing the proportion of those who receive mental-health services in a given year to almost 15 percent of the total adult population. Severe disorders like schizophrenia and manic-depressive illness affect about 3 percent of the adult population, and slightly more than 1 million citizens suffering from severe mental illnesses receive Social Security disability benefits (Horowitz & Scheid, 1999).

According to the National Institute of Mental Health, "Both the prevalence of SMI [serious mental illness] and resulting disability are clearly related to poverty status. SMI [is] over 2½ times as likely among adults in poverty than among those not in poverty, and proportionally more poor than nonpoor adults with SMI [have] resulting disability" (National Center for Health Statistics, 1992, p. 4). Sociologists are interested in the relationship between social factors like poverty and the incidence of mental disorders. Is mental disorder associated with social class and with conflicts over the distribution of social rewards? Does it occur more frequently in urban centers than in rural areas or suburbs? In what population groups is it most prevalent? Would changes in social conditions prevent or alleviate certain mental disorders?

The study of such relationships is complicated by the difficulty of ascertaining the prevalence of mental disorders. We can count the number of patients in mental hospitals and, somewhat less accurately, those receiving treatment in clinics and other outpatient facilities. It is far more difficult to obtain reliable statistics on the number being treated in private practice. Moreover, any number of people who would qualify as emotionally disturbed are not under treatment at all and therefore do not appear in most estimates of the incidence of mental disorders. Consequently, any statistics on treated mental disorders must be viewed as only a very rough estimate of the total number of people suffering from these problems.

Despite these difficulties, sociologists have reached several tentative conclusions about the relationship between mental disorders and patterns of inequality in a society. It should be noted that research on the impact of inequality is often conducted from a conflict perspective. Conflict theorists call attention to the ways in which inequalities of wealth and power produce inequalities in access to effective treatment for mental disorders. Underlying these inequalities is class conflict. The poor demand more services and better care from public institutions, while those who are better off believe that the poor bring their troubles on themselves and do not deserve expensive care facilities and treatment programs. Conflict theorists also emphasize that poverty itself is a social problem that can produce severe stress in those who experience it. Life in poverty is associated with higher exposure to crime and violence, which adds to the stress of everyday life. In some individuals such extreme stress can precipitate mental illness (Kozol, 1988; Snow, 1993).

Social Class and Mental Disorder

Long before sociologists began to make systematic studies of social conditions and mental disorders, the connection between the two had been recognized. It was only in the 1930s, however, that serious sociological study of this relationship began, and although the research results are not in perfect agreement, they offer some useful information.

One pioneering study (Faris & Dunham, 1938) investigated the residential patterns of 35,000 hospitalized mental patients in Chicago. The highest rates of mental disorder were found near the center of the city, where the population was poor, of very mixed ethnic and racial background, and highly mobile. Although this number included many cases of organic psychosis due to syphilis and alcoholism in the skid row districts, it also included a significantly high rate of schizophrenia throughout the area. Conversely, the lowest rates of mental disorder were found in stable, higher-status residential areas.

We now know that the early research was somewhat misleading in suggesting that psychoses are more likely to occur among people who are poor and live in rundown areas. It has been shown that people with schizophrenia and drug-induced organic disorders tend to inhabit the poorer areas of cities, partly because they usually have limited incomes and also because they feel more comfortable where there are people like themselves.

Another classic study, the Midtown Manhattan Study, went beyond treatment to include a random sample of 1,660 adult residents of midtown Manhattan (Srole et al., 1978). The researchers found that almost 23 percent were significantly impaired in mental functioning, including many people who were not under treatment. One of the factors investigated was socioeconomic status, not only that of the subjects but also that of their parents. Among subjects who were considered seriously impaired in mental functioning, the percentage with lower-class parents was twice the percentage of those with upper-class parents. This finding suggests that socioeconomic status has a strong influence on the mental health of children.

A similar study of a nonhospitalized population was conducted among residents of rural Sterling County in Nova Scotia (Leighton et al., 1963). Like the Midtown Manhattan Study, this one found high rates of untreated mental disorders. More recent research confirms this finding; for example, a study carried out in New Haven, Baltimore, and St. Louis reported that between 29 and 38 percent of the sample had had symptoms of mental illness (Robins et al., 1984).

It should be kept in mind that studies like these tend to come up with widely divergent estimates of the proportion of mentally ill individuals in various populations. Some of these differences are due to the use of different data-collection techniques and different definitions of mental illness. The studies are consistent, however, in reporting that only a minority of the cases observed have ever received treatment (Barker, Manderscheid, & Gendershot, 1992; Horowitz & Scheid, 1999; Regier et al., 1993).

These classic studies established the basic methods for estimating the incidence and prevalence of mental illnesses. In the United States, all measures of how many Americans have symptoms of various illnesses and how many of them receive treatment (or do not) are based on the selection of representative communities and the random selection of households within those communities. Individuals in these households are interviewed about their present and past mental histories. These epidemiological studies of mental illnesses are extremely costly and cannot be done every year, but they establish the baseline data on which a good deal of social policy directed at mental illness is based. Many nations, especially in poor regions of the world, do not have the resources to carry out such studies (Horowitz & Scheid, 1999).

The Drift Hypothesis. All the studies just described agree that psychosis in general and schizophrenia in particular are much more common at the lowest socioeconomic level than at higher levels. They do not indicate, however, whether most schizophrenic individuals were originally in the lowest class or whether they drifted down to it as the disorder worsened. In other words, they fail to make clear whether low socioeconomic status is primarily a *cause* or an *effect* of serious mental disorder.

Some researchers reject the social-stress hypothesis as an explanation of the preponderance of mental illness in the lower classes. Instead, they propose the *social-selection* or *drift hypothesis,* which holds that social class is not a cause but a consequence of mental disorder. In this view, mentally disordered people tend to be found in the lower classes because their illness has prevented them from functioning at a higher class level and they have "drifted" downward to a lower class. This interpretation is partially supported by a study of a population of over 16,000 individuals in southern Appalachia (Harkey, Miles, & Rushing, 1976), which found that the primary effect of psychological disorder is to retard upward mobility (although it does not necessarily contribute to downward mobility). A study of Dutch schizophrenics also supported the social-selection theory (Fox, 1989).

Studies like these, though not conclusive, provide evidence that low social class does not cause mental illness. Instead, a low social-class position is associated with mental disorders, most likely as a result of a process in which the mentally ill drift downward in society. A review of existing studies on this subject, together with an analysis of new data from repeated interviews with a large sample of Americans, lends further support to the drift hypothesis. Sociologists and mental-health experts on the study team found that a wide variety of mental illnesses impair individuals' ability to develop their skills and advance in the world of work, and thus prevent them from attaining social mobility. In short, it is more often the case that mental disorders produce low socioeconomic status than that low socioeconomic status produces mental disorder (Miech et al., 1999).

Most cities have rundown areas where people from other neighborhoods and outlying areas congregate. Often suffering from the consequences of multiple problems (poverty, homelessness, mental illness, alcoholism), these individuals feel less deviant in these areas than in more "respectable" parts of the city.

Mental Disorder and Urban Life

Whatever the precise relationship between mental illness and social class, there is no doubt that people who live in lower-class communities or neighborhoods, especially in central cities, experience high levels of stress. This aspect of their social environment can bring on bouts of mental illness. The presence of high rates of mental illness in urban settings leads many people to assume that there is a connection between city life and mental disorder. However, since there has been little research in this area, no conclusive test of this assumption is available. Investigation is made more difficult by the fact that mental disorder is more likely to be diagnosed and treated where facilities are readily accessible—which usually means in and around cities. Studies of treated mental disorder, therefore, are of limited usefulness in making urban-rural comparisons.

A feature of urban life that has received particular attention in studies of the causes of mental illness is crowding in the home. Research on this subject has generated considerable controversy. A survey of Chicago residents (Gove, Hughes, & Galle, 1979) measured both objective crowding (number of people per room) and subjective

Loss of a job or failure to pay the rent may leave families struggling to find their way on city streets.

crowding (excessive social demands and lack of privacy). The results indicated that household crowding has a number of adverse consequences, including poor mental health. However, this conclusion has been challenged by critics who contend that complaints of lack of privacy and excessive demands by others may themselves be signs of mental disorder (Booth, Johnson, & Edwards, 1980).

Recent research on crowding and child development offers substantial evidence that children growing up in crowded apartments, neighborhoods, and child care facilities can suffer a variety of disorders that may put them at risk for more severe mental disorders later in life. In a study of 10-to-12-year-old children of working-class parents living in India (Evans et al., 1998), the researchers found that chronic residential crowding is associated with difficulties in behavioral adjustment at school, poor academic achievement, and impaired parent-child relationships. Another study found that children in crowded homes and classrooms are more likely to develop behavior problems because they lack the coping abilities and experience that most adults have (Henderson, 1995).

Other Factors

A variety of other factors have been investigated in an attempt to discover their relationship to mental disorder. Among these are race and sex.

Race. Race does not appear to be a significant variable by itself. Instead, racial differences in mental health can be explained in terms of social class. Poor people, of whom a large proportion are black, are much more likely to be seen as needing hospitalization than members of the middle and upper classes, most of whom are white. The latter are more likely to be seen as needing outpatient psychotherapy. The poor are also much more likely to deal with public agencies, including mental-health centers, and to live in deteriorated urban environments (Gaw, 1993; Miech et al., 1999).

Sex. Although overall rates of mental illness are about the same for men and women (Regier et al., 1984), women are more likely than men to suffer from depression, anxieties, and phobias. In a classic study of this important subject, Phyllis Chesler (1972) suggested that the nature and incidence of mental disorder among women are a reflection of women's secondary status and restricted roles. Women are expected to conform to rigidly defined standards of behavior—to be passive, dependent, and emotional, for example, in accordance with traditional feminine roles. Since mental-health professionals are predominantly male, women who behave in nontraditional ways are more likely to be defined as mentally ill.

Chesler cites a study in which mental-health clinicians were asked to identify healthy male traits and healthy female traits. The researchers found that the standards of mental health for men and women differed according to traditional sex-role stereotypes. Thus, healthy women were considered to be unaggressive, submissive, excitable, and vain. Other studies cited by Chesler confirm that such attitudes do indeed serve as a basis for the decisions of mental-health professionals. For example, the major difference between female ex-mental patients who were rehospitalized and those who were not was that the former had refused to perform their domestic "duties"—cleaning, cooking, and the like. Women were also more likely to be called schizophrenics when they behaved in ways that are considered acceptable in men.

The question of whether men and women have different rates of psychosis has not been fully resolved. Men are thought to be more susceptible than women to schizophrenia; however, in a review of existing research, Dohrenwend and Dohrenwend (1975) found that half of the studies they investigated reported schizophrenia to be more prevalent among men, whereas the other half found it to occur more frequently among women. On the other hand, a study based on the criteria listed in *DSM-III* found significantly more men than women among schizophrenic patients (Lewine, Burbach, & Meltzer, 1984).

Although the evidence on schizophrenia, the most serious mental illness, is contradictory, there is widespread agreement among researchers that women tend to have significantly higher rates of depression than men and that men exhibit significantly higher rates of personality disorders. Women who are single parents and in the labor force have the highest rates of depression (Cockerham, 1998; Jamison, 1999; Mirowsky, 1985).

Institutional Problems of Treatment and Care

The treatment of mental disorders has undergone enormous changes in the past century and remains one of the most controversial aspects of mental health in all societies. In this section we will review the major approaches to the treatment of mental illness, as well as changes in mental-health institutions. We will see that although there has been a great deal of progress in treating mental illness, many problems remain, especially in creating and maintaining effective institutions for the treatment and care of the mentally ill (Dial et al., 1992; Horowitz & Scheid, 1999).

Methods of Treatment

The two major approaches to the treatment of mental disorders are psychotherapy (sometimes called insight therapy) and medical treatment in the form of psychotropic drugs or electroconvulsive therapy. Although these approaches are sometimes used simultaneously, they involve different groups of mental-health professionals, who often have difficulty coordinating the diagnosis and treatment of their patients. The problem of coordination will be discussed more fully in the Social Policy section of the chapter. In this section we will briefly review the most important methods of treatment.

Nonmedical Forms of Treatment. Patients who undergo psychotherapy are helped to understand the underlying reasons for their problems so that they can try to work out solutions. The process involves some form of interaction between the patient and the therapist or among patients in groups. Among the major forms of psychotherapy are psychoanalysis, client-centered therapy, and various types of therapy and support groups.

Developed by Sigmund Freud in the late nineteenth century, psychoanalysis seeks to uncover unconscious motives, memories, and fears that prevent the patient from functioning normally. Patients may use various methods of exploration and discovery, including dreams and free association. Client-centered therapy was developed by Carl Rogers in the 1940s. This approach emphasizes current problems rather than unconscious motives and past experiences. The patient sets the course of the therapy, while the therapist provides support. In therapy and support groups, people attempt to solve their problems through interaction with one another. Therapy groups are led by professionals; support groups are organized by people who have experienced the same problems as the other participants, for example, Alcoholics Anonymous, Overeaters Anonymous, and Gamblers Anonymous. Another important type of group therapy is family therapy, in which family members work with the help of a trained professional to overcome their difficulties.

Still another nonmedical approach, hypnosis, can help patients recall deeply repressed but significant memories that may be blocking their progress toward understanding and dealing with their problems. Hypnosis is often used successfully in the treatment of milder mental disorders but has not had a major impact on the treatment of psychoses.

Medical Approaches to Treatment.   Medical treatments, particularly chemotherapy and shock treatment, are applied to the most severe mental illnesses, such as schizophrenia and manic depression. Control over these treatments is in the hands of medical or clinical psychiatrists, whereas insight therapies are practiced by other professionals, including licensed psychologists, clinically trained social workers, and lay therapists. None of the latter is authorized to prescribe drugs, shock treatment, or hospitalization.

Before the late 1930s severe psychosis was treated in a variety of ways: by confining the patient in a straitjacket; by administering sedatives; by wrapping the patient in moist, cool sheets; or by immersing the patient in a continuous flow tub for hours at a time (Sheehan, 1982). Then a more drastic treatment was introduced: electroconvulsive therapy, in which an electric shock produces a convulsion and brief unconsciousness. This frightening and dangerous treatment has produced dramatic results with deeply depressed patients and some schizophrenics. However, the effects tend to be temporary, and it is not clear how much brain damage the treatment causes. Moreover, it often results in long-term memory loss.

In the 1940s and early 1950s shock treatment was used extensively, sometimes in coercive and excessive ways (Squire, 1987). The procedure was modified in the mid-1950s and made somewhat safer, but in the 1960s and 1970s it fell into disfavor as drug therapies became increasingly popular. Recently, interest in this form of treatment has revived, partly because drug therapies have turned out to be less effective than anticipated (Regier, 1991).

The other important medical approach to treatment, chemotherapy, involves treating patients with a variety of drugs, ranging from mild tranquilizers to antidepressants and antipsychotic agents. The development of antipsychotic drugs has made it possible to control the most incapacitating aspects of schizophrenia and paranoia. This, in turn, often permits the patient to return to the commuity, with occasional periods of hospitalization when stress or other problems cause more severe symptoms of the disorder to recur. But these powerful drugs cause side effects when they are administered over long periods (Regier, 1991). Of all the recent innovations in drug therapy, the administration of antidepressants, especially Prozac, has had the greatest impact and has relieved severe and debilitating symptoms in millions of people (Jamison, 1999).

Chemotherapy is also used in the treatment of anxiety. This usually involves the use of mild tranquilizers such as Valium and Xanax, the most frequently prescribed drugs today. It is generally believed that chemotherapy should be used in conjunction with some other form of therapy since drugs alone can rarely bring about significant long-term changes in behavior.

Changes in Mental-health Professions

In the largest survey of mental-health needs and access to medical care in many decades, researchers at the National Institute of Mental Health contacted more than 20,000 Americans, who were interviewed about their recent history of mental disorders and asked what they did when they had symptoms of mental illness and distress. The study showed that mental illness goes untreated in seven out of ten cases. Of people who did go to doctors or other mental-health professionals for treatment, those with severe mental illnesses were likely to be treated by psychiatrists and other highly trained mental-health professionals, whereas those with milder but still quite troubling problems (43 percent of this group) most often consulted their family physicians, who did not necessarily have special training in mental-health care. About 40 percent of those who sought medical help for mental illness said that they visited mental-health professionals, including psychiatrists, who can dispense psychotropic drugs, and psychologists and clinical social workers, who cannot dispense such drugs. Another 18 percent said that they visited a family friend, a member of the clergy, or a self-help group (Regier et al., 1993). These findings suggest that there is an urgent need for more research to find better ways to identify and treat individuals with severe untreated mental illnesses. They also indicate that family physicians require more training in dealing with mental-health issues.

In treating patients who seek professional help for mental disorders, psychiatrists increasingly find themselves in direct competition for patients with therapists who rely on insight methods or "talking cures." The latter include clinical psychologists, clinical social workers, and marriage and family counselors. These professions are growing far more rapidly than psychiatry, despite the fact that only psychiatrists with a licensed medical degree are legally permitted to write drug prescriptions, and only psychiatrists can supervise the treatment of hospitalized patients. The services of clinically trained social workers and psychologists cost less than two-thirds of the costs of psychiatric care, and insurance companies would rather pay these lower fees. Also, many insurance companies have reduced the number of therapy visits they will cover. When patients have to pay some of the fees, they, too, are more likely to choose the less costly form of treatment as long as their disorder does not involve symptoms that require drug therapy. Figure 3–2 shows the consequences of these trends: The number of clinical social workers and psychologists more than tripled between 1975 and 1990, while the number of psychiatrists leveled off at about 36,000.

Treatment Institutions

The forms of treatment described earlier are carried out in a variety of settings. Psychotherapy and other nonmedical forms of treatment generally occur in nonhospital settings such as psychologists' offices. Medical treatments, in contrast, often require

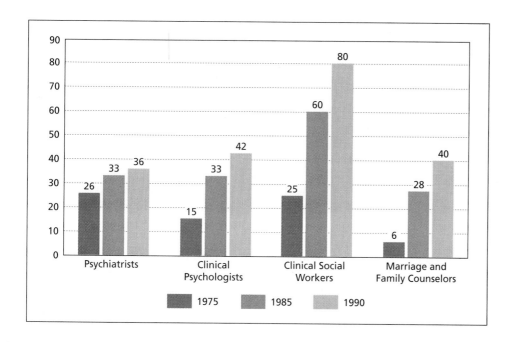

Figure 3–2 Growth in Number of Mental-Health Professionals (in thousands)

Source: Data from American Psychiatric Association; American Psychological Association; National Association of Social Workers; and American Association of Marriage and Family Therapists.

hospitalization. In addition, some patients are so seriously ill that they cannot be cared for outside a hospital or asylum. In this section we discuss issues related to the care of the mentally ill in hospitals and other institutions.

Mental Hospitals.   In the late nineteenth and early twentieth centuries, mental-health care meant, in practice, mental hospitals. During this period, the ties among members of extended families were being weakened as a result of increased mobility. The smaller nuclear family was less well equipped to care for its disabled members and began to look to the state for assistance (Curtis, 1986). Institutions like mental hospitals were developed to meet this need. In such institutions the insane were to be sheltered from a hostile world, kept from harming themselves or others, and given help and treatment. Hospitals were built in secluded spots and surrounded by high walls and locked gates. Within the walls, all the patient's needs were to be met. But the purpose of the hospital was not merely to protect patients from society and, if possible, to cure them; it was also to protect society from the patients. The old stereotype of the "raving lunatic" persisted, and gradually security came to be considered more important than therapy.

For the sake of economy and efficiency, the present system of enormous hospitals developed, each housing several thousand patients and staffed largely by aides whose main job is to keep things quiet on as low a budget as a state legislature can decently supply. Staffing these hospitals is a perennial problem. Salaries are usually low; working conditions are often unattractive or discouraging; and professionally trained personnel are almost irresistibly tempted by private hospitals, clinics, or private practice, where the rewards, both monetary and in terms of visible therapeutic achievement, are much greater. Consequently, public institutions must depend heavily on partially trained personnel, particularly attendants or nursing aides. These attendants, though not fully qualified, have the most contact with the patients, and typically they control most aspects of the patients' daily life, including access to doctors.

There is evidence that hospitalization may not always be the best solution to mental illness, even in good hospitals. Long-term studies have shown that patients who do not improve enough to be discharged within a short period are likely to remain hospitalized for a very long time, if not indefinitely. This effect is due in part to the inadequacies of the hospital. It also seems to be a consequence of hospitalization itself, a position taken by Erving Goffman (1961). Goffman developed the concept of the **total institution,** which may be defined as "a place of residence and work where a large number of like-situated individuals, cut off from the wider society for an appreciable period of time, together lead an enclosed, formally administered round of life" (p. xiii).

Goffman (1961) regarded the mental hospital as a prime example of a total institution. His field research and work in mental hospitals convinced him that because inmates are constantly subject to its control, the hospital profoundly shapes their sense of self. In general, mental hospitals downgrade patients' desire for self-esteem and emphasize their failures and inadequacies. Uniform clothing and furniture, a regimented routine, and the custodial atmosphere of the hospital make patients docile and unassertive. Since the psychiatric approach requires cooperation, staff members often encourage patients to view themselves as sick and in need of help. Any act of self-assertion or rebellion will probably be interpreted as further evidence of illness, and patients will be expected to take that view of themselves. Release from the hospital is often contingent on the patient's accepting, or appearing to accept, the official interpretation of his or her hospital and prehospital life. Goffman concluded that in most cases there is a high probability that hospitalization will do more harm than good.

In recent years Goffman's (1961) research has received heavy criticism. In particular, he has been criticized for not having conducted enough empirical research on enough hospitals to determine whether all mental hospitals could be called total institutions. Moreover, although Goffman's view has had a great influence on the way people think about mental hospitals (and jails), he is accused of having himself been influenced by the literary power of his ideas and images rather than by the force of empirical data (McEwen, 1988; Scull, 1988).

The classic study by Rosenhan (1973) mentioned earlier illustrates the conditions prevailing in many mental hospitals. This research project involved eight normal people, or pseudopatients, who were admitted to a mental hospital and diagnosed as schizophrenics. Their only symptom was a fabricated one: They said that they had heard voices on one occasion. Although the pseudopatients spent some time in the institution and were recognized as normal by their fellow inmates, the staff continued to think of them as schizophrenic. Some were released with the diagnosis of "schizophrenia in remission," and none was ever thought to be cured. In a follow-up study, a hospital that had heard of these findings was informed that over a period of three months some pseudopatients would attempt to gain admission to the hospital, and staff members were asked to judge which applicants were faking illness. Over the three-month period at least 41 patients were judged to be pseudopatients. In fact, none of those patients was faking.

The results of this study were widely cited as supporting the labeling theory, in that the diagnosis of illness—or health—was applied regardless of the actual condition of the patient. But here we are interested in what the pseudopatients observed while in the hospital. As much as possible, staff members were separated from patients by a glass enclosure; psychiatrists, in particular, almost never appeared on the wards. When pseudopatients approached staff members with questions, the most common response was to ignore the questions or mumble something—avoiding eye contact with the patient—and quickly move on. Patients were sometimes punished excessively for misbehavior, and in one case a patient was beaten. In sum, the atmosphere was one of powerlessness and depersonalization.

Community Psychology. The increased use of chemotherapy in the treatment of mental disorders caused a revolution in mental-health care. It began in the hospitals in the 1950s. As a result of the introduction of psychotropic drugs,

> thousands of patients who had been assaultive became docile. Many who had spent their days screaming subsided into talking to themselves. The decor of the wards could be improved: Chairs replaced wooden benches, curtains were hung on the windows. Razors and matches, once properly regarded as lethal, were given to patients who now were capable of shaving themselves and lighting their own cigarettes without injuring themselves or others or burning the hospital down. (Sheehan, 1982, p. 10)

But the revolution went far beyond hospital care. New "wonder drugs" like Thorazine made it possible to release hundreds of thousands of hospitalized patients (Sperry, 1995), who were supposed to receive outpatient treatment in their own communities.

Outpatient treatment for mental disorders is far from new, but until the 1960s it was confined largely to less severe disorders and to the upper and middle classes. With the passage of the Community Mental Health Centers Construction Act in 1963, the idea of easily accessible, locally controlled facilities that could care for people in their own communities—**community psychology**—was established.

The community psychology movement arose from two basic sources: (1) awareness that social conditions and institutions must be taken into account in dealing with individual mental-health problems; and (2) the idea that psychologists or psychiatrists should be able to contribute to the understanding and solution of social problems. The guidelines laid down for the centers provided for a wide range of mental-health care in the community and for coordination with, and consultative assistance to, other community agencies. Other nations, particularly Belgium and France, had had great success in developing residential treatment facilities for mentally ill individuals who were able to live among the general population.

The Community Mental Health Centers Construction Act set up a sophisticated support system to aid newly released patients, many of whom need considerable help in relearning the skills of everyday life and social interaction. The cornerstone of this system is the **halfway house,** a small, privately run residential community, usually located in an urban area, in which ex-patients are helped to make the transition from the hospital to normal life. They may receive therapy from a psychiatrist; they may be trained for a job and helped to obtain or keep one; and they are able to practice fitting into a community in which behavior is not subject to hospital regulations.

Under optimal conditions, halfway houses are capable of providing high-quality care; however, a variety of obstacles have prevented them from meeting the needs of many discharged mental patients. Operating almost in a vacuum—with no working relationship with the state mental hospitals from which they receive patients—many halfway houses soon had far more patients than they had staff or facilities to handle. This problem was exacerbated as hospitals rushed to reduce their patient loads long before community support systems were in place. In addition, halfway houses and other community mental-health centers faced the enormous problem of lack of funds. The insurance coverage of mentally ill patients tended to favor hospital care, and the coverage for mental problems was inferior to that available for physical illnesses. As a result, halfway houses, nursing homes, and other community mental-health facilities found it difficult to meet the growing demand for services.

Cost Shifting and the Two-class Mental-health System.   For over a century the public mental-health system, including state and local services, has subsidized the private mental-health system through the technique of cost shifting (see Chapter 2).

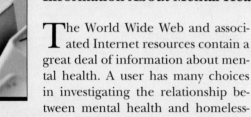

SOCIAL PROBLEMS ONLINE

Information About Mental Health and Homelessness

The World Wide Web and associated Internet resources contain a great deal of information about mental health. A user has many choices in investigating the relationship between mental health and homelessness. A good first site to visit is the National Institute of Mental Health's home page at **http://www.nih.nimh .gov.** This site contains links to NIMH publications on conditions that affect many homeless people, such as schizophrenia and alcoholism. The National Alliance for the Mentally Ill, which advocates medical treatment of mental illness, has a home page at **http://www .nami.org** that features links to publications and book reviews, many of which explore the interconnections between mental health and homelessness. It also presents updates on pending legislation, grassroots advocacy, and recent medical research.

A good website with a full range of links to resources on psychiatry, including discussion groups that touch on social problems such as homelessness, is Cyber-Psych at **http://www.webweaver.net/psych.**

Most of the web resources that are directly concerned with homelessness address the connections between poverty and lack of shelter, but several offer information on mental illness as well. The National Coalition for the Homeless has an interesting home page at **http://nch.ari.net/;** it emphasizes advocacy by the homeless and formerly homeless to "create the systemic and attitudinal changes necessary to end homelessness." It provides facts about homelessness and attempts to dispel some of the myths about mental illness and homelessness.

From Australia comes an invaluable resource for those who work with the homeless. The Homeless Handbook can be accessed at **http://www.infoxchange .net.au/hhb.** Containing chapters on alcohol and drugs, psychiatry, and first aid, this online book has practical information on symptoms and treatment for many of the medical problems associated with homelessness. For example, the chapter on psychiatry addresses schizophrenia, mania, acute and chronic psychosis, suicide, and psychiatric drugs. The web page also contains a good search tool for looking up topics quickly.

Since it provides mental-health services to people who cannot pay for them, including the uninsured, the public system has always tended to "absorb the private system's bad risks, difficult patients, and high-cost cases. Because the public system historically has been underfunded and has provided charity care, it has been perceived as inferior to the private care system" (Goldman, Frank, & McGuire, 1994, p. 74). And since severe mental illnesses like schizophrenia often reduce their victims to poverty, the public system has always been further burdened with the stigma of treating these individuals.

The resulting two-class system of care has persisted despite the change from a system dominated by large state mental hospitals to one of community mental-health care. The failure of community mental health is ironic since never before in the history of mental illness has it been possible to do so much to alleviate the suffering of the mentally ill through drug therapy and social services (National Advisory Mental Health Council, 1993). At present, however, the number of untreated indigent mentally ill people, many of whom are also chemically addicted, remains extremely large and is a significant social problem in many parts of the nation. To understand more about the origins of this problem, we turn to a discussion of released mental patients and the problem of homelessness.

Deinstitutionalization and Homelessness

We noted in the preceding section that beginning in the mid-1950s large numbers of mental patients were deinstitutionalized, or released from mental hospitals. The prominent medical sociologist David Mechanic (1990) notes that in the United States, "We have emptied out mental institutions, reducing the number of public mental hospital beds from a peak of 559,000 in 1955 to 110,000 today, but have not developed effective systems of community care" (p. 9). As Figure 3–3 shows, deinstitutionalization reversed a trend that had extended throughout the early twentieth century, in which the population of state mental hospitals increased fourfold. During that time mental hospitals were subjected to intense criticism, but the solutions proposed involved increasing the funding of hospitals, not the wholesale release of their inmates.

The trend toward deinstitutionalization is generally attributed to the introduction of **psychotropic drugs,** which greatly reduce the disruptive behavior of patients and make it possible to treat them outside of the hospital. However, some experts on mental-health care believe that other factors besides the drug revolution played a role

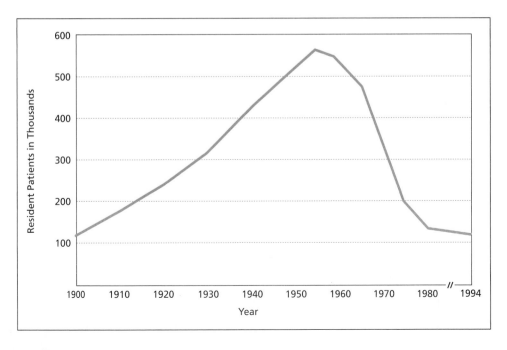

Figure 3–3 The Impact of Deinstitutionalization

Source: From "The Homelessness Problem" by E. I. Bassuk; © 1984 by Scientific American, Inc.; all rights reserved; also *Statistical Abstract,* 1999.

in deinstitutionalization. One was the expansion of federal health and welfare programs, which resulted in "the emergence of a new philosophy regarding what was possible and desirable in the provision of mental health care for the seriously mentally ill" (Gronfein, 1985, p. 450). In other words, although the advent of psychotropic drugs certainly played an important role in deinstitutionalization, they were not the cause of large-scale discharges. It would be more accurate to say that the use of psychotropic drugs reinforced a trend that began at about the same time in response to a combination of factors, including not only expanded federal welfare programs but also the fiscal crises that were developing in many states, as well as growing demands for protection of the rights of the mentally ill (Wilton & Wolch, 1996).

Throughout the 1960s and 1970s it was hoped that reductions in the hospital population would be accompanied by equivalent reductions in the incidence of mental disorders. This hope proved vain. Far from decreasing, the incidence of mental disorders increased. At the same time, the funding of community mental-health care was cut back. Of the 2,000 community mental-health centers planned in 1963, fewer than 1,000 have been established. As a result, hospital emergency rooms are often crowded with psychiatric patients. In addition, large numbers of former patients are homeless (Senate Committee on Finance, 1994).

The presence of deinstitutionalized mental patients among the homeless is due partly to their tendency to congregate in central-city neighborhoods, which are unable to provide the services they need. It has also been caused, in part, by the passage of laws designed to protect the rights of the mentally ill. Because only patients who are demonstrably dangerous may be involuntarily committed to mental hospitals, most mentally ill patients receive only brief, episodic care (Bassuk, 1984). Chronically disturbed people who are not dangerous to themselves or others are released into the community. Some find housing in single-room occupancy (SRO) hotels or cheap rooming houses, but these forms of housing are far less available today than they were in the 1950s and 1960s because landlords have either abandoned them or converted them into condominiums. As a result, mentally ill people often end up on the streets (Jencks, 1995).

The presence of mentally ill individuals among the homeless is highly visible and has contributed to the widespread impression that a large proportion of homeless people have mental disorders. It has been estimated that between 30 percent and 60 percent of the homeless are seriously mentally ill. Social-scientific research has found, however, that the majority of the homeless are individuals who have been caught in a cycle of low-paying, dead-end jobs that fail to provide the means to get off the streets (Snow, 1993). In one study, 164 homeless people in Austin, Texas, were tracked over a 20-month period. Approximately 10 percent were found to have psychiatric problems of varying degrees of severity. Even among this group, more than 50 percent registered for job referrals at the Texas Employment Commission at least once. The researchers concluded that the erroneous notion that the homeless are predominantly mentally ill is explained by four interconnected factors: undue emphasis on the causal role of deinstitutionalization, the medicalization of homelessness (i.e., viewing it as an illness instead of a social condition), the high visibility of the homeless mentally ill, and the difficulty of assessing the mental status of the homeless (Bassuk, Browne, & Bruckner, 1996; Jencks, 1994).

The fourth factor was emphasized by a New York State judge in a case involving a homeless woman who had been involuntarily hospitalized under a program to remove seriously disturbed people from New York City streets. The judge ordered the woman released on the ground that the city had failed to prove that she was mentally ill. (The ruling was subsequently reversed by a court of appeals.) "The issue for most homeless people," he said, "is not whether they are mentally ill, but housing" (quoted in Barbanel, 1987). The crisis in housing for low-income individuals and families will be discussed further in Chapters 8, 12, and 15.

Even though the proportion of mentally ill individuals among the homeless may have been exaggerated, there is no doubt that a frequent outcome of untreated mental

CURRENT CONTROVERSIES

Caring For the Homeless Mentally Ill

Although social scientists who conduct research on homelessness generally agree that only about 30 percent of the homeless are mentally ill, this segment of the homeless population presents special problems for policymakers. With society generally reluctant to build low-cost housing, homelessness is likely to remain a severe problem for the foreseeable future. But even if there were a crash program to build more adequate housing for homeless people, some critics argue that the mentally ill homeless would not avail themselves of it. Many think they would continue to wander the streets and sleep in railway stations, bus terminals, and alleys even if better shelters or housing were available.

In the existing shelters it is often those with histories of mental illness or alcohol and drug addiction—those who are hallucinating or high or who otherwise act in a somewhat bizarre fashion—who either discourage others from using the shelters or are themselves most frequently victimized. Most recommendations in this area of social policy, therefore, insist on the need to provide special shelters and housing units for the homeless mentally ill. Ideally these would be places where there could also be a concentration of health services, occupational therapy programs, and supported workshops (where people can work under conditions that tolerate their differences and support their individual needs). Where these types of community-based and comprehensive programs have been instituted, they have tended to be very successful. One of the major obsta-

cles to their growth, however, is the resistance of communities and neighborhoods to having such programs in their midst. Known as the NIMBY ("Not in My Back Yard") phenomenon, this is a serious obstacle to many types of social programs designed to address severe problems, but shelters and programs for the homeless mentally ill are especially vulnerable to such resistance.

The NIMBY attitude frequently delays the implementation of programs to address social problems such as homelessness among the mentally ill. People who claim that they want to see such problems dealt with but do not want to make any sacrifices themselves usually need to be confronted by neighbors who believe that the demands being placed on them are fair. On one hand, shelters and low-income housing for special populations are often proposed for poor or moderate-income neighborhoods, and even sympathetic residents come to feel that too much is asked of them while not enough is asked of more affluent residents elsewhere in the community or city. In more affluent communities, on the other hand, people tend to feel that they have more to lose in terms of property values and status, and they justify their resistance on these grounds. It takes long hours of persuasion, carefully designed programs, firm leadership that is committed to action, and adequate funding to overcome NIMBY attitudes. In the meantime the combination of local resistance and inadequate funding impedes progress toward providing housing and supportive programs for the homeless mentally ill.

disorder is rejection and homelessness. Homelessness usually is the final stage in a long series of crises and missed opportunities, the end result of a gradual process of disengagement from supportive relationships and institutions. The situation is especially severe for the mentally ill. They are isolated. Family members and friends have become tired and discouraged or are unable to help. Social workers are overburdened and cannot give them the attention they need, and the mentally ill themselves cannot communicate their needs adequately. In addition, the mentally ill encounter hostility from other residents of the urban communities in which they try to exist (Dickey et al., 1997).

As a result of experiences like these, the homeless, especially those who are mentally disturbed, tend to be extremely afraid of strangers. This is one explanation for the fact that they often reject offers of shelter and efforts to help them. The fear experienced by some homeless people is so great that it can be overcome only with effort and patience. However, much of the assistance offered to these individuals is perfunctory and uncaring, serving only to further isolate them from society. (See the Current Controversies feature above.)

It should be pointed out that mental illness can be a consequence of homelessness as well as a factor that leads to social isolation (Senate Committee on Finance, 1994). People who lose their homes suffer severe stress. They experience hunger, lack of sleep, and physical illnesses ranging from asthma to tuberculosis. In addition, they are "disorganized, depressed, disordered . . . immobilized by pain and traumatized by fear" (Kozol, 1988). To the uninformed observer, such individuals resemble the former mental patients who have also ended up on the streets, and their disordered appearance helps perpetuate the belief that all homeless people are crazy.

SOCIAL POLICY

Despite repeated urging from the Clinton administration over the past few years, at this writing Congress has not passed legislation to establish full parity between physical- and mental-health coverage. A 1996 federal parity law bars health plans from capping lifetime or annual benefits for mental-health treatment at a lower dollar figure than benefits for medical-surgical care. The law does, however, allow insurance plans to impose higher copayments and deductibles on mental-health coverage than on medical-surgical coverage. This legislation also permits health insurance plans to impose limits on inpatient and outpatient visits for mental-health problems that are not imposed on visits for physical illnesses (Aston,1999). In 1999 the Clinton administration attempted to jump-start legislation on this issue by granting mental-health insurance parity to 9 million employees of the federal government, as well as to employees who receive federal funding as part of their salaries.

The goal of eliminating the discrimination against mental illness that is inherent in existing health insurance plans—which helps produce the two-class system of mental-health care—is highly desirable, but insurance company executives fear that it could increase the costs of insurance paid by employers. Large corporations typically impose a $50,000 lifetime limit on mental-health care, whereas the limit for physical-health care may range from $750,000 to $1 million. Thus, health insurance experts fear that an unintended consequence of the legislation would be to actually reduce the number of people covered by any form of mental-health insurance (Pear, 1996a).

Mental-health advocacy groups in the United States cite a 1998 report to Congress by the National Advisory Mental Health Council that estimates that full parity would increase total health-care costs by less than 1 percent for managed-care plans and 4 or 5 percent for fee-for-service and preferred-provider plans. Insurance companies and their supporters in Congress remain unconvinced and are unwilling to assume the risks of higher Medicare payments that parity might entail (Aston, 1999).

Without adequate coverage for mental-health care, people who suffer from severe mental illnesses are often forced into poverty. Once on the streets they may be treated in public institutions, but in an era of shrinking budgets this, too, becomes problematic. State and municipal governments are often unwilling or unable to assume the burden of caring for the mentally ill. Some provide shelters for the homeless, but these cannot hope to replace the mental hospital or the halfway house. Shelters offer minimal medical, psychological, and social services. Generally understaffed, they are open only at night and cannot provide the supervision and support needed by disturbed individuals.

Some *re*institutionalization has occurred as a result of the public outcry over the plight of the homeless mentally ill. This is especially true of patients under constant medication, who need careful monitoring because their tolerance of and need for psychotropic drugs are constantly changing. If they receive adequate treatment outside, as well as inside, the hospital, this revolving-door system is reasonably effective. However, such situations are rare.

An important problem in caring for the mentally ill is the lack of coordination of treatment. Because of the division of mental-health care between insight therapists and medical practitioners, there is a widespread tendency to see psychotherapy and medical treatment as mutually exclusive. Yet a patient who is on medication needs to have enough insight to be able to take the medicine in the prescribed dosage at the correct intervals. It follows that there must be a high level of coordination of treatment between social workers and others in the patient's social world, on one hand, and the clinical personnel who prescribe medication and decide whether patients should be hospitalized, on the other.

Problems of treatment and supervision of nonhospitalized patients stem in part from certain characteristics of the organization of mental-health institutions. According to one expert (Meyer, 1985), the mental-health-care system lacks integration or structure. The various types of organizations that provide mental-health services differ greatly in the types of cases they handle, the way they are staffed and funded, the way they relate to other mental-health organizations, and many other respects. In addition, they are constantly changing, and they are continually under attack for failures both real and imagined. There is a need for what Meyer terms "institutional coordination" such as that which exists in education. Educational institutions also differ greatly, but they are held together by shared definitions of the nature of education, the requirements for teaching, the meaning of degrees and credit, and so on. Similar agreements are needed in the field of mental-health care—for example, agreements on the definition of treatable problems, appropriate professionals, funding responsibilities, and the like.

In the absence of a comprehensive approach to health care, including mental-health care, it is likely that there will be further deterioration in the treatment conditions for people with severe mental illnesses. This population currently depends heavily on the social safety net of public mental-health services (Goldman, Frank, & McGuire, 1994). However, decreasing insurance coverage will probably force more severely ill patients into an already heavily burdened public system. People with moderate mental illnesses like chronic depression, who need extensive rehabilitation or long-term care services, are even less likely to receive the care they need because of inadequacies in coverage and the fact that (since they usually are not indigent) they are ineligible for care in public institutions.

As the number of untreated and poorly treated mental patients increases, many experts anticipate that their problems will become so visible on the streets and in residential neighborhoods that an alarmed public will again realize the need for a balanced public and private approach to comprehensive mental-health-care coverage. This may be an overly hopeful scenario, however. The costs of such an approach would be extremely high and would require a far more generous spirit than now exists among American voters.

One promising approach to the problems of the severely mentally ill is being promoted by the national Alliance for the Mentally Ill. This program began in Wisconsin in the early 1970s and has been developed in a number of mental-health centers since then. It calls for a program of assertive community treatment (PACT) for people with severe and persistent mental illnesses like schizophrenia, bipolar disorder, and other psychoses. PACT uses a multidisciplinary team that provides comprehensive, client-centered care on a round-the-clock basis. Seventy-five percent of this care is provided in community settings, including homes, workplaces, restaurants, laundromats, and grocery stores. Models of assertive community-based care are also being developed in Great Britain and Australia. They are achieving considerable success because mental-health workers are reaching out to the mentally ill where they are and when they are in need, rather than waiting for them to appear in clinics or to be incarcerated.

Beyond Left & Right

Whose responsibility are the mentally ill? This question does not give rise to as many moral or ideological debates as some other social problems, but there are controversies nonetheless. In this chapter, for example, we have described the failure of the community mental-health-care movement. There was no ideological debate over the need to end the warehousing of mentally ill people in isolated state hospitals, especially when new drug therapies made it possible for them to live more normal lives. But where were they to live? In whose communities? Do we all share the responsibility for their care, or must the communities where the mentally ill are most numerous bear a greater share of the burden?

On the right, there is a tendency to insist on the responsibility of families to care for their mentally ill members. On the left, one hears demands for public funding of mental-health clinics. What are your views on the issue? Does the sociological analysis presented in this chapter help you go beyond the opposing viewpoints?

Family responsibility and adequate funding of public programs need not be incompatible policies. At some point the laws, which are based on social custom, insist that an adult person is no longer the sole responsibility of his or her family. However, lack of adequate funding for public mental-health programs remains a serious obstacle to providing care for such individuals. Clearly, there is a role for community and society that almost all of us can agree needs to be strengthened.

SUMMARY

- The mental disorders that cause severe social problems are the most extreme forms of mental illness, in which individuals become violent and irrational. Less threatening, but more widespread as a social problem, are severely ill individuals who are unable to care for themselves without specialized attention.

- There are three different explanations of mental illness: (a) the medical model, which simply asserts that mental illness is a disease with physiological causes; (b) the deviance approach, which asserts that mental illness results from how people considered mentally ill are treated; and (c) the argument that mental illness is not a disease but a way of defining certain people as being in need of isolation and "treatment."

- The American Psychiatric Association's *Diagnostic and Statistical Manual of Mental Disorders* has gone a long way toward standardizing the diagnosis of mental illness. However, many researchers believe that psychiatric diagnoses are arbitrary and amount to labels, describing behavior that is contrary to accepted social and psychological norms.

- Poverty is associated with high exposure to crime and violence, which creates stresses that can precipitate mental illness. In addition, lower-class social status is associated with a greater likelihood of being selected or labeled as mentally ill.

- According to the social-selection, or drift, hypothesis, low-class status is not a cause but a consequence of mental disorder. Mentally disordered people tend to be found in the lower classes because their illness has prevented them from functioning at a higher-class level.

- Research on the correlation between mental illness and such factors as urban life and crowding in the home has not produced conclusive results. Race also does not appear to be a significant variable by itself, but there are differences in the types of mental illnesses suffered by men and women.

- The two major approaches to the treatment of mental disorders are psychotherapy and medical treatment. The major forms of psychotherapy are psychoanalysis, client-centered therapy, and therapy and support groups. Medical treatments such as chemotherapy and shock treatment are applied to the most severe mental illnesses.

- Increasingly, psychiatrists are competing for patients with therapists who rely on insight methods. The services of the latter cost less and therefore are favored by insurance companies and many patients.

- Medical treatments often require hospitalization. Until the mid-twentieth century, this usually meant care in mental hospitals or asylums. However, long-term studies have shown that patients who do not improve enough to be discharged within a short period are likely to remain in the hospital indefinitely.

- The community psychology movement arose in the 1950s, partly as a result of the increased use of chemotherapy in the treatment of mental disorders.

Many patients were released from mental hospitals to be cared for in community mental-health centers or halfway houses. The large-scale deinstitutionalization of mental patients led to a variety of problems, including the tendency of such patients to end up among the homeless.

■ Legislative efforts are under way to reduce some of the disparities in insurance coverage between mental and physical illness. Treatment of patients both within and outside mental-health institutions is difficult to achieve, however, because of the lack of coordination of medical and nonmedical treatment.

KEY TERMS

mental disorder, p. 61
mental illness, p. 61
deinstitutionalization, p. 62

residual deviance, p. 67
total institution, p. 78
community psychology, p. 79

halfway house, p. 80
psychotropic drugs, p. 81

INTERNET EXERCISE

The web destinations for Chapter 3 are related to different aspects of mental illness. To begin your explorations, go to the Prentice Hall Companion Website: **http://pren.hall.com/kornblum.** Then choose **Chapter 3** (Mental Illness). Next, select **destinations** from the menu on the left side of the screen. There are a variety of sites to investigate. We suggest that you begin with **National Health Care for Homeless Council.** The *Current Controversies* feature in this chapter deals with caring for the homeless mentally ill. Even though only about 30 percent of the homeless are mentally ill, this segment of the homeless population presents special problems for policymakers. After accessing the NHCHC site, click on "Success Stories." Here you will find actual accounts of mentally ill

homeless women and men who have benefitted from the kind of work the NHCHC is doing. After you have explored the NHCHC site, answer the following questions:

■ Do you think that *deinstitutionalization* is responsible for the problem of the homeless mentally ill? Do you think these people belong in institutions? Why or why not?

■ The text discusses the relationship between inequality and mental illness. What are your reactions to the plight of people who suffer from mental illness *and* who are homeless? What recommendations would you make for revised social policy designed to deal with this problem?

4 Sex-related Social Problems

SEX-RELATED SOCIAL PROBLEMS

- The average age of male heterosexual sex offenders is under 40.

- Over 50 percent of prostitutes were raped as children.

- About 40 percent of street prostitutes have been exposed to AIDS.

- The National Opinion Research Corporation reports that 28 percent of its respondents admit that they have seen an X-rated movie in the last year.

Sex as a Social Problem
Tolerated Sex Variance
Asocial Sex Variance
Structured Sex Variance

Homosexuality
Social-scientific Perspectives on Homosexuality
Who Becomes a Homosexual?
Lesbianism
The Homosexual Subculture

Prostitution
Social-scientific Perspectives on Prostitution
Norms of Prostitution
Why Do People Become Prostitutes?
The Prostitute Subculture
The Impact of AIDS

Pornography
Social-scientific Perspectives on Pornography
Pornography and Censorship
Research on Pornography
Pornography and Public Opinion

Social Policy
Homosexuality
Prostitution
Pornography

Sex and sexuality are extremely controversial issues in American culture. The conflict over whether homosexuals should be allowed to marry or to serve in the military or whether pornography should be banned from the Internet, as well as the scandal surrounding the news that a prominent presidential adviser had consorted with a prostitute to whom he revealed inside political gossip, indicates the extent to which sexual behavior generates social conflict. But for much of the past century—until about 30 or 40 years ago—Americans' attitudes toward sexual behavior seemed fairly traditional and easy to define: Normal sex was that which led to the bearing of children in a socially legitimate family. Premarital intercourse might come within the narrowly defined range of acceptable behaviors, but only if it led to marriage fairly quickly. All other sexual acts, such as any act between consenting adults of the same sex, were condemned and prohibited. The possibility of allowing for variations in sexual tastes, or even the idea that such differences might be legitimate reflections of human individuality, was ignored. While many people pursued sexual adventures and found pleasure in sexual behaviors that differed from the generally accepted norms, those differences were not recognized as legitimate. The behaviors were condemned, and many people were persecuted for engaging in them.

Today attitudes toward sex are much more ambivalent and inconsistent, although sexual matters are discussed more openly. On one hand, a variety of sexual behaviors are portrayed in the media and elsewhere. On the other hand, many people are strongly opposed to greater sexual freedom, considering it abnormal or even degenerate. Many citizens oppose even basic sex education in schools. And in most states laws continue to prohibit not only nonheterosexual or nonmarital sexual acts but even some sex acts between husband and wife.

Although attitudes toward sex may be ambivalent, there can be no doubt that the past 50 years have seen immense changes in sexual behavior in the United States. To take just one example, 68 percent of women born between 1933 and 1942 report that they had no experience with sexual intercourse before age 18, whereas only 42 percent of women born between 1963 and 1974 make that claim (Laumann et al., 1994).

Despite these developments, many traditional attitudes are still present—not only in our laws but also in our behavior. For example, although more Americans are permissive about premarital, oral, and anal sex, they still prefer that such practices occur within the context of close and affectional relationships (Laumann et al., 1994; Schur, 1988). Couples who live together in what amount to trial marriages have "firm emotional ties, conventional standards regarding fidelity, and a definite social identity as a couple" (Hunt, 1974, p. 153). The role of traditional values has become especially pronounced in recent years as a result of the AIDS epidemic. Psychiatrists, public health workers, and law enforcement officials agree that there has been a significant decrease in casual or promiscuous sexual activity. Many gay men are limiting their sexual encounters, and straight men and women are avoiding one-night stands. Women typically carry condoms for their dates to use when and if they have sex, and some dating services require their members to undergo regular HIV testing. Rates of teenage pregnancy have declined to historic lows.

The changes in sexual attitudes and behaviors that have occurred in recent decades are not in themselves a social problem. The problem is that the resulting diversity leads to a great deal of conflict over how society should address issues related to sexual behavior. Among those issues are how to guarantee the rights of people with nontraditional lifestyles and how to understand and respond to sexual behaviors that deviate from widely held norms, particularly homosexuality and prostitution. The need to cope with AIDS, the most severe sex-related social problem of modern times, is a crisis on a global scale.

The spread of AIDS and the increased prevalence of other sexually transmitted diseases (e.g., herpes and syphilis), as well as the continuing problem of adolescent pregnancy, point to another problem associated with sexuality: the absence of "sexual literacy." In 1990 the Kinsey Institute and the Roper Organization asked 1,974 randomly selected adult Americans a series of 18 questions designed to test their basic knowledge about sex and human reproduction. The majority of those questioned answered 10 or more of the questions incorrectly (Reinisch, 1990). (See Figure 4–1.) The sexual ignorance revealed by this survey is itself a problem because of its consequences. But as the questions in Figure 4–1 indicate, the main problem with sexual illiteracy is that it prevents the nation's citizens from engaging in healthy and responsible sexual behavior and leads to ignorance about even more difficult social and biological issues.

Sex education is one means of addressing sexual ignorance, but to be effective such education must be more explicit than some parents consider acceptable.

A survey by the Kinsey institute and the Roper Organization found gaps in Americans' knowledge about sex. These are 5 of the 18 questions. The answers appear below with the percentage of people who answered correctly.

1. Nowadays, what do you think is the age at which the average or typical American first has sexual intercourse?
   a. 11 or younger   b. 12   c. 13   d. 14   e. 15   f. 16   g. 17   h. 18   i. 19   j. 20
   k. 21 or older   l. Don't know.

2. Of every 10 married American men, how many would you estimate have had an extramarital affair—that is, have been sexually unfaithful to their wives?
   a. Fewer than 1 of 10   b. One   c. Two   d. Three   e. Four   f. Five   g. Six
   h. Seven   i. Eight   j. Nine   k. More than 9 of 10   l. Don't know.

3. Of every 10 American women, how many would you estimate have had anal (rectal) intercourse?
   a. Fewer than 1 of 10   b. One   c. Two   d. Three.   e. Four   f. Five   g. Six
   h. Seven   i. Eight   j. Nine   k. More than nine   l. I don't know.

4. More than one of four (25 percent) of American men have had a sexual experience with another male during their teen or adult years.
   True   False   Don't know

5. A woman or teenage girl can get pregnant during her menstrual flow (her "period").
   True   False   Don't know

Answers

1. f or g	Percentage correct:	24%
2. d or e	Percentage correct:	25%
3. d or e	Percentage correct:	21%
4. True	Percentage correct:	21%
5. True	Percentage correct:	51%

Figure 4–1   Selected Questions from the Kinsey-Roper Survey on Sexual Literacy
Source: Copyright © 1990 by the New York Times Company. Reprinted by permission.

Sex as a Social Problem

We saw in Chapter 1 that a social condition becomes a social problem when many people agree that it threatens the quality of their lives and their most cherished values and that something should be done about it. In the case of sexual behavior, the social condition at issue is the great difference between the stated norms of our society and people's actual behavior. Sexual behavior that was once condemned is now considered acceptable by most people. Not long ago, for example, oral intercourse was considered immoral; today the majority of young people have engaged in it. Until recently masturbation was considered sinful and unhealthy; today it is widely assumed that masturbation is not only normal but also beneficial to sexual development, although Catholics, Mormons, and other religious groups preach against it.

Nevertheless, there are still sex-related acts or conditions that many people have difficulty accepting; among these are homosexuality, prostitution, and pornography. In the past such behavior was labeled "deviant," but we now avoid this term whenever possible because it implies that there is a normal and therefore proper form of sexual expression, and also because it entails the same stigma as "degenerate," "perverted," or "sick." We prefer instead to refer to these acts or conditions as sex-related social problems because of the degree of conflict they engender. A useful classification of such problems is that of Gagnon and Simon (1967), who divide them into three categories. We will use our own names for these categories: tolerated sex variance, asocial sex variance, and structured sex variance.

Tolerated Sex Variance

Tolerated sex variance includes such acts as heterosexual oral-genital contact, masturbation, and premarital intercourse. These acts "are generally disapproved, but . . . either serve a socially useful purpose and/or occur so often among a population with such low social visibility that only a small number are ever actually sanctioned for engaging in [them]" (Gagnon & Simon, 1967, p. 8). Except for premarital intercourse among teenagers, which has resulted in high rates of teenage pregnancy, these acts arouse little special interest, and outside of certain religious organizations there is little pressure for policies to regulate this behavior. The Church of Latter Day Saints (Mormons), the most rapidly growing religious group in the United States, condemns masturbation, and conservatives support bans on heterosexual "sodomy" of all kinds. In 1986, in *Bowers* v. *Hardwick,* the Supreme Court upheld Georgia's antisodomy laws, which apply both to heterosexuals and to homosexuals. Nevertheless, it is likely that over time these behaviors will become socially acceptable and cease to be regarded as social problems.

Asocial Sex Variance

Asocial sex variance includes incest, child molestation and sexual abuse, rape, exhibitionism, and voyeurism. These acts are usually committed by a lone individual or at most a small number of people. Although there are social influences on the incidence of such acts, they must be understood primarily from a psychological or social-psychological viewpoint. People who engage in such behavior do not have a social structure that recruits, socializes, and provides social support for these acts. Major forms of asocial sex variance—incest, rape, and child molestation—elicit widespread and strong disapproval even among other lawbreakers.

Incest.   **Incest,** or sexual relations between individuals who are so closely related that they are forbidden to marry by law or custom, is almost universally prohibited. "The incest taboo is universal in human culture. . . . All cultures, including our own, regard violations of the taboo with horror and dread. Death has not been considered too extreme a punishment in many societies. In our laws, some states punish incest with up to twenty years' imprisonment" (Herman & Hirschman, 1988, p. 735).

Weinberg (1955) found that in cases of father-daughter incest (i.e., in most cases of incest), the family is likely to be characterized by paternal dominance, with the father intimidating and controlling the other family members. When incest occurs between siblings, the parents are not dominant and do not prevent the children from engaging in sex play. In cases of mother-son incest, the family is characterized by maternal dominance, with the father either absent or extremely subservient. In all cases, Weinberg found, incest causes confusion in family roles and creates rivalries within the family. It also generates conflict in the child or children involved and disturbs other family members, who may be only subliminally aware of what is happening. Even when they are aware of it, family members keep the behavior a secret. Indeed, according to one expert, "The essence of incest is secrecy. Anything that breaks the silence . . . makes it more possible for victims and others to speak out" (Dr. Judith L. Herman, quoted in Kleiman, 1987, pp. A1, B5).

Research findings suggest that the common belief that incest occurs more frequently among people of low socioeconomic status is incorrect. Hunt (1974) found that incestuous acts are more common at higher socioeconomic levels. A study by Diana E. H. Russell (1986) also found that incest is more frequent in high-income families than in low-income ones. Higher rates of incest are reported for lower socioeconomic groups because "the poor, the ignorant, and the incompetent come to official attention, while people of higher socioeconomic status are able either to keep their acts hidden or, if discovered, to keep the discovery from becoming part of the official record" (Hunt, 1974, p. 347).

Child Molestation and Coercive Adult Sex.   In most societies, including our own, child molestation is feared and deplored and results in humiliation and loss of status for the adult involved. More than 2 million cases of child abuse are reported in the United States each year, and many more are unreported. Of the reported cases, some 150,000 to 200,000 involve new cases of sexual abuse. A 1998 study published in the *Journal of the American Medical Association* found that sexual abuse directed at young boys is common but is not reported nearly as often as abuse of girls (Morrison et al., 1997). Contrary to popular belief, molestation by heterosexuals is far more common than molestation by homosexuals. Moreover, most child molesters do not fit the stereotype of the "dirty old man"; the average age of male heterosexual sexual offenders is under 40. Nor do child molesters fit the image of the lurking stranger; most young girls who are molested know the man.

Adults also experience a great deal of coercive sexual contact. This fact emerged clearly from the survey of American sexuality mentioned earlier (Laumann et al., 1994), which asked respondents whether their first experience with sexual intercourse was something the respondent wanted to happen at the time, something he or she did not want to happen but went along with, or something forced on the respondent. The results are presented in Table 4–1. Another important finding, not shown in the table, is that far more younger women reported that their first experiences with sexual intercourse were not wanted than did older women, who tended to wait until marriage or shortly before marriage.

Rape.   Forcible rape—coercive coitus with another person—is a violent crime. As such, it will be discussed more fully in Chapters 6 and 7. Our concern here is with some of the psychosocial factors involved.

Many studies have found that rapists are usually young and unmarried; some studies also suggest that a disproportionate number of convicted rapists are physically handicapped in some way. Ostensibly, then, sexual deprivation is a key factor in rape. Most analysts believe, however, that the desire for sexual gratification is at most a secondary motive. In this view, rape is an act of aggression or sadism engaged in by males to bolster a weak self-image and to feel powerful (Acierno, Resnick, & Kilpatrick, 1997).

In recent years increasing attention has been focused on rape by an acquaintance, or date rape. Also termed **paraphyllic rapism,** it has been proposed to the American Psychiatric Association as a diagnosis for men who can achieve sexual pleasure only in the context of rape and coercion. Women's rights groups oppose the use of the latter term because it might be used to exonerate men who have been formally charged with forcible rape (Easton et al., 1997). These groups have also sponsored publicity campaigns to make women more aware of the danger of being raped by men who are known to them (Parrot & Bechhofer, 1991).

Various theories attempt to explain the relationship between rape rates and the social climate. One, suggested by Merton's theory of anomie (see Chapter 6), is that when heterosexual contact is valued but access to it is restricted, the rape rate will be higher. According to this hypothesis, the more sexually permissive a

TABLE 4–1   First Intercourse Wanted, Not Wanted, or Forced (percentages)

First Intercourse	Men	Women
Wanted	92.1	71.3
Not wanted but not forced	7.6	24.5
Forced	0.3	4.2
N	1,337	1,689

Source: Edward Laumann et al., *The Social Organization of Sexuality, 1994.* Reprinted by permission of Edward Laumann.

society is, the lower its rape rate will be. Another theory, advanced by feminists, holds that rape is a result of the patriarchal structure of American society, in which heterosexual love is expressed through male dominance and female submission.

Peggy Reeves Sanday (1984) studied patterns of rape in 186 tribal societies and found that cultures marked by high levels of male dominance and high levels of interpersonal violence had a high incidence of rape. These cultural traits may also help explain the high incidence of rape in the United States. Edwin Schur (1988) suggests that the extent to which sex is made into a desirable commercial commodity and viewed as an abstract pleasure (rather than part of an intimate relationship) also helps explain the incidence of rape.

Exhibitionism and Voyeurism. Minor forms of asocial sex variance are **exhibitionism** (deliberate exposure of one's sex organs) and **voyeurism** (watching people undressing or performing a sexual act). Flashers and peeping Toms may be annoying, but perhaps because they are not usually very threatening, their behaviors have not received much analysis.

Structured Sex Variance

Behaviors that are classified as **structured sex variance** are associated with relatively well-defined roles and social institutions. Although they are engaged in by large numbers of people, these behaviors run counter to prevailing norms and legal statutes and therefore are often perceived as problems that threaten the social order. Such behaviors are also associated with the development of unique subcultures. Three examples of this type of sex variance that we will examine in some detail are homosexuality, prostitution, and pornography. Of course, these are not the only sexual behaviors that are regarded as social problems, but it can be argued that they are the most visible and controversial sex-related social problems in our society.

Homosexuality

The brutal murder of college student Matthew Shepard, who was kidnapped, beaten, and left to die on a fence along a Wyoming highway (shown in the chapter-opening photo), along with many other incidents of homophobic violence and harassment against gay people in the United States and elsewhere indicate why homosexuality is a social problem. Although millions of homosexuals find immense satisfaction and fulfilment in their lives, controversies raised by antigay groups, discrimination against homosexuals, battles over the rights of same-sex partners, and struggles by gay people to win acceptance of same-sex marriages often force them into painful confrontations with some "straight" people. In one sense, homosexuals share the difficulties of any minority group, but the conflicts centering on sexuality and gender in the United States often compound the problems, as we will see in this section (Fulton et al., 1999; Morrison et al., 1997).

Homosexuality is a sexual preference for members of one's own sex. Some people are exclusively homosexual; others may engage in homosexual behavior only under special circumstances, such as imprisonment; still others have both homosexual and heterosexual experiences. Both males and females may be homosexual; female homosexuals are usually referred to as **lesbians.** Much more research has been done on male homosexuality than on lesbianism.

It is difficult to determine the number of homosexuals in the United States (Painton, 1993). An often-cited estimate based on the original research of Alfred Kinsey (Kinsey, Pomeroy, & Martin, 1948), which included 17,000 interviews, places the proportion of homosexual or lesbian Americans at 10 percent. Kinsey found that 37 percent of the male population had had physical contact to the point of orgasm with other men at some time between adolescence and old age. The extent to which respondents had engaged in homosexual behavior varied, with 10 percent of the sample reporting that they had been more or less exclusively homosexual for at least three years.

The most recent surveys of sexual behavior in the United States and other Western societies have found lower percentages, varying between 1 percent and 4 percent, of men who indicated that they had had homosexual relations in the year prior to the survey (Alan Guttmacher Institute, cited in Barringer, 1993b; Laumann et al., 1994; Schmidt, 1997). Gay-rights activists and survey research experts agree that although the Kinsey figures may be high estimates, the fluctuations in recent survey data suggest that sensitive questions about sexual behavior are subject to rather high levels of error because respondents may not feel comfortable about answering truthfully (Schmidt, 1997).

In our society homosexuality has alternately been regarded either as a sin or as the effect of some physical or mental disturbance; until the rise of the gay-rights movement in recent decades it was considered too shameful and indecent to be spoken of openly. Although society has become more tolerant of open discussions of homosexuality today, many prejudices still prevail. Surveys consistently show increasing public tolerance of homosexuality, but almost half of all Americans believe that homosexuals should be barred from certain jobs for which they may be qualified, particularly jobs involving young people (NORC, 1999). Elsewhere in the world, a similar picture of increasing acceptance and persistent problems of homophobia also prevails. In Europe, there is growing acceptance of homosexuality and gay people are far less closeted about their sexual identity than they were a generation ago. But in the Islamic world, although homosexuality is not uncommon, it is severely persecuted; in fundamentalist nations like Iran, it can result in harsh and even deadly sanctions. In India, gay communities are emerging in major cities, and in parts of Africa homosexuality is becoming more accepted. Throughout much of Africa, however, it remains a taboo subject and leads to clandestine, closeted behavior (Widmer, Treas, & Newcomb, 1998).

Lesbian and gay couples are demanding to be recognized as domestic partners in order to qualify for the employment benefits that other couples enjoy. They also want to be open about their unions and to have them accepted by mainstream society.

Social-scientific Perspectives on Homosexuality

In the early decades of the twentieth century, social scientists generally viewed homosexuality as a form of social pathology brought on by the disorganization of families and communities that were experiencing the effects of rapid urbanization and industrialization. Sociologists tended to regard homosexuality, along with prostitution, as an individual response to the disorganization of family life. Psychologists attempted to treat it as an illness with physiological causes.

Sigmund Freud and other founders of the psychoanalytic movement realized that many homosexuals are well-adjusted, productive adults. Freud also believed that homosexuality is a stage that all people pass through on the way to developing heterosexual desires. Homosexuals, in his view, have been "arrested" and have failed to develop further. The Freudian perspective on homosexuality did not become a dominant viewpoint, however. The majority of American social scientists continued to view homosexuality as an illness that should be cured through some kind of therapy.

Kinsey's study of the sexual behavior of American males (Kinsey et al., 1948) marked a turning point in the understanding of homosexuality from both a scientific and a popular point of view. This work was extraordinary because it was based on interviews with thousands of ordinary Americans rather than with people who had requested psychiatric treatment. It revealed a wide gap between sexual norms and actual behavior and questioned the idea that there is a clear dichotomy between heterosexual and same-sex attraction. Kinsey and subsequent sex researchers began to believe that sexual feelings toward same-sex friends are not abnormal or deviant and that homophobia is often a response to the severe conflict that people feel, but deny feeling, about this attraction and society's condemnation of it.

Despite the torrent of criticism that greeted Kinsey's studies when they first appeared, other social scientists soon published findings that supported his conclusion that homosexuals cannot be distinguished from nonhomosexuals in psychological terms. The most famous of these studies were conducted by psychologist Evelyn Hooker during the 1950s. Hooker showed that it is not possible to distinguish homosexuals from nonhomosexuals with any of the standard projective tests available in clinical psychology. She went on to show that alleged homosexual obsessions (with anonymous sex, for example), where they exist, are caused not by homosexuality itself but by stigmatization and rejection. If homosexuals are a deviant group in society, she reasoned, they are so not because of any inherent feature of homosexuality but because of their rejection by the larger society (Hooker, 1966).

Thomas Szasz (1994)—who, as we have seen, was one of the founders of labeling theory—carried this perspective a step further. He argued that psychiatrists and others who labeled homosexuality an illness were merely taking the place of the church in identifying homosexuals and punishing them for their deviant sexual behavior. The gay-rights movement of the 1960s and 1970s drew on this perspective with great effectiveness.

Most recent social-scientific research on homosexuality has focused on its collective features, such as the emergence of the gay-rights movement and its consequences (Bawer, 1994; Bell & Valentine, 1995). The famous 1969 police raid on Stonewall, a gay bar in Greenwich Village, marked the beginning of a new era of public organization of homosexual activities and concern about the civil liberties of gay men and lesbians. Efforts to alter public perceptions of homosexuality have met with some success in recent decades. While the majority of Americans continue to believe that homosexuality is "wrong" (NORC, 1999), they are nonetheless increasingly tolerant of homosexual behavior. For example, polls taken during government debates over acceptance of homosexuals in the military show the nation to be rather evenly split on the issue. Moreover, slightly over 50 percent of Americans believe that homosexuality is a feature of one's identity that cannot be changed, whereas about 30 percent feel that it is a voluntary "lifestyle choice" (with the remainder "not sure"). Those who believe that homosexuality is not a choice or mere preference but a deep-seated sexual orientation tend to be far more tolerant of the civil rights of homosexuals than do those who believe that it is a voluntary choice (Schmalz, 1993). Recent research among college students shows, however, that tolerant attitudes may not change more subtle forms of discrimination against gay men who do not conform to stereotypical male heterosexual behaviors (Aberson, Swan, & Emerson, 1999).

Although there is increasing tolerance, there is still significant division in the general population about the civil rights of homosexuals. This division is mirrored to some degree in gay and lesbian communities, where there is much debate about how forcefully to push for such changes as the legalization of gay marriage or the fairness of *outing*, that is, public identification of closet homosexuals who are politically or socially influential but have not acknowledged their gay identity.

New trends in social-scientific research do not necessarily replace older research. Thus, social scientists who study behavior that deviates from major social norms continue to investigate such questions as who becomes homosexual and what factors are associated with higher rates of homosexuality in some groups. Researchers who apply labeling theory to the study of sexual behavior continue to demonstrate the effects of stigmatization on homosexuals. And social scientists who study the institutions and conflicts that shape our perceptions of social problems tend to focus on the ongoing conflicts that occur over such issues as acceptance of homosexuality in the military and other social institutions.

Who Becomes a Homosexual?

To date there is no convincing evidence that homosexuality is biologically determined. Biologists tend to agree that evidence from studies of twins reared apart and from other research seems to indicate that there is a strong genetic component in sexuality, but this does not mean that there are direct links between specific sexual behaviors like homosexuality and genetic transmission (Pillard & Bailey, 1998). A large proportion of homosexuals find the origins of their sexual preference in their earliest experiences as children, and hence they tend to accept the hypothesis that homosexuality has a strong genetic component. Opponents of homosexuality, especially among conservative Christian groups, tend to reject biological explanations because they view homosexuality as a "lifestyle preference" that is voluntary and could be changed through therapy or religious conversion (Fulton, Gorsuch, & Maynard, 1999; Jones, 1999).

Sociologists, psychiatrists, and anthropologists argue that the social environment in which a person grows up plays as great a role in producing homosexuality as any biological factor. They emphasize that human sexual behavior is learned behavior. Human beings may or may not have a basic need for sex, but its expression is shaped by experience. However, psychiatrists and psychologists have not succeeded in identifying any early experiences that result in homosexuality. Certain situations do seem to be frequent in the case histories of homosexuals: The family often includes a dominant or seductive mother and a weak, detached, or overly critical father—factors that discourage the male child from identifying with male role models. Yet it is not clear why homosexuality develops only in some children who are reared under these conditions; many researchers, in fact, question whether homosexuality is caused by a pathological family situation at all.

One study of the process by which an individual becomes a homosexual (Troiden, 1987) emphasized the importance of labeling. The process of gaining a homosexual identity was divided into four stages: (1) sensitization, (2) dissociation and signification,* (3) coming out, and (4) commitment. In this model, the gay identity is subject

---

*These terms refer to the mental processes by which sexual feelings and/or activity are distinguished from sexual identity.

to modification at each stage, and the later stages do not inevitably follow the earlier ones. The third stage, coming out, marks the point at which the individual defines himself or herself as homosexual and becomes involved in the homosexual subculture. The specific means through which this occurs may vary, as can be seen in Table 4–2.

One important difference among homosexuals involves their willingness to come out, that is, to live openly as a homosexual. Some are completely candid about it. They may have relatively low-status and/or low-visibility jobs, which they are unlikely to lose because of their homosexuality. Or they may work in fields in which homosexuality is frequently taken for granted, such as the arts. Some are young people who have not yet made family and career commitments and believe that their sexual, psychological, and emotional needs are more important than their job or social position. These individuals are likely to be the most committed to a homosexual lifestyle. Many homosexuals, however, lead conventional lives that are simply homosexual counterparts of conventional heterosexual patterns: They have steady jobs and regular social lives that may center on groups of homosexual friends; they generally avoid public settings like gay bars (Bell & Weinberg, 1978). Some married homosexuals enjoy intercourse with their wives; a few are genuinely bisexual, enjoying the sex act with either male or female partners. Most are more comfortable in homosexual relationships but are married for the sake of domestic stability, companionship, and respectability.

A special category of homosexuality is situational, that is, homosexual activity that takes place in circumstances in which heterosexual contact is virtually impossible. This behavior is common in prisons, for example, where some of it can only be characterized as rape. Another form of situational, transitory homosexuality is that of delinquent youths who engage in homosexual prostitution with adult males. A. J. Reiss, Jr. (1964), found that some lower-class boys in large cities are taught this behavior by a peer group or gang whose older members know how to locate potential clients. These encounters occur at specific locations, such as certain street corners, parks, public toilets, or movie houses. A boy who engages in such behavior must belong to a group that accepts and encourages it, the group must indoctrinate him into it, and he must participate strictly for the money and never for sexual gratification.

TABLE 4–2   How Do Gay Men Define the Term "Coming Out?"[a]

	Responses	
	Percent	Number
To admit to oneself a homosexual preference, or decide that one is, essentially, homosexual	31	77
To admit to oneself a homosexual preference *and* to begin to practice homosexual activity	27	41
To start actively seeking out other males as sexual partners	9	13
First homosexual experience as a young adult (i.e., after middle teens)	8	12
A homosexual experience that triggers self-designation as homosexual	1	2
Other	3	5
	99	150

[a]Informants were asked to define what the term *coming out* meant to them—that is, how they would use the term.

Source: Richard Triden, "Becoming Homosexual," *Psychiatry: Journal for the Study of Interpersonal Processes* (November 1978), 42:362–373.

Only oral-genital fellatio, with the adult client acting as fellator, is permitted. The boy and/or his peer group will resort to violence if the adult does not conform to the established customs for such transactions. As long as the boy also conforms, he will not be defined as a homosexual and will not define himself as one.

Lesbianism

It is even harder to estimate the number of lesbians in the United States than it is to estimate the number of male homosexuals. Lesbians are less conspicuous, they are generally less publicly active and have fewer sex partners, they are less likely to "cruise" or to frequent bars, and they are less likely to be arrested. In addition, social norms make it easier to conceal female homosexuality. A single woman who does not date men is usually assumed to be uninterested in or afraid of sex rather than being suspected of lesbianism. Also, it is considered more acceptable for women to share an apartment or to kiss or touch in public than it is for men (Gallagher & Hammer, 1998). Finally, laws against homosexuality usually are concerned primarily with the activities of males.

Although as individuals female homosexuals are as diverse as male homosexuals, there are some general differences between the ways in which males and females manage homosexuality. Many of these differences appear to arise from differences in socialization. Homosexuals, as much as heterosexuals, are affected by society's expectations about the kinds of behavior that are appropriate for members of each sex. Well before a girl begins to experience homosexual tendencies, she is absorbing society's assumptions about how females should act—for example, that they should be less aggressive than males and that sex is permissible only as part of a lasting emotional relationship. Moreover, sexual experiences usually begin later for females than for males. A boy is likely to have a sexual experience to the point of orgasm—usually through masturbation—relatively early in adolescence, whereas for a girl the corresponding experience is likely to occur in late adolescence or early adulthood. It is therefore likely that a girl will learn to think in terms of emotional attachment and permanent love relationships before she develops any strong sexual commitment; when that commitment appears, whether heterosexual or homosexual, it does so in the context of love. Thus, for most of the lesbians studied by Gagnon and Simon (1973), the first actual sexual experience came late, during an intense emotional involvement.

These differences in development and socialization underlie many of the subsequent differences in the behavior of male and female homosexuals. The lower level of sexual activity among lesbians, for example, parallels the behavior of women in general. Lesbians typically come out at a later age than male homosexuals. When a lesbian does come out, she usually looks for one partner and remains with her as long as the relationship is satisfying. When she lacks a partner, she is less likely than a male to look for one-night stands and hence spends less time in the gay bars and other gathering places that are so important to male homosexuals.

As in the case of male homosexuality, a special category of lesbianism is found in prisons. Many women who are in prison have experienced severe abuse by male partners or parents and feel angry and estranged from men. In prison they form friendships that may lead to sexual relations, a pattern that may endure later in life (E. M. Miller, 1986).

The Homosexual Subculture

When we speak of the homosexual subculture, we are referring to the visible institutions of the gay community. *The Advocate,* "the national gay and lesbian newsmagazine," is an example of such an institution. An undetermined proportion of

SOCIAL PROBLEMS ONLINE

Gays on the Internet

The Internet carries a host of resources on issues of concern to gays, lesbians, and bisexuals. Perhaps the best place to start is the Queer Resources Directory, or QRD (**http://www.qrd.org/grd/**), an unabashed guide to available sites both in the United States and in other countries. The QRD is encyclopedic—it contains more than 16,000 files. Among the major areas covered are gay youth, families, and religion, as well as business, legal, and workplace issues. Queer Culture, History and Origins, at **http://www.qrd.org/culture/**, includes articles on the history of homosexuality and essays on gender and capitalism, as well as more lighthearted pieces on subjects like tax humor for gays.

The National Gay and Lesbian Task Force has a home page at **http://www.ngltf.org/gi.html** that tracks political issues of concern to lesbians and gays and suggests activities for those who want to advance their civil rights. Links to resources on political activism throughout the world can also be accessed from the QRD.

A website devoted to bisexuality—Bi the Way, at **http://www.gworld.org/friends/bitheway/**— offers reviews of bi-oriented literature, links to other related web pages, and opportunities for interactive conversation. Those who are interested in noninteractive dis-

cussions about homosexuality and bisexuality can subscribe to list serves such as **alt.homosexual, soc.bi, soc.motss,** or **alt.politics.homosexuality**.

The Ontario (Canada) Centre for Religious Tolerance, at **http://web.canlink.com/ocrt/hom_chur. htm**, explores the attitudes of Christian religious groups toward homosexuality. It includes information on the attitudes of 17 denominations with memberships of 1 percent or more of the populations of the United States or Canada. The page also addresses internal church conflicts and the incidence of homosexuality within churches. The Biblical Studies Foundation (**http://www. bible.org/**) features articles based on a literal reading of the Bible. The APA's and AMA's positions on homosexuality are available at **http://www .geocities.com/WestHollywood/ 1348/apa_ama.htm**.

The Family Research Council, which condemns homosexuality, has a home page at **http://www.frc.org**. Its online publications cover homosexuality, homosexual marriage, and gays in the military, among other topics. It has links to kindred groups such as the Sexual Health Internet Project (**http://www.shiproject. com**), which monitors from a conservative point of view the activities of groups that are sympathetic to gay and lesbian civil rights.

homosexuals remain in the closet; that is, they do not participate openly in the life of the gay community. It is the declared homosexuals who create the gay subculture and have mobilized to bring about changes in laws and social norms that would create a more tolerant climate for all homosexuals.

The homosexual subculture may be found in most big cities in the United States, which have large homosexual populations in neighborhoods such as Greenwich Village and Chelsea in New York City and the Castro district in San Francisco. Gay institutions in these communities, which provide services and serve as meeting places for homosexuals, include certain parks, restrooms, movie theaters, public bathhouses, gyms, and bars. Cities with large gay populations also support businesses—restaurants, boutiques, barbershops, bookstores, travel agencies, repair shops, and so forth—that cater primarily to a gay clientele. Certain doctors, dentists, and lawyers also have largely gay clienteles. The growth of such businesses has fostered a sense of community among homosexuals. In New York and San Francisco, for example, it is possible for a homosexual to live, work, shop, and be entertained in a largely gay milieu. In 1999 Chicago unveiled a commemorative statue for gay rights in the growing homosexual community on the city's north side, another indication of the political and cultural influence of gay people in major American cities.

Despite such progress, in the 1990s homosexuals have increasingly had to defend their identity in communities outside major metropolitan centers. In doing so they have often had to demonstrate that they exist in significant numbers even outside the publicly known gay communities. In 1993, for example, the arts commission of Cobb County, a suburb of Atlanta, Georgia, bowed to conservative pressure and declined to fund a theater group that had presented a play about AIDS that also dealt with homosexuality. The region's gay population, normally reluctant to call attention to itself, staged demonstrations to protest the decision. The purpose of such demonstrations is to show not only that homosexuals demand fair treatment but also that they are a subculture that is not isolated in a few major urban centers.

A major function of the homosexual subculture is to give its members a way to understand and accept their sexual orientation. This function is performed not only by gay bars and similar meeting places but also by some homosexual organizations. These groups work to abolish laws that discriminate against homosexuals and to persuade homosexuals themselves and society in general that there is nothing shameful or harmful about being homosexual. Since the advent of the AIDS epidemic, they have also worked to propagate knowledge about safe sex and to lend support to those stricken by the disease.

The Impact of AIDS.   Almost twenty years after AIDS was recognized as a new disease, AIDS activists fear that it has become part of the landscape. Because the disease is not seen as a significant threat among suburban white males, it seems to be receding from the forefront of concern, even though it is still the leading cause of death among young men. At the same time, recent advances in the medical treatment of AIDS involve expensive multidrug therapies, which are often beyond the reach of indigent AIDS patients. This is creating an ever-widening gap between those who can afford expensive treatment and those who cannot hope to receive the advanced medications and care, yet apathy in the larger population is hindering progress in addressing this problem. In voicing their concern, therefore, AIDS activists, many of whom are gay, are often speaking out for the needs of nongay groups as well.

The AIDS quilt is a strategy designed to capture public attention and remind people that anyone can be afflicted by the disease.

Within the homosexual population the AIDS epidemic has had profound effects. As it became increasingly evident that the dreaded virus can be transmitted through sexual intercourse and that certain sexual activities, such as anal intercourse, are particularly risky, many gay men felt compelled to modify their lifestyles. Large numbers of gay men have sought to establish monogamous relationships. This trend has accelerated demands for acceptance of gay marriage and for equal rights for same-sex partners. On the AIDS front, developments in drug therapy during the 1990s, along with massive education efforts among gay populations about the requirements for safe sex, have diminished the ravages of AIDS even as the disease claims an increasing number of lives in areas of the world where expensive drug therapies are far less accessible. A recent fear in the United States, however, is that renewed confidence in medical treatment for AIDS may be causing younger generations of gay men to again become careless in their sexual behavior (Rochman, 1999).

Prostitution

Prostitution can be defined as sexual relations on a promiscuous and mercenary basis with no emotional attachment; prostitutes make a living by selling sexual favors to anyone who will pay for them. Although most prostitutes are female, there are also male prostitutes. Both groups cater to a male clientele.

Prostitution has existed since the dawn of history—it is sometimes referred to as the oldest profession—but its place in society and the prevailing attitudes toward it have varied. In early societies it was often associated with religious rituals. Occasionally, secularized prostitution has been legitimized (somewhat reluctantly), as it is today in some parts of Nevada. The usual rationale for this is the belief that no matter what society attempts to do about prostitution, there will be prostitutes and men will patronize them; therefore it is better to have the practice out in the open, where it can be supervised to some extent. More often, especially during the past century, prostitution has been banned (with varying degrees of enforcement), and the female prostitute has been considered a fallen woman, degraded and disreputable.

Social-scientific Perspectives on Prostitution

Early American sociologists tended to study prostitution in association with the disruption of family and community life brought about by immigration and rapid urbanization. For example, W. I. Thomas's (1923) pioneering study, *The Unadjusted Girl*, conceived of prostitution as an outcome of parental neglect combined with the need for young girls to adjust to a competitive social environment. In the 1940s and 1950s social scientists increasingly viewed prostitution as a form of deviance from the dominant normative order. Sociologist Kingsley Davis (1937) suggested that prostitution exists because in situations in which men need sexual release and women need money, prostitution may appear preferable to the more difficult seduction process.

Much contemporary research takes the interactionist perspective (Sterk, 2000). Jennifer James's research on prostitution in Seattle showed that over half of the women interviewed who were prostitutes at the time of the study had been raped or otherwise sexually abused before becoming prostitutes (James & Meyerding, 1977). This finding and others similar to it suggest that once women have been sexually abused, they are more likely to be labeled or to label themselves morally degraded and that this condition is a likely precursor to self-identification as a prostitute (European Committee on Crime Problems, 1993).

Functionalist research on prostitution tends to look at the roles, statuses, and types of conflict that are typical of the prostitute's world. For example, in her research on how prostitutes learn their trade in brothels, Barbara Heyl (1978) has shown that a madam who is talented as a trainer of prostitutes can establish a status for herself in "the life" (as the world of prostitution is called) in which she functions as a teacher. This research, along with that of Christina and Richard Milner (1973), describes the actions of prostitutes, madams, pimps, their customers ("tricks" or "Johns"), the police, and the courts as forming an interrelated set of social institutions that create the life. These researchers tend to see prostitution as a social problem because of the degree of conflict it generates over its impact on certain parts of cities, the use of scarce law enforcement and judicial resources to arrest and try prostitutes, and related problems stemming from prostitution (Grasso, 1994; Sterk, 2000). Table 4–3 presents various social-scientific perspectives on prostitution.

Norms of Prostitution

Prostitutes are not a homogeneous group. There are several fairly well-defined levels of prostitution, with typical differences in education, fees, methods of attracting customers, and types of customers served. Fees for services vary not only according to the "class" of the prostitute but also according to the community or neighborhood in which the prostitution occurs.

The aristocrats among prostitutes are the *call girls* and *call boys.* This type of prostitute never solicits; clients come through personal references, and arrangements are usually made by telephone. The cost of the prostitute's services ranges from $200 to a great deal more for an evening, which may include dinner at an expensive restaurant. The clients come from the upper-middle and upper classes. Both call boys and call girls consider themselves totally distinct from other prostitutes and in fact never refer to themselves by that term (McNamara, 1994).

Unlike call girls, *female hustlers* solicit directly, working out of nightclubs and bars. They are paid less than call girls, receiving between $100 and $200 for turning a trick. They may have several clients each night.

A *house girl* works in a brothel and is an employee of the madam who runs the house. She must accept any client the madam assigns to her and is allowed to keep half of the fee ($100–$200) for each trick.

Looked down on somewhat by all other prostitutes is the *streetwalker,* who solicits customers wherever she can find them and charges about $20 a trick (typically fellatio). In small towns, under highly competitive conditions, or if she is desperate, a woman may charge less.

TABLE 4–3   Social-Scientific Perspectives on Prostitution

Perspective	Reasons for Prostitution	Why Prostitution Is a Social Problem
Functionalist	Exists because it is useful in societies as a way of coping with male sexuality.	Actually fills social needs but is a problem because many segments of society see it as a threat.
Conflict	Exists because women are oppressed and poor women especially are attracted to the life as a means of survival.	Perpetuates or increases gender conflict and represents another form of exploitation.
Interactionist	Exists because once they become part of the prostitute subculture, women base their identity and social life on that subculture.	Prostitutes become stigmatized and cannot leave the life without great difficulty.

Like most occupations, prostitution has various levels of prestige, with high-priced call girls at the top and the far more visible and lower-paid street prostitutes at lower levels.

Prostitutes at these various levels have little to do with one another; they work in different places and attract different clients. The only movement between the groups is generally downward: When a call girl begins to lose her looks and is in less demand, she may be forced to solicit directly; hustlers and house girls may eventually be reduced to walking the streets.

There is a similar hierarchy among male prostitutes, although there are fewer types. The most visible male prostitute is the hustler. Typically he wears a "masculine" uniform—Levi's, a leather jacket, and boots. To most of his clients, or scores, it is important to believe that the hustler is heterosexual, and in fact research has shown that the majority of hustlers are straight.

Researchers have found that sexual self-definition is extremely important to the male prostitute, whether he is a call boy, a hustler, a delinquent youth out to make a quick buck, or a "chicken" (child or teenage prostitute) (Elifson, Boles, & Sweat, 1993; McNamara, 1994). Some male prostitutes have no difficulty accepting their homosexuality, but those to whom a heterosexual self-image is necessary follow a clearly defined set of rules to maintain it. The first rule relates to motivation: The goal must be monetary; to seek sexual gratification would be an admission of homosexuality. The second rule relates to "masculinity": Although many male prostitutes, both straight and gay, will perform any sexual act for the right price, many straight hustlers set limits on what they will do with a client and perform only in the traditional masculine role.

In the face of the AIDS epidemic, prostitutes are under a great deal of pressure from law enforcement authorities and public health officials to practice safe sex, which usually means use of condoms and avoidance of anal intercourse. Research indicates that prostitutes are increasingly insisting on the use of condoms but that they are often pressured by tricks who are unwilling to do so (Sterk, 1989, 2000).

Why Do People Become Prostitutes?

If society considers prostitution unacceptable and degrading, why do people become prostitutes? It is usually assumed that because of society's disapproval, asking why someone becomes a prostitute is different from asking why someone becomes a lawyer. Robert Bell (1971) has suggested, however, that the answers to the two questions may not be so different and that more attention should be paid to the answers prostitutes give when they are asked why they entered their line of work. If good pay and association with glamorous people are acceptable reasons for becoming an administrator, why should they not apply to becoming a prostitute? Kingsley Davis (1937) noted that one might legitimately ask why more people do *not* become prostitutes—why so many people stick to such tedious jobs as secretaries or clerks when they could make more money in less time as prostitutes. Evidently society's norms work very strongly for most people who might otherwise consider a career in prostitution.

Some studies approach the question from a psychological perspective. They consider two things: the unique life history and psyche of an individual (to see what factors might predispose him or her to become a prostitute) and the psychological defenses or mechanisms the individual develops to maintain an acceptable self-image after becoming a prostitute.

Many investigators have related early sexual abuse to later prostitution. In studies of female prostitutes carried out during the 1970s, Jennifer James and Jane Meyerding (1977) found that a disproportionately high number of prostitutes had been raped as children. Fifty-seven percent of the prostitutes in the earlier study and 65 percent of those in the later study had been raped. In addition, many of the prostitutes in these sample populations (23 percent and 12 percent) had been sexually abused by their fathers. James and Meyerding concluded that although rape and incest cannot be viewed as the cause of female prostitution, they may play a part in its development: "To be used sexually at an early age in a way that produces guilt, shame, and loss of self-esteem on the part of the victim would be likely to lessen someone's resistance to viewing oneself as a saleable commodity" (p. 41).

In a study of teenagers from low-income families in four American cities, Williams and Kornblum (1985) found that young women who live in communities characterized by severe poverty and the visible presence of prostitutes tend to regard part-time prostitution as a means of obtaining money for clothes and entertainment. Eleanor Miller (1986) has studied the recruitment of young women from black, Hispanic, and white families into a deviant lifestyle that includes prostitution. A factor that Miller identifies as particularly important for black women is a familial structure known as the domestic network (Stack, 1974), in which a number of households are linked together by ties based on kinship, pseudokinship, and reciprocal personal and economic obligations. Domestic networks evolve out of numerous intersecting attempts to achieve financial and emotional security; they have no obvious nucleus or defined boundary. For this reason, it is relatively easy to recruit younger members of the network to engage in various illegal activities. Although parents and guardians usually disapprove of such behavior by their children, other members of the network who may engage in such activities—for example, stepsiblings, young aunts or uncles, or friends of these relatives—often have enough influence to counteract the parents' efforts.

Miller (1986) finds that the most frequent route to prostitution for Hispanic women is membership in peer groups in which drug use is common. In fact, for high proportions of women from all backgrounds, prostitution serves as a means of obtaining the money to buy drugs. Running away from home—often to escape from an incestuous relationship—also frequently leads to prostitution, regardless of the young woman's race, ethnicity, or social class. Miller points out that these routes to prostitution are not mutually exclusive and in fact often overlap; however, a dominant influence can usually be identified.

It should be noted that there is no evidence for a causal link between drug abuse and prostitution. However, there is a high correlation between the two conditions. In one study, 87 percent of female and 65 percent of male prostitutes had used drugs other than alcohol and tobacco in the past year (Marshall & Hendtlass, 1986). There is a strong tendency for street prostitutes to use illicit drugs, thereby conveying the impression of a causal relationship (Sterk, 2000).

Becoming a Prostitute.   Nanette Davis (1987) interviewed 30 prostitutes in correctional institutions. She found that her subjects typically had progressed through three stages: casual promiscuity, a transitional phase, and full-fledged prostitution. She concluded that the crucial influences in this process are those that lead a woman to identify herself as a person who has departed from the values and norms of society and to organize her behavior accordingly.

The first stage, a period of gradual drift from promiscuity to the first act of prostitution, might take several years but typically begins at an early age. Nineteen of Davis's subjects had had intercourse by age 13. The mean age for the first act of prostitution was 17.3, but the earliest age was 14. Most of the subjects' families were highly permissive, exercising little or no supervision, and peer group norms favored early sexuality. As a result, both opportunities for and encouragement of promiscuity were present in the girls' social environment.

During adolescence and even earlier, most of the girls were already considered "bad" by their parents and others. Twenty-three had been sentenced to correctional institutions during adolescence for truancy, sexual delinquency, or other reasons. At the institutions they met more experienced inmates who made prostitution seem prestigious. Since the girls were usually confused about their own identities, they were glad to learn a new and attractive role.

The girls who were not institutionalized generally experienced peer pressure to engage in prostitution. Some were encouraged by pimps, who provided clients and, apparently, the kind of secure relationship that the girls badly needed; this was the precipitating factor in their choice of prostitution as a career.

During the second stage, which Davis labeled "transitional deviance," the girl engaged in prostitution on an occasional basis but did not yet think of herself as a prostitute. She usually retained some commitments to the straight world—a job, marriage, and/or nonprostitute friends. Economic motivation became more important, together with loneliness or entrapment by the pimp. Eventually this stage culminated in some situation, such as arrest, that forced the girl to perceive herself unequivocally as a prostitute.

Professionalization is the final stage. Labeled as a prostitute by society and perceiving herself as one, the girl made sex her vocation and shaped her life around it. Most of Davis's subjects claimed that they would not want to go back to the "square" life, although some maintained that their prostitution was a transition to another career such as modeling or dancing. Only a few succeeded in maintaining a home with children.

In sum, it appears that the low-status prostitute typically drifts into the profession through a combination of circumstances, social conditions, and internalization of the label of prostitute. Rarely has she set out deliberately, through free choice, to become a prostitute.

The Prostitute Subculture

Like members of other subcultures, prostitutes usually develop their own specialized knowledge, language, folklore, and network of relationships, in this case with other prostitutes, pimps, customers, and the police. Becoming a prostitute means more than selling sex for money; it also means becoming part of a distinct, well-defined world.

A major part of the prostitute subculture involves the roles of those who participate in it. One important role, obviously, is that of the customer.* The prostitute learns to see the customer in strictly economic terms, as her source of income. This is facilitated by the attitude that the customer is basically corrupt—a belief that prostitutes adopt as a way of maintaining their self-image.

Another subculture figure who is important to many prostitutes is the pimp. A pimp lives off the earnings of one or more prostitutes and serves as manager, protector, and companion or lover. Virtually all streetwalkers have a pimp, who may be a husband or boyfriend and is usually referred to as "my man." Although in the past pimps often acquired customers for their "girls," today their responsibilities are primarily financial, and they almost never appear on the street except to check up on their women.

A study by two anthropologists (Milner & Milner, 1973) found that part of the attraction of pimping is the pimp's delight in exercising total control over women, who, he believes, should be completely subservient to men. This feeling might have been enhanced by the fact that many of the pimps studied were black and many of their prostitutes were white. Another considerable attraction, of course, is the chance to make a great deal of money while doing virtually nothing. The study found that pimps put great value on material possessions, lavish parties, expensive jewelry and clothing, and an elegant life free from strain and drudgery.

Although pimps exploit their prostitutes, it is clear that the women derive something from the relationship. A streetwalker's status in the subculture is derived from that of her pimp—how good-looking and well dressed he is and whether he drives an expensive car. The pimp takes care of business matters—paying bills, arranging bail and lawyers' fees when necessary, and so on. Without a pimp, the streetwalker is

*An insightful and often amusing account of a sociologist's first visit to a brothel is provided in Steward, "On First Being a John" (1972).

an "outlaw" and is likely to be harassed or threatened with assault and robbery. The pimp also gives his prostitutes a sense of family and a feeling of being taken care of. It has been pointed out that the relationship between a pimp and a prostitute is similar to the traditional husband-wife relationship, with the economic roles reversed. The prostitute makes the money, and the pimp gives her a sense of security and family.

Eleanor Miller (1986) describes the everyday life of street women as "characterized by alternating periods of hustling and partying; lying low, running, and furtive hustling; ill health or frequent court appearances and institutional confinement; and hustling as outlaw women, independent of street networks" (p. 139). During periods of "hustlin' and partyin'," street women feel a sense of "mastery, independence, individual accomplishment, and immediate reward" (p. 140). The fast life sometimes leads a woman to exceptional risks, however, and she may find herself "runnin'" or "sittin'." Depending on the seriousness of the crime she has committed, she may run to another state, often accompanied by her man, or just lie low for a while. During such periods the woman may feel "victimized, hopeless, vulnerable, and disillusioned" (p. 142).

"Sittin'" refers to temporary withdrawal from street life because of ill health or incarceration and may have the effect of increasing the woman's contacts with other members of the deviant network, including, sometimes, a new man. Finally, in some situations a street woman may attempt to hustle as an outlaw, that is, independently of a man. Periods of outlaw hustling tend to be short-lived, however, partly because "men" interfere and partly because the woman has difficulty reconciling solo street hustling with care of her children.

Violence Against Prostitutes.   At this writing, police in Vancouver, British Columbia, report that they believe a serial killer is stalking street prostitutes in that city. Across the border in Seattle, police believe that the killer may be the same one who is responsible for the deaths of more than 40 prostitutes there. Although this is an extreme case, violence against prostitutes is common. Any illegal or semilegal occupational group is vulnerable because when its members are victimized they cannot easily go to the authorities for protection. Male and female prostitutes are often victimized by violent clients and people who pretend to be clients in order to brutalize them. Indeed, one of the reasons for high rates of AIDS and other sexually transmitted diseases (STDs) among prostitutes is that they are often harassed and assaulted by their clients when they attempt to use condoms. But direct brutality, sadism, and assault are extremely worrisome occupational hazards of prostitution throughout the world.

In a recent study of street prostitutes and those who work in brothels, Australian sociologists Pricilla Pyett and Deborah Warr (1999) found that street prostitutes experience far higher levels of abuse and violence than do those who work in brothels and escort services. The street prostitutes were also far more likely to abuse addictive drugs, which in turn exposes them to greater risk of violence and disease. In Australia some brothels are licensed, and women who work in them are protected and obliged to refrain from drug use.

Prostitution and Globalization.   The boom in world travel, the spread of military bases into impoverished third-world regions, and the ease of disseminating information over the Internet have all contributed to a vast increase in various forms of what is known as "sex tourism." A decade ago the feminist sociologist Cynthia Enloe (1990) pointed out that military bases, with large numbers of single males, were associated with the development of prostitution and the exploitation of helpless women, who are often sold into prostitution by their desperate families. Today, as tourism has become the world's largest industry in terms of investment and revenue flow, sex tourism—including male and female prostitution, child prostitution, and every form of sexual service that can be imagined—has become a significant market, often concentrated in impoverished and war-torn regions of the world. (See the Critical Research feature on page 108.)

CRITICAL RESEARCH

Sex Tourism Exploits Vulnerable Populations

Sex tourism—travel to foreign lands in search of sexual pleasures that are illicit in one's own society—is only one branch of the global tourism industry, but it is a rapidly growing one and is associated with many other social problems, especially poverty, gender discrimination and sexism, child abuse, and crime. Sex tourism is thriving in poor Asian nations like South Korea, Thailand, Cambodia, the Philippines, and parts of India, but it can be found throughout the world (Enloe, 1996; Oppermann, 1998). For many poor nations, where tourism is a large business, it is extremely difficult to discourage or crack down on sex tourism because it generates so much cash for otherwise destitute individuals; moreover, the corrupt sex brokers who run the trade can easily bribe politicians and the police. Wherever sex tourism is flourishing, there is usually a pattern of collusion between local governments that are seeking a flow of foreign currencies and foreign businessmen eager to invest in travel for sexual commerce.

In her pioneering research on sex tourism, sociologist Cynthia Enloe observed the growth of the industry in Southeast Asia. She concluded that if it is to succeed, sex tourism requires third-world women to be economically desperate enough to enter prostitution; once they have done so, it is difficult to leave. The other side of the equation requires men from affluent societies to imagine that certain women, usually women of color, are more available and submissive than the women in their own countries. Sex tourism also involves male prostitution in many regions and puts vulnerable teenagers and young adults, male and female, at risk of AIDS and other sexually transmitted diseases.

Researchers warn that child prostitution is an especially exploitive and increasingly popular form of sex tourism. The United Nations estimates that in Asia alone there are over a million child sex workers (Gampell, 1999). One current strategy to combat sex

These teenage prostitutes in Thailand work in the global sex industry, which caters to tourists seeking sexual pleasure for pay.

tourism is to show ads condemning child prostitution on airplanes bound for cities with developed child sex markets. These ads inform those who might be thinking of buying the sexual services of children that their behavior is illegal, can land them in jail, and can cause them to be labeled as sexual offenders in their own nations as well. Major airlines are participating in efforts to reduce sex tourism, even as they profit immensely from the trade (Gampell, 1999).

The Impact of AIDS

We noted in Chapter 2 that prostitution is one of the means by which AIDS has spread among the heterosexual population. A study commissioned by the Centers for Disease Control has found that about 40 percent of street prostitutes have been exposed to AIDS (usually because their lovers are intravenous drug users); in contrast, fewer than 20 percent of call girls are AIDS carriers (Sterk, 1989). Rates of infection for male prostitutes are lower than for female street prostitutes, but risks increase dramatically with age (Elifson, Boles, & Sweat, 1993; Elifson & Sterk-Elifson, 1992).

The presence of AIDS among prostitutes poses numerous problems both for the individual and for society. When a prostitute discovers that she has been infected by HIV, she may be reluctant to seek medical and social assistance for fear of being arrested and imprisoned. Because she still needs to support herself, she may continue to hustle, thereby transmitting the virus to her customers. Although many prostitutes supply their clients with condoms, this practice is by no means universal and does not entirely eliminate the risk of transmission (Rubington & Weinberg, 1995).

Part of the difficulty of limiting the spread of AIDS stems from the attitudes of prostitutes and their customers. According to one streetwalker, "You can just as easy get it at home or on the streets. . . . There's no one-woman men or one-man women any more" (quoted in Winerip, 1988, p. B1). As for the customers, recent research indicates that there may be an increasing number of HIV-positive men who continue to frequent prostitutes, especially streetwalkers (Ayala, 1996).

Pornography

A third sex-related social problem is **pornography,** which may be defined as the depiction of sexual behavior in such a way as to excite the viewer sexually. Pornography has existed for centuries, but in recent decades it has come to be considered a social problem in many communities. The vast increase and unprecedented openness of its distribution, and its tendency to become concentrated in particular areas and thereby adversely affect whole neighborhoods, have caused serious disagreement about both what actually constitutes pornography and the wisdom of permitting or suppressing it (Zillman & Bryant, 1989).

As stated at the beginning of this chapter, sexual attitudes and behavior are learned. Among the things we learn is that anything "pornographic" is something other than an appropriate sex object that has the capacity to arouse us. This belief in the power of pornography is related to the view of sex as innate, overwhelming, and instinctual. Pornography is thought to be able to release the sexual beast in all of us (especially males) and to have "a magical capacity to push men into overt sexual action" (Gagnon & Simon, 1973, p. 261).

According to Gagnon and Simon, pornography deals with illicit sex; it does not describe conventional sexual activity that occurs within a marital relationship: "The rule is: If the activity is conventional, the context is not (the relationship, the motives, etc.); if the context is conventional, the activity is not" (p. 263). It is this illicit emphasis that makes pornography controversial.

An aspect of pornography that almost everyone agrees is a serious social problem is the exploitation of children in the production of pornographic materials (Zillman & Bryant, 1989). Many states have passed legislation that increases the penalties for those found guilty of producing or distributing pornographic materials that feature minors (Grasso, 1994). But the extremely rapid growth of the Internet during the 1990s has raised anew the fear that many children and adolescents will be exposed to sexually explicit materials or will enter into sexually exploitive conversations and even relationships with adults who wish to use the youths' photographs for pornographic purposes (Winner, 1994). The availability of pornography and explicitly sexual discussions on the Internet raises many problems of free speech versus the desire to protect minors from exploitation (Fiss, 1996; Strossen, 1995). There are never entirely satisfactory solutions to conflicting values, and the case of social control of the Internet is no exception. Technological solutions analogous to the V-chip, which allows parents to control children's access to cable pornography channels, are often implemented in schools, but home computers present more difficult challenges (Farnsworth, 1996).

Pornography is often associated with central-city "combat zones," but as this photo shows, it is found in rural settlements as well.

There are no reliable estimates of how many children are affected by sexual abuse that is connected to the production of pornographic books and films, but even a casual inspection of the materials available in a large city's pornography market will convince the reader that children are being photographed and filmed in sexual acts that clearly constitute abusive behavior. Advocates of legalized pornography claim that they are being victimized by allusions to crimes that involve only a small portion of their industry, but in the public mind the exploitation of children is the most serious charge against the pornography industry (Grasso, 1994). Women who are active in antipornography campaigns argue that much commercial pornography expresses violence against their sex, but this argument has not had nearly as great an impact on the courts or the media as the issue of exploitation of children.

Social-scientific Perspectives on Pornography

Conflict theorists are interested in pornography as an issue that reveals a great deal about changing moral values in the United States. The degree to which the law is used in instances in which the value issue is unclear is a primary concern: "When law becomes a vehicle to enforce a particular moral philosophy, there is the continual danger of its abuse, since the law does not reflect a consensus as to the appropriate social policy for the society, but the power of a particular group engaged in status politics" (Rist, 1975, p. 12).

The functionalist perspective on pornography is illustrated by the research of William Kornblum, Charles Winick, and Terry Williams in New York City's West Forty-second Street area (CUNY, 1978; Williams & Kornblum, 1994). Here the concentration of commercial sex establishments, adult bookstores, peep shows, topless bars, and adult movies created a de facto (i.e., not legal but tolerated) combat zone. This once notorious sex neighborhood discouraged the development of other businesses and forms of entertainment. From the perspective of those who wish to build up the city's economy, pornography is a form of urban blight; legislation has been passed in New York and other cities to limit the concentration of commercial sex establishments.

Another perspective on pornography is that of feminists, who believe it is degrading to women in particular and to all human beings in general (Jacobson, 1995; A. Lewis, 1994). Among the better-known university-based feminists is Catherine MacKinnon, who argues that pornography is a form of symbolic rape that threatens to engender actual violence against women. MacKinnon advocates placing a higher value on the protection of women than on the rights of free speech, and therefore she defends legal measures to limit the concentration of porn establishments, as has been attempted in Minnesota and New York City in recent years (A. Lewis, 1994; MacKinnon, 1993).

In a number of cities, groups affiliated with Women Against Pornography have led protests in downtown porn and commercial sex districts. Led by well-known writers like Susan Brownmiller, such groups assert that most pornography is aimed at a male audience that can only be negatively affected by the obvious violence directed against women in pornographic materials. Within feminist circles, however, there is considerable disagreement on these issues. Few feminists defend pornography, but there is vigorous debate over the concept of "sex workers," who may be prostitutes or porn models but are seen as exploited workers who need to be understood and defended by feminist activists (Leuchtag, 1995).

Pornography and Censorship

Any discussion of pornography must take into account the issue of censorship and, in the United States, the rights guaranteed by the First Amendment. Today this is a particularly sensitive issue. Serious arguments both for and against the suppression of pornographic material can be made. The arguments against limiting pornography include the following:

1. Censorship is damaging to artistic and literary efforts since experience has shown that works of sound artistic value are likely to be considered pornographic or obscene if they contain any explicit sexual material.

2. The vagueness of existing legal definitions of pornography gives too much latitude to judges and other authorities, enabling them to suppress material because they personally consider it offensive.

3. The reading or viewing of pornographic material is a private act that does no harm to society and therefore cannot legitimately be prohibited by society.

4. If pornography is freely available, sophisticated people with good judgment will soon become bored with it and turn to more worthwhile entertainment.

Those who argue against pornography claim that habitual exposure to pornographic materials is indeed harmful, particularly to young people and, therefore, to the society of which they are a part. They believe that when pornography becomes so widespread that people (presumably a majority) who want to avoid it find it extremely difficult to do so, it is legitimate for society to try to control it. This argument has prompted several attempts by the Supreme Court to define and control pornography. In 1976 the Court ruled that it is constitutional for municipalities to restrict the proliferation of pornographic theaters and bookstores through zoning regulations, which must be based on "community standards" regarding what types of materials are considered obscene. In 1987, however, the Court ruled that judges and juries that are deciding whether sexually explicit material is legally obscene must assess the social value of the material from the standpoint of a "reasonable person."

Research on Pornography

Unfortunately for the objectivity of these arguments, until recently very little empirical research has been done on either the effects of pornography or the extent of exposure to it. A few studies have been carried out, notably in connection with the work of the U.S. Commission on Obscenity and Pornography, reported in 1970. On the basis of these studies, the commission concluded (though not unanimously) that no social or individual harm can be traced directly to exposure to pornographic material. For example, there is no connection between pornography and street crime (assault, mugging, and the like), although it is linked to organized crime. On the basis of these findings, the commission recommended that most existing restrictions on pornography be relaxed. The rejection of the commission's findings and recommendations, both in the government and elsewhere, suggests the extent to which empirical study in this area must contend with deeply ingrained fears.

What exactly have studies of pornography revealed? For one thing, they have shown that some degree of exposure to pornographic material is quite common in our society and apparently has been for a long time. The General Social Survey, conducted annually by the National Opinion Research Corporation (NORC), reports that 28 percent of its respondents admit that they have seen an X-rated movie in the last year (NORC, 1999). Younger adults and people with some college education are more likely than older adults and people with only a high school education to have encountered sexual materials. Among men, but not women, geographic location makes a difference: The greatest exposure occurs in large metropolitan areas in the Northeast; the least exposure occurs in the northern central states.

Research has found that sexually explicit materials are often used by young adults and adolescents as a form of sex education (Kutchinsky, 1992). How many people become attracted to more violent, sadomasochistic, or juvenile pornographic material is less well understood. Studies conducted for the original Commission on Obscenity and Pornography in 1970 estimated that it was a far smaller number than the number of people who watch X-rated material—probably less than 10 percent of the entire population—but in absolute terms this translates into a large number of people who are attracted to the more problematic forms of pornography (Allen, Emmers, & Gebhardt, 1995).

The easy availability of all kinds of pornographic materials on the Internet presents a major change and creates a host of new controversies among opponents of pornography. The availability of explicit sexual materials to the home may have reduced somewhat the demand for pornographic products and services provided in specialized urban "combat zones," but it has also given children easier access to sexually explicit materials and exposed more children and adolescents to predatory advances by adults. Direct marketing of pornography on the Internet is a major business, one of the most successful forms of e-commerce to date and one that nets over a billion dollars of sales annually (Leland, 1999). Internet pornography has also led to efforts to censure or filter sexually explicit materials on the Internet, which in turn have raised issues of constitutional law, as we will see in the Social Policy section of the chapter.

Pornography and Public Opinion

The public has a complex and seemingly contradictory view of pornography. According to surveys conducted from 1978 to 1999 (NORC, 1999), most Americans appreciate the role of pornography as an outlet for bottled-up sexual impulses. However, at the same time they fear that pornography may lead to rape and other crimes, even though the evidence does not prove anything of the sort. In a survey of the major studies of pornography and crime, W. Cody Wilson (1971) pointed out that most sex crime offenders had significantly less experience with pornographic materials, as well as later introduction to such materials, in their youth than the control groups. Recent research on attitudes toward obscenity and pornography in Ohio communities shows that ideology has a great deal of influence. Individuals with more education and higher occupational status are less likely to consider sexually explicit materials obscene than older people with less education. Deeply held religious principles are highly correlated with a tendency to see sexual representations as obscene (Franks, 1999).

In 1990 the issue of pornography, and especially of what constitutes child pornography, spread to the art world. The highly controversial photographs of Robert Mapplethorpe, a homosexual artist and photographer who died of AIDS in 1989, became the subject of a precedent-setting trial in Cincinnati. The director of the Cincinnati Contemporary Arts Center was accused of the crime of obscenity for including in the Mapplethorpe exhibit photographs that depicted homosexual sex and nude children—actually, 7 photographs out of a total of 175. The director was acquitted of all charges in an emotional trial that had far-reaching implications for social policy, but at this writing the controversy continues; conservative critics like Senator Jesse Helms of North Carolina argue that taxpayers' money should not be used (through the National Endowment for the Arts and other public agencies) to support art that some people find obscene and offensive.

SOCIAL POLICY

Efforts to combat prostitution and pornography or to deny homosexuals their freedom of expression often resemble what Joseph Gusfield (1963) terms *symbolic crusades*. Debates over whether these behaviors should be permitted become struggles for status among different subcultures in American society. Like the controversies over abortion and birth control, efforts to force legislatures to permit or to ban these behaviors often serve the larger purposes of people involved in conservative, liberal, or feminist movements.

From a functionalist perspective, these battles prove that there is a great deal of dissension about sex-related social problems. All the parties are attempting to force the government to intervene because the norms and institutions that formerly controlled these behaviors have broken down. Interactionists argue, however, that each side is struggling to define the situation—that is, to have its version of reality become the dominant one, which in turn will lead to social policies that are favorable to its position. Conflict theorists argue that the struggles are inevitable since the various parties hold irreconcilable views. In recent years these debates have intensified as a result of the AIDS epidemic, focusing on issues of sexual morality and practical questions such as contact notification. (See Chapter 2.) Nevertheless, to a large extent they remain symbolic crusades with little promise of resolution.

Homosexuality

The furor over extending civil rights to gay individuals and couples continues in many regions of the United States. The issue of gay rights took a significant turn when the Supreme Court ruled in *Romer* v. *Evans* that Colorado's constitutional amendment barring legislation that protects homosexuals from discrimination was unconstitutional. But this decision does not represent a real gain for gay men and lesbians; it simply overturns a statute that barred such legislation. Discrimination in housing, jobs, and welfare benefits still exists.

The issues of same-sex marriage, gays in the military, and custody of children in same-sex households remain extremely controversial (Fineman, 1996). In North Carolina, for example, Fred Smith, a homosexual, lost custody of his two sons because he was living with a male partner (see the Current Controversies feature on page 114). The Defense of Marriage Act, which bars the federal government from recognizing same-sex unions, was passed by Congress and signed into law by President Clinton in 1996, largely because the majority of Americans continue to feel that same-sex marriages should not be condoned. However, a growing number of corporations, including Disney, Xerox, and IBM, now extend health insurance and other benefits to members of same-sex unions despite vociferous criticism from conservative organiza-

CURRENT CONTROVERSIES

Homosexuality and Child Custody

In 1993, in an immensely controversial decision, a state court in Virginia ruled that a two-year-old boy must be removed from the custody of his mother, a lesbian, and given to his grandmother. "The mother's conduct is illegal and immoral and renders her an unfit parent," the judge stated. The ruling was based on an earlier decision by the Virginia Supreme Court, which ruled that a parent's homosexuality is a legitimate reason for losing custody of a child, but other issues were involved as well. Among these were the child's best interests and the rights of parents, whether gay or straight.

The charges in the case were originally brought by the grandmother, who believed that the behavior of her daughter was damaging the health of the child. The authorities could intervene because in Virginia, as in about half of the states, oral sex between adults is a punishable offense. The grandmother also believed that the child would be emotionally confused throughout his life by the relationship between his mother and her female companion, whom he occasionally referred to as "Da Da."

Conservative groups were immensely pleased by the decision, believing it to be "fully in keeping with the historical norms and laws and mores of Western civilization" (quoted in Ayers, 1993, p. A16). Gay-rights advocates were outraged, however, claiming that the ruling violated the right of any parent, gay or straight, to raise his or her child. They pointed out that there was no evidence that the mother's lesbian relationship was having a detrimental effect on her child. Moreover, there is no reputable study showing that children raised by homosexual parents are more likely to become homosexuals themselves than children raised by heterosexual parents.

There have been several cases in which a heterosexual parent, after divorce from a homosexual partner, sued for custody of a child; these cases have been decided in various ways. The ruling just described was overturned by the Virginia Court of Appeals, providing further evidence that the law in this area is in considerable flux. Nevertheless, it seems clear that despite some progress on such issues as acceptance of homosexuals in the military, there remain major areas of conflict over the right of gay people to live their lives as they wish.

tions, and Vermont recently passed legislation granting same-sex couples all benefits given to heterosexual couples.

Laws that try to control homosexual behavior have come under attack as violations of constitutional rights and attempts to legislate private morality. Those who support such laws usually argue that they are necessary to protect young boys from seduction. They believe that legalizing homosexual behavior will encourage more people to become homosexual. Against this view must be set the loss suffered by society when homosexuals are legally or informally prevented from pursuing certain careers because of their sexual preference, together with the cost of the suffering imposed on them and their families by society's rejection.

The AIDS epidemic has raised the stakes in dealing with homosexual issues because it has revealed the need for open discussion of sexual practices among homosexuals and heterosexuals alike (Rochman, 1999). In the opinion of most gay social scientists, the only effective way to limit the spread of AIDS is through public education aimed at reducing high-risk sex, that is, through campaigns that promote safe sex practices. This approach runs the risk of creating even more negative attitudes toward homosexuals by publicizing their sexual activities and appearing to condemn them. Some communities and gay organizations have managed to publish guidelines for less risky sex without being either moralistic or judgmental. In contrast, governments at all levels have been unwilling to become involved in education about high-risk sex (Altman, 1987).

films, whatever their merits, are rated with an X, a symbol with strong negative connotations. Censorship of works of art may also lead to censorship of unpopular ideas, thereby threatening the foundations of democracy.

In the late 1980s, public policy regarding pornography focused on law enforcement efforts. In 1986 a federal advisory commission, the Attorney General's Commission on Pornography, called for a national assault on the pornography industry through a combination of more vigorous law enforcement and increased vigilance by citizens' groups. Stating that intensified enforcement should focus on child pornography and materials that portray sexual violence, the commission recommended that "knowing possession of child pornography" should be made a felony under state law. In 1990 the Supreme Court ruled that sale or possession of what a local court deems to be child pornography can be declared illegal in that community or jurisdiction. In its majority opinion, the Court held that the states are justified in passing such laws in an effort to "destroy a market for the exploitative use of children" and to protect the victims of child pornography.

Law enforcement officials have long maintained that the pornography industry has links to organized crime, and the commission arrived at the same conclusion: "Significant portions of the pornographic magazine industry, the peep show industry, and the pornographic film industry are either directly operated or closely controlled by [organized crime] members or very close associates" (Attorney General's Commission on Pornography, 1986; Grasso, 1994). Accordingly, in 1988 the Justice Department began to seek racketeering indictments against major distributors of pornographic materials. Many states are adding new muscle to their efforts to enforce laws against the production and marketing of child pornography (Grasso, 1994).

The Supreme Court's decision in *Roth* v. *United States* (1975) called for the application of "community standards" to this market, and city zoning laws permit restrictions on the concentration of businesses in certain areas. Cities have tried a number of strategies to prevent the proliferation of retail sex and porn shops and related businesses like massage parlors and peep shows. In Boston, a legal "combat zone" was established by laws that made it illegal to set up retail sex businesses anywhere else in the city. As the area was gradually improved through commercial investments, the porn shops were driven almost out of existence by rising rents and competition from other commercial uses. In Minneapolis and New York, local political leaders have attempted to follow Detroit's lead by passing laws that bar sex businesses from locating near churches or schools or within a designated distance from an existing shop. However, it remains to be seen how these efforts will fare in the face of legal challenges on First Amendment grounds.

Efforts to control access to pornography on the Internet are among the most controversial aspects of this social problem in the contemporary world. In 1999 the Senate began debating a bill that would order all schools that receive federal subsidies for Internet access (the so-called e-rate for Internet connections to schools) to run a filtering program that would automatically bar students' access to X-rated Internet sites. Meanwhile, computer makers began marketing filtering chips for home computers so that parents could have more control over what materials their children have access to at home. In 1998 Congress and the administration cooperated in the passage of the Child Online Protection Act, which is designed to keep minors from visiting sexually explicit commercial websites. But the Supreme Court had earlier struck down a similar 1996 law on the ground that it violated freedom of speech. The new law, which requires operators of such sites to get credit card numbers from customers to verify that they are 18 or older, has already been declared unconstitutional in a Pennsylvania federal district court and will come before the Supreme Court in coming months (Morrow, 1999).

The problem of pornography, in sum, is a complex one that involves not only issues of morality and freedom of speech but also such questions as how to prevent further deterioration of the quality of life in American cities. And it is no closer to a solution today than it has been at any time in the past 25 years. As is so often true in the formulation of policy on social problems, there is a need for more research not only on the consumption and effects of pornographic materials but also on sexual behavior in general.

Beyond Left & Right

It would be difficult to imagine an area of life in which there is more ideological and moral conflict in the United States than sexuality. People on the ideological right believe strongly that it is wrong to have sex outside of marriage, to engage in homosexual practices, or to consume pornography. Among people on the ideological left, there are perhaps more shadings of opinion, but the central attitude is one of tolerance: Sex of any kind between consenting adults is permissible; prostitution is not desirable but should at worst be treated as a victimless crime; pornography is protected by the right of free speech except where minors are concerned.

As you become more sociologically informed, must you become tolerant of behaviors that you do not condone? If you have liberal views on these issues, can you simply ignore the feelings of those who oppose your views? The answer to both questions is no. As sociologically informed citizens we can examine our own feelings and beliefs, set limits for ourselves, and seek to convince others through persuasion.

At the same time, we are learning that a society of people with diverse and strong opinions must still achieve social peace. Some compromises will be necessary. Look at our social policies to see how we arrive at compromises we can live with. For example, we are moving toward a society in which homosexual unions are granted more of the rights and benefits of heterosexual unions, but we do not seem ready to view gay marriage as legitimate. Our feelings about this issue will differ, but as sociologically informed people we will understand why the situation exists.

SUMMARY

- Social problems related to sex arise largely from changes and conflicts in attitudes toward human sexuality. Such problems are basically deviations from widely held norms of a particular society. In the United States there is a striking lack of "sexual literacy," which is itself a social problem because it prevents citizens from engaging in healthy and responsible sexual behavior.

- Sex-related social problems may be grouped into three categories: tolerated sex variance (masturbation, premarital intercourse, etc.), asocial sex variance (incest, child molestation, etc.), and structured sex variance (homosexuality, prostitution, and pornography).

- Homosexuality is a sexual preference for members of one's own sex. Sociologists have viewed homosexuality as a product of social disorganization, as an illness with physiological or psychological causes, as a product of societal labeling, and as a set of institutions in conflict with the institutions of straight society.

- It is not known what causes people to become homosexual. An important factor may be the social environment in which a person grows up. Recent research has emphasized the importance of the labeling of the individual as homosexual.

- Homosexuals differ greatly in the ways in which they satisfy their sexual desires and cope with the attendant problems, in their willingness to come out, in their ties to the straight world, and in their marital status.

- Lesbians are less conspicuous than male homosexuals and find it easier to conceal their sexual preference. They are more likely to view their relationships in terms of emotional attachment and tend to come out at a later age than male homosexuals.

- Gay institutions and businesses are concentrated in areas with a large homosexual population. These give homosexuals a way to understand and accept their sexual orientation.

- The AIDS epidemic has had a profound effect on the homosexual subculture. Homosexuals have come under a great deal of pressure to limit their sexual activity and to establish monogamous relationships.

- Prostitution is defined as sexual relations on a promiscuous and mercenary basis with no emotional attachment. In the past century, prostitution has generally been banned in the United States. There are several fairly well-defined types of prostitution, ranging from expensive call girls to streetwalkers, who solicit customers wherever they can find them.

- Psychological studies of why people become prostitutes focus on the individual's life history and psyche. Many investigators relate early sexual abuse to later prostitution. Prostitutes often come from broken homes and feel that they were unwanted or misunderstood as children.

- Women who become prostitutes typically progress through three stages: casual promiscuity, transitional deviance, and professionalization. Prostitutes have a subculture with its own language, folklore, and network of relationships. An important figure in this subculture is the pimp, who lives off the earnings of one or more prostitutes and serves as manager, protector, and lover.

- Prostitution is one of the means by which AIDS has spread among the heterosexual population. Infected prostitutes may continue to seek clients because they need to support themselves. Prostitutes are under a great deal of pressure to practice safe sex, but their customers are often unwilling to do so. Prostitutes also are frequently victimized by violent clients.

- Pornography may be defined as the depiction of sexual acts in such a way as to excite the viewer sexually. It is often perceived as a social problem not only because it offends conventional norms but also because it may have negative effects on neighborhoods in which it is sold.

- A major issue in connection with pornography is censorship. It is argued that censorship of pornography is damaging to artistic and literary efforts and that vague legal definitions give too much latitude to judges. Recent trials on charges of obscenity have shown that juries of conservative citizens are able to apply community standards in determining whether material that is sexually disturbing nevertheless has artistic merit.

- Research has shown that exposure to pornography is common in American society, often beginning at an early age, and that no social or individual harm can be traced directly to pornographic materials.

- Public policy regarding sex-related social problems remains generally restrictive. Although attitudes toward homosexuality have become more accepting, many gay-rights issues remain controversial. Prostitution is illegal almost everywhere in the United States, although there are many advocates of legalization. With respect to pornography, policy has focused on efforts to prevent the exploitation of children in the creation of such materials, as well as to limit access to them on the Internet.

KEY TERMS

tolerated sex variance, p. 92
asocial sex variance, p. 92
incest, p. 92
forcible rape, p. 93

paraphyllic rapism, p. 93
exhibitionism, p. 94
voyeurism, p. 94
structured sex variance, p. 94

homosexuality, p. 94
lesbians, p. 94
prostitution, p. 102
pornography, p. 109

INTERNET EXERCISE

The web destinations for Chapter 4 are related to different aspects of sex-related social problems. To begin your explorations, go to the Prentice Hall Companion Website: **http://prenhall.com/kornblum**. Then choose **Chapter 4** (Sex-Related Social Problems). Next, select **destinations** from the menu on the left side of the screen. There are a variety of sites to investigate. We suggest that you begin with **Sex Tourism**. The *Critical Research* feature in this chapter deals with how sex tourism exploits vulnerable populations. The Sex Tourism website provides an overview of the issues involved and describes different efforts to combat the problem. After you have explored the Sex Tourism site, answer the following questions:

- The text points out that child prostitution is an especially exploitive and increasingly popular form of sex tourism. What are your reactions to this problem? What do you think should be done about it?

- Research shows that wherever sex tourism is flourishing, there is usually a pattern of collusion between local governments and foreign businessmen who are eager to invest in travel for sexual commerce. How should American social policy deal with the problem of sex tourism?

5

Alcohol and Other Drugs

FACTS ABOUT

ALCOHOL AND OTHER DRUGS

- The rate of teenage smoking rose from 51.2 per 1,000 nonsmoking teens in 1988 to 77.0 in 1996.

- American adults consume an average of 33.9 gallons of beer, 3.01 gallons of wine, and 1.9 gallons of distilled spirits a year.

- Heavy drinking among men is most common between the ages of 21 and 30; among women it occurs most frequently between the ages of 31 and 50.

- Drinking by either a driver, a passenger, or a pedestrian is a factor in about 40 percent of all traffic fatalities.

- Drug use among young Americans, and among Americans overall, peaked in the late 1970s, declined until the early 1990s, and began rising again after 1993.

OUTLINE

The Nature of the Problem
Drug Abuse
Abuse, Addiction, and Dependence

Alcohol Use and Abuse
Problem Drinkers and Alcoholics
Who Drinks?
Drinking among Young People
Alcohol-related Social Problems
Treatment of Alcoholism

Illegal Drug Use and Abuse
Commonly Abused Drugs
Patterns of Drug Abuse
Drug Use and Crime
Drug Use and AIDS
Treatment of Drug Abuse

Social Policy

O urs is a drug-using society. We use drugs to ease pain, increase alertness, relax tension, lose weight, gain strength, fight depression, and prevent pregnancy. Americans of all ages and at all socioeconomic levels consume vast quantities of chemical substances every year. Most of these drugs are socially acceptable, and most people use them for socially acceptable purposes. Alcohol is a drug, as are caffeine and nicotine; these are commonly and widely used as aids to sociability and ordinary activity. But some drugs and some users of drugs are socially defined as unacceptable, and it is these drugs and users that constitute the drug problem.

The uses and abuses of alcohol and other drugs are discussed together in this chapter for a number of reasons. Through its personal and social effects, alcohol abuse is at least as harmful as the abuse of less socially accepted drugs. Moreover, many drugs, including alcohol, offer satisfactions that make them attractive to many people, but they can be habit forming, sometimes with destructive consequences to users, as well as to nonusers; thus there are controversies over the causes, consequences, and moral implications of their use. Efforts to control drug use—particularly the "War on Drugs" that has been a cornerstone of American social policy against substance abuse for over twenty years—are increasingly controversial among political leaders and social scientists.

We will see that strategies of interdiction and control are often associated with other social problems, such as violence, racism, and crime. Drastic measures to prevent drug cultivation and importation can also have negative effects on democratic institutions, both in the United States and abroad, with little evidence of success in diminishing drug supplies. Moreover, despite the nation's huge investments in antinarcotics policies, experts on addiction continually find that alcohol abuse is far more prevalent and damaging to individuals and society than any other form of substance abuse.

Other observers have noted that increased drug use in the 1960s and 1970s coincided with a period of social and political ferment that was especially prevalent among young people. Increasingly, adults in the dominant culture viewed young people as a separate cultural subgroup; and whereas alcohol use was interpreted as "part of growing up, as an act of socialization," some drug use was viewed as "growing away" instead (Gusfield, 1975, p. 9).

It should be kept in mind, however, that no matter what society thinks about certain drugs, many are dangerous to the user when consumed in steady doses over time. In addition, many drugs (especially alcohol, the opiates, and cocaine) are associated with antisocial behaviors. Thus, illness, crime, and interpersonal violence are significant aspects of the social problem of alcohol and drug abuse that must be dealt with regardless of how any particular drug is viewed at any given time.

The Nature of the Problem

From a pharmacological viewpoint, a *drug* is any substance, other than food, that chemically alters the structure or function of a living organism. So inclusive a definition, however, encompasses everything from vitamins and hormones to laxatives, snake and mosquito venom, antiperspirants, insecticides, and air pollutants. Obviously, this definition is too broad to be of practical value. Definitions that depend on context are more useful. In a medical context, for example, a drug may be any substance that is prescribed by a physician or manufactured expressly to relieve pain or to treat and prevent disease. In a sociological context, the term **drug** denotes any habit-forming substance that directly affects the brain or nervous system. More precisely, it refers to any chemical substance that affects physiological functions, mood, perception, or consciousness; has the potential for misuse; and may be harmful to the user or to society. In addition to the illicit drugs that attract so much attention, many pharmaceutical drugs are abused as narcotics (Lyman, 1996).

Although the last definition is more satisfactory for our purposes than the original, much broader one, it omits the social bias that has traditionally determined what substances are labeled drugs. When the members of a society have used a habit-forming substance for centuries, that substance may not be classified as a drug in that society even if it has been proven to be harmful. Alcohol and tobacco (nicotine) are examples of such substances, although there is a growing movement to classify nicotine as a drug (Ray, 1996).

Drug Abuse

We can define **drug abuse** as the use of unacceptable drugs and/or the excessive or inappropriate use of acceptable drugs in ways that can lead to physical, psychological, or social harm. (See the discussion of drug dependence later in this section.) With this definition, there can be little question that the abuse of both legal and illegal drugs is a social problem.

Like so many other social problems, drug use has both objective and subjective dimensions. The objective aspect is the degree to which a given substance causes physiological, psychological, or social problems for the individual or the social group—the family, the community, or the entire society. The subjective aspect is how people perceive the consequences of drug use and how their perceptions result in social action concerning drug use (norms, policies, laws, programs, etc.). Of course, these subjective perceptions may be based on objective evidence, but very often they are based on past practices and combinations of scientific and folk wisdom about a given substance. Aspirin, for example, is one of the most widely used drugs in the United States. From an objective standpoint we know that aspirin is often taken in excessive dosages for every real or imagined physical or mental discomfort. Aspirin can cause ulcers, gastrointestinal bleeding, and other ailments. But most Americans believe—this is the subjective aspect—that aspirin is a harmless drug that is dangerous only when taken in massive doses. Thus, aspirin use is part of our overall drug problem in objective terms but not in subjective terms. For many Americans, the same failure to allow objective facts to shape subjective perceptions is true in the case of alcohol, as we will see later in the chapter.

Other drugs are part of the social problem of drug use because they are perceived as problems even if the way they are used by certain people is not problematic in objective terms. Marijuana is an example. Objectively, there is little evidence that marijuana users damage themselves psychologically or physiologically, although researchers believe that marijuana may decrease the user's motivation to concentrate and learn complex material. Yet the subjective view of many Americans, especially those in policymaking positions, is that marijuana is a dangerous drug. This subjective viewpoint is incorporated into laws against marijuana use, and these laws, in turn, foster the illegal traffic in marijuana (House Committee on Government Operations, 1994; Lyman, 1996).

The discrepancy between the subjective viewpoint and objective reality comes to prominence quite often in American political affairs. In 1992, Bill Clinton's admission that he had tried marijuana as a student but had not inhaled became the subject of innumerable jokes during the presidential election campaign. The question of whether George W. Bush had used cocaine as a young man while "sowing his wild oats" was a persistent issue during the 2000 presidential primaries. In the meantime, thousands of Americans are in prison for possession of marijuana. Facing a backlash from an important segment of voters, only the bravest or most secure legislators would seriously consider supporting a bill to legalize or decriminalize the substance (Souder & Zimmer, 1998).

Other examples of this type of discrepancy could be added. The point is that drugs such as marijuana are treated as social problems within our society's dominant system of norms and institutions. Other drugs, such as alcohol and nicotine, are much less sharply defined as problems even though in objective terms their harmful consequences have been fully documented. In the past 25 years, as the harmful effects of smoking tobacco and heavy consumption of alcohol have been documented and have become a target of policies aimed at prevention and control, these behaviors have also begun to be defined as social problems. Nevertheless, these substances remain legal and continue to be sanctioned in many social settings.

Abuse, Addiction, and Dependence

The difficulty of separating the subjective and objective dimensions of drug use causes a great many problems of definition for experts in the field. The term *drug abuse* is widely used to refer to the objectively harmful consumption of drugs that are subjectively approved of, such as alcohol and tranquilizers. The term also refers to the use—in any amount—of drugs that are subjectively disapproved of, such as cocaine and marijuana, even if the objective facts about their effects in certain dosages do not indicate that they are harmful. Of course, almost all strongly addicting drugs, such as heroin, are harmful both to the user and to society at any level of use. But many other drugs whose use is considered abusive do not appear to be harmful when they are used sparingly or in small doses. Despite this ambiguity, the National Institute on Drug Abuse continues to support the use of the term, and we will use it in this chapter—except that we define drug abuse as *the use of a drug to an extent that causes harm to the user.*

Like the term *drug*, the term *addiction* is used rather loosely to refer to any habitual or frequent use of a drug, with or without dependence. In fact, addiction is a complex phenomenon that involves the drug user's physical and psychological condition, the type of drug, and the amount and frequency of use. Similarly, precise degrees of dependence are difficult to define because of the physiological and psychological complexity of drug use. Nevertheless, a limited consensus has developed among some experts, and certain definitions are considered acceptable. Physical dependence occurs when the body has adjusted to the presence of a drug and will suffer pain, discomfort, or illness—the symptoms of withdrawal—if its use is discontinued. The word

Drug problems are by no means limited to the United States or other modern nations. In prerevolutionary China, for example, opium addiction seriously weakened the society by depriving it of thousands of productive workers.

addiction is used to describe physical dependence; **psychological dependence** occurs when a user needs a drug for the feeling of well-being that it produces. The word **habituation** is sometimes used to mean psychological dependence.

In the diagnosis and treatment of alcoholism, the terms *dependence* and *abuse* are carefully defined in *DSM-IV*. These definitions are used to determine third-party payments for treatment and to legally determine the presence of alcohol problems. Criteria for alcohol dependence focus on cravings, withdrawal symptoms, and other behavioral measures of feelings associated with alcohol consumption. The criteria for abuse include drinking despite recurrent social, interpersonal, and legal problems resulting from alcohol use. In addition, *DSM-IV* highlights the fact that symptoms of certain disorders, such as anxiety or depression, may be related to the use of alcohol or other drugs (National Institute on Alcohol Abuse and Alcoholism, 1995).

It is important to note that not all drug use is considered abuse in the sense that it impairs health. A person who is suffering from an illness that requires treatment with morphine, for example, might be addicted but would not be considered an abuser. However, there can be no doubt that some drugs are not only physically addicting but also dangerous to society because they compel their users to seek ever larger quantities to maintain a high. These highly addictive drugs can be a major social problem in that thousands of otherwise productive people may disappear from the labor market or become involved in an underground drug economy. The classic example is the city of Shanghai before the Chinese Communist revolution of 1949. It has been estimated that almost 500,000 residents of Shanghai were addicted to opium and had to spend hours in smoking dens each day. Earlier in the twentieth century, thousands of Americans were addicted to a form of opium known as *laudanum,* which they used for headaches and menstrual cramps. In North America today, cocaine is a popular drug that is used in moderation by some people. But its more powerful, smokable form, known as *crack,* creates an intense desire for more of the drug and can be extremely addicting.

However one defines abuse and addiction, mere knowledge of patterns of use in the general population at a given moment and over time is an essential starting point. This is where social-scientific data play an important role. Monitoring of drug use by people who are arrested, large-scale surveys of alcohol and drug use, and national surveys of the incidence of mental illness—including drug- and alcohol-related disorders—are designed and carried out by professional social scientists. At their most basic level these surveys establish the prevalence of alcohol, tobacco, and illicit drug use in the general population, as shown in Table 5–1. **Prevalence** refers to the extent to which a behavior appears in the population to any degree at all; in other words, Table 5–1 shows the proportion of the population (high school seniors in this case) that has ever used the substance, regardless of frequency.

Drug prevalence data are especially helpful in comparing the popularity of specific drugs in a population or a segment of a population, such as teenagers. Questions that ask about the use of illicit drugs in the past month, as reported in Figure 5–1, are especially helpful in tracking trends in drug consumption over time. The figure shows a significant decrease in illicit drug use by teenagers and young adults between 1979 and 1992 and a slight increase since then. Figure 5–2 shows the increase in smoking among teenagers since 1988.

TABLE 5–1 Lifetime Prevalence Rates of Use of Different Drugs Among High School Seniors and the General U.S. Population Aged 12 and Over

	Percentage Ever Using Drugs	
Substance	High School Seniors	General Population
Alcohol	81.7%	81.9%
Cigarettes	65.4	70.5
Marijuana	49.6	32.9
Stimulants	16.5	4.5
Inhalants	16.1	5.7
Cocaine	8.7	10.5
Hallucinogens	15.1	9.6
Tranquilizers	7.2	3.2
Heroin	2.1	0.9

Source: Data from National Institute on Drug Abuse (NIDA), 1998; *Statistical Abstract,* 1999.

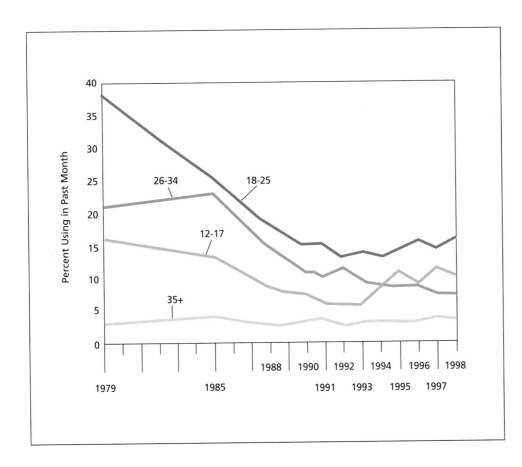

Figure 5–1 Illicit Drug Use by Age, 1979–1998

Source: National Household Survey on Drug Abuse, 2000.

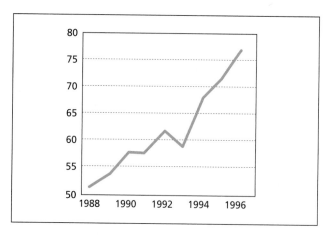

Figure 5–2 Number of Teenagers Who Smoke
Source: Data from Centers for Disease Control and Prevention.

Alcohol Use and Abuse

American adults consume an average of 33.9 gallons of beer, 3.0 gallons of wine, and 1.9 gallons of distilled spirits a year (*Statistical Abstract,* 1999). Despite these high rates of consumption, the problems associated with alcohol abuse—especially chronic inebriation, vagrancy, and drunken driving—arouse less interest and concern than the abuse, or even the use, of other drugs. In contrast to other drugs, alcohol is thoroughly integrated into Western culture. It may also be better adapted to our complex lifestyle because, in addition to relieving tension and reducing sexual and aggressive inhibitions, alcohol seems to facilitate interpersonal relations, at least superficially, whereas other drug experiences, even in groups, are often highly private.

In our society people have mixed feelings about alcohol. On one hand, alcohol creates warmth and high spirits and promotes interpersonal harmony and agreement ("Let's drink to that"). It has long been used in informal rituals (Christmas eggnog) and formal rites (wine as the blood of Christ) and has been important in the economies of many nations. The growing and harvesting of grapes, grain, and other crops used to produce alcoholic beverages, as well as the brewing, fermenting, distilling, and sale of alcoholic beverages, provide employment, trade, and tax revenues. On the other hand, the problems created by the abuse of alcohol are staggering. They include public drunkenness and disorderly behavior, traffic and industrial accidents, poor social functioning, broken marriages, child abuse, and aggravation of existing conditions such as poverty, mental and physical illness, and crime.

The perception of alcohol as a social problem varies with changes in American culture and increased knowledge about the effects of alcohol use. According to some sociologists, in the early decades of the twentieth century alcohol was a symbol that masked the larger social conflict between the working class, with its large immigrant component, and the upper class, which sought to control the workers and increase their productivity (Gusfield, 1963; Szasz, 1992). In recent years the American public has become more aware of the dangers associated with drinking—for example, the damage it can cause to an unborn fetus and the high correlation between highway accidents and driving while intoxicated. Alcohol is implicated in about 40 percent of all fatal highway accidents in the United States and approximately one-third of all homicides, drownings, and boating deaths. These problems have led to crusades against excessive drinking rather than against alcohol itself. In the 1990s both the Highway Safety Council and the Council for Accident Prevention have reported significant declines in traffic deaths due to drinking and in home accidents associated with alcohol consumption. These decreases seem to indicate that crusades against excessive drinking are having an impact, and their success will surely reinforce efforts to educate the public about its risks.

Problem Drinkers and Alcoholics

The National Longitudinal Alcohol Epidemiological Survey (1995) reported that 7.41 percent of adults in the United States meet current criteria for alcohol abuse or dependence. Alcohol addicts, or **alcoholics,** have an uncontrollable need for intoxication, and if this need is frustrated they will develop acute withdrawal symptoms like those of narcotics addicts—uncontrollable trembling, nausea, rapid heartbeat, and heavy perspiration. Some alcohol addicts have physiological symptoms after abstaining for only one day; in fact, alcohol withdrawal is even more likely to be fatal than narcotics withdrawal. Alcoholism may develop after ten or more years of problem drinking; however, many alcoholics go directly from total abstinence to chronic alcoholism. Such cases are believed to involve a complex set of physiological, psychological, and social factors.

Who Drinks?

Obviously, people are not alike in their drinking habits. Several factors seem to be related to whether, how much, and in what ways an individual uses alcohol. Among these are biological and socioeconomic factors, gender, age, religion, and cultural influences.

Biological Factors.   Alcoholism appears to be due in part to biological factors. So far, researchers who study the genetic factors linked to alcoholism are able to explain about half the risk for alcoholism faced by any given individual: "Recent genetic studies have demonstrated that close relatives of an alcoholic are four times more likely to become alcoholics themselves. Furthermore, this risk holds true even for children who were adopted away from their biological families at birth and raised in a nonalcoholic adoptive family, with no knowledge of their biological family's difficulties with alcohol" (Carson-DeWitt, 1999, p. 79). These findings are further supported by neurological studies showing that brain function is often different in alcohol abusers and their children. Studies of alcoholism and biogenetic factors also indicate that some ethnic groups, particularly Indians of the Western Hemisphere, have lower tolerances for alcohol than other groups do, putting them at greater risk for alcoholism, and that some Asian populations have highly negative physiological reactions to alcohol, which tend to diminish their risk of becoming alcoholics (Schuckit & Jefferson, 1999).

Socioeconomic Factors.   Drinking appears to be most frequent among younger men at higher socioeconomic levels and least frequent among older women at lower levels. Members of the higher socioeconomic classes drink to excess less often; heavier drinking is found at lower socioeconomic levels and among young people (Kandel, 1991). When drinking is analyzed by occupation, however, a different pattern emerges: Business and professional men are most likely to be heavy drinkers, whereas farmers are least likely to drink heavily. Among women, service workers drink most heavily.

Gender.   Recent decades have seen a dramatic increase in alcoholism among adult women. There are several possible explanations, but research has focused on the differences between female and male alcoholics. For both sexes, social factors—the presence of alcoholism in the family, childhood unhappiness, and trauma—are important influences. But for women, increasing rates of alcoholism seem to be related to their entry into the labor force in large numbers. One study found that married working women are more likely to become alcoholics than homemakers or single working women. Yet the statistics on female alcoholism may be misleading. As women have become more visible in society, their drinking patterns have become more visible. Perhaps researchers are only now learning to identify the female alcoholic, and many women may still be hiding their drinking problems at home. Moreover, even if there has been an increase in alcoholism among women, it remains true that women have far fewer drinking problems than men do.

Binge drinking—consumption of large amounts of alcohol over an extended period—is a particularly dangerous behavior pattern because it often leads to violence, auto accidents, and other major problems. Bingeing is at least three times more common among male drinkers and among heavy drinkers regardless of gender. But binge drinking by pregnant women is a particular problem because of the resulting danger to fetal health. Recent studies show that between 1991 and 1995 the prevalence of binge drinking by pregnant women increased significantly, from 0.7 percent to 2.9 percent, whereas the prevalence among nonpregnant women showed little change (11.3 percent vs. 11.2 percent) (Ebrahim, 1999).

Age.   Heavy drinking among men is most common at ages 21–30; among women, it occurs at ages 31–50. In general, older people are less likely than younger people to drink, even if they were drinkers in their youth. (Drinking among young people is discussed more fully in the next section.) Drinking among the elderly is a hidden social problem, however, especially because statistics on alcohol use suggest that drinking diminishes with age. As a larger portion of the population is elderly, the absolute number of problem drinkers in this population segment increases even if the proportion of heavy drinkers (five or more drinks per day) is lower than in other age groups.

Religion.   Regular churchgoers drink less than nonchurchgoers. However, within the former group, Episcopalians drink most heavily and conservative and fundamentalist Protestants drink most lightly. More Catholics than members of other religions are heavy drinkers, whereas fewer Jews are heavy drinkers. One study linked the low rate of problem drinking among Jews with informal processes of social control such as the association of alcohol abuse with non-Jews and a set of techniques for avoiding excess drinking under social pressure (Glassner & Berg, 1980).

Cultural Influences.   Among some groups, alcoholic beverages are normally drunk in moderate amounts at meals. Members of other groups drink after meals or on other occasions, sometimes to the point of drunkenness. It is the latter custom that seems to promote alcoholism, as is illustrated by a comparison of American Jews and Italian Americans, who customarily drink with meals and in the home, and Irish Americans, who are more likely to drink outside the home and/or not at meals. Most Jewish and Italian adults use alcohol and report having done so since childhood, but their rate of alcoholism is quite low; among the Irish, childhood drinking is less likely and alcoholism rates are much higher. One study (Vaillant, 1983) found that Irish Americans are seven times as likely as those of Mediterranean descent (e.g., Italians and Greeks) to be alcoholics.

The correlation between familial drinking patterns and alcoholism has been found to hold true for other groups as well. In ethnic groups in which drinking habits are established by cultural custom, alcohol abuse is rare. But in groups with ambivalent attitudes toward alcohol, including American Protestants and Native Americans, alcoholism rates are high; in particular, drinkers from groups in which alcohol is seldom used are most likely to encounter problems (Chafetz, 1972). In general, when children grow up with routine, comfortable exposure to alcohol within the family, they are very unlikely to become excessive drinkers when they become adults. Indeed, "the power of the group to inspire moderation of consumption is perhaps the most consistent finding in the study of addictive behavior" (Peele, 1987, p. 189).

In the past two decades there has been a marked decline in drinking, especially of hard liquor, in many segments of the American public. This is especially true among upwardly mobile members of the middle class. The consumption of distilled spirits declined dramatically during the 1980s, and the consumption of beer also fell. Despite these significant declines, however, rates of alcohol consumption in the United States remain extremely high, and newer products like wine coolers and specially promoted malt liquors threaten to diminish the downward trend in alcohol consumption.

Marketers of alcoholic beverages have attempted to address the problems associated with alcohol consumption through advertising that promotes "moderate" or "responsible" drinking. However, one study identified a number of problems with such ads (Dejong, Atkin, & Wallack, 1992). Slogans like "Know when to say when" and "Drink safely" tend to ignore or gloss over the fact that no level of alcohol consumption is completely risk free; moreover, they do not place sufficient emphasis on the need for some people—drivers, pregnant or nursing women, and people using other drugs—to abstain totally. The ads themselves often undermine the message they are trying to convey; for example, they reinforce the idea that beer consumption is a reward for hard work, a form of escape, a means of promoting romance, and a way of obtaining comradeship, acceptance, and social identity (Kilbourne, 1991; Postman et al., 1987). They also seem to imply that abstinence is not socially acceptable.

Drinking Among Young People

In the 1970s and 1980s there was a marked increase in alcohol consumption among teenagers and young adults. As early as 1974 Morris Chafetz noted that "the switch is on. Youths are moving from a wide range of other drugs to the most devastating drug—the one most widely misused of all—alcohol" (quoted in *Time,* April 22, 1974, p. 75). Today teenage and preteenage drinking is widespread; in fact, alcohol is the most widely used drug among young people. Recent national data demonstrate that 39.7 percent of Americans between the ages of 12 and 17 have used alcohol; the proportion of 12-to-17-year-olds who reported current alcohol use (at least once in the past month) stood at 20.5 percent in 1997 (*Statistical Abstract,* 1999).

Teenagers who are defined as problem drinkers include those who have had confrontations with teachers or the police because of their drinking. Of these, only a relatively small percentage can be defined as chronically alcoholic. Alcoholic teenagers differ from other adolescent drinkers in that they drink more often and consume greater quantities, often with the intention of getting drunk; they are also more likely to drink alone, to display aggressive or destructive behavior, and to have severe emotional problems.

The popularity of alcohol among young people is attributed to many factors, including the difficulty, expense, and danger of obtaining other drugs; low legal drinking ages; and the manufacture and advertisement of products that are especially appealing to the young, such as sweet wines and alcoholic beverages that resemble milk shakes. Alarmed at the increase in traffic fatalities caused by young drunk drivers, many states have passed laws in recent years that raise the minimum age for the purchase of alcoholic beverages.

Drinking among young people can also be construed as a rebellion against the adult world—an attempt to assert independence and imitate adult behavior. Some authorities believe that strict regulations on drinking only make it more appealing. Moreover, prohibition of drinking by the young is extremely difficult in a society in which alcohol is widely used and relatively easy to procure.

Many young people turn to alcohol for the same reasons that their parents do: to have a good time, to escape from the stress of everyday life, and to conform to social norms. A recent study compared teenage males who abstain with those who drink in varying amounts; it found that those whose fathers are nondrinkers are most likely to abstain, but that abstainers tend to have fewer close friends. Moreover, abstainers tend to become somewhat isolated from their peers, the large majority of whom consume alcohol at social gatherings (Leifman, Kuhlhorn, & Allebeck, 1995).

It is estimated that about 3 million people between the ages of 14 and 17 have problems related to the use of alcohol.

Alcohol-Related Social Problems

Excessive use of alcohol contributes to many different social problems: murder, family violence and divorce, suicide, ruined health, fetal death, and many more. The United States spends approximately $130 billion annually on problems related to alcoholism (Carson-DeWitt, 1999). In this section we briefly describe a few of these problems.

Health. On average, alcoholics can expect to live 10 to 12 fewer years than nonalcoholics. There are several reasons for this shortened life span. First, alcohol contains a high number of calories and no vital nutrients. Thus, alcoholics generally have a reduced appetite for nutritious food and inevitably suffer from vitamin deficiencies; as a result, their resistance to infectious diseases is lowered. Second, over a long period, large amounts of alcohol destroy liver cells, which are replaced by scar tissue; this condition, called cirrhosis of the liver, is the eighth most frequent cause of death (over 25,000 cases a year) in the United States (*Statistical Abstract,* 1999). Heavy drinking also contributes to heart ailments, and there is some evidence that alcohol contributes to the incidence of cancer. Finally, alcohol is implicated in thousands of suicides every year.

Drinking and Driving. Tests of the amount of alcohol in the blood of drivers involved in accidents have found a significant connection between alcohol and vehicular accidents. According to the National Institute on Alcohol Abuse and Alcoholism (1994), drinking by a driver, a passenger, or a pedestrian is a factor in about 40 percent of all traffic fatalities. The relationship between alcohol use and accident rates at different times of the day and week is shown in Figure 5–3.

Alcohol and Arrest Rates. In 1997, 1,724,300 arrests, or 11 percent of all nonserious crimes, involved drunkenness or an offense related to violations of the liquor laws (*Statistical Abstract,* 1999). These criminal acts were minor, such as breaches of the peace, disorderly conduct, vagrancy, and so on. In arrests for major crimes, drunkenness generally does not appear in the charges, although alcohol often contributes to

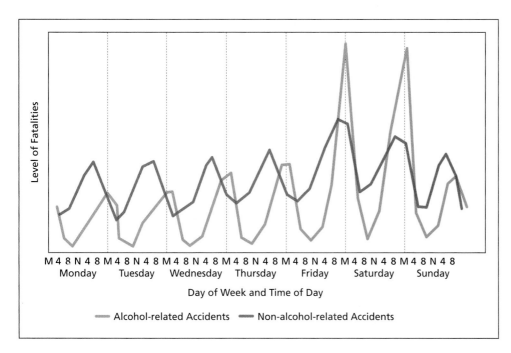

Figure 5–3 Number of Fatalities by Day of Week, Time of Day, and Alcohol Involvement

Note: Although the number of all fatalities decreased slowly during the 1980s, the same proportional relationships by day of the week and time of day held into the 1990s.

Source: U.S. Department of Health and Human Services, 1983.

criminal acts. In many homicide cases, alcohol is found in the victim, the offender, or both; each year thousands of homicides are linked to alcohol use. A significant percentage of male sex offenders are chronic alcoholics or were drinking at the time of the offense. The rates for drinking in relation to skilled property crimes, such as forgery, appear to be somewhat lower than the rates for violent and sex-related crimes.

The reasons for the high correlation of drinking with arrests for serious crimes are not fully understood. It has been pointed out that alcohol, by removing some inhibitions, may cause people to behave in unaccustomed ways. Also, as with other drugs, the need to obtain the substance may lead to theft or other property crimes and sometimes to violent crimes like armed robbery. Since chronic alcoholics may be unable to hold steady jobs, their financial difficulties are compounded, perhaps increasing the temptation to commit crimes. Also, the values and self-image of chronic heavy drinkers tend to change as their condition worsens. They are more likely to associate with delinquents or criminals, which may lead them to commit criminal acts themselves.

In addition to its link with serious crimes, alcoholism creates another problem; it places a major strain on the law enforcement system, which must process large numbers of petty offenders. Arrests, trials, and incarcerations of offenders cost taxpayers billions of dollars each year. And many of these arrests involve a small segment of the community—the neighborhood drunk or derelict who may be repeatedly arrested and imprisoned briefly during the course of a year.

Effects on the Family. If the only victims of alcoholism were the alcoholics themselves, the social effects would be serious enough; but other people, especially the families of alcoholics, also suffer. The emotional effect, which is part of any family crisis, is heightened when the crisis itself is socially defined as shameful. The effects of "acts of God," such as fires, illnesses, and accidents, on a family elicit sympathy, but those of alcoholism produce negative reactions. The children of an alcoholic parent frequently develop severe physical and emotional illnesses, and marriage to an alcoholic frequently ends in divorce or desertion. Finally, since alcoholics are often unable to hold jobs, the outcome may be poverty for their families.

Families of alcoholics often cease to function well because of a pattern known as **codependency.** The spouse of the problem drinker, and often the children as well, frequently participate in a pattern of interactions designed to excuse the problematic behavior. Without thinking about it, they may aid the drinker in his or her behavior through various forms of denial. They may even help supply the drinks in an effort to reduce conflict or ease pain. As a result of these activities, they may themselves become dependent on alcohol, despite its negative effects on the family. In many instances the children, too, become problem drinkers later in life.

Alcoholism and Homelessness.   Contrary to popular belief, only about 5 percent of all alcoholics and problem drinkers are homeless vagrants; most have jobs and families. Several theories have been advanced to explain the differences between the alcoholics who end up homeless and those who do not. Homeless alcoholics often want to separate themselves from their past, as well as to drink. Lack of social affiliation, a feeling that usually exists for a long time before the person finally becomes a derelict, is another likely cause. Homeless alcoholics have a strong need to escape from the realities of social life—an escape that is provided by chronic drinking (P. H. Rossi, 1989a).

Additional evidence suggests that in some cases alcoholism itself helps produce homelessness. In a study of homeless male alcoholics in Baltimore, 59 percent of those interviewed said that drinking itself had led them to become homeless (Shipley, Shandler, & Penn, 1989). Many other homeless men and women are alcoholics who formerly lived in single-room occupancy hotels; when the hotels were closed by urban redevelopment, they were cast out onto the streets (Kasinitz, 1989). Life on the streets for alcoholic men and women is extremely stressful and accounts for rates of heart disease that are three times higher than rates for normal populations at equivalent ages (Ober, Carlson, & Anderson, 1997). In the less developed regions of the world, there is also growing evidence that alcoholism is associated with a range of other social problems, including homelessness and the emergence of public drunkenness in urban centers (Beckman, 1995).

Treatment of Alcholism

Rehabilitation.   Alcoholism is increasingly viewed as an illness with a variety of psychological and physiological components; therefore, it is possible to rehabilitate, but not completely cure, many alcoholics (National Institute on Alcohol Abuse and Alcoholism, 1995). A variety of nonpunitive attempts have been made to assist alcoholics in overcoming their addiction or habituation and to help alcoholism-prone individuals to handle disturbing emotions and anxieties. The Comprehensive Alcohol Abuse and Alcoholism Prevention, Treatment and Rehabilitation Act of 1970 created the National Institute on Alcohol Abuse and Alcoholism (to coordinate federal government activities) and the National Advisory Council on Alcohol Abuse and Alcoholism (to recommend national policies). The act also provided grants to states for the development of comprehensive programs for alcoholism, grants and contracts for specific prevention and treatment projects, and incentives for private hospitals that admit patients with alcohol-related problems.

Traditionally, hospitals offered little beyond the "drying out" and release of alcoholic patients; they might treat a specific medical problem caused by alcohol but not alcoholism itself. The American Hospital Association now advocates hospital alcoholism programs and is attempting to utilize the resources of general hospitals in community treatment programs.

Alcoholics Anonymous.   The most impressive successes in coping with alcoholism have been achieved by Alcoholics Anonymous (AA). The effectiveness of this group in helping individual alcoholics is based on what amounts to a conversion. Alcoholics are led to this experience through fellowship with others like themselves, some of whom have already mastered their problem while others are in the process of doing so.

The organization insists that drinkers face up to their shortcomings and the realities of life and, when possible, make amends to people they have hurt in the past. The

SOCIAL PROBLEMS ONLINE

Youth and Alcohol on the Internet

The Internet is a valuable resource for exploring the social and medical problems associated with youthful alcohol consumption. The National Council on Alcoholism and Drug Dependence (NCADD) offers a concise but well-documented overview, Youth and Alcohol, which can be accessed at **http://www .ncadd.org/youthalc.html.** This site stresses the negative health and safety consequences of drinking by young people, as well as highlighting some of the usage patterns and attitudes of the young toward alcohol. Graphic illustrations of some of the same points can be found at **http://www.ria.org/findings/youth.htm,** the address of the Research Institute on Addictions.

The physiological effects of alcohol consumption, including those related to blood alcohol concentration, are detailed at **http://www.paranoia.com/drugs/ alcohol/.** The American Society of Addiction Medicine has a medical model of alcoholism, which can be found at **http://www. ncadd.org/defalc.html.** The address of Alcoholics Anonymous (AA), the world's largest organization concerned with alcoholism, is **http://www.alcoholics-anonymous.org.** Reflecting its

international breadth, AA presents a self-test on alcoholism, information for professionals, and a fact file in English, French, and Spanish.

The World Health Organization has an annotated list of its publications on European policy approaches to alcoholism control; several that address young people can be found at **http://www.who.org/programmes/pll/ dsa/newpub/sub.htm#you.** The Netherlands Institute for Alcohol and Drugs (NIAD) emphasizes a "harm reduction" approach to alcohol and drug abuse. Its site at **http://www. niad.nl** contains a wide range of international links to online academic journals, research institutes, news groups, and organizations interested in alcohol, tobacco, and drug use. Despite its emphasis, the links provided by NIAD represent an eclectic mix of approaches, ranging from strict prohibition to decriminalization.

The industry trade group DISCUS, the Distilled Spirits Council of the United States, has a policy of strong opposition to underage drinking. Its website, Underage Drinking: Perception Versus Reality (**http:// www.discus.org/underage.htm**), argues that the "number and proportion of youths drinking alcohol have declined significantly over the past ten years."

---

movement also concentrates on building up alcoholics' self-esteem and reassuring them of their basic worth as human beings. Since its founding in 1935, the group has evolved a technique in which recovered alcoholics support and comfort drinkers who are undergoing rehabilitation. This support is also available during crises, when a relapse seems likely, and on a year-round basis through meetings that the alcoholic may attend as often as necessary.

Alcoholics Anonymous has created special groups to deal with teenage and young adult drinkers. It has also established programs to aid nonalcoholic spouses and the children of alcoholics. Alateen, for example, is for young people whose lives have been affected by someone else's drinking. The alcoholic need not be a member of AA for relatives to participate in these offshoot programs, which developed out of the recognition that an entire family is psychologically involved in the alcohol-related problems of any of its members.

It appears that AA is the most successful large-scale program for dealing with alcoholism. According to the AA credo, it is essential for addicts to acknowledge their lack of control over alcohol use and to abstain from all alcoholic beverages for the rest of their lives. This approach sees alcoholism as an allergy in which even one drink can produce an intolerable craving for more. Although precise figures are not available, it seems that more than half the individuals who join AA with a strong motivation to cure themselves are rehabilitated (Chafetz & Demone, 1972). The voluntary nature of the program probably contributes to its success; however, it is unlikely that this approach, with its insistence on total abstinence, could be applied successfully to all alcoholics. This is especially true of alcoholics who reject the spiritual tenets of AA, which teach the recovering alcoholic to seek help from a "higher power," whatever that may mean to the individual. Alcoholics who are unwilling to accept these tenets can often find programs that are related to the 12 steps of the AA program but eliminate the spiritual aspects.

Antabuse.   Antabuse, a prescription drug, sensitizes the patient in such a way that consuming even a small quantity of alcohol causes strong and uncomfortable physical symptoms. Drinkers become intensely flushed, their pulse quickens, and they feel nauseated.

Before beginning treatment with Antabuse, the alcoholic is **detoxified** (kept off alcohol until none shows in blood samples). Then the drug is administered to the patient along with doses of alcohol for several consecutive days. The patient continues to take the drug for several more days, and at the close of the period another dose of alcohol is administered. The trial doses of alcohol condition the patient to recognize the relationship between drinking and the unpleasant symptoms. (Similar treatment programs depend on different nausea-producing drugs or electric shock to condition the patient against alcohol; this process is known as **aversion therapy** or **behavior conditioning.**)

Antabuse (or Disulfiram) has gained only limited acceptance in the treatment of alcoholics. Critics claim that its effect is too narrow and that this approach neglects the personality problems of the drinker. They also maintain that the drug does not work for people who are suspicious of treatment or have psychotic tendencies.

Other Programs.   A problem drinker or alcoholic who receives help while remaining in his or her family and on the job usually responds better than one who is institutionalized. Community care programs treat these problem drinkers, as well as their families, in an effort to improve their self-image and enhance their sense of security within the family.

Employee assistance programs, a relatively new development, have demonstrated considerable effectiveness in treating problem drinkers in the workplace. Their success depends on their availability on a scheduled basis and during crises, on the maintenance of absolute confidentiality, and on the development of rapport between the counselor and the patient as they explore underlying psychological problems such as loneliness, alienation, and poor self-image. Also important is the patient's desire to remain in the community and to continue working (Lyman, 1996).

The Johnson Intervention.   The Johnson intervention, a technique for intervening in the lives of alcoholics or drug abusers, is one of many "tough love" strategies that have emerged in recent years. In this approach, members of a person's social network confront the individual about the damage his or her drinking (or drug use) has caused and the action they will take if treatment is refused. In a study of its effectiveness, researchers found that those who had been subjected to the Johnson intervention were more likely to enter treatment than members of any of the other four groups studied. Moreover, people who were subjected to this intense pressure from family and friends were more likely to complete treatment than members of other groups who entered treatment (Loneck, Garrett, & Banks, 1996).

Illegal Drug Use and Abuse
Commonly Abused Drugs

The major categories of illegal drugs are constantly changing as culture and customs change. In eighteenth-century England, the use of tobacco was forbidden; anyone found guilty of consuming it could be punished by such extreme measures as amputation or splitting of the nose. In the United States, cocaine was introduced to the public early in the twentieth century as an additive to a new commercial soft drink,

Coca-Cola. Today the use of illegal drugs embraces an extremely diverse set of behaviors, ranging from recreational use of marijuana to heroin addiction. The most commonly used drugs today, in addition to alcohol, are marijuana, cocaine, the opiates (including heroin and morphine), hallucinogens, amphetamines, and barbiturates. Marijuana use was so widespread in the 1980s that the U.S. Department of Agriculture estimated that the plant ranked among the top five cash crops in some states. The use of cocaine has increased dramatically in recent years, and heroin continues to find a ready market in the United States. The spread of the smokable form of cocaine known as crack is the latest in the series of drug epidemics that have swept North America since World War II.

As the crack epidemic wanes, there are indications that heroin use is increasing. Heroin is especially popular among former cocaine addicts. In addition, some young people are again experimenting with psychedelic drugs like LSD and XTC. In short, trends in drug use change quite rapidly, but the most serious social problems associated with illegal drug use have always stemmed from drugs that cause severe psychological and physiological addictions, especially the opiates, cocaine, and amphetamines (Fields, 1999).

Marijuana. Like alcohol, marijuana is a social drug, one that is often used in social gatherings because it is thought to ease or enhance interaction. This accounts for its popularity among the young, who in the 1960s considered it the hallmark of rebellion, as well as among many members of the middle and upper classes. Because the use of marijuana is widespread and there is little evidence that it has detrimental long-term effects or leads to the use of stronger drugs, the federal government has shifted its enforcement efforts to the more clearly addicting drugs. At the same time, the eradication of marijuana crops in the western United States and the interdiction of bulk shipments from the Caribbean and Mexico have reduced supplies, and some dealers have turned to trafficking in more dangerous but less bulky drug products like crack cocaine.

Cocaine. Cocaine, which produces a sense of greater strength and endurance and a feeling of increased intellectual power, can cause paranoid psychoses when taken in large quantities over time. Until the 1980s, because of its high street price, cocaine was viewed as an upper-class indulgence, a pastime of celebrities like actor John Belushi (who died from an overdose). Over the past decade or more, cocaine use has become more prevalent in the middle and working classes.

Crack is a form of cocaine that can be smoked rather than ingested through the nasal passages. Commercial cocaine is "cooked" with ether or bicarbonate of soda to form a "rock" of crack. When it is smoked, crack produces an instant and extremely powerful rush that tends to last only about 15 minutes and to cause a strong desire for another rush. This form of cocaine is therefore highly addicting.

Crack is more expensive than cocaine in its powder form, and its use is often associated with an expensive lifestyle. Perhaps for this reason, some athletes, movie stars, and politicians who previously used cocaine have become addicted to crack, with disastrous consequences in some cases. At this writing there is evidence that the crack epidemic has peaked, but the violence associated with the distribution and sale of crack continues. In addition, the birth of sickly, low-weight babies with

Use of the smokeable form of cocaine known as crack led to a high frequency of neurological disorders and seizures among chronic users in the late 1980s and early 1990s.

cocaine addictions formed in utero is a serious problem in communities where the effects of the crack epidemic are still being felt.

Heroin.   Most heroin users experience a sudden, intense feeling of pleasure; others may feel greater self-esteem and composure. But because heroin slows brain functions, after the initial euphoria the addict becomes lethargic. The acknowledged relationship between crime and heroin addiction results not from the influence of the drug but from the suffering caused by the lack of it: Withdrawal symptoms are avoided at all costs. Since addicts are seldom employable and a single day's supply of heroin may cost more than $100, most of an addict's day is usually devoted to crime, especially property crimes.

The typical lower-class heroin addict is under 30, lives in an urban area, has serious health problems, and has a greatly reduced life expectancy. The addict frequently suffers from malnutrition, as well as from hepatitis, AIDS, and other infections caused by intravenous injection of the drug. In communities where heroin addicts are numerous and visible, there is often conflict over the advisability of providing free needles so that addicts will not be forced to share illegally purchased hypodermics and risk the mixing of blood that may contain the HIV virus.

Hallucinogens.   Hallucinogens, such as lysergic acid diethylamide (LSD), distort the user's perceptions. Despite frequent warnings about "bad trips," studies indicate that long-term adverse reactions to LSD occur primarily when the user has preexisting mental problems. There are no data to indicate that the drug can cause either physical or emotional dependence (Ray, 1996).

Amphetamines.   Amphetamines—called "uppers" because of their stimulating effect—are legal when prescribed by a physician, and many people become addicted to them through medical use. In some cases an overdose of one of these drugs can cause coma, with possible brain damage or even death. Amphetamine psychosis is likely to occur when amphetamines are used in high doses over a long period, and abrupt withdrawal may cause suicidal depression in a heavy user.

In young children, some amphetamine-type drugs actually decrease activity and may improve attention span. These drugs are often prescribed for hyperactive children and children diagnosed with attention deficit disorder. Ritalin, the drug most often prescribed in these cases, is the subject of a growing controversy among specialists in child development and education. International medical experts have criticized American physicians for prescribing pills to improve children's behavior without first attempting behavioral therapies. Parents often report that the medication has enormously positive effects on their children's performance in school and their social adjustment with peers. Still, the growing use of these drug therapies is alarming to some experts, who note that Americans took more than 350 million doses of Ritalin in 1996, an increase of 50 percent since 1994 (Kiernan, 1996; Murray, 1998).

Barbiturates.   Barbiturates depress the central nervous system. Prolonged barbiturate use and high dosages can cause physical dependence, with symptoms similar to those of heroin addiction. Indeed, many drug experts believe that barbiturate addiction is even more dangerous and more resistant to treatment and cure than heroin addiction.

A barbiturate overdose can cause poisoning, convulsions, coma, and sometimes death. In fact, in the United States barbiturates are a leading cause of accidental death by poisoning, largely because they tend to heighten the effect of alcohol. Taken in moderate doses, barbiturates, like alcohol, have a mildly disinhibiting effect; however, other personality changes show no consistent pattern. The barbiturate user may be calmed and relaxed—reactions that are normally associated with a depressant—or lively and convivial.

People frequently develop a habit of using both amphetamines and barbiturates, either together or alternately. Combined amphetamine and barbiturate use makes the normal rhythm of life, the alternation of rest and wakefulness, meaningless. It is replaced by chemical cycle of consciousness through "ups," produced by amphetamines, and "downs," produced by barbiturates. Such chemical regulation of activity, if prolonged, causes severe physical and psychological deterioration.

Patterns of Drug Abuse

Who Uses Drugs?   The opportunity to use drugs is among the most important factors in illicit drug use. The National Institute on Drug Abuse (1980) reports that acquaintance with a user precedes the first experience with drugs. Although most people who use drugs are likely to pass up the first opportunity to do so, they take advantage of subsequent opportunities. Among professionals, doctors are most likely to use drugs and to become addicted to them because they have the most knowledge about these substances, as well as access to them. For the general public, opportunity and lifetime experience with drugs (more than one or two "experiments") are strongly related to age. Older teenagers and young adults are more likely to use drugs than older adults, and the younger a person is at the time of the first opportunity, the more likely he or she is to eventually try the drug (Landry, 1996; Ray, 1996).

The study of drug use in the United States is a social-scientific undertaking of great magnitude. The data come from two major sources. The first source includes reports from public and private agencies that deal with arrest, hospitalization, treatment, or legal matters. These reports offer important evidence about trends in drug use among individuals arrested for crimes or admitted to hospital emergency rooms. But they do not tell us very much about the distribution of drug use in the general population. This information is obtained from large-scale national surveys, the second source.

In an annual survey, Monitoring the Future, conducted by the Institute of Survey Research at the University of Michigan, more than 16,000 high school seniors are given a self-administered questionnaire (to encourage honesty) about their substance use. Conducted annually since 1975, this survey is an essential barometer of drug use among young Americans. Like all surveys, however, it has its limitations; in particular, it does not sample young people who have dropped out of school, an important population in the study of drug use. Another important survey is the National Household Survey on Drug Abuse, which is sponsored by the National Institute on Drug Abuse. Other surveys that collect information on various aspects of substance use and abuse are quite common, but these two allow us to track patterns of use from year to year.

Data from the national surveys indicate that drug use among young Americans, and among Americans overall, peaked in the late 1970s, declined until the early 1990s, and began rising again after 1993—although by no means to the levels of the late 1970s. All surveys show that alcohol use among teenagers and young adults occurs at twice the rates of any other substance included in national prevalence studies. Analyses of the prevalence research and opinions about use also indicate that there is a pattern of "intergenerational forgetting" that helps explain these trends. As Lloyd D. Johnston, one of the key researchers in the University of Michigan drug studies, has pointed out, "Each new generation needs to learn the same lessons about drugs if they're going to be protected from them. Unless we do an effective job of educating the newer generations, they're going to be more susceptible to using drugs and have their own epidemic" (quoted in Wren, 1996, p. A11).

Johnston and other drug researchers note that there is an inverse, or negative, relationship between teenagers' disapproval of drugs and their use of drugs like marijuana. This relationship is shown in Figure 5–4, which traces the percentage of teenagers who admit to having used marijuana in the last year and the percentage who disapprove of drug use. Clearly, there is an inverse relationship between the two

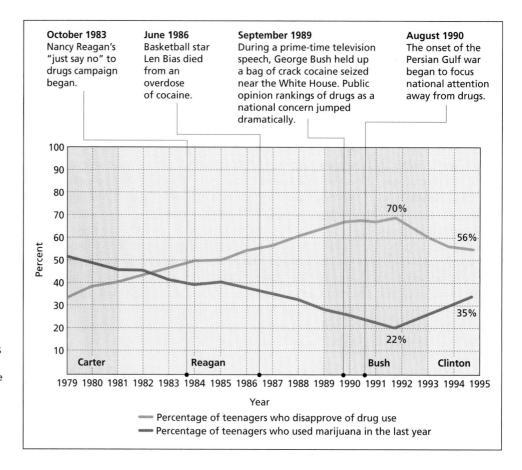

Figure 5–4 Attitudes on Drugs

This chart shows the percentage of twelfth-graders who used marijuana, the percentage of teenagers who say that drug use is socially unacceptable, and significant events involving drug use.

Source: Monitoring the Future Study, University of Michigan Institute for Social Research.

variables: The more teenagers disapprove of drugs, the less they tend to use or experiment with them. The changing curve of disapproval appears to be sensitive both to the campaigns of national leaders and to such events as the arrest of famous athletes who experiment with drugs. In 1999 the Partnership for a Drug Free America, one of the leading public education groups in the movement against drug use, reported a significant increase in the proportion of school-age children who said that drug use is "uncool." On a more pessimistic note, the proportion of students who report that they can easily obtain illicit drugs has not declined appreciably over the past decade.

Marijuana use is an inadequate indicator of teenagers' predisposition to use or experiment with drugs and alcohol more generally. As marijuana use has increased somewhat in recent years, use of cocaine by the same age groups has continued to decline. Also, separate campaigns against tobacco and alcohol may contribute to the belief that of all the possibilities, marijuana is the least dangerous. Frequent use of marijuana can have very negative consequences, especially for young people, because it has been shown to severely diminish the ability to concentrate in school; it can also have deleterious effects on the respiratory system similar to those of tobacco (Brook et al., 1999; Wren, 1996).

Surveys of drug use over time also provide information about its distribution by gender, socioeconomic status, and racial or ethnic background. Table 5–2, for example, clearly shows that there is more drug experimentation and use by men than by women (except among people with higher incomes, for whom levels of use by men and women are more similar). We can see in the table that people with lower incomes have a higher prevalence of illicit drug use in general, as well as a higher prevalence of marijuana and cocaine use. Other studies, however, have found opposite trends. A survey by Denise Kandel and her associates (Kandel, 1991) shows that affluent

TABLE 5–2 Prevalence Rates of Use of Selected Drugs Among Full-time Employed Men and Women Aged 18 to 40 in the General Population, by Sex and Personal Income

Annual Personal Income	Past Month Use of Any Illicit Drug		Past Month Use of Marijuana		Past Month Use of Cocaine	
	Male	Female	Male	Female	Male	Female
Less than $12,000	24.8%	8.4%	22.8%	7.7%	13.9%	5.8%
$12,000 to $19,999	19.6	9.3	18.9	7.4	10.0	7.3
$20,000 to 29,999	15.2	4.3	12.0	3.6	12.5	4.7
$30,000 or over	8.6	10.8	8.1	5.6	9.4	7.8

Source: Kopstein & Gfroerter, National Institute on Drug Abuse.

teenage students are substantially more likely to experiment with and use illicit drugs than those from modest and poor backgrounds. These differences in findings point to the difficulty of judging trends in illicit drug use from a particular survey, especially where students are concerned, since student surveys miss many people who are out of school and, possibly, in the labor force.

Surveys of various racial and ethnic groups show that the prevalence of drug use is higher among whites than among blacks, with Hispanics falling somewhere between the two. Table 5–3, which presents data on cocaine use by ethnic groups, shows these trends quite clearly for most age groups. The figures on annual use and use in the past month reveal that more white than black teenagers are probably frequent users, but this situation is reversed among older age groups. Among adults aged 26 to 34, for example, frequent cocaine users are a far smaller proportion of the population than individuals who have ever used the drug. And among black males in this age group, 5.0 percent had used cocaine in the past month, whereas 1.4 percent of white males had done so. These proportions correspond to the experience of people in black communities, for whom the presence of crack cocaine addicts is perceived as a far more serious problem than it is in white or Hispanic communities. But since there are so many more whites, these proportions indicate that the number of frequent cocaine users is far higher among whites than among blacks or Hispanics.

How Does Drug Use Spread? Most sociologists and social psychologists agree that drug use is a learned behavior that spreads through groups of peers who influence one another. In the pioneering study described in Chapter 1, Howard S. Becker (1963a) traced the career of a marijuana user, showing that users must learn how to smoke the drug and identify their reaction to it as pleasurable. If they are unable to make this identification, they stop using the drug. They also gradually learn that the social controls that work against marijuana use—limited supplies, the need to maintain secrecy, and the definition of drug use as immoral—either do not apply to the peer group or can be circumvented.

The popular view that marijuana is a stepping-stone to stronger drugs is not supported by research. Becker (1963a) found marijuana users to be "noncompulsive and casual" (p. 44), and the National Institute on Drug Abuse (1980) found that in 1979, 30 percent of high school seniors who were using marijuana tried other illicit drugs. Findings from Europe—especially Amsterdam, where marijuana and hashish are legal—confirm the U.S. research, which shows that a minority of marijuana users experiment with more dangerous drugs (Donohew et al., 1999; Ray, 1996).

In explaining the spread of heroin use, Hunt and Chambers (1976) developed a disease model of "initiators" and "susceptible communities" and suggested ways to

TABLE 5–3   Percentage Reporting Cocaine Use in Their Lifetime, the Past Year, and the Past Month, by Age Group, Race/Ethnicity, and Gender

Race/Ethnicity and Gender	Age Group (Years)				
	12–17	18–25	26–34	35+	Total
Sample Size					
White male	(1,142)	(805)	(1,095)	(886)	(3,928)
Black male	(523)	(325)	(412)	(327)	(1,587)
Hispanic male	(627)	(547)	(601)	(455)	(2,230)
White female	(1,107)	(930)	(1,499)	(1,199)	(4,735)
Black female	(561)	(466)	(781)	(615)	(2,423)
Hispanic female	(614)	(539)	(706)	(617)	(2,476)
A. Used Cocaine in Their Lifetime					
White male	1.4%	15.8%	29.6%	10.4%	13.4%
Black male	1.1	5.9	20.2	12.2	11.0
Hispanic male	2.1	14.8	18.7	8.8	11.3
White female	2.3	12.8	23.1	6.0	9.3
Black female	0.4	2.0	11.7	5.1	5.3
Hispanic female	3.3	7.1	7.9	3.0	4.8
B. Used Cocaine in the Past Year					
White male	0.8%	5.0%	4.4%	0.9%	2.0%
Black male	0.6	3.2	8.0	4.9	4.5
Hispanic male	1.4	6.1	6.4	1.4	3.5
White female	1.7	2.7	2.0	0.4	1.0
Black female	0.4	0.5	3.5	1.5	1.6
Hispanic female	1.5	1.2	1.5	1.2	1.3
C. Used Cocaine in the Past Month					
White male	0.3%	1.8%	1.4%	0.3%	0.7%
Black male	[a]	0.9	5.0	1.7	1.9
Hispanic male	0.9	3.8	2.2	0.8	1.7
White female	0.3	0.6	0.7	0.3	0.4
Black female	0.3	0.5	1.8	0.7	0.8
Hispanic female	0.5	0.5	0.4	0.6	0.5

[a]Low precision; no estimate reported.

Source: U.S. Department of Health and Human Services, 1996.

identify and contain the "contagious" individuals. Hunt and Forsland (1980) found that addicts who moved to a Wyoming community from other locations were "not part of a coherent pattern of growing use (as are native users)" (p. 213) and that discontinuity eventually developed between local users and the newcomers because the latter were "not related to the original friendship groups" (p. 214).

More recent research has provided additional evidence that "the most important direct influence on drug use is that of the peer cluster: 'gangs,' best friends, or couples" (Oetting & Beauvais, 1987, p. 133). However, other factors set the stage for involvement in drug-using peer groups. These include the individual's socioeconomic status and neighborhood environment and the influences of family, religion, and school. For example, drug use is more likely when the family is not intact, when the young person has problems in school, or when the family is forced to live in a neighborhood where young people have ready access to drugs and are exposed to deviant role models (Oetting & Beauvais, 1987). Research on the use of addictive drugs, especially crack cocaine, among women indicates that personal traumas such as severe abuse or the loss of an infant can lead to relapse in drug use or to initial use (El-Bassel, Gilbert, & Schilling, 1996).

If the individual's social milieu contributes significantly to drug use, what effect might a change in milieu have? American soldiers who were addicted to heroin in Vietnam were generally able to kick the habit rather easily when they returned home (Robins, 1973). This shows that people are able to abstain from an extremely addicting drug when their social milieu supports nonuse. It is also an example of the phenomenon that drug researchers term "maturing out," that is, the tendency of drug users to decrease their use of drugs of all kinds, including alcohol, beginning in their late 20s (Neff & Dassori, 1998).

Drug Use and Crime

The nature of drug-related crimes varies with the drug involved. According to the classic, and still definitive, study by the National Commission on Marihuana and Drug Abuse (1973), "The only crimes which can be directly attributed to marihuana-using behavior are those resulting from the use, possession, or transfer of an illegal substance." Neither marijuana nor low to moderate use of barbiturates is likely to promote violence, "although high dose use of [barbiturates] has been known to cause irritability and unpredictably violent behavior in some individuals" (p. 159). Amphetamine users, in contrast, seem disproportionately involved in violent crimes such as robberies and assaults, and it is possible that these crimes are "directly attributable to acute reactions to the drug" (p. 160).

Heroin and crack are the drugs most frequently associated with various kinds of criminal behavior. Heroin and crack addicts can rarely support their habit without resorting to crime. In addition, they often already have a criminal history (Inciardi, 1998; Williams, 1992). Studies show that the crimes committed to support a drug habit tend to be money-seeking crimes like shoplifting, burglary, and prostitution. Although these crimes may provide 40–50 percent of the addict's income for drug purchases, one study estimated that almost half the annual consumption of heroin in New York City is financed by selling the drug itself, along with the equipment needed to inject it (Inciardi, 1998). All these crimes, considered to be nonviolent in themselves, nevertheless are often accompanied by violence: "Muggings and armed robberies will be committed regularly by some addicts and occasionally by many; even in burglary, violence may result if the addict is surprised by the victim while ransacking the latter's home or store" (Wilson, 1977, p. 156). The relationship between heroin addiction and crime is supported by evidence that "when the drug users are active in a therapeutic program and presumably not using heroin, criminal activity decreases" (p. 156).

The crack epidemic is also associated with criminal activity. Because crack is produced from large volumes of commercial cocaine, it is expensive; like heroin, it often involves users in the sale of the drug itself or in criminal activities designed to raise money to buy it. In addition, there is evidence that in some communities crack use has led to increases in female prostitution and other crimes (Bourgois, 1995; Inciardi, 1998).

A great deal of evidence indicates that crack and cocaine dealers contributed to the sudden rise in the number of violent deaths and shootings of innocent bystanders in large U.S. cities in the late 1980s and early 1990s (Bourgois, 1989; Williams, 1989). As the crack business became more competitive, with more dealers seeking to serve a steady or somewhat decreasing number of customers, there was increasing violence in communities where retail drug markets thrive. Despite declining murder rates, due in part to an easing of the crack epidemic, we can expect to see continuing use of heavy weaponry in those communities since assault rifles and automatic rifles are readily available to drug dealers and distributors and those who attempt to rob them. (Gun control is discussed in Chapter 7.)

Over 80 percent of all prison inmates have a history of substance abuse, and about 50 percent of those arrested for crimes are drug users (Blanchard, 1999). This close association between crime and substance abuse does not prove that drug use actually causes crime. Other factors, such as early abuse, socialization into a criminal peer group, and the lure of seemingly easy gain, frequently help explain how an individual becomes involved in criminal activities. But drug and alcohol abuse is clearly a contributing or facilitating influence in the majority of cases. Crimes committed by heroin or crack addicts, however, can often be directly attributed to the individual's efforts to obtain money to purchase illicit drugs (Lyman, 1996). Despite this situation, few probationers and prison inmates are enrolled in substance treatment programs (Blanchard, 1999).

It is evident that there are new patterns of organized crime in the illicit drug trade. New organizations that are not associated with older crime "families" have sprung up in American cities. They frequently resort to extreme violence in controlling local drug dealing. In the 1990s there were numerous murders and other violent incidents among Dominican, Vietnamese, Chinese, Colombian, and Russian participants in the organized branches of the cocaine trade, as well as violent killings among native-born Americans of every description.

Drug Use and AIDS

We saw in Chapter 2 that a major means by which AIDS spreads among heterosexual populations is the sharing of needles and syringes by intravenous drug users. In large cities like New York and Moscow, AIDS is a leading cause of death among intravenous drug addicts.

Public health officials were slow to realize the extent of AIDS transmission among intravenous drug users. Hence, they were also slow to initiate educational and other programs that might hinder the spread of the disease in this population. Educational programs that focus on sexual practices are inappropriate for this group; drug treatment programs and efforts to prevent addiction in poor communities are needed (Sullivan, 1987).

Efforts to reach addicts face a number of obstacles. Since their activity is illegal, addicts are reluctant to come forward to be tested for AIDS. Public health workers lack credibility in the eyes of addicts, and attempts to employ ex-addicts in outreach programs encounter resistance from law enforcement personnel. Proposals to give addicts sterile needles on an experimental basis have also been thwarted in many areas. However, needle exchange programs have been tried successfully in New York City and San Francisco, and New York legalized the programs in 1992. Research by Don Des Jarlais and his coworkers in New York showed that as a result of needle exchange programs, especially for heroin users, use of unclean and possibly HIV-infected needles declined from 51 percent to 7 percent. In San Francisco, researchers found that by 1994 almost 64 percent of intravenous drug users had used a needle exchange program within the last year (Paone, Des Jarlais, & Caloir, 1995). These are extremely important findings, but their impact is limited by public opposition to programs that seem to condone drug use.

Outreach programs also face public opposition since it is often believed that narcotics addicts "deserve what they get." But perhaps the greatest obstacle is the attitude of the addicts themselves: "Ninety of 100 guys won't come in [for testing]," said one former addict. "They're either too high or else they're trying to score their fix. They don't want to know if they're sick" (quoted in Freedman, 1987, p. B7).

Treatment of Drug Abuse

Efforts to rehabilitate narcotics addicts have been impeded by the notion that "once an addict, always an addict." Until recently, statistical evidence supported this belief, and the prospects for returning addicts to normal living were bleak. However, drug use spreads through the peer group and may be reversed with a change in social milieu. And drug use does not necessarily follow a predictable course from experimentation to addiction; instead, it encompasses a wide range of behaviors that may include experimentation, occasional use, regular use, and heavy use (Lipton, 1996; Lyman, 1996). These behaviors stem from the interaction of many complex factors, and efforts to rehabilitate addicts have not always addressed all of them. For example, until very recently it was thought that crack was so highly addicting that existing treatment programs and methods could not be effective. However, researchers at the Addiction Research Center in Baltimore have found that crack is less addicting than nicotine but more addicting than alcohol. Nine out of ten people who experiment with cigarette smoking become addicted to nicotine; for crack, the figure is one out of six; and for alcohol, it is one in ten.

Crack addiction responds to the same treatment that other drugs require, but because it is especially appealing to people who are depressed and do not have strong social support from family and nonaddict friends, it is important to try to remove the crack addict from the social milieu in which the drug is used. This is the basic strategy of therapeutic communities.

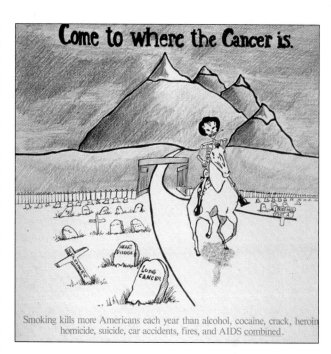

Smoking kills more Americans each year than alcohol, cocaine, crack, heroin homicide, suicide, car accidents, fires, and AIDS combined.

This public-service poster, originally a winner of a school contest, turns a familiar cigarette ad into a powerful warning.

Therapeutic Communities.   Therapeutic communities are a way to attack the high relapse rate of addicts who are detoxified and returned to the larger society. They enable individuals to reenter social life gradually and at their own pace. This reduces the shock of moving from a protective institutional environment to the much greater freedom of the outside world.

One of the most highly developed therapeutic community programs is operated by Phoenix House. In the Phoenix program, addicts who have completed their treatment are transferred to a Re-Entry House for gradual reintegration into everyday life. Educational facilities are part of the program and include training in vocational skills and preparation for entry into other educational programs.

The Phoenix House approach rests on two key precepts: that addicts must assume responsibility for their own actions, and that treatment should address psychological as well as physical difficulties. Phoenix House relies on ex-addicts, who are often more effective in breaking through the barriers of isolation and hostility. In addition, ex-addicts provide living proof that addiction can be overcome. In operation since 1968, the Phoenix House program has helped many addicts recover permanently.

Methadone Maintenance.   Methadone, a synthetic narcotic, has been tested extensively and is now used regularly in treatment programs for heroin addicts. In prescribed amounts it satisfies the addict's physical craving, preventing the agonizing symptoms of withdrawal. Although it does not produce a high, methadone is addicting and therefore offers not a cure but a maintenance treatment for addicts who do not respond to other types of therapy.

Many people, including addicts themselves, believe that methadone keeps addicts dependent on drugs and hence is useful only for a short time while the addict is weaned from heroin. Methadone treatment is sometimes regarded as a form of social control imposed by the dominant culture. (The substance is legally available only through approved programs, which require addicts to report to the treatment center for their daily dosage.) These ambivalent attitudes toward methadone treatment do not seem to deter potential clients. According to one survey, one of the major reasons cited by addicts for not entering treatment earlier was the absence of treatment facilities in their neighborhood (Lipton, 1996).

CRITICAL RESEARCH

The Critical View on Marijuana

Sociologist Lynn Zimmer is deeply embroiled in the drug wars. She and her colleague John Morgani are the authors of a highly acclaimed and criticized study, *Marijuana Myths/Marijuana Facts* (1997). Their research has made them critical of existing drug policies, especially as they apply to marijuana. As Zimmer explains it:

> This costly battle is a waste of government money and human capital. A friend of mine allows his teenage son to smoke marijuana. The boy gets intense nausea from the chemotherapy for his cancer, and marijuana works better than the medications prescribed by his physician. My accountant, a 35-year-old man with AIDS, smokes marijuana before dinner to stimulate his appetite and help him gain weight. A 77-year-old woman who lives near my mother smokes marijuana to treat her glaucoma.
>
> Under federal law and the laws of most states, these people are committing criminal offenses. In 1996, voters in California and Arizona passed referendums to prevent state law-enforcement officials from arresting people who use marijuana as a medicine. Washington State voters recently defeated a drug-policy referendum which, among its provisions, allowed patients access to medical marijuana. In exit polls, however, more than half of those voting "no" said they would have voted "yes" if the initiative had been for medical marijuana alone. Next year, voters in several other states will get to approve or reject proposals to decriminalize marijuana's use as a medicine. Public-opinion poll data available today suggests they overwhelmingly will approve. Still, unless federal law is changed, medical marijuana will remain illegal throughout the United States. (Souder & Zimmer, 1998, p. 24)

In the highly polarized climate surrounding drug policy, with "forcers" pitted against "legalizers," Zimmer comes in for a fair share of harsh criticism. Representative Mark Souder, vice chairman of the House Government Reform and Oversight Subcommittee on National Security, which has focused on the U.S. narcotics problem, argues that Zimmer and others who write favorably

Destruction of narcotics crops—in this case marijuana—is a strategy of the U.S. War on Drugs, which experts consider to be largely ineffective.

about medical marijuana are merely trying to put a "foot in the door" of drug legalization. For Souder, "the ballot box is the wrong place for decisions about efficacy and safety of medicines. The Food and Drug Administration, or FDA, was created to protect the public against snake-oil salesmen, and consumer-safety laws require proper labeling of ingredients and dosages. The sale of crude marijuana circumvents those protections."

For Zimmer and her colleagues, the medical marijuana controversy is merely one among many issues concerning marijuana use that have convinced her that some form of "harm reduction" model, such as that used in Holland, is a better way to deal with this substance. In Holland marijuana is illegal, although its use and possession are generally not prosecuted. The drug is sold in designated coffee shops, but those who abuse the controls over its sale can be prosecuted. Morgan and Zimmer's book shows that, contrary to the claims of opponents of legalization, the Dutch model is working well and has not been associated with increased marijuana use.

Among the nation's major social critics, there has

been some surprising support for Zimmer and Morgan's views. In a recent review of their work, the highly conservative critic William F. Buckley writes:

> Now it's one thing to say (I say it) that people shouldn't consume psychoactive drugs. It is entirely something else to condone marijuana laws the application of which resulted, in 1995, in the arrest of 588,963 Americans. Why are we so afraid to inform ourselves on the question?
>
> Surely legislators who write marijuana laws and judges who sentence marijuana users should inform themselves on these questions? It is terrifying and humiliating to remind ourselves that 10,000 people every week are arrested for marijuana handling because legislators do not pause over evidence as readily obtainable as is now the case in a book that is exemplary, in terms of research graphically presented and concisely rendered, on a large public question. It may be very dumb to use marijuana. But it is surely very wrong for those who inveigh on the question to fail to consult this little book. (1997, p. 63)

Narcotic Antagonists.   Narcotics users who are weaned from their physical addiction often have a psychological craving for drugs as soon as they return to their normal environment. The need to overcome this problem led scientists to develop **narcotic antagonists,** substances that negate the effects produced by the opiates. By counteracting the positive sensations produced by heroin, narcotic antagonists help motivated addicts overcome their psychological conditioning to the drug.

SOCIAL POLICY

Social policies that address drug and alcohol abuse take two main forms. One consists of control strategies—that is, attempts to help individuals or groups control their own behavior—coupled with efforts to build local institutions (e.g., residential treatment centers) that provide helping services. The other is law enforcement, meaning attempts to tighten the enforcement of existing laws or to enact new laws designed to deal with the problem more effectively. Since control strategies were discussed earlier, in the sections on treatment, this section will focus on law enforcement.

The simplest approach to a problem like drug abuse is to crack down on the sale or use of the drug. This was the rationale for Prohibition, in which the manufacture, sale, or transportation of alcoholic beverages was banned in 1919 by an amendment to the U.S. Constitution. Although Prohibition was repealed in 1933, the attitudes that gave rise to this approach are still in evidence. Chronic drinkers are still thrown in jail to dry out; people are still arrested for possession of a single marijuana cigarette; drug addicts still receive heavy jail sentences. In many places treatment is limited to incarceration.

Repeated arrests of chronic alcoholics merely perpetuate a revolving-door cycle. Offenders are arrested, processed, released, and then arrested again, sometimes only hours after their previous release. Each such arrest, which involves police, court, and correctional time, is expensive and may actually contribute to the labeling process in which an excessive drinker becomes an alcoholic and behaves accordingly.

In the 1980s there was considerable pressure for legislation to reduce the number of automobile accidents caused by drunken driving. In 1984 a Gallup poll found that 79 percent of Americans favored a national law that would raise the legal drinking age to 21 in all states because statistics indicate that a large percentage of drunken drivers are under 21. Shortly thereafter, President Reagan signed legislation that would deny some federal highway funds to states in which the drinking age is below 21. Now all states require a person to be 21 or older to purchase liquor and beer (other than 3.2 beer in some states).

In addition to attempting to prevent teenagers from driving while drunk, some states have instituted programs in which motorists are stopped for sobriety checks during holiday weekends. Others require first offenders to participate in education programs that stress that alcohol and driving do not mix. Critics of these efforts point out that most drunk drivers are not social drinkers who have overindulged but chronic alcoholics or problem drinkers. They claim that education programs will not change the behavior of these people; the alcohol addiction itself must be treated. On the other hand, groups like Mothers Against Drunk Driving (MADD) call for strict legal sanctions against people who drink and drive.

Both educational programs and law enforcement efforts seem to have had some effect: In 1985, 25.7 percent of all drivers involved in fatal crashes were found to be drunk, but by 1995 only 19.3 percent were drunk (*Statistical Abstract,* 1999). Authorities attribute this encouraging change to a number of policies, including direct campaigns against drunk driving, federal pressure on states to raise the drinking age, and the tendency of states to lower the amount of blood alcohol in definitions of drunkenness. But they also point out that much remains to be accomplished. Studies by the National Highway Safety Administration show that if more resources were directed at changing the drinking and driving habits of men between the ages of 21 and 35, the high level of annual traffic deaths attributable to drunken driving, currently about 17,500, could be reduced further (Ayers, 1994).

Many observers believe that the drug problem can be eased by revising drug laws so that they deal with issues more realistically and consistently. The most insistent demands for reform have focused on marijuana. It is considered illogical to classify marijuana with the far more dangerous hard drugs, and even people who do not favor legalization of marijuana may support reductions in the penalties for its possession and sale. (See the Critical Research feature on pages 144–145.) So far, however, there has not been a major shift in public opinion toward legalization of marijuana that would allow lawmakers to seriously consider such legislation.

With regard to hard drugs, some experts advocate revision of the law and, in some cases, legalization. One argument for the legalization of heroin is that it would drive down the price of the drug so that addicts would no longer be compelled to engage in crime to support their habit; the British system is cited in support of this position. The British view drug addiction as a disease that requires treatment, and they regulate the distribution of narcotics through physicians and government-run clinics. This system does not give addicts unlimited access to narcotics, but it eases the problem of supply. Those who oppose this approach fear that it might tempt people to experiment with drugs. Moreover, the British system is flawed because many addicts do not wish to register their addiction and prefer to find sources in the illegal drug markets (MacGregor, 1990).

What can be said about legalization is that each year more social scientists and law enforcement officials are taking its possibility seriously (Goode, 1999). As Harvard sociologist Nathan Glazer, a critic of liberal social policies, stated ten years ago, "Is it possible to reduce the intensity of the war against drugs, no great success to date, by some degree of legalization? I'm definitely on the side of let's talk about it" (quoted in Roberts, 1990, p. B1). It should be noted, however, that opposition to legalization is very strong in minority communities, where it is often seen as a form of surrender that is likely to trap even more poor minority people in addiction (Rangel, 1998).

The problem of enforcement at the national level is complicated by issues of foreign policy. Through economic and military aid, the United States supports the

Unintended Consequences

Drug Control in a Borderless World

The economies and political institutions of Mexico, Colombia, Peru, Bolivia, Barbados, and many other nations of the Caribbean and Latin America have been shaken by the rise of international markets for narcotic substances like cocaine. But the problem is not limited to the Western Hemisphere. In Europe and the nations of the former Soviet Union, the easy flow of drugs across relatively porous national frontiers is an ever-increasing problem of public health and national politics (Inciardi, 1998; Stares, 1996).

The relaxation of borders in Europe is a result of efforts to create a common market and improve the flow of goods and services among the European nations. A necessary step in this direction is to reduce border inspections, which has the unintended consequence of making the movement of illegal substances from one nation to another far easier. Marijuana grown in the Netherlands can be transported easily into France or Germany, which have more stringent laws about drug sales. And hard drugs like heroin and cocaine can pass more easily from Italy or Spain into southern France and then into the lucrative markets of central and eastern Europe and Russia.

In the Western Hemisphere it has proven to be extremely difficult to police national borders for drug shipments. As international trade among Canada, Mexico, and the United States has been encouraged as a result of the North American Free Trade Agreement (NAFTA), drug trafficking among these nations has been unintentionally facilitated. Recent scandals in Mexico, for example, reveal that there has been longstanding collusion between some of that nation's highest political officials and international drug dealers. Diminishing public funds for policing the international flow of narcotics also makes it more difficult to stem the flow of drugs across national boundaries.

governments of countries that are major suppliers of illegal drugs, particularly Colombia, Peru, and Bolivia. It has been suggested that the United States should suspend foreign aid to governments that do not cooperate with efforts to stop the flow of drugs into the U.S. market. Other suggestions include imposing trade sanctions on those countries or reducing military assistance. The arrest in 1996 of Mexico's top drug enforcement official on charges of drug trafficking, and the subsequent problems of U.S.–Mexican relations, illustrate the influence of narcotics control efforts on foreign policy. (See the Unintended Consequences feature above.)

An issue that has generated a great deal of controversy is the testing of public employees for drug use. Appeals court rulings have reversed lower court decisions that such testing violates the Fourth Amendment to the Constitution, which protects citizens against "unreasonable searches and seizures." Many private firms are imposing drug (including alcohol) testing on employees in sensitive positions. This trend has become especially prominent since the *Exxon Valdez* oil spill in 1989.

Today drug use remains one of the most serious social problems in the United States. At present there is no fully effective means of dealing with it; drug traffickers have succeeded in overcoming every obstacle placed in their way, and the demand for illegal drugs remains high. Some experts believe that there is no solution to the problem; others are convinced that it would be even worse without existing enforcement efforts. The Clinton administration committed itself to shifting the emphasis of drug policies away from interdiction of supplies, concentrating instead on education about the dangers of alcohol and drug use. These policies and the need for more adequate funding of alcohol and drug treatment programs remain the themes of substance abuse legislation, even as debates over medical uses of marijuana and mandatory drug testing in schools continue unabated.

Beyond Left & Right

Is there really a difference between the views of those on the left (liberals and others) and those on the right (conservatives of most descriptions) about drug and alcohol use and abuse? In fact, there are many differences, although there are no monolithic views on either side of the political spectrum. Too many people have had direct experiences with drug and alcohol problems for this to be a partisan issue. Nevertheless, there are some clear differences among major segments of the population. Think about these issues and choose among the following beliefs:

A. You believe that all kinds of mind-altering substances, from alcohol to most illegal drugs, are immoral and must be strongly prohibited. ———

B. You believe that what people want to drink or ingest is their own business, and the state should have no role in saying what they may buy or use. ———

C. You believe that mind-altering drugs like marijuana and LSD and the opiates and amphetamines are dangerous and need to be controlled, but you approve of moderate social drinking. ———

D. You believe that many drugs that are now illegal are no more or less dangerous than alcohol and should not be prohibited. ———

Do you agree with any of these strong but commonly held opinions? No doubt you do. *A* is likely to be a religious conservative, for example, a Southern Baptist or a follower of Islam. *B* could well be a libertarian who mainly desires less government and regulation; *B* could also be a conservative but more tolerant of different behaviors than *A*. *C* could be on the right or the left. The majority of Americans, spanning all political divisions, drink in moderation (or hope and pretend they do) but feel that society needs to control access to other illegal substances. *D*, who argues against the criminalization of marijuana and other mind-altering drugs, is likely to be on the political left. But some conservatives also support this position.

To go beyond all these differences and divisions one needs to go back to the facts about alcoholism or drug addiction. One needs to consider the ravages of alcohol in families and entire peoples, such as Native Americans. One needs to see the associations between alcohol and drug abuse and poverty and discrimination. These considerations lead to the idea that society as a whole, through its governmental institutions or its civic and community institutions, has a responsibility to devise policies to deal with the problems of alcohol and drug abuse.

SUMMARY

- In sociological contexts, the term *drug* refers to any chemical substance that affects body functions, mood, perception, or consciousness; has a potential for misuse; and may be harmful to the user or to society. Drug abuse is any use of unacceptable drugs and excessive or inappropriate use of acceptable drugs so that physical or psychological harm can result.

- The issue of drug use has objective and subjective dimensions. The objective aspect is the degree to which a given substance causes physiological, psychological, or social problems for the individual or the social group. The subjective aspect involves people's perceptions of the consequences of drug use and how those perceptions result in social action.

- The word *addiction* is used to describe physical dependence on a drug, in which the body has adjusted to its presence. The word *habituation* is sometimes used to mean psychological dependence, in which the user needs the drug for the feeling of well-being that it produces.

- Alcohol use is widely accepted in Western culture, even though its abuse creates many complex problems. There are many problem drinkers and alcoholics (alcohol addicts) in the United States. It is possible that the tendency to become an alcoholic is an inherited trait.

- Drinking is heaviest at higher socioeconomic levels, among men, among non-churchgoers, and in cultures whose members do not normally drink alcoholic beverages with meals. Alcohol is the drug that is most widely used by young people. Older people are less likely than younger people to drink, but as the proportion of elderly people in the population increases, so does the number of problem drinkers and alcoholics among them.

- Social problems related to excessive alcohol use include health problems, automobile accidents, criminal conduct, family disorganization, and homelessness.

- Attempts to help alcoholics overcome their addiction take a variety of forms, including group therapy (e.g., Alcoholics Anonymous), Antabuse programs, community care and employee assistance programs, and direct intervention (the Johnson intervention technique).

- The most commonly abused drugs are marijuana, cocaine and its derivative crack, the opiates, the hallucinogens, the amphetamines, and the barbiturates. Of these, by far the most widely used is marijuana.

- Drug use is largely a matter of opportunity. The younger one is at the time of the first opportunity to try a drug, the more likely one is to eventually try it.

- It is generally agreed that drug use is a learned social behavior. Users must learn how to use the drug and to identify their reactions to it as pleasant. The most important direct influence on drug use is that of the peer group. People can stop using drugs relatively easily if their social milieu does not encourage drug use.

- The drugs that are most frequently associated with criminal behavior are heroin and crack; many addicts cannot hold jobs and must resort to crime to support their habit. Use of crack is also associated with criminal activity and with high rates of murder and violence in large cities.

- The primary means by which AIDS is transmitted among heterosexual populations is the sharing of needles and syringes by intravenous drug users. Efforts to prevent the spread of the virus in this way face a number of obstacles, including legal barriers and public opposition.

- Approaches to the rehabilitation of addicts include therapeutic communities, where individuals prepare to reenter the larger society at their own pace; methadone maintenance, in which a synthetic narcotic is used to wean addicts from heroin; and the use of narcotic antagonists, substances that prevent the euphoria produced by opiates.

- Increased emphasis on law enforcement has not solved the problems associated with abuse of alcohol and other drugs. Many people advocate reform of the law, especially for marijuana use. Some also call for legalization of hard drugs, but this remains a highly controversial issue.

KEY TERMS

drug, p. 122
drug abuse, p. 122
addiction, p. 124
psychological dependence, p. 124

habituation, p. 124
prevalence, p. 125
alcoholics, p. 127
codependency, p. 131

detoxified, p. 134
aversion therapy, p. 134
behavior conditioning, p. 134
narcotic antagonists, p. 145

INTERNET EXERCISE

The web destinations for Chapter 5 are related to different aspects of alcohol and other drugs. To begin your explorations, go to the Prentice Hall Companion Website: **http://prenhall.com/kornblum.** Then choose **Chapter 5** (Alcohol and Other Drugs). Next, select **destinations** from the menu on the left side of the screen. There are a variety of sites to investigate. We suggest that you begin with **Alcoholics Anonymous.** After you have accessed this site, click on "AA Fact File." Here you will find a description of the program and the "Twelve Steps" that are its building blocks. The text points out that AA is the most successful large-scale program in dealing with alcoholism. Suppose you are a person who has a problem with alcohol. Click on "Is AA For You?" After you have explored the Alcoholics Anonymous site, answer the following questions:

- Imagining, once again, that you are a person who has a problem with alcohol, do you feel that Alcoholics Anonymous would be helpful? Why or why not?

- Do you know someone who may have a drinking problem and/or may be an alcoholic? According to the AA credo, it is essential for addicts to acknowledge their lack of control over alcohol use and to abstain from all alcoholic beverages for the rest of their lives. If you know someone who may have a problem with alcohol consumption, do you think this person would benefit from Alcoholics Anonymous? Would you be willing to confront this person regarding his/her use of alcohol? Why or why not?

6 **Crime and Criminals**

CRIME AND CRIMINALS

- In 1998 about 12.5 million violent and property crimes were committed in the United States.

- Crimes reported to the police make up about a third of actual offenses and about half of violent crimes.

- When weapons are involved, guns account for about 60 percent of murders.

- People under 25 account for over 58 percent of all arrests for property crimes.

- Women make up 16 percent of the total prison population in the United States.

OUTLINE

The Nature of Crime
Police Discretion
Problems of Accuracy

Types of Crimes and Criminals
Violent Personal Crimes
Occasional Property Crimes
Occupational (White-collar) Crimes
Corporate Crimes
Public-order Crimes
Conventional Crimes
Organized Crime
Professional Crimes
Juvenile Delinquency
Hate Crimes

Conditions and Causes of Crime
Biological Explanations of Crime
Gender and Crime
Age and Crime
Sociological Explanations of Crime

Controlling Crime
Retribution-Deterrence
Rehabilitation
Prevention

Social Policy
Conventional Crimes
Occupational and Corporate Crimes
Organized Crime
Public-order and Juvenile-justice Reforms

A mericans consistently rank crime among the most serious social problems in the United States. Depending on their concerns about such issues as health care or the state of the economy, they may rank these as more serious problems at a given moment. But for many decades crime has been ranked at or very near the top of the list of major social problems. For the past few years, during a period of sustained economic growth, some crime rates have decreased. The public's perception of crime as a serious social problem has similarly abated, although it remains high on any survey list. But at the same time, as we will see in this chapter, governments at all levels continue to invest heavily in crime control. As a result, the prison population in the United States has reached record proportions.

It is important to realize that at least some crime has existed in almost all societies. As the French sociologist Émile Durkheim (1950) pointed out, wherever there are people and laws, there are crime and criminals:

> Crime is present . . . in all societies of all types. There is no society that is not confronted with the problem of criminality. Its form changes; the acts thus characterized are not the same everywhere; but, everywhere and always, there have been men who have behaved in such a way as to draw upon themselves penal repression. . . . What is normal, simply, is the existence of criminality. (p. 65)

According to the *Uniform Crime Reports* (*UCR*) of the Federal Bureau of Investgation (FBI), between 1997 and 1998 there was a 6 percent drop in the rate of serious crime, following a 3 percent drop in 1996–1997 and a 3 percent drop in 1995–1996. The 1998 rate was 14 percent below the rate for 1994 and 20 percent below the rate for 1989 (*UCR*, 1999). These changes are widely regarded as encouraging but possibly deceptive. Violent crime decreased for adults and the elderly but increased among people under age 25. We will see in this chapter that there are some convincing explanations for these trends but that there is also a good deal of argument among experts about whether they are likely to continue. Another problem is that these statistics are based on reports provided by local police departments, which often contain errors of various kinds.

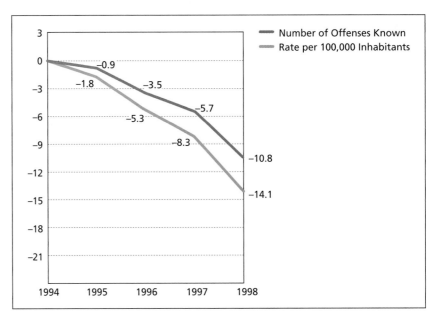

Figure 6–1 Crime Index Total (Percent Change from 1994)
Source: Federal Bureau of Investigation, *Uniform Crime Reports,* 1999.

One reason for the disagreement is that it is extremely difficult to measure actual rates of crime. An annual survey of American households by the U.S. Department of Justice asks respondents detailed questions about their experiences with crime. This survey, known as the National Crime Victimization Survey of the Bureau of Justice Statistics, reveals that the actual rates of violent personal and property crime are several times higher than the official rates presented in the Federal Bureau of Investigation's *Uniform Crime Reports,* which are based on crimes reported to the police. Many victims do not report crimes because they believe that nothing can be done or that the crime was unimportant. Sample surveys of Americans indicate that crimes reported to the police account for about 33 percent of actual offenses and about 50 percent of violent crimes (Bureau of Justice Statistics, 1996b; Reid, 1991).

Even with a large proportion of unreported crimes, statistics showed a rapid increase in crime in the early 1970s. The crime rate continued to increase in the late 1970s, but in the early 1980s it leveled off. Beginning in 1985 there was a steady increase in the absolute number of serious crimes and in the rate of crime per 100,000 inhabitants, which controls for any increase in population size that alone might result in more crime. These trends continued until the early 1990s, when, as just mentioned, the rate of serious crime began to decrease. The number of serious crime offenses reported to the police in 1998 was approximately 12,500,000, of which almost 60 percent were larceny or theft. Violent crimes, including murder, forcible rape, robbery, and aggravated assault, accounted for 12.4 percent of all known crimes in 1998 (*UCR,* 1999). (See Figures 6–1, 6–2, 6–3, and 6–4.)

Sociologists believe that the recent decline in crime rates is a result of the rapid increase in the number of prison inmates, the waning of the crack epidemic in

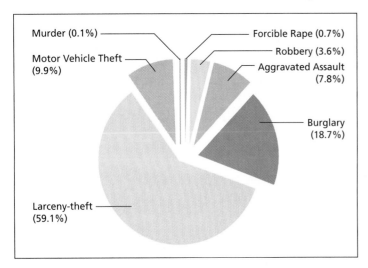

Figure 6–2 Crime Index Offenses, 1998 (Percent Distribution)*
*Percentages do not add up due to rounding.
Source: Federal Bureau of Investigation, *Uniform Crime Reports,* 1999.

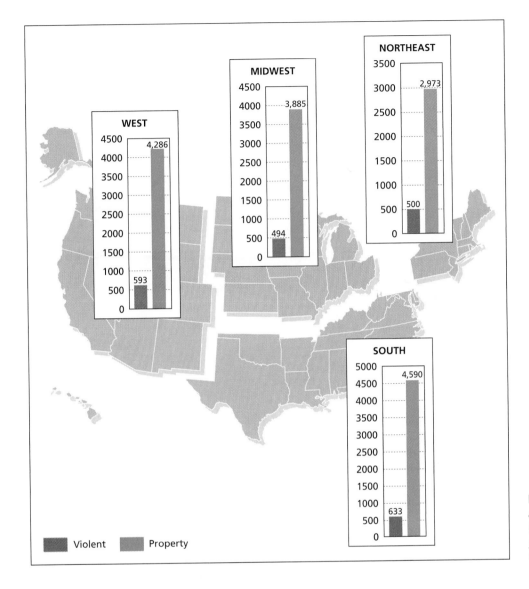

Figure 6–3 Regional Violent and Property Crime Rates, 1998 (Per 100,000 Inhabitants)

Source: Federal Bureau of Investigation, *Uniform Crime Reports,* 1999.

the largest metropolitan centers, and increases in police forces throughout the nation (Krauss, 1996). Nevertheless, although the deceleration of crime rates since the 1970s is most welcome, the rates remain higher that those in European nations.

The extent of the nation's crime problem is measured by the **crime index,** developed in the 1930s by the Committee on Uniform Crime Records of the International Association of Chiefs of Police. The crime index collects data on the most serious and most frequently occurring crimes—those that are most likely to come to the attention of the police. These include murder and nonnegligent manslaughter, forcible rape, robbery, aggravated assault, burglary, larceny-theft, motor vehicle theft, and arson. The statistics reported throughout this chapter are taken from the crime index.

Official statistics, of course, do not tell the whole story. It has never been easy, for example, to assess accurately the extent of organized and occupational (white-collar) crime. Exposures of scandals in government and business show that these types of crimes are far more widespread and pervasive than is generally realized. Not only is the rate of crime itself extremely high, but fear of crime, especially in large cities, significantly affects the lives of many people. Large numbers of Americans feel unsafe in their homes, neighborhoods, or workplaces. Many have stopped going to areas they used to go to at night, and fear of violent crime is widespread.

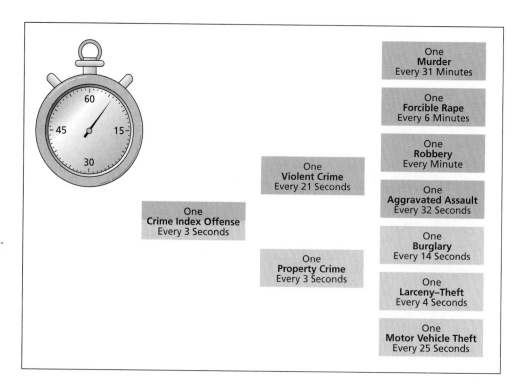

Figure 6–4 The Crime Clock, 1998

The Crime Clock should be viewed with care. Being the most aggregate representation of *UCR* data, it is designed to convey the annual reported crime experience by showing the relative frequency of occurrence of the Index offenses. This mode of display should not be taken to imply a regularity in the commission of offenses; rather, it represents the annual ratio of crime to fixed time intervals.

Source: Federal Bureau of Investigation, *Uniform Crime Reports,* 1999.

Sociologists who study the effects of media coverage of crime report that attitudes about safety in one's neighborhood and about going out at night in the city in which one resides vary directly with the rate of index crimes in that city; however, reports of crimes in other cities make people feel safe in comparison. The reports that are most closely correlated with fear of crime are those describing sensational murders in one's own city, that is, murders that are reported on the front pages of newspapers and on television. Less sensational murders, even in one's own city, do not have a measurable impact (Heath, 1984; Liska & Baccaglini, 1990). Of course, the crimes that are most likely to generate fear are those that directly affect one's family and friends, even if they are relatively minor. (Table 6–1 lists crime rates for selected cities.)

The Nature of Crime

There is no single, universally agreed-upon definition of crime. In the words of one of the world's foremost historians of crime, the late Sir Leon Radzinowicz, crime

> is something that threatens serious harm to the community, or something generally believed to do so, or something committed with evil intent, or something forbidden in the interests of the most powerful sections of society. But there are crimes that elude each of these definitions and there are forms of behavior under each of them that escape the label of crime. The argument that crime is anything forbidden, or punishable, under the criminal law is open to the objection that it is circular. But at least it is clear cut, it refers not to what ought to be but to what is, and it is an essential starting point. (Radzinowicz & King, 1977, p. 17)

According to this argument, a **crime** is any act or omission of an act for which the state can apply sanctions. This is the most frequently used definition of crime and the one we will use in this chapter. However, it should be kept in mind that definitions of crime are subject to changing values and public sentiments; moreover, as we will see

TABLE 6–1   Crime Rates, by Type—Selected Large Cities: 1997

(Offenses known to the police per 100,000 population. Based on Bureau of the Census estimated resident population as of July 1.)

City ranked by population size, 1997[a]	Crime index Total	Violent Crime					Property Crime			
		Total	Murder	Forcible Rape	Robbery	Aggra-vated Assault	Total	Burglary	Larceny—Theft	Motor Vehicle Theft
New York, NY	4,861.6	1,268.5	10.5	29.5	610.7	617.8	3,593.1	739.0	2,145.2	708.9
Los Angeles, CA	5,776.3	1,596.5	16.3	39.9	579.1	961.3	4,179.8	852.7	2,332.6	994.5
Chicago, IL	b	b	27.4	b	914.3	1,320.4	7,008.6	1,469.1	4,324.5	1,215.1
Houston, TX	7,263.6	1,174.5	14.1	43.9	452.2	664.3	6,089.1	1,330.5	3,604.2	1,154.4
San Diego, CA	4,985.6	827.7	5.7	32.5	220.2	569.4	4,157.9	689.9	2,553.9	914.0
Phoenix, AZ	9,608.0	884.9	14.9	36.5	317.7	515.8	8,723.0	1,793.5	5,256.5	1,673.2
Dallas, TX	9,335.8	1,383.8	19.4	69.0	522.0	773.4	7,952.0	1,647.3	4,693.3	1,611.4
San Antonio, TX	8,050.5	401.7	9.2	59.5	196.1	136.9	7,648.8	1,274.5	5,544.3	830.0
Detroit, MI	11,669.1	2,151.5	45.9	94.8	803.6	1,207.3	9,517.6	1,891.9	4,351.9	3,273.8
Honolulu, HI	6,067.4	299.5	3.9	29.2	137.9	128.5	5,768.0	994.6	4,138.5	634.9
San Jose, CA	3,870.2	736.6	5.1	44.6	108.0	578.8	3,133.6	521.2	2,144.2	468.2
Indianapolis, IN	6,743.4	1,132.3	18.7	71.0	427.9	614.8	5,611.1	1,474.2	3,146.9	990.0
San Francisco, CA	6,893.8	1,133.5	7.8	30.9	610.7	484.1	5,760.4	948.4	3,830.5	981.5
Baltimore, MD	10,783.3	2,420.3	43.4	66.7	1,199.2	1,111.1	8,363.0	1,722.5	5,363.2	1,227.2
Jacksonville, FL	8,252.6	1,343.3	10.7	86.3	337.2	909.1	6,909.3	1,756.9	4,382.6	769.8
Columbus, OH	9,735.9	933.5	13.1	108.5	484.0	327.9	8,802.4	2,097.6	5,594.9	1,109.9
Memphis, TN	10,041.7	1,856.7	21.6	147.1	822.0	865.9	8,185.0	2,426.9	3,961.0	1,797.2
Milwaukee, WI	7,587.0	1,053.0	19.4	48.8	565.3	419.4	6,534.1	1,084.8	4,129.5	1,319.8
El Paso, TX	6,960.2	791.3	3.9	36.7	174.0	576.7	6,168.9	530.6	5,055.5	582.8
Charlotte-Mecklenburg, NC	9,409.9	1,630.8	10.5	61.4	483.3	1,075.6	7,779.1	1,852.8	5,146.2	780.1
Boston, MA	6,817.4	1,420.8	7.7	63.1	491.5	858.5	5,396.5	774.9	3,228.7	1,392.9
Seattle, WA	10,350.7	914.1	9.0	39.8	380.3	485.0	9,436.6	1,487.4	6,655.0	1,294.2
Austin, TX	7,870.0	645.7	7.3	51.8	235.1	351.5	7,224.3	1,375.1	5,031.8	817.4
Nashville, TN	11,091.4	1,746.7	21.1	103.4	485.6	1,136.7	9,344.7	1,660.8	6,147.3	1,536.5
Washington, DC	9,827.2	2,023.8	56.9	41.2	850.5	1,075.2	7,803.4	1,316.3	5,056.3	1,430.8
Denver, CO	5,803.4	672.3	13.1	67.7	238.3	353.2	5,131.1	1,227.9	2,806.2	1,097.0
Cleveland, OH	7,455.5	1,458.6	15.5	128.5	772.6	542.1	5,996.9	1,640.3	2,880.4	1,476.2
New Orleans, LA	9,355.8	1,720.3	54.7	78.8	813.1	773.8	7,635.5	1,659.5	4,055.8	1,920.1
Tucson, AZ	9,965.8	1,052.8	10.3	59.9	297.6	685.1	8,913.0	1,424.3	6,085.4	1,403.3
Fort Worth, TX	7,317.8	902.5	15.5	55.5	293.4	538.2	6,415.4	1,375.4	4,187.1	852.9
Portland, OR	11,199.6	1,604.4	9.7	75.2	411.2	1,108.3	9,595.2	1,561.8	6,492.3	1,541.1
Oklahoma City, OK	11,655.6	1,073.0	12.5	86.6	295.9	677.9	10,582.7	2,071.4	7,547.6	963.7
Kansas City, KS	10,952.1	1,895.5	22.1	92.2	599.7	1,181.5	9,056.6	1,911.4	5,502.2	1,642.9
Long Beach, CA	4,898.2	944.5	12.6	28.1	415.1	488.8	3,953.7	964.3	2,039.5	949.9
Virginia Beach, VA	4,482.0	239.7	4.3	23.0	116.0	96.4	4,242.3	673.7	3,358.4	210.2

TABLE 6–1 (continued)

(Offenses known to the police per 100,000 population. Based on Bureau of the Census estimated resident population as of July 1.)

City ranked by population size, 1997[a]	Crime index Total	Violent Crime					Property Crime			
		Total	Murder	Forcible Rape	Robbery	Aggravated Assault	Total	Burglary	Larceny— Theft	Motor Vehicle Theft
Albuquerque, NM	11,118.3	1,317.1	11.4	62.6	401.1	841.9	9,801.2	1,982.0	6,021.4	1,797.8
Atlanta, GA	13,921.6	3,048.5	35.6	87.0	1,128.9	1,797.0	10,873.1	2,181.9	6,821.4	1,869.7
Fresno, CA	9,480.6	1,205.0	15.1	48.4	452.1	689.4	8,275.6	1,673.2	4,796.6	1,805.8
Miami, FL	12,828.8	2,813.7	26.3	48.2	1,153.0	1,586.2	10,015.2	2,283.5	5,771.0	1,960.6
Sacramento, CA	8,890.4	968.2	10.7	41.9	482.1	433.4	7,992.2	1,790.2	4,501.4	1,630.5
Tulsa, OK	7,472.2	1,204.3	10.5	72.8	240.3	880.7	6,268.0	1,666.5	3,629.1	972.4
St. Louis, MO	13,576.7	2,542.5	40.6	59.6	946.9	1,495.4	11,034.1	2,676.7	6,204.6	2,152.8
Oakland, CA	10,100.5	2,184.5	26.3	81.2	924.4	1,152.7	7,915.9	1,572.4	5,019.7	1,323.9
Minneapolis, MN	11,439.5	1,850.1	15.9	147.3	909.0	777.9	9,589.4	2,263.3	5,730.7	1,595.4
Pittsburgh, PA	5,817.7	786.4	14.2	49.5	436.8	285.9	5,031.3	950.9	3,283.2	797.2
Omaha, NE	7,236.2	1,385.4	8.8	50.0	232.6	1,094.0	5,850.8	899.8	3,964.8	986.2
Mesa, AZ	7,730.1	728.5	3.7	35.9	128.4	560.5	7,001.6	1,218.5	4,799.6	983.5
Toledo, OH	8,526.5	823.1	7.7	72.0	337.6	405.9	7,703.4	1,789.9	4,973.8	939.7
Wichita, KS	8,037.9	833.4	10.1	72.2	281.9	469.1	7,204.5	1,510.7	4,976.4	717.5
Buffalo, NY	8,095.4	1,284.5	14.7	73.6	702.6	493.6	6,810.9	1,915.4	3,656.7	1,238.8
Arlington, TX	6,621.7	797.4	4.0	41.8	173.6	577.9	5,824.3	1,007.0	4,141.5	675.8
Tampa, FL	12,260.1	2,663.8	11.7	88.4	846.7	1,717.1	9,596.3	2,202.6	5,983.7	1,410.0
Santa Ana, CA	4,035.9	675.2	9.0	30.5	327.6	308.1	3,360.7	537.6	1,925.2	897.9
Corpus Christi, TX	10,219.0	984.1	6.2	52.9	146.9	778.2	9,234.8	1,500.4	7,173.9	560.6
Anaheim, CA	4,187.9	678.1	5.2	34.5	280.3	358.0	3,509.8	783.7	2,045.3	680.8
Louisville, KY	6,906.7	1,112.2	22.4	46.3	559.0	484.5	5,794.5	1,620.9	3,150.0	1,023.6
Birmingham, AL	9,590.0	1,375.2	39.2	80.7	485.8	769.5	8,214.8	1,884.2	5,110.9	1,219.7
St. Paul, MN	7,909.7	886.6	8.9	85.2	308.3	484.2	7,023.1	1,487.2	4,558.6	977.3
Aurora, CO	6,188.4	621.1	6.4	83.5	187.7	343.5	5,567.4	867.1	3,890.7	809.5
Newark, NJ	10,728.0	2,734.7	21.6	64.3	1,302.5	1,346.4	7,993.3	1,728.2	4,091.3	2,173.9
Anchorage, AK	5,971.4	738.9	9.0	68.1	196.0	465.9	5,232.5	755.4	3,944.3	532.8
St. Petersburg, FL	8,939.1	2,098.4	8.4	80.2	500.9	1,508.9	6,840.7	1,612.7	4,520.1	708.0
Raleigh, NC	7,747.3	907.5	9.3	41.0	292.4	564.8	6,839.7	1,468.3	4,805.9	565.6
Norfolk, VA	7,598.8	974.1	22.2	55.6	476.8	419.5	6,624.8	1,018.8	5,086.0	519.9
Riverside, CA	5,881.2	1,008.2	9.3	39.1	305.1	654.6	4,873.1	1,117.4	2,856.8	898.9

[a] Resident population estimated by the FBI.
[b] The rates for forcible rape, violent crime, and crime index are not shown because the forcible rape figures were not in accordance with national Uniform Crime Reporting guidelines.

Source: Statistical Abstract, 1999.

shortly, factors like police discretion play a major role in the interpretation of particular behaviors as crimes.

The **criminal law** in any society prohibits certain acts and prescribes the punishments to be meted out to violators. Confusion frequently arises because although the criminal law prescribes certain rules for living in society, not all violations of social rules are violations of criminal laws. A swimmer's failure to come to the aid of a drowning stranger, for example, would not constitute a criminal act, although it might be considered morally wrong not to have done whatever was possible to save the victim, short of risking one's own life.

Many acts that are regarded as immoral are ignored in criminal law but are considered civil offenses. Under **civil law**—laws that deal with noncriminal acts in which one individual injures another—the state arbitrates between the aggrieved party and the offender. For example, civil law is involved when a person whose car was destroyed in an accident sues the driver responsible for the accident to recover the cost of the car. The driver at fault is not considered a criminal unless he or she can be shown to have broken a criminal law, for instance, to have been driving while intoxicated. Further confusion results from changes in social attitudes, which usually precede changes in criminal law. In some states, for example, old laws that are still on the books continue to define as criminal some acts that are no longer considered wrong by society, such as certain forms of sexual behavior between consenting adults.

Police Discretion

In addition to problems of definition, such as ambiguity about whether loitering is a crime, certain other factors contribute to the difficulty of knowing what crimes are committed in a particular society. A significant factor is the role of police discretion. In practice, the definition of criminality changes according to what the police believe criminal behavior to be. Given the thousands of laws on the books, police officers have considerable discretion about which laws to ignore, which laws to enforce, and how strongly to enforce them. This discretionary power, in turn, gives them many opportunities to exercise their own concept of lawful behavior in decisions about what complaints merit attention, whom they should arrest, and who should be released.

In an important study of police discretion, Michael K. Brown (1988) compared police activities in two Los Angeles Police Department (LAPD) districts and three suburban towns in the Los Angeles metropolitan region. On the basis of interviews with patrol officers and their supervisors, he concluded that "a police bureaucracy has a significant impact on the behavior of patrolmen. . . . Patrolmen in the two divisions of the LAPD are formalistic and more willing to make an arrest in a variety of incidents than patrolmen in small departments, who are consistently more lenient and less willing to invoke the force of the law in the same circumstances" (p. 275). When asked whether they would normally arrest disorderly juveniles on their beat, for example, 28 percent of veteran police officers with five years or more experience in the smaller departments said that they would not arrest the offenders, whereas 65 percent of the LAPD veteran officers said that they would arrest disorderly juveniles.

Police discretion has become a controversial issue in Los Angeles and other major cities. In Los Angeles, where there are more street gangs than in any other U.S. city, the police have developed a policy of issuing what are known as "gang injunctions." These local policy orders target specific gangs and their members. They order people wearing gang colors off the street, and they ban driving or congregating with other known gang members. This is a response to demands for action to prevent gang crimes. But the wide use of gang injunctions has drawn the criticism of citizens who are concerned about the curtailment of personal liberties and civil rights. The Supreme Court has so far refused to rule on the use of gang injunctions, but the controversy further demonstrates how police discretion can account for important

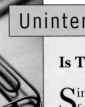

Is There a Case for Discretion?

Since at least 1986 many state and federal regulations severely restrict the discretion of judges in individual sentencing decisions. Perhaps the most controversial of these mandatory sentencing rules is California's "three strikes, you're out" law, under which offenders convicted of their third felony must be sentenced to life imprisonment. Many such laws are in effect throughout the nation, reflecting a more punitive public attitude toward offenders.

On one hand, it appears that mandatory sentencing has the desired effect of making it clear to criminals what the penalties for their actions will be. Criminologists James Q. Wilson and John DiIulio argue that this clarity is partly responsible for the recent decreases in some categories of crime. On the other hand, the majority of the million or more people incarcerated in federal and state prisons are there for drug-related crimes, often as a result of mandatory sentencing. Those convicted of selling crack cocaine have received far stiffer sentences than those convicted of selling powdered cocaine. According to the chief federal drug official, Lee Brown, this disparity in mandatory sentencing reflects class and racial bias since crack is used mainly in poor inner-city neighborhoods. Also controversial are reports that in Florida and other states violent offenders who are serving terms for rape or armed robbery, but not under mandatory sentences, have been released to make room in crowded prisons for drug offenders who are serving mandatory sentences.

Chief Justice William Rehnquist has called mandatory minimum sentences "a good example of the law of unintended consequences" (quoted in Brennan, 1995, p. 18). Recently the California Supreme Court decided that judges in lower courts have the right to disregard the three strikes rule if they believe that the mandatory sentence would represent "cruel and unusual punishment." So although there is strong public support for clarity in sentencing requirements and attention to the injuries suffered by victims, there is growing support among professionals and citizens alike for restoring some of the judicial discretion eliminated by mandatory sentencing rules.

---

differences in the enforcement of laws from one community to another (Lipsky, 1980; Shoop, 1998). (See the Unintended Consequences feature above.)

In a classic study of two groups of adolescents in the same high school, William Chambliss (1973) examined how the biases of the local police affected their treatment of middle- and lower-class delinquents. A group of middle-class boys (the Saints) had been truant almost every day of the two-year period during which they were studied. They drove recklessly, drank excessively, and openly cheated on exams. Yet only twice were members of the Saints stopped by police officers; even then, nothing appeared on their school records. The members of the other group (the Roughnecks) all came from lower-class families. Unlike the Saints, who had cars and could "sow their wild oats" in parts of town where they were not known, the Roughnecks were confined to an area where they could be easily recognized; they therefore developed a reputation for being delinquent.

The demeanor of the two groups of boys differed markedly when they were apprehended by the police. The Saints, who were apologetic, penitent, and generally respectful of middle-class values, were treated as harmless pranksters. The Roughnecks, who were openly hostile and disdainful toward the police, were labeled deviant. These results demonstrate that factors such as low income, unemployment, or minority status are not the only ones that have a bearing on the commission of juvenile crimes. Although these factors did account for a higher rate of detection and punishment, the rates of actual misbehavior in Chambliss's study were virtually the same for both groups. Differences in the official records of the two groups reflect the discretionary power of the police. Chambliss's experience with the empirical facts of police discretion and unequal application of state power has made him one of the nation's foremost critical criminologists (Chambliss, 2000).

Problems of Accuracy

Another factor that contributes to the problem of determining the level of crime in a society is that police statistics depend on police reports, which in turn depend on the level and quality of police personnel in a given area. Since police are assigned to lower-income communities in greater numbers, there is a tendency for police records to show higher crime rates for those communities and lower rates for more affluent areas.

If official data on crime are less than fully accurate on a limited scale, it is possible that similar problems undermine the accuracy of national crime statistics. The standard index of criminal activity in the United States is the *Uniform Crime Reports* (*UCR*), which supplies racial and economic profiles of people arrested for such crimes as murder, rape, assault, and robbery. Recent data support the long-held assumption that minority group members are more likely than nonminority individuals to be involved in crimes. Yet it must be remembered that *UCR* statistics cite only individuals who are apprehended. If, like the Saints in the Chambliss (1973) study, adult offenders in middle- and upper-class groups are rarely caught or punished, *UCR*-based data become inaccurate. Because it does not profile those who successfully evade apprehension and prosecution, the *UCR* fails to reveal the entire range of criminal activity in the United States.

Acting on this hypothesis, researchers have attempted to devise more reliable ways of tracking criminal activity. Self-report studies, which ask respondents to report their own criminal involvement through an anonymous questionnaire, have provided alternative data. Whereas minority groups have higher crime rates when judged by official data (such as juvenile or criminal court records or the *UCR* index), self-reporting techniques indicate that whites and nonwhites have similar rates of criminal activity. Thus, on one hand, the idea that race is a factor in criminality is called into question when different standards of measurement are used. On the other hand, some criminologists argue that although self-report studies question the distribution of crime in the population, they do not show significant differences in levels of crime from those shown in the *UCR* (Kempf, 1990; Maltz, 1999).

Another attempt to supplement *UCR* data has led to the development of **victimization reports.** These surveys, conducted by the Census Bureau, collect information from a representative sample of crime victims. Comparisons of *UCR* and victimization indexes reveal discrepancies in the data, and depending on which standard is used, different conclusions can be drawn about the correlation between crime and socioeconomic status (Reid, 1993). The *UCR* data reflect only crimes that are reported, yet many victims—through fear, ignorance, or alienation—do not file reports. Victimization surveys indicate that this is particularly true in low-income, high-crime areas. Certain crimes—especially sex-related crimes such as rape and child molestation—are underreported, and the statistics are distorted as a result.

In sum, it appears that the poor, the undereducated, and minority groups have become the victims of selective law enforcement, stereotyping, and misleading statistics. The rich and powerful, in contrast, have been insulated from these problems; they are so seldom sent to prison that when one of them is finally jailed for fraud, embezzlement, or tax evasion, it makes headlines. Some sociologists, noting the difficulty of obtaining accurate information on the incidence of these crimes, have contended that the upper classes may actually have a higher rate of crime than the lower classes (Pepinsky & Quinney, 1991; Reckless, 1973). It will be helpful to keep these contrasts in mind as we discuss the various types of crimes.

SOCIAL PROBLEMS ONLINE

Crime and Criminal Justice on the Internet

The Internet offers a plethora of resources on crime and the criminal justice system. Starting with the FBI at **http://www.fbi.gov/**, one can locate several sources of information about current and historical investigations. Clicking on Ten Most Wanted Fugitives brings up the Internet's version of the "wanted" poster. On the FBI's home page are links to monographs about the agency's most famous cases, including the capture of John Dillinger, investigations of Nazi saboteurs, and the Lindberg kidnapping. Press releases, hotlines on current unsolved crimes, congressional testimony, and downloadable files that contain statistics from the *Uniform Crime Reports* are available.

The U.S. Department of Justice, at **http://www.usdoj.gov/**, has a regularly updated home page with links to various agencies and projects. The Violence Against Women Office has a website at **http://www.usdoj.gov/vawo/** with information on the National Domestic Violence Hotline, copies of federal legislation and regulations, ongoing research reports and studies, and a Domestic Violence Awareness Manual targeted to federal employees but applicable to almost anyone. The Bureau of Justice Statistics, at **http://www.ojp. usdof.gov/bjs/welcome.html,** provides statistics, most in downloadable format, about crimes and their victims, drugs and crime, and the criminal-justice system. It also has links to other sources of data on crime.

The Federal Bureau of Prisons site can be accessed at **http://www.bop.gov/**. It provides statistics on the federal prison population (inmates and staff) broken down by age, ethnicity, race, sentences, types of offenses, and other variables. The bureau's Program Statements can be accessed, as can links to other pages, such as those of the Federal Prison Industries and the National Institute of Corrections. Research documents pertaining to the prison system are available, and most can be downloaded.

For a view from inside the jailhouse, there is a lively and innovative journal written for, by, and about inmates. The Journal of Prisoners on Prison at **http://www.synapse.net/~arrakis/jpp/jpp.html** is an academically oriented journal published since 1988 by prisoners whose purpose is "to bring the knowledge and experience of the incarcerated to bear upon more academic arguments and concerns." This remarkable publication offers insight and analysis from people for whom imprisonment is or has been the reality of their daily existence. Articles have appeared on Native Americans in the prison system, prison education, attitude and behavior modification, the death penalty, and other topics. Back issues are available online.

Types of Crimes and Criminals

In this section we review ten major types of crimes and criminals (Siegel, 1999). Seven of them have been classified by sociologists according to how large a part criminal activity plays in people's lives; that is, whether or not people see themselves as criminals and the extent to which they commit themselves to a life of crime. To these we add an eighth category, juvenile delinquency, and a ninth, corporate crimes. Two forms of illegal activity—occupational and organized crime—will receive more extensive treatment here because their social costs probably exceed those of all the others combined. Hate crimes, a tenth category, are not accorded official status in all states, but the increase in such crimes is an important exception to the recent decline in U.S. crime rates and a subject of much current debate.

Violent Personal Crimes

Violent personal crimes include assault, robbery, and various types of homicide—acts in which physical injury is inflicted or threatened. Although robbery occurs most often between strangers, murders are very often a result of violent disputes between friends or relatives. In 1998, 51 out of every 100 murder victims were related to or acquainted with their assailants, and murders initiated by arguments (as opposed to premeditated murders) accounted for 32 percent of all murders committed during that year. Murders and aggravated assaults, therefore, are usually considered unpremeditated acts. The offenders are portrayed in the media as normally law-abiding individuals who are not likely to engage in other criminal activities. Some murders may be contract murders, which are committed by hired killers and are often linked to organized crime. When weapons are involved, guns account for about 60 percent of murders (*UCR*, 1999). (Violent crimes are discussed more fully in Chapter 7.)

Shoplifting or "boosting" is one of the most common forms of juvenile crime.

Occasional Property Crimes

Occasional property crimes include vandalism, check forgery, shoplifting, and some kinds of automobile theft. These crimes are usually unsophisticated, and the offenders lack the skills of the professional criminal. Because occasional offenders commit their crimes at irregular intervals, they are not likely to associate with habitual lawbreakers. Nonprofessional shoplifters, for example, view themselves as respectable law-abiders who steal articles from stores only for their own use. They excuse their behavior on the grounds that what they steal has relatively little value and the "victim" is usually a large, impersonal organization that can easily replace the stolen article (Pepinsky & Quinney, 1991; Siegel, 1999).

Neither nonprofessional shoplifters nor nonprofessional check forgers are likely to have a criminal record. Like vandals and car thieves, they usually work alone and are not part of a criminal subculture; they do not seek to earn a living from crime.

Occupational (White-collar) Crimes

The phenomenon of occupational crime was defined and popularized by sociologist Edwin H. Sutherland, first in a 1940 article and then in his 1961 book *White Collar Crime*. Sutherland analyzed the behavior of people who break the law as part of their normal business activity: corporate directors who use their inside knowledge to sell large blocks of stock at tremendous profits; accountants who juggle books to conceal the hundreds of dollars of company funds that they have pocketed; firms that make false statements about their profits to avoid paying taxes. Such acts tend to be ignored by society. They rarely come to the criminal courts, and even then they are rarely judged as severely as other kinds of criminal activities. Since Sutherland first described it, the category of occupational crime has also come to include such acts as false advertising, violations of labor laws, price-fixing, antitrust violations, and black-market activities.

The occupational offender is far removed from the popular stereotype of a criminal. Few people imagine that a lawyer or stockbroker is likely to engage in illegal activities. Because of their respectable appearance, it is difficult to think of these offenders as criminals. In fact, occupational offenders often consider themselves respectable citizens and do everything possible to avoid being labeled as lawbreakers—even by themselves.

Sutherland's theory of **differential association** asserts that occupational criminality, like other forms of systematic criminal behavior, is learned through frequent direct or indirect association with people who are already engaging in such behavior. (We discuss this theory later in the chapter.) Thus, people who become occupational criminals may do so simply by going into businesses or occupations in which their colleagues regard certain kinds of crime as the standard way of conducting business.

A good example of occupational crime is the insider trading that frequently occurs in the securities industry. Some stockbrokers and major shareholders may be privy to inside information about an impending corporate merger or a change in the financial condition of a company that will affect the price of its stock. Brokers who possess such information are prohibited from either profiting from it themselves or selling it to others who may be able to profit from it. Nevertheless, in the 1980s the senior partners of several large brokerage houses were convicted of using inside information to make hundreds of illegal stock transactions worth many millions of dollars (Auletta, 1987).

Embezzlement. **Embezzlement,** or theft from one's employer, is usually committed by otherwise law-abiding people during the course of their employment. Embezzlement occurs at all levels of business, from a clerk who is stealing petty cash to a vice-president who is stealing large investment sums. Most cases are not detected, and companies are often unwilling to prosecute for fear of bad publicity. In 1998, 12,215 people were arrested for embezzlement (*UCR*, 1999).

Donald Cressey's (1953) book, *Other People's Money,* is a classic study of embezzlers. On the basis of interviews with convicted embezzlers, Cressey concluded that three basic conditions are necessary before people will turn to embezzlement. First, they must have a financial problem that they do not want other people to know about. Second, they must have an opportunity to steal. Third, they must be able to find a formula to rationalize the fact that they are committing a criminal act—such as "I'm just borrowing it to tide me over."

Fraud. **Fraud,** or obtaining money or property under false pretenses, can occur at any level of business and in any type of business relationship. A citizen defrauds the government by evading the payment of income taxes; workers defraud their employers by using company property or services for their personal benefit; an industry defrauds the public when its members agree to keep prices artificially high. The cost of fraud may run from a few cents to millions of dollars, and the methods may be as crude as the butcher's thumb on the scale or as sophisticated as the coordinated efforts of dozens of lawyers, executives, and government officials. In 1998 there were 268,351 arrests on charges of fraud (*UCR*, 1999).

Within this category, the incidence of crimes committed through computer technology has increased dramatically. Computer crimes are quite diverse, ranging from data diddling, or changing the data stored in a computer system, to superzapping, or making unauthorized use of specialized programs to gain access to data stored in a computer system. In 1999 the first conviction for creation of a computer virus (the Melissa virus) was handed down. No doubt many more will follow. And along with the boom in electronic commerce has come a rash of online fraud, which was estimated to have risen by 600 percent in 1999 (Mollman, 1999).

The U.S. government estimates the cost of white-collar crimes of all types at $40 billion a year; other estimates range as high as $100 billion, not including enforcement and court costs (Reid, 1991).

Corporate Crimes

Corporate crimes include, but are not limited to, environmental crimes, illegal credit card manipulations, insider trading in financial institutions, intimidation of competitors and employees, illegal labor practices, defrauding of pension plans, falsification of company records, bribery of public officials, and computer crimes. Because it is so often undetected or unpunished, there are no reliable estimates of the cost of corporate crime to the public (Sherrill, 1997; Weston, 1987).

Recent disclosures of corporate crime in the tobacco and food industries have commanded large headlines and been the subject of movies like *The Insider*. But measured in terms of loss of public and private funds, the single worst example of corporate crime in American history occurred toward the end of the 1980s (Sherrill, 1997). It is known as the savings and loan scandal, and in the early 1990s it was estimated that it would cost taxpayers up to $500 billion, not to mention the large amounts of unprotected savings lost by individuals. In fact, the seizure and sale of properties involved in the scandal eventually reduced the overall financial damage (Foust, 1993). However, to assess the impact of this crime one needs to realize that the total value of property reported stolen in other kinds of crimes each year amounts to about $15.4 billion. Even by a conservative estimate, the amount paid to recoup the losses due to the savings and loan scandal was over twice the total cost of property lost to all other forms of crime over the same period. Perhaps even more harmful than the actual financial losses were the political consequences. Since so many political figures were implicated, including members of the Bush family and the Clintons, the damage to the public's trust of government has been inestimable.

Public-order Crimes

In terms of sheer numbers, public-order offenders constitute the largest category of criminals; their activities far exceed reported crimes of any other type. Public-order offenses include prostitution, gambling, use of illegal substances, drunkenness, vagrancy, disorderly conduct, and traffic violations. These are often called *victimless crimes* because they cause no harm to anyone but the offenders themselves. Society considers them crimes because they violate the order or customs of the community, but some of them, such as gambling and prostitution, are granted a certain amount of tolerance.

Public-order offenders rarely consider themselves criminals or view their actions as crimes. The behavior and activities of prostitutes and drug users, however, tend to isolate and segregate them from other members of society, and these individuals may find themselves drawn into criminal roles.

Conventional Crimes

Conventional offenders tend to be young adults who commit robbery, larceny, burglary, and gang theft as a way of life. They usually begin their criminal career in adolescence as members of juvenile gangs, joining other truants from school to vandalize property and fight in the streets. As juvenile offenders they are not organized or skillful enough to avoid arrest and conviction, and by young adulthood they have compiled a police record and may have spent time in prison.

Conventional offenders could be described as semiprofessional since their techniques are not as sophisticated as those of organized and professional criminals, and they move into a criminal life only by degrees. For this reason, their self-concept as criminals develops gradually. By the time they have built up a criminal record, they have usually identified fairly strongly with criminality. The criminal record itself is society's way of defining these offenders as criminals. Once they have been so defined, it is almost impossible for them to reenter the mainstream of society.

Since only a small percentage of conventional crimes results in arrest, most offenders in this category are convinced that crime does pay. Moreover, the life of a successful criminal has a certain excitement, and many criminals are seduced into a life of crime by the excitement they experience in the criminal act itself (Siegel, 1999). Not only the sudden windfall of money but also the thrill of getting away with an illegal act and the release of tension after it has been committed can become part of the reward system (Katz, 1988). Because offenders associate mostly with other criminals, they develop a shared outlook that scorns the benefits of law-abiding behavior.

Organized Crime

Organized crime is a term that includes many types of criminal organizations, from large global crime syndicates that originated in Sicily and Italy (the Mafia), and more recently in Russia, to smaller local organizations whose membership may be more transient. Based on research in England, British sociologist Dick Hobb makes this observation:

> Contemporary serious crime groups possess the ability to splinter, dissolve, mutate, self-destruct, or simply decompose. For instance, I found that a group dealing in amphetamines splintered into both legal and illegal enterprise when a key member was arrested for a crime totally unconnected with their business. They were not bonded by some mysterious brotherhood of villainy, their collaboration was temporary and sealed with money. (Hobb, 1997, p. 57)

The groups that we usually think of as representing organized crime tend to be large and diversified regional or national units. They may organize initially to carry on a particular crime, such as drug trafficking, extortion, prostitution, or gambling. Later they may seek to control this activity in a given city or neighborhood, destroying or absorbing the competition. Eventually they may expand into other types of crime, protecting their members from arrest through intimidation or bribery of public officials.

Unlike other types of crime, organized crime is a system in which illegal activities are carried out as part of a rational plan devised by a large, often global organization that is attempting to maximize its overall profit. To operate most efficiently, organized crime relies on the division of labor in the performance of numerous diverse roles. Within a typical organized crime syndicate in a large metropolitan area, there will be groups in the stolen car and parts business, others in gambling, and still others in labor rackets. In each of these and other businesses there will be specific occupations like enforcer, driver, accountant, lawyer, and so on. Another major feature of organized crime is that the crime syndicate supplies goods and services that a large segment of the public wants but cannot obtain legally. Without the public's desire for gambling or drugs, for example, organized crime's basic means of existence would collapse.

In recent years the American FBI has investigated large and well-organized crime syndicates on the Mexican border that deal in international drug smuggling, as well as a growing number of Russian crime syndicates that have been caught moving large amounts of illegally gained money through U.S. and European banks (Shaw, 1999). These large, globally organized crime organizations derive huge profits from supplying illegal goods and services to the public. Their major source of profit is illegal gambling in the form of lotteries, numbers games, off-track betting, illegal casinos, and dice games. Much illegal gambling is controlled by organized crime syndicates that operate through elaborate hierarchies. Money is transferred up the hierarchy from the small operator, who takes the customer's bet, through several other levels until it finally reaches the syndicate's headquarters. This complex system protects the leaders, whose identities remain concealed from those below them. The centralized organization of gambling also increases efficiency, enlarges markets, and provides a systematic way of paying graft to public officials.

Closely related to gambling and a major source of revenue for organized crime is *loan sharking*, or lending money at interest rates above the legal limit. These rates can be as high as 150 percent a week, and rates of more than 20 percent are common. Profits from gambling operations provide organized crime syndicates with large amounts of cash to lend, and they can ensure repayment by threatening violence. Most of the loans are made to gamblers who need to repay debts, to drug users, and to small businesses that are unable to obtain credit from legitimate sources.

Drug trafficking is organized crime's third major source of revenue. Its direct dealings in narcotics tend to be limited to imports from abroad and wholesale distribution. Lower-level operations are considered too risky and unprofitable and are left to others.

Organized Crime and Corruption.   Organized crime could not flourish without bribery. By corrupting officials of public and private agencies, the syndicate tries to ensure that laws that would hamper its operations are not passed, or at least not enforced.

Corruption occurs at all levels of government, from police officers to high elected and appointed officials. It is especially effective with individuals in more powerful positions since they can prevent lower-level personnel from enforcing laws against organized crime activities. If the cooperation of the police chief can be obtained, for example, a police officer who tries to arrest gamblers may be shifted to another assignment or denied a raise or promotion. Other officers will quickly learn from this example.

In Sicily, where the Mafia retain a powerful grip over community leaders, social activists use photos of Mafia killings to stimulate local and international protest.

Professional Crimes

Professional criminals are the ones we read about in detective novels or see on television: the expert safecracker with sensitive fingers; the disarming con artist; the customer in a jewelry store who switches diamonds so quickly that the clerk does not notice; the counterfeiters who work under bright lights in the basement of a respectable shop. This class of criminals also includes the less glamorous pickpockets, full-time shoplifters and check forgers, truck hijackers, sellers of stolen goods, and blackmailers.

Professional criminals are dedicated to a life of crime; they live by it and pride themselves on their accomplishments. These criminals are seldom caught, and even if they are, they can usually manage to have the charges dropped or a sentence reduced. Meyer Lansky, a particularly successful thief who was a top figure in a national crime syndicate, spent only 3 months and 16 days in jail out of a criminal career that spanned over 50 years (Plate, 1975). These are the cleverest of all criminals, with the most sophisticated working methods.

Professional criminals tend to come from higher social strata than most people who are arrested for criminal activities. They frequently begin as employees in offices, hotels, and restaurants, with criminal life as a sideline. Eventually their criminal careers develop to the point at which they can make a living almost entirely from criminal activities. This phase usually starts at the same age at which conventional criminals are likely to give up crime. As criminologist E. M. Lemert put it, "Unemployment occasioned by old age does not seem to be a problem of con men; age ripens their skills, insights, and wit, and it also increases the confidence they inspire in their victims" (quoted in Quinney, 1979, p. 245). Most professional criminals enjoy long, uninterrupted careers because experience improves their skill at avoiding arrest. They often justify their activities by claiming that they are simply capitalizing on the fact that all people are dishonest and would probably be full-time criminals themselves if they had the ability and opportunity. Many are employed in operations carried on by organized crime syndicates.

Juvenile Delinquency

Historically, children have been presumed to lack the criminal intent to commit willful crimes; hence, juvenile law is designed primarily to protect and redirect young offenders rather than to punish them. There is a separate family court system for dealing with juvenile offenders, and their sentencing is limited. Within those limits, however, judges have wide discretion in dealing with youthful offenders and can choose the approach that they feel will be most effective.

In recent years there has been increasing dissatisfaction with the workings of juvenile law (Jacobs, 1990). Some critics contend that law enforcement authorities have too much latitude in interpreting juvenile behavior and that standards differ too much from one community to another. In addition, there is evidence that today's young criminals are much more sinister than yesterday's. Criminologist John DiIulio believes that the large number of juvenile criminals incarcerated today is producing a serious social problem for the near future. His research on the subject has convinced him that although the proportion of repeat offenders among juveniles has remained relatively constant over time, the level of violence in their crimes has escalated, even as violent crime among adults is decreasing. DiIulio and his coauthor William Bennett, a former head of the federal drug enforcement agency, argue that the nation's poor neighborhoods and prisons are producing a new breed of "super-predators," young men whose violent criminality will become one of the foremost social problems in coming decades (Bennett, DiIulio, & Walters, 1996; Traub, 1996). We will return to this immensely controversial theory in the next section, where we consider the causes of crime.

As noted in the preceding chapter, many young people become involved in drug commerce at the retail level, especially because as juveniles they often run somewhat less risk of incarceration than people over 18 years of age. Involvement in petty sales and other aspects of drug commerce puts juveniles at risk of addiction and, increasingly, of violent death. As the demand for cocaine and crack abates while law enforcement pressure continues, there is an escalation of violence, often involving automatic weapons, among drug dealers and their associates. Thus, in some large American cities the homicide rate among juvenile males has reached record levels.

Teenagers who are arrested on minor sales or possession charges often begin a career in and out of detention centers and jails, where they are initiated into the world of professional crime (Sullivan, 1989). Young women who become involved in the drug world and associated illegal hustling often trade sexual services for drugs and thus are recruited into the culture of prostitution. Although prostitution may not be considered a serious crime, it places young women at serious risk of violent death or injury and of sterility or death from sexually transmitted diseases.

Status offenses, such as running away and vagrancy, are a very common reason for arrests of juveniles. In 1998 about 117,089 juvenile runaways were arrested in the United States, of whom 58 percent were females (*UCR*, 1999). This is one of the few types of arrest in which the usual gender distribution is reversed. The reason so

Arrests in the War on Drugs often lead to felony convictions for youthful offenders. As a consequence of efforts to lengthen prison terms for people with multiple felony convictions, these early episodes could greatly increase the risk of eventual life imprisonment.

many girls are runaways is that they are far more likely than boys to be abused, both sexually and otherwise, in their homes.

Hate Crimes

It is perhaps appropriate to follow juvenile crimes with a discussion of hate crimes. Many of the most sensational recent crimes that were motivated by deep hatreds for people of other groups were committed by teenagers and young adults. The killings at Columbine High School in Colorado and those of James Byrd, Jr., in Texas and Matthew Shepard in Wyoming are hate crimes that most readers will remember vividly. Even when they do not result in murder and mayhem, these criminal acts reveal hatreds and violent propensities that go far beyond what we usually categorize as juvenile crime. Hatred of gays or people of other races and religions is widespread in all societies, but the propensity to express it through violent acts tends to be a phenomenon of youth and young adulthood. Yet the emotions that motivate the deeds are taken from the adults who socialize young people. Throughout the world—in Kosovo, Rwanda, Northern Ireland, Israel, Pakistan, Russia, the United States, and elsewhere—adult hatreds spawn violence, which is often carried out by the young.

In an exhaustive study of hate crimes, the FBI concluded that 61 percent of such incidents were based on race, 13 percent on sexual orientation, and another 10 percent on ethnicity or national origin. Intimidation, the single most frequently reported hate crime offense, accounts for 41 percent of the total; damage, destruction, or vandalism of property for 23 percent; simple assault for 18 percent; and aggravated assault for 13 percent (Gondles, 1999).

The 1994 Crime Act defines a hate crime as "a crime in which the defendant intentionally selects a victim, or in the case of a property crime, the property that is the object of the crime, because of the actual or perceived race, color, national origin, ethnicity, gender, disability, or sexual orientation of any person." Thirty-seven states have statutes addressing hate crime, and others have pending legislation in this area. But the major controversy surrounding the issue of hate crimes is whether the federal government needs a stronger law that sets greater penalties for crimes motivated by hatred against specific social groups. Since a great deal of contemporary violence is motivated by hatred of groups defined as "the others," we will return to this subject again in the Social Policy section of the next chapter.

Conditions and Causes of Crime

In this section we consider several explanations for crime, beginning with nonsociological ones and continuing with various sociological approaches based on the theoretical perspectives described in Chapter 1.

Biological Explanations of Crime

A medieval law stated that "if two persons fell under suspicion of crime the uglier or more deformed was to be regarded as more probably guilty" (Ellis, 1914; quoted in Wilson & Herrnstein, 1985, p. 71). This law and others like it illustrate the age-old and deep-seated belief that criminality can be explained in terms of certain physical characteristics of the criminal. An example of this point of view is the theory of crime advanced by an Italian physician, Cesare Lombroso, in the late nineteenth century.

Lombroso was convinced that there is a "criminal man" (or woman), a type of human being who is physically distinct from ordinary human beings. In the course of his examinations of convicts both before and after their deaths, he developed the concept of *criminal atavism*—the notion that criminality is associated with physical characteristics that resemble those of primitive humans and lower primates: a sloping forehead, long arms, a primitive brain, and the like. Lombroso believed, in short, that there was such a thing as a "born criminal." Although this explanation was wrong, it served to initiate scientific inquiry into the causes of crime.

In the twentieth century, Lombroso's theory and other biologically based explanations of crime have been discredited and supplanted by sociological theories. However, some theorists (e.g., Wilson & Herrnstein, 1985) defend the identification of biological characteristics that appear to be predisposing factors in criminal behavior rather than full explanations of it. They believe that certain inherited traits, such as an extra Y chromosome or a particularly athletic physique, may be correlated with a greater than average tendency to engage in criminal behavior.

Research on the possibility of a link between criminality and an extra Y chromosome has consistently found that no such relationship can be demonstrated. Nevertheless, biologists, medical researchers, and some behavioral scientists continue to search for possible genetic causes of crime. Efforts by the National Academy of Sciences and other prestigious scientific organizations to study the possible biological basis of crime have generated heated controversy and scientific debate, in part because biological research on crime usually fails, as sociologist Joan McCord points out, "to look at the social and psychological variables." McCord herself analyzed data from a long-term study of pairs of brothers in the Boston area between 1926 and 1933, comparing their criminal histories with each other and with those of subjects from similar backgrounds; she found no evidence of a genetic contribution to criminality (cited in Horgan, 1993). Although new efforts to establish genetic or other biological origins of criminality are also likely to fail, most sociologists agree with Troy Duster, who argues that such studies can help, because if they properly account for social variables such as racism and class inequality, they will counteract the notion of a biological basis for crime in the lower classes or among some racial groups (cited in Horgan, 1993).

Gender and Crime

Since nations began collecting systematic statistics on crime, analysts have realized that men are far more likely than women to commit crimes. Indeed, gender is one of the most obvious correlates of criminality. Although there are significant variations from one society to another, numerous studies of crime in different countries demonstrate that the gender gap is universal. Males are 5 to 50 times as likely to be arrested as females (Steffensmeier & Allan, 1996). As women have gained greater social equality with men in industrialized countries, however, the ratio of male to female arrests has decreased, although men still lead in most categories of crime. (See Figure 6–5.)

The different arrest rates for men and women seem to be a result of different patterns of socialization. In our society men have traditionally been raised to be more aggressive than women, and they have therefore been more likely to commit certain kinds of crimes. Women generally have been regarded more protectively by the police and the courts; therefore, they have been less likely to be arrested and, if arrested, less likely to be punished severely, especially if they are wives or mothers. Despite the persistent differences in arrest rates of women and men, with men more than eight times more likely to appear in official crime statistics, rates of crime by women have increased rapidly in the second half of the twentieth century. As more women are socialized under conditions of deprivation and abuse, we can expect that larger numbers will be recruited into street hustling, prostitution, and shoplifting, which in turn will account for increasing numbers of arrests (Friedman, 1993; Miller, 1986). Indeed, today women make up 16 percent of the total prison population in the United States, compared to only 7.7 percent in 1997 (Greenfield & Snell, 1999).

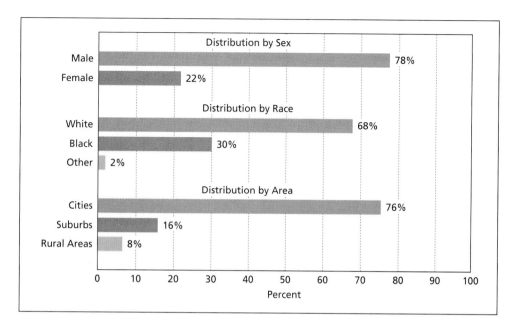

Figure 6–5 Total Arrests by Sex, Race, and Area, 1998

Source: Federal Bureau of Investigation, *Uniform Crime Reports,* 1999.

Age and Crime

Criminologists have found age to be more strongly correlated with criminal behavior than any other factor (McKeown, Jackson, & Valois, 1998). The age of the offender is closely related not only to crime rates but also to the types of crimes committed. Data from several nations, including England, Wales, and France, provide evidence that the correlation between age and crime holds across geographic boundaries (Gottfredson & Hirschi, 1995; Hirschi & Gottfredson, 1983).

Teenagers and young adults accounted for 45.4 percent of arrests in the United States in 1998, and 32.3 percent of all arrests were of people under the age of 21. A solid majority of arrests for property crimes—58.5 percent—were of people under 25 (*UCR,* 1999). Although young people may be arrested more than older offenders because the young are less experienced, it is clear that many teenagers and young adults, especially those who become involved in gang activities, are enticed by opportunities to commit various kinds of thefts. Automobile and bicycle thefts and vandalism are among the major juvenile crimes, although they are by no means limited to the young.

Is There a "Super-predator" Cohort? The rate of violent felonies committed by children aged 10 to 17 has increased for most of the past ten years, a trend that runs counter to the decrease in violence among adults in the United States (Belluck, 1996). Figure 6–6 shows the rate of arrests for violent crimes per 100,000 boys and girls aged 10 to 17. Even though it indicates that there have been slight declines in recent years, the rates remain extremely high. These high rates of violence are doubly disturbing because the size of this population cohort will increase over the next decade. High rates of crime in a growing segment of the population will result in increased violence in many neighborhoods and continue to swell the numbers of youthful inmates in detention centers and jails.

Criminologist John DiIulio and conservative social critic William Bennett believe that these ominous trends point to the emergence of a cohort of "super-predators" for whom there is probably no alternative but surveillance, arrest, and long-term incarceration. Other

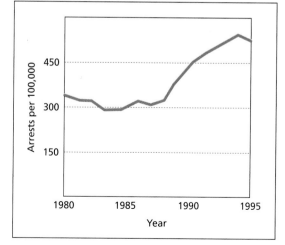

Figure 6–6 Arrests for Violent Crime per 100,000 Youths, Ages 10 through 17

Source: Data from Federal Bureau of Investigation.

criminologists agree with Marvin Wolfgang, who says, "I dislike the term 'super-predators.' They may have committed some hard crimes, but that doesn't mean that they will be forever hardened criminals, or that they have a 'criminal mind'" (quoted in Traub, 1996, p. 52). DiIulio agrees that many young offenders can be rehabilitated, but he also believes that among the waves of teenagers and young adults released from prisons over the next ten years there will be a large number who are so hardened to violence and so alienated from society that they will remain in the criminal underworld, where they will be especially violent. We will return to this issue in discussing rehabilitation strategies.

It is fortunate for society that some criminals give up crime in their late 20s or early 30s, for reasons that are not clear to criminologists (Gottfredson & Hirschi, 1995). Perhaps they marry and find their family life more rewarding than crime. For these individuals, family responsibilities seem to be a more powerful inhibitor of criminal behavior than rehabilitation or coercion. This "maturing out" is a subject of great interest to sociologists. In a study of the criminal careers of juvenile males in three urban communities of whites, African Americans, and Latinos, respectively, Mercer Sullivan (1989) found that as the boys grew older there was an increasingly marked convergence in their tendency to reduce their criminal activity in favor of increased income from legitimate sources. Sullivan attributes this change to their greater maturity, their recognition that sanctions were becoming more severe, and their perception that their opportunities to hold real jobs were better than they had been when they were younger.

Sociological Explanations of Crime

Demographic factors do not offer a complete explanation of crime. They do not, for example, explain why some juveniles and young adults drift into long-term criminal careers or why some young people never commit crimes. Nor do they tell us why some individuals, such as white-collar criminals, begin breaking laws during adulthood and middle age. Thus, in addition to demographic analyses of crime, sociologists have proposed at least four theoretical approaches to explain why some people become criminals and others do not.

The first theoretical approach to be discussed here has evolved from conflict theory; it claims that most crime is either a form of rebellion by members of lower social classes or a form of illegal exploitation by the rich and powerful. A second approach, derived from the functionalist perspective, holds that crime stems from the uncertainty about norms of proper conduct that accompanies rapid social change and social disorganization. A third major explanation applies the interactionist perspective to the study of how people drift toward criminal subcultures and become socialized for criminal careers. And in the next chapter we will add a fourth theory of crime, known as control theory, which views crime as a type of economic behavior that is based on criminals' perceptions of the likely consequences of their actions.

Conflict Approaches to the Study of Crime.   Conflict theorists identify inequalities of wealth, status, and power as the underlying conditions that produce criminal behavior. Groups in society that are more disadvantaged than other groups, such as the poor and racial minorities who experience discrimination, are thought to be likely to rebel against their situation. Criminality, in this view, is one way in which disadvantaged individuals act out their rebellion against society (Quinney, 1979).

Inequality and Crime. As noted earlier in the chapter, official statistics show a high incidence of crime among members of the lower socioeconomic classes. Those statistics have fueled a sociological debate over the relationship between social class and criminality. For much of the twentieth century many sociologists believed that people in lower socioeconomic classes were more likely than those in higher classes to commit crimes. In 1978 criminologists Charles R. Tittle, Wayne J. Villemez, and Douglas A. Smith (1978) analyzed existing studies of crime and class status to determine whether the inverse relationship between class status and the commission of crime always held. When they examined data from arrest records, they found evidence to support the prevailing view. But when they reviewed data from self-report studies, they found no link between class and crime. On the basis of these results, the investigators concluded that "it is time to shift away from class-based theories to those emphasizing more generic processes" (p. 654).

Cross-cultural research on crime suggests that rapid increases in inequality, rather than long-standing patterns of poverty and wealth (e.g., as in India), tend to produce increases in crime (Bunnell, 1995). For example, in the nations of the former Soviet Union there have been rapid increases in poverty and in the number of wealthy individuals, many of whom have made their fortunes in connection with organized crime or other criminal activity. This rapid social change, in which it is no longer clear what the rules of behavior are or whether laws will be enforced, tends to produce lawlessness and crime.

As the total U.S. prison population has grown to a record 1.8 million, the conflict perspective on crime gains new adherents. Joseph Califano (1998), former secretary of Health and Human Services, is an example. Today, he points out,

> One of every 144 American adults is in prison for a crime in which drugs and alcohol were involved. Thanks largely to alcohol and drug abuse, the rate of incarceration for American adults was 868 per 100,000 in 1996, compared with less than 100 per 100,000 for most European countries and 47 per 100,000 for Japan. If the current rate of increase continues, one in every 20 Americans born in 1997 will spend some part of his or her life in prison. This will be the case for one in every 11 men and one in every four black men. (p. 3)

Califano is highly critical of theories of crime that suggest that only punishment can deter people from committing crimes. He sees the failure of U.S. drug policy and the failure to provide adequate rehabilitation as major causes of the boom in prison populations—which, he believes, only increases the chances that people in prison will become criminal recidivists later in their lives. In other words, in Califano's view it is conflicts in American society over how to deal with drug and alcohol abuse that result in some types of crime and, more important, in the dramatic increases in the prison population. More critical theorists, however, still view major differences in income in a society as the most important contributor to crime (Anderson, 1992, 1999; Methwin, 1997).

Race and Crime. Every study of crime based on official data shows that blacks are overrepresented among those who are arrested, convicted, and imprisoned for street crimes. According to official statistics, blacks are arrested at higher rates than whites on charges of murder, rape, robbery, and other index crimes.

In any society one can find differences in crime rates among various racial and ethnic groups. Chinese and Japanese Americans have lower crime rates than other Americans; Hungarian immigrants to Sweden have higher crime rates than native Swedes; Scandinavian immigrants to the United States get into less trouble with the police than Americans of Anglo-Saxon descent (Reckless, 1973). In the case of black Americans, however, the differences are pronounced; for example, "If blacks were arrested for robbery at the same rate as are whites, there would be half as many robbers arrested in the United States" (Wilson & Herrnstein, 1985, pp. 461–462).

It is possible that the overrepresentation of blacks in official crime statistics is due to greater surveillance of black communities by the police and to the greater likelihood that blacks who commit crimes will be arrested and imprisoned. One expert has calculated that about 80 percent of the disproportion in the rates of imprisonment can be attributed to the disproportion in arrest rates (Blumstein, 1982). However, victimization surveys show that police and court bias cannot be the sole cause. Blacks are far more likely than whites to be victims of crime, and it is unlikely that

CRITICAL RESEARCH

Racial Profiling

David Cole and Kathryn Russell are two of the leading critical criminologists in the United States. Both have been documenting patterns of racial unfairness and discrimination in the criminal justice system. Cole's (2000) newest study, *No Equal Justice,* is a compendium of facts about racial injustice in arrest procedures, court proceedings, prison sentencing, and much more. Cole also suggests some timely policy changes that would begin to balance the scales of justice, which he shows are heavily weighted against non-white Americans.

Why, for example, do California blacks, who make up only 7 percent of the state's population, account for over 40 percent of the "third-strike" defendants sent to state prisons? Even when one accounts for greater poverty and higher crime rates among African Americans, these differences are way out of line. What happens, Cole demonstrates, is that patterns of racial profiling in arrests bring more minorities into the justice system. Lack of access to better legal services, along with patterns of bias in jury selection, help account for much higher conviction rates among people of color. Unequal sentencing accounts for longer prison terms for minority group members and thus for higher proportions in prison. These patterns of racial injustice are examples of what is known as *institutional racism.* They are discriminatory practices engaged in by the institutions of law, not acts of personal prejudice or racial bigotry. But their effects, according to Cole, are a major threat to American democracy.

Cole is particularly critical of the use of racial profiling in federal, state, and municipal police forces. This term refers to the tendency to view members of certain minority groups as more likely to commit crimes than the general population, and to use that assumption in making decisions about such procedures as traffic stops, personal searches, and customs investigations. The subject of racial profiling has become extremely controversial in many states in the past few years. Russell (1999) also conducts research on profiling and its racial bias. As she puts it, "The high number of blacks arrested are partially the result of police targeting them in the first place" (p. 12).

Are black Americans more likely to commit crimes, or are their higher arrest rates a function of discriminatory police profiling? The National Household Survey of Substance and Drug Abuse finds that roughly the same proportion of blacks and whites—12 to 13 percent—say that they use illegal substances. Yet 37 percent of those arrested for drug-related crimes such as trafficking or possession are black (Russell, 1999).

In many minority communities, feelings against racial profiling are profound and bitter. The phrase "driving while black" sums up much of the attitude; it seems as if merely being an African-American driver is a crime. Cole (2000) has gathered large amounts of data to support this perception. His data show that wherever police have broad discretion, they disproportionately stop and search minorities. The following are among the many examples he cites:

- Reviewing police videotapes, the *Orlando Sentinel* found that in 1992 in Volusia County, Florida, on a road where approximately 5 percent of the drivers are identifiably black or Hispanic, 70 percent of those stopped and 80 percent of those searched were black or Hispanic.

- Analyzing some 16 million driving records, the *Houston Chronicle* found that in 1995 blacks who traveled in white enclaves of Houston were twice as likely as whites to be ticketed for traffic offenses.

- In 1998 the American Civil Liberties Union reported that during a nearly three-year period 70 percent of the drivers stopped and searched on Interstate 95 in Maryland were African-American, whereas only 17.5 percent of the drivers and speeders on that road were black.

- A 1998 analysis of police records found that in Philadelphia African-Americans were subject to both car stops and pedestrian stops at rates that were disproportionate to their representation in the population.

- According to the New Jersey attorney general, 77 percent of the motorists stopped and searched by New Jersey state troopers are black or Hispanic, even though only 13.5 percent of the drivers on New Jersey highways are black or Hispanic.

- A 1999 ACLU analysis of Illinois traffic data found that Hispanics account for less than 8 percent of the state's population but for 27 percent of those stopped and searched by drug-interdiction units.

This evidence suggests that racial profiling is a nationwide problem (Cole, 2000).

these higher victimization rates are caused by whites who enter black neighborhoods to commit crimes (Wilson & Herrnstein, 1985). (See the Critical Research feature on page 172.)

A more plausible explanation is the disproportionately high percentage of blacks in the lower classes, which, as we saw earlier, are associated with higher crime rates. But economic disadvantage alone cannot fully account for the racial disparity in crime rates. The higher arrest rates for blacks persist even when socioeconomic status is taken into consideration. Moreover, offenders who commit numerous crimes begin to exhibit delinquent behavior early in life, before their outlook has been affected by such factors as inability to find a good job (Adler, Mueller, & Laufer, 1995).

Recent research by William Julius Wilson (1996) points to the growing isolation of some black communities from sources of jobs and income. This trend is especially marked in and around cities that have lost large numbers of manufacturing jobs, which once provided a relatively decent livelihood for African-American and other minority workers. In communities where legal employment is in short supply, people often turn to illegal activities. Census statistics, however, suggest some encouraging signs: In 1995 the poverty rate for African Americans dropped below 30 percent; in addition, the homicide rate among blacks dropped from over 40 per 100,000 in 1990 to about 30 in 1995 (Holmes, 1996a). These important social indicators may be signs of more improvements to come, a subject to which we return in Chapter 9.

The Functionalist View: Anomie Theory. Anomie theory, also known as the goals-and-opportunities approach, is favored by many scholars, notably Robert K. Merton (1968). Merton argues that a society has both approved goals and approved ways of attaining them. When some members of the society accept the goals (e.g., home ownership) but do not have access to the approved means of attaining them (e.g., earned income), their adherence to the approved norms is likely to be weakened, and they may try to attain the goals by other, socially unacceptable means (e.g., fraud). In other words, criminal behavior occurs when socially approved means are not available for the realization of highly desired goals.

Anomie, the feeling of being adrift that arises from the disparity between goals and means, may vary with nationality, ethnic background, bias, religion, and other social characteristics. Some societies emphasize strict adherence to behavioral norms—the case in Japan, for example—and for them the degree of anomie may be fairly low. Others place relatively more emphasis on the attainment of goals and less on their being attained in socially approved ways. Merton (1968) maintains that the United States is such a society. Identifying anomie as a basic characteristic of American society, he lists several kinds of common adaptations. One of these, innovation, consists of rejecting approved practices while retaining the desired goals. This seems to characterize the behavior of certain lower-class gang members, who have adoped socially approved goals but abandoned socially approved methods of attaining them.

This rejection of approved practices occurs widely in groups with the greatest disjuncture among goals, norms, and opportunities. In this country it is most often found among those who have the greatest difficulty in obtaining a good education or training for high-paying jobs, particularly members of disadvantaged minority groups. Higher crime rates among such groups are not automatic, but they can be expected when the goals that people internalize are dictated to them by a society that at the same time erects barriers to the attainment of those goals by approved means. If more attainable goals were set for people in lower socioeconomic classes, presumably there would be less disjuncture between goals and means and, hence, less anomie. For example, if low-cost rental housing were more widely available as a goal, more poor people could see how even low-wage jobs would improve their lives. When only luxury homes are available (and shown as models on television), the poor sense the futility of conventional jobs or other approved means.

Since the initial formulation of the anomie approach, research seems to have provided at least some support for its basic premise, although there are types of crimes that it fails to explain adequately, such as assault for purposes other than monetary gain. This omission is related to the question that is most frequently raised about Merton's theory: Are financial success and material possessions only middle-class goals? Do members of the lower classes have different values and aspirations? Many sociologists believe that people in the lower classes tend to hold two sets of beliefs simultaneously. That is, they share the norms and values of the larger society but are forced to develop standards and expectations of their own so that they can deal realistically with their particular circumstances. For example, people in the lower classes share with the affluent the view that crime is bad, but they lack conventional means to attain such goals as secure jobs. They may consider illegal "hustles" as an alternative means to some goals, especially when these crimes seem justified by the behavior of others outside their communities whom they observe buying drugs or sex or other illicit goods and services. It is not surprising, therefore, that studies have supported Merton's view that anomie, rather than poverty itself, is a major cause of crime and delinquency.

Interactionist Approaches: Differential Association and Delinquent Subcultures. Interactionist explanations of criminal behavior focus on the processes by which individuals actually internalize the norms that encourage criminality. This internalization results from the everyday interaction that occurs in social groups. Interactionist theories differ in this respect from anomie theory, which sees criminal behavior as the result of certain aspects of social structure. Two examples of interactionist theories of criminality are Edwin Sutherland's theory of differential association and the subcultural approach to the study of juvenile delinquency.

Differential Association. Introduced by Sutherland in 1939, the approach known as *differential association,* with some later modifications, still seems to explain the widest range of criminal acts. According to this theory, criminal behavior is a result of a learning process that occurs chiefly within small, intimate groups—family, friends, neighborhood peer groups, and the like. The lessons learned include both the techniques for committing crimes and, more important, the motives for criminal behavior. The law is defined not as a set of rules to be followed but as a hindrance to be avoided or overcome.

Briefly stated, the basic principle of differential association is that "a person becomes delinquent because of the excess of definitions favorable to violation of law over definitions unfavorable to violation of law" (Sutherland & Cressey, 1960, p. 28). People internalize the values of the surrounding culture, and when their environment includes frequent contact with criminal elements and relative isolation from noncriminal elements, they are likely to become delinquent or criminal. The boy whose most admired model is another member of his gang or a successful neighborhood pimp will try to emulate that model and will receive encouragement and approval when he does so successfully.

Although a child usually encounters both criminal and noncriminal behavior patterns, these encounters vary in frequency, duration, priority, and intensity. The concepts of frequency and duration are self-explanatory. *Priority* means that attitudes learned early in life, whether lawful or criminal, tend to persist in later life, although this tendency has not been fully demonstrated. *Intensity* refers to the prestige of the model and the strength of the child's emotional ties to that person.

Delinquent Subcultures and Conflicting Values. The legal definition of crime ignores the effect of social values in determining which laws are enforced. Although judges and prosecutors use criminal law to determine the criminality of certain acts, the process of applying the law involves class interest and political power: One group imposes its will on another by enforcing its definition of illegality. For example, authorities are not nearly as anxious to enforce laws against consumer fraud as they are to enforce laws against the use of certain drugs. Consumer fraud is often perpetrated by powerful business interests with strong political influence. The drug user, on the other hand, usually lacks power and public support.

The issue of class interests is especially relevant to the study of delinquent subcultures. Albert K. Cohen (1971), for example, viewed the formation of delinquent gangs as an effort to alleviate the difficulties gang members encounter at the bottom of the status ladder. Gang members typically come from working-class homes and find themselves measured, as Cohen put it, with a "middle-class measuring rod" by those who control access to the larger society, including teachers, businesspeople, the police, and public officials. Untrained in such "middle-class virtues" as ambition, ability to defer gratification, self-discipline, and academic skills, and therefore poorly prepared to compete in a middle-class world, they form a subculture whose standards they can meet. This delinquent subculture, which Cohen described as nonutilitarian, malicious, and negativistic, "takes its norms from the larger culture, but turns them upside down. The delinquents consider something right, by the standards of their subculture, precisely because it is wrong by the norms of the larger culture" (p. 28).

Other sociologists do not believe that the formation of delinquent subcultures is a frustrated reaction to exclusion by the dominant culture. Instead, they see delinquency as a product of lower-class culture. A study of street gangs by Walter Miller (1958), for example, identified six "focal concerns" of lower-class culture that often lead to the violation of middle-class social and legal norms:

1. *Trouble.* Trouble is important to the individual's status in the community, whether it is seen as something to be kept out of or as something to be gotten into. Usually there is less worry about legal or moral questions than about difficulties that result from the involvement of police, welfare investigators, and other agents of the larger society.

2. *Toughness.* Toughness comprises an emphasis on masculinity, physical strength, and the ability to "take it," coupled with a rejection of art, literature, and anything else that is considered feminine. This is partly a reaction to female-dominated households and the lack of male role models both at home and in school.

3. *Smartness.* In the street sense of the term, *smartness* denotes the ability to outwit, dupe, or "con" someone. A successful pimp, for example, would be considered smarter than a bank clerk.

4. *Excitement.* To relieve the crushing boredom of ghetto life, residents of lower-class communities often seek out situations of danger or excitement such as gambling or high-speed joyrides in stolen automobiles.

5. *Fate.* Fate is a major concern because lower-class citizens frequently feel that important events in life are beyond their control. They often resort to semimagical resources such as "readers and advisers" as a way to change their luck.

6. *Autonomy.* Members of this group are likely to express strong resentment toward any external controls or exercise of coercive authority over their behavior. At the same time, however, they frequently seem to seek out restrictive environments, perhaps even engineering their own committal to mental hospitals or prisons.

Research by Gerald Suttles (1970) and Elijah Anderson (1992, 1999) on the street corner culture of delinquents and other groups provides evidence of continuity in these values. Anderson, for example, writes that lower-class life has an internal coherence that is seldom appreciated by the casual observer. Both show that teenagers and young adults in lower-class street corner groups

Through their dress and styles of behavior, these members of a teenage gang in England assert their loyalty to an adolescent subculture and their opposition to norms of conventional adult society.

make careful distinctions based on trust and confidence. They may be labeled street people by the larger society, but among themselves they continually rank each other according to notions of respect and trust derived from their life on the street.

Controlling Crime

Efforts by the police, courts, and other agencies to control crime need to be understood as part of society's much larger system of social control (Wouters, 1999). In its broadest sociological sense, **social control** is the capacity of a social group, which could be an entire society, to regulate itself according to a set of "higher moral principles beyond those of self-interest" (Janowitz, 1978, p. 3). The Ten Commandments are a good example of what is meant by such values as they are translated into norms of everyday life. All of a society's ways of teaching the young to conform to its values and norms (i.e., *socialization*), together with the ways in which people in a society reward one another for desired behaviors, contribute to social control. But every society also includes members who deviate from its norms, even strongly held norms like the prohibition against murder or thievery. Viewed in terms of the problems created by such deviance, social control can be defined somewhat more narrowly as "all the processes by which people define and respond to deviant behavior" (Black, 1984, p. xi).

Techniques of social control range from informal processes such as gossip, ridicule, advice, and shunning to the formal processes embodied in the actions of the police, courts, corrections officers, and others who work in the criminal-justice system and in related systems like the mental-health and juvenile-justice systems. These formal systems of social control, established by government, are so important and complex and subject to so much study and debate that in this chapter we will focus on them more than on the informal processes. Nevertheless, it is important to recognize that without the great array of informal controls that exist in every community and society, none of the formal systems would be of much use. If the police and the courts and other formal institutions of social control are at all effective, it is because most people are law-abiding and these institutions need deal only with a relatively small minority (which may still be a very large number in absolute terms).

Most formal systems of social control rely on coercion rather than on reward. Surely this is true of courts and prisons. But it is not true by definition. In a prison or other correctional facility a person can be rewarded for behavior that is defined as positive and as having favorable consequences for the individual and for society. The fact that coercion and punishment often far outweigh persuasion and reward reflects the different goals society has incorporated into its institutions of criminal law, that is, police, prosecution, and corrections. As we examine how these formal institutions of social control operate (and sometimes fail to operate), we need to remember that formal efforts to control crime can be classified under four headings: retribution-deterrence, rehabilitation, prevention, and reforms in the criminal-justice system. The last category includes efforts to improve society's ability to deal with all kinds of crime; it will be discussed in the Social Policy section of the chapter.

Retribution-Deterrence

Retribution and deterrence—"paying back" the guilty for their misdeeds and discouraging them and others from committing similar acts in the future—have historically been the primary focus of efforts to control crime. Only relatively recently has rehabilitation of offenders—attempts to give them the ability and motivation to live in a law-abiding and socially approved manner—gained wide acceptance. The correctional system, however, is still largely punitive. Although retribution no longer follows the "eye for an eye, tooth for a tooth" formula (in which slanderers had their tongues cut out, thieves had their hands amputated, and rapists were castrated), the retributive orientation can be seen in public demands for longer sentences for such crimes as murder.

The punishments meted out to murderers, forgers, and other offenders are meant to serve several purposes. Besides the often-cited goals of preventing crime and rehabilitating offenders, punishment serves to sustain the morale of those who conform to society's rules. In other words, law-abiding members of society demand that offenders be punished partly to reinforce their own ambivalent feelings about conformity. They believe that if they must make sacrifices to obey the law, someone who does not make such sacrifices should not be allowed to "get away with it." Even those who view criminals as sick rather than evil, and who call for the "treatment" of offenders to correct an organic or psychological disorder, are essentially demanding retribution.

In recent years the public's desire for more retribution has resulted in pressure in many states to restore capital punishment and to restore more punitive, as opposed to rehabilitative, forms of correction. In 1995, for example, Alabama reinstituted the penal practices of chain gangs and rock breaking, practices that were far more common in southern prisons a century ago than they are today.

Some criminologists, such as James Q. Wilson (1977, 1993), have suggested that society needs the firm moral authority derived from stigmatizing and punishing crime. Although Wilson grants that prisoners must "pay their debts" without being deprived of their civil rights after release from prison and without suffering the continued indignities of parole supervision and unemployment, he stresses the moral value of stigmatizing crime and those who commit it: "To destigmatize crime would be to lift from it the weight of moral judgment and to make crime simply a particular occupation or avocation which society has chosen to reward less (or perhaps more) than other pursuits. If there is no stigma attached to an activity, then society has no business making it a crime" (1977, p. 230).

Laws that establish penalties for crimes are enacted by the states and by the federal government. But concern for the rights of citizens faced with the power of the state to enforce laws and inflict punishment is a prominent feature of the United States Constitution. The Fourth Amendment guarantees protection against "unreasonable searches and seizures"; the Fifth Amendment guarantees that citizens shall not be compelled to testify against themselves or be tried more than once for the same crime (double jeopardy) or be deprived of due process of law; the Sixth Amendment guarantees the right to a public trial by an impartial jury, the right to subpoena and confront witnesses, and the right to legal counsel; the Eighth Amendment prohibits "cruel and unusual punishment" and "excessive" bail or fines.

The trend toward "hard time" incarceration for both teenage and adult offenders is becoming popular throughout the United States. It has yet to be determined whether these measures actually reduce recidivism.

It is important to note these points because they are at the heart of conflicts about how fairly laws are enforced and how impartially justice is meted out. In the controversy over capital punishment, for example, opponents argue that it has become a form of cruel and unusual punishment. Others argue that because those who are condemned are often unable to afford adequate counsel, they have been deprived of their rights under the Sixth Amendment. Whatever one believes about such controversies, it is clear that the Constitution establishes the basis for protection of individual rights but also leaves much discretion to citizens and lawmakers to establish the ground rules for how justice is to be carried out.

The role of the sociologist in these debates is to help establish a scientific basis for decision making. In the highly controversial area of retribution, this often means attempting to assess the efficacy of punishment, that is, whether it achieves the goal of deterrence for which it is usually established. For example, there is little or no social-scientific evidence that the death penalty acts as a deterrent. Criminologist Hans Zeisel (1982) compared murder rates in states that have had the death penalty continuously, states that have had it intermittently, and states that have not had the death penalty at any time. (See Figure 6–7.) He reached the following conclusion:

> These curves show with great clarity, first, that the homicide rate fluctuates dramatically over the course of the years; second, that these fluctuations are startlingly similar in all groups of states and therefore obviously independent of the availability of the death penalty. As if to underscore that independence, the latest surge in the homicide rate begins about the time we began executing again after a decade during which the death penalty was in limbo. (p. 60)

Zeisel and others also cite the negative effects of the severe anti-drug-dealing and anti-gun-possession laws put into effect in New York during the 1970s. In the years since these laws were passed, there have been significant increases in rates of drug dealing and arrests on drug and gun possession charges, despite much higher penalties for these offenses (Califano, 1998). Critics of such findings point out that very

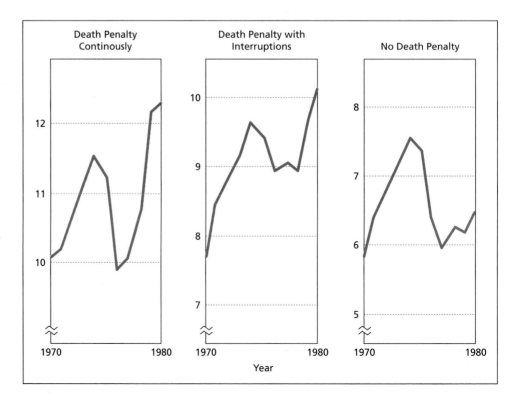

Figure 6–7 Homicide Rates in States With and Without the Death Penalty, 1970–1980 (Rate per 100,000 Population)

States that had the death penalty continuously: Arizona, Arkansas, Connecticut, Florida, Georgia, Montana, Nebraska, Nevada, Oklahoma, Texas, Utah, Virginia. States without the death penalty: Alaska, Hawaii, Iowa, Maine, Michigan, Minnesota, New Jersey, North Dakota, West Virginia, Wisconsin, Washington, D.C. The remainder of the states had the death penalty with interruptions.

Source: From H. Zeisel, *The Limits of Law Enforcement,* 1982, published by the University of Chicago. Reprinted by permission of the University of Chicago.

often criminals ask themselves before committing a crime, "Will I be punished if I am caught, and how severe will the punishment be?"

Research on the deterrent effects of punishment for crimes other than murder is made extremely difficult by the fact that very few perpetrators of these crimes are actually caught and sentenced. For many decades researchers have been able to show that whatever the punishment, a high likelihood of arrest is the greatest deterrent to crime. However, the arrest rate for property crimes is only 17.4 percent, and for all index felonies it is only about 21 percent (*UCR*, 1999). These rates are based on crimes reported to the police. Since far more crimes are committed than are known to the police, the actual rates are even lower.

Rehabilitation

The idea of rehabilitating offenders, which has developed only during the past century and a half, rests on the concept of crime as a social aberration and the offender as a social misfit whose aberrant behavior can be modified to conform to society's norms—in other words, "cured." As yet there are no clear guidelines concerning the form of rehabilitation that will be most effective with a particular kind of offender. Rehabilitation usually includes varying amounts of counseling, educational and training programs, and work experience. In the past the programs that have had the most success have been those that prepare criminals to enter the world of legitimate work and help them actually secure and hold jobs after incarceration. However, such ambitious programs are unlikely to be implemented on a large scale.

By the 1990s both the ideal and the practice of rehabilitation in prisons and among paroled offenders had reached a low point in what has historically been a cyclical process. Efforts to institute rehabilitation programs often follow efforts to increase the severity of sentencing. When it is shown that longer sentences and harsher punishment do not prevent crime or repeated offenses, society tends to shift toward efforts to rehabilitate criminals (Adler, Mueller, & Laufer, 1995; Friedman, 1993).

Studies of **recidivism**—the probability that a former inmate will break the law after release and be arrested again—have found no conclusive evidence that various approaches to rehabilitation, such as prison counseling programs or outright discharge, are more effective in reducing recidivism rates than more punitive alternatives. All that can be said is that some of the rehabilitation experiments undertaken to date—in particular, those that include extensive job training and job placement—have been more successful than others.

In an in-depth study of the juvenile-justice system and rehabilitation, sociologist Mark Jacobs (1990) found that professionals in the system—court officials, parole officers, psychologists, correctional administrators, and others—often believe that they must "screw the system" to make it rehabilitate rather than do further harm to juvenile offenders and young "persons in need of supervision." (The latter is a court-designated category of juveniles who are judged by their parents and others to be highly at risk of falling into a criminal subculture; courts can order these children to be placed in foster homes or residential care facilities even if they have committed no crimes.)

Jacobs's (1990) study showed that rehabilitation is hampered by a maze of organizations and regulations. Juveniles are shuttled from one jurisdiction or program to another and are often the victims of inadequately funded training programs and haphazard supervision by overburdened caseworkers. Given the extreme splintering of the system—family courts, juvenile courts, schools, parents, parole officers, correctional officers, psychologists, and many more—the young offender is often deprived of the rehabilitation to which he or she is entitled. And no coherent set of laws holds anyone in the system accountable for the youth's rehabilitation; that is, no single institution, group, or person can be said to be at fault. In such a no-fault society, Jacobs argues, rehabilitation will remain a distant ideal.

The nature of the prison system itself is a major hindrance to rehabilitative efforts. Prisons remove offenders from virtually all contact with society and its norms and subject them to almost continual contact with people who have committed crimes ranging from murder and petty larceny to homosexual rape and fraud. Often inmates are abused by their guards. A notorious case, probably indicative of more widespread patterns of abuse, was revealed in a 1992 court ruling against 119 former officials and guards at a Georgia prison for women; inmates were able to prove that they had been subjected to sexual abuse and rape over a period of several years (Applebome, 1992).

Within prison walls, offenders are punished by being deprived of liberty, autonomy, heterosexual contacts, goods and services, and the security that is normally obtained from participation in ordinary social institutions. At the same time, prisoners create a social order of their own. Adherence to the norms of prison life, which may be necessary for both mental and physical well-being, further separates inmates' goals and motivations from those of the larger society and makes it more difficult for them to benefit from whatever rehabilitative measures are available.

The most common type of rehabilitation program consists of work training. However, prison work is generally menial and unsatisfying, involving such jobs as kitchen helper or janitor. The difficulty of rehabilitating offenders in prison has led to various attempts to reform them outside prison walls. This approach seems to have several benefits. Treating offenders without exposing them to all the deficiencies of the prison system not only reduces the antisocial effects of prolonged exposure to a criminal society but also reduces the cost of custodial facilities and personnel. This makes treatment resources more available to those who seem to have the best prospects for rehabilitation. Perhaps the oldest and most widely used system of this kind is the *work release* program, in which prisoners are allowed to leave the institution for part of the day or week to work at an outside job. Although this type of program was first authorized in Wisconsin in 1913, it has become widely used only since the mid-1950s. Today many states and the federal government have authorized various kinds of work release programs.

The idea of releasing convicted felons into society, even for limited periods, has met with considerable opposition, but in general such programs seem to work well. Besides removing convicts from the criminal society in the prison, work release programs reimburse the state for some of the costs of supporting them and also allow the prisoners to support their dependents, thereby helping them stay off the welfare rolls. In addition, a work release program is a practical step toward reintegrating offenders into society since many of those who successfully complete the program retain their jobs after release. In fact, in a classic study Martinson (1972) found that the most effective single factor in rehabilitating offenders is a program of training for work following release; work during the prison term itself; and above all, job placement and training during probation.

At present there are two competing tendencies in corrections in the United States with regard to work and occupational training. On one hand, state prison systems are seeking to put prisoners to work, usually at unskilled jobs, on contracts with private businesses that will reduce soaring prison costs. On the other hand, there has been a decrease in the number of job training programs that prepare inmates for productive work after incarceration (Califano, 1998; Gondles, 1999).

The controversy over youthful offenders, especially the issue of whether there are "super-predators" among those now in prison or soon to enter prison for the first time, raises further questions about what kinds of corrections are most appropriate for this segment of the criminal population. So far it does not appear that more punitive programs, or "boot camps," are more effective than others. In addition, it is extremely costly to keep teenagers in prison or detention; the costs range from $20,000 to $90,000 per year, depending on the state and the particular form of incarceration (Belluck, 1996). Many states, therefore, are experimenting with programs in which youthful offenders can attend school or job training while in prison or in lieu of prison.

Programs like these are controversial because violent offenders are expected to do "hard time." In consequence, a few states (New Jersey, Texas, Florida, and California) have created residential training schools for juvenile offenders. This is an old concept that is being modified with new techniques for supervision, mentoring, and training. Although such programs may not work for the most violent or hardened young criminals, many penologists believe that when young inmates can be released to their communities with new skills and education, more positive options are open to them and they are less likely to drift back into a criminal lifestyle (Sadd & Grinc, 1996). But many young offenders return to extremely troubled families and peer groups. The more contact they have with professionals who can help them find alternatives to a violent home or neighborhood group, the better their chances—and society's—of avoiding crime and violence (Belluck, 1996).

Prevention

The idea of preventing crime and delinquency before they occur is an attractive one, but like rehabilitation it is difficult to implement. Aside from the deterrent effect of punishment, crime prevention is customarily defined in three different ways: (1) the sum total of all influences and activities that contribute to the development of a nondeviant personality; (2) attempts to deal with conditions in a person's environment that are believed to lead to crime and delinquency; and (3) specific services or programs designed to prevent further crime and delinquency.

Programs based on the first definition include measures designed to improve the social environment, such as improved housing and job opportunities for ghetto dwellers. Although one of their goals may be the reduction of crime and delinquency in the target area, this is rarely their primary goal. Moreover, studies of youths involved in antipoverty programs have not demonstrated a positive correlation between such participation and reduced delinquency rates. The most positive results are found in evaluations of Job Corps and other education, job-training, and social-skills programs in which young people at risk are given a chance to leave their neighborhood peer groups.

The second definition includes efforts based on Sutherland's theory of differential association (Sutherland & Cressey, 1960), such as efforts to reduce children's exposure to the antisocial and/or illegal activities of people around them, to improve their family life, and to create a viable and conforming social order in the community itself. Several projects of this sort have been attempted; some, like the Chicago Area Project (to be discussed shortly), have had notable success.

Most crime prevention programs attempt to work within the third definition—prevention of further delinquency and crime. They include well-established approaches such as parole, probation, and training schools, as well as more experimental programs. It is difficult to compare these approaches with those attempted under the other two definitions since they deal with quite different sets of circumstances.

An early prevention program, the Chicago Area Project, was established in the mid-1930s in the Chicago slums, where immigrant families were no longer able to control their children because of a weakening social order. The project sought to develop youth welfare programs that would be viable after the project leaders had left. It was assumed that local youths would have more success than outside workers in establishing recreation programs (including summer camping), community improvement campaigns, and programs devoted to teaching and assisting delinquent youths and even some adults who were returning to the community after release from prison. The project not only demonstrated the feasibility of using untrained local youths to establish welfare programs but also indicated a possible decrease in the delinquency rate (Kobrin, 1959). This model has been used successfully in many communities to diminish gang violence.

It is difficult to prove the effectiveness of preventive measures. Although they seem to fail at least as often as they succeed, the difficulty may lie more in the specific kinds of services offered than in the concept of prevention itself. When delinquency prevention seems to fail, there are often signs that there were some beneficial effects, even if they were not of the desired magnitude. It should be kept in mind that most of the programs described here are experimental and have not been attempted on a large scale. Delinquency prevention needs further research and more government funding (Hagedorn, 1988; Williams & Kornblum, 1994).

According to Charles Silberman (1980), one of the major problems with programs designed to control juvenile delinquency is that they place too much emphasis on methods of policing, more efficient courts, and improved correctional programs, and too little emphasis on community programs that give families the support they need to deal with delinquency:

> If a community development program is to have any chance of success, those in charge must understand that the controls that lead to reduced crime cannot be imposed from the outside; they must emerge from changes in the community itself and in the people who compose it. Hence the emphasis must be on enabling poor people to take charge of their own lives—on helping them gain a sense of competence and worth, a sense of being somebody who matters. (p. 430)

SOCIAL POLICY

In their efforts to reduce crime, governments at all levels experience more frustration than success. In a few short periods, such as the present period of relative and sustained affluence in the United States, crime rates have fallen, or at least the rates of some crimes have, but such lulls have been temporary. As crime historian Lawrence M. Friedman (1993) points out, crime is far too complicated and diverse and too firmly embedded in American culture to be controlled and eliminated. Whenever one kind of crime is reduced, criminals invent others. And social change is constantly at work on the criminal-justice system, producing a recurrent pattern of criminalizing, decriminalizing, and recriminalizing certain behaviors.

President Clinton and Attorney General Janet Reno appeared to have understood this history of failed wars on crime. In their first round of proposed anticrime legislation, they did not proclaim a great new offensive in the war on crime or make sweeping promises. Nor did the candidates in the 2000 presidential election make grand anticrime gestures. Their proposals tended to center on increased funding to enable local law enforcement agencies throughout the nation to hire more police officers. Clinton and Gore urged stricter laws to control the sale of handguns and to ban the sale of automatic weapons. They also advocated measures to punish corporate crime and attempted to shift the War on Drugs away from efforts to control the supply coming into the United States to greater emphasis on public education and drug treatment. New policy initiatives will no doubt depend on more basic changes in crime rates.

The fact that important decreases in some categories of violent crimes were announced in recent years also calmed public fear of crime somewhat. For the first time in recent memory, in fact, the public rated educational quality above crime and drugs as the foremost issue facing the nation in coming years. Crime remains a major concern of Americans, especially the elderly and residents of central cities, but according to the National Opinion Research Center (NORC), citizens are beginning to question such policies as mandatory sentences, the "three strikes" policy, and some aspects of the War on Drugs, which have resulted in large increases in the prison population (NORC, 1999).

Social policies to control crime or punish criminals are not formulated only at the federal level. States and municipalities often take the lead in promoting new approaches and policies. Examples include the reinstitution of capital punishment and chain gangs in some states and new rehabilitative programs in others. In this review of social policy we will

discuss trends and reforms in policies aimed at conventional, occupational, and organized criminals and then examine proposed changes in the juvenile-justice system.

Conventional Crimes

In 1998 about 12.5 million violent and property crimes were committed in the United
States. Of these, only about 21 percent were cleared by arrests, and even fewer ended
in convictions, making crime an attractive pursuit for many people (*UCR*, 1999). Even
the relatively small number of people apprehended presents an almost insurmountable burden for existing correctional systems. Court calendars and prison cells are so
overloaded that there is continual pressure to find ways to reduce sentences or to create new forms of corrections. One of the most controversial, yet widespread, strategies
is **plea bargaining,** in which the offender agrees to plead guilty to a lesser charge and
free the courts from the need to conduct a jury trial. By this means most of those who
are convicted of serious crimes receive shortened sentences. Plea bargaining has been
criticized for allowing dangerous criminals to receive mild sentences. It has been estimated, however, that if the plea-bargaining process were reduced to even 80 percent
of serious crimes, the number of trials would double and put an enormous strain on
the court system (Reid, 1993).

The prison system is also experiencing severe strains. By 1999, because of the increase in drug arrests in many parts of the United States, prison populations had
reached record levels (see Figure 6–8). The U.S. rate of imprisonment of 460 people
per 100,000 is higher than that of any other nation (Califano, 1998).

More than 100,000 juveniles are incarcerated on any given day, despite the fact
that they make up a smaller proportion of the total population than they did in the
1970s. Adult prison populations have also reached extremely high levels. However, of
the 5 million people in custody in all U.S. correctional systems, only about 20 percent
are in prisons. The majority are under community supervision through probation or
parole. (**Probation** is supervision of offenders who have not been sentenced to jail or
prison; **parole** is supervision of people who have been released from prison.) And although both probation and parole were originally intended for nonviolent offenders,
they are increasingly being used for those who have committed felonies because of
the costs of incarceration and the problems of overcrowded prisons.

Recidivism rates are quite high among felons who are placed on probation. Research
indicates that from half to two-thirds are rearrested, a situation that indicates the continuing need to develop a greater array of sentencing options and rehabilitation strategies while ensuring public safety (Adler, Mueller, & Laufer, 1995; Jenson & Howard,
1998). Faced with these problems, many states have been seeking alternatives to

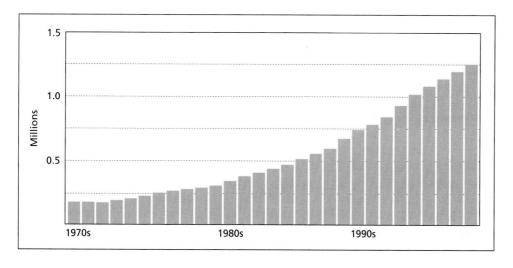

Figure 6–8 Total Population in
State and Federal Prisons
Source: Data from Bureau of Justice
Statistics.

conventional incarceration and parole. Community corrections, in which the offender provides a service to social-welfare agencies or neighborhood associations, is one approach. Another is house arrest and monitoring by electronic devices.

Occupational and Corporate Crimes

A variety of legal reforms have been proposed to curb occupational and corporate crimes. One approach would be to increase the penalties for such crimes. Frequently a company with a net worth of hundreds of millions of dollars faces a fine of only $50,000, and its executives may be fined only $5,000, upon conviction for fraud or price-fixing. Large corporations can regard such penalties as an acceptable risk. One way to increase fines is simply to raise the dollar amount of the penalty; another is to make the penalty a fixed percentage of the company's profits. It is widely believed that the ten-year prison sentence received by junk bond dealer and stock manipulator Michael Milken in 1990 was a signal to other white-collar criminals that the era of light sentences had ended.

Another aspect of legal reform involves changing laws to make them less easy to break. For example, complicated tax laws full of alternatives and loopholes may invite cheating. Streamlining the laws might both discourage cheating and make it easier to detect when it does occur. The law could also be reformed to make accomplices in occupational crimes vulnerable to court action, so that for each crime many more corporate employees would face punishment.

Obviously, stronger enforcement must accompany legal reform if it is to be meaningful, and this means more money and personnel for enforcement agencies. To detect more income tax cheating, for example, the IRS must hire more auditors. To detect more white-collar crime, the FBI must devote more resources to investigations in this area. Similarly, once a case against occupational offenders has been won in court, the judge must be willing to invoke the full penalty allowed under the law.

These two approaches—legal reform (particularly tougher penalties) and stronger enforcement—would probably deter much occupational crime. More than most other types of crimes, occupational crimes involve calculation, planning, and the weighing of gains against costs. Increasing the costs, as well as the risk of detection, might lead occupational criminals to conclude that honesty is more profitable.

Organized Crime

It is particularly hard to fight organized crime, for several reasons. A major one is the difficulty of obtaining proof of syndicate activities that will be accepted in court. Witnesses rarely come forward; either they fear retaliation or they themselves are too deeply implicated. Since the top levels of the syndicate's hierarchy are so well insulated from those below them, witnesses are rarely able to testify against them. Documentary evidence is equally rare since the transactions of organized crime are seldom written down. Finally, corruption hinders effective prosecution of organized crime.

Despite these obstacles, in recent decades the FBI has made immense progress in its battle against organized crime; today numerous reputed syndicate leaders are under indictment or in jail. Experts credit this breakthrough to a number of factors, of which the most prominent is the fact that the FBI now devotes about one-quarter of its personnel to combating organized crime. Other important factors are using undercover agents in long-term investigations, pooling the resources of agencies that formerly competed with one another, and giving the FBI jurisdiction in narcotics cases. Especially significant has been the use of sophisticated surveillance techniques and computer technology. The witness protection program, in which witnesses are offered new identities, support, and protection in moving away from their organized-crime contacts, has also proven successful in a number of instances. An example is the successful arrest and conviction of mob boss John Gotti and his son, both major organized-crime figures who were notorious for flouting the law.

Public-order and Juvenile-justice Reforms

Many criminologists and legal authorities agree that there are too many laws that make certain behaviors (such as truancy) illegal only for children, as well as too many laws that address nonviolent victimless crimes like adultery, homosexuality, prostitution, and drunkenness. Offenders in both categories account for 40 percent of the caseload in both juvenile and adult courts. In addition, abuse at home often causes juveniles to become runaways. When they are apprehended for this offense, they spend even more time in juvenile detention. The large number of arrests of juvenile runaways has led experts such as Edwin M. Schur (1973) to advocate a thorough reform of the concept of juvenile justice that would tolerate a broader range of behaviors and define as crimes only specific antisocial acts.

The conservative mood of the nation during the 1980s made such reforms unlikely; instead, the Crime Control Act of 1984 tightened existing laws, relaxed restrictions on evidence-gathering activities, and allocated more funds to the construction of prisons and detention facilities. At the same time, there was little effort to decriminalize juvenile status crimes, despite evidence that status offenders do not inevitably go on to commit serious crimes as adults (Silberman, 1980).

By the early 1990s rates of juvenile crimes and the number of juveniles in criminal detention had risen dramatically. These trends, combined with the impact of some highly sensational juvenile crimes, have tended to blur the distinction between juvenile and adult offenders. In 1996, for example, a 12-year-old boy became the youngest inmate of a high-security prison. He and his 13-year-old accomplice had been convicted of dropping a small child from a 14-story building in Chicago. The sentencing itself, carried out under a new Illinois law, was an example of the trend toward judging serious juvenile crimes on the same basis as adult crimes.

Fears of an increase in juvenile crimes are supported by statistical evidence, and victims of these crimes are calling for tougher penalties (Gest, 1996). But the trend toward greater punitiveness has its critics, who believe that putting young offenders in prison will simply produce more super-predators (Males, 1996).

In addition to proposals directed at law enforcement agencies, some small-scale community-based approaches have been attempted. An example is the House of Umoja in Philadelphia. This program, which combines surrogate family relationships with job opportunities and placement counseling for youths, has virtually eliminated street violence in a ghetto neighborhood. A similar program in Ponce, Puerto Rico, provides a wide range of services to an entire community; one of its achievements has been to cut the delinquency rate in half despite a rapidly growing teenage population (Kornblum & Boggs, 1984). Maryland, New York, and other states are also experimenting with programs that provide intensive home surveillance and counseling for delinquents from high-crime and poor neighborhoods.

Despite these and other measures, many experts agree that the problem remains far from a solution. None of the approaches taken so far has been shown to be successful (Reid, 1993). As a result, public policy toward serious juvenile crime is in a state of considerable confusion, and opinions on what can be done vary widely. As the rate of juvenile violence rises throughout the nation, policymakers are debating the causes and the possible remedies. The Department of Justice's position is that the problem is caused by the breakdown of family and community controls and that until these are strengthened there is little that federal funds can accomplish. However, members of the Congressional Select Committee on Children argue that the rate of poverty among children has increased to 20 percent at the same time that there have been immense cuts in child welfare services (32 percent), juvenile delinquency prevention programs (55 percent), and drug and mental-health treatment programs (30 percent). Most law enforcement officials believe that without more resources to address joblessness, lack of education, and lack of housing and recreational facilities and to provide drug treatment on demand, there will be little overall improvement in the juvenile crime situation (Diesenhouse, 1990; Males, 1996).

Beyond Left & Right

There are many differences among people on the liberal left and the conservative right concerning crime and its control. Liberals believe that crime is caused by social-structural factors, such as poverty, and recommend rehabilitative strategies for offenders. Conservatives stress personal responsibility and the rights of crime victims. Are there no areas of common ground? Yes, there are. Sociology offers some important ones, especially if one thinks globally.

Indeed, on the global level the differences between left and right diminish, at least when confronted by the threat of organized criminal attacks on the rule of law. If a society like Russia or Italy or even, in some specific cases, the United States cannot protect its citizens against criminal victimization and organized crime, it can no longer claim to be the legitimate representative of its people, nor can it guarantee order within its borders or contribute to world peace. These are fundamental issues of human existence. Without the rule of law, the distinctions between left and right are absurd. A sociological analysis of global crime shows us that policies to address the threat of criminal victimization are vital to economic and social well-being at all levels of society.

SUMMARY

- The criminal law prohibits certain acts and prescribes punishments to be meted out to offenders. In practice, the definition of criminality changes according to what law enforcement authorities perceive as criminal behavior.

- Researchers have attempted to find more reliable ways of tracking criminal activity. Self-report studies and victimization surveys provide useful data; both are used to supplement the FBI's *Uniform Crime Reports*.

- Violent personal crimes include assault, robbery, and the various forms of homicide. Robbery usually occurs between strangers, murder between friends or relatives.

- Occasional property crimes include vandalism, check forgery, shoplifting, and so on. Offenders are usually unsophisticated and unlikely to have a criminal record.

- Occupational, or white-collar, crimes are committed by people who break the law as part of their normal business activity. They include such acts as embezzlement, fraud (including computer crimes), and insider trading in the securities industry. Occupational offenders have a respectable appearance and often consider themselves to be respectable citizens.

- Corporate crimes include a variety of illegal practices of private corporations, including environmental crimes, insider trading, illegal labor practices, defrauding of pension plans, and the like. Such crimes are extremely difficult to control.

- Public-order offenses include prostitution, drunkenness, vagrancy, and the like. They are often called victimless crimes because they cause harm only to the offender.

- Conventional criminals commit robbery, burglary, and other crimes as a way of life, usually beginning their criminal careers as members of juvenile gangs.

- Organized crime is a system in which illegal activities are carried out as part of a rational plan devised by a large organization for profit. The profits come largely from supplying illegal goods and services to the public.

- Professional criminals are dedicated to a life of crime and are seldom caught. They include safecrackers, check forgers, and blackmailers.

- Teenagers and young adults account for almost half of all arrests in the United States. The majority of arrests for property crimes are of people under 25 years of age. In addition, many young people become involved in drug commerce at the retail level. Status offenses like running away and vagrancy are another common reason for arrests of juveniles, especially young women.

- Hate crimes are crimes in which the defendant intentionally selects a victim, or in the case of a property crime, the property that is the object of the crime, because of the actual or perceived race, color, national origin, ethnicity, gender, disability, or sexual orientation of any person. They are often carried out by young people, acting on emotions taken from the adults who socialize them.

- Various explanations of the causes and prevalence of crime have been suggested. They include biological explanations; demographic factors (including gender and age); and sociological explanations based on conflict theory, functionalism, and interactionism.

- Conflict approaches to the study of crime see inequalities of wealth, status, and power as the underlying conditions that produce criminal behavior. These inequalities are thought to explain the overrepresentation of blacks in official crime statistics.

- The functionalist explanation of crime is based on anomie theory, in which crime is considered to be the result of a disparity between approved goals and the means of achieving them.

- Interactionist explanations include differential association, in which criminal behavior is said to be learned from family and peers, and theories about the origin and character of delinquent subcultures.

- Efforts to control crime take four forms: retribution-deterrence, rehabilitation, prevention, and reform of the criminal-justice system. Retribution-deterrence focuses on punishing the criminal and attempting to deter others from committing similar crimes. The idea of rehabilitating offenders rests on the concept of cure; the most successful form of rehabilitation is work release. Programs to prevent crime and delinquency include parole, probation, training schools, and more experimental programs.

- Proposals for reform of the criminal- and juvenile-justice systems include imposing harsher and more specific penalties for conventional crimes, increasing the penalties for occupational and corporate crimes and improving law enforcement in this area, and repealing laws dealing with status and public-order offenses. Recently there has been increased emphasis on punishment and incapacitation as opposed to rehabilitation. However, higher rates of imprisonment have resulted in severe overcrowding of the prison system, leading to proposals like community corrections and house arrest.

KEY TERMS

crime index, p. 153
crime, p. 154
criminal law, p. 157
civil law, p. 157
victimization reports, p. 159
differential association, p. 161

embezzlement, p. 162
fraud, p. 162
organized crime, p. 164
status offenses, p. 166
anomie, p. 173

social control, p. 176
recidivism, p. 179
plea bargaining, p. 183
probation, p. 183
parole, p. 183

INTERNET EXERCISE

The web destinations for Chapter 6 are related to different aspects of crime and criminals. To begin your explorations, go to the Prentice Hall Companion Website: **http://prenhall.com/kornblum**. Then choose **Chapter 6** (Crime and Criminals). Next, select **destinations** from the menu on the left side of the screen. There are a variety of sites to investigate. We suggest that you begin with **Racial Profiling in America**. This site is sponsored by the American Civil Liberties Union. The *Critical Research* feature in this chapter deals with the problems associated with this extremely controversial practice. After you reach the opening page of the ACLU site, click on "Tales of DWB" (Driving While Black). Here you will be able to read about *actual cases* involving racial profiling and associated acts of discrimination. If you have time, there are various "news stories" accessible from this site that highlight this debatable procedure. You may wish to take a look at a few of them. After you have explored the Racial Profiling site, answer the following questions:

- What are your reactions to the practice of racial profiling? Do you think that this procedure violates people's rights? Why or why not?

- Do you think that the benefits of racial profiling outweigh the costs? Why or why not?

7 Violence

VIOLENCE

- Between 1820 and 1945, human beings killed 59 million other human beings—one every 68 seconds—in wars, murders, quarrels, and skirmishes.

- According to official statistics, approximately 16,914 murders were committed in 1998, as well as 93,103 rapes, 974,402 aggravated assaults, and 446,625 robberies.

- In 1998, 69 percent of those arrested for murder were between the ages of 17 and 34.

- At least 750,000 children are physically abused each year, and many die as a result.

- The rate of death due to firearms is from three to six times the rate in Western nations with comparable levels of industrial and urban development.

OUTLINE

The Concept of Violence

Explanations of Violence
The Biological Viewpoint
Frustration-Aggression and
   Control Theories
Violence as a Subculture
Violence as Rational Choice
The Influence of the Mass
   Media

Criminal Violence
Criminal Homicide
Hate Crimes
Assault and Robbery
Rape

Family Violence
Child Abuse
Spouse Abuse
Elder Abuse

**Gangs, Guns,
and Violent Death**

Social Policy

Gun Control

Media Violence

**Dealing with Family
Violence**

**Race, Poverty, and
Violence: The Unfinished
Agenda**

In the industrial nations, rates of interpersonal violence have decreased over the past few years. Murder rates are moving downward. More people are employed, a condition that is always associated with lower rates of violence. At the same time, however, fear of violence is heightened by sensational incidents of school violence and terrorism. And on the world stage, intergroup violence is an ever more serious social problem. "Ethnic cleansing," or warfare based on ethnic and national hostilities, is widespread in Southeast Asia, the former Soviet Union, and Africa. In this chapter we narrow our focus from crime in general to particular acts of violence, their prevalence, their possible causes, and efforts to control violence in the United States and elsewhere in the world.

Despite signs of progress, the level of deadly violence remains higher in the United States than in any other urban industrial nation. Although rates of interpersonal violence may be higher in a few poorer nations, no major industrialized nation has homicide rates as high as those in the United States. For black men in the United States, the chances of living beyond age 40 are worse than in the poorest nations of the world, mainly because of the toll taken by violence. The widespread availability of guns and the contribution of drugs to violence are important factors in this situation, but those who study the problem also point to the pervasiveness of violence in our culture. Increasingly frequent incidents of aggressive driving, often referred to as "road rage," increases in fights at sports events and school outings, rising rates of family violence, and outbreaks of deadly violence in workplaces such as post offices have drawn attention to the underlying levels of interpersonal violence that result in spectacular and grisly headlines (Elvin, 1999).

Much violent action throughout the world is not recognized as such. This is particularly true of violence associated with the rise or expansion of a political party or social movement; most groups try to forget, justify, or disguise their use of violence for these purposes. Whereas extralegal violent acts like murder, rape, or gang wars elicit public condemnation, other forms of violence are accepted or even praised, for example, those that occur in war. Similarly, in troubled times and in frontier areas, vigilante activities are often approved by the local community as the only available means of maintaining order. In general, violence by or on behalf of the state is less likely to be condemned than violence by private citizens or violent acts in defiance of authority.

Despite the relative stability of its institutions, the United States has witnessed more violent behavior than other Western industrial nations. According to official statistics, approximately 16,914 murders were committed in 1998, as well as 93,103 rapes, 974,402 aggravated assaults, and 446,625 robberies (*UCR*, 1999). (See Figure 7–1.) The significance of violence and the need to find means to control and prevent it are apparent.

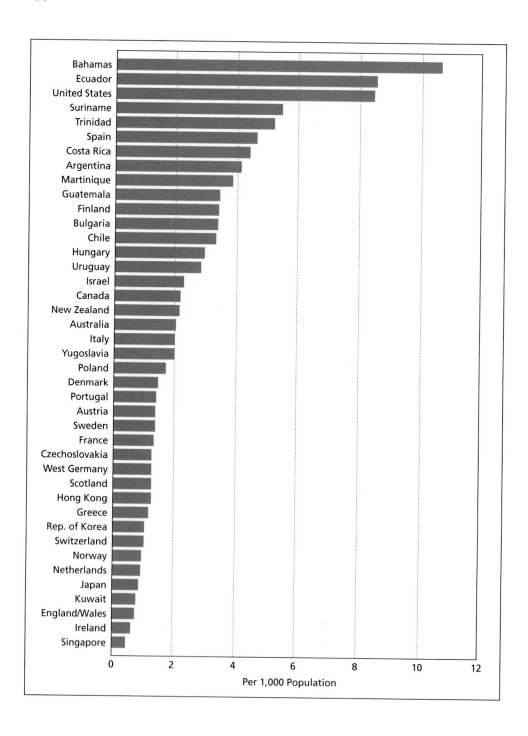

Figure 7–1 Homicide Rates, Selected Countries

Source: Reis & Roth, 1993.

The Concept of Violence

The word **violence** has a generally negative connotation; it has been defined as "behavior designed to inflict injury to people or damage to property" (Graham & Gurr, 1969, p. xiv). It may be considered legitimate or illegitimate, depending on who uses it and why and how it is used. Some special uses of violence, particularly in athletic activities like football and hockey, are so socially accepted that they are usually perceived not as violence but as healthy and even character-building behaviors.

Also not generally thought of as violence is **structural violence,** that is, "the dominance of one group over the other, with subsequent exploitative practices" (Galtung, 1971, p. 124). The threat or potential of violence is usually sufficient to keep the dominated group "in its place," but its effect on social relations is very much like that of overt violence. This aspect of violence will not be discussed at length in this chapter, but it should be noted that a dominated group's recognition that it has experienced structural violence may engender overt group violence such as civil disorder and rebellion, as can be seen in Northern Ireland.

Sociologists recognize that *violence* is an ambiguous term whose meaning is often established through political processes (Skolnick, 1998). What a society classifies as violent is likely to depend largely on who provides the definitions of violence and has the resources to publicize and enforce them. War is a classic example: The actions of one's own side are generally viewed as honorable, whereas the other side is described as the aggressor and its violent acts are viewed as atrocities. Similarly, within a nation, accusations of violent behavior are exchanged by those in power and their relatively powerless adversaries: "Within a given society, political regimes often exaggerate the violence of those challenging established institutions. The term *violence* is frequently employed to discredit forms of behavior considered improper, reprehensible, or threatening by specific groups which, in turn, may mask their own violent response with the rhetoric of order or progress" (Skolnick, 1969, p. 4).

Although we think of ourselves as a peace-loving people, we continually resort to violence in defense of what we consider our vital interests. The American Civil War was among the bloodiest in world history.

Former math professor Theodore Kaczynski, suspected of being the Una-bomber who, over the course of several years, sent lethal letter bombs to individuals throughout the nation. He may be an example of a new type of serial killer with an extremely high degree of technical skill and a homicidal obsession.

Several writers have attempted to justify the use of violence by a colonized people against the colonial regime or by the have-nots against the haves. Frantz Fanon (1968), the Caribbean French psychiatrist whose experiences in the Algerian war made him a revolutionary, spoke of violence as a "cleansing force" that frees the spirit and restores self-esteem; it unifies the people and teaches them to assert themselves against any attempt at tyranny, even by their own leaders. Herbert Marcuse (1964) wrote about the revolutionary potential of people who have been denied full participation in the social life of advanced industrial nations—"the substratum of the outcasts and outsiders, the exploited and persecuted of other races and other colors, the unemployed and the unemployable" (p. 256).

The concept of violence thus has many dimensions. A useful distinction can be made between **institutional violence,** or violence exercised on behalf of or under the protection of the state, and the **noninstitutional violence** of those who are opposed to established authority. Violence in both of these categories may be either constructive or destructive; but institutional violence is usually presumed to be legitimate until proven otherwise, whereas people who engage in noninstitutional violence are punished. Thus, wars or violent police actions are usually considered legitimate because they are conducted under the aegis of the state; violent protests and demonstrations, revolutionary activity, civil disorders, and violent criminal activity are not. Although this difference is partly a matter of the difference in power between the "ins" and the "outs," it is also based on the traditional idea that the state may do some things that an individual citizen may not do in order to meet its responsibility for protecting the general welfare. It is when the state is seen to be using force for purposes contrary to the general welfare that noninstitutional violence—sabotage, terrorism, rebellion, or revolution—is likely to occur.

Explanations of Violence

The Biological Viewpoint

Homo sapiens, self-proclaimed to represent the pinnacle of evolution, is in fact the earth's most dangerous living species. Between 1820 and 1945, human beings killed 59 million other human beings—one every 68 seconds—in wars, murders, quarrels, and skirmishes (Boelkins & Heiser, 1970). Violence is also commonplace in many American homes. In recent years the volume of reports of child abuse and complaints to the police of domestic violence has been high enough to prompt Congress to hold numerous hearings on the subject (Berry, 1995; Gelles, 1996). Even before the sensational trial of O. J. Simpson brought family violence and spouse abuse to national attention, professionals who work with families in distress were warning that violence is an everyday occurrence in far too many families.

Is violence simply part of human nature? Since it is such a common occurrence, some social scientists have argued that human aggressive tendencies are inherent or instinctual. According to this view, only social organization keeps violent tendencies under control. Other experts argue that aggression is natural but violence is not. In an exhaustive review of research on the causes of interpersonal violence, a panel of experts convened by the National Academy of Sciences concluded that there is no solid evidence to support neurological or biological explanations of violent behavior. The panel did note, however, that findings from studies of animals and humans point to several features of the nervous system as possible sources of such explanations and recommended continued research (Reiss & Roth, 1993). Given the weight of evidence in favor of social and psychological explanations of violent behavior, this recommendation drew considerable criticism from social scientists (Kornblum, 1993).

In her response to the report, Dorothy Nelkin (1995), a well-known evaluator of scientific panels, argued that "biology is not destiny" and "it is not necessary to explain through biology why a child exposed to poverty and racism might become violent." The real source of violence, she believes, can be found in the growing inequality in the United States and other societies. This is an important sociological viewpoint, to which we will return in this and later chapters.

Frustration-Aggression and Control Theories

Some theorists have argued that violence is a form of aggression that results from frustration. An unfulfilled need produces the frustration, and the frustration is vented in aggression. The strength of the impulses, needs, or wishes that are blocked determines the amount of frustration experienced, which in turn determines the degree of aggression. Failure, lack of affection, and poverty are suggested as possible causes of frustration. The frustration-aggression theory has been described as the easiest and most popular explanation of social violence of all kinds, including riots, political turmoil, robberies, and juvenile delinquency (Berkowitz, 1993). The main problem with this theory is that it fails to explain why frustration leads to aggression in some instances and not in others; moreover, frustration-aggression can be defined so broadly that it can cover almost any conceivable situation.

Related to the frustration-aggression theory is the control theory, which states that a person's ability to restrain or control impulsive behavior is correlated with the existence of close relationships with significant others. In this view, people may resort to violence when their attempts to relate to others in their own fashion are frustrated. The fact that violence is significantly more prevalent among ex-convicts, alcoholics, and others who are out of the mainstream of society and estranged from family and friends is also cited as evidence for the control theory. Thus, from this standpoint, murderers are likely to be "egocentric, impulsive, rebellious, or sadistic persons who cannot control their emotions" (Lunde, 1975, p. 39).

Of course, not all people who fit this description become murderers, nor do all murderers fit this description. One study suggested that there are actually two common personality types among murderers. One is undercontrolled: The person is unable to restrain aggressive impulses, has "never developed internal taboos against lashing out when provoked, and [has] few inhibitions about satisfying . . . acquisitive or sexual desires aggressively." The second is the exact opposite: an overcontrolled person who inhibits aggressive impulses almost completely and for whom "even socially acceptable outlets for aggression, such as swearing or pounding on a table, [are] off-limits" (Lunde, 1975, p. 39). Such people are said to repress their anger or hostility to the breaking point, until they suddenly and unpredictably explode.

It is difficult to demonstrate the validity of the control theory since most murders and many other violent crimes are spontaneous, and their causes are not always clear. The lack of close relationships could simply be one factor among many that lead to violent behavior. The control theory does, however, suggest one explanation of why violent crimes are increasing in frequency. In the past, various social factors—generally accepted moral standards; church membership; smaller, more intimate communities—

aided in the development of controlled personalities. As a result of the erosion of these traditional social controls, people feel isolated and are more likely to resort to violence.

Violence as a Subculture

Many sociologists believe that violence is a learned behavior, one that is acquired through the process of socialization. Accordingly, aggressive or violent actions are most likely to occur in a culture or subculture in which violence is accepted or encouraged. Originally devised to explain juvenile gang behavior, the subculture theory has also been seen as the key to violence in general. In this model, members of violent subgroups have a low threshold for provocation, perceiving threats to their integrity in situations that would not be perceived as such by members of the dominant society. The norms of these groups require a combative response to provocation (Felson & Tedeschi, 1993).

It has also been suggested that all American males participate to some extent in a subculture of violence; the relatively low rate of violent acts by women is cited as evidence. Eugene C. Bianchi (1974), for example, sees professional football as a metaphor for America's "physical brutality, profit-maximizing commercialism . . . authoritarian-military mentality, and sexism" (p. 842). He notes that school and family join in forming "male children into competitors and achievers" (p. 843).

If violence is a consequence of social learning, frustration is not a prerequisite for violent behavior. Rather, violent habits are acquired through imitation or as a result of reinforcement of aggressive behavior. Along these lines, it has been shown that physically aggressive parents tend to have physically aggressive offspring. In addition, laboratory studies indicate that children who observe adults displaying physical aggression will be more aggressive in their later play activities than children who are not similarly exposed (Bandura, 1986). On the basis of this and much other research, social scientists conclude that physical punishment by parents is more likely to encourage physical violence in children than to discourage it. Violence frustrates the child and provides a model to imitate and learn from. Nevertheless, the majority of American parents continue to believe that because they were spanked occasionally and did not become violent criminals, they should use physical punishment on their children when it is called for. Survey research data show that 65 percent of Americans approved of spanking in 1998, a small decrease since the mid-1940s, when 74 percent did so. But these numbers mask major differences in the propensity to use physical punishment by people in different social classes and with different levels of education. Poll data show that about 40 percent of college-educated Americans disapprove of spanking, whereas only 20 percent of those who did not complete high school disapprove (Rossellini, 1998).

The subculture theory asserts that aggression is a byproduct of a culture that idealizes a tough, "macho" image. This theory developed from analyses of official statistics, which suggest that certain subcultures have higher rates of violent crime than other segments of society. But as we suggested in Chapter 6, the stereotype that most acts of aggression are committed by young, minority males is erroneous because official statistics do not register the actual incidence of crime. Moreover, since the statistics do not reflect the attitudes or ideologies of individual offenders, it is difficult to discover the motives for their crimes. Data collected for the National Commission on the Causes and Prevention of Violence indicated that interpersonal violence received a low rate of approval in all socioeconomic groups (Reiss & Roth, 1993).

A study of British men who had been convicted of acts of hostile aggression found that none of the men had committed their crimes to protect their reputation or win peer approval. The highest percentage of the crimes sprang from the aggressor's desire to inflict harm on the victim (Berkowitz, 1993). Indeed, crime, including violent crime, can be seductive for some perpetrators, who obtain a thrill from exercising power over another person or inflicting pain. Although these seductions fortunately do not apply to most people, some fall under the spell of violence and crime; for them, behavior that seems sick or irrational to most people may be explained by the desire to capture the thrill of causing pain or getting away with a violent act (Katz, 1988).

In sum, people who commit acts of hostile aggression seem to share not an adherence to external subcultural norms but rather a similar set of psychological traits that can be found in any social, economic, or ethnic group.

Violence as Rational Choice

Although the implications of violence for human life and society seem wholly irrational, in many instances violent behavior can be interpreted as a rational means of attaining otherwise impossible ends. Rational-choice theory looks at all forms of human behavior for evidence of the actor's conscious or unconscious weighing of costs versus benefits (Hechter, 1987). Thus, rational-choice theorists would ask how criminals weigh the chance of punishment against the likelihood of gain from breaking the law. Although it would seem that crimes that involve terror and bloodshed are highly irrational acts committed by crazed individuals, in fact in many cases a rational strategy is at work.

Such crimes as extortion, kidnapping, and blackmail are often accompanied by the threat of violence. They are referred to as **strategic crimes,** however, because the violent act is one move in a complex game played by the criminal, the victim, and law enforcement agencies (Laver, 1982). In these games, the criminals often wish to achieve their goals without resorting to maximum violence, but they must be prepared to use maximum force to convince the authorities that they are serious. To take just one example, "The successful kidnapper is the one who is perfectly prepared to kill the hostage and who can get this point across to his victim" in such a way that the law enforcement agencies involved will agree to meet the kidnapper's demands (p. 91).

The rational-choice approach is limited as an explanation of violence, but it is useful in situations in which it is important to understand what the violent actor hopes to gain. It stresses the importance of communication in cases of kidnapping, siege, and the like. Without communication, the strategic criminal and the authorities cannot reach an agreement that would prevent further violence. An example is the standoff between the FBI and David Koresh, the leader of the Branch Davidian cult, which eventually led to the tragic deaths of many cult members in a fire that engulfed their fortified compound near Waco, Texas, in 1993. It is for this reason that the media often play such a crucial role in situations like hijackings, in which hostages are held until the terrorist's demands are met. In fact, the role of the media in violence of all kinds is significant and controversial, as will become clear in the next section.

The Influence of the Mass Media

Over the past 40 years, hundreds of studies have attempted to show what, if any, relationship there is between viewing violence on television and acting violently. There are literally thousands of social-scientific articles on the subject, many of which are based on about 200 actual empirical studies, but the results remain inconclusive. Studies of children's responses to TV or movie violence tend to show that (1) children imitate behavior they see on television; (2) they are more likely to imitate behavior that is rewarded than behavior that is punished; (3) from the frequency of violence on television they learn that it is normal; and (4) from watching violence on a steady basis they may become desensitized to violence (Leland, 1995). There is other evidence that suggests that the most aggressive children and adults are most likely to have strong imitative reactions to TV or movie violence.

George Gerbner (1990, 1996), one of the foremost TV researchers in the world, argues that the question of whether television causes violence misses the point. He believes that TV violence stimulates a number of responses that go beyond simple aggression and include insecurity, mistrust, and gloom. Television and movie violence, he believes, is used to define who can get away with what against whom, who is likely to be a victim and who a victimizer.

Although none of these positions is based on definitive research, it is clear that some films on television and in the movies have actually stimulated copycat violence. Young people have been burned while copying the types of fires started by Beavis and Butt-head; Britain and Ireland banned the 1994 film *Natural Born Killers* because of imitative murders in the United States; the list could include many other recent films that have been implicated in violent acts (Leland, 1995). Violent video games need to be considered as well. Here, too, the research results are inconclusive, but games like Mortal Kombat have been found to raise levels of aggression and hostility in children and adults who play them frequently (Ballard & Wiest, 1996).

The influence of the mass media, particularly television, in the reporting of protests, demonstrations, civil disorders, and other forms of potentially violent activity is another important issue. There are two questions here: Do the media distort the facts by stressing the violent aspects of news events, and does the presence of media reporters tend to increase the possibility that violence will occur? The answer to both questions may be yes, in some instances. Distortion and provocation are difficult concepts to measure, however, and the matter is far from settled (Gerbner, 1996). There is reason to fear that the extensive publicity given to school shootings, bomb scares, prison riots, and political assassinations is contagious, inspiring other attempts to engage in similar behavior.

In this regard there is a growing tendency to look carefully at local TV programming. Many people, especially in minority communities, are increasingly critical of the emphasis on violent crimes and on violent behavior in general. These critics cite research by Robert Putnam that shows that the more television a person watches, the more he or she is likely to overestimate the crime rate and express distrust of other people (Budiansky, 1996). These and other criticisms of media violence are causing many to support the V-chip, a controversial technological means of controlling young people's access to TV violence (B. Carter, 1996). We consider this subject more fully in the Social Policy section of the chapter.

It is an oversimplification, of course, to assume that any portrayal of violence will tempt spectators to act out what they have seen. Both the context of the stimulus and the attitude of the viewer must also be considered. The desire to imitate what is seen on the TV or movie screen is likely to depend largely on how it is presented, although we still lack hard evidence on what the relevant variables are. Similarly, the emotional condition of individual viewers will predispose them to react in different ways. Scenes of a prison riot are likely to evoke quite different reactions from a high school dropout who feels oppressed by the system than they would from an ambitious young executive.

Criminal Violence

Statistically, violent crimes are the least prevalent types of crime. According to the FBI's *Uniform Crime Reports* (*UCR*, 1999), murder, robbery, aggravated assault, and forcible rape account for 12.2 percent of all reported crimes; the remainder are property crimes and status offenses. But although violent crime is not the most common type, it is the most frightening. People who return to a burglarized home often report feeling revulsion at the thought of strangers handling their personal possessions; the intrusion itself is felt as a defilement. But the defilement of one's body in a violent attack is a far more terrifying prospect. More than any other crime, it threatens one's integrity and sometimes one's life.

In this section we examine three types of violent crime: homicide, assault, and rape. Later in the chapter we discuss the violence that occurs in families and the possible links between violence and gangs.

Criminal Homicide

Criminal homicide takes two forms: **Murder** is defined as the unlawful killing of a human being with malice aforethought; **manslaughter** is unlawful homicide without malice aforethought. In practice, it is often difficult to distinguish between them. Someone may attack another person without intending to kill, but the attack may result in death. Depending on the circumstances, one case might be judged to be murder and another to be manslaughter. Often the deciding factor is the extent to which the victim is believed to have provoked the assailant.

Paradoxically, most murderers do not have a criminal record. Of course, there are those who use actual or threatened violence as tools in a criminal career, but these are exceptions. As a rule, professional criminals try to keep violence—especially killing—to a "necessary" minimum because of the "heat" it would bring from the law. Most murderers do not see themselves as real criminals, and until the murder occurs, neither does society. Murderers do not conform to any criminal stereotype, and murder does not usually form part of a career of criminal behavior.

Murder does, however, follow certain social and geographic patterns. Reported murders occur most often in large cities. The murder rate for large metropolitan areas is 7 per 100,000 people, compared to 5 per 100,000 in rural counties and 4 per 100,000 in cities outside metropolitan areas (*UCR*, 1999). The incidence of murder is unevenly distributed within cities; as Donald T. Lunde (1975) has pointed out, "Most city neighborhoods are just as safe as the suburbs" (p. 38). There are also regional differences; for example, murder is more likely to occur in the South, even though it is one of the more rural parts of the country. This seems to be a result of the culture of the region, which tends to legitimize personal violence and the use of weapons.

Most murderers are men, who generally are socialized to be more violent than women and to use guns for recreation or for military purposes; guns are the most common murder weapon. Most murderers are young; in 1998, 69 percent of those arrested for murder were between the ages of 17 and 34. The victims are young, too; in 1998, 54 percent were between the ages of 20 and 34 (*UCR*, 1999). More than half of all murder victims are members of minority groups. Most of the time, the killer and the victim are of the same race. In 1998, 87 percent of white murder victims were slain by white offenders, and 94 percent of black victims were slain by black offenders (*UCR*, 1999).

More significant than the demographic characteristics of murderers and their victims is the relationship between them. Several studies have indicated that this relationship is generally close; often the murderer is a member of the victim's family or an intimate friend. A high proportion of murderers are relatives of their victim, often the spouse. Victim studies suggest that there is a great deal of unreported domestic violence and that the majority of violent crimes are committed by family members, friends, or acquaintances (Reid, 1991). One study found that

> more than 40 percent of murder victims are killed in residences. . . . More women die in their own bedrooms than anywhere else. One in every five murder victims is a woman who has been killed there by her spouse or lover. Husbands are most vulnerable in the kitchen; that's where wives are apt to pick up knives to finish family arguments.
>
> The other half of murders involving close relatives include parents killing children, children killing parents, or other close relatives killing each other. These victims usually die in the living room from gunshot wounds. Another 6 percent of murders [are] between more distant relatives. (Lunde, 1975, pp. 35–36)

Most murders occur during a quarrel between two people who know each other well. Both the murderer and the victim may have been drinking, perhaps together, before the event; as noted in Chapter 5, many homicides are alcohol-related. Even though many homicides occur during the commission of other crimes, these killings, too, are usually unpremeditated—a thief surprised by a security officer, a bank robber confronted by an armed guard, and so on. In addition, some homicides involve police officers, many of whom are killed in the line of duty. In 1960, 48 law enforcement officials were killed in the states and territories of the United States. This number reached a peak of 134 in 1975 and stood at 61 in 1998 (*UCR*, 1999).

The mentally ill commit murder at the same rate as the general population, but serial killers are almost always psychotic—either paranoid or sexual sadists (Nocera, 1999). These murderers may hear voices commanding them to kill, think they are superhuman or chosen for a special mission, or kill to avert imagined persecution. Sadists may torture before killing and/or mutilate their victims afterwards. Unlike most murderers, psychotic killers are seldom acquainted with their victims, who are often representatives of a type or class—rich businessmen, for example, or young middle-class women.

Mass Murders. There is some evidence that mass murders (in which four or more people are killed by the same person in a short time) are becoming more frequent. Although the number fluctuates from year to year, some of the worst cases of the century have occurred since 1980.

On July 18, 1984, James Oliver Huberty, a recently fired security guard, opened fire in a McDonald's restaurant, killing 21 people and injuring 20 others. Before the 1995 Oklahoma City bombing, this was the worst massacre by a single person in a single day in U.S. history. In 1989, Theodore ("Ted") Bundy, an articulate and rather charming drifter, was executed for the murder of numerous children and teenagers throughout the United States. These two cases, one a psychotic who murdered in a fit of rage, the other a cool but also psychotic individual who organized a series of killings (and therefore is known as a serial killer), illustrate quite well the types of people who commit mass murders. Generally, a mass murderer like Huberty kills in a fit of spontaneous rage, whereas a serial killer is highly organized and seeks to perfect a murder technique that will prevent detection and apprehension. Most serial killers have deep emotional problems concerning sexuality and describe the act of violence itself as thrilling and compelling (Holmes & DeBurger, 1987; Levin & Fox, 1985; Reid, 1991).

Workplaces like post offices, banks, and factories are increasingly frequent scenes of mass murders or outbreaks of lethal violence, apparently because of a buildup of rage in a person who fits the profile of a potential mass murderer. Unfortunately, it is extremely difficult to know beforehand whether a person fits that profile. There is a need, therefore, for greater vigilance and more open lines of communication in the workplace (Nigro & Waugh, 1996).

School Violence. Parents and students in the United States and other industrial nations have been alarmed by recent episodes of extreme violence in and around schools. Most of these have occurred in the United States. Schools were once viewed as safe and nurturing environments for children, but school shootings in Arkansas, Colorado, Alaska, Kentucky, and Washington, among others, have changed this perception for the worse. Deborah Prothrow-Stith (1996), an expert on adolescent violence, points out that there has always been a certain amount of school violence due to bullies or cliques. But recent outbreaks of violence in and around schools have been far more lethal than those experienced by earlier generations.

But how serious is school violence, and what are its causes? Another question, which critical sociologists and social commentators frequently ask in response to sensational coverage of violent incidents, is, What are the consequences of school violence for the quality of life and for the rights of students in schools?

Even before the incident in Littleton, Colorado, in which 15 people were killed, poll data indicated that the American public perceived fighting, violence, and gangs as one of the top three most serious problems in public schools. An estimated 2.7 million violent crimes take place annually either at school or near schools, according to data from the National Crime Victimization Survey (Nolin, Davies, and Chandler, 1996). Reports from the Bureau of Justice Statistics offer evidence that for youths aged 12 to 15, 37 percent of violent crime victimizations take place on school property. National school safety reports since the early 1990s show that each month about 28,000 high school students and about 5,000 teachers are attacked while in school. Findings from a National School Boards Association study conducted in 1994, again before the most sensational events in Littleton and Paducah, Kentucky, indicate that 80 percent of surveyed school officials believe that violence in schools had increased in the past five years (Futrell, 1996).

Despite the emotion it generates, there is as yet no national standard or system for reporting school violence. To address this problem, several national studies based on polling and sampling techniques have been initiated. Chief among these is the Youth Risk Behavior Survey (YRBS), which asks a large national sample of teachers and students a standard set of questions about their experiences with school violence. Several government-funded studies of adolescent health and school-related violence have recently been completed, including the Safe School Study, the National Adolescent Student Health Survey, and the School Health Policies and Programs Study. All of these are too recent to allow for reporting on trends in school violence, but they do establish baseline measures against which future trends can be measured. Congress and the president have also passed or proposed policies to deal with violence; these are discussed in Chapter 13.

The shocking events in Littleton have received a great deal of attention because Columbine High School was perceived as a safe haven, a middle- and upper-middle-class school far from the impoverished and racially diverse inner-city communities where higher levels of school violence are too often taken for granted. The enormous death toll and the evident hatred that had stimulated it produced panic, a reaction that, though understandable, stifles or inhibits the very strategies that educators suggest for dealing with the problem. These strategies hinge on efforts to implement greater openness in communication among students and teachers, more direct discussion of cliques and rivalries in school, more emphasis on negotiation skills, and enhancement of self-esteem and tolerance. (See the Critical Research feature on page 200.)

A law enforcement officer comforts a young girl as students are led through backyards of a residential area near the scene of a school shooting at Columbine High School in Littleton, Colorado.

Hate Crimes

As noted in Chapter 6, the term *hate crime* is used to refer to incidents that appear to have been motivated by feelings about race, religion, sexual orientation, ethnicity and national origin, or disability. Table 7–1 shows the proportions of hate crimes directed against different groups in the latest year for which statistics are available. As in the case of school violence, the measurement of hate crime is not standardized throughout the United States or the world, but recent efforts by the U.S. government, particularly the FBI, to make hate crime a major category of analysis are changing that situation. Note also that most of the hate crimes included in the table are based on individual offenses or offenses committed by small groups. Typically, the hate crimes that come to the attention of the public are extremely brutal crimes such as the killing of Matthew Shepard because he was gay or the dragging death of James Byrd,

CRITICAL RESEARCH

Crisis of Youth Violence or Adult Panic ?

Sensational and drastic acts of violence, such as the shootings and suicides at Columbine and other high schools, result in copycat violence, calls for urgent legislation, sermons about wayward youths, and a host of other immediate reactions. Critical sociologists, however, warn about over-reaction. They warn that tragic violence can distort realities. Panic can stifle more constructive responses and worsen the underlying problems by denying students' rights and gagging their voices. Harvard research fellow Wendy Kaminer and University of California sociologist Mike Males exemplify this critical view. Here is how Kaminer (1999) applies her critical viewpoint on youth, school, and violence:

> Fearful of violence and drugs, intolerant of dissent or simple nonconformity, public school officials are on the rampage. They're suspending and expelling even grade school students for making what might be considered, at worst, inappropriate remarks, dressing oddly, or simply expressing political opinions. Efforts to strip students of rights are hardly new, but they have been greatly accelerated in recent months by hysteria about school violence and "terroristic" threats.
>
> In Ohio a third-grader was suspended after writing a fortune cookie message, "You will die an honorable death," which he submitted for a school project. (A terroristic threat? Or an innocent, well-intentioned remark by a child who watches martial-arts videos?) Eleven high school students in Ohio were suspended for contributing to a gothic-themed web site. In Virginia a 10th-grader was suspended for dying his hair blue. In Missouri, high school junior Dustin Mitchell was suspended and required to perform 42 days of community service with the local police department for offering a flippant opinion on school violence in an Internet chat room (when asked if a tragedy like the Littleton shootings could happen in his school, Mitchell responded "yes").
>
> Those students who dare to use their speech rights to protest such draconian restrictions on speech are liable to be punished severely. In Texas, 17-year-old high school student Jennifer Boccia was suspended for wearing a black armband to school to protest restraints on free speech that followed the shootings in Littleton. Boccia was also reprimanded

In the aftermath of school violence, young people who choose to dress and act in nonconforming ways often face hostility from more conforming adults and peers.

by her school principal, Ira Sparks, for daring to tell her story to the media; she was told that if she wanted to clear her record, she should refrain from speaking to the media before discussing her remarks with school officials. Boccia made a federal case of it and won a settlement from her school vindicating her First Amendment rights. The landmark 1969 Supreme Court decision *Tinker* v. *Des Moines Independent Community School District* upholding the right to wear a black armband to school to protest the Vietnam War has not been overruled, but its assertion that students do not leave their First Amendment rights at the schoolhouse door has not been honored either. (p. 11)

Kaminer and Males both point out that despite sensational juvenile violent acts, the trends in youth violence have actually been quite favorable in recent years. Males (1998) observes,

> The sharp increase in teenage murder and violent crime from 1984 to 1992 occurred only among inner-city populations stressed by poverty, job loss, isolation, and growth in warring gangs. States which separate statistics by ethnicity, such as California, show that violence and homicide among white (non-Latino) teenagers actually declined over the last two decades. A white California teenager is only one-fifth as likely to be murdered as a black fifty-year-old. So concentrated is youth homicide that two or three Los Angeles zip codes account for more than the entire state of Minnesota. (p. 22)

The most frightening myth, Males believes, is "that kids today are more murderous and that the nation faces rising hordes of 'adolescent super-predators.'"

Magazine covers and "experts," Males argues, "trumpet that teenagers everywhere are slaughtering in record blood-lust. Not true" (p. 22).

Do these critical sociological viewpoints suggest that school violence is not a social problem? On the contrary. They simply warn that demonizing youth in response to sensational episodes of violence is not justified by the facts. Depriving students of their liberties, they assert, will further alienate many young people who expect to be able to voice criticisms of society in their schools. We have seen that the American public is genuinely worried about school violence and that the facts about its prevalence support their concern, especially if it is directed at violence in disadvantaged communities. The role of critical sociology, however, is to channel that concern away from panic and toward policies based on genuine conditions.

TABLE 7–1   Hate Crimes, 1997

Bias Motivation	Offenses	Percent[a]	Bias Motivation	Offenses	Percent[a]
Total	9,861	100.0	Anti-Islamic	31	2.1
Race, total	5,898	59.8	Anti-other religious group	173	11.7
Anti-White	1,267	21.5	Anti-multireligious group	26	1.8
Anti-Black	3,838	65.0	Anti-atheism, agnosticism, etc.	3	0.2
Anti-American Indian/ Alaskan native	44	0.7	Sexual orientation, total	1,375	13.9
Anti-Asian/Pacific Islander	437	7.4	Anti-male homosexual	912	66.3
Anti-multiracial group	312	5.2	Anti-female homosexual	229	16.7
Ethnicity/national origin, total	1,083	11.0	Anti-homosexual	210	15.3
Anti-Hispanic	636	58.7	Anti-heterosexual	14	1.0
Anti-other ethnicity/ national origin	447	41.3	Anti-bisexual	10	0.7
Religion, total	1,483	15.0	Disability, total	12	0.1
Anti-Jewish	1,159	78.2	Anti-physical	9	75.0
Anti-Catholic	32	2.2	Anti-mental	3	25.0
Anti-Protestant	59	4.0	Multiple bias	10	0.1

[a]Percentages may not total 100 because of rounding.

Source: Statistical Abstract, 1999.

Jr., because he was black. In fact, most hate crimes take the form of harassment and threats, which may not be reported to the authorities.

On a global basis, however, a great deal of violence due to hate is more systematic and often genocidal, as in Africa or the Balkans. On a global level, the most deadly combinations of social problems are inequalities of power and wealth, on one hand, and ethnic or racial divisions within the population, on the other. In the case of the Tutsis and Hutus in Rwanda, for example, both populations were largely impoverished, but whenever one gained power, the other suffered abuses and violence. Eventually the hatred engendered by this pattern of abuse resulted in widespread terror and genocide, much of which was witnessed by the entire world on television. The same basic situation prevailed in Kosovo. Hatred between Serbs and Albanian Kosovars was longstanding. It was severely aggravated, however, by Serbian policies of expansion and "ethnic cleansing" of the Albanians from their properties.

Hate-based episodes of ethnic cleansing, widespread rape and torture, mass killings, and systematic genocide increasingly take place on a world stage. The "community of nations," and especially the more powerful nations, are asked to intervene to prevent catastrophe. Should they do so? This is one of the most vexing and difficult social policy issues confronting the United Nations and the United States today, and we will return to this question in the Social Policy section of the chapter.

Assault and Robbery

Murder and assault are similar. **Assault** is a threat or attempt to injure. Murder, therefore, is a form of aggravated assault in which the victim dies. Often an extreme case of assault becomes murder accidentally; it may depend on the weapon used or the speed with which the injured person receives medical attention. Since murder and assault are similar kinds of crimes, most observations about murder also apply to assault. However, a person who commits assault is somewhat more likely to have a criminal record than one who commits murder.

Robbery may be defined as taking another person's property by intimidation. It accounts for almost one-third of all reported crimes of violence (*UCR*, 1999). A robbery in which violence was actually used is recorded as an assault. Unlike murder or assault, robbery usually occurs between strangers; it is also the only major violent crime that is likely to occur between members of different races or classes.

Rape

Forcible rape is the act of forcing sexual intercourse on another person against his or her will. **Statutory rape,** for which the penalties are less severe, is the act of having sexual relations with someone who is below a particular age established by state law. Although most arrests are for statutory rape, forcible rape attracts the most attention.

In the past, forcible rape was an extremely difficult crime to prove. Evidence requirements—bruises or torn clothing, eyewitnesses, or medical proof of intercourse—were unrealistic. Relatively few rapes occur in front of witnesses, and recent findings indicate that many rapists experience sexual dysfunction, which makes it less likely that rape can be verified by the presence of semen. Such difficulties discouraged victims from reporting the crime, and those who did press charges often encountered additional problems. Defending attorneys sought to discredit the plaintiff's testimony by suggesting that she had provoked or cooperated with her assailant. In some cases the victim's previous sexual behavior was used to imply that she was promiscuous and, hence, not a reliable witness. Women who had suffered from the trauma of rape often found themselves the further victims of unresponsive and even hostile court proceedings. Many victims also feared revenge by the rapist.

These conditions persisted as long as rape was viewed as an exclusively sexual crime. The perpetrator of the "crime of passion" was thought to be driven by overwhelming and uncontrollable desire. Rapists were believed to be different from other people who commit violent crimes. This is only partially true; unlike murderers and those who commit assault, rapists often have a long history of criminal offenses. These offenses, however, tend to be for crimes other than rape (Reiss & Roth, 1993). This relatively high rate of criminal involvement suggests that the rapist's motivation may be violent rather than sexual. A team of Massachusetts researchers found that the rapist's anger, need for power, and desire to control the victim are significant factors. Sex itself does not always seem to motivate the rapist, although in some cases it may. Most often, sex becomes the means through which the assailant expresses hostility and power over his victim (Felson & Krohn, 1990).

Defining forcible rape as a crime of violence rather than one of passion helps place it in the proper perspective and invalidates the idea that the victim can initiate the crime by arousing desire in the rapist. It also suggests that women are not the only victims of this crime; men can also be raped, either by other men or by women. The old stereotypes of men as masters and women as objects of desire and domination worked to the disadvantage of both male and female rape victims. The women's movement and changing attitudes have led to a new understanding of this crime. Although rape laws still vary from state to state, the nationwide trend is to revise existing statutes in favor of the victim. Corroboration by a witness is no longer necessary, and the plaintiff's sexual history is admissible only if it involves previous contact with the accused; moreover, although women are still the most likely victims of rape, men are now entitled to press charges against their attackers.

Rape victims are generally treated with more consideration and sensitivity today than they were in the past. Round-the-clock medical and counseling services are available, and police units staffed with specially trained personnel help victims overcome the trauma of the experience. As a result of these measures, more victims are willing to seek justice. Nevertheless, rape remains one of the most underreported of all crimes. According to the FBI, many women are too embarrassed or afraid to report a rape. They feel shamed by the attack and do not want others to know about it. Many also fear that the assailant will attack them again if they report the incident to the police.

Victim studies show that the vast majority of forcible rapes are not reported to the police. In fact, in 1995 the federal government more than doubled its annual estimate of rapes or attempted rapes. The new data came from the government's National Crime Victimization Survey (see Chapter 6), which was redesigned to ask respondents specifically whether they had been raped or sexually assaulted (rather than asking about attacks of any kind, without mentioning rape). In reporting on the newly designed survey, the Bureau of Justice Statistics estimated that there are 500,000 sexual assaults on women each year, including 170,000 rapes and 140,000 attempted rapes; fewer than 100,000 of these incidents are reported to the police. It is important to note that these figures do not necessarily indicate an increase in the frequency of

RPEP
Rape Prevention Education Program

Women don't cause acquaintance rape. Rapists do.

But there are things you can do to reduce the risks of being raped by someone you know.

1 STAY away from men who: put you down a lot, talk negatively about women, think that "girls who get drunk should know what to expect," drink or use drugs heavily, are physically violent, don't respect you or your decisions.

2 SET sexual limits and intentions. Communicate them early and firmly.

3 DON'T pretend you don't want to have sex if you really do.

4 STAY sober.

5 DON'T make men guess what you want. Tell them.

6 REMAIN in control. Pay your own way. Make some of the decisons.

7 LISTEN to your feelings.

8 FORGET about being a "nice girl" as soon as you feel threatened.

9 LEARN self-defense. Know how to yell. Take assertiveness training.

10 TAKE care of yourself. Don't assume others will.

For more information, please phone 893-3778 A service of the Women's Center and Police Department, University of California, Santa Barbara

➡

In the 1990s, date or acquaintance rape became a major concern on many university campuses and in communities across the nation.

rape. They are a result of asking victims more directly about their experiences (Hall, 1995).

Date Rape.   **Date rape,** or **acquaintance rape,** is forcible sex in which the victim is known to the offender. Although the victim has agreed to engage in some form of social interaction with the offender, she has not agreed to sexual intercourse. When a woman is raped on a date, she is much less likely to report the incident than if she were raped by a stranger (Hall, 1995).

Studies have found that between 11 percent and 25 percent of college women have been forced to have sexual intercourse by their boyfriends. As many as 35 percent of male college students report that they have become so sexually aroused on a date that they have forced themselves on the woman or felt that they were capable of doing so (National Victim Center, 1992). Often date rape on college campuses takes the form of gang rape, usually at parties and after heavy drinking or use of other drugs. In recent years a number of drugs known as "date rape drugs" have been used in an illicit fashion to decrease inhibition. Drugs that are often slipped to unknowing victims include rohypnol ketamine hydrochloride, often called Special K, and most recently gamma hydroxy butyrate (GHB), also known as liquid ecstasy (*Alcoholism & Drug Abuse Weekly,* 1998).

Until recently, colleges and universities were totally unprepared to respond to date rape; but as incidents are given greater publicity, college administrators are adopting measures designed to prevent these acts and are providing counseling and other resources to the victims.

Family Violence

Child Abuse

Child abuse is a serious problem in the United States. At least 750,000 children are physically abused each year, and many die as a result. Between 15 percent and 18 percent of mothers and between 6 percent and 10 percent of fathers interviewed in random sample surveys say that they were physically abused as children (Berry, 1995; Finkelhor & Meyer, 1988). One important survey compared two-parent families in the mid-1970s, when child abuse became a national issue, and similar families in 1985, after ten years of publicity and efforts to prevent violence directed at children. In the earlier sample, 14 percent reported incidents of severe violence worse than slapping or spanking, including beating with an object, kicking, and hitting with fists; ten years later about 11 percent reported such behavior. This is an extremely small reduction, given the increased attention to the problem, and recent studies indicate that child abuse has not declined appreciably since the mid-1980s, if at all (Berry, 1995).

Child abuse may be defined as a deliberate attack on a child by a parent or other caregiver that results in physical injury. A major obstacle to research on this topic is concern for the traditional rights of parents, who have the right to inflict physical violence on their children (Justice & Justice, 1990). The most universal type of physical violence is spanking and other kinds of corporal punishment by parents.

If parents are to be responsible for raising and training children, they need to exercise a certain degree of authority, including the right to punish. Our culture strongly defends the right of parents to govern their children as they see fit, and it has traditionally approved of corporal punishment for this purpose ("Spare the rod and spoil the child"). Thus, one of the first court cases in which an outside agency successfully intervened to protect an abused child was the 1866 *Mary Ellen* case, in which the plaintiff was the Society for the Prevention of Cruelty to Animals.

Increased concern with children's rights has changed this picture somewhat. Child labor laws, actions of the Society for the Prevention of Cruelty to Children, and changes in the handling of juvenile delinquents have helped reinforce these rights. However, the rights of parents and the preservation of the family unit are still regarded as primary concerns, even when in any other situation the nature of the injury would warrant criminal investigation and possible prosecution. Indeed, even in some of the worst cases, the traditional autonomy of the family unit prevents the authorities from intervening or even learning about the problem. Some researchers estimate that only one case in three is ever discovered (Reiss & Roth, 1993).

The victims of child abuse appear to be fairly evenly distributed over all age groups and between the sexes, although there are some changes in sex distribution during different stages of childhood and adolescence. At least half the victims have been abused prior to a reported incident. A significant proportion of children seem to invite abuse through provocative behavior, although this plays a much smaller role in explaining attacks on children than the cultural norms discussed earlier. Of all cases of abuse, almost 90 percent are committed by the child's parent or guardian (Gelles, 1996).

A family in which there is child abuse typically has one or more of the following characteristics:

1. There is only one parent.
2. The parent's socioeconomic status and level of education are low.
3. The parent is highly authoritarian.
4. The family includes four or more children and has received some kind of public assistance within a year of the abuse.
5. The family changes its place of residence frequently.

Although these characteristics are found in many poor families, it is important to note that any correlation between abuse and poverty is biased by the fact that the behavior of the poor is more likely to be reported in official records than that of members of other classes, who are better equipped to conceal their activities. However, some specific problems, such as stress, anxiety, and alcohol abuse, are particularly prevalent in poor families.

Because studies based on official statistics have an inherent bias against the poor, the findings of a classic longitudinal study by Brandt Steele and Carl Pollock (1974) are of interest. For five and a half years the researchers, both psychiatrists, studied 60 families in which significant child abuse had occurred. These families were not chosen by any valid sampling technique and therefore cannot be regarded as statistically representative; they were merely families that happened to come to the attention of the investigators. They did, however, span a wide range of socioeconomic and educational levels, and they included urban, rural, and suburban residents. The information the researchers obtained led them to conclude that poverty, alcoholism, unemployment, broken marriages, and similar social and demographic factors are less significant than previous studies had seemed to indicate. Instead, Steele and Pollock found a typical personality pattern among abusive parents: The parent demands a high level of performance from the child at an age when the child is unable to understand what is wanted and unable to comply; and the parent expects to receive from the child a degree of comfort, reassurance, and love that a child would ordinarily receive from a parent. When the expected performance and nurturance are not forthcoming, the parent retaliates the way a small child might, with violence; but in this case the violence is not by the weak against the strong but by the strong parent against the weak, defenseless child.

It is important to note that *in every case studied,* Steele and Pollock found that the abusive parents had themselves been subject to similar unreasonable demands in childhood, and in a few cases they found evidence of the same experience among the grandparents. More recent research confirms that child abuse is far more likely in families in which one or both parents have a history of abuse as children and there are other symptoms of family dysfunction, including alcohol and substance abuse (Clarke et al., 1999).

Spouse Abuse

On a rainy day in March 1992, Shirley Lowery, a Milwaukee bus driver, was stabbed to death by the man from whom she had fled a few days before. She was attacked as she hurried into the county courthouse to seek an injunction against her former companion, whom she accused of beating and raping her and threatening her life. Like many abusive husbands and boyfriends, her companion could not tolerate the idea of her leaving him. Lying in wait for her in the courthouse hallway, he stabbed her 19 times with an 8-inch butcher knife.

Violence between spouses has long been acknowledged and even tolerated as part of domestic life. Wives are the most frequent victims, although cases of battered husbands are sometimes reported. Very often the victims are seriously injured, yet, as with violence directed against children, the traditional autonomy of the family, together with the traditional subordination of women within the family, has made the authorities reluctant to intervene. Only recently has spouse abuse become an issue of social concern, and it is still difficult to assess its frequency and its impact on American family life.

Spouse abuse is a form of violence that actually demands the use of profiling by the police. The FBI's most recent research reports on family violence and police responses points out that in the vast majority of cases the dispute is not two-sided:

> Domestic abuse is about one person dominating and controlling another by force, threats, or physical violence. The long-term effects of domestic violence on victims and children can be profound. A son who witnesses his father abuse his mother is more likely to become a delinquent or batterer himself. A daughter sees abuse as an integral part of a close relationship. Thus, an abusive relationship between father and mother can perpetuate future abusive relationships.
>
> Battering in a relationship will not improve on its own. Intervention is essential to stop the reign of terror. When intervention is lacking, the results can be dire: An average of 1,500 American women are killed each year by husbands, ex-husbands, or boyfriends.

Yet until fairly recently, the FBI report continues,

> police officers rarely ventured into the private domain of the marital relationship. At most, officers responding to calls for help attempted to calm things down and arrange for one party to leave the home for the evening. While such an approach provided a short-term solution, it rarely helped bring about an end to the violence.
>
> During the 1980s, this response began to change as communities implemented more aggressive strategies to address domestic abuse. Many law enforcement agencies began to explore new ways for officers to respond to domestic violence calls. Gradually, the focus shifted from merely "maintaining the peace" to arresting offenders, protecting victims, and referring battered women to shelters and other community resources available to help victims of domestic violence. (Marvin, 1997, p. 13)

Even when faced with constant violence, a surprising number of women make no attempt to leave the men who abuse them. Lenore Walker (1977) has suggested that this passivity is a form of fatalism. A pattern of dependency, of "learned helplessness," is established early in many women's lives:

It seems highly probable that girls, through their socialization in learning the traditional woman's role, also learn that they have little direct control over their lives no matter what they do. . . . They learn that their voluntary responses really don't make that much difference in what happens to them. Thus, it becomes extremely difficult for such women to believe their cognitive actions can change their life situation. (pp. 528–529)

Other experts have described wife abuse as "a complicated and cumulative cycle of tension, belittlement, violence, remorse, and reconciliation that can lead to a paralysis of will and extinction of self-respect" (Erlanger, 1987, p. 1). This "battered women's syndrome," they claim, is a result of the deliberate undermining of a woman's sense of independence and self-worth by a possessive, overly critical man. "There is a sense of being trapped," one victim reports. "You live in terror and your thinking is altered" (quoted in Erlanger, 1987, p. 44).

The sustained public attention given to the trial of O. J. Simpson brought to prominence the situation of battered women and the question of how to protect women who have left abusive relationships. We return to this issue in the Social Policy section of the chapter.

Research has uncovered a high correlation between child abuse and spouse abuse. Between 30 percent and 40 percent of the time, a man who abuses his wife also abuses his children (Berry, 1995; Erlanger, 1987). Thus, a battered wife may remain with her husband in an attempt to protect the children. Conversely, the children may try to intervene and defend their mother, thereby causing the father to turn on them.

Elder Abuse

A form of violence that has recently come to public attention is abuse of the elderly by members of their own families, sometimes referred to as "granny bashing." Abuse of the elderly may take other forms besides outright violence, such as withholding of food, theft of savings and Social Security checks, and verbal abuse and threats. Accurate data on elder abuse are not available, and it is difficult to prove that such violence has occurred. Elderly people bruise easily and fall often, and physicians are not trained to detect abuse in elderly patients. Moreover, because social scientists have only recently begun to study this type of violence, little is known about its causes. It is possible that family members are simply unable to cope with the problems of an aging parent or grandparent but are unwilling to place the parent in a nursing home. As the proportion of elderly people in the population increases, it can be expected that the frequency of elder abuse will also increase.

Gangs, Guns, and Violent Death

Why is the homicide rate in the United States as much as 20 times the rate in other industrialized nations? (See Figure 7–1.) There is no one answer, but important explanations may be found in an analysis of changing patterns of juvenile violence, the increased firepower available to violent people, and the inability of American society to agree on appropriate controls on lethal weapons.

In many sensational headlines, one reads of brutal violence by juvenile gangs in large cities. In an especially infamous case in New York City, a gang of youths described as a "wolf pack" raped and nearly murdered a female jogger in Central Park. In Los Angeles, the Crips and Bloods are said to be especially violent gangs engaged in the distribution of crack cocaine. In Chicago and elsewhere, violence is attributed to the activities of armed gangs of various kinds. In the 1980s and early 1990s there was an upsurge of gang activity and gang-related violence in smaller cities and suburban areas, most often associated with drug dealing. More recently, skinheads and

SOCIAL PROBLEMS ONLINE

Information About Guns and Violence on the Internet

The relationships among guns, violence, and crime are hotly debated in American society, and the Internet reflects that debate; most sites dealing with the issue are highly opinionated. The Violence Policy Center (**http://www.gunfree.inter.net/vpc/welcome.html**), based in Washington, D.C., is a nonprofit educational foundation working "to stem the tide of firearms violence engulfing the nation." It treats gun violence as a public health issue and not solely as a crime problem, pointing out that the majority of deaths from guns result from suicide, not homicide. The center supplies fact sheets on the firearm industry, gun safety and violence prevention, and women and firearm violence, as well as an extensive bibliography on guns and violence. It weighs in on the gun control side of the constitutional debate with its publication "Second Amendment: No Right to Keep and Bear Arms."

Another group that wants to restrict the proliferation of guns in America is the Pacific Center for Violence Prevention (PCVP) at **http://www.pcvp.org/**. It works to prevent youth violence in California but has useful resources on the relationships between alcohol and violence and between guns and violence that are applicable to the nation as a whole. It provides fact sheets on the economics of violence and publications that report on recent decreases in youth violence ("Violence and Latino Youth") and offenders under the age of 18 in the California adult correctional system.

The National Rifle Association, America's oldest and largest lobby group for gun owners, maintains a home page at **http://www.nra.org/** with links to its Institute for Legislative Action, which advises members whom to vote for and what to lobby for. It also provides a series of fact sheets on the NRA's reading of the Second Amendment that strongly argue for the right of all citizens to bear arms. Its Crimestrike web page features several publications that emphasize the role of gun ownership in preventing crimes against property.

The American Firearms Association (AFA), at **http://www.globescope.com/afa**, advertises itself as "working to reconcile the Second Amendment with common sense." It believes that the "Second Amendment guarantees Americans an individual right to own guns, but that it does not preclude fair gun control measures which seek to safeguard society." The AFA's website presents its position paper on the Second Amendment, as well as a paper that is highly critical of the NRA's "armed populace" doctrine.

other groups of teenagers and young adults have committed hate crimes, often involving violent attacks on homosexuals, Jews, and Asian immigrants. Today much lethal gang violence is associated with the sale and use of crack cocaine or other illicit rugs, especially in some smaller cities and towns and in specific inner-city communities (Males, 1998).

Between 1960 and 1990 the rate of offenses involving dangerous weapons, especially handguns, increased from less than 50 per 100,000 people to well over 100. Although the rate has decreased recently, largely because of a decline in gang-related shootings, Figure 7–2 shows that weapons offenses vary greatly by state; the highest rates are found in the South and Southwest and in urban areas in the Northeast. Figure 7–3 shows that the rate of death due to firearms is from three to six times the rate in Western nations with comparable levels of industrial and urban development. Although gun possession and deaths from guns are problems that extend well beyond the phenomenon of youth gangs, early involvement in crime, gangs, and weapons possession among teenagers, of whom the large majority come from poverty-stricken and socially isolated neighborhoods, is a strong signal that creative programs to combat poverty and neglect are urgently needed in communities throughout the nation.

Gangs range from the peer groups that hang out on street corners to the well-organized, hierarchical gangs of crime syndicates. The latter often include contract

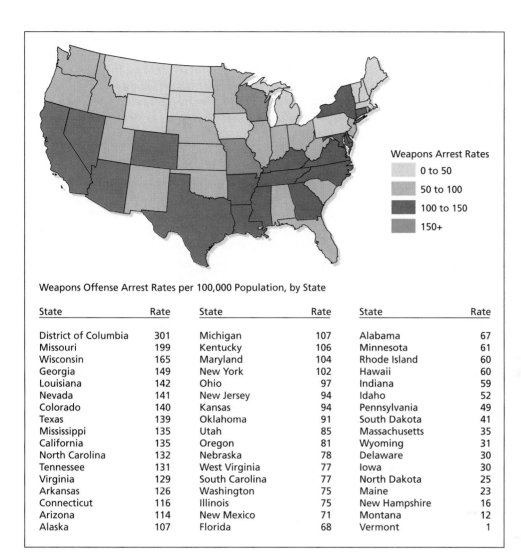

Weapons Offense Arrest Rates per 100,000 Population, by State

State	Rate	State	Rate	State	Rate
District of Columbia	301	Michigan	107	Alabama	67
Missouri	199	Kentucky	106	Minnesota	61
Wisconsin	165	Maryland	104	Rhode Island	60
Georgia	149	New York	102	Hawaii	60
Louisiana	142	Ohio	97	Indiana	59
Nevada	141	New Jersey	94	Idaho	52
Colorado	140	Kansas	94	Pennsylvania	49
Texas	139	Oklahoma	91	South Dakota	41
Mississippi	135	Utah	85	Massachusetts	35
California	135	Oregon	81	Wyoming	31
North Carolina	132	Nebraska	78	Delaware	30
Tennessee	131	West Virginia	77	Iowa	30
Virginia	129	South Carolina	77	North Dakota	25
Arkansas	126	Washington	75	Maine	23
Connecticut	116	Illinois	75	New Hampshire	16
Arizona	114	New Mexico	71	Montana	12
Alaska	107	Florida	68	Vermont	1

Figure 7–2 Weapons Offense Rates by State

Source: Greenfield & Zawetz, 1995.

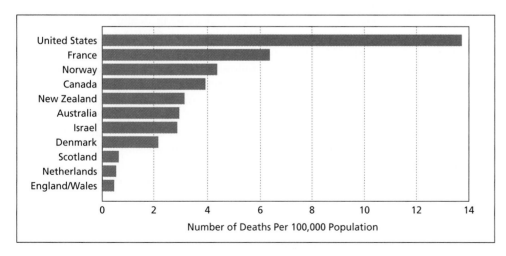

Figure 7–3 Death Rates from Firearms, Selected Countries (Average Annual Deaths per 100,000 Population)

Source: Data from *Statistical Abstract,* 1999.

killers, professional murderers who kill for money. But killings related to organized crime account for only a small percentage of all murders. Do deaths caused by other types of gangs account for the remainder? This does not seem to be the case.

Juvenile and young-adult gangs often begin as street corner cliques and become incorporated into a larger gang confederation. These organizations are often located in poor, segregated communities, where much of their activity is dedicated to the defense of local territory, or turf. But experts on the sociology of gangs are quick to point out that there are many types of juvenile gang structures and many different types of gang activity, not all of which are violent or criminal.

In a thorough study of gang confederations in Milwaukee, John M. Hagedorn (1988; Hagedorn, Torres, & Giglio, 1998) found that while gangs in large cities like Los Angeles, Chicago, and New York have been present more or less continuously for generations, in smaller cities and suburban areas gangs may be a new phenomenon. And simply because a community does not have recognizable gangs does not mean that gangs may not form in the near future. Much depends on relations between teenagers and the police, on the drug trade and its control, and on how young people perceive the need (or lack of it) to defend their turf from other teenagers. Thus, in Milwaukee, although there is some fighting, especially as young men strive to gain prestige within the gangs, there is relatively little gang warfare or homicide attributable to gang warfare. In Chicago, in contrast, there seems to be far more gang-related homicide, especially among Hispanic gangs.

A large majority of the gang members Hagedorn (1988) interviewed admitted owning at least one handgun. He concludes that the problem of violence and homicide is related more to the increasing availability of guns and the involvement of some gangs in the illegal drug industry than to inherent features of the gangs themselves; this conclusion is shared by most students of gang behavior. Martin Sanchez-Jankowsky (1991), one of the nation's foremost authorities on violent gangs, notes that contrary to what some members of the public—and some sociologists—think, gang members typically do not like violence and the risks to personal safety that it entails. But most gang members believe that "if you do not attack, you will be attacked." This worldview implies that much gang violence is premeditated with the goal of taking the opponent by surprise. In addition, Sanchez-Jankowski notes, "the injuries incurred as a result of organizational violence [in the gang] become the social cement that creates group bonds in a deviant individualist setting." Overall, he concludes, gang violence "is understood to be the instrument used to achieve objectives that are not achievable in other ways" (p. 177).

Another study of gang activity and involvement in drug dealing supports Hagedorn's conclusions and reinforces the idea that high rates of lethal violence are attributable more to the widespread use of guns than to the presence of gangs themselves. Terry Williams (1989) spent three years following the activities of a mobile drug "crew" in New York. This small and highly entrepreneurial gang was in the retail crack business. Its success depended on discipline—on ensuring that members did not become too high to function in their jobs or so careless that they became victims of violent robberies. Williams, like Hagedorn, documents the widespread and routine possession of handguns, but he also notes the increasing availability of more powerful automatic weapons and submachine guns.

As noted earlier, rates of gun violence, homicide, and aggravated assault reached their peaks in the early 1990s. It is likely that the waning of the crack epidemic is part of the reason for the recent declines in those rates. But the United States had extremely high homicide rates even before the advent of crack; drugs alone, therefore, do not provide a sufficient explanation. The availability of easily concealed handguns, together with the traditions of interpersonal violence that date from the frontier period of American history, probably accounts for much of the deadly violence in the United States.

Franklin E. Zimring (1985), one of the nation's foremost experts on guns and gun control, states that the "proportion of all households reporting handgun ownership has increased substantially over a twenty-year period" (p. 138). On the basis of survey research, Zimring and associates estimate that between one-fourth and one-third of all American households have one or more handguns (Zimring & Hawkins, 1997). This represents an enormous increase since the late 1950s, when the proportion was probably well below one in ten households. Studies of the relationship between handgun possession and homicide find that when people arm themselves out of fear and a desire for protection, there is also an increased risk of fatalities from accidents involving guns, as well as homicides caused by mistaken recourse to fatal force—as in the tragic case of a Japanese exchange student in New Orleans who was killed when he approached the wrong house in search of a party to which he had been invited (Reiss & Roth, 1993).

SOCIAL POLICY

Despite the decrease in violent crimes in the United States in recent years, political leaders and the public remain committed to further efforts to reduce violence. As we have seen, rates of teenage violence are extremely high, and more violence can be expected as these cohorts move through their crime-prone years. Rates of family violence also remain high, as can be seen in sensational cases of child abuse and murder. The American public is clearly justified in its demand that society "do something" about violent crime. However, exactly what should be done is much less clear, as shown in the controversies over gun control, media violence, and ways of dealing with family violence.

Gun Control

In recent decades there has been increasing demand for stricter federal supervision of the purchase and sale of firearms, particularly the cheap handguns that are readily available in many areas. However, opponents of gun control legislation, represented primarily by the National Rifle Association (NRA), constitute one of the most powerful interest groups in the nation. The NRA draws much of its strength from areas of the nation where hunting is popular and there is a strong feeling that people need to be able to protect themselves and their families. Members of the NRA claim that gun control measures would violate the "right to bear arms" that is contained in the Second Amendment to the United States Constitution. This is a strong position and one that most political leaders are unwilling to challenge directly.

Opponents of gun control claim that the decision to commit murder has nothing to do with possession of a gun; a killer can stab, strangle, poison, or batter a victim to death. Gun control, therefore, would make little difference. Although this argument sounds logical, it ignores the lethal potential of guns, which are about five times more likely to kill than knives, the next most commonly used murder weapon. And since most murders are spontaneous results of passion rather than carefully planned acts, it follows that the easy availability of guns is likely to increase the death rate in criminal assaults. In most cases murders are a result of three factors: impulse, the lethal capacity of the weapon, and the availability of the weapon. Strict gun control would eliminate or at least reduce the latter two factors.

Record levels of gun violence in 1999 seemed likely to turn public opinion firmly against supporters of the free market in firearms. Columbine (15 dead, 23 wounded), the Wedgwood Baptist Church in Fort Worth (8 dead, 7 wounded), the North Valley Jewish Community Center near Los Angeles (5 wounded), Atlanta (9 dead, 13 wounded), Honolulu (7 dead), and Seattle (2 dead, 2 wounded) received intensive media coverage. But even as political leaders and the majority of the public joined the outcry against widespread availability of heavy firepower, the National Rifle Association experienced its largest jump in membership ever. And in fact, public opinion on the basic issues of gun control was altered, but not dramatically (Birnbaum, 1999).

A significant majority of the American public has long favored tighter controls over firearms that stop short of a complete ban on handguns. This support for gun control correlates most closely with the nation's murder rate. Throughout the1980s and 1990s the murder rate varied between about 8 and 10 per 100,000. Table 7–2 demonstrates that high poll numbers favoring gun control in the early part of the period correlate to a high murder rate (associated with the crack cocaine epidemic, among other factors). The lower figures in the mid-1980s correlate with a lower murder rate. When the murder rate increased in the early 1990s, support for gun control moved upward again. Most likely, the low figures reported before the Columbine incident reflect the recent substantial drop in the murder rate to under 7 per 100,000 (Gillespie & Lynch, 1999; Kleck, 1999).

In 1993, in response to what had come to be perceived as a national epidemic of gunshot injuries and deaths, as well as the earlier shooting of President Reagan and his press secretary Matthew Brady, Congress finally passed the Brady Act and other legislation to limit the access of felons to handguns and assault weapons. In 1996 Congress attempted to repeal the ban on assault weapons, but the repeal was vetoed by President Clinton. This veto became an important issue in the 1996 presidential election because many voters, especially women, strongly favored gun control. In the campaigns leading up to the 2000 presidential election, gun control figured as a major issue as the Democrats attempted to capitalize on their efforts to close loopholes in the Brady Act, especially those concerning sales of weapons at gun shows and auctions; the Republicans attempted to maintain the support of gun advocates while not seeming to be influenced by the NRA and thereby alienating the majority that favors gun control.

Not all antigun, antiviolence policy is made at the federal level. Many states and municipalities have recognized that the alarming increase in the number of youths

---

TABLE 7–2 Responses to Gallup Poll on Gun Control

"In general, do you feel that the laws covering the sale of handguns should be made more strict, less strict, or kept as they are now?"

Date	More Strict	Less Strict	Kept as Now	No Opinion
1999	68%	6%	25%	1%
1993	72	5	22	1
1988	64	6	27	3
1986	60	8	30	2
1981	65	3	30	2
1980	59	3	30	2
1975	69	3	24	4

Source: The Gallup Poll, Statistical Assessment Service, 1999.

aged 10 to 17 who are arrested for violent crimes demands more creative approaches than simply trying them in adult courts and locking them up with adult prisoners. In the wake of the rash of killings in 1999, California passed both a ban on assault weapons and a "gun a month" law that limits handgun purchases to one every 30 days. A new Connecticut law allows police to seize firearms from anyone accused of threatening "imminent personal injury" by two "credible persons," although that phrase has not been defined by the courts at this writing. And Illinois passed a law penalizing parents who keep guns in unlocked locations at home. New Jersey legislators are debating a bill that may require gun makers to sell "smart" guns that allow only their owners to fire them—even though such guns may not be available for years. Four states, however, took pro-gun policy action. Maine legislators rejected a bill similar to the one passed in Illinois. Even more significant, officials in Louisiana and Texas took action to stop product liability lawsuits against gun makers (blocking a suit against manufacturers filed earlier by New Orleans). Texas also rejected a bill requiring background checks at gun shows. And Nevada lawmakers approved a measure allowing concealed weapons to be carried in public buildings except airports and schools (Biddle, 1999).

Laws that limit product liability lawsuits are particularly troubling for gun control advocates because this is the newest and, from their perspective, most promising strategy in the battle to limit the use of firearms. At the national level, the Department of Housing and Urban Development (HUD) has taken up lawsuits against gun manufactures in the name of residents of public housing projects who have suffered inordinate numbers of shootings because of the failure of gun manufacturers to limit the lethal firepower of the weapons they put on the market. In California the state supreme court has granted municipalities the right to bring suits against gun makers. This opens the way for court battles against gun makers similar to the strategies used successfully by the states against tobacco companies.

But as can be seen from the pro-gun laws passed by some states, the power of gun advocates remains strong in many parts of the nation. In many congressional and legislative districts, especially in the South and West, there are lawmakers who are in office because the NRA mobilized pro-gun voters on election day. With 3 million dedicated members and an annual budget of $137 million, the NRA is one of the nation's largest and wealthiest cause-oriented groups (Birnbaum, 1999). But activists on both sides of the issue agree that the NRA is fighting at best a holding action against the rising tide of public opinion in favor of more gun control.

While the political debate has continued, there have been quite successful efforts to decrease the number of available guns in high-risk communities—that is, places where there have been recent histories of high murder rates and deaths of bystanders. Since 1991 Congress and the Justice Department have cooperated in instituting experimental programs to decrease the number of guns carried in "high risk places at high risk times" (Sherman, Shaw, & Rogan, 1995). Perhaps the most important of these is the Kansas City Gun Experiment, part of the Justice Department's Weed and Seed program in which local authorities were given wide latitude in planning strategies to reduce gun violence. The Kansas City experiment attempted to show a relationship between seizures of guns and reduced crimes committed with guns. A target police beat, covering a neighborhood where homicides were 20 times above the national average, was selected. The beat was patrolled by officers with special training in detecting people who were carrying weapons. On another beat, similar in demographic and crime characteristics, the police continued to use their traditional methods. After 29 weeks of operations, statistics showed that gun crimes had dropped significantly on the beat with the special patrols. Drive-by shootings also decreased, as did homicides of all kinds. In patrolling the beat, the police concentrated on likely gun carriers in special hot spots, where crimes had often been committed in the past. Since the focus was on crimes committed with guns, it is not

Opponents of gun control often fear that banning any type of weapon, including assault weapons, would eventually result in government control even over hunting rifles. They claim that possession of guns is necessary for self-defense and is protected by the Second Amendment to the Constitution.

surprising that there was little difference between the two beats in other violent crimes or in property crimes.

From a policy standpoint, the most important conclusion of the experiment is that "the police can increase the number of guns seized in high crime areas at relatively modest cost" (Sherman, Shaw, & Rogan, 1995, p. 9). Specially trained patrols seize about three times as many guns over a similar period as do traditional police patrols. Similar programs of community policing and gun interdiction (funded by private foundations, as well as by the federal government) are likely to become a major area of antiviolence policy in high-crime communities throughout the nation.

An important issue related to gun control is the extent to which women who are heads of households will choose to arm themselves with handguns for protection. Since the number of female-headed households is rising rapidly, any increase in the propensity of women to arm themselves could raise the overall level of handgun ownership to 50 million in the next decade. But research shows that women are still far more reluctant than men to purchase handguns; female-headed households are half as likely to have handguns as male-headed households (Zimring, 1985). This suggests that the outcome of the political battle over handguns may eventually depend on how both sides manage to appeal to female voters.

Media Violence

Although a direct link between violent behavior and media depictions of violence has never been established, there is a great deal of evidence that the two are related. In a historic 1972 study, the U.S. Surgeon General's Study of Television and Social Behavior, the researchers concluded:

> The causal relationship between televised violence and antisocial behavior is sufficient to warrant appropriate and immediate remedial action. The data on social phenomena such as television and violence and aggressive behavior will never be clear enough for all social scientists to agree on the formulation of a succinct statement of causality. But there comes a time when the data are sufficient to justify action. That time has come. (Quoted in Bogart, 1972–1973, p. 521)

It should be possible, through either legislation or voluntary regulation, to reduce the incidence of killings and the reliance on shoot-and-slug formulas, especially in movies and TV programs. The media have agreed to devote the first hour of prime-time television—from 8 P.M. to 9 P.M., called the family hour—to programming that is considered suitable for family viewing, with the more violent programs being shown at later hours. Although network broadcasters have made efforts to reduce the level of violence, the proliferation of cable channels, which often show violent crimes in their entertainment programs, has more than offset this improvement (Budiansky, 1996).

Since the early 1970s a team of researchers at the University of Pennsylvania has provided counts of media violence. These counts show that despite the family hour, rates of televised violence have not fallen and in fact have increased steadily. Children's television is even more violent than adult programming (Donnerstain & Linz, 1987; Hirsch, 1987). The most recent policy effort to address the increase in televised violence is the V (violence)-chip. This computer chip is designed to allow parents to program their TV sets so that children cannot watch certain channels or programs while the parents are at work or out of the house. The Clinton administration approved legislation that requires manufacturers to equip future TV sets with the chip.

Although the results of research on the effects of televised violence on viewers are ambiguous, large segments of the American public are convinced that there is a connection between high levels of televised violence and aggressive behavior by viewers of violent programs.

In addition, the TV industry voluntarily devised a system for rating shows according to their sexual and violent content. Both of these measures face court challenges on the ground that they restrict freedom of expression. Nevertheless, polls show that the public favors the V-chip technology (Budiansky, 1996).

The ready availability of videotapes has become a matter of widespread concern in recent years. Children and teenagers routinely obtain videotapes of movies that feature extreme violence, including dismemberment and sexual mutilation, and watch them without their parents' knowledge. Some organizations have taken a stand against easy access to violent films; they have called for legislation that requires prominent display of Motion Picture Association of America ratings of videotapes and, in some cases, for bans on the sale or rental of certain types of cassettes. To date, however, few states have enacted such requirements. It is fair to say that most attacks on media content are directed against sexuality and against depictions that are thought to legitimize homosexuality and pre- and extramarital sex, rather than against violence. After the 1999 killings, however, the film industry began a serious effort to decrease the number of violent incidents portrayed in films, but the results of this effort have yet to be assessed.

Dealing with Family Violence

Child abuse is widely recognized as a serious national problem. In recent decades there have been numerous efforts, by both government and private agencies, to increase public awareness of the problem and to prevent it where possible. The Child Abuse Prevention and Treatment Act was passed by Congress in 1974 to help states and communities organize programs for parents who abuse their children. Also in 1974, the National Institute of Mental Health established a national center in Denver to study the problem more thoroughly and to set up a national commission to resolve the complicated legal problems and recommend changes in federal and state laws. Grant programs have also been funded to identify the causes of child abuse and to provide treatment through self-help programs and lay therapy. Increasingly, states are requiring social workers and psychologists to report all cases of known or suspected child abuse to child protection authorities in their communities.

To break the cycle of abuse, some therapy groups have attempted to teach parenting techniques to mothers and fathers who were abused children themselves. The clinic workers try to supply these parents with alternative outlets for their frustration and anger and encourage them to call for help whenever they feel tempted to strike their children. Parents are also encouraged to seek meaningful relationships with other adults and not to invest their children's behavior with so much significance.

C. Henry Kempe, who initiated the first treatment programs for parents at the Denver Child Abuse Center, found that 80 percent of the children could be returned to their parents "without risk of further injury, if their parents received intensive help [while the child lived in a foster home] and if there was a follow-up program after the child went home" (MacLeod, 1974, p. 719).

In recent years greater efforts have been made to address child abuse that results from abusive parental relations. In contentious custody battles, for example, there is often a history of abuse in the family that may extend to kidnapping and further violence once the couple is separated. In 1990, therefore, Congress passed a joint resolution that urged the courts not to grant custody or other rights to a violent parent. Also, in a 1993 study, the National Institute of Justice found that prosecutors throughout the United States pursue far fewer cases of physical abuse than of sexual abuse. A variety of measures to address this imbalance were advocated, but the researchers concluded that a great deal of public education is necessary to convince Americans that physical abuse is as dangerous as sexual abuse (Smith, 1995).

Like child abuse, spouse abuse has received increased public attention in recent years. This problem is usually dealt with at the local rather than the national level. For example, in the 1970s many municipalities created shelters for battered wives, and others formed crisis intervention teams that attempt to negotiate with or "cool out" couples who are engaging in physical conflict. The need for both shelters and active intervention has not been met on a large scale, however, because of lack of public funds.

More recently there has been a trend toward efforts to prevent spouse and child abuse by encouraging neighbors, friends, and family members themselves to notify the authorities when they have reason to believe that abuse is likely or is occurring. However, even when the authorities know that abuse is occurring in a particular household, they are often unable to act, especially in cases of child abuse. One problem, as noted earlier, is that there is little agreement on where child protection ends and rights to family privacy begin. Another is the lack of coordination among agencies dealing with spouse and child abuse—the former is treated as a routine police matter and the latter as a concern of child welfare agencies. Increasing cooperation among police investigators, medical professionals, and social workers has therefore become a high priority in many communities.

Race, Poverty, and Violence: The Unfinished Agenda

The link between socioeconomic inequalities and the level of violence in society has been demonstrated in numerous studies. At the end of the 1960s, the National Commission on Civil Disorders (the Kerner Commission), after studying rioting in more than 150 cities, warned that the United States was moving toward "two separate societies, one black, one white—separate and unequal." Another commission, the National Commission on the Causes and Prevention of Violence (the Violence Commission), was appointed in 1968 after the assassinations of Dr. Martin Luther King, Jr., and Senator Robert Kennedy. It concluded that violence occurs when groups in a society are denied access to opportunities to obtain a decent living and to participate in the decisions that affect their lives. A third presidential commission, the Commission on Law Enforcement and Administration of Justice (the Katzenbach Commission), also concluded that "the roots of violence and disorder lie deep in the social fabric of American society, in its traditions, inequalities, and conflicts and ineffective governance" (Ball-Rokeach & Short, 1985).

These three major federal studies marked a shift from an emphasis on the psychological disorders underlying violence to a more sociological understanding of its origins. The redress of legitimate grievances and the equitable sharing of the American pie became more important considerations in formulating policy than the search for personality profiles or biological predispositions that would explain violent behavior. The growing conservatism of American society has not altered this fundamental shift.

In the 1990s policymakers with various ideological perspectives once again began debating the issues of crime control that had been raised in the 1960s and 1970s. The primary question was how to decrease rates of crime and violence by increasing the share of wealth available to those at the bottom of the social order. (See the Current Controversies feature below.) But social scientists are discovering that they need to

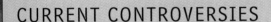

CURRENT CONTROVERSIES

The Myth of Black Violence

It is widely believed, not only by the public but also by the media and the government, that blacks—especially young black males—are more prone to violence than whites. Official statistics seem to confirm this view: Although blacks make up 13 percent of the population, they account for 43 percent of those arrested for murder, rape, and nonnegligent manslaughter. In addition, the victims of violent crime are far more likely to be black. Homicide is the primary cause of death for younger black men, as well as for black women under the age of 40.

Official statistics may be misleading, however. They reflect official attitudes and behavior, particularly the greater likelihood that black offenders will be arrested. Victim surveys provide more accurate information than arrest reports about crimes committed. Thus, although the FBI reports that the proportion of blacks arrested for aggravated assault is more than three times greater than the proportion of whites, the National Crime Survey finds that the actual proportions are very similar.

If rates of violence are comparable among blacks and whites, why are the consequences of violence, in terms of both imprisonment and death by violence, so much more severe for blacks than for whites? One explanation is the double standard of police protection. Police are seven times more likely to charge black teenagers than white teenagers with felonies, and the courts are more likely to imprison black teenagers. More telling, perhaps, is the belief that violent behavior is normal in inner-city black neighborhoods; arrest and imprisonment occur only if violence reaches extreme levels. In cases of domestic violence, for example, law enforcement officials do not intervene until a serious injury or fatality occurs. A similar pattern can be seen in the police response to assault and homicide among black males, including gang members (Garza, 1999). In recent research on differences in sentencing by race, criminologist Gary Kleck and associates analyzed data from repeat offenders in Florida's courts. They found "a significant and substantial race effect. The disadvantage of black defendants is particularly strong for drug offenses and for property crimes that have relatively high victimization rates for whites (larceny, burglary). Race is less consequential for violent and weapons-related offenders" (Crawford, Chiricos, & Kleck, 1998, p. 481).

The myth of black violence, with its consequences in actual experience, flies in the face of two of the nation's most cherished ideals: equal protection of the law and social equality. It is further evidence of the need for policies that address the correlation between social inequality and violence rather than stereotyping any particular group.

develop more varied policy recommendations that also address serious problems of media violence, the targeting of enforcement and rehabilitation programs to communities with the greatest need, and the role of educators in combating the epidemic of juvenile violence.

Beyond Left & Right

There are no simple views on violence from the perspectives of the left and the right. However, people on the pro-NRA right, who are part of the broader conservative population, often believe that if society makes guns illegal, only criminals will have guns. People who oppose ready availability of guns are not always on the left, but the antigun lobby does tend to attract people from the liberal side of the political spectrum. Issues like the ban on assault weapons or the requirement of waiting periods for gun purchases often lead to bitter quarrels among people who take these opposing positions. But must the question of reducing gun violence always lead to such a complete division? Are people who defend the right to bear arms always to blame for the easy availability of handguns? Are those on the left always bound to restrict the rights of gun owners in their zeal to control gun violence?

Fortunately, new policies are emerging that do not lead to these unresolvable disputes. The Weed and Seed program described in the Social Policy section is a case in point. Forceful action to prevent criminal gun possession in high-crime neighborhoods is a sophisticated sociological approach to violence at the community level. Of course, not all gun control policies are free from controversy, as can be seen in the case of the Brady Act and the ban on assault weapons. But a sociological perspective can at least help us understand how to devise successful antiviolence policies with minimum infringement on the rights of innocent people.

SUMMARY

- Violence may be considered legitimate or illegitimate, depending on who uses it and why and how it is used. Sometimes a distinction is made between institutional violence, which is exercised on behalf of or under the protection of the state, and noninstitutional violence, which is exercised by those who are opposed to established authority.

- Biological explanations of violence are based on the idea that there are instinctive violent or destructive urges in all humans. The frustration-aggression theory holds that an unfulfilled need produces frustration, which is then vented in aggression. A related view is the control theory, in which the ability to control impulsive behavior is correlated with the existence of close relationships with other people.

- Many sociologists believe that violence is a learned behavior and that violent actions are most likely to occur in a culture or subculture in which violence is accepted. In this theory, violent behavior is learned by imitation and is a byproduct of a culture that values toughness.

- Rational-choice theorists have explored the role of violence in so-called strategic crimes like extortion, kidnapping, and blackmail. In such instances, violent behavior can be interpreted as a rational means of attaining otherwise impossible ends.

- The role of the mass media in fostering violent attitudes has been a subject of considerable research. Although the findings are inconclusive, there is enough evidence to justify concerns that some individuals imitate violent acts observed on television. It is also thought that the reporting of civil disorders and other forms of violence by the mass media may increase the possibility that further violence will occur.

- Murder is the unlawful killing of a human being with malice aforethought. Most murderers are young men; more murders occur in cities than in rural areas; and in a large proportion of the cases, the relationship between murderer and victim is a close one. Mass murderers are either psychotics who murder in a fit of rage or serial killers who are also psychotic but are cool and well organized. Recent outbreaks of violence in and near schools are a source of alarm in the United States and other industrial nations. The rising rate of hate crimes is also cause for concern.

■ Robbery may be defined as the taking of another person's property by intimidation. It usually occurs between strangers.

■ Forcible rape is the act of forcing sexual intercourse on another person against his or her will. In recent years rapes by offenders who are known to the victim—date or acquaintance rape—have become a matter of concern, especially on college and university campuses.

■ Child abuse, sometimes leading to death, is a serious problem in the United States. Many abusive parents were themselves abused in childhood. Spouse abuse is also common and appears to be highly correlated with child abuse.

■ The much higher rate of homicide in the United States than in other industrialized nations is sometimes attributed to violence by juvenile gang members, but the available evidence indicates that it is not the presence of gangs per se but the ready availability of guns that accounts for the prevalence of lethal violence in American cities.

■ Policymakers do not agree on what should be done to reduce or eliminate violent crime. Although most Americans favor gun control (i.e., supervision of the purchase and sale of firearms), opponents of such measures are powerful and well organized and have succeeded in preventing the passage of meaningful legislation in this area. There are signs that the dominance of the gun lobby is weakening, but legislators and the public are still divided on this issue. Efforts to reduce the level of media violence have also met with little success.

■ Family violence is widely recognized as a serious national problem, and there have been numerous efforts to increase public awareness of it and to prevent it where possible. There is a need for greater cooperation among police investigators, medical professionals, and social workers who deal with families in which abuse occurs.

■ The relationship between socioeconomic inequality and violence has been the focus of recent analyses of violence and debates over policies directed toward its abatement. Numerous important studies have demonstrated the need for the redress of legitimate grievances and a more equitable sharing of values and resources if the overall level of violence in American society is to be reduced.

KEY TERMS

violence, p. 191
structural violence, p. 191
institutional violence, p. 192
noninstitutional violence, p. 192
strategic crimes, p. 195

murder, p. 197
manslaughter, p. 197
assault, p. 202
robbery, p. 202
forcible rape, p. 202

statutory rape, p. 202
date rape, p. 204
acquaintance rape, p. 204
child abuse, p. 204

INTERNET EXERCISE

The web destinations for Chapter 7 are related to different aspects of violence. To begin your explorations, go to the Prentice Hall Companion Website: **http://prenhall.com/kornblum**. Then choose **Chapter 7** (Violence). Next, select **destinations** from the menu on the left side of the screen. There are a variety of sites to investigate. We suggest that you begin with **Families First: Youth Violence**. In Chapter 7, the *Critical Research* feature is entitled "Crisis of Youth Violence or Adult Panic?" Sociologists warn that tragic violence can distort realities, that panic can stifle more constructive responses, and that these reactions can worsen the underlying problems by denying students' rights and gagging their voices. The **Families First** site is designed to help parents and other interested parties understand youth violence. After you access the site, there are a number of icons along the left margin that you may click on, including "Facts and Figures on School Violence," "Warning Signs," and "Why Might Youth Be Expressing Violence More Frequently?" After you have explored the Families First site, answer the following questions:

■ Do you think there is a crisis of youth violence in our society, or is this perception fueled by what the text refers to as "adult panic"?

■ If you were a policymaker, what approach would you recommend in reaction to the recent episodes of youth violence?

8

Poverty Amid Affluence

POVERTY

- The poorest 20 percent of U.S. households received 4.2 percent of all income in 1997.

- Twenty percent of children under the age of 18 are living in poverty.

- The median household income of two-parent families with children was $54,395 in 1997; that of female-headed families with children was only $21,023.

- Twenty-four percent of the black population and 25 percent of people of Spanish-speaking descent have incomes below the official poverty line, compared with 8.4 percent of the white population.

- About 1.35 million children—nearly 2 percent of the nation's total—are homeless.

OUTLINE

The Haves and the Have-nots
The Rich
The Poor

Poverty and Social Class

The Nature of Poverty
The Poverty Line
Who Are the Poor?

Concomitants of Poverty
Health Care
Education
Housing and Homelessness
Justice

Explanations of Persistent Poverty
Structural Explanations
Cultural Explanations

Social Policy
Reform of "Welfare as We Know It"
Dependency, Work, and Responsibility
Single Mothers: A Special Case
Moving to Opportunity?

Although at the turn of the twenty-first century the United States is enjoying an economic boom of record proportions, the gap between rich and poor is widening. Worldwide, the gap between rich and poor is also a cause of growing concern. Of the 6 billion people on the planet, about 1.2 billion are so poor that they must subsist on the equivalent of a dollar a day or less. Although the poor in the United States do not routinely face starvation or the possibility of economic catastrophes like famine, the decline of their health and the growing precariousness of their access to the means of existence results in a wide array of social problems.

We will see in this chapter that there are wide ideological differences among the various policies proposed for dealing with poverty. There are also many different explanations for the persistence of poverty amid growing affluence. But despite the differences in ideology, most observers of inequality in the United States would agree with a recent statement by Senator Edward M. Kennedy: "As a society we must answer an increasingly urgent question. What can we do to close the widening gap in income and skills that leaves too many Americans unable to participate fully in the American Dream?" (quoted in Stevenson, 2000, p. 3).

By almost any standard measure, the United States ranks as one of the wealthiest nations in the world. The gross domestic product (GDP)—the total market value of all final goods and services produced within the United States in one year—is over $8.5 trillion. If we divide the GDP by the total population to derive the per capita GDP, a crude but commonly used measure of the comparative wealth of nations, we find that the United States ranks well above most other countries, with a GDP of over $31,000 per person. Other advanced industrial nations, such as France, Germany, Denmark, and the United Kingdom, fall below this figure by $8,000 or more (*Statistical Abstract*, 1999).

In the United States, wealth is concentrated in the hands of a relatively small number of people, while many other Americans can barely make ends meet or are living in poverty. American households have a median income of approximately $37,000; about 44 percent enjoy incomes above $50,000 (*Statistical Abstract*, 1999). Indeed, we will see in this chapter that the gap between the rich and the poor has widened in the past decade, that the level of living of most

In many third world countries, poverty is increasing as unemployment and population growth out-strip economic development.

Americans has been declining, that the concentration of wealth in the hands of a few fortunate people has been increasing, and that policymakers are engaged in an intense debate over how to address the problem of persistent poverty. In the first section of the chapter we briefly examine the consequences of the inequality that characterizes American society. Later we explore some theories that attempt to explain the presence of poverty in one of the world's most affluent nations, as well as social policies aimed at reducing or eliminating poverty.

Although this chapter focuses on poverty in the United States, it is important to note that a growing gap between the haves and the have-nots exists throughout the world. One-fifth of the world's people live in the richest nations (including the United States), and their average incomes are 15 times higher than those of the one-fifth who live in the poorest nations. In the world today there are about 157 billionaires and about 2 million millionaires, but there are approximately 100 million homeless people. Americans spend about $5 billion per year on diets to lower their caloric intake, while 400 million people around the world are undernourished to the point of physical deterioration (Conway, 1999). These growing disparities between rich and poor throughout the world have direct effects on the situation of the poor in the United States because many jobs are "exported" to countries where extremely poor people will accept work at almost any wage. The increase in world poverty also contributes to environmental degradation and political instability and violence, which drain resources that might be used to meet a nation's domestic needs.

The experience of poverty is based on conditions in one's own society. People feel poor or rich with reference to others around them, not with reference to very poor or very rich people elsewhere in the world. The experience of living in the United States as a teenager in a family for which every penny counts—and there is rarely enough money for new clothes or a family car or trips outside of town—can be as difficult to bear as life in poverty anywhere. That the poor in the United States are relatively better off than the poor in Bangladesh is of little comfort.

The Haves and the Have-nots

Although equality of opportunity is a central value of American society, equality of outcome is not (Cox & Alm, 2000). Most Americans believe everyone should have the same opportunity to achieve material well-being (equality of opportunity). They do not object to inequality in the actual situation of different groups in society (equality of outcome). Thus, the middle-class standard of living is the norm that is portrayed over and over again in media representations of American lifestyles. But this image ignores both the handful of extremely rich Americans and the tens of millions who share only minimally in the nation's affluence. To observe inequality and understand its impact, we need only compare a few aspects of the lives led by the affluent and the poor in our society.

The affluent live longer and better and can afford the best medical care in the world, the finest education, and the most elegant possessions. In addition, by discreetly influencing politicians, police officers, and other public officials to promote or defend their interests, they can obtain social preference and shape government policies. This capacity to purchase both possessions and influence gives the extremely wealthy a potential power that is grossly out of proportion to their numbers.

For the poor, the situation is reversed. Although America's poor people seldom die of starvation and generally have more than the hopelessly poor of the third world, they lead lives of serious deprivation compared not only to the wealthy but to the middle class as well. This relative deprivation profoundly affects the style and quality of their lives. It extends beyond mere distribution of income and includes inequality in education, health care, police protection, job opportunities, legal justice, housing, and many other areas. The poor are more frequently subject to mental illness than other Americans. They require more medical treatment and have longer and more serious illnesses. Their children are more likely to die than those of the more affluent, and their life expectancy is below the national average. They are more likely to become criminals or juvenile delinquents, and they contribute more than their share of teenage pregnancy, alcoholism, and violence to American society.

The Rich

Economist Paul Samuelson has provided a vivid metaphor for the disparity in the distribution of income in the United States: "If we made an income pyramid out of a child's blocks, with each layer portraying $1,000 of income, the peak would be far higher than the Eiffel Tower, but almost all of us would be within a yard of the ground" (quoted in Blumberg, 1980, p. 34). Whatever measure or standard is used, the implications are the same: The rich own more, earn more, and use more—much, much more—and they have been doing so for a long time.

Net worth, a frequently used measure of wealth, refers to the value of savings and checking accounts, real estate, automobiles, stocks and bonds, and other assets minus debts. Surveys by the Federal Reserve Board suggest that 1 percent of all households hold over one-third of all personal wealth. The distribution of income is even more unequal: The wealthiest 20 percent of households received 47.2 percent of all income in 1997, while the poorest 20 percent received 4.2 percent (*Statistical Abstract*, 1999).

The United States has a long history of attempting to redistribute wealth through taxation and other policies. These policies have been instituted for three reasons: (1) The wealthy get more out of the economic system and can afford to pay more taxes; (2) they have a greater investment in the economic system and should pay more to maintain it; (3) redistributing some income from the rich to the poor is fair and just in a democratic society. It was ideas like these that led to the establishment in the 1930s of President Franklin D. Roosevelt's New Deal, which, together with the Great

Society legislation proposed by President Lyndon B. Johnson in the 1960s, created most of this country's welfare institutions and programs.

The United States is now considered a **welfare state,** meaning that a significant portion of the GDP is taken by the state to provide certain minimum levels of social welfare for the poor, the aged, the disabled, and others who would not be able to survive under conditions of market competition. In a welfare state, governments at all levels attempt to smooth out the effects of recessions and economic booms through such devices as graduated income taxes, public-sector employment, economic incentives for private firms, unemployment insurance, and the transfer of some wealth from the rich to the poor.

In general, the competition for resources—not only income and wealth but also what they can buy (health care, comfortable housing, expensive education, etc.)—heavily favors the rich. For example, people in upper income brackets have many legal ways to avoid taxes. If they purchase real estate, they can obtain substantial tax reductions for mortgage interest payments at the same time that the property is increasing in value. In addition, the wealthy can make tax-free investments that are not available to those who are less well-off. The income from municipal bonds—which are commonly sold in denominations of $5,000—does not have to be reported on tax returns.

Several other aspects of the welfare state's programs have turned out to be what is sometimes called **wealthfare,** or subsidies for the rich. For example, government import-export policies are designed to protect certain industries, such as textiles or steel, and the jobs of their employees. However, when the government limits imports of a certain product, competition is stifled and consumers must pay the prices demanded by domestic manufacturers. When the government agrees to rescue failing corporations, as it has done with railroads, banks, and aerospace companies, the owners of substantial portions of the corporations' capital are most likely to benefit. It can be argued that the poor are relative losers in these situations since less government money is available for social programs. Similarly, when government revenues are raised through such means as sales taxes on gasoline, those with less money effectively bear a greater share of the burden because the proportion of tax they pay is higher relative to their smaller incomes than it is for the rich. As shown in Figure 8–1, as a result of changes in state tax policies during the 1990s, revenues obtained from individual income taxes have decreased dramatically while sales taxes on consumer goods, which disproportionately tax those who can afford them least, have been increasing.

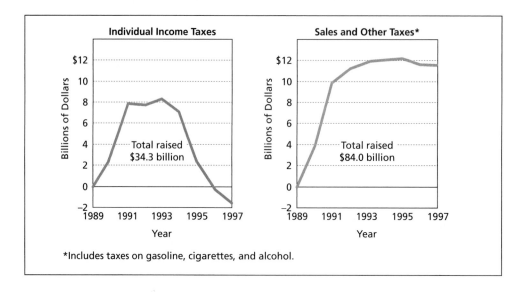

Figure 8–1 Yearly Rise or Fall in Total Revenue for All 50 States as a Result of Tax Changes Made Since 1989 (in 1997 Dollars)

Source: Center on Budget and Policy Priorities.

*Includes taxes on gasoline, cigarettes, and alcohol.

Are the Rich a Social Problem?   During the presidential election campaigns of the 1990s, the Democrats seemed to score heavily against their Republican opponents by accusing some of them of fostering a "public be damned, let me enrich myself" attitude among wealthy Americans. The Democrats pointed to the encouragement the rich receive from the so-called "trickle-down" theory of economics, which states that policies that benefit businesses or wealthy individuals will stimulate economic activity and thereby create more jobs. Although the Clinton administration made some very modest gains in correcting the public image of "government for the rich," frequent news stories continually remind us, for example, that the 400 richest Americans have amassed a total net worth of $1 trillion more than the gross domestic product of China (Galewitz, 1999). At the same time, increasing numbers of low-wage workers have seen the value of their earnings diminish even in a period of low inflation. The gains of the rich and the losses of the nonrich are clearly shown in Table 8–1. Note the extraordinary growth in income share—119.7 percent—of the 1 percent of American households with the highest income.

We will return to this issue in the discussion of corporate power in Chapter 14. Here it is sufficient to point out that although there is no consensus in American society that the rich themselves are a social problem, there is evidence of concern that the ethic of individual success and enrichment may hamper efforts to develop new policies to address the problems of poverty (Reich, 1998).

The Poor

While the rich are able to take advantage of various ways of improving their situation, the poor face an entirely different set of circumstances. They are part of a society that has the means to greatly alleviate poverty but, instead, has adopted policies that actually increase the percentage of the poor. In the words of a pastoral letter issued by a committee of Roman Catholic bishops in 1984, "The level of inequality in income and wealth in our society . . . today must be judged morally unacceptable" (quoted in Briggs, 1984). Many social scientists believe that the situation of the poor is likely to become still worse. There are several reasons for this, including technological changes that eliminate certain kinds of jobs, the reluctance of the middle and upper classes to share their wealth with less fortunate members of society, and the general attitude of Americans toward poverty.

TABLE 8–1   **Proportion of Income Received by Each Fifth of Households, 1977 and 1999**

Household Groups	Share of All Income*		Average After-tax Income (estimated)		Change
	1977	1999	1977	1999	
One-fifth with lowest income	5.7%	4.2%	$10,000	$8,800	▼ 12.0%
Next lowest one-fifth	11.5	9.7	22,100	20,000	▼ 9.5
Middle one-fifth	16.4	14.7	32,400	31,400	▼ 3.1
Next highest one-fifth	22.8	21.3	42,600	45,100	▲ 5.9
One-fifth with highest income	44.2	50.4	74,000	102,300	▲ 38.2
1 percent with highest income	7.3	12.9	234,700	515,600	▲ 119.7

* Figures do not add up to 100% due to rounding.

Source: Congressional Budget Office data analyzed by Center on Budget and Policy Priorities.

Many people believe that the poor are largely to blame for their own poverty. The argument is as follows: "The poor as a class consists of the unemployed, who are responsible for their condition because they will not work. If they could be persuaded to work for a living or were forced to take jobs, poverty could be eliminated. What we have now is a group of freeloaders who are getting by on welfare." The inaccuracy of this argument is evident when one examines the data on poverty and work.

Of the 35.5 million people who were classified as living below the official poverty line in 1998, 14.1 million (20 percent) were children under the age of 18; another 3.4 million (10.5 percent) were over 65 years old (*Statistical Abstract,* 1999). Millions more were female heads of households with children younger than 18 and no husband present, or were ill, disabled, or going to school; of the remainder, the majority worked either full or part time in the previous year, but their wages were not sufficient to elevate them above the poverty threshold.

Members of minority groups are especially likely to be included among the poor. The median income of minority families is about 60 percent of that of white families (*Statistical Abstract,* 1999), and unemployment rates for black and Hispanic workers average about double the rate for white workers. (See Figures 8–2 and 8–3.)

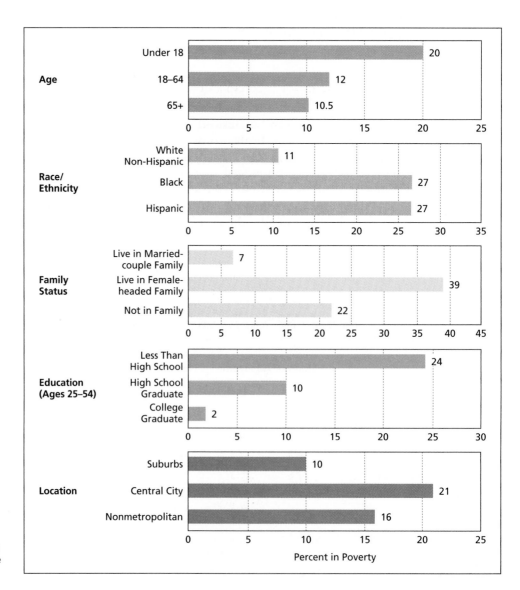

Figure 8–2 Poverty Rates of Persons, by Selected Characteristics

Source: W. P. O'Hare, "Poverty Rates of Persons by Selected Characteristics," *Population Reference Bureau Bulletin* 51 (Washington, D.C.: Population Reference Bureau, 1996).

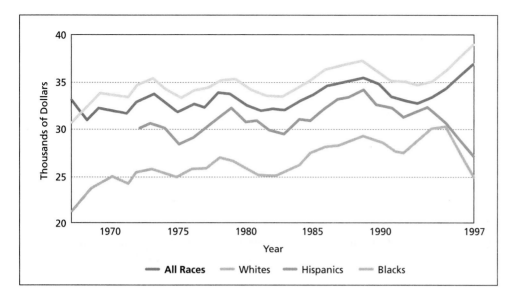

Figure 8–3   Median Household Income (in Constant Dollars, Adjusted for Inflation)

Source: Data from U.S. Bureau of the Census.

Of enormous significance for the so-called **working poor** is the fact that real wages (i.e., wages measured in constant dollars) have declined since the late 1980s. In 1997 the median household income was $37,005. In 1989, as shown in Figure 8–3, it peaked at over $37,415; for the next few years it declined steadily. The most recent data show a small increase in median household income for all groups. So far, the increases of the 1990s have not brought incomes back to the levels of a decade ago.

Poverty and Social Class

In every society people are grouped according to their access to the things that are considered valuable. These groupings of people are variously called classes, status groups, or strata, depending on the classification scheme used. Whatever the name, the phenomenon being described is **social stratification**—a pattern in which individuals and groups are assigned to different positions in the social order, positions that enjoy varying amounts of access to desirable goods and services.

The stratification of individuals and groups according to their access to various occupations, incomes, and skills is called **class stratification.** A social class is a large number of people who have roughly the same degree of economic well-being; people enter or leave a given class as their economic fortunes change. Marxian social theory emphasizes this form of stratification. For Marx and his followers, the basic classes of society are determined by ownership or nonownership of the means of production of goods and services. The owners are called capitalists, and those who must sell their labor to the capitalists are the workers.

Marx referred to members of capitalist societies who are poor and not in the labor force as the **lumpenproletariat.** This class is made up of people at the margins of society who either have dropped out of the capitalist system of employment or have never been part of it at all. Marx thought of the lumpenproletariat as comprising the criminal underworld, street people, the homeless, and all the other categories that make up the dregs of humanity. He believed that capitalism would always impoverish the working class because the owners of capital would seek to exploit the workers to the fullest extent possible, and as a result the lumpenproletariat would expand and become ever more dangerous to the stability of capitalist societies.

The German sociologist and historian Max Weber was critical of the Marxian perspective. Weber accepted most of the Marxian analysis of economic classes, but he did not believe that capitalism would inevitably cause the expansion of the lumpenprole-tariat. Moreover, he pointed out that other valued things besides wealth are distrib-uted unequally in modern societies. For example, status (or prestige) and power are both highly valued, and their distribution throughout society does not always coin-cide with the distribution of wealth. People who have made their money recently, for example, are often accorded little prestige by capitalists who made their money much earlier.

In their studies of the American system of social stratification, social scientists have developed a synthesis of the Marxian and Weberian approaches. They have devised designations like upper class, upper-middle class, middle class, working class, and poor, which combine the Marxian concept of economic class with the Weberian con-cept of status.

Sociologists have pointed out that the ways in which we distinguish among these class levels have both *objective dimensions,* which can be measured by quantifiable vari-ables such as income or membership in certain clubs, and *subjective dimensions,* which are the ways in which we evaluate ourselves and others (and the way we feel about people in the various objective classes). Objectively, we base our estimations of social-class position more or less on the Marxian model. Major employers and powerful po-litical leaders are assigned to the upper class. Managers of large firms and relatively wealthy people with successful businesses and professional practices are in the upper-middle class. People who are employed as middle-level managers and lower-paid pro-fessionals (e.g., technicians) are in the middle class. People who work in factories or depend on hourly wages are assigned to the working class. People who lack steady work or drift back and forth between legitimate employment and other ways of ob-taining income are the poor.

The subjective dimension of social class becomes evident when people are asked to identify the class to which they belong. For example, the proportion of people who classify themselves as poor is considerably lower than the proportion who are so classi-fied by the Census Bureau. (See Table 8–2.) Part of the reason for this is that many poor people have low-paying jobs and hesitate to identify themselves as poor even when they are; they place themselves in the working class. Moreover, as Mary R. Jack-man and Robert W. Jackman (1983) have pointed out, respondents who do identify themselves as poor might not do so if the same category were labeled "lower class" (Gilbert, 1993).

All the categories mentioned earlier are used to discuss the American stratification system, but they are extremely difficult to define scientifically. The designations "middle

TABLE 8–2 Distribution of Responses to Class-identification Question (for Total Sample, by Race and Sex)

	Poor	Working	Middle	Upper Middle	Upper	Other	No Social Classes	Don't Know	Not Ascertained	Total Number
Total Sample	7.6%	36.6%	43.3%	8.2%	1.0%	1.3%	0.5%	1.5%	0.2%	1,914
Whites	4.8	35.8	46.4	9.0	1.0	1.1	0.5	1.3	0.2	1,648
Blacks	27.7	41.5	22.1	1.5	1.5	2.6	0.5	2.6	0.0	195
Other*	14.1	39.1	32.8	7.8	0.0	1.6	0.0	3.1	1.6	64
Men	5.4	41.4	40.5	8.5	1.1	1.4	0.9	0.5	0.4	802
Women	9.2	33.1	45.2	8.0	0.9	1.2	0.2	2.2	0.1	1,112

*This category includes Asians, Hispanic Americans, and American Indians.

Source: Mary and Robert Jackman, "Distribution of Responses to Class Identification," *Class Awareness in the United States.* By permission of the University of California Press, Berkeley.

class" and "working class" are especially problematic. In the 1950s and 1960s, when the GDP doubled each decade, it appeared that the distinctions between the working and middle classes were becoming blurred and meaningless. For a period of about 20 years, it seemed that the United States and Canada were experiencing a convergence in social classes as more and more people shared in the benefits of expanding wealth. Workers—defined in the Marxian sense—were adopting lifestyles that seemed to make them indistinguishable from the middle class of salaried employees and professionals. In that period only the extremes of social stratification were easy to identify: the wealthy at the top and the poor at the bottom. Otherwise, the incomes of most Americans were giving them access to what sociologist David Riesman called the "standard package" of goods and services available in a wealthy society (Riesman, Glazer, & Denney, 1950). That package included a home, a car, and such consumer goods as TV sets, air conditioners, and washing machines (Blumberg, 1980).

The development of welfare state institutions in the United States from the 1930s to the end of the 1960s supported the notion that the classes were converging toward a generalized level of affluence. The growing strength of labor unions allowed workers to bargain for higher wages and better benefits than ever before. The growth of mass educational institutions made education available to more people and provided training for new jobs and professions. Social-welfare programs like Social Security, workfare, food stamps, Medicare and Medicaid, affirmative-action programs, youth programs, unemployment insurance, and many other kinds of government support seemed to offer the hope that the degree of inequality in American society would be reduced still further. However, events of the 1980s and 1990s reversed the trend toward greater affluence for all. We will return to this subject in later sections of the chapter.

The Nature of Poverty

Poverty is a deceptively simple term to define. Certainly the poor have less money than other people. In addition, the money they do have buys them less. The poor must often purchase necessities as soon as they have cash (e.g., when a welfare check arrives). They cannot shop around for sales or bargains, and they are often victimized by shopkeepers who raise their prices the day welfare checks are delivered. When they buy on credit, the poor must accept higher interest rates because they take longer to pay and are considered poor credit risks. Inflationary price increases affect the poor first, and more severely. The cost of essential consumer goods, ranging from rice and sugar to toilet tissue and soap, may rise suddenly (e.g., when energy costs increase as a result of a crisis in the Middle East), but the wages of the lowest-paid people and government income assistance payments rise slowly if at all.

For most people, poverty simply means not having enough money to buy things that are considered necessary and desirable. Various formal definitions of poverty have been offered. John Kenneth Galbraith (1958) stressed the sense of degradation felt by the poor and concluded that "people are poverty stricken when their income, even if adequate for survival, falls markedly behind that of the community" (p. 245). Poverty may mean a condition of near starvation, bare subsistence (the minimum necessary to maintain life), or any standard of living measurably beneath the national average. To deal more effectively with poverty as a social problem, a generally agreed-upon, scientifically based, and more specific definition is needed.

The Poverty Line

Official U.S. government definitions of poverty are based on the calculation of a minimum family "market basket." The U.S. Department of Agriculture regularly prepares estimates of the cost of achieving a minimum level of nutrition, based on average food prices. It is assumed that an average low-income family of four must spend one-third of its total income on food; thus, by multiplying the family food budget by four, the government arrives at a poverty income that can be adjusted for the number of people in the household and for changes in the cost of food. The official, food-based poverty line can also be adjusted to account for the tendency of rural people to supplement their incomes with subsistence agriculture and gardens. The official measure is also corrected each year or even more often for changes in the cost of living as measured by the consumer price index (CPI). In 1999 this inflation-corrected, official poverty line for a family of four was $16,600. By this measure, 35 million people, or 12.9 percent of the U.S. population, were below the poverty line.

SOCIAL PROBLEMS ONLINE

Poverty and Welfare on the Internet

There are several websites on the Internet with data and analyses of poverty in the United States, as well as debates about welfare policies. To get a numerical account of poverty and wealth in America, start at the U.S. Census Bureau's home page at **http://www.census.gov**/. Click on Subject A–Z and then on P to find Poverty in the menu. Information concerning poverty areas, historical poverty tables (1959–1989), poverty thresholds by family size and number of children, and the like can be found there. For related areas check Income and Wealth.

The Census Bureau also offers links with organizations such as the Institute for Research on Poverty, which is located at **http://www.ssc.wisc.edu/irp**. It is a university-based center (University of Wisconsin, Madison) whose mission is to research "the causes and consequences of poverty and social inequality in the United States." Clicking on the Online Publications section of the institute's home page brings up a menu of choices, such as Newsletters, Discussion Papers, Special Reports, and so forth. One site to visit is the Institutional Index to Poverty-related Sites, which provides an alphabetical link with organizations committed to research and analysis of poverty and welfare policy.

The National Center for Children in Poverty, at **http:/cpmcnet.columbia.edu/dept/nccp**/, has updated information and ongoing research on the effects of changes in welfare policy on the lives of poor children and their communities. Also, the Children's Defense Fund, at **http://www.tmn.com/cdf/index.html**, which "pays attention to the needs of poor, minority, and disabled children," has a section of Facts & Figures that presents updated information on the costs of raising children, as well as ongoing demographic data for different ethnic and racial groups in the United States. Finally, the University of Berkeley Data Archives & Technical Assistance Center, at **http://ucdata.berkeley.edu**/, provides data sets on a variety of subjects related to welfare and poverty.

For summaries of welfare reform and its impact on adolescents, health care, immigration, and the like, browse the Welfare Information Network at **http://www.welfareinfo.org**/. Clicking on Overall Summaries will offer a link with other organizations and analyses of welfare and poverty issues. The National Association of Community Action Agencies, at **http://www.nacaa.org**/, has a home page with a section called National Dialogue on Poverty. There one can find the analyses and recommendations of different communities and think tanks from a public forum held in 1996. Finally, for help with research on different issues related to poverty and welfare, browse the Social Work and Social Services web sites at **http://www.gwbssw.wustl.edu/~gwbhome/websites.html**.

The Urban Institute, **http://www.urban.org**/, is a policy research organization that investigates social and economic problems. The Hot Topics section of the home page offers reports and papers to those interested in doing research. The Cato Institute, at **http://www.cato.org**, is a think tank that emphasizes market-based rather than government-driven policies. Its home page has a search engine that allows one to type, for example, "welfare" to access several hotly debated articles on the subject. Similarly, for research papers and data related to welfare and poverty, visit the Brookings Institution at **http://www.brook.edu**/.

This official poverty measure was developed in 1965 by Mollie Orshansky, an economist at the Social Security Administration, who reasoned that the only acceptable measure of the adequacy of a person's level of living is food consumption. But although this definition was accepted as the official means of establishing a poverty line, there has been continuing controversy and debate over definitions of poverty and their implications for social policy.

During the Reagan administration, conservative social scientists and policymakers were critical of the way poverty is measured. In particular, they argued that if benefits provided to the poor, such as food stamps, Medicaid, and housing, are included in the calculation of income, the extent of poverty is much less than is generally believed. Others have argued that the CPI overestimates the impact of rising prices on the poor. These differences in measurement could affect whether millions of Americans are classified above or below the official poverty line.

But those who believe that the existing poverty measures actually underestimate the size of the poor population also have strong arguments on their side. First, there is the argument that taxes, alimony, out-of-pocket health-care expenses, and many work-related expenses should be excluded from the income figures used to determine poverty status because this money cannot be used to purchase food and other necessities of life. Second, the official poverty definition does not take into account regional differences in the cost of living and therefore neglects hundreds of thousands of poor people in high-cost cities like Washington, D.C., while overestimating the number of poor people in rural areas, where the cost of living is lower. Finally, many researchers and advocates for the poor note that the poverty threshold is extremely low and that people living well above that level are still quite poor. Recent polls show that most Americans favor raising the poverty line by up to 25 percent. Had this been done in 1999, the number of "officially poor" Americans would have been closer to 50 million than to the 35 million reported (Uchitelle, 1999).

Poverty scholar Patricia Ruggles (1990) has observed that according to official definitions of poverty, a single mother of three who works full time and earns $5 an hour is not officially poor. Yet her rent, child care costs, and taxes would probably account for 80 percent of her weekly income, leaving her with about $40 a week to pay for food, medical care, clothing, and everything else. According to Ruggles, this anomaly is due to changes in American living standards that have occurred since the official formula for calculating the poverty line was established. When the poverty formula was first developed, such conveniences as telephones and indoor plumbing were not part of Americans' expectations of a minimally adequate level of living. And at that time far fewer children lived with one parent and far fewer women were employed. Child care, a significant expense for most working families (and essential if a single parent is to work), was not the major and necessary expense it is today. With these factors in mind, Ruggles suggests that the official food-price-based estimate of the poverty line should be recalculated at regular intervals on the basis of changing definitions of minimal consumption.

The idea that poverty is relative rather than absolute is nothing new. Forty years ago Victor Fuchs (1956) proposed that any family may be classified as poor if its income is less than half of the median family income. By this definition, about 20 percent of the population would be considered poor. Contrary to the Orshansky formula or any arbitrary income standard, the use of such a relative standard implies that poverty will exist as long as income distribution

The most common cause of poverty is the breakup of a couple, which often leaves the woman unable to work because she must care for a young child.

remains unequal. And in fact, the proportion of poor people in America has tended to remain stable when measured by the Fuchs formula.

Who Are the Poor?

Since the passage of the Social Security Act (1935), which established federal old-age pensions (Social Security), unemployment insurance, and aid to dependent children, the nation has made great strides in its effort to combat poverty. Although it remains true that far too many citizens live in poverty, it is not true, as some argue, that programs to combat poverty have had negative effects or no effect at all (Murray, 1984). Figure 8–4 shows clearly that over the same period poverty among people under the age of 18 has been increasing. Table 8–3 shows that other nations, such as Ireland, the United Kingdom, France, and Israel, also have large numbers of poor children, but these nations dramatically reduce their rates of child poverty through government assistance. As William O'Hare (1996), a noted expert on the demographics of poverty, points out, "These findings suggest that the public sector in other developed countries does more than the United States to lift poor children out of poverty" (p. 37). The primary reason for child poverty is birth into a single-parent family or the breakup of a two-parent family. It is worthwhile, therefore, to look more closely at the link between poverty and single-parent families.

Poverty and Single-parent Families.   Of all children under the age of 18 in the United States, 19.2 percent are living in poverty. The situation is especially severe for children in single-parent families headed by women. The median household income of two-parent families with children was $54,395 in 1997; that of female-headed families with children was only $21,023 (*Statistical Abstract*, 1999).

Black and Hispanic female-headed families (over 30 percent of all black families) are especially likely to be living in poverty (Jencks & Swingle, 2000). About 37 percent of black and 36 percent of Hispanic children under the age of 18 were classified as poor in 1997 (*Statistical Abstract*, 1999).

Single female parents are part of a much larger trend toward diversity in family structure, a trend to which we return in Chapter 12. Poor women who are raising

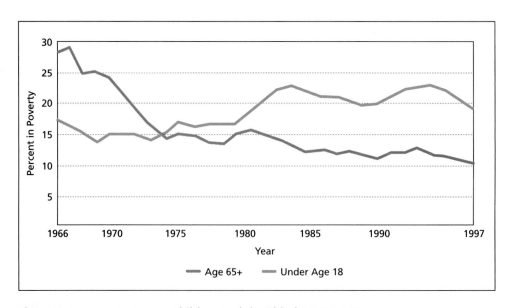

Figure 8–4   Poverty Among Children and the Elderly, 1966–1997

Source: Statistical Abstract, 1999. W. P. O'Hare, "A New Look at Poverty in America," *Population Reference Bureau Bulletin* 51 (Washington, D.C.: Population Reference Bureau, 1996).

TABLE 8–3   Child Poverty in 17 Developed Countries Before and After Government Assistance, Mid-1980s to Early 1990s

| Country* | Percent of Children in Poverty | | Percent of Children Lifted out of Poverty by Gov't Programs |
	Before Assistance	After Assistance	
United States	25.9	21.5	17
Australia	19.6	14.0	29
Canada	30.2	12.0	60
Israel	23.9	11.1	54
United Kingdom	29.6	9.9	67
Italy	11.5	9.6	17
Germany	9.0	6.8	24
France	25.4	6.5	74
Netherlands	13.7	6.2	55
Norway	12.9	4.6	64
Luxembourg	11.7	4.1	65
Belgium	16.2	3.8	77
Denmark	16.0	3.3	79
Switzerland	5.1	3.3	35
Sweden	19.1	2.7	86
Finland	11.5	2.5	78

*Ranked by poverty rate after assistance.

Source: L. Rainwater and T.M. Smeeding, 1995, *Doing Poorly: The Real Income of American Children in a Comparative Perspective.* Working Paper no. 127, Luxembourg Income Study, Maxwell School of Citizenship and Public Affairs, Syracuse University.

their children without the immediate aid of husbands, however, are a special target for moral crusaders and social policymakers alike. In 1996 Congress passed the Personal Responsibility and Work Opportunity Reconciliation Act of 1996, more widely known as "welfare reform." This legislation was largely targeted toward the parents of children in households whose incomes fall below the poverty line. Single female parents who were formerly entitled to monthly payments or assistance through the Aid to Families with Dependent Children(AFDC) program were required to obtain jobs or enroll in work training programs to qualify for supplemental assistance through their state governments. These state payments are subsidized by federal government grants. We will describe some of the changes brought about by welfare reform shortly. Few policy changes have received more attention or generated more confusion or ideological controversy. (See the Critical Research feature on page 234.)

Advocates of welfare reform, including both Republicans and Democrats, point to dramatic decreases in the number of people, especially female single parents, receiving various types of "welfare" payments. They may also cite abundant examples of people who have succeeded in finding real employment. These individuals often gain greater self-esteem and pride from their jobs than they ever experienced in the far more passive but frustrating life lived from one AFDC check to another. But have these far-reaching changes actually improved the lives of female single parents? The answers are not fully known, but much of the data suggests that a great deal of caution should accompany the generally enthusiastic welcome that welfare reform has received so far.

Single Mothers Making Ends Meet

"**I** really like my work, but the money is not enough. People work me really hard, and there's nowhere to be promoted to unless I get more school. So sometimes it's depressing. I feel like I do a good job though, and I like to have contact with all these people."

The speaker is a 23-year-old woman from San Antonio with three preschool-aged children. Her job has helped her stay off public assistance for over a year. She is speaking to social scientists Kathryn Edin and Laura Lein (1997), whose research on how single parents survive on and off public assistance ("welfare") is considered the most sophisticated and critical analysis of the subject currently available. Edin and Lein repeatedly interviewed a roughly matched sample of single mothers receiving public assistance ($n = 214$) and a somewhat smaller sample ($n = 165$) of single mothers who had gone to work and were no longer on the welfare rolls. The women lived in a number of different cities and one rural area in the United States.

Edin and Lein's overall finding is that none of the single mothers could raise their children on the "official" incomes they received. Welfare payments were too low by about 40 percent of the eventual budgets the women achieved. So were the wages of the entry-level jobs of the working women. All had to develop additional survival strategies. These include finding sources of low-cost clothing for their children, working at off-the-books jobs, and doing favors for friends and relatives in return for "loans." The list of creative ways the women found to obtain money and nourish their children physically and emotionally is almost endless.

Despite their creative survival strategies, the women on public assistance and at low-wage work experienced a range of hardships. Recipients of public assistance were more likely to experience a day at the end of the month before welfare checks were issued when they had no food in the house. On the other hand, low-wage workers were far more likely to forgo visits to a doctor for their children because they had no health insurance and could not afford to pay a doctor's fee. Other hardships, such as homelessness or lack of phone service, are shared more or less equally by welfare recipients and low-wage workers, as shown in the accompanying table.

Edin and Lein are not criticizing welfare policies or welfare reform from an ideological perspective. Their

This single mother has worked her way up to become a manager of a fast-food restaurant. But many of her peers are struggling to get by at minimum-wage jobs.

criticism is based on empirical data. They conclude their study by suggesting that it is reasonable to predict that the children of the women in their study are likely to suffer higher rates of delinquency, school leaving (dropping out), teenage pregnancy, and incarceration than their parents' generation did. "These problems," the authors assert, "which may not become fully evident for a generation, will certainly prove far more costly in the long run than the 'welfare problem' Americans have complained so bitterly about during the 1980s and . . . 1990s."

Some Material Hardships Experienced by Single Female Parents on Public Assistance and at Low-Wage Work

Hardship	Public Assistance	Low-wage Work
No food	31%	15%
Can't afford doctor visit	7	40
Utilities shut off	17	21
Phone off or no phone	34	30
Homeless	16	15

Source: Adapted from Edin & Lein (1997).

Boosted by a booming economy, welfare officials have found it far less difficult than anticipated to find jobs for clients. Caseloads have dropped by over 50 percent in many states. At the same time, the earnings and employment of poor people have increased. But a study by the Center on Budget and Policy Priorities (1999) offers evidence that the poorest families—those headed by single women—have fallen more deeply into poverty. The study analyzed census data that show that between 1993 and 1995 the income (including such benefits as food stamps) of the poorest fifth of families with children headed by single mothers rose by an average of almost 14 percent, or just over $1,000. Between 1995 and 1997, however, the same population's income fell by nearly 7 percent, or an average of $580 per family. About 2 million families, encompassing about 6 million parents and their children, are affected. The incomes of the poorest single-mother families, the 10 percent with the lowest incomes, fell by almost 15 percent between 1995 and 1997.

Much of the decline seems to be due to a decrease in subsidies for low-income children and their mothers. In 1995, for instance, some 88 percent of poor children received food stamps. By 1998 the figure had dropped to 70 percent. Families that are technically eligible for assistance seem not to receive it once they leave the welfare rolls, often because women are intimated about requesting aid or because it is being withheld by states and municipalities.

Child care is often a major obstacle for single mothers who want to work and could be successfully employed. Parents in the labor force most find ways to cope with the unpredictable time demands of children. Most single parents have access to some form of daily child care, often local day care centers or reliance on friends and, especially, on grandmothers. Indeed, recent studies show that 1 in 10 grandparents is either taking full responsibility for rearing a grandchild or providing regular day care. And fully 4 in 10 who are not providing these major services say that they see their grandchildren every week. (Lewin, 2000). But what happens when the child is ill or when it snows or when children are having difficulties in day care or in school? Then it becomes necessary for the working parent to have other resources to draw on. Figure 8–5 shows that paid sick leave, paid vacation, or both are luxuries for poor working women who were formerly dependent on AFDC welfare payments. Note also that women who were on AFDC for 60 months or more, or five years, are the most likely to find jobs with no leave or flexibility and to have no grandparents' services to draw on. This segment of the female single-parent population reports the most trouble keeping the jobs they are required to accept to maintain their households (Heymann & Earle, 1997).

Paternal involvement and child support enforcement are other major areas of concern for poor mothers struggling to work and raise children simultaneously. The 1996 legislation includes tough language about paternity and child support enforcement, but so far there appear to have been only sporadic increases of enforcement at the state level. Too often men are unable to pay court-ordered child support payments, and there is little provision in the act to allow fathers to replace cash payments with services like child care or transportation. Negative incentives abound but are fitfully enforced, while positive incentives and programs to increase the employability and income of fathers of low-income children are underfunded (Wolk & Schmahl, 1999).

Poverty and Minority Groups.   It should be noted that although whites are by far the largest group among poor families, blacks and other racial minorities are overrepresented. For example, 24 percent of the black population and 25 percent of people of Spanish-speaking descent have incomes below the official poverty level, compared with 8.4 percent of the white population. The median income of white families is $46,754, whereas that of black families is $28,662 and that of Hispanic families is $28,142 (*Statistical Abstract*, 1999).

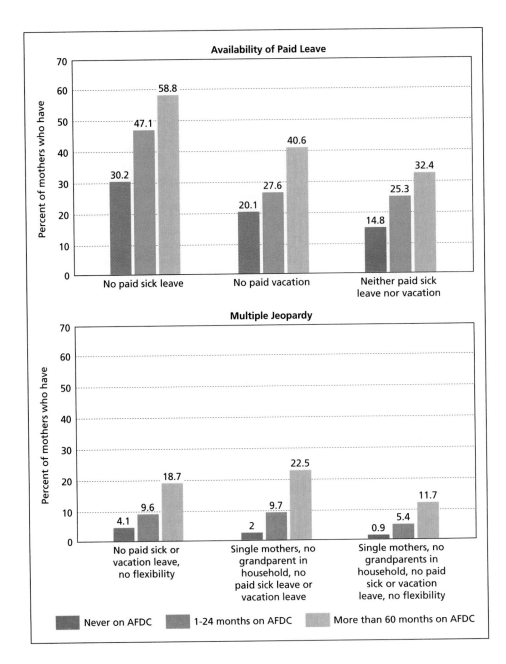

Figure 8–5 Leave and Job Conditions for Working Parents

Source: A. Earle and S. J. Heyman, "Working Conditions Faced by Poor Families and the Care of Children, *Focus,* Summer-Fall 1997, pp. 56–59. Reprinted with permission of the Institute for Research on Poverty, University of Wisconsin-Madison.

Several factors are thought to be responsible for the lower earning power of blacks and other minority workers. For one thing, they are less likely to be well educated; among blacks and Hispanics over the age of 25, 24.0 percent and 44.5 percent, respectively, have not completed high school (*Statistical Abstract,* 1999). However, from the 1970s to the end of the 1900s the gap in educational attainment between whites and blacks narrowed for people under the age of 25.

The discrimination experienced by blacks, Chicanos, Puerto Ricans, Native Americans, and other minority groups in housing, education, and health care exacerbates the effects of low income. Members of these groups are often forced to pay higher rents and to live in dilapidated or deteriorating dwellings, and the quality of predominantly minority schools is often inferior to that of predominantly white schools. In these and other areas, the disparity between blacks and whites in both opportunity and treatment is evident. (These problems are discussed more fully in Chapter 9.)

Poverty and Geography.   Although urban poverty is probably more familiar to most people, about one fifth of poor people live in rural areas and another third in suburban areas. Rural poverty is not as visible as urban poverty. Separated from the mainstream of urban life, the rural poor are largely hidden on farms, on Indian reservations, in open country, and in small towns and villages. Unemployment rates in rural areas are far above the national average. Largely because of the technological revolution in agriculture and other occupations, poorly educated, unskilled workers have been left with no means of support.

The majority of the rural poor are white, but a high percentage of southern blacks, Native Americans, and Mexican Americans are poor as well. During the 1980s, poverty and economic inequality increased among rural Americans because of downturns in agriculture, mining, and rural manufacturing. Thus, the most recent statistics indicate that people living in rural areas have lower incomes, higher poverty rates, higher unemployment, and lower educational attainment than those living in metropolitan areas (Pollard & O'Hare, 1990). Certain areas that have historically been poor, such as many counties in Appalachia, much of the Mississippi Delta, and the arid regions of the Southwest outside of the cities and irrigated farming areas, as well as many other rural areas, showed further declines in the 1980s. Those declines were accompanied by increases in the correlates of poverty: infant mortality, family dissolution, out-migration of the younger and better educated population, and malnutrition (Harrington, 1987).

Among the rural poor are migrant workers who, following the harvest, live in tarpaper shacks with few possessions. The rural poor also include Native Americans on reservations, who often lead lives of destitution and regimentation, with decisions made for them by faraway bureaucrats. Other poor populations in rural areas are out-of-work coal miners and farmers and farm workers who cannot compete with automated production techniques.

Attempting to escape poverty, many of the rural poor migrate to urban areas, where they discover that the problems of the countryside are magnified. In the cities, lack of money is aggravated by higher living costs, overcrowded and inadequate housing, poor nutrition, insufficient medical care, unsanitary health conditions, and other serious problems. The desired jobs are unobtainable since the demand for unskilled labor has declined drastically. In addition, as businesses move to the suburbs, transportation to work becomes unavailable or too expensive. As a result, rural immigrants frequently end up on the urban welfare rolls.

The Dependent Poor.   Americans have an ambivalent attitude toward poverty. We recognize that the poor are not always responsible for their situation, yet those who must turn to public assistance (sometimes referred to as the dependent poor) are often pictured as lazy, shiftless, or dishonest. Their private lives are scrutinized, and the constant presence of social workers and welfare investigators in their homes denies them the basic right of privacy.

A significant proportion of the dependent poor are people who have struggled with disabilities from childhood. Many people who have not studied poverty closely fail to understand the outstanding importance of this fact. Approximately 1 million poor children in the United States receive Supplemental Security Income (SSI) because they have disabilities. As Figure 8–6 shows, the largest proportion are mentally retarded. Slightly over 8 percent have attention deficit hyperactivity disorder (ADHD), a disability that often severely impedes the educational attainment of children from poor families. Although childhood disabilities are not unique to poor families,

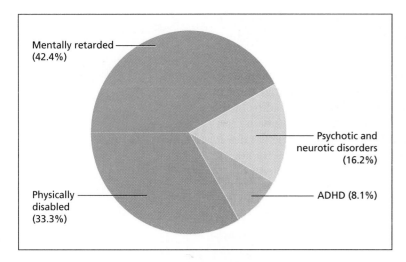

Figure 8–6 Children with Disabilities Receiving Supplemental Security Income (SSI)

Source: Meyers, Lukemeyer, & Smeeding, *Focus,* (Newsletter of the Institute for Research on Poverty, University of Wisconsin-Madison) 19, no. 1, Summer-Fall, 1997, p. 51.

children in low-income households are more likely to be chronically ill or disabled because of the environmental risks of low-income neighborhoods, as well as deficiencies in nutrition and health care. Moreover, not only does childhood disability correlate highly with later adult dependence, but it can also create extreme hardship for single parents already burdened by the basic effects of poverty (Meyers, Lukemeyer, & Smeeding, 1997).

While many poor parents face the difficulties of dealing with children's disabilities, all poor people who depend to some degree on public assistance are victims of myths and misconceptions like the following:

Myth 1: The vast majority of the poor are blacks or Hispanics. Poverty rates are higher among blacks and Hispanics than among other racial/ethnic groups, but they do not make up the majority of the poor. Non-Hispanic whites are the most numerous racial/ethnic group in the poverty population.

Myth 2: People are poor because they do not want to work. Half of the poor are not in the working ages: About 40 percent are under age 18; another 10 percent are age 65 and older. Many poor people have jobs, but earn below-poverty wages. Many poor individuals cannot work because of a serious disability or because they must care for family members.

Myth 3: Poor families are trapped in a cycle of poverty that few escape. The poverty population is dynamic—people move in and out of poverty every year. Only 12 percent of the poor remain in poverty for five or more consecutive years.

Myth 4: Welfare programs for the poor are straining the federal budget. Social-assistance programs for low-income families and individuals accounted for about 14 percent of federal expenditures for fiscal year 1996. A much larger share of the budget goes to other types of social assistance, such as Social Security, which mainly go to middle-class Americans.

Myth 5: The majority of the poor live in inner-city neighborhoods. Less than half of the poor live in central-city areas, and less than one-quarter live in high-poverty inner-city areas. Over one-third of the poor live in the suburbs, and more than one-fifth live outside metropolitan areas.

Myth 6: The poor live off government welfare. Welfare, as we have seen, accounts for a diminishing proportion of the income of poor adults. Social Security contributes about 22 percent of the income of the poor. Nearly half of the income received by poor adults comes from wages or other work-related activity.

Myth 7: Most of the poor are single mothers and their children. Female-headed families represent just 38 percent of the poor. About 34 percent of the poor live in married-couple families, 22 percent live alone or with nonrelatives, and the remainder live in male-headed families with no wife present.

Myth 8: Antipoverty programs are designed to reduce poverty. Most welfare programs are geared to sustain the poor, not pull them out of poverty. Only about 10 percent of the welfare budget goes to education and training programs designed to help people improve their earning potential. (O'Hare, 1996, p. 11)

The Working Poor—Event Poverty.   Perhaps the most pernicious myth about the poor is that they do not share the work ethic of the middle class—that they are lazy or shiftless and would much rather be on welfare than work. Many studies have shown that the poor strongly share the work ethic and regret being on welfare (Jencks & Swingle, 2000). The research indicates that there are no differences between the poor and the nonpoor in life goals and willingness to work; the differences are that the poor lack confidence in their ability to succeed, and hence they accept welfare or low-wage work as a necessity.

Contrary to popular conceptions, the large majority of the poor are in male-headed families in which at least three-fourths of the family's income is derived from work. This large group is known as the *working poor*. These families are poor primarily because the men have limited skills, making it difficult for them to compete in the job market, and as a result their incomes from work are not sufficient to lift them above the poverty level.

Note that in a family with two wage earners who have jobs that pay slightly more than the minimum wage—say, $6 an hour—the workers' combined annual income would be about $25,000 a year (assuming that each works 50 weeks a year). After taxes, this income would be reduced, although a family with children would qualify for the Earned Income Tax Credit, which would more than offset deductions for Social Security and payroll taxes, except it would not be paid until after the end of the tax year. In any case, this family would barely be making enough to be above the poverty level of about $17,000 a year for a family of four.

Very often such families are prone to what is known as *event poverty*. In the event of illness, loss of one of the jobs, marital discord, or pregnancy, for example, the family could easily lose half its income and then plunge well below the official poverty level (Ellwood, 1996).

Immigration and Poverty.   In many of the world's wealthier nations, an increasing proportion of the poor are immigrants. This is certainly true in the United States. Almost 25 percent of the increase in poverty since the early 1970s has occurred among recent immigrants and their children. Although the majority of Hispanics are neither impoverished nor immigrants, poor people from Mexico, Central America, and the Caribbean are among the largest immigrant groups today. Many live in the poorest city neighborhoods and rural counties. Most of the adults work full time, often in the lowest-paying and most undesirable jobs. Most lack health insurance, and many fear that changes in welfare laws will make it impossible for them to send their children to school or to receive the same benefits as others who pay taxes.

The issue of whether poor and unskilled immigrants drive down the wages of the working poor and represent a burden to taxpayers generates a great deal of controversy. It is often used by politicians who wish to capitalize on the resentment some Americans already feel toward immigrants. In 1994, for example, California voters passed Proposition 187, which asserted that the state's welfare benefits were a "magnet" for immigrants from Mexico and made illegal immigrants ineligible for state aid, including public education (Rodriguez, 1999). Although it was quickly declared unconstitutional by the California supreme court, the idea of denying access to food stamps and other forms of public assistance remained popular and was incorporated as a highly controversial policy of the 1996 welfare reform act.

In 1997 a panel of experts convened by the prestigious National Academy of Sciences released a comprehensive study that examined the impact of immigration on the U.S. economy as a whole and on low-wage workers in particular. The study found that "the vast majority of Americans are enjoying a healthier economy as a result of the increased supply of labor and lower prices that result from immigration" (quoted in Pear, 1997, p.1). The analysis also showed, however, that competition from low-wage immigrant workers "lowered the wages of high school dropouts by about 5 percent, which accounts for about 44 percent of the total decline in wages of high school dropouts from 1980 to 1994" (p. 24).

Concomitants of Poverty

"Poverty," said George Bernard Shaw, "does not produce unhappiness; it produces degradation." Most Americans take for granted a decent standard of living—especially good health care, decent education and housing, and fair treatment under the law. In this section we will examine the impact of poverty in each of these areas.

Health Care

The poor are less healthy than the rest of the population, by almost every standard. For example, the mortality rates for poor infants are far higher than those for infants in more affluent families, and poor women are much more likely to die in childbirth. Poor women are also far more likely to give birth to their children in a municipal hospital. Inadequately housed, fed, and clothed, the poor can expect to be ill more often and to receive less adequate treatment. The health problems of the poor are not limited to physical ailments. Rates of diagnosed psychosis are higher among the poor, and they are more likely to be institutionalized and to receive shock treatment or chemotherapy in lieu of psychotherapy.

Of all the population groups in the United States, the poor are the least likely to have health insurance. In their analysis of the impact of welfare reform on poor households, Christopher Jencks and Joseph Swingle (2000) found that "health insurance coverage has fallen for almost all groups, including single mothers, since the early 1990s." Health insurance coverage for single-parent families fluctuated between 81 percent and 82 percent from 1987 to 1993. But by 1998 it averaged only 79 percent. "The reason for declining coverage is clear," the authors note. "When a single mother goes on welfare, she is automatically enrolled in Medicaid. In 1993, when the welfare rolls peaked, 40 percent of all single mothers said they had Medicaid. As the rolls fell, Medicaid coverage fell too." As a result, by the end of the 1990s only about 33 percent of single mothers had Medicaid coverage. As single mothers took "workfare jobs" or found jobs themselves in the labor force, private coverage increased somewhat. But that increase was not sufficient to offset the decline in Medicaid.

Not only do the poor have unequal access to health services and receive less adequate treatment, but there is evidence that they often view sickness and health differently than middle-class people do. The poor are less likely to identify symptoms of a variety of physical and mental illnesses, and as a result they may seek treatment only after the illness has become serious. When they do see a doctor, the treatment they receive may be cursory. Doctors are less likely to advise a poor patient to stay home from work until completely recovered (Edin & Lein, 1997).

Since the inception of Medicare and Medicaid in 1965, the poor have had greater access to various medical resources. But there are problems with almost all insurance programs: Coverage is often inadequate, it begins only after a specified deductible expense has been reached, and many people do not know exactly what is covered. Recent reductions in funding for Medicare are resulting in further curtailment of medical benefits for the poor. Throughout the nation the drive to reduce Medicare costs and close public hospitals is reducing access to health care and hospitals, especially for immigrants.

Other federal programs have established health-care centers in impoverished communities, but they are not sufficient to solve the health-care problems of the poor. Because most such programs allocate federal funds to match funds provided by a state or local government, they frequently are underfunded precisely where they are needed most. Moreover, each program and agency has different requirements, deadlines, and goals, resulting in a mass of regulations and interminable waiting periods before services are obtained. Finally, these programs do little to solve the overall health problems of the poor, who are victims of malnutrition, higher rates of disease, inadequate housing, sanitation, and rodent control, and even inadequate clothing.

Education

In every respect poor children get less education than those born into more affluent families. They receive fewer years of schooling, have less chance of graduating from high school, and are much less likely to go to college. They are apt to be taught in overcrowded classrooms, often by inexperienced teachers, and to receive little if any individual attention. Moreover, most teachers come from a middle-class background and have little training in working with disadvantaged children. They bring to the job the expectation that poor children will read, speak, and behave poorly and perform poorly on tests and that their parents and home life do not encourage academic achievement. It is not surprising that these expectations become self-fulfilling prophecies.

In recent decades considerable research has been devoted to the question of how effective preschool programs are in counteracting the effects of poverty. A review of that research concluded that children who attended preschool programs had higher intelligence scores at the age of 6, were less likely to be assigned to special-education classes, were less likely to be held back, and were less likely to drop out or be classified as delinquents (Brooks-Gunn & Hearn, 1982).

A study of children of teenage mothers in Baltimore (Brooks-Gunn & Furstenberg, 1987) found that maternal welfare status affects schooling in preschool and high school. Among children in preschool programs, those from welfare families make fewer gains. However, if the mother moves off welfare, the child is less likely to fail in subsequent years. This finding is especially important in view of the fact that the percentage of children living in poverty has increased dramatically in recent decades, so that the population at risk of school failure is higher than ever.

The low educational attainment of poor children tends to perpetuate poverty. In general, the less educated have lower incomes, less secure jobs, and more difficulty in improving their economic condition. Children of parents with less than a high school education generally do not do as well in school as children whose parents have completed high school. Thus, the cycle in which poverty and education are linked is passed from one generation to the next.

Housing and Homelessness

The poor are likely to live in housing that is overcrowded, infested with vermin, in need of major repairs, lacking basic plumbing facilities, and inadequately heated. More than half of such housing is in rural areas. Poor people who live in cities are unable to move around and utilize the city's resources but are often forced to move from one bad situation to another because of fire, crime, and other misfortunes. They are isolated and segregated both economically and racially.

Racial segregation increases when middle- and upper-income families leave the city. Cities also lose businesses when more prosperous citizens leave, and consequently their tax revenues decline. This leaves poor residents with fewer jobs and less adequate police protection and other services. Suburban zoning requirements, such as minimum lot sizes, are designed to attract newcomers who add more in taxes than they require in services. Suburban restrictions on multiple-dwelling structures have the same purpose: to prevent low-income housing from being erected and to keep out low-income and minority families.

People who live in their cars while they work at jobs that do not pay enough for them to afford local housing are homeless. So are people sleeping over the warm air of exhaust grates in the alleys of urban office buildings. Women seeking safety from abusive spouses by sleeping with their children in a local women's shelter may have a home, but during the time they are in the shelter they, too, are homeless. A recent analysis of national census and survey data found that about 1.35 million children—nearly 2 percent of the nation's total—are homeless (Bernstein, 2000). As these examples suggest, it is extremely difficult to actually count the homeless or even to adequately describe all the forms it can take (Burt, 1994). In an effort to fill in some of the knowledge gaps, the U.S. Department of Housing and Urban Development conducted a survey in shelters, soup kitchens, and other programs; some of the results are shown in Figure 8–7.

One notable finding of the survey is the disproportionate number of African-American men among the homeless. Note also the relatively high proportion of veterans compared to the entire population. Insufficient income and lack of a job, both aspects of the homeless person's poverty status, rather than lack of available housing, appear to be the major obstacles to finding a home. Not shown in the charts is the fact that the same survey found that the majority of the homeless had worked for pay

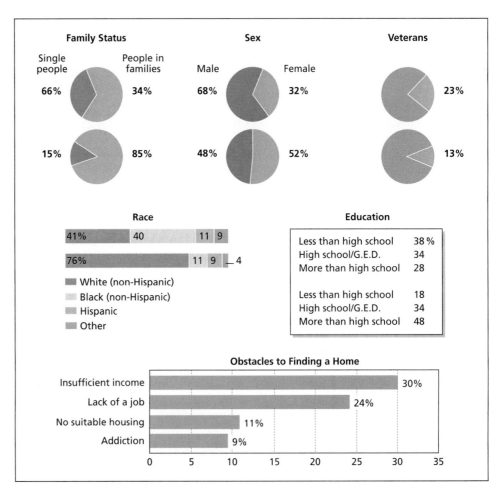

Figure 8–7   Characteristics of the Homeless Population, Compared to U.S. Adult Population

Source: Adapted from Slobin, 1999. Copyright © 1999 by The New York Times Company. Reprinted by permission.

in the past month, another indication that the combination of low wages and lack of affordable housing prevents many people from securing more permanent shelter. As housing prices move beyond the reach of the homeless and as their ability to move up the income ladder weakens, the demand for affordable housing will only increase.

Rehabilitation of existing structures has been advocated as one solution to the housing problem, one in which the poor need not be uprooted from familiar surroundings. But the cost of rehabilitating antiquated structures in deteriorating neighborhoods is too high, and the potential return on the investment too low, to appeal to private builders. Because poor families cannot afford rentals or purchase prices that would be profitable to owners and builders, it is extremely difficult to induce private industry to provide low-income housing. Each year, therefore, the lack of housing for the poor becomes more serious, a subject to which we return in Chapter 15.

Justice

As noted in Chapter 6, poor people are more likely than members of the middle and upper classes to be arrested, indicted, convicted, and imprisoned, and they are apt to be given longer sentences for the same offenses. Conversely, they are less likely to receive probation, parole, or suspended sentences. Also, adolescents who are poor are more apt to be labeled juvenile delinquents. Children from affluent families who commit crimes are likely to be sent to a psychiatrist and left in their parents' custody; poor children who commit crimes are likely to be sent to a correctional institution.

Because of the position of poor people in society, the crimes that they are most likely to commit (property theft and assault) tend to be the ones that are most disapproved of by those who make the laws—the middle and upper classes. These crimes also tend to be the most visible and widely publicized ones. Members of the middle and upper-middle classes tend to commit white-collar crimes—embezzlement, price-fixing, tax evasion, bribery, and so on. Although these crimes involve much more money than street crimes or property theft and may even pose a greater threat to social institutions, they tend not to be regarded as serious by the criminal-justice system. Moreover, white-collar crimes are rarely publicized. Even if they are arrested, prosperous citizens are more likely to be able to afford bail, to know their rights, to be competently defended, and to receive brief sentences. But an indigent defendant who is unable to post bail may be kept in jail for months.

Under the law, every accused person has the right to be represented by counsel, and some cities, counties, and states provide public defenders. But many large cities and a majority of the states lack public-defender services, and in federal courts there are neither paid defenders nor funds to compensate court-appointed counsel, who serve on a voluntary basis. When public defenders and court-appointed lawyers are provided, they may not have the financial resources or time required for extended investigations.

Inadequate defense is one of the reasons that the poor are more likely to be convicted and, if they are, to receive more severe sentences than those who are better off. And poor individuals who have been arrested and convicted are likely to be sentenced to overcrowded jails, where few inmates can be truly rehabilitated. Upon release, they bear a stigma that makes it difficult to find or hold a job.

Explanations of Persistent Poverty

Structural Explanations

Structural explanations of poverty incorporate elements of both the functionalist and the conflict perspectives described in Chapter 1. They attribute poverty to the functioning of the dominant institutions of society, such as markets and corporations.

Abandonment of inner-city housing in the 1970s and 1980s helped create the low-income housing crisis of the 1990s.

When these major social structures change, conflicts arise as large numbers of people attempt to adjust to new conditions and new forms of social organization. For example, in a society that is dominated by agrarian production and agricultural markets, the poor tend to be people who lack land or whose land is unsuitable for farming. Or they may be people who have been forced off their land and have come to towns and cities to look for work. In industrial societies, the poor tend to be those who have been unable to acquire the skills or knowledge that would enable them to find and keep jobs in factories or other businesses.

During various periods of American history, some groups migrated to the cities in an attempt to escape from an impoverished rural life. Others migrated when they were forced off the land by the mechanization of farming, by the consolidation of farms into larger units, and by the pressure of competition with large agribusinesses. All these changes in the social structure of farming created a class of poor people who were forced to sell their labor for whatever wages they could obtain. Since the Civil War, entire population groups, including U.S.-born blacks and Appalachian whites with neither land nor marketable skills, have been forced into the cities, where they compete with newly arrived immigrants and other groups for menial, low-paying jobs.

The Marxian structural explanation would add to the causes of poverty just mentioned the case of the impoverished industrial worker. The poor, according to the Marxian view, increasingly are industrial workers who have been displaced from their jobs through the efforts of capitalists to find ever-cheaper sources of labor, to automate their production systems and thereby eliminate the need for workers, or to move their factories out of the country altogether. This trend, which is characteristic of all unregulated capitalist societies, creates a "reserve army of unemployed," which, in its desperate search for income of any kind, drives down wages for all workers.

Contemporary social scientists may not agree with Marx's theory, but they tend to agree that changes in macrosocial patterns of growth have a lot to do with increasing poverty. Nobel Prize-winning economist James Tobin (1994), for example, points out that earlier in this century, when U.S. society was undergoing rapid industrialization and urbanization, the "rising economic tide" reduced poverty by increasing employment and providing the revenue needed to invest in education, housing, jobs, and greater income security for the elderly. Now, with slow economic growth, there are fewer "good jobs" to lift people out of poverty and less money to invest in the programs needed to help poor families achieve upward mobility.

Closely related to structural explanations like that offered by Tobin are those that emphasize the dual market for labor. In studies of the migrations of blacks and other groups to the cities, sociologists have found that there is a dual labor market in which favored groups are given access to the better jobs—those that offer secure employment and good benefits. Other groups, usually minority groups and migrants, are shunted into another segment of the labor market in which the jobs pay extremely poorly and offer no security or benefits (Bonacich, 1976; Piore, 1979; Wilson, 1996a).

Still another structural explanation of poverty maintains that the state, through its efforts to eliminate poverty, actually causes it. This explanation has both radical and conservative proponents. The radicals argue that whereas low wages and unemployment cause a great deal of poverty, the state's welfare and relief programs actually perpetuate it. They claim that the state uses programs like unemployment insurance to prevent rebellions by the poor that might otherwise challenge the existing capitalist order; yet it does not use its power to ensure that all citizens can work for a decent wage (Piven & Cloward, 1972). Arguing in a somewhat similar vein but from a conservative point of view, George Gilder (1981) claims that poverty in America is generally caused by well-meaning but misguided liberal welfare policies, which rob unemployed workers of the initiative to develop new, marketable skills and also rob society of capital that should be invested in new businesses to produce new wealth and new jobs. The high proportion of the poor who work or are actively seeking work constitutes a strong argument against this claim.

These structural theories discuss the causes of poverty and the origins of the lower class in terms of the structure of the society in which the poverty occurs. Other theories, to which we now turn, attempt to explain the perpetuation of poverty. They examine why certain individuals, families, and groups tend to remain poor even in good economic times and in spite of what appear to be ample opportunities for education and personal advancement.

Cultural Explanations

Cultural explanations of poverty are based on the interactionist perspective in sociology. In this view, through the ways in which they are brought up and socialized and through their interactions in everyday life, people become adapted to certain ways of life, including poverty. These ways of life persist because they become part of a group's culture.

Proponents of the cultural approach argue that a "culture of poverty" arises among people who experience extended periods of economic deprivation. Under these conditions, new norms, values, and aspirations emerge and eventually become independent of the situations that produced them, so that eliminating the problem does not eliminate the behaviors that have been developed to deal with it. The result is a self-sustaining system of values and behaviors that is handed down from one generation to the next (Lewis, 1968; Murray, 1984; Rector & Lauber, 1995).

The idea that there is a culture of poverty that arises among chronically poor individuals and families is highly controversial. William J. Wilson (1996a), a noted expert on inner-city poverty, rejects the concept, claiming that it is a global label that does not fit in many instances. But he recognizes that long spells of poverty may have long-term consequences for children and grandchildren: "As the disappearance of work has become a characteristic feature of the inner-city ghetto, so too has the disappearance of the traditional married-couple family" (p. 31). He attributes this decline in family norms to the despair felt by the poor, especially impoverished men. This despair also leads to higher rates of suicide, homicide, incarceration, and addiction, which in turn decrease the pool of eligible men in poor communities.

A culture-of-poverty explanation for the decline in two-parent families in the inner city and among poor people elsewhere would argue that children in poor families are socialized to believe that it is permissible to father babies and not take responsibility for them or that it is acceptable to spend long periods on welfare. Wilson's (1996a) research finds little evidence that such norms are widespread. Instead, poor people in inner-city ghettos and elsewhere share the same values and express the same aspirations as more affluent Americans, but their confidence in attaining them is greatly diminished by their negative life experiences. They may develop certain styles of language and expression that look like a separate culture to outsiders, but this, according to Wilson, hardly qualifies as a culture of poverty.

Sociologist Herbert J. Gans (1995) is also critical of the culture-of-poverty thesis. Gans stresses the heterogeneity of the poor, noting that some are in families that have been poor for generations, while others are poor only periodically; some have become so used to coping with deprivation that they have trouble adapting to new opportunities; and some are beset by physical and emotional illnesses. He is critical of the idea that culture is holistic, that no element of it can be changed unless the entire culture is altered. Instead, he argues that behavior results from a combination of cultural and situational influences.

Gans (1995) maintains that the ultimate solution to the problem of poverty lies in the discovery of the specific factors that constrain poor people in reacting to new opportunities when these conflict with their present cultural values. He and Wilson (1996a) believe that we must examine the kinds of changes needed in our economic system, social order, and power structure and in the norms and aspirations of the affluent majority that permit a poor class to exist. These are all themes that emerge again in considerations of social policy and poverty.

SOCIAL POLICY

As has been evident throughout this chapter, the extent of poverty in the world's most affluent society is a matter of continuing controversy. So is the question of what can be done about it. This question is intimately bound up with attitudes toward the poor themselves: Are the poor to blame for their own poverty? Do they avoid work? Would providing more jobs for the poor do any good? One's views on these issues have a lot to do with one's opinions about government intervention on behalf of the poor.

Reform of "Welfare as We Know It"

As noted earlier, the 1996 welfare reform bill ended the 60-year-old program known as Aid to Families with Dependent Children, originally part of the landmark Social Security Act of 1935 (Cancian, 1996). Under the new legislation, no longer are parents whose household incomes fall below a given level (depending on the size of the household) entitled to federal funds administered through state and county welfare agencies. Instead, the states receive block grants, large sums of money earmarked for specific purposes, to be used for assistance to the poor. The payments people receive are no longer termed Aid to Families with Dependent Children (AFDC). Instead, they are referred to as Temporary Assistance to Needy Families (TANF).

As in the past, the cash amounts vary widely from one state to another, with Mississippi and Alabama on the low end and California and New York on the high end. The critical difference, however, is that federal requirements now specify that after two years of welfare payments under the new system, an able-bodied recipient must enroll in a training program or find work. The federal law also places a five-year limit on all payments to individual households in an attempt to prevent "chronic" welfare dependency. As long as the states conform to the broad mandates of the new federal program, they may shape the actual program of work requirements, monthly payments, and other policies to suit their own specific needs. Although the states are under intense pressure to shift welfare recipients to paid work, they may use block grant funds to create jobs or to supplement wages that do not bring the recipient up to a minimum monthly income.

We have seen in this chapter that despite years of a booming economy, which has helped many former welfare clients find decent jobs, the picture for the poorest segments of the population has not improved. Does this mean that the welfare reforms are actually harming poor people, especially poor children? How social scientists answer this question depends to a great extent on their ideological positions on the left-right spectrum. On the right, social scientists often claim that welfare reform is working extremely well. It has reduced welfare rolls by almost half in many states. Most important from the conservative perspective, it is claimed that the reforms discourage welfare dependency by increasing work opportunities and reducing family breakdown. Supporters of the new system also claim that work rather than welfare dependency builds independence and self-esteem. They note that there is a 20 percent exception in the laws that allows the states to waive the rules for the neediest clients, so that flexibility and the possibility of humane treatment are built into the law (Besharov & Germanis, 1999).

Liberal critics of welfare reform argue that the new system is increasing the number of homeless people and people who lack health insurance, and that it is, in effect, a form of government enforcement of underpaid work. "At first glance," writes Frances Fox Piven (1999), "the campaign to reform welfare seemed to be entirely about questions of the personal morality of the women who subsist on the dole. The problem was, the argument went, that a too generous welfare system was leading women to spurn wage work for lives of idleness and for what Senator Orrin Hatch called 'the deep, dark pit of welfare dependency.'" Piven argues that the reforms drew on popular stereotypes and prejudices toward " black and Latina minorities who were widely understood to be the main beneficiaries of welfare, and also tapped the energy and excitement evoked by talk of women and sex and sin." She believes that the real motivation behind welfare reform was to enforce low-wage work. She and other critics of both the old and the new welfare systems believe that education and job creation are vital to getting people off the dole. To them, the ironies of the new system are clear:

> A good many Americans are frustrated by low and declining wages and overwork. They are anxious that their family life is eroding now that neither parent has time to do the cooking and caretaking that sustains families. They have been encouraged to vent their frustrations on welfare. In the process, they are supporting a reconfiguration of policy that will worsen the terms of their own work and wear away at their own families while gripping them ever more tightly in the cultural vise that compels low wage work no matter the terms. (p. 32)

Piven (1999), Gans (1995), and many other welfare critics on the left side of the political spectrum argue that with all its faults, AFDC was a relatively small federal program. It never cost more than about 1 percent of the federal budget, and fewer than 5 million people were on the rolls. They maintain that beginning in the early 1980s, the welfare poor were targeted as examples of the failure of liberal antipoverty policies. To afford tax cuts and budget reductions before the economic boom of the late 1990s, it was necessary to cut programs for the most vulnerable and politically powerless segments of the population. The poor are foremost among these groups. So are immigrants, whose benefits are also scheduled for cuts under the new policies being formulated in many states. The idea that some people could subsist on payments that transferred funds from the more well-to-do to the poor, and that in some cases they could live that way for years without any work requirement, became an easy target for those who wished to decrease federal spending. On this last point, conservative social scientists would certainly agree. From their perspective, the liberals who were critical of the old AFDC program failed to make adequate reforms when they had control of Congress.

Unintended Consequences

Effects of Welfare Reform

Christopher Jencks and colleagues at Harvard's Kennedy School of Public Policy are continually reviewing new studies of the welfare reform policies. Here are some of their observations:

More single mothers are working. That is the good news. The bad news is that a large minority of the women who leave the welfare rolls do not find or keep jobs. Follow-up studies show that most mothers who leave the welfare rolls find jobs, but a large minority do not. Moreover, some of those who find jobs soon lose them and do not appear on the welfare rolls. Between 1987 and 1996, about 10 percent of all single mothers fell into this category. By 1998 the proportion had climbed to 12 percent.

Incomes are rising at the top but not at the bottom. Most social-scientific and journalistic accounts of welfare reform in different states or cities provide abundant evidence of successful transitions to work, often after many years of welfare dependence. Kathryn Edin and Laura Lein's (1997) empirical work on poor women's incomes demonstrates that even the more successful job holders experience economic hardship and often must resort to the help of family and friends.

Doubling up? Liberal critics of welfare reform often speculate that when single mothers cannot make ends meet, they will increasingly move in with relatives. So far, the doubling-up hypothesis is not confirmed. The proportion of single mothers living with relatives has not increased.

Less health insurance coverage. As we saw earlier in the chapter, there have been significant increases in the proportion of poor people, especially single mothers, who are not covered by health insurance. Once people leave welfare to begin working, they may not be eligible for Medicaid even though their employer does not offer health insurance.

More marriage? Conservatives hoped that welfare reform would encourage morality, especially through encouragement of marriage and discouragement of single motherhood. The results suggest otherwise. Wisconsin, for example, began welfare reform efforts early. It has reduced its welfare rolls more than any other large state, yet the proportion of Wisconsin children born to single mothers has not fallen. In fact, "the proportion climbed from 27.1 percent in 1994 to 28.5 percent in 1998—an increase of 1.4 points—at a time when the increase for the nation as a whole was only 0.2 points."

Aside from these economic and moral considerations, two facts stand out: "First, almost all mothers who are working tell interviewers that they prefer work to welfare. Second, many working mothers report problems finding satisfactory child care." Reports provide a great deal of anecdotal evidence that young children are being left alone, sometimes for long periods. "These reports suggest that welfare reform could end up helping parents but hurting their children. Because we have no reliable system for monitoring children's well-being, we will probably never know how welfare reform affected them." (Jencks & Swingle, 2000, p. 49)

Jencks and others who are evaluating the impact of welfare reform are especially cautious about the fact that so far the policies have been implemented in a favorable economic climate. No one knows what might happen if unemployment rates began to rise and an economic contraction was under way. In addition, Jencks issues this warning:

Some single mothers can't manage both employment and parenthood simultaneously. Even those who have the energy and skill to juggle work and parenthood often earn so little that they cannot make ends meet without additional help. If such help is not available, the long-term impact of welfare reform on both single mothers and their children could well turn out to be like the long-term impact of deinstitutionalization on the mentally ill: good for some but terrible for others. This is a worst-case scenario. But it is a possibility we should bear in mind as states keep cutting their welfare rolls. (Jencks & Swingle, 2000, p. 51)

So what is the truth about welfare reform? The answer is that there is no single truth. Different state policies are still being evaluated. Positive claims based only on reduction of the welfare rolls should never be taken as the full measure of the program's success. Neither should claims based on the experience of the poorest of the poor. Far more careful evaluation of the actual conditions of life of parents and children in the new welfare systems are required. In the meantime, it is important for social scientists to conduct politically neutral analyses of the empirical facts. The results of one such analysis are presented in the Unintended Consequences feature on page 248.

The United States also attempts to provide a safety net of social-insurance programs for all taxpayers and their dependents, not only those who are already quite poor. Some social-insurance programs are intended to compensate for loss of income, regardless of income level or need. Through unemployment insurance, for example, cash benefits are paid for short periods to insured workers who are involuntarily unemployed. Unemployment insurance was created by the same act of Congress that established the Social Security system; however, the responsibility for administering unemployment insurance was delegated to the states, which were given broad latitude in setting eligibility standards and levels of benefits. As a result, the amount and duration of unemployment benefits vary greatly from one state to another. In Massachusetts, a worker who is unemployed after paying into the system beyond the minimum period is eligible for more than $200 a week for 15 weeks. In South Carolina, a worker who has paid into the system is eligible for only $150 per week for 9 weeks (Edelhoch, 1999).

Other forms of social insurance include workers' compensation programs, which provide wage replacements to insured workers who suffer occupational injuries, and veterans' compensation plans, which issue benefits to disabled veterans to make up for their loss of earning potential. Social Security payments to the elderly also fall into this category. Cash income-support programs are provided for unemployable people, those who are not covered by any form of social insurance, and those with special needs. Veterans' pensions fall into this category.

Income-in-kind programs provide goods and services, such as food, housing, and medical care, to the poor. These programs include public housing and urban renewal, health plans like Medicare and Medicaid (see Chapter 2), and food supplements like the commodity distribution program (which distributes surplus farm products to poor households) and food stamps (which in effect provide discounts on food purchases).

Dependency, Work, and Responsibility

Critics of welfare programs on both the left and the right increasingly agree that welfare policies should not establish disincentives to work, nor should they reward vice or encourage people to regard public funds as a long-term substitute for work (Jencks, 1992; Wilson, 1996a). And while there is still a good deal of debate over the degree to which various welfare programs actually do create these negative results, there is also much agreement that welfare payments to families with dependent children ought to encourage recipients to seek job training as well as employment. This view was incorporated into the 1996 welfare reform act, which requires states to provide education and job training programs and provides federal funding to help pay for these opportunities.

Training programs require federal and state funding and do not necessarily lead to longer-term employment for trainees. Trainees must have access to care for their children. Also, the majority of former welfare recipients are hired in public-sector jobs in schools and other agencies. As public budgets are cut, it becomes more and more difficult to secure an adequate number of jobs for former welfare recipients. These problems make the issue of welfare and work an ongoing challenge to policy-makers.

In his thorough review of antipoverty policies in the United States and other nations, William J. Wilson (1987) notes that the countries that rely least on public assistance (e.g., Sweden and West Germany) instead emphasize such policies as family and housing allowances, child care services, and various types of work incentives. Thus, the cornerstone of their antipoverty policies is employment policies that make it easier for adults to manage their work and family lives without undue strain on themselves and their children (Kamerman & Kahn, cited in Wilson, 1987).

How should the United States address the dependency issue? One answer frequently given by social scientists and policymakers is that a serious effort should be made to increase the income of low-wage workers so that the working poor, by far the largest category of poor households, will not be forced to live in poverty. Another, similar approach would be to provide incentives for people on welfare to work if they are able to do so.

As noted earlier in the chapter, a person who works full time all year at the minimum wage cannot earn enough to keep even a two-person family above the poverty line. To support a family of four, a worker must earn 60 percent more than the minimum wage (Ellwood, 1987). There are a variety of possible approaches to this problem. One recommended approach is income supplements, which could include wage subsidies, medical protection, and expansion of the earned income tax credit (EITC). The EITC was instituted in 1975 as a means of reducing the total tax bill of low-income taxpayers with dependent children. Originally the credit was 10 percent of earned income up to $4,000, with a smaller credit for amounts between $4,000 and $8,000, but in the 1980s it was extended to somewhat higher incomes. If the credit exceeds the amount of tax due, an eligible individual can receive a payment from the Internal Revenue Service. In some respects, therefore, the EITC can be viewed as a negative income tax.

Numerous proposals have been made to modify or extend the EITC. In one approach, a household could designate a principal earner whose wages would be subsidized if they were below a specified level; this would increase the reward for working. Another suggestion is to expand the EITC and allow it to vary by family size; this would help protect larger families and encourage low-income workers with families to return to work. A third approach is to convert the current tax deduction for children into a refundable tax credit.

Moving to Opportunity?

One of the most difficult problems in attempting to improve the condition of the poor is what to do about people living in highly concentrated or segregated poor neighborhoods. We saw earlier that the ghetto poor of central cities are a minority of all poor households, but they are highly visible and therefore are the focus of a great deal of attention, much of it negative and mean-spirited (Gans, 1995; Wilson 1996a). As long as large numbers of people live in inner-city neighborhoods where there has been a drastic loss of jobs and opportunity, it will be difficult for workfare or any other training and work approaches to make much of a difference. And decreases in welfare payments, Medicare services, and disability payments are likely to increase the economic and social stress in these impoverished areas of urban America.

A policy innovation that holds promise is a set of experimental programs designed to move people from areas of concentrated poverty to communities where they will have more opportunity. These programs were motivated in large part by an important court decision about what is known as the Gautreah project in Chicago. The city of Chicago and the state of Illinois were ordered to assist residents of public housing in an extremely poor neighborhood to move to better neighborhoods outside the inner city. Evaluations of how the families who moved fared in the job market and in schools were generally favorable (Rosenbaum et al., 1996). In consequence, the federal Department of Housing and Urban Development (HUD) has developed a program known as Moving to Opportunity. Although the program is still in the evaluation stage, families that are selected to move to new housing in neighborhoods with better job and educational opportunities are showing statistically significant gains in important social indicators, especially family income. If these results hold up in further evaluations of these experimental initiatives, HUD is seeking broader support for a new set of housing and relocation strategies to help poor people in segregated, low-income enclaves to move to opportunity. But will these goals receive legislative support? Much will depend on the public's understanding of poverty and its causes and on its support for improving the conditions under which poor people suffer.

Beyond Left & Right

Critics of welfare reform often divide into warring camps on the left and the right, with vastly different interpretations of why poverty exists and what can be done about it. Do you think the poor are to blame for their own misery? Do you think that the poor are often victims of structural conditions like lack of jobs or inadequate education? The first type of opinion tends to put you on the right, the second on the left. Of course, you can subscribe to both of these views. That would put you in the confused majority on the complicated issues of poverty and policy.

How can we move beyond the punitive policies proposed by those on the right, the too costly or coddling measures advocated by those on the left? Perhaps the answers will be found in our experience with the new welfare reform legislation. If benefits are cut and poor people suffer even more as a consequence, that may motivate some clearer thinking on both sides. Few Americans want to see mothers with babies sleeping on the streets or crying outside government offices. As vulnerable people on the margins of an enormously affluent society, the poor are often made to suffer before wiser policies are formulated to meet their needs. But opportunities for adequate child care, decent education, and job training do not negate the widely shared desire that we end welfare dependency by asking people who are able to do so to work for their incomes. We can begin to go beyond the left-right impasse by achieving a better balance between work requirements and opportunities to meet those requirements.

SUMMARY

- Although the United States ranks among the wealthiest nations in the world, many Americans are living in poverty. During the 1980s and 1990s the gap between the rich and the poor widened.

- The United States has a long history of attempting to redistribute wealth through taxation and other policies. In so doing, however, it has actually provided more opportunities for the rich to get richer than for the poor to escape from poverty.

- More than 35 million people live below the official poverty line. They include children, elderly people, single mothers, ill or disabled individuals, and students, as well as people who work either full or part time at poverty-level wages.

- The stratification of individuals and groups according to occupation, income, and skills is called class stratification. The Marxian view of stratification holds that classes are determined by economic measures. This view has been supplemented by those of Weber and his followers, who pointed out that other valued things besides wealth, such as status and power, are distributed unequally in modern societies. American society can be divided into five main classes: the upper class, the upper-middle class, the middle class, the working class, and the poor.

- Poverty can be defined in a variety of ways. It can mean a condition of near starvation, bare subsistence, or any standard of living that is measurably below the national average. Official definitions of the poverty line are based on the consumer price index. Alternative measures have been proposed that take into account changing definitions of minimal consumption.

- A large proportion of the poor are children, many of them in single-parent families. Blacks and other racial minorities are overrepresented among the poor. Poor people living in rural areas include migrant workers, Native Americans on reservations, and farmers. Many of the poor are working at low-paying jobs.

- Concomitants of poverty include poor health and unequal access to health services, inadequate education,

substandard housing and homelessness, and discrimination in the criminal-justice system.

- Structural explanations of poverty attribute it to dominant social institutions such as the dual market for labor. The cultural explanation holds that extended economic deprivation creates a culture of poverty, with its own norms and values. The situational approach interprets the behavior of the poor as an adaptation to their environment.

- The 1996 welfare reform bill replaced AFDC with a system of block grants to the states to be used for assistance to the poor. After two years of welfare payments under the new system, able-bodied recipients must enroll in a training program or find work. Evaluations of the new system find that more single mothers are working, but a large minority of the women who leave the welfare rolls do not find or keep jobs. They also find that the incomes of the poorest of the poor are not rising, and that increasing numbers of poor people lack health insurance.

- Proposals for alleviating the problems of people who work at low-wage jobs include modifying or extending the earned income tax credit (a means of reducing the total tax bill of low-income taxpayers with dependent children), enabling single mothers to work part time while receiving welfare payments, and reforming the child-support system so that fathers are held accountable for the support of their children.

KEY TERMS

welfare state, p. 224
wealthfare, p. 224
working poor, p. 227

social stratification, p. 227
class stratification, p. 227
lumpenproletariat, p. 227

INTERNET EXERCISE

The web destinations for Chapter 8 are related to different aspects of poverty. To begin your explorations, go to the Prentice Hall Companion Website: **http://prenhall** **.com/kornblum**. Then choose **Chapter 8** (Poverty Amid Affluence). Next, select **destinations** from the menu on the left side of the screen. There are a variety of sites to investigate. We suggest that you begin with **Welfare Reform: Department of Housing and Urban Development (HUD).** If you have time, you may also wish to access the **Office for Social Justice** site, which also deals with welfare reform. The *Unintended Consequences* feature in this chapter focuses on the effects of welfare reform. Christopher Jencks and his colleagues at Harvard University's Kennedy School of Public Policy present a number of observations about welfare reform policies. The two sites just recommended will provide you with a variety of information about recent welfare reform in the United States. After you have explored these sites, answer the following questions:

- Jencks and others who are evaluating the impacts of welfare reform are cautious about the fact that, thus far, the new policies have been implemented in a favorable economic climate. What are your personal reactions to welfare reform?

- Do you think that welfare benefits should be available in American society? Who should be eligible for these benefits? If you were a policymaker, how would you configure a welfare program so that recipients have feasible incentives to work?

9 **Racism, Prejudice, and Discrimination**

PREJUDICE AND DISCRIMINATION

- In 1998, 16.3 percent of whites aged 25 and over had not completed high school; the comparable figures for blacks and Hispanics were 24.0 percent and 44.5 percent, respectively.

- Sixty-nine percent of black and 75 percent of Hispanic children attend predominantly minority schools.

- Almost 79 percent of black households have inadequate assets in re- serve to allow them to survive for at least three months at an income of $968 a month.

- Although blacks account for only 12 percent of the population, they make up about 42.7 percent of the prison population.

O U T L I N E

The Meaning of *Minority*

Defining Racism, Prejudice, and Discrimination

Origins of Prejudice and Discrimination
Prejudice and Bigotry in the Individual
Prejudice and Bigotry in Social Structures
Cultural Factors: Norms and Stereotypes

Institutional Discrimination
Education
Housing
Employment and Income
Justice

Some Consequences of Prejudice and Discrimination

Social Policy
Job Training
Affirmative Action
Education for Equality
Some Trends and Prospects

Throughout the world, prejudice, discrimination, and intergroup ha- treds often result in bloodshed, genocide, mass expulsions in the name of "ethnic cleansing," and anguish for millions of people. Com- pared to the Nazi Holocaust or the recent genocidal wars in Rwanda or to the mass expulsions in nations of the former Yugoslavia, the degree of prejudice and discrimination found in the United States seems relatively mild. But when we read about Ku Klux Klan activities or violence directed against recent immigrants or bias crimes against Jews or the presence of hate groups and hate speech on the Internet, it becomes clear that the effort to maintain civility and cooperation among distinct racial and ethnic groups in modern societies is always a challenge (Massey & Denton, 1993).

The United States prides itself on its ethnic and racial diversity and on the progress it has made since the Civil War toward greater tolerance and racial har- mony. At the same time, when one looks at the conditions of life in inner-city ghettos or on Indian reservations and at the continuing struggle against racial and ethnic hatreds, it becomes clear that the gains have been modest. In the early twentieth century the United States was still characterized by deep racial and eth- nic divisions. Its educational and economic institutions were marked by sharp pat- terns of racial and ethnic exclusion, its communities rigidly segregated along racial lines. Indeed, when he surveyed the situation of prejudice and discrimina- tion in the 1930s and 1940s, the eminent Swedish social scientist Gunnar Myrdal called the situation of "poor and suppressed" minorities in the land of freedom and opportunity "the American dilemma." Although much has changed since that time, racial and ethnic prejudice is still a significant problem in many areas of American life. And we will see in this chapter that many aspects of inequality in our society are the results of past patterns of racial and ethnic discrimination (Wegner, 1993; Wilson, 1996a).

Although the constitutional bases for racial equality were established in the 1860s and 1870s with the ratification of the Thirteenth, Fourteenth, and Fif- teenth Amendments, it was not until the mid-twentieth century that the rights guaranteed by these amendments began to be exercised effectively. Starting with Supreme Court decisions that affected specific, small areas of life, black Americans

This scene in an ethnic neighborhood highlights the growing ethnic and racial diversity of the American population.

began to work their way toward equality. A major legal breakthrough came in 1954 with the historic decision in *Brown* v. *Board of Education of Topeka* that "separate educational facilities are inherently unequal." The Supreme Court later applied this "separate cannot be equal" doctrine to a wide range of public facilities.

The Civil Rights Act of 1964 was another important step. Unlike the civil rights acts passed in 1957 and 1960, the 1964 act provided a means for fighting discrimination in employment and public accommodations and for denying federal funds to local government units that permitted discrimination. There followed the comprehensive Voting Rights Act of 1965 and a federal prohibition against housing discrimination in the Civil Rights Act of 1968. Subsequent affirmative-action orders by President Lyndon B. Johnson aided the enforcement of these new laws; in addition, the Johnson administration set up new programs, such as Head Start, to counter the effects of discrimination.

But the discrepancy between legal equality and actual inequality remained. The impatience of some American blacks developed into anger, and in August 1964 a riot erupted in Watts, a black section of Los Angeles. By the time the wave of violent protest set off by the Watts riot subsided, it had struck almost every major urban center in the country. In 1967, following especially destructive riots in Newark and Detroit, President Johnson appointed the National Advisory Commission on Civil Disorders (1968) to investigate the origins of the disturbances and to recommend ways to prevent or control them in the future. Its findings suggested that there had been very little change since Myrdal's study. Describing the basic causes of the disorders, the commission stated,

> The first is surely the continuing exclusion of great numbers of Negroes from the benefits of economic progress through discrimination in employment and education, and their enforced segregated housing and schools. The corrosive and degrading effects of this condition and the attitudes that underlie it are the source of the deepest bitterness and at the center of the problem of racial disorder. (p. 203)

The commission concluded that "our nation is moving toward two societies, one black, one white—separate and unequal" (p. 1).

Although the situations of other minority groups—Native Americans, Chicanos (Mexican Americans), Hispanic Americans (especially Puerto Ricans and Cubans), Asian Americans, and some white ethnic groups—have received less intensive study, they are similar to that of black Americans. One form of discrimination to which these other groups are particularly vulnerable is harassment at the voting booth, largely because of some individuals' inadequate command of English. The 1975 extension of the Voting Rights Act attempted to alleviate this problem by requiring cities with sizable "language minority" populations to provide bilingual ballots in elections; it also permanently banned the use of literacy tests as a prerequisite for voting.

In recent years there has been a major influx of immigrants from Far Eastern countries, especially Korea, Vietnam, and Cambodia. Their experience has shown that small groups with education, business experience, and some funds, coupled with cultural values that stress family cohesion and extremely hard work, have little difficulty in adapting to their new environment (Kim, 1983). On the other hand, large populations that gather in concentrated settlements, as Vietnamese immigrants have done in Texas and California, have been targets of racial hostility. Thus, it appears that the larger a group and the more segregated it is, the more hostility it encounters (Portes, 1995; Portes & Rumbaut, 1990).

In the same vein, Stanley Lieberson (1990) argues that when an immigrant group is small, it is relatively easy for it to develop an occupational niche or specialty, as the Greeks and the Chinese have done in the restaurant industry. He cites a study that showed that 14.8 percent of Greek immigrants were working in the restaurant industry and 9.4 percent of Swedish immigrants were carpenters. But when an immigrant population grows, it becomes far more difficult for it to retain control of an occupational niche and expand it enough to accommodate newcomers. Later arrivals, therefore, are more dependent than earlier immigrants on the general labor market.

The situation of immigrant groups highlights the problems of minority status in the United States. But before we can discuss these problems in detail, we must gain a clearer understanding of the meaning of the term *minority* as it is commonly used today.

The Meaning of *Minority*

In his last State of the Union address, in January 2000, President Clinton referred to the probability that sometime during the twenty-first century the United States will become a nation of minorities, without a majority group. But he was referring to the increasing numbers of Latinos, Asians, and other groups, not to the sociological meaning of the term *minority*. From the standpoint of social problems, the most significant minorities are those that do not receive the same treatment as other groups in society. But how and why does such a situation come about? Before we can begin to answer these questions, it is important to define three terms that are central to the discussion: *racial minorities, ethnic minorities,* and *assimilation.*

Racial minorities are groups of people who share certain inherited characteristics, such as eye folds or brown skin. Many experts believe that the biologically determined racial groups into which humanity is divided—caucasoid, mongoloid, and negroid—are strictly social categories and that the actual hereditary differences among them are meaningless (Alland, 1973; Gould, 1981). **Ethnic minorities** are made up of people who share cultural features, such as language, religion, national origin, dietary practices, and a common history, and who regard themselves as a distinct group. When members of either a racial or an ethnic minority take on the characteristics of the mainstream culture by adapting their own unique cultural patterns to those of the majority, as well as by intermarrying, **assimilation** occurs.

It should be noted that the term *minority* as used here does not refer to a group's numerical strength in the population. This is true even though in most cases minority groups lack both numerical superiority and other means of counteracting unequal treatment.

All minority groups have their own particular characteristics, but the following are sociologically significant (Feagin, 1996; Simpson & Yinger, 1985):

1. Minorities are subordinate segments of a complex society.

2. Minorities tend to have special physical or cultural traits that are seen as undesirable by the dominant segments of the society.

3. Minorities develop a group consciousness or "we feeling."

4. Membership in a minority is transmitted by a rule of descent—one is born into it—which can impose the minority status on future generations even if by then its special physical or cultural traits have disappeared.

5. Members of a minority, whether by choice or by necessity, tend to practice **endogamy**—that is, to marry within the group.

There is no clear line between totally dominant and totally minority groups; rather, any given group can be placed at some point along a continuum of "minorityness." Various immigrant groups in the United States have moved along this continuum, edging progressively closer to equality and shedding some or all of their distinctive minority characteristics. It should be emphasized, however, that the physical distinctiveness of racial minorities has made the attainment of assimilation and equality much more difficult for them than for other immigrant groups, which are defined largely by cultural traits. Thus, racial minorities have tended to remain minorities much longer than nonracial minorities.

The characteristics just listed apply somewhat less accurately to nonracial and nonethnic minority groups. The aged, for example, constitute a minority group in terms of both absolute numbers and the treatment they receive, yet they are not born into it. Membership in the homosexual minority is not transmitted from one generation to another. Nevertheless, these groups share the major characteristics of minorities: subordinate status, special traits, and increasingly, group self-awareness.

Subordinate status is the principal characteristic of a minority group. In almost any society the desire for some goods, whether tangible or intangible, exceeds the supply, and groups within the society are likely to compete for them and for the power to control them. The groups that gain the most power dominate the other groups, controlling their access to the desired goods and often to other goods—social, economic, political, and personal—as well. The dominant group need not be the most numerous; it must merely be able to prevent other groups from effectively challenging its power.

Once established, however, the dominant-subordinate relationship is not fixed for all time. Either through the efforts of the subordinate group itself or as a result of changing legal or economic conditions, power relationships can be altered. We can see in our own society that women are not as subordinate as they were only a generation ago. Similarly, in southern counties where blacks considerably outnumber whites, extensive voter registration has enabled the formerly subordinate blacks to become politically significant. On a broader scale, most of the former colonial areas of Africa and Asia are independent nations, and some countries that formerly lacked influence, such as Japan and China, are now world powers.

Despite these examples of long-term change, it is usually very difficult for members of a subordinate group to attain a share of power and influence. The dominant group naturally wants to protect its privileged position. Among the weapons it uses to do so are prejudice and discrimination.

Defining Racism, Prejudice, and Discrimination

Racism is behavior, in word or deed, that is motivated by the belief that human races have distinctive characteristics that determine abilities and cultures. Racists believe in this erroneous concept of race; they also believe that their own race is superior and therefore ought to dominate or rule other races. Racism may be an attribute of an individual, or it may be incorporated into the institutions (social structures and laws) of an entire society. Nazi Germany, South Africa under apartheid, and the United States before the civil rights era of the mid-twentieth century are examples of societies and nations that incorporated racist beliefs in their social institutions. Societies that have attempted to eliminate racism from their institutions continue to struggle with the legacies of their racist histories. These legacies often appear in the form of prejudices, discrimination, and incidents of overt racism—such as the killing of a black man, James Byrd, Jr., by white supremacists who chained him to the back of a truck and dragged him along the ground until he died. Although the townspeople of Jasper, Texas, where the incident occurred, were shocked by the ghastly killing, the murder revealed the continuing presence of extreme racism in the United States.

Discrimination is "the differential treatment of individuals considered to belong to a particular social group" (R. M. Williams, 1947, p. 39). To treat a member of a subordinate group as inferior is to discriminate against that person. Members of the dominant group tend to use one standard of behavior among themselves and a different standard for any member of a subordinate group.

Discrimination is overt behavior, although it may sometimes be difficult to observe—as in tacit agreements among real estate agents to steer members of minority groups to particular blocks or neighborhoods. To justify the behavior to themselves, people tend to rationalize it on the ground that those whom they discriminate against are less worthy of respect or fair treatment than people like themselves (a perspective

Throughout the world, including the United States, there is an alarming resurgence of groups like the Ku Klux Klan, which advocate policies that would maintain the dominance of one race or ethnic group over others.

to which we return later in the chapter). Moreover, people tend to be *ethnocentric*—to see their own behavioral patterns and belief structures as desirable and natural and those of others as less so. These two tendencies usually result in **prejudice**—an emotional, rigid attitude—against members of the subordinate group (Simpson & Yinger, 1985).

But while prejudices are attitudes, not all attitudes are prejudices. Both share the element of *pre*judgment—the tendency to decide in advance how to think about a situation or event. Unlike other attitudes, however, prejudice involves an emotional investment that strongly resists change. Prejudiced people tend to be so committed to their prejudgments about a particular category of people that even in the face of rational evidence that the prejudgment is wrong, they will maintain their prejudice, even defend it strongly, and denounce the evidence.

It is important to note that prejudice need not always involve antipathy. One can be prejudiced in favor of a person or group, with a similar degree of disregard for objective evidence. Prejudice is based on attitude; it is a tendency to think about people in a categorical, predetermined way. Discrimination, on the other hand, involves behavior. It is overt unequal treatment of people on the basis of their membership in a particular group. Prejudice and discrimination are closely related, and both are often present in a given situation.

Robert Merton (1949) outlined four possible relationships between prejudice and discrimination: unprejudiced and nondiscriminatory (integration), unprejudiced and discriminatory (institutional discrimination), prejudiced and nondiscriminatory (latent bigotry), and prejudiced and discriminatory (outright bigotry). (See Table 9–1.) Although it is possible to be both completely free of prejudice and completely nondiscriminatory—or, on the other hand, to be a complete bigot—most people fall somewhere between these two extremes. It is possible to be prejudiced against a particular group but not to discriminate against it; it is also possible to discriminate against a particular group but not to be prejudiced against it.

For example, the builders of a new, expensive cooperative apartment house may not be personally prejudiced against Jews, but they may refuse to sell apartments to Jewish families—that is, they may discriminate against Jews—out of fear that the presence of Jewish families would make it more difficult to sell the remaining apartments. This is a clear case of institutional discrimination (the lower-left cell in Table 9–1). Or the reverse may occur: In a corporation that holds a government contract, and hence is subject to federal equal employment opportunity regulations, the personnel director may be very prejudiced personally against both blacks and women but may hire a black woman as a management trainee—that is, not discriminate against her—to comply with the law. This is an example of latent bigotry (the upper-right cell).

Suppose the builders were confronted with a different situation: a black family attempting to buy one of their apartments. They might very well discriminate out of

TABLE 9–1   A Typology of Prejudice and Discrimination

Prejudice (the Attitude)	Discrimination (the Behavior)	
	Yes	No
Yes	Outright bigotry	Latent bigotry
No	Institutional discrimination	Integration (both psychological and institutional)

Source: Adapted with permission of The Free Press, a Division of Simon & Schuster, Inc. from *Social Theory and Social Structure* by Robert K. Merton. Copyright © 1949, 1957 by The Free Press; renewed 1977, 1985 by Robert K. Merton.

both personal prejudice and concern for profits—a case of outright bigotry (the upper-left cell). On the other hand, there can be situations in which legal controls prevent latent bigotry from affecting such behaviors as the sale of a house to a black family but cannot prevent social isolation of the family after the sale. These examples point up the difficulty of keeping personal prejudices from leading, sooner or later, to some form of discrimination, particularly if a significant number of people share the same prejudice.

Origins of Prejudice and Discrimination

We have said that prejudice and discrimination are weapons used by a dominant group to maintain its dominance. It would be a mistake, however, to see them as always, or even usually, consciously used weapons. Unless the subordinate group mounts a serious challenge to the dominant group, prejudice and discrimination are likely to seem part of the natural order of things. Their origins are numerous and complex, and to explain them it is necessary to consider both the felt needs of individuals and the structural organization of society. Do patterns of prejudice and discrimination result from the aggregation of individual attitudes and behaviors, or are these attributes of individuals shaped by the society of which they are members? In fact, neither argument excludes the other; both are possible. To blame prejudice and discrimination wholly on warped personalities or wholly on oppressive social structures is to oversimplify.

Prejudice and Bigotry in the Individual

Frustration-Aggression. At one time or another most human beings feel frustrated. They want something, but because of events or other people they cannot get it. This can lead to anger and to aggression, which may be expressed in any of several ways. The most obvious way is to strike at the source of the frustration, but often this is impossible; frustrated individuals do not know the source or are subjectively unable to recognize it or are in a position in which they cannot risk such an action. Whatever the reason, the results are the same: They are unable to vent their anger on the real source of their frustration.

Instead, the aggression is often directed at a safer and more convenient target, usually one that somewhat resembles the real source of the frustration. In other words, the aggression is displaced onto a **scapegoat.** When this displacement is not limited to a particular person but is extended to include all similar people, it may produce a more or less permanent prejudice.

For example, suppose a middle-aged man who has been working for 20 years at the same job is told by his young supervisor that his job will soon be eliminated as a result of automation. The man is understandably angry and frightened. But if he were to vent his aggression on the supervisor, he would almost certainly be fired. That evening, as he is telling his woes to friends at the local bar, a young man comes in for a beer. The middle-aged man accuses the youth, and "all you lazy kids," of being a good-for-nothing and ruining the country, and only the intervention of the bartender prevents him from assaulting the young man.

It is fairly clear that this man has displaced his aggression toward his young supervisor onto all young people. Rather than dealing with the supervisor and the whole range of factors that led to the elimination of his job, he blames the problems of the country on young people; that is, he uses them as a scapegoat. (Frustration-aggression theory is also discussed in Chapter 7.)

Projection. Another source of prejudice and discrimination is **projection.** Many people have personal traits that they consider undesirable. They wish to rid themselves

Professor John Salter and other sit-ins at a lunch counter in Jackson, Mississippi, were sprayed with mustard, catsup, and sugar by a crowd of white teenagers. Civil disobedience and peaceful protests such as sit-ins made an enormous contribution to changing patterns of segregation in the United States in the 1950s and 1960s.

of those traits, but they cannot always do it directly—either because they find the effort too difficult or because they are unable to admit to themselves that they possess those traits. They may relieve their tension by attributing the unwanted traits to others, often members of another group. This makes it possible for them to reject and condemn the traits without rejecting and condemning themselves. Since the emotional pressures underlying projection can be very intense, it is difficult to counter them with rational arguments.

An often-cited example of projection is white attitudes toward black sexuality. Historically, many whites saw blacks as extremely promiscuous and uninhibited in their sexual relations, and there was much concern about protecting white women from sexual attacks by black men. Actually, white men enjoyed virtually unlimited sexual access to black women, particularly slaves. White society, however, regarded overt sexuality as unacceptable, and it is likely that white men felt some guilt about their sexual desires and adventures. To alleviate their guilt, they projected their own lust and sexuality onto black men—a much easier course than admitting the discrepancy between their own values and behavior.

Prejudice and Bigotry in Social Structures

The emotional needs of insecure individuals do not explain why certain groups become objects of prejudice and discrimination. To understand this, we need to look at some larger social processes.

As noted earlier, in many societies the demand for more than the available supply of certain goods gives rise to a competitive struggle, which usually results in the dominance of one group and the subordination of others. Even if the initial competition is for economic goods, the contest is ultimately a struggle for power and, hence, a political process. Once established, political dominance is likely to be reinforced by economic exploitation. Slavery and serfdom are the most obvious forms of exploitation, but "free" workers may also be exploited. Migrant farm workers, illegal aliens, and unorganized clerical and service workers are examples of the latter.

Economic exploitation is one form of discrimination practiced by the dominant group against a subordinate group. Historically, the subordinate group has consisted of unskilled workers. In the case of African Americans, for example, unskilled jobs were plentiful and available (at low wages) before the 1940s. With the development of protective labor legislation (e.g., minimum wage, antidiscrimination, and workers' compensation laws), employers could no longer use the subordinate group as a source of cheap labor. African Americans were systematically denied jobs as white-dominated unions maintained control over skilled jobs and employers sought cheaper unskilled labor by transferring basic manufacturing operations abroad (Bonacich, 1976).

Discrimination can take many other forms. Some of these are practical: Members of the subordinate group may be legally prevented from owning property or voting or may be terrorized into submission, as often happened to strikers early in the labor movement. Some forms of discrimination are symbolic, as when African Americans were refused service in restaurants before the civil rights movement. All are aimed, consciously or unconsciously, at keeping the subordinate people "in their place."

Cultural Factors: Norms and Stereotypes

Social Norms. A **social norm** is a commonly accepted standard that specifies the kind of behavior that is appropriate in a given situation. It is relevant to our discussion because, although it does not tell us why prejudice and discrimination begin, it helps explain how and why they are perpetuated.

Social norms are learned in a process that begins almost at birth. Small children soon learn what kind of behavior elicits the approval of their parents and what kind is likely to elicit a rebuke. The same process continues as they encounter other significant adults. Gradually children internalize the values and norms of their society. They receive approval from parents and other adults, and later from their peers, when they behave in socially acceptable ways; they experience disapproval when they do not.

A good example of a social norm that pertains to minority-majority relations is **homogamy,** the requirement that one must marry a person similar to oneself in religion, social class, and race or ethnicity. This has been a particularly strong norm in the United States for race. Before the civil rights movement of the 1960s, many states had laws that prohibited racial intermarriage. Racially mixed couples often encountered severe hostility, and many felt compelled to move to places like Greenwich Village in New York City or Hyde Park in Chicago, where there were similar couples and they could feel less "deviant."

Recent research shows, however, that the norm of homogamy is far weaker today than it was even 20 years ago. The rate of marriage between blacks and whites in the United States is accelerating rapidly. So are the rates of intermarriage for Asians and Native Americans. (It is far more difficult to measure intermarriage rates among Hispanics because Hispanics may be of any race.) The trends shown in Figure 9–1 continued to accelerate throughout the 1990s (Lind, 1998). Social scientists point out that many black women say that because of the lack of suitable African-American husbands—as a result of incarceration, early death, and chronic unemployment—they have little choice but to marry outside of their race (Holmes, 1996b). But since rates

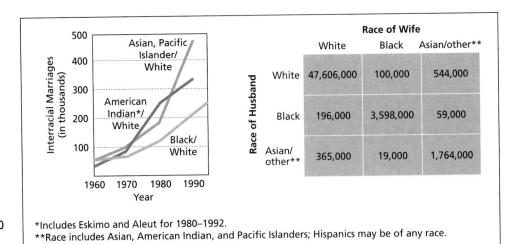

Figure 9–1 Interracial Marriages, United States, 1960–1990

Source: Data from U.S. Bureau of the Census.

*Includes Eskimo and Aleut for 1980–1992.
**Race includes Asian, American Indian, and Pacific Islanders; Hispanics may be of any race.

	Race of Wife		
Race of Husband	White	Black	Asian/other**
White	47,606,000	100,000	544,000
Black	196,000	3,598,000	59,000
Asian/other**	365,000	19,000	1,764,000

of intermarriage are also rising for other ethnic and racial groups, it does appear that the norms that once made such marriages almost taboo are weakening significantly.

Stereotyping. Still another source of prejudice and discrimination is **stereotyping,** or attributing a fixed and usually unfavorable or inaccurate conception to a category of people. Whereas social norms are concerned primarily with behavior and only indirectly with attitudes, stereotyping is basically a matter of attitude.

Usually a stereotype contains (or once contained) some truth, but it is exaggerated, distorted, or somehow taken out of context. Stereotyping has much to do with the way humans normally think. We tend to perceive and understand things in categories, and we apply the same mental process to people. We build up mental pictures of various groups, pictures made from overgeneralized impressions and selected bits of information, and we use them to define all members of a group regardless of their individual differences. Thus, we come to assume that all Native Americans are drunks, all African Americans are lazy, all residents of Appalachia or the Ozarks are hillbillys, all Puerto Ricans are short, all Italians are gangsters, all Jews are shrewd, all English people are reserved, all Swedes are blond, all Frenchmen are amorous, all old people are senile, and so forth. None of these generalizations will stand up to even perfunctory analysis, yet many people habitually use them in thinking about minority groups. For example, social scientists in the United States believe that young black males are victimized by stereotypes that portray them as violent and swaggering. In studies of the "cool pose" of inner-city black men, Robert Majors finds that this essentially defensive posture is often misinterpreted as a threatening pose, even by black middle-class individuals, and can lead to discrimination and prejudice (cited in Goleman, 1992). (See the Critical Research feature on page 265.)

It should be noted that stereotyping is not confined to any particular group, nor is it unique to the United States. Throughout the world it follows well-established patterns based on in-group/out-group distinctions and hostilities (Paul, 1998).

The three approaches just described—psychological, social-structural, and cultural—should not be viewed as mutually exclusive. As Milton Yinger (1987) has pointed out, human problems like racial disharmony are best viewed from all three of these perspectives, not just one.

The body language and clothing style of many inner-city young men, known as "the cool pose," often leads to labeling these teenagers as members of a "dangerous underclass."

CRITICAL RESEARCH

Stigmatizing Minority Women as "Welfare Queens"

Critical social scientists have often taken a leading role in combating one of the most pernicious myths about people in need in U.S. society—the myth of the "welfare queen." Patricia Hill Collins, a leading feminist social scientist, attacks this myth as a "script" that is often played out for political advantage in the media or during campaign appearances. The poor woman, Collins observes, "is portrayed as being content to sit around and collect welfare, shunning work and passing on her bad values to her offspring. The welfare mother represents a woman of low morals and uncontrolled sexuality" (quoted in Gilliam, 1999, p. 49).

In attacking the former system of Aid to Families with Dependent Children, candidate Ronald Reagan often recited a story about a woman from Chicago's South Side who was arrested for welfare fraud. "She has," he claimed, "80 names, 30 addresses, 12 Social Security cards and is collecting veteran's benefits on four nonexisting deceased husbands. And she is collecting Social Security on her cards. She's got Medicaid, getting food stamps, and she is collecting welfare under each of her names." Collins and other critical sociologists note that such statements by extremely influential American leaders served to embed in the consciousness of Americans the image of the lavishly living, Cadillac-driving welfare queen.

Collins and others point out as well the racial coding implicit in this stereotype. Poor women of all races are blamed for their impoverished condition, but the stereotype suggests that African-American women commit the most flagrant violations of American values. The story line of the welfare queen myth taps into stereotypes about women's uncontrolled sexuality and African Americans' laziness.

Collins argues that the welfare queen myth, which was used so effectively against poor women in the welfare reform debates, is merely one of many persisting racist myths. "For example," she observes, "African-American male rates of incarceration in American jails and prisons remain the highest in the world, exceeding even those of South Africa. Transcending social class, region of residence, command of English, ethnic background, or other markers of difference, all black men must in some way grapple with the actual or potential treatment by the criminal justice system" (1997, p. 341). They must also deal with persistent images of themselves as criminals or potential criminals. As mothers, daughters, wives, and lovers of black men, Collins observes, "black women also participate in this common experience." Stigmatizing images also extend to "children from poor communities and homeless families, [who] are unlikely to attend college, not because they lack talent, but because they lack opportunity" because myths about their lack of ability are used to justify lower investment by society in their education. For Collins, one of the key issues is how minority group members can gain enough power in society so that they can collectively oppose those who willingly perpetuate damaging and stigmatizing myths like that of the "welfare queen."

Institutional Discrimination

If discrimination is a socially learned behavior of members of dominant groups, designed to support and justify their continued dominance, it is reasonable to expect that it will be built into the structure of society. To members of a society who are socialized to believe that members of certain groups "just are" to be treated as inferiors, it would be perfectly natural to formulate public policies and build public institutions that discriminate against them.

To some extent this is exactly what has happened in the United States. If many blacks, Chicanos, Native Americans, Puerto Ricans, women, and members of other minority groups do not have equal protection of the law in their dealings with public institutions, it is not necessarily because of the conscious prejudices of public officials. Such **institutional discrimination** is an unconscious result of the structure and functioning of the public institutions and policies themselves.

For example, people living near reservations often believe that Native Americans are lazy and incompetent, unable to exercise initiative or do anything to improve their often deplorable condition. What such people fail to realize is the degree to which this apparent incompetence is a result of the way Native Americans are governed. Their ability to handle their own affairs has been hampered by an administrative structure that denies them opportunities to learn new ways of doing things while simultaneously rendering old tribal ways ineffective. As Gary D. Sandefur and Marta Tienda (1988) have written,

> Native Americans collectively have been victims of discrimination and persecution throughout the history of the development of the United States. The contemporary expression of subjugation and discrimination has changed considerably from the blatant destruction experienced a century ago. . . . Despite substantial increases in educational attainment over the past few decades, many Native Americans remain unprepared to compete in a highly technical and bureaucratized world of work. Consequently, there persist income and employment differentials relative to comparably schooled whites. . . . To the

Many young Americans experience racial integration for the first time in their lives when they join the armed services.

extent that job possibilities on reservations remain limited while large shares of Native Americans reside on them, the prospects for economic parity with whites probably will not be realized. (pp. 8–9)

It should be noted that Native Americans are by no means a homogeneous group. They have been lumped into a single category ("Indians"), but in fact they constitute a variety of peoples with vastly different cultures. Despite the poverty and hardship they have experienced on segregated reservations and the racism they often experience outside them, many of these groups have succeeded in preserving their traditional identities while adapting to the ways of the larger society.

Since it would be difficult to discuss all categories of institutional discrimination against all minority groups, we will focus on four major categories: education, housing, employment and income, and social justice. But the patterns we describe will apply to other categories as well, such as health care and consumer issues.

Education

A question that generates a great deal of emotion in the United States is whether black, Puerto Rican, Chicano, and Native American children should attend the same schools as white children. This question underlies such issues as busing to achieve racial balance, high-quality education for all, and public tax support for private schools.

Americans take public school systems very seriously. Undoubtedly, one reason is that in this country education has generally been seen as the road to social and economic advancement. It is almost an article of faith that American children should get more education than their parents and achieve higher social and economic status. (This subject is discussed in detail in Chapter 13.)

Since the 1940 census, which was the first to ask about educational attainment, the average number of years of school completed by all Americans has increased steadily. (See Figure 9–2.) Despite these gains, members of minority groups still have less chance of finishing high school or attending college than do whites. In 1998, 16.3 percent of whites aged 25 and over had not completed high school; the comparable figures for blacks and Hispanics were 24.0 percent and 44.5 percent, respectively (*Statistical Abstract*, 1999). Thus, although Figure 9–2 indicates a significant gain in educational parity since World War II, large differences remain. The greatest difference is

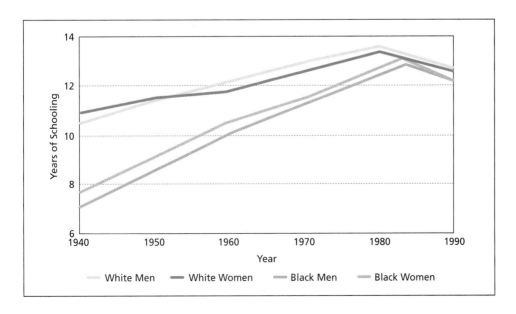

Figure 9–2 Average Years of Schooling Completed by Persons Age 25–29, by Race and Sex, 1940 to 1990

Source: Data from Farley, Bianchi, & Colasanto, 1979; and *Statistical Abstract*, various years.

TABLE 9–2   Mean Earnings, by Highest Degree Earned

Characteristic	Total Persons	Not a High School Graduate	High School Graduate Only	Some College, No Degree	Level of Highest Degree				
					Associate's	Bachelor's	Master's	Professional	Doctorate
All persons	$29,514	$16,124	$22,895	$24,804	$29,872	$40,478	$51,183	$95,148	$77,445
White	30,515	16,596	23,618	25,442	30,509	41,439	52,475	97,487	79,947
Black	21,909	13,185	18,980	22,105	25,527	32,062	40,610	51,104	—*
Hispanic	20,766	15,069	19,558	20,825	25,478	33,465	46,556	—*	—*

*Base figure too small to meet statistical standards for reliability of a derived figure.

Source: Statistical Abstract, 1999.

in the attainment of a college diploma plus graduate training. In 1998, among Americans aged 25 and over, only 14.7 percent of blacks and 11.0 percent of Hispanics had completed four years of college or more, compared to 25.0 percent of whites (*Statistical Abstract,* 1999).

We have long assumed that higher education leads to higher income. There is no doubt that among people working at this time, the more highly educated usually receive substantially higher salaries than those with little education. Evidence also suggests that even better than a sheepskin is a white skin, for minority group members at all levels of education earn less than their nonminority counterparts. (See Table 9–2.) As educational requirements for the labor force increase, it becomes ever more urgent for members of minority groups to enter colleges and universities (Evangelauf, 1992). Despite recent gains, minority enrollment rates are lower than they would be under conditions of equality.

Unequal Access to High-quality Schooling.   Throughout the United States school administrations are under pressure to raise standards and increase performance, especially in underachieving schools, which are often found in communities with high proportions of low-income black and Hispanic households. The causes of this situation and policies to address it are among the most hotly contested issues in American public life at this time. We will deal in more detail with educational issues in Chapter 13. Relevant here is the issue of minority segregation and poor schools, along with the retreat from policies to achieve school desegregation.

In its decision in *Brown* v. *Board of Education* the Supreme Court mandated integration "with all deliberate speed" but was vague on actual remedies to be used. The decision effectively wiped out **de jure segregation**—segregation required by law—and by finding that "separate but equal" schooling was inherently unequal, it set in motion decades of sporadic efforts to achieve more racially balanced classrooms. To do so, states and municipalities had to address **de facto segregation,** segregation resulting from housing patterns, economic inequalities, gerrymandered school districts, and the departure of middle-class families from communities with increasing rates of minority households and poor or mediocre schools (Orfield & Eaton, 1996).

Throughout much of the last 30 years, busing of students, primarily minority students, to schools outside their neighborhoods has been the primary remedy for desegregation. Today, however, busing is largely considered to have been a failure. At the same time, no alternative strategies are being implemented to achieve school desegregation. Demands for higher standards and higher achievement are not generally matched with increases in funding for schools in lower-income minority neighborhoods. Public schools in the United States are typically funded from local property taxes, so wealthier communities can afford to pay higher salaries to teachers and hire more experienced teachers than can financially strapped inner-city schools. States often attempt to correct this imbalance with supplemental funding, but the results are extremely mixed.

A recent study by the Harvard Project on School Desegregation found that resegregation of the races is increasing. This is true despite the growing diversity of minority enrollments as a result of recent immigration (discussed in Chapter 16). Resegregation is occurring most rapidly in the South, but the races are increasingly separate in schools in other regions as well. The study also found that over the past three decades the following changes have occurred (Cutler, Glaeser, & Vigdor, 1999; Orfield & Eaton, 1996):

- Enrollment of Hispanic students has increased 218 percent, and nearly 75 percent of Latino schoolchildren attend predominantly minority schools.

- Enrollment of black students has risen 22 percent, and 69 percent of African-American children attend schools where at least half the students are from minority groups.

- Enrollment of white students has declined by 16 percent, and the vast majority of white students attend schools that are 80 percent or more white. This finding holds even for white students who live in generally nonwhite areas (often because of white enrollment in private schools). At the same time, black and Hispanic students generally remain in black- and Hispanic-majority schools even when they live in the suburbs.

- Schools with mostly black and Hispanic students are 11 times more likely to be in areas with concentrated poverty than their peers in predominantly white schools.

- Poverty compounds the problems of segregation and is linked to lower classroom performance and achievement. The research shows that schools with many poor children lack advanced courses and well-qualified teachers. Such schools are more likely than others to have children who drop out, suffer from untreated health problems, and do not attend college.

- The research reveals that black students are most likely to go to majority-black schools in the following states, in order of severity: Michigan, Illinois, New York, New Jersey, and Maryland. The top states for Hispanic student concentration are, in order, New York, Texas, New Jersey, California, and Illinois.

Housing

School desegregation is an extremely difficult issue to address when such a high proportion of minority and nonminority people live in segregated neighborhoods to begin with. Housing segregation—the separation of minority groups into different regions, cities, neighborhoods, blocks, and even buildings—has diminished somewhat in recent years as a result of immigration into formerly segregated neighborhoods, but as we will see in this section, it remains a serious obstacle to the achiement of racial and ethnic harmony (Quillian, 1999).

In an important study of trends in residential segregation and poverty in the United States, sociologists Douglas Massey and Nancy Denton (1993) found that although some decrease in housing segregation has occurred in urban regions, the largest cities, including Chicago, Cleveland, Detroit, New York, and St. Louis, have failed to significantly reduce housing segregation. The figures in Table 9–3 are percentages based on a calculation of how many of each city's African-American residents would have to move out of their segregated neighborhoods to achieve an even distribution of their

TABLE 9-3 Trends in Black-White Segregation in 30 Metropolitan Areas with Largest Black Populations, 1970–1990

Metropolitan Area	1970	1980	1990
Northern areas	(Percentages)		
Boston	81.2%	77.6%	68.2%
Buffalo	87.0	79.4	81.8
Chicago	91.9	87.8	85.8
Cincinnati	76.8	72.3	75.8
Cleveland	90.8	87.5	85.1
Columbus	81.8	71.4	67.3
Detroit	88.4	86.7	87.6
Gary–Hammond–E. Chicago	91.4	90.6	89.9
Indianapolis	81.7	76.2	74.3
Kansas City	87.4	78.9	72.6
Los Angeles–Long Beach	91.0	81.1	73.1
Milwaukee	90.5	83.9	82.8
New York	81.0	82.0	82.2
Newark	81.4	81.6	82.5
Philadelphia	79.5	78.8	77.2
Pittsburg	75.0	72.7	71.0
St. Louis	84.7	81.3	77.0
San Fransisco–Oakland	80.1	71.7	66.8
Average	84.5	80.1	77.8
Southern areas			
Atlanta	82.1%	78.5%	67.8%
Baltimore	81.9	74.7	71.4
Birmingham	37.8	40.8	71.7
Dallas–Ft. Worth	86.9	77.1	63.1
Greensboro–Winston-Salem	65.4	56.0	60.9
Houston	78.1	69.5	66.8
Memphis	75.9	71.6	69.3
Miami	85.1	77.8	71.8
New Orleans	73.1	68.3	68.8
Norfolk–Virginia Beach	75.7	63.1	50.3
Tampa–St. Petersburg	79.9	72.6	69.7
Washington, DC	81.1	70.1	66.1
Average	75.3	68.3	66.5

Source: Reprinted by permission of the publisher from *American Apartheid: Segregation and the Making of the Underclass* by Douglas S. Massey and Nancy A. Deuton, Cambridge, Mass., Harvard University Press. Copyright © 1993 by the President and Fellows of Harvard College.

numbers throughout the city's neighborhoods. Poverty, unemployment, homicide, AIDS, and many other problems of urban centers are heightened by the segregation of racially distinct and poor households in blighted urban communities. This study confirms what many others have shown: Failure to enforce federal laws against housing discrimination continues to produce rates of black segregation that are far higher than those experienced by any other group in U.S. history.

A practice that contributes to high rates of segregation is **racial steering,** in which real estate brokers refuse to show houses outside of specific areas to minority buyers. Before the landmark judicial decisions of the 1950s, racial steering was enforced through *restrictive covenants*—agreements among home owners not to sell their property to people who were designated as undesirable. Although restrictive covenants are now illegal, racial and ethnic steering still occurs unofficially in many all-white neighborhoods. Because it operates below the surface, with no written agreements, racial steering is difficult to detect or prevent (Farley, 1996; Farley, Bianchi, & Colasato, 1979).

Massey and others who study racial and ethnic segregation assert that more *audit research* is needed to show lawmakers that racial steering and other forms of discrimination exist and that laws against them must be enforced far more rigorously. In audit research, a black or minority couple is sent to real estate agents and shown (or not shown) certain types of housing. Then a white couple is sent to the same agents and the results are compared; this process is repeated many times with different agents to determine whether a systematic pattern of discrimination exists (Massey & Denton, 1993).

The housing problems of another minority group, Native Americans, provide further examples of how segregation and faulty application of social policies worsen an already difficult situation. Until the early 1960s Indians were excluded from plans for public housing. They lived on reservations, where some had adequate housing, especially on the more well-to-do reservations, but many more lived in tarpaper shacks, draughty log houses, ragged tents, abandoned automobile bodies, and hillside caves. When public housing did become available on the reservations, failure to build adequate housing with federal funds, often due to corruption, resulted in poor and extremely depressing housing conditions in the new buildings (Nagel, 1996).

The problem of inadequate housing on Indian reservations is related to the federal government's long-standing policy of taking Native American children away from their homes to be educated in boarding schools. This had the effect of weakening the family. Depressed by the destruction of their families and convinced of their powerlessness, some Native American tribes have difficulty developing the patterns of leadership needed to argue their case effectively with the government or to develop their own communities (Sandefur, 1996; Sandefur & Tienda, 1988).

Employment and Income

The idea of work as a way to improve one's social status is deeply ingrained in American culture. Although it is no longer as pervasive as it once was, the work ethic still holds that if you really want a job you can find one, and that if you work hard you will make money. The corollary to this is the notion that if you are wealthy, you deserve your wealth because you worked for it, and if you are poor, it is because you are lazy. Thus, one hears the argument that if only blacks and Puerto Ricans and Native Americans would make an effort to find jobs and stick to them, they could improve their lot in life. This view ignores the fact that discrimination is no less prevalent in employment than it is in education and housing.

In some ways discrimination in employment is a direct result of discrimination in education. We have already noted the relationship between income and education. Since today the chances of finding even an entry-level job without a high school diploma are slim, lack of education means that many minority group members will spend their lives underemployed or unemployed (Wilson, 1987). This, in turn, means a low income, resulting in inferior housing, with the likelihood of a poor education for the next generation, and so on—a cycle of discrimination that is built into the system.

Is there any escape from this situation? What about jobs that do not require much formal education, jobs that one learns mostly through apprenticeship and are represented by many labor unions?

Historically, labor unions have been in the forefront of battles for civil rights, but union locals often resisted minority demands for membership. William Gould (1968) pointed out a basic conflict between the rhetoric of union leadership and established union policies and practices. Unions, like other institutions, are resistant to internal changes or economic sacrifices to accommodate the demands of minority workers. There are only so many jobs to go around, and those who have them want to keep them. This has meant that union-sponsored job training programs are generally closed to minority workers. Progress in opening apprenticeship and training programs has been slow. Although in 1983 blacks accounted for 26 percent of union members, by 1990 this figure had fallen below 24 percent. This negative trend has been reversed in recent years with renewed effort by organized labor to bring in new members.

The employment problem among minority groups is particularly devastating for young black and Hispanic men. In the absence of legitimate means of getting ahead, many turn to various forms of illicit activity. In addition, without hope for a steady income, they often find it economically impossible to form stable families. And this situation shows few signs of improving; the employment gap between young white men and black and Hispanic youths increased in the 1990s despite the narrowing of the educational gap.

Recent research has shown that focusing on income differences can be deceptive. Although it is true that in the past 20 years there has been a trend toward income parity among African Americans, some Latino populations, and whites, the same is not true for assets, such as first and second homes and other costly material possessions or capital-generating investments. In their influential research on asset inequality, Melvin Oliver and Thomas Shapiro (1995) found that about a third of Americans own almost no assets other than a car. The asset gap is far wider for African Americans, Puerto Ricans, and urban Mexican Americans. Although there is a growing black middle class whose members do own property and have bank accounts and pension funds, it is far outnumbered by those who own almost nothing and have no assets to fall back on during hard times. Asset inequality has a profound impact on intergenerational inequality. People with property and investments can will their estates to their children so that they have some material advantages as they establish homes of their own. This is not possible for those with no assets, whatever their ethnic or racial background.

Table 9–4 shows the proportions of black, Hispanic, and white households that live "on the edge." By this the authors mean households with zero or negative net financial worth (the value of all possessions, bank accounts, and so forth, other than weekly income). The data show that fully 60 percent of black and 54 percent of Hispanic households have no assets and that almost 79 percent of black households have inadequate assets in reserve to allow them to survive at an income of $968 a month for at least three months. These data suggest that there is a rather large number of white households in the same precarious situation but that far higher proportions of black and Hispanic households live on the edge of possible financial disaster.

Research on impoverished ghetto neighborhoods by William J. Wilson (1996) emphasizes that the economic and social distance between the small middle class and the poor is widening. Blue-collar manufacturing work once helped create a relatively secure black and Latino middle class. As manufacturing has disappeared from many

TABLE 9–4   Net Financial Assets (NFA) of Households, by Race

	Households with 0 or Negative NFA	Households without NFA for 3 months*	Households without NFA for 6 months*
Sample	31.0	44.9	49.9
Race			
White	25.3	38.1	43.2
Black	60.9	78.9	83.1
Hispanic	54.0	72.5	77.2

*NFA reserves to survive at the poverty line of $968 per month.

Source: Adapted from Oliver & Shapiro, 1995.

metropolitan areas, finding a decent job is often a matter of good basic education and interpersonal skills. Inadequate schools and the growing isolation of poor African Americans in segregated inner-city neighborhoods make it difficult for young people to learn the vocabulary and mannerisms of the dominant white middle class. In consequence, many employers have had negative experiences with African Americans, especially young men, and tend to be wary of employing them.

Wilson (1996) also notes that some employers are simply racist and discriminate because of their own prejudices. But as Table 9–5 shows, employers often come to feel that poor African-American males from ghetto neighborhoods lack a work ethic or basic educational skills. Employers' perceptions vary from one type of work to another, but often they share the notion that black males' lives are complicated by other social problems and that they do not understand what employers require in a new worker. Wilson and others who have studied this problem call for social policies that provide more opportunities for young men and women from segregated communities to find jobs at which they can succeed, and opportunities to get more training for

TABLE 9–5   Employers' Observations About Why Inner-City Black Males Cannot Find or Retain Jobs Easily

Frequency of Responses, by Employers' Profession

Rationale	Customer Service	Clerical	Craft	Blue Collar	All Employers
Lack of job skills	9.0%	7.1%	12.5%	17.6%	11.7%
Lack of basic skills	44.5	37.5	37.5	36.8	38.5
Lack of work ethic	25.0	48.0	25.0	52.9	36.9
Lack of dependability	13.6	14.3	12.5	22.0	16.8
Bad attitude	15.9	16.1	25.0	19.1	17.3
Lack of interpersonal skills	18.2	10.7	0	3.0	8.9
Racial discrimination	15.9	14.3	0	13.2	13.4

Source: From *When Work Disappears* by William Julius Wilson. Copyright © 1996 by William Julius Wilson. Reprinted by permission of Alfred A. Knopf Inc.

work (Reich, 1992; Wilson, 1996a). (We return to these subjects in the Social Policy section of the chapter.)

During the 1980s and 1990s a debate raged among social scientists over whether the concentration of black and Puerto Rican people in inner-city ghettos, where they are isolated from better jobs and educational opportunities, has produced an "underclass," that is, a class of people who not only are poor and undereducated but are being enticed into petty crime and welfare dependency because of their limited access to legitimate opportunities. Until very recently, William J. Wilson (1996) was the chief proponent of this thesis. But fearing that the term *underclass* lumps together too many different categories of impoverished people and threatens to become a pejorative label, he and others have abandoned the term even while many other social scientists continue to assert its validity.

Justice

Philosopher and social theorist Cornel West (1994) recounts an all-too-familiar tale of the daily injustices faced by African Americans and other nonwhites. While driving to a college lecture, he remembers, "I was stopped on fake charges of trafficking cocaine. When I told the police officer I was a professor of religion, he replied, 'Yeh, and I'm the Flying Nun. Let's go, nigger!'" (p. xv). Such degrading experiences with the police and other street-level authorities enrage members of minority groups, who know that those who are poor and powerless may receive far worse treatment in the justice system.

The American system of justice is based on two premises that are relevant to this issue: (1) Justice is blind—racial, ethnic, economic, or social considerations are irrelevant in the eyes of the law—and (2) any accused person is considered innocent until proven guilty in a court of law. But do these assumptions apply equally to everyone?

As noted in Chapter 6, minority groups are overrepresented in official arrest records, and it seems probable that in general they are more likely to be arrested and charged with a crime, whether or not they are guilty. The higher arrest rates among minorities are due partly to the higher arrest rates among the poor in general (who, as noted earlier, include a disproportionate number of minority group members), but there is considerable evidence that discrimination plays a role in who is arrested.

Following arrest, the obstacle of the bail system must be overcome. It is here that the American criminal-justice system may be most discriminatory. To begin with, bail involves money: Those who have it can usually arrange to be released after arrest and await their trial in freedom, subject only to the limitations of the bail agreement. Those who do not have money are punished, in effect, because of the long delay between arrest and trial in many jurisdictions (particularly in big cities). They are compelled to wait in jail—often for months, sometimes for more than a year—until their case comes up. This borders on punishment before conviction and certainly runs counter to the precept of presumed innocence (Feagin, 1996). Even those who can pay bail can rarely afford costly legal counsel, and those who are detained have little opportunity to prepare a defense. This inequality in the administration of justice extends to the sentencing process. Although blacks account for only 12 percent of the population, they make up about 42.7 percent of the prison population (*Statistical Abstract*, 1999); whites are much more likely to be released on their own recognizance or given suspended sentences.

In capital crimes, the probability that minority offenders would be more likely to receive the death penalty—because of the effects of prejudice and inability to afford good legal counsel—prevented the Supreme Court from reinstituting capital punishment for many decades. In 1977, however, the Court reversed its position and the death penalty was reinstated. Since then the issue of racial bias in the application of the death penalty has also reappeared in many states.

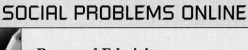

SOCIAL PROBLEMS ONLINE

Race and Ethnicity

The Internet carries several web sites that provide discussions and analyses of ethnic and racial issues. The Race and Ethnic Studies Institute at Texas A&M University, **http://resi.tamu.edu/**, has a Publications section that presents abstracts of articles on education and minorities. Clicking on Other Resources opens a menu that includes the Minority Affairs Forum, which is devoted to education about issues in such areas as immigration, affirmative action, bilingual education, and race relations. Another interesting website is the Balch Institute for Ethnic Studies, **http://www.libertynet.org,** which is concerned with the reduction and prevention of intergroup tensions and violence. Clicking on The Electronic Information Center brings up several connections to resources on race and ethnicity, as well as links to other research organizations.

For information about antibias education and other research-oriented websites on civil rights, race, ethnicity, and "trouble spots around the world," visit the Southern Institute at Tulane University, **http://www.tulane.edu/%7Eso-inst.** Its home page provides access to discussion groups, databases, and research publications.

Those interested in the growing debate over the nature of racial categories and the need to recognize mixed-race individuals as a separate racial group should access Interracial Voice, an electronic publication at **http://www.webcom.com/~intvoice/**.

The Media Resources Center of Moffitt Library at the University of California at Berkeley carries a home page titled The Movies, Race, and Ethnicity (**http://www.lib.berkeley.edu/MRC/EthnicimagesVid.htm**), which provides videographies, bibliographies, and full-text articles of a sample of Hollywood films that emphasize issues faced by African Americans, Asians, Latinos, Jews, and Native Americans.

Several web resources are concerned with discrimination in American society. The National Fair Housing Advocate, **http://www.fairhousing.com/**, keeps track of legal cases that involve housing discrimination throughout the nation. It links organizations that call for fair-housing practices, and it provides updated information on federal guidelines, job openings, articles, news, and so forth. The Legal Information Institute at Cornell University, **http://www.law.cornell.edu/topics/civil_rights.htm**, has a Civil Rights and Discrimination home page that provides legal information on civil and constitutional rights, employment discrimination, human rights, and the latest judicial decisions.

The National Employment Lawyers Association (NELA) has a conference home page at **http://www.nela.org/nela/nelaweb.htm**. It presents news, discussion, and analysis of issues about discrimination, employment law, international labor standards, and the like. For an extensive link to directories, as well as articles about discrimination against blacks and Latinos, the Catholic Mobile (Alabama) Resources for the Study of Discrimination Against African-Americans, at **http://www.mcgill.pvt.k12.al.us/jerryd/cm/black.htm**, and the Catholic Mobile Resources for the Study of Discrimination Against Latinos/Chicanos, at **http://www.mcgill.pvt.k12.al.us/jerryd/cm/latino.htm**, offer current and historical information about race relations in the South.

The National Association for the Advancement of Colored People (NAACP), the nation's largest civil-rights organization, at **http://www.naacp.org/**, has Issue Alerts, with late-breaking news on issues that affect people of color. For comprehensive access to organizations, demographic data, affirmative action updates, and other research networks on black issues, see the African American Web Sites (**http://home.earthlink.net/%7Eanthony/africa.htm**). For Asians, the Student Information Processing Board at MIT has a home page of Asian American Resources at **http://www.mit.edu:8001/afs/athena.mit.edu/user/i/r/irie/www/aar.html**. Finally, the Latinos Web, at **http://www.catalog.com/favision/resource.htm**, offers a wide selection of research data and has links to organizations that advocate for the Latino community, such as the Institute for Puerto Rican Policy, the Mexican American Legal Defense Fund, and the National Association of Latino Elected Officials.

The European Research Centre on Migration and Ethnic Relations (Ercomer) is a university-based research institute in the Netherlands that promotes "peaceful co-existence, justice, and harmony in inter-ethnic relations." Ercomer's home page at **http://www.ruu.nl/ercomer/** offers access to summaries of research papers and monographs, as well as other projects.

David C. Baldus, the nation's leading expert on the subject and the author of numerous studies that have influenced the courts, notes, "Some people are being sentenced to death based on race, and I find that morally and legally objectionable" (quoted in Eckholm, 1995, p. B1). In fact, studies by Baldus and others show that the race of the defendant is not significant in explaining whether the death penalty is applied in murder trials. What is highly significant is the race of the victim. About half of the people murdered in the United States each year are black, but since 1977, 85 percent of those sentenced to death have killed a white person.

In the important case of *McCleskey* v. *Kemp* (1987), it was argued that the death sentence of a black defendant convicted of killing a white police officer should be revoked because there was evidence of systematic discrimination in similar cases. In a five-to-four decision, the Supreme Court denied the appeal. More recently, in 1994 Congress rejected a requirement that federal sentencing guidelines for the death penalty must be based on quantitative studies of racial patterns in sentencing in capital cases and that these findings must be given important courtroom standing. But for Baldus and others who study patterns of racial preference in sentencing, the issue is not to increase the number of executions for murderers of black people but to end racial biases of all kinds in the administration of justice (Eckholm, 1995).

Some Consequences of Prejudice and Discrimination

The harmful effects of prejudice and discrimination are not limited to minority groups. As the Supreme Court noted in its decision in *Brown* v. *Board of Education of Topeka,* the lives of members of the dominant group are also stunted by the artificial barriers and warped perceptions that such social divisions create. Here, however, we will consider the effects on the subordinate group since they are usually more serious.

What happens to people who must live with institutionalized discrimination and the prejudice that accompanies it? There are, of course, effects on the individual personalities of minority group members. And both individuals and groups develop protective reactions against prejudice and discrimination.

First, consider the effects of discrimination on individual personalities. In his ground-breaking work, *Children of Crisis,* Robert Coles (1968) documented some of the effects on the first black children to attend desegregated schools in the South. These children were subjected to blatant discrimination and bitter prejudice, including mob action against them and their parents. For several months Coles observed the children, focusing on how they depicted themselves and their world in drawings. His account of the drawings of one black girl, Ruby, is fascinating. For months Ruby would never use brown or black except to indicate the ground. However, she distinguished between white and black people:

> She drew white people larger and more lifelike. Negroes were smaller, their bodies less intact. A white girl we both knew to be her own size appeared several times taller. While Ruby's own face lacked an eye in one drawing, an ear in another, the white girl never lacked any features. Moreover, Ruby drew the white girl's hands and legs carefully, always making sure that they had the proper number of fingers and toes. Not so with her own limbs, or those of any other Negro children she chose (or was asked) to picture. A thumb or forefinger might be missing, or a whole set of toes. The arms were shorter, even absent or truncated. (p. 47)

At the same time, Jimmy, a white classmate, always depicted blacks as somehow related to animals or extremely dirty and dangerous. After about two years of contact with Ruby and other black children in his school in New Orleans, Jimmy grew less fearful of blacks, and the change was reflected in his drawings. Coles concluded that children were conditioned to fear and distrust members of the other race, but that with continuing friendly contact, these prejudices were broken down and the children eventually helped change their parents' attitudes as well. To this day Ruby Bridges, now a grown woman with children of her own, and Dr. Coles are friends who share a strong bond, having struggled together for social justice. Coles recently wrote a children's book about Ruby's experiences (Judson, 1995).

The most common reaction against inequality during the past few decades has been public protest. Following the success of the Montgomery bus boycott of 1955 and 1956 (when blacks stopped riding buses until discriminatory seating rules were eliminated), a broad social movement for desegregation emerged. Initially led by Martin Luther King, Jr., the movement was directed against laws that enforced or created a statutory inequality—that is, an obstruction maintained for the purpose of denying minority groups the rights and privileges enjoyed by other Americans. In the 1960s, however, as progress slowed and resistance increased, minority protests sometimes took more violent forms. Anger, frustration, and rage provoked urban riots across the country. Often the catalyst was the arrest of a black by white police officers, who served as visible symbols of the attitudes of the white majority. At no time, however, did a majority of blacks approve of the violent protests (National Advisory Commission on Civil Disorders, 1968).

By the mid-1970s the frequency of riots had diminished considerably. The recession during this period caused both whites and blacks to suffer from high unemployment rates and inflation, and expectations of progress were reduced. Moreover, the end of the Vietnam War and the draft caused a general decline in protest movements. There may also have been a sense that riots had reached the limits of their effectiveness and that more deliberate, better organized efforts were necessary. In addition, it is possible, as Frances Piven and Richard Cloward (1997) have theorized, that welfare rolls were increased in response to the riots and that this had the effect of mollifying blacks.

A different kind of racism is often experienced by young upper-class blacks. This type of prejudice is considerably more subtle and more difficult to confront than open bigotry. It may take the form of excessive highway stops by police or patronizing comments (e.g., "Blacks are not good swimmers because their bodies are less buoyant than those of whites") or simple lack of awareness (e.g., "I never think of you as black"). Blacks are still prevented from renting apartments or buying homes in certain neighborhoods, and racist incidents in schools and restaurants are common. In the words of one young black woman, "The old racism seems . . . ever ready to resurface with a vengeance" (Russell, 1987, p. 2).

Research by sociologist Joe R. Feagin (1991) in major metropolitan areas also documents the persistence of discrimination and prejudice against middle-class blacks in public places. Feagin's black respondents mentioned case after case of avoidance by whites; of rejection or extremely poor service in public establishments; of verbal epithets, public harassment, and other threats. Feagin also found, however, that black citizens are increasingly asserting their rights even in embarrassing social situations and demanding redress and apologies from business owners.

The consequences of prejudice can also be seen in the events following the collapse of communism and the easing of the cold war. In many areas these stunning changes also rekindled nationalist passions. The conflicts among different nationality groups in the former Soviet Union, Bosnia, and other nations remind us again of the fierce power of ethnic and racial sentiments and their ability to violently disrupt political and economic institutions. In the United States, growing tensions among different groups have also caused outbreaks of violence. Even before the series of arson fires in black churches in 1996, the FBI had reported that crimes motivated by racism and bias against minority groups (including homosexuals and religious groups) were becoming more frequent. And sociologist Jack McDevitt found in analyzing 452 cases of crimes motivated by prejudice that the majority (57 percent) involved "turf defense"; that is, they occurred when people walking or driving or working in a neighborhood were attacked for being different from those living there (cited in Goleman, 1990).

SOCIAL POLICY

In response to the demands of blacks and other minority groups for a more equal share in the benefits of the American way of life, various programs have been instituted to alleviate the effects of prejudice and discrimination. In this section we examine some of the approaches and goals of these programs and evaluate their effectiveness.

Job Training

A persistent political demand in the United States today is the need to reduce taxes and shrink the size and responsibilities of government. These demands make it increasingly difficult for governments to take the initiative in creating employment and training programs. At the same time, major U.S. corporations have been "downsizing," or eliminating as many jobs as possible, to increase their profitability. This tends to create situations in which more qualified workers compete with less well-trained or experienced ones for a limited number of jobs. Members of minority groups, especially blacks and Puerto Ricans, Mexicans in some states, and Native Americans—all groups that have experienced discrimination in the past—suffer the most severe consequences of these changes. Since welfare reform on a significant scale depends on the availability of jobs for those attempting to make the transition from welfare to work, it is difficult to imagine how workfare programs can succeed without an improvement in overall economic conditions.

Recent setbacks cannot erase the programs' positive contributions. Besides those who received job training and secured higher-paying jobs, many people improved their skills in other ways. Some entered counseling programs and went to school and hence were able to keep their jobs; others qualified for high school equivalency diplomas, thereby improving their chances of finding employment.

Affirmative Action

The most controversial policy designed to redress past institutional discrimination is **affirmative action.** This term refers to policies based on a body of federal law originating in the 1964 Civil Rights Act that bans discrimination on the basis of race, religion, sex, or national origin in such areas as employment, education, and housing. Affirmative-action programs require institutions that have engaged in discriminatory practices to increase opportunities for women and members of minority groups (Kahlenberg, 1996). The policy is controversial because, with the goal of correcting past patterns of discrimination, institutions such as universities and businesses must make special efforts to recruit minority applicants, and those efforts may in effect represent discrimination against white applicants.

Affirmative-action policies are also controversial because they often appear to divide both majority and minority groups into those who support the policy and those who believe that it represents a form of "reverse discrimination." This is true not only in the United States but also in South Africa, Europe, and other regions of the world (Alexander & Jacobsen, 1999).

In an effort to enable members of minority groups to receive the same educational opportunities as whites, beginning in 1965 the federal government required schools to establish goals for minority enrollment and, in some cases, to set quotas that specify the number of minority students to be admitted each year. These policies met with considerable opposition. Charging that affirmative action is reverse discrimination, critics focused on the Supreme Court case of Alan Bakke, a white student who was refused admission to the medical school of the University of California at Davis even though his grades were higher than those of many black students who were admitted under an affirmative-action program.

The fight against the medical school's program was led by Jewish organizations, which viewed quota systems as a threat to the advancement of Jews in American society. Emphasis on educational achievement had caused the relatively small Jewish population to be overrepresented at institutions of higher education, even though they had been subject to quotas in the past. Many Jews feared that quotas would again limit their access to colleges and universities to roughly the same small proportion as their numbers in the general population.

Those who support affirmative action cite a major difference between discriminatory quotas and policies designed to extend the opportunities available to victims of past discrimination. Describing affirmative action as a societal commitment to bringing blacks and other minority groups to a position of equality in the professions, they adamantly deny charges of reverse discrimination. The few whites who lose the opportunity to attend professional schools because of affirmative-action programs are, they argue, victims not of racism but of an effort to eradicate racism from the college and university environment (Kahlenberg, 1996).

The Supreme Court's decision in the *Bakke* case straddled these opposing points of view. The medical school's system was struck down, but the Court did not extend its ruling to all preferential admission systems. Affirmative action in college and professional school admissions remained in effect and continued to generate a great deal of rancorous conflict and political agitation, especially from conservative opponents of the policy. In 1996 California voters passed a statewide referendum, known as Proposition 209, that ended affirmative-action programs in public college admissions and in government hiring and contracts. A similar referendum passed in Washington State, and even earlier Texas had begun to dismantle affirmative-action programs in colleges and universities. On the other hand, a referendum against affirmative action was soundly defeated in Houston in 1998, and other states have failed to pass similar legislation, a sign that Americans remain extremely divided over what do to redress past patterns of racial and gender discrimination (Staples, 1999).

Three years after Proposition 209 was passed in California, data on college admissions revealed a precipitous drop in enrollments of Latino and black students in the more prestigious colleges in the University of California system and even lower minority enrollments in professional schools. In 1999, therefore, the state's Civil Liberties Union brought suit against the state on behalf of minority high school students. The suit was filed on behalf of four black and Hispanic students at Inglewood High School in Los Angeles, which offers only three advanced-placement courses. Inglewood's student population is 97 percent black. Beverly Hills High, which is 91 percent white, offers 14 advanced-placement courses. Surprisingly, University of California Regent Ward Connerly, a conservative African American who championed Proposition 209 and other initiatives like it throughout the nation, has joined the supporters of the suit. Although he opposes any form of affirmative-action quota system or preferential selection, he and others are appalled by the drastic results of Proposition 209 and realize that other measures, such as more effective high school preparation and better outreach to gifted minority students, are still needed (Alexander & Jacobsen, 1999). At the same time, staunch opponents of affirmative action in California are continuing to mobilize support for the proposition and seek to ban outreach and recruitment efforts that encourage minorities and women to compete for jobs, contracts, and college admissions (Staples, 1999).

Although it is too soon to know the fate of affirmative-action policies, it seems likely that preferential selection systems of any kind will continue to come under attack, at least in public institutions like universities and agencies of government. The same is not entirely true of private businesses. Major corporations like Texaco and Bell Atlantic have affirmative-action recruitment policies for women and minorities and will maintain those policies because they fear negative publicity and wish to please all segments of the vast markets they serve. This may not be true of all corporations, but it has been a pattern for many of the large corporations that operate in global markets.

Although affirmative-action policies remain under attack, efforts to redress past patterns of discrimination will no doubt continue. In 1997, for example, southern African-American farmers were successful in suing the government for past discrimination in farm loans, which deprived hundreds of independent minority farmers of the opportunity to make a living from the land. Under the agreement reached between the United States and the black plaintiffs, each farmer is entitled to receive $50,000 tax free and to have his or her federal loan debts erased. The debts average $100,000. Farmers with the most damaging claims can seek more compensation through arbitration, the courts, or the Department of Agriculture's administrative process (Cannon, 1999).

Analyses of employment data show that even at exactly the same levels of education and training and even with the same college grade point averages, white male college graduates earn 10 to 15 percent more per hour than comparable female, black male, or Asian male graduates (Weinberger, 1998). As social scientists continue to document persistent patterns of discrimination in opportunities and in the treatment of minorities, efforts to correct these inequities will persist.

Education for Equality

In an influential study titled *American Apartheid,* Massey and Denton (1992) demonstrated that native-born blacks are (and have always been) far more segregated than any other racial or ethnic group in the United States. Persistent patterns of housing discrimination, documented in careful studies by the federal government during the 1980s, show that real estate agents, banks, local governments, and even the federal government have engaged in a variety of discriminatory housing practices or have failed to enforce legislation designed to guarantee freedom of choice in housing decisions. The extremely high rates of racial segregation in U.S. communities are reflected in increasing segregation in public schools (Celis, 1993c).

A study released in late 1993 by researchers at the Harvard School of Education (including Gary Orfield) confirms what many observers feared: The lack of vigorous enforcement of antidiscrimination legislation and the increasing segregation of blacks and some Hispanic groups in U.S. cities have resulted in a reversal of the 20-year trend toward decreasing school segregation (cited in Celis, 1993c). These dramatic findings are likely to stimulate renewed efforts to develop policies to promote desegregation. Although few groups wish to resort to busing, it is likely that in many cities there will be renewed attempts to bus children to achieve racial integration. In addition, an increasing number of state courts will hear lawsuits challenging school-funding formulas that favor segregated suburban school districts over those with higher concentrations of poor minority residents. At this writing, such suits are pending in more than 25 states.

Recognition of the problems of segregated and unequal schooling is also likely to spur efforts to increase funding for preschool programs that address the needs of children in communities where segregation and discrimination have produced persistently high rates of school failure. **Head Start** is a blanket term that refers to federally funded preschool programs aimed at preparing disadvantaged children for school. They are quite popular among parents, administrators, and education activists.

At its inception in the 1960s and during its early years, Head Start was a showcase program. Early studies found improvements of 8 to 10 points in the IQs of 480 children in a Head Start program conducted in Baltimore in the summer of 1965 (Levitan, 1968). These immediate, measurable gains in cognitive achievement heralded an enormous expansion of Head Start operations and a push for year-long programs throughout the country. From small beginnings, Head Start grew until it cost several hundred million dollars a year, served approximately 400,000 children, and was widely supported.

The initial goals of Head Start and its early popularity obscured some basic flaws. First, although the concept of early intervention was popular among researchers on child development, and their research did in fact suggest that there is real potential for intellectual improvement through early-childhood training, there remain few unchallenged guidelines for exactly what is to be taught, how, when, and by whom. Second, it is argued that Head Start does too little, too late, to be effective. According to this view, the most important period in a child's emotional, social, and intellectual development is the first three years of life, when the child begins to acquire language and learns to manipulate his or her surroundings. Parents, not teachers, therefore, are the most important educators, and for intervention to be effective, it must begin during infancy in the child's own home. (These issues are discussed further in Chapter 13.)

Although funds for Head Start were not cut during the 1980s, when many other social programs were scaled back, funding has not been sufficient either to expand the programs or to train and adequately compensate needed personnel. In consequence, of the 2.5 million poor preschool-age children in the United States, only one in five is currently enrolled in Head Start or an equivalent high-quality preschool program. Although an increasing proportion of high-income parents are sending their children to the best preschool programs they can find and afford, low-income parents, whose children are most in need of such programs, are finding them unavailable or fully enrolled. To meet the pressing need for more openings for low-income minority

Project Head Start, a preschool enrichment program for disadvantaged children, was begun in the 1960s. Evaluations of the achievements of children from Head Start programs indicate that such programs have lasting beneficial effects that more than justify their expense.

children, foundations and child advocacy groups are demanding a major expansion of Head Start programs. Because the federal government had a major budget surplus in 2000, advocates of Head Start began making efforts to convince legislators to expand the programs and to greatly increase the number of after-school centers for disadvantaged children as well. It is not clear at this writing what the results of that effort will be. (See Figure 9–3.)

Some Trends and Prospects

What lies ahead for minority groups? Most experts agree that minorities will have to continually struggle to hold on to past gains in the face of increased racism in American society. Today minority groups find it difficult, if not impossible, to maintain the foothold they have gained in the job market through affirmative-action and equal employment opportunity programs. Government jobs, which make up a sizable portion of minority employment opportunities, are becoming less numerous. When the federal government eliminates functions and departments, the number of blacks and Hispanics with secure public-sector jobs decreases markedly.

The minority employment picture is even more dismal in the private sector. Even when government regulatory commissions are fully funded, discrimination in hiring and employment is more difficult to uncover and correct in the private sector than in the public sector. With only partial funding and a relaxation of regulation and

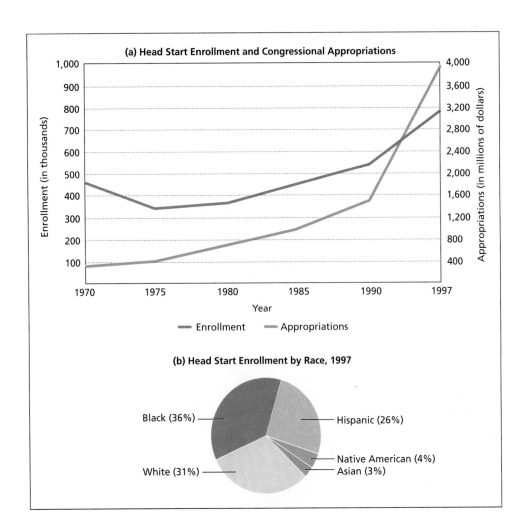

Figure 9–3 The Growing Importance of Early Childhood Education

Source: Data from *Statistical Abstract,* 1999.

enforcement, it becomes even harder to combat discrimination—the more so as competition among racial groups increases at the lower end of the labor market.

There is also renewed controversy over the efficacy of bilingual education programs. Designed to bridge the cultural gap that Spanish-speaking children experience in English-speaking schools, as well as to facilitate learning, bilingual education programs have been sponsored both by the federal Department of Education and by various state departments of education. At present such programs are in danger of being curtailed, if not entirely eliminated.

CURRENT CONTROVERSIES

Immigration

Should legal immigration to the United States be curtailed? Are immigrants a threat to the social mobility of African Americans and other minority groups that experienced racism and discrimination earlier in U.S. history? Should immigrants qualify for the same social benefits as citizens? These and many related questions are high on the political and policy agenda in the United States. Welfare reform policies single out illegal immigrants, and in some cases legal immigrants, for restrictions of benefits. Congress is now debating a new round of restrictions on the flow of legal immigrants into the United States.

Immigration is also a burning issue in many other nations, especially in western Europe, where anti-immigration sentiment is on the rise and is inspiring the hopes of nativist political parties, just as it is in the United States. *Nativism* is the idea that only native-born persons deserve the full benefits of citizenship and that foreigners are a danger to the stability of the society. Nativism is an old issue in nations with histories of immigration. But why is it undergoing such a resurgence now? Many of the answers to these questions depend on some knowledge of the current immigration situation in the United States and other countries.

The U.S. Immigration Act of 1986 increased the quotas of immigrants significantly and at the same time attempted to decrease the flow of illegal immigration from Mexico and other nations (Portes & Rumbaut, 1990). Legal immigration increased from a level of about 60,000 per year to more than 900,000 (counting refugees, who are included under another law). Some of the major supporters of the increased quotas were employers represented by the U.S. Chambers of Commerce and the National Association of Manufacturers. The employers were frank in their argument that the nation needed the energies and motivation of workers who were willing to produce well at low wages. But in the ensuing decade it proved difficult to decrease the flow of illegal immigrants. At the same time, legal immigrants made their presence felt quite dramatically in certain areas of the country, particularly in the Northeast, Florida, California, and Texas.

Social scientists who study U.S. immigration argue that the combined flow of legal and illegal immigrants is not enough, in a nation with a low overall birthrate, to significantly disrupt the economy, and in fact it can be a spur to economic growth (Waldinger, 1996). Although this may be true, increasing numbers of citizens in California and other immigrant-receiving areas feel otherwise, and this perception of economic and social competition from immigrants has clearly stimulated the rise of nativist feelings.

At this writing it is not clear how restrictive immigration policies will become in the United States. Congress will again consider immigration reform and will no doubt again debate measures designed to decrease immigration, both legal and illegal. But an unusual coalition is emerging, made up of representatives of high-technology industries, civil rights groups, immigrant and ethnic associations, and some conservative research organizations, all of which argue in favor of continued high levels of immigration (Schmitt, 1996). So while it is not clear how restrictive the new immigration policies will become, it is apparent that immigration is changing the nature of minority affairs in the United States. There are so many new groups representing different ethnic and racial backgrounds in the nation's largest cities that simple distinctions like "black and white" are less and less relevant, and the building of new coalitions among older and newer minorities is a major political trend.

Native Americans fare no better than members of other minority groups in education and health care. Operating under a severely restricted budget, the Bureau of Indian Affairs can no longer provide adequate social-welfare services to the thousands of Native Americans who live on reservations. Native Americans also face serious divisions within their own tribes as opposing factions struggle over the issue of how mineral rights on their lands should be handled.

In response to attacks on affirmative action, school desegregation, and many other policies designed to integrate American society, and perhaps as a consequence of continuing immigration into the nation's large cities, minority groups are increasingly developing a form of "identity politics." (See the Current Controversies feature on page 283.) This trend emphasizes the need for a minority group to recognize its own culture within the larger society and to work to develop strong schools, strong neighborhoods, and new forms of employment. Critics of identity politics fear that it will further divide the United States into competing ethnic and racial groups (Gitlin, 1996). But others, like Cornel West (1994), argue that "without some redistribution of wealth and power, downward mobility [especially of minority group members] will continue to drive people into desperate channels" (p. 116).

Beyond Left & Right

Conservatives tend to dislike affirmative action because it often discriminates against individuals who themselves are not responsible for past patterns of racism and discrimination. Liberals want to redress old patterns of racial and ethnic inequality and argue that when other considerations are equal, race or descent may be valid criteria for allocating scarce resources like scholarships.

Where do you stand on these difficult issues? Most likely you are among the majority who would like to see less racism and discrimination and more equality but are also opposed to "reverse discrimination." So what solutions do sociologists propose?

William J. Wilson and many others argue for race-blind social policies that will not create reverse discrimination but will address past patterns of racism and the inequalities they engendered. Such policies would create jobs where there is high unemployment and increase educational and training opportunities wherever people need them, thus dealing with the needs of people on a class basis rather than in terms of their race or ethnic status. Many conservatives have doubts about any government-sponsored program to deal with inequality, but they are more willing to entertain such race-blind policies than those directed at particular groups.

SUMMARY

- The United States has a long history of inequality. Although much progress has been made toward legal equality as a result of the civil rights movement, inequality remains a significant problem in American society.

- Racial minorities are made up of people who share certain inherited characteristics. Ethnic minorities are made up of people who may share certain cultural features and who regard themselves as a unified group. The principal characteristic of any minority group is subordinate status in society.

- Racism is behavior motivated by the belief that human races have distinctive characteristics that determine abilities and cultures. Discrimination is the differential treatment of individuals on the basis of their perceived membership in a particular social group. It is overt behavior. People rationalize it on the ground that those against whom they discriminate are less worthy of respect or fair treatment than people like themselves. This reasoning results in prejudice against the subordinate group.

- Prejudice and discrimination have several sources. Among these are individual psychological factors, including frustration-aggression (which involves displacing anger onto a scapegoat) and projection (in which people attribute their own undesirable traits to others). Other factors include social structure (especially economic competition and exploitation) and the norms and stereotypes of a particular culture.

■ Institutional discrimination is discrimination that is built into the structure and form of society itself. In the United States this kind of discrimination is especially evident in the educational system. Here the most prominent issue is achievement in school. Desegregation through busing is largely considered to have been a failure, but no alternative strategies have been suggested.

■ Another area in which institutional discrimination is evident is housing. Housing segregation is widespread, with the clearest division being between whites in the suburbs and blacks and other minority groups in the cities. Among the causes of housing segregation is racial steering by real estate agents.

■ Discrimination is also prevalent in employment, often as a direct result of discrimination in education. Those who lack education are often underemployed or unemployed, which results in low incomes and the likelihood of a poor education for the next generation. Even when their educational levels are similar, however, blacks and members of other minority groups are often paid less than whites.

■ Members of minority groups are more likely than whites to be arrested and charged with a crime. Following arrest, they face discrimination under the bail system, in which those who lack the money to post bail must wait in jail for their cases to come to trial.

■ Prejudice and discrimination have a number of harmful consequences. Among the most destructive is lack of self-esteem among those who are discriminated against. Other reactions are separatism and protest, sometimes leading to riots. There are many indications that racism and racial stereotypes persist, including violence directed against blacks, as well as more subtle forms of racism like patronizing remarks.

■ The gains made by minority groups since the 1960s faced major challenges in the 1990s and continue to do so. Affirmative action and equal employment opportunity have come under attack. Efforts to increase educational equality through preschool programs have been more successful, and advocates of Head Start are seeking to convince legislators to expand the program.

KEY TERMS

racial minorities, p. 257
ethnic minorities, p. 257
assimilation, p. 257
endogamy, p. 258
racism, p. 259
discrimination, p. 259

prejudice, p. 260
scapegoat, p. 261
projection, p. 261
social norm, p. 263
homogamy, p. 263
stereotyping, p. 264

institutional discrimination, p. 266
de jure segregation, p. 268
de facto segregation, p. 268
racial steering, p. 271
affirmative action, p. 278
Head Start, p. 281

INTERNET EXERCISE

The web destinations for Chapter 9 are related to different aspects of racism, prejudice, and discrimination. To begin your explorations, go to the Prentice Hall Companion Website: **http://prenhall.com/kornblum**. Then choose **Chapter 9** (Racism, Prejudice, and Discrimination). Next, select **destinations** from the menu on the left side of the screen. There are a variety of sites to investigate. We suggest that you begin with **The Immigration Superhighway**. When you access this site, look for "Articles" and then click on "Immigration Debate." The *Current Controversies* feature in this chapter focuses on the question of whether legal immigration to the United States should be curtailed. In this feature, the text points out that it is not clear how restrictive new immigration policies will become. Further, it is apparent that immigration is changing the nature of minority affairs in the United States. The "Immigration Debate" article within the Immigration Superhighway site offers a number of different points of view on the subject. After you have explored this site, answer the following questions:

■ Do you believe that immigration to the United States should be curtailed or encouraged? Why?

■ What special interest groups in our society benefit from legal immigration?

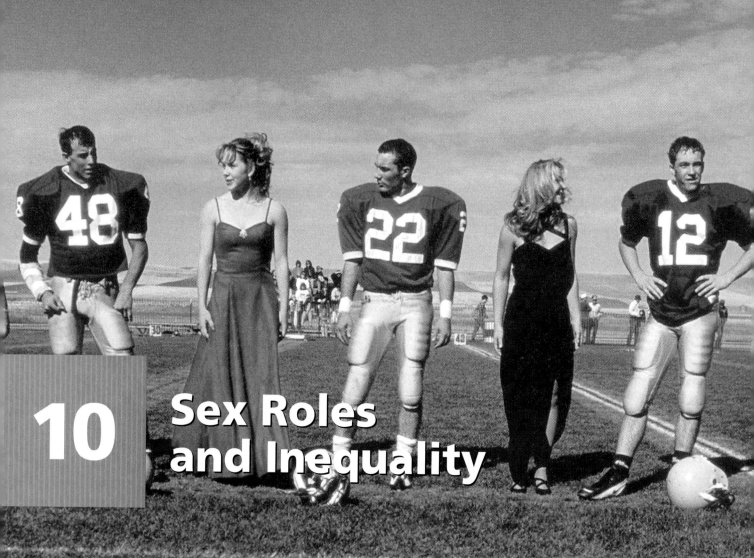

10 Sex Roles and Inequality

FACTS ABOUT

SEX ROLES AND INEQUALITY

- In 1998 the median earnings of women who worked full time were about 76 percent of those of men.

- Women are three times as likely as men to have had interruptions in their work history because of child-bearing, child care, illness, disability, and unemployment.

- Victimization surveys reveal that an estimated 115,000 women were raped in 1997, and another 79,000 were subjected to unsuccessful rape attempts.

- Jobs held mainly by women are paid at rates that average 20 percent below those for equivalent jobs held mainly by men.

OUTLINE

Traditional Sex Roles

The Nature of Sexism
Power and Male Hegemony
Stereotyping
Sexism and Employment
Sexual Harassment
Homemaking
The Women's Movement

Sources of Sexism
Socialization
Education
The Family
Language and the Media
Organized Religion
Government
The Legal System

Social Policy
Changes in Child-rearing
   Practices
Changes in the Educational
   System
Changes in the Legal System
Reproductive Control
Social Policy and the
   Women's Movement
Changes in Men's Roles

Over the past several decades, women have made many notable gains. They are increasingly entering occupations that were traditionally dominated by men—28.9 percent of mathematical and computer scientists are women, for example, as are 28.6 percent of lawyers and judges. Moreover, the gap between the earnings of men and women is narrowing. In 1998 the median earnings of women who worked full time were about 76 percent of those of men, compared to 68 percent in 1985 (*Statistical Abstract*, 1999). The remaining gap can be explained largely by differences in education and work experiences. A significant obstacle to income equality is the fact that women are three times as likely as men to have had interruptions in their work history because of childbearing, child care, illness, disability, and unemployment.

On the world scene, women's opinions and desires are taking on ever greater significance. Delegates to the 1995 international conference in Beijing focused with great intensity on such problems as "the feminization of poverty," "women's human rights," "violence against women," and the changing situation of women in a globalizing economy (Mbere, 1996). Participants from the United States and other industrialized nations returned home with a new understanding about how powerful the growing influence of women's networks are becoming throughout the world (Simpson, 1996). In many impoverished regions, it is the efforts of women to form economic cooperatives, develop women's reproductive health clinics, and carry forward the fight for women's political rights that provide the greatest impetus to positive social change and economic development. But in these and many other regions, the extent to which women remain subordinate to men, a subordination that is often reinforced by religious norms, remains a severe obstacle to further development.

Despite the gains of recent decades, sex discrimination and stereotyping continue to limit the opportunities of women. Globally, woman are beset by hunger and violence far more than men. In the United States, women are still shunted into the "girl's ghetto": housekeeping; retail trades; insurance; real estate; and service positions such as secretary, receptionist, telephone operator, and clerk. About 59 percent of working women in the United States are employed in these kinds of jobs (Hartmann, 1994). There are 9 female senators and 56 female

TABLE 10–1 Median Weekly Earnings of Full-time Wage and Salary Workers, 1997

Occupation	Women	Men
Total[a]	$24,973	$33,674
Executive, administrators, and managerial	33,037	50,149
Professional specialty	35,417	50,402
Technical and related support	27,576	37,705
Sales	21,392	35,655
Admin. support, incl. clerical	22,474	29,442
Precision production, craft and repair	21,649	31,496
Machine operators, assemblers, and inspectors	17,683	26,969
Transportation and material moving	21,024	28,227
Handlers, equipment cleaners, helpers, and laborers	15,774	21,475
Service workers	15,964	22,335
Private household	12,648	[b]
Service, except private household	16,120	22,359
Farming, forestry, and fishing	17,301	17,394

[a]Includes persons whose longest job was in the Armed Forces.
[b]Base less than 75,000

Source: Adapted from *Statistical Abstract,* 1999.

representatives in the U.S. Congress. In both chambers the numbers doubled during the 1990s, but few women think the present proportions are sufficient, especially since women make up more than 50 percent of the population. Even when women are in the same professions or occupations as men, their salaries are lower; subtle and persistent discrimination in employment and salaries is still widespread. (Table 10–1 shows the wage gap for selected occupations.)

In the 1970s and early 1980s, efforts to combat these inequalities centered on ratification of the Equal Rights Amendment to the U.S. Constitution. However, by the June 30, 1982, deadline for ratification, only 35 of the required 38 states had ratified the amendment. The amendment was reintroduced in Congress in 1983, but in the House of Representatives it fell six votes short of the two-thirds majority needed to send it to the states for ratification. Thus, women do not yet have legal assurance of equal rights in American society.

Traditional Sex Roles

In Chapter 9 we suggested that prejudice—a predisposition to regard a certain group in a certain way—often becomes the justification for discriminatory behavior. That is, if we believe that a certain group is "inferior" or "different," we can easily defend less-than-equal treatment of its members. We also suggested that the norms of society are an important source of prejudice and discrimination. If an entire society is prejudiced against a certain group and discriminates against it, such actions will be accepted as natural and right by most members of that society.

Until fairly recently, it was widely accepted that the only desirable roles for a woman were wife, mother, and homemaker and that her entire life should revolve around them. The roles themselves emphasized that a woman should be nurturing and skilled in the emotional aspects of personal relationships. A man, on the other hand, was expected to be a leader and provider, a highly rational person who would not let emotions get in the way of action. These expectations often caused men to deny their emotions and thus made them less able to enjoy many aspects of life in their families and communities.

Betty Friedan (1963) was one of the first contemporary feminists to identify and criticize the traditional view of female roles, which she labeled "the feminine mystique":

> The feminine mystique says that the highest value and the only commitment for women is the fulfillment of their own femininity. It says that the great mistake of Western culture, through most of its history, has been the undervaluation of this femininity. It says this femininity is so mysterious and intuitive and close to the creation and origin of life that man-made science may never be able to understand it. But however special and different, it is in no way inferior to the nature of man; it may even in certain respects be superior. The mistake, says the mystique, the root of women's troubles in the past, is that women envied men, women tried to be like men, instead of accepting their own nature, which can find fulfillment only in sexual passivity, male domination, and nurturing maternal love. . . . The new mystique makes the housewife-mothers, who never had a chance to be anything else, the model for all women . . . a pattern by which all women must now live or deny their femininity. (p. 43)

So pervasive was this view, and so thoroughly was it internalized by both men and women, that Friedan called women's dissatisfaction with their traditional roles "the problem that has no name."

Today many people think of the traditional roles of women and men as somewhat outdated. At the time that Friedan (1963) wrote her book, the traditional roles formed the basis for social behavior. Women were considered too delicate to do "men's work" and therefore were legally denied many career and job opportunities. Men were supposed to be dominant and unemotional, to "act like a man." For women, chastity and fidelity were considered major virtues; for men, promiscuity was considered natural. Women and men were thought to be different and hence were treated differently by social institutions—including the government and the legal system. The entire range of social norms and values reflected different standards of behavior for men and women, which few people questioned.

This double standard is not unique to our society. In many Latin American and Muslim countries, the status of women is far more subordinate than in our own. Few women in those societies have the freedom that men have or are able to pursue careers outside the home. And although women in eastern European countries have greater equality with men, disparities exist there as well. For example, most of the physicians in Russia are women, but female physicians receive lower pay than male physicians.

This traditional hierarchy is extremely resistant to change. Women and men are shaped by the culture in which they are raised, so that most adults are thoroughly indoctrinated or socialized for the roles their culture has prescribed for them. Change is suspect because it threatens their identity. Thus, many women oppose attempts to give them equal status with men. It was a women's organization—

In traditional Muslim society, women are not permitted to show their face or other parts of their body outside the home. Although many women accept this norm and feel that it protects them, others believe that it conflicts with their desire for greater equality in their society.

Stop-ERA, led by Phyllis Schlafly—that led the battle to prevent ratification of the Equal Rights Amendment.

It seems clear that there is considerable variation in the types of behavior that are considered appropriate for men and for women and that to a large extent these behaviors reflect the values of a particular society more than any innate or "natural" qualities. Whereas it was once supposed that behavioral differences between men and women are innate, today we know that these differences are largely learned through socialization. And although it was once believed that there are universal standards of masculine and feminine behavior, in fact the standards in other societies are very different from our own (Richmond-Abbott, 1992).

In the 1950s, sex researcher John Money and his colleagues found that the best predictor of a person's sexual identity is not his or her physiological sex but the sex he or she was assigned at birth. Specifically, male children who had been incorrectly identified as female and raised as females, or female children who had been raised as males, identified themselves as members of the other sex even after their true physical sex became known to them (Money et al., 1955). For reasons such as this, many researchers use the term **gender identity** to refer to a person's sexual self-image and to distinguish it from physiological sex.

The role of biological factors in determining sex roles and sexual behavior is again becoming one of the most exciting and controversial fields of research on gender and sexuality (Horton, 1995). This research is particularly relevant in disputes over whether homosexuality is a lifestyle choice or an expression of immutable genetic traits. Recent research by Simon Le Vay and Dean Hamer, for example, offers partial evidence for genetic explanations of sexual behavior; they discovered certain differences in the hypothalmus—a small region at the base of the brain known to influence sexual behavior—between homosexual and heterosexual individuals (Hamer & Copeland, 1995; Le Vay, 1995). Although there are no definitive answers, it is becoming quite clear that biological and social influences on gender and sexuality must be better understood.

Alice Rossi (1984) argues that "gender differentiation is not simply a function of socialization. . . . It is grounded in a sex dimorphism that serves the fundamental purpose of reproducing the species. . . . Theories that neglect these characteristics of sex and gender carry a high risk of eventual irrelevance" (p. 1). Rossi considers the biological differences between the sexes to be a major source of "masculine" and "feminine" traits, but she writes that "masculine qualities and feminine qualities do not preclude each other in the same person, although that combination is still not prevalent in American society" (p. 14).

Jan Morris, a respected British author and social commentator who was one of the first people to undergo a sex-change operation, offers the following insight:

> We are told that the social gap between the sexes is narrowing, but I can only report that having, in the second half of the 20th century, experienced life in both roles, there seems to be no aspect of existence, no moment of the day, no contact, no arrangement, no response, which is not different for men and women. . . . I discovered that even now men prefer women to be less able, less talkative, and certainly less self-centered than they are themselves. (quoted in Bleier, 1984, p. 80)

Morris's description of her experiences is an apt illustration of the phenomenon that has come to be known as sexism.

The Nature of Sexism

Sexism is the counterpart of racism and ageism, which are discussed in Chapters 9 and 11, respectively. It may be defined as the "entire range of attitudes, beliefs, policies, laws, and behaviors discriminating against women (or against men) on the basis of their gender" (Safilios-Rothschild, 1974, p. 1). In this section we will describe several factors that contribute to sexism around the world and in the United States.

Power and Male Hegemony

Sociologists who study gender relations call attention to persisting patterns of male dominance throughout the institutions of modern societies. R. W. Connell (1995), for example, has analyzed how dramatic inequalities in the distribution of power in societies often deprive women of opportunities to realize their full potential. Connell's research shows that wherever possible, males attempt to preserve their hegemony (controlling power) over women. In relations marked by hegemony, domination by one group, class, or gender over another is achieved by a combination of political and ideological means. Although political power or coercion is always important, ideologies can be equally important. In gender relations these ideologies differ from one culture to another. In parts of the Islamic world, male dominance is enforced by religious principles that emphasize female dominance over the home and male dominance over the world outside the home. In parts of the United States, ideologies that portray men as soldiers, athletic heros, and managerial leaders, and women as homemakers and nurturant spouses, reinforce male dominance.

Connell's (1995) work shows that in much of the industrialized world men still have much greater access to cultural prestige, political authority, corporate power, individual wealth, and material comforts than women. Individual men or small groups may be confused or insecure about these inequalities. Others, such as gay men or men with feminist ideals, may join with women in rejecting male hegemony. But despite all the recent feminist criticism and despite all the documented struggles by women to assert their equality and make gains in the workplace, men continue to be dominant. With some notable exceptions (the occasional woman boss or female political leader), male-female relations are structured so that women are subordinate. This subordination is reinforced by the symbolic equation of masculinity and power.

One of the unfortunate aspects of ideologies that support male dominance is that even people who are victimized by them tend to believe that they are true. Thus, many women have attitudes that are prejudicial to women, causing them to undervalue the work of other women and to set up psychological barriers to their own achievement. Matina Horner (1970) found that many women were motivated to avoid success, fearing that the more ambitious and successful they became, the less feminine they would be. Recent research on the influence of stereotypes focuses on how women may become obsessed with their appearance and their efforts to please males or to live up to an image of femininity that is largely created by men. Sharlene Hesse-Biber (1996) attributes the rise of problems like anorexia and compulsive dieting to the commercialization of images of women's bodies and the prevalent notion that one cannot be too thin.

Power held by men creates significant barriers to equality since men still hold most positions of authority in American society. Although it appears that affirmative-action policies and efforts to combat sexual harassment have made male managers more sensitive to gender issues in the workplace, incidents like the Tailhook scandal—in which former Navy Lieutenant Paula Coughlin and at least 82 other women were assaulted by navy and marine fighter pilots at the 1991 Tailhook convention—are reminders of how serious the situation can become in organizations with a dominant male culture (Faludi, 1994; Francke, 1994).

In her study of gender and sex roles, sociologist Cynthia Epstein (1993) found that there have been many positive changes in corporations and the professions but that inadvertent and at times open hostility toward women remains a problem in many organizations. The continuing presence of sexism is revealed by the fact that white males still hold about 95 percent of the top management jobs in major corporations (Silver, 1990).

Women are demonstrating their ability to serve as soldiers in combat, but recent scandals concerning harassment have kept problems of gender relations in the armed forces in the public spotlight.

Stereotyping

As we saw in Chapter 9, one source of prejudice and discrimination is stereotyping—attributing a fixed and usually unfavorable and inaccurate conception to a category of people. Stereotypes often make it easier to justify unequal treatment of the stereotyped person or group.

Among the traditional stereotypes about women is the belief that they are naturally passive, domestic, and envious. It is this set of stereotypes that Friedan (1963) lumped together and labeled "the feminine mystique." However, Marc Fasteau (1974) has pointed out that there is a "masculine mystique" as well—a set of stereotypes about men that limits their ability to function fully and effectively. The masculine stereotype is that all men are tough, unemotional, and dominant; and however unrealistic and inaccurate this stereotype is, many men (and women) believe it. Many men avoid performing traditionally "female" tasks, such as washing dishes or working as a secretary, for fear that their masculinity will be questioned. And men who might prefer the role of homemaker feel compelled to seek careers in business because they have been socialized to believe that domestic work is not masculine.

Not only does the masculine stereotype limit the freedom of men to engage in any activity or occupation they choose, but it also limits their personal relationships. Many men believe that they cannot discuss their feelings with other men. Instead, they tend to be extremely competitive. They also feel compelled to try to dominate women instead of relating to them as equals (Benokraitis & Feagin, 1986; Gould, 1974; Kimmel & Messner, 1992). (See Chapter 6 for a discussion of the effects of male socialization on crime patterns.)

Sexism and Employment

Sexism is perhaps most evident in the employment status of women. Women are concentrated in lower-status jobs at the low end of the pay scale. The vast majority of retail clerks, typists, and secretaries are women, whereas men account for by far the largest proportions of corporate directors, white-collar administrators, and blue-collar supervisors. It could be claimed that these differences are due to differences in educational attainment. However, as Table 10–2 shows, this is not the case. For the past several decades men and women have received the same amount of schooling. Although men hold more bachelor's and graduate degrees than women do, more men than women drop out of high school, so that the average educational attainment is the same in each group (England & Farkas, 1986; England, Herbert, & Kilbourne, 1994).

The difference in the average number of years of work experience is a more useful explanation of the income gap between men and women. Various studies (e.g., Corcoran & Duncan, 1979; Mincer & Polachek, 1974; Sandell & Shapiro, 1978) have found that between one-quarter and one-half of the income gap can be accounted for by interruptions in the work histories of women. Corcoran and Duncan (1979) found that the most important factor is the number of years a worker has been with his or her current employer, especially the years during which the employee receives training.

Table 10–2 indicates that since 1970 there have been significant increases in the proportion of women in formerly male occupations like engineering, economics, and public service. Note, however, that occupations like secretary, teacher, and nurse continue to be dominated by women. And recent research shows that despite their increased ability to enter male-dominated occupations, women in those occupations still earn 20 percent less, on the average, than men.

This type of pay inequity, as well as unequal access to certain jobs, has given rise to debates over "comparable worth"—the idea that the pay levels of certain jobs should be adjusted so that they reflect the intrinsic value of the job; holders of jobs of comparable value would then be paid at comparable rates. This concept is discussed in more detail in the Social Policy section of the chapter.

Wage and job discrimination are illegal under the Equal Pay Act of 1963 and the Civil Rights Act of 1964, yet they continue to exist. About 3,000 charges of sex discrimination are filed with the Equal Employment Opportunity Commission each year. One way that such discrimination works was demonstrated by Levinson (1975) in a study of job inquiries. Levinson selected several classified advertisements in newspapers and defined the jobs as "male" or "female," depending on their present sex composition. Male researchers inquired by telephone about the traditionally female jobs (e.g., secretary), and female researchers inquired about traditionally male jobs (e.g., auto mechanic). Then the procedure was reversed: The researchers of each sex called to inquire about jobs that were considered appropriate for them. Levinson found that in 35 percent of all cases there was clear-cut sex discrimination. Male inquirers for a secretarial job, for example, were told that the job had been filled, whereas subsequent female callers were encouraged to apply. Sometimes the discrimination was more blunt. For example, women callers were told that "we don't hire girls as fuel attendants." Frequently male inquirers for "sex-inappropriate" jobs were encouraged to apply for higher-level management positions, whereas female callers were told to apply for lower-level jobs. Clearly, sex typing of jobs is a major part of sex discrimination.

In sum, there is a significant earnings gap between men and women in the American labor force. This is evident in Table 10–3, which shows women's earnings as a

TABLE 10–2 Proportion of Jobs in Selected Occupations Held by Women, 1970 and 1998

Occupation	1970	1998
	(Percent)	
Bartender	27	59
Chemist	17	29
Doctor	11	37
Economist	14	45
Farmer	7	17
Industrial engineer	3	26
Lawyer, judge	6	33
Librarian	84	85
Nurse	91	94
Police, detective	5	14
Psychologist	43	61
Public official	24	59
Secretary	98	98
Teacher	74	74

Source: Data from Program for Applied Research, Queens College; *Current Population Survey.*

TABLE 10–3 Pay of Women Employed Full Time, Year Round, as a Percentage of Pay of Men for Selected Years

Year	Women's Earnings As Percentage of Men's
1968	58.5
1972	57.4
1976	60.0
1980	60.5
1983	64.3
1985	65.0
1988	67.8
1990	71.8
1992	75.4
1995	75.5
2000	80.0

Source: Adapted from England and Farkas, 1986; Hacker, 1999.

percentage of men's. It can also be seen in Table 10–4, which compares indicators of gender inequality in the United States and in selected European nations. Although the United States has significantly higher proportions of women, both single and married, in its labor force and enrolled in higher education, it has not achieved greater income equality than the other nations; in fact, it lags behind Austria and Great Britain (Davis & Robinson, 1991). Between 1950 and 1980, the sex difference in earnings remained remarkably constant, with women's median earnings about 60 percent of men's. Although the sex gap in pay has decreased since 1980—women's earnings now average about 75.5 percent of men's—there is still a long way to go before full equality is achieved.

Sexual Harassment

Among the most persistent and difficult aspects of sexism is sexual harassment, as noted earlier in the Tailhook example. The tumultuous Senate hearings on the confirmation of Clarence Thomas as a Supreme Court justice focused national attention on the range of behaviors that may be viewed as forms of sexual harassment. The charges leveled against Thomas by Anita Hill, a former employee, included making lewd and suggestive comments, requesting sexual favors, and similar behaviors that are often labeled "flirtation" when they occur outside the workplace. Partly as a result of the Hill-Thomas controversy and partly as a consequence of women's continual struggle against harassment, people throughout the nation have been drawn into a national debate over its nature and significance.

The controversy has focused on serious forms of harassment, including date rape, as well as on behaviors that are viewed as annoying if not dangerous. In 1993, for example, the students and faculty of Antioch College in Ohio published a set of written rules that require verbal consent at every stage of sexual intimacy. Although the rules have been the subject of much satire and derision, they represent a model for dealing with a highly sensitive and often taboo subject.

Such episodes are bringing people closer to a consensus about the norms of conduct between men and women. An increasing number of Americans are recognizing that one person's joke or offhand comment can create another's hostile environment.

TABLE 10–4 Indicators of Gender Inequality, Various Countries

Indicator	Austria	Germany	Great Britain	United States
Percent women employed	47.8	49.4	49.9	66.0
Percent women employed full time	35.1	35.0	29.7	49.8
Percent married women employed	42.0	44.8	46.3	59.9
Percent college students who are female	41.1	41.9	37.3	51.7
Women's annual earnings as percent of men's for full time only	71.5	59.9	64.0	61.9

Source: Nancy J. Davis and Robert V. Robinson, "Men's and Women's Consciousness of Gender Inequality," *American Sociological Review* 56 (1991), pp. 72–84.

In an attempt to provide a less subjective description of sexual harassment, the Michigan Task Force on Sexual Harassment developed the following definition:

> [**Sexual harassment**] includes continual or repeated verbal abuse of a sexual nature, including but not limited to graphic commentaries on the victim's body, sexually suggestive objects or postures in the workplace, sexually degrading words used to describe the victim, or propositions of a sexual nature. Sexual harassment also includes the threat or insinuation that lack of sexual submission will adversely affect the victim's employment, wages, standing, or other conditions that affect the victim's livelihood. (Stover & Gillies, 1987, p. 1)

Although sexual harassment has been a common feature of work and community life for well over a century, the problem came under public scrutiny only recently as a result of court decisions and government attempts to punish offenders. (See Figure 10–1.) Many thousands of complaints of sexual harassment are filed each year in agencies at all levels of government; of these, less than 10 percent are filed by men (Richmond-Abbott, 1992). The formal complaints represent a small fraction of the incidents of harassment that occur in workplaces, schools, community associations, and public settings (Hippensteele & Pearson, 1999).

Even rape, the most brutal form of violence against women short of murder, is significantly underreported, often because women fear the stigma of having been raped more than they desire justice. Data from the FBI show that in 1997 just over 96,000 rapes were reported to local police departments; of those incidents, just over 40,000 resulted in arrests. But victimization surveys reveal that an estimated 115,000 women were raped in 1997, and another 79,000 were subjected to unsuccessful rape attempts, for a combined total that is twice the number of reported rapes (Hacker, 1999). (See the Critical Research feature on page 296.)

Homemaking

In a review of research on changing sex roles and housework, sociologist Janet Z. Giele (1988) observes that women continue to bear the primary responsibility for child care and housework even if they are employed. In the past 20 years men with working wives have begun to take on a greater share of this burden, but inequalities remain. Time budget studies show that when one measures solo time spent with children, fathers average 4.5 hours a week and mothers 19.6 hours; however, men with working wives who themselves support nontraditional sex roles spend significantly more time with their children than do men who lack such ideals. Researchers have also noted that wealth permits working couples to displace housework and child care responsibilities onto hired domestic helpers, which may ease their burden but also increases inequalities of race and class in their communities.

Elsewhere in the world, especially in Asia, Africa, and many parts of Latin America, homemaking remains a predominant concern of women. Indeed, while they may be involved in producing or selling goods and services, third-world women are also responsible for much of the work that sustains life in rural villages and small towns. In consequence, experts often point to the need for literacy programs and reproductive and public health instruction as vital to the future of women's efforts to become fully empowered citizens of their nations. These demands were

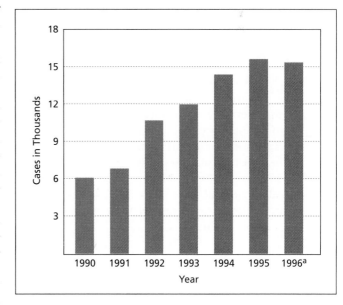

Figure 10–1   Reported Incidents of Sexual Harrassment, 1990–1996

[a]Preliminary.

Source: Organization for Economic Cooperation and Development.

CRITICAL RESEARCH

Catharine MacKinnon: Anti-Harassment Warrior

Law school professor, scholar, and pioneering social scientist Catharine A. MacKinnon is no stranger to controversy. Indeed, in some circles she is seen as the embodiment of the strident feminist activist. This is not a label she accepts, but she is far more concerned about winning support for her battle against the harassment of women in all walks of life than in being known as a nice person or a sweet and gentle woman.

One of the reasons MacKinnon is so controversial is that she is relentless in her opposition to pornography and its concentration in retail districts of cities and towns. Her campaign against pornography has resulted in the enactment of laws in some cities, notably Minneapolis and New York, that restrict retailers' ability to market pornographic materials. Recently she has taken her battle against pornography to so-called virtual pornography on the Internet. MacKinnon knows the risks to freedom of speech but prefers to speak out against pornographic exploitation:

> Real acts must be performed, usually on women, to make visual pornography. Real acts are typically performed by men when they use it. Real acts are inflicted upon many women every day as a result of its consumption. Andrea Dworkin and I, with others, have exposed the active role of pornography in sex inequality. The acts are real, not a conceptual game. The empirical evidence, including testimony from experience, is clear. Not all consumers of pornography act out aggressively, but many do, and not only the predisposed. Not all come to believe that women are lesser forms of life and live to be raped, but many do, including so-called normal men. How many can we afford? No one learns respect for women from pornography. (MacKinnon, 1995, p.7)

MacKinnon's major contribution to the laws against gender discrimination may lie in her successful struggle to convince the courts that sexual harassment and a sexualized work environment are actually forms of discrimination against women (and, in some cases, against men). Before the publication of MacKinnon's articles and book (*Sexual Harassment of Working Women*, 1979), most judges (the vast majority of whom were

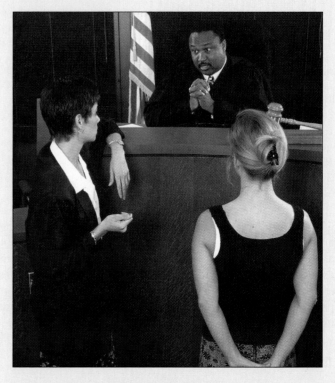

Catharine McKinnon's pathbreaking attacks on sexual harassment have been taken up by other lawyers throughout the nation.

males) "took male privilege for granted, accepted men's sexual overtures toward women as natural compliments, rather than as hostile discrimination. A supervisor's retaliation was seen as an understandable, if somewhat cowardly, response to an embarrassing personal rebuff."

MacKinnon's book examined the conduct of sexual relations in modern society and found exploitation and inequality to be extremely widespread. "Sexual harassment, in this view, was not simply an abuse of an employment position or an effort to exploit women's inferior status in the workplace. Rather, it was part of a broader dynamic. Sexual harassment disadvantages women as a gender," argued MacKinnon; "the harm comes in a social context in which women's economic survival and sexual exploitation are constructed and joined to women's detriment." MacKinnon argues, therefore, that an antidiscrimination law should do more than merely pick out and condemn policies that were based on inaccurate or outmoded stereotypes. It should seek instead to eliminate the subordination of women. "With inequality 'sexualized,' and sexuality reinforcing gender inequality, sexual exploitation was seen as central to other forms of oppression of women by men."

Sexual Harassment of Working Women contributed to the eventual judicial recognition of sexual harassment as a form of sex discrimination, and it changed the perception of sexual harassment from a workplace hazard to a form of sexual abuse. It also changed the way in which constitutional equal protection law was taught in law schools.

MacKinnon's critics see her as one of the creators of "political correctness," or what they see as oversensitivity to issues of gender and race so that people are encouraged to eliminate any references to sex, appearance, race, or ethnicity from their everyday speech. But MacKinnon's greatest victory is the recognition that sexual overtures can indeed be intended as hostile. This point is now firmly fixed in law. For MacKinnon and her allies, if this means that men (and some women) will have to refrain from making jokes about each other's bodies or looks or sexual feelings it is a small price to pay for greater equality (Olsen, 1999).

voiced over and over again by delegates to the Beijing conference mentioned earlier, and they will continue to appear wherever the condition of rural women is addressed (Mbere, 1996).

The Women's Movement

The women's movement in the United States was officially founded in 1848, when a women's rights convention held in Seneca, New York, was attended by 300 women and men, many of whom, like Elizabeth Cady Stanton and Lucretia Mott, were active in the abolitionist movement. The Seneca convention endorsed a platform that called for the right of women to vote, to control their own property, and to obtain custody of their children after divorce. After women won the right to vote in the 1920s, the women's movement receded from public consciousness until the 1960s, a decade characterized by considerable activism and numerous social movements (Richmond-Abbott, 1992).

The resurgence of the movement in the 1960s occurred in a context of widespread social change. In 1963, the year in which Friedan's *The Feminine Mystique* appeared, the President's Commission on the Status of Women published its recommendations for equal opportunity in employment. In 1964 Congress passed the Civil Rights Act, which included a provision (Title VII) that made it illegal to discriminate against women in promotion and hiring. But the Equal Employment Opportunity Commission (EEOC), established to enforce Title VII, was unwilling to serve as a watchdog for women's rights. As a result, in 1966 a pressure group, the National Organization for Women (NOW), was founded. Its stated purpose was "to take action to bring women into full participation in the mainstream of American society *now,* exercising all the privileges and responsibilities thereof in truly equal partnership with men."

Attitudes about gender roles have undergone a major transformation since the resurgence of the women's movement. Although, as we have seen, significant inequalities and double standards continue to exist, they are far less sharply defined than they were in earlier decades. Survey researchers find, for example, that in the 1930s about 75 percent of all Americans disapproved of a woman earning money if she had a husband who was capable of supporting her. By 1978 that proportion had declined to 26 percent. In 1957 as many as 80 percent of respondents to opinion polls agreed that a woman who remained unmarried "must be 'sick,' 'neurotic,' or 'immoral.'" By 1994 the proportion who agreed with this idea had fallen to less than 20 percent (NORC, 1998). Many of these changes in attitudes were due to the impact of the women's movement and the changing nature of women's economic participation.

During the 1970s, women's political participation also increased steadily. The National Women's Political Caucus was founded in 1971; as a result of its efforts, 40

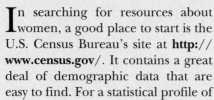

SOCIAL PROBLEMS ONLINE

Information About Women on the Internet

In searching for resources about women, a good place to start is the U.S. Census Bureau's site at **http:// www.census.gov/**. It contains a great deal of demographic data that are easy to find. For a statistical profile of the population, which includes data on women, go to the bureau's population profile (**http://www.census .gov/population/www/pop-profile**). The profile is divided into several short essays with colorful graphs on a number of topics, such as labor force participation and family arrangements, almost all of which compare women and men. Return to the bureau's home page and click on the Subjects A to Z box for a list of more than 100 categories. For example, W shows an entry for women-owned businesses that is linked to a page with data on minority- and women-owned enterprises categorized by gross receipts, number of employees, and annual payroll. The data are further divided by geographic area, industry, size of firm, and legal form of organization. Other areas that highlight the demographic differences between men and women include Household and Families, Immigration, and Poverty. The U.S. Department of Labor Women's Bureau (**http://dol.gov/dol/wb/**) offers labor-related statistics.

The Feminist Internet Gateway (**http://www. feminist .org/gateway/1_gatway.html**) has what it calls a "mediated listing of the best on the 'net" that provides links to web resources, both domestic and international. Among other topics covered are global feminism;

women and girls in sports; violence against women; and feminist arts, literature, and entertainment. For users interested in political organizations there is a link to the National Organization for Women (NOW), at **http://www.now.org**, which features calls for action, press releases and the NOW newspaper, as well as a history of the organization. A more conservative political organization is the Eagle Forum (**http://www.eagle forum.org/**).

Users interested in women's health issues can access Women's Health Interactive through the Feminist Internet Gateway or at **http://www.womens-health.com/** for interactive sessions led by health-care professionals. A typical session was a nutrition conference titled Menopause, Heart Disease, & You. These conferences occur regularly and are archived for later perusal. The Feminist Internet Gateway also has a compilation of list services with instructions on how to subscribe for discussions on topics pertaining to gender issues.

The University of Maryland's Women's Studies program has a web page at **http://www.inform.umd.edu: 8080/EdRes/Topic/WomensStudies/**. Downloadable reports on such issues as the glass ceiling, women's status in higher education, women in the work force, sex discrimination, and sexual harassment can be accessed there. For a comparative study of women's reproductive freedom, with a discussion of pertinent laws and policies in Brazil, China, Germany, India, Nigeria, and the United States, go to **http://www.echonyc.com/ ~jmkm/wotc.html**.

percent of the delegates to the 1972 Democratic political convention were women. Continued lobbying by women's political groups resulted in President Carter's appointment of more women to top positions in the government and judiciary than ever before. In 1981 President Reagan appointed the first woman to serve on the Supreme Court, and in 1997 President Clinton appointed the first female secretary of state.

In the late 1970s and early 1980s, the women's movement encountered increasing opposition, and its momentum slowed. The Equal Rights Amendment failed to obtain ratification by the required number of states. Opposition to more liberal abortion laws was well organized and vocal, and the movement faced severe challenges in several other areas. Nevertheless, reproductive choice remained a dominant theme of the movement, one that could unite women with diverse interests; this was evident in the massive free-choice rally in Washington, D.C., in 1988, which drew more than 500,000 marchers. With the election of President Clinton in 1992, the movement gained greater influence in Washington, and women voters played an important part in Clinton's reelection in 1996. However, in the face of a relatively unsympathetic Congress, feminist leaders feel that the movement needs to place far greater emphasis on mobilizing women to demand active government intervention in such areas as pay equity and protection against abuse (Hartmann, 1995a).

Sources of Sexism

We have described some of the causes of the subordination of women from a historical viewpoint and indicated some of the major inequities that women face in our society. In this section we will discuss in some detail the processes by which American institutions reinforce and perpetuate sexism.

Socialization

In her book *The Second Sex,* the famous French philosopher and sociologist Simone de Beauvoir (1961) described how as children women are often socialized for roles in which they are not expected to compete with men in any way. Often, she observed, women are discouraged from studying more challenging subjects like mathematics, science, and philosophy. Instead, they are expected to learn the domestic skills of cooking and running a household and the emotional skills of soothing children's and men's bruised feelings. These observations signal the immense importance of sex role socialization in forming our attitudes and behavior as men and women.

Socialization is the process whereby we learn to behave according to the norms of our culture. It includes all the formal and informal teaching that occurs in the home and in the school; among peers; and through agents of socialization like radio, television, the church, and other institutions (Kornblum, 2000). As Janet Chafetz (1974) has suggested, through socialization people internalize to varying degrees the roles, norms, and values of their culture and subculture, which become their guides to behavior and shape their deepest beliefs.

Most socialization takes place in the course of interaction with other people; how others react to what we do will eventually influence how we behave. We are also socialized through popular culture—largely through television, films, and books. Socialization may be consciously imposed, as in compulsory education, or it may be subtle and unconscious, conveyed in the nuances of language. According to Eleanor Maccoby and Carol Jacklin (1977), common myths about sex differences, such as "girls are more suggestible than boys" and "boys are more analytical than girls," reinforce sex role socialization.

In her review of research on gender socialization in families, Marie Richmond-Abbott (1992) notes,

> As infants become toddlers, parental interaction with them continues to be sex-differentiated. In certain studies, both parents emphasized achievement for boys and urged them to control their emotions. Both parents characterized their relationship to their daughters as having more warmth and physical closeness. They believed the daughters were more truthful and showed a reluctance to punish them. They discouraged rough-and-tumble play for girls and doll play for boys. They were more likely to let boys be independent. (p. 69)

Some research emphasizes the importance of peer socialization in schools and neighborhoods. Barrie Thorne (1994), for example,

As First Lady, Hillary Rodham Clinton was criticized for being too assertive whenever she attempted to apply her legal expertise to matters of public policy. When she ran for U.S. senator in New York, she got a chance to put her policy proposals to the test of a political campaign on her own behalf.

TABLE 10–5 Proportion of Degrees Awarded to Women

	B.A.s	Ph.D.s	M.D.s
	(Percent)		
1960	38.5	10.5	5.5
1970	43.1	13.3	8.4
1980	49.0	29.7	23.4
1996	55.1	45.4	40.9
	Law	M.B.A.s	Engineering
	(Percent)		
1960	2.5	3.6	0.4
1970	5.4	3.6	0.8
1980	30.2	22.4	9.3
1996	43.5	37.6	16.1

Source: A. Hacker, "The Unmaking of Men," *New York Review of Books,* October 21, 1999. pp. 25–30. Used with permission.

spent many hours watching children and adolescents interacting in school classrooms and play yards. She notes that whereas adolescent girls usually dream of love and intimacy, "the heterosexual marketplace all too often involves exploitation. Active efforts to get and keep a boyfriend lead many young women to lower their ambitions, and the culture of romance perpetuates male privilege" (p. 170).

Education

Education represents a more formal type of socialization. Considering how much time children spend in school, the socialization they receive there inevitably affects how they behave. Several studies have indicated that, by and large, schools reinforce traditional sex role stereotypes and socialize children into traditional sex roles.

In recent years much emphasis has been placed on ridding the schools of bias against female achievement and increasing gender equality. Greater emphasis on girls' sports and on more equal participation in the school's political activities and newspapers, for example, attests to increased concern for sex role equality. But some major problems remain. For example, women continue to achieve less well than men in math and science, and far fewer women than men are recruited into the ranks of engineers and scientists. Table 10–5 confirms these facts. Note that since 1960 the numbers of women receiving degrees in law and medicine, academic Ph.D.s, and even business have risen dramatically, while engineering degrees have increased at a far slower rate.

A 1992 study by the American Association of University Women (AAUW) found that girls and boys start school with similar levels of skill and confidence but that by the end of high school, girls trail boys in science and math. After reviewing more than 100 articles and reports of research conducted during the past ten years, the authors reached several conclusions:

Teachers pay less attention to girls than to boys.

Girls lag in math and science scores, and even those who do well in these subjects tend not to choose careers in math and science.

Reports of sexual harassment of girls are increasing.

Textbooks still ignore or stereotype women and girls and omit discussion of pressing problems such as sexual abuse.

Some tests are biased against females and thereby limit their chances of obtaining scholarships.

Black girls are particularly likely to be ignored or rebuffed in schools.

Clearly, continued efforts are needed to address these inequalities of socialization if more women are to be attracted to the sciences.

An especially insidious form of sex segregation occurs during career counseling, which often channels young people into careers on the basis of sex rather than ability. Counselors frequently advocate traditionally female occupations for young women who are qualified and eager to enter so-called male preserves. A girl who is a good math student may be told to go into teaching; a boy with equal skills may be directed toward engineering. However, more recent research indicates that there have been quite positive changes in adolescent girls' attitudes about what they can achieve and that young women are more aware of the opportunities they can compete for in formerly male-dominated fields like law enforcement and business (Richmond-Abbott, 1992).

The Family

Although many women report great satisfaction as mothers and homemakers, this traditional role often gives a woman a subordinate status within the home, limits her freedom, and leaves her feeling unfulfilled (Richmond-Abbott, 1992). Some researchers argue that more feminist researchers distort the extent to which women are dissatisfied with their homemaking roles. They believe that many women would appreciate the opportunity to devote more time to mothering and homemaking. Although this perception is surely true for a certain proportion of women with children, it does not apply to the growing number of women who are single parents, who must work to survive. And Heidi Hartmann (1994) of the Institute for Women's Policy Research points to the following data from the Bureau of Labor Statistics:

> While the number of women who collect any kind of paycheck has nearly doubled, climbing to 57 million over the past 20 years, the number of women working at two or more jobs has quintupled, soaring from less than 650,000 to over 3 million. Similarly, the number of women working in their own businesses has nearly tripled, rising from 1.38 million to over 4 million; more than a third of those holding multiple jobs worked in their own businesses. (p. 16)

As a result of these changes, more and more women are facing the challenge of balancing work and family roles.

Even in many nontraditional marriages in which there is a great degree of equality between husband and wife, the husband often has a more privileged position. One study found that even when both members of a couple are professionals, the woman is often forced into a somewhat subordinate position because it is assumed that the man's career is more important or more likely to be successful than the woman's. As a result, wives in professional pairs are less likely than their husbands to be satisfied with their careers (Crittenden, 1999).

Language and the Media

The language used in the media (and in textbooks) often reinforces traditional sex role stereotypes through overreliance on male terms and a tendency to use stereotypic phrases in describing men and women. The use of male pronouns in referring to neutral subjects—"The typical doctor enjoys his leisure"—also implies that women are excluded from an active social life.

Whereas sexism in everyday language is subtle and unconscious, in advertising it is often blatant. According to sociologist Barbara Ehrenreich (1992), the importance of sexist themes in advertising and the way in which advertisements capitalize on women's anxieties about their appearance are revealed by the fact that over the past 30 years 1.6 million women have undergone breast enlargement operations, often with dubious medical results.

Typically, far fewer women than men are portrayed in the media as employed, although more than half of all women work outside the home. Few women are shown in executive positions; instead, they play largely decorative roles. Moreover,

This kind of advertisement is what feminist sociologists have in mind when they point to the problem of sexism in advertising.

the vast majority of buying decisions are portrayed as being made by men, particularly decisions involving major purchases like cars. Recent advertising campaigns have sought to attract the growing population of female executives by presenting successful businesswomen and female scientists to endorse products. But the patterns of sexism in advertising remain strong: Sex appeal and sexual stereotypes are still used to sell many products.

Organized Religion

Women attend church more frequently, pray more often, hold firmer beliefs, and cooperate more in church programs than men do; yet organized religion is dominated by men (Hurty, 1998; Mills, 1972). In their theological doctrines and religious hierarchies, churches and synagogues tend to reinforce women's subordinate role. Explicit instructions to do so can be found in the Bible: "A woman must be a learner, listening quietly and with due submission. I do not permit a woman to be a teacher, nor must woman domineer over man; she should be quiet. For Adam was created first, and Eve afterwards; and it was not Adam who was deceived; it was woman who, yielding to deception, fell into sin." (Timothy 2:11–15).

Historically, organized religion has reinforced many secular traditions and norms, including the traditional view that men are primary and women secondary and that a woman's most important role is procreation. In Judaism, women are required to obey fewer religious precepts than men because less is expected of them. Orthodox Jewish males recite a prayer each morning in which they thank God that they are not women. The Catholic church still assumes authority over a woman's sexual behavior, forbidding the use of birth control devices because they prevent reproduction.

Most churches bar women from performing the most sacred rituals or attaining the highest administrative posts. The consequences of this practice have been summed up as follows:

> As long as qualified persons are excluded from any ministry by reason of their sex alone, it cannot be said that there is genuine equality of men and women in the church. . . . By this exclusion the church is saying that the sexual differentiation is—for one sex—a crippling defect which no personal qualities of intelligence, character, or leadership can overcome. In fact, by this policy it is effectively teaching that women are not fully human and conditioning people to accept this as unchangeable fact. (Daly, 1970, p. 134)

In recent decades there have been some changes. The movement to allow women to hold leadership positions in churches and synagogues has had some success: In more liberal denominations (e.g., Episcopalians, Presbyterians, and Reformed Jews), women may be ordained as ministers and rabbis. Within the Catholic church there are groups of women devoted to changing the norm against female priests, but they encounter severe resistance from traditionalists in the Catholic hierarchy (Farrell, 1991; Witt, 1999).

Government

The federal government has a long history of discrimination against women. A 1919 study by the Women's Bureau (a federal bureau created by Congress) found that women were barred from applying for 60 percent of all civil-service positions, notably those involving scientific or other professional work. Women were placed in a separate employment category, and their salaries were limited. The professionals in the Women's Bureau, for example, were required under an act of Congress to receive half the salaries received by men for doing the same work in other federal agencies.

Although discrimination against women has received less overt support from the government in recent years, patterns of discrimination still exist at all levels of government. In state and local governments, for example, women face a "glass ceiling" that causes them to be underrepresented in high-level jobs and concentrated in lower-level, nonexecutive positions. The 1964 Civil Rights Act, which prohibited discrimination on the basis of sex, specifically excluded federal, state, and local governments from its provisions. Thus, women who work for the government are concentrated in clerical or service-type jobs, whereas most administrative posts are held by men (Nussbaum, 1999).

The Legal System

There are many legal barriers to sexual equality. For example, many state labor laws passed during the late nineteenth and early twentieth centuries set work standards that were designed to protect all workers; they established the maximum hours people could be required to work, the maximum weights they could be required to lift, and so on. The Supreme Court found, however, that such restrictions were unconstitutional in the case of male workers because they violated constitutional liberties. Women, on the other hand, could still be subject to these restrictions. In its decision in *Lochner* v. *New York* (1908), which upheld a state law limiting the number of hours women factory workers could work, the Court stated,

Attorney General Janet Reno (left) and Secretary of State Madeleine Albright are the two highest-ranking women cabinet members in the history of the U.S. Government.

> History discloses the fact that woman has always been dependent on man. He has established his control at the outset by superior physical strength, and this control in various forms, with diminishing intensity, has continued to the present. . . . Differentiated by these matters from the other sex, [woman] is properly placed in a class by herself, and legislation designed for her protection may be sustained, even when like legislation is not necessary for men, and could not be sustained.

This decision in effect legalized and perpetuated state laws that differentiated between men and women. As late as 1965, the EEOC stated that state laws designed to protect women were not discriminatory.

A related issue is sexual harassment on the job. As noted earlier in the chapter, this harassment is widespread and usually intentional. It includes touching and staring at a woman's body, requesting sexual intercourse, and sometimes actual rape. Verbal abuse and derogatory language are common. In one study, half the respondents reported that they had been victims of physical harassment and 70 percent had been subjected to various types of sexual comments or suggestions (MacKinnon, 1979). Although there are legal prohibitions against sexual harassment in the workplace, laws of this type are hard to enforce because it is often difficult to define a particular incident as sexual harassment. Another serious problem with existing laws is that a woman who files a complaint may have to endure years of procedures and hearings before she can win a chance at redress.

The problem of legal differentiation between men and women exists in other areas as well. Some state educational institutions are permitted to exclude women, either from their student bodies or from their faculties. Many technical high schools admit only boys; many high schools prohibit pregnant or married girls from attending but admit unmarried fathers or married boys.

Credit for low-income women is another area in which past patterns of discrimination have led to strange and unintended social change. The Equal Credit Opportunity

Act, passed in 1974, makes it illegal to discriminate against women in many types of credit transactions. As a result, it is now somewhat easier for women to qualify for home loans as single parents or widows. At the same time, the laws have made it possible for credit card companies to flood the market with easy credit, even for very poor Americans, many of whom are single mothers. Between 1983 and 1995 the percentage of all U.S. families holding a credit card rose from 65 percent to over 77 percent, and the average monthly balance in constant dollars rose from $751 to $1,852. In the mid-1990s about 36 percent of poor families had credit cards, with an average monthly balance of $1,380. In essence, in the United States the problem is not lack of credit but the dangers of too easy access and the temptation to run up unmanageable bills as part of the struggle to make ends meet (Bird, Hagstrom, & Wild, 1999).

On a global scale, however, lack of access to credit remains a major challenge for women and social policymakers. A pioneer in this regard is Dr. Muhammad Yunus, founder of the Grameen (meaning "rural") Bank. This bank lends small amounts of money to women who wish to start businesses or build new homes. It began when Yunus found himself surrounded by begging women, to whom he loaned $30 rather than giving the money away. He then began working with women to establish a rotating credit fund. Eventually his activities became the Grameen Bank, which now has more than 1,000 branches in 34,000 villages and makes loans totaling about $369 million a year, with repayment rates higher than those of commercial banks in the United States. "The woman who has completed the loan," Dr Yunus observes, "is completely different. The whole world was telling her, 'You are no good, you are a woman.' Now comes the First Lady [Mrs. Clinton] to talk about it. It is a validation of what they are doing." The Grameen Bank model of small loans has been replicated in many areas of the developing world and in the United States as well, notably in Arkansas, where then Governor Bill Clinton helped start the Arkansas Development Bank (Purdum, 1995; Wahid, 1999).

SOCIAL POLICY

Changes in Child-rearing Practices

Perhaps the greatest obstacle to equality of the sexes is the "motherhood ethic"—the idea that women are most fulfilled as mothers and that children, particularly young children, require a mother's constant attention if they are to grow up healthy and well adjusted.

It is evident that children need loving, consistent care and attention and the chance to build a relationship with one or two caring adults who are present on a regular basis. However, there is no evidence that those adults must be female. In fact, the absence of male figures can be harmful to a growing and developing child (Bronfenbrenner, 1981). Many social scientists have found that an important prerequisite for full sexual equality is for fathers to share equally in the process of child rearing (and homemaking in general). This does not mean that all fathers or all mothers must do exactly half the work involved in raising children and keeping house. But political activists who organize efforts to reduce gender-based discrimination argue that society should encourage men to contribute as much to family life as women do.

Several steps could be taken to make it easier for men and women to share domestic tasks. For example, parental leaves could enable men or women who want to take some time to raise a child to do so without losing their jobs. Another approach is to upgrade the importance of part-time work by institutionalizing many of the benefits of full-time work, such as unemployment insurance and seniority. This would make it easier for men and women to share the responsibilities of supporting the family and taking care of the home and children.

In 1990 Congress passed a family and medical leave act that would have guaranteed unpaid leave with job security to men and women in firms with 50 or more employees. President Bush vetoed this legislation. However, during his campaign for the presidency Bill Clinton made family leave one of his key campaign promises. As soon as he was elected, Congress again passed the Family Leave Act, and Clinton signed the legislation. The major issue in child care policy at this writing is whether mothers who are being pushed into minimum wage jobs can obtain high-quality care for their children. Recent research indicates that the outlook is rather bleak. A team of social scientists at Berkeley and Yale interviewed almost 1,000 poor mothers who had been obliged to find jobs. In early 2000 they issued a report on the first phase of a four-year examination of mothers and children under the new system. Their findings showed that children in workfare families were generally being placed in low-quality child care settings that were frequently unclean and relied heavily on television and videos to occupy the children's time. The majority of the mothers did not take advantage of child care subsidies because they did not know they were available or did not think that they could be used to pay the neighborhood babysitter or because the funds were being withheld by local authorities.

The mothers themselves, the study found, showed a high incidence of depression—up to three times the national average—a factor that can have a negative impact on infants' and toddlers' early social development and learning. Results like these cannot, of course, be applied to all low-income mothers, but the preliminary findings warn that high-quality child care remains a major social policy issue for welfare reformers (Garrett, 2000).

There is always controversy over institutional day care for young children. It is well known, for example, that babies and children in large, impersonal residential institutions are often noticeably retarded in many aspects of their development. It has also been noted that communally raised children such as those of the Israeli kibbutzim—although they usually grow up to be well-adjusted adults—tend to be somewhat lacking in imagination and personal ambition. There is little doubt, however, that a well-staffed, well-organized day care center can offer children opportunities and stimuli for exploration and discovery that may be considerably greater than those available at home. Well-trained teachers are alert to children's developing interests and abilities and know how to encourage them, and there is a greater variety of play equipment than in most private homes.

Changes in the Educational System

To eliminate sexism in education, teachers and school administrators must become more sensitive to their own stereotypes about boys and girls (or men and women) and treat members of both sexes equally—for example, by paying equal attention to male and female students and not assigning tasks according to traditional sex role stereotypes. One way to counteract the idea that only women take care of children is to attract more male teachers for the lower grades. Another is to eliminate traditional occupational and role stereotypes from the standard curriculum.

During the 1980s, progress toward greater equality in education slowed. In 1984, for example, the Supreme Court ruled in *Grove City College* v. *Bell* that legislation prohibiting sex discrimination in education applied only to programs receiving federal aid, not to entire institutions. This ruling allowed colleges to bar women from certain courses or to deny them equal athletic opportunities with men. The *Grove City* decision was reversed by an act of Congress in March 1988. Schools and other institutions that accept federal funds are required to end discrimination in all of their programs and activities.

As noted in the preceding chapter, laws that challenge or eliminate affirmative action for minorities and women have been passed in California, Florida, Washington State, and elsewhere in the United States since the mid-1990s. At this writing, however, it is by no means clear how far-reaching this retreat from the goals of affirmative action will be. Many educators are especially concerned about the impact on the entry of women into science programs. In recent years there have been some vigorous efforts to recruit women and minorities into such programs, but these efforts are threatened by the retreat from affirmative action (Barinaga, 1996; Steinberg, 1996). During the 2000 presidential election campaign, moderates in both major parties warned that full-scale retreat from affirmative action would be a major blow to the goal of an inclusive society (Ford, 1999). Thus, affirmative action, like abortion, remains one of the most divisive political issues in the United States.

Changes in the Legal System

Many laws and statutes discriminate against women. Some states, for example, still require that women be given longer sentences than men for the same crimes, on the assumption that female criminals require more rehabilitation; conversely, many states treat women offenders more leniently than men, on the assumption that women require the state's protection. In Alabama women were excluded from jury duty until 1966, when a federal court ruled that this practice was unconstitutional. However, the Supreme Court has upheld the right of states to keep women from being automatically selected for jury duty: In many states women must volunteer or they will not be called.

Title VII of the Civil Rights Act of 1964 forbids discrimination on the basis of sex. However, as we have seen, wage and job discrimination against women remains widespread. Complicated rules for filing discrimination complaints, a huge backlog of cases, lack of enthusiasm in enforcing the act, and loopholes in the act itself have all reduced its effectiveness. Despite these obstacles, in 1988 women in California won a major victory against sex discrimination in employment. In a multimillion-dollar settlement, the State Farm Insurance Company agreed to pay damages and back pay to thousands of women who had been refused jobs as insurance sales agents over a 13-year period. The women had been told that a college degree was required for sales agents, even though men who lacked a degree were hired.

One area in which some progress has been made toward greater equality is known as **comparable worth.** The concept of "equal pay for comparable work," rather than "equal pay for equal work," has won some support in recent years. This concept holds that the intrinsic value of different jobs can be measured and that jobs that are found to be of comparable value should receive comparable pay. It is intended to correct the imbalance in earnings caused by the fact that many women hold jobs in relatively low-paying fields. Comparable worth received a major boost in 1983 when a federal judge ordered Washington State to raise the wages of thousands of women employees. Although the decision was appealed, it drew national attention to the fact that jobs held mainly by women are paid at rates that average 20 percent below those for equivalent jobs held mainly by men (Goodman, 1984).

Critics of the comparable-worth concept claim that there is no such thing as an intrinsic value of any job. A job is "worth" what a person is paid for doing it. Discrimination may or may not be present, but many other factors go into determining the wages of all workers. Moreover, comparable worth could turn out to be very costly; in the Washington State case, which was eventually settled out of court, the state increased the salaries of 35,000 employees, at a total cost of $482 million. By 1990 the average salary for all jobs in Washington State had increased by 20 percent from the

1986 level as salaries were adjusted to ensure comparable worth. The gap in wages between men and women had been reduced from 20 percent to 5 percent (Hartmann, 1995a; Kilborn, 1990). As we have seen in this chapter, however, there remains a substantial gap overall between men's and women's wages in some occupations, and women's wages lag behind men's in all occupations. In consequence, pay equity, or comparable worth, is an issue that continues to arise in discussions of social problems and their solutions (Gahr, 1999).

Reproductive Control

Abortion is probably the single most controversial social and political issue in the United States. Reproductive rights are controversial in many other parts of the world as well, although the specific cultural practices and behaviors involved may differ. In France, for example, authorities have approved the use of "morning after" contraceptives on an emergency basis for teenagers in schools, something that would be unheard of in the United States, where more conflicted attitudes about sexuality divide the population. In much of Europe, abortion is an issue but not one that results in major political movements or violence against doctors, as it has in the United States.

Antiabortion laws were passed in the mid-nineteenth century, when "certain governments and religious groups desired continued population growth to fill growing industries and new farmable territories" (Sanford, McCord, & McGee, 1976, p. 217). Another reason given for the passage of these laws was to protect women against the danger of crude "backstreet" operations. Yet women continued to have abortions, legal or otherwise, and many deaths and injuries resulted. Those who could afford the services of expensive doctors stood a better chance of survival than poorer women, who had to risk highly unsanitary and often degrading conditions.

In the mid-1950s, agitation against the existing laws caused a few states to permit abortions under limited circumstances. Women could apply for abortions, but the decisions were made by doctors and hospitals. As a result of bureaucratic red tape and high costs, patients who could afford private physicians were able to benefit most from the reformed laws, while many poorer women continued to have few alternatives to illegal abortions.

In 1970 New York State allowed abortion almost on demand, followed within the next two years by Alaska, Hawaii, and Washington State. Many women took advantage of this situation, and mortality and injury rates, as well as the number of illegal abortions, began to drop. Responding to the proven success and safety of legal abortions and continued pressure for federal legislation, the Supreme Court affirmed the legality of abortion in 1973.

In recent years the antiabortion movement has suffered some setbacks because of the Clinton administration's strong support for pro-choice policies. In 1994, for example, the Supreme Court ruled that organizers of violent protests against abortion clinics may be prosecuted under federal racketeering laws. Nevertheless, the movement continues to pursue strategies whose effect is to make it more difficult for women to have abortions. Since the Court's landmark ruling in *Roe* v. *Wade* (1973), more than 1,000 bills dealing with abortion have been introduced in Congress, mostly designed by pro-life activists in the interest of curtailing access to abortion and other reproductive services. As a result of these and other activities of antiabortion groups, the "choice" to have an abortion is not always feasible for many women. For instance, 94 percent of nonmetropolitan U.S. counties have no abortion provider, and 86 percent of family planning clinics report regularly experiencing at least one form of harassment by protesters. It is no surprise, therefore, that abortion remained a central concern of voters in the 2000 presidential election.

Related to reproductive control is the availability of sex education and contraception. Clearly, the need for abortion decreases as education and the availability of contraceptive devices increase. Many pregnancies among young women could be prevented by education about birth control. As former Surgeon General Joycelyn Elders pointed out in her 1993 confirmation hearings, sex education in the United States is vague or haphazard. Many poor women have less access to sex education and contraception than other women.

A 1995 study by Kenneth Chew and colleagues at the University of California found that half of the fathers of babies born to women between the ages of 15 and 17 were 20 or older. In other words, young women are often at risk of pregnancy not from peers but from older men, a problem that experts believe calls for stricter enforcement of statutory rape laws and far more attention to practical education about sexuality and birth control in low-income communities, where this problem is most severe (Steinhauer, 1995).

Social Policy and the Women's Movement

The 1980s were a time of setbacks for the women's movement, especially in affirmative action, day care, and the politics of equal rights (Faludi, 1999). But the fundamental social changes that created an environment in which the women's movement could flourish are unlikely to be reversed. Women's participation in the labor force is not expected to return to the lower rates that characterized the 1950s and 1960s. Thus, women can be expected to continue to make progress toward occupational parity with men. There are signs of continued progress in other areas, too. More women are planning careers in traditionally male fields such as business, medicine, law, and engineering, and some denominations now ordain women clergy.

In coming years the women's movement is likely to focus on single-parent families and, within this group, the special needs of low-income, female-headed families. With half of all marriages ending in divorce and about one-fourth of all households headed by single parents or unrelated individuals, it is certain that the politics of child care and aid to children will be at the forefront of feminist concerns (Hartmann, 1995b; Simpson, 1996).

On a global level, what Jessie Bernard (1987) refers to as the "feminist enlightenment" has made significant progress in recent years. Women throughout the world have benefited in many ways, ranging from improved health and education to expanded economic and political opportunities. Much of this progress can be attributed to the role of the United Nations as a platform for issues of concern to women. Throughout the late 1970s and the 1980s, women became increasingly skilled at using the United Nations' information and communication systems effectively. These efforts continue to build momentum throughout the developing world (Mbere, 1996).

Changes in Men's Roles

The issues of women's rights have often eclipsed the need for men to examine and change their own sex roles. Inspired by the successes of women, however, many men are exploring the roles that have also limited them in the past, and they are discovering a new freedom in moving toward sex role egalitarianism. Although the shift in male attitudes appears mainly among educated men in their 20s and 30s (Kimmel & Messner, 1992), there is reason to believe that sex role stereotyping among men of all ages is changing. The growing presence of women in the work force is leading to greater egalitarianism as women become breadwinners and men participate more freely in child rearing and housework. Progress in this direction is slow, however; even when they work outside the home, women still do most of the food shopping and cooking (Burros, 1988; Robinson & Godbey, 1996).

The opening up of fields that have traditionally been "male" or "female" to members of both sexes is likely to remain an important goal of the women's movement

Unintended Consequences

Greater Equality Increases Domestic Burdens

"You know how in a new relationship you give and you give," said Marie Benedict, a 35-year-old hotel concierge from La Costa, California, who is in the midst of a divorce. "You try to be superwoman. I worked and I did everything. My husband did nothing."

National survey research shows that the situation is similar for the large majority of working women. Although the burden of trying to be a superwoman was not the main reason Benedict gave for the failure of her marriage, the stress and unfairness she felt certainly contributed to the couple's problems. The women's movement is dedicated to ending the double standard that specifies that women must bear the majority of domestic responsibilities even if they are full-time workers. In the past 30 years the movement has made a great deal of progress toward ending discriminatory policies that prevent women from entering occupations that were formerly reserved for men, and it has made much progress in changing how women think of themselves—as people who can pursue a career and compete with men, for example—yet the traditional sex roles of domestic life are proving extremely difficult to change.

Recent polls have consistently found that although more women are in the work force and have less time at home, they are still the primary caregivers and meal planners in their households. Over 90 percent of women report that they do most or all of the cooking and kitchen cleanup. Among married couples, less than 20 percent of men report that they do most of the shopping. These studies show that more men are taking on household responsibilities, but the proportions who do so remain small (Robinson & Godbey, 1996).

The strength of the norm that requires women to take primary responsibility for the home can be seen in the case of Houston Oiler David Williams. Williams missed an important game to be with his wife for the birth of their first child. "It was the most unbelievable thing that I've ever seen and I wouldn't have missed it for anything in the world," he said. Team officials threatened to discipline Williams for "wimping out," claiming that showing up for the game was equivalent to going to war. Eventually, however, they were forced to back down in the face of widespread public protest.

From the perspective of social policy, the persistence of the double standard is a fascinating unintended consequence of the women's movement and one that is difficult to resolve through further policies. Greater gender equality in the labor force without concomitant progress toward sharing domestic roles has increased the stress and fatigue felt by women. But since the problem lies at the level of the couple and the family, it does not lend itself to direct policy solutions.

and civil-rights organizations throughout the United States. Labor shortages in some parts of the nation are also likely to encourage employers to actively recruit women for nontraditional occupations. Clearly, policy initiatives in the area of comparable worth and efforts to combat gender discrimination will continue to occupy legislators at every level of government, and there will surely be increased concern about how to fund these policies (England, Herbert, & Kilbourne, 1994). An unintended consequence of the conflict between desired policies and the ability to make the actual changes is that women continue to shoulder more than their fair share of domestic responsibilities. (See the Unintended Consequences feature above.)

Issues like abortion often divide a group into conservatives and liberals. There are no easy ways to resolve conflicts over sexual norms or over "the right to choose" abortion versus "the right to life." But in many areas of gender relations that seem highly conflicted, there is room to establish a common ground of reasoned social policy. Consider the storm over welfare reform, for example. Poor women throughout the nation are

Beyond Left & Right

facing new work requirements. Often they will also face the problem of obtaining adequate child care. Conservatives have been loath to commit sufficient funds to pay for the new demands that will be placed on the already overburdened system of public day care. Liberals often fixate on government solutions to problems like this even though there may be alternatives in nongovernment institutions. A sociological approach must emphasize the need to look at child care funding in the context of different communities. What resources are currently available in the public and private sectors? How can private and public funds be used to increase these resources? Thinking along these lines will avoid ideological battles and may produce some improvement in the availability of care for the nation's needy children.

SUMMARY

- Until fairly recently it was widely accepted that the only desirable roles for a woman were wife, mother, and homemaker; men were required to be leaders and providers. Today those roles are viewed as outdated or as representing only some of the roles that may be adopted by people of either sex.

- The types of behavior that are considered appropriate for men and women reflect the values of a particular society. They are largely learned as a person is socialized into his or her culture.

- Sexism is the range of attitudes, beliefs, policies, laws, and behaviors that discriminate against the members of one sex. One source of sexism is the persistence of male dominance in the institutions of modern societies. Sexism also stems from popular stereotypes about women and men. It is especially evident in employment and contributes to the earnings gap between men and women. It can also take the form of sexual harassment. The women's movement has striven to eliminate sexism from American society, and there is evidence that it has had an impact on attitudes about gender roles.

- The primary source of sexism is socialization, particularly in the family, where children are treated differently on the basis of their sex. More formal socialization occurs in school, where traditional sex role stereotypes are reinforced. Later the role of homemaker often perpetuates a woman's subordinate status, and even in two-earner marriages the husband may have a more privileged position.

- Other sources of sexism are language and the media, which reinforce stereotypes; organized religion, in which women have a subordinate role; and a legal system that assumes that men are wage earners and women are homemakers.

- A significant step toward sexual equality would be for fathers to share equally in child rearing and homemaking. This could be encouraged by upgrading part-time work and providing day care for preschool children. Changes are also needed in the educational process so that children of both sexes are treated equally. In 1993 Congress passed the Family Leave Act, which allows employees of either sex to take unpaid leave to care for family members; the legislation was signed by President Clinton. At present an important issue is access to affordable, high-quality child care.

- Many laws and statutes discriminate against women. Job discrimination on the basis of sex is forbidden by law, but for the most part such laws have not been strongly enforced. Some efforts to counteract job discrimination have focused on the concept of comparable worth, or measuring the intrinsic value of jobs and paying holders of jobs of comparable value at comparable rates.

- Another area in which legislation plays an important role is abortion. Abortion laws have been greatly liberalized since the 1950s, but the issue remains highly controversial.

- In the future the women's movement is likely to focus on single-parent families and the special needs of female-headed, low-income families . In addition, the presence of large numbers of women in the labor force can be expected to produce continued pressure for greater equality between the sexes, although such pressure appears to have the unintended consequence of increasing the total burden of responsibility borne by women.

KEY TERMS

sexism, p. 290
gender identity, p. 290
sexual harassment, p. 295

socialization, p. 299
comparable worth, p. 306

INTERNET EXERCISE

The web destinations for Chapter 10 are related to different aspects of sex roles and inequality. To begin your explorations, go to the Prentice Hall Companion Website: **http://prenhall.com/kornblum**. Then choose **Chapter 10** (Sex Roles and Inequality). Next, select **destinations** from the menu on the left side of the screen. There are a variety of sites to investigate. We suggest that you begin with **Harassment Hotline, Inc.** The *Critical Research* feature in this chapter focuses on the work of Catharine Mackinnon, whom the text refers to as an "anti-harassment warrior." MacKinnon is the author of *Sexual Harassment of Working Women*. The Harassment Hotline, Inc. site offers a variety of links to many sexual-harassment-related websites. Try clicking on "Capstone Communications." Take the online interactive quiz concerning sexual harassment. After you have explored the Harassment Hotline, Inc. site, answer the following questions:

■ Do you believe you have ever been victimized by sexual harassment, or do you know someone who has? If you have experienced sexual harassment, how did it make you feel? If you know someone who has had this experience, make a point of asking them how they felt.

■ Your college or university probably has a sexual harassment policy. Locate this document and read it carefully. Do you think enough is being done in your school to combat sexual harassment?

11 An Aging Society

VOUCHERS DON'T CURE

National Council of Senior Citizens

I'm OLD Not Stupid

VOUCHERS DON'T CURE

AGING AND AGEISM

■ In 1900 there were 3.1 million Americans over the age of 65; in 1995 there were more than 35.5 million.

■ Older men are almost 12 times more likely to commit suicide than are older women.

■ There are about 1.7 million people in nursing homes.

■ Over 27 percent of blacks aged 65 and over live below the poverty line.

■ In 1998 the average monthly Social Security benefit for retired workers was $780.

O U T L I N E

Aging as a Social Problem

Perspectives on Aging

The Elderly in America Today
Age Stratification
Who Are the Elderly?
Ageism

Dimensions of the Aging Process
Physiological Aspects
  of Aging
Psychological Dimensions
  of Aging
Social and Cultural
  Dimensions of Aging

Concomitants of Aging
Victimization of the Elderly
Elder Abuse
Health Care and the Aged
Economic Discrimination
Family Problems

Retirement

Death

Social Policy
Housing
Health Care
Retirement and Social
  Security

The aging of baby boom cohorts is creating a worldwide surge in the proportion of elderly people in nations throughout the world. People who were born in the 1940s and 1950s, and are now in their early 50s or soon will be, are poised to enter late adulthood. As they begin to feel their age physically and socially, these changes exert major influences on their societies (Riley, 1996). Among these influences are the likelihood of increased conflict between the generations over scarce public resources; increasing immigration to offset the loss of large numbers of retired people from national labor forces; and changing attitudes toward youth, infirmity, and death (Kristof, 1996). In the United States, as we will see in this chapter, the elderly exert an increasing influence over social policy, in large part because of their special needs and concerns.

As Table 11–1 shows, the phenomenon of an aging population is hardly limited to the United States. In fact, whereas the proportion of Americans over age 65 is expected to reach 18 percent in 2023, in Italy, Japan, and Germany this high percentage will be reached in only a few years. In this context it is important to realize that throughout most of the world's history the proportion of people over 65 never exceeded 2 or 3 percent. Now people over 65 account for 14 percent of the population in the developed nations, and the percentage may be as high as 25 percent 30 years from now. The number of people over 65 in the industrialized nations is projected to increase by about 90 million, while the number of people under 65 will fall by an estimated 40 million (Peterson, 1999).

The main factors that affect a population's general "youth" or "age" are changes in the fertility rate, the infant mortality rate, and the life expectancy of people at older ages. In social terms, age is one of the major factors in determining groupings and role assignments in a society. How old people are plays a large part in how they feel about themselves and what society expects of them. And the way in which a society thinks about its aged members depends very much on the value its culture attaches to age as opposed to youth. Our culture places a high value on youth, and consequently it tends to devalue aging because it is associated with changes in physical appearance that detract from the image of youth. This is a feature of most Western cultures, but it is particularly prevalent in the United States.

TABLE 11–1 Estimated Time in Which Proportion of Population Over Age 65 Will Reach 18 Percent, Selected Countries

Italy	2003
Japan	2005
Germany	2006
United Kingdom	2016
France	2016
Canada	2021
United States	2023

Source: M. Peyser, "Home of the Gray," *Newsweek,* March 1, 1999, pp. 50–53. ©1999.

In our culture, role assignments tend to be based on arbitrarily defined age ranges. One must attend school from age 6 to age 16. One cannot vote until age 18. The law dictates when a person may marry, sign a lease, run for office, and so on—all on the basis of age. Beginning around age 65, people are designated as "old" and encouraged to withdraw from the mainstream of life, regardless of their mental capabilities, motivations, or health. The new status is a "roleless" one, involving no power, no responsibilities, and few rewards (Riley, Kahn, & Foner, 1994).

Aging as a Social Problem

Aging places stress on society, as well as on the individual. A major source of structural strain in societies is the long-term failure of social institutions to accommodate the increasing proportion of the population that is elderly. For example, the family has failed to adapt to the presence of older members, and there is considerable strain in the labor force as younger workers find their careers blocked and older ones are forced to leave their jobs before they are ready to do so. The result, according to Matilda White Riley (1987), senior sociologist in the U.S. Office on Aging, is that "human resources in the oldest—and also the youngest—strata are underutilized, and excess burdens of care are imposed upon strata in the middle years" (p. 10).

The social problems associated with certain age groups, especially the very young and the very old, are aggravated by three factors, which all have an impact on the roles assigned to people of different ages (Vincent, 1995): labeling, the concept of work as the basis of personal value, and economic deprivation. These three factors are inextricably linked, and each reinforces the others. Labeling leads to discrimination against older workers, which reduces their responsibility while they are still on the job and forces them to retire. Characterized as weak and incompetent, older people often lose their self-confidence and begin to conform to the stereotype. Retirement often removes people from the mainstream of life and diminishes their status and social contacts, consigning still-vital people to a vaguely defined position on the fringe of society. In a world where one's job is the basis of one's worth and acceptance, retired people are relegated to a position of low esteem. Individuals who once described themselves as accountants, salespeople, or secretaries are suddenly and arbitrarily looked on as noncontributors, a status that reduces both their incomes and their responsibilities.

In the past several decades, the economic status of the aged as a group has improved markedly; the average income of older people is about 90 percent of that of younger adults (Palmer & Gould, 1986). The elderly are not a homogeneous group, however, and the situation of those who live alone is not as comfortable as that of couples. The very old (those over 85) and members of minority groups are less well off than white, "young-old" couples. Moreover, although on the whole the elderly are faring much better than they have in the past, this improvement is due largely to public policies designed to alleviate the problems faced by aging individuals. Such policies do not reach the entire older population. Thus, there are still large numbers of older people who experience economic insecurity because of their vulnerability to major costs, such as medical expenses that are not fully covered by insurance (Blieszner & Bedford, 1995). We will return to some of these issues later in the chapter.

Much of what we say about the elderly also applies to young people who are not yet in the labor force. Young people in American society are frequently dependent on others for support and lack the power to assert their needs as citizens. In most states, for example, it is unlawful for people under the age of 21 to purchase alcoholic beverages, yet they can be drafted for military service and may vote in national elections. This is not to argue that young people should drink or that the laws should be changed, but it points to the inconsistency in society's treatment of the young as dependent in some cases and responsible in others.

The problems of different age groups are a vast subject in the social sciences, and it will be necessary in this chapter to dwell primarily on those that confront the aged. As our aging society produces an ever larger population of elderly people, the problems of the elderly become increasingly evident and require more attention from both researchers and policymakers.

Perspectives on Aging

Aging as a social problem is often studied from the point of view of one or more of the basic perspectives described in Chapter 1. From the functionalist perspective, for example, aging is a problem because the institutions of modern society are not working well enough to serve the needs of the dependent aged. The extended family, which once allowed elderly people to live out their lives among kin, has been weakened by greater social mobility and a shift to the nuclear family as the basic kinship unit. (See Chapter 12.) The elderly are rendered useless as their functions are replaced by those of other social institutions. As grandparents, for example, older people once played an important part in socializing the young, teaching them the skills, values, and ways of life of their people. Now those functions are performed by schools and colleges, for it is assumed that the elderly cannot understand or master the skills required in today's fast-changing world. Instead, they must be cared for either at home or in institutions like old-age homes, which remove this burden from the productive members of society.

Many older people cherish the opportunity to spend time with children and participate in their education.

Interactionists take a different view. They see the term *elderly* as a stigmatizing label; it suggests that older people are less valuable because they do not conform to the norms of a youth-oriented culture. Interactionists view the elderly as victims of **ageism**—forms of prejudice and discrimination that are directed at them not only by individuals but also by social institutions. The remedy is to fight ageism in all its forms. (Ageism is discussed more fully later in the chapter.)

Finally, conflict theorists believe that the problems of the elderly stem from their lack of power to shape social institutions to meet the needs of people who are no longer in their productive years and have not accumulated the means to preserve their economic and social independence. In this view, the aged must resist the debilitating effects of labeling and the loss of their roles by banding together in organizations, communities, and voting blocs that will assert their need for meaningful lives and adequate social services. (Table 11–2 summarizes the major sociological perspectives on aging.)

The Elderly in America Today

Research on nomadic societies has found that in some situations, especially in times of scarcity or when they impede the group's mobility, elderly individuals may be badly mistreated and even encouraged to die (Cox, 1990). Explorers and anthropologists have also cited instances of mistreatment in some tribal societies. But in many settled agrarian societies, the status of adults actually increases with age. In many African and Asian nations, for example, decisions about land tenure, kinship, and ceremonial

TABLE 11-2 Major Sociological Perspectives on Aging

Perspective	Why Aging Is a Social Problem
Functionalist	Social institutions do not adequately serve people as they grow older (e.g., the family is no longer capable of providing adequate care).
Interactionist	The elderly are stigmatized and are victims of ageism because they do not conform to the norms of a culture that emphasizes youthfulness.
Conflict	The problem of the elderly is their relative lack of power; when they organize for political action, they can combat ageism.

affairs are the province of the aged. In the United States and most Western countries, the productive and cultural roles of the aged have been weakened by industrialization and the migration of family members to cities. In this sense, then, the problems of the aged are part of the larger complex of social changes known as **modernization,** which has been described as the transformation of societies to urbanized and industrialized ways of life based on scientific technologies, individualized rather than communal or collective roles, and a cosmopolitan outlook that values efficiency and progress. Thus, many of the problems faced by the aged in America today are social problems that arise from the nature of modern Western society.

Modernization produces far-reaching changes in societies, but clearly the terms *modernization* and *progress* are not equivalent. With modernization come new social problems and, sometimes, new solutions. Modernization is usually associated with increasing length of life, but this is a positive change only when the quality of life is also enhanced. For many people, however, as the life span increases, so does the pain associated with old age.

Technological and scientific advances have reduced the infant mortality rate and eliminated or provided cures for many formerly fatal diseases. Since many of these advances, such as antiseptics and antibiotics, occurred within a short time (often within this century), record numbers of people began living to old age. As the population of elderly people increased, modern societies all over the globe began to deal with poverty and illness among their elderly citizens. Pension plans, Social Security, and medical-care systems had to be developed to address their needs.

From the earliest periods of human prehistory (before written evidence of human civilization appeared) to the present, the average life expectancy has increased by about 40 years. In prehistoric times a person could expect to live into his or her early 40s; now life expectancy is approaching 80 in some societies. Great surges in life expectancy occurred with the transition from hunting-and-gathering to agrarian societies, with the development of modern techniques of sanitation and water supply, and with the discovery of the causes of diseases and of antibiotics and techniques for preventing many major illnesses. In the past 20 or 30 years, however, there has been a deceleration of the rate of increase in life expectancy (Riley, 1989). There are biological limits to how long humans can live, and although there may be small shifts in life expectancy in the future, we cannot project past advances indefinitely.

We can, however, project increases in the number of elderly people who are alive but unwell. As more people live longer, the proportion with major medical problems increases, as does the need for costly medical care. Although most of us wish to live longer lives, the negative side is that we are likely to suffer longer and more as we do so. For society as a whole, this means an increased need to improve the quality of life for the most elderly among the population and to find ways to care for a growing number of frail and ill elderly people (Blieszner & Bedford, 1995).

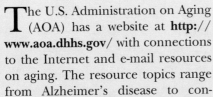

SOCIAL PROBLEMS ONLINE

Information About Aging on the Internet

The U.S. Administration on Aging (AOA) has a website at **http://www.aoa.dhhs.gov/** with connections to the Internet and e-mail resources on aging. The resource topics range from Alzheimer's disease to consumer information to legal services to state and local agencies. Social scientists will be interested in the links to demographic centers, data sets, and statistical information. A short statistical profile of older Americans, with graphs and maps, can be found on the U.S. Census Bureau's web page, at **http://www.census.gov/socdemo/www/ agebrief.html**.

A branch of the AOA, the National Aging Information Center (**http://www.ageinfo.org/**), provides several charts and graphs of emerging trends in the population over age 65. It also offers downloadable statistics from several sources, including the census and its own downloadable reports. The Maxwell School of Syracuse University has a Center for Policy Research (**http://www-cpr.maxwell.syr.edu/oth-inst.htm**), which provides several links to other sites of interest, with brief summaries of the types of data sets included. The page is rich with connections to U.S. and western European research institutions.

For a comparative approach to attitudes and treatment of the elderly from different cultures, Senior Japan's web page, at **http://www.mki.co.jp/senior/seni.html**, presents a snapshot of issues that affect people over the age of 50 in Japan. The Institute for Local Government Studies in Denmark (**http://www.akf.dk/eng/weak-eld.htm**) has published a survey of attitudes that Danish elderly people hold about themselves.

The American Psychiatric Association offers several pamphlets about the mental and physical health of the elderly. Among the topics covered are Alzheimer's disease, dementia, nutritional problems, and the tendency for the elderly to be overmedicated. They can be read and downloaded at **http://www.iacnet.com/health/09348252.htm**.

One of the largest and most important nongovernment organizations in the United States is the American Association of Retired Persons (AARP), at **http://www.aarp.org/**. Counting the 33 million elderly Americans as its "constituents," AARP offers several services on its web pages. Of interest to students of social problems are several short reports of survey data. In a partisan but not inaccurate manner, they track public opinion about issues that affect older Americans. As part of its education and mobilizing efforts, AARP posts up-to-the-minute news briefs on public policy questions such as Social Security. It also offers a Mini-Focus Webplace that addressses consumer issues of interest to its members, such as fraud in telemarketing.

Urbanization, like advances in medical and other technologies, is another major change associated with modernization. The increasing tendency for people to live in cities and for cities and metropolitan regions to dominate the life of modern societies has also affected the lives of the elderly. It has created new jobs for mobile workers who are willing to relocate from rural areas or small towns to large cities or from the older industrial cities of the North and Midwest to the newer urban centers of the Sunbelt. The resulting migration has led to differing concentrations of elderly and younger people in different parts of the nation. Figure 11–1 illustrates quite dramatically how decreases in employment in rural areas and in the older manufacturing cities have created high concentrations of elderly people in counties throughout the Midwest and Plains states.

In counties with high proportions of elderly residents, such as Smith County, Kansas, there is a need for creative entrepreneurs who are willing to help their elderly neighbors remain independent as long as possible. In many rural counties in the Midwest, a variety of services are provided for elderly people, such as minor home repairs, errands, or monitoring of medical needs. These enable older people to live happily on their own and may be harbingers of trends elsewhere in the nation (Barringer, 1993c).

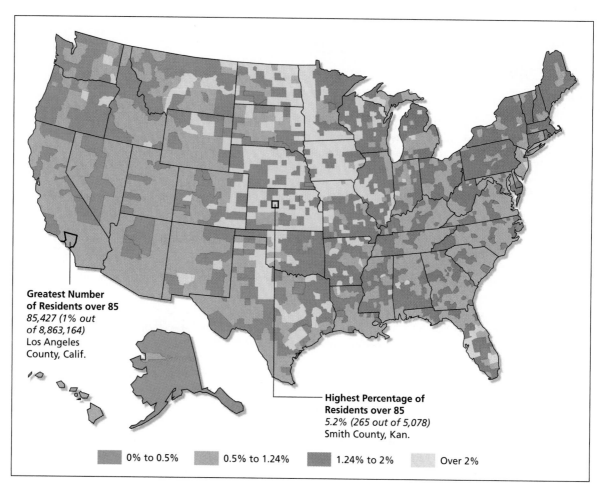

Greatest Number
of Residents over 85
*85,427 (1% out
of 8,863,164)*
Los Angeles
County, Calif.

**Highest Percentage of
Residents over 85**
5.2% (265 out of 5,078)
Smith County, Kan.

| 0% to 0.5% | 0.5% to 1.24% | 1.24% to 2% | Over 2% |

Figure 11–1   Percentage of Residents Over 85, by County, United States
Source: Data from U.S. Census Bureau.

Age Stratification

Matilda White Riley and Joan Waring (1976; Riley, 1996) have described the process of **age stratification.** Age, they point out, operates like race or class in segregating people into different groups or strata. Like the class system, age stratification limits the kinds of roles that the members of each group can hold. Some degree of age stratification seems acceptable and even inevitable. People are attracted to their peers and to those with whom they share common experiences and concerns, and certain activities seem to attract members of particular age groups. However, "Many of these age-related differences in access to the good things in life are violations of societal ideas of equity or harmony. They inhibit communication and understanding between generations. They can create a sense of relative deprivation or inadequacy and feelings of hostility with reference to other age strata" (Riley & Waring, 1976, p. 363).

Age stratification may produce some of the disengagement that is so common among elderly people in America. Young people who are denied jobs and opportunities to play rewarding roles often react by engaging in deviant behaviors, including crime. Old people may react by becoming dependent or uninvolved or by manifesting the kinds of behavior that are labeled senile.

Age stratification may also lead to age segregation and conflict. From childhood we are segregated into age groups, classes, and clubs; the retirement community, restricted to people of specified ages, continues this process. In the wake of age segregation come suspicion, mistrust, and hostility. The young lack confidence in their elders; the old often fear the young. Isolation of age groups and intergenerational conflicts are common.

It is possible that many conditions that exist today will be reversed in the future. For example, the middle-aged have traditionally enjoyed a better position than the elderly. But that position could be eroded as a result of a combination of factors, including a lower median wage for male heads of households, larger percentages of infants born out of wedlock and children living in female-headed households, and higher educational attainment among individuals currently approaching old age (Riley, 1987). The effect of these trends may counteract the "normal" relationship between the old and the middle-aged and perhaps produce new forms of tension between generations.

Who Are the Elderly?

Anyone over 65 is commonly considered old. Recently, however, social scientists have begun to identify specific groups within the growing population of the elderly (Perls, 1995). People between the ages of 65 and 75, who are still inclined to be healthy and active, are called the "young-old." Those over 75, a group that is more likely to require support services, are the "old-old." Those over the age of 85 may be termed the "oldest old." Another group, the "frail elderly," consists of those over 65 who, because of poor health or economic problems, cannot carry out the basic activities of life without help. Assistance may range from full-time nursing care to the delivery of a hot meal each day or help with shopping or cleaning.

As noted at the beginning of the chapter, rapid increases in the proportion of elderly people are occurring throughout the world. Figure 11–2 indicates that the proportion of people over 65 is growing most rapidly, but the increase in the proportion of the "oldest old" is also quite steady and is projected to continue into the new century. The global elderly population currently grows by about 800,000 a month and is expected to exceed 7 percent of the total population before 2010 (Kristof, 1996).

Figure 11–3 compares the increase in people over 65 in the developing and developed nations. Note that this figure presents the trend in growth rates rather than changes in the overall size of the elderly population, as in Figure 11–2. The graph reveals that in both the industrialized and the developing nations there has been no

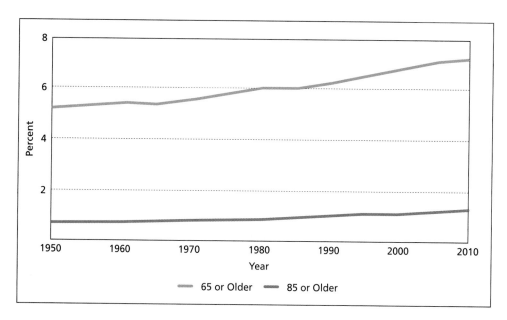

Figure 11–2 Percentage of World Population Aged 65 or Older and Aged 85 or Older

Source: United Nations Population Division. Copyright © 1996 by The New York Times Co. Reprinted by permission.

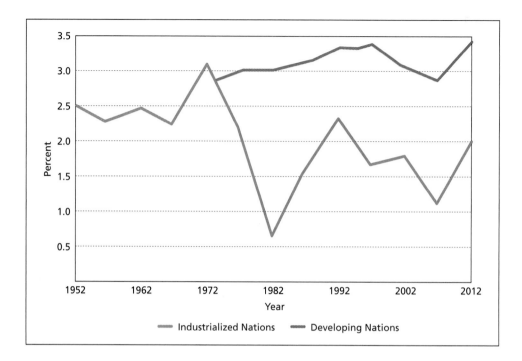

Figure 11–3 Percentage of Annual Growth of the Population Aged 65 and Older in Industrialized and Developing Countries
Source: U.S. Census Bureau.

period since the 1950s without some growth in the elderly population, but in some decades this growth has been far lower than in others. The sharp decrease in the elderly growth rate between 1972 and 1982 in the industrialized world is explained by a very low birthrate in many Western nations during World War I; the sharp rise projected for the second half of the new century's first decade will reflect the entry of the post–World War II baby boom cohorts into the ranks of the aged. The graph also indicates that elderly growth rates in the developing world are expected to accelerate to an even higher level (well above 3 percent annual growth) in the first decade of the new century.

Although the oldest elderly people in the United States now number about 4.2 million, or about 12 percent of those over age 65, projections indicate that this figure is likely to increase to almost 22 percent by the middle of the twenty-first century. This will occur because by about 2010 the post–World War II baby boom generation will be entering this age group. Thus, as time goes by, far larger numbers of Americans will be elderly. (See Table 11–3.)

The elderly portion of the American population grows larger in each decade. In 1900 there were 3.1 million Americans over the age of 65; in 1995 there were more than 35.5 million. More important, the proportion of the population over 65 has more than tripled, increasing from 4.1 percent in 1900 to 13 percent in 1999, and it is continuing to increase. Demographers in the U.S. Census Bureau estimate that in the twenty-first century the elderly will be the fastest growing segment of the population as the huge baby boom generation enters its later years. (See Figure 11–4.)

Two-thirds of the elderly live in urban areas, many in central cities. For them, the problems of aging are complicated by the problems of the urban environment: crime, decaying neighborhoods, the shortage of affordable housing, and congestion. (See Chapter 15.)

Although most elderly people live in urban areas, they also represent the highest proportion of the population of small towns. This phenomenon is a result of the patterns of migration that have occurred since World War II, when many people moved from farms to small towns. Many of those people

TABLE 11–3   Percent of total population 65+, 1950 to 2050 (projected)

Year	Percentage
1950	8.1
1965	9.5
1984	11.8
1995	13.1
2010	13.8
2030	21.2
2050	21.8

Source: Adapted from *Our Aging Society, Paradox and Promise,* edited by Alan Pifer and Lydia Bronte, by permission of W.W. Norton & Company, Inc. Copyright © 1986 by Carnegie Corporation of New York.

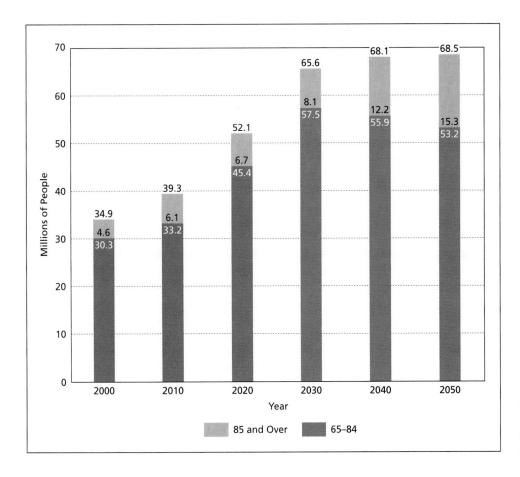

Figure 11–4 Projections of the Elderly Population, by Age: 2000–2050 (in Millions)

Source: U.S. Census Bureau, 1989.

are now elderly. In turn, their children have relocated from small towns to suburbs or cities. Another important pattern of migration is the movement of retired people to the West and South. In some parts of the United States, such as Miami and south Florida and parts of Arizona and southern California, the elderly have become a dominant group and exert considerable political influence. We are likely to see more growth in these areas as the elderly proportion of the population continues to expand (Hooyman & Kiyak, 1999).

Ageism

Many attitudes that are prevalent in modern society contribute to *ageism,* the devaluation of the aged. One of these is the inordinate value placed on youthful looks, especially for women (Epstein, 1993). Older adults do not meet the standards of youthful beauty, and many people may be repelled by the appearance of the aged. Another source of ageism is the belief that the old are useless; since they do not work and cannot reproduce, they serve no purpose. Those who do hold jobs are resented for occupying a position that a young person probably needs. Because it is so deeply rooted in the social and psychological fabric of our culture, ageism is extremely difficult to eliminate. Ageism as a social problem is also confounded with sexism. Feminist social scientists ask, with reason, whether ageism would be the problem it is in U.S. society if men outlived women instead of the reverse (Friedan, 1993).

Ageism prevails in the government. The Administration on Aging, an agency of the Department of Health and Human Services, has low status and limited access to decision makers. When Congress makes budget cuts, programs for the aged are a frequent target. When states and municipalities have to cut their budgets because of recession or regional depression, they often reduce programs for the aged, as well as those for the poor. The elderly fare no better in business and industry. Although the Age Discrimination in Employment Act of 1967 prohibits discrimination against workers between the ages of 40 and 65, little is done to enforce it. Critics have pointed out that the law itself exhibits ageism since it does nothing for workers over the age of 65, who probably need even more protection.

Ageism is reflected in the practice of mandatory retirement. This takes a heavy toll on the health, self-respect, social status, and economic security of older people. Retirement isolates the old from the mainstream of American life. The daily social contacts of the working world are gone, and reduced income may bring reduced mobility or prevent participation in social activities. The status of a productive worker is replaced by a new status with low prestige and a negative image. Mandatory retirement can thus be considered the most serious and pervasive form of ageism.

The mass media play a part in promoting ageism. Just as women and minority groups must contend with negative images in the media, so must old people. Television, which does so much to shape and maintain attitudes, persists in portraying the elderly as weak in both body and mind and as a burden on their relatives—or else as unnaturally wise or kindhearted. Newspapers and magazines also contain ageist images. Howard P. Chudacoff (1989) found that only in the past 50 years have newspapers and other communications media begun to stress "age-appropriate behavior." Song lyrics, for example, are often concerned about looking young and not looking old.

There is recent evidence, however, that the aging of the American population may be resulting in some value shifts. In an opinion survey that asked a series of questions

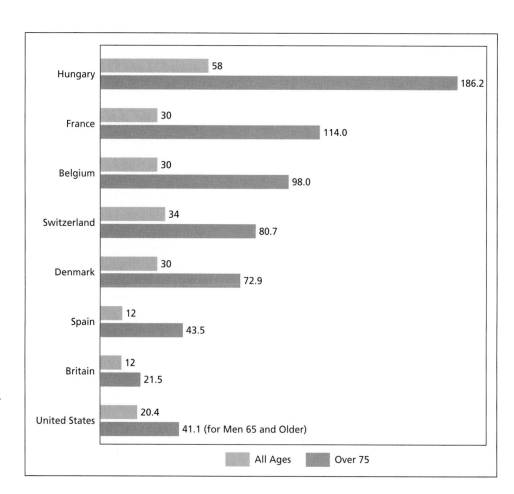

Figure 11–5 Suicide Rates (per 100,000) for Men of All Ages and for Men Aged 75 and Older, Various Countries

Source: Data from the World Health Organization.

about changing values, "respect for the aged" was chosen by 91 percent of the respondents as the most important single value to pass on to younger generations, a higher percentage than those who chose "hard work" or "patriotism" or "consideration for others" (Kristof, 1996).

The difficulties of the old in modern societies are mirrored by their higher-than-average suicide rate. As Figure 11–5 demonstrates, throughout the developed world the suicide rates of elderly males are far higher than the average number of suicides per 100,000 in the general population. And elderly men are far more likely to kill themselves than are women. The suicide rate for women is similar in all age groups, although it is somewhat higher for elderly women than the average for all women. But for men the differences are enormous. Older men are almost 12 times more likely to commit suicide than are older women.

Although declining health, loss of status, and reduced income play a part in suicides by the elderly, lack of relationships with family, friends, and coworkers seems to exert the most consistent influence (Hooyman & Kiyak, 1999). An analysis of suicides by elderly people in Pinellas County, Florida, over a period of nine years indicated that widowed males were more likely to commit suicide than any other group of old people. Elderly women were more likely to have extended family ties, friends, and club memberships that provided social restraints against suicide. Elderly men who enjoyed these kinds of contact were less likely to commit suicide. This finding mirrors the classic finding by Émile Durkheim (1951/1897), one of sociology's founders, that people of any age who lack social attachments are more likely to commit suicide than people with active social lives among family and friends.

Dimensions of the Aging Process

Physiological Aspects of Aging

Chronological Aging.   Chronological aging, the simple accumulation of years, is a largely automatic process. We know from our own observations, however, that not everyone ages at the same rate. Some people look and act middle-aged before they leave their 20s, whereas some 50-year-olds radiate the vitality and health that are usually associated with youth.

The dramatic increase in life expectancy and the growing population of older people in America have stimulated interest in the aging process and its causes. The field of study and practice known as **gerontology** has grown. Among other concerns, gerontologists attempt to identify the physical causes and effects of the aging process and to control the factors that diminish the rewards of a long life.

Primary and Secondary Aging.   There are two categories in the aging process: primary aging, the result of molecular and cellular changes, and secondary aging, an accelerated version of normal aging (Medina, 1996) that is caused by environmental factors: lack of exercise, stress, trauma, poor diet, and disease.

The effects of primary aging are seen in the characteristics that we associate with advancing years, such as gray hair, wrinkles, and increased susceptibility to disease. As the body ages, its systems degenerate. The brain, for example, loses thousands of cells daily from birth onward. Some of the body's systems, like the skin, are able to regenerate their cells, although they do so less effectively with each passing year. Others, like the kidneys, lack regenerative powers and eventually wear out. More significant, however, is the fact that there is a general decline in the body's immune defenses, which fight off infections like pneumonia. As a result, elderly people often die of diseases that would not usually be fatal to younger people (Posner, 1995).

Aging is a gradual process; not all of the body's systems age at the same rate. The process of decline usually starts relatively early in life. By the mid-20s the skin begins to lose its elasticity and starts to dry and wrinkle; by 30 the muscles have begun to shrink and decrease in strength. As time passes, the capacity of the lungs is reduced, and less and less air is drawn into the body; circulation slows and the blood supply decreases; bones become brittle and thin; hormonal activity ebbs; and reflexes become slower. Aging is not a disease in itself, but it does increase susceptibility to disease. In old age, therefore, disease becomes chronic rather than episodic.

Some researchers are convinced that each of us carries a personal "timetable" for aging within our cells, a timetable that is controlled by our genes. Others believe that secondary aging factors are also involved. The role of stress is particularly important. One of the most salient age-related changes is the decline in homeostatic capacity—the ability to tolerate stress. This makes older people more susceptible to stress, and it takes them longer to return to normal after being exposed to a stressful situation.

The reduced capacity to cope with stress is a result of primary aging; stress itself is an agent of secondary aging. Together they may be responsible for many of the illnesses that plague the elderly. Older people are confronted by numerous stress-producing situations, including widowhood, the death of friends and family members, and loss of status and productivity. Studies have demonstrated that such illnesses as leukemia, cancer, and heart disease often strike in the wake of stress-producing life changes (Rowe & Kahn, 1998).

There is evidence that many of the effects of aging are neither inevitable nor irreversible. For example, reduced oxygen intake, diminished lung capacity, and slow circulation—and related mental and physical problems—are results not just of age but also of the inactivity that may come with it. New developments in drug therapy and exercise are producing some dramatic changes in health and well-being among elderly populations. An annual federal survey of 20,000 people aged 65 and over showed a steady decrease in chronic disabilities in the 1980s and early 1990s. In part this is occurring because of new medications that can diminish depression and chronic pain. Gerontologists are increasingly pursuing a preventive strategy to slow the aging process and ensure that a longer lifespan is a blessing rather than a painful and expensive curse. The preventive strategy accepts biological aging as a given but assumes that physical and mental decline, disability, and disease can be staved off or delayed through medical advances, diet, and exercise (Smolowe, 1996).

Psychological Dimensions of Aging

The aging process produces psychological effects as well as physical ones. Social factors also influence the psychological consequences of aging. Self-concept and status are particularly important as aging occurs. One theory views older people as trapped in a shrinking social environment—their world grows smaller and smaller as they leave work, as their friends and relatives die, and as their mobility decreases; at the same time, their social status changes and they become less influential and less important.

New roles always require some adjustment, but for the elderly this adjustment is complicated because their new roles are poorly defined; there are few role models or reference groups on which they can pattern their behavior. Because of the nebulous quality of their new status, older people become dependent on labels and on the opinions of others for their self-definition. In our society the labels applied to the old are consistently negative because they are based on an ethic that equates personal worth with economic productivity (Newman, 1988; Riley, Kahn, & Foner, 1994).

This negative labeling is one of the causes of the psychological difficulties experienced by the aged. The old tend to rely on the image imposed on them, even though that image is a negative one. They internalize it, and eventually their self-image and behavior correspond to the weak, incompetent, useless image that has been forced on them. It is widely believed, for example, that intellectual ability declines with age. As a consequence, many people are reluctant to place older individuals in positions of authority or to retrain or reeducate them. Research has shown, however, that this belief is incorrect. Reflexes and responses slow down, but in the absence of organic problems intellectual capacity remains unchanged until very late in life.

False assumptions about the inevitability of the condition known as *senility* account for much of this misunderstanding. Contrary to what many people believe, the human brain does not necessarily deteriorate with age. It is not unusual for the brain to function well for over nine decades. At age 86, Artur Rubinstein played the piano better than ever, and George Burns continued cracking jokes at machine-gun speed until he died at the age of 100.

Negative attitudes about the elderly cause many people to consider an older person senile when in fact that person is merely depressed. Depression can cause such symptoms as confusion and loss of certain intellectual abilities. Even elderly people who do become senile do not immediately lose all their capacity for intellectual functioning. Rather, they undergo progressive memory loss. This may be accompanied by gradual decreases in the abilities to calculate, think abstractly, imagine, speak fluently, or orient oneself in time and space. Eventually this deterioration affects the entire personality, but it is a gradual process (Rowe & Kahn, 1998).

Social and Cultural Dimensions of Aging

The Aged as a Minority Group.   Social gerontologists frequently refer to the aged as a minority group, pointing out that the elderly exhibit many characteristics of such groups. (See Chapter 9.) Like members of racial and ethnic minorities, the elderly are victims of prejudice, stereotyping, and discrimination. They are thought to be inflexible, a burden on the young, and incompetent workers. However, some social scientists argue that although the elderly share many of the characteristics of minorities, they are not a true minority group. Unlike traditional minority groups—such as blacks, Native Americans, and Jews—the elderly do not exist as an independent subgroup; everyone has the potential to become old. Some gerontologists suggest that it would be more accurate to describe the elderly as a "quasi-minority" (Barron, 1971), reflecting their unique position in our society (Blieszner & Bedford, 1995).

The potential power of this quasi-minority is enormous. Not only are the elderly increasing in numbers and as a proportion of the population, but they themselves are changing significantly. As can be seen from their turnout at elections, they are a political force to be reckoned with. People over 65 vote at higher rates than the total voting-age population. Thus, as the population grows older, political leaders will be unable to ignore the power wielded by the elderly at the ballot box. In addition, many people remain active in voluntary associations even into their 80s. They play a much larger role in organizational life than most younger people assume (Riley, 1996).

Myths and Stereotypes About the Elderly.   Popular culture characterizes old people as senile, lacking in individuality, tranquil, nonproductive, conservative, and resistant to change. These beliefs persist despite abundant evidence to the contrary. Many of the myths about older workers, for example, were disproved when they were drawn into the labor force during World War II. Other studies have demonstrated that the elderly are no more difficult to train than the young; in addition, they have a lower than average absentee rate and compare favorably with younger workers in accident rates and productivity.

Some of the most pernicious myths about the elderly are directed against older women. In our society women become devalued much sooner than men; therefore, in old age women tend to have a more negative image than men. Among the most common and damaging stereotypes are the following:

1. *Health.* Older women are seen both as hypochondriacs and as having more health problems than older men. A number of investigations, including the noted Duke Longitudinal Study of Aging, have shown that there are neither objective nor subjective differences in physical health between men and women. In fact, elderly women are more likely than younger women to avoid seeking necessary medical care, and elderly men are more likely than younger men to go to a doctor (Blieszner & Beford, 1995).

2. *Marriage.* In a society in which women have traditionally achieved worth only through marriage, widowhood or remaining single are viewed in a very negative light. Older women in particular are characterized as "mateless." This reflects the fact that females tend to outlive males; moreover, older men who want to remarry after the death of a spouse have a greater chance of finding a partner their own age or younger.

3. *Widowhood.* According to a popular stereotype, a widow continues to base her identity on that of her dead husband. This is generally untrue; older women demonstrate a strong sense of personal identity.

4. *The rocking-chair image.* Older women are characterized as grandmotherly types who confine their interests to knitting and rocking by the fireside. A number of studies have shown that there is little difference between the leisure activities of older men and those of older women or between those of people in their middle and later years (Blieszner & Bedford, 1995).

One of the most widely accepted stereotypes about the old is that they are sexually inactive because of both lack of desire and lack of ability. A number of studies have proved that this view is incorrect (Smolowe, 1996). Research has shown that although sexual interest and activity tend to decline with age, sex continues to play an important role in the lives of older people. However, elderly men enjoy more sexual interest and activity than elderly women. The principal reason for this distinction is that elderly men are more likely to have a readily available, socially sanctioned, and sexually capable partner.

Many age-related changes in sexual behavior have their antecedents in middle age. Women who have been sexually active throughout their adult lives continue to enjoy sexual activity in old age. Those who have had a less than satisfactory sex life tend to use age as an excuse for avoiding sex (Riley, 1990).

Concomitants of Aging

Victimization of the Elderly

The media often portray the old as victims of fraud and violence. Although this kind of reporting may alert the elderly to potential dangers, it also serves to reinforce their image as weak, incompetent, and easy targets. The elderly themselves do not share this view—only about 6 percent of people aged 65 and older believe that they are "very likely" to be victims of violent crimes (NORC, 1998).

Because many elderly people live in high-crime areas, they run a risk of being victimized. When this does happen, they suffer more than members of other age groups. They are likely to sustain more serious injuries during a physical assault and to recover more slowly. Often alone and isolated, old people may lack friends and family members who can provide the emotional support that helps dispel the fear and depression that often follow victimization.

Elderly people are frequent victims of a wide variety of business crimes that prey on their desire for security and comfort. Phony home-repair schemes, medical quackery, mail fraud, and schemes to bilk the elderly of their savings abound in areas where there are high proportions of older people living in private homes or apartments. Law enforcement authorities cannot accurately state the amount of loss caused by such swindles, but it is estimated to total hundreds of millions of dollars annually.

Elder Abuse

In the United States and other aging societies there is growing awareness of mental and physical abuse of elderly people. (See Chapter 7.) This is especially true in societies where employment opportunities and upward mobility for the working-age population are decreasing. These conditions are highly correlated with deteriorating care and even abuse of the elderly. In recent testimony before Congress, it was estimated that there are at least 1.5 million cases of physical abuse of elderly people in the United States each year, and many experts view this as a conservative estimate because it does not include mental cruelty or severe neglect, which can be as damaging as physical abuse. While much of the abuse reported to authorities occurs in private households, a significant proportion of reported cases occur in nursing homes and other institutional settings ("Elder Abuse and Family Violence," 1996).

Health Care and the Aged

Today individuals either do not encounter the infectious diseases that formerly killed people of all ages, or if they do, they survive them. They live longer, and in their later years, as their health declines, they become more prone to chronic illnesses, which develop over a long period and are often expensive to treat. Thus, the elderly tend to require increasing amounts of costly medical care, which they may be unable to afford. To complicate matters further, physicians have a tendency to lump together elderly people in a single category, even though an 80-year-old person may be "younger" physiologically and in better health than a 65-year-old person with numerous health problems. Because physicians view older patients largely in terms of chronological age, they often do not give them the same level of care that they give to younger patients (Wilkes & Schuchman, 1989).

Many people assumed that with the passage of Medicare and Medicaid the problem of health care for the elderly would be eliminated. These programs have alleviated some health-related problems, but they have not been completely successful; thousands of elderly people still lack adequate care. The failure of comprehensive medical care reform in 1994 has created uncertainty about the future of health services for the elderly. The elderly poor are especially vulnerable to projected cuts in services and state requirements that they enroll in managed-care systems to maintain their eligibility (Wolfe, 1996). But perhaps the greatest uncertainty at this writing centers on the fate of the elderly poor who are legal residents of the United States but are not citizens. The Welfare Reform Act of 1996 threatens to bar them from Medicaid coverage, although Congress is likely to reexamine this aspect of the new law. As the number of elderly people in the United States and other industrialized nations continues to increase, the problems of funding adequate health coverage for the elderly, for whom long-term care is often a necessary and costly requirement, remains a major social policy issue.

For those who are covered by Medicare and Medicaid, these programs are extremely important. Thirty-five percent of Medicaid expenditures are for the care of elderly people. Medicare covers most hospital costs but only half of physicians' bills; the charges that are not covered can quickly become an enormous financial burden. Moreover, most nursing-home care is not covered, nor are prescription drugs, dental care, hearing aids, eyeglasses, and many other health services. About two-thirds of the elderly have private health insurance in addition to Medicare, but even they can encounter high medical costs if they become seriously ill (Hooyman & Kiyak, 1999).

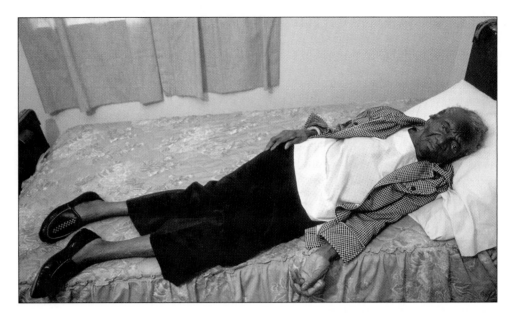

Multiple jeopardy: Many elderly people, especially women and members of minority groups, experience disproportionate levels of poverty and neglect as they become old and frail.

Although the problem of medical care for the aged is inextricably linked to the national crisis in health services, some aspects of the problem are unique to the aged. One of these is institutionalization. There are about 1.7 million people in nursing homes—often not because they require constant attention but because no alternative services are available (*Statistical Abstract,* 1999). Unnecessary institutionalization of the elderly is costly in terms of both public spending for Medicare and Medicaid and the negative psychological effects on the occupants.

Economic Discrimination

Older workers are frequent targets of job discrimination. The most common form of discrimination at work is mandatory retirement, a life-altering experience with social, economic, and emotional effects. The practice of mandatory retirement gives companies a tool for cutting labor costs. In a tight economy a company can simply retire its older employees, who earn higher salaries, and replace them with younger workers, who usually are paid less.

Older workers also encounter job discrimination when seeking new employment. The 1967 Age Discrimination in Employment Act is designed to protect workers between the ages of 40 and 65 and has not succeeded in eliminating discrimination against those over 65. Employers can no longer advertise for applicants "under 30," but a phrase like "one to three years' experience" accomplishes the same goal. When they do obtain interviews, older workers are often rejected as "overqualified," a euphemism for "too old." For these reasons, older unemployed workers remain jobless longer than younger ones.

The Social Security system has been modified so that the retirement age will increase in the next few years. However, the purpose of the change was to reduce financial pressure on the program, not to counteract economic discrimination against the elderly. In fact, it can be argued that public policies toward the aged should be reexamined in light of the improved economic situation of older people today (Palmer & Gould, 1986; Riley, Kahn, & Foner, 1994). A key issue in American society is how to devise social policies that extend income and medical benefits to the needy elderly while asking those who are affluent to assume a larger share of their own support.

Multiple Jeopardy.   To be old, black (or Hispanic or Native American), and female in U.S. society is to experience multiple jeopardy—to face more hardships than one would face if one were in just one or two of these categories.

Although the elderly as a group have fared better economically in recent years than they did in the past, this is not true of aged blacks. In a report to the House Committee on Aging, the National Caucus and Center on Black Aged (1987) pointed out that elderly blacks are three times as likely to be poor as elderly whites—in fact, 26 percent of blacks aged 65 and over live below the poverty line. (See Table 11–4.) Moreover, their health is poorer than that of whites, and they have fewer contacts with social-service workers. Their old age is a bitter culmination of the discrimination they have suffered all their lives. Most are ineligible for Social Security because their jobs were menial ones that were not covered by the program. Their health is poor because of inadequate diet and the effects of stressful work. In addition, a high percentage of black women live alone.

Figure 11–6 shows that poverty among the elderly is not much worse in the United States than in the United Kingdom, Germany, or Norway, but compared with advanced nations like Sweden or Canada, the United States has a long way to go. The figure reveals another, even more ominous situation, however: The poverty rate among children is higher in the United States than in any of the other nations. Since poverty among children is associated with a wide range of problems, including poor health, crime, and underachievement in school, it is likely that the effects of childhood poverty will in many cases persist throughout life, making it more difficult to reduce poverty among the elderly.

Women of all races face disadvantages in old age. As they move away from the ideal of female attractiveness established by a youth-oriented society, they are increasingly devalued. There are more than 20 million elderly women in America (*Statistical Abstract*, 1999), and many of them have financial problems. Because their salaries were lower than those of men, their pensions and Social Security benefits are also lower.

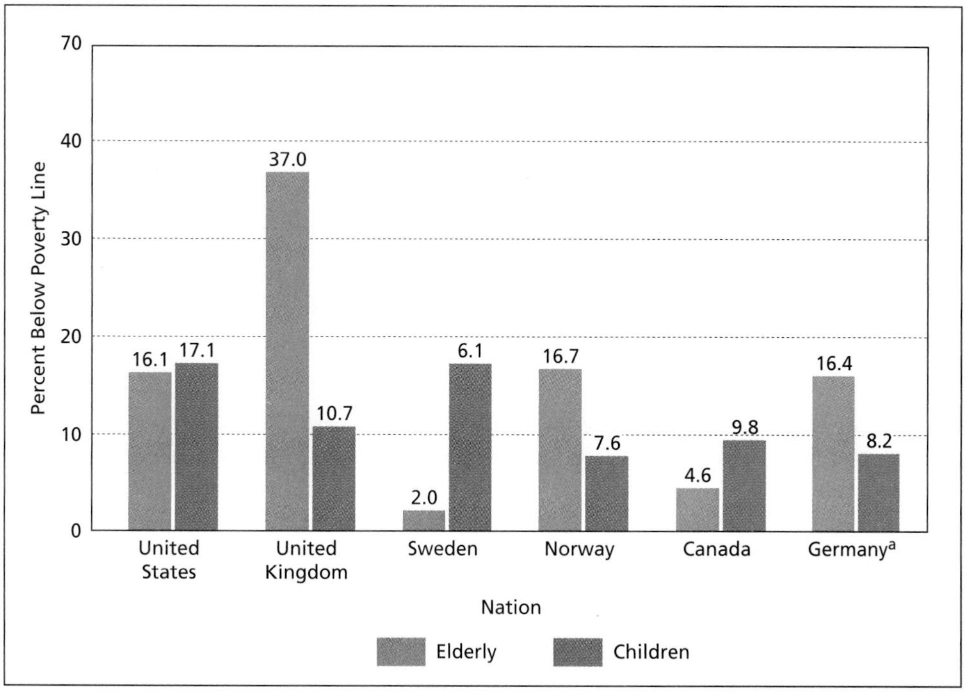

TABLE 11–4   Poverty by Race for Persons Aged 65 or Older (in thousands)

Race	Total Number	Over 65	Percent
White	24,376	2,569	9.9
Black	9,116	700	26.0
Hispanic	8,388	384	23.8
All Races	35,574	3,376	10.5

Source: Statistical Abstract, 1999.

Figure 11–6   Comparative Rates of Poverty, Using U.S. Poverty Line as Measure

[a]Former West Germany only.

Source: Adapted from T. M. Smeeding, "Social Thought and Poor Children," *Focus,* Institute for Research on Poverty, 1990, Vol. 12, No. 3. By permission of the author.

The Social Security system gives no credit for homemaking, the principal occupation of most women until recent decades. Older women who want to work suffer the double burdens of age and sex discrimination.

Family Problems

One of the most pervasive myths about the aged is that they are abandoned by their children. In reality, however, the majority of old people who live alone do so voluntarily; they often wish to live near their children but not with them. However, many elderly people do live with one of their children, and those who do not live with their children see them frequently (Blieszner & Bedford, 1995).

The institutionalized elderly are not typical. They represent a special population who are, on the average, a decade older than most elderly people; in addition, they suffer severe chronic physical or mental ailments. Most of them have outlived their spouses and relatives; many have also outlived their children.

Placing an aged relative in an institution is usually a difficult experience. Most families have endured severe personal, social, and economic stress in attempting to avoid doing so; the decision is made reluctantly. The spouse usually is very old, and the adult children are approaching their later years and often are subject to competing demands from ill spouses or their own children (Perls, 1995).

The problems of caring for the elderly at home are complicated by the fact that as more people live to an extremely old age, the total family unit also ages. People aged 65 may have to provide 24-hour care for parents aged 90 while experiencing economic and health problems of their own. There may be two generations of elderly people in one family, requiring different degrees of care. Moreover, the mobility that is characteristic of Americans may leave parents and their adult children separated by thousands of miles, making home care impossible (Perls, 1995).

The high divorce rate, the growing number of single-parent families, and the trend toward smaller families also affect the possibilities for home care for the aged. Future generations of old people may lack relatives to care for them, or they may have weak family ties.

Changes in the roles of women also affect how the old are treated. Historically, tending the elderly was the task of daughters or daughters-in-law, who were full-time homemakers. As more women work outside the home, they are less available to care for aged parents. Yet women who work full time are still more likely than men to be expected to care for elderly parents, a situation that can greatly increase the stress and physical burdens of working women.

Today the American family has fewer children but the same number of grandparents and great-grandparents as in earlier decades. Also, multiple patterns of kinship have been created by divorce and remarriage. In addition to tensions between parents and growing children, there are tensions between aging parents and adult offspring.

Retirement

Retirement is a fairly recent concept. Before the advent of Social Security and pension plans, few workers could afford to stop working. As a result, people worked into old age, often modifying the nature of their work to match their diminished strength.

From the point of view of society as a whole, retirement creates problems because those who are no longer in the labor force are dependent on the wealth produced by those who are still working. Figure 11–7 shows that over the next 25 years there will be major increases in the ratio of retirement-age people to working-age adults. In fact, the United States will fare rather better than nations like Japan, Austria, and Germany, where the number of retirees may severely tax the ability of the working population to

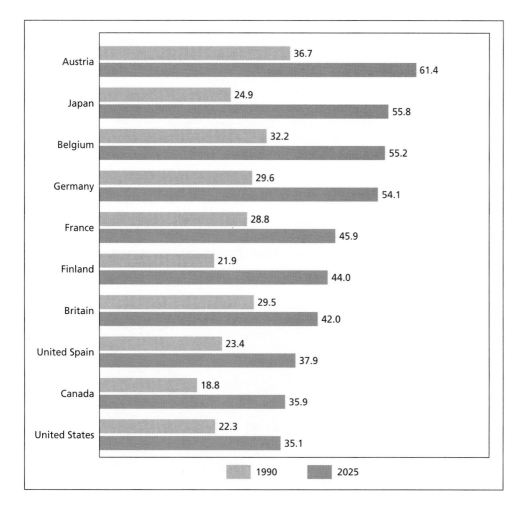

Figure 11–7 Ratio of Retirement-age People to 100 Working-age Adults, 1990 and 2025

Source: Nicholas D. Kristof, "Aging World, New Wrinkles," *The New York Times,* September 22, 1996, pp. 1, 5. Data from Organization for Economic Cooperation and Development.

produce adequate surpluses. But even in the United States, the problem of increasing dependency ratios poses a threat to the Social Security and Medicare systems, a problem to which we return in the Social Policy section of the chapter.

One measure that might reduce the rate of increase in economic dependency is to extend the average working years of older workers. Such measures are more popular than one might imagine. Significant numbers of workers would prefer to continue working as long as possible even if they could be assured of financial security in retirement. Even when people have retired from jobs they disliked, they have trouble adjusting to their new status. Part of the difficulty lies in the lack of role models and reference groups. As noted earlier in the chapter, this is a problem that all older people must cope with, even the fortunate few who have financial security and good health.

Death

Death and age have always been closely linked, but today death is almost exclusively the fate of the old. This association has some significant implications. Although the old have always died, the dying have not always been old. Only in recent decades has death occurred mainly among the elderly. Because of the link between old age and death in modern industrial societies, the social issues related to death involve aging as well. In fact, one reason that the old are avoided and isolated is their association with death.

Social scientists study death in terms of its psychological and social impact. Their research indicates that the old, perhaps because of a natural process of disengagement, have less fear of death than the young. There are also indications that during the process of dying a distinct pattern of feelings and behavior emerges. This *dying trajectory* differs from one person to another and from one situation to another.

The best-known description of the dying trajectory was proposed in the now-classic work of Elisabeth Kübler-Ross (1969, 1975). Kübler-Ross believes that the dying process is characterized by five stages: (1) denial and isolation, (2) anger and resentment, (3) bargaining and an attempt to postpone death, (4) depression and a sense

CRITICAL RESEARCH

Dying with Dignity

One of the most unusual episodes in the sociology of old age is the story of Brandeis University professor Morris Schwartz. Much to his surprise, Schwartz became one of the most respected contemporary voices on issues of life and death. And it is all because a former student took the trouble to renew their friendship and to listen to what his former professor had to say.

One night in the summer of 1994, Mitch Albom, a sports columnist at the *Detroit Free Press*, saw Professor Schwartz on the Ted Koppel show, speaking about his terminal illness and his journey toward death. Although it had been 16 years since they last spoke, Albom had promised to stay in touch and felt guilty about not having done so. After seeing Schwartz on television, he made the long trip to the Boston area, where his former mentor lived. To his great joy he found not a gasping, embittered dying person but a mentally sharp teacher who welcomed him fondly. Schwartz, Albom soon learned, had found that facing death allowed him to "see things with incredible clarity." His lingering death, during which he was surrounded by former students and loved ones, inspired the professor to teach his "final course . . . in living."

Albom (1999) visited Schwartz, whom everyone called Morrie, every Tuesday for the next several months. He recorded his insights about life and death and compiled them into a book titled *Tuesdays with Morrie*, which became a best seller. It was featured on the "Oprah Winfrey Show," and a TV movie of the story was made. By now the book has been on the best-seller list for over two years and has reached millions of people with its message.

Morrie Schwartz had many lessons to teach about

confronting death. Chief among them is that death is part of life and must be experienced fully. It is not something to be ashamed of, to be whispered about, as is too often the case. For Schwartz, the end of life is a time to dwell on "love, responsibility, spirituality, awareness." To do so, despite his increasing weakness and pain, the former professor surrounded himself with the people and things he loved and, according to Albom, essentially wrapped himself in a cocoon of human activities, conversation, interaction, and affection. He even hosted his own "living funeral" to give his family and himself the rare opportunity to hear and say the things that they all felt needed to be said. Schwartz's criticism of the American way of death was thus countered by the offer of a loving and deeply personal example of how death can be dignified, spiritual, and enlightening.

of loss, and (5) acceptance. Some social scientists have pointed out that Kübler-Ross's research involved primarily young people with terminal illnesses and that the stages she identified may not always apply to the elderly—especially the very old, who sometimes claim to be ready for death well before it is clear that they are dying (Retsinas, 1988).

By understanding the dying process, physicians, caretakers, friends, and family members can make the experience easier for the dying person. Being informed of one's true condition is very important to the terminally ill (Callahan, Meulen, & Topinkova, 1995). Several studies suggest, however, that current practices in hospitals and nursing homes offer almost no possibility of a good and meaningful death. Critically ill patients are usually treated as though they were already dead. Their autopsies are planned; they are sometimes kept in hallways or supply closets; their relatives may be approached for a donation of organs. In contrast, **hospices**—special institutions designed for the terminally ill—are as comfortable and homelike as possible and are staffed by personnel who are trained in working with the dying. A hospice may be a place, a set of services, or both. Hospices increasingly emphasize home health services for the dying, including visiting nurses, on-call physicians, and counselors. Home care enables many people to live their final days in familiar surroundings close to their loved ones.

The underlying problem addressed by the hospice movement is discussed in Chapter 2: Today, because of the availability of life-prolonging medical technology, people are increasingly faced with choices about how to die. Surveys indicate that most people would prefer to die at home. Being at home with one's family seems to provide a greater chance for "death with dignity"; being institutionalized implies loss of control and individuality.

Federal laws that allow Medicare reimbursement for home hospice care went into effect in 1983. This policy encouraged more people to choose home care for the dying. In consequence, the number of hospice patients has more than doubled, from 101,000 in the early 1980s to more than 300,000 in 1999 (*Statistical Abstract*, 1999). While this figure indicates the increasing popularity of dying at home, it masks the extreme stress many individuals and families may experience as they attempt to provide around-the-clock care in their homes (Pipher, 1999).

"Death with dignity" has become a popular phrase as people confront the issues of relegating the old and the terminally ill to institutions and to a life sustained by machines. (See the Critical Research feature on p. 332.) Often the use of these technologies amounts to prolonging dying rather than maintaining life. Widespread concern about these problems is further evidence of the need for hospices and home health care for the aged.

SOCIAL POLICY

The primary social-policy issues concerning the elderly are housing, health care (including controversies over the right to die), and retirement and Social Security.

Housing

From 1980 to the present, the proportion of elderly people living alone increased only slightly, by less than 1 percent, but since the number of people over 65 in the population increased from about 24 million to more than 32 million, the total number of people living alone increased to almost 10 million. Of these, women constitute the vast majority (Rowe & Kahn, 1998; *Statistical Abstract*, 1999). Isolation and loneliness, and the depression these may engender, become serious problems for the solitary elderly, especially when their ability to get out and see others decreases.

Most elderly people who live with their children or other younger relatives do so for financial reasons or because of declining health. Most older people prefer to live in their own homes but near family members. However, as they and their homes age, problems arise that are increasingly difficult to cope with. At the same time, their income tends to decrease and their health-care needs tend to increase, further reducing their ability to live independently.

Despite these problems, most older people want to continue living where they are. Not only do they view it as demeaning to move to a retirement community or an "old folks' home," but their housing choices may be limited by long waiting lists or lack of appropriate housing in a particular area. Among people aged 65–74, only about 2 percent are in nursing homes; of those aged 75–84, the figure is 6 percent. But according to federal surveys, 23 percent of those over 85 are in nursing homes. Because so many more people in the last group suffer from dementia or physical infirmities, an increasing proportion will require nursing-home or comparable care, which in turn will require an increase in public funds from the present level of about $18 billion.

In 1998 the federal government approved the first major increase in housing subsidies, rent vouchers, and special housing programs for disabled elderly people. Some of these funds—approximately $700 million in 1999—will take the form of grants to nonprofit organizations throughout the nation, to be used to build and rehabilitate more than 8,000 apartment units for older people whose income falls below the official poverty line. According to New York's Housing and Urban Development Commissioner, Andrew Cuomo, although this funding is an encouraging sign of change in housing policies for the indigent elderly, the number of elderly people continues to increase faster than the amount of affordable housing (cited in Janofsky, 1998).

Health Care

The problem of providing health care for the aged must be viewed in the context of the rapid expansion of the elderly population. Between 1900 and 1980, the number of Americans over the age of 65 grew eightfold while the population as a whole tripled. By 2030, nearly one-quarter of the U.S. population will be over 65 (Eckholm, 1990). Moreover, more than 3 million elderly people are among the "oldest old"—those over 85—currently the fastest-growing age group in the nation. These people are most likely to be mentally or physically impaired and, hence, most in need of care that they cannot afford.

As a result of these trends, Medicare, the federal program that provides health care for the elderly, is in financial trouble. The basic problem is that Medicare payments to doctors, hospitals, and other health-care facilities are increasing at a faster rate than the revenues coming into the fund from payroll taxes (Medicare is part of the Social Security system). This accounts for proposals that would require elderly people in higher income brackets to pay taxes on the Medicare benefits they receive, to pay for a larger share of their medical care, and to obtain a second opinion before undergoing major surgery. These recommendations are opposed by representatives of the black elderly, who believe that blacks suffer disproportionately from cutbacks in Medicare and Medicaid coverage. They recommend instead that greater emphasis be placed on cost containment and preventive measures (National Caucus and Center on Black Aged, 1987).

Some observers believe that a more comprehensive policy toward health care for the elderly is needed. In the meantime, greater planning and steps to distribute income to living family members so that it is not absorbed by long-term care are becoming a ritual of aging in many families. Many elderly people fear that they will lose all their savings if they are placed in a residential care institution, be it a nursing home or a long-term-care facility. Recent changes in the Medicare laws protect elderly people from losing all of their savings if their spouse is institutionalized. Typically, however, the elderly person lives alone, and it is still common for insurance plans, including Medicare, to insist that an individual's assets be used to pay the costs of nursing home or hospital care above Medicare's contribution. As a result, many elderly are creating "living trusts" in which they cede ownership of their assets to their children or beneficiaries but retain the right to use those assets to pay for their living expenses.

In the 2000 presidential election, the elderly represented a major swing vote, capable of defeating or electing a candidate about whom they have strong feelings. This is one reason that issues related to Social Security and medical care, such as subsidies for prescription drugs, continue to play a major role in political campaigns at both the national and state levels. The American Association of Retired Persons (AARP), the largest single lobbying organization in the United States, exerted considerable influence over congressional elections in key states with high proportions of elderly residents, and it is likely that AARP and other organizations will continue to exert a powerful influence on social policies that affect the elderly. It is equally likely, therefore, that generational conflict over who pays the bills for Social Security and Medicare will increase in years to come.

Retirement and Social Security

The Social Security system was not designed to be the main source of income for the elderly. It was originally intended as a form of insurance against unexpected reductions in income due to retirement, disability, or the death of a wage-earning spouse. However, the system has become a kind of government-administered public pension plan. Many people do not have pensions, investments, or sufficient savings to support them in retirement, and this, coupled with the practice of mandatory retirement, has made Social Security the main source of income for the elderly.

Perhaps the greatest flaw in the Social Security system is that its benefits are too small for the purpose they must serve. In 1998 the average monthly benefit was $780 for retired workers, $733 for disabled workers, and $749 for widows and widowers (*Statistical Abstract,* 1999). This is far from an adequate income.

Social Security is financed by fixed wage and payroll taxes based on the first $60,600 of annual income. This means that lower-paid workers pay a higher proportion of their income in Social Security taxes than higher-paid workers do. Social Security benefits, however, are based on the amount of tax paid, not on a percentage of total income. Thus, the poorest workers will remain the poorest after retiring.

The Social Security system also discriminates against women. At age 65 a woman is entitled to benefits equal to half of those received by her husband, even if she has never worked outside the home. If she has been employed and has paid Social Security taxes, she can receive benefits on her own account or through her husband. But she cannot do both. Since most husbands work longer than their wives, most women can collect higher Social Security payments by drawing from their husbands' accounts.

The most fundamental criticism of the Social Security system is that it denies that the elderly can and should remain productive. Under current policies, large numbers of people are maintained outside the labor force to make room for younger workers. This is a costly approach, and the costs are increasing as the proportion of older people in the population increases.

CURRENT CONTROVERSIES

Do We Have a Right to Die?

Probably the most controversial doctor in the United States today is Jack Kevorkian, the so-called Michigan suicide doctor. It seems that whenever he uses his painless death apparatus to inject a willing patient with a lethal drug, he is featured in the national news and either imprisoned or threatened with imprisonment. Kevorkian's actions raise a larger issue for public debate: Do individuals have the right to kill themselves, and do doctors or other medical professionals have the right to allow them to do so or even to assist them? As more elderly people in this and other aging nations endure lingering and painful illnesses, these questions will be asked with increasing frequency.

The ancient Hippocratic norms of medical practice deny doctors the right to hasten death. But these norms are changing as a growing number of terminally ill patients plead with medical workers for alternatives to life-prolonging procedures that may actually increase their physical and mental suffering.

Thomas Szasz (1992), himself one of the more controversial critics of mental and medical care in the United States, strongly advocates the right of suicide. He is, however, careful to point out the difference between a right to act and the idea that an action should be valued by all. "The right to do X," he writes, "does not mean that doing X is morally meritorious. We have the right to divorce our spouse, vote for a politician we know nothing about, eat until we are obese, or squander our money on lottery tickets." Thus, he argues that the "right to suicide" does not mean that suicide is morally desirable: "It only means that agents of the state have no right or power to interfere, by prohibitions or punishments, with a person's decision to kill himself" (pp. 161–162). In his view, the state and all others who wish to keep a particular person from committing suicide must be content to use persuasion to try to make that person change his or her mind.

Clearly, these ideas are extremely controversial. Those who believe in the sanctity of life are quick to argue that for the state to condone assisted suicide or the individual's right to commit suicide by any means is an abdication of the obligation to value human life, be it that of an unborn fetus or an aging, terminally ill individual (Wilson, 1994). Szasz (1992) and others who support the right to die admit that Kevorkian is performing a public service by raising the issue for public debate. They also believe that ultimately an individual of any age ought to have access to the drugs or other means that would allow death to be an individual choice, not one that must be assisted by a "death doctor."

In 1997 the Supreme Court ruled that the "right to die" is not a constitutional right. This decision allowed Congress to pass laws that effectively nullify Oregon's "right to die" statutes, even though Oregon had previously held referendums on the issue (Kaminer, 2000). In 1998 Dr. Jack Kevorkian administered a lethal injection to Thomas Youk, who was suffering from a painful terminal illness. For assisting in this suicide Kevorkian was convicted of second-degree murder and sentenced to 10 to 25 years in prison.

Both the sentencing of Dr. Kevorkian and the recent political battles over the "right to die" have also highlighted the pervasive problem of chronic pain and inadequate approaches to palliative care. Many health professionals point out that the greatest fear of terminally ill patients is the suffering their illness will cause for family members, but they also fear the extreme pain that often accompanies such illnesses. Until recently patients did not have adequate access to pain-reducing drugs or to care oriented toward making their last days as comfortable as possible. Gradually, with the rise of hospice care and greater attention to pain and its treatment, this situation is changing.

At this writing there is debate about how much of the federal government's budget surplus should be invested in shoring up the Social Security system and how much income people between the ages of 65 and 70 who are receiving Social Security benefits should be allowed to earn without losing their benefits. A variety of measures have been proposed to maintain the viability of Social Security and Medicare, all of which would require some additional revenues in the form of taxes, private investment, or both. One can be certain, however, that in the next few years policies will be established to reassure those now entering the labor force that when they retire they, too, will receive Social Security income and Medicare benefits.

What right do people have to take their own lives? What right do governments have to intervene in such a private decision? Today people on the right often ask the first question, usually out of a concern that suicide, doctor-assisted or otherwise, represents yet another step toward the devaluation of life itself. People on the left are more prone to ask a version of the second question out of a desire to preserve the autonomy of the individual when faced with suffering. Curiously, however, the issues of the right to die and assisted suicide find people on the left arguing against government intervention and people with more conservative views arguing against individual autonomy. (See the Current Controversies feature on page 336.)

Beyond Left & Right

The majority of elderly people, many of whom are disturbingly close to the realities of these issues, tend to avoid these left-right ideological divisions. Their behavior in choosing living wills and "do not resuscitate" orders suggests that the desire to avoid needless suffering when faced with the inevitability of death is a normal and practical human response. Their behavior does not in itself argue for a right to die, but it does suggest that many would take the position that these matters are best resolved by individuals, their doctors, and their immediate family.

SUMMARY

- The United States is an aging society, and this fact has a major impact on social institutions as well as on the lives of individuals. The social problems of the aged are aggravated by three factors: labeling, the concept of work as the basis of personal value, and economic deprivation.

- From the functionalist perspective, aging is a social problem because the institutions of modern society are not meeting the needs of the dependent elderly. Interactionists believe that the elderly are stigmatized because they do not conform to the norms of a youth-oriented culture. Conflict theorists view the problems of the elderly as stemming from lack of power to shape social institutions to meet their needs.

- Many of the problems faced by the aged in America today arise from the nature of modern Western society, in which their productive and cultural functions have been disrupted by modernization.

- Age stratification is the segregation of people into different groups or strata on the basis of their age. It limits the kinds of roles that the members of each group can hold, and it can lead to conflict.

- The number of aged people in the United States is increasing, and so is the proportion of the population that is over the age of 65. Two-thirds of the elderly live in urban areas.

- Ageism is bias against the aged. It arises largely from the belief that the old are useless because they do not work and cannot reproduce, and it is common in government, business and industry, the medical profession, and the media.

- The aging process can be divided into primary aging and secondary aging. Primary aging is a result of molecular and cellular changes. Secondary aging is an accelerated version of normal aging caused by environmental factors like stress or poor diet.

- The psychological difficulties of the aged stem largely from the fact that their new status is poorly defined, and they therefore tend to accept the negative labels that are applied to them. For example, it is widely believed that intellectual ability declines with age, but this belief is incorrect. Intellectual capacity remains unchanged until very late in life, and senility affects only 1 percent of elderly people.

- The aged exhibit many characteristics of minority groups. In particular, they are victims of prejudice, stereotyping, and discrimination. They are also increasingly subject to mental and physical abuse. Among the popular stereotypes about the elderly are the portrayal of older women as hypochondriacs, the negative view of widowhood, the rocking-chair image, and the belief that the old are sexually inactive.

- The aged are more prone to chronic illnesses but less able to pay for medical care. Despite the passage of Medicare and Medicaid, many elderly people still lack adequate health care. A major geriatric health issue is unnecessary institutionalization.

- Older workers often experience economic discrimination, both in the form of mandatory retirement and when they seek new employment. Older women and members of minority groups face additional hardships.

- Most older people want to live near their children, and many live with them. Many families, however, are ill equipped to care for elderly parents, making institutionalization the only alternative for those who are unable or unwilling to live alone.

- Workers who retire have trouble adjusting to their new status. They lack role models and reference groups; many must also cope with reduced income.

- Social scientists have studied the dying trajectory—the pattern of feelings and behavior that emerges during the dying process. They have identified five stages: denial, anger, bargaining, depression, and acceptance. The hospice movement attempts to provide special institutions for the terminally ill, as well as home health services for the dying.

- There is no coherent housing policy for the aged, and existing health-care programs are costly and inadequate. The Social Security system has also been a target of criticism because it discriminates against women and against elderly people who continue to work; moreover, the payments are too low to support those who lack other sources of income.

KEY TERMS

ageism, p. 315
modernization, p. 316

age stratification, p. 318
gerontology, p. 323

hospices, p. 333

INTERNET EXERCISE

The web destinations for Chapter 11 are related to different aspects of aging. To begin your explorations, go to the Prentice Hall Companion Website: **http://prenhall .com/kornblum**. Then choose **Chapter 11** (An Aging Society). Next, select **destinations** from the menu on the left side of the screen. There are a variety of sites to investigate. We suggest that you begin with **Euthanasia World Directory-ERGO. (ERGO** (stands for Euthanasia Research and Guidance Organization.) After you access the open-

ing page, click on "Who's Who and What's What." The *Current Controversies* feature in this chapter is entitled "Do We Have a Right to Die?" Among the topics of discussion in this feature is Dr. Jack Kevorkian's recent imprisonment for second-degree murder. The ERGO site provides a wealth of information about the Kevorkian case, albeit from the perspective of an organization supporting euthanasia. If you are interested in taking a look at opposing points of view, all you need to do is enter "euthanasia" in your favorite search engine on the Internet. There are many sites to choose from. After you have explored the ERGO site and any others concerning euthanasia and the right to die, answer the following questions:

- Do you support or oppose euthanasia? To what do you attribute your beliefs in this regard?

- Do you believe that Dr. Jack Kevorkian was rightfully convicted? Why or why not?

- Do you support physician-assisted suicide? Why or why not?

12 The Changing Family

THE CHANGING FAMILY

- In 1999, only 30 percent of families with wage earners conformed to the traditional concept of the family, in which the husband worked in the paid labor force while the wife cared for the home.

- Almost 32 percent of all children under the age of 18 are now living with a single parent.

- In 1997 half as many couples divorced as got married, representing a divorce rate of 4.3 per 1,000.

- Teenage birthrates have fallen by almost 50 percent in the past 40 years.

- In 1995, 11.6 million mothers were legal custodians of their children under the age of 21; of them, 4.3 million actually received child support in that year.

OUTLINE

The Nature of Families
Adequate Family Functioning
Effects of Women's
   Employment
The Black Family

Divorce
Stepfamilies
Explanations of Trends
   in Divorce Rates
The Impact of Divorce
Cohabiting Couples

**Postponement
of Marriage**

**Changing Norms
of Parenthood**
Births to Unmarried Women
Teenage Pregnancy
Gay and Lesbian Families

Homeless Families

Reproductive Issues
Advances in Reproductive
   Technology
The Morning-after Pill

Social Policy
Divorce Law
Efforts to Reduce Teenage
   Pregnancy
Child Care and Family
   Support

D o children still chant the old jump-rope rhyme "First comes love, then comes marriage, then comes Mary with the baby carriage"? If so, they are clearly behind the times. As a national news magazine pointed out in an issue devoted to the "state of the American family," a likely sequel to the traditional rhyme is that Mary and John break up two or three years after having the baby. John moves in with Sally and her two boys; the baby stays with Mary, who marries Jack (who is divorced and has three children). Before the baby can understand what is going on, he or she has a family made up of a mother, a father, a stepfather, a stepmother, five stepbrothers and stepsisters, and four sets of grandparents (biological and step).

If this sounds confusing to you, imagine what it takes for young children to make sense of all these relationships. Yet such "confusion" is becoming more normal all the time: About one-third of all children born in the 1980s will probably live with a stepparent before they reach the age of 18 (Kantrowitz & Wingert, 1990; Sweet & Bumpass, 1987). But do these changes mean that the family is on the verge of collapse or that the traditional two-parent family is a thing of the past?

In every recent presidential election campaign—and the 2000 contest was no exception—"family values" has been a hot issue. Conservatives attack liberals for their tolerance of alternative family forms, especially gay marriage and single parenthood. Liberals assert that the conservatives' attacks are a smoke screen to divert attention from the relatively low levels of assistance given to struggling families by the institutions of government. These debates are not likely to disappear in the foreseeable future, especially as the diversity of family forms in the United States and throughout the world continues to increase. And the debate tends to emerge in a variety of situations. For example, the popular TV show "The Simpsons" has been a target of much criticism by conservatives, but those who defend the show claim that despite their outrageous behavior the Simpsons actually represent the contemporary nuclear family (Cantor, 2000).

No matter how they view the consequences of change in families, sociologists agree that the family is here to stay as a social institution (Gelles, 1995; Skolnick & Skolnick, 1994). They also agree that what Americans understand by "family" is becoming far more diverse. Alongside the more traditional two-parent nuclear families, there will be an increasing number of families with one parent or with stepparents, as well as gay and lesbian families. A major question, to which we will turn in the Social Policy section of the chapter, is to what extent laws and other government policies can help people in families of all kinds realize their full potential as human beings.

Marriages may end in divorce, and children may be raised by one parent or by other relatives; yet society continues to regard the nuclear family as the norm. In another society an extended-family system might remain the norm despite the frequent dispersal of such families into nuclear units. A social problem arises only when the pressure for change can no longer be accommodated within the limits of existing social structures or when those who want to maintain those structures fear that they cannot do so. Often these pressures result in changes in the norms themselves. For example, as divorce rates rise, we no longer condemn couples whose marriages are about to break up; instead, we alter our norms for marriage. We encourage couples to work out their problems, but if divorce is inevitable we accept it and sanction another, relatively new norm—remarriage.

As the social institution that organizes intimate relationships among adults and socializes new generations, the family is frequently singled out as the source of many social problems. Functionalist theorists argue that the inability of certain groups, especially the poor and immigrants, to maintain their traditional structures in new societies causes their children to seek alternative relationships—for example, in gangs, criminal groups, or other deviant peer groups. Interactionists study patterns of interaction within the family for clues to why some family members drift toward deviant careers. They often find that certain kinds of families, especially those headed by women or those in which the couple does not marry and conform to conventional norms of family formation, are stigmatized as the source of social problems like teenage pregnancy and welfare dependency. For conflict theorists, the family is a source of social problems when the values that are taught within it conflict with those of the larger society. But regardless of their theoretical perspective on the family, sociologists tend to focus on what can be done by other institutions in society, particularly social-welfare institutions, to maintain and reinforce family stability.

In this chapter we will examine various types of problems and policy initiatives related to family structure. But first it is important to gain a clear understanding of the nature of families.

The Nature of Families

A **kinship unit** is a group of individuals who are related to one another by blood, marriage, or adoption. Within the kinship group there is usually a division of authority, privilege, responsibility, and economic and sex roles. Definitions of kinship differ from one society to another. In some societies the basic kinship group is the **nuclear family**—a father, a mother, and their children, living apart from other kin (or, increasingly, a single parent and his or her children). In other societies a more common type of kinship group is the **extended family**—parents, children, grandparents, aunts, uncles, and others living together or in very close proximity. In the typical extended family, parents may retain authority over their married sons and daughters, who maintain their nuclear family units within the larger extended-family kinship structure. Increasingly, societies exhibit another type of kinship group, the **modified extended family,** in which the individual nuclear families live separately but the extended family remains a strong kinship organization through a combination of interpersonal attachments and various forms of economic exchanges and mutual aid.

The nuclear family is the predominant kinship group in hunting-and-gathering societies and in industrial societies, whereas the extended family is more likely to be

The nuclear family unit, consisting of mother, father, and children, is common not only in modern industrial nations but in many hunting-and-gathering societies as well. In fact, the traditional Eskimo family kinship system is organized in much the same way as the American nuclear family.

found in agrarian societies. However, almost all societies, regardless of their level of economic and political development, are organized around a system of modified extended kinship units within which the nuclear family is a more or less autonomous unit. In societies in which the extended kin system is the dominant family type, married couples generally choose to live within the family network established by either the man's or the woman's kinship group. In societies in which the nuclear family is dominant, newly married couples are expected to set up a household that is relatively independent of both the maternal and the paternal kinship groups while maintaining ties to both extended families.

Industrialization seems to promote the development of smaller family units that are more mobile, both geographically and socially: Although extensive ties with relatives may be maintained, the nuclear family becomes the basic familial unit as the extended family loses its major functions. Functionalist theorists proposed that industrialization, the growth of cities, and modern technology and its demands for a highly educated and mobile labor force brought about a decrease in the economic functions of the extended family and an increase in the functions of the nuclear family (Goode, 1959; Parsons, 1943). However, after years of empirical research on changing family structure in different types of societies, sociologists no longer believe that there is a unilinear trend from extended to nuclear family forms that accompanies industrialization and urbanization (Skolnick & Skolnick, 1994). There is evidence that nuclear families predominated in preindustrial periods and that extended-family forms persist in some industrial societies even with increases in nuclear-family organization. Changes in family form and function in the United States and other large contemporary societies suggest that many different family forms are possible and will coexist under different economic and social conditions (Huber & Spitze, 1988).

Regardless of type, all families are characterized by an organization of roles. If the family is to function adequately, its members must perform those roles in ways that are compatible both with the expectations of other family members and with the standards of their society.

Adequate Family Functioning

All families are continually undergoing change because they must constantly adapt to a family cycle of development in which the roles of all family members change (Galinsky, 1999; Minuchin, 1974; Rossi & Rossi, 1990; Williams, 2000). For example, most families go through the stages of early marriage, child rearing, the empty nest, and retirement. During each stage and in the periods of transition from one stage to the next, the family faces the challenge of maintaining stability and continuity, that is, functioning adequately.

Failure to function adequately could lead to problems within the family. Such failure is usually involuntary, resulting from either external or internal crises. External crises such as war and economic recession disrupt the family from the outside. The absence of a parent during military service changes both that parent's roles and those of the other parent; unemployment of a parent who usually works can be unsettling not only because other family members are likely to be anxious about their unexpected economic insecurity but also because the unemployed parent suffers a loss of self-esteem and/or authority. It is extremely difficult to maintain loving relationships when the family is experiencing severe economic hardship; in a recent survey, 57 percent of those questioned said that lack of money was a major cause of their divorce (A. C. Carter, 1996).

Internal crises arise within the family—for example, when a family member suffers from a serious physical or mental disorder. Many families adjust to the need to take on the roles of the handicapped member and the responsibility of caring for him or her. However, this added burden may cause strain. Marital infidelity can be another source of internal crisis, particularly if it is seen as a threat to the family. The same can be said for a major change in the roles of family members. For example, a parent who suddenly decides to work outside the home instead of staying home with the children may cause other family members to feel threatened or confused.

These stresses and other interpersonal problems may reduce the family to an "empty shell," one that is held together not so much by feelings of warmth and attraction as by outside pressures. Within the shell, members of the family feel no strong attachment to one another; they neglect mutual obligations and in general keep communication to a minimum (Cuber & Haroff, 1965; Okun, 1996).

Several factors contribute to the continuation of empty-shell marriages. Habit and fear of change play a role, as do economic constraints. In addition, both partners may feel that divorce or separation would be wrong or might harm the children. There is also usually some social pressure to stay together; in many areas, social life for adults more or less presupposes married couples. Also, some marriage counselors assume that their job is to preserve the marriage, even though their clients might be happier unmarried (Okun, 1996).

Although about half of all marriages begun during the 1980s and early 1990s will end in divorce, another half will not. Since the breakup of marriages is more often associated with social problems, less attention is devoted to marriages that remain vital throughout the partners' lives. Indeed, with all the stresses and changes that couples must endure, and given the greater acceptance of divorce, it is almost miraculous that so many marriages remain satisfying, that is, that each partner feels fulfilled emotionally, sexually, and socially

All couples argue, but conflict is a daily routine for some, and their home life tends to be tense and unhappy. Family researchers are often surprised at how long such conflicted relationships may last.

even with advancing age. Sociologists are only beginning to understand what makes marriages long-lasting and vital, but clearly economic influences on the married couple are of great importance (Cherlin, 1996; Hackstaff, 1999).

Effects of Women's Employment

In the traditional concept of the American family, the husband worked in the paid labor force and the wife worked—unpaid—at home. In 1960, about 60 percent of American families still conformed to this model. By 1999, only about 30 percent did so (*Statistical Abstract*, 1999). What had been accepted as the norm for generations has become an exception. Today over 70 percent of American women with children under the age of 18 work outside the home (*Statistical Abstract*, 1999). Figure 12–1 shows trends in the labor force participation rate (the percentage of a population actively working or seeking work) for married women in families in which the husband is present in the home. Note especially the dramatic increase in the proportion of women with children under age 6 who are now in the labor force (63.7 percent) from the level recorded in 1960 (18.6 percent). Much of the conflict over family issues and over the sharing of domestic and economic roles stems from this major change.

Many women entered the labor force to use the skills they had learned in college and out of a new sense of identity stimulated by the women's movement. Many others found jobs simply because they needed the money. For both groups, the reversals of economic trends that occurred in the late 1970s and early 1990s were major blows. Economic opportunities became less abundant, and debt replaced savings. The cost of living outstripped disposable income, and people found themselves working harder than ever just to keep from falling behind. In many cases women were hit hardest by these economic recessions. Often they were single parents, but even working wives experienced severe stress and anxiety. As Katherine Newman (1988) found in her extensive interviews of middle-class women, "Having experienced the benefits of middle-class life in their own childhoods, they felt they owed it to their

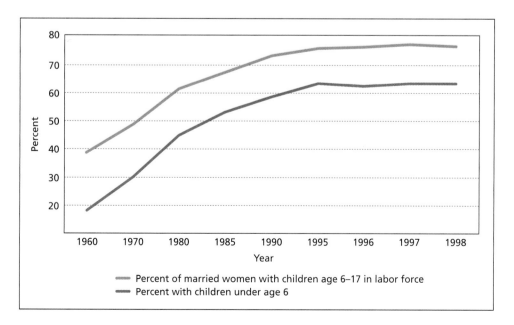

Figure 12–1 Employment Status of Married Women with Children, 1960–1998
Source: Data from *Statistical Abstract,* 1999.

kids to reciprocate across the generations. Downward mobility made it almost impossible to follow through" (p. 215).

Most sociologists agree that the movement of women out of the home and into the labor force is one of the most important social trends of the second half of the twentieth century (Furstenberg & Cherlin, 1991). It has caused an upheaval in traditional male and female roles in the family, as well as in other social institutions, as couples struggle to balance the demands of work and family life.

Despite this massive transformation, attitudes about working mothers have not changed as fast as the statistics. In her study of women who became mothers after the massive movement of American women into the labor force, sociologist Kathleen Gerson (1985) found that most expected or hoped to be able to stay home and care for their young children as their mothers had done. Those whose mothers had been full-time workers expected to be workers themselves and typically welcomed the challenges of work and motherhood. But for all working mothers, Gerson found that inequalities in the workplace, lack of support for their domestic roles (in the form of family sick leave, for example), and lack of support from their spouses made their decision to enter the labor force while their children were young a very difficult (but increasingly necessary) one.

Several studies have concluded that if the wife works outside the home as a matter of choice, the marriage is as happy or happier than it would be if she chose to remain at home; if she works out of necessity, marital happiness suffers. The relative value of working by choice and remaining at home varies at different stages of the family life cycle: When there are preschool children, happiness seems greater if the wife remains at home; when the children are in elementary school, working by choice seems to produce greater happiness; after the children enter high school, the value of the two choices seems about equal. However, when the wife works out of necessity, marital happiness is lower in all cases (Gelles, 1995; Skolnick & Skolnick, 1994).

Most evidence does not support the traditional view that women are fulfilled by a domestic role. Surveys on this issue tend to show that the lives of both career women and full-time homemakers include a mixture of satisfactions and problems (NORC, 1999). Although many working women have a strong sense of independence and enjoy their work, they have more complicated, hectic lives than full-time homemakers, who have more time for themselves but may suffer from boredom, stagnation, and lack of independence and money.

In a landmark study of women's attitudes about work and marriage, Arlie Hochschild (1990) found that women who work have less time for themselves and often think of the work they do in the home as a kind of "second shift." Some women resent the extra work and the time spent juggling the responsibilities of job and home; others take the situation for granted. In a study of middle-class men's reactions to the problem of the "second shift," Kathleen Gerson (1993) found that many men are beginning to shoulder more of the responsibility for domestic tasks like child care. And recent statistics from the U.S. Census Bureau show that an increasing number of men are becoming "house husbands," at least in the sense that almost one out of five married men is minding preschool children at home—although these statistics do not reflect their feelings about the matter or the quality of their child care.

A more problematic finding of Gerson's study is that a significant proportion of the men she interviewed were becoming what she calls "autonomous males." They appear to have decided that it is too difficult to adjust to the demand for greater equality or to find wives with more traditional views; instead, they are choosing to avoid lasting relationships in favor of the single life. This is an international trend. Research on the Italian family, for example, finds that more men are choosing to marry later in life and remaining in their family of origin for more of their adult years. This is placing new strains on the family and resulting in a rapid decline in birthrates (Bohlen, 1996).

Juggling Work and Family Responsibilities.

A common theme in all urban industrial societies is the difficulty of juggling work and family responsibilities, especially for women (Jacobs & Gerson, 1998). Table 12–1 shows that since 1970 there has been an increase in the numbers of women and men working more than 50 hours a week. This segment of the labor force is the most stressed, and those with children have the greatest difficulty in coping with domestic and work responsibilities. But the data also show that on the average women are working fewer hours a week than men, even though the percentage in the 50 hours or more category has doubled since 1970.

Polls often reveal that women with young children would prefer to stay home rather than work but that economic conditions and the desire to achieve and maintain a middle-class lifestyle often oblige both parents to work, sometimes at more than one job (Lamanna, 1997). Table 12–2 offers another perspective on these issues. Although the traditional belief that young children suffer if their mother works was shared by a strong majority as late as the 1970s, this consensus has declined rapidly as more women have actually experienced both work and mothering. The table also shows that married women of childbearing age, many of whom always did work for a variety of reasons, never quite shared the traditional view; by the 1990s, less than a third believed that preschool children suffer if their mother works outside the home (Rindfuss, Brewster, & Kavee, 1996).

Since couples often delay marriage while seeking greater economic security, in some cases the woman may have advanced further in her career than her husband when their children are very young, and the father may stay home to care for them. This imbalance in the traditional norm—male as provider, woman as caregiver—has created stresses in some marriages and innovative role changes in others (Cherlin, 1992). It should be noted that new telecommunications technologies allow for flexible solutions to the problem of role juggling, permitting more husbands to spend time at home as caregivers. Even so, families are increasingly shifting work and family roles, especially in the early years of marriage and child rearing. For example, the husband may return to school to upgrade his skills while the wife works full time, creating a situation in which the husband becomes the primary parent during those years. These may not be dominant trends, but they are showing up in family statistics. However, more women than men still choose to sacrifice long-term career goals and take part-time jobs so that they can spend more time in child rearing.

Some observers believe that the increasing amount of part-time work helps employers rather than employees. Part-time work is not well paid and usually does not include fringe benefits. In service industries, it results in a low-paid, floating work force that is highly advantageous to employers (Spain, 1996). The employers are, in effect, exploiting the pressure placed on women by the conflicting demands of family responsibilities and economic need.

TABLE 12–1 Trends in Hours Worked Last Week, 1970–1997, by Sex, Nonfarm Wage and Salary Workers

	Mean Hours Last Week	Percent Working Less Than 30 Hours per Week	Percent Working 50+ Hours per Week
Men			
1997	42.5	9.6	25.2
1970	43.5	4.5	21.0
Women			
1997	36.7	20.5	10.8
1970	37.0	15.5	5.2

Source: Jacobs & Gerson, 1998.

TABLE 12–2 Proportion Agreeing That a Preschool Child Suffers if the Mother Works: Total Adult Population and Currently Married Women of Childbearing Age, United States, 1970–1991

Year	Total Population		Married Women of Childbearing Age	
	Percent	Number	Percent	Number
1970	NA	NA	73	5,535
1977	68	1,498	58	280
1985	55	1,499	37	242
1986	52	1,442	37	244
1988	48	985	32	140
1989	48	974	40	143
1990	49	900	38	134
1991	48	996	34	167

NA = not available

Source: Rindfuss, Brewster, & Kavee, 1996.

One consequence of the difficulties couples encounter in juggling work and family roles is that marital happiness often decreases when children are born. Contrary to the common belief that children bring joy to a household, the added stress of caring for a child and managing new financial burdens can be a shock to couples who are not prepared for the realities of parenthood. As a result, growing numbers of couples are postponing childbirth or deciding not to have children at all, as shown by the relatively low birthrates among middle-class couples in most industrial nations (Spain, 1996). These trends also explain why social policies such as family leave are extremely popular among couples with young children, who are facing the stresses of work and family role conflicts and desire some help from the larger society (Deckman & Marni, 1996).

The Black Family

For most of the second half of the twentieth century, indicators of family well-being have been alarmingly negative for African Americans (Jencks & Peterson, 1991; Moynihan, 1965). In fact, as recent research by William J. Wilson and others points out, many of the problems of African-American families are concentrated in segregated inner-city communities. The drastic decline in husband-wife families in these economically and socially depressed communities is, however, "part of a process that now affects all racial and ethnic groups in the United States" (Wilson, 1996a). Almost 32 percent of all children under the age of 18 are now living with a single parent, a figure that includes about 62 percent of all black children, 36 percent of all Hispanic children, and 27 percent of all white children (*Statistical Abstract*, 1999). The proportion of black single families has remained high for almost three decades, whereas it has only recently soared for whites: "Between 1980 and 1992," Wilson notes, "when the rate of births outside of marriage increased nationally by 54 percent, it rose 94 percent for whites and only 9 percent for blacks" (p. 87).

Much of this variation is explained by differences in opportunities and behavior. In African-American communities, rates of marriage vary positively with education; better-educated women are far more likely to marry than less educated women. Among whites, the relationship is reversed: White women with more education are less likely to marry than those with less education. "The positive association between education and marriage among African Americans," Wilson (1996) observes, "is in part due to the extraordinarily low rate of marriage among less educated black Americans, many of whom are concentrated in inner-city neighborhoods" (p. 88).

Figure 12–2 is from Wilson's (1996) study of family poverty and work problems, known as the Urban Poverty and Family Life Study, in inner-city Chicago. It shows that only 28 percent of the African-American parents aged 18 to 44 are currently married, compared with 75 percent of the Mexican parents, 61 percent of the white parents, and 45 percent of the Puerto Rican parents in the same age groups. Wilson and his colleagues also found that inner-city Mexican and white single fathers are, respectively, 2.6 and 3 times more likely to marry after the birth of their first child than are black single fathers. Although these are extreme differences, they are part of a major trend in the United States and other industrial nations. There was a weakening of marriage norms during the second half of the twentieth century; thus, "shotgun marriages" and the insistence that males take parental responsibility for the children they have fathered are weakening, although the trend has been most extreme among African Americans (Lester, 1996; Mare & Winship, 1991).

Most social scientists agree that the single most important cause of these historic changes has been the sudden and almost complete disappearance of work in inner-city communities for less educated minority males (and, to a somewhat lesser extent, for white males as well). Unless they can reasonably be expected to help support a new family, young fathers are increasingly considered to be poor prospects for marriage, and marriage norms seem to be weakening as a result of these economic

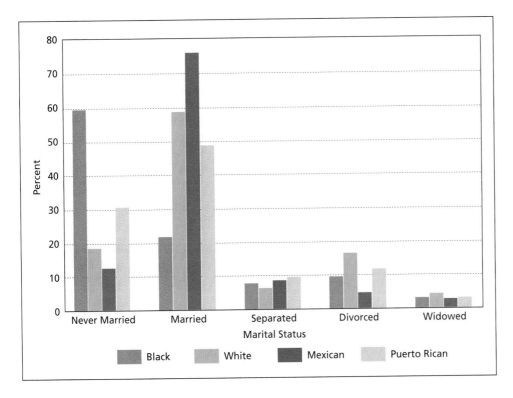

Figure 12–2 Marital Status of all Urban Poverty and Family Life Study Respondents in Census Tracts with 20 Percent or More Families in Poverty

Source: From *When Work Disappears* by William Julius Wilson. Copyright © 1996 by William Julius Wilson. Reprinted by permission of Alfred A. Knopf Inc.

considerations. Wilson (1996) and others find this to be especially true among African Americans and far less so among more recent arrivals to the inner city, such as Mexicans, but the trend is occurring to varying degrees in all population groups.

The population of males of marriageable age who are not developing marketable skills and are at risk of becoming involved in illegal activities in their impoverished neighborhoods is a major source of the decline in family strength in the inner city (Oppenheimer, 1994; Wilson, 1966a). Table 12–3 shows that the proportion of

Despite the dramatic rise in single-parent families, especially among African Americans, the extended family is still a thriving institution of African-American life.

| **TABLE 12-3** | High School Dropouts, by Race and Hispanic Origin: 1975–1997 |

(In percent. As of October)

	1975	1980	1985	1989	1990	1991	1992	1993	1994	1995	1996	1997
Total[a]	15.6	15.6	13.9	14.4	13.6	14.2	12.7	12.7	13.3	13.9	12.8	13.0
White	13.9	14.4	13.5	14.1	13.5	14.2	12.2	12.2	12.7	13.6	12.5	12.4
Male	13.5	15.7	14.7	15.4	14.2	15.4	13.3	13.0	13.6	14.3	12.9	13.8
Female	14.2	13.2	12.3	12.8	12.8	13.1	11.1	11.5	11.7	13.0	12.1	10.9
Black	27.3	23.5	17.6	16.4	15.1	15.6	16.3	16.4	15.5	14.4	16.0	16.7
Male	27.8	26.0	18.8	18.6	13.6	15.4	15.5	15.6	17.5	14.2	17.4	17.5
Female	26.9	21.5	16.6	14.5	16.2	15.8	17.1	17.2	13.7	14.6	14.7	16.1
Hispanic[b]	34.9	40.3	31.5	37.7	37.3	39.6	33.9	32.7	34.7	34.7	34.5	30.6
Male	32.6	42.6	35.8	40.3	39.8	44.4	38.4	34.7	36.1	34.2	36.2	33.2
Female	36.8	38.1	27.0	35.0	34.5	34.5	29.6	31.0	33.1	35.4	32.7	27.6

[a]Includes other races, not shown separately.

[b]Persons of Hispanic origin may be of any race.

Source: Adapted from *Statistical Abstract,* 1999.

African-American males aged 18–24 who are not in school and have not finished high school ("dropouts") reached its lowest point in 1992, close to the beginning of the economic boom of the 1990s. By the end of the decade the proportion had begun to increase again. This pattern probably reflects the availability of jobs for young minority workers, but it is disturbing because, as Wilson and others have shown, lack of education is a major contributor to single parenthood and family instability.

We can infer, therefore, that income and education are major factors in explaining black-white differences in the marital status of men: "If, instead of their own income distribution, black men had the income distribution of white men, their marital status distribution would . . . be more like that of white men" (Jaynes & Williams, 1989, p. 530).

In sum, insofar as the black family is distinctive, it is probably a consequence, for the most part, of the special intensity and duration of the poverty and discrimination suffered by African Americans. (See Chapters 8 and 9.) In effect, the problems of the black family are symptomatic of larger social problems. Therefore, we will not undertake a detailed study of the black family as such but will consider the evidence and possible causes of problems among families in general, bearing in mind that some of these occur with particular frequency among poor blacks.

Divorce

All but unheard of in the nineteenth century and still rare before World War I, divorce and remarriage have become commonplace in American society. From the early 1930s until the late 1950s, divorce rates in the United States remained fairly constant—about 1.3 per 1,000 people. As late as 1966, the divorce rate was still only 2.5. But in 1997, half as many couples got divorced as married—1.16 million divorces and 2.38 million marriages—representing a divorce rate of 4.3 per 1,000 people (*Statistical Abstract,* 1999). This trend is partially responsible for the significant increase in the proportion of female-headed and single-person households in the U.S. population.

The traditional correlation between socioeconomic and educational levels and the frequency of divorce is no longer as true as it once was. For example, divorce used to be much more likely among people with a high school education than among those who had completed college, and more frequent among the poor than among members of the middle and upper-middle classes. But in recent years the divorce rate has risen among college-educated couples and those in higher socioeconomic groups.

The highest rate of divorce, amounting to about one-third of all divorces, occurs in the first three years of marriage. This widely known fact leads many people to believe that having children "cements" a marriage and adds to marital happiness. Sociological research conducted in the 1950s documented this popular belief, but it also demonstrated that the facts are otherwise: Having babies early in a marriage does not make a couple happier and often makes them less happy (Skolnick & Skolnick, 1994). In subsequent decades, people still believed that children "cement" marriages, even though the empirical evidence showed that having children increases the strains on a couple's time, energy, money, and other resources; thus, couples who are not happy in their relationship often become less so when babies arrive (Ross & Huber, 1985). One implication of this research is that couples who can plan the arrival of their children have a better marriage and family prognosis than those who cannot.

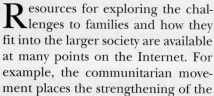

SOCIAL PROBLEMS ONLINE

Families and the Internet

Resources for exploring the challenges to families and how they fit into the larger society are available at many points on the Internet. For example, the communitarian movement places the strengthening of the traditional nuclear family at the forefront of its political and intellectual agenda. Representative and sophisticated analyses of the state of the family can be accessed from the Civic Practices Network's (CPN) home page at **http:/www.cpn.org**. A collaborative and nonpartisan project, CPN is dedicated to building a movement for "new citizenship" and "civic revitalization."

A more traditional approach to family problems is through the legal system. Resources on family law are provided by the University of Indiana's law school at **http://www.law.indiana.edu**. There are links there to other web sites such as the "Freedom to Marry" group, which supports same-sex marriages, and a site that offers family dispute resolution advice. An overview of family law can be accessed on "Legal Net" (**http:// www. legal.net/family.htm**).

Those interested in adoption law and reforms can follow the latest changes in that field, as well as get practical advice on adoption at several sites. Adoptive Families of America is the "largest non-profit organization in the United States bringing together people interested in adoption and resources to support adoption," and it has a home page at **http://www .AdoptiveFam.org/** that provides an online catalog of "resources for Adoption, Children, Parenting, and Multicultural Awareness." The AdoptioNetwork (**http:// www.adoption.org**) has a number of links in addition to such features as statistical profiles of domestic and international adoptions. Included on their page are U.S. presidential policy statements on adoption and related issues.

News articles for, about, and by foster parents can be accessed at the Foster Parent Home Page at **http:// worldaccess.com/FPHP/news.htm**. They include debates on orphanages, surveys on child abuse and neglect, and analyses of media coverage of foster care. Articles are archived.

Families have changed over time and are different across cultures. The University of Manitoba's anthropology department has an online and interactive tutorial, "Kinship and Social Organization," at **http://www .umanitoba.ca/faculties/arts/anthropology/kintitle.html** that is engaging and informative. Other sociological references to the family can be viewed at **http://www .trinity.edu/%7Em-kearl/family.html**.

On a global scale, research on changing patterns of marriage and divorce in 72 nations shows that the changes associated with modernization, especially the rapid growth of urban populations (urbanization), increasing levels of employment in salaried and hourly-wage positions, and increased levels of education, are also associated with higher divorce rates. The phenomenon of divorce appears to be closely linked to modernization, regardless of the particular religion that is dominant in a nation. Also, contrary to much speculation, global research indicates that women's increasing participation in the labor force is not associated with higher rates of divorce (Lester, 1996).

Stepfamilies

Nearly 40 percent of families in the United States are stepfamilies, and the number is growing continually. Today about 15 million children are growing up in "blended" families. Since stepmothers typically bear much of the emotional burden in these families, research is focusing on their problems and how they manage relationships with their own children and their stepchildren. Recent studies indicate that stepmothers typically work quite hard to be good parents to their stepchildren while maintaining open lines of communication with the children's natural parents—not always an easy task (Orchard & Solberg, 1999). Although these findings attest to the strength of marriage and family norms, it is also true that combining children in a new family often adds conflict and tension to family life, and this in turn is sometimes seen as a cause of the relatively high divorce rate for such marriages (Ahlburg & De Vita, 1992).

Explanations of Trends in Divorce Rates

An examination of all the forces that put pressure on marriage would be beyond the scope of this chapter, but we can point out some of them. Most frequently cited is the change from extended to nuclear families. Another factor is the extent to which functions that were formerly performed by the family have been assumed by outside agencies. Still other factors are the relaxation of attitudes about divorce, the reformation of divorce laws so that divorces are easier to obtain, and the growing number of educated women who can earn a living independently of their husbands. (The general change in role expectations for women is discussed in Chapter 10.)

The change to a smaller family unit, coupled with the mobility of many modern families, places more responsibility on a husband and wife for the satisfaction of each other's emotional needs. Where once there were plenty of relatives or long-term neighbors at hand to whom the partners could turn for companionship, today spouses are more dependent on each other.

The decrease in family size has been accompanied by a decrease in family functions. Food production, education, entertainment, and other activities that were once centered in the home are now performed by outside agencies. This emotional satisfaction becomes increasingly important as the bond that holds a marriage together. If that emotional bond weakens and the couple feels incompatable, there are fewer economic and other social forces to take its place (Gelles, 1995).

Because of the greater social tolerance of divorce, partners who might once have resigned themselves to an unhappy marriage, or quarreled constantly yet stayed together, may now feel more inclined to get a divorce. Women—at least educated women—are better able to earn an adequate living. The increasing acceptance of sexual activity outside of marriage also contributes to the likelihood of divorce. In addition, a child of divorced parents is no longer likely to suffer embarrassment, pity, or discrimination in school. Finally, the chances for remarriage, especially for men, are fairly high.

The Impact of Divorce

Divorce, even when it is desired by both partners, is almost always accompanied by considerable emotional and financial strain. This is especially true for women, who often have to work and care for children without adequate economic and psychological help from their partners. Because more jobs are open to them, well-educated women are better able to cope with the effects of divorce and in fact may choose not to remarry. Other women have more limited options. Most husbands do not continue to support their families after divorce, although they are often legally required at least to pay child support. Divorced mothers, therefore, are frequently forced into poverty and dependence on public assistance; the leading cause of dependence on welfare (formerly known as Aid to Families with Dependent Children) is divorce or desertion (Ellwood, 1988). And because it is assumed that divorced people will soon remarry, adequate social supports are not provided to single parents.

There are about 1.2 million divorces in the United States each year. Of these, approximately 50 percent involve couples who have one or more children (*Statistical Abstract*, 1999; Sweet & Bumpass, 1987). The majority of these divorces occur in marriages of less than ten years' duration; as a result, young children, who are most dependent and vulnerable, are especially likely to feel the impact of divorce. Although divorce has become a common event and children of divorced parents may no longer feel the stigma they once did, there is no question that in the vast majority of families in which divorce occurs it is an extremely difficult experience for children, as well as for adults.

Children may experience divorce as the end of life as they knew it, as a falling apart and a severe disruption of their existence. They feel fear, anger, depression, and confusion. Often they blame themselves for contributing to their parents' difficulties. Over a longer period, children (and, typically, their mothers) experience divorce as a severe diminution in their material well-being; one of the leading causes of poverty among children is the dissolution of their parents' marriage. They may also become "latchkey children," far more responsible for their own care after school and for the care of their siblings than they might have been had there not been a divorce.

Much research focuses on families with preschool children in the period immediately following a divorce. The lifestyle of these families often becomes chaotic—meals are eaten at irregular times, the children's bedtimes are erratic, and so forth. The separated spouses experience anxiety, occasional depression, and personal disorganization, and the children tend to be bewildered and frightened. Other research has found that children whose parents are divorced are twice as likely as children from intact families to need professional help for an emotional, behavioral, mental, or learning problem (Weissbourd, 1996).

In an important study of the effect of divorce on children, Wallerstein and Blakeslee (1989) tracked 60 families with a total of 131 children for 10 to 15 years after divorce. Although some of the children were better off than they would have been in an unhappy intact family, for most of them the divorce had serious consequences. A significant finding was that many divorced parents are unable to meet the challenges of parenting and instead depend on the children to help them cope with their own problems. The result is an "overburdened child" who must not only handle the normal stresses of childhood but also help a parent avoid depression.

Divorce has a major psychological impact on adults as well. In a classic study, Robert Weiss (1979) observed single parents for several years and identified three common sources of strain: (1) responsibility overload—single parents must make all the decisions and provide for all the needs of their families; (2) task overload—working, housekeeping, and parenting take up so much time that there is none left to meet unexpected demands; and (3) emotional overload—single parents must constantly give emotional support to their children regardless of how they feel themselves.

This and other research suggests that the number of parents in the home is not as crucial as the functioning of the member who is present (Lamanna, 1997).

Other consequences of divorce that can create problems include the increase in the number of single people in the population, more complicated family relationships when divorced people remarry, and the right of grandparents to see their grandchildren. The basic social problem created by the high divorce rate, however, is that the other institutions of society (e.g., schools and economic institutions) remain geared to the traditional family. These institutions are now under pressure to adapt to the needs of single people and single-parent families—for example, to provide more care for children of working parents, more flexible working hours, and more welfare services.

Cohabiting Couples

Most common among people under the age of 25 and over the age of 65, cohabitation has been increasing at a rate of approximately 15 percent a year for the past decade or more. Among younger people, living together is most popular in college towns, where students may have more opportunities to experiment with intimate living arrangements (Wolf, 1996). There are more than 3.5 million cohabiting couples in the United States, and this arrangement is even more popular in some western European nations. Although some cohabiting couples may see living together as a form of trial marriage, others regard it as an alternative to conventional marriage; this is especially true of elderly unmarried couples. In one study, John Z. Zhao (1995) interviewed 177 Canadian cohabiting couples and followed them over time to study the connections between premarital cohabitation and marital instability. He concluded that premarital cohabitation was related to a higher risk of divorce. Other research has confirmed this result, but the research record is by no means definitive at this time. One hypothesis under study is that the greater tendency of former cohabiting partners to divorce may be due to a slightly less conventional attitude and less willingness to make commitments, rather than to any aspect of cohabitation itself (Skolnick & Skolnick, 1994; Zhao, 1995).

Postponement of Marriage

Postponement of marriage became more common in the decades following World War II as young people chose to concentrate on education and careers. Today American woman are postponing marriage longer than ever before. The median age of women who marry for the first time is 24.5 years. Men also are marrying later than at any time since 1900, with a median age at first marriage of 26.7 years. (See Figure 12–3, which shows trends in age at first marriage from 1890 to 1990.) One result of this trend, coupled with the high divorce rate, is that more than one American adult in ten lives alone.

Postponement of marriage has a variety of implications for the family. One is a decrease in the average number of children per family—the longer marriage is postponed, the fewer children the couple is likely to have when they eventually do marry. Advances in reproductive technologies and medical care during pregnancy have made it possible for more women to have children while in their 40s, and there has been an increase in the number of women who bear their first child late in their reproductive years. Even in such cases, however, the family is likely to have only one or at most two children.

When couples have children relatively late in life, they also become grandparents later and for a shorter time than those who marry and have children earlier. (This is especially true for men, who have a shorter life expectancy than women.) Postponement of marriage is also correlated with an increase in the proportion of childless couples since many people who marry late choose not to have children for personal

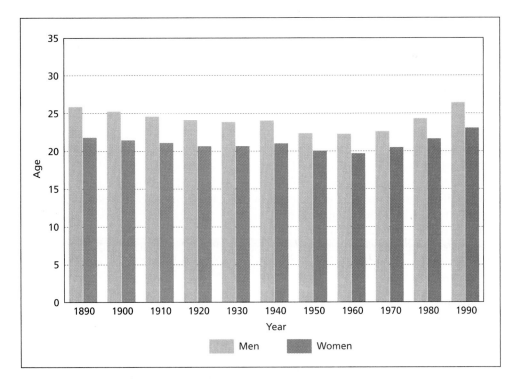

Figure 12–3   Median Age at First Marriage for Men and Women

Source: Data from U.S. Census Bureau.

or economic reasons or because the risk of birth defects increases with the age of the mother.

As a demographic trend, postponement of marriage has a significant effect on the population as a whole. A change of only two years in the median age at first marriage can make a vast difference in the number of married couples in the population in a given year. Moreover, since men tend to marry women who are younger than themselves, women who postpone marriage become caught in a "marriage squeeze": The number of women who would like to marry is greater than the number of available men (Biblarz & Raftery, 1999; Rossi & Rossi, 1990).

Changing Norms of Parenthood

Births to Unmarried Women

Anthropologist Bronislaw Malinowski (1941) noted that in most so-called primitive societies there is a social dogma to the effect that "every family must have a father; a woman must marry before she may have children; there must be a male in every household" (p. 202). In other words, it is expected that every child will be provided with a legitimate father who will act as its protector and guardian.

Actually, there are societies in which marriage is not always a social prerequisite for parenthood. In parts of West Africa, for example, a woman may bear a child out of wedlock, and no stigma will be attached to her or to the child as long as the father's identity is reasonably certain. It is not sexual activity out of wedlock that is frowned on but promiscuity.

In our society, many of the stigmas traditionally associated with premarital pregnancy have been reduced. Relatively few children of unmarried women are given up for adoption. Nevertheless, premarital pregnancy is still frowned on, generally because it indicates that sexual intercourse has occurred out of wedlock; the stigma is removed only if the couple is willing to marry before the child is born. Society still expects children to be provided with two recognized parents, and failure to meet this norm may result in various degrees of social condemnation. One form of condemnation is the legal classification of the child as illegitimate.

It is important to keep this legal aspect in mind when considering the social problem of illegitimacy. Granted that the one-parent family faces special problems—especially in a society in which the nuclear family is the norm—those problems are in themselves no different whether the single parent is unmarried, widowed, or divorced. Many of the distinctive difficulties of the unwed mother and her child, at least in the United States, are a matter of legal status.

In recent years there has been a growing trend toward enactment of stricter child-support laws and stronger enforcement of such laws. Single mothers do not often have the resources to pursue deadbeat fathers. In consequence, under the leadership of the federal government and some states, like Wisconsin, new efforts are being made to enforce compliance with court orders of child support for all children, regardless of the parents' marital status, a subject to which we will return shortly (Meyer & Bartfeld, 1996).

Many sociologists view the weakening of marital norms as one of the greatest and most negative changes in the family as a major institution of modern society. According to many experts, growing up fatherless is never a desirable condition (Popenoe, 1996). Others point out, however, that many nontraditional families provide children with a degree of love and nurturing that is lacking in families where the father is present but is struggling with a problem such as alcoholism or unemployment. Thus, the controversy over "family values" continues in sociology as well as in the popular media (Lamanna, 1997; Reigot, 1996).

Teenage Pregnancy

The very good news about teenage fertility and childbearing is that in the United States teenage birthrates have recently fallen to a level not witnessed in four decades. The lingering bad news is that teenagers are still having babies in greater numbers than their counterparts in other urban industrial nations.

Figure 12–4 shows that teenage birthrates have fallen by almost 50 percent in the past 40 years. Births to minority teenagers, which were higher at the beginning of the

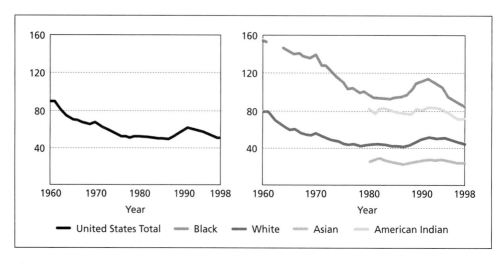

Figure 12–4 Birthrates for Ages 15 to 19 Years (per 1,000 women)
Source: Data from National Center for Health Statistics.

period, are falling steadily. They remain highest among African Americans. Birthrates are still high among all U.S. teenagers compared to rates in other nations. The United States ranks with Indonesia, the Phillippines, and Turkey as the nations with the highest teenage birthrates, whereas the rates in Japan, France, Germany, and Britain are significantly lower. These nations also provide their teenagers with far more sex education, more access to birth control, and superior health institutions.

The U.S. state with the lowest teenage birthrate has a rate about equal to the highest rate in the developed world outside the United States. Figure 12–5 shows that although no state stands up well in international comparisons, Vermont has a rate of about 27, whereas states in the South and Southwest have extremely high rates of teenage fertility.

A persistent issue in the United States today is whether young women who become pregnant should be allowed to have abortions. In 1990 the National Institute of Child Health and Human Development reported the results of a study of black teenagers who came to family planning clinics in Baltimore for pregnancy tests. The young women were divided into three groups: those who chose to have an abortion, those who bore the child, and those who turned out not to be pregnant. The groups were followed for two years. The researchers found that 90 percent of the group who had abortions and 79 percent of those whose pregnancy tests were negative graduated from high school or stayed in school. Among those who bore children, 68 percent dropped out of school. The study also found that 4.5 percent of those who chose abortion experienced an adverse psychological effect, compared to 5.5 percent of those who bore children. Opponents of abortion criticized the study, contending that two years was not a long enough period to produce meaningful results and that "postabortion stress syndrome" often does not show up until five years after the abortion.

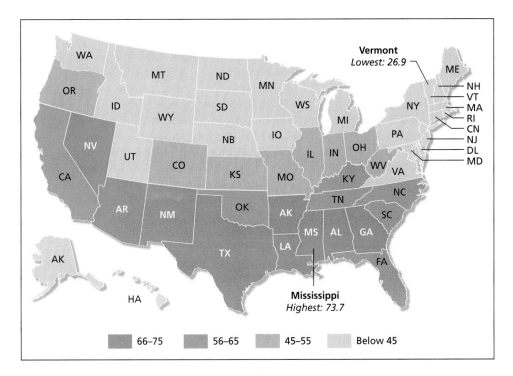

Figure 12-5   Birthrates by State for Ages 15 to 19 Years (per 1,000 women)

Source: Data from National Center for Health Statistics.

Gay and Lesbian Families

Throughout the United States, and especially in California, New York, and Chicago, the number of same-sex marriages is on the rise. But the issue of whether these marriages can be legal according to the laws of given states remains extremely controversial. In 1989 the San Francisco city council passed an ordinance that legalized such marriages, but legislation elsewhere in the nation has been far less favorable. In 1996 Congress passed the Defense of Marriage Act, which allows states to pass laws against same-sex marriages but does not oblige them to do so (Butler, 1998). Despite this measure, Hawaii became the first state to permit gay and lesbian marriages. At this writing, however, the issue continues to generate debate and fierce political fights. In California, for example, voters recently approved a referendum, Proposition 22, that grants legal status only to marriages between males and females (Gale, 2000). Colorado's legislature had already passed a similar measure. Despite these laws, gay and lesbian activists continue to press for equality before the law and to demand recognition of same-sex marriages.

Almost as controversial are the recent decisions by major corporations like Disney and Xerox to extend health and other insurance benefits to the domestic partners of gay and lesbian employees, causing some conservative groups to threaten boycotts against these corporations. In the context of the AIDS crisis, these decisions represent an important moral stance because they could lead to high medical insurance costs. On the other hand, the new policies require employees to declare their sexual preference and document their partnerships before benefits can be extended to their partners. This can have negative consequences if the employee faces homophobia in the workplace.

The AIDS epidemic has led homosexual couples to consider longer-term relationships and, in doing so, to desire children of their own. Of course, people form long-term relationships for many reasons, but clearly AIDS is a consideration. Recent research has shown that people with AIDS are most likely to obtain support from present or former lovers, especially a spouse or domestic partner. The family of origin often fails to provide the support that one might expect because parents are ashamed of their child's homosexuality and AIDS or refuse to accept the domestic partner into the family (Ayala, 1996; Kadushin, 1996).

Many homosexual couples consider themselves to be married, and an estimated one-third of lesbians and one-fifth of gay males have children from previous heterosexual marriages (Bell & Weinberg, 1978; Richmond-Abbott, 1992). As reproductive technologies become increasingly effective, more lesbian couples are able to have children through artificial insemination. In addition, although laws in many states make it difficult for homosexuals to adopt children, many have succeeded in doing so. As a result, the number of same-sex couples with children is steadily increasing. In a recent review of 40 studies of children of same-sex couples sponsored by the American Psychological Association, researchers found that children of gay unions are just as likely to be well adjusted as children of heterosexual unions. The children of gay and lesbian couples play the same games, have similar likes and dislikes, and score equally well on intelligence tests. They do suffer, however, from a sense that society rejects their parents and that their friends may not understand their home situation. On the other hand, they are no more likely to be confused about sexual identity than children of heterosexual parents (Shapiro, 1996).

Homeless Families

Although homelessness has been recognized as a serious social problem since the early 1980s, only recently has it become evident that many of the homeless are families—usually mothers living on the streets with their children. No one knows exactly how many homeless families there are in the United States, but Martha Burt (1994) of the Urban Institute, the nation's leading expert on counting the homeless, estimates the total number at over 40,000, depending on the time of year, the state of the economy, and the availability of low-cost housing. Christopher Jencks (1994) has pointed out, however, that the number could vary quite widely, depending on how one defines homelessness. For example, families that live in public housing projects, where the lease may be held by a mother or grandmother, are often at risk of becoming homeless as a result of family disputes or crackdowns by authorities. So on a given night, the number of homeless families who are seeking aid may vary according to the climate of enforcement in a community, and the total number of homeless families may vary according to how long families must live in shelters or on the streets before they are considered to be homeless (Burt, 1994). In a recent study of homelessness, the U.S. Department of Housing and Urban Development interviewed more than 4,000 homeless individuals and families and found that 70 percent of homeless families who receive housing assistance and secure adequate shelter are able to improve their family's health, stabilize their economic and social condition, and move on to better housing on their own (*Alcoholism & Drug Abuse Weekly*, 1999).

This homeless family having their Thanksgiving dinner in the shadow of the Capitol symbolizes the plight of poor families who can no longer afford adequate shelter.

The plight of homeless families is illustrated by a case described by sociologist Jonathan Kozol (1988): Laura, a Hispanic woman, lives with her four children in a welfare hotel in New York City. The plaster on the walls in the hotel is covered with a sweet-tasting, lead-based paint; Laura's 7-year-old son is suffering from lead poisoning. The bathroom plumbing has overflowed and left a pool of sewage on the floor, and a radiator valve periodically releases a spray of scalding steam. Laura's 4-month-old daughter has contracted scabies, a serious skin disease. Laura has taken her children to a clinic, but because she cannot read, she is unable to follow instructions about their care that have been sent to her through the mail. She also was unable to read a request for information from her welfare office, and her welfare payments have been cut off as a result.

The families who are most at risk of becoming homeless are those who have experienced a crisis such as divorce or desertion, resulting in a drastic reduction of income and, hence, inability to pay for shelter. Studies have indicated that a large majority of homeless families do not have relatives, parents, or close friends to whom they can turn for support (Committee on Health Care for Homeless People, 1988). In addition, many homeless women with children are victims of family violence and may initially seek refuge in shelters for battered women. This suggests the need for more extensive public programs to provide emergency shelter for adults with children. These and related issues will be discussed more fully in Chapter 15.

Reproductive Issues

Advances in Reproductive Technology

In England in 1994 a woman who was over 60 and well past menopause gave birth to a child after artificial insemination. The birth immediately became the subject of an immense controversy. As Arthur Caplan (1992), one of the world's foremost students of bioethics, has noted, advances in reproductive technology have created an unprecedented number of moral dilemmas. These dilemmas are likely to become even more vexing as reproductive technology becomes more powerful.

The possibilities and choices associated with human reproduction have been greatly expanded as a result of new reproductive technologies, which permit women and men to deal with fertility control and childbearing in ways that were never before possible. However, they may also create new problems and raise thorny moral issues both for individuals and for society. We will describe several such technologies in this section. Each of them raises moral issues because each to some degree removes reproduction from the control of biology and fate and places reproductive decisions more squarely in the hands of individuals and society.

Amniocentesis.   Amniocentesis, a technique for drawing fluid from the uterus in the first trimester of pregnancy, makes possible genetic tests that can detect Down syndrome and a few other potentially severe birth defects. Since the risks of these problems increase with a woman's age, amniocentesis allows women in their 30s and early 40s to feel more confident about becoming pregnant and enables working women to have healthy children relatively late in their careers. However, the knowledge that one is carrying a fetus that will have severe birth defects or a genetic disease leads to the question of whether to terminate the pregnancy through abortion.

Implanted Contraceptives.   Opponents of birth control believe that contraception leads to more casual attitudes toward sex and to the devaluation of human life. These are similar to arguments about abortion, but contraceptives that can be implanted in a woman's body raise additional issues. These devices have been used in some cases in which judges have ordered that women under sentence must prevent themselves from becoming pregnant until they can demonstrate to the court that they are responsible enough to bear children. Such orders have angered women's groups and civil rights organizations, as well as traditional opponents of birth control.

Fertility Drugs.   Fertility drugs (e.g., Clonapin) allow previously infertile women to become pregnant, but there have been a number of cases in which the drugs have been implicated in multiple pregnancies—triplets, quadruplets, quintuplets, and more. Large multiple pregnancies can be harmful to the mother and greatly increase the risks of premature birth, birth defects, and fetal death. Doctors can use noninvasive sonar (sonograms) to track the development of multiple fetuses; they can even selectively abort fetuses so that the mother need not bear more than one or two babies. Again, the fertility drugs create unanticipated problems that require additional technologies and raise the difficult moral questions of choice and abortion.

Artificial Insemination and In-utero Implants.   To avoid certain reproductive difficulties, doctors can fertilize a woman's ovum with sperm from her husband or from a sperm bank. They can even implant in her uterus an ovum that has been fertilized outside a human body. These techniques allow women without husbands to have children. They also allow infertile couples to have children who carry the genes of at least one of their parents. These methods entail significant moral choices, such as whether to intentionally become a single parent. The procedures also widen the possibilities of surrogacy, currently among the most controversial aspects of reproductive technology.

The Morning-after Pill

The so-called morning-after pill, RU-486, causes a fertilized egg to detach itself from the uterine lining and be eliminated from the woman's body. This effective pill, developed in France, is available in Europe but is not marketed in the United States because of conservative opposition to any form of postcoital contraceptive (Mundy, 1999). However, Princeton University's Office of Population Research maintains a website (**www.not-2-late.com**) and a telephone hotline (1-888-NOT2LATE) that offer advice about another "morning after" treatment: a strong and perfectly legal dose of ordinary birth control pills that works before pregnancy occurs, preventing a fertilized egg from implanting itself in the uterus. This treatment will not terminate an established pregnancy or harm a fetus. The Office of Population Research estimates that it could reduce unintended pregnancies by 50 percent if it were more widely available.

SOCIAL POLICY

Social policies related to problems of families can be divided into four major categories: divorce law and alimony, efforts to reduce teenage pregnancy, programs to assist low-income families, and child care and family support.

Divorce Law

In the 1950s and 1960s, as attitudes toward divorce became more liberal, there was a growing demand for changes in state divorce laws. Laws that permitted divorce only in extreme cases—adultery, for example—were challenged in many states. Beginning with California in 1970, many states liberalized their divorce laws and moved toward the concept of no-fault divorce. No-fault divorce laws allow judges to decide on such issues as child custody and division of property without blaming one partner or the other; this eliminates the need for children to testify about parental behavior and thus be dragged into a bitter court battle in addition to the pain they are already suffering. Many states followed California's lead, instituting no-fault laws and allowing couples to petition for divorce under compatible (previously agreed-on) terms.

The no-fault approach does not entirely eliminate strife. In many instances the courts must still adjudicate conflicting claims and settle rancorous custody battles. However, contrary to the claims of critics who believed that no-fault policies would lead to an increase in divorce rates, comparative research shows that divorce rates have not increased disproportionately in states with liberal divorce laws (Cherlin, 1992).

The Ongoing Debate Over Divorce Law.   Several states are considering measures that would make it more difficult, rather than easier, for couples to divorce, especially if they have children. Leaders of this movement argue that no-fault laws in most states have not produced lower divorce rates, happier families, or less suffering for children of divorced parents. They also believe that liberal divorce laws may weaken trust in other people and in the institutions of society (Galston, 1996; Stanton, 1996). Their opponents argue that genuine concern for children might result in more support for child care provisions so that fewer women and children would experience the economic insecurity that often follows separation and divorce (Ehrenreich, 1996).

Alimony and Child Support.   **Alimony**—the money paid by one partner for the support of the other, usually by the husband to the wife—has been closely tied to the concept of fault in divorce proceedings. In the absence of no-fault provisions, the main purpose of a divorce trial has been to fix blame on one party or the other and to make the guilty party (usually the husband) pay a certain amount over and above that which would ordinarily have been paid; if the fault rested with the wife, she would receive less than the ordinary amount. However, when a decree of divorce can be granted without the need to punish either partner, alimony can be awarded on the

CRITICAL RESEARCH

Life Without Father

Family research expert David Popenoe (1996) is on a sociological crusade to convince Americans that families without fathers create a host of disadvantages for children. Unlike many who speak of "family values," Popenoe is not motivated by religious fervor or conservative ideologies. He considers himself a liberal who has simply seen the truth: Kids without dads are at a disadvantage throughout their lifetimes. The consequences of fatherlessness, according to Popenoe, are juvenile delinquency, abuse, economic hardship, male children with little sense of how to become mature men, and much more.

Popenoe's research demonstrates that the primary reason why growing numbers of fathers are abdicating their role and not staying in the family is the decrease in the proportion of couples who marry. This decrease has a variety of causes. According to Popenoe, his research demonstrates that relaxation of norms requiring that a couple marry before having children is largely responsible for the rise of single-parent households. But even when couples marry, the high rate of divorce is another sign that commitment to making marriages work, especially on the part of men, has been declining.

Marriage as a social institution has been weakened. "Involved fathers," he writes, "are indispensable for the good of children and society; and our growing national fatherlessness is a disaster in the making" (1996, p. 2). "An especially troubling trend is that males today show a reluctance even to acknowledge children that they do not see or support" (p. 25). He further states that "the end result is that fathers are vanishing from family life and only mothers are left to care for the children" (p. 51).

Why don't men see these problems? Why don't more men take responsibility for the children they have fathered and the women they have left with all the

burdens and joys of family life? Of course, many men are responsible fathers, but too many, Popenoe argues, have become radical individualists, convinced that by following their own star they are doing the best for themselves.

Popenoe's research has been criticized for not paying enough attention to the good parenting that often occurs in single-parent families. Noted feminist social scientist Judith Stacey (1993) faults Popenoe for not placing enough emphasis on changes in the economy, particularly the decline of good blue-collar jobs, which deprives many men of satisfactory ways of providing for their families. This lack of jobs is a major theme in the writings of William Julius Wilson, as we have seen elsewhere in the chapter. But Popenoe shows courage in raising his voice to say that his evidence convinces him, and should convince others, that social policies designed to help families should pay greater attention to absent fathers and their abdication of family responsibilities.

more realistic basis of financial need and ability to provide. Theoretically, this means that it would no longer be unusual for a man to receive alimony from his ex-wife if she has greater earning power; also, a woman with no children would not necessarily be granted alimony or would receive alimony only temporarily, to give her time to become self-supporting.

Children often suffer economically as a result of divorce. In 1995, the most recent year for which data are available, 11.6 million mothers were legal custodians of their children under the age of 21; of them, 4.3 million actually received child support in that year. In fact, 6.2 million of these women were supposed to receive child support, an indication that there are almost 2 million fathers who either are slow in making their payments or are not making any payments at all (*Statistical Abstract,* 1999). In view of statistics like these, a high priority of family courts is to track down ex-husbands who fail to pay for the support of their children. In a 1988 decision, the United States Supreme Court ruled that fathers who fail to make payments because of financial problems must prove to authorities that they indeed lack adequate funds. Since then the federal government and many states have instituted tougher policies on enforcement of child-support payments. (See the Critical Research feature on page 362.)

Efforts to Reduce Teenage Pregnancies

One motivation for the passage of the 1996 Welfare Reform Act was the desire to change policies that seemed to reward early childbearing by single mothers. By withdrawing the entitlement provisions from the welfare program, for example, conservative lawmakers hoped to allow states to deny payments to teenage mothers or to provide them only under certain conditions. The underlying reasoning was that welfare payments encourage women, especially teenagers, to have babies that they might not otherwise have. Most sociologists who study this issue believe that this reasoning is flawed. Before the passage of the 1996 law, welfare benefits varied widely from one state to another. Under the "welfare incentive" theory, one would expect to find higher teenage birthrates in the states with the highest welfare payments, but this was never true (Luker, 1996).

Sex education and access to birth control have been shown to reduce rates of teenage pregnancy. As we saw earlier, these rates have fallen to their lowest levels in 40 years in the United States but are still far higher than those in European countries. Sexually active women clearly are using more birth control more effectively over time, but the reverse seems to be true for women who are not sexually active. And whereas the pregnancy rates are almost twice as high for sexually active teenagers, the level of sexual activity has actually tripled over a generation; thus, were it not for the effects of birth control and sex education, the pregnancy rates would be even higher than they are (Alan Guttmacher Institute, 1994).

Despite the substantial social-scientific evidence, it is unlikely that there will be federal support for increased access to birth control or sex education directed toward teenagers. These issues are deadlocked by ideological differences in Congress and in many state legislatures. It is likely, however, that there will be new policy initiatives to make unmarried fathers more responsible for the support of their offspring. It is also possible that the cuts in aid for poor families, including those headed by teenage or young adult women, may begin to produce lower rates of teenage pregnancy. Some observers believe that even if previous welfare laws did not actually create incentives, society is becoming less tolerant of teenage pregnancy, and this change itself may lead to lower rates of pregnancy among teenage girls (Popenoe, 1996). On the other hand, some fear that new, more restrictive welfare laws may result in higher teen abortion rates and less support for children in single-parent families (Abramowitz, 1996; Luker, 1996).

Child Care and Family Support

Samuel Preston (1984), a well-known sociologist and demographer, has made an eloquent plea for a coherent public policy to assist low-income families with children:

> If we care about our collective future rather than simply about our futures as individuals we are faced with the question of how best to safeguard the human and material resources represented by children. . . . Rather than assuming collective responsibility, as has been done in the case of the elderly, U.S. society has chosen to place almost exclusive responsibility for the care of children on the nuclear family. Marital instability, however, has much reduced the capacity of the family to care for its own children. Hence insisting that families alone care for the young would seem to be an evasion of collective responsibility rather than a conscious decision about the best way to provide for the future. (p. 44)

CURRENT CONTROVERSIES

Family Support and Day Care

About 80 percent of American infants and school-age children have working mothers. The rapid increase in the number of working mothers adds to the urgency of the need to find high-quality child care during working hours. About 50 percent of working mothers report that they are unable to find satisfactory child care (Ford Foundation, 1990). At the same time, deep divisions in government about how best to establish and fund child care present major obstacles to new policies.

The 1996 Welfare Reform Act, which shifted the primary responsibility for welfare policy to the states, has resulted in cuts in food stamps and medical benefits, as well as in direct aid to single-parent families with young children. At the same time, there are increased demands for participation in work or training programs in lieu of welfare payments to reduce longer-term dependency on dole systems. The catch here, of course, is that welfare recipients need adequate day care services or after-school programs if they are to join the labor force without leaving their children unattended. Indeed, many fear that this problem will increase the incidence of child neglect and abuse in poor families that cannot afford adequate day care (Gelles, 1995; Luker, 1996). Moreover, the pressure to fund day care in communities throughout the nation is placing unprecedented burdens on private charities as well as state and federal budgets (Salter, 1996). For example,

the Mission Day Care Center in San Francisco, which served about 300 poor children, was forced to close because it lost its annual $50,000 grant from the United Way. Most of the children are now cared for in less secure and less reliable situations. Although it is too soon to tell what the policy response to this situation will be, it may be that a number of ghastly events must occur before a climate of support for adequate child care can develop (Abramovitz, 1996).

The Ford Foundation and other private philanthropic organizations have also called attention to the urgent need to improve existing day-care services. In California, for example, the California Child Care Resource and Referral Network has found that training new workers in the basics of child development and child care is an extremely high-priority need. There is also a serious problem of frustration and burnout among child care workers, many of whom work 12-hour days with few breaks and have little contact with other practitioners and professionals. The network estimates that "every year some 60 percent of home-based providers [in California] close their operations" (Ford Foundation, 1990, p. 8). The network is seeking to develop a system of peer support, training, and assistance from local resources to improve this situation. Throughout the nation the problem of adequate funding and training of day care providers and centers is becoming a growing social problem and an increasing challenge to policymakers.

Preston's (1994) comments are echoed in Hillary Clinton's book, *It Takes a Village*, which applies the African adage "It takes a village to raise a child" to issues of child care and family life. The point here is that communities and governments need to assist parents in caring for their children. Such assistance might include medical care, day care for the children of working parents, early childhood education, after-school learning programs, summer recreation, and so on. Family expert David Popenoe (1995) observes that if communities are to provide such support, they, too, must be strengthened. "The seedbed of social virtue is childhood," he writes. "Social virtue is in decline in the United States for two main reasons—a decline in family functioning and a decline in community functioning." But, echoing what many conservative leaders say about these issues, Popenoe adds that it is not clear how communities can be strengthened, but it is clear that individual men and women bear the responsibility for becoming good parents. "As individuals," he states, "we should seek to stay married, stay accessible to our children, stay active in our local communities, and stay put" (p. 98).

While the debates about "family values" and community responsibility for raising children continue to engage pundits and political leaders throughout the United States, the fact remains that for more and more families child care services in the community are becoming a necessity of family life (Loupe, 1996). Today 30 percent of working mothers are placing preschool children in organized day care, an all-time high. The "workfare" demand incorporated into the 1996 Welfare Reform Act will send increasing numbers of mothers with young children into the labor force in coming years, and that, too, will swell the demand for day care. Thus, there is little question that day care funding and day care policies (e.g., licencing and regulation) will become an increasingly important area of social policy at all levels of government.

One of the brightest areas of change is the Family Leave Act, which was passed by Congress during President Clinton's first term in office. This measure requires businesses to allow leaves, with or without pay, to mothers and fathers of newborn children. Before the passage of the act there was no national policy that mandated specific family-related benefits for all workers (*Congressional Digest,* 1993). Vast changes in the composition of the work force, especially the dramatic increase in the number of women with young children, have clearly spurred interest in policies like family leave. Nevertheless, the future of policies in this area is not clear. Will voters call for policies that extend family leaves for longer periods? And as baby boom parents enter their waning years, will there be greater demand for family leaves to take care of elderly and ill parents? Proponents of these policies point to the nations of western Europe, which have far more liberal family leave policies and far more extensive child care institutions than does the United States. There is little doubt that child care and the needs of families will remain active areas of social policy debate and legislation in the coming years. These issues are discussed further in the Current Controversies feature on page 364.

Beyond Left & Right

Few issues arouse more passionate debate than those bearing on families and family responsibilities. People on the liberal side of the political spectrum tend to worry about the fate of single parents and their children, especially in poor families with evident unmet needs. People on the right may be equally concerned about poor mothers and their children, but they tend to believe that if more people took responsibility for their own actions there would be fewer such cases. And so the debate over individual versus social responsibility continues without much resolution.

A sociological view of the issue is more pragmatic. What does the research show? If there are children with serious unmet needs for day care, early education, and protection against abuse, where will the resources come from? This may sound like a liberal approach since it directs attention toward the children in need and does not necessarily speak to issues of responsibility, but eventually all of society's leaders, whether they are in universities or in legislatures, are called on to "do something" about social problems. When social policies are discussed, the facts often make a big difference in cutting through the ideological barriers. No one wants to see children suffer. On the other hand, no one wants policies that make problems worse. Thus, whenever practical solutions to problems of the family are discussed, sociologists and other social scientists attempt to provide facts, evaluations of existing approaches, and unimpassioned answers to ease the tensions aroused by angry debates over values.

SUMMARY

- A kinship unit is a group of individuals who are related by blood, marriage, or adoption. It may be a nuclear family (a father, a mother, and their children living apart from other kin), an extended family (parents, children, grandparents, and others living together or in close proximity), or a modified extended family (nuclear families living separately but maintaining interpersonal attachments and economic exchanges within the extended family).

- Families must adapt to a cycle in which the roles of their members change from one stage of development to the next. During each stage the family faces the challenge of maintaining stability and continuity. External or internal crises may reduce the family to an empty shell, in which family members feel no strong attachment to one another and neglect mutual obligations.

- Among the most important social trends of the second half of this century is the movement of women out of the home and into the work force. As a result, only about one-fifth of all married couples are supported by the husband alone.

- Some studies have shown that a wife's job may enhance family well-being, especially if the wife works outside the home as a matter of choice. Some women resent their "second shift" of work at home after working at a job, but others take it for granted.

- Although there are certain fairly consistent differences between black and white families—in particular, a larger proportion of poor, female-headed families among blacks—most of these differences are probably due to poverty and discrimination.

- The divorce rate has risen dramatically since the mid-1960s, reflecting severe pressures on the institution of marriage. Among them are the change from extended to nuclear families and the reduction in the number of functions performed by the family. In addition, because of the increased social tolerance of divorce, more couples are willing to get a divorce rather than continue an unhappy marriage.

- The problems associated with divorce include emotional and financial strain, particularly for women. Divorced mothers are frequently forced to accept public assistance. Children often become bewildered and frightened and may need professional help for emotional and other problems.

- Postponement of marriage has become common in the United States and has a variety of implications for the family: fewer children per family, an increase in childlessness, and a shortage of available men for women who wish to marry.

- Rates of teenage pregnancy have fallen to their lowest levels in 40 years. However, teenagers in the United States are still having babies in greater numbers than their counterparts in other urban industrial nations. Another sign of changing norms is the increasing number of gay and lesbian couples who are raising children, either their own or adopted.

- The possibilities and choices associated with human reproduction have been greatly expanded as a result of technological advances.

- Social policy to address divorce has consisted chiefly of reforms in divorce laws. Since 1970 no-fault divorce laws have been adopted in a number of states. These have alleviated some of the problems associated with divorce, but others remain. In particular, the courts are unable to enforce alimony and child-support settlements, with the result that many divorced women and their children suffer economic hardship.

- The 1996 Welfare Reform Act includes provisions designed to discourage teenage pregnancy. Sex education and access to birth control have been shown to reduce rates of teenage pregnancy, but these approaches lack widespread public support.

- There is a growing need for child care services for families in all social classes. The Family Leave Act is a step in that direction, but the future of policy in this area is unclear.

KEY TERMS

kinship unit, p. 342
nuclear family, p. 342
extended family, p. 342

modified extended family, p. 342
alimony, p. 361

INTERNET EXERCISE

The web destinations for Chapter 12 are related to different aspects of the changing family. To begin your explorations, go to the Prentice Hall Companion Website: **http://prenhall.com/kornblum**. Then choose **Chapter 12** (The Changing Family). Next, select **destinations** from the menu on the left side of the screen. There are a variety of sites to investigate. We suggest that you begin with **Teenage Pregnancy-Kidsource**. After you reach the opening page, click on "Search" and then enter "teenage pregnancy." Then click on the first entry, which is a "fact sheet" on teenage pregnancy constructed by Kidsource. In discussing this topic, the text mentions the controversy regarding how recent changes in welfare laws will affect teen pregnancy. There are many other sites dealing with teenage pregnancy that are accessible from the Kidsource-Teenage Pregnancy page. After you have explored the issues thoroughly, answer the following questions:

■ The text points out that under the so-called "welfare incentive" theory, one would expect to find higher teenage birthrates in the states with the highest welfare payments, but this was *never* true. What do you think will be the impact of the Welfare Reform Act of 1996 on the incidence of teenage pregnancy?

■ If you were a policymaker, what suggestions would you make for reducing the incidence of teenage pregnancy in the United States? How would you propose dealing with *existing* teenage pregnancy?

13 Problems of Education

FACTS ABOUT

EDUCATION

- Over 99 percent of all American children between the ages of 5 and 19 are enrolled in school.

- The estimated lifetime earnings of high school graduates are at least $200,000 higher than those of dropouts.

- In inner-city neighborhoods it is not uncommon for public school classes to include more than 30 students.

- Among classroom teachers in public schools only about 2 in 10 use computers daily with students, and about 4 in 10 never use the machines in their classrooms at all.

OUTLINE

Sociological Perspectives on Education
Functionalist Approaches
Conflict Approaches
Interactionist Approaches

Education and Equality: The Issue of Equal Access
Black Students
Hispanic Students
Preschool Programs
Desegregation
Educational Attainment Today

School Reform: Problems of Institutional Change
Schools as Bureaucracies
Classroom and School Size
School Choice
The "Technological Fix"
Teachers' Professionalism and Unions
School Violence

Social Policy
Educational Conservatism and "Back to Basics"
Humanism and "Open Education"
Access to Higher Education
Trends and Prospects

In democratic nations education is viewed as the primary means of addressing a host of social needs and social problems. The schools are expected to prepare new generations to be good citizens and reliable, capable workers. Schooling is expected to produce young people who can enter the labor force with the necessary skills in literacy, computation, and written expression. Higher education in colleges, universities, and professional training institutions is expected to produce young adults who can become scientists and professionals and leaders in business and other institutions of society.

But these ambitious expectations hardly exhaust the list of demands placed on educators. Schools and institutions of higher education are expected to address and solve problems of inequality. They are not expected to make everyone equal—all societies recognize that people are born with differing interests and abilities—but they are expected to provide equal opportunities to learn and to gain the skills and experiences society requires. And as if these demands were not enough, the schools are also expected to address other social problems, such as racism, sexism, and violence. Given all these expectation and hopes, it is somewhat ironic that we can consider education to be a social problem. We do so, however, because of the very high expectations we have for education and because so many observers believe, rightly or wrongly, that the schools are failing to meet these demands.

No wonder the issues that affect schools in the United States are staggering. Almost every aspect of schooling is subject to controversy. At present there is a debate about national education standards, school choice, school privatization, prayer in school, weapons in schools, standards for teachers, the impact of technology, classroom and school size, and much more. School reform figured prominently in the 2000 presidential election and will no doubt be an issue in every state and local election for years to come. But one of the ironies in all of the controversies that swirl around the schools, including those in higher education, is that people tend to like their own schools and to place the blame for "educational failure" elsewhere (NORC, 1999).

Each time schoolchildren recite the Pledge of Allegiance, they are affirming the values of American citizenship. One of the primary functions of the educational system is to produce citizens who are aware of their rights and responsibilities in a democracy.

The "failure" of the American educational system is a complex issue that is defined differently by different groups in society, depending on the goals of the group in question. For example, parents at all social-class levels are demanding that the schools do a better job of preparing students to work and live in a technologically sophisticated society. Various minority groups want schools to prepare their children to compete in American society yet, at the same time, not strip them of their cultural identity—or, in the case of Hispanics, of the language they learn at home. Educational policymakers believe that schools must do more to increase the overall level of student achievement. Many teachers, on the other hand, believe that parents should play a greater role in their children's education. And an increasing minority of parents are choosing to teach their children at home, a trend known as "homeschooling."

In all of the controversies surrounding public education, there is little agreement even among experts. From a social-scientific viewpoint, part of the problem of knowing whether U.S. schools are truly failing to produce well-educated students lies in the difficulty of conducting comparative research. Comparative studies must hold constant social variables such as language and social class, and this is never entirely possible. However, one recent study succeeded in administering standardized tests in different languages and in controlling for social class.

The Third International Mathematics and Science Study (TIMSS) is the largest and most rigorous international comparison of education ever undertaken. It has many components, including studies of student performance, extensive interviews with parents about their children's schools and their performance in them, analysis of teacher-training systems, comparisons of different nations' educational policies, and much more. In an earlier phase of the study, the primary researcher, Harold W. Stevenson (1992), and his team looked at differences in performance on standardized tests between students in the United States and Asia (China, Japan, and Taiwan). They found that "the test results confirm what has become common knowledge: schoolchildren in Asia perform better academically than do those in the U.S." (p. 71). In mathematics, for example, first-graders in U.S. schools did not perform as well as comparable children in Asian schools, although students in some of the better U.S. schools had scores that were similar to theirs. By the fifth grade, however, the U.S. students had fallen quite far behind their Asian counterparts; students at only one school in the U.S. sample scored as high as students at the worst school in the Asian sample. Interviews with parents in the different nations indicated that Asian parents are far more demanding of their children and far less likely to accept poor or mediocre school performance than American parents are.

Later phases of the TIMMS reserarch centered on comparisons among the United States, Germany, and Japan. Among the many findings, the authors note that sorting students by ability (tracking) is far more prevalent and begins earlier in the United States than in Germany or Japan (where tracking is banned entirely in the primary grades). This may help account for differences in parents' acceptance of their children's school performance and the lower average standards set by U.S. parents (Stevenson, 1998).

Another study, which compared schools in the United States and selected European nations, found quite different results (Organization for Economic Cooperation and Development, cited in Celis, 1993b). When test scores of U.S. students from 16 public school systems in inner-city, suburban, and rural districts were compared to similar sets of scores from schools in 16 European, Canadian, and Australian systems, the results showed that U.S. students outperformed students in 12 other nations. In math, U.S. students scored ahead of students in only 2 other nations, but in science they scored in the middle range, along with students in Canada, France, England, Scotland, and Spain. This international study also found that U.S. colleges, especially community colleges, do a better job of preparing students for a changing labor market than do institutions of higher education in the other nations studied. And although only 15.5 percent of U.S. college and university degrees are awarded in the sciences, compared to 32 percent in Germany and 26 percent in Japan, far higher proportions of all students attend colleges and universities in the United States than in those nations; hence, the absolute number of science students in the United States is high and is continuing to increase.

The controversy over scholastic achievement scores is another example of how difficult it is to determine whether the schools are actually failing. Since the early 1960s there appears to have been a decline in the verbal and mathematical skills of high school students as measured by the Scholastic Aptitude Test (SAT), a standardized college entrance examination administered to high school students throughout the nation. But there are conflicting opinions on the significance of the drop in mean SAT scores. Many educators believe that the lower scores indicate an increase in the number of underprepared students who take the test. The scores reflect a decrease in student achievement (and, hence, a decrease in the effectiveness of public schooling). Others, however, argue that the SAT and other standardized tests measure what used to be taught rather than what is currently taught, that they are unimportant or irrelevant, that they may be valid for groups but are not valid for individuals, and so on. The most recent national assessment of educational achievement has shown some encouraging improvement in students' math scores (Applebome, 1997). Nevertheless, the level of student achievement remains a subject of widespread debate.

Education and the push for national standards figured prominently in the 2000 presidential election campaign. So did the claim, originally made by Al Gore, that schools need to be "wired" into the Internet. As these issues illustrate, not only the goals of education but also the means of achieving them are subjects of heated debate. Should schools be more open to new ideas and teaching methods, or should they focus more on the traditional curriculum—"the basics"? Indeed, what *are* the basics? Do they consist simply of reading, writing, and arithmetic, or do they include learning how to get along with others and how to communicate effectively? Are the basics the same for all students? These are only some of the fundamental questions that are being asked about public education in the United States today. There are many others. Should more qualified and effective teachers receive merit pay? Should the school year be longer? Should there be a standardized national curriculum? There is even some question about whether education should be a public institution. Perhaps high-quality private schooling should be encouraged by means of a government-sponsored voucher system that would refund to households the amounts they spend on public education through taxes. Such refunds could take the form of educational vouchers that could be used to pay for private schooling (Ballantine, 1993).

The United States has led the world in establishing free public education for its people. Per capita public expenditures on education are higher in the United States than in any other nation. Education is compulsory in the United States; the requirements differ from one state to another, but usually children must attend school until age 16. As a result, over 99 percent of all American children between the ages of 5 and 19 are enrolled in school, and about 75 percent of American adolescents remain in class full time through the final year of secondary school (*Statistical Abstract,* 1999). Moreover, the number of students enrolled in higher education has increased rapidly in this century (Trow, 1966).

So what is wrong? Why is the educational system under attack? How does this impressive record constitute a "failure"? These questions can be answered in different ways, depending on the sociological perspective from which they are viewed.

Sociological Perspectives on Education

As might be expected, there are vast differences in the analyses of public education by sociologists who approach the subject from different theoretical perspectives. Functionalists stress stability and consensus; in their view, education is, or should be, one of several interdependent parts that work together to create a smoothly functioning society whose members all share the same basic values and beliefs. Conflict theorists argue that schools reproduce the society's system of inequality and class stratification in new generations of children (McLeod, 1995). They focus on the coercive aspects of education; they see society as divided into dominant and subordinate groups, with education being used as a tool to promote the interests of the dominant group while teaching the subordinate groups to accept their situation. Interactionists take still another approach: They examine how expectations of students' performance actually determine that performance and can result in labels that shape the students' future. Each of these perspectives gives rise to different approaches to the study of public education.

Functionalist Approaches

From a functionalist perspective, problems in the educational system are a symptom of social disorganization. The educational system is geared to students from stable homes and communities. It is not well equipped to handle the problems of students from disorganized homes—for example, where there is divorce or cultural conflict. Such students are often depressed and angry, have trouble concentrating on their schoolwork, and therefore have difficulty achieving in school (Ballantine, 1993). According to social-disorganization theorists, these students are more likely to join deviant peer groups, such as gangs, that reinforce their negative attitudes toward school.

Also related to functionalism is the theory that educational problems stem from deviance from generally accepted norms of achievement. In this view, schools are agents of social control whose tasks are to reinforce society's values and to control deviance through discipline. This perspective can also be applied to the question of whether schools themselves produce deviance by setting unreachable standards for many students. In a study of boys in a British secondary school, for example, the researcher found that working-class students were unable to understand or appreciate the middle-class value orientation of the school. The school, in turn, was unable to modify its middle-class bias and, hence, was unable to deal with the working-class students' attitudes. The result was the development of a deviant group of alienated working-class youths (Willis, 1983).

Another functionalist approach focuses on the problems of shaping educational institutions to meet the requirements of changing economies and cultures. Institutional theorists look, for example, at how established bureaucracies in educational institutions militate against decentralization and other types of organizational reform (Hannaway, 1993). Studies of educational institutions often look at how changes in curriculum and other school programs designed for special populations (e.g., underachievers) can best be implemented (Drevitch, 1994).

Conflict Approaches

Viewed from a conflict perspective, the problems of education stem from conflicting views of the goals of education. The dispute over whether the schools should teach a universal curriculum in a single language or, instead, help preserve the cultural identities of minority students through bilingual education is an example.

Conflict theory has two main currents—Marxian and non-Marxian. The Marxian view stresses the goal of reducing social stratification and increasing equality. It argues that schools reflect the values of groups in society that are content with the status quo or favor even less equality. In a classic statement of this position, Samuel Bowles wrote that compulsory education in the United States developed to meet the needs of a capitalist economy for skilled and disciplined workers and, while doing so, to justify the unequal social status of workers and capitalists (Bowles & Gintis, 1977). Other investigators, who are not necessarily Marxian theorists but whose research confirms some aspects of Bowles's theory, point to unequal access to education, especially higher education, and inequalities in the resources available to schools in different states or districts (Lavin & Hyllegard, 1996).

The non-Marxian version of the conflict perspective, which is referred to as the *value conflict approach*, focuses on intergroup conflicts that arise out of the desire to maintain or defend a group's status in a particular community. This leads to conflicts over such issues as busing to achieve school desegregation. A case in point is the intense conflict that developed in Boston over efforts to desegregate that city's public schools through busing. One study of this conflict (Buell, 1982) emphasized the concept of the "defended neighborhood," a community that actively resists abrupt change. In more recent research, Gary Orfield also attributes the failure of school desegregation to the persistent segregation of communities. Housing segregation contributes to the resegregation of schools through white flight and the exclusion of minority families from housing markets in better school districts (Orfield & Eaton, 1997).

Interactionist Approaches

According to the interactionist perspective, schools label students "achievers," "underachievers," or "rebels," and these labels follow them throughout their lives. For some students, schools are "factories for failure." A well-known study of ghetto education found, for example, that "a 'slow learner' had no option but to continue to be a slow

TABLE 13–1   Perspectives on Education

Basic Perspective	Research Approach	View of Education as a Social Problem	Policy Recommendations
Functionalism	Social disorganization	Schools cannot help students who come from disorganized backgrounds or have low IQs	Requiring schools to work more closely with parents or guardians, or in some cases take their place
	Deviant behavior	Problems stem from deviance by some groups from accepted norms of achievement	Greater discipline; remedial education for nonachieving students; cracking down on weapons in school
	Institutional	There are difficulties in shaping educational institutions to meet changing economic or cultural needs	Allowing parents greater choice in schools
Conflict theory	Class conflict	Those with wealth and power try to ensure that their children get high-quality education; those with little wealth and power cite evidence that their children are shortchanged	Channeling adequate resources to the schools to improve the quality of education for the poor and educationally disadvantaged
	Value conflict	Problems stem from tensions between different groups over the goals of education	Allowing different groups to achieve their educational goals while also achieving basic competency
Interactionism	Labeling	Schools label students as "achievers," "underachievers," or "rebels"	Elimination of labeling practices such as ability tracking

learner, regardless of performance or potential" (Rist, 1973, p. 93). According to labeling theorists, teachers form expectations about students early in the school year, and in various ways these expectations are communicated to the students themselves. The students tend to perform in ways that meet the teacher's expectations, thereby reinforcing them.

Research by Stanford Dornbusch and his colleagues at Stanford University shows that students also use labels like "slacker" and "nerd" to categorize one another and to explain how they sort themselves into cliques that perform quite differently in social and academic settings (cited in Leslie, 1996).

The various perspectives on education as a social problem and the kinds of policy recommendations generated by each one are shown in Table 13–1.

Education And Equality: The Issue of Equal Access

It is well known that educational attainment (number of years of school completed) is strongly correlated with socioeconomic status (Campbell et al., 1996). Educational researcher Robert Slavin (1997) notes,

> Among 4th graders whose parents graduated from college, 70 percent were reading at or above the basic level. This drops to 54 percent for children of high school graduates and 32 percent for children of high school dropouts. Among children whose homes had magazines, newspapers, encyclopedias, and at least 25 books, about 70 percent scored at or above basic; among those without these resources, fewer than half scored this well. Differences in mathematics, writing, and science are similar. Further, performance differences increase as students get older. (p. 3)

An egalitarian society has a responsibility to provide equal access to high-quality education for all its citizens. Critics claim that American society has failed to meet this

In recent years Native Americans have become increasingly upset over what they perceive as a lack of commitment by the federal government to improving the quality of education on reservations, which are administered by the Federal Bureau of Indian Affairs. Educational attainment of Native Americans is among the lowest for any minority group in the nation.

responsibility, particularly for minority groups. This criticism has become especially sharp as the composition of student populations has changed. Since the 1960s, increasing numbers of blacks, Hispanics, and other minority groups have become concentrated in central cities while whites have moved to the suburbs. In some metropolitan areas, as a result, over 90 percent of the students in public schools are black or Hispanic. And since central-city schools often have fewer resources than suburban schools, the quality of education available to black and Hispanic central-city residents tends to be lower than that available to white suburban residents.

Nor are urban minorities the only slighted populations. Native Americans and Alaskan Inuit have also suffered as a consequence of inadequate education and lack of access to high-quality educational institutions. Both groups live in remote rural areas, where educational choices are extremely limited. In addition, Native Americans have been forced to depend on reservation schools, which they consider to be inferior (Fuller & Elmore, 1996).

Black Students

A major factor in the lower educational attainment of blacks than of whites is the fact that before World War I about 90 percent of all blacks in the United States lived in the southern states (Orfield & Eaton, 1997). The South was then (and remains to some extent) less affluent than the North. The data in Figure 13–1 show that most southern states and some western ones continue to spend far less per student than school systems in the Northeast. Since black students are disproportionately concentrated in the Deep South, one effect of this difference is that blacks (and poor southern whites) receive only about 70 percent of the amount of schooling received by whites in more advantaged areas of the nation.

In the North, educational opportunities for blacks and whites are more equal, but inequalities between schools in poor black communities and those in more affluent white suburbs tend to perpetuate differences in educational attainment. Early in the twentieth century, northern-born blacks were rapidly closing the educational gap between themselves and whites, but the gap widened again after 1915. The reasons for this reversal are complex. An important factor was the competition between black children and the children of European immigrants, who tended to come from better educated families and thus enjoyed an advantage over blacks, whose parents had migrated from the South. Another factor, beginning in the Great Depression and continuing to the present, was the higher rate of unemployment among blacks. The employment status of parents has a great deal to do with the educational attainment of their children because children of low-income parents are more likely to drop out of school (Slavin, 1997). A third factor was segregation. Segregation tends to increase disparities between groups, not only because minority schools, which are usually located in central cities, have fewer highly qualified teachers and other resources, but also because students in those schools do not learn the values, work habits, and skills they need to compete effectively in the larger society (Darling-Hammond, 1998; Orfield, 1991).

Hispanic Students

Another minority group that has faced difficulties in gaining equal access to education is Hispanic Americans. This large group (which accounts for over 10 percent of the U.S. population and is growing much faster than the population as a whole) is highly concentrated in metropolitan areas. The educational attainment of Hispanic students is lower than the average for all students. A significant factor in this differ-

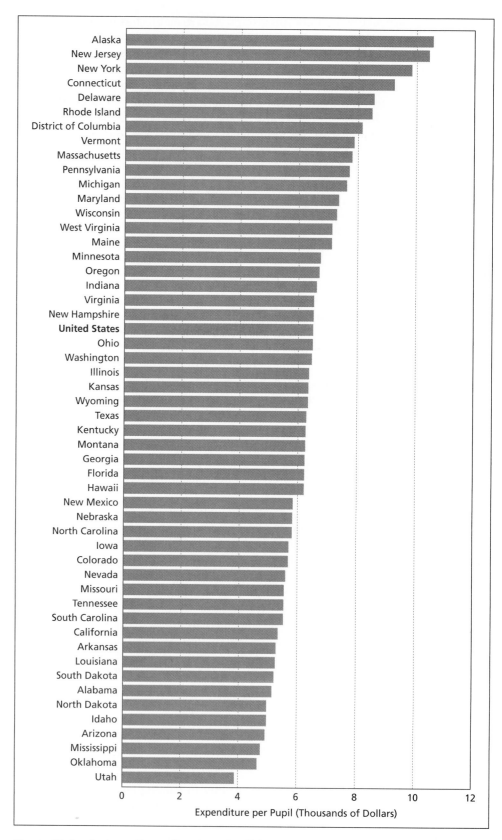

Figure 13–1 Average Expenditure per Pupil, by State, 1998
Source: Data from *Statistical Abstract,* 1999.

ence is the fact that Hispanic students who have recently arrived in the United States either do not speak English at all or do not speak it well enough to succeed in school. An especially important factor is that Hispanic students, like blacks, have experienced the effects of de facto segregation and poor schools, a problem that is particularly acute in large metropolitan areas (Orfield & Eaton, 1997).

Since the late 1960s, a primary goal of education for Hispanic students has been to improve their ability to use English without allowing them to fall behind in other subjects. One technique for achieving this is bilingual/bicultural education, in which students are taught wholly or partly in their native language until they can function adequately in English, and in some cases longer. This approach has received the support of the federal Office of Civil Rights, which requires that schools take "affirmative steps" to correct minority students' deficiencies in the English language in order to receive federal funds.

Bilingual/bicultural education is a subject of intense debate, particularly in California and other states with large Hispanic populations (Colvin, 1996). On one side are those who believe that preserving the language and culture of minority groups is a worthwhile, even necessary, goal of public education. On the other are those who believe that minority students must be "immersed" in English-language instruction if they are to be prepared to compete effectively in American society. Minority parents themselves often disagree on which approach best serves their children.

Preschool Programs

While ideological controversies have swirled around education in elementary and secondary schools, more pragmatic policies have been developed and tested at the preschool level. For example, the Perry Preschool Project studied 123 black children from low-income families in a neighborhood on the south side of Ypsilanti, Michigan. The children, all of whom had IQs between 60 and 90, were randomly divided into an experimental group that received a high-quality preschool program and a control

Among the most important goals of good preschools anywhere in the world are to help very young children feel comfortable in the classroom environment and to develop social skills, such as cooperation, attention, and sharing.

group that received no preschool program. Information about all the participants was collected and examined annually from the ages of 3 to 11 and again at the ages of 14, 15, and 19. The information included data on their families; their abilities, attitudes, and accomplishments; their involvement in delinquent and criminal behavior; and their patterns of employment and use of welfare assistance. Members of both groups were tested and interviewed; the testers and interviewers were not informed of the group membership of the participants in the study.

The preschool program to which 58 of the children were assigned was "an organized educational program directed at the intellectual and social development of young children" (Berrueta-Clement et al., 1984, p. 8). It was staffed by a team of four highly trained teachers. Most of the children participated in the program for two years, at the ages of 3 and 4.

The results of the Perry project were dramatic. Preschool education improved cognitive performance in early childhood; improved scholastic achievement during the school years; decreased rates of delinquency, crime, use of welfare services, and teenage pregnancy; and increased high school graduation and college enrollment rates. (See Table 13–2.) According to the researchers, "These benefits considered in terms of their economic value make the preschool program a worthwhile investment for society" (p. 1).

Perhaps the most significant outcome of the Perry project was its effect on educational attainment: Two out of three of the students in the preschool group graduated from high school; the comparable rate for the non–preschool group was one out of two. As noted earlier, failure to graduate from high school is a major obstacle to later educational progress and an important factor in many job and vocational-training opportunities.

The Perry Preschool Project is an outstanding example of how social-scientific research can play a vital role in public policy. Despite its desire to cut social spending, the Reagan administration admitted that the Perry results were impressive and justified the continuation of Head Start. Nevertheless, at present only one in five preschool-age children in families below the poverty line attends a high-quality preschool program.

TABLE 13–2   Major Findings at Age 19 in the Perry Preschool Study

Category	Number Responding	Preschool Group	Non-preschool Group
Employed	121	50%	32%
High school graduation (or its equivalent)	121	67%	49%
College or vocational training	121	38%	21%
Ever detained or arrested	121	31%	51%
Females only: teen pregnancies, per 100	49	64	117
Functional competence (APL Survey: possible score 40)	109	24.6	21.8
Percent of years in special education	112	16%	28%

Source: From Berrueta-Clement, J. R., Schweinhart, L. J., Barnett, W. S., Epstein, A. S., and Weikart, D. P., 1984, "Changed Lives: The Effects of the Perry Preschool Program on Youths Through Age 19." *Monographs of the High/Scope Educational Research Foundation*, 8, 2. Ypsilanti, MI: High/Scope Press. Reprinted by permission.

Desegregation

Efforts to alleviate some of the problems discussed in this section have centered on racial integration, or, more accurately, desegregation. Much of the pressure for change in this area has come from court rulings and legal mandates.

Desegregation effectively began with the Supreme Court's 1954 ruling in *Brown* v. *Board of Education of Topeka, Kansas,* which was based in part on the argument that segregation had negative effects on black students even when their school facilities were equal to those of white students. Black students in segregated schools knew that their schools were inferior and were likely to believe that they themselves were inferior as well. To avoid the formation of such a negative self-concept, the Supreme Court decided that black children should associate with white children as early as possible and should be taught by both white and black teachers.

In the 1980s the pace of desegregation slowed, especially in the Northeast. As noted in Chapter 9, there are a number of cities in which the distribution of the white and nonwhite populations places severe limits on the extent to which schools can be desegregated. Research by Douglas Massey and Judith Denton (1993) on the persistence of residential segregation suggests that without stronger enforcement of fair-housing laws and other measures to reduce racial segregation, it will be extremely difficult to accelerate the pace of school desegregation. The situation is aggravated by the tendency of middle-class urban residents to enroll their children in private schools. Nevertheless, many school systems throughout the country have adapted successfully to the demand for desegregated public schools.

In 1991 the Supreme Court held that the Oklahoma City schools could be permitted to cease busing children to meet the requirements of a 1972 desegregation order. The Court ruled that school systems could be released from busing orders once they have taken "all practicable steps" to eliminate segregation. The Harvard Project on School Desegregation notes that during the Reagan administration there was an explicit policy not to pursue school districts that failed to make progress toward desegregation. The administration also largely abandoned busing because it believed that "compulsory busing of students in order to achieve racial balance in the public schools is not an acceptable remedy" (Orfield & Eaton, 1997, p. 17).

There are continuing challenges to desegregation plans in cities and suburbs throughout the United States. At the heart of the problem is the fact that many suburban school districts are predominantly white, whereas those of central cities often have high proportions of black and Hispanic students. At present there is little political support for desegregation plans that include suburban communities. On the one hand, there is much fear that forced desegregation within cities will continue to stimulate white flight to the suburbs; on the other, politicians are fearful that suburban desegregation would cause them to lose the vital support of suburban voters (Orfield & Eaton, 1997).

Educational Attainment Today

The gap in educational attainment between blacks and whites has narrowed considerably since the turn of the century, mainly as a result of the increase in the minimum amount of education received by almost all Americans. In 1960 almost 44 percent of whites and 76 percent of blacks between the ages of 25 and 29 had not finished high school. By 1985 the proportions had declined to 13 percent of whites and 17 percent of blacks. The same trends apply to college education. In 1960 only 8.2 percent of whites and 2.8 percent of blacks aged 25–29 had completed college. By 1985 the proportions were 23.2 percent for whites and 16.7 percent for blacks. Considering their extremely low "cultural capital" at the beginning of desegregation, blacks made extraordinary gains in this period. More recently, however, cuts in support for low-income

SOCIAL PROBLEMS ONLINE

Education and the Internet

For information about education on the Internet, a good place to start is "Education Week on the Web" (http://www.edweek.org/). It contains weekly updates and news articles, "Teacher Magazine" online, and special reports of interest to policymakers, all of which are archived. "Class IV Publications," a publishing company devoted to keeping teachers "informed and connected" at http://www.clasIV.com, features abundant links to other web sites and an expanding resource of online education sites.

The Putnam Valley (NY) school system (http://putwest.boces.org/) has a host of links to other Internet sites concerned with K–12 education. They include U.S. government resources at the White House and the Department of Education (http://www.ed.gov), government resources from outside the United States, think tanks, and miscellaneous reports and academic papers.

For higher education resources there are web pages devoted to community colleges and traditional four-year institutions. The American Association of Community Colleges has a home page at http://www.aacc.nche.edu that provides historical overviews of community colleges and brief statistical profiles of the institutions, students, and curricula. The Western Interstate Commission for Higher Education (http://www.wiche.edu/wiche.htm) promotes educational resources in the western states. Its "Policy and Information" pages analyze educational attainment and inequality issues, with an emphasis on data that would be useful to policymakers.

The National Education Association (NEA), at http://www.nea.org, and the American Federation of Teachers (AFT), at http://www.aft.org, both represent the interests of teachers and have web pages targeted to their members. Both websites contain membership information such as model labor contracts, but they also look at debates on educational policy and provide links to other education sites.

The National Parent Teachers Association (PTA) has its home page at http://www.pta.org, where researchers can find programs and publications related to policy questions. Reports on current topics such as the push for national standards are available for downloading. The "American Prospect" (http://epn.org/prospect/spencer.html) has an online series on educational reform and computer technology with articles and conference speeches. People for the American Way (http://www.pfaw.org/educa.htm) advocates "effective public education and to defend the freedom to learn from censorship and other threats from the Religious Right." Its web page features reports on school library censorship, efforts to introduce creationism in public schools, and opinion pieces on school voucher programs. On the conservative side of the spectrum is the Center for Education Reform (http://edreform.com), which advocates school voucher plans. It offers a sample of editorials and reports.

---

students have reduced enrollments of both minority and nonminority students (Lavin & Hyllegard, 1996).

Rates of school leaving (dropout rates) remain higher among inner-city blacks and Hispanics than among whites, and alienation from school causes many minority teenagers and young adults to finish their schooling in high school equivalency programs. Despite this serious problem, however, the educational gap between blacks and whites continues to narrow.

It is argued that the higher dropout rates among minority students are caused by the fact that they do not receive enough help at home. This is known as the cultural-disadvantage argument. Although minority enrollments are higher today than at any time in the past, the parents of these students have less education than the parents of white students and therefore are less able to assist their children.

Although the primary cause of dropping out is poor academic performance, students often drop out of high school because of the difficulties they encounter in trying to cope with school and family and work roles at the same time. They may be married and/or pregnant or working at a regular job (this increases the likelihood of dropping out by more than one-third). Whatever the cause, dropping out has a number of serious consequences. The earnings of school dropouts are considerably lower than those of high school graduates. This disadvantage continues throughout life: The estimated lifetime earnings of high school graduates are at least $200,000 higher than those of dropouts. Most dropouts believe that leaving school before graduating was a poor decision, and an estimated 40 percent eventually return to the educational system (Pallas, 1987).

At the college level, educational attainment for low-income members of minority groups is hindered by lack of financial aid as a result of cutbacks in federally funded student assistance. Cutbacks in federally funded assistance in the 1980s, particularly the emphasis on loans rather than outright grants, put a college education out of reach for many minority students. The disparities in educational attainment between white and minority students are a matter of concern to those who believe that equality of educational attainment is basic to other kinds of social equality. For them, encouraging students to finish high school, developing systems of school financing that provide equal resources for all schools, and ending segregation are important policy goals.

School Reform: Problems of Institutional Change

The primary obstacle to significant changes in the educational system is that educational institutions have a built-in tendency to resist change. To some extent this is a useful quality: Schools tend to conserve society's values and do not yield easily to educational fads. Nevertheless, they must be able to change in response to changes in other major institutions. Such changes are highly visible, and several have been mentioned in other parts of this book. The family, for example, has changed dramatically as increasing numbers of women have entered the labor force. Economic institutions also are changing as jobs that require specialized skills replace jobs that require little training. These and other changes in American society call for adults with skills and outlooks different from those that were typical of their parents' generation. The schools are largely responsible for preparing students for these new adult roles.

The nature of schools themselves is a major barrier to change. Schools have been compared with total institutions—prisons, mental hospitals, and other institutions in which a large group of involuntary "clients" is serviced by a smaller group of employees (Ballantine, 1993). A central problem of such institutions is the maintenance of order and control, a concern that leads to the development of elaborate sets of rules and monitoring systems. Although schools are not total institutions in that not all their "clients'" activities take place within their boundaries, they exhibit one of the key traits of total institutions: The administrators tend to place a high priority on maintaining their authority.

Schools as Bureaucracies

According to Daniel Bell (1973),

> It is a truism of sociology that the initial patterns of any social system, like the first tracks through a virgin forest, shape its future modes. Traditions become established, routines are set, vested interests develop, innovations either are

resisted or must conform to the adaptive patterns laid down at the start, and an aura of legitimacy surrounds the existing ways and becomes in time the conventional wisdom of the institution. (p. 402)

This aptly describes the situation of education in what Bell calls "postindustrial" society.

Ann Parker Parelius and Robert J. Parelius (1987) have documented the extent of bureaucratization in the American educational system. They point out that increases in bureaucratization are associated with increases in organizational size and complexity. This is certainly true of American school systems. The one-room schoolhouse has become a complex system characterized by an increasingly specialized division of labor. Today's schools have large administrative staffs that include a variety of specialists such as community relations experts and guidance counselors. Even the teachers are specialists—for example, in a certain age group or, at the high school level, in a particular subject.

Another bureaucratic characteristic of modern school systems is the development of an elaborate hierarchy of authority. (See Figure 13–2.) The relationships

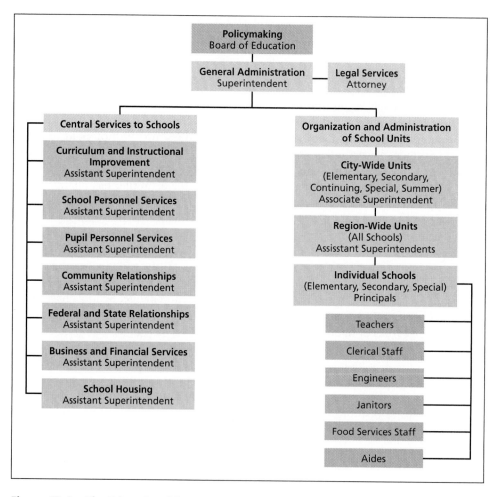

Figure 13–2 The Educational Bureaucracy

Source: From *Encyclopedia of Education,* Vol. 8, ed. Lee C. Deighton. Crowell Collier and MacMillan, Inc. © The Gale Group. Reprinted by permission of the Gale Group.

among people at various levels of the hierarchy have an important effect on educational policy at the district and school levels. In big-city school systems, for example, there may be several administrative layers between the superintendent and the schools themselves. In such cases the superintendent may be unable to control the implementation of policies. A similar situation exists at the classroom level. Teachers have considerable autonomy in how they run their classrooms; if they choose to, they can resist innovation simply by not following the directives of school boards and principals.

In the 1996 presidential election campaign, Republican candidate Bob Dole criticized the teachers' unions as a major obstacle to school reform. This attack backfired, however, as it appeared that in many communities there were good lines of communication and cooperation between local school officials and representatives of the teachers' union. Both parties were accustomed to working together to lobby against cuts in state and local school budgets. And since, as noted earlier, the majority of Americans like their own schools and believe that the problems of school failure lie elsewhere, the attack on teachers and their unions damaged the Republican cause (Applebome, 1995).

Classroom and School Size

For teachers and their unions, especially in large cities and less affluent districts, a primary issue in school reform is classroom size. Teachers simply find it far easier to provide high-quality instruction in classrooms where there are no more than 25 students. Project Star, a systematic longitudinal study conducted in the Tennesee schools, confirmed that smaller classes yield better results (Bracey, 1995). Throughout the United States, the average class size is 23 in the primary grades. Over 80 percent of teachers and school administrators believe that a class size of 17 is ideal. For many decades parents who could afford to do so have enrolled their children in private schools with small classes, especially where the alternative was urban public schools with large classes. In inner-city neighborhoods it is not uncommon for classes to include more than 30 students, with much crowding and inadequate learning materials like textbooks (Bell,1998; Bracey, 1999). Educators argue that calls for reform that do not address declining learning environments in impoverished communities are useless (Drevitch, 1994; Meier, 1995).

Another reform movement calls for smaller schools in order to address the problems of large, impersonal, bureaucratic schools (Meier, 1991; Sizer, 1992). Veteran school reformers like Theodore Sizer of the Coalition for Essential Schools and Deborah Meier—an innovative and charismatic school principal who has achieved success in inner-city schools—argue that the reforms included in the Goals 2000: Educate America Act are motivated by a "top-down" desire to impose national standards, which will increase reliance on standardized testing and further reduce the educational responsibilities of teachers, parents, and students. They argue that educational reform should begin at the school level and that large, impersonal schools need to be divided up into smaller schools, where administrators and teachers know every student and where parents and teachers can have a greater voice in decisions about how the school should operate.

Recent research on the relationship between high school size and student performance shows that scores are higher in schools with fewer than 600 students and lowest in high schools with more than 900 students. Large schools are a particular problem in inner-city communities with high proportions of poor and minority students (Bracey, 1998).

School Choice

Efforts to create smaller schools, schools with special approaches to learning, or schools that promote a particular religious orientation invariably become enmeshed in the ongoing debate over school choice (Alexander, 1996; Fuller & Elmore, 1996). People who are dissatisfied with the public schools or seek special educational opportunities for their children are often attracted to proposals for expanding the array of choices parents have, including parochial and secular private schools. Republican candidates at all levels of government often favor a system of vouchers that parents could "spend" in sending their children to any kind of academically accredited school they wish. Social-scientific research offers little support for the belief that school choice improves performance. After reviewing the evidence to date, educational researchers Salvatore Saporito and Annette Lareau (1999) concluded, "Indeed, if there is a single, consistent finding in the empirical literature on school choice it is that students from poorer families or with less educated parents are less likely than middle class families to apply to—or participate in—public choice programs" (p. 1).

The Christian Coalition advocates a system such as the one used in Georgia, known as the Hope scholarship program, in which the state offers money to students with a B or better average to attend the college or university of their choice. Under this proposal, the successful Georgia model would be extended to the high school and primary grades as a way of increasing the choices open to parents and thereby increasing enrollments in Christian schools, as well as in other private schools. Other, more liberal educators often argue for greater choice in the selection of public schools. Members of the movement for smaller schools, for example, often advocate the creation of special schools, known as charter schools, which are innovative in their use of resources and yet are funded as public schools. As the array of choices within the public school system widens, they argue, there will be more pressure on the conventional schools to become more competitive and to improve their educational methods (Meier, 1991).

The "Technological Fix"

Much of the pressure for change in the schools has developed out of the typically American belief in the value of technology. The "technological fix," it is widely believed, can solve any problem. Thus, it is commonplace to attempt to apply such techniques as cost accounting, systems analysis, closed-circuit television, and computer technology to educational problems. Although the evidence does not support the notion that technology can solve the problems of public education, some technological initiatives have had positive consequences. According to Parelius and Parelius (1987), "Students have more and better materials, a greater variety of courses, increased freedom to choose among diverse educational alternatives, and a less authoritarian relationship with teachers and administrators." However,

> there are some important ways in which the school has remained impervious to technological advances. . . . The basic classroom unit of the school has remained fundamentally unchanged. The role structure consisting of one teacher to a room full of students is still with us. . . . The teacher is still concerned with discipline . . . students are still expected to be obedient, punctual, and docile. . . . Blackboard and chalk, paper and pen remain the primary tools. . . . This mode of interaction has successfully resisted change for a long period of time. (p. 84)

The latest technological innovation to assume the dubious status of a "techno-fix" is the networked computer. At various times former Speaker of the House Newt

CRITICAL RESEARCH

Closing the Digital Divide in the Classroom

In a speech to educators in Washington, D.C., Secretary of Commerce William Daley (1999) called attention to the gap in technology skills between young people from more affluent homes, who have computers and Internet access, and those from low-income, often black or Hispanic, families who have none. "All this," he warned, "is creating what can be called a digital divide. And it is a divide that is growing. But we can't let this happen. Computer skills are just too important for getting a good job in today's economy. And without enough skilled people from all walks of life, we risk letting a 21st century opportunity become a 21st century social problem" (p. 25). During the economic boom years of the 1990s, Secretary Daley noted, about one-third of the jobs created were in "high-tech" industries in which basic computer and Internet skills are required of all entry-level workers.

In Austin, Texas, home to the main campus of the University of Texas and a major center of the new technologies, one can see the impressive homes of new millionaires who recently made their fortunes in high-technology companies and stocks. But according to researchers at the university, one-third of the work force is trying to live on $350 a week. Workers in hotels, restaurants, and hospitals have been particularly hard hit. Even teachers are finding it harder to make ends meet. All together, only 20 percent of Austin's work force is employed in technology-related areas. "The message is, if you're not part of the computer economy, you're a loser," says Gary Chapman, director of the 21st Century Project at the University of Texas–Austin (quoted in Holstein, 2000, p. 44).

Are educational institutions the answer to closing the new digital divide, at least for young people? In Austin at least, the answer is "not yet." Local computer companies donate computers to learning centers, libraries, and unemployment offices in the city's needy neighborhoods. But community leaders do not believe that these efforts even begin to close the gap. "It's not simply a question of putting the computers in there and expecting people to be able to use them," says Ana Sisnett, executive director of Austin Free-Net. "You have to have people to help them and the technical support to keep the machines up and running" (quoted in Holstein, 2000, p. 44).

Social scientists and political leaders alike are concerned that the "digital divide," the relative lack of access by poor and minority families to computers and the Internet, will worsen existing patterns of inequality.

Schools are expected to play a major role in teaching students to use the new technologies, and when they do not, they are faulted. Efforts are being made to flood the schools with hardware, software, and Internet connections, but often the technologies sit idle. Teachers are accused of being afraid of computers or unwilling to learn how to use them. As noted in the text, the facts seem to point to other problems.

According to Stanford educational researcher Larry Cuban,

Although information technologies have transformed most corporate workplaces, our teachers' schedules and working conditions have changed very little. They teach five classes a day, each 50 to 55 minutes long. Their five classes contain at least three different preparations; that is, for the math teacher among our five, there are two classes of introductory algebra, two of geometry, and one calculus class. In those five classes, she sees 140 students a day. Colleagues in other districts, depending on how affluent the district is and how determined the school board and superintendent are to keep class size down, may see 125 to 175 students a day. (quoted in Holstein, 2000, p. 44)

Cuban's research indicates that teachers are often extremely frustrated by the new technologies, but not because they do not feel comfortable using them or because they do not want to incorporate them in their teaching. The problems often stem from lack of opportunity to do the work it takes to develop curriculum plans and test the new computer systems, which are often unreliable, break down when students use them, and are quickly obsolete because of the pace of technological change. The answer, Cuban and many other educators and community activists feel, is greater investment in the human side of the technology, in providing the person-power needed to teach students and parents how to use the technologies.

Bashing teachers for not doing more with technology in their classrooms may give us cute media one-liners. What the one-liners miss, however, are the deeper, more consequential reasons for what teachers do every day. What corporate cheerleaders, policymakers, and vendors who have far more access to the media ignore are teachers' voices, the enduring workplace conditions within which teachers teach, inherent flaws in the technologies, and the ever-changing advice of their own experts. (quoted in Holstein, 2000, p. 44)

Gingrich, President Clinton, and Vice-President Gore have urged educational systems to add more computers and networks to their classrooms. But what is the basis for this strong advocacy of computers in education?

Part of the frenzy to wire classrooms for computers and Internet access comes from the fact that throughout the nation an estimated $4 billion per year is being spent doing just that—primarily in more affluent suburban schools (Kaplan & Rogers, 1996). Chris Whittle's Edison Project, which features the same kind of technological approach, has drawn a great deal of national and international attention (Mosle, 1993). The project aims to open a chain of for-profit schools that will use high-technology computers and satellite link-ups to create schools that are more efficient and successful than public schools. Although Whittle's grandiose claim that he could transform American education has received immense attention, his plan has failed to prove its feasibility in two communities where it was introduced in the early 1990s.

Although there is a growing computer gap between wealthier and poorer school districts, many inner-city districts that lack computers and teachers trained to use them must deal with even greater problems, such as overcrowded classrooms, inadequate facilities, and lack of basic textbooks. Research in the United States shows that among classroom teachers in public schools only about 2 in 10 use computers daily with students, and about 4 in 10 never use the machines in their classrooms at all. And even when the computers are being used, it is most often for low-end applications and word processing. The most frequent explanation for this behavior is that teachers do not know how to use computers and that many are "technophobes," afraid of new technologies. But the research shows that 7 out of 10 of the same teachers routinely use computers at home to write to friends, search the Internet, and much more (Cuban, 1999). It appears to be far easier to interest legislators in buying unproven computer and telecommunications systems for schools than in training teachers to apply these technologies to learning (Matthews, 1996). (See the Critical Research feature on page 385.)

Teachers' Professionalism and Unions

Another factor that affects school operations is the increased popularity of teachers' unions. Membership in teachers' trade unions like the National Education Association and the American Federation of Teachers has risen significantly since midcentury—from less than 10 percent of all teachers in the early 1960s to over 30 percent at present. These unions seek to improve the status and material well-being of their members, but they also support a range of policies directed toward reform of the educational system. Among other things, they demand smaller classes, more resources for the handicapped and slow learners, and more funds for in-service training for teachers. On the other hand, they often oppose policies whose goal is to improve the competence and motivation of public school teachers (discussed in the next section). For this reason, critics of the unions claim that they are more interested in maintaining the status quo than in genuine educational reform.

Partly because of the unions' efforts to professionalize and partly as a result of economic factors, there is renewed interest in teaching as a career. A study by the Cooperative Institutional Research program at UCLA has found a significant increase in the proportion of college students who want to become elementary or secondary school teachers. (See Figure 13–3.) The increase is attributed to widespread publicity about educational reforms, higher salaries for starting teachers, and awareness of an impending shortage of teachers. Education is now the third most popular undergraduate major (after business and the social sciences), and enrollments of education majors have been increasing.

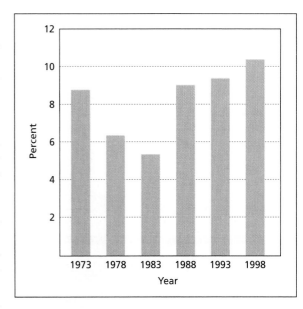

Figure 13–3   Percentage of College Freshmen Expressing Interest in Teaching Careers, 1973–1998

Source: A. W. Astin, S. A. Parrott, W. S. Korn, and L. T. Sax, *The American Freshman: Thirty Year Trends* (Los Angeles: Higher Education Research Institute, UCLA, 1997); also L.T. Sax, A. W. Astin, W. S. Korn, and K. M. Mahoney, *The American Freshman: National Norms for Fall 1998* (Los Angeles: Higher Education Research Institute, UCLA, 1998).

School Violence

Television coverage of the killings and suicides at Columbine High School in Littleton, Colorado, in 1999 brought school violence into homes throughout the world. But Columbine was only one of a series of tragic episodes of violence that have shaken Americans' confidence in the security of their children in schools that were once thought to be safe havens for learning and social development. The American public perceives fighting, violence, and gangs as the three most serious problems of public schools. An estimated 2.7 million violent crimes take place each year either at school or nearby (Hill & Drolet, 1999). Physician and violence prevention expert Deborah Prothrow-Stith (1996) observes that "violence in schools is certainly not new, almost every adult remembers the school bully. But today's school violence is increasingly lethal" (p. 154).

To explain why extremely violent episodes are occurring in schools, social scientists and others have often cited, among many possible causes,

> (a) failure of parents to supervise their children; (b) violence in the media; (c) access to guns and other lethal weapons; (d) harassment of students who are nonconformists; (e) the influence of religious cults and "outsider" groups; and (f) low self-esteem brought on by social isolation. Much attention has been focused on the influence of violent video games such as Doom that law enforcement agencies and the military use to desensitize recruits to killing and to sharpen their marksmanship skills. (Guetzloe, 1999, p. 21)

Faced with increases in violence among students, many school systems have installed metal detectors and imposed severe punishments on students caught bringing weapons to school.

Many observers believe that the underlying problem is that the role of the teacher no longer commands automatic respect because students do not care whether their teachers approve of their behavior. When large numbers of students are frustrated and alienated and their parents are uninvolved in their education, only the most forceful, experienced teachers are able to remain in control of their classes.

Solutions such as installing metal detectors and hiring additional security guards have been attempted, and these measures may help prevent violence by outsiders, but they do not convey authority to teachers. Educators are searching for ways to empower teachers who are intimidated by violent students. Several possibilities have been suggested: creating smaller high schools, or "schools within schools"; encouraging employers to require high school transcripts; expecting more from students than mere attendance; and encouraging dropouts to return to school as adults. The last suggestion is especially attractive because adult high school students often become role models for younger students, and their presence tends to reduce the amount of disorder in the schools they attend. On the more discouraging side of the picture is the fact that, even by the most conservative estimates, 3.3 million children experience domestic violence each year. These individuals, in turn, are most likely to commit violent acts against their peers (Szyndrowski, 1999).

Efforts to prevent school violence are beginning to achieve some success, even though episodes of violence continue to make headlines. In Chicago schools, the frequency of violent incidents fell consistently and dramatically over four years because of the city's decision to increase funding for school security. Between 1989–1990 and 1993–1994, the schools employed more security officers to supplement those supplied by the Chicago Board of Education. According to school principals, the biggest deterrent to violence is the presence of adults, especially parents, in the schools. But

Chicago school principals also instituted such changes as school uniforms, more student activities, and programs designed to change students' behavior such as peer mediation and conflict resolution (Williams, 1995).

Elsewhere in the United States gang violence often spills into the schools. For example, in 1996 a student in an Alexandria, Virginia, school was knifed in a gang-related dispute (Welsh, 1996). Episodes like this continue to place school violence at the forefront of concerns about education, and there has been a significant increase in the number of metal detectors installed in urban schools to prevent students from carrying weapons. However, as the Chicago experience demonstrates, when funds are invested in strategies to decrease school violence the effects can be dramatic.

SOCIAL POLICY

The public school is the nation's largest educational institution, offering basic education to the greatest number of children. However, as noted earlier in the chapter, public education has been subject to criticism on a number of fronts. The policy recommendations arising out of such criticism take two main forms, depending on whether their proponents have conservative or liberal views on educational policy.

Of all American social institutions, education is most subject to intentional change through social policy. Schools and educational systems are also attractive targets for critics. Those who believe American society has become too secular may advocate prayer in the schools. Others, who believe the schools have a responsibility to steer children away from the dangers of AIDS or early pregnancy, may advocate more thorough sex education. Still others, who lament the supposed failure of the schools to produce adequately trained students, may come up with proposals for educational reform.

As mentioned earlier, a popular scheme among conservative critics is a plan to provide parents with vouchers that would allow them to choose among public and private schools that offer all kinds of educational options. The theory is that increased competition among schools to attract students would improve the schools' efficiency or cost effectiveness while stimulating a more open market for educational practices. The main criticism of voucher plans is that they are likely to be used most effectively by more highly educated and affluent parents, leaving the poorer schools to less well-equipped parents; this would worsen the existing situation of stratification and inequality in education.

An alternative to school vouchers is reform of the property tax system for funding schools in the United States. Most public school systems are funded through a levy on residential property known as the school tax. In municipalities throughout the nation, property owners have become increasingly loath to pay higher taxes on their homes to fund increases in teachers' pay or improvements in the local schools. In large cities, where revenues from property taxes are lower, this system is largely responsible for inequities in funding between suburban and urban schools and explains the fact that urban schools often lack the art, music, athletic, and science programs that are usually found in suburban schools. In the past, state education budgets were used to offset these differences, but as states cut back on public spending, the schools in poorer central-city communities suffer inordinately. Moreover, as homeowners age, they often become less favorable toward higher school taxes, especially since their own children are no longer in school. In consequence, school reform without reform of educational funding systems is not likely to progress very far.

There are some signs of change, however. Michigan, for example, is leading the way toward improving the quality of education in poor communities without increasing taxes in affluent communities. In 1994 voters in that state approved a new school-funding system based primarily on sales taxes rather than on property taxes. Social scientists are watching Michigan schools carefully to see if educational quality improves in poor school districts as a result of this important fiscal change (Celis, 1994).

Educational Conservatism and "Back to Basics"

Educational conservatives believe that the job of the school is to preserve the culture of the past and transmit it to successive generations. This means that schools must concentrate on "essentials"—that is, a set of fundamental subjects and skills—and that all students must be expected to master them. It also means that schools are agencies of social control and as such should stress order, discipline, and obedience.

This point of view has been expressed in a variety of ways since the 1930s, when the debate between "essentialists" and "progressivists" drew national attention. After World War II it was alleged that the schools were failing to safeguard the values of "Americanism"; after the launching of the Sputnik I satellite by the former Soviet Union in 1957, American education was blamed for neglecting subjects that were vital to national survival. Critics claimed that instead of concentrating on mathematics, history, foreign languages, and other disciplines, high schools encouraged students to divert themselves with trivial subjects like ceramics, stagecraft, and table decorating.

The back-to-basics movement found support in the 1983 report of the National Commission on Excellence in Education (*A Nation at Risk*), which called for longer school hours, more homework, and more discipline. It also proposed that teachers receive salary increases based on merit rather than seniority, on the assumption that this would motivate teachers to do a better job in the classroom. The commission recommended that high schools concentrate on what it termed the "Five New Basics": English, mathematics, science, social studies, and computer science. It also recommended that schools and colleges adopt more rigorous standards and higher expectations for academic performance, on the theory that students will learn more in a more challenging environment.

This recommendation has spurred the trend toward experimentation with year-round schooling. In Los Angeles about 40 percent of the high schools are on a year-round schedule in which overcrowding is reduced by shorter school days, overlapping schedules, and a longer school year (Goldberg, 1996). New York and Miami are also experimenting with this approach to ease overcrowding in schools whose enrollments have been swollen by the influx of immigrant families in the past two decades. But year-round schooling is not especially popular in parts of the nation where overcrowding is not an issue. An even more widespread response to the demand for more challenging school environments is the push for national standards (Hirsch, 1996; Mosle, 1996).

The Fight Over National Standards.   At this writing, the issue of national educational standards has assumed center stage among all the many education issues discussed here. National standards and the development of national curriculum goals were major issues in the 2000 presidential election campaign. If national standards are enacted by Congress, the federal government would set minimum standards, establish curriculum guidelines, and develop a set of examinations to assess students' and schools' progress toward meeting the standards. But opponents of national standards are mounting a vigorous counteroffensive.

Opponents of a national curriculum fear that the imposition of standards at a national level will result in a vague set of criteria and goals that could hamper local efforts to achieve educational excellence. The National Congress of Parents and Teachers, which represents local parent-teacher associations (PTAs) at the national level, opposes a national curriculum because the idea is untested and raises more questions than it resolves (Celis, 1993a).

California, Kentucky, South Carolina, and Vermont have already passed legislation that establishes school standards, and educators in those states believe that the statewide standards do not prevent local schools from developing innovative educational programs of their own. However, in England, where a national curriculum has been implemented by the government, teachers have staged protests against standardized national exams, claiming that they do not reflect their own educational goals or adequately test students' abilities (Schmidt, 1993). Educators in the United States point to these protests as evidence that a national curriculum will not solve the problems of American education. Thus, the debate over national standards is likely to continue for the foreseeable future, especially since the demand for higher standards will highlight the disparities in funding between rich and poor school districts (Council of State Governments, 1998; Slavin, 1997).

Humanism and "Open Education"

A more liberal view of educational policy is based on the intellectual tradition known as **humanism.** In this view, the basic aim of education is to promote the maximum self-development of each individual learner, paying specific attention to differences among individuals' interests, needs, abilities, and values. Learning should be as "open" and meaningful as possible, with each learner establishing the goals of his or her own education.

In the United States this approach gave rise to the movement that came to be known as progressivism. **Progressivism,** which began in the early 1900s and gathered momentum in the 1920s and 1930s, is associated with the educational philosophy of John Dewey. Dewey believed that education should stress the expression of individuality and learning through experience. It should not be imposed from outside but should originate with the needs and interests of the learner. As Dewey (1916) defined it, education is "that reconstruction or reorganization of experience which adds to the meaning of experience, and which increases ability to direct the course of subsequent experience" (p. 126).

Dewey's views were central to the development of progressivism, which emphasized vocational training, "daily-living skills," and a "child-centered curriculum." They fell into some disfavor in the post–World War II period, but interest in humanistic education reappeared in the 1960s. In the course of the decade, numerous critiques of mainstream educational thought appeared—books with titles like *How Children Fail* (Holt, 1965), *The Way It Spozed to Be* (Herndon, 1968), *An Empty Spoon* (Decker, 1969), and *Death at an Early Age* (Kozol, 1967). In differing ways, each attacked what its author saw as rigid authoritarianism and systematic suppression of genuine learning in American schools.

The outgrowth of this criticism was a call for **open education,** or individualized instruction, based on the approach used in British elementary schools. The goal was independent, self-paced learning. Interest in open education became widespread in the 1970s; it was seen as the best way to make use of children's natural curiosity and to give them individualized attention. However, there is little evidence that open education improved students' intellectual achievement, and it has not proven to be a useful approach at the high school level.

Access to Higher Education

Another area of education in which significant policy innovations have been made in recent decades is the public university. The public two-year (or community) college is assuming a central role in current educational policy. President Clinton and many state governors emphasized the need to create more opportunities for students to gain access to higher education even after they have been out of high school for some years (Applebome, 1996). The community colleges are emerging as primary training and retraining institutions, helping people adapt to rapid economic changes in many regions of the United States. As opposed to many other nations, where apprenticeship programs are a primary route to careers for young people who do not attend universities, in the United States the community college and the four-year public university provide training and transition to adult careers.

Georgia's much-publicized Hope scholarship program, which provides higher-education funds for students who maintain a B or better average, is becoming a policy model that may be replicated elsewhere in the nation. More controversial, but perhaps of greater long-term importance, is the open-admissions program pioneered by the City University of New York (CUNY). Research has shown that students who gain access to higher education through open admissions make lasting gains in their jobs and incomes, which more than repay the expense of their education through the taxes they contribute over their working lives (Lavin, Alba, & Silberstein, 1981; Lavin & Hyllegard, 1996).

A careful analysis of the open-admissions program (Lavin, Alba, & Silberstein, 1981) found that more white than minority students took advantage of the program and that ethnic segregation among the university's 17 campuses increased. Nevertheless, the overall effect of open admissions was an increase in the equality of educational opportunity. "Black open-admissions graduates outnumbered black regular graduates," the authors report, "so that the program more than doubled the number of black students who received a degree of some kind" (p. 271). "The open-admissions policy has altered forever historic patterns of ethnic access to the University. . . . The thousands of minority students who have entered and graduated from the University since open admissions was inaugurated insure that black and Hispanic students will, in the future, look to the University as a source of opportunity for them" (pp. 276–277).

In recent years the demands on students who are entering colleges like those in the CUNY system—demands that they be better prepared in math, science, and English—have prompted a general tightening of admission requirements. This new policy is controversial because funds to pay for the added costs are not available at present and because the additional requirements mean that it will take students longer to obtain an undergraduate degree. At CUNY, new policies that will require students to pass stiff assessment tests and also require them to take remedial courses before they can enroll have been pushed through by supporters of Mayor Rudolph Giuliani. David Lavin (2000) and other prominent researchers who have studied the CUNY open-admissions system note that the new requirements will make it much more difficult for underprepared students to actually obtain needed remediation and eventually graduate from college.

Trends and Prospects

Current trends in educational policy include efforts to improve the quality of public school teaching, a longer school year in some communities, and school choice.

The need to provide more incentives for teachers has received widespread recognition, and teachers' salaries have increased in recent years; the average salary for elementary and secondary school teachers is now $39,385. There have also been demands that teachers receive higher pay and promotions based on merit, but with few exceptions there has been little progress toward this goal at either the federal or the state level. On the other hand, it is generally agreed that the quality of teachers must be improved, and there has been a great deal of discussion of such issues as improving education courses, standardized testing of teachers, and establishment of more rigorous requirements for certification. It has been suggested that a "master teacher" rank could be created that would recognize and reward outstanding teachers; however, teachers' unions fear that criteria other than ability and dedication might be used in designating master teachers.

On a more general level, although there has been much debate about the need to devote more resources to public education, the prospects are not bright. As mentioned, federal support for higher education (especially financial aid for students) has been greatly reduced. At the same time, the idea of a voucher system has not generated much support.

Throughout this book we have seen many instances of the importance of education in a technologically advanced and rapidly changing society. We have also noted that teaching is becoming more attractive as a career choice among first-year students. But if education is to meet the challenges facing it and if young people are to seriously consider teaching as a vocation, increased funding is necessary.

Beyond Left & Right

So many hopes are pinned on education and schools are asked to do so many things to assist in the socialization of the young—from teaching them the "basics" to providing physical and moral education of all kinds—that it is little wonder that education is such a contested area of life in democratic societies. There are, however, some areas of convergence between people on the left and right sides of the debate over school reform. For example, there is increasing consensus that schools need to raise their standards, although as yet there is little consensus about whether the federal and state governments should be the proper enforcers and monitors of these standards. Also, those on the left and the right generally agree that more universal access to higher education is necessary if Americans are to cope with changing economic and technological conditions. But again, there is not yet consensus on how to fund either elementary education or public colleges and universities. People of all ideological persuasions are seeking alternatives to the inadequate property tax system for funding the schools, and in time we may indeed see political, if not ideological, agreement on pragmatic means to fund the education that our society's students will need in coming decades.

SUMMARY

- The American educational system is subject to criticism for failing to produce competent, educated adults and for failing to reduce or eliminate inequality.

- Functionalist theorists believe that problems of public education arise because schools are not equipped to deal with students who come from disorganized homes. Also related to functionalism is the belief that the educational problems of certain groups stem from deviance from generally accepted norms of achievement. The institutional approach focuses on the problems of shaping educational institutions to meet the needs of changing economies and cultures.

- The conflict perspective sees educational problems as stemming from conflicting views about the goals of education. The class conflict approach argues that schools reflect the values of the dominant groups in society.

This approach focuses on intergroup conflicts over such issues as busing to achieve desegregation.

■ According to labeling theorists, schools attach labels like "achiever" or "rebel" to students, and those labels follow them throughout their lives.

■ Because educational attainment is strongly correlated with socioeconomic status, an egalitarian society has a responsibility to provide equal access to education for all its citizens. Although the educational gap between whites and minority groups has narrowed considerably, inequalities of access remain, especially in higher education.

■ It has been shown that a high-quality preschool program can significantly affect subsequent educational achievement and attainment. As a result, the national Head Start program has been continued.

■ The American educational system is highly bureaucratized, a fact that acts as a major barrier to educational change. Even the typically American belief in the "technological fix" encounters obstacles in the bureaucratic organization of school systems. Research has shown that smaller school and class size improves students' performance but that school choice programs do not.

■ Educational policy recommendations take two main forms. Educational conservatives believe schools should focus on "essentials" or "the basics." They recommend increased attention to academic subjects, more homework and testing, and firmer discipline; some call for a national curriculum and standards. Liberal, or "humanist," educators believe schools should promote the maximum self-development of each individual learner. They call for individualized instruction, greater flexibility in curriculum planning, and increased opportunities for educational innovation.

■ An important policy innovation is open admissions, meaning that any student with a high school diploma may attend a public university. This approach has not found widespread acceptance, although it appears to have increased equality of educational opportunity at one large university.

■ There is growing recognition of the need to improve the quality of public school teaching, but as yet there has been little progress toward this goal. Other current trends in educational policy include lengthening the school year in some communities and increasing opportunities for school choice.

KEY TERMS

humanism, p. 391
progressivism, p. 391
open education, p. 391

INTERNET EXERCISE

The web destinations for Chapter 13 are related to different aspects of problems surrounding education. To begin your explorations, go to the Prentice Hall Companion Website: **http://prenhall.com/kornblum.** Then choose **Chapter 13** (Problems of Education). Next, select **destinations** from the menu on the left side of the screen. There are a variety of sites to investigate. We suggest that you begin with **The Digital Divide**. The *Critical Research* box in this chapter is titled "Closing the Digital Divide in the Classroom." The *digital divide* refers to growing concern about the widening gap in technology skills between young people from more affluent homes, who have computers and

Internet access, and those from low-income, often black or Hispanic, families who have none. The **Digital Divide** website is sponsored by the Public Broadcasting System (PBS).

After you have accessed the main page, you will find a number of icons to click on, including *News* and *Themes*. These areas of the site will provide you with a more detailed history of the concept of the digital divide. If you have time, you may also wish to click on *Race* and *Gender* to develop a more complete understanding of how this widening gap affects the members of different minority groups. After you have explored the Digital Divide site, answer the following questions:

■ Do you have access to the Internet at home? If you are employed, do you have access at your workplace? Even if the answer is "No" in both of these instances, you probably have access at one of the computer terminals at the college or university you are attending. As pointed out in the *Critical Research* box and in the Digital Divide website, the members of minority groups are far less likely to have access to the Internet in comparison with more affluent individuals. Moreover, some of these people have *no knowledge* of the Internet other than what they see or hear on television. What are the liabilities today of not being able to use Internet technologies?

■ Some social critics believe that the digital divide will be the key ingredient in separating the "haves" from the "have-nots." What do you think can be done to avoid this eventuality? Try to make some specific suggestions for dealing with this problem.

14 Problems of Work and the Economy

WORK AND THE ECONOMY

- The worth of some multinational corporations, as measured by overall stock value (capitalization), is greater than the annual gross domestic products of entire nations.

- In 1960, over 28 percent of all workers were employed in manufacturing jobs. By 1998, this figure had dropped to about 14 percent.

- Between 1940 and 1990, the proportion of married women in the labor force rose by 10 percentage points per decade.

- At least 100,000 Americans die of job-related diseases each year.

OUTLINE

The American Free-Enterprise System

Global Markets and Corporate Power
Multinational Corporations
Global Factory, Global Sweatshops

Effects on American Workers
From Manufacturing to Services
Women in the Global Labor Market
Technology and Specialization

Problem Aspects of Work
Job Insecurity
Job Stress
Alienation
Unemployment
Occupational Safety and Health

Consumers and Credit
Problems of Debt Entanglement
Possessions and Self-expression

Social Policy

C orporations, workers, and consumers are not social problems, but some of the changes that affect them clearly are. Employees and businesses in the U.S. economy today are faced with enormous challenges. Among these are the need to cope with many effects of economic globalization and the way in which corporations and businesses adjust to global change. New forms of global business have major effects on workers in the United States and throughout the world. They help account for new patterns of wealth and power and for the growing gap between the affluent and those who are struggling to make ends meet. Also, many problems of consumers in today's economy stem from the wish to own ever more diverse and attractive goods and services, on one hand, and difficulties in actually paying for what they want, on the other. We deal with the subject of consumer debt in the last section of the chapter.

The American Free-Enterprise System

When people refer to the American free-enterprise system, they are talking about an economic system known as **capitalism** (Friedman, 1962; Gilder, 1981; Kuttner, 1997). The central social institutions of capitalism are **markets,** which regulate the worldwide flow of an almost infinite array of goods and services. Markets in a pure free-enterprise system are regulated by the demand for specific goods and services and the competition among suppliers to furnish them at a price that will be attractive to buyers. In fact, however, almost all markets in nations throughout the world are regulated by acts of governments. These regulations usually attempt to protect buyers in such areas as the safety of products (e.g., rules about food and drug purity and airline maintenance). Other regulations seek to ensure that markets remain competitive and are not dominated by a handful of giant companies known as monopolies.

In other cases, governments may try to affect the prices charged for various goods by imposing import taxes. These levies usually seek to give locally made products a price advantage over products imported from outside the nation. The

North American Free Trade Agreement of 1992 (NAFTA), for example, is essentially an arrangement in which the United States, Mexico, and Canada agree not to impose import taxes on goods and services flowing among these countries. The riots in Seattle during the 1999 meetings of the World Trade Council brought many of the controversial aspects of the attempt to regulate world trade to national and international TV audiences.

Capital refers to equipment of all kinds and to hourly or salaried labor. Capitalists are people who use capital to produce goods and services in the hope of making a profit, that is, by selling their product at a market price somewhat higher than the costs of the equipment and labor used to create it. A capitalist who creates a new business venture is known as an **entrepreneur.** In the pure form of free-enterprise capitalism, the entrepreneur assumes all the risks and expects to make as much profit as possible with as little regulation as possible. In actual practice, most entrepreneurs try to minimize their risks in many different ways.

Formation of a corporation is one major way of minimizing risk. Corporations are chartered by governments to conduct business with limited liability to the owners of the business. **Limited liability** means that only the assets of the corporation are liable to seizure in the case of economic failure or wrongdoing. The entrepreneur's personal assets are not liable if the corporation fails. This protection is vital to the existence of corporations and makes it possible for them to raise funds for expansion by selling shares of their business in the financial markets (stocks and bonds). Since they become part owners of the corporation, the shareholders are not liable for what the corporation does beyond the risk of losing their investment in the business. The fact that governments grant limited liability to corporations is one way that the public, through its elected representatives, can try to make corporations responsible for their actions: Governments can revoke their charters if they violate federal or state laws.

Not all corporations sell shares to the public, but those that do are among the largest and most powerful economic entities in the world. Indeed, the global reach of large corporations, as well as their increasing power throughout the world, is often associated with social problems like environmental pollution, sudden unemployment in specific regions, the use of child labor in poor nations, and many others. It is also true that corporations often create opportunities for economic development and new jobs in formerly impoverished regions.

Inspired by the Marxian dream of a classless society in which everyone owns the means of production (i.e., capital), Communist nations like the former Soviet Union attempted to abolish free enterprise, competitive markets, and profits and replace them with a planned economy in which government commands determined the flow of goods and services. The decline of the Soviet Union is attributed primarily to the failure of this "command" economic system, which created untold opportunities for corruption and waste.

Capitalist business practices are by no means free of problems, including ruthless dealings, exploitation of the powerless, and their own forms of corruption. Even when they are successful in generating economic growth and new employment opportunities, in a global marketplace success in one region may come at the expense of workers in another, a subject we introduce in the next section.

Global Markets and Corporate Power

We hear a great deal about the effects of globalization, but the term and its meanings are often not defined. By **economic globalization,** social scientists refer to the growing tendency for goods and services to be produced in one nation or region and consumed in another, and for the companies that produce those goods and services to engage in business activities in many different regions of the world. This trend is not new, but it is accelerating. Commodities like sugar, coffee, tobacco, and tea were early entrants in the global marketplace of the eighteenth and nineteenth centuries. Sugarcane, for example, was produced on slave plantations in the Caribbean, made into raw sugar and rum, and traded in the northern colonies of what is now the United States and Canada for lumber and other products, which were brought back to the rapidly industrializing nations of Europe. Much of the early economic growth of England, France, and Holland, as well as their competition to establish colonies, was stimulated by this global trade.

In today's global economy the major changes from older patterns of worldwide economic activity are due to the far greater speed of modern communications and transport. Fish produced in massive salmon farms in Chile, for example, can be on American dinner tables the next day. Information about prices and investment opportunities can travel with electronic speed over computer networks. Television can make a corporation like Coca-Cola, which has ventures everywhere, lose vast sums of money when there is a health scare about its products in one European nation (Belgium). Many of the social problems that globalization entails are due to the overwhelming influence of multinational corporations, both in the less developed nations, where they increasingly do business, and in their home nations.

Multinational Corporations

Few aspects of globalization are more controversial than the operations and even the existence of **multinational** (or transnational) **corporations.** The definition of these entities is extremely broad. They may produce many different kinds of goods and services, but they are all large corporations (often with many subsidiary corporations) that have their headquarters in one country but pursue business activities and profits in one or more foreign nations (Gordon, 1996; Kuttner, 1991). In this sense multinationals have existed at least since the international banking houses of the Italian Renaissance. American firms like Singer, United Fruit, and Firestone have had extensive foreign operations—and political influence—since the late nineteenth century. For the most part, however, these were national companies with secondary foreign operations.

The sharp rise in foreign investments and the concentration of financial resources that followed World War II led to the development of transnational corporations. These companies are international organizations that operate across national boundaries, whatever their country of origin may be. Their size, wealth, influence, and diversity of operations have grown enormously. The annual sales of companies like GM, ITT, and the "Seven Sisters" of the petroleum industry exceed the gross national product of many nations—not just the poorer countries of the third world, but highly industrialized countries like Switzerland and South Africa as well. Increasingly, therefore, the term *multinational* is used to emphasize the fact that these corporations operate outside national boundaries almost as if they were nations unto themselves.

For decades the multinational auto companies, such as GM and Ford, have been producing thousands of cars in Europe for sale in the expanding European markets. They have had less success in the growing Asian markets, which are dominated by Japanese manufacturers. Now the Japanese multinational manufacturers, especially Toyota, Nissan, and Honda, are increasing the production of cars in the United States, using Japanese methods and parts. These and other multinational companies try to create an image of themselves not as Japanese or American but as world companies that are above nationalistic sentiments. Although the multinationals will certainly continue to grow and to account for an increasing share of the world's production of goods and services, they are widely criticized for operating outside the control of any nation. They can rapidly move their activities from one nation to another, and their worth, as measured by overall stock value (capitalization) can be greater than the an-

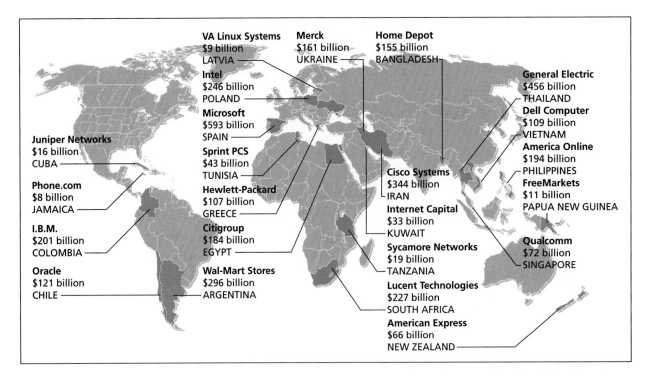

Figure 14–1 Gross Domestic Products of Selected Countries and Companies Whose Market Capitalizations Are About Equal to Them

Source: Morgenson, 1999. Copyright © 1999 by the New York Times Co. Reprinted by permission.

nual gross domestic products of entire nations (see Figure 14–1). One way in which multinational corporations are a source of social problems is that they tend to move quickly to areas where labor costs are lowest, often to the detriment of workers left behind in the nations where they began their operations.

Global Factory, Global Sweatshops

Multinational corporations are transforming the world's economy by focusing on rapidly developing markets and on labor forces in the less developed nations, which have an oversupply of workers in their manufacturing sectors and an undersupply of highly skilled workers with technological training. No longer confined to producing their products in just one country, the multinationals have created a "global factory" that is made possible by two kinds of technology: high-speed transportation and component production (Barnet, 1980). The first enables companies to get raw materials, finished products, communications, and so on from one point to another anywhere in the world. The second divides the production process into component operations that can be carried out anywhere, thereby allowing multinational companies to take advantage of the worldwide supply of cheap labor. For example, U.S. baseball manufacturers send the materials for their product—leather covers, yarn, thread, and cement—to Haiti, where the baseballs are assembled for wages far below those paid for similar work anywhere in the United States (Galbraith, 1998).

Critics of U.S. multinationals have been especially vocal in condemning the practice known as **outsourcing**—locating plants that produce goods for American markets in third-world nations where the firm can take advantage of lower wage rates. This practice in effect "exports" manufacturing jobs from the United States to the third world, greatly reducing the number of industrial jobs available for American workers. In recent years, however, a countertrend has become evident: Multinational firms are increasing their investments in the United States. Sony of Japan has purchased CBS Records; Germany's Daimler-Benz owns the Chrysler automobile company; Japanese and German automobile manufacturers have opened plants in the United States to assemble their cars, often using parts manufactured abroad. These arrangements are considered preferable to outsourcing because they keep jobs in the United States. But many foreign-based multinationals resist union contracts and the resulting higher wages and benefits (DiFazio, 1999).

In addition to engaging in outsourcing, multinational corporations attempt to sell their products in third-world markets. As the populations of those nations increase and their standard of living also rises (albeit much more slowly), they represent a vast untapped source of profits. However, multinationals increasingly produce high-technology products and services intended for markets with much greater buying power. Accordingly, many observers (e.g., Rohatyn, 1987) argue that it is necessary to develop more buying power in the third world. This, in turn, requires that workers in those nations be paid higher wages and not have to work in "sweatshops," in which they are essentially forced to endure conditions that would not be tolerated in affluent nations.

Many of the protesters in Seattle in 1999 were responding to revelations that major multinational corporations, or local companies under contract to them, hire child labor at extremely low wages. The United Auto Workers (1996) points out, for example, that the Nike Corporation subcontracts with local employers for about 75,000 Asian workers to make Nike shoes. In some cases 11-year-old workers, who earn about $2.20 a day, are producing sneakers at a cost of about $6 a pair. The sneakers are then sold in the United States for $80.00 or more and are advertised by celebrities like Michael Jordan, who earns about $20 million a year for selling his image to Nike.

Those who argue that the United States should apply trade sanctions, such as import duties, against nations that exploit their workers believe that wages in Latin America, Asia, and the Middle East will increase only if the rights of workers are protected from repression by their governments and powerful businesses. Workers must have the right to bargain collectively for wages, pensions, and health and other benefits. But representatives of China, Pakistan, India, and many other less developed nations where multinationals are active argue that insistence on workers' rights and other protections would drive labor costs up and diminish one of the few advantages poor nations have in the global marketplace. They claim that proponents of labor standards are protectionists who "stand against the trading interests of the developing countries" in order to "advance their own economic interests" (Bhagwati, 1999).

Effects on American Workers

For the American worker, the growth of multinationals and global markets means that a steadily decreasing number of employers have come to dominate the labor market. This has had several effects. Chief among them is the fact that as unions cope with increasingly large and centralized corporations, they, too, tend to become large and centralized, and their leadership tends to become oligopolistic (Gordon, 1996). The growth of multinationals is also associated with the tendency to export capital and jobs overseas, where labor is cheaper and more plentiful. American manufacturing workers have been most seriously affected by this trend. In 1960, over 28 percent of all U.S. workers were employed in manufacturing jobs. By 1998, this figure had dropped to about 14 percent (*Statistical Abstract*, 1999).

During the 1970s and 1980s, U.S. plants, factories, mills, and other industrial facilities suffered as capital was diverted abroad. Unable to maintain their competitive edge, many manufacturing facilities closed. Especially hard hit were plants in the nation's older, single-industry cities and towns, most of which were located in the manufacturing belt of the Midwest. When rubber mills in Akron and steel mills in Youngstown and the Pittsburgh area shut their doors, the local economies were devastated. With few secondary industries to fall back on, these cities experienced severe economic and social upheavals during the recessions of the mid-1970s and early 1980s and 1990s.

The biggest losers in the decline in manufacturing have been industrial towns and cities in the Northeast and Midwest. Manufacturing cities like Gary, Indiana, once the nation's most important producer of steel, have been hit hardest. In the 1970s the Gary steel mills employed almost 28,000 workers in relatively well-paid jobs with good benefits. Today fewer than 8,000 workers are employed in the Gary mills. Nevertheless, modernization of the steel industry, leading to greater efficiency and quality control, may produce a turnaround. Steel exports are rising, and steel companies' profits are improving.

Over the past generation or so there have been three unprecedented changes in the American labor force, largely because of transformations in the global economy. First is the shift from manufacturing to service employment. Second is the enormous increase in the number of women working outside the home—women of all ages and from all kinds of family backgrounds. Third is the emergence of new technologies and unprecedented economic growth in the past ten years, much of it related to the global influence of the U.S. economy.

From Manufacturing to Services

Because people work for so much of their lives, it is important to try to understand the social problems related to work. Later in the chapter we will discuss four: unemployment, automation, alienation, and occupational safety and health. In this section we will explore four patterns of change in the nature of work in the United States that have accompanied the shift from a manufacturing-based to a service-based economy.

The impact of the transition from an agricultural economy to an industrial one dominated by large corporations and government organizations can be gauged from a few figures. In 1900, 27 percent of the total labor force consisted of farm workers and 18 percent of white-collar workers. In 1998, a little over 3 percent of the labor force consisted of farming, forestry, and fishing workers, whereas slightly over 53 percent were white-collar workers (*Statistical Abstract,* 1999).

White-collar workers—professional, managerial, clerical, and sales personnel—are the largest occupational category in the nation, surpassing the blue-collar group since 1956. Most of the new white-collar jobs are professional and clerical. The number of clerical personnel has increased by more than 500 percent since 1900 and now accounts for about 17 percent of all employed people (*Statistical Abstract,* 1999). Clerical workers now vie with skilled and semiskilled workers as the largest occupational group in the labor force.

The decline in farm employment since the turn of the century has been as dramatic as the rise in white-collar employment. Farm workers—farmers, managers, and farm hands—once the largest occupational category in the United States, are now the smallest.

Blue-collar workers have witnessed enormous changes in the nature of their work. A declining proportion of the overall labor force, manual workers still constitute a very large segment of the work force but are employed in a changing array of jobs. The proportion of unskilled laborers has decreased. Similarly, the slight overall net gain in service occupations masks some important changes within that category. People employed as private household workers now account for less than 1 percent of the total labor force; in 1900 they accounted for 5 percent. In contrast, the proportion of other service personnel—hotel workers, waiters, barbers, and others—has risen to about 13 percent of all employed people; in 1990 it was 4 percent.

CRITICAL RESEARCH

The Maquilladora Effect

The effects of the North American Free Trade Agreement (NAFTA) are most obvious along the border between the United States and Mexico. In Tijuana, Matamoros, Juarez, and other Mexican border towns one can see hundreds of new factories where U.S. corporations and their Mexican subsidiaries are manufacturing products or parts of products for export to the United States and other countries. These are known as the *maquilladora* industries. They employ more than 1.23 million Mexican workers, often under conditions that would not be accepted in the United States and at beginning wages that average $35 a week. The maquilladora factories are bringing new economic growth to the poor Mexican border regions, where even $35 a week can be far more than agricultural work would pay. But critical research shows that unless Mexican workers can win legal protection of their right to form unions and bargain for better wages and working conditions, the promised economic growth cannot occur.

The accompanying chart shows that the number of maquilladora plants grew enormously between 1980 and 1999, from about 500 to more than 3,000. So did the number of employees, from less than 200,000 before NAFTA to more than a million. But average wages decreased from about $600 a month to slightly over $400 because the rapid growth in jobs attracted waves of men and women to the border towns from impoverished urban and rural neighborhoods to the south. These newcomers are willing to work for lower wages

A typical scene outside a maquilladora installation on the U.S.-Mexican border. Unlike their fellow Chrysler workers in the United States, these Mexican auto workers do not yet have the right to bargain collectively to improve their wages and working conditions.

than more experienced workers, and the net effect is that average wages are driven down. In the absence of regulations that establish adequate minimum wages or effective unions to fight for the workers' interests, this situation is unlikely to change in the near future—which is what American union activists point to when they criticize the trade agreement (Stevenson, 1999).

A number of American unions, notably the Oil, Chemical and Atomic Workers Union, are working to form cross-border coalitions with Mexican unionists to fight to reverse the wage gap between American and Mexican workers (Bacon, 1997). These coalitions of

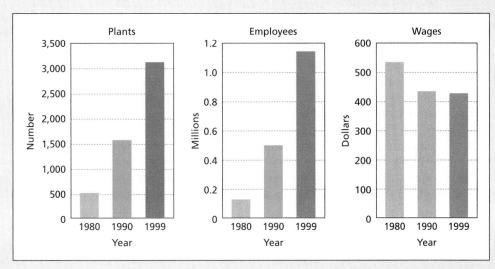

Plants, Employees, and Wages of Maquilladora Industries, 1980–1999

All figures are for January of each year. Wages includes management.

Source: Stevenson, 1999.

union organizers, local religious groups and their leaders, and active citizens are opposed by the companies and their allies. The contest is not evenly balanced. In 1994, for example, the director of Sony's maquilladora in Nuevo Laredo, across the border from Laredo, Texas, fired 18 workers who tried to run for office against entrenched officials of the plant union, a branch of the government-affiliated Confederation of Mexican Workers. After the firings, workers sat in at the plant gate. With full cooperation from local political leaders, Sony brought in riot police, who beat the workers. The dissidents then organized an independent union and tried, unsuccessfully, to register it with the government. And even though the NAFTA agreement includes clauses that promise to protect workers' rights, the U.S. government took no action other than forming a committee to study the situation.

As cross-border coalitions call attention to undemocratic practices like those invoked against the Sony workers, there is hope for positive change. The odds facing maquilladora workers and cross-border activists are improving because of changes in both the Mexican and the U.S. labor movements. In Mexico, the powerful alliance of government and employer-dominated unions is beginning to fracture, which is enabling more independent unions to have some organizing successes. On the U.S. side, the AFL-CIO's leadership is also overcoming its reluctance to support dissident groups across the border. Union organizer Ed Feigen believes that the AFL-CIO "not only can't stand in the way of these new initiatives, it doesn't want to. The door is open now. Our problem these days is making things happen fast enough" (quoted in Bacon, 1997, p. 4).

The momentous shift from an economy dominated by manufacturing employment to one dominated by jobs in services of all kinds results in improvements in some work-related social problems and at the same time brings on new ones to deal with. For example, accidents and deaths on the job are far more prevalent in an economy dominated by agriculture and extractive industries, such as mining and lumbering, or one in which there are large numbers of workers in heavy industries, such as metals production and auto and truck manufacturing. The rate of accidental deaths at work in 1960 was 21 per 100,000 workers, but by 1998, with the rise of service work as the leading form of employment, that rate had declined to 4 per 100,000 workers. Mining remains the most dangerous work environment in the United States, with 24 deaths per 100,000 workers, followed closely by agriculture, with 21. In service work, on the other hand, the rate of accidental deaths is about 1 per 100,000 each year (*Statistical Abstract*, 1999). Note also that societies with a *service economy* or *postindustrial economy* (terms that social scientists often use to refer to the labor market of mature industrial societies that export many of their manufacturing jobs abroad) do not entirely lose their manufacturing infrastructure. There are still mines, railroads, auto plants, and many other sources of blue-collar work, but they are a declining proportion of the total and are no longer setting the pace of social change in their societies.

The decline in union membership is a good indication of this change. In 1960, at the height of their influence in the United States, about 27 percent of employees in the private sector were members of trade unions. Today about 11 percent are union members, a reflection of the shift from manufacturing work, which was always more heavily unionized, to white-collar service work, which, with the exception of government work, is less unionized. This rate varies from one state to another. In Michigan, Illinois, and Ohio, states with higher proportions of manufacturing jobs, at least 18 percent of private-sector employees are union members, whereas in Georgia, Utah, and Mississippi, states with so-called "right to work" laws that make it much harder for unions to organize workers, less than 10 percent are union members. These differences are extremely important because unions help workers obtain not only higher pay but also health and other benefits that nonunion workers often do not have. Thus, the proportion of families with health insurance is higher for union families than for nonunion ones. Indeed, the loss of union jobs to global manufacturing sites outside the United States has resulted in more jobs with lower average pay and fewer

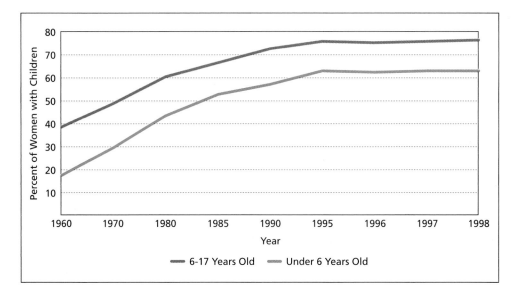

Figure 14–2 Labor Force Participation of Married Women, 1960–1998

Source: Data from *Statistical Abstract*, 1999.

benefits, a major cause of the growing gap between workers whose share of the national income is stagnant and those who benefited most from the economic boom of the 1990s. (See the Critical Research feature on page 403.)

Another aspect of the shift from manufacturing to services is the growing importance of what is known as "contingent" work, work that is not based on written employment contracts and regular hours. This problem is particularly serious for female workers.

Women in the Global Labor Market

The labor force, as defined by the federal government, consists of all people 16 years of age or over (excluding those in institutions[1]) who worked one hour for pay during one survey week (the employed) plus those who did not work during the survey week, do not have a job, and are actively seeking work (the unemployed). The most significant trend in the labor force is the inclusion of married women and the exclusion of older men.

Many social scientists argue that after the shift from manufacturing to service work, the single most significant trend in the labor force in the twentieth century was the enormous increase in women as paid workers. A century ago women and men rarely did the same work. Although there were always women in the labor force, much of the work they did was unpaid and in the home, usually involving extremely long hours. Married women were expected to remain at home. Between 1940 and 1990, however, the proportion of married women in the labor force—that is, the percentage working or looking for work—rose by 10 percentage points per decade. As we see in Figure 14–2, today the proportion is nearly 70 percent. Not shown in the figure is the fact that over 80 percent of women who have bachelor's degrees are in the labor force, a rate that is rapidly approaching that of men (Tienda, 1999).

Among African-American women, William J. Wilson notes,

> Noncollege black women had very little chance during the first half of this century to take a job other than as a domestic servant. After 1960, demand increased for clerical and service workers. Black women were able to take those positions, so much so that by 1980, only a small percentage of black women

---

[1]Prisons, asylums, and nursing homes.

were domestic household servants. But, ironically, just as blacks and Hispanics started to move into those clerical positions, changing demand began to reduce opportunities as bank tellers, typists, and so on. Now, folks who don't have college degrees face a new challenge because the areas that were opening up are starting to lose. Yet it's far better then it was. (Quoted in Tienda, 1999, p. 48)

Over the past 20 years the sheer number of people in the U.S. labor force has increased dramatically, again largely because of the rapid influx of women. In 1970 there were 78 million men and women in the labor force; now there are more than 130 million, of whom well over 40 percent are female. But for many of these workers, and especially for women, the costs of maintaining the home and raising children make it necessary to hold more than one job. About 6 percent of both women and men are multiple job holders. When asked why they must work two jobs, 31 percent of men say that they do so to pay regular household bills. But among women who maintain families themselves, over 40 percent say that they hold a second job to pay the bills, and the percentage rises to 52 percent of black female chief breadwinners and 39 percent of Hispanic women in the same situation (*Statistical Abstract*, 1999).

Some women who are second job holders need that job because the first job is part time and does not provide sufficient earnings to make ends meet. Twenty-one million Americans were working fewer than 35 hours a week in 1998, and in fact were averaging 21 hours a week. The majority of these part-timers were women. When questioned about why they were working part time, about 6.6 million men and women said that they were in school, but 5.5 million, again mostly women, said that they were part-timers because of family obligations, including problems with child care (*Statistical Abstract*, 1999). Here the problem is balancing work and family roles. As economist Juliet Shor concludes, "The major barrier is the structure of jobs. We have not been able to make good jobs compatible with child-rearing roles. The labor market is inflexible" (quoted in Tienda, 1999, p. 48). The massive entry of women into the labor market, sociologist Marta Tienda (1999) observes, is partly because of the need for child care: "Because we rely on other women to take care of our children, two women can enter the labor force for every one that takes on a new job. When women go to work, we buy child-care services, more takeout food and other services, all of which are driving economic growth in a profound way. It also means that we are fueling stratification [inequality]" (p. 48).

Finally, it should be noted that even though women are employed in greater numbers than ever before, their jobs are vulnerable during economic recessions; and although many women are highly motivated to work, outside employment has not released most of them from household and family tasks. As we saw in Chapters 10 and 12, a married woman typically works many hours at home in addition to holding an outside job.

Technology and Specialization

Much of the growth in the U.S. economy in the 1990s was fueled by the rise of new technologies, especially in computers, telecommunications (including Internet applications), biotechnologies, and e-commerce. As noted earlier, improved coordination of global production systems through faster transport of materials, goods, and people makes it possible to export manufacturing jobs overseas while creating more managerial, information resources, and finan-

As the proportion of women in the labor force has increased, so has the frequency with which women with dependent children experience layoffs and unemployment.

cial positions in the metropolitan centers of North America, Europe, and Asia. But even more significant is the rapid growth in applications of computer technologies. Every year the percentage of U.S. workers who use computers daily at their jobs increases dramatically. Between 1993 and 1998, this percentage rose from 46 percent to 50 percent, which translates into 12.5 million more computer users at work. In 1998, 56.5 percent of women, who are more likely to have white-collar jobs than are men, worked regularly with computers, far above the national average. Although the most common application was word processing, increasing proportions of women and men are using computers for a wider variety of tasks, often involving the World Wide Web.

Technology. Computer and telecommunications have spawned an astounding array of new Internet-related businesses, such as Amazon.com and iVillage.com. The growth of many of these was made possible by intense speculation in technology stocks at the end of the 1990s and well into 2000, but it is still too soon to know the many implications these new businesses will have for workers and consumers. One effect is clear, however: The number of self-employed people is growing rapidly. Much of this growth is made possible by the rise of new technology-based businesses (which require web page designers, programmers, and other technical specialists). The telecommunications technologies also allow many more people to create and manage their own home businesses, and thus to make their living at home. In 1998, 10 million people reported that they were self-employed (*Statistical Abstract*, 1999).

In the next few decades, new technologies will continue to fundamentally change the character of work in America. Many people fear—not unrealistically—that the principal change will be a reduction in the number of jobs. In this regard, sociologists Stanley Aronowitz and William DiFazio argue that for many millions of people in the older Western industiral nations, which are experiencing a combination of high rates of job elimination through automation and extensive exporting of less skilled work to low-wage regions of the world, there will be a "jobless future." Increasingly, they and others predict, new entrants to the labor force who do not have essential skills will undergo long spells of unemployment and circulation through training programs, but their work histories will not enable them to become secure in a middle-class lifestyle (Aronowitz & DiFazio, 1994; Rifkin, 1995). Critics of this viewpoint note that the American economy has continued to produce millions of new jobs at all skill levels despite the undeniable displacement and change caused by automation (Kasarda, 1995; Wetzel, 1995).

Specialization. Specialization is a long-term trend in the labor market. The vast majority of people in the labor forces of urban industrial societies are employees of small or large companies or of public administrations. For them, too, computer and other technologies are changing the nature of their work and the types of jobs available to them. Specialization, however, began long before the advent of computers. As the number of goods and services increases, so does job specialization. As the complexity of production processes increases with product diversity, so does job specialization.

As mentioned earlier, there are four broad categories of employment (white-collar, blue-collar, service, and farm workers). Within these categories, of course, there are literally thousands of jobs. The *Dictionary of Occupational Titles*, published by the Department of Labor, lists more than 22,000 jobs—a total that contrasts sharply with the 325 recorded by the 1850 census. The vast difference indicates the increasing specialization of labor and the complexity of its divisions.

Specialization has several important implications. First, lower-echelon workers who were trained only for a single, narrow job and who lose it may have difficulty in finding another like it. Second, these workers often feel that they are merely adjuncts to a machine or a process, with little chance to develop and use more than minor skills or abilities. This feeling often leads to dissatisfaction with work. For high-level managers,

Economics on the Internet

For those who wish to investigate the state of the U.S. economy, the federal government provides several indispensable resources. The Bureau of Labor Statistics's website (**http://stats.bls.gov/blshome.html**) displays several boxes that provide a window on the world of work. Click on Economy at a Glance to view statistics on current employment trends. More sophisticated data are available at DATA, as are links to other statistical sites. Research papers, many in downloadable form, are accessible through Publications and Research Papers.

The Department of Labor's web page (**http://www.dol.gov**) supplies other labor-related data, including reports on occupational injury and illness rates, as well as a link to the Economics and Statistics Administration, which is a source for much of the statistical, economic, and demographic information collected by the federal government.

Information on how the nation's banking system works is available from the Federal Reserve's home page at **http://www.bog.frb.fed.us/**. The page provides an informative and easy-to-understand guide to the Federal Reserve, along with congressional testimony, press releases, statistics, research papers, and the all-important minutes of the Federal Open Market Committee. International financial data are featured on the web pages of the International Monetary Fund (**http://www.imf.org/**) and the World Bank (**http://www.worldbank.org/**). The Organization for Economic Cooperation and Development (OECD) at **http://www.oecd.org/** has extensive data on social indicators such as health and education. It also provides downloadable reports on various aspects of economic development.

Virtually the entire gamut of subjects covered by the academic discipline of economics is just a click away at the WWW Virtual Library on Economics (**http://www.netec.wustl.edu/WebEc/**). Besides sections on the nuts and bolts of the discipline, such as micro- and macroeconomics, there are online courses and a Reference Shelf. One of the best resources for demystifying the "dismal science" can be found at the home page of the Left Business Observer (**http://www.panix.com/~henwood/LBO_home.html**). There, current debates and news stories are explained in plain and often witty prose. The site also offers numerous links to resources from the business, financial, academic, and political worlds. Economic policy debates take center stage at the web pages of the Center on Budget and Policy Priorities (**http://epn.org/cbpp.html**). They emphasize how government programs affect low- and middle-income people and offer reports on such topics as the federal budget, the minimum wage, and welfare reform. The American Enterprise Institute (**http://www.aei.org/**) advocates restricting government involvement in business affairs.

the increase in specialization has created problems of coordination and cooperation that present great challenges (Braverman, 1974).

Problem Aspects of Work

What are the effects of the new technologies? According to sociologist Shoshanna Zuboff (1982), managers and employees whose jobs are controlled by factory computer systems come to believe that their effective "boss" is the computer. In some cases unionized employees have protested the new forms of hidden computer supervision. Workers in the Bell system, for example, blamed computer technology for eroding the family culture of "Ma Bell." They equated the computer with oversupervision, stress, and excessive discipline.

Computer control not only affects workers but also alters the structure of the organization. For one thing, most computer-based operations require a separate data-processing staff. Computer specialists are different from many of the other people in a factory. They have skills that the others do not understand, and their job is not actually to produce the product but to provide efficient means of producing it. Computer technology, therefore, creates a new interdependence between the workers who are directly concerned with the end product and those who are concerned with data processing, whose job is to help accomplish the other workers' goal. People with high status in the organization but no technical expertise must cooperate with the technical experts, such as programmers and systems analysts, who have no supervisory authority—a relationship that is unique to modern organizations.

Such cooperation is not easy. Aronowitz and DiFazio (1994) note that technologies like computer-assisted design are eliminating highly skilled jobs in architecture and engineering because computers can now accomplish many drafting and design tasks that once employed thousands of technical workers who were gradually moving up through the ranks of the technological elite. They also note that the workers who remain after their colleagues have been replaced by technological systems are not necessarily more contented; they must live with the lingering fear that new technologies will eventually eliminate their jobs as well.

It seems that the new technologies may exacerbate some conditions that produce job dissatisfaction. Work will probably become increasingly demanding and precise. These changes will continue to increase demands by employers for a more highly educated and competent labor force. They also give rise to increased job insecurity and job stress.

Job Insecurity

Despite almost ten years of high employment rates, more people in the United States are staying at their jobs (see Figure 4–3). In good economic times, when jobs seem more plentiful, we usually see higher rates of voluntary job leaving. People quit their jobs to find better ones. But although employment was far higher in 1999 than in 1989 or 1979, fewer people are leaving their jobs voluntarily (Mason-Draffen, 1999). The lower rate indicates that more people feel insecure about the economy and about their chances of improving their situation through a voluntary job search. The combination of falling wages and increased job loss that the blue-collar, non-college-educated work force experienced in the 1980s has spread to higher-wage white-collar men and to middle-wage women. Insecurity has been worsened by a decline in the wealth of middle-class families and a decrease in employer-provided health insurance, pensions, and other benefits. Faced with a labor market that is offering more contingent work of various kinds, workers seem to be holding on to their jobs more out of insecurity than out of satisfaction with wages, benefits, and working conditions (Mishel, Bernstein, & Schmitt, 1996).

Job Stress

As more people work multiple jobs, are employed on a contingent basis, or experience the sometimes frantic environment of high-tech companies, their physical and mental lives are often negatively affected (Ross, 2000). A 1999 survey of workers' problems conducted by the National Institute for Occupational Safety and Health (NIOSH) found that job stress, because of irregular workloads, uncertain work expectations, loss of control over the pace of work because of increased computerization, poor social environments, and overall job insecurity, was reaching alarming levels. "We've identified this as a top priority issue," Linda Rosenstock, the institute's director, said. "The U.S. public is reporting very high levels of stress at work, and often reporting it's the largest source of stress they face. Shifting work patterns due to the global economy are aggravating these issues" (quoted in Grimsley, 1999, p. 1D).

Gary Namie, an organizational psychologist who operates a web site for workers with job stress, said that in one month 14 people who contacted the site said that they

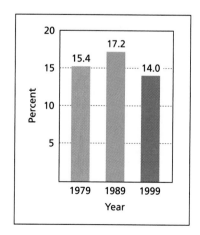

Figure 14–3 Job-leaving Rates, 1979–1999*

*Percentage of unemployed who quit jobs voluntarily

Source: Based on data from Mason-Draffen, 1999.

were considering suicide. "Stress is not to be taken lightly," Namie said. "Stress can kill. Stress is real. It's not imaginary. It has a biological basis. It's unconscionable that someone should sacrifice their health for the sake of a paycheck" (quoted in Grimsley, 1999, p. 1D). According to NIOSH, stress can be alleviated by ensuring that workloads are appropriate for workers' capabilities, clearly defining workers' roles and responsibilities, improving communication, providing opportunities for social interaction, and establishing work schedules that are compatible with other life responsibilities (cited in Grimsley, 1999).

Alienation

When people go to work, they sacrifice some personal freedom and assume some risk. A job demands that a person put his or her time at another's disposal. It may also mean spending money and time on commuting and enduring physical hazards and discomforts, psychological traumas, boredom, and frustration. In return, workers can expect varying amounts of pay and fringe benefits, job security, meaningful work, opportunities for advancement, flexibility in work time, decent surroundings, and positive interactions with peers and supervisors. Each of these factors affects job satisfaction. In recent decades there have been many changes in these factors. A new generation of workers, raised in the affluence of the 1950s and 1960s and well educated, has brought new ideals to the workplace. Daniel Yankelovich (1978) calls them the New Breed. New Breed workers, while still interested in the traditional concerns of salary and benefits, also place great emphasis on individuality and independence. They are less loyal to their employers.

The concept of **flexitime,** or sliding work hours, is very appealing to these workers—so appealing, in fact, that one survey showed that many workers are willing to remain in jobs they dislike because their schedules are flexible (Danesh, 1991). But although flexitime and other creative approaches are appealing and have shown some success, it is more usual for workers in the United States and Europe to feel squeezed between the fear of displacement, on one hand, and the demand that they work longer hours under greater stress, on the other. Critics of the automated, postindustrial society argue that these conditions are likely to cause new outbreaks of industrial strife and to stimulate alienated workers to form unions (Gordon, 1996; Moore, 1996).

Marx and other nineteenth-century social critics attacked the assignment of people to activities that have no meaning for them. Factory workers, they charged, are merely part of a productive process, lacking control over either the process or the product. Workers who lose the capacity to express themselves in their work will experience **alienation.**

In modern work situations, several elements combine to produce a sense of alienation. The primary source today is the clash between a person's self-image and the requirements of his or her job. Those who believe that they need the companionship of others may feel stifled by a job that does not allow them to socialize with fellow workers. Some people may be alienated by jobs that offer little opportunity for personal judgment. Others may see themselves as independent and decisive but find that their bosses are constantly and closely supervising them. The symptoms of alienation are not necessarily confined to blue-collar workers. Alienation may occur in any hierarchy that limits autonomy and the chance to use individual skills. Thus, white-collar workers often feel estranged from their employers and the long-term interests of their companies.

Are the causes of alienation different for different types of workers? Are white-collar workers, such as accountants or engineers, affected by the same factors as blue-collar workers, such as assemblers or welders? A study of nearly 800 workers by the Survey Research Center at the University of Michigan (cited in Gruenberg, 1980) found that although intrinsic sources of job satisfaction are important to all workers regardless of their educational background, such external satisfactions as wages and

The "underground economy" includes many types of businesses that do not report their transactions or pay taxes. An example is the peddler who buys wholesale merchandize and resells it on the street.

vacation time are more important for blue-collar workers. This emphasis on what they get out of the job rather than on what they put into it may reflect the low level of job satisfaction felt by most blue-collar workers.

Attempts to Make Work More Satisfying.   Many jobs are simply dull. For workers who already earn enough to live adequately, additional income cannot always offset the meaninglessness of these jobs. This applies particularly to younger workers, who are likely to be better educated and less concerned than their predecessors about job security. They particularly resent work that they consider trivial and boring, and they want to control the circumstances of their labor.

Some organizations have tried to enhance job satisfaction. One approach, called human relations, focuses on the social context of work and seeks to improve communication in the organizational hierarchy. Numerous corporations have conducted surveys in which employees are asked to criticize their jobs. Even when problems cannot feasibly be corrected, tensions seem to be at least temporarily relieved when employees are allowed to let off steam.

Social scientists like Robert Schrank (1978) and Tom Jurevich (1984) have suggested that piecemeal solutions are inadequate. The only way to reduce dissatisfaction with jobs that are intrinsically dull, unchallenging, or beneath the workers' abilities is to grant them some of the privileges that already sweeten management and professional positions: flexible schedules, a feeling that their opinions are valued, opportunities to socialize more freely during the workday, and more breaks. However, such changes are unlikely in today's intensely competitive business environment (Gordon, 1996; Kuttner, 1997).

Unemployment

Until recently, to be unemployed in America was to be out of the cultural and social mainstream. The economic recessions of the early 1980s and early 1990s, however, made unemployment commonplace. High inflation combined with high interest and mortgage rates and sagging consumer spending threw an increasing number of people out of work, especially in the manufacturing and construction sectors of the economy.

Prolonged joblessness causes serious psychological and social damage. A significant part of today's work force has been denied not only the benefits of a regular and sufficient income but also the emotional rewards of a steady job: the sense of self-worth that comes from doing a job well and having others value that performance; the sense of community fostered by daily association with colleagues; in sum, the feeling that one is participating in society and contributing to it. The unemployed person, whether involuntarily retired, partially or intermittently out of work, or chronically unemployed, is denied many of these rewards. (For problems of the involuntarily retired person, see Chapter 11.)

The Intermittently and Chronically Unemployed.   In a competitive society, job insecurity is common. Even when the unemployment rate is low, many people are unemployed for part of the year and others are underemployed. More serious, however, is chronic unemployment. At this writing, in a period of economic prosperity in the United States, the national unemployment rate is about 4 percent, the lowest level since the 1960s. But when economic downturns, or recessions, occur, the unemployment rate rises. Many of the unemployed will be young and/or nonwhite. In general, the unemployment rate for blacks and other minority groups is twice as high as the rate for whites. The chronically unemployed and their children rarely acquire the capacity to break out of the unemployment pattern without some state or federal help. Many of them are high school dropouts, and their low educational attainment equips them only for low-skilled jobs. These young men and women may not yet have family obligations, but they are nonetheless reluctant to take dead-end jobs as domestics or kitchen workers. (See Chapters 8–10 for fuller discussions of the relationships among discrimination, unemployment, and poverty.)

Frictional Unemployment and Permanent Displacement.   Many workers undergo short spells of unemployment; they may be temporarily laid off from a factory job or may leave one job to search for another that is different or better. Economists call this *frictional unemployment* because it is a normal consequence of labor force mobility or brief economic changes in local labor markets. But a great deal of unemployment results in the permanent displacement of workers. Permanent displacement is extremely serious because often the employee must find work in an entirely different industry or field, which often necessitates retraining of some kind.

The "Invisible" Unemployed and the "Discouraged" Worker.   As stated earlier, the labor force is made up of people aged 16 or over (excluding those in institutions) who worked one hour for pay during the survey week plus those who did not work during the survey week, do not have a job, and are actively seeking work. By definition, all other people over the age of 16 are not in the labor force and therefore are not included in government unemployment reports. This definition persistently understates the size of the labor force and the volume of unemployment. First, it excludes unemployed people who, though able and willing to work, did not actively seek work during the survey week. A second factor is the failure of the official data to reflect adequately the underemployment of people with part-time jobs. R. A. Nixon (1968) estimated that a more accurate measure of unemployment would be about double the official rate.

The problem of "invisible" unemployment becomes more serious in recessions, when the average duration of unemployment increases; eventually many people stop looking for jobs altogether because they think it will be impossible to find one. These are known as "discouraged" workers, people who are out of work not because of personal disadvantages, such as being too old or too young, untrained, or overeducated, but because industries and manufacturers have cut back production and eliminated a large number of jobs. The Bureau of Labor Statistics estimates that the recession of the early 1990s caused about 1 million people to drop out of the labor force in a single year (Rackham, 1991).

Consequences of Unemployment.   What are the consequences of being without work? A classic study of 105 unemployed men in Detroit showed that the chief characteristic is extreme isolation (Wilensky, 1966). Half the men in the study had no close friends, half never visited neighbors, and few belonged to organizations or engaged in organized activities. These findings were in sharp contrast to the social life of an equal-sized sample of employed men. Such data tend to support the thesis that work is necessary if one is to be, in a full sense, "among the living." When work ties are cut, participation in community life declines and the sense of isolation grows. Thus, those with the most tenuous work connections—the retired, the elderly, those who have been squeezed out of the labor market, and those who seldom get into it—are often isolated from their communities and from society at large.

Further studies on the emotional and social effects of long-term unemployment were conducted by D. D. Braginsky and B. M. Braginsky in 1975. This research was confined to high-status unemployed men who had been thrown out of work in the recession of the mid-1970s. The subjects consisted of two groups, one a control group of employed white-collar men and the other a group of jobless men between the ages of 23 and 59. Almost half of the jobless men were college graduates; many had been engineers and company managers. The researchers found that such men undergo a "social transformation"; the trauma of unemployment causes a change of attitude that persists even after they are reemployed. Loss of one's job is commonly interpreted as a judgment of incompetence and worthlessness. In the Braginsky study the unemployed men expressed these feelings. Their self-esteem was lowered, and they felt alienated from society. They experienced depression, a common reaction to loss. Most suffered deep shame and avoided their friends. Many of those who did find new jobs did not fully recover their self-esteem.

As more and more women have entered the labor force, the consequences of unemployment for women have become more important, particularly for women who are single parents, who are divorced or separated, and whose families are dependent on their earnings. Katherine S. Newman (1988) found that middle-class women who are divorced "typically have to make do with 29 to 39 percent of the family income they had before divorce" (p. 202). When these women are in the labor force and experience layoffs and unemployment, it is often difficult for them to support their families while looking for new jobs. Typically they had interrupted their careers for marriage and child rearing, and they are less competitive in the labor market than men, who have been working more or less continuously. In this regard it is worthwhile to point out that the single greatest reason that women go on welfare is the "double jeopardy" situation of loss of spouse and loss of job (Newman, 1988; Reskin & Hartman, 1986).

Occupational Safety and Health

People have long been concerned about the physical toll exacted by work. Medical writings reveal that even in ancient Rome physicians recognized an unusually high frequency of lung disease among metalworkers, miners, and weavers of asbestos cloth. During the Renaissance each craft was known to have its unique maladies. But the industrial revolution created a new wave of deadly occupational hazards. From the beginning, the American labor movement made safety one of its top priorities, waging a constant battle for better work environments. Yet despite this long history of concern and awareness, occupational health remains a serious problem. Figure 14–4 presents the ten most dangerous occupations, some of which have fatality rates 10 or 20 times

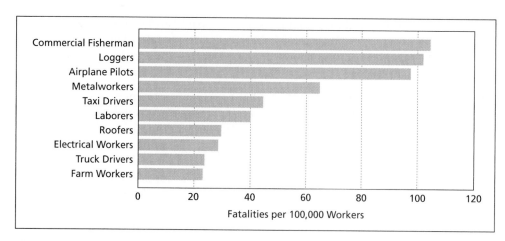

Figure 14–4   Fatality Rates of Ten Most Dangerous Occupations

Note: The average fatality rate in 1995 was 5/100,000 workers.

Source: Bureau of Labor Statistics, 1995.

the average. These tend to be male-dominated occupations, which explains why about 90 percent of those killed on the job are men (Nordheimer, 1996).

Industrial accidents are only part of the problem. Proponents of occupational health have widened their focus to include illnesses as well as accidents, and they have concentrated on preventing work-related diseases rather than merely treating or compensating workers for them. The situation is grim: At least 100,000 Americans die of job-related diseases each year.

Perhaps the greatest health hazards come from the chemicals industry. Chemicals, which are involved in the manufacture of almost every product we use, can also produce cancer. Workers who are exposed to certain chemicals have an unusually high

Health scandals and extremely high rates of injury in the meatpacking industry at the turn of the last century helped convince Americans of the need for government health and safety regulations. Shown here is a "dressing room" in a meatpacking plant in 1882.

rate of malignancies. They frequently suffer from other health problems as well, such as nervous disorders and sterility; their children may suffer from birth defects.

Occupational health is an issue that is loaded with moral, medical, and economic questions. Industries cite the enormous impact that needed changes will have on the entire economy as the cost of occupational health is passed along to consumers in the form of higher prices. Others argue that compulsory adherence to proposed health regulations will put them out of business or force them to relocate to other countries. Many workers, more fearful of imminent unemployment than of future illness, agree with their employers and take their chances in the workplace. Others, realizing that their interests as consumers and citizens may outweigh their economic stake, join the ranks of consumer activists.

As workers in the United States and other industrialized nations organize to deal with occupational safety issues, there is more incentive for industries to locate in low-wage regions of the world, whose impoverished populations are far less capable of recognizing dangers and less likely to complain to employers about dangerous working conditions (Rifkin, 1995). That even more workers do not question the conditions in which they work and the desirability of what they produce is perhaps attributable in part to their high level of indebtedness, which has resulted from extensive use of consumer credit. Since the relationship between consumers and credit is an important one, we devote the next section to this subject.

Consumers and Credit

The United States is a consumer society, one with an economy based on the activities of numerous corporations that depend on the disposable income, or buying power, of consumers. A consumer society requires a large middle and upper class with enough leisure time to enjoy the use of many goods and services that are not strictly necessary (although they may be perceived as such). Americans are proud of their access to an abundance of consumer goods and often contrast that abundance with the scarcities that are common in many other nations, especially those in less developed regions of the world.

There are several drawbacks to a consumer-based economy, however. Among these are the dominance of large corporations and franchise operations and the unplanned spread of shopping malls. Smaller businesses find it extremely difficult to compete with better financed, more efficient, highly profitable businesses. Indeed, franchise chains like McDonald's and Burger King have come close to wiping out the mom-and-pop restaurant and the roadside stand, traditional symbols of business independence.

The activities of franchise operations and major corporations like General Motors and IBM are accompanied by massive advertising campaigns. "Early to bed, Early to rise, Advertise, Advertise, Advertise" is the advice of McDonald's former advertising director (Boas & Chain, 1976). The communications media are inundated by advertising messages, so much so that advertising slogans have become part of our everyday conversation. ("Getting there is half the fun," an executive may comment ruefully as she arrives late for a meeting. "Don't leave home without it," a father may say to his son as he hands him an umbrella.) It cannot be denied that advertising plays a crucial role in a consumer society (Ritzer, 1993), but some observers are concerned about its effects on other aspects of social life. For example, the growth and development of TV and radio stations have been based primarily on their effectiveness as vehicles for advertising, which is their main source of income. To what extent does the dependence of the media on advertisers influence the content of the news and other information they broadcast? These are areas of active social-scientific research (Gans, 1979).

Problems of Debt Entanglement

The effects of a consumer society on other aspects of cultural and social life are a matter of concern to social scientists and others who caution that it leads to excessive materialism, a tendency to judge people by their possessions, and other negative consequences like waste and planned obsolescence. But perhaps the most serious flaw of a consumer society is the fact that it requires the ready availability of credit. Large-scale production of consumer goods depends on a steady flow of profits, which in turn requires that purchases be made constantly, not just whenever the consumer has a windfall or can accumulate enough through savings—hence the widespread use of consumer credit in the United States.

Since the 1950s the United States has been transformed from a cash to a credit society. Outstanding installment debt has grown from $29 billion in 1955 to more than $600 billion today. Although this enormous increase in consumer credit has been a boon to the U.S. economy, it has given rise to a new and pervasive social problem: debt entanglement and bankruptcy. This problem has received little attention either from social scientists or from policymakers; yet it is one of massive proportions. Each year more than 10 million workers have their wages garnisheed to meet their unpaid debts; many others are sued by their creditors for defaulting. The problem is particularly severe for low-income unskilled workers, who are predominantly black and Puerto Rican.

Figure 14–5 shows the dramatic increase in individual bankruptcies since 1980. Researchers have found that half of all bankruptcies are due to financial failure on the part of average homeowners, particularly female heads of households. A study of bankruptcies in the United States (Sullivan, Warren, & Westbrook, 1989, 1995) disproved a number of common myths. Using records of 1,529 consumer bankruptcy filings in three states, the researchers showed that contrary to the popular notion that "credit card junkies" are abusing the credit system, these people account for less than 2 percent of bankruptcies. Most people who go bankrupt are homeowners who can no longer pay their debts, often because of family dissolution or medical emergencies. About 10 percent are individuals who invested in risky financial ventures. However, these account for about 25 percent of the total debt of bankrupt individuals because often they were quite rich and defaulted on large loans.

The researchers also offered many recommendations for reducing the rate of bankruptcies, including measures to monitor consumer debt and income ratios far

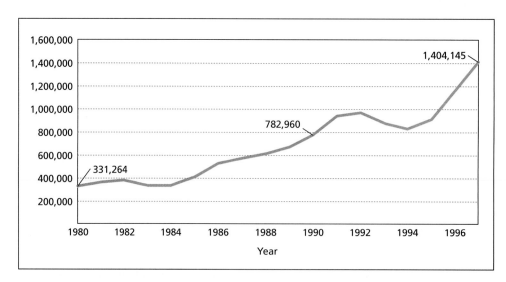

Figure 14–5 Bankruptcies Filed, 1980–1996
Source: Administrative Office of the U.S. Courts.

As marketing techniques improve, consumers' desire for goods increases, and, often, so does their level of indebtedness.

more effectively than the consumer credit industry does at present. But they also pointed to the need for more, not less, regulation in the economically more dangerous areas of banking and finance. This is a key point to which we will return in the Social Policy section of the chapter.

Possessions and Self-expression

A consumer society fueled by purchases of goods and services produced by profit-hungry corporations and sold with the aid of elaborate advertising campaigns; a society of debtors often forced into default, with wages garnisheed and mortgages foreclosed—these images suggest a hopelessly materialistic culture pursuing a path that will inevitably lead to its own destruction. Is this a valid picture of American society?

There can be no doubt that material possessions play an important role in most people's lives. As we have seen in this chapter, the corporations that produce and distribute material things significantly influence the lives of workers and consumers. We have noted elsewhere that poverty can be defined in terms of the degree to which a household does or does not possess the objects that make life comfortable.

A full discussion of the significance of material possessions for social life and organization is beyond the scope of this book. It is worth mentioning, however, that emphasis on material objects is not unique to modern societies. Throughout the world people express their identity as humans by using artifacts—they wear clothes, cook food, eat with utensils, live in houses, and sleep in beds (Csikszentmihalyi & Rochberg-Halton, 1981). Objects tend to be valued "not because of the material comfort they provide but for the information they convey about the owner and his or her ties to others. . . . A battered toy, an old musical instrument, a homemade quilt provide meaning that is more central to the values of people than any number of expensive appliances or precious metals" (p. 239). Yet this fact does not change people's behavior: "The habit of acquisition and the addiction to consumption will motivate their expenditure of energy even though these are not the source of their most significant rewards" (p. 239).

Nor is individual acquisitiveness the only route to debt entanglement. Entire communities and towns can become mired in such serious debt that, like Orange County, California, they must seek protection from their creditors under the bankruptcy laws.

This relatively affluent county south of Los Angeles County includes the original Disneyland. But despite the conservatism of its citizens, Orange County was spending far more on its schools, libraries, sports fields, parks, and other amenities than it was taking in from its citizens, who are extremely loath to pay high taxes. In consequence, the county supervisor began selling municipal bonds and using the cash generated in this way to invest in highly speculative stock funds. Eventually the county's losses reached almost $2 billion, leading to the most significant public bankruptcy case in U.S. history (Davis, 1995; Sterngold, 1995). The notorious Orange County bankruptcy has challenged financial and political policymakers everywhere to act more responsibly in investing public funds, and the issue of how to reduce public debt has taken a central place in recent policy debates.

SOCIAL POLICY

Economic policies developed by the states, the federal government, and in some cases private corporations or nonprofit agencies must respond to a number of changes in the United States and in the rest of the world. The first, and perhaps most significant, of these is the end of the cold war. With little prospect of war between superpowers, there is much less justification for defense budgets of $280 billion to $300 billion a year. We will see in Chapter 18 that increased political instability in many parts of the world means that defense and national security remain important concerns and costly government functions. Nevertheless, recent cuts in defense spending make possible a modest increase in spending on social programs.

The second major change in economic affairs is often termed *globalization* and refers to the ever greater economic interdependence of nations. This trend led to the passage of NAFTA in 1993 and the emergence of the European Union in the 1990s. NAFTA is intended to move the nations of North America (Canada, the United States, and Mexico) closer to a condition of free trade—that is, trade that is not hampered by tariffs and import or export quotas. Free trade can stimulate economic growth, but as we saw earlier, it can also have grave consequences for companies and workers in industries that undergo rapid change as a result. For example, Mexican peasants who grow corn fear that they will be wiped out by competition from U.S. agribusinesses, while U.S. auto workers fear that their jobs will be lost to Mexican workers whose wages average less than half of theirs.

Congress recently voted to grant Most Favored Nation trading status to China, a policy that the administration supported but many prolabor members of Congress opposed. The major labor unions, especially those of the auto workers and steelworkers, vigorously oppose this and related policies because they believe that China violates workers' rights and does not permit workers to join democratic labor unions. They also claim that child labor and forced prison labor are tolerated in China (*Solidarity*, March-April 2000).

Protests and demonstrations over free trade in a global economy, such as those that rocked Seattle in 1999, will continue to influence economic policies not only in the United States but elsewhere in the world as well. Whether Democratic or Republican, the U.S. administration is likely to push for more free trade and fewer international tariffs. At the same time, it will be under continuing pressure from those most likely to be hurt by this policy: unions, farmers, and businesses with strong investments in domestic markets (Yang & Satchell, 1999).

Increasing the availability of health insurance and other benefits for workers in part-time and temporary working situations would be an enormous policy change in the United States. This is not currently on the agenda of congressional leaders or leaders of either party. The lack of health insurance for workers at the lower end of the income hierarchy remains a glaring social policy issue and a major problem for those who wish to continue reforming welfare regulations.

Reform of the welfare laws continues to be the most important aspect of economic and social policy in the United States. These major social policy changes were part of the Republican party's agenda and were included in the Democratic party's platform during the 1996 presidential election campaign. They were motivated by a desire to reduce federal spending and debt, as well as to encourage welfare recipients to enter the labor force. As we have seen in earlier chapters, the effects of the reforms are beginning to be felt throughout the nation. There will be enormous changes in the lives of poor Americans and many others because of the elimination of Aid to Families with Dependent Children and changes in home relief, food stamps, and Medicaid. (See the Unintended Consequences feature below.) In most major cities, where people are being obliged to work in order to continue receiving welfare benefits, there is a shortage of job opportunities for unskilled people. As long as the economy remains strong, there will be few protests about the policy changes. But in a recession,

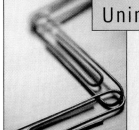

Unintended Consequences

Welfare Reform and Job Creation

In March 1997 President Clinton urged officials in federal agencies to take the lead in hiring welfare recipients, who are now obliged to work in order to qualify for their benefits. "Government can help," he said, "to move people from welfare to work by acting the way we want all employers to act—demanding high performance from workers but going the extra mile to offer opportunity to those who have been on welfare and want to do something more with their lives." Despite the president's optimism, it was clear to most observers that this initiative faces some extremely difficult obstacles. After all, the president himself had recently noted that he had reduced the number of civilian employees in the branches of government under executive control by 13 percent and that the federal work force would continue to shrink as efforts to balance the federal budget continued (Herbert, 1997).

Clearly there is a contradiction between two presidential policies here, just as there are contradictions in Congress's efforts to oblige poor welfare recipients to go to work without addressing the problems of how to create the jobs and child care arrangements that will make "workfare" a reality. But the unintended consequences do not stop with the poor themselves. In many communities with high concentrations of poor families, it is feared that reductions in food stamps, health-

care funding, and family budgets will have adverse effects on local businesses and schools as well. In communities where there are large numbers of poor Latino families, membership in the local churches and enrollments in parochial schools have declined (Sexton, 1997). There are also reports that small food stores and other retail businesses are closing in neighborhoods and communities that are already economically depressed.

Typically, in neighborhoods where 40 percent or more of the residents live in households whose annual income falls below the official poverty level (i.e., below $16,400 for a family of four), welfare payments have been a major source of revenue and have sustained many landlords, small businesses, medical offices, day care centers, and other local entrepreneurs. Although in theory the welfare reforms should produce more workers who are earning more and bringing more cash into these neighborhoods, it will take some time for these effects to be felt, if they are felt at all. This dilemma once again calls attention to the need for more entry-level, low-skill jobs in locations accessible to large numbers of welfare recipients. The welfare reforms of 1996 did not intend to make job creation a renewed area of social and economic policy, but they appear to be having that effect as too many poor people compete for too few low-paying jobs.

welfare reform in the absence of job-creating strategies is likely to cause many economic and social hardships, which in turn are likely to stimulate attempts to revise the welfare reform law passed in 1996.

Beyond Left & Right

Economic affairs often divide people in ways related to their own pocketbooks. On the right, there is a tendency to favor social policies that cost as little as possible, rely on the forces of supply and demand, and insist on individual initiative. On the left, there is a tendency to support policies that use the power of government to shape economic outcomes. The desire to create jobs for the poor, for example, is a liberal one, whereas the desire to cut welfare grants and oblige people to work for their incomes is a more conservative policy stance. During recessions, when the poor compete for low-skill job opportunities, it is likely that people on the left and the right will arrive at a compromise over the need for job-creating policies, both in private business and in the public or civic voluntary sectors of the economy (schools, parks, hospitals, etc.). Such a compromise will not settle the ideological dispute over market forces versus government initiatives, but in the practical effort to ease suffering and give more people more meaningful work, it is likely that some middle ground will be found. Not to do so is to invite great social unrest.

SUMMARY

- When people refer to the free-enterprise system, they are talking about an economic system known as market capitalism. Markets regulate the worldwide flow of goods and services. Almost all markets are regulated by acts of governments that attempt to protect buyers and ensure that markets remain competitive.

- *Capital* refers to equipment and labor; capitalists, or entrepreneurs, invest in labor and equipment to produce goods and services in the hope of making a profit. Corporations are a means of reducing the risk to entrepreneurs by limiting their personal liability in the event of a business failure.

- By *economic globalization* social scientists refer to the growing tendency for goods and services to be produced in one nation or region and consumed in another and for the companies that produce them to engage in business activities in many different regions of the world.

- A controversial aspect of globalization is the growth of multinational corporations—international organizations that operate across national boundaries. Multinational corporations are widely criticized for operating outside the limits of any nation's ability to control their conduct. They have contributed to the emergence of a global factory in which the production process is divided into component operations that can be carried out anywhere in the world.

- For the American worker, the growth of corporate power means a decreasing number of employers and a growing tendency to export capital and jobs overseas. Many U.S. manufacturing facilities have closed, especially in the nation's older cities and towns.

- Work in the United States underwent major changes in the twentieth century. The greatest change was the transition from an agricultural economy to an industrial one, with the result that today white-collar workers are the largest occupational category in the nation.

- With respect to the age and sex composition of the labor force, the most significant trend is the inclusion of married women and the exclusion of older men. Older men are being eliminated from the labor force primarily because of educational and occupational obsolescence.

- Another significant trend is the increasing specialization of labor. The total number of jobs in the American economy has increased steadily, but in the past decade low-wage jobs were created at a much higher rate than high-wage jobs.

- New technologies have had a variety of effects on the workplace. Managers and employees whose jobs are controlled by computers sometimes feel that the computer is their boss. Computer control can also alter the structure of the organization. Some analysts believe that these trends will lead to a jobless future for many new entrants into the labor force who lack essential skills.

- The chief sources of job satisfaction, in addition to monetary compensation, are individuality, independence, and a sense of accomplishment. The absence of these factors can lead to dissatisfaction and alienation. Blue-collar workers place more emphasis on external satisfactions than white-collar workers.

- Official definitions underestimate the size of the labor force and the volume of unemployment. They exclude unemployed people who did not actively seek work during a particular week, and they fail to reflect the underemployment of part-time workers who would like to work full time. A disproportionate number of the unemployed are young and/or nonwhite. Among the consequences of unemployment is a sense of isolation, which produces depression.

- The problem of occupational health involves industrial accidents and job-related diseases; perhaps the greatest health hazards are found in the chemicals industry.

- The United States is a consumer society; its economy is based on the activities of numerous corporations that depend on the buying power of consumers. A serious flaw of a consumer society is that it requires the ready availability of credit. The enormous increase in consumer credit has created serious debt entanglement.

- Economic policies must respond to several major changes in the United States and in the rest of the world, of which the most significant is the globalization of economic activity. These changes have led to reductions in military spending and the passage of NAFTA. The welfare reform act of 1996 is having a major impact on debates over economic policy and may lead to renewed efforts to create jobs for workers with low skill levels.

KEY TERMS

capitalism, p. 397
markets, p. 397
capital, p. 398
entrepreneur, p. 398

limited liability, p. 398
economic globalization, p. 398
multinational corporations, p. 399
outsourcing, p. 400

flexitime, p. 410
alienation, p. 410

INTERNET EXERCISE

The web destinations for Chapter 14 are related to different aspects of problems surrounding work and the economy. To begin your explorations, go to the Prentice Hall Companion Website: **http://prenhall.com/kornblum.** Then choose **Chapter 14** (Problems of Work and the Economy). Next, select **destinations** from the menu on the left side of the screen. There are a variety of sites to investigate. We suggest that you begin with **History of Maquilladoras**. The *Critical Research* box in this chapter deals with the "Maquilladora Effect," describing the impact of the North American Free Trade Agreement in terms of the number of Mexican workers employed by American companies. The *History of Maquilladoras* site provides a variety of links to other sites and information that will further acquaint you with the history of Mexican workers in Ameri-

can society. It was pointed out in the text that unless Mexican workers can win legal protection of their right to form unions and bargain for better wages and working conditions, the promised economic growth cannot occur. Try clicking on *Workers in maquilladoras from Tijuana to Juarez are fighting back against NAFTA-driven exploitation.* Then click on *Union wins recognition at Taiwanese computer plant in Mexican maquilladora.* After you have explored the History of Maquilladoras site, answer the following questions:

- Do you think that the wage gap between American and Mexican workers reflects a social problem, or is it just a "personal problem" of the maquilladora workers?

- Do you support the efforts of the maquilladora workers to unionize? Why or why not?

15 **Urban Problems**

FACTS ABOUT

CITIES

- According to U.N. population projections, by 2015 New York City will be the world's eleventh-largest city, outstripped by Tokyo, Bombay, Lagos, Shanghai, Jakarta, São Paulo, Karachi, Beijing, Dhaka, and Mexico City.

- Throughout American history no population group has experienced such persistent residential segregation in urban areas as African Americans.

- The fastest-growing urban communities are on the edges of metropolitan areas.

- Estimates of the total number of homeless people range from 600,000 to 7 million.

OUTLINE

An Urbanizing World

The American City
Urban Growth
  and Social Problems
Antiurban Bias
The Composition
  of Urban Populations

Theories of Urbanism
Wirth's Theory
Compositionalism
Subcultural Theory

Metropolitan Growth
The Transportation Boom
The Impact
  of Suburban Growth

Problems of Cities
Deconcentration
Relocation of Manufacturing
Financial Problems
Government

Shelter Poverty, Homelessness, and Neighborhood Distress
Shelter Poverty
Homelessness
Distressed Neighborhoods

Social Policy
Housing
Homelessness

Many of the social problems we have discussed so far—poverty, mental illness, AIDS, drug abuse, violence, and others—are especially serious in the nation's cities, not because city people are less moral than rural people but because cities, especially large cities, act as magnets for those who deviate from the norm and seek the company of others like themselves. Often this deviance is what makes cities so fascinating and creative, and it helps explain the attraction of city life for musicians, actors, artists, and people who wish to escape from what they see as the stultifying sameness of rural areas or suburban communities. But the attraction of the city for people who are different and who seek the greater tolerance and anonymity of urban life also increases the concentration of people who are ill and need help. The legacy of racism and racial and class segregation also leaves the cities with much higher concentrations of poor people than would be expected if these social problems were evenly distributed through the population.

At this time a controversy rages over how much responsibility the nation as a whole has for dealing with the problems that are concentrated in the cities. As many cities become de facto poorhouses, they require additional help from states and from the federal government. To better appreciate why this is so and why the policies that have been suggested to address this situation are controversial, it is worthwhile first to step back and consider what we understand by cities and by such terms as **rural** and **urban.**

The U.S. Bureau of the Census defines the **urban population** as all persons living in places with 2,500 or more inhabitants that are legally incorporated as cities, villages, boroughs, and towns (*Statistical Abstract*, 1999). An **urbanized area,** in the official census definition, "comprises one or more places [e.g., incorporated cities or towns] and the adjacent densely settled surrounding territory that together have a minimum population of 50,000 persons" (p. 4). Metropolitan regions usually include a number of urbanized areas, as well as less densely settled areas, on their fringes. Rural areas are those that are not classified as urban.

The distinction between urban and rural is important in the social sciences because many studies of social problems attempt to determine whether a particular condition is more serious in urban or in rural areas. It is not difficult to define

423

these words in abstract terms, but such definitions are not readily applicable to the real world. Today there is no longer a clear distinction between rural and urban life. **Urbanism**—a way of life that depends on industry, mass communication, a mobile population, and mass consumer markets—has penetrated even to rural places. For example, whereas the farm was once considered the epitome of rural life, today an increasing proportion of farms are large-scale agribusinesses, and the small farm is an endangered species. Farming communities are linked to major metropolitan regions by interstate highways, and the residents watch the same TV shows as people in the densely settled inner cities. In other words, it is not a question of whether a place is rural or urban but of the extent to which urbanism has influenced it.

An Urbanizing World

The urban revolution is a worldwide phenomenon, as can be seen in the changing ranking of cities. In 1950, the New York metropolitan area was the largest in the world. It was the third largest in 1995, although still the largest in the United States. But according to U.N. population projections, it will be in about eleventh place by 2015, outstripped by Tokyo, Bombay, Lagos, Shanghai, Jakarta, São Paulo, Karachi, Beijing, Dhaka, and Mexico City (Crossette, 1996).

In the developing world, people are leaving rural villages to seek their futures in cities. In sociological terms, this is a dominant trend of the modern era. In the more affluent regions of the world, as already noted, the majority of the population are city dwellers. But in much of Latin America, Asia, and Africa, the wrenching shift from country to city life is still occurring. Cities are growing at astounding rates, their populations doubling in a generation or less. Many Latin American cities are quite old, often older than the oldest U.S. cities, but the urbanization of rural populations is continuing. In Africa, many cities are only beginning to experience explosive growth. The rural-to-urban transition in Africa will be a major trend of the twenty-first century.

Figure 15–1 highlights the shift toward a predominantly urban world: By 2025 the vast majority of people will live in cities. The rural-urban transformation was largely completed in Europe and North America before 1975 but is now occurring rapidly in Latin America. The population projections shown in Figure 15–1 suggest that a similar transformation will occur in Asia and Africa in the next two decades. Not shown in the figure is the fact that China's urban population jumped from 19 percent to 28 percent between 1960 and 1992 and has been growing at 4.8 percent each year since that time. This means that the urban population of China today is probably almost half the entire Chinese population of 1.2 billion. Sub-Saharan Africa is experiencing even more explosive urban growth. Its urban population is increasing by 4.5 percent per year, which means that soon Africa, too, will be a continent dominated by cities rather than by agricultural and pastoral populations.

This rapid urban growth presents enormous problems for developing nations, which are still struggling to address the persistent poverty of their rural villages. Urban populations are extremely dependent on investments in transportation, education, and health-care institutions, as well as in the basic infrastructure of vital services (water, sewage, electricity, communications, and the like). When people are moving to cities in search of jobs and other types of economic opportunity (in education or expanding markets, for example), the resulting growth in person-power helps alleviate some social problems. In many of the developing nations, however, urban newcomers have great difficulty in finding work and making ends meet. The city beckons with the opportunity for escape from rural poverty, but once in the city many find that they lack the skills required to survive in the new and entirely strange urban social world.

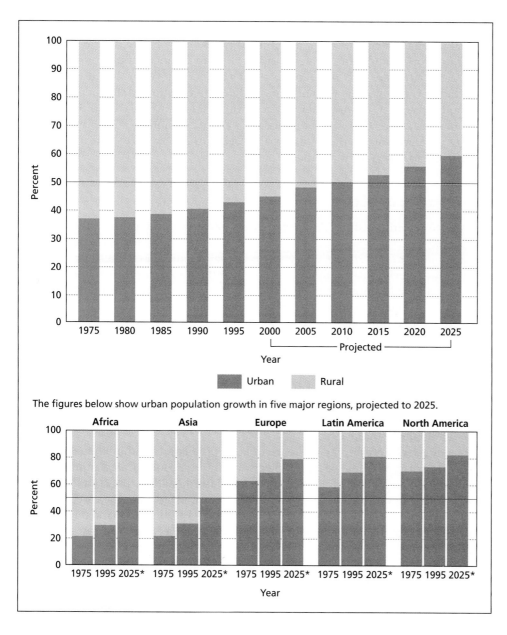

Figure 15–1   Percentage of World's Population Living in Urban Areas

*Projections

Source: B. Crossette, "Hope and Pragmatism for U.N. Cities Conference," *New York Times,* June 3, 1996, p. A3. © 1996 by the New York Times Co. Reprinted by permission. Data from the United Nations.

Thus, while many of the consequences of this urban transformation are positive, in that people who can no longer earn a living on the land are finding new opportunities for education and work in the cities, many other consequences are negative. Crowding, poverty, lack of adequate housing, and the threat of gangs and violence are only some of the social problems new urban migrants experience in very rapidly growing cities. And the cities themselves are often overwhelmed by the sheer mass of the new arrivals. Urban infrastructures—water, sewage, transportation, lighting, and medical care facilities, to name a few—are often inadequate to meet the new demands. India, for example, is the world's second most populous country and has more than 3,000 cities and towns, but only 8 of them have sewage treatment plants. Nor is this problem unique to India. The World Resources Institute estimates that 90 percent of the raw sewage from urban areas in developing nations is seeping into streams and oceans. The World Bank estimates that by 2010, 1.4 billion people will not have safe drinking water or sanitation (cited in Crossette, 1996).

In a world where social, economic, and environmental interconnections are ever more apparent, the conditions of life in metropolitan regions are an important issue for the developing and more affluent nations alike. In the more affluent industrial nations, older cities are also undergoing rapid change as jobs are lost to lower-wage areas and new populations with new needs demand attention while budgets for services and infrastructure investment are cut. In addition, in the United States, as in other nations where cities are no longer the centers of industrial production, vast changes are occurring in the nature of the social problems these cities must face as they attempt to cope with rapid social change.

The American City

Until the nineteenth century the United States was an agrarian country; the few existing cities were scarcely more than market towns. Increasingly efficient transportation and communication and the effects of industrialization caused the bulk of urban growth. Just as technological innovations, such as the use of cast iron in building construction and the invention of the elevator, made it possible for a city to expand vertically, more efficient modes of transportation, such as horse-drawn buses and railroads, made it possible for cities to expand horizontally as well. Railway lines and telegraph wires crossed the continent, closely tying cities to the nation's agricultural heartland. In turn, these improved methods of communication promoted westward expansion and the development of new cities. Many towns were built around railroad lines. Urban growth provided a larger market for agricultural products, which motivated farmers to invent new ways of growing and harvesting crops in order to increase efficiency and minimize expense. The resultant technological advances contributed to the development of the city.

As cities grew, however, the existence of large populations within limited amounts of space began to present special problems. Living in a concentrated community focuses attention on matters of mutual concern and need, matters that even the individualistic American was unable to ignore. Lighting, fire protection, the care of streets, crime prevention, sewage disposal, water, community health, and marketing facilities all became part of the community consciousness and, hence, the concerns of municipal governments.

Urban Growth and Social Problems

It was not until the twentieth century that adequate water supply and waste disposal systems were finally developed. Before then, cities were notorious for death rates that were substantially higher than those in rural areas, with larger cities suffering higher rates than smaller ones. Writing in 1899, Arnold Weber (1968) attributed this "excessive urban mortality . . . to lack of pure air, water, and sunlight, together with uncleanly habits of life induced thereby." He went on to say, however, that there was "no inherent external reason why men should die faster in larger communities than in small hamlets, provided they are not too ignorant, too stupid, or too individualistic to cooperate in the securing of common benefits" (p. 348). In fact, innovations in medicine and sanitation did improve the conditions of early urban life.

Antiurban Bias

Perhaps as a result of the congestion and corruption just described, antiurban sentiment became a tradition in American culture. Public sentiment against cities has generally echoed the antiurban bias of Thomas Jefferson, who compared "the mobs of great cities" to sores on the human body (Kennedy, 2000).

American literature, particularly in the nineteenth century, extolled the virtues of the self-sufficient farmer in an agricultural paradise, evoking memories of simpler, happier, more innocent times. The city has often been perceived as contrary to the "natural" relationship between the person and the environment. Although the image of a sacred city—Jerusalem or Rome—occasionally appears, it is the image of the sinful city—Sodom and Gomorrah or "Gay Paree"—that predominates. Heresy and vice are associated with the city; virtue and justice live in the country. This is true in literature throughout the world, and it remains a common theme in North America.

In recent years the spread of AIDS and highly addictive drugs like crack have reinforced the negative image of the nation's largest cities, especially New York, Los Angeles, and Miami. It is very likely that the negative view of large central-city areas reflects the continuing tradition of antiurban thought, which is only reinforced by current problems that are concentrated in the cities. To make matters worse, the city is often viewed as a temporary place of settlement, a central place of concentration for immigrants and rural newcomers where one attempts to gain a foothold in society before moving to the suburbs, where there is a bit of greenery and one can visit the city but is not obliged to live there.

Respondents to polls about quality of life and preferred place of residence consistently voice the opinion that life in central cities is less attractive for most people than life in suburbs and small cities (NORC, 1998). One consequence of these negative opinions about central-city life is the continual growth of suburbs and the gradual loss of population in the nation's older cities. As a result, according to Eli Ginzberg (1993), one of the nation's foremost analysts of urban social policy, "The core of urban life has shifted dramatically from the city center to the metropolitan area, with a growing proportion of the population living and working in the suburbs and in the outlying metropolitan areas" (p. 36). But Ginzberg notes that this change can be overstated since almost one-third of the nation's citizens continue to reside in communities and neighborhoods in the inner city.

The Composition of Urban Populations

The majority of Americans live in large metropolitan areas. There they encounter a very different environment from that provided by small towns or rural communities. Urban life gives rise to subcultures, social institutions, and personality traits that are not found in rural settings (Fischer, 1976); sociologists who study urbanism seek to explain these phenomena. In our discussion of urbanism we will stress the special consequences of life in cities both for individuals and for their communities.

Minority Migration.   Today's cities are populated largely by the descendants of rural Americans and immigrants from other countries who came in search of better jobs, higher wages, improved schooling for their children, cultural and political freedom, and a generally higher level of living. The migration to the cities began in colonial times but accelerated in the 1920s, when the drop in foreign immigration forced America's cities to look to the rural heartland for cheap labor. Attracted by the prospect of ready employment in the industrial cities of the Northeast, Midwest, and South, large numbers of rural blacks moved to urban areas.

This migration considerably altered settlement conditions in the larger urban communities. Unlike the foreign migrants, who had settled in mixed urban enclaves and begun to intermarry and disperse, the blacks who moved to northern cities settled in neighborhoods that quickly became, and remained, all black. Whereas earlier foreign immigrants gradually increased their incomes and moved out of the immigrant neighborhoods, the black settlements were more permanent, creating cities within cities. The tendency of the wealthy to move to the suburbs had already been established among the cities' white populations, and it was increased by the urban segregation of blacks. Although today blacks are moving into suburban communities in record numbers, they remain disporportionately represented in the central cities. As a result, their upward mobility has been severely limited, and the precedent has been set for the increased economic and cultural segregation found in the cities. (See Chapter 9.)

Many U.S. cities have seen a continual influx of foreign immigrants over the past four decades. Miami, Los Angeles, New York, and Houston now have large concentrations of immigrants, many of whom have come from Latin America, the Caribbean, and Asia. At present about 800,000 legal immigrants from these regions are admitted to the United States each year, and an uncounted number of illegal entrants arrive as well. In cities with older segregated ghettos adjacent to newer immigrant neighborhoods, there are increasingly frequent episodes of conflict between the newcomers and established residents. On the other hand, there are also many instances of intergroup cooperation and renewed economic growth in these rapidly changing urban communities (Portes & Rumbaut, 1990; Winnick, 1991). We will return to this subject in Chapter 16.

Voluntary and Involuntary Segregation.   Residential segregation may take either of two forms: (1) voluntary segregation, in which people choose to live with others similar to themselves (e.g., the ethnic, artistic, or homosexual neighborhoods of large cities), and (2) involuntary segregation, which occurs when various segments of the population (e.g., blacks, Jews, or the aged) are forced by social or economic circumstances to live in specific areas of the city. Although at first most immigrant groups chose to live together in urban enclaves, the situation of urban blacks and other minorities today is largely one of involuntary segregation. Within black neighborhoods there is further segregation according to income. Phoebe Cottingham (1975) found that segregation of families by income within black communities resembles the segregation of whites within white communities.

Throughout American history no population group has experienced such persistent residential segregation in urban areas as African Americans (Massey & Denton, 1993). Although white immigrant groups such as the Irish, Italians, and Poles were segregated in earlier periods, only African Americans have experienced high rates of segregation throughout the nation's history. Nor are recent trends encouraging. Table 15–1 shows that the mean racial segregation index for U.S. cities has decreased only slightly over the past 20 years or more. (The index of segregation indicates the percentage of the black population that would have to move for a city to achieve a nonsegregated racial distribution—that is, one in which the probability that a black person is living on a given block would be equal to the proportion of blacks in the city as a whole.) The younger cities of the West are less segregated than those in the rest of the nation, and smaller cities are less segregated than larger ones; but segregation in the nation's largest cities is a continuing problem (Kasarda, 1993).

For most city dwellers, residential segregation means a limited choice of lifestyles. This is especially true for minority groups and poor whites—particularly the elderly—and is caused as much by a negative self-image as by racial and economic segregation. It is difficult for the poor, the aged, and others to escape from undesirable or dangerous urban areas. As a consequence, these people cannot be described as entirely voluntary residents of a particular neighborhood. As neighborhoods decline, all people whose daily activities take them into these areas face the hardships brought about by loss of capital and lack of support facilities and community services.

TABLE 15–1   Mean Measures of Segregation (Index of Dissimilarity): United States, 1970–1990

	1970	1980	1990
All cities	63.6	66.8	60.3
Region			
Northeast (12)	63.3	71.3	66.0
Midwest (23)	63.4	70.0	66.0
South (40)	65.9	71.4	64.1
West (25)	60.1	53.8	46.1
Size			
Less than 250,000 (45)	62.1	62.7	56.0
250,000–499,999 (33)	63.6	68.2	61.2
500,000–999,999 (16)	66.5	70.7	64.9
1 million and over (6)	66.2	79.5	75.1
Age[a]			
Pre-1900 (45)	65.4	71.3	66.6
1900–1940 (40)	62.9	66.3	58.5
1950 and later (15)	59.6	54.3	45.9

[a]City age is defined as the year in which the city achieved 50,000 in population, which is the basis for metropolitan central-city status.

Note: The number of cities in each category is shown in parentheses.

Source: John D. Kasarda, "Cities as Places Where People Live and Work: Urban Change and Neighborhood Distress," in H. G. Cisneros, ed., *Interwoven Destinies: Cities and the Nation* (New York: Norton, 1993). © 1993 by The American Assembly. Used by permission of W. W. Norton & Company, Inc.

Douglas Massey, the foremost U.S. expert on urban racial segregation, argues that residential segregation of African Americans contributes to unemployment, educational inequality, high rates of criminal victimization, and drug addiction. He advocates much stronger enforcement of the antidiscrimination clauses of the Fair Housing Act as a way to attack persistent segregation (Massey & Denton, 1993). We will return to this point in the Social Policy section of the chapter.

Theories of Urbanism

As mentioned earlier, the propensity for large numbers of people to live in cities and for urban ways of life to become dominant throughout a society is known as urbanism. In rapidly changing regions of the world, such as large portions of Africa and Latin America, cities are growing at even greater rates than they are in North America and Europe. Does life in cities and the spread of urban areas over the globe account for other social problems, such as crime, the breakup of families, and intergroup conflict? Do urban people differ in some fundamental way from those who live in rural areas? Such questions have been the subject of much research and theory and are summarized in the three theories of urbanism to which we now turn.

Wirth's Theory

Several theories of urbanism have been proposed. The oldest and most influential is that of Louis Wirth, whose basic argument is that cities increase the incidence of both social and personality disorders. He described the city as "a relatively large, dense, and permanent settlement of socially heterogeneous individuals" (quoted in Fischer, 1976, p. 29). Borrowing extensively from the teachings of another sociologist, Georg Simmel, Wirth argued that the urban environment literally assaults the city dweller with multiple and intense stimuli. The pressures of this overabundance of stimulation force urban dwellers to adapt in order to maintain their mental equilibrium. Wirth contended that the resultant adaptation has negative effects. The mechanisms that permit the city dweller to withstand the shock of multiple stimuli also cause him or her to become insulated from other people. As a result, the typical city dweller "becomes aloof, brusque, impersonal in his dealings with others, and emotionally buffered in his human relationships" (p. 31). When such withdrawal fails to counter the effects of overstimulation, people experience "psychic overload," which produces irritation and anxiety.

The effects of psychic overload are illustrated by the following remarks of a frustrated urban resident: "You must understand this is a cramped place. Sometimes it feels like, well, like everything has been put through a trash compactor. Density like this annuls certain clauses in the social contract; it begets those dull, middle-distance stares, a defense mechanism. Some of us don't even acknowledge our next-door neighbors" (Jaynes, 1988, p. 29). Wirth asserted that this interpersonal estrangement loosens the bonds that unite people. In some cases these bonds are completely severed, and the result is antisocial and alienated behavior. When people are left without emotional support or societal restraint, they begin to act out their fantasies. According to Wirth, this explains the intense creativity and technological advancement, as well as the psychopathic and criminal behavior, that are prevalent in cities. Each extreme is a result of looser social restraints and interpersonal relationships (Abbott, 2000).

Another byproduct of city life is the economic process of competition and specialization, which results in community differentiation. Usually this differentiation is most visible in the division of labor, although it exists in other forms as well—for example, in separate districts for businesses, residences, and entertainment. In urban environments people often assume many different roles during an average day, roles that involve social interaction with coworkers, neighbors, close friends, and family. According to Wirth (cited in Fischer, 1976), the very multiplicity of people and places that compete for an urban dweller's time and attention weakens social bonds. As people continue to enter into primary relationships outside the family, the family becomes less important. Since many of these relationships are scattered across the city, neighbors also play a less significant role. In Wirth's opinion, such loosening of social ties produces an alienated condition, or anomie, a weakening of the norms that govern acceptable social behavior.

Once the personal approach to preserving societal norms has been weakened, other attempts to control social behavior must be made. Most often, these take the form of complaints to impersonal government authorities. Wirth believed that such impersonal control can never fully replace the power and moral strength of small primary groups. Therefore, he considered cities—with their inclination toward individualism, estrangement, stress, and especially social disorganization—as societies in which social relationships are weak. Such weakness may indeed provide more freedom for individuals, but it also leads to social disruption and personality disorders (cited in Fischer, 1976).

Compositionalism

Wirth's theory is not accepted by all urban sociologists. Herbert Gans, among others, has challenged Wirth's ideas about the effects of urbanism on personal behavior. *The Urban Villagers,* Gans's (1984) classic study, is a closeup view of life in the Italian neighborhoods of the West End of Boston shortly before they were torn down in the name of "urban renewal." Gans shows that many families were deeply committed to a life spent largely within the neighborhood. That is, they were immersed in the life of the Italian-American community and were not at all like the disorganized slum dwellers of Wirthian theory. The forms of deviance found in the neighborhood—gang activity and some organized crime—did not result from social disorganization. Nor were these neighborhoods dominated by impersonal institutions such as housing authorities, as Wirthian theory would predict.

Gans (1984) used these findings and those from similar community studies in immigrant neighborhoods to conclude that personal behavior is shaped by the social life of specific neighborhoods and communities, not by the larger social forces described by Wirth under the heading of urbanism. Fischer (1976) called this a *compositional theory* of urbanism. The difference between the two theories rests on opposing views of how the city affects the existence of small groups. Compositionalists see the city as a mosaic of social worlds—intimate social circles with their roots in kinship, ethnicity, neighborhoods, occupations, and lifestyles. Whereas Wirth believed that the pressures of the city disrupt these worlds, drawing people away from close associations with family and neighbors, compositionalists believe that these worlds persist undiminished in an urban setting. Gans contends, in fact, that the closeness of these social worlds envelops individuals and protects them from the pressures of city life. Compositionalists cite economic position, cultural characteristics, and marital and family status as the determinants of personal behavior. The strength of these attributes, rather than the size or density of the community at large, molds a person's social and psychological experience.

Subcultural Theory

Fischer's (1976, 1995) own theory of urbanism agrees with the Wirthian theory in acknowledging that cities produce major social-psychological effects. Fischer, however, believes that these effects occur not because existing social groups break down but because cities foster new ones. Known as the *subcultural theory*, Fischer's argument suggests that the most socially significant consequence of an urban community is the promotion of diverse subcultures—culturally distinct groups such as college students, Chinese Americans, artists, and homosexuals. In New York's Greenwich Village or San Francisco's Castro district, for example, there are communities of gay men and women who create a local culture of tolerance for homosexuality. In addition, they create institutions of homosexual thought and expression—newspapers, theater, cabarets—in which the norms of the straight world are suspended to a degree and other sexual norms are encouraged or discussed. People who are homosexual feel more free to express themselves in such communities and to form close relationships with one another.

In contrast to Wirth, who held that no significant primary social relationships can be achieved in an urban environment, Fischer (1976, 1995) believes that people in cities live in meaningful social worlds. More important, subculturists contend that large communities attract immigrants precisely because of this distinctively urban phenomenon. In Fischer's view, urbanism intensifies subcultures, partly through critical mass: A large city is more likely than a small community to attract a sizable proportion of a given subculture. This process operates for artists, academics, bohemians, corporate executives, criminals, and computer programmers, as well as for ethnic or racial minority groups. Subcultural intensification also occurs through multigroup contact. In a densely populated environment, subcultures are constantly bumping into one another. Sometimes these groups coexist; in other instances tensions mount. When one subculture finds another annoying, threatening, or both, a common reaction is to embrace one's own social world even more firmly.

Large cities promote the emergence of diverse subcultures, which add to the enjoyment of life for many city people.

Few episodes in recent urban affairs better illustrate subcultural processes than the Elián Gonzalez case. When Elián and his mother, along with several others, fled from Cuba in 1999, their boat sank and only the 6-year-old boy survived. He was taken in by Cuban-American relatives in Miami. His father in Cuba attempted to gain custody of the boy, but the Miami relatives refused to allow him to be repatriated on the ground that Elián would suffer severe hardship if he was raised in communist Cuba. The confrontation between the politically powerful Cuban Americans and the federal government highlighted the emergence of Miami's Cuban community as one of the nation's largest and most influential urban subcultures. Opposition to the government's efforts to return Elián to his father ran so high that some of the most impassioned members of the community even spoke of having a separate foreign policy and seceding from the United States (Bragg, 2000).

Metropolitan Growth

The mass migration from the farms to the cities in the nineteenth century has been described as a rural-urban flow. But in the twentieth century, with most of the U.S. population living in or near urban areas, the pattern of flow has changed from rural-urban to intermetropolitan. In 1910 the Bureau of the Census identified 25 **metropolitan districts.** This term was designed to assist in the measurement of urban populations, which even then could no longer be contained within the traditional urban political boundaries. These districts varied in size from the largest (New York, with 616,927 acres of land and 6,474,568 people) to the smallest (Portland, Oregon, with a population of 215,048 and a land area of 43,538 acres). Through this approach, the unity of such urban areas as the Twin Cities of Minnesota, the cities of

San Francisco Bay, and the two Kansas Cities along the Missouri-Kansas border was recognized. The importance of the urban clusters around Philadelphia, New York, and Boston also became apparent.

Since 1983 the U.S. Bureau of the Census has defined the urban population according to residence in three categories of urban settlement. The largest of the three, the **consolidated metropolitan statistical area (CMSA),** refers to large metropolitan complexes within which are recognized subcenters that may themselves have large core areas, called **primary metropolitan statistical areas (PMSAs).** Dallas and Fort Worth and the urban areas surrounding them, for example, are classified as a CMSA, but statistics are also published separately for the Dallas and Forth Worth PMSAs. **Metropolitan statistical areas (MSAs)** have a large urban nucleus (a city of 500,000) and surrounding communities that are closely linked to it through economic and social activities. Indianapolis, Indiana, is an MSA, as is Little Rock–North Little Rock, Arkansas.

How do "metropolitan" and "urban" areas differ? An urban area usually contains a large population within a limited area. A metropolitan area contains several urban communities, all of which are located in close proximity to one another. For example, the greater New York metropolitan area contains not only New York City but also Long Island, Westchester County, and parts of New Jersey (including Newark) and Connecticut.

Table 15–2 shows how many new metropolitan areas have emerged since 1960, as well as the enormous increase in the amount of land in the United States that is included in such areas. Some of them have become socially and economically interrelated, forming urbanized regions or, in some cases, an urban corridor such as Boston–New York–Philadelphia–Washington. Figure 15–2 shows the largest metropolitan regions in the United States. Note the dramatic growth of regions in the South and West, in marked contrast to those in the Midwest and Northeast. With the exception of Minneapolis–St. Paul, many of the latter experienced population declines in the 1970s and modest increases, often due to the influence of immigration, in the 1980s. Although they are not growing rapidly, metropolitan regions in the Northeast remain the largest on the continent. Social scientists often use the term **megalopolis** to refer to these large areas (Garreau, 1991, 1996; Gottmann, 1978).

The development of megalopolitan areas has large-scale effects on the environment and on other parts of the continent. The energy consumed in the major megalopolitan regions of the United States, especially the BosWash (Boston-to-Washington) corridor, contributes enormously to acid rain and other problems in the Northeast and elsewhere. Air pollution and the demand for shrinking supplies of water in the SanSan (San Diego–San Francisco) megalopolitan strip are reaching

TABLE 15–2 Metropolitan and Nonmetropolitan Area Population: United States, 1960–1990

	1960	1970	1980[a]	1990[a]
Metropolitan areas				
Number of areas	212	243	268	268
Population (1,000)	112,885	139,480	176,663	197,467
Percent change over previous year shown	—	23.6	—	11.8
Percent of total U.S. population	63.0	68.6	78.0	79.4
Land area, percent of U.S. land area	8.7	10.9	19.0	19.0
Nonmetropolitan areas, population (1,000)	66,438	63,822	49,879	51,243

[a]Areas are as defined December 31, 1992.

Source: Statistical Abstract, 1993.

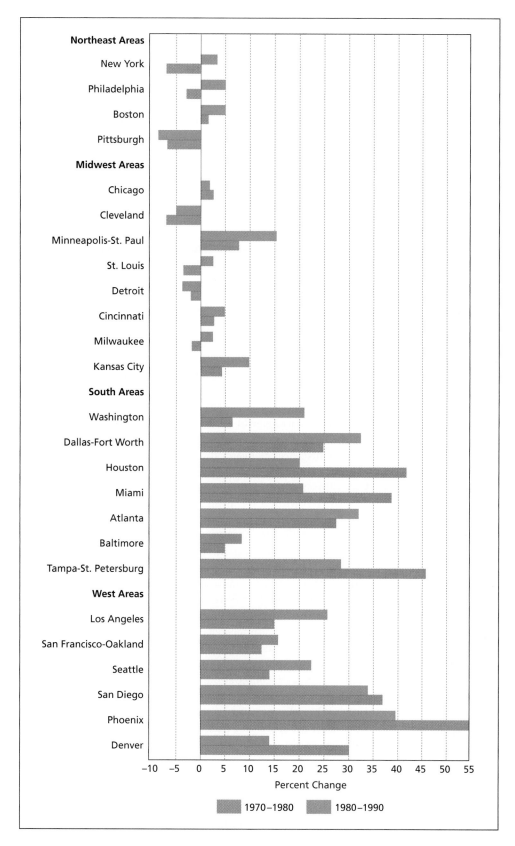

Figure 15–2   Percent Population Change in Largest Metropolitan Areas in 1980–1990, Compared to 1970–1980

Source: Reynolds Farley, *State of the Union: America in the 1990s*, Vol. 2: *Social Trends.* ©1995 Russell Sage Foundation. Used with permission of the Russell Sage Foundation.

emergency proportions. Development along major auto routes between urban areas within the megalopolitan regions is also a growing problem as urban growth threatens to choke out green space and result in unplanned urban sprawl.

In the leading nations of western Europe, especially Holland, France, Germany, and Denmark, investment in rail transport, high-speed trains, and improved bus transportation promises to limit the unplanned effects of megalopolitan development, but similar investments in the urban transportation infrastructure have not been made in the United States. On the other hand, as we will see in Chapter 17, the United States has succeeded in implementing air pollution controls that are more stringent than those of European nations, and these controls have had highly positive effects, although air pollution remains a serious problem in major urban regions.

The Transportation Boom

Relatively primitive communication and transportation facilities and the need for defensive fortifications forced ancient and medieval cities to be compact, and the movement of their inhabitants was restricted to a relatively small area. This was also true for cities in the United States throughout most of the nineteenth century, when walking was the chief mode of transportation. After 1870, however, several major advances, beginning with the horse-drawn streetcar, allowed urban residents the luxury of living up to 5 miles from their place of business. The day of the commuter had dawned. Electric trolley lines and streetcars were introduced in the 1880s and 1890s, extending the commuting distance to about 10 miles. When rapid-transit electric trains were introduced around the turn of the century, the distance doubled once again. The movement to the suburbs had begun.

The trend toward suburbanization began in earnest with the introduction of commuter railways. As wealthy third- and fourth-generation urbanites retreated from the central city, putting ever larger distances between their residences and their places of business, the separation between low-income and high-income neighborhoods increased markedly. Quick to follow the trend, commercial institutions began their own redistribution process. The first to vacate the central city were convenience-goods and service establishments, the businesses that are most dependent on the type of customer who was rapidly moving to suburbia. As these businesses and various manufacturing concerns were leaving the central city, professional service organizations were moving in, creating a central business district made up of administrative, communications, financial, and other businesses that serviced the entire metropolitan region.

By the 1930s the automobile had made suburban development a major factor in the economic, social, and political life of the United States. Motor vehicle registration increased from 8,000 in 1900 to 26,352,000 in 1930, representing an increase from approximately 1 automobile for every 10,000 people to 1 per household (Flink, 1976; Glaab & Brown, 1967). The automobile altered the shape of urban expansion. Whereas previous suburban growth had developed along railroad lines and other public transport systems, the automobile permitted much more dispersed growth. By 1930 urban sprawl was well under way.

The growth of the outlying rings of metropolitan areas occurred so dramatically that by 1930 suburbs were growing two and a half times faster than central cities. In 1910, only 15.7 percent of the total U.S. population lived in metropolitan areas. Between 1960 and 1965, the growth rate for the United States as a whole was 7.1 percent; the growth rate for nonmetropolitan rings increased by 14.5 percent, markedly faster than the increase within the central cities,

High-speed trains like France's TGV are increasingly common in Europe and Japan, but not in the United States, where investments in air and highway travel have been seen as more important than investment in rail transit.

which was only 7.9 percent (Glaab & Brown, 1967). And during the 1970s and early 1980s, there was a large shift of population from the central cities to the suburbs.

Edge Cities.   In the 1980s urban growth entered a new stage. On the perimeters of metropolitan areas, large urban clusters emerged, dense and more focused than the conventional suburb. Sometimes referred to as "edge cities," these new developments rival downtown areas in size and surpass them as sources of jobs. An example of this trend is Tysons Corner. Once a crossroads village in rural northern Virginia, Tysons Corner is now a burgeoning business and shopping center on the edge of the Washington, D.C., metropolitan area. Seventy thousand people work in Tysons Corner, but little else happens there; community life and institutions are almost entirely lacking (Stevens, 1987). Nevertheless, as shown in Figure 15–3, there are many existing edge cities in the Washington, D.C., area, as well as some emerging ones. These new centers for office buildings, shopping malls, and in some cases light manufacturing are surrounded by suburban and exurban communities and are often located near major transportation nodes like Dulles International Airport.

Many other metropolitan regions, notably Los Angeles, Phoenix, Atlanta, Dallas, and northern New Jersey, are experiencing an explosive growth of edge cities as well. Since many of these new areas of economic growth are relatively inaccessible to poor inner-city residents, the mismatch between jobs and population is becoming a pressing urban social policy issue (Garreau, 1996; Kasarda, 1995).

The Impact of Suburban Growth

Public policy, especially in the areas of urban renewal and highway construction, has encouraged suburbanization, often to the detriment and/or destruction of central-city neighborhoods. Financial opportunities—particularly Federal Housing Authority or Veterans Administration mortgages—make buying a house more attractive and easier in the suburbs than in the aging residential areas of the central city. Since a large proportion of a mortgage payment is interest and therefore is tax deductible, simple economics makes it expedient for many American families to move to the suburbs.

Federal financing for home ownership, primarily in the suburbs, is much more accessible than funds for rental housing in the city. This has tended to produce increasing social-class segregation, with lower-income minorities concentrated in the cities and more affluent whites in the suburbs. Explicit efforts to add higher-quality rental housing to the stock of inner-city housing have had mixed results. Public housing, almost all of it built before the 1980s, has added about 1.3 million apartment units to the existing stock of lower-cost rental housing, but about 15 percent of those units are troubled by high rates of drug abuse, crime, and violence (Bratt, 1989; Williams & Kornblum, 1994). Except in the very few cases in which careful planning made it possible to achieve successfully integrated projects, public housing policies have merely managed to keep lower-income people in the city, thereby strengthening patterns of segregation. Moreover, it has been almost impossible for the cities to obtain federal funds for mass transportation projects. By encouraging highway construction rather than strengthening mass transportation, the government encourages industry to leave the city, thereby eliminating a major portion of the central city's tax base.

The steady growth of suburbs has posed many problems for the older cities, particularly in their internal structure and composition. With the increasing differentiation between the central city and the suburban ring and the subsequent outflow of population and industry, America's cities face social and economic problems of seemingly insurmountable proportions. As urban history shows, the steady flight to the suburbs by business, industry, and residents—all eager for less expensive and more comfortable quarters—has made renovation and rehabilitation of the central city both

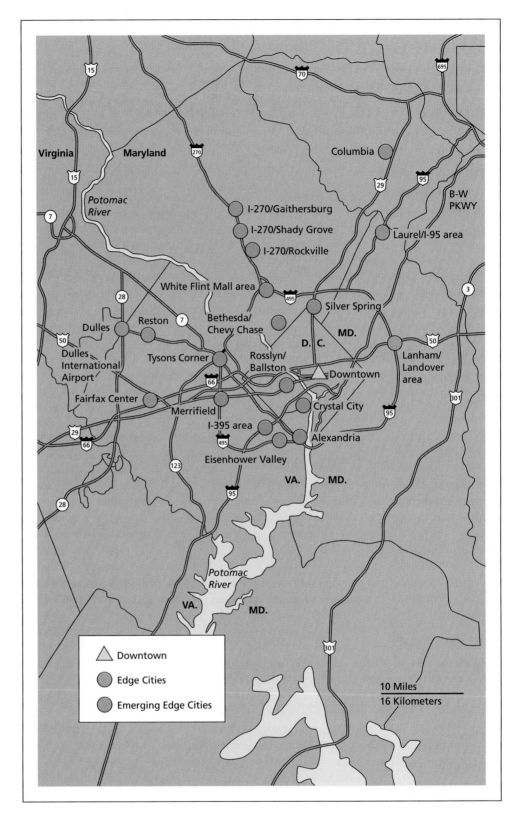

Figure 15–3 Edge Cities in the Washington, D.C., Area

Source: From *Edge City* by Joel Garreau. Used by permission of Doubleday, a division of Random House, Inc.

SOCIAL PROBLEMS ONLINE

Urban Problems and the Internet

The problems of cities are addressed at several sites on the Internet. Wayne State University in Detroit (**http://www.cus.wayne.edu/**) has a web page that features programs concerning a variety of topics such as business assistance, children and families, neighborhood development, and demographics and mapping. Its Urban Safety Program highlights the problems of crime and safety and offers the opportunity to join an urban safety discussion group in which experts can be queried and issues debated. Statistics and technical reports, as well as tips on safety and crime prevention, are available for downloading.

The University of Toronto offers a website for its Global Urban Research Initiative (GURI) at **http://www.chass.utoronto.ca:SOSO/guri/Welcome.html,** with text in English, Spanish, and French. The site has numerous links to other organizations and electronic magazines. It also has connections to e-mail lists for those interested in sociological approaches to urbanism and political geography. The U.S. Department of Housing and Urban Development sites can be accessed from GURI, as can news services from Africa, the Middle East, and Latin America. University and research institutes in Europe, the Americas, Africa, Australia, and Asia round out the available resources.

A good source for housing information is CHAPA, the Citizens' Housing and Planning Association, of Boston. Its web page, at **http://www.chapa.org/chapa_hm.html**, has selections on the latest federal and state housing news, updates on legislation, and research reports and handbooks. For a look at European policies on housing and homelessness, York University in Britain provides a web page for its Centre for Housing Policy (**http://www.york.ac.uk/inst/chp/Welcome.html**). Newsletters from the centre give an overview of some of the ways in which British and U.S. policies differ.

difficult and expensive. In many older metropolitan areas, particularly those in the Northeast, the abandonment of urban neighborhoods to the poor, who are ill equipped to move long distances, has led to the proliferation of slums, causing both the economic base and the actual population of the city to decline. Although the suburbs, the nearby towns, and all of their residents belong to the same metropolitan area as the urban centers, they escape responsibility for the financial burdens they place on the cities.

It is important to recognize that suburbs are no longer as homogeneous as they once were (or were thought to be). Long characterized as bedroom communities, suburbs today mix rural villages with business districts and pockets of poverty and homelessness with areas of middle-class comfort and wealth. Nor are suburbs immune to the kinds of problems that are usually associated with cities, such as traffic congestion and lack of affordable housing.

Problems of Cities

Modern cities are constantly undergoing change and restructuring. Economic change is especially significant in urban areas. As new industries are born and old ones die, entire neighborhoods and communities may be lost and new ones created elsewhere. In the 1950s, for example, economic growth in cities like San Francisco, New York, and Seattle was based on seaport industries. But automation in the handling of goods (especially the use of containers and trucks) greatly diminished the need for workers in the ports. Many port cities still serve as transshipment centers, but far fewer workers are needed to perform this function. Some cities have made up for the loss in seaport employment by building major jetports. Still, economic and social change is so rapid that cities are continually racing to adapt and attract new industries. In the meantime they continue to attract newcomers, many of whom bring more than their share of troubles.

These major social changes affect urban centers more drastically than they do other communities, and they often create a variety of urban problems. Among these are deconcentration, relocation of manufacturing, and financial problems, all of which are complicated by the division of government responsibility between cities and suburbs. These problems will be discussed in this section. Two other serious problems, the lack of affordable housing and the increase in homelessness, will be discussed in the next section.

Deconcentration

A primary cause of central-city decay is **deconcentration:** the flight to the suburbs of middle- and upper-middle-class families; the influx of poor minority groups, the chronically unemployed, the aged, and others who tend to be more of a liability than an asset to central-city budgets; the retreat of commerce and industry from the taxing jurisdiction of central cities; the disparity between the requirements of available jobs in the central city and the skills of the resident labor force; and the daily flow into the city of suburban residents, who utilize public facilities without paying for their upkeep. All these circumstances strain the budgets of the central cities at a time when their revenues are decreasing and their public service obligations have increased substantially.

The decade between 1920 and 1930 was a period of pronounced deconcentration, or suburbanization, in the United States. In subsequent decades the population within the suburban rings increased significantly more than the population of the central cities. By the 1960s suburbanization accounted for almost all the growth within metropolitan areas, and today the growth of central cities is still smaller than that of the outer fringes. But this does not mean that there is no population change inside the cities. On the contrary, as more affluent households move from inner cities to suburban areas, new populations are constantly arriving, especially from other nations. Thus, although population figures may not show them as growing, the inner cities are in fact subject to major population shifts (Kasarda, 1993).

As people left the cities during the period of most intense suburbanization, business and industry quickly followed. The years from 1954 to 1977 saw the construction of more than 15,000 suburban shopping centers and regional shopping malls, which by 1978 were responsible for more than half of the total annual retail sales in the United States (Kasarda, 1978, 1993). From 1975 to 1980, central cities continued to lose population while the suburbs continued to gain new residents, as did nonmetropolitan regions. The 1980 census showed that during that period the cities lost 6.3 million residents, of whom 5 million moved to the suburbs and 1.3 million to nonmetropolitan areas.

The 1990 census confirmed that the fastest-growing urban communities are on the fringes of metropolitan areas. During the 1980s there was a significant shift of jobs and people to the outer counties of metropolitan regions. In New York, for example, the population of the outer counties grew by 13 percent while that of the inner counties grew by just 2 percent. In many metropolitan regions the rapid growth of suburban communities attracts jobs that were formerly located in the urban core. Table 15–3 shows that metropolitan areas continue to absorb most of the growth of the nation's population, accounting for almost 80 percent of the total. Not shown in the table is the fact that within these areas, the populations of inner cities are generally either declining or remaining stable. The vast majority of the growth is in newer suburbs and edge cities on the outskirts of metropolitan regions.

TABLE 15-3   Metropolitan and Nonmetropolitan Population, United States, 1980–1996

	Total Population (in thousands)			Percent Change	Percent of Total Population	
	1980	**1990**	**1996**	**1980–1996**	**1990**	**1996**
Metropolitan	177,361	198,249	211,874	6.9	79.7	79.9
Nonmetropolitan	49,180	50,465	53,410	5.8	20.3	20.1
Total	226,541	248,714	265,284			

Source: Data from *Statistical Abstract,* 1999.

In addition to the movement to the suburbs, there has been a tremendous shift of population from the Snowbelt cities of the North and East to the Sunbelt cities of the South and West—Houston, San Antonio, Phoenix, and others. And as the population has moved, so have jobs, a fact that has added to the problems of the older, larger cities in the northern industrial states. But life is not always sunny in the Sunbelt cities either. In California, for example, severe drought and increasing overpopulation, lack of affordable housing, and earthquakes have tarnished the image of Southern California as the embodiment of the American Dream. Although the large-scale influx of immigrants continues to produce growth in the Los Angeles metropolitan area, it is likely that the region will experience continuing economic problems because of the end of the cold war and the decline in defense production, as well as the effects of environmental catastrophes ranging from earthquakes to brush fires and mudslides (Davis, 1990).

Elsewhere in the Sunbelt there are other major urban problems. In their studies of Houston, Joe R. Feagin (1988) and Robert D. Bullard (1988) found that by the end of the 1980s the long period of prosperity in that city, fueled by steady demand for higher-priced oil, had ended. Recession and increasing racial segregation had replaced the upbeat free-enterprise image projected by the city's business leaders. Like many cities in the Southwest and the Northeast, Houston had overbuilt its downtown office centers in anticipation of more white-collar jobs and had failed to invest enough of its resources in upgrading schools and health-care facilities in the inner city.

Relocation of Manufacturing

Manufacturers benefit from suburban relocation because they can minimize their transportation and freight costs by locating near suburban highway systems. Accordingly, manufacturing firms have left the inner cities in large numbers. To a certain extent, their departure has been balanced by an influx of new types of business establishments that offer specialized goods and services. Legal, government, and professional complexes and service organizations such as travel agencies, advertising firms, and brokerage houses have all become more numerous in recent decades. Yet although the percentage of white-collar jobs has increased in the central cities, it has increased much faster in the outlying suburban areas.

Especially dramatic has been the rise of high-tech manufacturing centers like Silicon Valley in California and the Route 128 region near Boston. Among the industries that have found it advantageous to operate in these areas are manufacturers of office and computing machines, communication equipment, electronic components and accessories, and engineering and scientific instruments, as well as computer and data-processing services and research and development labs. These industries are dependent on intensive, sophisticated technical research, and hence the new manufacturing zones are almost always located near major universities like the Massachusetts Institute of Technology. High-tech firms have created large numbers of new jobs, especially high-paying jobs in science, engineering, and management. One result is a growing demand for expensive housing in the surrounding communities, which tends to increase the average price of housing in the area and displace lower-income residents (Kasarda, 1995).

Financial Problems

Property assessments are the primary source of tax revenues for city governments. As a result of the exodus of industry to the suburbs, the real estate tax base of most central cities has been greatly reduced. Population shifts within the boundaries of metropolitan areas have further increased the financial pressures on central cities. For the larger metropolitan areas, the increased concentration of low-income groups in the inner cities demands a larger investment in welfare and other social programs. Many cities, fearful of losing residents and businesses to the suburbs, also need to invest in large-scale physical rehabilitation and redevelopment projects.

The economic gap between healthy suburbs and distressed cities has worsened in recent years, despite signs of improvement in some areas. Many urban specialists fear that cities with financial difficulties will channel funds away from essential services, such as streets, water and sewage systems, and mass transportation facilities, to finance their debts and meet operating costs.

Related to the problem of finances is the poor condition of the infrastructure (i.e., physical facilities) of many cities. Most American cities grew rapidly after World War II, especially in the 1950s. Large investments were made in public transportation, bridges, and highway systems to serve rapidly growing and increasingly affluent urban populations. But by the 1980s much of this infrastructure had begun to wear out. Estimates made by the federal government in the early 1980s indicated that billions of dollars would be needed to repair and rebuild crumbling city facilities. In the

Large tracts of urban real estate have been abandoned because of high crime rates or the inability of tenants to make rent payments. Public-private partnerships using federal housing funds have provided these formerly homeless families with their first decent, afforable housing.

CRITICAL RESEARCH

Destructive Urban Design

Sociologist Lyn Lofland (1998) is a leading critic of the way architecture and urban design are used to eliminate certain forms of interaction or contact among people. Lofland's research supports the thesis that cities spawn subcultures but questions the assumption that such groups normally interact. In fact, her findings show how frequently city space is used to prevent or control interaction.

In her critical research on trends in constructing urban spaces, Lofland (1998) studies five types of design, which she terms *megamononeighborhoods, autoresidences, autostreets, antiparks,* and *megastructures.* Each of these has a negative effect on interaction among urban residents.

Megamononeighborhoods are huge and relatively homogeneous complexes of buildings and roads devoted to a single use. Typical examples are industrial parks; hospital complexes; and above all, residential tract developments. Although these huge places may have public space in the form of small parks or streets, they rarely encourage interaction among strangers.

When people do use them, they are usually already friends from a subunit of the megastructure.

Autoresidences are tracks of houses, usually built since the auto boom of the postwar years, in which the main message given to the passerby is that "cars live here." There are many garages, and the "houses appear to have been designed for the sole purpose of housing automobiles" (Lofland, 1998, p. 201). Such places have little space for public sociability, people watching, public solitude, or any of the features of urban space that encourage people of different backgrounds to gather together.

"In a nation where automobiles appear to have their own houses," Lofland writes, "it is both logical and unsurprising that they should also have nearly exclusive claim to so many traffic arteries—that is, that streets should be or become autostreets" (Lofland, 1998, p. 201). On autostreets there is an emphasis on ease of driving and a deemphasis on ease of walking, sitting, bike riding, strolling with children, or other pedestrian activities.

Antiparks are research parks, business parks, green patches in malls that are closed off to public use, and

The Renaissance Center in downtown Detroit has an imposing beauty from a distance, but it is also an example of "destructive" urban design due to its fortresslike isolation from surrounding streets and neighborhoods.

other nonpublic park spaces or spaces that resemble parks but are not actually designed to be used as public parks. These are often found in and around mega-mononeighborhoods.

Finally, megastructures are huge developments in cities that are designed to capture much business use, and perhaps residential use as well, but to discourage other members of the public from visiting them. As the pioneering urban critic Jane Jacobs (1961) observed in her classic book, *The Death and Life of Great American Cities,* megastructures create an "all or nothing" form of urban life. One is either inside the great building complex or outside. There are no edges and spaces in and around these structures that encourage the easy mixing of strangers, so one is either an insider or an outsider. Lofland agrees that such urban design is destructive to interaction and therefore antipublic.

mid-1980s many observers warned that the decay of the country's roads, bridges, sewers, and rail and water systems had reached alarming proportions. These warnings were reinforced by an increase in the frequency of accidents caused by train derailments and collapsing bridges and overpasses. At the same time, however, the federal budget deficit rose to record levels, precluding large-scale federal investment in infrastructure projects.

In the 1990s there were numerous natural calamities such as flooding in cities and towns of the Mississippi, Ohio, and Missouri valleys; earthquakes and brush fires in California; and hurricanes in the Gulf states. These added to the burden of financing the repair and maintenance of urban infrastructures. Since the majority of the nation's metropolitan population lives in disaster-prone regions, it is likely that natural disasters and their consequences will become more frequent in coming years as both the population and the surface area of these metropolitan centers continue to grow. (See the Critical Research feature on page 441.)

Government

A major cause of the problems of cities today is the inequitable distribution of economic resources and costs of public services between the cities and higher levels of government. Of every $100 the U.S. government collects in taxes, it spends about $16 on national defense, $23 on Social Security, $14 on income security (federal pensions, unemployment insurance, food and nutrition assistance, etc.), and $20 on interest on the national debt. It spends less than $1 to run the federal government, $7 on health-care services and research (not including Medicare), $2 on transportation (especially highways), and a little over $1 on criminal-justice assistance to states and cities (*Statistical Abstract,* 1999). Although crime and overcrowded prisons are deemed to be major social problems by residents of metropolitan regions, one can see from these figures that very little of the tax revenue collected at the federal level is returned to municipalities to help them cope with these problems. In consequence, suburbs with affluent residents who pay high property taxes can afford adequate protection, whereas inner cities with poorer residents, which have much less revenue from property taxes, must depend on the meager return from federal taxes to tackle not only crime but also poor education, inadequate health care, and other major problems.

In addition, many urban social problems extend beyond the jurisdiction of any single local government, and often cross state boundaries as well. Such concerns as air and water pollution require control over entire areas rather than strict observance of municipal boundaries. This is also true for major waterways, mass transit, and water supplies. The situation for recreational facilities, public institutions like libraries and museums, and public services like police and fire protection is less clear. The benefits of all these services are not restricted to a single municipal jurisdiction. On the other hand, they are not equally distributed throughout the entire metropolitan area. Who, then, is to pay how much for these necessary services?

City governments have been forced to bear the financial burden for municipal services even though those services are extensively utilized by suburban residents. Thousands of visitors flock to city museums and parks every day, placing additional burdens on sanitation and public-health facilities and transportation systems, all of which must be paid for out of municipal funds. In this way city residents assume the tax burden for their suburban neighbors. Numerous social scientists have pointed out that regardless of its political boundaries, a metropolitan area is in fact a single economic entity, with an integrated labor market, a unified transportation system, and a closely interrelated set of housing markets. Dividing this entity into separate local economies results in inefficiency and duplication of services.

In extreme cases, the discrepancies between municipal boundaries and social needs can have dire consequences. This is illustrated by East St. Louis, Illinois, which has been described as "a textbook case of everything that can go wrong in an American city." Once a prosperous blue-collar town of stockyards and meat-packing plants beside the Mississippi River, in the 1990s East St. Louis was "a city at rock bottom, a partly inhabited ghost town whose factories and theaters and hotels and auto dealerships and gas stations and half its schools are mostly burned-out shells" (Wilkerson, 1991, p. A16). Although riverboat gambling has brought some new jobs and income, the city remains mired in poverty. The causes of this situation include a rapidly declining tax base and the fact that even though East St. Louis borders on St. Louis, it is a separate municipality in another state.

Shelter Poverty, Homelessness, and Neighborhood Distress

Shelter Poverty

As noted in Chapter 8, the majority of America's poor live in substandard, deteriorated housing that has been rejected by people who can afford better. This is especially true of poor members of minority groups, who inhabit substandard housing either because they cannot afford anything better or because discrimination keeps them where they are. As a result, people with higher incomes live in new housing in the suburbs while the poor live in older central-city housing. Shelter poverty, it should be noted, also occurs among affluent families when sudden unemployment decreases their income while mortgages and other housing costs remain the same. But shelter poverty is most prevalent among families at or below the poverty line.

Some experts argue that many sections of cities that are severely run down can be rehabilitated. Others claim that this does nothing to solve social problems. The standard procedure in most urban renewal or redevelopment programs involves the mass removal of slum housing. To accomplish this, the residents of the area must be removed first. Since most urban renewal projects result in more expensive housing, the residents are for the most part unable to return to their former neighborhoods. Those who can afford to return find that the characteristics that made the neighborhood their own—churches, schools, family, and friends—are no longer there. The majority of those who are dislocated as a result of urban renewal move to nearby areas that will probably be cleared in future renewal projects.

Instead of providing adequate housing at a low cost, most urban renewal drives the poor out of rehabilitated areas because too often the redeveloped housing is intended for people with high incomes. Low-cost housing for low-income residents has never been financially feasible. Meanwhile, federal public housing policy often ensures the development of a "federal slum." By preventing the working poor from living in the housing projects, the government restricts the projects to the very poor, people on welfare, broken families, and the disabled.

It should be noted that much public housing is far better than the dilapidated, decaying buildings it replaced. However, the problem of segregation of the poor remains; in addition, the quality of the neighborhoods in which the housing projects are located is often substandard. Critics of public housing point out that "even when dwelling units occupied by the poor are not overcrowded, contain their own kitchens and bathrooms, and may even be in somewhat decent repair, they are set in a dismal environment. They are surrounded by abandoned buildings and located on streets that are unsafe and littered with trash" (Salins, 1986, pp. 24–25). A major reason for this situation is that more affluent communities tend to oppose even small additions of low-income housing to their neighborhoods.

Homelessness

A frequent consequence of shelter poverty is homelessness. People who cannot afford rent increases may end up among the large number of homeless people in the nation's big cities. Moreover, many young families who would have purchased a house a decade ago are forced to stay in rental housing. This development has tended to push rents up and squeeze lower-income people out of the rental market; because of the lack of space in public housing, the result, for many, is homelessness.

Another trend that has contributed to the housing problem is *gentrification,* the return of affluent, single people and childless couples to selected central-city neighborhoods. As these new urban residents restore and renovate buildings and upgrade apartments in decaying neighborhoods, poor residents are forced to seek living space in other parts of the city. If they are unable to find housing they can afford, they, too, may end up among the homeless.

We have noted at several points in this book that homelessness has become a major social problem in recent years. As a result of numerous factors, including deinstitutionalization of mental patients, the increasing concentration of poor people in central cities, the lack of low-cost housing, and the displacement of poor families by urban renewal and gentrification, there has been a large and visible increase in the number of homeless people who wander through public places in central cities. The size of the homeless population is extremely difficult to assess. Not only are homeless people virtually impossible to keep track of, but estimates of their numbers tend to reflect the interests of the organizations that provide them.

In the late 1980s and early 1990s, Republican administrations tended to support estimates of the homeless population that varied around the 600,000 level. The Clinton administration, drawing on the expertise of demographer Martha Burt, sociologist Peter Rossi, and other social scientists with long experience in measuring and counting homeless populations, revised these figures upward. The administration's report concluded that on an annual basis (as opposed to any given night) as many as 7 million Americans are homeless (Burt, 1992; DeParle, 1994; Rossi, 1989b).

In 1999 the Department of Housing and Urban Development (HUD) released the results of its most ambitious survey yet of the nation's homeless population (*Alcoholism & Drug Abuse Weekly,* 1999). This study shows that most people who are homeless have suffered severe hardship—physical and sexual abuse, childhood trauma, poverty, disability, and disease—but are successful in escaping from homelessness when they receive help from assistance programs. The report found that when homeless people receive housing assistance and needed services, such as health care, substance abuse treatment, and mental-health services, 76 percent of those living in families and 60 percent of those living alone are able to move into better living situations, provided that such situations are available. The study highlights the need for housing and supportive services for the nation's homeless population. During the economic boom of the 1990s that population was reduced somewhat, but it remains high in depressed inner-city neighborhoods and impoverished rural areas.

There have always been homeless groups in the United States: hoboes, unemployed migrants, and the like. For them homelessness was either a chosen lifestyle or a more or less temporary condition. Today's homeless people are a more serious problem. Not only is the homeless population larger than ever before, but it includes a much wider range of groups—deinstitutionalized mental patients and displaced families, chronic alcoholics, destitute drug addicts, Vietnam veterans, unemployed laborers, and others. This large population has placed a heavy burden on the public and private shelters and other social services of American cities. In some cities existing shelters and other facilities are woefully inadequate, and as a result homeless people have sought refuge in bus terminals and train stations. Policies for dealing with homelessness are discussed further in the Social Policy section of the chapter.

Distressed Neighborhoods

As a consequence of the flight of more secure middle-class people from the central cities over the past 20 years or more, there has been an increase in what social scientists call **neighborhood distress.** In discussing this problem, it is important to note that it is extremely difficult to define precisely what constitutes a neighborhood. The Census Bureau divides urban regions into **census tracts,** areas that are relatively homogeneous in population, socioeconomic status, and living conditions. Census tracts, which have an average population of 4,000 people, are equivalent to urban neighborhoods for analytical purposes.

In the largest central cities of the United States, there are slightly over 14,000 census tracts. Analyses of the characteristics of inner-city tracts reveal that in many there have been sharp increases in the degree of neighborhood distress. According to social scientists such as John Kasarda, one of the nation's leading analysts of urban social change, neighborhood distress is measured by several characteristics (Kasarda, 1993; Ricketts & Sawhill, 1988):

Poverty—the rate of poverty in the tract

Joblessness—the proportion of out-of-school males aged 16 and older who work fewer than 26 weeks a year

Female-headed families—the proportion of families headed by a female with children under the age of 18

Welfare recipiency—the proportion of families that receive public assistance

Teenage school dropouts—the proportion of people aged 16 to 19 who are not enrolled in school and are not high school graduates

Distressed neighborhoods are not the same as poverty tracts, although the two have much in common. Poverty tracts are census tracts in which at least 20 percent of the residents fall below the poverty line; in extreme poverty tracts, at least 40 percent do so. When the concepts of distressed neighborhoods and poverty tracts are combined, the following definitions emerge (Kasarda, 1993):

Distressed tracts—census tracts that fall 1 standard deviation or more (that is, 30 percent or more) below the mean (based on the 1980 census) on all five measures listed earlier

Severely distressed tracts—census tracts with extremely high rates of teenage school dropouts, causing them to fall 1 standard deviation above the 1980 national tract average on this measure (used in defining severely distressed tracts because completing high school is essential for gaining employment in the nation's rapidly changing economy)

Census Tracts	1970	1980	1990
Total number of tracts	12,584	13,777	14,214
(% of city total)	100.0	100.0	100.0
Poverty tracts	3,430	4,713	5,596
(% of city total)	27.3	34.2	39.4
Extreme poverty tracts	751	1,330	1,954
(% of city total)	6.0	9.7	13.7
Distressed tracts	296	1,513	1,850
(% of city total)	2.4	11.0	13.0
Severely distressed tracts	166	562	566
(% of city total)	1.3	4.1	4.0

Table 15–4 Number of Census Tracts, by Poverty and Distress Status: 100 Largest Central Cities, 1970–1990

Source: Data from U.S. Census Bureau, 1990.

Table 15–4 indicates that since 1970 there has been a dramatic increase in the number of census tracts in the 100 largest U.S. cities that are classified as poverty tracts or extreme poverty tracts. The increase in distressed tracts has also been significant, but between 1980 and 1990 the rate of increase was slower than in the previous decade. The number of severely distressed tracts increased only slightly in the same period after rapid growth between 1970 and 1980.

Kasarda's (1993) research also shows that there has been an alarming concentration of households in extreme poverty tracts and distressed tracts in the nation's 100 largest cities. From 1970 to 1990 the number of people in distressed tracts increased from about 1 million to 5.7 million, or from about 2 percent of the total population of those cities to about 11 percent. Worse still is the growing concentration of minorities in distressed central-city tracts. Whereas 2.2 percent of non-Latino whites live in such areas, 29.7 percent of non-Latino African Americans and 13.2 percent of Latinos live in distressed tracts in the nation's 100 largest cities.

It is difficult to overstate the consequences of this concentration of poor people in distressed neighborhoods. These are likely to be the areas with the highest rates of drug sales and addiction, violent crime, and housing abandonment. Twenty years ago residents of most of the census tracts that are now characterized by poverty and neighborhood distress could find manufacturing jobs nearby. Today the jobs are gone, and the economic future of these areas is extremely uncertain. Although some communities outside central cities also suffer from high rates of poverty and related social problems, the most important test of policies to address urban social problems will be whether they are able to improve conditions of life in the distressed neighborhoods of the inner cities, for improvements there will result in overall improvements for all residents of urban areas.

SOCIAL POLICY

Intentionally or unintentionally, social policies instituted by governments at all levels, and especially by the federal government, have encouraged suburban sprawl and contributed to the problems of rural areas and inner cities (Brown, 1997; Lofland, 1998). Policies that subsidize mortgages for buyers of private homes favor the suburbs over denser apartment neighborhoods. Policies that favor highway and road construction over mass transit encourage the growth of communities at the edges of metropolitan areas but make it more difficult for people without adequate personal transportation to reach jobs and educational opportunities. To correct these biases, recent administrations have developed policies that encourage economic development, housing construction, and transportation alternatives in inner-city areas and the older suburbs that surround them. In larger cities like Chicago, New York, St. Louis, Atlanta, and many others, these policies have helped spur economic and social revitalization of the city center.

Throughout the nation, residential land values in cities are significantly higher than in the suburbs, indicating that a central location is desirable to many people. Housing in the central cities, particularly in high-rise apartment complexes, is very expensive. The fact that a central location still has a high economic value is the best evidence that the central city can be restored. Indeed, many urban sociologists view restoration projects in central-city neighborhoods—such as Capitol Hill in Washington, D.C.; Old Town and New Town in Chicago; Pioneer Square in Seattle; and Olympic Park in Atlanta—as indications of a revival of central-city life. Others are encouraged by the growth of luxury apartments and condominiums in and around the business districts of urban centers.

However, as noted earlier, the revitalization of neighborhoods by the upper-middle class is not always beneficial to all concerned. In particular, the poor and the elderly are often victims of this trend as their apartment buildings are converted into condominiums or cooperatives and they come under intense pressure to leave homes and neighborhoods that they can no longer afford. In addition to the return of the middle class, therefore, if today's cities are to be fully revitalized, some of the businesses that moved to the suburbs will have to return.

To some extent this has happened already. Large regional capitals like New York, Boston, Louisville, Philadelphia, and Baltimore have undergone a transition to new industries based on light manufacturing of high-technology goods and the provision of new services, especially in finance, insurance, international trade, air freight, and research and development. The influx of new workers, often in higher-paying jobs, has stimulated leisure industries in these cities as well (Garreau, 1991).

An example of the kind of redevelopment that is occurring in some urban centers is the Times Square project in New York City. This project has pooled funds from public and private sources to redevelop the Times Square area as a combined entertainment, wholesale marketing, and office complex. The project is controversial, however, because it has the potential to drive up rents in the area, thereby displacing low-income residents. Moreover, the plan calls for the preservation of the historic theaters on Forty-second Street, although public support of the arts, including the theater, has decreased significantly in recent years. In 1994 the Disney Corporation announced that it would open a major cultural development center in Times Square, a sign of the project's potential for eventual success. This announcement quieted some critics of the project, who argue that, like many other urban redevelopment plans, it emphasizes the building of structures at the expense of the building of institutions such as theater companies or musical production organizations (Goldberger, 1996; Zukin, 1991). Today the new Times Square is attracting millions of domestic and foreign visitors annually and has become a focus of economic growth in the central city.

Housing

During the 1980s the federal government eliminated or drastically reduced many programs that had provided housing assistance to American families for 50 years. The Reagan administration believed that the forces of supply and demand, operating independently of government incentives and subsidies, would meet the need for moderate- and low-income housing. In effect, this amounted to the lack of a housing policy at the federal level.

At the state and local levels, in contrast, some new initiatives emerged in the late 1980s and early 1990s. Local governments began setting up funds to provide housing assistance to low- and moderate-income families, encouraging private and public partnerships for developing low-cost housing and earmarking certain taxes (e.g., offshore oil taxes or real estate transfer taxes) for financing housing programs. These policies can be seen as part of the increased emphasis of many state governments on economic revitalization.

At the federal level, the public housing properties under the fiscal control of HUD, in cooperation with local managing authorities, are continually subject to changes in policy. The Clinton administration pursued a policy of tearing down dangerous and deteriorated high-rise housing in favor of low-rise garden apartments or single homes. It hoped to demolish some 100,000 units of the old housing and sought funding to cover the costs of replacing it. Unless replacement housing becomes available quite soon, however, this policy runs the risk of contributing still further to the problem of homelessness (Adler & Malone, 1996) if there is a serious downturn in the economy.

Homelessness

In 1987 Congress passed the Stuart B. McKinney Homeless Assistance Act, which allocated hundreds of millions of dollars to house homeless people; in 1988 the federal government initiated a $2 billion program to create emergency housing for the homeless in states and cities where the need is greatest. Both actions, though clearly necessary, are unlikely to address the long-term problems that have produced a

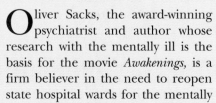

CURRENT CONTROVERSIES

Reinstitutionalization Versus Community Care

Oliver Sacks, the award-winning psychiatrist and author whose research with the mentally ill is the basis for the movie *Awakenings,* is a firm believer in the need to reopen state hospital wards for the mentally ill homeless who now sleep on city streets, in parks and rail terminals, and in temporary shelters. These troubled people were supposed to be cared for in community mental-health centers, halfway houses, and group homes, but in too many cases they are not. To alleviate their suffering, he proposes making room for them in state hospitals, where they can obtain proper treatment.

On a related front, William J. Bennett, former director of the Bush administration's antidrug programs, advocates the creation of orphanages for children in drug-infested neighborhoods. "We may just have to . . . find some way to get children out of the environment which they're in, to go to orphanages, to go to Boys Town, to expand institutions like that, where they will be raised and nurtured," he declared in a speech to an antidrug organization (quoted in Kosterlitz, 1990, p. 2120).

Many sociologists support Bennett's view. Joyce A. Ladner, for example, has conducted extensive studies of foster care and adoption and notes that "we're seeing increasing numbers of children who are not getting adequate care and for whom adequate care is not an imminent possibility" (quoted in Kosterlitz, 1990, p. 2120). Society, she says, must cease to believe blindly in an ideal family life that often does not match reality and must put more children in group settings that offer safety and stability.

Those who oppose the movement toward reinstitutionalization warn of a return to the era of the "snake pit" and the grim, underfunded, understaffed orphanage. They point out that many mental hospitals and orphanages were shut down because they had become dumping grounds for society's most troubled and neglected members. The ideals of community care, patients' rights, and the mainstreaming of people with mental disabilities or histories of neglect may be threatened if society again resorts to "warehousing" its most problematic citizens. Advocates of community-based care believe that cities and towns need more support in their efforts to add to the insufficient number of small, local care programs and facilities. They see the reinstitutionalization movement as a return to the past.

What is a concerned citizen to think? On the one hand, respected medical professionals such as Sacks advocate a return to institutionalization. On the other hand, many experts continue to hold out hope for community-based care and mainstreaming. Yet these are not necessarily mutually exclusive policies. One could advocate an increase in well-funded and well-staffed orphanages and mental hospitals while at the same time pressing for more community-based facilities. The problem, of course, is that mental hospitals and community care facilities are competing for public and private funds. For the care of dependent children without parents, for example, the federal government now makes available about $256 million a year, but an estimated $1 billion a year is needed if real progress is to be made toward providing adequate care. Competing budget demands make it unlikely that such funds will be provided.

serious lack of adequate housing for the poor. Shelters and temporary quarters need to be augmented; but without increased investment in low- and moderate-income housing, it is likely that gentrification, along with the "normal" calamities of arson and urban blight, will continue to add to the homeless population.

In addition to the need for shelter, there are special needs among the homeless that have only recently been recognized and addressed by policymakers. Foremost among these is the spread of AIDS. It is estimated that between 15 percent and 20 percent of shelter residents are infected with the AIDS virus and have such symptoms as diarrhea, weight loss, chronic fevers, and pneumonia. Although they account for a small proportion of the homeless population, they present a major problem because they need hospice care and cannot be integrated with the residents of public shelters. A similar situation exists with respect to the mentally ill, as we saw in Chapter 3. (Some experts believe that the mentally ill and homeless children should be cared for in institutions, a proposal that is discussed in the Current Controversies feature on page 448.)

Before he became Secretary of Housing and Urban Development, Andrew Cuomo was responsible for many of the studies that arrived at more realistic (and higher) estimates of the annual homeless population. The research showed that lack of shelter and homelessness are often caused by a complex of problems, including mental illness, drug abuse, poverty, racism, and cuts in government spending. According to former HUD Secretary Cisneros, "Homelessness has become a structural problem in America: chronic, continuous, large scale, complex" (quoted in DeParle, 1994, p. A1). In an effort to address this massive social problem, HUD proposes to undertake an aggressive housing development program and to revise the McKinney Act so that services to homeless people would be delivered by nonprofit groups rather than by federal or local governments. As noted earlier, however, these efforts are severely hampered by the lack of sufficient funds in the federal budget.

Dislike of city life is not a monopoly of people on the conservative end of the political continuum, who typically live in suburban or small-town residential environments. Many people on the liberal side also dislike urban life, preferring to live in exurban or rural areas such as Vermont or the Pacific Northwest. Although those on the left are more likely to support efforts to improve conditions of life in the inner cities, they often send their children to private schools and buy vacation homes far from the stresses of the central city. There are many important exceptions to these observations, but this behavior illustrates one of the main problems of the inner city: Its neighborhoods, often racially segregated, are not seen as desirable living environments. Increasingly, therefore, policymakers on both sides of the ideological divide recognize society's pressing need to address the plight of inner-city communities. The strategy of creating empowerment zones to attract new businesses is popular with policymakers on both the left and the right, but these zones have yet to prove their worth in the difficult task of revitalizing economically depressed communities in the inner cities.

Beyond Left & Right

SUMMARY

- The U.S. Bureau of the Census defines the urban population as all persons who are living in places with 2,500 or more inhabitants that are legally incorporated as cities, villages, boroughs, and towns. Many social problems, such as poverty, mental illness, drug abuse, and violence, are especially serious in the nation's cities.

- The urban revolution is a worldwide phenomenon. Throughout the world, rapidly growing cities are experiencing social problems such as crowding, poverty, lack of adequate housing, and the threat of gangs and violence.

- Most urban growth has been caused by increasingly efficient transportation and communication and the effects of industrialization. Urban growth has stimulated technological advances, but it has also created various social problems, as well as a strong antiurban bias among a large proportion of the American public.

- The population of U.S. cities today consists largely of descendants of immigrants from other countries and from rural areas of the nation. Cities continue to receive large numbers of immigrants from other countries, and conflict between the newcomers and residents of older ghettos is frequent.

- Residential segregation, both voluntary and involuntary, is common in urban areas. African Americans have been subject to the highest and most persistent rates of segregation throughout the nation's history.

- The three main theories of urbanism are the Wirthian theory, the compositional theory, and the subcultural theory. The Wirthian theory holds that cities increase the incidence of social and personality disorders because city dwellers must adapt to a multitude of intense stimuli. The compositional theory views the city as a mosaic of social worlds that protect individuals from the pressures of city life. The subcultural theory suggests that urban life promotes diverse subcultures.

- Many urban areas are not single cities but what the Census Bureau terms metropolitan statistical areas and consolidated metropolitan statistical areas. The core areas of these urban centers are primary metropolitan statistical areas. The term *megalopolis* is often applied to a region that contains several metropolitan areas.

- The growth of metropolitan areas has been associated with the development of new forms of transportation, including the streetcar, the commuter railway, and especially the automobile. These hastened the trend toward suburbanization, which was also encouraged by urban renewal and highway construction programs and by federal programs that encourage home ownership.

- In the 1980s urban growth entered a new stage. On the perimeters of metropolitan areas, large urban clusters emerged, denser and more focused than the conventional suburb. Sometimes referred to as edge cities, these new developments rival downtown areas in size and surpass them as sources of jobs.

- As suburbs and edge cities have grown, the central cities have decayed. A primary cause of decay is deconcentration, the flight of middle-class families to the suburbs coupled with the influx of poor minority groups, the unemployed, and the aged to the central cities. Business and industry have also moved to the suburbs; in the cities, manufacturers have been replaced by establishments that offer specialized goods and services. Unskilled or semiskilled jobs have been transferred to the suburbs, and white-collar jobs in the cities are filled by skilled personnel, leaving unskilled central-city residents with fewer opportunities for employment.

- The exodus of industry to the suburbs has significantly reduced the real estate tax base of most central cities. At the same time, the increase in the low-income population of the cities creates additional financial burdens. This situation has resulted in serious financial problems for large cities. Related to this problem is the deterioration of the infrastructure, or physical facilities, of many cities, which has been made even worse by natural calamities like hurricanes, brush fires, and earthquakes. The financial problems of cities are exacerbated by the inequitable distribution of economic resources and costs between the cities and higher levels of government.

- Housing is a major problem in the central cities. Many urban residents are shelter poor, meaning that they must pay so much for housing that they no longer have enough money for other necessities. Shelter poverty is most prevalent among the poor, who are forced to live in substandard, deteriorated housing. Urban renewal or redevelopment programs involve removing such housing, thereby displacing the poor, and replacing it with housing for people with higher incomes. Housing projects for the poor, on the other hand, quickly turn into slums.

- Gentrification, the renovation of decaying neighborhoods by affluent residents, has displaced poor city dwellers and added to the homeless population. This large population has placed a heavy burden on public and private shelters and other social services in American cities.

- Over the past 20 years there has been an increase in what social scientists call neighborhood distress. Distressed neighborhoods are characterized by high rates of poverty, joblessness, female-headed families, welfare recipiency, and teenage school dropouts. Such areas are also likely to have the highest rates of drug sales and addiction, violent crime, and housing abandonment.

- Many of America's oldest cities are undergoing a process of revitalization as members of the upper middle-class return, together with new industries. Nevertheless, there is still an urgent need for social policies to improve conditions of life in the inner cities.

KEY TERMS

rural, p. 423
urban, p. 423
urban population, p. 423
urbanized area, p. 423
urbanism, p. 424
metropolitan districts, p. 431

consolidated metropolitan statistical
    area (CMSA), p. 432
primary metropolitan statistical areas
    (PMSAs), p. 432
metropolitan statistical areas (MSA),
    p. 432

megalopolis, p. 432
deconcentration, p. 438
neighborhood distress, p. 445
census tracts, p. 445

INTERNET EXERCISE

The web destinations for Chapter 15 are related to different aspects of urban problems. To begin your explorations, go to the Prentice Hall Companion Website: **http://prenhall.com/kornblum**. Then choose **Chapter 15** (Urban Problems). Next, select **destinations** from the menu on the left side of the screen. There are a variety of sites to investigate. We suggest that you begin with the following two sites: **The Devil in Deinstitutionalization** and **Community Mental Health Care.** The *Current Controversies* box in this chapter deals with the issues surrounding reinstitutionalization of the mentally ill versus caring for them through community-based programs. The *Devil in Deinstitutionalization* site shows how the movement to release

mental-health clients from the "snakepits"of the 1960s has failed. The Community Mental Health site will provide you with a glimpse of how community-based care works and the prospects for this alternative in the future. After you have explored these two sites, answer the following questions:

- Do you agree that the movement to deinstitutionalize the "snakepit" mental hospitals of 30 years ago has failed? Do you support reinstitutionalization?

- Do you think community-based mental-health care is a better alternative for dealing with the mentally ill in comparison with reinstitutionalization? Why?

16 Population and Immigration

POPULATION AND IMMIGRATION

- The world's population reached 5.8 billion in 1999.

- If the world's population continues to grow at the current rate, it will double in 45 years.

- The United States uses 352 million Btu's of energy per person per year. The comparable figure for India is 12.

- An estimated 500,000 females are missing from China's annual birth statistics.

- The United States receives about 800,000 immigrants and refugees each year.

OUTLINE

The World's Population
Measures of Population
   Growth
The Demographic Transition
Rising Expectations
Food and Hunger

The U.S. Population

Population Control
Family Planning
ZPG
Population Control in LDCs

Immigration and Its Consequences
Immigration to the United
   States: A Brief History
Recent Trends in Immigration
   to the United States
Urban Concentration
   of Immigrants
Undocumented Immigrants

Social Policy

I n many parts of the United States, and in other nations as well, changes in population because of alterations in rates of births or deaths or patterns of immigration lead to major social problems. In the United States there is a low rate of natural population increase but a high rate of immigration. Immigration thus accounts for much (but by no means all) of the overall growth of the U.S. population. It is often difficult to assimilate new immigrants into American society. The newcomers require special education and health care and other services that may strain already tight municipal budgets. Yet, were it not for immigration, nations like the United States would have growing labor shortages. Immigration also helps alleviate the effects of severe population pressure in other parts of the world. Indeed, in most nations the problem is not low rates of natural growth but high rates of reproduction and population increase.

The World's Population

Although humanity has flourished for more than 2 million years, the rapid and problematic rise in population that concerns us in this chapter is a feature of the last 300 years. The average population growth rate before 1650 is thought to have been about two-thousandths of a percent per year, and the world's population in that year is estimated to have been 500 million. Thereafter the rates and numbers leap: By 1900 the annual growth rate had reached fully half of 1 percent, and a billion people had been added to the world's population. Between 1900 and 1940 the rate rose to 1 percent; by 1960, to 2 percent. The numerical total reached 2.5 billion in 1950 and 5.8 billion in 1999. (See Figure 16–1.) If the world's population continues to grow at the current rate, it will double in a mere 45 years.

Measures of Population Growth

Before we discuss the significance of these figures, a few definitions are in order. A commonly used measure of population growth is the **crude birthrate,** or the number of births per 1,000 population. A crude birthrate of 20, for example,

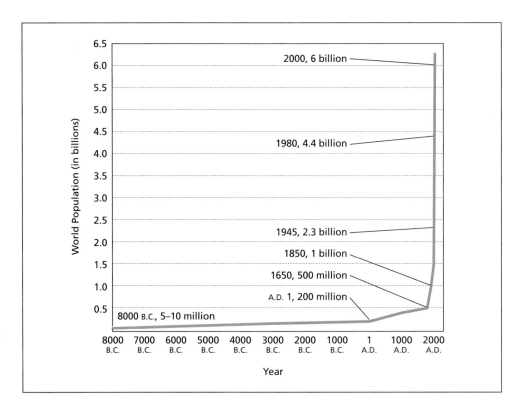

Figure 16–1 World Population Growth from 8000 B.C. to A.D. 2000

Source: Data from Office of Technology Assessment.

means that each year a given group of 1,000 people will produce 20 babies. This does not tell us what percentage of the population is of childbearing age or how many people can afford to raise children. It also does not tell us how long these 20 babies are likely to live—in particular, whether or not they will live long enough to produce children. Similarly, a crude death rate of 10 indicates only that among a group of 1,000 people 10 will die every year. Again, this figure tells us nothing about the distribution of deaths— whether they occurred among old people or among those of childbearing age.

The differential between the (crude) birthrate and the death rate is called the **rate of population growth (natural increase)** and is usually expressed as a percentage. (Population growth is also affected by migration to and from the particular unit, a factor that can be ignored for the purposes of this discussion.) In our hypothetical 1,000-person group, in which 20 people were added by birth and 10 removed by death, the total population at the end of the year is 1,010—a growth rate of 1 percent.

Taken as a whole, the peoples of the world are not reproducing at a higher rate than in the past, but more people are living to the age of fertility and beyond. In effect, more babies are surviving to produce babies themselves. This change is traceable to several causes: enormous advances in sanitation, disease control, and public health; our increased ability to compensate for excessive cold, heat, and other dangers to life in our environment; and our greater power to prevent or quickly counteract the effects of famine, drought, flood, and similar natural disasters.

Most nations have population growth rates of 0.1 percent to 3.0 percent, with the older, more industrialized nations grouped at the low end and the less developed nations at the high end. (See Table 16–1.) If a nation's population growth rate is negative, more people are lost through death than are gained through birth and immigration, and the

TABLE 16–1 Changes in Population, Selected Countries

Country	Rate of Natural Increase (Percentage)
China	1.0
South Korea	1.0
Japan	0.2
India	1.9
United States	0.6
United Kingdom	0.2
France	0.3
Nigeria	3.0
Argentina	1.1
Philippines	2.3
Peru	2.2
Kenya	2.0
Mexico	2.2
Sudan	2.1
Brazil	1.4

Source: Population Reference Bureau, 1998 World Population Data Sheet.

total population can be expected to decline over time. When a nation's population growth rate is 2 percent or more, as is true for many of the less developed nations, this is considered "explosive" population growth. If it were to continue unabated, such a rate would cause the population to double in 35 years or less. (A growth rate of 1 percent will cause a population to double in 70 years.) There is, however, evidence from some sub-Saharan nations of a decline in fertility because of greater availability of contraceptives and increased education of women (Caldwell et al., 1992).

For the less developed nations, growth rates of 1 percent are unlikely to occur in the near future. Growth in the developing regions of the world is expected to taper off in coming decades, but in these populations the momentum of growth caused by large numbers of young people who will be attaining childbearing age is expected to result in large numerical increases. Figure 16–2 shows that populations in the developing nations are expected to almost double, from about 4.19 billion today to 7.8 billion at midcentury. We will see shortly, however, that the experience of the industrialized nations indicates that fertility can be controlled even without large-scale use of contraception, and that in many of the wealthier nations of the world fertility rates have actually declined to levels below that required to replace the population (Davis et al., 1987).

Russia seems to be developing an unusual case of potential population decline. In 1990 2.2 children were born, on average, to each woman, but since then this figure has fallen to slightly more than 1.4. In addition, the declining economy and other social problems have led to a dramatic increase in the death rate. During the 1990s, deaths in Russia exceeded births by nearly 800,000 annually, making Russia the first industrial country to experience a sharp population decrease for reasons other than war, famine, or disease (Specter, 1994).

The Demographic Transition

Lower death rates are closely associated with the spread of technological change and higher living standards, which constitute part of a process known as the **demographic transition.** In this process, a population shifts from an original equilibrium in which a high birthrate is more or less canceled out by a high death rate, through a stage in which the birthrate remains high but the death rate declines, to a final equilibrium in which the birth and death rates are lower but the population is much larger. The first stage is characteristic of peasant and primitive populations before large-scale improvement in sanitation, health care, and the like. This is followed by a period of

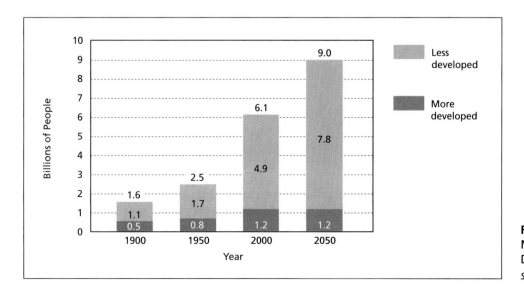

Figure 16–2 Population in More Developed and Less Developed Regions, 1900–2050

Source: Gelbard et al., 1999.

rapid population growth as traditional values about family size, together with the lack of birth control techniques, keep the birthrate high while technological advances produce a steady decrease in the death rate, especially of infants. In the final stage, which is characteristic of industrialized societies, values change, the birthrate declines, and rates of natural increase slow.

The demographic transition first occurred in northwestern Europe. During a period of about 100 years in the eighteenth and nineteenth centuries, death rates decreased by about 60 percent while birthrates remained at their traditional high levels. Then, toward the end of the nineteenth century, fertility began a long-term decline. Figure 16–3 illustrates this process in the case of Sweden.

Wherever industrial technology has taken hold on a local level, the third stage of the demographic transition has followed—from northwestern Europe to North America, Australia, and New Zealand and later through the rest of Europe. Today the populations of Japan, Singapore, Taiwan, Hong Kong, and two or three other such areas have reached the final phase, and they have tended to reach it much more quickly (in about 30 years) than the northern European nations did.

On the other hand, large areas of Asia, Africa, and Latin America remain in the middle phase, with sustained high birthrates and reduced death rates. In this century, and very dramatically since World War II, the amazingly effective adoption of Western methods in medicine and public health on a mass basis, usually involving international aid programs, has resulted in a rapid decline in mortality. Within a span of about 25 years, death rates fell from approximately 40 per 1,000 to 20 or less. But fertility remains high, often over 40 per 1,000, and the growth rate reaches 3 percent in some places. Adults live longer, and more of the young survive to have children; there are no new frontier lands to draw off excess population. In these societies population growth often outstrips economic and social development, producing poverty and social unrest.

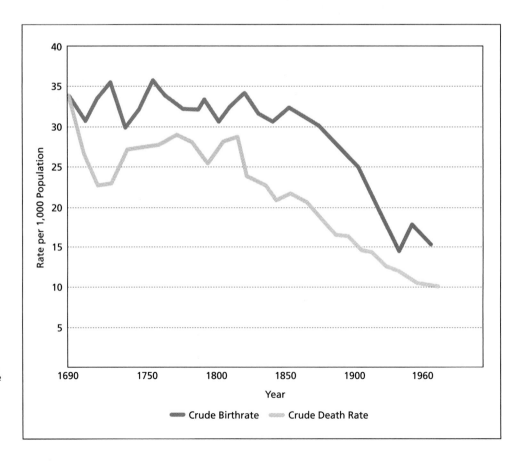

Figure 16–3 Crude Birth and Death Rates for Sweden, 1690–1960

Note: This chart exemplifies the classic demographic transition, in which death rates and birthrates eventually become more or less equal and the rate of population growth stabilizes. Many less developed nations have birth and death rates similar to those in the center of the chart, where crude death rates are declining and birthrates remain high—a formula for population explosion.

Source: Matras, 1973. Courtesy Armand Colin Éditeur, Paris.

SOCIAL PROBLEMS ONLINE

Population and the Internet

The Internet provides considerable data on population, migration, and other areas of interest to demographers. A useful starting point for research is the World Wide Web Virtual Library on demography and population studies, maintained by the Australian National University, **http://coombs.anu.edu.au/ResFacilities/DemographyPage.html.** The library has links to national government, academic, and national and international nongovernmental organizations, with home pages devoted to demography. A search might begin at the United Nations Population Fund **(http://www.unfpa.org/)** website, where the annual *State of World Population* reports are available. The United Nations Development Programme at **http://www.undp.org/** has links to statistical sources and other features, such as the "poverty clock" that records the increase in the world's poor population.

An online bibliographic resource is maintained by the Princeton University Office of Population Research. Browsable versions of its publication *Population Index* are available for issues since 1986 at **http://popindex.princeton.edu/.** A user-friendly search interface makes it easy to locate specific citations or to do free-text searches. The U.S. government provides data and reports about demographic trends in the United States on the Census Bureau web page **(http://www.census.gov/).**

The Population Council is one of the largest international nongovernmental organizations (NGOs) involved in research and advocacy about issues affecting the world's population. Its home page is located at **http://www.popcouncil.org/.** It contains recent publications and working papers, news releases, and links to development and population resources, as well as to other international NGOs.

Migration and the social problems associated with it are addressed by the European Research Centre on Migration and Ethnic Relations (ERCOMER) in the Netherlands. Centre publications, reports on conferences, and links to numerous other research and advocacy groups are available at the ERCOMER website at **http://www.ruu.nl/ercomer/index.html.**

Zero Population Growth disseminates its views at **http://www.zpg.org/.** For an opposing assessment of population trends and the threat of overpopulation, go to the United Nations International Conference on Population and Development's 1994 Cairo Conference home page **(http://www.mbnet.mb.ca/linkages/cairo.html).** Texts of official documents along with reports from several news services can be accessed there.

Several nations that are still in the middle phase of the demographic transition border the United States on the south. Among them are the countries of the Caribbean and Central America, Mexico, Haiti, the Dominican Republic, and Puerto Rico. Their inhabitants are subject both to the stresses of overpopulation and to the influence of American popular culture through television and mass consumer markets. Not only are these countries poor, but they are often ruled by violent and repressive regimes—all of which produces migration to the United States. Currently the United States admits about 800,000 immigrants annually, an increase from about 600,000 in the late 1980s and a direct result of the 1986 Immigration Reform and Control Act, which established higher immigration quotas. (The implications of this increase will be discussed later in the chapter.) The United States remains a land of opportunity for immigrants because of its slow rate of population growth. Here, except for the baby boom during and after World War II, births have outpaced deaths only to a modest degree.

The birthrate in the industrialized nations had begun to drop before the institution of organized family planning programs. The organized programs have certainly accelerated the process, however, especially in the United States: They have made information and contraceptives more widely available, led to the repeal of laws against the use of contraceptives, and influenced opinion in favor of birth control. Thus, in contrast to the 1800 figure of about 55, the crude birthrate in the United States stood at 16 in 1990. In the 1970s the total fertility rate (the average number of children born per woman throughout the childbearing years) fell below 2.1, the rate required to maintain the population at the same level. In 1800 the total fertility rate was 7.0, an extremely high rate that reflected the demand for farm labor and the high value placed on having many children (Davis, 1986b; Preston, 1987).

In his thorough analysis of low population growth rates in the non-European industrialized nations (Canada, United States, Japan, Australia, and New Zealand), demographer Samuel Preston (1987) concludes that "the recent fall in fertility is related to declining proportions married, increased use of contraception and abortion, and a reduction in family size desires" (p. 44). Of these factors, Preston identifies delay or indefinite postponement of marriage as the most important. He finds, for example, that fertility decreased in Japan well before the widespread use of contraception and well before the large-scale entry of women into the labor market. The critical factor was postponement of marriage—Japanese parents were requiring their grown children to delay marriage until they had accumulated the resources to support a child or two.

Rising Expectations

Not only do people in less developed and politically troubled countries look to the United States as a land of opportunity, and therefore attempt to migrate here to improve their situation, but in the less developed countries (LDCs) themselves there has been considerable improvement in the living standards of a portion of the population. This improvement has led to a state of mind known as rising expectations, the belief that if conditions have already begun to improve, the trend will continue and a larger portion of the population should be able to share in its benefits.

This process began in the late 1950s and early 1960s, when many LDCs, particularly in sub-Saharan Africa and Southeast Asia, gained independence from the former colonial powers (Geertz, 1963). Turning their attention to efforts to improve the lives of their generally isolated, rural populations, governments embarked on campaigns for favorable terms of trade and direct aid from the developed nations. Ever greater

In many rural parts of the world, a single communal television set contributes to the villagers' rising expectations for material well-being.

sums were invested in education, health care, transportation, and communication. These investments ultimately resulted in changing expectations among the populations of the LDCs as newly educated and healthier multitudes were exposed to the media and all the information about culture and standards of living that they convey (Martine, 1996).

It is important to distinguish between the **standard of living** of a population, which is what people want or expect in the way of material well-being, and the **level of living,** which is what people actually obtain. In many less developed countries and nations of the former Soviet bloc, there is a wide gap between the two, and this produces frustration and political instability. These problems make economic and social development in the poor regions of the world even more problematic.

Literacy rates are a good indicator of the likelihood that poor and powerless populations may be rapidly gaining a new perspective on their situation. Illiteracy has been decreasing steadily, from an estimated 32.5 percent of the total world population in 1970 to 28 percent in 1997 (United Nations Development Programme, 1997). These figures, of course, do not show the tremendous disparities in literacy that persist. For example, Cuba enjoys a 96 percent literacy rate and Chile's literacy rate is 93.4 percent, whereas the figure for Egypt is 48.4 percent, for India 52.1 percent, and for Pakistan 35.0 percent (*Brittanica Book of the Year,* 1995).

While literacy and the wide-ranging awareness that it fosters have increased, mushrooming populations have tended to more than absorb the sums devoted to their well-being, creating a significant lag in the fulfillment of their rising expectations. Per capita energy consumption is a good indication of the quality of life of a population, and by this measure stark disparities remain: The United States, by far the world's largest consumer of energy, uses about 352 million Btu's of energy per person per year, compared to France (166), Mexico (59), the United Kingdom (171), Colombia (33), and India (12) (*Statistical Abstract,* 1999). The extremely high U.S. rate reflects the nature of American industry, transportation, and housing. The typical middle-class, generally suburban American lifestyle presumes considerable use of gasoline, as well as the consumption of extremely large quantities of paper, steel, synthetic chemicals, aluminum, and so forth, all of which require high levels of energy for their production.

The fact is that the gaps in living standards between the have and have-not societies have actually widened. In such a situation, rising expectations are associated with a wide spectrum of social problems, including political instability and backwardness, neocolonialism, and terrorism, as well as renewed international migrations by the poor. This is especially true in the heavily indebted nations of Asia, Africa, and Latin America.

Food and Hunger

Almost three-quarters of a billion people are hungry in a world where there is plenty to eat. Every 3.6 seconds someone somewhere dies of hunger; and children account for 75 percent of these deaths (**www.thehungersite.com**; *Population Today,* 2000). The irony of this situation is that although there may not be much food in their villages or enough food to go around in a particular region, food is actually plentiful in the world today. The fundamental problem is the maldistribution of available food (United Nations Development Programme, 1997). In Western Europe and North America, the average person's diet supplies about 3,500 calories a day. In much of Africa south of the Sahara and in South Asia, average caloric intake is less than two-thirds of this total. (See Figure 16–4.) An adult working at heavy labor, as many agricultural workers in developing nations do, needs over 3,500 calories a day, but this total is relatively rare in those nations. Thirty-five countries, including almost half the nations of Africa, have food supplies that afford their populations an average of less

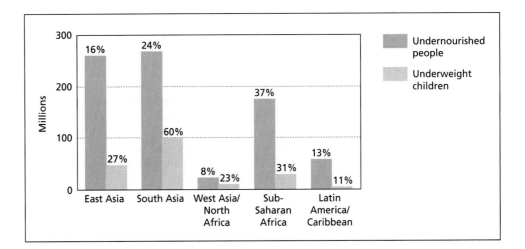

Figure 16–4 Undernourishment, Selected Regions

Source: Conway, 1997. United Nations Administrative Committee on Coordination, Committee on Nutrition, 1992.

than 2,200 calories a day. According to estimates by the Food and Agriculture Organization (1996), an affiliate of the United Nations, about 800 million people, almost 15 percent of the world population, eat less than 2,000 calories a day. This hungry population is chronically undernourished and experiences the lowered resistance to diseases that comes with semistarvation.

One of the paradoxes of world hunger is that food supplies have been increasing over the past 20 years while the cost of food has been decreasing. There are adequate supplies of food at relatively low prices, but the poorest segments of many populations in the developing nations cannot afford it. Their wages have fallen too low to enable them to buy available food, or at least the combinations of foods that would prevent malnutrition and related illnesses (Conway, 1997). Changes in the technologies of food production, some of which are extremely controversial (see Chapter 17), have been increasing world food production and promise to do so well into the future. As populations in the poorest nations continue to grow rapidly, it becomes especially difficult for these nations to feed their poor children, but often political violence, civil strife, and corruption, which divert food aid, are more responsible for malnutrition than absolute shortages. (This insight has only recently been supported by sound social-scientific data. See the Critical Research feature on page 461 for more details about the seminal work in this area by Nobel-prize-winning economist Amartya Sen, whose research on famines and food entitlement has established the connections between starvation and available food supplies.)

The U.S. Population

Current trends in the U.S. population may be summarized by three striking features: slow growth, population redistribution, and increasing immigration. In 1800 the country's crude birthrate may have been as high as 55, but it soon declined, reaching a low of 18 in the 1930s, before the post–World War II baby boom. After another low point in the 1970s, the birthrate began rising again. The total fertility rate reached 3.7 between 1955 and 1957 and fell to 1.8 in 1976, well below the 2.1 rate needed for the population to replace itself, assuming current death rates. Whereas fertility among whites alone was even lower than 1.8 during this period, the rate for ethnic and racial minority groups was 2.3 (U.S. Bureau of the Census, 1980). Present population growth is due mainly to immigration and to births to children of the baby boom generation. And as that generation continues to grow older, issues of security in retirement and old age will undoubtedly receive increasing attention (Roberts, 1995; U.S. Bureau of the Census, 1996).

CRITICAL RESEARCH

Starvation in the Midst of Plenty

Amartya Sen, 1998 Nobel prize-winner in economics, has conducted research that contributes to saving millions of lives in the impoverished regions of the world. Sen's research on the causes of famines in the world shows that nations which neglect the poor often do so in the midst of economic good times. This neglect may cause millions to die of malnutrition and even famine. Sen's most famous research is about the great famine which struck Bengal, India in 1943. His investigation into the causes of the famine shows that the catastrophe which claimed over a million lives was due to a sudden rise in food prices, fueled by a boom in the distant urban economy of the region which drove food prices up in the rural areas where the food was actually produced. Societies that attend to the poorest of the poor can save their lives, promote their longevity and increase their opportunities through education and productive work. Societies that neglect the poor, on the other hand, may inadvertently allow millions to die of famine—even in the middle of an economic boom, as occurred during the great famine in Bengal, India, in 1943, the subject of Sen's most famous case study. Sen demonstrated that the Bengal famine was caused by an urban economic boom that raised food prices, thereby causing millions of rural workers to starve to death when their wages did not keep up. And why didn't the government react by dispensing emergency food relief? Sen's answer was enlightening. Because colonial India was not a democracy, he said, the British rulers had little interest in listening to the poor, even in the midst of famine. This political observation gave rise to what might be called Sen's Law: shortfalls in food supply do not cause widespread deaths in a democracy because vote-seeking politicians will undertake relief efforts; but even modest food shortfalls can create deadly famines in authoritarian societies.

Sen has placed great emphasis on poor societies that have achieved high standards in health and education. Costa Rica, for example, which has an average annual income that is only about one-fourth the U.S. level, boasts a life expectancy of 76 years—almost identical to the U.S.'s. Reason: Costa Rica disbanded its army in 1949 and focused public spending on basic health and education. Brazil, by contrast, has almost the same average income as Costa Rica, but a life expectancy that

Amartya Sen, a scholar from India whose work has produced a new understanding of the catastrophes that plague people, won a Nobel Prize in economics in 1998.

is 10 years lower. Brazil has greater social inequalities, and much of the population lives in deep poverty.

Sen's observations have been taken to heart in the valuable Human Development Report issued annually by the United Nations Development Programme. That document features a Human Development Index that ranks countries by a combination of three factors: average income, educational attainment, and life expectancy. Thus, Costa Rica ranks 62nd from the top in average income but much better, at 39th, in the Human Development Index. These rankings convey Sen's powerful message: Annual income growth is not enough to achieve development. Societies must pay attention to social goals as well, always leaning toward their most vulnerable citizens, and overcoming deep-rooted biases to invest in the health and well-being of girls as well as boys. In a world in which 1.5 billion people subsist on less than $1 a day, this Nobel Prize can be not just a celebration of a wonderful scholar but also a clarion call to attend to the urgent needs and hopes of the world's poor.

Source: Sachs, 1998, p. 61. © 1998 Time Inc. Reprinted by permission.

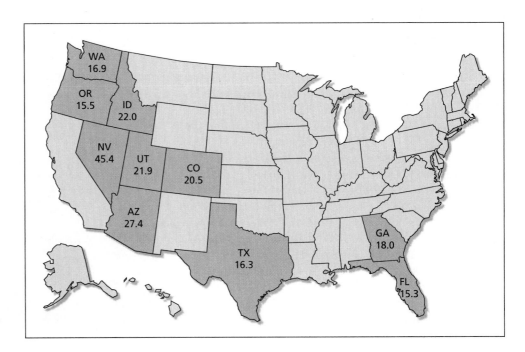

Figure 16–5 Ten Fastest-Growing States, Percent Population Change, 1990–1998

Source: Statistical Abstract, 1999.

Slow population growth means that people's hopes can still be high, and many migrate in search of new opportunities. Recent decades have seen increased migration to the Sunbelt and western states. In 1950, for example, 26 percent of the population lived in the Northeast and 13 percent lived in the West. By 1990 these percentages had shifted to 20 and 21 percent, respectively. Figure 16–5 shows that, with the exception of Georgia and Florida, the ten fastest-growing states are still located in the Southwest and West. California is no longer growing at the boom rates it experienced in the 1960s and 1970s, but Nevada has taken up much of the slack. Note that the Pacific Northwest, with its rapidly growing technology industries, is experiencing quite rapid growth even though it is not technically in the Sunbelt.

Another significant change in the U.S. population in recent years is the increase in age and income disparities between old and new ethnic groups. The median incomes of Russian, Polish, and Italian Americans are among the highest in the nation, whereas those of Spanish-speaking groups, especially Puerto Ricans, are the lowest. Conversely, the proportion of people under 18 years of age is lowest among the old ethnic groups, whereas the Spanish-speaking groups include the highest proportion. What this means is that the fastest-growing ethnic minorities in the United States are also among the poorest segments of the population.

Finally, slow growth has been a factor in the dramatic persistence of immigration to the United States, and differences in fertility between old and new ethnic groups have a significant impact on the composition of the population. Immigration also raises a number of complex policy issues, as will become clear later in the chapter.

Population Control

Efforts to control population growth can take any of three basic approaches: (1) Reduce the rate of growth of the population, (2) control fertility to achieve a zero rate of population growth, or (3) achieve a negative rate of growth and thus reduce the size of the population. Obviously, all three of these approaches involve reduction of the birthrate. However, even when it is agreed that births should be limited, there is much less agreement on how fast and to what extent limits should be imposed—indeed, on whether or not they should be imposed at all (i.e., whether limits on family size should be voluntary or involuntary). Efforts to limit births raise a number of moral and ethical questions, but the costs of not making such efforts could be catastrophic.

Family Planning

Voluntary efforts to limit births customarily take the form of family planning. Essentially, a family planning program allows couples to have the number of children they want. Although this policy usually entails helping couples limit childbearing, it can also involve helping couples who want children and have been unable to have them. The stress is usually placed on the good of the family—especially the health of the mother and children and the ability to provide education and other desired advantages.

In the United States, the family planning movement owes much to the energy and dedication of a nurse named Margaret Sanger, who hoped to free women from the burdens of unlimited childbearing. In 1916 she opened the nation's first birth control clinic (and was jailed for doing so). Later court decisions permitted physicians to prescribe birth control for health reasons; these were the first in a series of decisions that permitted the sale and advertisement of contraceptive materials and the dissemination of information about birth control. By 1965 some 85 percent of married women in the United States had used some method of birth control (Ehrlich et al., 1977).

ZPG

In 1968, in response to widespread concern about population growth, an organization known as Zero Population Growth, Inc. (ZPG) was founded. Its goal was to promote an end to population growth as soon as possible through lowered birthrates, both in the United States and in other nations. It would achieve this goal by educating the public about the dangers of uncontrolled population growth and by taking political action to encourage policies that reduce growth rates.

The organization has been active in promoting access to birth control and legalized abortion, and it has had a definite effect on attitudes toward family size and population control. However, ZPG has encountered some opposition on social and economic grounds. It is argued, for example, that halting population growth would greatly change the age composition of the population, creating a larger proportion of older people and thereby adding to the problems of an already overburdened society. Moreover, a nongrowing population implies a nongrowing economy, and it is often assumed that a continually growing economy is necessary for the maintenance of a high standard of living.

It should be noted that family planning and population control are not synonymous. Family planning has historically dealt with the needs of individuals and families, not those of societies. Kingsley Davis (1971) has pointed out some fundamental weaknesses of the family planning approach as a means of large-scale population control. Chief among them is its basic assumption that the number of children couples want is the number they should have. In a poor country with a growth rate of 3 percent per year, a family of five or six children, which is probably desired by most couples, will be anything but desirable for the economic health of the country—or for the family's own chances of economic betterment. In addition, the strongly medical emphasis of the usual family planning program can limit its large-scale effectiveness, particularly in developing countries, where doctors and nurses are usually scarce (Smil, 1997).

Population Control in LDCs

In less developed countries, efforts at population control have, in a few rare but instructive cases, used compulsory methods of birth control. One such method is sterilization of parents who have had a specified number of children. India adopted such a plan in 1976, with financial incentives to encourage volunteers and, in some states, fines and other penalties for births after the third child. In one year more than 8 million sterilizations were performed. As might be expected, this program met with great resistance. Although no one disputed the need to curb the rate of population growth, the Indian government was severely criticized for what was considered a compulsory, rather than a strictly voluntary, policy; in fact, the policy contributed to the defeat of the government of Indira Gandhi.

China's population program differs in some important ways from that of any other country. China, whose population is now more than 1 billion, has adopted a policy of one child per family for urban dwellers; the goal is a 40 percent reduction in population size by 2050. Couples are strongly urged not to have more than one child unless both parents were only children themselves, and birth control information and materials are readily available. At the same time, the bearing and rearing of children are supported through such policies as paid maternity leave, time off for breast-feeding, free nursery care, and all needed medical attention (Li, 1995).

This far-reaching policy has already slowed China's population growth significantly, but not without enormous social consequences. Political unrest has increased in the cities, where the policy is far more easily implemented than in the countryside. Far worse, recent studies of the policy's effects indicate that couples are seeking ways to determine the gender of unborn infants so that they can abort female fetuses. The traditional culture of China favors boys over girls to such a degree that many couples believe that they must have a male child at all costs. Although no one knows exactly how many female infants are aborted or killed, and some Chinese authorities dispute Western analyses of the situation, the fact remains that the excess of recorded live male births over female births is far greater in China than in any other society. This suggests that various forms of abortion, infanticide, and secret adoptions are occur-

ring. Demographers who have studied the situation closely believe that about half of the estimated 500,000 females missing from the annual birth statistics may have been secretly adopted by foreigners through illicit adoption agencies, but no one knows the fate of the others. Clearly, these are serious, even if unintended, consequences of China's drastic population reduction policy (Johannson & Nygren, 1991).

Nothing as drastic as China's population control policy has ever been attempted before (except in cases of war or genocide), and only a nation with a very authoritarian and highly controlled population can successfully implement such a policy. Thus, for the time being, voluntary birth control seems to be a more realistic—and more desirable—approach in LDCs. Indeed, family planning programs are the primary form of population control in most of these countries, sometimes supplemented by other social and economic policies. The main thrust of these programs is the provision of birth control information along with educational programs that demonstrate the economic benefits of smaller

Many Asian nations have entered the low-growth phase of the demographic transition. In China, however, strict measures designed to discourage couples from having more than one child are highly controversial.

families. Many programs are directed toward women who have already borne three or more children.

Fertility control in Brazil stands in marked contrast to China's experience (Martine, 1996). As shown in Table 16–2, Brazil's population growth, as measured by the fertility rate, was extremely high in the 1960s but has fallen precipitously in recent years and is now similiar to the slower growth rates of the European industrial nations. This decrease in fertility is not solely a consequence of economic development and greater affluence. Northeast Brazil is by far the poorest region of the nation, yet even here there have been dramatic decreases. Experts on the demography of Brazil concur that there is no single explanation for these momentous changes.

Brazil has no government fertility control policy like that of China, nor does it have a national policy for making contraception widely available. Studies show that the contraceptive choices made by people in Brazil are similar to those made by people in the United States, but with some important exceptions. Women bear most of the responsibility for contraception and tend to rely on birth control pills or, once they have had the desired number of children, on sterilization. An extremely small proportion of couples report that they rely on condoms. Abortion is not legal, except in cases of rape or risk to the mother's life, and is not reported in official statistics, but research in urban areas has found high rates of illegal abortions. Most important, however, is the desire to limit births. Where does this desire originate? In Brazil, as elsewhere, people's aspirations for a lifestyle in which they can afford consumer goods and raise fewer children with a decent level of education, health care, and material comfort seem to be a major factor. Contributing to these aspirations are the increased education of women and the influence of the mass media, especially television (Martine, 1996).

In the 1960s and 1970s it appeared that nations like Brazil were doomed to experience a population explosion, leading to drastic overpopulation. These recent changes and the research that explains their causes highlight some of the ways in which population growth may be controlled in other areas of the world, without the kinds of drastic and authoritarian measures that have been undertaken in China.

TABLE 16–2 Total Fertility Rate, Brazil and Northeast Region of Brazil, 1960–1995

Years	Brazil	Northeast
1960–65	6.00	7.44
1965–70	5.75	7.11
1970–75	4.97	6.77
1975–80	4.17	5.97
1980–85	3.37	4.76
1985–90	2.82	3.97
1990–95	2.48	3.50

Source: Martine, 1996.

Immigration and Its Consequences

Throughout the world people in poor nations dream of moving to richer ones. Most often they do not wish to uproot themselves entirely but hope to be temporary sojourners, working at the better-paying jobs that are said to be available there. If they can save and send money home, they may someday be able to return to a better life in their homeland.

Immigration to the United States has reached levels unmatched since early in this century. But the movement of people from poor to richer lands is occurring elsewhere as well. There has been an influx of people into Germany and France from poorer areas to the south, especially Turkey and northern Africa. In the Middle East there has been a great movement of temporary workers from Egypt to the richer and underpopulated nations of Saudi Arabia and Kuwait. Before the 1991 war in that region, many of the immigrant workers were Palestinians or Yemenites. In Japan there are Korean immigrants, and in Australia there are immigrants from many Asian nations. But the United States leads the world in total number of immigrants.

In fact, it is often said that the United States is a nation of immigrants. Since the earliest days of European settlement, North America has attracted people from all over the world. Some, like the black slaves from Africa, were brought against their will. Many other groups came in search of new opportunities and freedom from oppression. Over two centuries the tides of immigration brought people of different races, different religions, different cultures, and different political views to these shores. This diversity of peoples has become one of the most important aspects of American culture. Tolerance of differences, struggles against racial oppression, arguments about the assimilation of immigrants, the variety of diet and dress and music— all can be traced to the unique contributions of people of many different national origins and cultures.

But immigration has also contributed to some of the problems that plague American society. Beginning with the exclusion of Native Americans from their original lands, immigration has led to ethnic and racial conflict; competition among nationality groups for a piece of the pie; debates about immigration policy, illegal immigration, and the exploitation of illegal aliens; and the stresses and costs associated with educating and caring for newcomers. These and other issues can become severe social problems when they are not addressed in a timely fashion. To better understand why this is so, we will begin with a summary of the major periods of immigration to the United States.

Immigration to the United States: A Brief History

The Early Colonial Period (to 1790).   During the colonial period, the major population groups in North America other than Native Americans had come from Great Britain and accounted for 77 percent of the total population. African and native-born slaves of African origin accounted for 19 percent, German immigrants for 4 percent, Irish immigrants for 3 percent, and Dutch immigrants for 2 percent (Bogue, 1985). There were many other immigrant groups in the population, but their numbers were much smaller.

Old Northwest European Migration, 1820–1885.   Large-scale immigration to the new nation known as the United States began again in 1820 and was dominated by people from England and other areas of northwestern Europe until about 1885. In this wave of immigrants, the largest groups came from northern and western Europe, especially Germany, Ireland, and England. The proportion of immigrants from Ireland reached high levels in the 1840s and 1850s as a result of severe famine and economic catastrophe in Ireland. German immigration reached a peak in the years after 1848, when popular revolutions in Germany failed and many Germans sought asylum or greater political freedom in the United States.

The most significant nonwhite immigrant group during this period was the Chinese, many of whom settled on the West Coast or in the Rocky Mountain states, along with a smaller number of Japanese. Many of the Chinese immigrants were brought in by labor contractors who were seeking low-wage workers for the construction of railroads.

The Intermediate Migration from Southern and Eastern Europe (1885–1940).
Because of the breakup of the Austro-Hungarian and Ottoman empires and the resulting political upheavals, many thousands of people from southern and eastern Europe found their way to the United States. The major immigrant groups during this period were Italians, Poles, Hungarians, Serbians, Croatians, Greeks, and Jews from all of these nations and from Russia. During this period waves of nativist feeling (anti-immigrant or antiforeigner sentiment) swept across sections of the United States. Among other things, nativism gave rise to the oriental exclusion movement, which flourished between 1882 and 1907 and resulted in sporadic violence against Chinese and Japanese Americans and the passage of legislation in some states that stopped further immigration of Asians.

At the same time, large numbers of Mexican immigrants began streaming into the Southwest, the West, and portions of the Midwest. These immigrants often joined

The upper photo, taken about 1900, shows immigrants waiting to leave Ellis Island after many hours of screening and processing. In an effort to modernize its procedures, the U.S. Immigration and Naturalization Service is testing a new system in which processing takes place before arrival in the United States, and each new immigrant is issued a pass that resembles a credit card.

relatives and friends in parts of California and the Southwest, where Mexicans had been living long before these regions became part of the United States.

During this period Congress passed the Immigration Act of 1921, which for the first time in American history established quotas and strict controls over the admission of new immigrants, imposing an overall quota of 150,000 per year. Before 1921 there had been no specific limits on immigration to the United States, and well over 20 million immigrants had arrived since the early nineteenth century.

The Post–World War II Refugee Period (to 1968). By the end of World War II, hundreds of thousands of Europeans had lost their homes and property and many were refugees. Some, like Jews and Roman Catholic activists, were fleeing religious persecution. In 1945 Congress agreed to admit 185,000 immigrants per year, many of whom would be European refugees.

The New Immigration (1968–Present). In 1968 Congress again voted to increase immigration quotas, establishing totals of 170,000 per year from the Eastern Hemisphere and 120,000 from the Western Hemisphere. Priority would be given to immigrants who were political or religious refugees or who had close relatives living in the United States. (This is known as the principle of family unification.) In 1980 Congress increased the overall quota to 280,000 per year, not including additional refugees and special categories that might be designated in the future (e.g., the *marielitos*, former political prisoners from Cuba). The increases in immigration quotas in recent decades have given rise to a new pattern of immigration to the United States, with the largest flows of people coming from Asia and Latin America.

Recent Trends in Immigration to the United States

Figure 16–6 shows that since the 1970s the rate of legal immigration to the United States has accelerated. The major cause of this trend has been the gradual liberalization of immigration laws, which have set increasingly larger annual quotas. From an annual total of slightly under 400,000 in 1970, the United States is now receiving about 800,000 immigrants and refugees each year (Massey, 1995).

Between 1971 and 1993, approximately 9.3 million new immigrants arrived in the United States. Of these, the largest share came from the Americas (Mexico, Canada, the Caribbean, and Latin America). Asia—especially the Philippines, Korea, and China—contributed the next largest share, and Europe, which accounted for the bulk of earlier immigration to the United States, was a distant third. (See Figure 16–7.)

Neither the increase in immigration nor the specific composition of the immigrant population is a social problem in itself. But there are groups in American society that oppose immigration and are hostile toward immigrants, and the resulting conflicts and tensions can be a problem for immigrants and for the regions or cities that receive

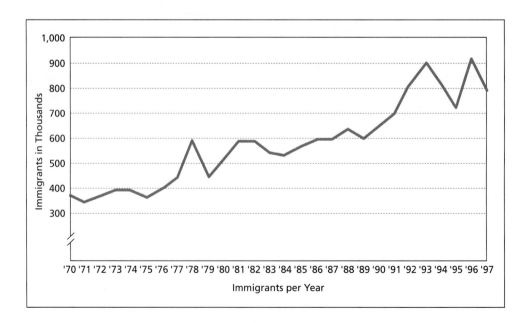

Figure 16–6 Legal Immigration to the United States, 1980–1997

Beginning in 1992, totals include persons who were granted permanent residence under the legalization program of the Immigration Reform and Control Act of 1986.

Source: Data from *Statistical Abstract,* 1999.

them. Since new immigrants tend to settle near other immigrants, these tensions can run especially high in regions with large immigrant populations. Also, not all immigrants enter legally. The presence of illegal aliens, or undocumented immigrants, is one of the most severe social problems associated with immigration. In the remainder of this section, therefore, we will consider the social problems caused by the uneven distribution of immigrants in the United States and the special problems of undocumented immigrants.

Urban Concentration of Immigrants

The vast majority of the immigrants who arrive in the United States tend to remain in only a few cities and regions. New York, Los Angeles, Miami, Chicago, and their metropolitan regions are the preferred destinations of almost half of the nation's immigrants. Mexicans tend to congregate in the Southwest and Vietnamese in Texas, but the major urban centers of the West and East Coasts absorb far more than their proportional share of new immigrants.

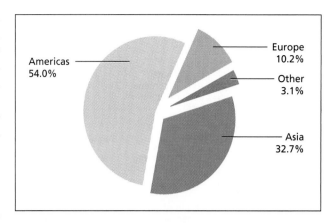

Figure 16–7 Sources of Immigration to the United States (percent of total), 1971–1993

Source: Massey, 1995. Used with the permission of the Population Council.

The concentration of new immigrants in a few metropolitan regions greatly adds to the problems of both immigrants and nonimmigrants in those areas. This concentration, especially of Spanish- and Chinese-speaking newcomers, leads to the formation of large non-English-speaking enclaves, where education becomes a problem and the economic and social assimilation of the newcomers may create difficulties for native-born citizens. Increasingly frequent attacks against immigrants and members of minority groups and the rise of nativist and anti-immigrant feelings in many parts of the United States are another consequence of the concentration of immigrants in certain localities (Brimelow, 1995).

The phenomenon of **chain migration,** the primary cause of this urban concentration, refers to the tendency of immigrants to migrate to areas where they have kin and others from their home communities. Although there may be opportunities for them in nearby cities and towns, they often remain in the place of original settlement because of the presence of people who share their culture and language and can help them adjust to their new social environment. Figure 16–8 shows the wide differences in sources of immigrants to various regions of the United States. New Jersey, for example, receives its highest numbers of immigrants from Italy and Cuba, whereas California receives most of its immigrants from Mexico and the Philippines.

The uneven distribution of immigrants greatly adds to the costs of education and health care in the cities in which they become concentrated. Since many immigrants arrive without any form of health insurance and do not speak English well enough to qualify for employment, schools and adult education programs are taxed to the maximum. These expenses of the cities are not usually compensated for by the federal government, even though the entry of immigrants is regulated by federal legislation.

A problem that affects the immigrants in these urban centers is the intense competition and, at times, direct hostility they encounter from nonimmigrants or immigrants who have lived there for long periods. For example, Koreans tend to establish businesses (especially wig stores, fruit and vegetable stores, and other retail businesses) in segregated minority communities, where costs are lower. They thus become a new ethnic and racial group in those communities. Often they encounter anger and hostility from residents who believe that the Koreans are not sensitive to their needs and their local culture (Kim, 1981). This is a theme explored by the African-American filmmaker Spike Lee in his movie *Do the Right Thing.* Elsewhere in the nation—along the Gulf coast of Texas, where Vietnamese shrimp fishermen have

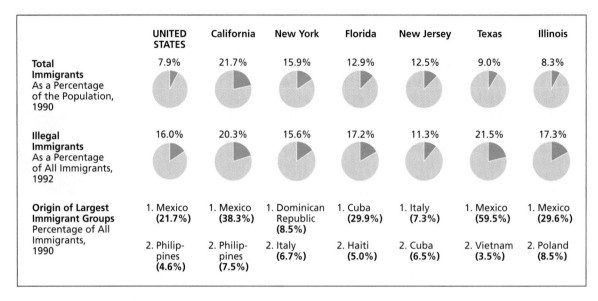

	UNITED STATES	California	New York	Florida	New Jersey	Texas	Illinois
Total Immigrants As a Percentage of the Population, 1990	7.9%	21.7%	15.9%	12.9%	12.5%	9.0%	8.3%
Illegal Immigrants As a Percentage of All Immigrants, 1992	16.0%	20.3%	15.6%	17.2%	11.3%	21.5%	17.3%
Origin of Largest Immigrant Groups Percentage of All Immigrants, 1990	1. Mexico (21.7%)	1. Mexico (38.3%)	1. Dominican Republic (8.5%)	1. Cuba (29.9%)	1. Italy (7.3%)	1. Mexico (59.5%)	1. Mexico (29.6%)
	2. Philippines (4.6%)	2. Philippines (7.5%)	2. Italy (6.7%)	2. Haiti (5.0%)	2. Cuba (6.5%)	2. Vietnam (3.5%)	2. Poland (8.5%)

Figure 16–8 National Origin and Legal Status of Immigrants to Six States in the United States

Source: Dugger, 1997. Copyright © 1995 by the New York Times Co. Reprinted by permission. Data from "Keys to Successful Immigration," edited by Thomas J. Espenshade and published by the Urban Institute Press.

come into conflict with native-born fishermen, or in the Southwest, where Mexican immigrants are often discriminated against by earlier settlers—the difficulties of life as a stranger in a strange land are amplified by prejudice and violence.

In response to the hostility they often encounter, children and adolescents in the new groups often form defensive gangs. Those who do not wish to join gangs may be considered deviant and isolated by their peers. But some immigrant groups, notably the Chinese and Koreans, attempt to shelter their children from the problems of urban street life by imposing a strict set of values and high expectations for achievement in school (Caplan et al., 1989). Children of Asian immigrants make rapid strides in American schools, often achieving the highest honors in their high schools and on standardized achievement tests. Indeed, the school achievement of Asian Americans is now so high that many of the brightest Asian students have come to believe that they are subject to admission quotas in private universities, an experience exactly analogous to that of high-achieving children of Jewish immigrants two generations ago (Cowan & Cowan, 1989).

Undocumented Immigrants

Figure 16–8 presents some estimates of the proportion of illegal immigrants in selected regions of the United States. Clearly, there are important differences: States like New Jersey rank low in illegal immigration, and border states like California and Texas receive high proportions of illegal entrants. These estimates are based on the best available data, but no one knows with great accuracy how many undocumented immigrants actually arrive. Every year the U.S. Immigration and Naturalization Service (INS) locates more than 1.2 million illegal immigrants, many of whom are deported. The INS estimates that there are approximately 2.7 million illegal immigrants now residing in the United States. By far the largest percentage are people from Mexico and Central America who have illegally crossed the border between Mexico and the United States, but recent alien arrest statistics suggest that the number of illegal Asian and European immigrants is also increasing. The shocking case of the *Golden Venture*, the ship carrying smuggled Chinese immigrants that ran aground in rough seas off Long Island, brought the black market in illegal immigrant workers to national attention in 1993. (This incident is portrayed in the photo at the beginning of the chapter.)

Authorities in New York City estimate that there are as many as 30,000 undocumented immigrants there, a situation that poses some unique problems (Lorch, 1991). Undocumented immigrants are easily exploited by ruthless individuals who know that these immigrants cannot readily go to the authorities when they have been victimized. But illegal aliens from China have an especially difficult time. To be transported the great distance from China to the United States and to be smuggled into the New York area, many promise to pay as much as $50,000 to professional smuggling rings. Once in New York they often have no means of repaying this debt, and because they cannot qualify for regular work or any social benefits, they are at the mercy of the people who brought them into the city. The smugglers often insist that the immigrants work at illegal activities, such as collecting gambling debts, or that they work in local restaurants at extremely low wages. If they attempt to leave in search of better opportunities elsewhere, they may be killed. In essence, this practice has created a new form of slavery.

Nor is the situation much easier for illegal immigrants from Mexico and Central America. Often they pay large sums to smugglers, known as coyotes, who attempt to direct them across the border. Very often they are captured and lose both their chance to work in the United States and the hard-earned funds they gave to the smugglers. If they do gain entry into California or Texas and manage to find work, their status is quite precarious since employers must report them if they are discovered not to have proper documents. Thus, employers who continue to hire them or disregard the evident forgery of their documents also tend to exploit them by paying pitifully low wages and expecting inordinate amounts of work.

It is not clear exactly what effect illegal residents have on the U.S. economy. They may take some jobs away from native-born residents, but they also perform functions that citizens are reluctant to do—"dirty work" or stoop labor on row crops, for example—and they help maintain some industries by accepting lower wages and inferior working conditions. This may hold back progress on wages and working conditions for others, but the survival of such industries stimulates growth in associated services, actually creating more jobs. Indeed, it appears that migrants—who can generally be laid off or discharged more easily than citizens—play a vital, if equivocal, role in many advanced nations, cushioning the native-born population from economic uncertainty (Piore, 1979). And when an increasing proportion of adults are retired—as an estimated 20 percent of U.S. adults will be in 2035—the taxes paid by employed legal immigrants become extremely important (Rothstein, 1993).

In a study of rural Mexican communities that typically send many immigrants, legal and illegal, to the southwestern United States, Wayne A. Cornelius (1989) found that people there are knowledgeable about changes in U.S. immigration laws and how they affect their chances of finding work and of being apprehended by the authorities. In his extensive interviews, Cornelius found no evidence that immigrants or likely immigrants were changing their behavior, despite the knowledge that it has become more difficult to gain entry to the United States. He did find that more people were planning to become documented temporary farm workers, but he found no decrease in the number who intended to try to immigrate illegally. He also found that more

Increased immigration results in the creation of new ethnic communities in the cities where immigrants arrrive in large numbers. Shown here is "Little Hong Kong" in Flushing, New York, a point of entry for many immigrants from the Far East.

women intended to try to enter the United States, a fact that is confirmed in the statistics of immigration authorities, which show a steady increase in the number of undocumented Mexican women who attempt to cross the border.

SOCIAL POLICY

On the world stage, population policies are often hammered out at world congresses such as the historic International Conference on Population and Development, held in Cairo in 1994 (McIntosh & Finkle, 1995). Individual nations are, of course, free to pursue their own population policies, as we have seen in China, but nations like the United States and England, agencies of the United Nations, and international development agencies like the World Bank all send delegates to world congresses in an effort to develop a broader policy consensus. Increasingly, therefore, these conferences are marked by lively debates about the sensitive issues of population growth and its control.

The 1994 Cairo conference was unusual for the role played by women in its deliberations. Although there was not always a consensus among the women delegates themselves on family planning issues, there was wide agreement that empowering women through increased literacy, grassroots economic development, and political rights would have a profound impact on population trends. The more women can control their fertility, the conference decided, the more they will be able to make choices that benefit themselves and their children, including limiting the number of children they choose to bear.

The United States and other major participants in these conferences take such recommendations quite seriously. Although they continue to promote contraception and family planning, the new policies of local development and female empowerment are also shaping the actions of aid agencies throughout the world.

In the United States, population-related policies focus mainly on immigration, particularly illegal immigration. Under current immigration laws it is a felony to transport or harbor an illegal immigrant. Until recently it was not against the law to employ such a person. This situation changed in 1986, when Congress passed the Immigration Reform and Control Act. Under the new law, employers are subject to civil penalties that range from $250 to $10,000 for each illegal alien they hire. Concerning people who are already living in the United States illegally, it is generally agreed that mass deportation is not feasible. Thus, the 1986 law offered legal status to illegal aliens who entered the United States before January 1, 1982, and have lived here continuously ever since. These undocumented aliens may qualify for permanent status (a green card), which in turn allows them to begin applying for U.S. citizenship and also allows them to freely leave and reenter the country.

The Immigration Reform and Control Act sought to stem the flow of illegal immigrants from Mexico and elsewhere through a number of reforms in existing laws. The bill included the employer sanctions just noted. It also sought to discourage illegal immigration by measures that would reduce the chances of finding work in the United States. In particular, it offered legal status to immigrants who claimed three months of prior agricultural work, thereby increasing the supply of legal labor for the big farms of southern California and decreasing the need for more casual, often illegal labor.

Although the political climate in which immigration issues are discussed is often troubled with doubts and conflict, with lower-income groups often opposed to

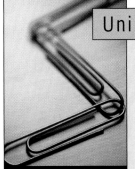

Unintended Consequences

Making Family Unification More Difficult

In 1996 Congress failed to win adequate support, even from some conservative members, for placing strict lower quotas on legal immigration to the United States. But in a less publicized piece of legislation, Congress imposed income requirements on sponsors of new immigrants that could make it far more difficult for poor immigrants already in the country to help members of their families immigrate under the terms of family unification.

Under the new law, the sponsor of an immigrant or an immigrant family must show that she or he is earning at least 125 percent of the poverty level ($20,500 for a family of four). Under the old law, there was no such requirement. The law's proponents argue that the measure will cut down on the number of new immigrants who apply for welfare benefits. But research by the Urban Institute on a random sample of immigrants shows that 40 percent did not earn enough in the previous year to sponsor an immigrant family member, compared to 26 percent of native-born Americans—who might also be of immigrant stock (Dugger, 1997).

Another clause in the new law permits immigrants to sue their sponsor for support until they either obtain U.S. citizenship or have worked and paid taxes for ten years. Again, the law's intent is to prevent immigrants from applying for welfare, but it also forces individuals to choose between attempting to unite their families and facing unknown future consequences. Some immigration experts believe that the law will actually encourage illegal immigration, on one hand, and, on the other hand, discourage family unification for many legal immigrants and naturalized U.S. citizens, who previously would have been able to arrange for their parents and children to join them. And as the federal government and many states begin to crack down on illegal immigrants and bar legal immigrants from certain forms of welfare eligibility, another consequence of the new anti-immigrant attitude is increased political mobilization of immigrants, who are becoming U.S. citizens in record numbers.

increased immigration, the extent to which immigration cuts across racial, ethnic, and class lines results in broad-based popular support for proimmigration policy. The principle of family unification—long a basic element of immigration policy—also explains why immigration legislation has public support. So many people are directly affected or have friends who are affected by efforts to unite families separated by immigration that opposition to the abstract idea of population growth is blunted by human concerns. But as shown in the Unintended Consequences feature above, new changes in immigration laws promise to make family reunification far more difficult for immigrants who are poor. Indeed, alterations in the U.S. welfare laws, as well as seemingly minor ones in the immigration laws, are creating enormous changes and some chaos among immigrant populations in the United States.

Welfare reform has hit legal immigrants especially hard. Laws passed by Congress in 1996 deny welfare benefits (including Medicaid and food stamps) to legal immigrants who are not citizens, many of whom are too old to work and rely on minimal welfare and health benefits. And to make matters more difficult for some immigrant families, new regulations announced by the federal government require immigrants to recite the citizenship oath even if they are disabled by Alzheimer's disease, severe mental retardation, or other mental disabilities. These regulations are being challenged in the courts, but they are in effect in some states.

Social-scientific evidence will play an important part in the debates about immigration policies. Recent research by sociologist Thomas J. Espenshade (1997) of Princeton and the Urban Institute, for example, shows that immigrants have made an extremely important contribution to New Jersey's economy. Although state taxpayers spend an average of $250 per year to defray the costs of education and health care for immigrants, the benefits to the state from immigrants' work, taxes, investments, and housing renewal far outweigh these costs. In California, where there are many poorer immigrants, the balance is not so favorable, but even the poorest immigrants contribute to the regional economy—often, unfortunately, as exploited, off-the-books domestics and workers in sweatshops. Clearly, the combination of new and more restrictive immigration laws and welfare reforms designed to reduce benefits to legal and illegal immigrants will have far-reaching effects.

Beyond Left & Right

There are no clear left and right viewpoints on immigration, but there are some people with strong views on the issues involved. Those on the right may be of the opinion that the United States is threatened by hordes of newcomers, some of whom will become burdens on the welfare rolls. But many other people with conservative views argue that immigrants are needed to provide low-wage workers, to compete with workers in other regions of the world, to do the work that people born here don't want to do. On the left there are also divisions. Some liberals argue that immigrants add new vitality to the society and its culture and that they are living reminders of the traditions of American democracy. But others on the left side of the political spectrum may voice concern about the possibility that immigrants drive down wages for native-born workers and compete with poor Americans for entry-level jobs, especially as welfare reform pushes more poor people into the job market.

Clearly, there are subdivisions within the major ideological divisions. In deciding where you stand, these disputes will help you realize that there are no easy solutions. But since immigrants are encouraged in a variety of ways to work in the United States and to strive to become U.S. citizens, it is reasonable to argue that people who are already citizens have some responsibilty for helping the newcomers achieve a better life, regardless of one's political ideology.

SUMMARY

- A common measure of population growth is the crude birthrate, or the number of births per 1,000 population. The differential between the crude birthrate and the death rate is the rate of population growth, or natural increase. Today more people are living to childbearing age, so that the world's population is growing faster than in the past and putting increased pressure on resources and the environment.

- The demographic transition is a process that consists of three stages: (a) a high birthrate canceled out by a high death rate, (b) a high birthrate coupled with a declining death rate, and (c) low birth and death rates. The process began in northern Europe in the eighteenth century and has occurred in all areas where industrial technology has taken hold on a local level. Today large areas of Asia, Africa, and Latin America remain in the middle phase of the demographic transition.

- An unintended effect of population growth, coupled with awareness of higher living standards, is the revolution of rising expectations, in which people develop higher expectations for their own future and that of their children. Literacy rates serve as an indicator of rising expectations. Although literacy rates have increased in many countries, the gaps in living standards between rich and poor societies have widened. Hunger and malnutrition are persistent problems in the less developed regions of the world.

- The main trends in the U.S. population are slow growth, population redistribution, and increasing immigration. Among the effects of these trends are the disproportionate representation of minority groups in the older central cities and increased age and income disparities between old and new ethnic groups.

- The population of the industrialized nations is growing at a relatively slow rate, and it appears likely that this rate can be maintained through voluntary population control (e.g., family planning). Zero Population Growth, Inc., and other organizations have been active in promoting access to birth control and legalized abortion.

■ In some less developed countries, compulsory birth control has been attempted and has met with considerable resistance. In these countries the most effective policies provide not only birth control devices but also economic and social incentives to limit family size.

■ The United States is often described as a nation of immigrants; since the earliest years of European settlement, it has attracted people from all over the world. Since the 1970s the rate of legal immigration to the United States has accelerated. The largest numbers of immigrants have come from Asia and Latin America.

■ A problem related to immigration is the uneven distribution of immigrants among cities and regions in the United States. Almost half settle in New York, Los Angeles, Miami, or Chicago, greatly adding to the costs of education and health care in those cities.

■ Immigrants in urban centers encounter intense competition and, at times, direct hostility. Their children may form defensive gangs or be isolated by their peers. Some immigrant groups shelter their children from street life and encourage them to achieve in school.

■ Millions of undocumented immigrants are currently residing in the United States, and more arrive each year. Undocumented immigrants are easily exploited by employers and others. Their effect on the U.S. economy is not clear, but it appears that they cushion the native-born population from economic uncertainty.

■ Population-related policies in the United States focus mainly on immigration. It is illegal to transport or employ undocumented immigrants. Illegal aliens who entered the country before 1982 and have lived here continuously ever since may qualify for permanent status. The principle of family unification is a basic element of immigration policy, but recent changes in immigration laws have made it more difficult for low-income immigrants to bring other members of their family to the United States.

KEY TERMS

crude birthrate, p. 453
rate of population growth
(natural increase), p. 454

demographic transition, p. 455
standard of living, p. 459

level of living, p. 459
chain migration, p. 469

INTERNET EXERCISE

The web destinations for Chapter 16 are related to different aspects of population and immigration. To begin your explorations, go to the Prentice Hall Companion Website: **http://prenhall.com/kornblum**. Then choose **Chapter 16** (Population and Immigration). Next, select **destinations** from the menu on the left side of the screen. There are a variety of sites to investigate. We suggest that you begin with **Federation for American Immigration Reform;** after you have accessed this page, click on **Numbers, USA.** The *Unintended Consequences* feature in this chapter deals with how family unification is becoming more difficult due to income requirements imposed by Congress on sponsors of new immigrants. The *Numbers, USA* site will acquaint you with the arguments associated with immigration reform. After you have explored the site, answer the following questions:

■ Do you think the United States should have strict immigration quotas? Why or why not?

■ Do you support or oppose congressional legislation that makes it more difficult for poor immigrants who already live in the United States to sponsor other members of their families who also wish to come to this country?

17 Technology and the Environment

TECHNOLOGY AND THE ENVIRONMENT

- A mechanical robot can replace three or more workers.

- Over 98 percent of American households have at least one television set.

- Americans drive their cars over 1.5 trillion miles per year, using about 70 billion gallons of gasoline in the process.

- In urban areas almost half of the carbon monoxide in the air comes from motor vehicles.

- Radioactive wastes must be stored safely for up to 1,000 years before they become harmless.

OUTLINE

Defining Technology

Technology and Global Inequality
The Digital Divide

Technological Dualism

Controlling Technology
Autonomous Technology
Automation
Whistle-blowers
Bureaucracy and Morality

Technology and Institutions

Technology and the Natural Environment

Environmental Stress
Origins of the Problem
Air Pollution
Water Pollution
Solid-waste Disposal
Other Hazards

The United States and the World Environment

Social Policy
Appropriate Technology
Technology Assessment
Policy on Global Warming
Environmental Action

M uch of what we hear on the news about globalization—of economic relations, cultural behavior, and much more—has come about because of technological revolutions in transportation and communications (Winner, 1997). But globalization is not a recent phenomenon. The technological and organizational revolutions of the past 200 years are sweeping away social boundaries that were built up over 5 millennia; in some ways the world has become, as futurist Marshall McLuhan put it, a "global village." Two previous cultural transformations were also based on technological changes, but they occurred at a relatively slower pace. Between the shift from hunting to farming and the shift from village to urban civilizations based on industrial production and low-cost energy, there were some 5,000 years of social and scientific progress. Today momentous changes are brought about by technology in each new generation, so that science itself seems overwhelmed by the pace and scale of technological change.

The most common view of technology among physical and social scientists is that every major innovation has both freed humanity from previous hardships and created new, unanticipated problems. Thus, technology is seen as a double-edged sword. Although most of us benefit immensely from technological progress, technology itself can be viewed as a social problem. In this chapter, therefore, we will look at research and theories about the social impact of technology, as well as particular phases of technological change.

Of all the many ways in which technology has changed our lives, probably none has more far-reaching consequences than its impact on the earth's environment. The problems of possible global warming, acid rain, toxic waste disposal, and water and air pollution are direct consequences of technological advances. The way we use energy has an enormous impact on the earth's ecological systems. The technologies of production, climate control, transportation, and agriculture transform the physical shape of the planet and lead to environmental stress. In this chapter, therefore, we will examine how technologies can become social problems and how they contribute to problems in the natural environment.

Defining Technology

The dictionary definition of **technology** is "the totality of means employed by a people to provide itself with the objects of material culture." In this sense, technology is a way of solving practical problems; indeed, it is often viewed as the application of scientific knowledge to the problems of everyday life. But neither the dictionary definition nor the view of technology as applied science places enough emphasis on its organizational aspects. Langdon Winner (1977, 1986) has provided a useful set of dimensions for understanding the broader meaning of technology:

1. Technological tools, instruments, machines, gadgets, which are used in accomplishing a variety of tasks. These material objects are best referred to as *apparatus*, the physical devices of technical performance.

2. The body of technical skills, procedures, routines—all *activities* or behaviors that employ a purposive, step-by-step, rational method of doing things.

3. The *organizational* networks associated with activities and apparatus (Winner, 1977, pp. 11–12).

Technological change refers to changes in any or all of the major dimensions of technology listed here. Some technological changes have revolutionary significance in that they alter the basic institutions of society. Thus, the industrial revolution—that is, the development of factories and mass production—has drastically altered the organization of a number of noneconomic institutions, including the family, religion, the military, and science itself.

Not all technological change is revolutionary, however. Some innovations spur minor adjustments in other sectors of society or among small numbers of people. Nor does technological change always consist of a single major invention. Daniel Bell (1973), perhaps the most prominent sociologist in this field, defines technological change as "the combination of all methods [apparatus, activities, organization] for increasing the productivity of labor and capital" (p. 188). This is a valuable definition because it stresses the combination of methods that alter production, rather than single innovations. After all, the technological revolution that took place in American agriculture from the end of the nineteenth century to World War II involved hundreds of major inventions and the skills and organization to support them. The combination of all these factors allowed the United States to make the transition from an agrarian society to an urban industrial society in less than one century.

Technology and Global Inequality

Are new technologies increasing the gap between haves and have-nots throughout the world? The potential consequences of lack of access to technologies are a subject of lively debate and new research. The *Human Development Report* of the United Nations Development Programme (1999), which focuses on these issues, notes that "the fusion of computing and communications—especially through the Internet—has broken the bounds of cost, time, and distance, launching an era of global information networking. In biotechnology the ability to identify and move genetic materials across species types has broken the bounds of nature, creating totally new organisms with enormous but unknown implications" (p. 57). These technologies are creating new markets and new fortunes, many of which are dominated by individuals and corporations in the wealthier nations, especially the United States.

After reviewing all the trends, the authors of the *Human Development Report* conclude, "The global gap between haves and have-nots, between know and know-nots, is widening" (United Nations Development Programme, 1999, p. 57). Figure 17–1 shows that access to the Internet, the home of the telecommunications revolution, is

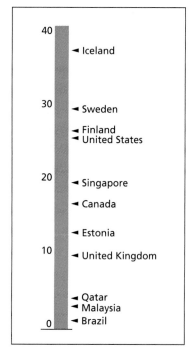

Figure 17–1 Internet Users as a Percentage of the National Population

Source: United Nations Development Programme, 1999.

largely reserved for selected segments of the populations of the wealthier nations. Note also, as indicated in Figure 17–2, that in many parts of the world people do not have access to telephones, let alone computers and the Internet. In fact, almost one-quarter of the world's nations have not achieved the basic measure of telephone access of 1 phone per 100 people.

Information and the technologies that convey it can be a positive force for social change, but too often they are not delivering on their potential. Existing patterns of inequality prevent more equal access to computers and even to telephones. People in developing nations, for example, suffer from the most serious infectious diseases. Yet medical personnel in those nations often lack access to the information they need to combat those diseases. The average U.S. medical library subscribes to about 5,000 journals, many of which are also available online to people with computers and Internet access. Nairobi University's medical library, long regarded as the best medical school library in East Africa, has only 40 medical books and a dozen journals, and students at the university have extremely limited access to the Internet, with its online journals and technical discussions. This one example could be multiplied by hundreds of other situations in which people in the third world suffer because of their limited access to new technologies that hold so much promise for the betterment of their lives.

The Digital Divide

In the United States, the gap between those with access to computers and the Internet and those without such access is often referred to as the **digital divide.** Poor families are far less likely to be among the two-thirds of American households that are active on the Internet. But this divide, still immense in the third world, is narrowing quickly in the United States. Efforts to give children time on computers in schools have greatly reduced the gap. In 1998 approximately 89 percent of U.S. schools gave their students Internet access. That figure was 65 percent in 1996. For schools in which two-thirds or more of the students are eligible for a free school lunch (a measure of attendance by poor children), 80 percent had Internet access, compared to 53 percent in 1996 (*Statistical Abstract,* 1999).

These are extremely encouraging statistics, but one might reasonably ask how important the Internet is in students' overall education. In fact, there are few hard data on this subject. Many parents and political leaders believe that Internet access is a sort of passkey to success in the global economy, but research on this issue lags behind speculation. It is clear, however, that students who master the more technical aspects of computers and their applications have more career options than those who do not. From that perspective, narrowing the digital divide is a significant accomplishment (Williams-Harold, 2000).

Technological Dualism

The phrase **technological dualism** refers to the fact that advances in technology can have both positive and negative impacts. Consider the following examples.

Technology and Jobs.   Technological innovation is causing drastic and extremely rapid changes in the types of work available to Americans. Between 1975 and 1990, for example, employment in the production of computers increased by about 89 percent. Employment in the production of food and kindred products remained about the same, and employment in textile mill products decreased by about 20 percent (*Statistical Abstract,* 1993). These changes are due to the increasing importance of advanced technology.

At this writing, the unemployment rate in the United States is about 4 percent, the lowest since the 1960s, although this still means that more than 6 million American

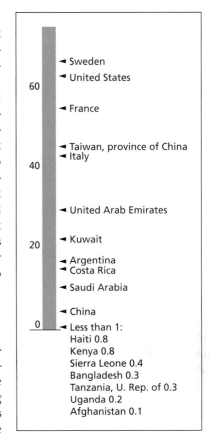

Figure 17–2   Teledensity— Telephone Main Lines per 100 People

Source: United Nations Development Programme, 1999.

workers are looking for work, especially in manufacturing sectors of the economy. Many of these workers will never find employment in their original industries because the jobs will have been eliminated by automation. Americans with secure jobs will benefit from the increased productivity of the entire labor force; but the fate of the displaced workers depends heavily on policies and programs that offer opportunities for retraining and further education. Thus, technology has had both positive and negative effects.

Telecommunications and the Global Village.   The revolution in telecommunications has already made the United States a single community for some purposes. In 1950, 9 percent of American households had TV sets, which were turned on for an average of 4.6 hours a day. Today over 98 percent of U.S. households have at least one TV set, and the average American watches about 4½ hours of TV a day (*Statistical Abstract*, 1999). In 1915 it cost $20 to call San Francisco from New York. Today, because of microwave satellite technology, it costs only a few cents. Because of these new forms of communication, it is much easier to maintain extended family ties today than in earlier decades. And we can all, or almost all, watch the same sporting events or political speeches, and this may strengthen our sense of shared citizenship. But what about literacy? Is the revolution in communication making reading obsolete? The United States publishes more books than ever before, but the reading ability of American children seems to have suffered, partly because of the distraction of television. As more and more TV services develop, will earlier traditions of entertainment and urban living be maintained?

In an era when increasing numbers of people are using sophisticated telecommunications technologies to fax their mail and memos, to do library searches, and to

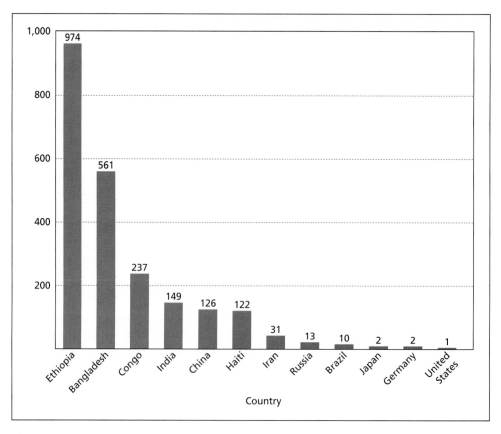

Figure 17–3   Ratio of Population to Vehicles, Selected Countries

Source: Automobile Manufacturers Association.

communicate via computer terminals throughout the world, there is a growing population of telecommunications have-nots. People in inner-city ghettos and in remote rural areas who are poor and cannot afford telephones, to say nothing of computers, are in danger of being pushed even further toward the margins of society because of their lack of access to new technologies. In the most rural areas of the nation, telephone companies estimate that as many as 200,000 households are not connected by phone wires. Often these residents cannot pay the initial installation expenses. Congress and state public service commissions are investigating the problem in the hope of finding a way to subsidize telephone service for poor, remote communities (Johnson, 1991; Schiller, 1996).

Automobility.   Periodic shortages of gasoline and increasingly frequent traffic jams in metropolitan areas have not cooled America's love affair with the private automobile. Americans drive their cars over 1.5 trillion miles per year. It takes about 70 billion gallons of gasoline a year to fuel private cars and 29.5 billion more to fuel trucks (*Statistical Abstract,* 1999). Figure 17–3 demonstrates that the United States leads the world in the number of cars on its roads, with at least one automobile for every person in the nation. Ecologists worry that as the number of automobiles increases throughout the world, there will be a concomitant increase in pollution, which could further endanger human populations. Places like Mexico City are already so congested and polluted that the prospect of additional automobile pollution is staggering. The United States has tended to seek a technological fix for the problem by encouraging the development of electric cars rather than supporting the development of alternative forms of transportation such as railways (Tunali, 1996).

Controlling Technology

Some critics of technology are convinced that it has become an autonomous force in society—that it is less and less subject to the control of democratic political institutions. A more hopeful view stresses social adaptation to technological innovation. In this section we will explore these contrasting views of technology.

Autonomous Technology

The theme of technology run amok appears frequently in movies, books, and other fictional works. But these fictional nightmares are based on real experiences or real possibilities for future problems. The biological and genetic manipulations depicted in the immensely popular film *Jurassic Park,* with its lesson that fooling Mother Nature can be extremely dangerous and morally questionable, unfolded shortly before scientists in Scotland succeeded in cloning a sheep, proving that the technology to reproduce exact replicas of human beings already exists. To many people, cloning as a scientific possibility is even more frightening than the more farfetched but equally possible (in theory) possibility of producing living dinosaurs.

The computer named Hal that ran the space mission in the film *2001* malfunctioned and had to be taken over by its human crew. This is, of course, a satirical view of computers' domination of human life, but how often do we read about computer mistakes that result in bureaucratic disasters affecting hundreds, perhaps thousands, of people? We depend on machines, which are all too frail and fallible, yet we know that machines do not literally have lives of their own. People make machines and operate them, not vice versa. How can it be, then, that technology has achieved a seeming independence from human control, as many critics argue?

The answer, according to Winner (1986, 1997) and others, is not that individual machines exercise tyranny over human subjects but that the technological order—the complex web that connects the various sectors of technology, such as communication, transportation, energy, manufacturing, and defense—has enmeshed us in a web of dependency. People who live in simple societies meet their basic survival needs with a fairly small number of tools and a simple division of labor. To accomplish such goals as building a shelter, gathering and growing food, and warding off enemies, they have evolved a set of tools that families and other groups manufacture and use as the need arises. The lives of these people are dominated by the need to survive, and technology simply provides the means for doing so. In modern industrial societies, however, most people spend most of their productive hours working to meet the quotas, deadlines, and other goals of large organizations. Each of the corporations, government bureaucracies, and other organizations that together make up the technological order produces goods and services that people want or need. These organizations do so not with a few tools but with a complex array of machines and skills. As a whole, the technological order supplies the basic necessities of life, along with innumerable extras. But in the process, much of the life of society has been diverted from meeting the needs of survival to meeting the requirements of technology.

We have seen elsewhere in this book that military technology accounts for a large proportion of the federal budget. The devastating bombing of the Serbian forces in Kosovo in 1999 demonstrated to many Americans that this technology was worth the expense. But the allied victory and the evident effectiveness of the weapons systems inspired many observers to ask why the nation could not use its technological knowhow to improve schools and health care and solve other social problems. In attempting to answer such questions, Daniel Bell (1991) notes that smart bombs and computer-assisted weapons are technologies designed to meet well-defined and very narrow objectives. He warns that "'solutions' to the social problems (if solutions are possible) spring from the different values people hold" (p. 23).

Most sociologists do not see technology as autonomous. They argue that we have been drawn into the momentum of technological change but are not sure where it is taking us. In the following pages we will discuss this theme as it applies to particular technologies.

Automation

A classic example of the difficulty of understanding the interaction between technology and human values is automation, the replacement of workers by a nonhuman means of producing the same product. People may lose jobs because of automation, but should we fight to keep these jobs, many of which may be among the dirtiest and most dangerous ones in industrial facilities? On the other hand, the greatly feared displacement of workers by machines may or may not increase productivity and thus create new wealth, which could be channeled into the "higher" work of humans: health care, education, caring for the aged, and so on.

In fact, the stereotypical image of automation, in which a worker is replaced by a mechanical robot, is actually occurring throughout the industrialized world. Each of these machines replaces at least three workers because it can work continuously, whereas human workers must be replaced every eight hours. But most robots replace more than three workers, even though they must be tended by highly trained maintenance personnel. Thus, automation increases the productivity of the economy since a constant or decreasing number of workers can turn out more of a desired product. The question remains, however, of whether the new wealth generated by higher productivity will be used to benefit the entire society or only individuals who are already wealthy.

The direct replacement of workers by machines is the most dramatic and perhaps the most widely held image of automation. Evidence suggests, however, that the contemporary effects of automation as measured by increasing productivity, defined as output per hour of labor, have been much less than the stereotypical image of robots that replace workers would suggest. According to one estimate, productivity due to machines (as opposed to organization) improved at a fairly consistent annual rate of about 2.5 percent between 1919 and 1953 (Solow, 1959; cited in Bell, 1973). In the 1960s the pace of automation increased somewhat, but no major change occurred in the 1970s. In the 1980s, although the U.S. economy continued to create new jobs, the impact of automation reduced the number of new jobs in the manufacturing sector, especially automobiles and steel. (See Chapter 14.) In the 1990s, however, employment in the production of computing equipment and other digital technology grew rapidly.

Whistle-blowers

So many of the proposed solutions to technological problems are themselves new technologies that opportunities abound for abuse and personal profit through their application. People who see abuses of new technological systems often run grave personal risks when they attempt to expose them. These individuals are known as **whistle-blowers.**

Within any organization, certain ways of doing things, beliefs about the environment in which the group operates, and ideas about how individuals should behave become established. Whistle-blowers challenge some element of this body of procedures, beliefs, and norms in an effort to bring about change. At the least, they must endure snubs or ostracism by fellow workers. At the worst, they may be fired or even subjected to physical violence.

The difficulty of succeeding in such a situation can be appreciated by reviewing the experience of Peter Faulkner (1981), an engineer for a private nuclear engineering firm, who in 1974 publicized certain hazardous deficiencies in the design of nuclear power systems. Early in the 1970s Faulkner had become concerned about the fact that many systems that were being marketed contained design flaws that posed grave threats to the public and to the natural environment: "Overconfident engineering, the failure to test nuclear systems fully in intermediate states, and competitive pressures that forced reactor manufacturers to . . . sell first, test later" (pp. 40, 41) contributed to the persistence of these flaws.

Curious about whether his fellow engineers shared his concerns, Faulkner (1981) discussed his perceptions with them. From these discussions, he realized that many of them shared his view that poor management had led to the marketing of defective reactors. But most of his colleagues preferred to leave management problems to the executives, even though this resignation of responsibility contributed to the design flaws with which they were already familiar from their daily experience. Senior engineers informed him that utility executives "didn't want management advice—only technical assistance to get them over the next hill."

Frustrated by the indifference of his colleagues, Faulkner made the difficult and costly decision to present articles that criticized the industry to a Senate subcommittee and a scientific institute. Dissemination of critical papers clearly violated the ethics of the nuclear industry and of the engineers within it, but Faulkner acted to further what he considered to be a higher goal—public safety. Within two weeks he had been interviewed by the company psychiatrist, who wanted to learn whether Faulkner had been motivated by some deep-seated hostility to embarrass his firm. A week later he was fired.

The explosion of the space shuttle *Challenger* in January 1986 is sometimes attributed to a similar situation: failure to listen to whistle-blowers in the company that manufactured the shuttle's solid-fuel booster rockets. It is true that engineers repeatedly warned of the danger of engine seal failure in very cold weather, that they were overruled by their superiors, and that when they testified at congressional hearings on the disaster they were either fired or "promoted" to meaningless positions.

However, the situation was much more complex than these facts suggest. The pressure to go ahead with the fatal launch was enormous, and subsequent investigations revealed that other aspects of the shuttle program, particularly safety procedures, were seriously deficient. As Charles Perrow (1984) points out in his book *Normal Accidents*, modern technological systems are extremely complex, and despite the best intentions of managers and employees, information is often lost or suppressed because of lack of coordination between different parts of the system. The tragic example of the space shuttle illustrates the need for more thorough technology assessment, which will be discussed in the Social Policy section of the chapter.

Bureaucracy and Morality

As noted earlier, technology consists not only of machines but also of procedures and organizations. Today much of the productive activity that occurs in complex societies takes place in large bureaucratic organizations. With their orientation toward specified goals, their division of labor into narrowly defined roles, and their hierarchical authority structures, such organizations are supremely efficient. But like technology in general, some of the qualities of large organizations that make them so productive and valuable can also cause harm. For example, in a hierarchical system individuals may commit immoral acts because they are not personally responsible for the consequences of those acts, which are carried out under the direction of superiors.

The list of immoral acts committed on the instructions of superiors in large organizations is long. Writing as London was being pounded by Nazi bombs during World War II, George Orwell (quoted in Milgram, 1974) described the irony of one such situation:

> As I write, highly civilized human beings are flying overhead, trying to kill me. They do not feel any enmity against me as an individual, nor I against them. They are only "doing their duty," as the saying goes. Most of them are kind-hearted law abiding men who would never dream of committing murder in private life. On the other hand, if one of them succeeds in blowing me to pieces with a well-placed bomb, he will never sleep any the worse for it. (pp. 11–12)

Stanley Milgram called attention to the fact that when an immoral task is divided up among a number of people in a large organization like an air force or a bomb factory, no one person, acting as an individual, actually decides to commit the act, perceives its consequences, or takes responsibility for it. It is easy for each participant to become absorbed in the effort to perform his or her role competently. It is also psychologically easy to reduce guilt with the rationalization that one's duty requires the immoral behavior and that one's superior is responsible in the end.

In a famous series of experiments conducted at Yale University, Milgram (1974) studied the conditions under which people forsake the universally shared moral injunction against doing harm to another person in order to obey the instructions of someone in a position of authority. Subjects entered the laboratory assuming that they were to take part in a study of learning and memory. One person was designated a "learner" and the other a "teacher." The experimenter explained that the purpose of the study was to observe the effect of punishment on learning, and then the "learner" was strapped into a chair and electrodes were attached to his wrist. Next, the "learner" was told that the task was to learn a list of word pairs and that for every error he would receive an electric shock of progressively greater intensity. The "teacher," who had been present for this interchange, was escorted to another room and seated at the controls of a large shock generator. Each time the "learner" gave a wrong answer, the "teacher" was to flip the next in a series of 30 switches designed to deliver shocks in 15-volt increments, from 15 to 450, starting at the lowest level. (See Figure 17–4a.)

In reality, the "learner" was an actor who received no shock but registered greater discomfort as the supposed intensity of the shocks increased. Grunts gave way to verbal complaints, to demands for release from the experiment, and then to screams. The true purpose of the experiment was to study the behavior of the "teachers." They were affected by the cries and suffering of the "learners"—especially in high-proximity situations—but whenever they hesitated to deliver a shock, the experimenter ordered them to continue. In one form of the experiment, almost two-thirds of the subjects administered the maximum shock of 450 volts. (See Figure 17–4b.) Interviews with these subjects (who had been carefully selected to represent a cross section of society) revealed that they tended to adjust to their task by absorbing themselves in its technical details, transferring responsibility to the experimenter, and justifying their actions in the name of scientific truth (Milgram, 1974).

Milgram's experiments generated a great deal of controversy and contributed to the establishment of rules for governing federally funded social-science research that uses human subjects. At the same time, there has not been any significant debate about the implications of his findings for society. Should people be taught that disobedience to authority under some conditions is necessary? This is the situation faced by whistle-blowers, who actually overcome their feelings of subservience to technologically oriented bureaucratic hierarchies.

Technology and Institutions

Sociologists who study technology and the effects of technological change most often concern themselves with the adaptation of social institutions to changing technology or, conversely, the adaptation of technology to changing social institutions. The best-known statement of these relationships is William F. Ogburn's **cultural lag** theory, first stated in the 1920s. According to Ogburn (1957), a founder of the study of technology in the United States, "A cultural lag occurs when one of two parts of culture which are correlated changes before or in greater degree than the other part does, thereby causing less adjustment between the two parts than existed previously" (p. 167).

A classic example of cultural lag involves the failure of social-welfare legislation over a period of 30 or 40 years to adjust to the introduction of new industrial machinery in the United States at the end of the nineteenth century. The frequency of industrial accidents was increasing during that period because operators were not adequately protected from the rapidly moving wheels of the new machines. The loss of life and limb generally meant financial disaster for workers' families because under existing law, employers could not easily be held liable. As a result, compensation was meager and slow to come. Only when worker's compensation and employer liability were introduced early in the twentieth century was this maladjustment, which had led to much impoverishment and suffering, finally corrected (Ogburn, 1957).

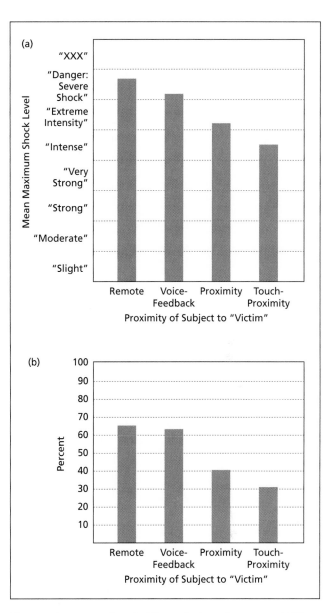

Figure 17–4 Results of Milgram's Experiments on Willingness to Obey People in Authority

Part (a) shows the extent to which proximity to the "victim" affected the subject's willingness to administer the maximum shock. Part (b) shows the percentage of obedient subjects under varying degrees of proximity to the "victim." The subject is the person administering the shock; the "victim" is an accomplice to the experimenter. The voltage levels indicated in (a) ranged from 15 for "slight shock" to a maximum of 450 for "XXX." No actual shocks were administered.

Source: S. Milgram, *Obedience to Authority.* © 1974 by Stanley Milgram. Reprinted by permission of HarperCollins Publishers, Inc.

Typically, social institutions and technology adjust and readjust to each other in a process that approaches equilibrium, unless one or the other alters so radically that a lag develops. In the history of transportation technology, radical changes have occurred relatively often. Witness the impact of the steamboat, the railroad, the automobile, and the airplane. Sometimes mere refinements in existing technology can devastate the social arrangements that had grown up in response to older machines and procedures. This is what occurred in the railroad town of Caliente (not its real name) when diesel power replaced steam in the 1940s. A classic study by Cottrell (1951) describes the results.

Caliente had been settled at the turn of the century, when the railroad was built, and it owed its existence almost entirely to the railroad. When the line was put through, the boiler of a steam engine could withstand high pressures and temperatures for only short periods. A locomotive had to be disconnected from service roughly every 100 miles, and Caliente was located in the middle of the desert for this purpose.

Over the years the community had invested considerable sums in its own future. Railroad workers and others had put their life savings into mortgages; merchants had built stores; and the town had constructed a hospital, a school, and a park. But the diesel engine undermined the economic base of the town, saddling its residents with devalued property and no means of supporting themselves. Diesel engines require much less maintenance and many fewer stops for fuel and water than steam engines do. Thus, the railroad employees who lived in Caliente either lost their jobs or were transferred; the town had become irrelevant from the point of view of the railroad. In the American free-enterprise system, the profitability of the railroad determined the fate of the town. The railroad was under no obligation to cushion the social impact of its move, and the state did not offer any assistance; so the town died.

The construction of interstate highways after World War II had the opposite effect. The width, straightness, and limited access of interstates permit greater traffic flow and higher speeds than are possible on conventional roads. The highways therefore expanded the potential markets of retail service businesses located near them. Improved markets, in turn, tend to increase employment in retail and service occupations. The promise of new jobs attracts new residents from areas with less opportunity. Thus, a study of the impact of interstate highways on nonmetropolitan counties between 1950 and 1975 was able to establish an association between highway construction and population and economic growth along the interstate corridor (Lichter & Fuguitt, 1980).

Ogburn's (1957) theory of cultural lag and other sociological research on adaptation to technological change are often considered examples of technological determinism, the crude theory that technological innovation dictates changes in social institutions and culture (Winner, 1997). But Ogburn demonstrated that in many instances cultural change occurs long before technological change. Such technological lags are major challenges to modern science and engineering. For example, American culture has come to depend on the availability of relatively cheap fossil fuels. As supplies dwindle or become more difficult to secure for political reasons, technological breakthroughs are needed to maintain the supply of low-cost energy. Thus, if physicists and engineers could control the nuclear fusion reaction (in which hydrogen atoms are fused into helium, releasing vast amounts of energy) so that its energy could be captured, Americans might once again have a source of plentiful, cheap fuel.

Fusion research is still in its early stages, however. Upon completion, the most powerful fusion reactor yet designed will be able to generate only about 3 percent as much wattage as the best fission reactors (Bernstein, 1982). If economically feasible fusion reactors are to be built, the nation must invest in the training of additional physicists and technicians, as well as research facilities and equipment. But because fusion research drains huge sums from the pool of money available for energy research, many critics argue that the federal government should diversify its research grants. They believe that other technologies, such as solar energy, may become much more economical than fusion as researchers solve the problems that contribute to their cost. Public debate of this nature is an important part of the process of overcoming technological lag (Read, 1994).

The pressure to discover cheap and efficient routes to the control of nuclear fusion has led scientists to either falsify data or almost entirely neglect the rules of scientific inquiry. This seems to have occurred in the late 1980s in the case of two chemists, one in Utah and the other in England, who shocked the scientific world with the announcement that they had discovered a fusion reaction that did not require immense quantities of energy. While the team was garnering lucrative research contracts from firms that were hoping to profit from the discovery, efforts to replicate the cold fusion experiment were made in laboratories throughout the world. None of those efforts was successful. In a study of this scientific scandal, the research physicist Frank Close (1991) warns that the pressure to make discoveries and to bring in profits for universities and research institutes can create an incentive for unscientific manipulations of data or serious lapses in scientific judgment. The cold fusion fiasco illustrates why the norms of science are valuable and need to be protected (U.S. Congress, 1996).

Technology and the Natural Environment

In recent decades the American public has been increasingly concerned about the impact of pollution on its air and water (Dunlap & Scarce, 1991). This concern has led to research and speculation about our ability to control the sometimes harmful effects of certain technologies on the natural environment. Barry Commoner (1992), one of the best-known authorities on this subject, has described the fundamental problem in terms of a clash between the speed of change in human civilization and the pace of change in the cycles of the natural environment; he has also noted that most vital natural resources are rapidly being exhausted.

According to Commoner (1992), human civilization has been changing and becoming more complex at an accelerating rate. The ideas, facts, and procedures that make up science and technology at any given time serve as a platform for future progress. A single technological advance such as the wheel, the internal-combustion engine, or the semiconductor may form the basis of an enormous range of inventions. As the ability of humans to exploit the resources of the earth has grown, so has the size of human populations.

These two developments—accelerated technological and scientific change and rapid population growth—are causing pollution and depletion of the natural environment as never before. Natural cycles of purification can absorb only a limited amount of certain artificial substances before ecological damage is done. Water pollution occurs when streams, rivers, lakes, and oceans can no longer purify themselves. When wind, rain, and snow can no longer remove the particles deposited in the air by machines of various kinds, pollution is the result (Commoner, 1992; Toolan, 1998). In these cases the speed at which technology creates pollutants exceeds the pace at which nature can absorb them. The spectacular fires and pollution that spewed from Kuwait's burning oil wells after the Persian Gulf war were stark reminders of the destructive forces unleashed by humans and the urgent need to control them.

As recreational vehicles take more people off the roads and onto deserts, dunes, and frozen lakes, the negative impacts multiply.

Sometimes technologies that seem benign and that we take for granted as part of everyday life have unanticipated consequences. Earlier in this century pesticides and herbicides revolutionized agriculture, making it much more productive. Subsequent research has linked many of these chemicals to the destruction of fish and birds and to certain cancers in humans. Along the same lines, for years we used aerosol containers for purposes ranging from personal hygiene to applying whipped cream to ice-cream sundaes. In the mid-1970s the suspicion that a propellant used in aerosol cans was eroding the atmospheric ozone layer, which protects us from harmful radiation, led to the use of different propellants.

Perhaps the central question is this: Can we control such harmful effects before it is too late? In many cases the technology exists to control environmental damage, but powerful interests do not wish to shoulder the cost of doing so. Here the problem becomes one of creating a political consensus around a solution. In other cases the technology needed to get us out of jams that earlier inventions have helped put us into does not yet exist. Thus, advanced economies around the world are consuming energy in the form of oil, which is becoming depleted and for which an adequate substitute has not yet been found. Any technological solution to this and other problems will almost inevitably contribute to a whole new generation of crises.

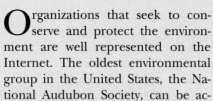

SOCIAL PROBLEMS ONLINE

Environmental Information on the Internet

Organizations that seek to conserve and protect the environment are well represented on the Internet. The oldest environmental group in the United States, the National Audubon Society, can be accessed at **http://www.audubon.org/**. Its web page provides legislative updates, information about the organization, and educational campaigns. Virtual nature walks feature text and graphics about local flora and fauna from the society's sanctuaries, such as Florida's Corkscrew Swamp.

The Sierra Club "promotes conservation of the natural environment by influencing public policy decisions." Its website at **http://www.sierraclub.org/** offers online copies of its magazines, *Planet* and *Sierra,* that inform the reader about urban ecology, as well as endangered species and natural wonders. The web page also addresses momentous issues such as global warming.

The activist group Earth First! (**http://www.imaja .com/imaja/change/environment/ef/earthfirst.html**) defines its mission as working to save "the earth's remaining sacred natural land and its inhabitants from the destructive greed of corporations." Its photo gallery illustrates several aspects of environmental destruction and highlights its campaigns to save old-growth forests in the United States and rainforests throughout the world. Its gopher site allows the user to download research articles about the environment, as well as pieces about the history and politics of this influential group.

The Nature Conservancy (**http://www.tnc.org/**) preserves wetlands and other environmentally sensitive and threatened areas by purchasing them or controlling their use. Its web page provides links to a library, the magazine *Nature Conservancy,* and descriptions of programs in the United States, the Caribbean, and South America.

Envirolink, at **http://www.envirolink.org/**, is an Internet site with links to other environmental groups throughout the English-speaking world. It includes a daily update of news stories about ecological issues.

Organizations that are critical of the mainstream environmental movement on the grounds that it overestimates ecological damage or encourages unwarranted government involvement include the Science & Environmental Policy Project (SEPP) (**http://www.his .com/sepp/**) and the Heartland Institute (**http://www .heartland.org/envpubs.html**), which both offer downloadable reports. SEPP targets its publications toward the scientific community and the media.

Environmental Stress

An investigation of winter fish kills in Wisconsin lakes led to the unexpected conclusion that they were caused by snowmobiles. Heavy snowmobile use on a lake during the winter compacts the snow and makes the ice opaque. This reduces the amount of sunlight that reaches underwater plants, which need it for photosynthesis. As the plants' oxygen production declines, they die, and their decomposition consumes considerable amounts of the oxygen left in the water. As a result, the fish are asphyxiated.

As this example suggests, we can best understand environmental stress as the interaction of three systems: the natural environment, the technological system, and the social system. The fish, ice, oxygen, and plants are all elements of the natural system. The snowmobile is an element of the technological system. The fact that this vehicle is produced, marketed, and used is a product of the social system—as is the fact that no one is held responsible for the fish kills.

Taking a broader perspective, we can define the natural system as containing these elements and their interrelationships: air, water, earth, solar energy, plants, animals, and mineral resources. Our technological system includes transportation, farming, electricity-generating facilities, manufacturing processes and plants, various methods for extracting mineral resources, and the actual consumption and disposal of the products of these processes. Our social system includes attitudes, beliefs and values, and institutional structures. And as with the fish and the snowmobiles, so in larger matters we must look to our social and technological processes for the origins of the problems in the natural system.

Origins of the Problem

The term **environmental stress** refers to what society does to the environment. Examples include discharging substances into the air, water, and soil; producing heat, noise, and radiation; removing plants and animals; and physically transforming the environment through drilling, damming, dredging, mining, pumping, and so on (Ehrlich & Ehrlich, 1991; MacDonald, 1996). Environmental stress is not synonymous with pollution, although pollution is perhaps its most familiar form. Webster's dictionary defines *pollution* as "a state of being impure or unclean, or the process of producing that state." **Environmental pollution,** therefore, is "the presence of agents added to the environment by society in kinds and quantities potentially damaging to human welfare or to organisms other than people" (Ehrlich et al., 1977, p. 542).

Four concepts are basic to understanding environmental stress: interdependence, diversity, limits, and complexity (Ophuls, 1977). *Interdependence* literally means that everything is related to, and depends on, everything else; there is no beginning or end to the web of life. *Diversity* refers to the existence of many different life and life-support forms. A basic principle of ecology is that the greater the diversity of species, the greater the probability of survival of any given one. *Limits* are of several kinds. First, there is a finite limit to the growth of any organism. Second, there is a limit to the numbers of a given species that an environment—including other organisms—can support. Finally, there is a finite limit to the amount of materials available in the earth's ecosystem.

Complexity refers to the intricacy of the relationships that constitute the web. Because of this complexity, interventions in the environment frequently lead to unanticipated and undesired consequences. For example, DDT (dichloro-diphenyl-trichloro-ethane) was once repeatedly sprayed over large areas of land to eliminate various disease-carrying or crop-destroying insects. To an impressive degree it succeeded. But DDT is a long-lasting chemical, and its effects are not limited to insects. Much of it was washed from farmlands and forests into rivers and oceans, where it was taken up by smaller organisms at the bottom of the food chain. Eventually, as small creatures consumed tiny plants and larger creatures consumed smaller ones, several species of fish-eating birds accumulated so much of the poison that their eggs developed very thin shells, which consistently broke before hatching. These species were in grave danger of extinction, although the users of DDT never intended such a result (Ehrlich & Ehrlich, 1991). Only federal restrictions on the use of DDT prevented the elimination of these bird species.

One of the major difficulties in dealing with environmental stress, therefore, is the number of problems involved and the extent to which they are interrelated. This will become clear as we explore the specific problems and the efforts that have been made to combat them.

Air Pollution

If the atmosphere is not overburdened, natural processes will cleanse it and preserve its composition. Through photosynthesis, for example, green plants combine water with the carbon dioxide that we and other organisms exhale, and they produce oxygen and carbohydrates. But these natural processes, like other resources, have limits. They can remove only a limited quantity of harmful substances from the air; and if pollution exceeds their capacity to do so, the air will become progressively more dangerous to those who breathe it.

Human activities are overtaxing the atmosphere. Although the specific nature of air pollution varies from one locality to another (as a function of geography, climate, and type and concentration of industry), we can identify some of the common components. These include organic compounds (hydrocarbons); oxides of carbon, nitrogen, and sulfur; lead and other metals; and particulate matter (soot and fly ash).

In urban areas almost half of the carbon monoxide in the air comes from motor vehicles. The remainder comes from the burning of fossil fuels (oil and coal) in power-generating plants, airplanes, and homes; airborne wastes from manufacturing processes; and the burning of municipal trash. (See Table 17–1.) Certain chemical processes frequently render these pollutants more dangerous after they reach the atmosphere. In the presence of sunlight, the emission of hydrocarbons and nitrogen oxides (primarily from cars) produces the photochemical soup, called smog, that envelops many of our cities; and various oxides combine with water vapor in the atmosphere to produce corrosive acids that eat away the surface of many buildings.

TABLE 17–1 Air Pollutant Emissions, by Pollutant and Source (in thousands of tons)

Source	Particulates	Sulfur Dioxide	Nitrogen Oxides	Volatile Organic Compounds	Carbon Monoxide	Lead
Fuel combustion, stationary sources	1,101	17,259	10,724	860	4,817	496
Industrial processes	861	1,664	804	1,527	4,779	2,251
Waste disposal and recycling	296	50	103	449	1,242	646
Highway vehicles	268	320	7,035	5,230	50,257	19
Miscellaneous[a]	30,469	13	346	858	9,568	(NA)

[a]Includes emissions from forest fires and various agricultural activities, fugitive dust from paved and unpaved roads and other construction and mining activities, and emissions from natural sources.

Source: Statistical Abstract, 1999.

Effects on Human Health. The effects of chronic air pollution are of great significance for human health in the long run. Continued exposure to air pollutants and their accumulation in the body—essentially a slow poisoning process—increases the incidence of such illnesses as bronchitis, emphysema, and lung cancer (MacDonald, 1996). Air pollution also causes severe eye, nose, and throat irritations, and poor visibility as a result of smog has been cited as a factor in both automobile and airplane accidents.

Economic Effects. Air pollution has economic effects as well. Accelerated deterioration of property increases maintenance and cleaning costs; blighted crops mean lost income for farmers and higher food prices for consumers; pollution-caused illnesses erode productivity, reduce workers' earnings, and raise the cost of medical care for everyone. The sulfur emitted from the smokestacks of factories and power plants in the United States would be worth millions of dollars if it could be recovered.

Ecological Effects. Finally, air pollution may have a dangerous long-term effect on the earth's ecosystem. For example, several studies suggest that fluorocarbon gases, commonly used in spray cans and refrigerating systems, may be breaking down the earth's protective ozone layer (Yoon, 1994). (The ozone layer surrounds the earth from an altitude of 8 to 30 miles above sea level; it screens out many of the sun's harmful rays.) Fluorocarbon molecules, according to these studies, are not broken down in the earth's lower atmosphere but continue to rise to a much higher altitude. Here they are broken up by high-intensity radiation and begin to chemically destroy ozone molecules. Destruction of the ozone layer would lead to a much higher worldwide incidence of skin cancer and crop failure; there would also be changes in the world's climate.

Concern about ozone depletion was heightened by the finding that the ozone layer above Antarctica decreases by roughly 40 percent each October, shortly after sunlight reappears following the Southern Hemisphere's winter months. The significance of this phenomenon is unclear, but some scientists believe that it may mean that the earth's ozone layer will be depleted more rapidly than expected (Brown & Postel, 1987).

A particularly troublesome form of air pollution, and one that has attracted increasing attention in recent years, is **acid rain.** This term refers to rainfall that contains large concentrations of sulfur dioxide, which is emitted by utility and industrial plants in many parts of the nation. Acid rain has a highly detrimental effect on forests and lakes, causing severe damage to trees and to fish and other forms of aquatic life and polluting water supplies.

The Global-warming Controversy. Of all the many aspects of pollution and environmental stress, perhaps none alarms scientists and environmental groups as much at present as the possibility of dangerous warming of the planet because of continued high levels of carbon emissions into the atmosphere. Created primarily by the burning of fuel by humans, the amount of carbon dioxide in the atmosphere is estimated to have increased by 15 percent to 25 percent since 1800 and is expected—assuming that we do nothing to prevent it—to reach twice the preindustrial level by 2050 (Read, 1994).

Each ton of carbon emitted into the air produces 3.7 tons of carbon dioxide. During 1988 about 5.6 billion tons of carbon were produced by the combustion of fossil fuels. The United States was responsible for about one-fifth of this total (Flavin, 1990). Third-world countries burn fossil fuels at far lower rates than industrialized nations, but many of the former meet their energy needs by burning wood, straw, and similar fuels, which also emit carbon. And as countries such as South Korea become more and more industrialized, they increase their use of fossil fuels. At the same time, the felling and burning of forests in tropical countries adds between 1 billion and

2 billion tons of carbon emissions to the worldwide total. Growing populations and the associated demand for energy, land, and other resources mean that carbon emissions—and, hence, the amount of carbon dioxide in the atmosphere—are likely to increase for the foreseeable future. Some scientists are concerned that the buildup of carbon dioxide in the atmosphere could produce a "greenhouse effect." That is, the carbon dioxide would trap heat near the earth's surface, raising the average temperature of the atmosphere. Such overheating, even by a few degrees, could melt the polar ice caps, with calamitous results.

At present there is widespread consensus among earth and environmental scientists that global warming is a real and present danger (Hesman, 2000). Still, there is continued debate about the basic causes of the trend and its implications. In 1995 a respected group of climatologists sponsored by the United Nations agreed that their findings do point to a dangerous warming trend (Stevens, 1996). But some business and conservative groups deny that there is an impending crisis (Moore, 1995). United Nations conferences on global warming held since 1996 have failed to arrive at a firm agreement to begin a program for reducing greenhouse gas emissions, especially from heavily industrialized nations like the United States (Reiner, 1999). (We return to this subject in the Social Policy section of the chapter.)

Radioactivity.   The two large explosions that occurred on April 26, 1986, at the nuclear power plant in Chernobyl in the former Soviet Union released a cloud of radioactive gases over central and northern Europe. People in these regions experienced the highest levels of radioactive fallout ever recorded there. Two weeks later, minor airborne radioactivity was detected throughout the Northern Hemisphere (Flavin, 1987).

Many environmental scientists fear that the health of people in the former Soviet Union and Europe could be severely affected by this event for decades. Radioactivity is the most dangerous form of air pollution because it increases the probability that people will develop various kinds of cancer. Moreover, in the Chernobyl accident, 135,000 people had to be evacuated from populated areas within 20 miles of the plant. Thus, the problems of airborne radioactivity, together with the need to evacuate huge populations when accidents occur, have raised severe problems for the nuclear power industry throughout the world. Nor are such problems limited to recent years. Thousands of U.S. military personnel and civilians were exposed to high levels of radiation during the 1950s, when tests of nuclear explosions were conducted. The Clinton administration adopted a policy of making these events public so that the injured parties may seek compensation, and confidence in the government's ability to control hazardous technologies can be restored.

Water Pollution

Water is constantly moving through what is known as the hydrologic cycle. It is found in the atmosphere as vapor; it condenses and falls to the earth as rain, snow, or dew; it percolates underground or runs off the surface as streams, rivers, and finally oceans; it evaporates into the atmosphere as vapor once again; and the cycle continues. While on the ground, water may be absorbed into the roots of plants and, through the leaves, eventually evaporate back into the atmosphere; or it may be drunk from streams by animals or people and evaporated or excreted back into the earth or air. Or it may sink into underground reservoirs and be stored for millions of years.

It is quite possible for water to be used more than once as it passes through a single round of the hydrologic cycle, if it is sufficiently purified between uses by natural or artificial means. However, we render much of our water unfit for reuse because of various kinds of pollutants: raw and inadequately treated sewage, oil, synthetic organic chemicals (detergents and pesticides), inorganic chemicals and mineral substances, plant nutrients, radioactivity, and heat. We therefore face a dual crisis: The amount of water available to us could be insufficient for our demands, and what is available could be polluted.

Just as air can cleanse itself if not overburdened, so, too, can rivers, lakes, and oceans. But we have been discharging wastes, directly or indirectly, into our waterways in amounts that prohibit natural purification. In fact, some 25 percent of the U.S. population is not served by sewage treatment facilities. The bacteria in untreated sewage render the water unfit for drinking, swimming, and many industrial uses. Finally, the use of oxygen to decompose the waste reduces the life-support capacity of the water, with a consequent decline in the number and variety of fish. As the population grows, the problem of waste disposal will become even more acute.

Current farming practices, such as extensive use of nitrate and phosphate fertilizers, also seriously impair water quality. Rain and irrigation cause the runoff of large quantities of these materials into rivers and lakes. The fertilizers work in water much as they do on land, producing algae "blooms"—huge masses of algae that grow very quickly and then die. As with the decomposition of sewage, the decay of these blooms consumes oxygen, thereby killing fish and other animals that have high oxygen requirements. As the algae decay, they settle at the bottom of the water, along with various compounds of nitrogen and phosphorus. At one time the bottom of Lake Erie was covered by a layer of muck from 20 to 125 feet thick. Only intensive efforts by environmentalists to stop pollutants from being discharged into the lake and adjoining waterways saved Lake Erie from total destruction.

Long-lasting pesticides and radioactive substances are especially dangerous because they accumulate in the tissues of animals that eat them. One reason this poses such a serious problem is the process known as biological magnification, whereby the concentration of a given substance increases as it ascends the food chain. This can be an especially serious danger in the vicinity of nuclear plants, where safe levels of radioactivity in the surrounding waters may still produce high levels of radioactivity in plankton. Those levels, in turn, can multiply to produce extremely high levels of radioactive contamination in birds and fish that eat these microorganisms (Ehrlich & Ehrlich, 1991).

Another form of water pollution is thermal pollution. The effluents of many factories and generating plants—especially nuclear power plants—are warmer than the rivers and lakes into which they flow, and when discharged in quantity they may raise the water temperature by as much as 10 to 30 degrees Fahrenheit. Such thermal pollution can be ecologically devastating. Because most aquatic animals are cold-blooded, they are at the mercy of the surrounding water temperature. If the temperature rises beyond an organism's capacity for metabolic adjustment, the animal will die. Because larvae and young animals are far more susceptible to slight temperature variations than mature organisms and because rises in temperature also interfere with the spawning and migratory patterns of many organisms, thermal pollution may exterminate some aquatic populations through reproductive failure.

Solid-waste Disposal

We do not really "consume" most products, despite our reputation as a consumer society. It is more accurate to say that we buy things, use them, and then throw them away. Thus, we have several hundred million tons of solid wastes to dispose of every year, including food, paper, glass, plastic, wood, abandoned cars, cans, metals, paints, dead animals, and a host of other things. The annual cost of disposing of such waste amounts to billions of dollars.

The two principal methods of solid-waste disposal are landfills and incineration. Although landfills are supposed to meet certain sanitary standards, violations are

The United States lags behind other industrial nations in efforts to deal with the problem of solid-waste disposal. The accumulation of garbage in landfills like this site in Alaska is becoming one of the nation's most critical environmental problems.

common. Improperly designed municipal incinerators are major contributors to urban air pollution. In addition, many cities use the ocean as a dumping ground. New York City's practice of dumping tons of refuse into the ocean each day has made a "dead sea" out of a large area in the Atlantic (O'Connor & Stanford, 1979).

The large-scale introduction of plastics and other synthetics has produced a new waste disposal problem: Whereas organic substances are eventually decomposed through bacterial action, plastics are generally immune to biological decomposition and remain in their original state when they are buried or dumped. If they are burned, they become air pollutants in the form of hydrocarbons and nitrogen oxides.

In the 1980s the waste disposal problem took on new urgency as many landfill sites filled up and fears of groundwater contamination caused many communities to forbid the opening of new sites on their land. In 1987, in a notorious illustration of the seriousness of the problem, a barge filled with garbage from Long Island spent several weeks searching the East Coast for a site that would accept its load of waste. Currently many states are trying to export their solid wastes elsewhere, primarily to states that are attempting to develop commercial landfill operations. In the meantime, however, there is a growing shortage of disposal sites as older ones are filled or closed as a result of community protests (MacDonald, 1996).

Environmental Racism.   Solid-waste dump sites are often located near low-income neighborhoods on the outskirts of metropolitan regions or in rural areas (Board, 1996). Because these neighborhoods are also quite likely to be home to members of minority groups, there is a growing tendency for solid-waste dumping to be a particular problem for African Americans and Latinos. Many local activists and residents of these neighborhoods term such dumping *environmental racism.* This issue is increasingly recognized, especially among African Americans, as a serious social problem that they experience to a far greater extent than would be expected if the dumping sites were located on a more equitable basis (Kenny, 1996). Low-income people—especially poor African Americans and Mexicans—have far higher levels of illnesses because of contamination of their water and gardens by toxic runoff from these dump sites.

Toxic Wastes.   There is, in addition, the problem of toxic wastes or residues from the production of plastics, pesticides, and other products. These residues have typically been buried in ditches or pits. The famous case of Love Canal, near Niagara Falls, arose when toxic residues that had been dumped into the unfinished canal seeped into the surrounding area and contaminated both the soil and the water, creating severe health hazards for local residents. In 1978 Love Canal was declared an environmental disaster area, and more than 200 families were evacuated from the neighborhood. In early 1985, after more than six years of litigation, 1,300 former residents were awarded payments totaling $20 million in compensation for health problems (including birth defects and cancers) suffered as a result of the contamination of their neighborhood by toxic wastes. In 1991, 13 years after the discovery of the contamination and the beginning of cleanup efforts, some houses in the Love Canal area were declared habitable again.

Radioactive Wastes.   The United States currently produces about 20 percent of its electricity in nuclear power plants. These plants pose a special problem because the radioactive fuel in the reactor's core must be replaced periodically. The spent fuel must be deposited somewhere under extremely well-protected conditions because it is highly dangerous and can contaminate surrounding water and lands. In the last two decades, as tons of nuclear waste have accumulated in temporary storage sites, the U.S. government has spent over $4 billion on efforts to create a system for permanent storage.

Radioactive wastes must be stored safely for up to 1,000 years before they become harmless. During that time, any alteration in the seismological conditions of the burial site could disturb the radioactive material and contaminate the area. A large facility under Yucca Mountain in Nevada is being constructed, but disputes about its safety (e.g., in an earthquake) have cast some doubt on whether the facility will eventually be approved. There is also a major controversy over how the radioactive wastes would be transported to the site (Suplee, 1995). Most people who think about the problem want the wastes to be disposed of properly, but few are willing to have trucks or trains carry these hazardous materials through their communities.

Other Hazards

Besides the environmental problems just noted, other threats to our well-being arise from the indiscriminate use of technological knowledge. These include land degradation, noise pollution, chemical hazards, and the undesirable consequences of certain large-scale engineering projects.

Land Degradation. Any local ecosystem, such as a forest, swamp, or prairie, is a complex matrix of interrelated and interacting organisms and processes, one that both supports its own patterns of life and contributes to those of the larger regional, continental, and planetary ecosystems. Serious alteration of a local ecosystem, therefore, can affect the balance of life in a larger area. Yet through greed and/or ignorance of ecological principles, we have diminished or destroyed the capacity of large land areas to support life. We are only beginning to recognize the possible consequences.

Huge deserts can be created by misuse of the environment. In 1952, 23 percent of the earth's total land area was classified as desert or wasteland; by 1984, an estimated 35 percent of the earth's land area was threatened by desertification. Recent research on the expansion of arid lands and deserts shows that overgrazing by domesticated animals, dependence on wood for fuel, and depletion of soil nutrients by crops produce desertification. When natural cycles of drought and wet seasons interact with human overuse, the rate of desertification can increase drastically (Stevens, 1994). It takes from 300 to 1,000 years to produce 1 inch of topsoil under the most favorable conditions. Many areas of the earth are now losing topsoil at the rate of several inches per year because of management techniques that expose the soil to wind and water erosion. Such irreparable losses are intolerable in view of the world's increased need for arable land.

Shorelines like this one in Turkey are fouled with garbage, a global environmental problem.

Noise Pollution. Noise is a dysfunctional consequence of technology. It is produced by airplanes, cars, buses, trucks, motorcycles, motorboats, factory machinery, dishwashers, garbage disposals, vacuum cleaners, television, radio, phonographs, air conditioners, jackhammers, bulldozers, and much else. Noise, which can be harmful even when it is not consciously heard, directly affects physical and emotional well-being. Studies have shown that people today suffer from greater hearing losses with increasing age than in the past and

These barges are used to transport salmon smolts downstream past dams that prevent salmon from migrating. Efforts like these have been inadequate to sustain salmon populations, and environmentalists and many political leaders are calling for destruction of the dams.

that noise contributes significantly to the tension of daily life, sometimes even precipitating stress-related illnesses like peptic ulcer and hypertension (Monroe, 1996). Hearing loss caused by excessive noise now affects about 10 million people in the United States, especially those who work in loud environments or who listen to extremely loud music on earphones. There is also evidence from recent studies that noise from nearby airports can adversely affect the reading scores of schoolchildren (Maxwell & Evans, 1997).

Chemicals. Pressure to get new products on the market has resulted in the widespread use of various pesticides and herbicides without adequate testing of their long-run cumulative effects. It has also led to the massive use of plastics and other synthetics, which create serious problems of disposal, and untested industrial chemicals like vinyl chloride gas. (Less than 2 percent of industrial chemicals have been tested for possible side effects.) Moreover, there has been a proliferation in the variety and amount of food additives—chemicals that are used in processing food and sometimes cause allergic reactions. Little is known about the long-term effects of continual ingestion of these substances, either alone or in combination.

Large-scale Engineering Projects. Humans have always taken immense pride in their ability to change the face of the earth in ways that are deemed beneficial. However, they frequently fail to anticipate and assess the associated costs. Thus, a new dam is hailed both as an engineering masterpiece and because it opens up new lands for agriculture, settlement, and recreation. Less often recognized is that although a dam may permit the controlled distribution of water to desired locations, it also results in water loss through evaporation. Moreover, large dams have caused earthquakes because of the tremendous pressure exerted by the billions of gallons of water they store.

Strip mining also poses hazards to the environment. Much of the coal in the United States lies deep within the earth and must be obtained by underground mining. However, there is also a great deal of coal lying close enough to the surface for strip mining, in which the top layers of soil are removed so that the coal can be excavated. Although strip mining is cheaper and safer than underground mining, it causes much greater harm to the environment. Vast areas of land are denuded of all living things and scarred by huge, ugly trenches. Because the topsoil is removed during the strip-mining process, healthy plant life cannot return for centuries. And because the soil balance is disturbed, water supplies in the area may be irreparably damaged; increased erosion at the mining site can cause both local and distant water sources to become contaminated by sediment, dissolved acids, and other pollutants.

The United States and the World Environment

William C. Clark (1989) has written, "Our ability to look back on ourselves from outer space symbolizes the unique perspective we have on our environment and on where we are headed as a species. With this knowledge comes a responsibility not borne by the bacteria: the responsibility to manage the human use of planet earth" (p. 47). Because Americans are among the wealthiest, the most educated, and the most polluting of the earth's peoples, environmental scientists often argue that they bear a large share of the responsibility for wise management of the planet.

The difference in living standards between the United States and most other countries is enormous. In stark contrast to the hunger that prevails in many poor nations,

The Global Food Fight

Monsanto Chemical Corporation is widely considered to be a global villain, threatening the security of the food eaten in many parts of the world. Just a few years ago Monsanto was riding a favorable wave of investment in genetically modified crops. Genes introduced into seeds produced by Monsanto's subsidiaries could resist fungus, rot, and the extreme heat and drought that are common in many parts of the agricultural world. How, then, did the company become a global villain? The answer depends on one's political and environmental values, but any sociologist with a research background in social movements can easily explain how it is that so many environmental groups now line up in opposition to Monsanto and other global producers of genetically modified crops.

Humans have been genetically modifying crops for centuries. The very process of crop domestication is a form of genetic selection and modification imposed by humans on plants. So why do the genetically modified soy and corn seeds that Monsanto produces terrify so many people in nations outside the United States?

> The first protests against genetic modification took place in America in the late seventies, when activists from a group called Science for the People destroyed frost-resistant strawberries and delayed the construction of Princeton's molecular-biology building. Then they fizzled out. Americans, by and large, trust the FDA to keep the levels of toxicity in their daily bread down to a psychologically manageable level and don't worry too much about the source of the goodies that fill their horn of plenty. The great grain factories of the Midwest work their magic far from the places most people visit to enjoy nature. In much of Europe, though, nature and agriculture go hand in glove, occupying the same physical and social space. Europe's layered patchwork of farming and culinary landscapes has taken shape over 2,500 years, altered by small and large migrations, the conquest and loss of colonies, wars, and revolutions. Europeans feel strongly about what they eat: Food is a matter of identity as well as economy, culture as well as nurture. (Margaronis, 1999, p. 11)

Monsanto compounded the problem by developing and promoting genetically modified foods that contain what is known as a "terminator gene." This gene makes the seed produced by the plant infertile, which means that it cannot be replanted but is, according to the

Two members of Greenpeace scale a building to hoist a banner protesting a conference on genetically modified foods held in Montreal in January 2000.

company, perfectly safe to eat. The reason for inserting the terminator gene is that the plants also have other genetic modifications invented by Monsanto. The company believes that if farmers are allowed to keep seeds with these modifications, they will not need to buy Monsanto seeds again. Since the genes are forms of information that the company has patented, it feels that it has the right to make the seeds infertile as well so that farmers will be obliged to buy more seeds in coming years. In short, Monsanto is protecting its investment. Environmentalists are extremely concerned, however, that genetically modified plants may spread their genes into other plants or that eating genetically modified foods may have long-term consequences that research has not yet uncovered. For their part, many farmers are incensed about the terminator genes, which make it impossible for them to use seeds from their own crops. All of this has made it relatively easy for Greenpeace and other environmental action groups to mobilize a food security movement in Europe in which Monsanto is cast as the major villain and U.S. food crops are attacked. Here is an instance in which global marketing of new technologies has backfired, largely, critics claim, as a result of arrogance and greed.

the increased affluence of the United States and other developed countries has made possible a steady increase in per capita consumption of meat and other nutritious foods. In fact, Americans consume, on the average, four times as much food per person as people in poor nations. This is not to say that all Americans are overfed. The poor in the United States, like those in poor countries, are plagued by hunger, malnutrition, and disease (Brown, 1998).

Not only do most Americans eat much more food than people in most other parts of the world, but the food they eat includes a much larger proportion of meat than of grain. By contrast, three-fourths or more of the food energy in the diet of Asians comes directly from grain (Ehrlich & Ehrlich, 1991). Vast quantities of grain—one-third of total world production—are fed to livestock in the United States and other developed countries to produce meat. It is sometimes claimed that this practice is immoral because the grain that is fed to livestock in the United States could be used to nourish hungry people elsewhere in the world (Brown & Eckholm, 1974; Brown & Young, 1990).

It is true that the United States exports large amounts of grain to all parts of the world. Some of these exports are part of international aid programs that help alleviate the problem of hunger in the poorer nations; in fact, some of the world's least developed nations depend heavily on this aid. But it remains true that the developed nations consume a disproportionate share of the world's food resources. (See the Critical Research feature on page 497.)

Figure 17–5 compares energy and resource consumption in major regions of the world. It shows that with only 5 percent of the world's population, the United States consumes 25 percent of the world's fossil fuel and produces 72 percent of its hazardous waste. Since the high-consumption American lifestyle is emulated in many developing nations, it is difficult to imagine how conservation can become a stronger value than it is today (Bender & Smith, 1997).

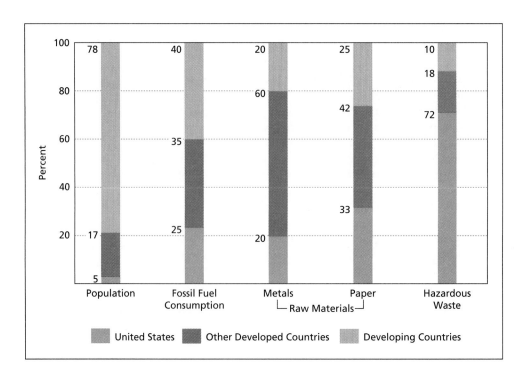

Figure 17–5 Share of Population, Resource Consumption, and Waste Production

Source: Natural Resources Defense Council.

The significance of these facts is twofold. The industrialized nations consume a disproportionate share of total food and energy resources, leaving comparatively little for the majority of the world's population. This is one explanation—though by no means the only one—for the desperate plight of people in the least developed nations. The other major effect of the dominant position of the United States in the world economy is that it contributes to environmental problems both at home and abroad. As the world's most industrialized nation, the United States "exports" technologies that can contribute substantially to the environmental

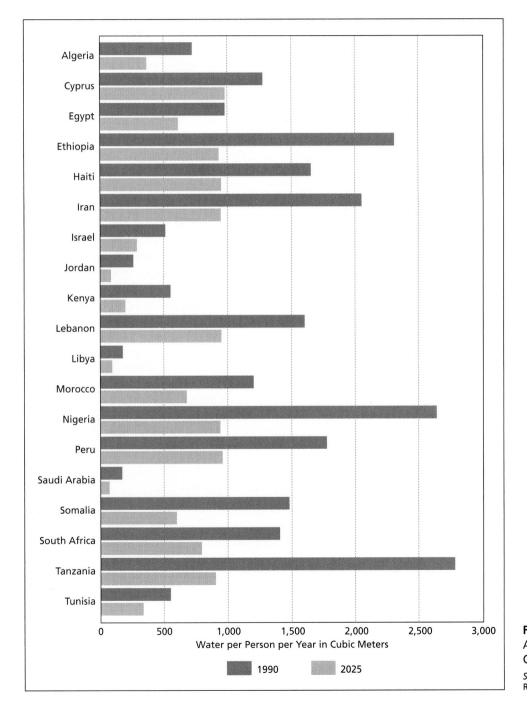

Figure 17–6 Estimates of Availability of Water: Various Countries, 1990 and 2025

Source: Homer-Dixon, Boutwell, & Rathjens, 1993.

problems of other nations. A vivid example is the disaster that occurred in Bhopal, India, in December 1984, in which a deadly gas, methyl isocyanate, escaped from a Union Carbide storage tank, killing more than 2,000 people and injuring about 100,000 others.

In sum, as populations increase in size and affluence, the complexity of social organization, the imbalances in energy and food budgets, the depletion of resources, and the difficulty of correcting these problems also increase. If the United States is to maintain its position as a world leader, it must take the lead in developing a way to control environmental problems.

The United States and other affluent nations can use their resources to help control the growth of the world's population. Through their own aid and through cooperation with agencies of the United Nations and the World Bank, they can help poorer nations develop more adequate and sustainable water supplies. Ecologists estimate that unless continued action is taken, water shortages in arid areas of the world may produce serious regional conflicts and even warfare (Homer-Dixon, Boutwell, & Rathjens, 1993). (Areas of growing water shortage are shown in Figure 17–6.)

SOCIAL POLICY

As is evident from much of the discussion in this chapter, issues of environmental control and restoration often overlap with policies designed to reduce the negative effects of new technologies. The growing fields of technology assessment and risk assessment, for example, contributed to the sensational debates that culminated in the defeat of legislation to fund research and development of a commercial supersonic passenger airplane in the United States (Hall, 1982; Ormes, 1973). Public fears about the effects of sonic booms were not allayed by the results of scientific assessments, and the proposal was defeated. England and France went on to produce a supersonic jet, the Concorde, which has shown that sonic boom effects can be controlled. Social policies that deal with technologies and their environmental consequences are extremely controversial—especially when potentially lucrative products are involved—and point up the significance of scientific assessment of the environmental impact of proposed technologies.

Appropriate Technology

Appropriate technologists advocate major changes in technology itself. In most cases **appropriate technology** is smaller-scale technology. Thus, Amory Lovins (1977, 1986) argues that we need to reexamine our basic way of life and the energy needs that go with it. Renewable energy sources such as wind and solar energy, which can be harnessed by families and communities, are preferable to such sources as nuclear power, which is polluting, requires massive amounts of capital, and is controlled by large corporations (Read, 1994).

The appropriate technologists are often accused of advocating an impractical retreat to a simpler way of life. In answer to this charge, they argue that their alternatives sound impractical because most people assume that continued economic and institutional expansion is necessary. A closer examination of social needs would make smaller-scale technology seem more appropriate. Appropriate technologists also point out that they do not oppose all technology, only large-scale technology that has unfavorable social consequences.

Technology Assessment

Technology assessment is a complex area of scientific and political research. Its complexity stems in part from the fact that it requires an interdisciplinary approach if it is to succeed. Physical scientists, social scientists, and policymakers generally speak their own technical languages and have their own perspectives and methods. Often these do not lend themselves to cooperation, and the assessment of a particular technology is limited to a single scientific discipline. Recently, however, a new professional cadre of interdisciplinary scientists has emerged. They are known as *risk professionals* and are skilled in the use of physical and social-scientific methods of assessing and evaluating technological systems (Jasanoff, 1986).

A more fundamental problem in technology assessment is the fact that it is easier to assess the risk of failure in a piece of hardware or a set of mechanisms within a technological system than the risk of failure in the entire system. Thus, in his path-breaking study of accidents in major technological systems such as air traffic control, dams, and nuclear power plants, Charles Perrow (1984) concluded that "the dangerous accidents lie in the system, not in the components" (p. 351).

During the 1980s and 1990s the pressure for deregulation of many industries resulted in less funding for technology assessment and a greater likelihood of accidents and failures in complex technological systems. This is not to say that there is no justification for deregulation, just that, given the expanding risk to people and to the environment, the need for better technology assessment and more forceful regulation is increasing.

Policy on Global Warming

The 1997 UN conference on global warming held in Kyoto, Japan, drafted a historic international agreement on reducing the emission of greenhouse gases. Targets for the developed and less developed regions of the world were established after much debate and compromise. The draft agreement was the result of years of negotiation and debate among environmental activists and UN delegates. In April 1998 the European Union members officially ratified and signed the Kyoto treaty. They accepted an 8 percent reduction of carbon emissions over the next 13 years. The United States, whose delegation had tentatively accepted a 7 percent reduction, still has not ratified the agreement, and the likelihood of its doing so is slight because of Republican opposition in the Senate, which must ratify any treaty agreements. Japan, Australia, Brazil, Canada, Norway, and Monaco signed in 2000. Argentina and Pacific island nations had signed earlier. It is not clear at this writing, before the 2000 presidential elections, what if any action the U.S. government is likely to take on the agreement (*Business Week,* 1999; Kronenwetter, 1999).

Environmental Action

The Clean Air Act of 1970 established the Environmental Protection Agency (EPA) and empowered it to set and enforce standards of air quality. The EPA has since been given authority over most matters that involve environmental quality.

During the 1980s, environmental policy was hampered by the conflicting desires of a society that wished to preserve and improve environmental quality but not to discourage economic growth or distort energy prices. In 1981, as the time for revision of the Clean Air Act approached, the EPA interpreted the law as encouraging *both* economic growth and improved air quality. It proposed less stringent ambient-air standards (e.g., for the amount of carbon monoxide that may be emitted by cars and trucks) in an attempt to reach a compromise between the desire for clean air and the need to control energy costs.

In the 1990s environmental quality and regulation again became popular causes. Under the leadership of Vice-President Albert Gore, a recognized expert on environmental policy, the Clinton administration took steps to tighten regulations concerning air pollution, solid-waste disposal, and drainage of wetlands. Such steps are not always popular. For example, after the Mississippi River floods in the summer of 1993, the administration attempted to discourage the rebuilding of some levees and the restoration of some farmland on flood plains, a policy that outraged many residents of the area. In the West, the administration's policies on preserving old-growth timber and restricting grazing on public lands angered many people whose livelihood depended on relatively cheap access to those natural resources. On the other hand, some states, especially California, have become impatient with Congress's reluctance to pass more stringent air-quality legislation and have developed standards of their own. California's air-quality standards require greater control of pollution emissions from gasoline engines and have spurred the development of prototypes of an electrically powered automobile. (See the Current Controversies feature below.)

In recent years, laws regarding the dumping of toxic wastes have been enforced more strictly by government agencies at all levels. There has also been an attempt to cope with the destruction of the earth's ozone shield. Although the depletion of the ozone layer continues, the seriousness of the problem is a matter of debate. Indeed, the difficulty of determining how serious an environmental problem actually is remains a major obstacle in environmental policymaking. Nowhere is this situation more evident than in the controversy over global warming and the policies intended to solve the problem once its severity has been determined.

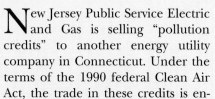

CURRENT CONTROVERSIES

Market Approaches to Pollution

New Jersey Public Service Electric and Gas is selling "pollution credits" to another energy utility company in Connecticut. Under the terms of the 1990 federal Clean Air Act, the trade in these credits is encouraged as a way of reducing emissions of smog-producing pollutants. The act establishes what is essentially a free market in pollution: It allows companies that can reduce their emissions below the level required by law to sell their "surplus" emissions to other companies, which find it cheaper to buy the right to pollute than to curtail their own emissions.

The New Jersey utility was able to reduce its emissions of nitrogen oxides by 2,400 more tons than the law required by making certain adjustments in its coal-burning plants. The Connecticut utility bought 500 tons of pollution rights from the New Jersey company so that some of its customers could continue to use old boilers that produce more air pollution than the law allows. In essence, the purchase of pollution credits allows cleanups to occur where they can be made as cheaply as possible.

Similar market solutions to pollution problems are being developed in many parts of the United States, but they are not without their critics. Some environmental groups object to the exchange of pollution credits for sulfur dioxide emissions because these emissions cause acid rain, which destroys forests and habitats. Others object to the idea that any form of excessive pollution can be considered legitimate just because it is offset by the antipollution efforts of another entity. These trades are also complicated by changes in wind direction. Pollution that has been "bought" by another company cannot drift back to the location where the original cleanup occurred without negating the purpose of the pollution credit system. Despite these criticisms, however, the creation of markets in pollution rights is a major new policy approach to curbing pollution (Flavin, 1996; Wald, 1994).

A largely unheralded piece of environmental legislation, the Emergency Planning and Community Right to Know Act, passed in 1986, is proving to be an effective tool in local struggles against polluters. In 1991, for example, the town of Baton Rouge, Louisiana, was able to force the American Cyanamid Corporation to reduce its pollution of the region. The community obtained data showing that the company was responsible for at least 25 percent of the 750 million pounds of toxic chemicals poured into the local environment each year. The facts were gathered by the EPA under the mandate provided by the act.

There are some loopholes: Small businesses with nine or fewer employees are exempt from the regulations, and large companies that claim to be recycling dangerous chemicals may not be reporting the extent to which they release pollutants into the environment. Nevertheless, information gathered under the provisions of the act is increasingly being used by communities to pressure polluters to change their ways—an example of successful environmental policy based on the free flow of information (Schneider, 1991).

The problems of environmental pollution and land degradation are more serious in poor and minority communities than elsewhere. This is true in the United States, as well as in third-world nations. A famous example occurred in Chikpo, India, where local women chained themselves to trees to prevent their forest from being cut down by government and commercial agencies. Such social movements are having an increasing impact on environmental policies around the globe (Martínez-Alier & Hershberg, 1992). In the United States, the Clinton administration invoked the 1965 Civil Rights Act on behalf of poor African-American residents in Mississippi and Louisiana who have been subjected to far more than their fair share of toxic waste dumping and other pollution hazards like pesticides. Since state policies are supported in part by federal funds, the Civil Rights Act, which bans discrimination in federally supported projects, may help minority residents gain redress for past harm and greater protection against polluters in the future (Cushman, 1993).

Despite the attention focused on environmental problems in recent years, there is still a need for public education about the state of the environment, how it got that way, and what can be expected to happen in the future. People must be persuaded to change their attitudes and learn that the earth's resources are not limitless. This entails a distinct change in values. Since there are limits to both the amount of goods we can produce and the amount of waste the earth can absorb, we must abandon the concept that more is better. We must also strive for a relatively equal distribution of our limited supply of life-supporting and life-enhancing goods among all the earth's inhabitants.

Beyond Left & Right

Do companies have the right to pollute or exterminate endangered species to save jobs? People on the ideological right often answer this question with a qualified yes. Those on the left often say no, arguing instead that environmental restoration will add new, less damaging jobs to the economy. In some parts of the world these debates are extremely rancorous; the same is true of disputes over timber cutting in the western part of the United States.

Another view of environmental problems suggests that no matter what our politics are, we are the problem. Most people who live in affluent nations consume large quantities of gasoline and other consumer goods. Unless we begin to understand the global consequences of our consumption, it is argued, we will never reduce the level of stress on the environment. This is an argument based on facts. However, although it goes beyond left-right debates, it is not very popular with large segments of the American public.

SUMMARY

- Technology has three dimensions: the apparatus, or physical devices, used in accomplishing a variety of tasks; the activities involved in performing these tasks; and the organizational networks associated with activities and apparatus.

- Existing patterns of inequality in different regions of the world prevent more equal access to new technologies. In the United States, the gap between those with access to computers and those who lack such access is referred to as the digital divide.

- Advances in technology can have both positive and negative effects. When technology has adverse side effects, people tend to blame the technology itself rather than the combination of economic, social, and technical factors.

- The concept of autonomous technology is a recurrent one in American social thought. One element in this concept is the idea that technology has become independent of human control. Most writers on the subject do not believe this is the case. Instead, they argue that the social order has become interwoven with the technological order to such an extent that we have become enmeshed in a web of dependency.

- In bureaucratic organizations individuals may commit immoral acts because they are not personally responsible for the consequences of those acts, which are carried out under the direction of superiors. Whistle-blowers are individuals who place their personal moral concerns in opposition to the activities of an organization. They often suffer as a result of their efforts.

- The best-known statement about the relationship between technology and institutions is Ogburn's theory of cultural lag. According to Ogburn, a cultural lag occurs when one of two correlated parts of a culture changes before or in greater degree than the other, thereby causing less adjustment between the two parts than existed previously. Typically, social institutions and technology readily adjust and readjust to each other, but sometimes one or the other changes radically and a lag develops.

- Environmental stress results from the interaction of the environment, the technological system, and the social system. This interaction produces air and water pollution, problems of solid-waste disposal, and other hazards. A difficulty in dealing with environmental stress is the number of problems involved and the extent to which they are interrelated.

- Americans consume, on the average, four times as much food per person as people in less developed countries. Energy resources and consumption are also distributed unevenly throughout the world, with energy use in the United States amounting to about one-quarter of the worldwide total. To satisfy their high standard of living, Americans put enormous stress on the environment. Many observers believe that the United States should take the lead in efforts to reverse the effects of environmental stress throughout the world.

- Appropriate technologists advocate changes in large-scale technologies that have unfavorable social consequences. Technology assessment and risk assessment use both physical and social-scientific methods in studying the social consequences of existing and proposed technologies.

- A number of laws designed to control or reduce the harm being done to the environment have been passed since the 1960s, and some progress has been made. The 1997 UN conference on global warming drafted an international agreement on reducing the emission of greenhouse gases. The Clinton administration took steps to tighten regulations concerning air pollution, solid-waste disposal, and drainage of wetlands; and it invoked the 1965 Civil Rights Act to combat excessive exposure to pollution hazards in minority communities. However, there is a need for additional public education about the environment and further efforts to change people's attitudes about the depletion of the earth's resources.

KEY TERMS

technology, p. 478
digital divide, p. 479
technological dualism, p. 479
whistle-blowers, p. 483

cultural lag, p. 485
environmental stress, p. 489
environmental pollution, p. 489
acid rain, p. 491

appropriate technology, p. 500
technology assessment, p. 501

INTERNET EXERCISE

The web destinations for Chapter 17 are related to different aspects of technology and the environment. To begin your explorations, go to the Prentice Hall Companion Website: **http://prenhall.com/kornblum**. Then choose **Chapter 17** (Technology and the Environment). Next, select **destinations** from the menu on the left side of the screen. There are a variety of sites to investigate. We suggest that you begin with a comparison of two sites: **Monsanto Biotech Primer** and **Farm for Profit.** The *Critical Research* box in this chapter, "The Global Food Fight," deals with the controversy over Monsanto Chemical Corporation's research on genetic modification of crops. Quite obviously, the Monsanto website takes a "pro" stance toward this issue. The *Farm for Profit* site offers an alternative and very critical view. After you have compared the contents of these two sites, answer the following questions:

■ The text points out that humans have been genetically modifying crops for centuries, but the Monsanto project appears to be in a category by itself. Now that you are more familiar with the issues involved, are you concerned about the prospect of further biotechnological alterations by Monsanto and other similar companies?

■ What are your reactions to Monsanto's arguments about genetic modification of crops? Do you think that these measures rate a clean bill of health, or is there cause for concern?

18 War and Terrorism

WAR AND TERRORISM

- During World War II almost 17 million soldiers and 35 million civilians were killed.

- It is estimated that between 75,000 and 100,000 Iraqi soldiers died in the Persian Gulf war.

- In 1998 almost 2.3 million veterans were receiving compensation from the U.S. government for war-related disabilities. Of these, 161,000 were totally disabled.

- Between 1975 and 1982, 627,000 Southeast Asians fled their homes to take refuge in the United States.

- If a 1-megaton bomb struck the ground in downtown Detroit, it would dig a crater 1,000 feet across and 200 feet deep and would level all buildings within a radius of 1.7 miles.

OUTLINE

The Nature of the Problem
Direct Effects of War
Indirect Effects of War
Effects of Nuclear War

Military Technology and the Conduct of War
Controlling Warfare

Theories About War and Its Origins
Ethological and Sociobiological Theories
Clausewitz: War as State Policy
Marx and Lenin on War
Institutional and International Perspectives

Terrorism: Undeclared War

Social Policy
Arms Control: A Promise Unfulfilled
Alternatives to the Arms Race
Dealing with Terrorism

With the fall of the Berlin wall and the collapse of the Soviet empire in 1989, many observers of world affairs thought for a brief period that a new era of world peace might be at hand. Others, more familiar with the problems of nationalism and regional conflicts, were far more pessimistic. Unfortunately, the pessimists' view has been confirmed (Denitch, 1996; Urquhart, 2000). Wars in Chechnya and Bosnia, ethnic cleansing in Kosovo, genocide in Rwanda and East Timor, nuclear bomb tests in India and Pakistan, and the increased fear that international terrorists could obtain nuclear arms are all evidence of the fragility of world security. They are also reminders of the ever-present threat of large-scale violence and the cataclysmic social change that often accompanies war and terrorism.

The twentieth century has been called the Century of Total War, both because of the vast increase in the human capacity for waging war and because the possibility of wars that involve the entire globe is inherent in the rise of nations with global political ambitions (Aron, 1955). Although the end of the cold war has somewhat lessened the threat of global war and nuclear holocaust, it also seems that the spread of advanced weapons around the globe, the rise of smaller nuclear powers such as Iraq and North Korea, and the worsening of environmental and ethnic problems have increased the threat of wars of all kinds in many parts of the world (Kennedy, 1993).

What can be done to reduce the likelihood of war and terrorism? No one can answer this question with certainty. Much may depend on how well individual citizens understand the causes and consequences of war and on how effectively they participate in debates over policies designed to control the arms race and limit the use of force in settling national differences.

In the first section of the chapter we will examine the impact of wars on those who fight them and on civilians, both those at home and those trapped in war zones. We will continue with a survey of some of the theories of war that have been proposed by social scientists and others. The chapter will conclude with a summary of attempts by governments and private citizens to prevent outbreaks of war and terrorism.

The Nature of the Problem
Direct Effects of War

For those who experience its tragic devastation, war is the most serious social problem one can imagine. Over the centuries warfare has taken millions of lives. According to one estimate (Sorokin, 1937), between 1100 and 1925 about 35 million soldiers were killed in some 862 wars in Europe. Other investigators have calculated that between 1816 and 1965 alone, about 29 million soldiers were killed in 33 major European conflicts (Singer & Small, 1972). And these figures do not include the untold millions of civilians who perished as well. By any standard, the twentieth century was the deadliest in human history. During World War I, 8 million soldiers and another 1 million civilians died. The casualties of World War II were even higher: Almost 17 million soldiers and 35 million civilians were killed. In the Soviet Union, the generation of men old enough to fight in World War II was decimated. In the Persian Gulf war it is estimated that between 75,000 and 100,000 Iraqi soldiers died, but the impossibility of knowing exact casualty figures is a reminder of how devastating that war—and the ensuing boycotts—was for Iraq.

Long after peace is declared, many soldiers bear the scars of their battlefield experiences. For every American soldier who died in battle in the major wars of this century, between two and four others received nonfatal wounds (Newspaper Enterprise Association, 1983). Many of the wounded have required medical care for months or years, and many have been so badly injured that they have not been able to hold a job or return to a normal way of life. In 1998 almost 2.3 million veterans were receiving compensation from the U.S. government for war-related disabilities. Of these, 161,000 were totally disabled (*Statistical Abstract,* 1999). The poor are especially likely to be recruited into dangerous military roles. Several studies have shown that during the Vietnam War, battle deaths and injuries were more common among lower-class soldiers than among those from the middle or upper classes (Badillo & Curry, 1976; Janowitz, 1978; Zeitlin, Lutterman, & Russell, 1973).

Not all war-related disabilities are physical. War takes a psychological toll as well. During and after World War II, Harvard sociologist Samuel Stouffer and his colleagues (1949) conducted the first major study of war stress. They found correlations between psychological stress and several types of combat experience. For example, soldiers stationed close to the front lines—who were constantly exposed to the threat of injury or death to themselves and their friends, the hardships of life on the battlefield, the value conflicts involved in killing others, and inability to control their own actions—suffered psychological stress to a greater extent than others. In the decades since Stouffer's research, mental-health experts have identified posttraumatic stress disorder (PTSD) as a common aftereffect of battle. People suffering from PTSD feel generally irritable, depressed, and unhappy and have nightmares and flashbacks of war experiences. One study of Vietnam War veterans found that 36 percent of all men exposed to heavy combat during the war displayed PTSD for an average of ten years after their tour of duty (Kadushin, 1983).

The psychological impact of the Vietnam War may have differed from that of earlier American wars because it was a guerrilla war. That is, the enemy blended in with the civilian population and therefore seemed to be everywhere and nowhere at the same time.

Oil wells burn out of control in Kuwait at the end of the Iraqi occupation. The Persian Gulf War was notable for the extent to which environmental terrorism was used as a political and social weapon.

These conditions may have been responsible for the unusually high levels of violence against civilians that characterized the war, as well as for the mistreatment of prisoners and the use of such weapons as napalm, which killed civilians and the enemy indiscriminately. Soldiers who saw or engaged in these forms of violence suffered from psychological disorders to a greater extent than those who did not.

Indirect Effects of War

In addition to the killing and the wounding, war disrupts the lives of the civilians whose homeland has become a battleground. Often it leads to mass migrations of people who are trying to escape from danger or persecution or are looking for new opportunities. Between 1975 and 1982, for example, 627,000 Southeast Asians fled their homes to take refuge in the United States (*Statistical Abstract*, 1983), and thousands more were accepted by other nations. When refugees arrive in a new country, their problems are not over. As we noted in Chapter 9, they often encounter prejudice, unemployment, and difficulty in adjusting to a new culture.

Another major cause of wartime migration is government policy. During and after World War II, a number of European states forced whole populations to move. During the war, the German government ordered hundreds of thousands of ethnic Germans to move back to Germany from the eastern European nations that Germany had invaded. After the war, under the terms of the Potsdam Treaty, many more Germans were required to move from various eastern European nations to areas within the redrawn borders of Germany.

Some of the indirect effects of war are not as easy to calculate as the numbers of refugees. For example, it is impossible to measure the economic damage caused by war. Billions of dollars must be diverted from productive uses, first into arms and then into the effort to repair the damage caused by arms. Even less quantifiable is the impact of war on how people think. World War I left in its wake widespread disillusionment with traditional values. To the men in the trenches, patriotism lost much of its appeal. After the war many people were pessimistic about the future of civilization and were alienated from their former way of life.

Long after ceasefires have been negotiated, the consequences of war are felt among displaced refugees like these victims of the conflict in Kosovo in 1999.

Liberated Kuwait is a good example of the longer-term political and social effects of even a "successful" war. The nation's people remain badly divided in their feelings about the ruling elite, some of whom chose to stay and resist while many more lived in luxury outside the country during the Persian Gulf war. Critics of the elite have called for a more democratic form of government. Similarly, in the former Yugoslavia, uneasy truces cannot heal the hatreds caused by ethnic expulsions and intergroup brutality.

Effects of Nuclear War

In the past 100 years, wars have become less frequent but more intense as military technology has become more lethal. The development of nuclear weapons in the 1940s contributed to peace among the major powers, but if peace breaks down, a war of almost unimaginable destructiveness could ensue. Some idea of the nature of that destruction is provided by accounts of the bombing of Hiroshima, Japan, during World War II.

On the morning of August 6, 1945, as the people of Hiroshima were preparing to go to work, an American aircraft flew over the city. Seconds later a nuclear bomb exploded 2,000 feet above the center of the city. Even though the 12.5-kiloton device was tiny by modern standards, its effect was devastating. The force and heat of the blast annihilated tens of thousands of people almost instantly and delivered a deadly dose of radiation to thousands of others; within three months some 130,000 would be dead.

Many of those who survived were burned and maimed. One woman, who had been with some junior high school boys about a mile from the center of the blast, was knocked unconscious. "When I came to, I looked around," she said in a recent interview. "The boys had been so cute before, but now their clothes were burned off and they were nearly naked. Their skin was cut up and ripped off. Their faces were peeling off as well." She herself was so hideously deformed that her own parents urged her to show mercy to her husband and leave him. "At that time, I cried every day, wishing that I had died immediately," she said. She added that she did not seek compensation from the United States. "I just want [Americans] to feel sorry and to try to abolish nuclear weapons" (quoted in Kristof, 1995, pp. 1, 12).

Nuclear bombs more than 1,600 times more powerful than the one that destroyed Hiroshima have now become a standard part of the weapons systems of the major world powers. The U.S. Office of Technology Assessment (1979) has described the impact that a single nuclear device about 80 times more powerful than the Hiroshima bomb would have on a city like Detroit. A 1-megaton bomb that struck the ground in downtown Detroit would dig a crater 1,000 feet across and 200 feet deep and would level all buildings within a radius of 1.7 miles. If the attack occurred during the day, when the downtown area is crowded with workers, more than 200,000 people would be killed within seconds. The number of deaths would double if the bomb were set to explode in the air over the city, although the damage to buildings would be reduced.

Some two-thirds of the energy of a nuclear explosion is converted into heat, which travels away from the blast in a searing flash that lasts for several seconds. In Detroit, heat from a ground burst could kill and injure about 275,000 people within a distance of about 7.5 miles from ground zero, the point of the explosion. In addition, fires set by the heat would engulf much of the city, taking still more lives.

Besides causing massive physical damage, nuclear blasts release radiation, which in large doses leads to radiation sickness and death within a few weeks. In smaller doses, radiation increases the rate of cancer in the exposed population. Most of the people exposed to the direct radiation of a ground burst in Detroit would already have been killed by the blast. However, the radioactive dust thrown up by the explosion could be blown hundreds of miles downwind into Canada or over Lake Erie to Pittsburgh and beyond. People who lived within about 100 miles of Detroit who could not be evacuated or housed in fallout shelters would probably receive a fatal dose within the first week.

Even if Detroit were the only city struck by a nuclear attack, the disaster would severely strain the nation's resources. The hospital beds remaining in the Detroit area could serve only about 1 percent of the survivors. Moreover, the several thousand beds in burn centers throughout the nation could accommodate only a tiny portion of the burn victims. Tens of thousands of people would need shelter, food, and other forms of support.

The specter of global nuclear war has lessened since the fall of the Soviet empire. The United States, Russia, and Ukraine have agreed to dismantle or otherwise disable their missiles, but vast destructive nuclear capabilities remain in place around the globe. The possibility that nuclear bombs will be obtained by nations in unstable areas of the world such as Southeast Asia, North Korea, and the Middle East keeps the threat of nuclear war alive. Even a limited nuclear war would create human catastrophes on a scale not hitherto experienced, to say nothing of the environmental damage and destruction such wars would cause for years afterward, even in regions beyond the boundaries of the original conflict. These concerns, as well as the possibility that nuclear weapons could be used by terrorists, suggest that it is premature to celebrate the end of the threat of nuclear war. Experts in the field agree that efforts to control the proliferation of nuclear weapons are as vital today as they ever were (Lifton & Mitchell, 1995).

Military Technology and the Conduct of War

Throughout human history the actual conduct of war has been closely linked to the nature of existing military technology. The introduction of bronze (and later iron) weapons, the use of horses and chariots in warfare, the invention of gunpowder, and the development of the armored tank are just a few of the technological "improvements" that have affected the nature of warfare and the relative dominance of different human groups.

As the technologies of war have become ever more deadly, the ravages of war have become ever greater. Thus, in the battle of Marathon in 490 B.C., the Athenians killed about 6,400 Persians. Similarly, when rebellious British tribes slaughtered an entire Roman legion in A.D. 62, the casualties totaled fewer than 7,000. These battles were fought hand to hand with swords, axes, spears, and the like. However, with the invention of gunpowder in the Middle Ages, it became possible to eliminate large numbers of enemy forces at a distance. From that time on, war became steadily more deadly and involved larger numbers of troops and higher casualties.

In the second half of the nineteenth century, as a result of the industrialization of England and other European nations, the scale and impact of warfare increased dramatically. Although technological advances like the invention of armor plate and large field cannons increased the firepower of armies, new weaponry did not change the conduct of war as much as did the use of more modern means of transport, especially railroads and steamships, which made possible the movement of enormous numbers of troops to the battlefront. Armies began to count their soldiers by the millions rather than the thousands: "The ideal of every man a soldier, characteristic only of barbarian societies in time past, became almost capable of realization in the technologically most sophisticated countries of the earth" (McNeill, 1982, p. 223).

The advent of tanks and bombs made possible even greater carnage, and the death tolls of modern wars reflect this fact: 10.5 million people died in World War I and another 52 million in World War II. It is estimated that in an all-out nuclear war, more than 160 million people would be killed outright and countless millions more would die as a result of the lingering effects of radiation, destruction of the natural environment, and massive social disorganization.

It is important to recognize that changes in the organizational dimension of military technology have been at least as important as advances in military apparatus. (See Chapter 17 for a discussion of the three major dimensions of technology.) A notable example is the introduction of the phalanx by the ancient Greeks. In this form of military organization, foot soldiers were arrayed in ranks in a wedge-shaped formation so that the enemy had only a few targets to strike at. Each row of men in the phalanx was furnished with longer spears than those in front of them, so that several rows could strike at the enemy simultaneously. A phalanx could also defend itself against projectiles by crouching under a "roof" of interlocked shields. When skillfully used, the phalanx was virtually invincible, as can be seen in its use by Alexander the Great in conquering the Persian Empire.

A more recent example of change in military organization is the bureaucratization of military administration. Beginning in Europe between 1300 and 1600, taxes were collected on a regular basis for the support of standing armies. In the seventeenth century, the Dutch discovered that long hours of repeated drill made armies more efficient in battle and created a strong esprit de corps. It soon became evident that "a well-drilled army, responding to a clear chain of command that reached down to every corporal and squad from a monarch claiming to rule by divine right, constituted a more obedient and efficient instrument of policy than had ever been seen on earth before" (McNeill, 1982, p. 117).

One result of the increased efficiency and effectiveness of armies was an increase in the influence of military institutions on social organization. An example from the twentieth century is Japan's development of a war economy before World War II. The entire course of Japan's modernization was guided by the management of the national effort to achieve military power (McNeill, 1982).

During World War II and in subsequent decades, the rate of change in military technology—in both apparatus and organization—increased dramatically. As William McNeill (1982) points out,

> The accelerated pace of weapons improvement that set in from the late 1930s, and the proliferating variety of new possibilities that deliberate invention spawned, meant that all the belligerents realized by the time fighting began that some new secret weapon might tip the balance decisively. Accordingly, scientists, technologists, design engineers, and efficiency experts were summoned to the task of improving existing weapons and inventing new ones on a scale far greater than ever before. (p. 357)

The outcome of this process of technological advance was the present situation of immense destructive power and, for the first time, the possibility of annihilating the human species (Lifton & Mitchell, 1995).

Controlling Warfare

Despite the increasing scale, sophistication, and destructiveness of modern warfare, there has been some progress toward controlling the conduct of war. As was evident in the UN and congressional debates before the Persian Gulf war, a body of international law deals with armed conflicts. It includes a complex set of rules that defines the rights and privileges of those who fight and that attempt to protect noncombatants. Table 18–1 lists some of the specific actions that have been declared war crimes under international law.

Underlying this body of law is the ancient concept of the "just war." This doctrine, which developed out of the shared culture of Greek and Roman civilization, has two

TABLE 18–1 **War Crimes**

1. Making use of poisoned or otherwise forbidden arms or munitions.

2. Treachery in asking for quarter or simulating sickness or wounds.

3. Maltreatment of corpses.

4. Firing on localities which are undefended or without military significance.

5. Abuse of or firing on a flag of truce.

6. Misuse of the Red Cross or similar emblems.

7. Wearing of civilian clothes by troops to conceal their identity during the commission of combat acts.

8. Improper utilization of privileged (exempt, immune) buildings for military purposes.

9. Poisoning of streams or wells.

10. Pillage.

11. Purposeless destruction.

12. Compelling prisoners of war to engage in prohibited types of labor.

13. Forcing civilians to perform prohibited labor.

14. Violation of surrender terms.

15. Killing or wounding military personnel who have laid down arms, surrendered or are disabled by wounds or sickness.

16. Assassination, and the hiring of assassins.

17. Ill-treatment of prisoners of war, or of the wounded and sick—including despoiling them of possessions not classifiable as public property.

18. Killing or attacking harmless civilians.

19. Compelling the inhabitants of occupied enemy territory to furnish information about the armed forces of the enemy or his means of defense.

20. Appropriation or destruction of privileged buildings.

21. Bombardment from the air for the exclusive purpose of terrorizing or attacking civilian populations.

22. Attack on enemy vessels which have indicated their surrender by lowering their flag.

23. Attack or seizure of hospitals and all other violations of the Hague Convention for the Adaptation of Maritime Warfare of the Principles of the Geneva Convention.

24. Unjustified destruction of enemy prizes.

25. Use of enemy uniforms during combat and use of the enemy flag during attack by a belligerent vessel.

26. Attack on individuals supplied with safe-conducts, and other violations of safeguards provided.

27. Breach of parole.

28. Grave breaches of Article 50 of the Geneva Convention for the Amelioration of the Condition of the Wounded and Sick in Armed Forces in the Field, of 1949, and Article 51 of the Geneva Convention of 1949 Applicable to Armed Forces at Sea: "wilful killing, torture or inhuman treatment, including biological experiments, wilfully causing great suffering or serious injury to body or health, and extensive destruction and appropriation of property not justified by military necessity and carried out unlawfully and wantonly."

29. Grave breaches of the Geneva Convention Relative to the Treatment of Prisoners of War, of 1949, as listed in Article 130: "wilful killing, torture or inhuman treatment, including biological experiments, wilfully causing great suffering or serious injury to body or health, compelling a prisoner of war to serve in the forces of the hostile Power, or wilfully depriving a prisoner of war of the rights of fair and regular trial prescribed" in the Convention.

30. Grave breaches of the Fourth Geneva Convention of 1949, as detailed in Article 147: "wilful killing, torture or inhuman treatment, including biological experiments, wilfully causing great suffering or serious injury to body or health, unlawful deportation or transfer or unlawful confinement of a protected person, compelling a protected person to serve in the forces of a hostile Power, or wilfully depriving a protected person of the rights of fair and regular trial prescribed in the present Convention, taking of hostages and extensive destruction and appropriation of property, not justified by military necessity and carried out unlawfully and wantonly." In addition, conspiracy, direct incitement, and attempts to commit, as well as complicity in the commission of crimes against the laws of war are punishable.

Source: Gerhard von Glahn, Law Among Nations, 2nd ed., Copyright © 1970 by Allyn & Bacon. Reprinted by permission.

major branches: justification for going to war (*jus ad bellum*) and justifiable acts in wartime (*jus in bello*). *Jus in bello* is concerned with whether or not a particular war is being fought "justly." It sets limits on the means of violence (e.g., the use of particularly inhumane weapons) and on the injury or damage done to civilians.

The rules of *jus in bello* are difficult to enforce and are frequently violated. In the Vietnam War, for example, the United States used chemical defoliants that harmed human, animal, and plant life. American planes bombed North Vietnamese population centers, and both sides tortured and assassinated civilians. The most notorious American attack on civilians was the massacre of between 175 and 400 noncombatants, including infants, at the hamlet of My Lai in March 1968. For this crime one American officer was convicted and sentenced to life imprisonment, but he was released after serving two years in prison (Beer, 1981).

Further instances of disregard for international law were seen in the Persian Gulf war. In Kuwait, the Iraqi invaders used torture and terrorism. In addition, by pouring crude oil into the Gulf and setting fire to the Kuwaiti oilfields, they added an extremely ominous form of violence, environmental terrorism, to the arsenal of war tactics.

Theories About War and its Origins

In the 45 years since nuclear weapons were developed, war has become a much riskier policy than ever before because local wars fought with conventional weapons could escalate into destruction on a vast scale. Just because the stakes have risen so high, however, does not mean that the chances of a nuclear holocaust are remote. The United States, still the only nation that has ever used nuclear bombs in war, has threatened to use nuclear weapons at least 11 times since 1946. These instances include the Berlin crisis of 1961, the Cuban missile crisis of 1962, and twice during the Vietnam War. Because warfare has become so dangerous and the world's military powers have built up huge stockpiles of both conventional and nuclear arms, many people have begun to study the causes of war in the hope of promoting peace. We turn now to a discussion of some of the theories that have been proposed to account for war.

No single theory can fully explain any given war. Nevertheless, a number of theories have shed light on some of the forces that contribute to war. For the purposes of this discussion, we will not consider rebellions, riots, and other forms of violence that take place within the borders of nations. Instead, we will adopt a narrow definition of war as a violent conflict between nations. We will first consider the view that human beings are aggressive by nature.

Ethological and Sociobiological Theories

According to some scientists, humans have their primate ancestors to thank, at least in part, for the existence of war. During earlier phases of human evolution, aggressive behavior may have improved the odds of survival and become encoded in the genes of a growing number of individuals. Ethologists and sociobiologists believe that a predisposition to aggression may have been transmitted genetically from one generation to the next. One of the best-known proponents of this view is the ethologist Konrad Lorenz (1981). Like other ethologists, Lorenz has focused his research on the behavior of animals other than humans. From this work he has concluded that aggression is an instinct in humans, as it is in lower animals. Lorenz links aggression with territoriality. Just as animals defend their nests, burrows, and ranges, humans fight wars to defend their nations. It follows from this explanation that because war results from a natural urge, it is probably inevitable.

Many sociobiologists (scientists who study genetic influences on human behavior) also believe that humans have inherited a predisposition to engage in warfare.

However, they are also well aware of the influence exerted by culture. In the view of the noted sociobiologist Edward O. Wilson, learned ways of doing things guide much of human behavior, but genetic tendencies also have a persistent influence. Although aggression may have been adaptive for humans thousands of years ago, Wilson (1975) believes that aggressive tendencies must be controlled if humans are to avoid global suicide.

Lorenz, Wilson, and their followers have been attacked by critics who argue that comparisons of human behavior with that of lower animals are suspect. Among humans, the motivation to fight is a learned response to symbols, such as speeches, flags, propaganda, and other stimuli. Thus, human warfare is far more complex than fighting among animals. Moreover, there is no evidence that instinct plays any role in human aggression (Montagu, 1973). In sum, the critics deny that genes influence human behavior in general and warfare in particular; instead, they explain behavior in terms of learned responses.

Clausewitz: War as State Policy

In seeking to account for war in terms of genetically influenced tendencies, Lorenz and Wilson have viewed humans who make war as individuals independently motivated by their biological nature. In fact, however, soldiers fight in a social context, and their actions are governed largely by the dictates of military organizations. The freedom of military leaders to direct their armies is constrained by other institutions in society, such as the government, industry, the press, and religious organizations. Finally, even if the leaders of a nation's institutions were to agree among themselves, they would not have a free hand. Political and economic forces that cross national boundaries determine what strategies are available to win a war and whether war itself is a practical tactic in a given situation.

One of the most influential theories of war, proposed in 1832 by the Prussian general and military philosopher Carl von Clausewitz, took into account some of these aspects of the social context of war. During the century before Clausewitz wrote, most of the nations in Europe had been governed by monarchs who had the power to wage war if the use of military force would serve their interests. For this reason, Clausewitz focused on the role of the monarch and described war as an alternative to diplomacy, engaged in for the purpose of gaining land, prestige, and other benefits. According to Clausewitz, war is strictly a means to an end, to be used only if its benefits outweigh its costs. The resources of the whole nation should be mobilized for just one purpose: victory (Rapoport, 1968). Thus, Clausewitz explained war in terms of the rational decisions of monarchs rather than irrational elements of human nature like a predisposition for aggression.

To support his claim that monarchs were the key actors in wars, Clausewitz adopted a fairly simple view of how societies function. He assumed, for instance, that the job of the military was to serve the monarch, regardless of the ambitions of military leaders. Thus, the interests of the military and the monarch were the same. In addition, Clausewitz did not foresee that by the end of the nineteenth century wealthy merchants and industrialists would be able to exert a strong influence on military policy. His functionalist approach to war and politics (i.e., the assumption that the military would always perform its function and serve the monarch) was weakened by the conflict inherent in the rise of powerful elites who could afford to marshall their own armed forces and challenge the power of the monarchy.

In the contemporary world, the social control of the armed forces remains a serious problem in many nations. In this regard it is encouraging to note that in Latin America, a region that for decades was dominated by military dictatorships, there has been a drastic decline in the prevalence of military rule. In 1979 at least seven Latin American nations, including Brazil, Argentina, and Chile, were ruled by military dictators; in 1989 there was only one military dictatorship—in Suriname (Brookes, 1991). At present the worst effects of war and violence in Latin America are being experienced in Colombia. The civil war there is complicated by the warring factions' involvement in the international drug trade. The United States has been sending technical and military support to help the embattled Colombian government combat the drug factions, but many observers fear that U.S. involvement will escalate the conflict and drag American forces into a deepening civil war (Guillermoprieto, 2000).

Marx and Lenin on War

Early in the twentieth century, Vladimir Ilyich Lenin built on the ideas of Karl Marx to propose a new theory of war, one that took into account some of the social changes that had transformed European societies since Clausewitz's time. According to Marx, two competing social classes were developing in all industrializing societies. The bourgeoisie owned the means of production—that is, land, factories, and other resources needed to produce the necessities of life. The other class, the proletariat, sold its labor to the bourgeoisie in return for wages that barely enabled its members to survive. Marx believed that political leaders acted as the agents of the bourgeoisie in their struggle to improve business conditions and keep the proletariat under control.

Marx predicted that as capitalist economies grew, their need for raw materials, labor, and new markets in which to sell finished goods would increase as well. Lenin claimed that the competition among Britain, France, Germany, and other major powers to establish colonies around the world during the nineteenth and early twentieth centuries was evidence that Marx's prediction was correct. Acting in the interests of the bourgeoisie—rather than in those of the monarch or nation, as Clausewitz had argued—the major powers were locked in a fierce competition for colonies. It was this competition that led to World War I, according to Lenin. In essence, the war pitted the national ruling classes against one another; the workers had nothing to gain by taking up arms (Rapoport, 1968). The basis of war, then, is economic competition among national ruling classes. Lenin contended that the violent overthrow of the bourgeoisie by the proletariat would eventually remove this motivation for warfare.

Institutional and International Perspectives

Marx and Lenin believed that economic interests shape most social phenomena, including warfare, but a number of social scientists have argued that noneconomic factors must also be considered. These explanations can be grouped into two types. The first takes the individual nation as the unit of analysis and looks inside societies at the relationships among institutions like the military, government, and business. The second group of explanations focuses on institutions and patterns of behavior that cut across national boundaries. According to this perspective, organizations such as the United Nations, as well as international treaties and trade networks, are among the factors that influence the likelihood of war or peace. We will begin with the first set of explanations, looking within nations at the institutional forces that may be responsible for war.

Institutional Forces Within Nations. Most social scientists believe that during much of the twentieth century the influence of military leaders on government policy has grown in the United States and many other nations. Many also view that growth as a threat to peace. They maintain that keeping a large, well-equipped military force at the ready makes it easier for political leaders to choose war rather than negotiation as a tactic for handling international conflicts (Barton, 1981). Supporters of military interests, on the other hand, argue that a powerful military discourages other nations from starting wars.

With the rise of aggressive totalitarian societies in Europe during the 1930s, social scientists began to analyze the growing influence of the military on domestic affairs. Harold Lasswell (1941) predicted the rise of "garrison states," in which military leaders impose dictatorial power on society, channel a growing share of the nation's resources into weapons production, and win public support through propaganda.

After World War II, a few critics voiced alarm at the newly won power of the military in the United States. In *The Power Elite,* C. Wright Mills (1956) argued that by the mid-1950s military leaders were

> more powerful than they have ever been in the history of the American elite; they have now more means of exercising power in many areas of American life which were previously civilian domains; they now have more connections; and they are now operating in a nation whose elite and whose underlying population have accepted what can only be called a military definition of reality. (p. 198)

During the war, military officers had met with heads of corporations to coordinate industrial output with military needs. America's political leaders were weak partners in this collaboration because they did not have the expertise to challenge the decisions of corporate and military leaders. Since the war, according to Mills, military institutions had "come to shape much of the economic life of the United States" (p. 222). In effect, the U.S. economy has not returned to its peacetime production patterns. Military and industrial leaders have ensured that a significant portion of the national budget is allocated to preparation for war.

Although Mills doubted the ability of political leaders to control corporate and military elites, others have argued that government officials are indeed a powerful force in defining defense policy. In fact, according to Seymour Melman (1974), the president and top officials of the Pentagon and other federal agencies have the final say in most military decisions that are important to them. Melman has challenged the Marxist explanation of war as a tool used by the rich to solve certain problems of capitalist economies. In his view, managers at the top of the federal government have often made decisions that served their own interests but damaged the economy and the interests of the rich. Pentagon policy during the Vietnam War, for example, resulted in high rates of inflation and diverted money that corporate executives could have invested for other purposes.

Because high government and military officials have so much control over military policy, their values and their beliefs about their nation's rivals are important. For example, in many respects the planning for Operation Desert Shield began after the failed attempt to rescue the hostages held in Iran during the Carter administration. At that time, military planners began to develop a more sophisticated approach to desert warfare. They developed the theory of the mobile strike force, and the technologies that would eventually be used against the Iraqis were moved from the laboratory to production lines. The end of the cold war and of the perceived Russian threat in Europe allowed planners to view the North Atlantic Treaty Organization (NATO) forces as the nucleus of an army that could be deployed in the Middle East, and that is indeed what occurred during the 1991 war. In the thinking of military strategists, therefore, the political and economic climate of the world has become as important as technology and personnel.

In addition to military, political, and economic elites, there is another actor that affects the likelihood of war—the public. When Clausewitz wrote about warfare, public opinion did not matter much. Monarchs and ministers conducted diplomacy and war without interference from the populace. In the twentieth century, however, many states have become much more democratic. As a result, political leaders must take public opinion into account in setting foreign policy. In some cases public opinion actually favors war, especially when sentiments of **nationalism**—identification with the

With the end of the cold war, the United States, as the remaining superpower, is called upon to use its influence to resolve regional conflicts such as the long and bitter one between Protestants and Catholics in Northern Ireland. Shown here is former U.S. Senator George Mitchell, who served as mediator in negotiations between the two sides.

idea of nationhood and exaltation of the nation's culture and interests above those of all other states—are strong. In the early years of this century, powerful nationalistic feelings in Germany, a number of eastern European countries, Great Britain, and other nations helped make peace seem dishonorable and war a feasible option.

Today renewed nationalism in eastern Europe, Serbia and Croatia, the former Soviet Union, and Israel and the Middle East poses a serious threat to prospects for world peace—not because of the balance of terror between the United States and the Soviet Union but because the possibility of civil wars and nationalist movements leads to increased fear of terrorism and greater political instability. Moreover, local wars can draw in the larger nations, as occurred during World War I and could occur again in the Middle East.

The International Context of War and Peace.   So far we have limited our discussion to national institutions and domestic forces that tend to preserve or threaten peace. However, no discussion of the causes of war would be complete without some attention to the international context. The world is made up largely of independent sovereign states, each with its own interests. Because the supply of natural resources, power, prestige, and other valued commodities is limited, nations inevitably compete with one another. There is no central authority powerful enough to resolve all international conflicts peacefully. Nevertheless, a number of forces do reduce incentives to wage war. (See the Critical Research feature on page 519.)

One such force is international cooperation. The League of Nations and later the United Nations are examples of international institutions designed to promote cooperation among nations. A key function of these organizations is the settlement of disputes. The United Nations, for example, has helped restore peace in three wars between Israel and the Arabs, in the Korean conflict, in the Greek civil war, in Bosnia, and in a number of other conflicts. It has often failed to resolve clashes that involve the superpowers, however. The United States, Russia, and other major nations are often unwilling to give up some of their power to arbitrators, especially on issues of vital national interest. Moreover, research on international organizations has cast doubt on their value as peacekeepers in general.

Although the United States and other nations are often drawn into global conflicts in the role of peacekeepers, recent research indicates that such third-party intervention has been largely unsuccessful. Almost invariably the peacekeeping force has been unable to withdraw after successfully restoring peace between the combatants. This pattern does not appear to be due to personal or organizational failure on the part of the peacekeepers. Instead, it stems from the explosiveness of the conflicts themselves, the problems faced by peacekeepers in attempting to maintain neutrality, the difficulty of coordinating in-the-field mediation with diplomacy, and the lack of a workable model for peacekeeping. All of these problems were encountered in Bosnia, Rwanda, Somalia, and Sierra Leone. But the desire to do something to ease bloody conflicts and to provide humanitarian aid continues to motivate third-party peacekeeping efforts and to improve their effectiveness in some instances (Rudolph, 1995; Walker, 1996).

CRITICAL RESEARCH

Globalization and the Hope of World Peace

As General Secretary of the United Nations, Kofi Annan has commissioned extensive research on UN interventions to stop the slaughter of innocent victims. In this research he and the institution he leads have been subjected to harsh criticism, particularly for the failures of peacekeeping missions in Kosovo and Rwanda. But criticism is what the UN leader asked for. No social organization, especially a world body as fraught with problems as the United Nations, can improve its effectiveness without sound evaluations of its actions. One aspect of globalization is that the world has shrunk as a result of the instant flow of TV and other images from one nation to another. When innocent populations are threatened with disaster, either from wars or from natural causes, there is an outcry from all directions to "do something" to help. Many other political considerations also come into play, but it is clear that world events now take place with far greater public awareness than ever before. In consequence, in the past decade the United Nations has intervened in Iraq, Bosnia, Cambodia, Somalia, Rwanda, Haiti, the Great Lakes region of East Africa, Nigeria, Sierra Leone, East Timor, and many other places (Urquhart, 2000).

The research Annan has commissioned at the United Nations takes a hard look at these interventions. It faults not only the United Nations but many of the leading nations of the world as well. The two most extensive research reports evaluate UN operations in Kosovo in 1998 and in Rwanda during the 1994 genocide (United Nations, 1999a, 1999b). The Rwanda report notes that the genocidal violence began only four months after the disastrous intervention of U.S. Rangers in Somalia, and there was little or no enthusiasm in the United States or elsewhere for substantial military intervention in Rwanda. Annan, then head of the UN's peacekeeping department, approached more than 100 governments around the world in a vain attempt to gather troops to head off the looming genocide. The evaluation report concludes that with 5,000 troops, the genocide that cost the lives of more than 400,000 people, the majority women and children, could have been avoided. In Kosovo, too, intervention came too late to prevent ethnic cleansing and the destruction of many cities and countless lives.

The research points to one basic problem facing the United Nations and the world's nations as they consider intervention in potential disasters. The problem is that the United Nations has no constitutional authority to gather troops and enforce measures to bring

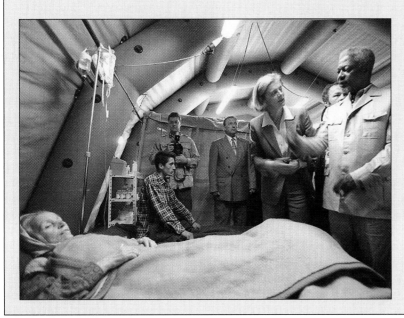

UN Secretary General Kofi Annan (right) and his wife meet with an ethnic Albanian patient from Kosovo at a field hospital set up by the French humanitarian organization Doctors Without Borders during the conflict there in 1999.

about peace. No nation wishes to give up its sovereignty: "No government wants to set up a system which may, at some point in the future, be invoked against itself"(Urquhart, 2000, p.19). In the United States, Senator Jesse Helms has often threatened to lead a movement to pull the United States out of the United Nations if that body seriously proposes any set of rules requiring its members to contribute military resources for its discretionary use. He and other opponents of the United Nations are willing to consider participation in peacekeeping missions on an individual basis but are far from willing to work out anything that begins to look like a world government with its own military resources. While this attitude prevails, Annan's research concludes, the prospects of guaranteeing human security around the world remain rather dim.

International trade is another force that tends to promote peace. When influential citizens benefit economically from peaceful relations, support for war is diminished. Moreover, trade promotes a common outlook as well as common interests; trading partners are usually political partners. Today world trade is dominated by market economies such as those of Japan, Europe, and the industrialized nations of the West. As the former communist nations of eastern Europe develop market economies and economic growth transforms more of the nations of the Pacific Rim into economic competitors of the advanced nations, global competition is likely to increase, making it even more necessary to have international peacekeeping institutions and effective international law. This is especially true as the renewed influence of nationalism throughout the world threatens to produce greater instability and terrorism.

Terrorism: Undeclared War

Violent terrorist acts—kidnapping, torture, bombings, and the like—are often committed by a nation or by a political movement to call attention to its cause and to shake people's faith in the ability of the government to eliminate the threat. The movement may be a revolutionary one that seeks far-reaching change in the government or hopes to gain control over the state. But not all terrorism is revolutionary in nature. The terrorism of cocaine barons in Colombia (known as **narcoterrorism**) is designed to take revenge on the authorities and to intimidate them into lax enforcement of the law. The terrorism of governments like that of Nigeria against their own people (known as repressive terrorism or **state terrorism**) is also not associated with revolutionary movements (Mazrui, 1996).

But **revolutionary terrorism** is the most common form, and it often leads to the other types. In Peru, for example, the revolutionary terrorist group Túpac Amaru opposes the government but also protects cocaine traffickers in return for funds to support the movement. In the Middle East, revolutionary Arab terrorist groups like Hammas have been enlisted by heads of state, such as Saddam Hussein and Muammar Quaddafi, to conduct repressive terrorist acts. In Northern Ireland, terrorism is motivated by the desire of the Irish Republican Army and its nonmilitary civil party, Sinn Fein, to achieve independence from England, but the Protestant minority fears independence, and the resulting political stalemate has often erupted in terrorist violence.

In recent decades, terrorism has become one of the most dangerous threats to world order. In its effects, and sometimes in its causes, terrorism is comparable to more traditional forms of war. It destabilizes governments, preys on innocent victims, and involves large amounts of financial and human resources. Yet unlike war, which openly pits opponents against each other in a recognized trial of strength, terrorism is covert. It seeks to sway the masses through intimidation.

SOCIAL PROBLEMS ONLINE

Information About War and Terrorism

War, revolution, and terrorism garner considerable attention on the Internet. For a current look at international violence, start with the daily newspaper. The daily edition of the *New York Times* (**http://www.nytimes.com**) can be accessed by following a simple registration procedure. The site also maintains an archive of past stories. Most of the other major national newspapers can be found by entering their names on any one of the major search engines. Foreign newspapers often offer a slightly different slant than U.S. papers. Because it serves the international business community, the *Financial Times* offers wide-ranging coverage of trouble spots throughout the world; it can be accessed at **http://www.ft.com** after registering.

The Central Intelligence Agency (CIA) does more than engage in cloak-and-dagger activities. Its web pages (**http://www.odci.gov/cia/ciahome.html**) offer lists of online publications, including its *World Factbook*, which provide basic information about geography, population, demographics, and governments (including names of chiefs of state and cabinet members). An atlas of the Balkans and a *Handbook of International Economic Statistics* are other resources that can help make sense of the changing international situation.

Stanford University's Hoover Institution on War, Revolution and Peace at **http://www-hoover.stanford.edu/homepage** analyzes social, political, and economic change from a largely conservative viewpoint. Selections from its *Hoover Digest* are available for reading or downloading and cover both domestic and international issues related to "principles of statecraft, the art of government, and relations among nations during war, revolution, and peace." From a more liberal perspective, the Carnegie Endowment for International Peace seeks to "invigorate and extend both expert and public discussion on a wide range of international is-

sues," including worldwide migration, nuclear nonproliferation, regional conflicts, multilateralism, and the use of force. It provides a catalog of publications and an index of its magazine *Foreign Policy*, with articles from several issues. It can be accessed at **http://www.ceip.org/**.

The Center for Democracy and Technology (**http://www.cdt.org/index.html**) features resources that are critical of U.S. and other government efforts to restrict free speech and the flow of information in the name of countering terrorism. It disseminates information about Internet censorship and privacy issues and offers interesting scenarios on how the Internet can and cannot be used to further terrorism.

Peace Brigades International has a web page at **http://www.igc.apc.org/pbi/** that offers links to humanitarian, human rights, and peace and justice organizations in the Caribbean, Latin America, North America, Europe, Australia, and New Zealand. Most of the organizations offer newsletters and publications that describe political, economic, and social conditions in specific countries or regions. Several groups provide opportunities for becoming active in human rights campaigns or other activities that promote peace and justice.

Those interested in research on feeding the world's hungry and relieving international poverty may access InterAction, "a coalition of more than 150 nonprofit organizations advocating for humanitarian assistance to the world's poor." Its web page is located at **http://www.interaction.org/**. It offers an informative set of background briefing papers on the crisis in central Africa, as well as links to the United Nations's "ReliefWeb." Further information about Africa that places its various crises in historical and geopolitical context can be accessed at the University of Pennsylvania's African Studies web page (**http://www.sas.upenn.edu/African_Studies/AS.html**).

Until recently the United States was relatively free of terrorism. The bombings of the federal office building in Oklahoma City and the World Trade Center in New York City; the letter bombs mailed by the so-called Unabomber; and, some would argue, the terrorism perpetrated by agencies of the U.S. government against the Branch Davidians in Waco, Texas, in 1993 are examples of recent cases of terrorism in the United States. These acts suggest that terrorism is increasing not only in the

United States but throughout the world. Surely the potential for terrorism is growing, spurred by increases in ethnic and national hostilities around the world. On the other hand, the number of terrorist incidents fluctuates greatly from one period to another. In 1999, for example, with peace talks progressing well in the Middle East and Northern Ireland, acts of terrorism in these global hot spots were at a low ebb. At the same time, just before the worldwide celebrations of the new millennium, antiterrorist agents arrested 13 suspected terrorists who had been trained in the camps of terrorist leader Osama Bin Ladin in Afghanistan, thereby possibly averting what could have been major acts of violence during the celebrations (Meed, 2000).

Fluctuations in the number of terrorist acts can be caused by many factors. Chief among these are events in the more troubled areas of the world. The prospect of lasting peace in the Middle East or a resolution of the conflict in Northern Ireland could produce major decreases in the total number of terrorist acts; conversely, any worsening of conditions in these and similar areas could lead to higher rates of terrorism (Long, 1990; U.S. Congress, 1993).

In addition to its origins in political radicalism, terrorism may spring from various kinds of cults that have much in common despite differing ideologies. In March 1997, Americans were shocked when 39 members of the cult known as Heaven's Gate were discovered in a mass suicide in an affluent San Diego suburb (Bruni, 1997). As in earlier instances of mass murder and suicide, these were linked to the charismatic appeal of deranged leaders who were believed to possess supernatural powers. The history of David Koresh and the Branch Davidians in Waco follows the same pattern. The more convinced members were of the leader's power, the more isolated they felt from the rest of society. A collective paranoia developed as they perceived themselves to be targets of society's hate. In both cases these feelings led to acts of irrational violence (Niebuhr, 1995).

As noted earlier, terrorism can be perpetrated by agencies of the state. Adolph Hitler and Josef Stalin practiced state terrorism, using brutality, fear, and legalized murder on an overwhelming scale to subjugate the masses. The attack and fire that destroyed the Branch Davidian compound suggest that that tragedy may also be considered an episode of state terrorism. Whereas victims of other forms of terrorism may hope to be rescued by government or police forces, victims of state terrorism can have no such hope. Indeed, the extreme nature of state terrorism has led many people to argue that violent rebellion is a justifiable reaction.

The terrorist recruit is often well educated and young, with an upper-middle- or middle-class background. As individuals, terrorists want to save the world, although their concept of salvation is based on a limited set of inflexible beliefs. The terrorist believes that purity of motive justifies whatever methods are employed. In this detachment from reality, coupled with total willingness to surrender life itself for the cause, terrorists become dehumanized. They see themselves as catalysts, worthless in themselves, through which social change can be accomplished (Hassel, 1977).

In this process, the victim, who in the terrorist's mind is merely a pawn in the struggle for societal reform, is stripped of human rights and identity. The terrorist wants to punish society, to force it to accept his or her demands. The terrorist preys on both known and unknown victims, assured that—as representatives of an abhorrent society—the victims are responsible for society's wrongs and unworthy of compassion. Because any society is the combined achievement of thousands of individuals and many generations, the injustice of terrorist thinking is obvious. Terrorists' victims are innocent people whose lives are destroyed by fanatical intolerance.

Those who suffer as a result of terrorist acts can be divided into two groups. The first are random victims, people who are simply in the wrong place at the wrong time. Bombings, hijackings, and the spontaneous seizing of hostages victimize whoever happens to be available. Other members of society are intimidated by the casualness of this kind of terror, and the terrorist hopes that they will pressure their government to meet his or her demands. The other category of victims includes individuals who are singled out because of their prominence. They, too, become dehumanized symbols: All politicians bear the blame for whatever political injustices the terrorist perceives; all businesspeople are held personally responsible for commercial waste and greed. The civilians who have been killed or injured in bombings by terrorist groups as part of the Palestinian-Israeli conflict are an example of the first category; the prominent computer scientists targeted by the Unabomber and the murdered Israeli leader Yitzhak Rabin are examples of the second.

SOCIAL POLICY

Although stockpiles of nuclear arms in the world's most powerful nations remain high and the possibility of the spread of nuclear arms to less developed nations continues to pose a threat to world peace, for the first time since the development of these terrible weapons there is hope for a reduction in the threat of nuclear war. This hope comes mainly from the progress already made in limiting conventional weapons and from the rapidly changing world situation, particularly the end of 45 years of "cold" war between the superpowers.

In 1990 the United States, the (then) Soviet Union, and the major nations of Europe agreed to limit the number of tanks, combat planes, artillery pieces, and combat-ready ground forces held by NATO and by the Soviet Union and its former satellites in eastern Europe. Basically, this pact meant that the Soviet Union began to remove its military threat to Europe and that the United States began to withdraw its forces stationed in Europe. We will see shortly that arms reductions talks between the United States and Russia continue.

On a less promising note, in 1999, by a vote of 51 to 48, the U.S. Senate rejected the global nuclear test ban treaty that President Clinton had signed in 1996 and had promised to shepherd through the Senate, where a two-thirds vote was needed for ratification. Earlier the Senate had passed a treaty banning chemical weapons, but this time it failed to heed world opinion or the urgings of the administration (Schwartz, 2000).

Arms Control: A Promise Unfulfilled

The history of disarmament since nuclear weapons were invented consists of a series of limited agreements that have, until very recently, allowed the arms race to continue almost unabated. This is not to say that negotiations to achieve total disarmament have not been attempted. In August 1945, the first resolution passed by the United Nations set up the International Atomic Energy Commission and instructed it to propose plans for the complete elimination of nuclear weapons. Because the Soviet Union had not yet built a bomb, it vetoed the commission's proposal, which called for arms control first and prohibition at some time in the future. (Control would permit certain levels of weapons; prohibition would ban them entirely.)

In the early 1950s, France, Great Britain, Canada, the United States, and the Soviet Union again tried to reach a general arms control agreement. In talks that lasted for several years, these nations reached a consensus on several issues, including the date at which total prohibition of nuclear weapons should take effect and how they should inspect one another's defense sites. However, disagreements on verification led to a deadlock that could not be resolved.

Despite their failure to ban nuclear weapons, the major powers have succeeded in formulating a number of treaties that limit certain weapons and regulate the spread of others. The first of these accords was the Nuclear Test–ban Treaty, which was signed in 1963. This agreement forbade all nuclear tests under water, in outer space, and on the ground, but it did not prohibit underground tests.

In addition to the test-ban treaty, agreements prohibiting the spread of nuclear weapons to Antarctica, Latin America, Mexico, and outer space were signed between 1959 and 1967. In 1968, the Nuclear Nonproliferation Treaty was ratified by the UN General Assembly. This treaty was designed to stop the flow of nuclear weapons to nations that did not already have them. However, the agreement did nothing to slow the production of nuclear weapons by nations that *did* have them.

Since the nonproliferation treaty was signed, the United States has entered into a series of negotiations with the former Soviet Union to limit strategic arms, that is, weapons that are considered essential to a nation's offense or defense. Two agreements emerged from the Strategic Arms Limitation Talks (SALT). The SALT treaties were flawed in a number of ways. First, they did not bind any nuclear powers except the Soviet Union and the United States. Other nations that possess the bomb, such as France and Great Britain, were not obligated by the terms of these treaties. Second, the limits on offensive weapons were set above existing levels, thus allowing for continued expansion of both nations' arsenals. Third, and even more detrimental to arms control, was the total lack of restrictions on improvements to existing weapons. Both nations were free to build greater accuracy, speed, and range into their missiles. Finally, the agreements did not prevent the two superpowers from developing new weapons like the cruise missile.

In December 1987 the United States and the Soviet Union signed a treaty to eliminate all shorter- and medium-range nuclear missiles—those with a range of 300 to 3,400 miles—from their arsenals within three years. The treaty also set forth procedures to be followed in eliminating the missiles, as well as rules governing inspection by both sides.

But as the wars in the Middle East, Bosnia, and Kosovo demonstrate, the arms race will very likely become a serious problem not so much for the superpowers as for regions of the world where nationalism and conflicts over borders threaten peace (Karp, 1994). Advances in technology create the temptation to build weapons that could provide at least a temporary advantage. Most military experts agree that the performance of America's highly sophisticated weapons systems—including computer-guided "smart bombs," infrared sighting systems, the Patriot antimissile missiles, and other arms developed and produced in large quantities during the 1980s—have turned the world toward a new arms race based primarily on the quest for effective conventional weapons.

In the debates that took place in the United States over whether to attack the Iraqi forces in Kuwait, the threat posed by Iraq's nuclear and chemical weapons and the superiority of its armed forces in the Middle East were powerful arguments in favor of quick intervention. The allied victory over Iraq left the Middle East in a highly uncertain state, however. The 1993 Chemical Weapons Convention was signed by 160 nations, but weaknesses in the control and inspection provisions and the tendency for renegade nations in the developing world to resort to chemical weapons make these deadly forms of nonnuclear arms a persistent threat to regional peace.

Another serious problem created by smaller regional wars is the legacy they leave behind in the form of unexploded ammunition and buried land mines. Rich nations like Kuwait have professional demolition experts to clear the land of thousands of buried mines. Poor nations like Somalia and Angola must endure unpredictable explosions that take the lives and limbs of thousands of poor farmers. In Afghanistan, the Soviets laid 12 million mines during the war in the 1980s. Similar situations exist in Cambodia and in many African nations. Since many of the land mines were made in the United States, this nation bears much of the responsibility for establishing better control over the sale of deadly military technology (Donovan, 1994).

Alternatives to the Arms Race

War and the arms race are social problems in themselves, and they leave even greater social problems in their wake, as can be seen in the devastation, poverty, and environmental and political damage in the Middle East after the liberation of Kuwait. If we fail to make progress on these issues, the other problems discussed in this book may become footnotes to the history of social conditions "before the war." Yet many proposed solutions seem idealistic in the current political context. One such proposal is renewed pressure by the public for an end to the testing and deployment of nuclear weapons through support for arms control treaties as they have been negotiated in the past. However, the superpowers have tended to word the treaties in such a way that they exclude any new weapons systems that are under development while the agreement is being negotiated (Bee, 1995; Crossette, 1995).

In most societies the use of violence to resolve conflicts among citizens is held to be not only illegal but also immoral. Hence, violent acts are punished by both legal and moral sanctions. When violence breaks out between nations, however, few such sanctions are available to address it. According to some arms control advocates, the world needs much more effective ways to regulate violence and the types of behaviors (e.g., arms buildups) that make violence more destructive when it occurs.

Dealing with Terrorism

Terrorist acts, especially kidnappings and the holding of hostages, often attract worldwide attention. Indeed, terrorists use violence and drastic actions to attract media attention to their cause, as well as to intimidate civilians and show governments that they can exert power. Although public sentiment often favors negotiating with terrorists to win the release of captives, the usual official policy is not to give in to terrorist demands (Bremer, 1988; Clawson, 1988). Policies that have proven somewhat effective include the following: Governments should use boycotts and other measures to put pressure on states that sponsor terrorism; negotiators may promise anything to terrorists but not keep the promises after the captives have been released because promises made under threat are not valid; terrorists should be treated as criminals; the cooperation of journalists and media personnel should be enlisted to deprive terrorists of media attention; substantial rewards should be offered for information about and capture of terrorists; and an international campaign against terrorists should be undertaken with the help of a network of experts on the subject.

An informed public that will cooperate with antiterrorist policies is extremely important in combating this social problem. During the 1991 Persian Gulf war, for example, there were predictions of widespread terrorism, especially against air travelers; and although the traffic on commercial flights was drastically reduced because of this fear, the cooperation of the public with searches and stringent antiterrorist measures at airports was credited with preventing more violence than actually occurred. However, although these policies help diminish the spread and effectiveness of terrorism, much larger forces are at work that seem to be increasing the likelihood of terrorist acts. (See the Unintended Consequences feature on page 526.)

The Oklahoma City terrorism trial raises questions about why the United States does not pass laws that require tagging explosives with an identifying chemical that would make it far more difficult to use commonplace materials like fertilizer as explosives for mass destruction. The National Rifle Association and other pro-weapons groups oppose such laws on grounds of individual freedom and self-protection (Guterl, 1996). Other experts on domestic terrorism argue that the United States

Unintended Consequences

Terrorism and the Internet

The 1995 bombing in Oklahoma City and the 1997 Heaven's Gate mass suicide are tragic events that also cast a negative light on the Internet. The Oklahoma City bombing called attention to the proliferation of explicitly racist, anti-Semitic, white power, and terrorist-related sites on the World Wide Web. The Heaven's Gate suicides called attention to the equally robust growth of fringe religious groups, UFO enthusiasts, and many other seemingly apocalyptic or doomsday groups whose messages are easily accessible on the Internet.

For those who are intent on keeping cyberspace as free from censorship as possible, these are problems that threaten the future of this exciting new communication channel. For those concerned about exerting social control, however, the Internet is an increasingly problematic communications medium. In 1997, for example, the U.S. Parole Commission ruled that in certain cases federal parolees can be barred from using a computer to access the Internet (Johnson, 1997). But for every website that represents a potential threat to social order, there are at least ten times as many others that deal with benign subjects, from news of new allergy treatments to the latest weather report. Still, these recent events, as well as the problem of protecting minors from indecent advances by adults, have tarnished the Internet's image.

David Gelernter (1997), a noted Yale University computer scientist who was one of the Unabomber's victims, observes that the connection between the Internet and terrorism, the appeal of cults, and other social problems is not unusual or unexpected. He notes that since the Heaven's Gate cult "ran a Web-page design business, they may have trolled for new members by sending E-mail to likely targets. They believed an alien spaceship was hiding behind the Hale-Bopp comet; they may have got the news over the Net, where rumors spread fast." But before they used the Internet, they recruited people into the cult through posters and other old-fashioned techniques. It is tempting to blame technology, Gelernter notes, but if people are confused about what to believe about good and evil, or God and humanity, why blame that on the Internet rather than face the real problem? It is clear, however, that as with all technologies that expand the possibilities for human communication and persuasion (especially movies, radio, and television), the subject of how and whether to control some forms of activity and speech on the Internet will continue to be a social policy issue for the foreseeable future.

should ban private armies and militias, but given the fierce lobbying that accompanies any effort to control sales of personal weapons, it is doubtful that the nation has the political will to accomplish this goal (Dees & Zelikow, 1995).

Beyond Left & Right

Should the United States be more forceful in banning the kinds of weapons that are used in domestic terrorism, such as assault rifles and unidentifiable explosives? Most people on the liberal side of American politics would agree that they should. Many on the conservative side would not. They may not believe in the spread of arms and private armies any more than others do, but they often fear the growing power of the federal government. How can this stalemate be resolved?

The answer seems to be on a case-by-case basis. First ban assault weapons; then pass laws calling for the addition of "taggants" to fertilizers and other materials that can be used as deadly explosives. Perhaps it takes tragedies like the Oklahoma City bombing to gain a consensus across the political spectrum, and even that consensus will not last long. Each victory in the effort to check the spread of weapons of terror needs to be gained when the "right" conditions are present. Such victories require the assent of people of all political persuasions—all, of course, except those who would resort to terror themselves.

SUMMARY

- The direct effects of war include extensive death and destruction. In addition, many soldiers suffer lasting physical and psychological injuries.

- Indirect effects of war include disruption of the lives of people whose homeland has become a battleground. War also leads to mass migrations of people who are trying to escape persecution or seeking new opportunities. In addition, war causes immeasurable economic damage.

- The development of nuclear weapons has contributed to peace among the major powers. However, if peace breaks down, a war of unprecedented destructiveness could ensue. The effects of a nuclear war would include not only widespread death and massive physical damage but also radiation sickness and increased rates of cancer. Nuclear warfare would also severely strain the resources of governments, destroy the ability of societies to function, and damage the environment–perhaps irrevocably.

- Throughout human history the actual conduct of war has been closely linked to the nature of existing military technology. As the technologies of war have become ever more deadly, the ravages of war have increased. Changes in the organizational dimension of military technology have been at least as important as advances in military apparatus.

- There has been some progress toward controlling the conduct of war. A body of international law that deals with armed conflicts includes rules that define the rights and privileges of those who fight and that attempt to protect noncombatants. However, these rules are difficult to enforce and are frequently violated.

- Among the theories that have been proposed to account for war is the view that humans have a predisposition for aggression that has been transmitted genetically from one generation to the next. This view is challenged by those who believe that the motivation to fight is a learned response to symbols.

- According to the nineteenth-century military philosopher Carl von Clausewitz, war is used by monarchs as an alternative to diplomacy to gain land, prestige, and other benefits. Marx and Lenin, on the other hand, believed that economic competition leads national ruling classes (as opposed to workers) to wage war on one another.

- Noneconomic explanations of war are of two basic types: those that look at relations among institutions within a society and those that focus on relations among nations. In the former category is the belief that a strong, influential military affects the likelihood that a nation will go to war. This view is expressed in Lasswell's prediction of the rise of "garrison states," in which military leaders have dictatorial power, and in Mills's warning of the power of the "industrial-military complex." An opposing view holds that government officials do indeed define military policy. In modern times, public opinion has also been an important factor in military policy decisions.

- Among the forces that reduce incentives to wage war are international organizations and international trade. As international economic competition increases, the need for international peacekeeping institutions will also increase.

- Terrorism has reached alarming proportions in recent decades. Terrorist acts may be spurred by revolutionary fervor, the collective paranoia of followers of a deranged leader, or the attempts of a state to repress its citizens. Transnational terrorism is committed by independent agents who are essentially autonomous.

- Victims of terrorist acts are of two types: random victims and individuals who are singled out because of their prominence. In both cases the victim is dehumanized in the eyes of the terrorist and used as a symbol of political or other injustice.

- Policies aimed at reducing the buildup of arms have focused on international arms control treaties. These agreements have limited certain weapons and regulated the spread of others, reducing the chance that a minor incident will lead to a full-scale war. However, the arms race will continue in regions where nationalism and conflicts over borders threaten peace.

- The usual official policy toward terrorism is not to give in to terrorist demands and to treat terrorists as criminals. However, while this policy may diminish the spread and effectiveness of terrorism, other forces seem to be increasing the likelihood of terrorist acts.

KEY TERMS

nationalism, p. 517

narcoterrorism, p. 520

state terrorism, p. 520

revolutionary terrorism, p. 520

INTERNET EXERCISE

The web destinations for Chapter 18 are related to different aspects of war and terrorism. To begin your explorations, go to the Prentice Hall Companion Website: **http://prenhall.com/kornblum**. Then choose **Chapter 18** (War and Terrorism). Next, select **destinations** from the menu on the left side of the screen. There are a variety of sites to investigate. We suggest that you begin with **Terrorism and the Internet.** The *Unintended Consequences* box in this chapter deals with terrorist activities on the Internet/World Wide Web. This problem threatens cyberspace freedom and raises questions about future government-imposed controls on the Internet. The *Terrorism and the Internet* website will better acquaint you with the issues involved in this controversy. After you have explored this site, answer the following questions:

■ Do you think that certain controls on the Internet are necessary? For example, imagine that the perpetrators of the Oklahoma City bombing incident had a website that encouraged people to engage in terrorist acts. Do you think that the existence of such a site is a social problem? How should this kind of behavior be dealt with?

■ Do you think that censorship of the Internet is a problem? If so, how could reasonable controls on terrorist activities on the Internet be imposed without sacrificing freedom of speech? If controls are needed, how should the government go about imposing them?

acquaintance rape   See *date rape.*

acquired immune deficiency syndrome (AIDS)   A chronic and often fatal disease in which the normal immunological defenses of the body deteriorate, making the sufferer prey to a host of infectious diseases, particularly pneumonia, tuberculosis, and certain forms of cancer.

addiction   Physical dependence on a drug.

affirmative action   Programs that systematically increase opportunities for women and members of minority groups that have been the victims of past economic and social discrimination.

age cohort   A group of people who were born in the same period.

ageism   Devaluation of the aged and the resultant bias against older people.

age stratification   The process by which people are segregated into different groups or strata on the basis of age.

AIDS-related complex (ARC)   A complex of symptoms that many health scientists believe is indicative of the early stages of AIDS.

alcoholic   A person who is addicted to alcohol.

alienation   A condition experienced by workers who lose the capacity to express themselves in their work.

alimony   The money paid by one partner for the support of the other after they have obtained a divorce.

amphetamine   A drug that has a stimulating effect; known as "speed" or "uppers" in street language.

anomie   A weakening of the norms that govern acceptable social behavior; a disparity between approved goals and the approved means of obtaining them.

appropriate technology   A policy perspective that advocates less complex and smaller-scale technological solutions than those offered by large-scale corporate and government institutions.

asocial sex variance   Sexual acts that are strongly disapproved of and are usually committed by one individual or at most a small number of people.

assault   An attempt to injure or kill a human being.

assimilation   The process by which members of a racial or ethnic minority group take on the characteristics of the mainstream culture by adapting their cultural patterns to those of the majority group and by intermarrying.

authority   Power that has been routinized within a social organization.

automation   Computer-controlled production methods; also, the replacement of workers by a nonhuman means of producing the same product.

aversion therapy   A treatment program that employs nausea-producing drugs or electric shock to condition a patient against alcohol.

baby boom generation   The portion of the U.S. population born during the years immediately following World War II.

barbiturate   A drug that depresses the central nervous system; known as "downers" in street language.

behavior conditioning   See *aversion therapy.*

breakdown   A condition in which obedience to a set of rules results in no reward or in punishment; a manifestation of social disorganization.

bureaucracy   An organization in which activities are divided into precisely defined roles arranged in a hierarchy or chain of command.

capitalism   A system for organizing the production of goods and services that is based on markets, private property, and the business firm or company.

census tract   A relatively homogenous area with respect to population, socioeconomic status, and living conditions.

chain migration   The tendency of immigrants to migrate to areas where they have kin and others from their home communities.

child abuse   A deliberate attack on a child by a parent or other caregiver that results in physical injury.

civil law   Laws that deal with noncriminal acts in which one individual injures another.

class stratification   The stratification of individuals and groups according to their access to various occupations, income, and skills; see *social stratification.*

codependency   A pattern in which members of a problem drinker's family participate in a pattern of interactions designed to excuse the problematic behavior.

community psychology   An approach to the treatment of mental disorders that makes use of easily accessible, locally controlled facilities that can care for people in their own communities.

comparable worth   The idea that the pay levels of certain jobs should be adjusted so that they reflect the intrinsic value of the job; holders of jobs of comparable value would then be paid at comparable rates.

computer crimes   Illegal manipulation of computer technology to commit robbery, fraud, and other crimes.

conflict perspective   A sociological perspective based on the belief that social problems arise out of major contradictions in the way societies are organized, which create conflict between those who have access to the "good life" and those who do not.

conglomerate   A combination of firms that operate in greatly diversified fields.

consolidated metropolitan statistical area (CMSA)   The largest urban areas in the United States, comprising two or more closely linked major cities or primary metropolitan statistical areas, such as Dallas–Fort Worth or New York City–northern New Jersey–Long Island.

control group   The subjects who do not receive the "treatment" in an experiment.

conventional crimes   Crimes that are committed by semiprofessional criminals as a way of life.

cost shifting   The tendency for the costs of treating people with serious illnesses to be transferred from one insurance system to another.

crime   An act or omission of an act for which the state can apply sanctions.

crime index   A set of data on the most serious, frequently occurring crimes: murder and nonnegligent manslaughter, forcible rape, robbery, aggravated assault, burglary, larceny-theft, motor vehicle theft, and arson.

criminal law   A subdivision of the rules governing society that prohibits certain acts and prescribes punishments to be meted out to violators.

cross-sectional data   Data based on a questionnaire given to a sample on a single occasion.

crude birthrate   The number of births per 1,000 population.

cultural lag   A condition in which one of two correlated parts of a culture changes before or in greater degree than the other, thereby causing less adjustment between the two parts than existed previously.

culture conflict A condition in which people feel trapped by contradictory rules; a manifestation of social disorganization.

date rape Forcible sex in which the victim is known to the offender.

debt entanglement The accumulation of large, and frequently unpayable, amounts of personal debt by consumers who have purchased most of what they own by using consumer credit.

deconcentration The situation created by the flight of middle-class families from the central city to the suburbs, together with the influx of poor minority groups, the unemployed, and the aged to those areas.

de facto segregation Segregation that is a result of housing patterns, economic patterns, and other factors.

deinstitutionalization The discharge of patients from mental hospitals directly into the community.

de jure segregation Segregation that is required by law.

demographic transition The process in which a population shifts from an original equilibrium in which a high birthrate is canceled out by a high death rate, through a stage in which the birthrate remains high but the death rate declines, to a final equilibrium in which the birth and death rates are lower but the population is much larger.

demography The subfield of sociology that studies how social conditions are distributed in human populations and how those populations are changing.

dependency ratio The relationship between the number of working people and the number of nonworking people in a population.

detoxification A treatment in which an alcoholic is kept off alcohol until none shows in blood samples.

deviance Behavior that departs from an accepted norm.

differential association An explanation of crime that holds that criminal behavior is a result of a learning process that occurs chiefly within small, intimate groups that value such behavior.

discrimination The differential treatment of individuals who are considered to belong to a particular social group.

domestic network A familial network consisting of a number of households linked together by ties based on kinship, pseudokinship, and reciprocal personal and economic obligations.

drift hypothesis See *social-selection hypothesis*.

drug A chemical substance that affects body function, mood, perception, or consciousness; has a potential for misuse; and may be harmful to the user or to society.

drug abuse The use of unacceptable drugs, and excessive or inappropriate use of acceptable drugs, so that physical, psychological, or social harm can result.

drug dependence The compulsion to use a drug, whether the cause is physical or psychological.

dying trajectory The pattern of feelings and behavior that emerges during the process of dying.

educational attainment The number of years of school completed by an individual.

embezzlement Theft from an employer by an employee with privileged access to company finances.

endogamy A norm stating that a person brought up in a particular culture should marry within the cultural group.

ethnic minority A minority group made up of people who may share certain cultural features and who regard themselves as a unified group.

ethnography The close observation of interactions among people in a social group or organization.

exhibitionism Deliberate exposure of one's sex organs in public.

experimental group The subjects who receive the "treatment" in an experiment.

extended family A kinship unit that consists of parents, children, grandparents, and other related individuals who are living together.

field research See *participant observation*.

flexitime An approach to work hours that allows employees to arrive and depart from the job when they choose, as long as they work during specific core hours and for a certain amount of time per week.

forcible rape The act of forcing sexual intercourse on a woman of legal age.

formication The illusion that insects or snakes are crawling on or in the skin.

fraud Obtaining money or property under false pretenses.

future shock A general sense of anxiety or confusion about the future and, at times, the present, caused by the constant need to adapt one's way of life to new ways of doing things.

gender identity A person's sexual self-image, as distinguished from physiological gender.

gentrification Revitalization of urban neighborhoods by professionals and other upper-middle-class people.

gerontology The study of the physical causes and effects of the aging process.

gross domestic product (GDP) The total market value of all final goods and services produced in the economy in one year.

habituation Psychological dependence on a drug.

halfway house A small residential community, usually under private auspices and most often in an urban area, in which for a period of weeks or months ex-patients are helped to adjust from hospital to normal life.

hallucinogen A drug that distorts the user's perceptions.

Head Start A blanket term that refers to federally funded preschool programs aimed at preparing disadvantaged children for school.

health maintenance organization (HMO) A prepaid group practice that provides complete medical services to subscribers in a specific region.

homogamy The requirement that one must marry a person similar to oneself in religion, social class, and race or ethnicity.

homosexuality A sexual preference for members of one's own sex.

hospice An institution designed for terminally ill patients.

human immunodeficiency virus (HIV) The virus that causes acquired immune deficiency syndrome (AIDS).

incest Sexual relations between individuals who are so closely related that they are forbidden to marry by law or custom.

infrastructure Public facilities such as water, sewage, transportation, lighting, and medical care facilities.

insider trading Illegal trading of securities on the basis of "inside," or privileged, information that is not known to the public.

institution A more or less stable structure of statuses and roles devoted to meeting the basic needs of people in a society.

institutional coordination The concept that health-care institutions, particularly those that treat the mentally ill, should be more closely connected and coordinated in their efforts to help their patients.

institutional discrimination Discrimination that occurs as a result of the structure and functioning of public institutions and policies.

institutionalization The process through which the way a social institution works is changed—generally by passing new laws.

institutional violence Violence exercised on behalf of or under the protection of the state.

institution building Research that attempts to show how people reorganize their lives to cope with new conditions, often creating new kinds of organizations and, sometimes, whole new institutions.

juvenile delinquency A violation of the law committed by a person under 18 years of age; usually a status offense.

kinship unit A group of individuals who are related to one another either by bloodlines or by some convention equivalent to marriage.

labeling theory The view that social problems arise because certain groups or individuals, for their own profit, name or label other groups or individuals as demonstrating problems or deviant behavior.

lesbian A female homosexual.

level of living What people actually obtain in the way of material well-being.

living will A legal or quasi-legal document drawn up by an individual that instructs the family, the physician, and other health-care providers on what course to take should the individual who has written the document become incapacitated and unable to conduct his or her own affairs.

longitudinal data Data derived from comparisons of matched samples over time.

lumpenproleteriat A term used by Karl Marx to refer to the segment of the poor in a capitalist society who are not part of the labor force but are on the margins of the society, often subsisting through criminal and black-market activities.

mainstreaming Educating a handicapped child in an ordinary public school classroom.

malpractice Physically harmful mistreatment of a patient by a physician.

manslaughter Unlawful killing of a human being without malice aforethought.

market An economic institution that regulates exchange behavior through the establishment of different values for particular goods and services.

Medicaid An assistance program financed from tax revenues and designed to pay for the medical costs of people who cannot afford basic health care.

medical group A group practice, typically consisting of a general practitioner or internist sharing facilities with a number of different specialists.

Medicare A public health insurance program paid for by Social Security taxes and designed to cover some of the medical expenses of people aged 65 and over.

megalopolis See *standard consolidated statistical area.*

mental disorder Psychological or organic problems in the mental functioning of an individual that may require medical treatment but do not require hospitalization.

mental illness Psychological or organic problems in the mental functioning of an individual that are considered serious enough to require hospitalization.

merger The combining of separate businesses into a single enterprise.

metropolitan district An area that contains several urban communities, all of which are in close proximity to one another.

metropolitan statistical area An urban area that comprises a medium-sized city or two or more closely linked smaller cities, for example, Indianapolis, Indiana, or Little Rock–North Little Rock, Arkansas.

modernization The transformation of societies to urbanized and industrialized ways of life based on scientific technologies, individualized rather than communal or collective roles, and a cosmopolitan outlook that values efficiency and progress.

modified extended family A family structure in which the individual nuclear families live separately but the extended family remains as a strong kinship organization through a combination of interpersonal attachments among its members and various forms of economic exchanges and mutual aid.

multinational corporation An economic enterprise that is based in one country and pursues business activities in one or more foreign countries.

murder Unlawful killing of a human being with malice aforethought.

narcotic antagonist A substance that negates the effects produced by opiates.

nationalism Identification of the masses with the nation and exaltation of its culture and interests above those of all other states.

nativism The idea that only native-born individuals deserve the full benefits of citizenship in a nation and that foreigners are a danger to the stability of the society.

neighborhood distress A condition in which a neighborhood is characterized by high rates of poverty, joblessness, female-headed families, welfare recipiency, and teenage school dropouts.

noninstitutional violence Violence exercised by individuals and groups that are opposed to established authority.

nuclear family A kinship unit that consists of a father, a mother, and their children, living apart from other kin.

occasional property crimes Crimes such as vandalism, check forgery, and shoplifting that are usually committed by individuals who lack professional criminal skills.

occupational (white-collar) crimes Crimes such as embezzlement, fraud, and price-fixing that are committed in the course of business activity.

oligopoly The control of a commodity or service in a given market by a small number of companies or suppliers.

organized crime A system in which illegal activities are carried out as part of a rational plan devised by a large organization that is attempting to maximize its overall profit.

oriental exclusion The attempt by settlers in the western United States to exclude Asians from the country or from local labor markets in order to reduce competition for jobs.

outsourcing Locating of American manufacturing plants that produce goods for American markets in third-world nations, where the manufacturing firm can take advantage of lower wage rates.

paraphyllic rapism A term that has been proposed to the American Psychiatric Association as a diagnosis for men who can achieve sexual pleasure only in the context of rape and coercion.

parole Supervision of people who have been released from prison.

participant observation A research technique in which the sociologist participates directly in the social life of the individuals or groups under study.

plea bargaining An arrangement in which an offender agrees to plead guilty to a lesser charge than that of which he or she was originally accused in return for a lighter sentence.

political crime Activities such as treason, sedition, and civil disobedience that in the eyes of the state threaten the existing social order and could do the nation serious harm if unchecked.

pornography The depiction of sexual behavior in such a way as to sexually excite the viewer.

postindustrial society A society whose organizing principle is the dominance of theoretical knowledge.

power The ability of an individual or group to impose its will on others.

prejudice An emotional, rigid attitude toward members of a particular group that is maintained despite evidence that it is wrong.

prevalence The extent to which a behavior appears in the population to any degree at all.

primary metropolitan statistical area (PMSA) Urban areas that comprise one major city and the adjacent, closely linked suburbs; for example, New York City.

probation Supervision of offenders who have not been sentenced to jail or prison.

problem drinker A person whose frequent drinking interferes with his or her health, interpersonal relationships, and economic functioning.

professional crimes Crimes such as safecracking and counterfeiting that are committed by expert criminals who are dedicated to a life of crime.

projection A means of releasing tension that involves attributing one's own undesirable traits to some other individual or group.

prostitution Sexual relations on a promiscuous and mercenary basis with no emotional attachment.

psychological dependence A condition in which a user needs a drug for the feeling of well-being that it produces.

psychotropic drugs Pharmaceutical drugs used in the management of stress, mental disorders, and mental illness.

public-order crimes Activities that are considered to be crimes because they violate the order or customs of the community.

racial minority A minority group made up of people who share certain inherited characteristics.

racial steering The deliberate refusal of real estate brokers to show houses to minority buyers outside specific areas.

racism Behavior, in word or deed, that is motivated by the belief that human races have distinctive characteristics that determine abilities and cultures.

rate of population growth (natural increase) The differential between the crude birthrate and the death rate.

recidivism The probability that a former inmate will break the law after release and be arrested again.

residual deviance Deviance from social conventions that are so completely taken for granted that they are assumed to be part of human nature.

right to die The belief that a terminally ill patient has the right to refuse medical treatment that may be artificially prolonging his or her life.

robbery The act of taking another person's property by intimidation.

role A certain set of behaviors that are expected of and performed by an individual on the basis of his or her status or position in society.

rural A term used to describe a sparsely populated area that is mostly used for agriculture, forestry, or other exploitation of resources.

safe sex practices Sexual behaviors and techniques, such as monogamy and the use of condoms, that are designed to prevent the transmission of AIDS and other venereal diseases.

sample A number of people who represent the behavior and attitudes of the larger population from which they are selected.

scapegoat A person or group that becomes a target of aggression displaced from the real source of the aggressor's frustration.

secondary deviance A term applied to behavior that elaborates on a deviant act in order to reinforce the role of deviant.

social control The capacity of a society or social group to regulate itself according to a set of higher moral principles beyond those of self-interest.

social disorganization The condition that results when the expectations or rules by which society is organized fail to function effectively.

socialization The process by which individuals develop into social beings.

social mobility The movement of an individual from one socioeconomic level to another.

social norm A social standard that specifies the kind of behavior that is appropriate in a given situation.

social pathology A term applied to the "illness" of individuals or social institutions that fail to keep pace with changing conditions and thereby disrupt the healthy functioning of the social "organism."

social policy A formal procedure designed to remedy a social problem.

social problem Behavior that departs from established norms and social structures because individual and collective goals are not being achieved; a condition that a significant number of people believe should be remedied through collective action.

social stratification A pattern in which individuals and groups are assigned to different positions in the social order, with varying amounts of access to the desirable things in the society.

standard consolidated statistical area (SCSA) Two or more SMSAs that have become socially and economically interrelated.

standard metropolitan statistical area (SMSA) A large population nucleus and surrounding communities that are integrated with it economically and socially; according to the Census Bureau, one or more central counties, with at least 50,000 inhabitants, plus outlying counties with close economic and social ties to the central counties (e.g., a certain level of commuting).

standard of living What people want or expect in the way of material well-being.

status A socially defined position in a group or organization.

status offense An act that is illegal if it is performed by a person under 18 years of age.

statutory rape The act of having sexual relations with a person who is below a particular age established by state law.

stereotyping Attributing a fixed and usually unfavorable or inaccurate conception to a category of people.

sting A law enforcement technique in which people suspected of a criminal activity are given the opportunity to engage in that activity and are subsequently arrested by law enforcement officials.

strategic crimes Crimes such as extortion, kidnapping, and blackmail in which the threat of violence is used as a strategic ploy in a complex "game" played out by the criminal, the victim, and the law enforcement agency.

stress Physical or mental tension produced by the demands of environmental factors or by internal (perceived) behavioral requirements.

structural violence Dominance of one group over another, with subsequent exploitive practices.

structured sex variance Sexual behavior that runs counter to prevailing norms and legal statutes but is engaged in by large numbers of people and associated with relatively well-defined roles and social institutions.

supply-side economics The theory that if the side of the economy that supplies goods and services is stimulated, unemployment will decrease and prices will drop.

surrogacy The practice in which a woman, for a monetary fee, is artificially inseminated with the sperm of a man married to another woman who has been unable to bear children. After carrying the child and giving birth, the surrogate mother usually gives custody of the child to the biological father and his wife.

survey research A method for gathering information from a number of people, known as a *sample*, who represent the behavior and attitudes of the larger population from which they are selected.

technology The apparatus or physical devices used in accomplishing a variety of tasks, together with the activities involved in performing those tasks and the organizational networks associated with them.

technology assessment A policy perspective that emphasizes the need for scientific study of new technologies in order to anticipate their consequences for the physical and social environment.

tolerated sex variance Sexual acts that are generally disapproved of but either serve a socially useful purpose and/or occur so often among a population with such low social visibility that few people are sanctioned for engaging in them.

total fertility rate The average number of children born per woman throughout the childbearing years.

total institution A place where a large number of individuals, cut off from the wider society for an appreciable period, together lead an enclosed, formally administered round of life.

transnational terrorism Terrorism perpetrated by agents who are not affiliated with a recognized government.

trickle-down theory The theory that any measures taken to aid business or wealthy individuals will stimulate consumer demand and economic activity, thus providing jobs and opportunities for the poor and the unemployed.

underground economy Exchanges of goods and services, both legal and illegal, that are not monitored, recorded, or taxed by government.

urban A term used to describe a densely settled area where manufacturing, commerce, administration, and a great variety of specialized services are available.

urbanism A way of life that depends on heavy industry, mass communication, a mobile population, and other characteristics generally associated with life in urban areas.

urbanized area According to the Census Bureau, a city (or cities) of 50,000 or more inhabitants plus the surrounding suburbs.

urban population According to the Census Bureau, all persons in places of 2,500 inhabitants or more that are incorporated as cities, villages, boroughs, or towns.

victimization report A Census Bureau survey that collects information from a representative sample of crime victims.

victimless crime A crime that causes no physical harm to anyone but the offender; a public-order crime.

violence Behavior designed to cause physical injury to people or damage to property.

violent personal crimes Crimes in which physical injury is inflicted or threatened.

voyeurism Watching people undressing or performing a sexual act.

wealthfare The opportunities provided by government that enable the rich to become richer.

welfare state A nation in which a significant proportion of the gross domestic product is taken by the state to provide minimal social welfare for the poor, the aged, the disabled, and others who would not be able to survive under conditions of market competition.

whistle-blower A person who risks his or her reputation to reveal dangers in technology or in the application of technology.

working poor People with full-time jobs whose wages are insufficient to raise their incomes above the official poverty line.

zero population growth The condition that exists when a generation produces only enough children to replace itself (assumes no immigration).

ABBOTT, A. 2000. *Deportment and Discipline: Chicago Sociology at One Hundred.* Chicago: University of Chicago Press.

ABERSON, C. L., D. J. SWAN, & E. P. EMERSON. 1999. "Covert Discrimination Against Gay Men by U.S. College Students." *Journal of Social Psychology,* 139: 323.

ABRAMOWITZ, M. 1996. *Regulating the Lives of Women: Social Welfare Policy from Colonial Times to the Present,* rev. ed. Boston: South End Press.

ACIERNO, R., H. S. RESNICK, & D. G. KILPATRICK. 1997. "Prevalence Rates, Case Identification, and Risk Factors for Sexual Assault, Physical Assault, and Domestic Violence in Men and Women," part 1. *Behavioral Medicine,* 23: 53–66.

ADLER, F., G. O. W. MUELLER, & W. S. LAUFER. 1995. *Criminology,* 2nd ed. New York: McGraw-Hill.

ADLER, J., & M. MALONE. 1996, November 4. "Toppling Towers." *Newsweek,* pp. 70–71.

AHLBURG, D. A., & C. J. DE VITA. 1992. "New Realities of the American Family." *Population Bulletin,* 47, no. 2. Washington, DC: Population Reference Bureau.

AITKEN, P. V., JR. 1999. "Incorporating Advance Care Planning into Family Practice." *American Family Physician,* 59: 605.

ALAN GUTTMACHER INSTITUTE. 1994. *Sex and America's Teenagers.* New York: Planned Parenthood Federation of America.

ALBOM, M. 1998. *Tuesdays with Morrie.* Garden City, NY: Doubleday.

Alcoholism & Drug Abuse Weekly. 1998, August 17. "Federal, State Leaders Take Closer Look at Date-rape Drugs," p. 6.

Alcoholism & Drug Abuse Weekly. 1999, December 20. "HUD Study Gives Comprehensive View of Homeless Population's Needs," p. 4.

ALEXANDER, A., & K. JACOBSEN. 1999. "Affirmative Action: A Critical Reconnaissance." *International Journal of Urban and Regional Research,* 23: 593.

ALEXANDER, K. 1996, January 5. "Christian Coalition Pushes for School Choice." *Atlanta Constitution,* p. F2.

ALLAND, A. 1973. *Human Diversity.* Garden City, NY: Doubleday.

ALLEN, B. 1999. "The Social Construction of What?" *Science,* 285: 205.

ALLEN, M., T. EMMERS, & L. GEBHARDT. 1995. "Exposure to Pornography and Acceptance of Rape Myths." *Journal of Communication,* 45: 5–26.

ALTMAN, D. 1987. *AIDS in the Mind of America.* Garden City, NY: Doubleday Anchor Books.

ALTMAN, L. K. 1999, August 31. *New York Times,* pp. D5, F5.

AMERICAN PSYCHIATRIC ASSOCIATION. 1994. *Diagnostic and Statistical Manual of Mental Disorders,* 4th ed. Washington, DC: American Psychiatric Association.

ANDERSON, E. 1992. *Streetwise.* Chicago: University of Chicago Press.

ANDERSON, E. 1999. *Code of the Street.* New York: Norton.

ANDERSON, O. 1989. *The Health Services Continuum in Democratic States.* Ann Arbor, MI: Health Administration Press.

ANTONOVSKY, A. 1974. "Class and the Chance for Life." In L. Rainwater, ed., *Inequality and Justice.* Hawthorne, NY: Aldine.

APPLEBOME, P. 1992, November 14. "Jailers Charged with Sex Abuse of 119 Women." *New York Times,* pp. 1, 7.

APPLEBOME, P. 1995, September 4. "G.O.P. Efforts Put Teachers' Unions on the Defensive: 'Reform' Issues at Stake." *New York Times,* p.1.

APPLEBOME, P. 1996, February 21. "Governors Want New Focus on Education." *New York Times,* p. B7.

APPLEBOME, P. 1997, February 28. "National Tests Show Students Have Improved in Math." *New York Times,* p. A15.

ARON, R. 1955. *The Century of Total War.* Boston: Beacon Press.

ARONOWITZ, S., & W. DIFAZIO. 1994. *The Jobless Future: Sci-tech and the Dogma of Work.* Minneapolis: University of Minnesota Press.

ASTON, G. 1999, June 14. "Plan to Boost Mental Health Parity Gains Advocates' Support." *American Medical News,* p. 5.

ATKINS, R. M. 1999. "Controlling Costs Without Mismanagement." *Behavioral Health Management,* 19: 12.

ATTORNEY GENERAL'S COMMISSION ON PORNOGRAPHY. 1986. *Final Report.* Washington, DC: U.S. Government Printing Office.

AULETTA, K. 1987. *Greed and Glory on Wall Street.* New York: Warner Books.

AYALA, V. 1996. *Falling Through the Cracks: AIDS and the Urban Poor.* Bayside, NY: Social Change Press.

AYERS, B. D., JR. 1993, September 9. "Judge's Decision in Custody Case Raises Concerns." *New York Times,* p. A16.

AYERS, B. D., JR. 1994, May 22. "Big Gains Are Seen in Battle to Stem Drunken Driving." *New York Times,* pp. 1, 24.

BACON, D. 1997, July. "Evening the Odds: Cross-border Organizing Gives Labor a Chance." *The Progressive,* pp. 29–33.

BADILLO, G., & D. CURRY. 1976. "The Social Incidence of Vietnam Casualties: Social Class or Race?" *Armed Forces and Society,* 2: 397–406.

BALLANTINE, J. H. 1993. *The Sociology of Education: A Systematic Analysis,* 3rd ed. Upper Saddle River, NJ: Prentice Hall.

BALLARD, M. E., & J. R. WIEST. 1996. "Mortal Kombat: The Effects of Violent Videogame Play on Males' Hostility and Cardiovascular Responding." *Journal of Applied Social Psychology,* 26: 717–730.

BALL-ROKEACH, S., & J. F. SHORT, JR. 1985. "Collective Violence: The Redress of Grievance and Public Policy." In L. A. Curtis, ed., *American Violence and Public Policy.* New Haven, CT: Yale University Press.

BANDURA, A. 1986. *Social Foundations of Thought and Action.* Upper Saddle River, NJ: Prentice Hall.

BARBANEL, J. 1987, November 13. "Homeless Woman Sent to Hospital Under Koch Plan Is Ordered Freed." *New York Times,* pp. A1, A21.

BARINAGA, M. 1996. "Backlash Strikes at Affirmative Action Programs." *Science,* 271: 1908–1910.

BARKER, P. R., G. MANDERSCHEID, & I. G. GENDERSHOT. 1992. "Serious Mental Illness and Disability in the Adult Household Population: United States, 1989." In R. W. Manderscheid & M. A. Sonnenschein, eds., *Mental Health, United States, 1992.* Washington, DC: Center for Mental Health Services and National Institute of Mental Health.

BARNET, R. J. 1980. *The Lean Years.* New York: Simon & Schuster.

BARRINGER, F. 1993, March 7. "Where Many Elderly Live, Signs of the Future." *New York Times,* p. L20.

BARRON, M. L. 1971. "The Aged as a Quasi-minority Group." In E. Sagarin, ed., *The Other Minorities.* Lexington, MA: Ginn.

BARTON, J. H. 1981. *The Politics of Peace: An Evaluation of Arms Control.* Stanford, CA: Stanford University Press.

BASSUK, E. L. 1984, July. "The Homelessness Problem." *Scientific American,* pp. 40–45.

BASSUK, E. L., A. BROWNE, & J. C. BRUCKNER. 1996. "Single Mothers and Welfare." *Scientific American,* 275: 60–68.

BAWER, B. 1994, June 13. "Notes on Stonewall: Is the Gay Rights Movement Living in the Past?" *New Republic,* pp. 24–27.

BAYER, R. 1987. *Homosexuality and American Psychiatry: The Politics of Diagnosis,* 2nd ed. Princeton, NJ: Princeton University Press.

BECKER, H. S. 1963. "Becoming a Marijuana User." In *Outsiders: Studies in the Sociology of Deviance.* New York: Free Press.

BECKMAN, V. 1995, July/August. "Alcohol and Social Change." *World Health,* pp. 22–23.

BEE, R. J. 1995. *Nuclear Proliferation: The Post-cold-war Challenge.* New York: Foreign Policy Association.

BEER, F. A. 1981. *Peace Against War: The Ecology of International Violence.* San Francisco: Freeman.

BELL, A. P., & M. S. WEINBERG. 1978. *Homosexualities: A Study of Diversity Among Men and Women.* New York: Simon & Schuster.

BELL, D. 1973. *The Coming of Post-industrial Society: A Venture in Social Forecasting.* New York: Basic Books.

BELL, D. 1991, March 16. "The Myth of the Intelligent Society." *New York Times,* p. 23.

BELL, D., & G. VALENTINE, eds. 1995. *Mapping Desire: Geographies of Sexualities.* London: Routledge.

BELL, J. D. 1998, June. "Smaller = Better?" *State Legislatures,* pp. 14–19.

BELL, R. R. 1971. *Social Deviance.* Homewood, IL: Dorsey Press.

BELLUCK, P. 1996, November 17. "The Youngest Ex-cons: Facing a Difficult Road Out of Crime." *New York Times,* pp. 1, 40.

BENDER, W., & M. SMITH. 1997. "Population, Food and Nutrition." *Population Bulletin,* 51, no. 4. Washington, DC: Population Reference Bureau.

BENNETT, C., B. LEAKE, C. LEWIS, J. FLASKERUD, & A. NYAMATHI. 1993. "AIDS-Related Knowledge, Perceptions, and Behaviors Among Impoverished Minority Women." *American Journal of Public Health,* 83: 65–71.

BENNETT, W. J., J. J. DIIULIO, JR., & J. P. WALTERS. 1996. *Body Count.* New York: Simon & Schuster.

BENOKRAITIS, N. V., & J. R. FEAGIN. 1986. *Modern Sexism: Blatant, Subtle and Covert Discrimination.* Upper Saddle River, NJ: Prentice Hall.

BERGTHOLD, L. 1990. *Purchasing Power in Health: Business, the State, and Health Care Policies.* New Brunswick, NJ: Rutgers University Press.

BERKOWITZ, L. 1993. *Aggression: Its Causes, Consequences, and Control.* Philadelphia: Temple University Press.

BERNARD, J. 1987. *The Female World from a Global Perspective.* Bloomington: Indiana University Press.

BERNSTEIN, J. 1982, January 3. "Recreating the Power of the Sun." *New York Times Magazine,* pp. 14–17, 52–53.

BERNSTEIN, N. 2000, February 1. "Study Documents Homelessness in American Children Each Year." *New York Times,* p. A12.

BERRIOS, G. E. 1995. *The History of Mental Symptoms: Descriptive Psychopathology Since the Nineteenth Century.* New York: Cambridge University Press.

BERRUETA-CLEMENT, J. R., L. J. SCHWEINHART, W. S. BARNETT, A. S. EPSTEIN, & D. P. WEIKART. 1984. *Changed Lives: The Effects of the Perry Preschool Program on Youths Through Age 19.* Ypsilanti, MI: High/Scope.

BERRY, D. B. 1995. *The Domestic Violence Sourcebook: Everything You Need to Know.* Los Angeles: Lowell House.

BESHAROV, D. J., & P. GERMANIS, 1999. "Making Food Stamps Part of Welfare Reform." *Policy & Practice of Public Human Services,* 57: 6–12.

BHAGWATI, J. N. 1999, August 14. *USNewswire.*

BIANCHI, E. C. 1974, September 18. "The Superbowl Culture of Male Violence." *Christian Century,* pp. 842–845.

BIBLARZ, T. J., & A. D. RAFTERY, 1999. "Family Structures, Educational Attainment, and Socioeconomic Success: Rethinking the 'Pathology of Matriarchy.'" *American Journal of Sociology,* 105: 321–365.

BIDDLE, R. 1999, October. "Gun Spree." *Reason,* p. 13.

BIRD, E. J., P. A. HAGSTROM, & R. WILD. 1999, Spring. "Credit Cards and the Poor." *Focus,* pp. 40–43.

BIRENBAUM, A. 1995. *Putting Health Care on the National Agenda.* Westport, CT: Praeger.

BIRNBAUM, J. 1999, December 6. "Under the Gun." *Fortune,* pp. 211ff.

BLACK, D. 1984. *Toward a General Theory of Social Control.* Orlando, FL: Academic Press.

BLAKESLEE, S. 1994, April 20. "Poor and Black Patients Slighted, Study Says." *New York Times,* p. B9.

BLANCHARD, C. 1999, Winter. "Drugs, Crime, Prison and Treatment." *Spectrum: The Journal of State Government,* pp. 26–28.

BLIESZNER, R., & V. H. BEDFORD. 1995. *Handbook of Aging and the Family.* Westport, CT: Greenwood Press.

BLUMBERG, P. 1980. *Inequality in an Age of Decline.* New York: Oxford University Press.

BLUMSTEIN, A. 1982. "On the Racial Disproportionality of the United States' Prison Population." *Journal of Criminal Law and Criminology,* 73: 1259–1281.

BOARD, P. 1996. "Contaminated Lands." *New Scientist,* 152: 44–45.

BOAS, M., & S. CHAIN. 1976. *Big Mac: The Unauthorized Story of McDonald's.* New York: New American Library.

BOELKINS, R. C., & J. F. HEISER. 1970. "Biological Bases of Aggression." In D. Daniels, M. Gilula, & F. Ochberg, eds., *Violence and the Struggle for Existence.* Boston: Little, Brown.

BOGART, L. 1972–1973. "Warning: The Surgeon General Has Determined That TV Violence Is Moderately Dangerous to Your Children's Mental Health." *Public Opinion Quarterly,* 36: 491–521.

BOGUE, D. J. 1985. *The Population of the United States: Historical Trends and Future Projections.* New York: Free Press.

BOHLEN, C. 1996, March 1. "At 30-something, Leave Home? Mamma Mia, No! Italian Men Choosing to Live with Their Parents." *New York Times,* p. A4.

BONACICH, E. 1976. "Advanced Capitalism and Black/White Race Relations in the United States: A Split Labor Market Interpretation." *American Sciological Review,* 41: 34–51.

BOOTH, A., D. R. JOHNSON, & J. EDWARDS. 1980. "In Pursuit of Pathology: The Effects of Human Crowding." *American Sociological Review,* 45: 873–878.

BOURGOIS, P. 1995. *In Search of Respect: Selling Crack in El Barrio.* Cambridge: Cambridge University Press.

BOWLES, S., & H. GINTIS. 1977. *Schooling in Capitalist America.* New York: Basic Books.

BOZETTE, S. A. 1998. "The Care of HIV-infected Adults in the United States." *New England Journal of Medicine,* 339: 1897–1904.

BRACEY, G. W. 1995, September. "Research Oozes Into Practice: The Case of Class Size. Project STAR in Tennessee." *Phi Delta Kappan,* pp. 89–90.

BRACEY, G. W. 1998, January. "An Optimal Size for High Schools?" *Phi Delta Kappan,* p. 406.

BRACEY, G. W. 1999, November. "Reducing Class Size: The Findings, the Controversy." *Phi Delta Kappan,* p. 246.

BRAGG, R. 2000, April 1. "Stand over Cuban Highlights a Virtual Secession of Miami." *New York Times,* p. A1.

BRAGINSKY, D. D., & B. M. BRAGINSKY. 1975, August. "Surplus People: Their Lost Faith in Self and System." *Psychology Today,* pp. 68–72.

BRATT, R. G. 1989. *Rebuilding a Low-income Housing Policy.* Philadelphia: Temple University Press.

BRAVERMAN, H. 1974. *Labor and Monopoly Capital: The Degradation of Work in the Twentieth Century.* New York: Monthly Review Press.

BREMER, L. P., III. 1988, May. "Terrorism: Myths and Reality." *Department of State Bulletin,* p. 63.

BRENNAN, M. 1995, November 13. "A Case for Discretion." *Newsweek,* p. 18.

BRIGGS, K. A. 1984, November 12. "Catholic Bishops Ask Vast Changes in Economy of U.S." *New York Times,* p. 1.

BRIMELOW, P. 1995. *Alien Nation: Common Sense About America's Immigration Disaster.* New York: Random House.

BRONFENBRENNER, U. 1981. "Children and Families." *Society,* 18: 38–41.

BROOK, J. S., L. RICHTER, M. WHITEMAN, & P. COHEN. 1999. "Consequences of Adolescent Marijuana Use; Incompatibility with the Assumption of Adult Roles." *Genetic, Social, & General Psychology Monographs,* 125: 193.

BROOKES, J. 1991, March 24. "Latin American Armies Looking for Work." *New York Times,* p. E2.

BROOKS-GUNN, J., & F. F. FURSTENBERG, JR. 1987. "Continuity and Change in the Context of Poverty: Adolescent Mothers and Their Children." In J. J. Gallagher & C. T. Ramey, eds., *The Malleability of Children.* Baltimore, MD: Brookes.

BROOKS-GUNN, J., & R. P. HEARN. 1982. "Early Intervention and Developmental Dysfunction: Implications for Pediatrics." *Advanced Pediatrics,* 29: 497–527.

BROWN, D. I. 1997. "Enhancing the Spatial Framework with Ecological Analysis." In M. Micklin & D. L. Poston, Jr., eds., *Continuities in Sociological Human Ecology.* New York: Plenum Press.

BROWN, L. R., & E. P. ECKHOLM. 1974. *By Bread Alone.* New York: Praeger.

BROWN, L. R., & S. POSTEL. 1987. "Thresholds of Change." In L. Brown, ed., *State of the World 1987: A Worldwatch Institute Report on Progress Toward a Sustainable Society.* New York: Norton.

BROWN, L. R., & J. E. YOUNG. 1990. "Feeding the World in the Nineties." In L. R. Brown, ed., *State of the World 1990: A Worldwatch Institute Report on Progress Toward a Sustainable Society.* New York: Norton.

BROWN, M. K. 1988. *Working the Street: Police Discretion and the Dilemmas of Reform.* New York: Russell Sage.

BROWN, S. P. A. 1998, October. "Global Warming Policy: Some Economic Implications." *Economic Review,* p. 26.

BRUNI, F. 1997, March 29. "A Cult's 2-decade Odyssey of Regimentation." *New York Times,* p. A1.

BUCKLEY, W. F., JR. 1997, December 8. "Marijuana Myths/Marijuana Facts" (book review). *National Review,* p. 63.

BUDIANSKY, S. 1996, March 4. "Local TV: Mayhem Central." *U.S. News & World Report,* pp. 63–64.

BUELL, E. H. 1982. *School Desegregation and Defended Neighborhoods: The Boston Controversy.* Lexington, MA: Lexington Books.

BULLARD, R. D. 1988. *Invisible Houston: The Black Experience in Boom and Bust.* College Station: Texas A&M Press.

BUNNELL, J. E. 1995. "Global Crime Calls for Global Partnerships." *FBI Law Enforcement Bulletin,* 64: 6–7.

BUREAU OF JUSTICE STATISTICS. 1996. *National Crime Victimization Survey, 1995: Preliminary Findings.* Washington, DC: U.S. Department of Justice.

BURROS, M. 1988, February 24. "Women: Out of the House but Not Out of the Kitchen." *New York Times,* pp. A1, C10.

BURT, M. 1992. *Over the Edge: The Growth of Homelessness in the 1980s.* Washington, DC: Urban Institute Press.

BURT, M. 1994. *Methods for Counting the Homeless.* Washington, DC: Urban Institute Press.

BURT, M. R. 1995. "Critical Factors in Counting the Homeless." *American Journal of Orthopsychiatry,* 65: 334–340.

Business Week. 1999, October 18. "What Price Pollution? Leave That to a Global Market," p. 26.

BUTLER, C. J. 1998. "The Defense of Marriage Act: Congress' Use of Narrative in the Debate Over Same-sex Marriage." *New York University Law Review,* 73: 841–879.

CALDWELL, J. C., I. O. ORUBULOYE, & P. CALDWELL. 1992. "Fertility Decline in Africa: A New Type of Transition?" *Population and Development Review,* 18: 211–242.

CALIFANO, J. A. 1998, February 21. "A Punishment-only Prison Policy." *America,* pp. 3–6.

CALLAHAN, D. 1994. "From Explosion to Implosion: Transforming Healthcare." In W. Kornblum & C. D. Smith, eds., *The Healing Experience: Readings on the Social Context of Health Care.* Upper Saddle River, NJ: Prentice Hall.

CALLAHAN, D. 1995. "Once Again, Reality: Now Where Do We Go?" *Hastings Center Report,* 25: 33–37.

CALLAHAN, D. 1997. "Dying Well in the Hospital: The Lessons of SUPPORT (Study to Understand Prognosis and Preferences for Outcomes and Risks of Treatment)." *Journal of Applied Gerontology,* 16: 267–270.

CALLAHAN, D., R. T. MEULEN, & E. TOPINKOVA. 1995. "Introduction: Special Issue on Resource Allocation and Societal Responses to Old Age." *Ageing and Society,* 15: 157–161.

CAMPBELL, J. R., P. L. DONAHUE, C. M. REESE, & G. W. PHILLIPS. 1996. *NAEP Reading Report Card for the Nation and the States.* Washington, DC: National Center for Education Statistics, U.S. Department of Education.

CANCIAN, M., & L. GORDON. 1996, Fall. "Making Mothers Work." *Dissent,* pp. 73–75.

CANNON, A. 1999, January 18. "Settling Up Old Debts." *U.S. News & World Report,* p. 29.

CANTOR, P. A. 2000. "The Simpsons: Atomistic Politics and the Nuclear Family." In *Political Theory.* Thousand Oaks, CA: Sage.

CAPLAN, A. 1992. *If I Were a Rich Man Could I Buy a Pancreas?: And Other Essays on the Ethics of Health Care.* Bloomington: Indiana University Press.

CAPLAN, N., J. K. WHITMORE, & M. H. CHOY. 1989. *The Boat People and Achievement in America: A Study of Family Life, Hard Work, and Cultural Values.* Ann Arbor: University of Michigan Press.

CARMODY, D. 1992, January 30. "Coverage of Smoking Linked to Tobacco Ads." *New York Times,* p. D22.

CARSON-DEWITT, R. S. 1999. "Alcoholism." *Gale Encyclopedia of Medicine,* p. 79.

CARTER, A. C. 1996, November 18. "Why Money Is the Leading Cause of Divorce." *Jet,* pp. 34–36.

CARTER, B. 1996, February 7. "A New Report Becomes a Weapon in Debate on Censoring TV Violence." *New York Times,* p. C11.

CELIS, W., III. 1993a, August 1. "The Fight Over National Standards." *New York Times, Education Life,* pp. 14–16.

CELIS, W., III. 1993b, December 9. "International Report Card Shows U.S. Schools Work." *New York Times,* pp. A1, A26.

CELIS, W., III. 1993c, December 14. "Study Finds Rising Concentration of Black and Hispanic Students." *New York Times*, pp. A1, B6.

CELIS, W., III. 1994, March 17. "Michigan Votes for Revolution in Financing Its Public Schools." *New York Times*, pp. A1–A21.

CENTER ON BUDGET AND POLICY PRIORITIES. 1999, August 28. "Off Welfare, but Poorer." *The Economist*, p. 23.

CHAFETZ, J. S. 1974. *Masculine, Feminine, or Human? An Overview of the Sociology of Sex Roles*. Itasca, IL: Peacock Press.

CHAFETZ, M. E. 1972. *Alcohol and Alcoholism*. Rockville, MD: National Institute on Alcohol Abuse and Alcoholism.

CHAFETZ, M. E., & H. W. DEMONE, JR. 1972. *Alcoholism and Society*. New York: Oxford University Press.

CHAMBLISS, W. 1973. "The Saints and the Roughnecks." *Society*, 2: 24–31.

CHAMBLISS, W. J. 2000. *Power, Politics and Crime*. Boulder, CO: Westview Press.

CHERLIN, A. J. 1992. *Marriage, Divorce, Remarriage*, 2nd ed. Cambridge, MA: Harvard University Press.

CHERLIN, A. J. 1996. *Public and Private Families: An Introduction*. New York: McGraw-Hill.

CHESLER, P. 1972. *Women and Madness*. New York: Avon.

CHUDACOFF, H. P. 1989. *How Old Are You?* Princeton, NJ: Princeton University Press.

CLARK, W. C. 1989, September. "Managing Planet Earth." *Scientific American*, p. 47.

CLARKE, J., M. D. STEIN, M. SOBOTA, M. MARISI, & L. HANNA. 1999. "Victims as Victimizers." *Archives of Internal Medicine*, 159: 1920.

CLAWSON, P. 1988. "Terrorism in Decline?" *Orbis*, 32: 263–276.

CLOSE, F. 1991. *Too Hot to Handle*. Princeton, NJ: Princeton University Press.

CLYMER, A. 1996, April 24. "Senate Passes Health Bill with Job-to-Job Coverage." *New York Times*, pp. A1, B6.

COCKERHAM, W. C. 1998. *Medical Sociology*, 7th ed. Upper Saddle River, NJ: Prentice Hall.

COHEN, A. K. 1971. *Delinquent Boys*. New York: Free Press.

COLE, D. 2000. *No Equal Justice*. New York: New Press.

COLES, R. 1968. *Children of Crisis*. New York: Dell.

COLLINS, P. H. 1997, Winter. "Comment on Hekman's 'Truth and Method: Feminist Standpoint Theory Revisited' (p. 341)." *Signs*, pp. 375–382.

COLVIN, R. L. 1996, April 8. "Battle Heats Up Over Bilingual Education." *Los Angeles Times*, p. A1.

COMMITTEE ON HEALTH CARE FOR HOMELESS PEOPLE. 1988. *Homelessness, Health, and Human Needs*. Washington, DC: National Academy Press.

COMMONER, B. 1992. *Making Peace with the Planet*. New York: New Press.

Congressional Digest. 1993. "Current Family Leave Policies," p. 72.

CONNELL, R. W. 1995. *Masculinities*. Berkeley: University of California Press.

CONWAY, G. 1997. *Food for All in the Twenty-first Century*. Ithaca, NY: Cornell University Press.

CONWAY, G. 1999. "Food for All in the 21st Century." *Social Research*, 66: 351.

CORCORAN, M., & G. J. DUNCAN. 1979. "Work History, Labor Force Attachment, and Earnings Differences Between the Races and Sexes." *Journal of Human Resources*, 14: 3–20.

CORNELIUS, W. A. 1989. "Impact of the 1986 U.S. Immigration Law on Emigration from Rural Mexican Sending Communities." *Population and Development Review*, 15: 689–705.

COTTRELL, W. F. 1951. "Death by Dieselization: A Case Study in the Reaction to Technological Change." *American Sociological Review*, 16: 358–365.

COUNCIL OF STATE GOVERNMENTS. 1998, Fall. "School Finance: State Efforts to Equalize Funding Between Wealthy and Poor School Districts." *Spectrum: The Journal of State Government*, p. 20.

COWAN, N. M., & R. S. COWAN. 1989. *Our Parents' Lives: The Americanization of Eastern European Jews*. New York: Basic Books.

COX, H. 1990. "Roles for Aged Individuals in Post-industrial Societies." *International Journal of Aging and Human Development*, 30: 55–62.

COX, W. M., & R. ALM. 2000, January 24. "Why Decry the Wealth Gap?" *New York Times*, pp. A25, A29.

CRAIG, L. A. 1993. *Health of Nations: An International Perspective on U.S. Health Care Reform*, 2nd ed. Washington, DC: Congressional Quarterly.

CRAWFORD, C., T. CHIRICOS, & G. KLECK. 1998. "Race, Racial Threat, and Sentencing of Habitual Offenders." *Criminology*, 36: 481.

CRESSEY, D. R. 1953. *Other People's Money: A Study in the Social Psychology of Embezzlement*. Montclair, NJ: Patterson Smith.

CRITTENDEN, D. 1999. *What Our Mothers Didn't Tell Us: Why Happiness Eludes the Modern Woman*. New York: Simon and Schuster.

CROSSETTE, B. 1995, May 15. "U.S. Ready to Seek Worldwide Ban on Nuclear Arms Tests." *New York Times*, p. A7.

CROSSETTE, B. 1996, June 3. "Hope, and Pragmatism, for U.N. Cities Conference." *New York Times*, p. A3.

CSIKSZENTMIHALYI, M., & E. ROCHBERG-HALTON. 1981. *The Meaning of Things: Domestic Symbols and the Self*. Cambridge: Cambridge University Press.

CUBAN, L. 1999, August 4. "The Technology Puzzle." *Education Week*, p. 68.

CUBER, J. F., & P. HAROFF. 1965. *Sex and the Significant Americans*. Baltimore, MD: Penguin Books.

CUNY (CITY UNIVERSITY OF NEW YORK). 1978. *West 42nd Street: "The Bright Light Zone."* New York: City University of New York, Graduate School and University Center.

CURTIS, W. R. 1986, Fall. "The Deinstitutionalization Story." *Public Interest*, 85: 34–49.

CUSHMAN, J. H. 1993, November 19. "U.S. to Weigh Blacks' Complaints About Pollution." *New York Times*, p. A16.

CUTLER, D. M., E. L. GLAESER, & J. L. VIGDOR. 1999. "The Rise and Decline of the American Ghetto." *Journal of Political Economy*, 107: 455.

DALEY, W. M. 1999, July. "Bridging the Digital Divide." *Presidents & Prime Ministers*, p. 25.

DALY, M. 1970. "Woman and the Catholic Church." In R. Morgan, ed., *Sisterhood Is Powerful*. New York: Random House.

DANESH, A. H. 1991. *The Informal Economy: Underground Economy, Moonlighting, Subcontracting, Household Economy, Unorganized Sector, Barter, Ghetto Economy, Second Economy: A Research Guide*. New York: Garland.

DARLING-HAMMOND, L. 1998, Spring. "Unequal Opportunity: Race and Education." *Brookings Review*, pp. 28–33.

DAVIS, K. 1937. "The Sociology of Prostitution." *American Sociological Review*, 2: 744–755.

DAVIS, K. 1971. "Population Policy: Will Current Programs Succeed?" In D. Callahan, ed., *American Popular Debate*. Garden City, NY: Doubleday.

DAVIS, K. 1986. "Low Fertility in Evolutionary Perspective." *Population and Development Review*, 12 (Suppl.): 48–65.

DAVIS, K., M. S. BERNSTAN, & R. RICARDO-CAMPBELL. 1987. "Below-replacement Fertility in Industrial Societies: Causes, Consequences, Policies." *Population and Development Review*, 12 (Suppl. 5).

DAVIS, M. 1990. *City of Quartz: Excavating the Future in Los Angeles*. New York: Verso.

DAVIS, M. 1995, January 30. "Bankruptcy on the Backs of the Poor." *The Nation*, pp. 121–122.

DAVIS, N. 1987. "The Prostitute: Developing a Deviant Subculture." In J. H. Henslin, ed., *Studies in the Sociology of Sex*. Upper Saddle River, NJ: Prentice Hall.

DAVIS, N. J., & R. V. ROBINSON. 1991. "Men's and Women's Consciousness of Gender Inequality." *American Sociological Review*, 56: 72–84.

DECKER, S. 1969. *An Empty Spoon*. New York: Harper & Row.

DECKMAN, M., & E. MARNI. 1996. "Balancing Work and Family Responsibilities: Flexitime and Child Care in the Federal Government." *Public Administration Review*, 56: 174–179.

DEES, M. S., JR., & P. ZELIKOW. 1995, May 7. "Ban Private Military Groups." *New York Times*, sec. 4, p. 15.

DEJONG, W., C. K. ATKIN, & L. WALLACK. 1992. "A Critical Analysis of 'Moderation' Advertising Sponsored by the Beer Industry: Are 'Responsible Drinking' Commercials Done Responsibly?" *Milbank Quarterly*, 70: 661–677.

DENITCH, B. 1996. *Ethnic Nationalism: The Tragic Death of Yugoslavia*, rev. ed. Minneapolis: University of Minnesota Press.

DEPARLE, J. 1994, February 17. "Report to Clinton Sees Vast Extent of Homelessness." *New York Times*, pp. A1, A20.

DES JARLAIS, D. C. 1987, April 26. "Addicts Will Change if They Get the Word." *Newsday*, p. 8.

DEWEY, J. 1916. *Democracy and Education*. New York: Macmillan.

DIAL, T. H. 1992. "Training of Mental Health Providers." In R. W. Manderscheid and M. A. Sonnenschein, eds., *Mental Health, United States, 1992*. Washington, DC: Center for Mental Health Services and National Institute of Mental Health.

DICKEY, B., W. FISHER, C. SIEGEL, F. ALTAFFER, & H. AZENI. 1997. "The Cost and Outcomes of Community-based Care for the Seriously Mentally Ill." *Health Services Research*, 32: 599–615.

DIESENHOUSE, S. 1990, July 8. "A Rising Tide of Violence Leaves More Youths in Jail." *New York Times*, p. E4.

DIFAZIO, W. 1999. "Created Unequal: The Crisis in American Pay." *American Journal of Sociology*, 105: 904.

DOHRENWEND, B. P., & B. S. DOHRENWEND. 1975. "Sociocultural and Social-Psychological Factors in the Genesis of Mental Disorders." *Journal of Health and Social Behavior*, 16: 369.

DONNERSTEIN, E., & D. LINZ. 1987. "Sexual Violence and the Media: A Warning." In A. Wells, ed., *Mass Media and Society*. Lexington, MA: D. C. Heath.

DONOHUE, R. L., R. H. HOYLE, R. R. CLAYTON, W. F. SKINNER, S. E. COLON, & R. E. RICE. 1999. "Sensation Seeking and Drug Use by Adolescents and Their Friends: Models for Marijuana and Alcohol." *Journal of Studies on Alcohol*, 60: 622.

DONOVAN, W. 1994, January 23. "One Leg, One Life at a Time." *New York Times Magazine*, pp. 26–29.

DREVITCH, G. 1994. "Where Do You Stand?" *Scholastic Update*, 126: 13–14.

DUGGER, C. W. 1997, March 16. "Immigrant Study Finds Many Below New Income Limit." *New York Times*, pp. 1, 39.

DUNLAP, R. E., & R. SCARCE. 1991. "Environmental Problems and Protection." *Public Opinion Quarterly*, 55: 651–672.

DURKHEIM, É. 1950. *Rules of the Sociological Method*, 8th ed. S. A. Solvay & J. H. Mueller, trans.; G. E. G. Catlin, ed. New York: Free Press.

DURKHEIM, É. 1897/1951. *Suicide, a Study in Sociology*. New York: Free Press.

EASTON, A., J. SUMMERS, J. TRIBBLE, P. B. WALLACE, & R. S. LOCK. 1997. "College Women's Perceptions Regarding Resistance to Sexual Assault." *Journal of American College Health*, 46: 127.

EBRAHIM, S. H. 1999. "Comparison of Binge Drinking Among Nonpregnant Women, United States, 1991–1995." *Journal of the American Medical Association*, 281: 1360.

ECKHOLM, E. 1990, March 27. "An Aging Nation Grapples with Caring for the Frail." *New York Times*, pp. A1, A18.

ECKHOLM, E. 1995, February 24. "Studies Find Death Penalty Tied to Race of Victims." *New York Times*, pp. B1, B4.

EDELHOCH, M. 1999. "Welfare Reform in South Carolina: 'Roughly Right' Social Policy." *Social Policy*, 29: 7–15.

EDIN, K., & L. LEIN. 1997. *Making Ends Meet: How Single Mothers Survive Welfare and Low Wage Work*. New York: Russell Sage.

Educational Leadership. 1997, December. Pp. 6–11.

EDWARDS, L. P. 1927. *The Natural History of Revolution*. Chicago: University of Chicago Press.

EHRENREICH, B. 1992, February 17. "Stamping Out a Dread Scourge." *Time*, p. 88.

EHRENREICH, B. 1996, April 8. "In Defense of Splitting Up." *Time*, p. 80.

EHRLICH, P. R., & A. H. EHRLICH. 1991. *Healing the Planet: Strategies for Resolving the Environmental Crisis*. Reading, MA: Addison Wesley.

EHRLICH, P. R., A. H. EHRLICH, & J. P. HOLDREN. 1977. *Ecoscience: Population, Resources, Environment*. San Francisco: Freeman.

EL-BASSEL, N., L. GILBERT, & R. F. SCHILLING. 1996. "Correlates of Crack Abuse Among Drug-using Incarcerated Women: Psychological Trauma, Social Support, and Coping Behavior." *American Journal of Drug and Alcohol Abuse*, 22: 41–56.

"Elder Abuse and Family Violence: Testimony Presented Before the U.S. Senate Special Committee on Aging." 1996. *Journal of Elder Abuse and Neglect*, 8: 81–96.

ELIFSON, K., J. BOLES, & M. SWEAT. 1993. "Risk Factors Associated with HIV Infection Among Male Prostitutes." *American Journal of Public Health*, 82: 79–83.

ELIFSON, K. W., & C. STERK-ELIFSON. 1992. "Someone to Count On: Homeless Male Drug Users and Their Friendship Relations." *Urban Anthropology*, 21: 235–251.

ELLWOOD, D. T. 1987. *Divide and Conquer: Responsible Security for America's Poor*. New York: Ford Foundation.

ELLWOOD, D. T. 1988. *Poor Support: Poverty in the American Family*. New York: Basic Books.

ELLWOOD, D. T. 1996, May–June. "Welfare Reform as I Knew It: When Bad Things Happen to Good Policies." *The American Prospect*, pp. 22–30.

ELVIN, J. 1999, October 4. "Road Rage, Stadium Rage, Work Rage; What Next?" *Insight on the News*, p. 35.

ENGLAND, P., & G. FARKAS. 1986. *Households, Employment, and Gender: A Social, Economic, and Demographic View*. New York: Aldine de Gruyter.

ENGLAND, P., M. S. HERBERT, & B. S. KILBOURNE. 1994. "The Gendered Valuation of Occupations and Skills: Earnings in 1980 Census Occupations." *Social Forces*, 73: 65–100.

ENLOE, C. 1990. *Bananas, Beaches, and Bases: Making Feminist Sense of International Politics*. Berkeley: University of California Press.

ENLOE, C. 1996, March–April. "Spoils of War." *Ms. Magazine*, p. 15.

EPSTEIN, C. F. 1993. *Women in Law*, 2nd ed. Urbana: University of Illinois Press.

ERIKSON, K. T. 1972. *Everything in Its Path: Destruction of Community in the Buffalo Creek Flood*. New York: Simon & Schuster.

ERIKSON, K. T. 1995. *A New Species of Trouble*. New York: Norton.

ERLANGER, H. S. 1987, November 8. "A Widening Pattern of Abuse Exemplified in Steinberg Case." *New York Times*, p. 1.

ESPENSHADE, T. J., ed. 1997. *Keys to Successful Immigration*. New York: Urban Institute Press.

EUROPEAN COMMITTEE ON CRIME PROBLEMS. 1993. *Sexual Exploitation, Pornography and Prostitution of, and Trafficking in, Children and Young Adults: Recommendations*. Strasbourg: Council of Europe Press.

EVANGELAUF, J. 1992, January 22. "Minority-group Enrollment at Colleges Rose 10% from 1988 to 1990, Reaching Record Levels." *Chronicle of Higher Education*, pp. 70–71.

EVANS, G. W., S. J. LEPORE, B. R. SHEJWAL, & M. N. PALSANE. 1998. "Chronic Residential Crowding and Children's Well-being: An Ecological Perspective." *Child Development*, 69: 1514.

FALK, D. M. 1999, August 16. "ADA Rulings Look Good to Businesses." *National Law Journal*, 21: B9.

FALUDI, S. 1994, February 16. "Going Wild?" *New York Times*, p. A21.

FALUDI, S. 1999. *Stiffed: The Betrayal of the American Man*. New York: Morrow.

FANON, F. 1968. *The Wretched of the Earth*. New York: Grove Press.

FARIS, R. E. L., & H. W. DUNHAM. 1938. *Mental Disorders in Urban Areas*. Chicago: University of Chicago Press.

FARLEY, R. 1996. *The New American Reality*. New York: Russell Sage.

FARLEY, R., S. BIANCHI, & D. COLASSANTO. 1979. "Barriers to the Racial Integration of Neighborhoods: The Detroit Case." *Social Indicators Research*, 6: 439–443.

FARNSWORTH, C. H. 1996, February 28. "Chip to Block TV Gore Popular in Canada Tests." *New York Times*, p. A2.

FARRELL, S. 1991. "Womanchurch." Unpublished doctoral dissertation, City University of New York Graduate School.

FASTEAU, M. F. 1974. *The Male Machine*. New York: McGraw-Hill.

FAULKNER, P. 1981. "Exposing Risks of Nuclear Disaster." In A. F. Westin, ed., *Whistle Blowing!* New York: McGraw-Hill.

FEAGIN, J. R. 1988. *Free Enterprise City: Houston in Political and Economic Perspective*. New Brunswick, NJ: Rutgers University Press.

FEAGIN, J. R. 1991. "The Continuing Significance of Race: Anti-black Discrimination in Public Places." *American Sociological Review*, 56: 101–117.

FEAGIN, J. 1996. *Racial and Ethnic Relations*, 5th ed. Upper Saddle River, NJ: Prentice Hall.

FELSON, R. B., & M. KROHN. 1990. "Motives for Rape." *Journal of Research in Crime and Delinquency*, 27: 222–241.

FELSON, R. B., & J. T. TEDESCHI. 1993. *Aggression and Violence: Social Interactionist Perspectives*. Washington, DC: American Psychological Association.

FIELD, R. 1999, September. "The New Civil War: The Psychology, Culture, and Politics of Abortion." *Sex Roles: A Journal of Research*, p. 479.

FIELDS, S. 1999, October 4. "Deadly Heroin Makes a Comeback." *Insight on the News*, p. 48.

FINEMAN, H. 1996, June 3. "Dulling a Sharp Wedge." *Newsweek*, p. 30.

FINKELHOR, D., & L. MEYER. 1988. *Nursery Crimes*. Newbury Park, CA: Sage.

FISCHER, C. S. 1976. *The Urban Experience*. New York: Harcourt Brace Jovanovich.

FISCHER, C. S. 1995. "The Subcultural Theory of Urbanism: A Twentieth-year Assessment." *American Journal of Sociology*, 101: 543–578.

FISS, O. M. 1996. *The Irony of Free Speech*. Cambridge, MA: Harvard University Press.

FLAVIN, C. 1987. "Reassessing Nuclear Power." In L. R. Brown, ed., *State of the World 1987: A Worldwatch Institute Report on Progress Toward a Sustainable Society*. New York: Norton.

FLAVIN, C. 1990. "Slowing Global Warming." In L. R. Brown, ed., *State of the World 1990: A Worldwatch Institute Report on Progress Toward a Sustainable Society*. New York: Norton.

FLAVIN, C. 1996. *Climate of Hope: New Strategies for Stabilizing the World's Atmosphere*. Washington, DC: Worldwatch Institute.

FLINK, J. 1976. *The Automobile and American Culture*. Cambridge: Massachusetts Institute of Technology Press.

FOOD AND AGRICULTURE ORGANIZATION. 1996. *Sixth World Food Survey*. Rome: Food and Agriculture Organization.

FORD, G. 1999, August 8. "Inclusive America Under Attack." *New York Times*, sec. 4, p. 4.

FORD FOUNDATION. 1990. "Increasing the Quantity and Quality of Child Care." *Ford Foundation Letter*, 121: 1–9.

FOUST, D. 1993, March 8. "'Now They're Really Down to the Dregs.' Resolution Trust Corp.'s Remaining Properties." *Newsweek*, p. 80.

FOX, R. 1989. *The Sociology of Medicine*. Upper Saddle River, NJ: Prentice Hall.

FOX, R. 1992. *Spare Parts: Organ Replacement in American Society*. New York: Oxford University Press.

FOX, R. 1997. *Experiment Perilous*. New Brunswick, NJ: Transaction.

FRANCKE, L. B. 1994, November. "The Legacy of Tailhook." *Glamour*, pp. 214–217.

FRANKS, J. B. 1999. "The Evaluation of Community Standards." *Journal of Social Psychology*, pp. 253–255.

FREEDMAN, S. G. 1987, April 8. "New AIDS Battlefield: Addicts' World." *New York Times*, pp. B1, B7.

FREUDENHEIM, M. 1999, April 9. "A New Strain on the Cost of Health Care." *New York Times, Business*, pp.1, 17.

FRIEDAN, B. 1963. *The Feminine Mystique*. New York: Dell.

FRIEDAN, B. 1993. *The Fountain of Age*. New York: Simon & Schuster.

FRIEDMAN, L. M. 1993. *Crime and Punishment in American History*. New York: Basic Books.

FRIEDMAN, L. N. 1978. *The Wildcat Experiment: An Early Test of Supported Work in Drug Abuse Rehabilitation*. Washington, DC: U.S. Government Printing Office.

FRIEDMAN, M. 1962. *Capitalism and Freedom*. Chicago: University of Chicago Press.

FUCHS, V. 1956. "Toward a Theory of Poverty." In *Task Force on Economic Growth and Opportunity. The Concept of Poverty*. Washington, DC: U.S. Chamber of Commerce.

FULLER, B., & R. F. ELMORE, eds. 1996. *Who Chooses? Who Loses?: Culture, Institutions, and the Unequal Effects of School Choice*. New York: Teachers College Press.

FULTON, A. S., R. L. GORSUCH, & E. A. MAYNARD. 1999. "Religious Orientation, Antihomosexual Sentiment, and Fundamentalism Among Christians." *Journal for the Scientific Study of Religion*, 38: 14–23.

FURSTENBERG, F., & A. CHERLIN. 1991. *Divided Families*. Cambridge, MA: Harvard University Press.

FUTRELL, M. H. 1996. "Violence in the Classroom: A Teacher's Perspective." In A. M. Hoffman, ed., *Schools, Violence, and Society*. Westport, CT: Praeger.

GABAY, M., & S. M. WOLFE. 1997, September–October. "Nurse-Midwifery: The Beneficial Alternative." *Public Health Reports*, pp. 386–395.

GAGNON, J. H., & W. SIMON. 1967. "Introduction: Deviant Behavior and Sexual Deviance." In J. H. Gagnon and W. Simon, eds., *Sexual Deviance*. New York: Harper & Row.

GAGNON, J. H., & W. SIMON. 1973. *Sexual Conduct: The Social Sources of Human Sexuality*. Hawthorne, NY: Aldine.

GAHR, E. 1999, August. "Pay Equity Iniquity." *American Enterprise*.

GALBRAITH, J. K. 1958. *The Affluent Society*. Boston: Houghton Mifflin.

GALBRAITH, J. K. 1998. *Created Unequal: The Crisis in American Pay*. New York: Free Press.

GALE, E. 2000, February 28. "Churches Take Stake in Prop. 22." *Los Angeles Times*, sec. B, p. 1.

GALEWITZ, P. 1999, September 24. "Combined Worth of America's 400 Richest Surpasses $1 Trillion." *Journal News*, p. 1D.

GALINSKY, E. 1999. *Ask the Children: What American Children Really Think About Working Parents.* New York: Morrow.

GALLAGHER, J., & J. HAMMER. 1998, February 17. "Gay for the Thrill of It." *The Advocate*, pp. 32–37.

GALSTON, W. 1996. "Braking Divorce for the Sake of Children." *The American Enterprise*, 7: 36.

GALTUNG, J. 1971. "Peace-thinking." In Lepawsky, Buehrig, & Lasswell, eds., *The Search for World Order.* Upper Saddle River, NJ: Prentice Hall.

GAMPELL, J. 1999, May 31. "Getting Your Kicks, Without Kidding Around." *Time*, pp. 8ff.

GANS, H. 1979. *Deciding What's News.* New York: Pantheon Books.

GANS, H. 1984. *The Urban Villagers*, 2nd ed. New York: Free Press.

GANS, H. J. 1995. *The War Against the Poor.* New York: Basic Books.

GARREAU, J. 1991. *Edge City: Life on the New Frontier.* New York: Doubleday.

GARREAU, J. 1996, Summer. "Civilization Comes to the Suburbs." *New Perspectives Quarterly*, pp. 23–26.

GARRETT, K. 2000. "Welfare Children Still Hurting, Study Says." *Los Angeles Times*, February 7, p. 3.

GARZA, M. 1999, October. "Gang Bang." *Reason*, p. 15.

GAW, A. C. 1993. *Culture, Ethnicity, and Mental Illness.* Washington, DC: Psychiatric Press.

GEERTZ, C. 1963. "The Integrative Revolution." In C. Geertz, ed., *Old Societies, New States.* New York: Free Press.

GELBARD, A. *Population Bulletin* (Population Reference Bureau), vol. 54.

GELERNTER, D. 1997, March 30. "A Religion of Special Effects." *New York Times*, p. E11.

GELLES, R. J. 1995. *Contemporary Families: A Sociological View.* Thousand Oaks, CA: Sage.

GELLES, R. 1996. *The Book of David: How Preserving Families Can Cost Children's Lives.* New York: Basic Books.

GERBNER, G. 1990. *Violence Profile.* Philadelphia: Annenberg School of Communications.

GERBNER, G. 1996, Fall. "TV Violence and What to Do About It." *Nieman Reports*, pp. 10–13.

GERMOND, J. W., & J. WITCOVER. 1999, May 22. "Outbreak of Pragmatism in the GOP?" *National Journal*, p. 1430.

GERSON, K. 1985. *Hard Choices: How Women Decide About Work, Career, and Motherhood.* Berkeley: University of California Press.

GERSON, K. 1993. *No Man's Land: Men's Changing Commitment to Family and Work.* New York: Basic Books.

GEST, T. 1996, March 25. "Crime Time Bomb." *U.S. News & World Report*, pp. 28–30.

GIELE, J. Z. 1988. "Gender and Sex Roles." In N. J. Smelser, ed., *The Handbook of Sociology.* Newbury Park, CA: Sage.

GILBERT, D. L. 1993. *The American Class Structure: A New Synthesis*, 4th ed. Belmont, CA: Wadsworth.

GILDER, G. 1981. *Wealth and Poverty.* New York: Basic Books.

GILLESPIE, N., & M. W. LYNCH. 1999, October. "Same as It Ever Was." *Reason*, p. 17.

GILLIAM, F. D. 1999, Summer. "The 'Welfare Queen' Experiment." *Nieman Reports*, p. 49.

GINZBER, E. 1993. "The Changing Urban Scene: 1960–1990 and Beyond." In H. G. Cisneros, ed., *Interwoven Destinies: Cities and the Nation.* New York: Norton.

GITLIN, T. 1996. *The Twilight of Common Dreams.* New York: Henry Holt.

GLAAB, C. N., & A. T. BROWN. 1967. *A History of Urban America.* New York: Macmillan.

GLASSNER, B. 2000. *Culture of Fear: The Assault of Optimism in America.* New York: Basic Books.

GLASSNER, B., & B. BERG. 1980. "How Jews Avoid Alcohol Problems." *American Sociological Review*, 45: 647–664.

GLAUSIUSZ, J. 1999, January. "The Chasm in Care." *Discover*, pp. 40–42.

GOCHMAN, DAVID S., ed. 1997. *Handbook of Health Behavior Research.* New York: Plenum.

GOFFMAN, E. 1961. *Asylums: Essays on the Social Situation of Mental Patients and Other Inmates.* Garden City, NY: Doubleday.

GOLDBERG, C. 1996, September 24. "Notion of Year-round Schooling Is Slow to Win Over Los Angeles." *New York Times*, pp. A1, D25.

GOLDBERGER, P. 1996, October 15. "The New Times Square." *New York Times*, pp. C11–C12.

GOLDMAN, H. H., R. G. FRANK, & T. G. McGUIRE. 1994. "Mental Health Care." In E. Ginzberg, ed., *Critical Issues in U.S. Health Care Reform.* Boulder, CO: Westview.

GOLEMAN, D. 1990, May 29. "As Bias Crime Seems to Rise, Scientists Study Roots of Racism." *New York Times*, pp. C1, C5.

GOLEMAN, D. 1992, April 21. "Black Scientists Study the 'Pose' of the Inner City." *New York Times*, pp. C1, C7.

GOLEMAN, D. 1993, March 17. "Mental Disorders Common, but Few Get Treatment, Study Finds." *New York Times*, p. C13.

GONDLES, J. A., JR. 1999a, August. "Hate Crime: Not New, but Still Alarming." *Corrections Today*, p. 6.

GONDLES, J. A., JR. 1999b, October. "A New Look at an Old Idea." *Corrections Today*, p. 6.

GOODE, E. 1998, May–June. "Strange Bedfellows: Ideology, Politics, and Drug Legalization." *Society*, pp. 18–28.

GOODE, E. 1999, June 1. "For Good Health, It Helps to Be Rich and Important." *New York Times*, Science, pp. 1, 9.

GOODE, W. J. 1959. "The Sociology of the Family." In R. Merton, L. Broome, & L. Cottrell, eds., *Sociology Today.* New York: Free Press.

GOODIN, R. E., ed. 1995. *The Theory of Institutional Design.* Cambridge: Cambridge University Press.

GOODMAN, W. 1984, September 4. "Equal Pay for 'Comparable Worth' Growing as Job-discrimination Issue." *New York Times*, p. B9.

GORDON, D. M. 1996. *Fat and Mean: The Corporate Squeeze of Working Americans and the Myth of Managerial "Downsizing."* New York: Martin Kessler Books.

GORDON, D. R. 1994. *The Return of the Dangerous Classes: Drug Prohibition and Policy Politics.* New York: Norton.

GOTTFREDSON, M. R., & T. HIRSCHI. 1995. "National Crime Control Policies." *Society*, 32: 30–37.

GOTTMANN, J. 1978. "Megalopolitan Systems Around the World." In L. S. Bourne & J. W. Simmons, eds., *Systems of Cities: Readings on Structure, Growth, and Policy.* New York: Oxford University Press.

GOULD, R. E. 1974. "Measuring Masculinity by the Size of the Paycheck." In J. H. Pleck and J. Sawyer, eds., *Men and Masculinity.* Upper Saddle River, NJ: Prentice Hall.

GOULD, S. J. 1981. *The Mismeasure of Man.* New York: Norton.

GOULD, W. B. 1968. "Discrimination and the Unions." In J. Larner and I. Howe, eds., *Poverty: Views from the Left.* New York: Morrow.

GOVE, W. R., M. HUGHES, & O. R. GALLE. 1979. "Overcrowding in the Home: An Empirical Investigation of Its Possible Consequences." *American Sociological Review*, 44: 59–79.

GRAHAM, H. D., & T. R. GURR, eds. 1969. *Violence in America: Historical and Comparative Perspectives. A Report to the National Commission on the Causes and Prevention of Violence.* New York: Bantam Books.

GRASSO, K. L. 1994. *Criminal Child Sexual Abuse and Exploitation Laws in Eight Midwestern States: Recommendations for Legislative Change.* Washington, DC: The Center.

GREENFELD, L. A., & T. L. SNELL. 1999. *Women Offenders.* Washington, DC: Bureau of Justice Statistics, U.S. Department of Justice.

GREENFELD, L. A., & M. W. ZAWITZ. 1995. *Weapons Offenses and Offenders.* Washington, DC: Bureau of Justice Statistics, U.S. Department of Justice.

GREENLEY, J. R. 1972. "Alternative Views of the Psychiatrist's Role." *Social Problems*, 20: 252–262.

GRIMSLEY, K. D. 1999, January 18. "Survey: 26% of Workers 'Burned Out or Stressed' by Jobs." *Journal News*, p. 1D.

GROB, G. N. 1985, May–June. "The Transformation of the Mental Hospital in the United States." *American Behavioral Scientist*, 28: 639–654.

GRONFEIN, W. 1985, June. "Psychotrophic Drugs and the Origins of Deinstitutionalization." *Social Problems*, 32: 437–454.

GRUENBERG, B. 1980. "The Happy Worker: An Analysis of Educational and Occupational Differences in Determinants of Job Satisfaction." *American Journal of Sociology*, 86: 247–271.

GUETZLOE, E. 1999. "Violence in Children and Adolescents—A Threat to Public Health and Safety: A Paradigm of Prevention." *Preventing School Failure*, 44: 21.

GUILLERMOPRIETO, A. 2000, April 27. "Colombia: Violence Without End?" *New York Review of Books*, pp. 31–39.

GUSFIELD, J. R. 1963. *Symbolic Crusade: Status Politics and the American Temperance Movement.* Urbana: University of Illinois Press.

GUSFIELD, J. R. 1975. "The Futility of Knowledge?: The Relation of Social Science to Public Policy Toward Drugs." *Annals of the American Academy of Political and Social Sciences*, 417: 1–15.

GUTERL, F. 1996, January. "The Chemistry of Mass Murder." *Discover*, p. 7.

HACKER, A. 1999, October 21. "The Unmaking of Men." *New York Review of Books*, pp. 25–30.

HACKSTAFF, K. B. 1999. *Marriage in a Culture of Divorce.* Philadelphia: Temple University Press.

HAGEDORN, J. M. 1988. *People and Folks: Gangs, Crime, and the Underclass in a Rustbelt City.* Chicago: Lake View Press.

HAGEDORN, J. M., J. TORRES, & G. GIGLIO. 1998. "Cocaine, Kicks, and Strain: Patterns of Substance Use in Milwaukee Gangs." *Contemporary Drug Problems*, 25: 113–145.

HALL, P. 1982. *Great Planning Disasters.* Berkeley: University of California Press.

HALL, R. 1995. *Rape in America, a Reference Book.* Santa Barbara, CA: ABC-Clio.

HAMER, D., & P. COPELAND. 1995. *The Science of Desire: The Search for the Gay Gene and the Biology of Behavior.* New York: Simon & Schuster.

HANNAWAY, J. 1993. "Political Pressure and Decentralization in Institutional Organizations: The Case of School Districts." *Sociology of Education*, 3: 147–163.

HARKEY, J., D. L. MILES, & W. A. RUSHING. 1976. "The Relation Between Social Class and Functional Status: A New Look at the Drift Hypothesis." *Journal of Health and Social Behavior*, 17: 194–204.

HARRINGTON, M. 1987. *The New American Poverty.* New York: Henry Holt.

HARTMANN, H. 1994, December. "Women Working a Third Shift." *Working Woman*, p. 16.

HARTMANN, H. 1995a, Spring. "Feminism After the Fall." *Dissent*, pp. 158–159.

Hartmann, H. 1995b, May 1. "A Program to Help Working Parents." *The Nation,* pp. 592ff.

Hassel, C. V. 1977. "Terror: The Crime of the Privileged—An Examination and Prognosis." *Terrorism,* 1: 128.

Heath, L. 1984. "Impact of Newspaper Crime Reporting on Fear of Crime." *Journal of Personality and Social Psychology,* 47: 263–276.

Hechter, M. 1987. *The Foundations of Group Solidarity.* Berkeley: University of California Press.

Henderson, Z. P. 1995, Summer. "Children Need Space." *Human Ecology Forum,* pp. 20–23.

Herbert, B. 1997, March 10. "The Artful Dodger." *New York Times,* p. A15.

Herman, J. L., & L. Hirschman. 1988. "Father-Daughter Incest." *Signs: Journal of Women in Culture and Society,* 2: 735–756.

Herndon, J. 1968. *The Way It Spozed to Be.* New York: Simon & Schuster.

Hesman, T. 2000, March 4. "Climate Change Record in Subsurface Temperatures: Recent Heat May Indicate Faster Warming." *Science News,* p. 148.

Hesse-Biber, S. J. 1996. *Am I Thin Enough Yet?: The Cult of Thinness and the Commercialization of Identity.* New York: Oxford University Press.

Heyl, B. S. 1978. *The Madam as Entrepreneur: Career Management in House Prostitution.* New Brunswick, NJ: Transaction Books.

Heymann, S. J., & A. Earle. 1997, Summer-Fall. "Working Conditions Faced by Poor Families and the Care of Children." *Focus,* pp. 56–59.

HHS (U.S. Department of Health and Human Services, Public Health Service). 1990a. *Healthy People 2000.* Washington, DC: U.S. Government Printing Office.

HHS (U.S. Department of Health and Human Services, Public Health Service). 1990b. *Research on Children and Adolescents with Mental, Behavioral, and Developmental Disorders.* Rockville, MD: National Institute of Mental Health.

HHS (U.S. Department of Health and Human Services). 1996. *National Household Survey on Drug Abuse: Main Findings 1994.* Rockville, MD: U.S. Department of Health and Human Services, Public Health Service, Substance Abuse and Mental Health Services Administration.

Hill, S. C., & J. D. Drolet. 1999. "School-related Violence Among High School Students in the United States, 1993–1995." *Journal of School Health,* 69: 264.

Hilts, P. J. 1990, May 1. "Spread of AIDS by Heterosexuals Remains Slow." *New York Times,* pp. C1, C12.

Himmelstein, D. U., S. Woolhandler, I. Hellander, & S. M. Wolfe. 1999. "Quality of Care in Investor-owned vs. Not-for-Profit HMOs." *Journal of the American Medical Association,* 282: 159.

Hippensteele, S., & T. C. Pearson, 1999, January–February. "Responding Effectively to Sexual Harassment." *Change,* pp. 48-54.

Hirsch, E. D., Jr. 1996. *The Schools We Need: And Why We Don't Have Them.* New York: Doubleday.

Hirsch, K. 1987. "Media Violence and Audience Behavior." In A. Wells, ed., *Mass Media and Society.* Lexington, MA: D. C. Heath.

Hirschi, T., & M. Gottfredson. 1983. "Age and the Explanation of Crime." *American Journal of Sociology,* 89: 552–584.

Hobb, D. 1997. "Professional Crime: Change, Continuity and the Enduring Myth of the Underworld." *Sociology,* pp. 57–73.

Hochschild, A. R. 1990. *The Second Shift.* New York: Avon Books.

Holmes, R. A., & J. DeBurger. 1987. *Serial Murder.* Newbury Park, CA: Sage.

Holmes, S. A. 1996a, November 18. "Quality of Life Is Up for Many Blacks, Data Say." *New York Times,* pp. A1, B10.

Holmes, S. A. 1996b, July 4. "Study Finds Rising Number of Black-White Marriages." *New York Times,* p. A16.

Holstein, W. J. 2000, February 21. "A Tale of Two Austins." *U.S. News & World Report,* p. 44.

Holt, J. 1965. *How Children Fail.* New York: Dell.

Homer-Dixon, T. F., J. H. Boutwell, & G. W. Rathjens. 1993, February. "Environmental Change and Violent Conflict." *Scientific American,* pp. 38–45.

Hooker, E. 1966. "The Homosexual Community." In J. O. Palmer and M. J. Goldstein, eds., *Perspectives in Psychopathology: Readings in Abnormal Psychology.* New York: Oxford University Press.

Hooyman, N. R., & N. A. Kiyak. 1999. *Social Gerontology: A Multidisciplinary Approach.* Boston: Allyn & Bacon.

Horgan, J. 1993, February. "Genes and Crime." *Scientific American,* pp. 24, 26, 29.

Horner, M. 1970. "Femininity and Successful Achievement: A Basic Inconsistency." In J. M. Bardwick, ed., *Feminine Personality and Conflict.* Belmont, CA: Brooks/ Cole.

Horowitz, A. V., & T. L. Scheid, eds. 1998. *A Handbook for the Study of Mental Health.* New York: Cambridge University Press.

Horton, R. 1995, July 13. "Is Homosexuality Inherited?" *New York Review of Books,* pp. 36–41.

House Committee on Government Operations. 1994. *Drugs in the 1990's: Emerging Trends.* Hearing before the Information, Justice, Transportation, and Agriculture Subcommittee of the Committee on Government Operations, House of Representatives, 103rd Cong., 2nd sess., May 25. Washington, DC: U.S. Government Printing Office.

Huber, J., & G. Spitze. 1988. "Trends in Family Sociology." In N. J. Smelser, ed., *The Handbook of Sociology.* Newbury Park, CA: Sage.

Hunt, L. G., & C. D. Chambers. 1976. *The Heroin Epidemic.* Holliswood, NY: Spectrum Books.

Hunt, L. G., & M. A. Forsland. 1980. "Epidemiology of Heroin Use in Cheyenne, Wyoming: 1960–1977." In R. Faulkinberry, ed., *Drug Problems of the 70's: Solutions for the 80's.* Lafayette, LA: Endac Enterprises/Print Media.

Hunt, M. 1974. *Sexual Behavior in the 1970s.* New York: Dell.

Hurty, K. S. 1998, August 8. "Women of Faith Shepherds of Equality." *Arizona Republic,* p. D.

Jackman, M. R., & R. W. Jackman. 1983. *Class Awareness in the United States.* Berkeley: University of California Press.

Jacobs, J. 1961. *The Death and Life of Great American Cities.* New York: Vintage.

Jacobs, J. A., & K. Gerson. 1998. *Who Are the Overworked Americans?* London: Routledge.

Jacobs, M. D. 1990. *Screwing the System and Making It Work.* Chicago: University of Chicago Press.

Jacobson, D. 1995. "Freedom of Speech Acts? A Response to Langton." *Philosophy and Public Affairs,* 24: 64–79.

James, J., & J. Meyerding. 1977. "Early Sexual Experience as a Factor in Prostitution." *Archives of Sexual Behavior,* 7: 31–42.

Jamison, K. R. 1999. *Night Falls Fast: Understanding Suicide.* New York: Knopf.

Janofsky, M. 1998, November 29. "U.S. Bolsters Housing Aid for the Elderly." *New York Times,* p. 29.

Janowitz, M. 1978. *The Last Half Century: Societal Change and Politics in America.* Chicago: University of Chicago Press.

Jasanoff, S. 1986. *Risk Management and Political Culture.* New York: Russell Sage.

Jaynes, D. J., & R. M. Williams, Jr., eds. 1989. *A Common Destiny: Blacks and American Society.* Washington, DC: National Academy Press.

Jaynes, G. 1988, February 13. "Where Are You? A Nameless Man in a Grim World." *New York Times,* p. 29.

Jencks, C. 1992. *Rethinking Social Policy: Race, Poverty, and the Underclass.* Cambridge, MA: Harvard University Press.

Jencks, C. 1994, April 21. "The Truth About Homelessness." *New York Review of Books,* pp. 20–27.

Jencks, C. 1995. *The Homeless.* Cambridge, MA: Harvard University Press.

Jencks, C., & P. E. Peterson, eds. 1991. *The Urban Underclass.* Washington, DC: Brookings Institution.

Jencks, C., & J. Swingle. 2000, January 3. "Without a Net." *The American Prospect,* p. 37.

Jenson, J. M., & M. O. Howard. 1998. "Youth Crime, Public Policy, and Practice in the Juvenile Justice System: Recent Trends and Needed Reforms." *Social Work,* 43: 324–335.

Johannson, S., & O. Nygren. 1991. "The Missing Girls of China: A New Demographic Account." *Population and Development Review* 17: 35–52.

Johnson, D. 1991, March 18. "Where Phone Lines Stop, Progress May Pass By." *New York Times,* p. A12.

Johnson, G. 1997, March 30. "Old View of the Internet: Nerds. New View: Nuts." *New York Times,* sec. 4, p. 1.

Jones, S. L. 1999, October 4. "The Incredibly Shrinking Gay Gene." *Christianity Today,* p. 53.

Judson, G. 1995, September 1. "Child of Courage Joins Her Biographer." *New York Times,* pp. B1, B5.

Jurevich, T. 1984. *Chaos on the Shop Floor.* Philadelphia: Temple University Press.

Justice, B., & R. Justice. 1990. *The Abusing Family.* New York: Plenum.

Kadushin, C. 1983. "Mental Health and the Interpersonal Environment: A Reexamination of Some Effects of Social Structure on Mental Health." *American Sociological Review,* 48: 188–198.

Kadushin, G. 1996. "Gay Men with AIDS and Their Families of Origin: An Analysis of Social Support." *Health and Social Work,* 21: 141–149.

Kahlenberg, R. D. 1996. *Class, Race, and Affirmative Action.* New York: Basic Books.

Kaminer, W. 1999, December 20. "The War on High Schools." *American Prospect,* p. 11.

Kaminer, W. 2000, January 3. "When Congress Plays Doctor." *American Prospect,* p. 8.

Kandel, D. B. 1991. "The Social Demography of Drug Use." *Milbank Quarterly,* 69: 365–414.

Kantrowitz, B., & P. Wingert. 1990, Winter–Spring. "Step by Step." *Newsweek,* pp. 24–34.

Kaplan, D. A., & A. Rogers. 1996, April 22. "The Silicon Classroom." *Newsweek,* pp. 60–61.

Karp, A. 1994. "The Arms Trade Revolution: The Major Impact of Small Arms." *Washington Quarterly,* 17: 65–77.

Kasarda, J. 1978. "Urbanization, Community, and the Metropolitan Problem." In D. Street, ed., *Handbook of Contemporary Urban Life.* San Francisco: Jossey-Bass.

Kasarda, J. D. 1993. "Cities as Places Where People Live and Work: Urban Change and Neighborhood Distress." In H. G. Cisneros, ed., *Interwoven Destinies: Cities and the Nation.* New York: Norton.

Kasarda, J. D. 1995. "Industrial Restructuring and the Changing Location of Jobs." In R. Farley, ed., *State of the Union: America in the 1990s, Vol. 1: Economic Trends.* New York: Russell Sage.

Kasinitz, P. 1989. "Three Books About the Homeless." *Dissent,* 36: 566–569.

Katz, J. 1988. *Seductions of Crime: Moral and Sensual Attractions in Doing Evil.* New York: Basic Books.

Katz Rothman, B. 1994. *The Encyclopedia of Childrearing.* New York: Henry Holt.

Kempf, K., ed. 1990. *Measurement Issues in Criminology.* New York: Springer-Verlag.

KENNEDY, P. 1993. *Preparing for the 21st Century.* New York: Random House.

KENNEDY, R. 2000. *Burr, Hamilton, and Jefferson: A Study in Character.* New York: Oxford University Press.

KENNY, C. 1996. "Black Environmentalism in the Local Community Context." *Environment and Behavior,* 28: 267–282.

KILBORN, P. T. 1990, May 31. "Wage Gap Between Sexes Is Cut in Test, but at a Price." *New York Times,* pp. A1, D22.

KILBORN, P. T. 1998a, April 22. "Doctors' Pay Regains Ground Despite the Effects of H.M.O.'s." *New York Times,* pp. A1, A20.

KILBORN, P. T. 1998b, August 30. "The Uninsured Find Fewer Doctors in the House." *New York Times,* p. 14.

KILBOURNE, J. 1991, Spring–Summer. "Deadly Persuasion: Seven Myths Alcohol Advertisers Want You to Believe." *Media & Values,* pp. 10–12.

KIM, I. 1981. *New Urban Immigrants: The Korean Community in New York.* Princeton, NJ: Princeton University Press.

KIM, I. 1983. *Urban Newcomers: The Koreans.* Princeton, NJ: Princeton University Press.

KIMMEL, M. S., & M. A. MESSNER. 1992. *Men's Lives.* New York: Macmillan.

KING, E. A. 1999, September. "15 Myths About Adolescent Suicide." *Education Digest,* pp. 68–71.

KINSEY, A. C., W. B. POMEROY, & C. E. MARTIN. 1948. *Sexual Behavior in the Human Male.* Philadelphia: Saunders.

KLECK, G. 1999. "There Are No Lessons to Be Learned from Littleton." *Criminal Justice Ethics,* 18: 2.

KLEIMAN, D. 1987, September 28. "The Last Taboo: Case on L.I. Pierces the Silence on Incest." *New York Times,* pp. A1, B5.

KOBRIN, S. 1959. "The Chicago Area Project—A 25-year Assessment." *Annals of the American Academy of Political and Social Sciences,* 322: 20–29.

KOLATA, G. 1992, March 4. "New Insurance Practice: Dividing Sick from Well." *New York Times,* pp. A1, A15.

KORNBLUM, W. 1993. "Following the Action with Violence Research. Review of Albert J. Reiss, Jr., & Jeffrey A. Roth, eds., *Understanding and Preventing Violence.*" *Contemporary Sociology,* 22: 344–346.

KORNBLUM, W. 2000. *Sociology in a Changing World,* 5th ed. Fort Worth, TX: Harcourt.

KORNBLUM, W., & V. BOGGS. 1984, Winter. "New Alternatives for Fighting Crime." *Social Policy,* pp. 24–28.

KOSTERLITZ, J. 1990, September 8. "No Home, No Help." *National Journal,* p. 2120.

KOZOL, J. 1967. *Death at an Early Age.* Boston: Houghton Mifflin.

KOZOL, J. 1988. "The Homeless and Their Children," *The New Yorker,* January 25, pp. 65ff; February 1, pp. 36ff.

KRISTOF, N. D. 1995, August 6. "The Bomb: An Act That Haunts Japan and America." *New York Times,* pp. 1, 12.

KRISTOF, N. D. 1996, September 22. "Aging World, New Wrinkles." *New York Times,* pp. 1, 5.

KRONENWETTER, E. 1999, October 25. "U.S. to Renew Push on Emissions Trading as Nations Meet for Climate Change Meeting." *Oil Daily.*

KÜBLER-ROSS, E. 1969. *On Death and Dying.* New York: Atheneum.

KÜBLER-ROSS, E. 1975. *Death: The Final Stage of Growth.* Upper Saddle River, NJ: Prentice Hall.

KUTCHINSKY, B. 1992. "The Politics of Pornography Research. Comment on S. A. Childress." *Law and Society Review,* 26: 447–455.

KUTTNER, R. 1991. *The End of Laissez-faire: National Purpose and the Global Economy After the Cold War.* New York: Knopf.

KUTTNER, R. 1997. *Everything for Sale: The Virtues and Limits of Markets.* New York: Knopf.

LAMANNA, M. A. 1997. *Marriages and Families: Making Changes in a Diverse Society.* Belmont, CA: Wadsworth.

LANDRY, M. J. 1996. *Overview of Addiction Treatment Effectiveness.* Rockville, MD: U.S. Department of Health and Human Services.

LARANA, E., H. JOHNSTON, & J. R. GUSFIELD, eds. 1994. *New Social Movements: From Ideology to Identity.* Philadelphia: Temple University Press.

LASSWELL, H. D. 1941. "The Garrison State." *American Journal of Sociology,* 46: 455–468.

LAUMANN, E. O. 1996. "Formative Sexual Experiences." In M. D. Smith, J. A. Gagnon, & T. Smith, eds., *Early Sexual Experiences: How Voluntary? How Violent?* Menlo Park, CA: Henry J. Kaiser Family Foundation.

LAUMANN, E. O., J. H. GAGNON, R. T. MICHAELS, & S. MICHAELS. 1994. *The Social Organization of Sexuality: Sexual Practices in the United States.* Chicago: University of Chicago Press.

LAVER, M. 1982. *The Crime Game.* Oxford: Martin Robertson.

LAVIN, D. E., R. D. ALBA, & R. A. SILBERSTEIN. 1981. *Right Versus Privilege: The Open Admissions Experiment at the City University of New York.* New York: Free Press.

LAVIN, D. E., & D. HYLLEGARD. 1996. *Changing the Odds: Open Admissions and Life Chances.* New Haven, CT: Yale University Press.

LAVIN, E. D. 2000. Personal communication.

LEIFMAN, H., E. KUHLHORN, & P. ALLEBECK. 1995. "Abstinence in Late Adolescence—Antecedents to and Covariates of a Sober Lifestyle and Its Consequences." *Social Science and Medicine,* 41: 113–121.

LEIGHTON, D. C., J. S. HARDING, D. B. MACKLIN, A. M. MACMILLAN, & A. H. LEIGHTON. 1963. *The Character of Danger.* New York: Basic Books.

LELAND, J. 1995, December 11. "Violence, Reel to Reel." *Newsweek,* pp. 46–47.

LELAND, J. 1999, October 11. "More Buck for the Bang; How Sex on the Internet Has Transformed the Business of Pornography." *Newsweek,* p. 73.

LESLIE, C. 1996, July 8. "Will Johnny Get A's?" *Newsweek,* p. 72.

LESTER, D. 1996. "Trends in Divorce and Marriage Around the World." *Journal of Divorce and Remarriage,* 25: 169–171.

LESTER, D. 1997. "Correlates of Worldwide Divorce Rates." *Journal of Divorce and Remarriage,* 26: 215–219.

LEUCHTAG, A. 1995. "The Culture of Pornography." *The Humanist,* 55: 4–6.

LE VAY, S. 1995. *The Sexual Brain.* Cambridge: Massachusetts Institute of Technology Press.

LEVIN, J., & J. A. FOX. 1985. *Mass Murder: America's Growing Menace.* Newbury Park, CA: Sage.

LEVINSON, R. M. 1975. "Sex Discrimination and Employment Practices. An Experiment with Unconventional Job Inquiries." *Social Problems,* 22: 533–543.

LEVITAN, S. A. 1968. "Head Start: It Is Never Too Early to Fight Poverty." In *Federal Programs for the Development of Human Resources.* Washington, DC: U.S. Congress, Joint Economic Committee, Subcommittee on Economic Progress.

LEWIN, T. 2000, January 6. "Grandparents Play Big Part in Grandchildren's Lives, Survey Finds." *New York Times,* p. A16.

LEWINE, R. R., D. BURBACH, & H. Y. MELTZER. 1984. "Effect of Diagnostic Criteria on the Ratio of Male to Female Schizophrenic Patients." *American Journal of Psychiatry,* 14: 84–87.

LEWIS, A. 1994, March 13. "The First Amendment, Under Fire from the Left." *New York Times Magazine,* pp. 40–45.

LEWIS, O. 1968. *The Study of Slum Cultures—Backgrounds for La Vida.* New York: Random House.

LI, J. 1995. "China's One-child Policy: A Case Study of Hebei Province, 1979–88." *Population and Development Review,* 21: 563–586.

LICHTER, D. T., & G. V. FUGUITT. 1980. "Demographic Response to Transportation Innovation: The Case of the Interstate Highway." *Social Forces,* 59: 492–511.

LIEBERSON, S. 1980. *A Piece of the Pie: Black and White Immigrants Since 1980.* Berkeley: University of California Press.

LIEBERSON, S. 1990. *From Many Strands,* 2nd ed. New York: Russell Sage.

LIFTON, R. J., & G. MITCHELL. 1995. *Hiroshima in America: Fifty Years of Denial.* New York: Putnam.

LIND, M. 1998, August 16. "The Beige and the Black." *New York Times,* sec. 6, p. 38.

LIPSKEY, M. 1980. *Street Level Bureaucracy: Dilemmas of the Individual in Public Services.* New York: Russell Sage Foundation.

LIPTON, D. S. 1996. *The Effectiveness of Treatment for Drug Abusers Under Criminal Justice Supervision.* Washington, DC: U.S. Department of Justice, Office of Justice Programs, National Institute of Justice.

LISKA, A. S., & W. BACCAGLINI. 1990. "Feeling Safe by Comparison: Crime in the Newspapers." *Social Problems,* 37: 328–337.

LOFLAND, L. 1998. *The Public Realm: Exploring the City's Quintessential Social Territory.* Chicago: Aldine.

LONECK, B., J. A. GARRETT, & S. M. BANKS. 1996. "A Comparison of the Johnson Intervention with Four Other Methods of Referral to Outpatient Treatment." *American Journal of Drug and Alcohol Abuse,* 22: 233–246.

LONG, D. E. 1990. *The Anatomy of Terrorism.* New York: Free Press.

LORBER, J. 1994. *Paradoxes of Gender.* New Haven, CT: Yale University Press.

LORCH, D. 1991, January 3. "Immigrants from China Pay Dearly to Be Slaves." *New York Times,* pp. B1, B2.

LORENZ, K. Z. 1981. *The Foundations of Ethology.* New York: Springer-Verlag.

LOUPE, D. 1996, April 25. "Day-care Centers Gaining Favor with Employed Moms." *Atlanta Constitution,* p. D2.

LOVINS, A. B. 1977. *Soft Energy Paths: Toward a Durable Peace.* San Francisco: Friends of the Earth.

LOVINS, A. B. 1986. *Energy Unbound: A Fable for America's Future.* San Francisco: Sierra Club.

LUKER, K. 1996. *Dubious Conceptions: The Politics of Teenage Pregnancy.* Cambridge, MA: Harvard University Press.

LUNDE, D. T. 1975, July. "Our Murder Boom." *Psychology Today,* pp. 35–42.

LYMAN, M. D. 1996. *Drugs in Society: Causes, Concepts, & Control,* 2nd ed. Cincinnati: Andersen.

MACCOBY, E. E., & C. N. JACKLIN. 1977. "What We Should Know and Don't Know About Sex Differences." In E. S. Morrison and V. Borsage, eds., *Human Sexuality: Contemporary Perspectives.* Palo Alto, CA: Mayfield.

MACDONALD, G. J. 1996. "Assessing the U.S. Environment: Environmental Quality. The Twenty-fourth Annual Report of the Council on Environmental Quality." *Environment,* 38: 25–26.

MACGREGOR, S. 1990. "Could Britain Inherit the American Nightmare?" *British Journal of Addiction,* 85: 863–872.

MACKINNON, C. A. 1979. *Sexual Harassment of Working Women.* New Haven, CT: Yale University Press.

MACKINNON, C. 1993. *Only Words.* Cambridge, MA: Harvard University Press.

MACKINNON, C. 1995, March 13. "Online Fantasies." *Time,* pp. 7–9.

MACLEOD, C. 1974, June 8. "Legacy of Battering." *The Nation,* pp. 719–722.

MALES, M. 1996, February. "Crackdown on Kids." *The Progressive,* pp. 24–26.

MALES, M. 1998, July–August. "Disowning the Future." *Tikkun,* pp. 22–25.

MALINOWSKI, B. 1941. *The Sexual Life of Savages in North-western Melanesia.* New York: Halcyon House.

MALTZ, M. D. 1999. *Bridging the Gap in Police Crime Statistics.* Washington, DC: Bureau of Justice Statistics.

MARE, R. D., & C. WINSHIP. 1991. "Socioeconomic Change and the Decline of Marriage for Blacks and Whites." In C. Jencks & P. E. Peterson, eds., *The Urban Underclass.* Washington, DC: Brookings Institution.

MARGARONIS, M. 1999, December 27. "The Politics of Food." *The Nation,* p. 11.

MARMOR, T. R. 1994. *Understanding Health Care Reform.* New Haven, CT: Yale University Press.

MARMOT, M. G. 1998, Fall. "Contribution of Psychosocial Factors to Socioeconomic Differences in Health." *Milbank Quarterly,* pp. 403–449.

MARMOT, M. G., M. G. SHIPLEY, & G. ROSE. 1984. "Inequalities in Death: Specific Explanations of a General Pattern." *The Lancet,* 1: 1003–1006.

MARSHALL, N., & J. HENDTLASS. 1986, Spring. "Drugs and Prostitution." *Journal of Drug Issues,* 16: 237–248.

MARTINE, G. 1996. "Brazil's Fertility Decline, 1965–1995." *Population and Development Review,* 22: 47–76.

MARTÍNEZ-ALIER, J., & E. HERSHBERG. 1992. "Environmentalism and the Poor." *Items* (Social Science Research Council), 46: 1–5.

MARTINSON, R. 1972, April 29. "Planning for Public Safety." *New Republic,* pp. 21–23.

MARVIN, D. R. 1997, July. "The Dynamics of Domestic Abuse." *FBI Law Enforcement Bulletin,* pp. 13–19.

MARX, K. 1867/1962. *Capital: A Critique of Political Economy.* Moscow: Foreign Languages Publishing House.

MARX, K., & F. ENGELS. 1848/1969. *The Communist Manifesto.* New York: Penguin.

MASON-DRAFFEN, C. 1999, July 26. "Jobs? Yes. Security? No." *Newsday,* p. C1.

MASSEY, D. 1995. "The New Immigration and Ethnicity in the United States." *Population and Development Review,* 21: 631–652.

MASSEY, D. S., & N. A. DENTON. 1993. *American Apartheid: Segregation and the Making of the Underclass.* Cambridge, MA: Harvard University Press.

MATCHA, D. A. 1999. *Medical Sociology.* Needham Heights, MA: Allyn & Bacon.

MATRAS, J. 1973. *Populations and Societies.* Upper Saddle River, NJ: Prentice Hall.

MATTHEWS, R. 1996, October 17. "Cyberspace Not the Answer to Education Woes." *Atlanta Journal,* p. A18.

MAZRUI, A. A. 1996. "The New Dynamics of Security: The United Nations and Africa." *World Policy Journal,* 13: 37–42.

MBERE, N. 1996. "The Beijing Conference: A South African Perspective." *SAIS Review,* 16: 167–178.

MCEWEN, C. 1988. "Continuities in the Study of Total and Non-total Institutions." In *Annual Review of Sociology.* Newbury Park, CA: Sage.

MCINTOSH, C. A., & J. S. FINKLE. 1995. "The Cairo Conference on Population and Development." *Population and Development Review,* 21: 223–260.

MCKEOWN, R. E., K. L. JACKSON, & R. F. VALOIS. 1998. "The Frequence and Correlates of Violent Behaviors in a Statewide Sample of High School Students." *Family and Community Health,* 20: 38–54.

MCLEOD, J. 1995. *Ain't No Makin' It,* 2nd ed. Boulder, CO: Westview Press.

MCNAMARA, R. P. 1994. *The Times Square Hustler: Male Prostitution in New York City.* Westport, CT: Praeger.

MCNEILL, W. H. 1982. *The Pursuit of Power: Technology, Armed Force, and Society Since A.D. 1000.* Chicago: University of Chicago Press.

MECHANIC, D. 1990, September 16. "Promise Them Everything, Give Them the Streets," *New York Times Book Review,* p. 9.

MEDINA, J. J. 1996. *The Clock of Ages: Why We Age, How We Age, Winding Back the Clock.* Cambridge: Cambridge University Press.

MEED, I. 2000. "Islamist Leader Osama Binladin." *Middle East Economic Digest,* 12:19.

MEIER, D. 1991, March 4. "Choice Can Save Public Education." *The Nation,* pp. 253ff.

MEIER, D. 1995, January. "How Our Schools Could Be." *Phi Delta Kappan,* pp. 369–373.

MELMAN, S. 1974. *The Permanent War Economy: American Capitalism in Decline.* New York: Simon & Schuster.

MERTON, R. K. 1949. *Social Theory and Social Structure.* New York: Free Press.

MERTON, R. K. 1968. *Social Theory and Social Structure,* 3rd ed. New York: Free Press.

METHWIN, E. J. 1997, July–August. "Mugged by Reality." *Policy Review,* pp. 32–39.

MEYER, J. W. 1985, May–June. "Institutional and Organizational Rationalization in the Mental Health System." *American Behavioral Scientist,* 28: 587–600.

MEYERS, M. K., A. LUKEMEYER, & T. M. SMEEDING. 1997, Summer–Fall. "The Cost of Caring: Childhood Disability and Poor Families." *Focus,* p. 52.

MIECH, R. A., A. CASPI, T. E. MOFFITT, B. R. ENTNER WRIGHT, & P. A. SILVA. 1999. "Low Socioeconomic Status and Mental disorders: A Longitudinal Study of Selection and Causation During Young Adulthood." *American Journal of Sociology,* 104: 1096.

MILGRAM, S. 1974. *Obedience to Authority: An Experimental View.* New York: Harper-Collins.

MILLER, E. M. 1986. *Street Women.* Philadelphia: Temple University Press.

MILLER, W. B. 1958. "Lower Class Culture as a Generating Milieu of Gang Delinquency." *Journal of Social Issues,* 14: 5–19.

MILLS, C. W. 1956. *The Power Elite.* New York: Oxford University Press.

MILLS, V. K. 1972. "The Status of Women in American Churches." *Churches and Society,* 63: 50–55.

MILNER, C., & R. MILNER. 1973. *Black Players: The Secret World of Black Pimps.* London: Michael Joseph.

MINCER, J., & S. POLACHEK. 1974. "Family Investments in Human Capital: Earnings of Women." *Journal of Political Economy,* 82: S76–S108.

MINUCHIN, S. 1974. *Families and Family Therapy.* Cambridge, MA: Harvard University Press.

MIROWSKY, J. 1985. "Depression and Marital Power: An Equity Model." *American Journal of Sociology,* 87: 771–826.

MISHEL, L., J. BERNSTEIN, & J. SCHMITT. 1996, November–December. "The State of American Workers." *Challenge,* pp. 33–43.

MOLLMAN, S. 1999, December. Web Resources. *PC/Computing,* p. 82.

MONEY, J., 1955. "An Examination of Some Basic Sexual Concepts: The Evidence of Human Hermaphroditism." *Bulletin of the Johns Hopkins Hospital,* 97: 301–319.

MONROE, J. 1996. "How Noise Pollution Affects Us." *Current Health,* 22: 30–31.

MONTAGU, A. 1973. "The New Litany of 'Innate Depravity,' or Original Sin Revisited." In A. Montagu, ed., *Man and Aggression,* 2nd ed. New York: Oxford University Press.

MOORE, M. 1996. *Downsize This!* New York: Crown.

MOORE, T. G. 1995. *Global Warming: A Boon to Humans and Other Animals.* Stanford, CA: Hoover Institution.

MORGENSON, G. 1999, December 26. "A Company Worth More Than Spain?" *New York Times,* sec. 3, p. 1.

MORRISON, T. G., L. D. MCLEOD, M. A. MORRISON, D. ANDERSON, & W. E. O'CONNOR. 1997. "Gender Stereotyping, Homonegativity, and Misconceptions About Sexually Coercive Behavior Among Adolescents." *Youth & Society,* 28: 351–383.

MORROW, J. 1999, February 15. "Watching Web Speech." *U.S. News & World Report,* p. 32.

MOSLE, S. 1993, January 18. "Dim Bulb." *New Republic,* pp. 16ff.

MOSLE, S. 1996, October 27. "The Answer Is National Standards." *New York Times Magazine,* p. 45.

MOUW, R., D. JONES, S. SPENCER, & M. S. VAN LEEUWEN. 1999, October 4. "Just Saying 'No' Is Not Enough." *Christianity Today,* p. 50.

MOYNIHAN, D. 1965. *The Negro Family: The Case for National Action.* Washington, DC: U.S. Department of Labor.

MUNDY, L. 1999, September 19. "Dialing for Deliverance." *Washington Post Magazine,* p. 6.

MURRAY, C. 1984. *Losing Ground: American Social Policy, 1950–1980.* New York: Basic Books.

MURRAY, J. B. 1998. "Psychophysiological Aspects of Amphetamine-Metamphetamine Abuse." *Journal of Psychology,* 132: 227–238.

NAGEL, J. 1996. *American Indian Ethnic Revival.* New York: Oxford University Press.

NATIONAL ADVISORY COMMISSION ON CIVIL DISORDERS. 1968. *Report of the National Advisory Commission on Civil Disorders.* Washington, DC: U.S. Government Printing Office.

NATIONAL ADVISORY MENTAL HEALTH COUNCIL. 1993. "Health Care Reform for Americans with Severe Mental Illness." *American Journal of Psychiatry,* 150: 1447–1465.

NATIONAL CAUCUS AND CENTER ON BLACK AGED. 1987. *The Status of the Black Elderly in the United States.* Report for the Select Committee on Aging, House of Representatives, U.S. Congress. Washington, DC: U.S. Government Printing Office.

NATIONAL CENTER FOR HEALTH STATISTICS. 1992. *Serious Mental Illness and Disability in the Adult Household Population: United States, 1989.* Hyattsville, MD: National Center for Health Statistics, U.S. Department of Health and Human Services.

NATIONAL COMMISSION ON EXCELLENCE IN EDUCATION. 1983. *A Nation at Risk: The Imperative for Educational Reform.* Washington, DC: U.S. Government Printing Office.

NATIONAL COMMISSION ON MARIHUANA AND DRUG ABUSE. 1973. *Drug Use in America: Problem in Perspective,* 2nd Report. Washington, DC: U.S. Government Printing Office.

NATIONAL INSTITUTE ON ALCOHOL ABUSE AND ALCOHOLISM. 1994, July. "Alcohol-related Impairment." *Alcohol Alert,* p. 1.

NATIONAL INSTITUTE ON ALCOHOL ABUSE AND ALCOHOLISM. 1995a. "The Collaborative Study on the Genetics of Alcoholism." *Alcohol Health and Research World,* 19: 228–236.

NATIONAL INSTITUTE ON ALCOHOL ABUSE AND ALCOHOLISM. 1995b, October. *Diagnostic Criteria for Alcohol Abuse and Dependence.* Washington, DC: U.S. Government Printing Office.

NATIONAL INSTITUTE ON DRUG ABUSE. 1980. *Highlights from the National Survey on Drug Abuse: 1979.* Washington, DC: U.S. Government Printing Office.

"National Longitudinal Alcohol Epidemiological Survey." 1995. *The Lancet,* 345: 850.

NATIONAL VICTIM CENTER. 1992. *Rape in America: A Report to the Nation.* Charlotte, SC: National Victim Center.

NEFF, J. A., & A. M. DASSORI. 1998. "Age and Maturing Out of Heavy Drinking Among Anglo and Minority Male Drinkers: A Comparison of Cross-sectional Data and Retrospective Drinking History Techniques." *Hispanic Journal of Behavioral Sciences,* 20: 225–241.

NELKIN, D. 1995, September 28. "Biology Is Not Destiny." *New York Times,* p. A27.

NESS, R. B., & L. H. KULLER, eds. 1999. *Health and Disease Among Women: Biological and Environmental Influences.* New York: Oxford University Press.

NEWMAN, K. 1988. *Falling from Grace.* New York: Free Press.

NEWMAN, K. 1999. *No Shame in My Game.* New York: Knopf.

NEWSPAPER ENTERPRISE ASSOCIATION. 1981. *The World Almanac and Book of Facts: 1983.* New York: Pharas Books.

NIDA (NATIONAL INSTITUTE ON DRUG ABUSE). n.d. *High School and Youth Trends.* NIDAInfofax.

NIEBUHR, G. 1995, April 26. "Assault on Waco Sect Fuels Extremists' Rage." *New York Times,* p. A20.

NIGRO, L. G., & W. L. WAUGH. 1996. "Violence in the American Workplace: Challenges to the Public Employer." *Public Administration Review,* 56: 326–333.

NIXON, R. A. 1968. "An Appreciative and Critical Look at Official Unemployment Data." In M. Herman, S. Sadofsky, & B. Rosenberg, eds., *Work, Youth, and Unemployment.* New York: Crowell.

NOBLE, H. B. 1999, April 27. "Health Care Systems in U.S. Called Separate and Unequal." *New York Times,* p. F12.

NOCERA, J. 1999, September 27. "Sometimes, a Serial Killer Is Just a Serial Killer." *Fortune,* p. 60.

NOLIN, M. M., E. DAVIES, & K. CHANDLER. 1996. "Student Victimization at School." *Journal of School Health,* 66: 216–221.

NORC (NATIONAL OPINION RESEARCH CENTER). Annual. *General Social Survey, Cumulative Codebook.* Chicago: University of Chicago Press.

NORDHEIMER, J. 1996, December 22. "One Day's Death Toll on the Job." *New York Times,* sec. 3, pp. 1, 10.

NUSSBAUM, K. 1999, February. "Bye Bye to Pinkie Rings." *Working USA,* pp. 54–64.

OBER, K., L. CARLSON & P. ANDERSON. 1997. "Cardiovascular Risk Factors in Homeless Adults." *Journal of Cardiovascular Nursing,* 11: 50–60.

O'CONNOR, J. S., & H. M. STANFORD. 1979. "Chemical Pollutants of the New York Bight." In J. S. O'Connor and H. M. Stanford, eds., *Chemical Pollutants of the New York Bight: Priorities for Research.* Boulder, CO: National Oceanic and Atmospheric Administration.

OETTING, E. R., & F. BEAUVAIS. 1987, Spring. "Common Elements in Youth Drug Abuse: Peer Clusters and Other Psychosocial Factors." *Journal of Drug Issues,* pp. 133–151.

OGBURN, W. F. 1957. "Cultural Lag as Theory." *Sociology and Social Research,* 41: 167–174.

O'HARE, W. P. 1996. "A New Look at Poverty in America." *Population Bulletin,* (Population Reference Bureau), vol. 51.

OKUN, B. F. 1996. *Understanding Diverse Families: What Practitioners Need to Know.* New York: Guilford Press.

OLIVER, M. L., & T. M. SHAPIRO. 1995. *Black Wealth/White Wealth: A New Perspective on Racial Inequality.* New York: Routledge.

OLSEN, F. 1999, December 15. "The Outsider." *American Lawyer,* pp. 37–43.

OPHULS, W. 1977. *Ecology and the Politics of Scarcity.* San Francisco: Freeman.

OPPENHEIMER, V. C. 1994. "Women's Rising Employment and the Future of the Family in Industrial Societies." *Population and Development Review,* 20: 293–342.

OPPERMANN, M., ed., 1998. *Sex Tourism and Prostitution: Aspects of Leisure, Recreation, and Work.* New York: Cognizant Communication.

ORCHARD, A. L., & K. B. SOLBERG. 1999. "Expectations of the Stepmother's Role." *Journal of Divorce and Remarriage,* 31: 107–124.

ORFIELD, G. 1991. *The Closing Door: Conservative Policy and Black Opportunity.* Chicago: University of Chicago Press.

ORFIELD, G., & S. E. EATON. 1996. *Dismantling Desegregation: The Quiet Reversal of Brown v. Board of Education.* New York: New Press.

ORMES, I. 1973. *Clipped Wings.* London: William Kimber.

PAINTON, P. 1993, April 26. "The Shrinking Ten Percent: Battelle Study Affects Political Clout of Gays." *Time,* pp. 27–29.

PALLAS, A. M. 1987. *School Dropouts in the United States.* Washington, DC: U.S. Department of Education, Office of Educational Research and Improvement.

PALMER, J. L., & S. G. GOULD. 1986, Winter. "The Economic Consequences of an Aging Society." *Daedalus,* pp. 295–323.

PAONE, D., D. C. DES JARLAIS, & S. CALOIR. 1995. "Operational Issues in Syringe Exchanges: The New York City Tagging Alternative Study." *Journal of Community Health,* 20: 111–123.

PARELIUS, A. P., & R. J. PARELIUS. 1987. *The Sociology of Education,* 2nd ed. Upper Saddle River, NJ: Prentice Hall.

PARROT, A., & L. BECHHOFER. 1991. *Acquaintance Rape: The Hidden Crime.* New York: Wiley.

PARSONS, T. 1943. "The Kinship System of the Contemporary United States." *American Anthropologist,* 45: 22–38.

PAUL, A. M. 1998, May–June. "Where Bias Begins: The Truth About Stereotypes." *Psychology Today,* pp. 52–57.

PAYER, L. 1988. *Medicine and Culture: Varieties of Treatment in the United States, England, West Germany, and France.* New York: Henry Holt.

PEAR, R. 1996, September 21. "Experts Foresee Health Plan Shift for Mental Care." *New York Times,* pp. 1, 7.

PEAR, R. 1997a, May 18. "Academy Report Says Immigration Benefits the U.S." *New York Times,* p. 1.

PEAR, R. 1997b, April 30. "Employers Told to Accommodate the Mentally Ill." *New York Times,* pp. A1, D22.

PEAR, R. 1998, August 9. "Government Lags in Steps to Widen Health Coverage." *New York Times,* pp. 1, 22.

PEAR, R. 1999a, November 14. "Annual Spending on Medicare Dips for the First Time." *New York Times,* p. 1.

PEAR, R. 1999b, October 4. "More Americans Were Uninsured in 1998, U.S. Says." *New York Times,* pp. A1, A24.

PEDERSEN, D. 1999, July 26. "Is Your HMO Too Stingy? Under a Texas Law, They Rope 'em and Throw 'em." *Newsweek,* p. 56.

PEELE, S. 1987. "A Moral Vision of Addiction: How People's Values Determine Whether They Become and Remain Addicts." *Journal of Drug Issues,* 17: 187–215.

PEPINSKY, H. E., & R. QUINNEY. 1991. *Criminology as Peacemaking.* Bloomington: Indiana University Press.

PERLS, T. T. 1995, January. "The Oldest Old." *Scientific American,* pp. 70–75.

PERROW, C. 1984. *Normal Accidents: Living with High Risk Technologies.* New York: Basic Books.

PETERSON, P. G. 1999. *Gray Dawn: How the Coming Age Wave Will Transform America—and the World.* New York: Times Books.

PEYSER, M. 1999, March 1. "Home of the Gray." *Newsweek,* pp. 50–53.

PHILLIPS, M. 1998, October 25. "Forget Psychiatry, Stop Psychopaths." *New York Times,* p. 19.

PILLARD, R. C., & J. M. BAILEY. 1998. "Human Sexual Orientation Has a Heritable Component." *Human Biology,* 70: 347–366.

PIORE, M. J. 1979. *Birds of Passage.* New York: Cambridge University Press.

PIPHER, M. 1999. *Another Country: Negotiating the Emotional Terrain of Our Elders.* New York: Riverhead Books.

PIVEN, F. F. 1999, September. "The Welfare State as Work Enforcer." *Dollars & Sense,* p. 32.

PIVEN, F. F., & R. A. CLOWARD. 1972. *Regulating the Poor: The Functions of Public Welfare.* New York: Random House.

PIVEN, F. F., & R. A. CLOWARD. 1977. *Poor People's Movements: Why They Succeed, How They Fail.* New York: Pantheon Books.

PIVEN, F. F., & R. A. CLOWARD. 1982. *The New Class War: Reagan's Attack on the Welfare State and Its Consequences.* New York: Pantheon Books.

PIVEN, F. F., & R. CLOWARD. 1997. *The Breaking of the American Social Contract.* New York: New Press.

PLATE, T. 1975. "Crime Pays." In P. Wickman & P. Whitten, eds., *Readings in Criminology.* Lexington, MA: D. C. Heath.

POLLARD, K., & W. P. O'HARE. 1990. *Beyond High School: The Experience of Rural and Urban Youth in the 1980's.* Washington, DC: Population Reference Bureau.

POPENOE, D. 1995. "The Roots of Declining Social Virtue: Family, Community, and the Need for a 'Natural Communities Policy.'" In M. A. Glendon & D. Blankenhorn, *Seedbeds of Virtue.* New York: Madison Books.

POPENOE, D. 1996. *Life Without Father: Compelling Evidence That Fatherhood and Marriage Are Indispensable for the Good of Children and Society.* New York: Free Press.

Population Today. 2000. p. 28.

PORTES, A. 1995. *The Economic Sociology of Immigration.* New York: Russell Sage.

PORTES, A., & R. G. RUMBAUT. 1990. *Immigrant America: A Portrait.* Berkeley: University of California Press.

POSNER, R. A. 1995. *Aging and Old Age.* Chicago: University of Chicago Press.

POSTMAN, N., C. NYSTROM, L. STRATE, & C. WEINGARTNER. 1987. *Myth, Men, and Beer: An Analysis of Beer Commercials on Broadcast Television, 1987.* Falls Church, VA: AAA Foundation for Traffic Safety.

PRESTON, S. H. 1984, December. "Children and the Elderly in the U.S." *Scientific American,* p. 44.

PRESTON, S. H. 1987. "The Decline of Fertility in Non-European Industrialized Nations." *Population and Development Review,* 12 (Suppl. 5): 26–47.

PROTHROW-STITH, D. 1996. "Communities, Schools, and Violence." In A. M. Hoffman, ed., *Schools, Violence, and Society.* Westport, CT: Praeger.

PURDUM, T. S. 1995, April 4. "Bengali Women Are Candid with Hillary Clinton." *New York Times,* p. A3.

PYETT, P., & D. WARR. 1999. "Women at Risk in Sex Work: Strategies for Survival." *Journal of Sociology,* 35: 183.

QUILLIAN, L. 1999. "Migration Patterns and the Growth of High-Poverty Neighborhoods." *American Journal of Sociology,* 105: 1.

QUINNEY, R. 1979. *Criminology,* 2nd ed. Boston: Little, Brown.

QUINNEY, R. 1986. *Providence, the Reconstruction of Social and Moral Order.* Cincinnati: Anderson.

RACKHAM, A. 1991, January 7. "Economic Downturn Creates Growth in Ranks of Overqualified or Discouraged Job Seekers." *Los Angeles Business Journal,* p. 27.

RADZINOWICZ, L. R., & J. KING. 1977. *The Growth of Crime: The International Experience.* New York: Basic Books.

RAINWATER, L. 1974. "The Lower Class: Health, Illness, and Medical Institutions." In L. Rainwater, ed., *Inequality and Justice.* Hawthorne, NY: Aldine.

RAINWATER, L., & T. M. SMEEDING. 1995. *Doing Poorly: The Real Income of American Children in a Comparative Perspective.* Working Paper no. 127, Luxembourg Income Study, Maxwell School of Citizenship and Public Affairs. Syracuse, NY: Syracuse University.

RANGEL, C. B. 1998. "Why Drug Legalization Should Be Opposed." *Criminal Justice Ethics,* 17: 2.

RAPOPORT, A. 1968. "Introduction." In Carl von Clausewitz, *On War.* Harmondsworth, Eng.: Penguin Books.

RAY, O. S. 1996. *Drugs, Society and Human Behavior,* 7th ed. St. Louis: Mosby.

READ, P. 1994. *Responding to Global Warming: The Technology, Economics and Politics of Sustainable Energy.* Atlantic Highlands, NJ: Zed Books.

RECKLESS, W. C. 1973. *The Crime Problem,* 5th ed. Upper Saddle River, NJ: Prentice Hall.

RECTOR, R., & W. F. LAUBER. 1995. *America's Failed $5.4 Trillion War on Poverty.* Washington, DC: Heritage Foundation.

REGIER, D. 1991. *Psychiatric Disorders in America: The Epidemiological Catchment Area Study.* New York: Free Press.

REGIER, D. A., J. K. MYERS, L. N. ROBINS, & M. KRAMER. 1984, October 3. "Preliminary Report to the National Institute of Mental Health." Cited in H. M. Schmeck, Jr., "Almost One in 5 May Have Mental Disorder." *New York Times,* pp. A1, D27.

REGIER, D., W. NARROW, D. RAE, R. MANDERSCHEID, B. LOCKE, & F. GOODWIN. 1993. "The De Facto U.S. Mental Health and Addictive Disorders Service System: Epidemiological Catchment Area Prospective One-year Prevalence Rates of Disorders and Services." *Archives of General Psychiatry,* 50: 85–94.

REICH, R. 1992. *The Work of Nations: Preparing Ourselves for 21st Century Capitalism.* New York: Knopf.

REICH, R. B. 1998, Winter. "Broken Faith: Why We Need to Renew the Social Compact." *Generations,* p. 19.

REID, S. T. 1991. *Crime and Criminology.* Fort Worth, TX: Harcourt Brace.

REID, S. T. 1993. *Criminal Justice,* 3rd ed. New York: Macmillan.

REIGOT, B. P. 1996. *Beyond the Traditional Family: Voices of Diversity.* New York: Springer.

REINER, D. 1999, December. "Progress at Buenos Aires?" *Environment,* p. 4.

REINISCH, J. M. 1990. *The Kinsey Institute New Report on Sex.* New York: St. Martin's Press.

REISS, A. J., JR. 1964. "The Social Integration of Queens and Peers" In H. S. Becker, ed., *The Other Side: Perspectives on Deviance.* New York: Free Press.

REISS, A. J., JR., & J. A. ROTH, eds. 1993. *Understanding and Preventing Violence.* Washington, DC: National Academy of Science Press.

RESKIN, B., & H. HARTMAN, eds. 1986. *Women's Work, Men's Work: Sex Segregation on the Job.* Washington, DC: National Academy of Sciences Press.

RETSINAS, J. 1988. "Are There Stages of Dying?" *Death Studies,* 12: 207–216.

RICHARDSON, D., & H. MAY. 1999. "Deserving Victims? Sexual Status and the Social Construction of Violence." *Sociological Review,* 47: 308.

RICHMOND-ABBOTT, M. 1992. *Masculine and Feminine: Gender Roles Over the Life Cycle,* 2nd ed. New York: McGraw-Hill.

RICKETTS, E., & E. SAWHILL. 1988. "Defining and Measuring the Underclass." *Journal of Policy Analysis and Management,* 7: 38–46.

RIES, R. 1994. *Assessment and Treatment of Patients with Coexisting Mental Illness and Alcohol and Other Drug Abuse.* Rockville, MD: U.S. Department of Health and Human Services, Substance Abuse and Mental Health Services Administration, Center for Substance Abuse Treatment.

RIESMAN, D., N. GLAZER, & R. DENNEY. 1950. *The Lonely Crowd.* New Haven, CT: Yale University Press.

RIESSMAN, C. K. 1983, Summer. "Women and Medicalization." *Social Policy,* pp. 3–18.

RIFKIN, J. 1995. *The End of Work: The Decline of the Global Labor Force and the Dawn of the Post-market Era.* New York: Putnam.

RILEY, J. C. 1989. *Sickness, Recovery and Death: A History and Forecast of Ill Health.* Iowa City: University of Iowa Press.

RILEY, M. W. 1987, February. "On the Significance of Age in Sociology." *American Sociological Review,* 52: 1–14.

RILEY, M. W. 1996. "Discussion: What Does It All Mean?" *The Gerontologist,* 36: 256–258.

RILEY, M. W., R. L. KAHN, & A. FONER. 1994. *Age and Structural Lag: Society's Failure to Provide Meaningful Opportunities in Work, Family, and Leisure.* New York: Wiley.

RILEY, M. W., & J. WARING. 1976. "Age and Aging." In R. K. Merton & R. Nisbet, eds., *Contemporary Social Problems,* 4th ed. New York: Harcourt Brace Jovanovich.

RINDFUSS, R. R., K. L. BREWSTER, & A. L. KAVEE. 1996. "Women, Work, and Children in the U.S." *Population and Development Review,* 22: 457–482.

RIST, R. C. 1973. *The Urban School: A Factory for Failure.* Cambridge, MA: Massachusetts Institute of Technology Press.

RIST, R. C. 1975. "Pornography as a Social Problem: Reflections on the Relation of Morality and the Law." In R. C. Rist, ed., *The Pornography Controversy: Changing Moral Standards in American Life.* New Brunswick, NJ: Transaction Books.

RITZER, G. 1993. *The McDonaldization of Society: An Investigation Into the Changing Character of Contemporary Social Life.* Newbury Park, CA: Pine Forge Press.

ROBERTS, S. 1990, January 25. "On the Question of Legal Drugs, a Vote for Maybe." *New York Times,* p. B1.

ROBERTS, S. 1995. *Who We Are: A Portrait of America Based on the Latest U.S. Census.* New York: Times Books.

ROBINS, L. N. 1973. *A Follow Up of Vietnam Drug Users.* Washington, DC: Special Action Office for Drug Abuse Prevention.

ROBINS, L. N., et al. 1984. "Lifetime Prevalence of Specific Psychiatric Disorders in Three Sites." *Archives of General Psychiatry,* 41: 949–958.

ROBINSON, J. P., & G. GODBEY. 1996. "The Great American Slowdown." *American Demographics,* 18: 42–46.

ROCHMAN, S. 1999, October 12. "Leaving Safety at the Bedroom Door." *The Advocate,* p. 18.

RODRIGUEZ, J. 1999, Summer. "Welfare Reform and Latinos: Immigration and Cultural Politics." *Nieman Reports,* p. 45.

ROHATYN, F. 1987, December 3. "What Next?" *New York Review of Books,* pp. 3–5.

ROSENBAUM, J. E., N. FISHMAN, A. BRETT, & P. MEADEN. 1996. "Can the Kerner Commission's Housing Strategy Improve Employment, Education, and Social Integration for Low-income Blacks?" *North Carolina Law Review,* 71: 1519–1566.

ROSENHAN, D. L. 1973. "On Being Sane in Insane Places." *Science,* 179: 250–258.

ROSS, A. 2000, January. "Techno-Sweatshops." *Tikkun,* p. 57.

ROSS, C., & J. HUBER. 1985. "Hardship and Depression." *Health and Social Behavior,* 26: 312–327.

ROSSELLINI, L. 1998, April 13. "When to Spank." *U.S. News & World Report,* pp. 52–57.

ROSSI, A. S. 1984. "Gender and Parenthood." *American Sociological Review,* 49: 1–19.

ROSSI, A. S., & P. H. ROSSI. 1990. *Of Human Bonding: Parent-Child Relations Across the Lifecourse.* New York: Aldine de Gruyter.

ROSSI, P. H. 1989a. *Down and Out in America: The Origins of Homelessness.* Chicago: University of Chicago Press.

ROSSI, P. H. 1989b. *Without Shelter: Homelessness in the 1980s.* New York: Priority Press.

ROTHSTEIN, R. 1993, Fall. "Immigration Dilemmas." *Dissent,* pp. 66–71.

ROVNER, J. 1999. "U.S. Senate Passes Patients' Bill of Rights." *The Lancet,* 354: 316.

ROWE, J. W., & R. L. KAHN. 1998. *Successful Aging: The MacArthur Foundation Study.* New York: Pantheon.

ROWLAND, D. 1994. "Lessons from the Medicaid Experience." In E. Ginzberg, ed., *Critical Issues in U.S. Health Care Reform.* Boulder, CO: Westview.

RUBINGTON, E., & M. S. WEINBERG. 1987. *Deviance, the Interactionist Perspective: Text and Readings in the Sociology of Deviance,* 5th ed. New York: Macmillan.

RUBINGTON, E., & M. S. WEINBERG. 1995. *The Study of Social Problems: Seven Perspectives,* 5th ed. New York: Oxford University Press.

RUDOLPH, J. R. 1995. "Intervention in Communal Conflicts." *Orbis,* 39: 259–273.

RUGGLES, P. 1990. *Drawing the Line: Alternative Poverty Measures and Their Implications.* Washington, DC: Urban Institute.

RUSSELL, D. E. H. 1986. *The Secret Trauma: Incest in the Lives of Girls and Women.* New York: Basic Books.

RUSSELL, K. 1999, August. "Is Crime 'Profiling' a Reasonable Premise?" *USA Today Magazine,* p. 12.

RUSSELL, K. K. 1987, June 14. "Growing Up with Privilege and Prejudice." *New York Times Magazine,* pp. 22ff.

SACHS, J. 1998, October 26. "The Real Causes of Famine." *Time,* p. 69.

SADD, S., & R. M. GRINC. 1996. *Implementation Challenges in Community Policing: Innovative Neighborhood-oriented Policing in Eight Cities.* Washington, DC: National Institute of Justice, U.S. Department of Justice.

SAFILIOS-ROTHSCHILD, C. 1974. *Women and Social Policy.* Upper Saddle River, NJ: Prentice Hall.

SALINS, P. D. 1986, Fall. "Toward a Permanent Housing Problem." *Public Interest,* pp. 22–34.

SALTER, S. 1996, March 10. "More Kids About to Fall Through the Cracks." *San Francisco Chronicle,* p. B11.

SANCHEZ-JANKOWSKI, M. 1991. *Islands in the Street: Gangs and American Urban Society.* Berkeley: University of California Press.

SANDAY, P. R. 1984. "The Socio-cultural Context of Rape: A Cross-cultural Analysis." In D. E. H. Russell, *Sexual Exploitation.* Newbury Park, CA: Sage.

SANDEFUR, G. 1996. *Changing Numbers, Changing Needs: American Indian Demography and Public Health.* Washington, DC: National Academy Press.

SANDEFUR, G. T., & M. TIENDA, eds. 1988. *Divided Opportunities: Minorities, Poverty, and Social Policy.* New York: Plenum Press.

SANDELL, S. H., & D. SHAPIRO. 1978. "A Re-examination of the Evidence." *Journal of Human Resources,* 13: 103–117.

SANFORD, W. C., J. McCORD, & E. A. McGEE. 1976. "Abortion." In Boston Women's Health Book Collective, eds., *Our Bodies, Ourselves.* New York: Simon & Schuster.

SAPORITO, S., & A. LAREAU. 1999. "School Selection as a Process: The Multiple Dimensions of Race in Framing Educational Choice." *Social Problems,* 46: 418.

SCHEFF, T. J. 1963. "The Role of the Mentally Ill and the Dynamics of Mental Disorder." *Sociometry,* 26: 436–453.

SCHILLER, H. I. 1996. *Information Inequality: The Deepening Social Crisis in America.* New York: Routledge.

SCHMALZ, J. 1993, March 5. "Poll Finds an Even Split on Homosexuality's Cause." *New York Times,* p. A14.

SCHMIDT, G. 1997. "The Social Organization of Sexuality: Sexual Practices in the United States." *Archives of Sexual Behavior,* 26: 327–333.

SCHMIDT, W. E. 1993, August 1. "Britain Flunks a Test of Its National Curriculum." *New York Times Education Life,* pp. 17–19.

SCHMITT, E. 1996, February 26. "In Immigration Bill Debate, Divisions and Odd Alliances." *New York Times,* p. A1.

SCHRANK, R. 1978, July. "How to Relieve Worker Boredom." *Psychology Today,* pp. 79–80.

SCHUCKIT, M. A., & T. C. JEFFERSON. 1999. "New Findings in the Genetics of Alcoholism." *Journal of the American Medical Association,* 281: 1875.

SCHUR, E. M. 1973. *Radical Nonintervention: Rethinking the Delinquency Problem.* Upper Saddle River, NJ: Prentice Hall.

SCHUR, E. M. 1988. *The Americanization of Sex.* Washington, DC: Temple University Press.

SCHWARTZ, S. 2000. "Outmaneuvered, Outgunned, and Out of View." *Bulletin of the Atomic Scientists,* 56: 24.

SCULL, A. T. 1988. "Deviance and Social Control." In N. J. Smelser, ed., *The Handbook of Sociology.* Newbury Park, CA: Sage.

SELIGMAN, B. B. 1968. *Permanent Poverty.* Chicago: Quadrangle.

SENATE COMMITTEE ON FINANCE. 1994. *Deinstitutionalization, Mental Illness, and Medications.* Hearing before the Committee on Finance, U.S. Senate, 103rd Cong., 2nd sess., May 10. Washington, DC: U.S. Government Printing Office.

SEXTON, J. 1997, March 10. "In a Pocket of Brooklyn Sewn by Welfare, an Unraveling." *New York Times,* pp. A1, B6.

SHAPIRO, J. P. 1996, September 16. "Kids with Gay Parents." *U.S. News & World Report,* pp. 75–79.

SHAW, C. R. 1929. *Delinquency Areas: A Study of the Geographic Distribution of School Truants, Juvenile Delinquents, and Adult Offenders in Chicago.* Chicago: University of Chicago Press.

SHAW, J. 1997. "Racketeer Influenced and Corrupt Organizations." *American Criminal Law Review,* 34: 931–982.

SHAW, J. 1999, October–December. "Laundering Moscow's Money." *Europe Business Review,* p. 20.

SHEEHAN, S. 1982. *Is There No Place on Earth for Me?* New York: Scribner.

SHERMAN, L. W., J. W. SHAW, & D. P. ROGAN. 1995. *The Kansas City Gun Experiment.* Washington, DC: National Institute of Justice, U.S. Department of Justice.

SHERRILL, R. 1997, April 7. "A Year in Corporate Crime." *The Nation,* pp. 1–9.

SHIPLEY, T. E., JR., I. W. SHANDLER, & M. L. PENN. 1989. "Treatment and Research with Homeless Alcoholics." *Contemporary Drug Problems,* 16: 505–526.

SHOOP, J. G. 1998. "Gang Warfare: Legal Battle Pits Personal Liberty Against Public Safety." *Trial,* 34: 12–16.

SIEGEL, L. 1999. *Criminology.* Belmont, CA. Wadsworth.

SILBERMAN, C. 1980. *Criminal Violence, Criminal Justice.* New York: Random House.

SILVER, L. 1990, August 14. "Study: Women, Minorities Post Little Corporate Gain." *Washington Post,* pp. A1, A5.

SIMPSON, G. E., & J. M. YINGER. 1985. *Racial and Ethnic Minorities: An Analysis of Prejudice and Discrimination,* 5th ed. New York: Plenum.

SIMPSON, P. 1996. "Beijing in Perspective." *Journal of Women's History,* 8: 137–146.

SINGER, J. D., & M. SMALL. 1972. *The Wages of War, 1816–1965: A Statistical Handbook.* New York: Wiley.

SIZER, T. R. 1992, November. "School Reform: What's Missing." *World Monitor,* pp. 20–24.

SKOLNICK, A. S., & J. H. SKOLNICK. 1994. *Family in Transition,* 8th ed. New York: HarperCollins.

SKOLNICK, J. H. 1969. *The Politics of Protest.* New York: Simon & Schuster.

SKOLNICK, J. H. 1998. "Race, Crime, & the Law." *Michigan Law Review,* 96: 1474–1485.

SLAVIN, R. E. 1997, December. "Can Education Reduce Social Inequality?" *Educational Leadership,* pp. 6–11.

SLOBIN, S. 1999, December 12. "Homeless in America: A Statistical Profile." *New York Times,* p. 3.

SMIL, V. 1997. *Cycles of Life: Civilization and the Biosphere.* New York: Freeman.

SMITH, B. E. 1995. *Prosecuting Child Physical Abuse Cases: A Case Study in San Diego.* Washington, DC: National Institute of Justice, U.S. Department of Justice.

SMOLOWE, J. 1996, Fall. "Older, Longer." *Time,* pp. 76–80.

SNOW, D. A. 1993. *Down on Their Luck: A Study of Homeless Street People.* Berkeley: University of California Press.

SOLOMON, A. 1999, October 24. "An Epidemic of Death." *New York Times Book Review,* p. 13.

SOROKIN, P. 1937. *Social and Cultural Dynamics: Vol. 3. Fluctuations of Social Relationships, War, and Revolution.* New York: American Book.

SOUDER, M., & L. ZIMMER. 1998, January 12. "Symposium." *Insight on the News,* pp. 24–28.

SPAIN, D. 1996. *Balancing Act: Motherhood, Marriage, and Employment Among American Women.* New York: Russell Sage.

SPECTER, M. 1994, March 6. "Climb in Russia's Death Rate Sets Off Population Implosion." *New York Times,* pp. 1, 18.

SPECTOR, M., & J. KITSUSE. 1987. *Constructing Social Problems.* Hawthorne, NY: Aldine de Gruyter.

SPERO, R. 1993, March. "Sidney Wolfe (Health Care Activist) (Interview)." *The Progressive,* pp. 32–35.

SPERRY, L. 1995. *Pharmacology and Psychotherapy: Strategies for Maximizing Treatment Outcomes.* New York: Brunner/Mazel.

SQUIRE, S. 1987, November 22. "Shock Therapy's Return to Respectability." *New York Times Magazine,* pp. 78ff.

SROLE, L., T. S. LANGNER, S. T. MICHAEL, P. KIRKPATRICK, M. K. OPLER, & T. A. C. RENNIE. 1978. *Mental Health in the Metropolis: The Midtown Manhattan Study,* rev. ed. New York: New York University Press.

STACEY, J. 1993. "Good Riddance to 'The Family': A Response to David Popenoe." *Journal of Marriage and the Family,* 55: 545–548.

STACK, C. 1974. *All Our Kin: Strategies for Survival in a Black Community.* New York: Harper Colophon.

STAFFORD, D. 1999, August 23. "Disabled Still Fighting for Right to Work." *Journal News,* p. 1D.

STANTON, G. T. 1996. "The Counter-revolution Against Easy Divorce: New Rumbling in the States." *The American Enterprise,* 7: 37–38.

STAPLES, B. 1999, "Affirmative Action." August 9. *New York Times,* p. A14.

STARES, P. B. 1996. *Global Habit: The Drug Problem in a Borderless World.* Washington, DC: Brookings Institution.

STARR, P. 1982. *The Social Transformation of American Medicine.* New York: Basic Books.

STARR, P. 1995, September 3. "Look Who's Talking Health Care Reform Now: Proposed Changes to Medicare and Medicaid." *New York Times Magazine,* pp. 42–43.

Statistical Abstract of the United States. Annual. Washington, DC: U.S. Government Printing Office.

STEELE, B., & C. B. POLLOCK. 1974. "A Psychiatric Study of Parents Who Abuse Infants and Small Children." In R. Helfer and C. Kempe, eds., *The Battered Child.* Chicago: University of Chicago Press.

STEFFENSMEIER, D., & E. ALLAN. 1996. "Gender and Crime: Toward a Gendered Theory of Female Offending." *Annual Review of Sociology,* 22: 459.

STEINBERG, S. 1996, March. "The Affirmative Action Debate." *UNESCO Courier,* pp. 17–21.

STEINHAUER, J. 1995, August 2. "Study Cites Adult Males for Most Teen-age Births." *New York Times,* p. A10.

STENCEL, S. 1973. "Resurgence of Alcoholism." *Editorial Research Reports,* 2: 989–1006.

STERK, C. 1988, May 7. "Cocaine and HIV Positivity." *The Lancet,* pp. 1052–1053.

STERK, C. 1989. "Prostitutes and Their Health," Unpublished doctoral dissertation, Erasmus University, Amsterdam.

STERK, C. E. 2000. *Tricking and Tripping: Prostitution in the Era of AIDS.* Putnam Valley, NY: Social Change Press.

STERNGOLD, J. 1995, April 28. "Ex-official Pleads Guilty in Orange County's Fall." *New York Times,* pp. A1ff.

STEVENS, W. K. 1987, October 12. "Defining the 'Outer City': For Now, Call It Hybrid." *New York Times,* p. A14.

STEVENS, W. K. 1994, January 18. "Threat of Encroaching Deserts May Be More Myth Than Fact." *New York Times,* pp. C1, C10.

STEVENS, W. K. 1996, August 6. "At Hot Center of Debate on Global Warming." *New York Times,* pp. B5–B6.

STEVENSON, H. W. 1992, December. "Learning from Asian Schools." *Scientific American,* pp. 70–76.

STEVENSON, H. W. 1998, March. "A Study of Three Cultures: Germany, Japan, and the United States—An Overview of the TIMSS Case Study Project." *Phi Delta Kappan,* pp. 524–530.

STEVENSON, M. 1999, September 26. "Hope and Hopelessness Permeate Mexico's Border Towns." *Journal News,* p. 1D.

STEVENSON, R. W. 2000, January 23. "In a Time of Plenty, the Poor Are Still Poor." *New York Times,* p. 3.

STEWARD, G. L. 1972. "On First Being a John." *Urban Life and Culture,* 1: 255–274.

STOUFFER, S. A., E. A. SUCHMAN, L. C. DEVINNEY, S. A. STARR, & R. M. WILLIAMS. 1949. *The American Soldier.* Princeton, NJ: Princeton University Press.

STOVER, P., & Y. GILLES. 1987, October 27. "Sexual Harassment in the Workplace." Conference report, Michigan Task Force on Sexual Harassment, Detroit.

STROSSEN, N. 1995. *Defending Pornography: Free Speech, Sex, and the Fight for Women's Rights.* New York: Scribner.

SULLIVAN, M. 1989. *Getting Paid.* Ithaca, NY: Cornell University Press.

SULLIVAN, R. 1987, October 22. "AIDS Deaths in New York Are Showing New Pattern." *New York Times,* p. B1.

SULLIVAN, T. A., E. WARREN, & J. L. WESTBROOK. 1989. *As We Forgive Our Debtors: Bankruptcy and Consumer Credit in America.* New York: Oxford University Press.

SULLIVAN, T. A., E. WARREN, & J. WESTBROOK. 1995. "Bankruptcy and the Family." *Marriage and Family Review,* 21: 193–215.

SUPLEE, C. 1995, December 31. "A Nuclear Problem Keeps Growing." *Washington Post,* pp. A1, A18.

SUTHERLAND, E. H. 1961. *White Collar Crime.* New York: Holt, Rinehart & Winston.

SUTHERLAND, E. H., & D. R. CRESSEY. 1960. *Principles of Criminology.* Philadelphia: Lippincott.

SUTTLES, G. 1970. *The Social Order of the Slum.* Chicago: University of Chicago Press.

SWEET, J. A., & L. L. BUMPASS. 1987. *American Families and Households.* New York: Russell Sage.

SZASZ, T. S. 1992, Summer. "The Fatal Temptation: Drug Prohibition and the Fear of Autonomy." *Daedalus,* pp. 161–165.

SZASZ, T. S. 1994. *Cruel Compassion: Psychiatric Control of Society's Unwanted.* New York: Wiley.

SZASZ, T. S. 1998, June. Letter. *Reason,* p. 11.

SZYNDROWSKI, D. 1999. "The Impact of Domestic Violence on Adolescent Aggression in the Schools." *Preventing School Failure,* 44: 9.

THOMAS, W. I. 1923. *The Unadjusted Girl.* Boston: Little, Brown.

THOMAS, W. I., & F. ZNANIECKI. 1922. *The Polish Peasant in Europe and America.* New York: Knopf.

THORNE, B. 1994. *Gender Play.* New Brunswick, NJ: Rutgers University Press.

TIENDA, M. 1999, May 16. "A Man's Place." *New York Times Magazine*, p. 48.

TITTLE, C. R., W. J. VILLEMEZ, & D. A. SMITH. 1978. "The Myth of Social Class and Criminality: An Empirical Assessment of the Empirical Evidence." *American Sociological Review*, 43: 643–656.

TOBIN, J. 1994. "Poverty in Relation to Macroeconomic Trends, Cycles and Policies." In S. H. Danziger and G. Sandefur, eds., *Poverty and Public Policy*. Cambridge, MA: Harvard University Press.

TOOLAN, D. S. 1998, May 13. "Earth Day with Bella, Barry and Friends." *America*, pp. 3–5.

TORREY, E. F., & M. T. ZDANOWICZ. 1999, April 19. "Hope for Cities Dealing with the Mental Illness Crisis." *Nation's Cities Weekly*, p. 2.

TRAUB, J. 1996, November 4. "The Criminals of Tomorrow." *The New Yorker*, pp. 50–65.

TROIDEN, R. R. 1987. "Becoming Homosexual." In E. Rubington and M. S. Weinberg, eds., *Deviance: The Interactionist Perspective*, 5th ed. New York: Macmillan.

TROW, M. 1966. "The Second Transformation of American Secondary Education." In R. Bendix and S. M. Lipset, eds., *Class, Status, and Power*, 2nd ed. New York: Free Press.

TUNALI, O. 1996. "A Billion Cars: The Road Ahead." *World Watch*, 9: 24–33.

TURK, A. T. 1978. "Law as a Weapon in Social Conflict." In C. E. Reasons and R. M. Rich, eds., *Sociology of Law: A Conflict Perspective*. Toronto: Butterworths.

UCHITELLE, L. 1999, October 18. "Devising New Math to Define Poverty." *New York Times*, pp. A1, A16.

UCR (UNIFORM CRIME REPORTS, FEDERAL BUREAU OF INVESTIGATION). Annual. *Crime in the United States*. Washington, DC: U.S. Government Printing Office.

UNITED NATIONS. 1999a, December 15. Report of the Independent Inquiry Into the Actions of the United Nations During the 1994 Genocide in Rwanda.

UNITED NATIONS. 1999b, November 15. Report of the Secretary-General Pursuant to General Assembly Resolution 53/55 (1998). Srebenica Report.

United Nations Chronicle. 1999, Spring. "Totally Amazing Mind, So Understanding and So Kind," pp. 24–25.

UNITED NATIONS DEVELOPMENT PROGRAMME. Annual. *Human Development Report*. New York: Oxford University Press.

URQUHART, B. 2000, April 27. "In the Name of Humanity." *New York Review of Books*, pp. 19–22.

U.S. BUREAU OF THE CENSUS. Decennial. *Census of Population*. Washington, DC: U.S. Government Printing Office.

U.S. BUREAU OF THE CENSUS. 1996. *How We're Changing: Demographic State of the Nation*. Washington, DC: U.S. Government Printing Office.

U.S. CONGRESS. 1993. *Proliferation Threats of the 1990's*. Hearing before the Committee on Governmental Affairs, U.S. Senate, 103rd Cong., 1st sess., February 24. Washington, DC: U.S. Government Printing Office.

U.S. CONGRESS, HOUSE COMMITTEE ON SCIENCE. 1996. *Scientific Integrity and Public Trust: The Science Behind Federal Policies and Mandates*. Washington, DC: U.S. Government Printing Office.

U.S. OFFICE OF TECHNOLOGY ASSESSMENT. 1979. *The Effects of Nuclear War*. Washington, DC: U.S. Government Printing Office.

VAILLANT, G. E. 1983. *The Natural History of Alcoholism*. Cambridge, MA: Harvard University Press.

VERHOVEK, S. H. 1995, July 30. "Young, Carefree and in Love with Cigarettes." *New York Times*, pp. 1, 24.

VINCENT, J. A. 1995. *Inequality and Old Age*. New York: St. Martin's Press.

VON GLAHN, G. 1970. *Law Among Nations*, 2nd ed. New York: Macmillan.

WAHID, H. M. 1999, October. "The Grameen Bank and Women in Bangladesh." *Challenge*, pp. 90–101.

WALD, M. L. 1994, March 16. "Eastern Utilities in Unusual Pact: A Smog Tradeoff." *New York Times*, pp. A1, B2.

WALDINGER, R. 1996. *Still the Promised City*. Cambridge, MA: Harvard University Press.

WALDINGER, R., & T. BAILEY. 1990. "The Continuing Significance of Race: Racial Conflict and Racial Discrimination in Construction." Unpublished paper, Center for Conservation of Human Resources, Columbia University, New York City.

WALKER, H. B. 1996. "The United Nations: Peacekeeping and the Middle East." *Asian Affairs*, 27: 13–19.

WALKER, L. 1977. "Battered Women and Learned Helplessness." *Victimology*, 2: 525–534.

WALKER, L. 1987, June 21. "What Comforts AIDs Families." *New York Times Magazine*, pp. 16ff.

WALLERSTEIN, J., & S. BLAKESLEE. 1989. *Second Chances: Men, Women and Children a Decade After Divorce*. New York: Ticknor & Fields.

WEBER, A. 1968. "Labor Market and Perspectives of the New City." In S. F. Fava, ed., *Urbanism in World Perspective: A Reader*. New York: Crowell.

WEGNER, J. W., ed. 1993. "The Urban Crisis: The Kerner Commission Report Revisited." *North Carolina Law Review*, 71: 406–421.

WEINBERG, S. K. 1955. *Incest Behavior*. New York: Citadel Press.

WEINBERGER, C. J. 1998, January. "Race and Gender Wage Gaps in the Market for Recent College Graduates." *Industrial Relations*, pp. 67–84.

WEISS, R. S. 1979. *Going It Alone: The Family Life and Social Situation of the Single Parent*. New York: Basic Books.

WEISSBOURD, R. 1996. *The Vulnerable Child: What Really Hurts America's Children and What We Can Do About It*. Reading, MA: Addison-Wesley.

WELLNER, A. S. 1999. "The Young and the Uninsured." *American Demographics*, 21: 72.

WELSH, P. 1996, October 13. "A Death in the Schoolyard: Violent Gangs and Meddling 'Reformers' Combine to Create a Tragedy in Alexandria." *Washington Post*, p. A18.

WEST, C. 1994. *Race Matters*. New York: Vintage.

WESTON, R., ed. 1987. *Combating Commercial Crime*. Sidney: Law Book Co.

WETZEL, J. R. 1995. "Labor Force, Unemployment, and Earnings." In R. Farley, ed., *State of the Union: America in the 1990s, Vol. 1: Economic Trends*. New York: Russell Sage.

WHITE, M. 1998, September 10. "Study Shows Care in the Community Is Working." *Community Care*, p. 4.

WHITE HOUSE DOMESTIC POLICY COUNCIL. 1993. *The President's Report to the American People*. New York: Simon & Schuster.

WHO (WORLD HEALTH ORGANIZATION). 1994. *Women and AIDS: Agenda for Action*. Geneva: World Health Organization.

WIDMER, E. D., J. TREAS, & R. NEWCOMB. 1998. "Attitudes Toward Nonmarital Sex in 24 Countries." *Journal of Sex Research*, 35: 349.

WILENSKY, H. L. 1966. "Work as a Social Problem." In H. Becker, ed., *Social Problems*. New York: Wiley.

WILKERSON, I. 1991, April 4. "Ravaged City on Mississippi Floundering at Rock Bottom." *New York Times*, pp. A1, A16.

WILKES, M. S., & M. SHUCHMAN. 1989, June 4. "What Is Too Old?" *New York Times Magazine*, pp. 58–60.

WILLIAMS, A. P., E. VAYDA, M. L. COHEN, C. A. WOODWARD, & B. M. FERRIER. 1995. "Medicine and the Canadian State: From the Politics of Conflict to the Politics of Accommodation?" *Journal of Health and Social Behavior*, 36: 303–321.

WILLIAMS, D. 1995, November. "Security Efforts Cut Chicago-school Violence." *Education Digest*, pp. 18–21.

WILLIAMS, J. 2000. *Unbending Gender: Why Families and Work Conflict and What to Do About It*. New York: Oxford University Press.

WILLIAMS, R. M., JR. 1947. *The Reduction of Intergroup Tensions*. New York: Social Science Research Council.

WILLIAMS, T. 1989. *The Cocaine Kids*. Reading, MA: Addison-Wesley.

WILLIAMS, T. 1992. *Crack House*. New York: Addison-Wesley.

WILLIAMS, T. M., & W. KORNBLUM. 1985. *Growing Up Poor*. Boston: D. C. Heath/Lexington Books.

WILLIAMS, T., & W. KORNBLUM. 1994. *The Uptown Kids: Struggle and Hope in the Projects*. New York: Putnam.

WILLIAMS-HAROLD, B. 2000, March. "Across the Great Divide." *Black Enterprise*, p. 30.

WILLIS, P. 1983. "Cultural Production and Theories of Reproduction." In L. Barton and S. Walker, eds., *Race, Class and Education*. London: Croom-Helm.

WILSON, E. O. 1975. *Sociobiology: The New Synthesis*. Cambridge, MA: Belknap Press.

WILSON, J. Q. 1977. *Thinking About Crime*. New York: Vintage Books.

WILSON, J. Q. 1993. *The Moral Sense*. New York: Free Press.

WILSON, J. Q. 1994, Winter. "Abortion: A Moral Issue." *Commentary*, pp. 78–89.

WILSON, J. Q., & R. J. HERRNSTEIN. 1985. *Crime and Human Nature*. New York: Simon & Schuster.

WILSON, W. C. 1971. "Facts Versus Fears: Why Should We Worry About Pornography?" *Annals of the American Academy of Political and Social Sciences*, 397: 105–117.

WILSON, W. J. 1987. *The Truly Disadvantaged: The Inner City, the Underclass, and Public Policy*. Chicago: University of Chicago Press.

WILSON, W. J. 1996a. *When Work Disappears: The World of the New Urban Poor*. Chicago: University of Chicago Press.

WILSON, W. J. 1996b, August 18. "Work." *New York Times Magazine*, pp. 26ff.

WILTON, R. D., & J. R. WOLCH. 1996. "The World of Homelessness According to Jencks." *Economic Geography*, 72: 82–88.

WINERIP, M. 1988, January 15. "Getting the Truth About the Ways of Streetwalkers." *New York Times*, p. B1.

WINNER, L. 1977. *Autonomous Technology: Technics-out-of-Control as a Theme in Political Thought*. Cambridge, MA: Massachusetts Institute of Technology Press.

WINNER, L. 1986. *The Whale and the Reactor: A Search for Limits in an Age of High Technology*. Chicago: University of Chicago Press.

WINNER, L. 1994, February–March. "Cyberpornography." *Technology Review*, p. 70.

WINNER, L. 1997, November–December. "Look Out for the Luddite Label." *MIT's Technology Review*, p. 62.

WINNICK, L. 1991. *New People in Old Neighborhoods: The Role of New Immigrants in Rejuvenating New York's Communities*. New York: Russell Sage.

WIRTH, L. 1927. "The Ghetto." *American Journal of Sociology*, 23: 57–71.

WITT, G. E. 1999, May 12. "Women Show Their Spiritual Side." *American Demographics*, p. 14.

WOFSY, C. 1987, April 26. "'Safe Sex'—Why It's Not a Sure Thing." *Newsday*, p. 7.

WOLF, R. 1996. *Marriages and Families in a Diverse Society*. New York: HarperCollins.

WOLFE, B. 1996, Spring. "A Medicaid Primer." *Focus*, pp. 1–6.

WOLK, J. L., & S. SCHMAHL. 1999. "Child Support Enforcement: The Ignored Component of Welfare Reform." *Journal of Contemporary Human Services*, 80: 526.

WORSHAM, J. 1999, February. "Pharmaceuticals Present a Paradox." *Nation's Business*, p. 52.

WOUTERS, C. 1999. "Changing Patterns of Social Controls and Self-controls." *British Journal of Criminology*, 39: 416.

WREN, C. S. 1996, February 20. "Marijuana Use by Youths Continues to Rise." *New York Times*, p. A11.

YANG, D. J., & M. SATCHELL. 1999, November 1. "Hell, No. We Won't Trade." *U.S. News & World Report*, p. 54.

YANKELOVICH, D. 1978, May. "New Psychological Contracts at Work." *Psychology Today*, pp. 46–50.

YINGER, M. 1987, Spring. "From Several Threads, Stronger Cords." *Oberlin Alumni Magazine*, pp. 10–13.

YOON, C. K. 1994, March 1. "Thinning Ozone Layer Implicated in Decline of Frogs and Toads." *New York Times*, p. C4.

ZEISEL, H. 1982. *The Limits of Law Enforcement*. Chicago: University of Chicago Press.

ZEITLIN, M., K. LUTTERMAN, & J. RUSSELL. 1973. "Death in Vietnam: Class, Poverty and the Risks of War." *Politics and Society*, 3: 397–406.

ZHAO, J. Z. 1995. "Cohabitation and Divorce in Canada: Testing the Selectivity Hypothesis." *Journal of Marriage and the Family*, 57: 421–427.

ZILLMAN, D., & J. BRYANT. 1989. *Pornography: Research Advances and Policy Considerations*. Hillsdale, NJ: Lawrence Erlbaum.

ZIMBARDO, P. G. 1972, April. "Pathology of Imprisonment." *Society*, 9: 4–8.

ZIMMER, L., & J. P. MORGAN, 1997. *Marijuana Myths/Marijuana Facts*. New York: Lindesmith Center.

ZIMRING, F. E. 1985. "Violence and Firearms Policy." In L. A. Curtis, ed., *American Violence and Public Policy*. New Haven, CT: Yale University Press.

ZIMRING, F. E., & G. HAWKINS. 1997. *Crime Is Not the Problem: Lethal Violence in America*. New York: Oxford University Press.

ZUBOFF, S. 1982, Winter. "Problems of Symbolic Toil." *Dissent*, pp. 51–62.

ZUKIN, S. 1991. *Landscapes of Power: From Detroit to Disney World*. Berkeley: University of California Press.

CHAPTER 1 2 Baron Wolman/Tony Stone Images 4 Victor Ayala 11 AP/Wide World Photos 14 The Image Bank 18 Najiah Feanny/SABA Press Photos, Inc. 23 *(top)* AP/Wide World Photos; *(bottom)* Patrick Forestier/Corbis Sygma Photo News

CHAPTER 2 26 Steven Peters/Tony Stone Images 30 Dan Habib/Impact Visuals Photo & Graphics, Inc. 42 Chris Steele-Perkins/Magnum Photos, Inc. 43 Chris Steele-Perkins/Magnum Photos, Inc. 45 Jacques Chenet/Woodfin Camp & Associates 50 Mark Richards/PhotoEdit 54 Howard Sochurek/Woodfin Camp & Associates

CHAPTER 3 60 Bruce Ayres/Tony Stone Images 63 Mary Ellen Mark Library 65 Mary Kate Denny/PhotoEdit 67 Greenlar/The Image Works 73 A. Ramey/Woodfin Camp & Associates 74 Rob Crandall/Stock Boston

CHAPTER 4 88 Steve Liss/Corbis Sygma 90 Bob Daemmrich/The Image Works 95 Blake Sell/Reuters/Corbis 101 J.L. Atlan/Corbis Sygma Photo News 104 Adam Scull/Rangefinders/Globe Photos, Inc. 108 Liaison Agency, Inc. 110 Tom McCarthy/PhotoEdit

CHAPTER 5 120 Sheila E. Masson/Archive Photos 124 Burt Glinn/Magnum Photos, Inc. 130 Bob Daemmrich/Stock Boston 135 Larry Mulvehill/Photo Researchers, Inc. 143 C. Smith/Coalition for a Smoke-Free City/NYC Department of Health 144 Ian Dryden/Liaison Agency, Inc.

CHAPTER 6 150 A. Ramey/Woodfin Camp & Associates 161 Smith/Monkmeyer Press 165 © Franco Zecchin 166 Chris Brown/SABA Press Photos, Inc. 175 Greig/Monkmeyer Press 177 Jon Levy/Liaison Agency, Inc.

CHAPTER 7 188 Corbis 191 Scala/Art Resource, NY, Courrier and Ives (sec. XIX) Battaaglia di Sharpsburg, 17 Settembre 1862; Museum of the City of New York, New York, U.S.A. 192 Michael Gallacher/Liaison Agency, Inc. 199 Hal Stoelze/Denver Rocky Mountain News/Corbis Sygma 200 Laima Druskis/Stock Boston 203 Rape Prevention Education Program, UCSB 214 David Woo/Liaison Agency, Inc. 215 Byron/Monkmeyer Press

CHAPTER 8 220 Bob Daemmrich/Stock Boston 222 Das/Monkmeyer Press 231 Alan S. Weiner/Liaison Agency, Inc. 234 Denise McGill/Springfield News-Leader 244 Marc Asnin/SABA Press Photos, Inc.

CHAPTER 9 254 Ovie Carter 256 Robert Fox/Impact Visuals Photo & Graphics, Inc. 259 Gerrit Fokkema/Woodfin Camp & Associates 262 UPI/Corbis 264 Mark Peterson/SABA Press Photos, Inc. 265 Kevin Fleming/Corbis 266 Richard Ellis/Corbis Sygma 281 Jacques Chenet/Woodfin Camp & Associates

CHAPTER 10 286 William Allard/NGS Image Collection 289 Steve McCurry/Magnum Photos, Inc. 292 Karen Kasmauski/Woodfin Camp & Associates 296 Bob Daemmrich/Stock Boston 299 Michael P. Farrell/Corbis Sygma 301 Johnny Crawford/The Image Works 303 Karin Cooper/Liaison Agency, Inc.

CHAPTER 11 312 Dennis Cook/AP/Wide World Photos 315 John Eastcott/The Image Works 328 Roger M. Richards/Liaison Agency, Inc. 332 Brandeis University Photography Department

CHAPTER 12 340 Jodi Buren/Woodfin Camp & Associates 343 John Eastcott/Yva Momatiuk/Photo Researchers, Inc. 344 Bob Daemmrich/The Image Works 349 Karen Kasmauski/Woodfin Camp & Associates 359 Bruce Young/Reuters/Corbis 362 Bruce Ayres/Stone

CHAPTER 13 368 Joseph Bailey/NGS Image Collection 370 Bill Bachman/Photo Researchers, Inc. 374 Jim Carter/Photo Researchers, Inc. 377 E. Crews/The Image Works 385 Porter Gifford/Liaison Agency 388 Chris Doerst/AP/Wide World Photos

CHAPTER 14 396 Peter Menzel/Stock Boston 403 Steven Starr/Stock Boston 406 Collins/Monkmeyer Press 411 Paul Fusco/Magnum Photos, Inc. 414 Corbis 417 AP/Wide World Photos

CHAPTER 15 422 Jim Pickerell/Stock Boston 431 Donna Binder/Impact Visuals Photo & Graphics, Inc. 434 Charles Nes/Liaison Agency, Inc. 440 *(left)* C. Vergara/Photo Researchers, Inc.; *(right)* Charles Wenselberg/AP/Wide World Photos 441 Chromosohm/Sohm/Stock Boston

CHAPTER 16 452 DeMaria/Corbis Sygma 458 Raghu Rai/Magnum Photos, Inc. 461 Findlay Kember/AP/Wide World Photos 464 Michal Heron/Pearson Education/PH College 467 *(top)* Corbis; *(bottom)* Yvonne Hemsey/Liaison Agency, Inc. 471 Mark E. Gibson/Visuals Unlimited

CHAPTER 17 476 Alex L. Fradkin/PhotoDisk, Inc. 487 Bayard Brattstrom/Visuals Unlimited 494 Conklin/Monkmeyer Press 495 Gianni Tortoli/Photo Researchers, Inc. 496 Michael Wickes/The Image Works 497 AP/Wide World Photos

CHAPTER 506 David Brauchli/AP/Wide World Photos 508 S. Compoint/Corbis Sygma 509 Peter Dejong/AP/Wide World Photos 518 Paul McErlane/AP/Wide World Photos 519 © AFP/Corbis

Name Index

Aberson, C. L., 97
Abramowitz, M., 363, 364
Acierno, R., 93
Adler, F., 173, 179, 183
Adler, J., 448
Ahlburg, D. A., 352
Aitken, P. V., Jr., 45
Alexander, A., 278, 279
Alexander, K., 384
Alland, A., 257
Allen, B., 14
Allen, M., 112
Altman, Dennis, 50, 114
Altman, L. K., 46
Anderson, Elijah, 171, 175
Anderson, Odin W., 52
Antonovsky, A., 49
Applebome, P., 180, 371, 383, 392
Aron, R., 507
Aronowitz, Stanley, 407, 409
Astin, A. W., 387
Aston, G., 84
Atkins, R. M., 33
Ayala, Victor, 3, 4, 47, 56, 109, 358
Ayers, B. D., 114, 146

Bacon, D., 403–404
Badillo, G., 508
Baldus, David C., 276
Ballantine, J. H., 371, 372, 381
Ballard, M. E., 196
Ball-Rokeach, S., 217
Bandura, A., 194
Barbanel, J., 82
Barker, P. R., 72
Barnet, R. J., 400
Barnett, W. S., 378
Barringer, F., 95, 317
Barron, M. L., 325
Barton, J. H., 516
Bassuk, E. I., 81, 82
Bawer, B., 96
Bayer, R., 71
Becker, Howard S., 20, 139
Bee, R. J., 525
Beer, F. A., 514
Bell, A. P., 98, 358
Bell, D., 96, 383
Bell, Daniel, 381, 478, 482–83
Bell, Robert, 104
Belluck, P., 169, 180
Bender, W., 498
Benedict, Marie, 309
Bennett, C., 115
Bennett, William J., 166, 169, 448
Benokraitis, N. V., 292
Berg, B., 128
Bergthold, L., 29
Berkowitz, L., 193, 194
Bernard, Jessie, 308
Bernstein, J., 486
Bernstein, N., 242
Berrios, G. E., 67
Berrueta-Clement, J. R., 378
Berry, D. B., 192, 204, 207
Besharov, D. J., 247
Bhagwati, J. N., 401
Bianchi, Eugene C., 194
Bianchi, S., 267
Biblarz, T. J., 355
Biddle, R., 213
Bird, E. J., 304
Birenbaum, A., 32, 35, 40, 50, 52–53
Birnbaum, J., 212, 213

Black, D., 176
Blakeslee, S., 331, 353
Blanchard, C., 141–42
Blieszner, R., 314, 316, 325, 326, 330
Blumberg, P., 223
Blumstein, A., 171
Boelkins, R. C., 192
Bogart, L., 214
Boggs, V., 185
Bohlen, C., 346
Bonacich, E., 244, 263
Booth, A., 74
Bourgois, P., 141
Boutwell, J. H., 499–500
Bowles, Samuel, 373
Bozette, S. A., 46, 49
Bracey, G. W., 383
Bragg, R., 431
Braginsky, B. M., 413
Braginsky, D. D., 413
Bratt, R. G., 435
Braverman, H., 408
Bremer, L. P., 525
Brennan, M., 158
Brewster, K. L., 347
Briggs, K. A., 225
Brimelow, P., 469
Bronte, Lydia, 320
Brook, J. S., 138
Brooks-Gunn, J., 241
Brown, Michael K., 157
Brown, S.P.A., 498
Bruni, F., 522
Budiansky, S., 196, 214, 215
Bullard, Robert D., 439
Bunnell, J. E., 171
Burros, M., 308
Burt, Martha, 242, 359, 444
Butler, C. J., 358

Caldwell, J. C., 455
Califano, Joseph A., 171, 178, 180
Callahan, D., 43, 333
Callahan, Daniel, 44–45
Campbell, J. R., 374
Cancian, M., 246
Cannon, A., 280
Cantor, P. A., 341
Caplan, Arthur, 359
Caplan, N., 470
Carmody, D., 52
Carson-DeWitt, R. S., 127, 130
Carter, A. C., 344
Carter, B., 196
Celis, W., III, 280, 370, 390, 391
Chafetz, Janet, 299
Chafetz, Morris E., 128, 129, 133
Chambers, C. D., 139
Chambliss, William, 158, 159
Chapman, Gary, 385
Cherlin, A. J., 345, 361
Chesler, Phyllis, 74
Chew, Kenneth, 308
Chudacoff, Howard P., 322
Clark, William C., 496
Clawson, P., 525
Close, Frank, 487
Cloward, Richard A., 11, 245, 276–77
Clymer, A., 55
Cockerham, W. C., 29, 49, 75
Cohen, Albert K., 175
Colassanto, D., 267
Cole, David, 172
Coles, Robert, 277
Collins, Patricia Hill, 265
Colvin, R. L., 377

Commoner, Barry, 487
Connell, R. W., 291
Conway, G., 222, 460
Cooley, Charles Horton, 13
Corcoran, M., 293
Cornelius, Wayne A., 471
Cottingham, Phoebe, 428
Cottrell, W. F., 486
Cowan, N. M., 470
Cowan, R. S., 470
Cox, H., 315
Cox, W. M., 223
Craig, L. A., 33, 53
Crawford, C., 217
Cressey, Donald R., 162, 174, 181
Crittenden, D., 301
Crossette, B., 424, 425, 525
Csikszentmihalyi, R., 417
Cuban, Larry, 385–86
Cuber, J. F., 344
Curtis, W. R., 78
Cutler, D. M., 269

Daley, William, 385
Daly, M., 302
Danesh, A. H., 410
Darling-Hammond, L., 375
Davis, Kingsley, 102, 104, 455, 463
Davis, M., 418
Davis, Nancy J., 294
Davis, Nanette, 105–106
Decker, S., 391
Deckman, M., 348
Dees, M. S., 526
Deighton, Lee C., 382
Dejong, W., 129
Demone, H. W., Jr., 133
Denitch, B., 507
Denton, Judith, 379
Denton, Nancy, 255, 269–71, 280, 428, 429
DeParle, J., 444
DesJarlais, Don, 57, 142
Dewey, John, 391
Dial, T. H., 75
Dickey, B., 83
Diesenhouse, S., 185
DiFazio, William, 401, 407, 409
DiIulio, John, 158, 166, 169, 170
Dohrenwend, Barbara Snell, 75
Dohrenwend, Bruce P., 75
Donnerstein, E., 214
Donohew, R. L., 139
Dornbusch, Stanford, 374
Drevitch, G., 372, 383
Dugger, C. W., 470
Duncan, G. J., 293
Dunlap, R. E., 487
Durkheim, Emile, 8, 151, 323
Duster, Troy, 168

Earle, A., 235, 236
Easton, A., 93
Ebrahim, S. H., 128
Eckholm, E., 276
Edelhoch, M., 249
Edin, Kathryn, 234, 240, 248
Edwards, L. P., 15
Ehrenreich, Barbara, 301
Ehrlich, A. H., 463, 489–90, 493, 498
Ehrlich, P. R., 463, 489–90, 493, 498
El-Bassel, N., 141
Elders, Joycelyn, 308
Elifson, K., 104, 109
Elvin, J., 189
England, P., 293, 294, 309
Enloe, Cynthia, 107–108

Epstein, Cynthia F., 291, 321
Epstein, W. S., 378
Erikson, Kai, 18
Erlanger, H. S., 207
Espenshade, Thomas J., 470, 473

Falk, D. M., 56
Faludi, S., 291
Fanon, Frantz, 192
Faris, R. E. L., 72
Farkas, G., 293, 294
Farley, Reynolds, 267, 271
Farnsworth, C. H., 109
Farrell, S., 302
Fasteau, Marc, 292
Faulkner, Peter, 483
Feagin, Joe R., 258, 274, 277, 439
Felson, R. B., 194
Fields, S., 135
Fineman, H., 113
Finkelhor, D., 204
Fischer, Claude S., 427, 430–31
Fiss, O. M., 109
Flavin, C., 491, 492, 502
Flink, J., 434
Forsland, M. A., 140
Foust, D., 163
Fox, R., 29, 35, 73
Franke, L. B., 291
Franks, J. B., 112
Freedman, S. G., 142
Freud, Sigmund, 75, 96
Freudenheim, M., 35
Friedan, Betty, 289, 292, 297, 321
Friedman, L. N., 21
Friedman, Lawrence M., 168, 179, 182
Friedman, Milton, 397
Fuchs, Victor, 231
Fuller, B., 375, 384
Fulton, A. S., 94, 97
Furstenberg, F., 346
Futrell, M. H., 199

Gabay, M., 41
Gagnon, J. H., 92, 99, 109
Gahr, E., 307
Galbraith, John Kenneth, 229, 400
Gale, E., 358
Galewitz, P., 225
Galinsky, E., 344
Galston, W., 361
Gampell, J., 108
Gans, Herbert J., 245–46, 247, 250, 415, 430
Garreau, Joel, 432, 435, 436, 447
Garrett, K., 305
Gaw, A. C., 74
Geertz, C., 458
Gelbard, A., 455
Gelernter, David, 526
Gelles, R., 192, 205, 341, 346, 352, 364
Gerbner, George, 195, 196
Gerson, Kathleen, 346–47
Gest, T., 185
Giele, Janet Z., 295
Gilbert, D. L., 228
Gilder, George, 245, 397
Gillespie, N., 212
Ginsberg, Eli, 427
Glaab, C. N., 434–35
Glahn, Gerhard von, 513
Glassner, Barry, 16, 128
Glausiuz, J., 45
Gochman, David S., 51
Goffman, Erving, 78
Goldberg, C., 390
Goldberger, P., 447
Goldman, H. H., 71, 85
Goleman, D., 70, 264, 278
Gondles, J. A., Jr., 167, 180
Goode, E., 31, 146

Goode, W. J., 343
Goodin, R. E., 10
Goodman, W., 306
Gordon, D. M., 399, 401, 410
Gordon, D. R., 11
Gottfredson, M. R., 169, 170
Gottmann, J., 432
Gould, R. E., 292
Gould, S. J., 257
Gould, William, 272
Gove, W. R., 73
Grasso, K. L., 103, 109, 110, 117
Greenfeld, L. A., 168, 209
Greenley, J. R., 70
Grimsley, K. D., 409–410
Grob, G. N., 62
Gronfein, W., 82
Gruenberg, B., 410
Guetzloe, E., 387
Guillermoprieto, A., 516
Gusfield, Joseph R., 12, 113, 121, 126
Guterl, F., 525

Hacker, A., 294, 295, 300
Hackstaff, K. B., 345
Hagedorn, John M., 182, 210
Hall, P., 500
Hall, R., 204
Hamer, Dean, 290
Hannaway, J., 372
Harkey, J., 73
Harrington, M., 237
Hartmann, Heidi, 287, 299, 301, 308
Hassel, C. V., 522
Heath, L., 154
Hechter, M., 195
Henderson, Z. P., 74
Herbert, B., 293, 418
Herman, Judith L., 92
Herndon, J., 391
Hesman, T., 492
Hesse-Biber, Sharlene, 291
Heyl, Barbara, 102
Heymann, S. J., 235, 236
Hill, S. C., 387
Hilts, P. J., 47
Himmelstein, D. U., 50, 51, 54
Hippensteele, S., 295
Hirsch, E. D., Jr., 390
Hirsch, K., 214
Hirschi, T., 169, 170
Hobb, Dick, 164
Hochschild, Arlie R., 346
Holmes, R. A., 198
Holmes, S. A., 173, 263
Holstein, W. J., 385–86
Holt, J., 391
Homer-Dixon, T. F., 499–500
Hooker, Evelyn, 96
Hooyman, N. R., 321, 327
Horgan, J., 168
Horner, Matina, 291
Horowitz, A. V., 62, 70, 71, 72–73, 75
Horton, R., 290
Huber, J., 343
Hunt, L. G., 90, 139, 140
Hunt, M., 92–93

Jacklin, Carol, 299
Jackman, Mary R., 228
Jackman, Robert W., 228
Jacobs, J. A., 347
Jacobs, Jane, 442
Jacobs, M. D., 166
Jacobs, Mark, 179
Jacobson, D., 110
James, Jennifer, 102, 104–105
Jamison, Kay Redfield, 64–65, 75, 76
Janofsky, M., 334
Janowitz, M., 10, 176, 508

Jasanoff, S., 501
Jaynes, D. J., 350
Jaynes, G., 429
Jencks, C., 82
Jencks, Christopher, 232, 239, 240, 248, 249, 359
Jenson, J. M., 183
Johannson, S., 464
Johnson, G., 526
Johnston, H., 12
Jones, S. L., 97
Jurevich, Tom, 411
Justice, B., 204
Justice, R., 204

Kadushin, C., 508
Kadushin, G., 358
Kahlenberg, R. D., 278, 279
Kaminer, Wendy, 200
Kandel, Denise, 127, 138
Kantrowitz, B., 341
Kaplan, D. A., 386
Karp, A., 524
Kasarda, John D., 407, 428, 435, 438, 440, 445–46
Kasinitz, P., 132
Katz, J., 163, 195
Katz Rothman, B., 41–42
Kavee, A. L., 347
Kempf, K., 159
Kenney, C., 494
Kilborn, P. T., 33–34, 34
Kilbourne, J., 129, 307
Kim, I., 257, 469
Kimmel, M. S., 292, 308
King, E. A., 64
Kituse, John, 15
Kleck, Gary, 212, 217
Kleiman, D., 92
Kolata, G., 40
Korn, W. S., 387
Kornblum, William, 105, 110, 182, 185, 193, 299, 435
Kosterlitz, J., 448
Kozol, Jonathan, 72, 359, 391, 435
Kristof, N. D., 313, 319, 323, 331, 510
Kronenwtter, E., 501
Kubler-Ross, Elisabeth, 332–33
Kutchinsky, B., 112

Ladner, Joyce A., 448
Lamanna, M. A., 347, 354, 355
Landry, M. J., 137
Larana, E., 12
Lareau, Annette, 384
Lasswell, Harold, 7, 517
Laumann, Edward O., 49, 89, 90, 93, 95
Laver, M., 195
Lavin, David E., 373, 380, 392
Leifman, H., 129
Leighton, D. C., 72
Lein, Laura, 234, 240, 248
Leland, J., 112, 195, 196
Lemert, E. M., 165
Lenin, Vladimir Ilyich, 516
Leslie, C., 374
Lester, D., 348, 352
Leuchtag, A., 111
Le Vay, Simon, 290
Levin, J., 198
Levinson, R. M., 293
Levitan, S. A., 281
Lewine, R. R., 75
Lewis, A., 110–11
Lewis, O., 245
Li, J., 464
Lichter, D. T., 486
Lieberson, Stanley, 257
Liefman, H., 129
Lifton, R. J., 511, 512
Lind, M., 263
Lipton, D. S., 143
Liska, A. S., 154

Lofland, Lyn, 17, 441, 442
Lombroso, Cesare, 167–68
Loneck, B., 134
Long, D. E., 522
Lorch, D., 471
Lorenz, Konrad, 514, 515
Loupe, D., 365
Lovins, Amory, 500
Lowery, Shirley, 206
Lukemeyer, A., 238
Luker, K., 363
Lunde, Donald T., 193, 197
Lyman, M. D., 122, 123, 134, 142, 143

Maccoby, Eleanor, 299
McCord, Joan, 168
McDevitt, Jack, 277
MacDonald, G. J., 489, 491, 494
McEwen, C., 79
MacGregor, S., 146
McIntosh, C. A., 472
McKeown, R. E., 169
MacKinnon, Catherine, 110–11, 296–97, 303
MacLeod, C., 216
McLeod, J., 372
McNamara, R. P., 103, 104
McNeill, William, 511–12
Mahoney, K. M., 387
Majors, Robert, 264
Males, Mike, 185, 200–201, 208
Malinowski, Bronislaw, 355
Maltz, M. D., 159
Marcuse, Herbert, 192
Mare, R. D., 348
Margaronis, M., 497
Marmor, Theodore, 29
Marmot, M. G., 31
Marshall, N., 105
Martine, G., 459, 465
Martinez-Alier, J., 503
Martinson, Robert, 180
Marvin, D. R., 206
Mason-Draffen, C., 409
Massey, Douglas S., 255, 269–71, 280, 379, 428, 429,
    468–69
Matcha, D. A., 29
Matras, J., 456
Matthews, R., 386
May, H., 14
Mazrui, A. A., 520
Mbere, N., 287, 308
Mechanic, David, 81
Medina, J. J., 323
Meed, I., 522
Meier, D., 383, 384
Melman, Seymour, 517
Merton, Robert K., 173, 260
Methwin, E. J., 171
Meyer, J. W., 85, 355
Meyerding, Jane, 104–105
Meyers, M. K., 238
Miech, R. A., 73, 74
Milgram, Stanley, 484–85
Miller, Eleanor M., 99, 105, 107, 168
Miller, Walter, 175
Mills, C. Wright, 517
Milner, C., 106
Milner, Christina, 103
Milner, Richard, 103
Minuchin, S., 344
Mirowsky, J., 75
Mishel, L., 409
Mollman, S., 162
Money, John, 290
Monroe, J., 496
Montagu, A., 515
Moore, M., 410
Moore, T. G., 492
Morgani, John, 144–45
Morgenson, G., 400
Morrison, T. G., 93, 94

Morrow, J., 117
Mosle, S., 390
Mouw, R., 115
Mundy, L., 360
Murray, C., 232, 245
Murray, J. B., 136

Nagel, J., 271
Neff, J. A., 141
Nelkin, Dorothy, 193
Ness, R. B., 42
Newman, Katherine S., 17, 324, 345, 413
Niebuhr, G., 522
Nigro, L. G., 198
Noble, H. B., 31
Nolin, M. M., 199
Nordheimer, J., 414

Ober, K., 132
O'Connor, J. S., 494
Oetting, E. R., 140
Ogburn, William F., 485, 486
O'Hare, William P., 226, 232, 238
Okun, B. F., 344
Oliver, Melvin, 272–73
Olsen, F., 297
Ophuls, W., 489
Oppenheimer, V. C., 349
Oppermann, M., 108
Orchard, A. L., 352
Orfield, Gary, 269, 280, 373, 375, 377, 379
Ormes, I., 500
Orshansky, Mollie, 231

Painton, P., 94
Pallas, A. M., 381
Palmer, J. L., 314, 328
Paone, D., 142
Parelius, Ann Parker, 382, 384
Parelius, Robert J., 382, 384
Parrot, A., 93
Parrott, S. A., 387
Parsons, T., 343
Paul, A. M., 264
Payer, Lynn, 35
Pear, R., 30, 38–39, 53, 84, 239
Pedersen, D., 55
Peele, S., 128
Pepinsky, H. E., 159, 161
Perls, T. T., 319, 330
Perrow, Charles, 484, 501
Peyser, M., 314
Phillips, M., 68
Pifer, Alan, 320
Pillard, R. C., 97
Piore, M. J., 244, 471
Pipher, M., 333
Piven, Frances Fox, 11, 245, 247, 277
Plate, T., 165
Pollard, K., 237
Pollock, Carl, 205
Popenoe, David, 362, 363, 365
Portes, A., 257, 283, 428
Posner, R. A., 323
Postman, N., 129
Preston, Samuel, 364–65, 458
Prothrow-Stith, Deborah, 198, 387
Purdum, T. S., 304
Putnam, Robert, 196
Pyett, Pricilla, 107

Quillan, L., 269
Quinney, Richard, 11, 165, 170

Rackham, A., 413
Rainwater, Lee, 49, 233
Rapoport, A., 515, 516
Rathjens, G. W., 499–500
Ray, O. S., 122, 136, 137, 139
Read, P., 491, 500
Reckless, W. C., 159, 171

Rector, R., 245
Regier, D., 61, 62, 72, 74, 76, 77
Reid, S. T., 159, 183, 197, 198
Reigot, B. P., 355
Reiner, D., 492
Reisman, David, 229
Reiss, A. J., Jr., 98, 185, 190, 193, 194, 203, 205, 211
Reskin, B., 413
Retsinas, J., 333
Richardson, D., 14
Richmond-Abbott, Marie, 290, 295, 297, 299, 301, 358
Ries, R., 62
Riessman, C. K., 42
Rifkin, J., 407, 415
Riley, J. C., 316
Riley, Matilda White, 314, 318–19, 324, 325, 326, 328
Rindfuss, R. R., 347
Rist, R. C., 110, 374
Ritzer, G., 415
Roberts, S., 146, 460
Robins, L. N., 72, 141
Robinson, J. P., 308
Robinson, Robert V., 294
Rochman, S., 102, 114
Rodriguez, J., 239
Rohatyn, F., 401
Rosenhan, D. L., 70, 79
Ross, A., 409
Ross, C., 351
Rossellini, L., 194
Rossi, Alice, 290, 344, 355
Rossi, Peter H., 132, 344, 355, 444
Roth, J. A., 190, 193, 194, 203, 205, 211
Rothstein, R., 471
Rovner, J., 40, 55
Rowe, J. W., 324, 325, 334
Rowland, D., 32
Rubington, E., 12, 13, 109
Rudolph, J. R., 518
Ruggles, Patricia, 231
Russell, Diana E. H., 93
Russell, K. K., 277
Russell, Kathryn, 172

Sachs, J., 461
Sacks, Oliver, 448
Sadd, S., 181
Safilios-Rothschild, C., 291
Salter, S., 364
Sanchez-Jankowsky, Martin, 210
Sanday, Peggy Reeves, 94
Sandefur, Gary D., 266, 271
Sanford, W. C., 307
Saporito, Salvatore, 384
Sax, L. T., 387
Scheff, Thomas, 67
Schmalz, J., 97
Schmidt, G., 95
Schmidt, W. E., 391
Schmitt, E., 283
Schrank, Robert, 411
Schuckit, M. A., 127
Schur, Edwin M., 90, 116, 185
Schweinhart, L. J., 378
Scull, A. T., 67, 79
Sexton, J., 418
Shapiro, J. P., 358
Shapiro, Thomas, 272–73
Shaw, C. R., 15
Sheehan, S., 76, 79
Sherman, L. W., 213–14
Sherrill, R., 162–63
Shipley, T. E., Jr., 132
Siegel, L., 161, 163
Silberman, Charles, 182, 185
Simmel, Georg, 429
Simpson, G. E., 257, 260
Simpson, P., 287, 308
Singer, J. D., 508
Skolnick, A. S., 191, 341, 343, 346, 351, 354
Skolnick, J. H., 191, 341, 343, 346, 351, 354

Slavin, R., 374, 391
Slobin, S., 242
Smeeding, T. M., 233, 238, 329
Smil, V., 463
Smith, B. E., 216
Smith, Douglas, A., 170
Smolowe, J., 324, 326
Snow, D. A., 72, 82
Sorokin, P., 508
Spain, D., 348
Specter, M., 455
Spector, M., 15
Spero, R., 50
Sperry, L., 79
Squire, S., 76
Srole, L., 72
Stacey, Judith, 362
Stack, C., 105
Stafford, D., 43
Stanton, G. T., 361
Staples, B., 279–80
Stares, P. B., 147
Starr, Paul, 29, 33, 52
Steele, Brandt, 205
Steffensmeier, D., 168
Sterk, Claire, 47, 102, 103, 104, 105
Sterngold, J., 418
Stevens, W. K., 435, 492, 495
Stevenson, Harold W., 370
Stevenson, M., 403, 404
Steward, G. L., 106
Stover, P., 295
Strossen, N., 109
Sullivan, Mercer, 170
Sullivan, R., 142
Sullivan, T. A., 166
Suplee, C., 495
Sutherland, Edwin H., 161, 174, 181
Suttles, Gerald, 175
Sweet, J. A., 341, 353
Swingle, Joseph, 232, 239, 240, 248
Szasz, Thomas, 66–67, 96, 126, 336
Szyndrowski, D., 388

Thomas, W. I., 13, 102
Thorne, Barrie, 299
Tienda, Marta, 266, 271, 405–406

Tittle, Charles R., 170
Toolan, D. S., 487
Torrey, E. F., 61
Traub, J., 166, 170
Triden, Richard, 98
Troiden, R. R., 97
Trow, M., 371
Tunali, O., 481
Turk, A. T., 11

Uchitelle, L., 231
Urquhart, B., 507, 519

Vaillant, G. E., 128
Verhovek, S. H., 51
Villemez, Wayne J., 170
Vincent, J. A., 314

Wahid, H. M., 304
Wald, M. L., 502
Waldinger, R., 283
Walker, H. B., 518
Walker, Lenore, 47, 206–207
Wallerstein, J., 353
Waring, Joan, 318
Warner, Kenneth E., 52
Warr, Deborah, 107
Weber, Arnold, 426
Weber, Max, 227–228
Wegner, J. W., 255
Weikart, D. P., 378
Weinberg, M. S., 12, 13
Weinberg, S. K., 92
Weinberger, C. J., 280
Weiss, Robert, 353
Weissbourd, R., 353
Wellner, A. S., 30
Welsh, P., 389
West, Cornel, 274, 284
Weston, R., 162
Wetzel, J. R., 407
White, M., 63
Widmer, E. D., 95
Wilensky, H. L., 413
Wilkerson, I., 443
Wilkes, M. S., 327
Williams, A. P., 53

Williams, D., 309, 389
Williams, J., 344
Williams, R. M., 259
Williams, Terry, 105, 110, 141, 182, 210, 435
Williams-Harold, B., 479
Willis, P., 372
Wilson, Edward O., 515
Wilson, James Q., 141, 158, 167–68, 171, 177
Wilson, W. Cody, 112
Wilson, William Julius, 17, 173, 244–46, 249, 250, 251, 272–74, 284, 336, 348–49, 350, 405
Wilton, R. D., 82
Winerip, M., 109
Winick, Charles, 110
Winner, L., 109, 478, 481, 486
Winnick, L., 428
Wirth, Louis, 15, 429–30, 431
Witt, G. E., 302
Wofsy, C., 115
Wolf, R., 354
Wolfe, B., 50, 327
Wolfgang, Marvin, 170
Wolk, J. L., 235
Worsham, J., 35
Wouters, C., 176
Wrenn, C. S., 137–38

Yang, D. J., 418
Yankelovich, Daniel, 410
Yinger, J. M., 258, 260
Yinger, Milton, 264
Yoon, C. K., 491

Zawitz, M. W., 209
Zeisel, Hans, 18, 178
Zeitlin, M., 508
Zhao, John Z., 354
Zillman, D., 109
Zimbardo, Philip G., 21–22
Zimmer, Lynn, 123, 144–45
Zimring, Franklin E., 211, 214
Znaniecki, Florian, 13
Zuboff, Shoshanna, 408
Zukin, S., 447

Subject Index

Abortion, 12, 41, 58, 307
Acid rain, 432, 477, 491
Acquaintance rape, 203
Addiction, defined, 24
Adoption, 464
Advertising, 302, 415
Affirmative action, 229, 256, 278–80, 282, 306
Africa, 29, 45, 95, 202, 295, 424, 456
African Americans (see Blacks)
Aged/aging:
   alcoholism and, 128
   defining elderly, 319–21
   demographic trends, 33
   elder abuse, 207, 327
   family problems and, 330
   health care for, 316, 327–28
   nursing homes and, 29
   perspectives on, 315
   physiological aspects of, 323–24
   population across countries, 314
   poverty and, 232–33
   psychological dimensions of, 324–25
   social and cultural dimensions of, 325–26
   suicide among, 322–23
   in U.S., 315–18
   victimization of elderly, 326–27
   voting power of, 325
Age Discrimination in Employment Act (1967), 322

Ageism, 321
Age stratification, 318–19
Aggressive behavior, 194–95, 261
Agrarian societies, 316, 343
Agricultural sector, 244, 402, 477, 478
AIDS (acquired immune deficiency syndrome), 3, 45–49, 48, 118
   drug abuse and, 46, 47, 108, 136, 142
   educational system and, 389
   effect on prostitution, 108–9
   exposure categories, 47
   gay people and, 46–47, 114
   heterosexuals and, 46–47
   insurance coverage and, 40
   newborns and, 27
   sexual behavior and, 90
   social policy on, 56–57
   treatment for, 48
   in urbanized areas, 142, 423, 427
   in U.S., 45
Aid to Families with Dependent Children (AFDC), 4, 233, 235, 246, 265, 353
Air pollution, 432, 490–92
Alateen, 133
Alcoholics Anonymous (AA), 75, 132–34
Alcohol use/abuse, 121–22, 124, 126–34
   addiction (alcoholism), 37, 66, 83, 127
   culture and, 126–29
   effect on family, 131–32
   homicide and, 197–98
   individuals who drink, 127–29

legal age and, 314–15
social policy on, 145–47
social problems with, 130–32
socioeconomic factors, 127
treatments for, 132–34
young people and, 129
Alimony, 361, 362
Alternative families, 341
Alzheimer's disease, 44
American Association of University Women (AAUW), 300
American Federation of Teachers, 387
American Medical Association (AMA), 53
American Psychiatrists Association (APA), 70–71
American Sociological Association, 22
Americans with Disabilities Act (ADA), 55–56
Amniocentesis, 360
Amphetamines, 136
Anal sex, 102
Angola, 524
Anomie, 173
Anorexia, 291
Antabuse, 134
Antiurban bias, 426–27
Anxiety, 124
Appropriate technology, 500
Arms control, 523–25
Artificial insemination, 359, 360
Asia, 29, 45, 295, 370, 456
Asians, 257
Assault, 202

Assimilation, 257, 258
Attention deficit hyperactivity disorder (ADHD), 237–38
Australia, 32, 107, 456, 458, 465
Autism, 62, 66
Automation, 482–83
Automobiles, 480, 481
"Autonomous males," 346
Aversion therapy, 134

Baby boom, 35–37, 460
Bail system, 274
Bakke case, 279
Bank credit, 303
Bankruptcy, 416
Barbiturates, 136–37, 141
Behavior conditioning, 134
Berlin crisis (1961), 514
Bigotry, 260, 262–64
Bilinqual/bicultural education, 377
Biology:
    of aging, 316
    alcoholism and, 127
    of crime, 167–69
    homosexuality and, 97
    mental illness and, 62, 66
    of suicide, 64
Birth control, 302, 308, 456, 463, 464
Birthrate, 320, 348, 354, 357, 457
Birth trauma, 66
Bisexuality, 98
Blacks, 272, 279, 357
    aged among, 334
    criminal behavior and, 171
    discrimination against, 236–37, 266–67
    drug use among, 140
    education and, 236, 267, 375, 379
    hopelessness, 242
    job exploitation of, 261
    life expectancy and, 30–31, 189
    marriage and, 48
    net financial assets, household, 273
    poverty rate among, 173, 226, 235–37, 350
    prostitute subculture and, 106–9
    racial equality and, 255–56
    segregation and, 428
    sex-role stereotyping and, 300
    single-parent households, 232
    urban migration, 244, 427
    violence and, 216–17
    voter registration, 258
    welfare stereotyping, 265
    women in work force, 405–6
Blended families, 352
Blue-collar workers, 402–3
Bolivia, 147
Bosnia, 277, 518, 519, 524
Bowers v. *Hardwick*, 92
Brady Act, 212
Brain damage, 66
Brazil, 461, 465
Brown v. *Board of Education of Topeka*, 256, 268, 276, 379
Bureaucracy, 381, 484–85
Bush administration, 448
Busing, 268

Cambodia, 519, 524
Canada, 32, 50, 52–53, 371, 399, 418, 523
Capital, 398
Capitalism, 397
Career counseling, 300
Carter administration, 517
Catholic church, 302
Censorship, 111, 116–17, 119
Census tracts, 445, 446
Central America, 239, 457, 470
Cerebral palsy, 66
Chain migration, 469
Chemical industry, 414
Chemotherapy, 76, 86

Chernobyl incident, 492
Chicago Area Project, 181–82
Childbirth, 41–42
Child care, 231, 235, 310, 364
Child-centered curriculum, 391
Child molestation, 93
Child Online Protection Act (1998), 117
Children, 341
    abuse of, 204–6, 216–17
    AIDS and, 47
    criminal behavior and, 169–70
    with disabilities, 238
    divorce and, 363
    education and, 282
    mortality and, 28, 32
    pornography and, 109–10, 112
    poverty and, 223, 232–33
    sexual molestation, 93, 159
    working mothers and, 345, 346
Child support, 362
Chile, 399, 459
China, 4, 258, 370, 401, 418, 424, 464
Chronically unemployed, 412
Chronological aging, 323
Church of Latter Day Saints (Mormons), 92
Cities:
    deconcentration and, 438–39
    financial problems, 440–42
    government and, 442–43
    problems of, 437–38
Civil law, 157
Civil rights, 97, 177–78, 255–56, 272
Civil Rights Act (1964), 256, 278, 293, 297, 303
    Title VII of, 306
Class, social
    alcohol use/abuse, 127
    child abuse and, 205
    criminal behavior and, 170
    delinquent subcultures and, 175
    health-care access and, 30–31, 49–50
    health-care problems and, 29
    health insurance and, 38
    mental health and, 72–73
    mortality rates and, 31
    poverty and, 227–29
    self-identification, 228
Class stratification, 227
Clean Air Act (1970), 501
Client-centered therapy, 75, 86
Clinton administration, 225, 298, 305
    anti-crime policy, 182
    drug policy, 147
    homelessness and, 444
    housing policy, 447
    mental health initiatives, 84
    policy contradiction, 419
    pro-choice policies, 307
Cocaine, 122, 135–36, 158, 520
Codependency, 131–32
Coercive adult sex, 93
Cohabitating couples, 354
Colombia, 147, 459, 520
Columbine shootings, 64
"Coming out," 98
Command economies, 398
Commission on Obscenity and Pornography, U.S., 111, 112
Communism, 10–11, 14, 398
Community Mental Health Centers Construction Act (1963), 79, 80
Community psychology, 79–80, 86
"Community standards" criteria, 117
Comparable worth, 306–7
Competition, economic, 429–30
Compositionalism, 430
Computers, 162, 385–86, 408–9
Condoms, 115
Confidentiality, 22, 25
Conflict perspective, 7, 10–12, 24
    on aging, 315, 316

on health care, 49–50
    Marxian theory and, 10–12
    mental illness and, 63
    on prostitution, 103
Conservatism, 22, 24
Consolidated metropolitan statistical area (CMSA), 432
Constitution, U.S., 255, 288
Consumer credit, 415–18
Consumer price index (CPI), 230, 231
Consumption, resource, 417, 493–94
Contraception, 360, 458, 463
Control group, 20
Control theory, 193–94
Conventional crimes, 163, 183
Corporate crimes, 162–63, 184
Corporations, 398 (*see also* Multinational corporations)
Corruption, 165, 398
Costa Rica, 461
Cost of living, 345
Cost shifting, 40, 80–81
Crack cocaine, 124, 135, 141, 143, 158
    gangs and, 207
Credit, 303, 415–18
Crime, 8–9, 24, 122 (*see also* Criminal violence; Murder)
    age and, 169–70
    alcohol use/abuse and, 130–31
    conditions and causes, 167–70
    conflict analysis of, 170–73
    controlling, 176–82
    defined, 154
    drug abuse and, 141–42
    functional analysis of, 173–74
    interactionist analysis of, 174–76
    nature of, 154–57
    occupational (white-collar) crimes, 161–62
    police discretion, 157–59
    prevention, 181–82
    rates by type/city, 155–56
    reporting accuracy and, 159
    social policy on, 182–85
    as social problem, 151–54
    types of, 160–67
    underclass and, 274
    violent, 151
Crime Act (1994), 167
Crime Control Act (1984), 185
Crime index, 152–53
Criminal atavism, 167
Criminal law, 157
Criminal violence, 196–202 (*see also* Murder)
    assault and robbery, 202
    hate crimes, 167, 199, 201–202, 208
    homicide and, 197–99, 207
    mass murder, 198
    rape, 93–94, 111, 159, 202–204
    school violence, 198–99
Croatia, 518
Cross-sectional data, 19
Cuba, 459
Cuban missile crisis (1962), 514
Cultural anthropology, 6
Cultural-disadvantage argument, 380
Cultural lag, 485–86
Culture:
    ageism and, 128–29
    alcoholism and, 128–29
    antiurban bias, 426–27
    criminal behavior and, 171
    health care and, 35
    mental disorders and, 70–71
    of poverty, 245–46
    of youth, 313–14

Date rape, 204
Day care, 305, 310, 364
DDT (dichloro-diphenyl-trichloro-ethane), 489–90
Death, 331–33
Death penalty, 178, 274

Death rate, 454
Debt, consumer, 416–17
Deconcentration, 438–39
De facto segregation, 268
Defended neighborhood, 373
Defense of Marriage Act, 113
Deinstitutionalization, 62–63
De jure segregation, 268
Delinquent subcultures, 174–76
Dementia, 64
Demographics, 19, 25
  age of world population, 319, 320
  health care and, 33, 35–37
  of murder, 197
  physicians services and, 34
  postponing marriage, 355, 458
Demographic transition, 455–58
Denmark, 221
Department of Health and Human Services (HHS),
  55, 57
Department of Housing and Urban Development
  (HUD), 213, 242, 251, 444
Dependency, 247, 249–50, 482
Dependent poor, 237–38
Depression, 62, 70, 124
  women and, 65, 74
Desegregation, 379
Detoxification, 134
Developed countries, 28
Deviance
  criminal, 8–9
  interactionist view of, 13–14
  Marxian conflict view of, 11
  mental illness as, 66–67
  transitional, 106
Diagnostic and Statistical Manual of Mental Disorders
  (DSM-III), 68, 86
  DSM-IV, 68–70, 124
Differential association, 161, 174, 181
Digital divide, 385–86, 479
Disabled/handicapped, 42–43, 55–56, 58
"Discouraged" worker, 412–13
Discrimination, 259 (*see also* Prejudice and
  discrimination)
Discrimination in Employment Act (1967), 328
Divorce, 330, 342, 350–54
  explanation for trends, 352
  impact of, 353–54
  social policy for, 361, 363
  stepfamilies, 352
Dominican Republic, 457
Down syndrome, 66
Drift hypothesis, 73, 86
Driving while drunk, 126, 129, 130, 146
Dropouts, school, 380, 381, 388
Drug abuse, illegal, 3, 4, 27, 134–45
  by age group, 125
  AIDS and, 46, 47, 108, 142
  defining problem of, 122–23
  dependence and addiction, 123–26
  drugs of preference, 134–37
  homelessness and, 83
  legalization argument, 123, 144–45, 146
  people involved in, 137–39
  prevalence of, 125
  social policy on, 145–47
  treatment programs for, 142–45
Drugs, defined, 122
Drugs, pharmaceutical, 122, 134, 324
Drug trafficking, 147, 164, 172, 207
Dying trajectory, 332
Dying with dignity, 332

Earned Income Tax Credit (EITC), 239, 250
Earning gap, 293, 306
Ecology, 491
Economic globalization, 398–99
Economics, 6 (*see also* Work; Work force)
  aged's status, 314
  consumer credit, 415–18
  elder discrimination and, 328–30

free-enterprise system, U.S., 397–98, 486
GDP per capita, U.S., 221
  homemaking and, 295
  illegal immigrants, 471
  pollution and, 491, 502
  population growth and, 463
  productivity and, 478, 482–83
  transition to service economy, 402, 404–5
  war and, 512, 516
Edge cities, 435, 436
Edison Project, 386
Education, 205 (*see also* School reform)
  access to, 374–75, 392
  attainment gap, 379–81
  conflict analysis of, 372–73
  family violence and, 205
  functionalist analysis of, 372
  high school dropouts, 205
  income and, 268
  interactionist analysis of, 373–74
  marriage and, 348
  poverty and, 241
  preschool programs, 377–78
  segregation and, 256, 373
  sex education, 89, 307
  sexism in, 293, 305–6
  sex-role stereotyping and, 300–301
  social policy on, 280–82
  unequal access to, 268–69
  welfare reform and, 249
Education for All Handicapped Children Act (1975),
  55
Elder abuse, 207, 327
Embezzlement, 162
Employment:
  education and, 256
  immigration and, 257
  prejudice and discrimination in, 271–74
  sexism and, 292
  welfare reform and, 233–35
Empty-shell marriage, 344
Endogamy, 258
Energy consumption, 459, 498
England, 371, 399, 487, 511
Entitlements, 23
Entrapment, 116
Entrepreneurs, 398
Environment, natural (*see also* Water supply)
  metropolitan growth and, 432
  pollution, 51, 398
  technology and, 487–89
Environmental Protection Agency (EPA), 501
Environmental racism, 494
Environmental stress, 489–96
  air pollution, 432, 490–92
  chemicals, 496
  engineering projects, large scale, 496
  government actions, 501–502
  land degradation, 495
  noise pollution, 495–96
  origins of problem, 489–90
  solid-waste disposal, 493–95
  water pollution, 425, 477, 487, 492–93
Environmental terrorism, 514
Equal Credit Opportunity Act (1974), 304
Equal Employment Opportunity Commission (EEOC),
  297, 303
Equal Pay Act (1963), 293
Equal Rights Amendment (ERA), 288, 298, 303
Ethical issues, 43–45, 48
Ethnic cleansing, 189, 255
Ethnic minorities, 257
Ethnocentricity, 260
Ethnography, 17
Europe, 52, 139, 278, 399, 456
Exhibitionism, sexual, 94
Experimental group, 20
Exports, 400
Extended family, 342
Extortion, 164
Extra-marital births, 355–56

Families, 341–42 (*see also* Divorce; Marriage)
  adequate functioning within, 344–45
  aged and, 330
  alcohol use/abuse and, 131–32
  drug use and, 140
  homelessness and, 358–59
  inner city decline and, 349–50
  nature of, 342–43
  prostitution and, 107
  shrinking size of, 352
  violence and, 204–7, 213–16
  without fathers, 362
  women's employment and, 345–48, 381
Families therapy, 76
Family Leave Act (1993), 305, 365
Family planning, 463
Family support, 364–65
Family unification, 473
"Family values," 365
Farm employment, 402
Federal Housing Authority, 435
Federal Reserve Board, U.S., 223
Fee-for-services, 33
Female hustlers, 103
Feminine mystique, 292
Feminists, 12, 40
  abortion rights, 41
  sex roles, 389
Fertility drugs, 360
Fertility rate, 313, 458, 460
Fetal alcohol syndrome, 27
Field observation, 19–20, 25
Field research, 20
Flextime, 410
Food production, 497
Food stamps, 229, 231, 235
Forcible rape, 202
France, 32, 52, 79, 221, 360, 371, 399, 459,
  465, 523
Fraud, 162
Free trade, 418
Frictional unemployment, 412
Frustration-aggression theory, 193–94,
  261
Functionalist perspective, 7–10, 24, 515–16
  on aging, 315, 316
  on criminal deviance, 8–9
  education, 372, 373
  family structure and, 342
  industrialization and, 343
  mental illness and, 63
  on pornography, 110
  on prostitution, 102–103
Fusion research, 486–87

Gallup Organization, 16
Gambling, 164
Gang rape, 204
Gangs, 140, 175
  drug trafficking and, 210
  guns and violent death, 207–8, 210–11
  police discretion and, 157–59
Gay marriages, 341
Gay-rights movement, 95, 96
Gays in the military, 113
Gender
  alcohol use/abuse, 127–28
  crime and, 168–69
  drug use and, 138–39, 140
  earnings gap, 293–94
  education and, 267, 305–306
  global inequalities, 294
  income and, 288
  mental health and, 74–75
  sexism and, 290–91
  weekly hours worked, 127–28
Gender identity, 290
Genetics, 127
Gentrification, 444
Germany, 52, 221, 259, 313, 370, 465
Gerontology, 323

Global economy, 398–99
  effect on U.S. workers, 401–402
  shifting work patterns, 400
  women in work force and, 405–406
Global factory, 400–401
Globalization, 477, 519–20
Global warming, 477, 491–92, 501
Goals 2000: Educate America Act, 383
Government, 442–43 (*see also* Political issues:; Social policy)
  corruption and, 165
  problems of cities and, 442–43
  sexism and, 302–303
Grandparents, 235, 354
Great Britain, 32, 52, 85, 221, 459, 523
Great Depression, 375
Greenpeace, 497
Group therapy, 75
Grove City College v. *Bell,* 305
Guns:
  control of, 4, 211–14
  gang violence and, 207–208, 210–11

Habituation, defined, 124
Haiti, 457, 519
Halfway houses, 80
Hallucinogens, 136
Hate crimes, 167, 201–202, 208
Haves and have-nots, 222, 223, 478
Head Start, 256, 281–82
Health care, global, 27–29
  indicators across nations, 28
Health care, U.S., 58
  air pollution, 491
  conflict perspective on, 49
  cost shifting and, 40
  elderly and, 316, 327–28, 330
  ethical issues, 43–45
  functional perspective on, 50–51
  high cost of, 32–37
  hospitals and, 33, 35
  interactionist perspective on, 51–52
  lifestyles and, 29, 51
  physicians in, 33–35
  poverty and, 240–41
  prescription drugs and, 35
  protective measures and, 37–40
  technology and, 44–45
  unequal access and, 30–32, 58
  uninsured in, 38–40, 58
Health-care proxy, 45
Health insurance, 33, 248, 418
  elderly and, 327–28
  uninsured in U.S., 38–40
  unions and, 404
Health maintenance organizations (HMOs), 38, 53, 54
Heroin, 123, 135, 136, 139–40, 141
High school dropouts, 350
High-tech firms, 440
Hill-Thomas controversy, 294
Hispanics, 272, 279
  discrimination against, 236–37
  drug use, 139, 140
  education and, 236, 267, 375, 377
  gang culture and, 210
  language barriers and, 370, 372, 377
  net financial assets, household, 273
  poverty rate among, 226, 235–37
  prostitution and, 105
  welfare reform and, 247
History, 6
Holland, 144, 399
Home care, 333
Homelessness, 3, 23, 444–45
  alcohol use/abuse and, 132
  deinstitutionalization and, 81–84
  and drug abuse, illegal, 83
  families and, 358–59
  government policy on, 444
  medicalization of, 82
  mental illness and, 62, 68, 80, 83

  poverty and, 241–43
  reinstitutionalization of mentally ill, 84–85
  single-female households and, 5
  social policy on, 448–49
Homeschooling, 370
Homogamy, 263
Homophobia, 96
Homosexuality, 12–14, 94–102, 96, 118 (*see also* Lesbians)
  AIDS and, 46–47, 114
  causes of, 97–99
  child custody and, 114
  defined, 94
  interactionist perspective and, 13
  labeling theory and, 70–71, 96
  minority status for, 94
  prison community and, 98
  social policy and, 113–15
  social-scientific perspectives on, 96–97
Homosexual subculture, 99–102, 431
  AIDS impact on, 101–102
  gays on Internet, 100
Hong Kong, 456
Hospices, 333
Hospital emergency rooms, 40
Hospitals, 33
House girl, 103
Household income (1977–99), 225
Housing, 82, 241–43
  for elderly, 334–35
  segregated, 256
  shelter poverty, 443–44
  social policy on, 447–48
  suburban, 435
Housing segregation, 269–71
Human Development Index, 461
Human immunodeficiency virus (HIV), 40, 46, 48, 90
Humanism, 391
Hunting and gathering societies, 316, 342
Hypnosis, 76

Immigration, 257–58, 283, 457
  consequences of, 465
  entrepreneurship and, 469–70
  population growth and, 460, 462
  poverty and, 239–40
  recent trends to U.S., 468–69
  school population and, 390
  segregation and, 269
  undocumented immigrants, 470–72
  urban concentration of immigrants, 469–70
  urban migration, 427–28
  U.S. history of, 466–68
Immigration Act (1921), 467
Immigration and Naturalization Service (INS), 470
Immigration Reform and Control Act (1986), 283, 457, 472
Incest, 92–93, 105
Incidence, 19
Income:
  of aged, 314
  disparities between ethnic groups, 462
  drug use and, 138–39
  education and, 268
  health insurance coverage and, 39–40
  by household (1977–99), 225
  inequality in, 248
  median household income, 227
  mental health and, 82–83
  minority groups and, 235–37, 272
  net financial assets, household, 273
  of physicians, 34
  prejudice and discrimination in, 271–74
  single-parent households, 235
India, 45, 95, 401, 459
Industrial accidents, 414, 485
Industrialization, 244, 343
Industrial societies, 342
Inequality: (*see also* Poverty)
  crime and, 170–71

  gender and, 294
  income and, 248
Infanticide, 464
Infant mortality, 28, 32, 313
Informed consent, 22, 25
Infrastructure, 424, 425, 440
Inner-city (*see* Urbanized areas)
"Ins" and "outs," 192
Institutional discrimination, 266–76
  defined, 266
  education and, 267–69
  employment and income, 271–74
  housing and, 269, 271
Institutionalization, 81–85, 328, 330
Institutional violence, 192
Institution building, 10
Institutions, 7
  health care in urbanized areas, 424
  mental illness and, 77–81
  social-welfare and, 22
  technology and, 485–87
  total, 78
  war and, 516–18
Interactionist perspective, 7, 12–14, 24
  on aging, 315, 316
  education and, 373–74
  family structure and, 342
  labeling and, 13–14
  mental health and, 63, 66–71
  on prostitution, 103
Interdependence, 489
Intermarriage, 263
International Conference on Population and Development, 29
Internet information:
  aging, 317
  AIDS, 48
  alcohol use/abuse and, 133
  crime/criminal justice, 160
  economics, 408
  education, 380
  families, 351
  gays and lesbians, 100
  guns and violence, 208
  mental-health and homelessness, 80
  population, 457
  pornography, 112, 117
  poverty and welfare, 230
  race and ethniciity, 275
  terrorism, 526
  urban problems, 437
  war and terrorism, 521
  women's issues, 298
Intravenous drug users, 136, 142
In-utero implants, 360
"Invisible" unemployed, 412
Iran, 95, 517
Iraq, 517, 519
Ireland, 191
Irish Republican Army, 520
Italians, 264
Italy, 313

Japan, 173, 258, 313, 370, 399, 456, 458, 465
Jews, 260, 264, 325
Job discrimination, 328
Job security, 409
Job training, 278
Johnson intervention, 134
Judaism, 302
Judicial discretion, 158
Justice, 243, 274, 276
Juvenile delinquency, 166–67, 182
Juvenile justice system, 179, 185

Kansas City Gun Experiment, 213
Kinship unit, 342–43
Klu Klux Klan, 259
Korean War, 518
Kosovo, 202, 482, 519, 524
Kuwait, 465, 510, 514, 524

Labeling, 13–14, 25
  aged and, 314, 315
  educational system and, 374
  homosexuality and, 96
  mental illness and, 67, 70–71, 79
  negative, 324
Labor unions, 272, 387, 403, 404
Land mines/unexploded ammunition, 524–25
Language, 257, 283, 301–302
  education and, 370, 372, 377
"Latchkey children," 353
Latin America, 29, 147, 289, 295, 424, 456
Laudanum, 124
Lead paint poisoning, 359
League of Nations, The, 518
Legal immigration to U.S., 468
Legal issues:
  Alcohol use/abuse, 314–15
  controlling warfare, 401–402
  divorce law, 361
  pornography industry and, 117
  right to work laws, 404
  sexism and, 117, 306–307
  sex roles and, 289
  sexual behavior and, 90
Legislation (*see specific items*)
Lesbians, 99, 118
  definition of, 94
  internet information, 100
Less developed countries (LDC), 28, 400, 455, 458
Level of living, 459
Liberals, 22, 24, 247
Life expectancy, 313
  health care and, 27–28, 30–31
  racial differences, 30–31
Limited liability, 398
Literacy rates, 459
Living trusts, 335
Living will, 45, 337
Loan sharking, 164
Lochner v. *New York*, 303
Longitudinal data, 19
Lumpenproletariat, 227

Mainstreaming, 55
Male hegemony and power, 291
Male prostitutes, 104
Malnutrition, 460
Malpractice litigation, 34–35
Managed care, 34, 53
Mandatory retirement, 322
Manslaughter, 197
Manufacturing, relocation of, 439–40
Maquiladora industries, 403–404
Marijuana, 135
  criminal deviance and, 141
  legalization argument, 123, 144–45
  spread of use, 139
  teenage use of, 137–38
Markets, 397, 401
Marriage, 113, 263, 326
  black community and, 348
  empty-shell, 344–45
  first marriage median age, 355
  gay couples and, 341
  gay/lesbian, 358
  marriageable male population, 349–50
  postponing, 354–55
  women's attitude toward, 346
  working women and, 345–48, 405
Marxian theory, 10–12, 24, 227–28, 373, 410, 516
Mary Ellen case, 204
Masculine mystique, 292
Masculinity, 104
Mass murder, 198
Masturbation, 91, 92, 99
Material possessions, 417–18
McCleskey v. *Kemp,* 276
Media:
  ageism and, 322
  consumer credit and, 415

sex-role stereotypes in, 301–302
  social construction and, 14
  social problems and, 16–17
  violence and, 16, 195–96, 214–15
Medicaid, 38–39, 55, 229, 231, 240, 327–28, 473
Medical libraries, 479
Medical sociology, 29, 52
Medicare, 31, 38–39, 229, 231, 240, 250, 327–28
Megalopolis, 432
Men:
  child rearing and, 304
  criminal behavior and, 168–69
  drug use among, 140
  in elderly population, 325–26
  exclusion from work force, 405
  life expectancy and, 30–31
  mental health and, 74–75, 86
  murder rates and, 197
  population trends and, 36
  power and male hegemony, 291
  sex roles, 288–90, 308–10
  suicide and, 64
Mental disorder, 61–62, 86
  children with, 238
  classification of, 68–70
Mental health:
  conflict perspective on, 71–75
  interactionist perspective on, 63, 66–71
Mental-health profession, 76–77
Mental hospitals, 78–79
Mental illness, 61
  conflict perspective on, 63
  defined, 61–62
  deinstitutionalization and, 62, 81–84
  deviance and, 66–67
  drift hypothesis and, 73, 86
  labeling and, 70–71
  living problems of, 67–68
  medical model of, 66, 86
  medical treatment for, 76, 86
  nonmedical treatment, 75–76
  poverty and, 223
  reinstitutionalization, 84–85
  social construction of, 66–71
  suicide and, 63–64
  treatment institutions, 77–81
  urban living and, 72–74, 423
Merton's theory of anomie, 93, 173–74
Methadone maintenance, 143
Metropolitan districts, 423, 431
Metropolitan growth, 431–34
  suburban growth and, 435–37
  transportation and, 434–35
Metropolitan statistical areas (MSAs), 432
Mexico, 147, 239, 418, 457, 459, 470
Middle-aged, 319
Middle class, 228–29, 345, 347, 409, 447
Midtown Manhattan Study, 72–73
Midwives, 41
Milgrim's morality study, 484
Military technology, 482, 511–12
Minimum wage, 250, 263
Minority groups, 257–58
  access to education, 375–77, 381
  AIDS and, 50
  disabled/handicapped as, 43
  discrimination against, 236–37
  elderly among, 325
  health care access and, 30–31
  homosexuals as, 94
  housing problems for, 271
  intermarriage and, 263–64
  labor unions and, 272
  language barriers and, 370
  multiple jeopardy, 329–30
  poverty and, 226, 235–37
  profiling and, 274
  school segregation and, 267, 373, 375
  single-parent households and, 348
  stereotyping, 264
  urban migration by, 427–28

violence in, 194
  welfare reform, 247
Modern functionalism, 10
Modernization, 317
Modified extended family, 342
Morning-after pill, 360–61
Morphine, 124
Mortality rates, 31
  firearms and, 209
  infant, 32
Most Favored Nation status, 418
"Motherhood ethic," 304
Mothers Against Drunk Driving (MADD), 146
Multinational corporations, 399–402
  outsourcing and, 400–401
  U.S. workers and, 401–402
Multiple jeopardy, 329–30
Murder, 131, 154, 173, 178
  defined, 197–99
  global rates of, 190
  rates of, 189

Narcoterrorism, 520
Narcotic Antagonists, 145
National Advisory Commission on Civil Disorders
  (1968), 256
National Center on Child Abuse, 19
National Commission on Excellence in Education, 390
National Education Association (NEA), 387
National Household Survey of Drug Abuse, 137
National Institute for Occupational Safety and Health
  (NIOSH), 409
National Institute of Child Health and Human
  Development, 357
National Institute of Health (NIH), 42
National Institute of Mental Health (NIMH), 22, 63,
  71, 76
National Institute on Drug Abuse, 123
Nationalism, 517
National Opinion Research Corporation (NORC),
  112, 182
National Organization for Women: (NOW), 297
National Rifle Association (NRA), 15–16, 211
National Women's Political Caucus, 297
Native Americans, 148, 257, 271, 284, 325, 374, 375
Natural history of social problems, 14–16, 25
Needle exchange, 136
Neighborhood distress, 445–46
Net worth, 223
New Zealand, 456, 458
Nigeria, 519, 520
Noninstitutional violence, 192
North American Free Trade Agreement (NAFTA),
  147, 398, 418
North Atlantic Treaty Organization (NATO), 517, 523
Nuclear family, 342, 343
Nuclear Nonproliferation Treaty (1968), 524
Nuclear power, 500
Nursing homes, 29, 33, 334, 335

Objective dimensions, 228
Occupational safety and health, 402, 404, 413–15
Open education, 391–92
Oral sex, 92
Organ donations, 333
Organized crime, 164–65, 184, 430
Outpatient treatment, mental, 79
Outsourcing, 400–401
Ozone depletion, 488, 491

Paid leave, 236
Pakistan, 401, 459
Paraphyllic rapism, 93
Parenthood, 355–59
  births of unmarried women, 355–56
  extra-marital births, 355–56
  gay/lesbian families and, 358
Parole, 183
Participant observation, 25
Part-time work, 347
Patient's rights law, 55

Peer groups, 13
Peer socialization, 299
Pension plans, 316
Permanent displacement, 412
Perry preschool project, 377–78
Persian Gulf War, 510, 512, 514, 517
Peru, 520
Pesticides/herbicides, 488, 493
Petroleum industry, 399
Phobias, 62
Physicians, 33–35, 137
Pimps, 106–107
Plea bargaining, 183
Police:
    antisolicitation laws and, 115
    discretion by, 157–59
Political issues:
    abortion, 41, 309
    criminal deviance, 186
    domestic terrorism, 526
    economic programs, 420
    family problems, 365–66
    gender relations, 309–10
    health care and, 57
    homosexuality and, 71
    immigration, 474
    mental health and, 86
    natural environment, 503
    poverty, 251
    prejudice and discrimination, 284
    reproductive care and, 42
    right to die, 337
    school choice, 384
    sexuality and, 118
    substance abuse and, 148
    urban problems, 449
    violence and, 218
Political science, 7
Pollution, environmental, 51, 487, 489, 502
Poor people, 225–27
Population, 33 (see also Urban population)
    controlling growth, 462–65
    food/hunger, 459–60
    in LDCs, 464–65
    measuring growth of, 453–55
    rising expectations, 458–59
    in U.S., 460, 461
    world growth, 454, 487, 500
Pornography, 109–13, 119
    censorship and, 111
    children and, 109–10, 112
    feminist perspective on, 110–11
    functional perspective on, 110
    gender-discrimination in, 296
    public opinion and, 112–13
    research on, 111–12, 119
    social policy on, 116–18
    social-scientific perspective on, 110–11
    and violence, 111
Postabortion stress syndrome, 357
Postindustrial society, 382
Postponing marriage, 354–55, 458
Posttraumatic stress disorder (PTSD), 508
Potsdam Treaty, 509
Poverty, 4–5, 229–332
    absolute v. relative, 231–32
    criminal behavior and, 171
    cultural explanations for, 245–46
    dependent poor, 237–38
    education and, 241
    elderly and, 328
    geography and, 237
    health care access and, 31
    homelessness and, 241–43
    immigration and, 239–40
    justice and, 243
    mental health and, 81, 86
    minority groups and, 235–37, 350
    multiple jeopardy, 329–30
    poor health and, 49–50
    sexual deviance and, 105

single-parent households, 232–35, 238
    SMI and, 71
    structural explanations of, 243–45
    underclass and, 274
    urbanized areas and, 423, 424, 425
    violence and, 216–18
Poverty line, 229–332, 329
Poverty tracts, 445, 446
Preindustrial periods, 343
Prejudice, defined, 260
Prejudice and discrimination, 255–56 (see also
            Institutional discrimination)
    aged and, 315
    blacks and, 255–56
    consequences of, 276–78
    gender-based and, 287, 304, 306
    justice and, 274, 276
    psychological origins of, 261–63
    sex-based, 303
    shelter poverty and, 443–44
    Social Security system and, 335
    social structures and, 262–63
    topology of, 260
    workplace and, 306
Premarital pregnancy, 355
Premarital sex, 89, 92
Preschool programs, 377–78
Prescription drugs, 35, 327
Primary and secondary aging, 323–24
Primary metropolitan statistical areas (PMSAs), 432
Prisons:
    convict rehabilitation, 180
    homosexuality in, 98
    population growth in, 171, 183, 274
    substance abuse and, 141–42
Privacy, 22, 25
Probation, 183
Productivity, economic, 478, 482–83
Professional crimes, 165–66
Program of assertive community treatment (PACT), 85
Progressivism, 391
Projection, 261
Promiscuity, 47, 105, 262, 355
Property crimes, 161
Property tax system, 389, 440, 442
Proposition 187, 239
Proposition 209, 279
Prostitution, 102–109, 118, 119
    drug abuse and, 105
    globalization and, 107–108
    homosexual, 98
    impact of AIDS on, 108–109
    legalization of, 115–16
    male prostitutes, 104
    norms of, 103–104
    organized crime and, 164
    progression into, 105–106
    reasons for engaging in, 104–105
    sexual tourism, 108
    social policy on, 115–16
    subculture within, 106–109
    violence and, 107
Psychiatry, 77, 86
Psychoanalysis, 75, 86
Psychological dependence, defined, 124
Psychology, 6
Psychotic personalities, 62
Psychotropic drugs, 81
Public education, 267, 371
Public opinion, 16–17, 112
Public-order crimes, 163
Puerto Rico, 457

Race:
    criminal behavior and, 171
    drug use and, 138–39
    equality and, 255–56
    mental health and, 74, 86
    segregation and, 428, 429
    violence and, 216–17
Racial minorities (see also Minority groups)

Racial profiling and, 172, 274
Racial steering, 271
Racism, 259, 277, 494
Radioactivity, 492, 493, 494–95
Rape, 93–94, 111, 159, 202–204, 295, 303
Rate of population growth (natural increase), 454
Rational choice theory, 195
Reagan administration, 23, 231, 379
Recidivism, 179, 183
Redistribution of wealth, 223
Rehabilitation, convict, 179–81
Reinstitutionalization of mentally ill, 84–85, 448
Religion, 302
Renewable energy sources, 500
Reproductive issues, 359–61
Research methods, 17–22
Residual deviance, 67
Restrictive covenants, 271
Retirement, 314, 322, 330–31, 335, 337
Retribution-deterrence, 176–79
Revolutionary terrorism, 520
Rich people, 223–24
Right to die, 336
"Right to work" laws, 404
Risk professionals, 501
Road rage, 189
Robbery, 202
Roe v. *Wade*, 41, 307
Roles, 7
Romer v. *Evans*, 113
Roth v. *United States*, 117
Rural v. urban, 423–24
Russia, 289, 455, 511, 518
Rwanda, 202, 255, 518, 519

Same-sex marriage, 113
Sample, 19
Saudi Arabia, 465
Scapegoat, 261
Schizophrenia, 62, 75, 79
Scholastic Aptitude Test (SAT), 371
School choice, 384
School reform, 381–89
    "back to basics" and, 390–91
    bureaucratic entrenchment and, 381–83
    classroom/school size, 383
    funding systems and, 389–90
    humanism/open education, 391–92
    institutional nature of, 381
    national standards and, 390–91
    teachers' professionalism and, 387
    technological fix for, 384–85
    trends and prospects, 392–93
School segregation, 269, 373, 379
School tax, 389
School violence, 189, 198–99, 387–89
Scotland, 371
Secondary deviance, 13–14
Segregation, 241, 256, 267, 268, 269–71, 318
Self-employed people, 407
Senility, 66, 325
Sen's Law, 461
Serbia, 518
Sex dimorphism, 290
Sex education, 89, 307, 389
Sexes (see Gender)
Sexism:
    education and, 300–301, 305–306
    employment and, 292
    government and, 302–303, 302–304
    homemaking and, 295, 297
    language and media, 301–302
    legal system and, 303–304, 306–307
    nature of, 290–91
    organized religion, 302
    power and male hegemony, 291
    reproductive control, 307–308
    socialization and, 299–300
Sex roles (See also Gender)
    family and, 346
    marriage and, 347

traditional, 288–90
Sexual abuse, 104, 110, 300, 444
Sexual behavior (*see also* Homosexuality; Pornography; Prostitution)
  asocial sex variance, 92–94
  elderly and, 326
  life styles and, 290
  marital fidelity and, 344
  religion and, 302
  structured sex variance, 94
  tolerated sex variance, 92
Sexual harassment, 291, 294–96, 303
Sexually transmitted diseases (STDs), 29, 107
Sexual tourism, 108
Shelter poverty, 443–45
Shoplifting (boosting), 161, 165
Sierra Leone, 518, 519
Singapore, 456
Single-parent households, 5, 232–35, 238, 330
  divorce and, 353–54
  minority groups and, 348, 349
Slavery, 262, 263, 466
Smart guns, 213
Smoking, 37, 51–52, 123
Social construction, 14
Social control, 176
Social-disorganization theory, 9–10
Social environment, 66
Social experiments, 20–22, 25
Socialism, 22
Socialization, 299–300
Social norms, 263
Social pathology, 9
Social policy, 22–24, 25
  aged and aging, 333–37
  AIDS and, 56–57
  arms control, 523–25
  child abuse and, 216–17
  disabled/handicapped, 55–56
  economic policies, 418–20
  environmental control, 500–502
  family violence and, 215–16
  gun control, 211–14
  health care and, 52–53
  homosexuality and, 113–15
  insurance reform, 53, 55
  managed care, 53
  media violence and, 214–15
  mental health initiatives, 84–85
  population and, 472–74
  pornography and, 116–18
  prejudice and discrimination, 278–84
  problems of family, 361–65
  prostitution and, 115–16
  public school system and, 389–93
  sexism and, 304–309
  substance abuse and, 145–47
  terrorism and, 525–26
  urban problems, 446–48
  welfare reform, 246–49
  women's movement and, 308
Social problems, 3–5, 24
  aging as, 313–15
  approaches to studying, 6
  defined, 4
  education, 369–72
  globalization and, 399
  health care as, 29–40
  intervention, societal, 4
  natural history of, 14–16
  overview of perspectives on, 7
  perspectives on, 5–6
  research methods on, 17–22
  sex roles and sexism, 287–88
  sexual behavior as, 91–92, 118, 119
  social construction and, 14
  substance abuse, 121–25
  urban growth, 426
  violence, 189–90
  war and terrorism, 507
Social psychology, 6

Social Security system, 37, 38, 43, 229, 328
Social-selection, 73, 86
Social stratification, 227, 318–19, 373, 389
Social-welfare institutions, 22
Sociopaths, 62
Sodomy, 92
Solar energy, 487
Solid-waste disposal, 493–95, 498
Somalia, 518, 519, 524
South Africa, 45, 259, 278, 399
Soviet Union (former), 45, 189, 277, 518, 523, 524
Spain, 371
Specialization:
  job, 407–408
  medical, 34
  urbanization and, 430
Spouse abuse, 206–207, 216
Standardized tests, 370
Standards of living, 458, 459
Starvation, 461
State terrorism, 520
Status, 7
Status offense, 166–67
Statutory rape, 202
Stepfamilies, 352
Stereotyping, 264
  blacks and, 265
  elderly and, 325–26
  gender-based, 292, 308
  media and, 302
  minority groups and, 264
  sex-discrimination and, 287
  sex-role, 308
  welfare reform and, 265
Sterilization, 465
Strategic Arms Limitation Talks (SALT), 524
Streetwalker, 103
Stress, 324, 344, 347, 409
Structural violence, 191
Subcultures:
  delinquent class, 175
  homosexuality, 99–102, 431
  within prostitution, 106–109
  urbanization theory and, 430–31
  violence and, 194–95
Subjective dimensions, 228
Suburban growth, 435–37
Suicide:
  aged and, 322–23
  assisted, 43–44
  mental illness and, 63–64
"Super-predator" cohort, 169–70, 201
Supplemental Security Income (SSI), 237, 238
Survey research, 19, 25
Sweatshops, global, 400
Sweden, 32, 52, 456
Switzerland, 399

Taiwan, 370, 456
Tariffs, 418
Taxes, 23, 223, 224, 389, 398
Teachers, 383, 386, 387, 393
Teaching careers, 387
Technological dualism, 479–81
Technology (*see also* Military technology)
  aging and, 316, 317
  appropriate technology, 500
  assessment of, 501
  automation, 482–83
  autonomous nature of, 481–82
  bureauacracy/morality and, 484–85
  controlling, 481
  defining, 478
  demographic transition and, 456
  economic growth and, 406–407
  educational system and, 384–85
  energy consumption, 486
  globalization and, 477
  inequality, global, 478–79
  institutions and, 485–87
  and jobs, 479

  in medicine, 43
  reproductive issues and, 316
  whistle blowers, 483–84
Teenage pregnancy, 90, 357, 363, 389
Telecommunications, 478, 480–81
Television, 195–96
Temporary Assistance to Needy Families (TANF), 246
"Terminator gene," 497
Terrorism, 520–23, 525–26
Thalidomide, 40–41
Therapeutic communities, 143
Third International Mathematics and Science Study (TIMS), 370
Third-strike defendants, 172
Tinker v. *De Moines Independent Community School District*, 200
Total institutions, 78
Toxic wastes, 494
Tracking, 370
Trade unions, 404
Transitional deviance, 106
Transportation, 424, 434–35, 477
"Trickle-down" theory, 225
Turkey, 465
Two-class mental-health system, 80–81

Ukraine, 511
Underclass, the, 274
Undocumented immigrants, 470–72
Unemployment, 411–13
Unemployment insurance, 229, 244
Uniform Crime Reports (UCR), 151
United Auto Workers (UAW), 401
United Kingdom (*see* Great Britain)
United Nations, 519
United States, 52, 266
  AIDS in, 45
  alcohol use/abuse in, 126–27
  anomie in, 173
  cities in, 426–29
  controlling illegal substances, 146–47
  criminal justice system, 180–81, 274
  diversity in, 255
  educational system in, 369–71
  elderly in, 315–18
  energy consumption, 459
  homosexual population in, 94
  immigration, 247–58
  population growth in, 453
  poverty in, 222
  sexual behavior changes in, 89
  social policy, 22
  substance abuse in, 121–22
  suffrage movement in, 4
  welfare state, 224, 229
  world environment and, 496–500
Urban design, 441–42
Urbanism, 424
Urbanization, 244, 317, 434
Urbanization theories, 429–31
  compositionalism, 430
  subculture theory, 430–31
  Wirth's theory, 420–21
Urbanized areas, 423–24 (*see also* Cities; Metropolitan growth)
  AIDS in, 142, 423
  decline and families, 349–50
  deinstitutionalized mental patients in, 82
  drug abuse in, 136, 423
  effects of immigration, 423–24
  elderly in, 320
  gang activity in, 207–208, 425, 430
  global perspective on, 424–25
  health-care institutions and, 424
  infrastructure, 424, 425
  inner-city dropout rate, 380
  mental health and, 72–74, 86
  poverty in, 425
  problems in cities, 437–38
  safe drinking water and, 425

Urbanized areas (*cont.*)
school size in, 383
telecommunications in, 481
U.S. cities, 426–29
Urban population, 423, 424, 425
minority migration, 427–28
percent of change (1970s v. 1980s), 433
segregation and, 428–29
shifts in, 440

Value conflict approach, 373
Value conflict theory, 12
V-chip, 109, 196
Vera Institute of Justice, 20
Victimization reports, 159
Vietnam War, 277, 508, 514
Violence, 16, 122 (*see also* Crime; Criminal violence;
School violence)
concept of, 191–92
explanations of, 192–96
family violence, 204–207
hate crimes and, 167
media and, 16, 195–96, 214–15
pornography and, 111
as rational choice theory, 194–95
schizophrenia and, 68
subculture of, 194–95
in urbanized areas, 423
against women, 287, 295
youth violence, 200–201
Voting Rights Act (1968), 256, 257
Voyeurism, 94

Wages, 400
War, 191
century of, 507
Clausewitz's functional analysis of, 515–16
controlling warfare, 512–14
direct/indirect effects of, 508–10
ethological/sociobiological theories on, 514–15
institutional and international perspective, 516–20
Marx-Lenin conflict theory and, 516
military technology and, 511–12
nuclear war, 510–11
Water supply, 425, 477, 487, 492–93, 499
Wealthfare, 224

Webster v. *Reproductive Health Services,* 41
Welfare reform, 233, 246–49
effects of, 248
job creation and, 419–20
minority stereotyping and, 265
Welfare Reform Act (1996), 327, 364, 365
Welfare state, 224, 229
White collar crimes, 161–62, 184
White-collar workers, 402, 407
Wildcat experiment, 20–21
Wirth's theory of urbanization, 420–21
Women:
ageism and, 321
bank credit and, 303–304
child rearing and, 304
criminal behavior and, 168–69
depression and, 65, 74
drug use among, 140
education, 300
in elderly population, 325–26
extra-marital births, 355–56
health care and, 40–42
homelessness and, 242
housing for, 324
in labor force, 309, 345, 381
life expectancy and, 31
mental health and, 74–75, 86
multiple jeopardy, 329–30
occupations held by, 293
population trends and, 36
pornography and, 110
poverty and, 5
premarital sex and, 89
religion and, 302
reproductive control, 307–308
sex roles and, 288–90, 330
spouse abuse, 206–207, 216
suffrage movement in U.S., 4
welfare reform and, 233–35
Women's Movement, 297–99
Work, 314
alienation from job, 410
computer control and, 408–409
family and, 348
inner cities and, 348–49
insecurity and, 409

job satisfaction, 411
stress and, 409–10
telecommunications technology and, 347
unemployment and, 411–13
women's attitude toward, 346
Workers' compensation laws, 263
Work ethic, 17, 273
Workfare, 365
Work force
automation and, 482
exclusion of older men, 405
in less developed countries, 400
multinationals and, 401–402
size of, 406
specialization in, 407–408
women in, 345–48, 381, 405–406
Working class, 229
Working mothers, 345, 346
juggling work and family, 347
preschool children and, 347
stepfamilies and, 352
Working poor, 38, 227, 239
Work Opportunity Reconciliation Act (1996),
233
Workplace:
gender issues in, 291, 306
job discrimination in, 328
occupational safety and health, 402, 404
sexual harassment in, 303
violence in, 198
World Health Organization (WHO), 45, 56, 64
World War I, 509, 511
World War II, 52, 509, 510, 511

Young people
alcohol use/abuse and, 129
criminal behavior, 163, 169–70, 185
drunk driving and, 146
in prison, 183
status offenses and, 166–67
violence among, 200–201
Yugoslavia (former), 510

Zero Population Growth Inc. (ZPG), 463
Zimbabwe, 45
Zimbardo's "prison" study, 21–22